THE EXISTENCE
AND ATTRIBUTES OF GOD

STEPHEN CHARNOCK

WITH HIS LIFE AND CHARACTER
BY WILLIAM SYMINGTON

TWO VOLUMES IN ONE

Volume 1

Baker Books

A Division of Baker Book House Co
Grand Rapids, Michigan 49516

Reprinted 1996 by Baker Books
a division of Baker Book House Company
P.O. Box 6287, Grand Rapids, MI 49516-6287

Originally published as
Discourses upon the Existence and Attributes of God
by Robert Carter & Brothers, 1853

Third printing, January 2000

Printed in the United States of America

ISBN: 0-8010-1112-4

For information about academic books, resources for
Christian leaders, and all new releases available from
Baker Book House, visit our web site:
http://www.bakerbooks.com

CONTENTS OF VOL. I

DISCOURSE I

ON THE EXISTENCE OF GOD

DISCOURSE II

ON PRACTICAL ATHEISM

DISCOURSE III

ON GOD'S BEING A SPIRIT

DISCOURSE IV

ON SPIRITUAL WORSHIP

DISCOURSE V

ON THE ETERNITY OF GOD

DISCOURSE VI

ON THE IMMUTABILITY OF GOD

DISCOURSE VII

ON GOD'S OMNIPRESENCE

DISCOURSE VIII

ON GOD'S KNOWLEDGE

DISCOURSE IX

ON THE WISDOM OF GOD

LIFE AND CHARACTER OF CHARNOCK

BY WM. SYMINGTON, D.D.

STEPHEN CHARNOCK, B.D., was born in the year 1628, in the parish of St. Katharine Cree, London. His father, Mr. Richard Charnock, practised as a solicitor in the Court of Chancery, and was descended from a family of some antiquity in Lancashire. Stephen, after a course of preparatory study, entered himself, at an early period of life, a student in Emmanuel College, Cambridge, where he was placed under the immediate tuition of the celebrated Dr. William Sancroft, who became afterwards Archbishop of Canterbury. Although there is too much reason to fear that colleges seldom prove the spiritual birthplaces of the youth that attend them, it was otherwise in this case. The Sovereign Spirit, who worketh where and how he wills, had determined that this young man, while prosecuting his early studies, should undergo that essential change of heart which, besides yielding an amount of personal comfort, could not fail to exert a salutary influence on all his future inquiries, sanctify whatever learning he might hereafter acquire, and fit him for being eminently useful to thousands of his fellow-creatures. To this all-important event we may safely trace the eminence to which, both as a Preacher and as a Divine, he afterwards attained,—as he had thus a stimulus to exertion, a motive to vigorous and unremitting application, which could not otherwise have existed.

On his leaving the University he spent some time in a private family, either as a preceptor or for the purpose of qualifying himself the better for discharging the solemn and arduous duties of public life, on which he was about to enter. Soon after this, just as the Civil War broke out in England, he commenced his official labors as a minister of the gospel of peace, somewhere in Southwark. He does not appear to have held this situation long; but short as was his ministry there, it was not altogether without fruit. He who had made the student himself, while yet young, the subject of saving operations, was pleased also to give efficacy to the first efforts of the youthful pastor to win souls to Christ. Several individuals in this his first charge were led to own him as their spiritual father. Nor is this a solitary instance of the early ministry of an individual receiving that countenance from on high which has been withheld from the labors of his riper years. A circumstance this, full of encouragement to those who, in the days of youth, are entering with much fear and trembling on service in the Lord's vineyard. At the time when they may feel impelled to exclaim with most vehemence, *Who is sufficient for these things?* God may cheer them with practical confirmations of the truth, that their *sufficiency is of God.*

In 1649, Charnock removed from Southwark to Oxford, where, through favor of the Parliamentary Visitors, he obtained a fellowship in New College; and, not long afterwards, in consequence of his own merits, was incorporated Master of Arts. His singular gifts, and unwearied exertions, so attracted the notice and gained the approbation of the learned and pious members of the University, that, in 1652, he was elevated to the dignity of Senior Proctor,—an office which he continued to hold till 1656, and the duties of which he discharged in a way which brought equal honor to himself and benefit to the community.

When the period of his proctorship expired, he went to Ireland, where he resided in the family of Mr. Henry Cromwell, who had been appointed by his father, the Protector, to the government of that country. It is remarkable how many of the eminent divines, both of England and Scotland, have spent some part of their time in Ireland, either as chaplains to the army or as refugees from persecuting bigotry. Charnock seems to have gone thither in the capacity of chaplain to the Governor, an office which, in his case at least, proved no sinecure. During his residence in Dublin, he appears to have exercised his ministry with great regularity and zeal. He preached, we are told, every Lord's day, with much acceptance, to an audience composed of persons of different religious denominations, and of opposite grades in society. His talents and worth attracted the members of other churches, and his connection with the family of the Governor secured the attendance of persons of rank. By these his ministrations were greatly esteemed and applauded; and it is hoped that to some of them they were also blessed. But even many who had no respect for his piety, and who reaped no saving benefits from his preaching, were unable to withhold their admiration of his learning and his gifts. Studying at once to be an "ensample to the flock," and to "walk within his house with a perfect heart," his qualities, both public and private, his appearances, whether in the pulpit or the domestic circle, commanded the esteem of all who were privileged to form his acquaintance. It is understood that the honorary degree of Bachelor in Divinity, which he held, was the gift of Trinity College, Dublin, conferred during his residence in that city.

The restoration of Charles, in 1660, put an end to Charnock's ministry in Ireland, and hindered his resuming it elsewhere for a considerable time. That event, leading, as it could not but do, to the re-establishment of arbitrary power, was followed, as a natural consequence, by the ejectment of many of the most godly ministers that ever lived. Among these was the excellent individual of whom we are now speaking. Accordingly, although on his return to England he took up his residence in London, he was not permitted to hold any pastoral charge there. Nevertheless, he continued to prosecute his studies with ardor, and occasionally exercised his gifts in a private way for fifteen years, during which time he paid some visits to the continent, especially to France and Holland.

At length, in 1675, when the restrictions of the government were so far relaxed, he accepted a call from a congregation in Crosby Square, to become co-pastor with the Rev. Thomas Watson, the ejected minister of St. Stephen's, Walbrook, who, soon after the Act of Uniformity, had collected a church in that place. Mr. Watson was an eminent Presbyterian divine, and the society which he was instrumental in founding became afterwards, under the ministry of Dr. Grosvenor, one of the most flourishing in the city, in respect both of numbers and of wealth. It may not be uninteresting here to insert a few brief notices respecting the place of worship which this congregation occupied, being the scene of Charnock's labors during a principal part of his ministry, and that in connection with which he closed his official career.

The place in which this humble Presbyterian congregation[a] assembled was a large hall of Crosby House, an ancient mansion on the east side of Bishopgate Street, erected by Sir John Crosby, Sheriff and Alderman of London, in 1470. After passing through the hands of several occupants, and, among others, those of Richard III., who thought it not unfit for being a royal residence, it became, about the

---

[a] The Society which met in Crosby Hall has been represented as a *congregational church*; but Wilson, in his History of Dissenting Churches, repeatedly speaks of it as *Presbyterian.—Vide* v. i. p. 330.

year 1640, the property of Alderman Sir John Langham, a staunch Presbyterian and Loyalist. A calamitous fire afterwards so injured the building, as to render it unsuitable for a family residence; but the hall, celebrated for its magnificent oaken ceiling, happily escaped the conflagration, and was converted into a meeting-house for Mr. Watson's congregation, of which the proprietor is supposed to have been a member. The structure, though greatly dilapidated, still exists, and is said to be regarded as one of the most perfect specimens of the domestic architecture of the fifteenth century now remaining in the metropolis. But, as an illustration of the vicissitudes such edifices are destined to undergo, it may be stated that Crosby Hall, after having witnessed the splendors of royalty, and been consecrated to the solemnities of divine worship, was lately—perhaps it is still— dedicated to the inferior, if not ignoble, uses of a wool-packer.

After saying so much about the building, a word or two respecting the congregation which assembled for years under its vaulted roof, may not be deemed inappropriate. It was formed, as we have already said, by the Rev. Thomas Watson, the ejected minister of St. Stephen's, Walbrook. This took place in 1662, and Charnock was Mr. Watson's colleague for five years. Mr. Watson was succeeded by the son of an ejected minister, the Rev. Samuel Slater, who discharged the pastoral duties with great ability and faithfulness for twenty-four years, and closed his ministry and life with this solemn patriarchal sentence addressed to his people:—"I charge you before God, that you prepare to meet me at the day of judgment, as my crown of joy; and that not one of you be wanting at the right hand of God." Dr. Benjamin Grosvenor succeeded Mr. Slater. His singular acumen, graceful utterance, lively imagination, and fervid devotion, are said to have secured for the congregation a greater degree of prosperity than it had ever before enjoyed. A pleasing recollection has been preserved, of perhaps one of the most touching discourses ever composed, having been delivered by him in this Hall, on *The Temper of Christ*. In this discourse the Saviour is introduced, by way of illustrating his own command that "repentance and remission of sins should be preached unto all nations, *beginning at Jerusalem*," as giving the Apostles directions how they are to proceed in carrying out this requirement. Amongst other things, he is represented as saying to them:—"Go into all nations and offer this salvation as you go; but lest the poor house of Israel should think themselves abandoned to despair, the seed of Abraham, mine ancient friend; as cruel and unkind as they have been, go, make them the *first offer* of grace; let them that struck the rock, drink first of its refreshing streams; and they that drew my blood, be welcome to its healing virtue. Tell them, that as I was sent to the *lost sheep of the house of Israel*, so, if they will be gathered, I will be their shepherd still. Though they despised my *tears* which I shed over them, and imprecated my *blood* to be upon them, tell them 'twas for their sakes I shed both; that by my tears I might soften their hearts towards God, and by my blood I might reconcile God to them. . . . . . . Tell them, you have seen the prints of the nails upon my hands and feet, and the wounds of the spear in my side; and that those marks of their cruelty are so far from giving me vindictive thoughts, that, if they will but repent, every wound they have given me speaks in their behalf, pleads with the Father for the remission of their sins, and enables me to bestow it. . . . . . . Nay, if you meet that poor wretch that thrust the spear into my side, tell him there is another way, a better way, of coming at my heart. If he will repent, and *look upon him whom he has pierced, and will mourn,* I will cherish him in that very bosom he has wounded; he shall find the blood he shed an ample atonement for the sin of shedding it. And tell him from me, he will put me to more pain and displeasure by refusing this offer of my blood, than when he first drew it forth." In Dr. Grosvenor's old age, notwithstanding that he was assisted, from time to time, by eminent divines, the congregation began to decline. After his death, the pastoral charge was held by Dr. Hodge and Mr. Jones successively, but, under the ministry of the latter, the church had become so enfeebled, that, on the expiration of the lease in 1769, the members agreed to dissolve, and were gradually absorbed in other societies.

From this digression we return, only to record the last circumstance necessary to complete this brief sketch. The death of Charnock took place July 27, 1680, when he was in the fifty-third year of his age. The particulars that have come down to us of this event, like those of the other parts of his history, are scanty, yet they warrant us to remark that he died in a frame of mind every way worthy of his excellent character and holy life. He was engaged, at the time, in delivering to his people, at Crosby Hall, that series of Discourses on the Existence and Attributes of God, on which his fame as a writer chiefly rests. The intense interest which he was observed to take in the subjects of which he treated, was regarded as an indication that he was nearly approaching that state in which he was to be " filled with all the fulness of God." Not unfrequently was he heard to give utterance to a longing desire for that region for which he gave evidence of his being so well prepared. These circumstances were, naturally enough, looked upon as proofs that his mighty mind, though yet on earth, had begun to "put off its mortality," and was fast ripening for the paradise of God.   From his death taking place in the house of Mr. Richard Tymns, in the parish of White-chapel, London, it may be inferred that his departure was sudden. The body was immediately after taken to the meeting-house at Crosby Square, which had been so often the scene of his prayers and preach-ing.   From thence, accompanied by a long train of mourners, it was conveyed to St. Michael's Church, Cornhill, where it was deposited hard by the Tower under the belfrey.   The funeral sermon was preached by his early friend and fellow-student at Cambridge, Mr. John Johnson, from these apposite words:—"Then shall the right-eous shine forth as the sun in the kingdom of their Father."

Such is an outline of the facts, as far as they are known, of the life of this great man.   There are none, it is true, of those striking occur-rences and marvellous incidents in the narrative, which attract the no-tice of the multitude, and which are so gratifying to those who are in quest of excitement more than of edification.   But, let it not be thought that, for this reason, the narrative must be destitute of the materials of personal improvement.   If the advantages to be derived from a piece of biography are at all proportioned to the degree in which the character and circumstances of the subject resemble those of the reader, a greater number, at least, may be expected to obtain benefit from a life, the incidents of which are more common, inasmuch as there are but comparatively few, the events of whose history are of an extraordinary and dazzling description.   "When a character," to use the language of a profound judge of human nature,[b] "se-lected from the ordinary ranks of life, is faithfully and minutely de-lineated, no effort is requisite to enable us to place ourselves in the same situation; we accompany the subject of the narrative, with an interest undiminished by distance, unimpaired by dissimilarity of circumstances; and, from the efforts by which he surmounted diffi-culties and vanquished temptations, we derive the most useful prac-tical lessons.   He who desires to strengthen his virtue and purify his principles, will always prefer the solid to the specious; will be more disposed to contemplate an example of the unostentatious piety and goodness which all men may obtain, than of those extraordinary achievements to which few can aspire; nor is it the mark of a supe-rior, but rather a vulgar and superficial taste, to consider nothing as great or excellent but that which glitters with titles, or is elevated by rank."

[b] Robert Hall.

Let us endeavor to portray the character of Charnock.

The mental qualities by which he was most distinguished as a man, were judgment and imagination. The reasoning faculty, naturally strong, was improved by diligent training and habitual exercise. In tracing the relations and tendencies of things, he greatly excelled; he could compare and contrast with admirable ease and beautiful discrimination; and his deductions, as was to be expected, were usually sound and logical. Judgment was, indeed, the presiding faculty in his, as it ought to be in all minds.

The more weighty qualities of intellect were in him united to a brilliant fancy. By this means he was enabled to adorn the more solid materials of thought with the attractive hues of inventive genius. His fine and teeming imagination, ever under the strict control of reason and virtue, was uniformly turned to the most important purposes. This department of mental phenomena, from the abuses to which it is liable, is apt to be undervalued; yet, were this the proper place, it would not be difficult to show that imagination is one of the noblest faculties with which man has been endowed— a faculty, indeed, the sound and proper use of which is not only necessary to the existence of sympathy and other social affections, but also intimately connected with those higher exercises of soul, by which men are enabled to realize the things that are not seen and eternal. Charnock's imagination was under the most cautious and skilful management—the handmaid, not the mistress of his reason—and, doubtless, it tended, in no small degree, to free his character from that cold and contracted selfishness which is apt to predominate in those who are deficient in this quality; to impart a generous warmth to his intercourse with others; and to throw over his compositions as an author an animating and delightful glow.

These qualities of mind were associated with habits of intense application and persevering diligence, which alike tended to invigorate his original powers, and enabled him to turn them all to the best account. To the original vigor of his powers must be added that which culture supplied. Charnock was a highly educated man. As remarked by the first editors of his works, he was not only " a person of excellent parts, strong reason, great judgment, and curious fancy," but " of high improvements and general learning, as having been all his days a most diligent and methodical student." An alumnus of both the English universities, he may be said to have drawn nourishment from each of these generous mothers. He had the reputation of being a general scholar; his acquisitions being by no means limited to the literature of his profession. Not only was his acquaintance with the original languages of Scripture great, but he had made considerable attainments in the study of medicine; and, indeed, there was scarcely any branch of learning with which he was unacquainted. All his mental powers were thus strengthened and refined by judicious discipline, and, as we shall see presently, he knew well how to devote his treasures, whether original or acquired, to the service of the Redeemer; and to consecrate the richest stores of natural genius and educational attainment, by laying them all at the foot of the Cross.

But that which gave the finish to Charnock's intellectual character, was not the predominance of any one quality so much as the harmonious and nicely balanced union of all. Acute perception, sound judgment, masculine sense, brilliant imagination, habits of reflection, and a complete mastery over the succession of his thoughts, were all combined in that comely order and that due proportion which go to constitute a well-regulated mind. There was, in his case, none of that disproportionate development of any one particular faculty, which, in some cases, serves, like an overpowering glare, to dim, if not almost to quench the splendor of the rest. The various faculties of his soul, to make use of a figure, rather shone forth like so many glittering stars, from the calm and clear firmament of his mind, each supplying its allotted tribute of light, and contributing to the serene and solemn lustre of the whole. As has been said of another, so may it be said of him—"If it be rare to meet with an individual whose mental faculties are thus admirably balanced, in whom no tyrant faculty usurps dominion over the rest, or erects a despotism on the ruins of the intellectual republic; still more rare is it to meet with such a mind in union with the far higher qualities of religious and moral excellence."

Nor were Charnock's moral qualities less estimable than his intellectual. He was a pre-eminently holy man, distinguished at once by personal purity, social equity, and habitual devotion. Early the subject of saving grace, he was in his own person an excellent example of the harmony of faith, with the philosophy of the moral feelings. Strongly he felt that while "not without law to God," he was nevertheless "under law to Christ." The motives from which he acted in every department of moral duty were evangelical motives; and so entirely was he imbued with the spirit, so completely under the power of the gospel, that whatever he did, no matter how humble in the scale of moral duty, he "served the Lord Christ." The regulating principle of his whole life is embodied in the apostolical injunction:—"Whatsoever ye do, do it heartily, as to the Lord, and not unto men." The various talents with which he was gifted by the God of nature, were all presided over by an enlightened and deep-toned piety, for which he was indebted to the sovereign grace of God in the Lord Jesus Christ. It was this that struck the key-note of the intellectual and moral harmony to which we have adverted as a prominent feature in his character. This at once directed each faculty to its proper object, and regulated the measure of its exercise. Devotion was the very element in which he lived and breathed, and had his being. Devout communion with Supreme Excellence, the contemplation of celestial themes, and preparation for a higher state of being, constituted the truest pleasures of his existence, elevated him far above the control of merely sentient and animal nature, and secured for him an undisturbed repose of mind, which was itself but an antepast of what awaited him in the unclouded region of glory. Nor was his devotion transient or occasional merely; it was habitual as it was deep, extending its plastic and sanctifying influence to every feature of character, and every event of life; dictating at once ceaseless efforts for the welfare of man, and intensest desires for the glory of God; and securing that rarest perhaps of all combinations, close communion with the future and the eternal, and the busy and conscientious discharge of the ordinary duties of every-day life.

His natural temper appears to have been reserved, and his manners grave. Regarding the advantages to be derived from general society as insufficient to compensate for the loss of those to be acquired by retirement, he cultivated the acquaintance of few, and these few the more intelligent and godly, with whom, however, putting aside his natural backwardness, he was wont to be perfectly affable and communicative. But his best and most highly cherished companions were his books, of which he had contrived to secure a valuable though select collection. With these he held frequent and familiar intercourse. Great part of his time, indeed, was spent in his study; and when the calls of unavoidable duty compelled him to leave it, so bent was he on redeeming time, that, not content with appropriating the hours usually devoted to sleep, he cultivated the habit of thinking while walking along the streets. So successful was he in his efforts of abstraction, that, amid the most crowded and attractive scenes, he could withdraw his mind easily from the vanities which solicited his attention, and give himself up to close thinking and useful meditation. The productions of his pen, and the character of his pulpit services, bore ample evidence that the hours of retirement were given neither to frivolous vacuity nor to self-indulgent sloth, but to the industrious cultivation of his powers, and to conscientious preparation for public duty. He was not content, like many, with the mere reputation of being a *recluse;* on the contrary, he was set on bringing forth the fruits of a *hard student.* There was always one day in the week in which he made it to appear that the others were not misspent. His Sabbath ministrations were not the loose vapid effusions of a few hours' careless preparation, but were rather the substantial, well-arranged, well-compacted products of much intense thought and deep cogitation. "Had he been less in his study," says his editors quaintly, "he would have been less liked in the pulpit."

To a person of these studious habits it may easily be conceived what distress it must have occasioned to have his library swept away from him. In that dreadful misfortune which befell the metropolis in 1666, ever since known as "the fire of London," the whole of Charnock's books were destroyed. The amount of calamity involved in such an occurrence can be estimated aright only by those who know from experience the strength and sacredness of that endearment with which the real student regards those silent but instructive friends which he has drawn around him by slow degrees; with which he has cultivated a long and intimate acquaintance; which are ever at hand with their valuable assistance, counsel and consolation, when these are needed; which, unlike some less judicious companions, never intrude upon him against his will; and with whose very looks and positions, as they repose in their places around him, he has become so familiarized, that it is no difficult thing for him to call up their appearance when absent, or to go directly to them in the dark without the risk of a mistake. Some may be disposed to smile at this love of books. But where is the scholar who will do so? Where is the man of letters who, for a single moment, would place the stately mansions and large estates of the "sons of earth" in comparison with his own well-loaded shelves? Where the student who, on looking round upon the walls of his study, is not conscious of a satisfaction greater and better far than landed proprietor ever felt on surveying his fields and lawns—a satisfaction which almost unconsciously seeks vent in the exclamation, "My library! a dukedom large enough!" Such, and such only, can judge what must have been Charnock's feelings, when he found that his much cherished volumes had become a heap of smouldering ashes. The sympathetic regret is only rendered the more intense, when it is thought that, in all probability, much valuable manuscript perished in the conflagration.

Charnock excelled as a *Preacher*. This is an office which, whether as regards its origin, nature, design, or effects, it will be difficult to overrate. The relation in which it stands to the salvation of immortal souls, invests it with an interest overwhelmingly momentous. Our former remarks will serve to show how well he of whom we now speak was qualified for acting in this highest of all the capacities in which man is required to serve. His mental and moral endowments, his educational acquirements, his habitual seriousness, his sanctified imagination, and his vigorous faith, pre-eminently fitted him for discharging with ability and effect the duties of a herald of the Cross. Of his style of preaching we may form a pretty accurate idea from the writings he has left, which were all of them transcribed from the notes of his sermons. We hence infer that his discourses, while excelling in solid divinity and argumentative power, were not by any means deficient in their practical bearing, being addressed not more to the understandings than to the hearts of his hearers. "Nothing,' it has been justly remarked, "can be more nervous than his reasoning, nothing more affecting than his applications." While able to unravel with great acuteness and judgment the intricacies of a nice question in polemics, he could with no less dexterity and skill address himself to the business of the Christian life, or to the casuistry of religious experience. Perspicuous plainness, convincing cogency, great wisdom, fearless honesty, and affectionate earnestness, are the chief characteristics of his sermons.

To this it must be added that his preaching was eminently evangelical. So deeply imbued with gospel truth were his discourses, that, like the Book of the Law of old, they might be said to be sprinkled with blood, even the blood of atonement. The Cross was at once the basis on which he rested his doctrinal statements, and the armory from which he drew his most forcible and pointed appeals to the conscience. His aim seems never once to have been to catch applause to himself by the enticing words of man's wisdom, by arraying his thoughts in the motley garb of an affected and gorgeous style, or by having recourse to the tricks of an inflated and meretricious oratory. His sole ambition appears to have been to "turn' sinners from the error of their ways;" and for this end he wisely judged nothing to be so well adapted as "holding forth the words of eternal life" in their native simplicity and power, and in a spirit of sincere and ardent devotion. His object was to move his hearers, not towards himself, but towards his Master; not to elicit expressions of admiration for the messenger, but to make the message bear on the salvation of those to whom it was delivered; not to please, so much as to convert, his hearers; not to tickle their fancy, but to save the soul from death, and thus to hide a multitude of sins.

The character of his preaching, it is true, was adapted to the higher and more intelligent classes; yet was it not altogether unsuited to those of humbler rank and pretensions. He could handle the mysteries of the gospel with great perspicuity and plainness, using his profound learning for the purpose, not of mystifying, but of making things clear, so that persons even in the ordinary walks of life felt him to be not beyond their capacity. The energy, gravity, and earnestness of his manner, especially when young, contributed to render him a great favorite with the public, and accordingly he drew after him large and deeply interested audiences—a circumstance which, we can suppose, was valued by him, not because of the incense which it ministered to a spirit of vanity, but of the opportunity it afforded him of winning souls to the Redeemer. When more advanced in life, this kind of popularity, we are told, declined, in consequence of his being compelled from an infirmity of memory to read his sermons, with the additional disadvantage of requiring to supply defect of sight by the use of a glass. But an increasing weight and importance in the matter, fully compensated for any deficiency in the manner of his preaching. If the more flighty of his hearers retired, others—among whom were many of his brethren in the ministry—who knew how to prefer solidity to show, crowded to supply their places. Reckoning it no ordinary privilege to be permitted to sit devoutly at the feet of one so well qualified to initiate them into the knowledge of the deep things of God, they continued to listen to his instructions with as much admiration and profit as ever.

It is as a *Writer,* however, that Charnock is best known, and this, indeed, is the only character in which we can now come into contact with him. His works are extensive, but, with a single exception, posthumous. The only thing published by himself was the piece on "The Sinfulness and Cure of Thoughts," which appeared originally in the Supplement to the Morning Exercise at Cripplegate. Yet such was the quantity of manuscript left behind him at his death, that two large folio volumes were soon transcribed, and published by his friends, Mr. Adams and Mr. Veal, to whom he had committed his papers. The Discourse on Providence was the first published; it appeared in 1680. The Discourses on the Existence and Attributes of God came next, in 1682. There followed in succession the treatises on Regeneration, Reconciliation, The Lord's Supper, &c. A second edition of the whole works, in two volumes, folio, came out in 1684, and a third in 1702—no slight proof of the estimation in which they were held.   Several of the treatises have appeared from time to time in a separate form, especially those on Divine Providence, on Man's Enmity to God, and on Mercy for the Chief of Sinners.   The best edition of Charnock's works is that published in 1815, in nine volumes, royal 8vo; with a prefatory Dedication, and a Memoir of the Author, by the Rev. Edward Parsons of Leeds.

All Charnock's writings are distinguished for sound theology, profound thinking, and lively imagination.   They partake of that massive divinity for which the Puritan Divines were in general remarkable, and are of course orthodox in their doctrinal statements and reasonings.   Everywhere the reader meets with the evidences and fruits of deep thought, of a mind, indeed, of unusual comprehension and energy of grasp, that could penetrate with ease into the very core, and fathom at pleasure the profoundest depths of the most abstruse and obscure subjects; while, from the rich stores of an exuberant and hallowed fancy, he was enabled to throw over his compositions the most attractive ornaments, and to supply spontaneously such illustrations as were necessary to render his meaning more clear, or his lessons more impressive.   In a word, for weight of matter, for energy of thought, for copiousness of improving reflection, for grandeur and force of illustration, and for accuracy and felicitousness of expression, Charnock is equalled by few, and surpassed by none of the writers of the age to which he belonged.   The eulogy pronounced by a competent judge on the Treatise on the Attributes, applies with equal justice to all his other writings:—"Perspicuity and depth; metaphysical subtlety and evangelical simplicity; immense learning, and plain but irrefragable reasoning, conspire to render that work one of the most inestimable productions that ever did honor to the sanctified judgment and genius of a human being."[c]

The correctness of the composition, in these works, is remarkable, considering that they were not prepared for the press by the author himself, and that they must have been originally written amid scenes of distraction and turmoil, arising out of the events of the times. The latter circumstance may account for the manly vigor by which they are characterized, but it only renders their accuracy and polish the more wonderful.   Refinement of taste and extensive scholarship can alone explain the chasteness, ease, and elegance of style, so free from all verbosity and clumsiness, which mark these productions. There were giants in literature in those days, and STEPHEN CHARNOCK was not the least of the noble fraternity.

Charnock may not have all the brilliancy of Bunyan, nor all the

[c] Toplady.

metaphysical acumen and subtle analysis of Howe, nor all the awful earnestness of Baxter; but he is not less argumentative, while he is more theological than any of them, and his theology, too, is more sound than that of some. "He was not," say the original editors of his works, "for that modern divinity which is so much in vogue with some, who would be counted the only sound divines; having tasted the old, he did not desire the new, but said the old is better." There is, therefore, not one of all the Puritan Divines whose writings can with more safety be recommended to the attention of students of divinity and young ministers. It is one of the happy signs of the times in which we live, that a taste for reading such works is beginning to revive; and we can conceive no better wish for the interests of mankind in general, and of our country in particular, than that the minds of our young divines were thoroughly impregnated with the good old theology to be found in such writings as those which we now take the liberty to introduce and recommend. "If a preacher wishes to recommend himself by the weight of his doctrines," to use the language of Mr. Parsons, "he will find in the writings of Charnock the great truths of Scripture illustrated and explained in the most lucid and masterly manner. If he wishes to be distinguished by the evangelical strain of his discourses, and by the continual exhibition of Christ and him crucified, he will here find the characters of Christ, and the adaptation of the gospel to the circumstances and wants of man as a fallen creature, invariably kept in view. If he wishes for usefulness in the Church of God, here he has the brightest example of forcible appeals to the conscience, and of the most impressive applications of Scripture truth, to the various conditions of mankind. And, finally, if he reads for his own advantage as a Christian, his mind will be delighted with the inexhaustible variety here provided for the employment of his enlightened faculties, and his improvement in every divine attainment."

Happy shall we be, if what we have written shall, by the blessing of God, prove the means of producing or reviving a taste for reading the works of our author, being fully convinced with a former editor, that, "while talent is respected, or virtue revered—while holiness of conversation, consistency of character, or elevation of mind, are considered as worthy of imitation—while uniform and strenuous exertion for the welfare of man is honored, and constant devotedness to the glory of God admired, the memory of CHARNOCK shall be held in grateful remembrance."

ANNFIELD PLACE, Glasgow, June, 1846.

TO THE READER

THIS long since promised and greatly expected volume of the reverend author upon the Divine Attributes, being transcribed out of his own manuscripts by the unwearied diligence of those worthy persons that undertook it,[a] is now at last come to thy hands: doubt not but thy reading will pay for thy waiting, and thy satisfaction make full compensation for thy patience. In the epistle before his treatise on Providence, it was intimated that his following discourses would not be inferior to that; and we are persuaded that, ere thou hast perused one half of this, thou wilt acknowledge that it was modestly spoken. Enough, assure thyself, thou wilt find here for thy entertainment and delight, as well as profit. The sublimeness, variety, and rareness of the truths here handled, together with the elegancy of the composure, neatness of the style, and whatever is wont to make any book desirable, will all concur in the recommendation of this. What so high and noble a subject, what so fit for his meditations or thine, as the highest and noblest Being, and those transcendently glorious perfections wherewith he is clothed! A mere contemplation of the Divine excellencies may afford much pleasure to any man that loves to exercise his reason, and is addicted to speculation: but what incomparable sweetness, then, will holy souls find in viewing and considering those perfections now, which they are more fully to behold hereafter; and seeing what manner of God, how wise and powerful, how great, and good, and holy is he, in whom the covenant interests them, and in the enjoyment of whom their happiness consists! If rich men delight to sum up their vast revenues, to read over their rentals, look upon their hoards; if they bless themselves in their great wealth, or, to use the prophet's words (Jer. ix. 23), "glory in their riches," well may believers rejoice and glory in their "knowing the Lord" (ver. 24), and please themselves in seeing how rich they are in having an immensely full and all-sufficient God for their inheritance. Alas! how little do most men know of that Deity they profess to serve, and own, not as their Sovereign only, but their Portion. To such this author might say, as Paul to the Athenians, "Whom you ignorantly worship, him declare I unto you" (Acts xvii. 23). These treatises, reader, will inform thee who He is whom thou callest thine,

[a] Mr. J. Wickens, and Mr. Ashton.

present thee with a view of thy chief good, and make thee value thyself a thousand times more upon thy interest with God, than upon all external accomplishments and worldly possessions. Who but delights to hear well of one whom he loves! God is thy love, if thou be a believer; and then it cannot but fill thee with delight and ravishment to hear so much spoken in his praise. David desired to "dwell in the house of the Lord," that he might there behold his beauty : how much of that beauty, if thou art but capable of seeing it, mayest thou behold in this volume, which was our author's main business, for about three years before he died, to display before his hearers! True, indeed, the Lord's glory, as shining forth before his heavenly courtiers above, is unapproachable by mortal men ; but what of it is visible in his works —creation, providence, redemption—falls under the cognizance of his inferior subjects here. And this is, in a great measure, presented to view in these discourses ; and so much, we may well say, as may, by the help of grace, be effectual to raise thy admiration, attract thy love, provoke thy desires, and enable thee to make some guess at what is yet unseen; and why not, likewise, to clear thy eyes, and prepare them for future sight, as well as turn them away from the contemptible vanities of this present life? Whatever is glorious in this world, yet (as the apostle, in another case) "hath no glory, by reason of the glory that excels" (2 Cor. iii. 10). This "excellent glory" is the subject of this book, to which all created beauty is but mere shadow and duskiness. If thy eyes be well fixed on this, they will not be easily drawn to wander after other objects: if thy heart be taken with God, it will be mortified to everything that is not God.

But thou hast in this book, not only an excellent subject in the general, but great variety of matter for the employment of thy understanding, as well as enlivening thy affections, and that, too, such as thou wilt not find elsewhere: many excellent things which are out of the road of ordinary preachers and writers, and which may be grateful to the curious, no less than satisfactory to the wise and judicious. It is not, therefore, a book to be played with or slept over, but read with the most intent and serious mind; for though it afford much pleasure for the fancy, yet much more work for the heart, and hath, indeed, enough in it to busy all the faculties. The dress is complete and decent, yet not garish nor theatrical; the rhetoric masculine and vigorous, such as became a pulpit, and was never borrowed from the stage; the expressions full, clear, apt, and such as are best suited to the weightiness and spirituality of the truths here delivered. It is plain he was no empty preacher, but was more for sense than sound, filled up his words with matter, and chose rather to inform his hearers' minds than to claw any itching ears. Yet we will not say but some little things, a word, or a phrase now and then he may have, which, no doubt, had he lived to transcribe his own sermons, he would have altered. If in some lesser matters he differ from thee, it is but in such as godly and learned men do frequently, and may, without breach of charity, differ in among themselves : in some things he may differ from us too, and, it may be, we from each other; and where are there any two persons who have in all, especially the more disputable points of religion, exactly the same sentiments,—at least, express themselves altogether in the same terms? But this we must say, that though he treat of many of the most abstruse and mysterious doctrines of Christianity, which are the subjects of great debates and controversies in the world, yet we find no one material thing in which he may justly be called heterodox (unless old heresies be of late grown orthodox, and his differing from them must make him faulty), but generally delivers, as in his former pieces,[b] what is most consonant to the faith of this and other, the best reformed churches. He was not, indeed, for that modern divinity which is so much in vogue with some who would be counted the only sound divines; having "tasted the old," he did not desire "the new," but said, "the old is better." Some errors, especially the Socinian, he sets himself industriously against, and cuts the very sinews of them, yet sometimes almost without naming them.

In the doctrinal part of several of his discourses thou wilt find the depth of *polemical* divinity, and in his inferences from thence, the sweetness of *practical;* some things which may exercise the profoundest scholar, and others which may instruct and edify the weakest Christian. Nothing is more nervous than his reasonings, and nothing more affecting than his applications. Though he make great use of schoolmen, yet they are certainly more beholden to him than he to them; he adopts their notions, but he refines them too, and improves them and reforms them from the barbarousness in which they were expressed, and dresseth them up in his own language (so far as the nature of the matter will permit, and more clear terms are to be found), and so makes them intelligible to vulgar capacities, which, in their original rudeness, were obscure and strange even to learned heads.

In a word, he handles the great truths of the gospel with that perspicuity, gravity, and majesty, which best becomes the oracles of God; and we have reason to believe, that no judicious and unbiassed reader but will acknowledge this to be incomparably the best practical treatise the world ever saw in English upon this subject. What Dr. Jackson did, to whom our author gave all due respect, was more brief and in another way. Dr. Preston did worthily upon the Attributes in his day; but his discourses likewise, are more succinct, when this author's are more full and large. But whatever were the mind of God in it, it was not his will that either of these two should live to finish what he had begun, both being taken away when preaching upon this subject. Happy souls! whose last breath was spent in so noble a work, praising God while they had any being (Psal. cxlvi. 2).

His method is much the same in most of these discourses, both in the doctrinal and practical part, which will make the whole more plain and facile to ordinary readers. He rarely makes objections, and yet frequently answers them, by implying them in those propositions he lays down for the clearing up the truths he asserts. His dexterity is admirable in the applicatory

[b] Treatise of Providence and of Thoughts.

work, where he not only brings down the highest doctrines to the lowest capacities, but collects great variety of proper, pertinent, useful, and yet, many times, unthought-of inferences, and that from those truths, which however they afford much matter for inquisition and speculation, yet might seem, unless to the most intelligent and judicious Christians, to have a more remote influence upon practice. He is not like some school writers, whe attenuate and rarefy the matter they discourse of to a degree bordering upon annihilation, at least, beat it so thin, that a puff of breath may blow it away; spin their thread so fine, that the cloth, when made up, proves useless, solidity dwindles into niceties, and what we thought we had got by their assertions, we lose by their distinctions. But if our author have some subtilties and superfine notions in his argumentations, yet he condenseth them again, and consolidates them into substantial and profitable corollaries in his applications; and in them his main business is, as to discipline a profane world for its neglect of God, and contempt of him in his most adorable and shining perfections, so likewise to show how the Divine Attributes are not only infinitely excellent in themselves, but a grand foundation for all true divine worship, and should be the great motives to provoke men to the exercise of faith, and love, and fear, and humility, and all that holy obedience they are called to by the gospel; and this, without peradventure, is the great end of all those rich discoveries God hath in his word made of himself to us. And, reader, if these elaborate discourses of this holy man, through the Lord's blessing, become a means of promoting holiness in thee, and stir thee up to love and live to the God of his praise (Ps. cix. 1), we are well assured that his end in preaching them is answered, and so is ours in publishing them.

Thine in the Lord,

EDW. VEEL.
RI. ADAMS.

DISCOURSE I

ON THE EXISTENCE OF GOD

PSALM xiv. 1.—The fool hath said in his heart, There is no God. They are corrupt, they have done abominable works, there is none that doeth good.

THIS psalm is a description of the deplorable corruption by nature of every son of Adam, since the withering of that common root. Some restrain it to the Gentiles, as a wilderness full of briers and thorns, as not concerning the Jews, the garden of God, planted by his grace, and watered by the dew of heaven. But the apostle, the best interpreter, rectifies this in extending it by name to Jews, as well as Gentiles, (Rom. iii. 9.) "We have before proved both Jews and Gentiles, that they are all under sin;" and (ver. 10–12) cites part of this psalm and other passages of scripture for the further evidence of it, concluding by Jews and Gentiles, every person in the world naturally in this state of corruption.

The psalmist first declares the corruption of the faculties of the soul, *The fool hath said in his heart;* secondly, the streams issuing from thence, *they are corrupt,* &c.: the first in atheistical principles, the other in unworthy practice; and lays all the evil, tyranny, lust, and persecutions by men, (as if the world were only for their sake) upon the neglects of God, and the atheism cherished in their hearts.

The fool, a term in scripture signifying a wicked man, used also by the heathen philosophers to signify a vicious person, נבל as coming from נבל signifies the extinction of life in men, animals, and plants; so the word נבל is taken, a plant that hath lost all that juice that made it lovely and useful.[a] So a fool is one that hath lost his wisdom, and right notion of God and divine things which were communicated to man by creation; one dead in sin, yet one not so much void of rational faculties as of grace in those faculties, not one that wants reason, but abuses his reason. In Scripture the word signifies foolish.[b]

Said in his heart; that is, he thinks, or he doubts, or he wishes. The thoughts of the heart are in the nature of words to God, though not to men. It is used in the like case of the atheistical person, (Ps. x. 11, 13,) "He hath said in his heart, God hath forgotten; he hath said in his heart, Thou wilt not require it." He doth not form a syllogism, as Calvin speaks, that there is no God: he dares not

---

[a] Isaiah xl. 7. נבל ציץ "the flower fadeth." Isaiah xxviii. 1.　　[b] Mais נבל and לאבחם put together. Deut. xxxii. 6. "O foolish people and unwise."

openly publish it, though he dares secretly think it.   He cannot raze
out the thoughts of a Deity, though he endeavors to blot those characters of God in his soul.   He hath some doubts whether there be a
God or no : he wishes there were not any, and sometimes hopes there
is none at all.   He could not so ascertain himself by convincing
arguments to produce to the world, but he tampered with his own
heart to bring it to that persuasion, and smothered in himself those
notices of a Deity; which is so plain against the light of nature, that
such a man may well be called a fool for it.

There is no God [c] לית שולטנא *non potestas Domini,* Chaldæ.   It is
not Jehovah, which name signifies the essence of God, as the prime
and supreme being; but Eloahia, which name signifies the providence
of God, God as a rector and judge.   Not that he denies the existence of a Supreme Being, that created the world, but his regarding
the creatures, his government of the world, and consequently his
reward of the righteous or punishments of the wicked.

There is a threefold denial of God,[d] 1. *Quoad existentiam;* this is
absolute atheism.   2. *Quoad Providentiam,* or his inspection into, or
care of the things of the world, bounding him in the heavens.   3.
Quoad naturam, in regard of one or other of the perfections due to
his nature.

Of the denial of the providence of God most understand this, not
excluding the absolute atheist, as Diagoras is reported to be, nor the
skeptical atheist, as Protagoras, who doubted whether there were a
God.[e]   Those that deny the providence of God, do in effect deny the
being of God; for they strip him of that wisdom, goodness, tenderness, mercy, justice, righteousness, which are the glory of the Deity.
And that principle, of a greedy desire to be uncontrolled in their
lusts, which induceth men to a denial of Providence, that thereby
they might stifle those seeds of fear which infect and embitter
their sinful pleasures, may as well lead them to deny that there
is any such being as a God.   That at one blow, their fears may be
dashed all in pieces and dissolved by the removal of the foundation :
as men who desire liberty to commit works of darkness, would not
have the lights in the house dimmed, but extinguished.   What men
say against Providence, because they would have no check in their
lusts, they may say in their hearts against the existence of God upon
the same account; little difference between the dissenting from the
one and disowning the other.

*They are corrupt, they have done abominable works, there is none that
doeth good.*   He speaks of the atheist in the singular, " the fool ;" of
the corruption issuing in the life in the plural; intimating that though
some few may choke in their hearts the sentiments of God and his
providence, and positively deny them, yet there is something of a
secret atheism in all, which is the fountain of the evil practices in
their lives, not an utter disowning of the being of a God, but a denial
or doubting of some of the rights of his nature.   When men deny
the God of purity, they must needs be polluted in soul and body,
and grow brutish in their actions.   When the sense of religion is

---

[e] אין אלהים " No God." Muis.   [d] Cocceius.   [e] Not owning him as the Egyptians called, θεον ευκοσμιον. Eugubin in cloc.

shaken off, all kinds of wickedness is eagerly rushed into, whereby they become as loathsome to God as putrefied carcases are to men.[f] Not one or two evil actions is the product of such a principle, but the whole scene of a man's life is corrupted and becomes execrable.

No man is exempted from some spice of atheism by the depravation of his nature, which the psalmist intimates, " there is none that doeth good :" though there are indelible convictions of the being of a God, that they cannot absolutely deny it ; yet there are some atheistical bubblings in the hearts of men, which evidence themselves in their actions. As the apostle, (Tit. i. 16,) " They profess that they know God, but in works they deny him." Evil works are a dust stirred up by an atheistical breath. He that habituates himself in some sordid lust, can scarcely be said seriously and firmly to believe that there is a God in being ; and the apostle doth not say that they know God, but they profess to know him : true knowledge and profession of knowledge are distinct. It intimates also to us, the unreasonableness of atheism in the consequence, when men shut their eyes against the beams of so clear a sun, God revengeth himself upon them for their impiety, by leaving them to their own wills, lets them fall into the deepest sink and dregs of iniquity ; and since they doubt of him in their hearts, suffers them above others to deny him in their works, this the apostle discourseth at large.[g] The text then is a description of man's corruption.

1. Of his mind. *The fool hath said in his heart.* No better title than that of a fool is afforded to the atheist.

2. Of the other faculties, 1. In sins of commission, expressed by the loathsomeness (*corrupt, abominable*), 2. In sins of omission (*there is none that doeth good*) he lays down the corruption of the mind as the cause, the corruption of the other faculties as the effect.

I. It is a great folly to deny or doubt of the existence or being of God : or, an atheist is a great fool.

II. Practical atheism is natural to man in his corrupt state. It is against nature as constituted by God, but natural, as nature is depraved by man : the absolute disowning of the being of a God is not natural to men, but the contrary is natural ; but an inconsideration of God, or misrepresentation of his nature, is natural to man as corrupt.

III. A secret atheism, or a partial atheism, is the spring of all the wicked practices in the world : the disorders of the life spring from the ill dispositions of the heart.

For the first, every atheist is a grand fool. If he were not a fool, he would not imagine a thing so contrary to the stream of the universal reason of the world, contrary to the rational dictates of his own soul, and contrary to the testimony of every creature, and link in the chain of creation : if he were not a fool, he would not strip himself of humanity, and degrade himself lower than the most despicable brute. It is a folly ; for though God be so inaccessible that we cannot know him perfectly, yet he is so much in the light, that

---

[f] Atheism absolute is not in all men's judgments, but practical is in all men's actions. The Apostle in the Romans applying the latter part of it to all mankind, but not the former ; as the word translated *corrupt* signifies.   [g] Rom. i. 24.

we cannot be totally ignorant of him; as he cannot be comprehended in his essence, he cannot be unknown in his existence; it is as easy by reason to understand that he is, as it is difficult to know what he is. The demonstrations reason furnisheth us with for the existence of God, will be evidences of the atheist's folly. One would think there were little need of spending time in evidencing this truth, since in the principle of it, it seems to be so universally owned, and at the first proposal and demand, gains the assent of most men.

But, 1. Doth not the growth of atheism among us render this necessary? may it not justly be suspected, that the swarms of atheists are more numerous in our times, than history records to have been in any age, when men will not only say it in their hearts, but publish it with their lips, and boast that they have shaken off those shackles which bind other men's consciences? Doth not the barefaced debauchery of men evidence such a settled sentiment, or at least a careless belief of the truth, which lies at the root, and sprouts up in such venomous branches in the world? Can men's hearts be free from that principle wherewith their practices are so openly depraved? It is true, the light of nature shines too vigorously for the power of man totally to put it out; yet loathsome actions impair and weaken the actual thoughts and considerations of a Deity, and are like mists that darken the light of the sun, though they cannot extinguish it: their consciences, as a candlestick, must hold it, though their unrighteousness obscure it, (Rom. i. 18.) "Who hold the truth in unrighteousness." The engraved characters of the law of nature remain, though they daub them with their muddy lusts to make them illegible: so that since the inconsideration of a Deity is the cause of all the wickedness and extravagances of men; and as Austin saith, the proposition is always true, the fool hath said in his heart, &c. and more evidently true in this age than any, it will not be unnecessary to discourse of the demonstrations of this first principle. The apostles spent little time in urging this truth; it was taken for granted all over the world, and they were generally devout in the worship of those idols they thought to be gods: that age run from one God to many, and our age is running from one God to none at all.

2. The existence of God is the foundation of all religion. The whole building totters if the foundation be out of course: if we have not deliberate and right notions of it, we shall perform no worship, no service, yield no affection to him. If there be not a God, it is impossible there can be one, for eternity is essential to the notion of a God; so all religion would be vain, and unreasonable to pay homage to that which is not in being, nor can ever be. We must first believe that he is, and that he is what he declares himself to be, before we can seek him, adore him, and devote our affections to him.[h] We cannot pay God a due and regular homage, unless we understand him in his perfections, what he is; and we can pay him no homage at all, unless we believe that he is.

3. It is fit we should know why we believe, that our belief of a God may appear to be upon undeniable evidence, and that we may give a better reason for his existence, than that we have heard our

h Heb. xi. 6.

parents and teachers tell us so, and our acquaintance think so. It is as much as to say there is no God, when we know not why we believe there is, and would not consider the arguments for his existence.

4. It is necessary to depress that secret atheism which is in the heart of every man by nature. Though every visible object which offers itself to our sense, presents a deity to our minds, and exhorts us to subscribe to the truth of it; yet there is a root of atheism springing up sometimes in wavering thoughts and foolish imaginations, inordinate actions, and secret wishes. Certain it is, that every man that doth not love God, denies God; now can he that disaffects him, and hath a slavish fear of him, wish his existence, and say to his own heart with any cheerfulness, there is a God, and make it his chief care to persuade himself of it? he would persuade himself there is no God, and stifle the seeds of it in his reason and conscience, that he might have the greatest liberty to entertain the allurements of the flesh. It is necessary to excite men to daily and actual considerations of God and his nature, which would be a bar to much of that wickedness which overflows in the lives of men.

5. Nor is it unuseful to those who effectually believe and love him;[i] for those who have had a converse with God, and felt his powerful influences in the secrets of their hearts, to take a prospect of those satisfactory accounts which reason gives of that God they adore and love; to see every creature justify them in their owning of him, and affections to him: indeed the evidences of a God striking upon the conscience of those who resolve to cleave to sin as their chiefest darling, will dash their pleasures with unwelcome mixtures.

I shall further premise this, That the folly of atheism is evidenced by the light of reason. Men that will not listen to Scripture, as having no counterpart of it in their souls, cannot easily deny natural reason, which riseth up on all sides for the justification of this truth. There is a natural as well as a revealed knowledge, and the book of the creatures is legible in declaring the being of a God, as well as the Scriptures are in declaring the nature of a God; there are outward objects in the world, and common principles in the conscience, whence it may be inferred.

For, 1. God in regard of his existence is not only the discovery of faith, but of reason. God hath revealed not only his being, but some sparks of his eternal power and godhead in his works, as well as in his word. (Rom. i. 19, 20), "God hath showed it unto them,"— how?[k] in his works; by the things that are made, it is a discovery to our reason, as shining in the creatures; and an object of our faith as breaking out upon us in the Scriptures: it is an article of our faith, and an article of our reason. Faith supposeth natural knowledge, as grace supposeth nature. Faith indeed is properly of things above reason, purely depending upon revelation. What can be demonstrated by natural light, is not so properly the object of faith; though in regard of the addition of a certainty by revelation it is so. The belief that God is, which the apostle speaks of,[l] is not so much of the bare existence of God, as what God is in relation to them that

<hr>

[i] Coccei Sum. Theol. c. 8. § 1. [k] Aquin. [l] Heb. xi. 6.

seek him, viz. a rewarder. The apostle speaks of the faith of Abel, the faith of Enoch, such a faith that pleases God: but the faith of Abel testified in his 'sacrifice, and the faith of Enoch testified in his walking with God, was not simply a faith of the existence of God. Cain in the time of Abel, other men in the world in the time of Enoch, believed this as well as they: but it was a faith joined with the worship of God, and desires to please him in the way of his own appointment; so that they believed that God was such as he had declared himself to be in his promise to Adam, such an one as would be as good as his word, and bruise the serpent's head. He that seeks to God according to the mind of God, must believe that he is such a God that will pardon sin, and justify a seeker of him; that he is a God of that ability and will, to justify a sinner in that way he hath appointed for the clearing the holiness of his nature, and vindicating the honor of his law violated by man. No man can seek God or love God, unless he believe him to be thus; and he cannot seek God without a discovery of his own mind how he would be sought. For it is not a seeking God in any way of man's invention, that renders him capable of this desired fruit of a reward. He that believes God as a rewarder, must believe the promise of God concerning the Messiah. Men under the conscience of sin, cannot tell without a divine discovery, whether God will reward, or how he will reward the seekers of him; and therefore cannot act towards him as an object of faith. Would any man seek God merely because he is, or love him because he is, if he did not know that he should be acceptable to him? The bare existence of a thing is not the ground of affection to it, but those qualities of it and our interest in it, which render it amiable and delightful. How can men, whose consciences fly in their faces, seek God or love him, without this knowledge that he is a rewarder? Nature doth not show any way to a sinner, how to reconcile God's provoked justice with his tenderness. The faith the apostle speaks of here is a faith that eyes the reward as an encouragement, and the will of God as the rule of its acting; he doth not speak simply of the existence of God.

I have spoken the more of. this place, because the Socinians[m] use this to decry any natural knowledge of God, and that the existence of God is only to be known by revelation, so that by that reason any one that lived without the Scripture hath no ground to believe the being of a God. The Scripture ascribes a knowledge of God to all nations in the world (Rom. i. 19); not only a faculty of knowing, if they had arguments and demonstrations, as an ignorant man in any art hath a faculty to know; but it ascribes an actual knowledge (ver. 10) "manifest in them;" (ver. 21) "They knew God;" not they might know him; they knew him when they did not care for knowing him. The notices of God are as intelligible to us by reason, as any object in the world is visible; he is written in every letter.

2. We are often in the Scripture sent to take a prospect of the creatures for a discovery of God. The apostles drew arguments from the topics of nature, when they discoursed with those that owned the Scripture (Rom. i. 19), as well as when they treated with those

m Voet. Theol. Natural. cap. 3. § 1. p. 22.

that were ignorant of it, as Acts xiv. 16, 17.   And among the philosophers of Athens (Acts xvii. 27, 29), such arguments the Holy
Ghost in the apostles thought sufficient to convince men of the existence, unity, spirituality, and patience of God.   Such arguments had
not been used by them and the prophets from the visible things in
the world to silence the Gentiles with whom they dealt, had not this
truth, and much more about God, been demonstrable by natural
reason : they knew well enough that probable arguments would not
satisfy piercing and inquisitive minds.[n]

In Paul's account, the testimony of the creatures was without contradiction.   God himself justifies this way of proceeding by his own
example, and remits Job to the consideration of the creatures, to
spell out something of his divine perfections.[o]   And this is so convincing an argument of the existence of God, that God never vouchsafed any miracle, or put forth any act of omnipotency, besides what
was evident in the creatures, for the satisfaction of the curiosity of
any atheist, or the evincing of his being, as he hath done for the
evidencing those truths which were not written in the book of nature, or for the restoring a decayed worship, or the protection or
deliverance of his people.   Those miracles in publishing the gospel,
indeed, did demonstrate the existence of some supreme power ; but
they were not seals designedly affixed for that, but for the confirmation of that truth, which was above the ken of purblind reason,
and purely the birth of divine revelation.   Yet what proves the
truth of any spiritual doctrine, proves also in that act the existence
of the Divine Author of it.   The revelation always implies a revealer,
and that which manifests it to be a revelation, manifests also the
supreme Revealer of it.   By the same light the sun manifests other
things to us, it also manifests itself.   But what miracles could rationally be supposed to work upon an atheist, who is not drawn to a
sense of the truth proclaimed aloud by so many wonders of the creation?   Let us now proceed to the demonstration of the atheist's folly.

It is a folly to deny or doubt of a Sovereign Being, incomprehensible in his nature, infinite in his essence and perfections, independent
in his operations, who hath given being to the whole frame of sensible and intelligible creatures, and governs them according to their
several natures, by an unconceivable wisdom ; who fills the heavens
with the glory of his majesty, and the earth with the influences of
his goodness.

It is a folly inexcusable to renounce, in this case, all appeal to
universal consent, and the joint assurances of the creatures.

Reason I. 'Tis a folly to deny or doubt of that which hath been
the acknowledged sentiment of all nations, in all places and ages.
There is no nation but hath owned some kind of religion, and, therefore, no nation but hath consented in the notion of a Supreme Creator and Governor.

1. This hath been universal.   2. It hath been constant and uninterrupted.   3. Natural and innate.

[n] Ibid.   [o] Job xxviii. 39, 40, &c.   It is but one truth in philosophy and divinity ;
that which is false in one, cannot be true in another ; truth, in what appearance soever,
doth never contradict itself.

First, It hath been universally assented to by the judgments and practices of all nations in the world.

1. No nation hath been exempt from it. All histories of former and latter ages have not produced any one nation but fell under the force of this truth. Though they have differed in their religions, they have agreed in this truth; here both heathen, Turk, Jew, and Christian, centre without any contention. No quarrel was ever commenced upon this score; though about other opinions wars have been sharp, and enmities irreconcilable. The notion of the existence of a Deity was the same in all, Indians as well as Britons, Americans as well as Jews. It hath not been an opinion peculiar to this or that people, to this or that sect of philosophers; but hath been as universal as the reason whereby men are differenced from other creatures, so that some have rather defined man by *animal religiosum*, than *animal rationale.* 'Tis so twisted with reason that a man cannot be accounted rational, unless he own an object of religion; therefore he that understands not this, renounceth his humanity when he renounceth a Divinity. . No instance can be given of any one people in the world that disclaimed it. It hath been owned by the wise and ignorant, by the learned and stupid, by those who had no other guide but the dimmest light of nature, as well as those whose candles were snuffed by a more polite education, and that without any solemn debate and contention. Though some philosophers have been known to change their opinions in the concerns of nature, yet none can be proved to have absolutely changed their opinion concerning the being of a God. One died for asserting one God; none, in the former ages upon record, hath died for asserting no God. Go to the utmost bounds of America, you may find people without some broken pieces of the law of nature, but not without this signature and stamp upon them, though they wanted commerce with other nations, except as savage as themselves, in whom the light of nature was as it were sunk into the socket, who are but one remove from brutes, who clothe not their bodies, cover not their shame, yet were they as soon known to own a God, as they were known to be a people. They were possessed with the notion of a Supreme Being, the author of the world; had an object of religious adoration; put up prayers to the deity they owned for the good things they wanted, and the diverting the evils they feared. No people so untamed where absolute perfect atheism had gained a footing. No one nation of the world known in the time of the Romans that were without their ceremonies, whereby they signified their devotion to a deity. They had their places of worship, where they made their vows, presented their prayers, offered their sacrifices, and implored the assistance of what they thought to be a god; and in their distresses run immediately, without any deliberation, to their gods: so that the notion of a deity was as inward and settled in them as their own souls, and, indeed, runs in the blood of mankind. The distempers of the understanding cannot utterly deface it; you shall scarce find the most distracted bedlam, in his raving fits, to deny a God, though he may blaspheme, and fancy himself one.

2. Nor doth the idolatry and multiplicity of gods in the world

weaken, but confirm this universal consent. Whatsoever unworthy conceits men have had of God in all nations, or whatsoever degrading representations they have made of him, yet they all concur in this, that there is a Supreme Power to be adored. Though one people worshipped the sun, others the fire,—and the Egyptians, gods out of their rivers, gardens, and fields; yet the notion of a Deity existent, who created and governed the world, and conferred daily benefits upon them, was maintained by all, though applied to the stars, and in part to those sordid creatures. All the Dagons of the world establish this truth, and fall down before it. Had not the nations owned the being of a God, they had never offered incense to an idol: had there not been a deep impression of the existence of a Deity, they had never exalted creatures below themselves to the honor of altars: men could not so easily have been deceived by forged deities, if they had not had a notion of a real one. Their fondness to set up others in the place of God, evidenced a natural knowledge that there was One who had a right to be worshipped. If there were not this sentiment of a Deity, no man would ever have made an image of a piece of wood, worshipped it, prayed to it, and said, "Deliver me, for thou art my God."[p] They applied a general notion to a particular image. The difference is in the manner, and immediate object of worship, not in the formal ground of worship. The worship sprung from a true principle, though it was not applied to a right object: while they were rational creatures, they could not deface the notion; yet while they were corrupt creatures it was not difficult to apply themselves to a wrong object from a true principle. A blind man knows he hath a way to go as well as one of the clearest sight; but because of his blindness he may miss the way and stumble into a ditch. No man would be imposed upon to take a Bristol stone instead of a diamond, if he did not know that there were such things as diamonds in the world: nor any man spread forth his hands to an idol, if he were altogether without the sense of a Deity. Whether it be a false or a true God men apply to, yet in both, the natural sentiment of a God is evidenced; all their mistakes were grafts inserted in this stock, since they would multiply gods rather than deny a Deity.

How should such a general submission be entered into by all the world, so as to adore things of a base alloy,[q] if the force of religion were not such, that in any fashion a man would seek the satisfaction of his natural instinct to some object of worship? This great diversity confirms this consent to be a good argument, for it evidenceth it not to be a cheat, combination or conspiracy to deceive, or a mutual intelligence, but every one finds it in his climate, yea in himself. People would never have given the title of a God to men or brutes had there not been a pre-existing and unquestioned persuasion, that there was such a being;—how else should the notion of a God come into their minds?—the notion that there is a God must be more ancient.[r]

3. Whatsoever disputes there have been in the world, this of the

[p] Isaiah xliv. 17.   [q] Charron de la Sagesse, Liv. i. ch. 7. p. 43, 44.   [r] Gassend. Phys. § 1, lib. iv. c. 2. p. 291.

existence of God was never the subject of contention. All other
things have been questioned. What jarrings were there among
philosophers about natural things! into how many parties were they
split! with what animosities did they maintain their several judgments! but we hear of no solemn controversies about the existence
of a Supreme Being: this never met with any considerable contradiction: no nation, that hath put other things to question, would
ever suffer this to be disparaged, so much as by a public doubt. We
find among the heathen contentions about the nature of God and the
number of gods, some asserted an innumerable multitude of gods,
some affirmed him to be subject to birth and death, some affirmed
the entire world was God; others fancied him to be a circle of a bright
fire; others that he was a spirit diffused through the whole world:[s]
yet they unanimously concurred in this, as the judgment of universal
reason, that there was such a sovereign Being: and those that were
skeptical in everything else, and asserted that the greatest certainty
was that there was nothing certain, professed a certainty in this.
The question was not whether there was a First Cause, but what it
was. It is much the same thing, as the disputes about the nature
and matter of the heavens, the sun and planets, though there be great
diversity of judgments, yet all agree that there are heavens, sun,
planets; so all the contentions among men about the nature of God,
weaken not, but rather confirm, that there is a God, since there was
never a public formal debate about his existence.[t] Those that have
been ready to pull out one another's eyes for their dissent from their
judgments, sharply censured one another's sentiments, envied the
births of one another's wits, always shook hands with an unanimous
consent in this; never censured one another for being of this persuasion, never called it into question; as what was never controverted
among men professing Christianity, but acknowledged by all, though
contending about other things, has reason to be judged a certain
truth belonging to the christian religion; so what was never subjected to any controversy, but acknowledged by the whole world,
hath reason to be embraced as a truth without any doubt.

4. This universal consent is not prejudiced by some few dissenters.
History doth not reckon twenty professed atheists in all ages in
the compass of the whole world: and we have not the name of any
one absolute atheist upon record in Scripture; yet it is questioned,
whether any of them, noted in history with that infamous name, were
downright deniers of the existence of God, but rather because they
disparaged the deities commonly worshipped by the nations where
they lived, as being of a clearer reason to discern that those qualities,
vulgarly attributed to their gods, as lust and luxury, wantonness and
quarrels, were unworthy of the nature of a god.[u] But suppose they
were really what they are termed to be, what are they to the multitude of men that have sprung out of the loins of Adam? not so much
as one grain of ashes is to all that were ever turned into that form
by any fires in your chimneys. And many more were not sufficient
to weigh down the contrary consent of the whole world, and bear

  [s] Amyrant des Religion, p. 50.   [t] Gassend. Phys. § 1, lib. iv. c. 2. p. 291.
  [u] Gassend. Phys. § 1. lib. iv. c. 7. p. 282.

down an universal impression. Should the laws of a country, agreed universally to by the whole body of the people, be accounted vain, because an hundred men of those millions disapprove of them, when not their reason, but their folly and base interest, persuades them to dislike them and dispute against them? What if some men be blind, shall any conclude from thence that eyes are not natural to men? shall we say that the notion of the existence of God is not natural to men, because a very small number have been of a contrary opinion? shall a man in a dungeon, that never saw the sun, deny that there is a sun, because one or two blind men tell him there is none, when thousands assure him there is.[x] Why should then the exceptions of a few, not one to millions, discredit that which is voted certainly true by the joint consent of the world? Add this, too, that if those that are reported to be atheists had had any considerable reason to step aside from the common persuasion of the whole world, it is a wonder it met not with entertainment by great numbers of those, who, by reason of their notorious wickedness and inward disquiets, might reasonably be thought to wish in their hearts that there were no God. It is strange if there were any reason on their side, that in so long a space of time as hath run out from the creation of the world, there could not be engaged a considerable number to frame a society for the profession of it. It hath died with the person that started it, and vanished as soon as it appeared.

To conclude this, is it not folly for any man to deny or doubt of the being of a God, to dissent from all mankind, and stand in contradiction to human nature? What is the general dictate of nature is a certain truth. It is impossible that nature can naturally and universally lie. And therefore those that ascribe all to nature, and set it in the place of God, contradict themselves, if they give not credit to it in that which it universally affirms. A general consent of all nations is to be esteemed as a law of nature.[y] Nature cannot plant in the minds of all men an assent to a falsity, for then the laws of nature would be destructive to the reason and minds of men. How is it possible, that a falsity should be a persuasion spread through all nations, engraven upon the minds of all men, men of the most towering, and men of the most creeping understanding; that they should consent to it in all places, and in those places where the nations have not had any known commerce with the rest of the known world? a consent not settled by any law of man to constrain people to a belief of it: and indeed it is impossible that any law of man can constrain the belief of the mind. Would not he deservedly be accounted a fool, that should deny that to be gold which hath been tried and examined by a great number of knowing goldsmiths, and hath passed the test of all their touch-stones? What excess of folly would it be for him to deny it to be true gold, if it had been tried by all that had skill in that metal in all nations in the world!

Secondly, It hath been a constant and uninterrupted consent. It hath been as ancient as the first age of the world; no man is able to mention any time, from the beginning of the world, wherein this notion hath not been universally owned; it is as old as mankind,

[x] Gassend. ibid. p. 290. [y] Cicero.

and hath run along with the course of the sun, nor can the date be fixed lower than that.

1. In all the changes of the world, this hath been maintained. In the overturnings of the government of states, the alteration of modes of worship, this hath stood unshaken. The reasons upon which it was founded were, in all revolutions of time, accounted satisfactory and convincing, nor could absolute atheism in the changes of any laws ever gain the favor of any one body of people to be established by a law. When the honor of the heathen idols was laid in the dust, this suffered no impair. The being of one God was more vigorously owned when the unreasonableness of multiplicity of gods was manifest; and grew taller by the detection of counterfeits. When other parts of the law of nature have been violated by some nations, this hath maintained its standing. The long series of ages hath been so far from blotting it out, that it hath more strongly confirmed it, and maketh further progress in the confirmation of it. Time, which hath eaten out the strength of other things, and blasted mere inventions, hath not been able to consume this. The discovery of all other impostures, never made this by any society of men to be suspected as one. It will not be easy to name any imposture that hath walked perpetually in the world without being discovered, and whipped out by some nation or other. Falsities have never been so universally and constantly owned without public control and question. And since the world hath detected many errors of the former age, and learning been increased, this hath been so far from being dimmed, that it hath shone out clearer with the increase of natural knowledge, and received fresh and more vigorous confirmations.

2. The fears and anxieties in the consciences of men have given men sufficient occasion to root it out, had it been possible for them to do it. If the notion of the existence of God had been possible to have been dashed out of the minds of men, they would have done it rather than have suffered so many troubles in their souls upon the commission of sin; since there did not want wickedness and wit in so many corrupt ages to have attempted it and prospered in it, had it been possible. How comes it therefore to pass, that such a multitude of profligate persons that have been in the world since the fall of man, should not have rooted out this principle, and dispossessed the minds of men of that which gave birth to their tormenting fears? How is it possible that all should agree together in a thing which created fear, and an obligation against the interest of the flesh, if it had been free for men to discharge themselves of it? No man, as far as corrupt nature bears sway in him, is willing to live controlled. The first man would rather be a god himself than under one :[z] why should men continue this notion in them, which shackled them in their vile inclinations, if it had been in their power utterly to deface it? If it were an imposture, how comes it to pass, that all the wicked ages of the world could never discover that to be a cheat, which kept them in continual alarms? Men wanted not will to shake off such apprehensions; as Adam, so all his posterity are desirous to hide themselves from God upon the commission of sin,[a] and by the

same reason they would hide God from their souls. What is the reason they could never attain their will and their wish by all their endeavors? Could they possibly have satisfied themselves that there were no God, they had discarded their fears, the disturbers of the repose of their lives, and been unbridled in their pleasures. The wickedness of the world would never have preserved that which was a perpetual molestation to it, had it been possible to be razed out.

But since men under the turmoils and lashes of their own consciences could never bring their hearts to a settled dissent from this truth, it evidenceth, that as it took its birth at the beginning of the world, it cannot expire, no not in the ashes of it, nor in anything but the reduction of the soul to that nothing from whence it sprung. This conception is so perpetual, that the nature of the soul must be dissolved before it be rooted out, nor can it be extinct while the soul endures.

3. Let it be considered also by us that own the Scripture, that the devil deems it impossible to root out this sentiment. It seems to be so perpetually fixed, that the devil did not think fit to tempt man to the denial of the existence of a Deity, but persuaded him to believe he might ascend to that dignity and become a god himself; Gen. iii. 1, "Hath God said?" and he there owns him (ver. 5), "Ye shall become as gods." He owns God in the question he asks the woman, and persuades our first parents to be gods themselves. And in all stories, both ancient and modern, the devil was never able to tincture men's minds with a professed denial of the Deity, which would have opened a door to a world of more wickedness than hath been acted, and took away the bar to the breaking out of that evil, which is naturally in the hearts of men, to the greater prejudice of human societies. He wanted not malice to raze out all the notions of God, but power: he knew it was impossible to effect it, and therefore in vain to attempt it. He set up himself in several places of the ignorant world as a god, but never was able to overthrow the opinion of the being of a God. The impressions of a Deity were so strong as not to be struck out by the malice and power of hell.

What a folly is it then in any to contradict or doubt of this truth, which all the periods of time have not been able to wear out; which all the wars and quarrels of men with their own consciences have not been able to destroy; which ignorance and debauchery, its two greatest enemies, cannot weaken; which all the falsehoods and errors which have reigned in one or other part of the world, have not been able to banish; which lives in the consents of men in spite of all their wishes to the contrary, and hath grown stronger, and shone clearer, by the improvements of natural reason!

Thirdly, Natural and innate; which pleads strongly for the perpetuity of it. It is natural, though some think it not a principle writ in the heart of man;[b] it is so natural that every man is born with a restless instinct to be of some kind of religion or other, which implies some object of religion. The impression of a Deity is as common as reason, and of the same age with reason.[c] It is a relic of knowledge after the fall of Adam, like fire under ashes, which sparkles as soon

[b] Pink. Eph. 6, p. 10, 11.   [c] King on Jonah, p. 16.

as ever the heap of ashes is opened.   A notion sealed up in the soul
of every man ;[d] else how could those people who were unknown to
one another, separate by seas and mounts, differing in various customs and manner of living, had no mutual intelligence one with
another, light upon this as a common sentiment, if they had not been
guided by one uniform reason in all their minds, by one nature common to them all: though their climates be different, their tempers
and constitutions various, their imaginations in some things as distant
from one another as heaven is from earth, the ceremonies of their
religion not all of the same kind; yet wherever you find human
nature, you find this settled persuasion.   So that the notion of a God
seems to be twisted with the nature of man, and is the first natural
branch of common reason, or upon either the first inspection of a man
into himself and his own state and constitution, or upon the first
sight of any external visible object.   Nature within man, and nature
without man, agree upon the first meeting together to form this sentiment, that there is a God.   It is as natural as anything we call a
common principle.   One thing which is called a common principle
and natural is, that the whole is greater than the parts.   If this be
not born with us, yet the exercise of reason essential to man settles
it as a certain maxim; upon the dividing anything into several parts,
he finds every part less than when they were altogether.   By the
same exercise of reason, we cannot cast our eyes upon anything in
the world, or exercise our understandings upon ourselves, but we
must presently imagine, there was some cause of those things, some
cause of myself and my own being; so that this truth is as natural
to man as anything he can call most natural or a common principle.

It must be confessed by all, that there is a law of nature writ upon
the hearts of men, which will direct them to commendable actions,
if they will attend to the writing in their own consciences.   This law
cannot be considered without the notice of a Lawgiver.   For it is but
a natural and obvious conclusion, that some superior hand engrafted
those principles in man, since he finds something in him twitching
him upon the pursuit of uncomely actions, though his heart be
mightily inclined to them; man knows he never planted this principle of reluctancy in his own soul; he can never be the cause of that
which he cannot be friends with.   If he were the cause of it, why
doth he not rid himself of it?   No man would endure a thing that
doth frequently molest and disquiet him, if he could cashier it.   It
is therefore sown in man by some hand more powerful than man,
which riseth so high, and is rooted so strong, that all the force that
man can use cannot pull it up.   If therefore this principle be natural
in man, and the law of nature be natural, the notion of a Lawgiver
must be as natural, as the notion of a printer, or that there is a printer, is obvious upon the sight of a stamp impressed.   After this the
multitude of effects in the world step in to strengthen this beam of
natural light, and the direct conclusion from thence is, that that
power which made those outward objects, implanted this inward
principle.   This is sown in us, born with us, and sprouts up with our
growth, or as one saith; it is like letters carved upon the bark of a

d Amyrant des Religions, p. 6–9.

young plant, which grows up together with us, and the longer it grows the letters are more legible.[e]

This is the ground of this universal consent, and why it may well be termed natural. This will more evidently appear to be natural, because,

1. This consent could not be by mere tradition. 2. Nor by any mutual intelligence of governors to keep people in awe, which are two things the atheist pleads; the first hath no strong foundation, and that other is as absurd and foolish as it is wicked and abominable. 3. Nor was it fear first introduced it.

First, It could not be by mere tradition. Many things indeed are entertained by posterity which their ancestors delivered to them, and that out of a common reverence to their forefathers, and an opinion that they had a better prospect of things than the increase of the corruption of succeeding ages would permit them to have. But if this be a tradition handed from our ancestors, they also must receive it from theirs; we must then ascend to the first man, we cannot else escape a confounding ourselves with running into infinite. Was it then the only tradition he left to them? Is it not probable he acquainted them with other things in conjunction with this, the nature of God, the way to worship him, the manner of the world's existence, his own state? We may reasonably suppose him to have a good stock of knowledge; what is become of it? It cannot be supposed, that the first man should acquaint his posterity with an object of worship, and leave them ignorant of a mode of worship and of the end of worship. We find in Scripture his immediate posterity did the first in sacrifices, and without doubt they were not ignorant of the other: how come men to be so uncertain in all other things, and so confident of this, if it were only a tradition? How did debates and irreconcilable questions start up concerning other things, and this remain untouched, but by a small number? Whatsoever tradition the first man left besides this, is lost, and no way recoverable, but by the revelation God hath made in his Word. How comes it to pass this of a God is longer lived than all the rest which we may suppose man left to his immediate descendants? How come men to retain the one and forget the other? What was the reason this survived the ruin of the rest, and surmounted the uncertainties into which the other sunk? Was it likely it should be handed down alone without other attendants on it at first? Why did it not expire among the Americans, who have lost the account of their own descent, and the stock from whence they sprung, and cannot reckon above eight hundred or a thousand years at most? Why was not the manner of the worship of a God transmitted as well as that of his existence? How came men to dissent in their opinions concerning his nature, whether he was corporeal or incorporeal, finite or infinite, omnipresent or limited? Why were not men as negligent to transmit this of his existence as that of his nature? No reason can be rendered for the security of this above the other, but that there is so clear a tincture of a Deity upon the minds of men, such traces and shadows of him in the creatures, such indelible

* Charleton.

instincts within, and invincible arguments without to keep up this universal consent. The characters are so deep that they cannot possibly be rased out, which would have been one time or other, in one nation or other, had it depended only upon tradition, since one age shakes off frequently the sentiments of the former. I cannot think of above one which may be called a tradition, which indeed was kept up among all nations, viz. sacrifices, which could not be natural but instituted. What ground could they have in nature, to imagine that the blood of beasts could expiate and wash off the guilt and stains of a rational creature? Yet they had in all places (but among the Jews, and some of them only) lost the knowledge of the reason and end of the institution, which the Scripture acquaints us was to typify and signify the redemption by the Promised Seed. This tradition hath been superannuated and laid aside in most parts of the world, while this notion of the existence of a God hath stood firm. But suppose it were a tradition, was it likely to be a mere intention and figment of the first man? Had there been no reason for it, this posterity would soon have found out the weakness of its foundation. What advantage had it been to him to transmit so great a falsehood to kindle the fears or raise the hopes of his posterity, if there were no God? It cannot be supposed he should be so void of that natural affection men in all ages bear to their descendants, as so grossly to deceive them, and be so contrary to the simplicity and plainness which appears in all things nearest their original.

Secondly, Neither was it by any mutual intelligence of governors among themselves to keep people in subjection to them. If it were a political design at first, it seems it met with the general nature of mankind very ready to give it entertainment.

1. It is unaccountable how this should come to pass. It must be either by a joint assembly of them, or a mutual correspondence. If by an assembly, who were the persons? Let the name of any one be mentioned. When was the time? Where was the place of this appearance? By what authority did they meet together? Who made the first motion, and first started this great principle of policy? By what means could they assemble from such distant parts of the world? Human histories are utterly silent in it, and the Scripture, the ancientest history, gives an account of the attempt of Babel, but not a word of any design of this nature. What mutual correspondence could such have, whose interests are for the most part different, and their designs contrary to one another? How could they, who were divided by such vast seas, have this mutual converse? How could those who were different in their customs and manners, agree so unanimously together in one thing to gull the people? If there had been such a correspondence between the governors of all nations, what is the reason some nations should be unknown to the world till of late times? How could the business be so secretly managed, as not to take vent, and issue in a discovery to the world? Can reason suppose so many in a joint conspiracy, and no man's conscience in his life under sharp afflictions, or on his death-bed, when conscience is most awakened, constrain him to reveal openly the cheat that beguiled the world? How came they to be so unanimous

in this notion, and to differ in their rites almost in every country? why could they not agree in one mode of worship throughout all the world, as well as in this universal notion? If there were not a mutual intelligence, it cannot be conceived how in every nation such a state-engineer should rise up with the same trick to keep people in awe. What is the reason we cannot find any law in any one nation to constrain men to the belief of the existence of a God, since politic stratagems have been often fortified by laws? Besides, such men make use of principles received to effect their contrivances, and are not so impolitic as to build designs upon principles that have no foundation in nature. Some heathen lawgivers have pretended a converse with their gods, to make their laws be received by the people with a greater veneration, and fix with stronger obligation the observance and perpetuity of them; but this was not the introducing a new principle, but the supposition of an old received notion, that there was a God, and an application of that principle to their present design. The pretence had been vain had not the notion of a God been ingrafted. Politicians are so little possessed with a reverence of God, that the first mighty one in the Scripture (which may reasonably gain with the atheist the credit of the ancientest history in the world), is represented without any fear of God.[f] An invader and oppressor of his neighbors, and reputed the introducer of a new worship, and being the first that built cities after the flood (as Cain was the first builder of them before the flood), built also idolatry with them, and erected a new worship, and was so far from strengthening that notion the people had of God, that he endeavored to corrupt it. The first idolatry in common histories being noted to proceed from that part of the world; the ancientest idol being at Babylon, and supposed to be first invented by this person: whence, by the way, perhaps Rome is in the Revelations called Babylon, with respect to that similitude of their saint-worship, to the idolatry first set up in that place.[g] 'Tis evident politicians have often changed the worship of a nation, but it is not upon record that the first thoughts of an object of worship ever entered into the minds of people by any trick of theirs.

But to return to the present argument, the being of a God is owned by some nations that have scarce any form of policy among them. 'Tis as wonderful how any wit should hit upon such an invention, as it is absurd to ascribe it to any human device, if there were not prevailing arguments to constrain the consent. Besides, how is it possible they should deceive themselves? What is the reason the greatest politicians have their fears of a Deity upon their unjust practices, as well as other men they intend to befool? How many of them have had forlorn consciences upon a death-bed, upon the consideration of a God to answer an account to in another world? Is it credible they should be frighted by that wherewith they knew they beguiled others? No man satisfying his pleasures would im-

[f] Gen. x. 9. " Nimrod was a mighty hunter before the Lord.   [g] Or if we understand it as some think, that he defended his invasions under a pretext of the preserving religion, it assures us that there was a notion of an object of religion before, since no religion can be without an object of worship.

pose such a deceit upon himself to render and make himself more miserable than the creatures he hath dominion over.

2. It is unaccountable how it should endure so long a time; that this policy should be so fortunate as to gain ground in the consciences of men, and exercise an empire over them, and meet with such an universal success. If the notion of a God were a state-engine, and introduced by some political grandees, for the ease of government, and preserving people with more facility in order, how comes it to pass the first broachers of it were never upon record? There is scarce a false opinion vented in the world, but may, as a stream, be traced to the first head and fountain. The inventors of particular forms of worship are known; and the reasons why they prescribed them known; but what grandee was the author of this? Who can pitch a time and person that sprung up this notion? If any be so insolent as to impose a cheat, he can hardly be supposed to be so successful as to deceive the whole world for many ages: impostures pass not free through the whole world without examination and discovery: falsities have not been universally and constantly owned without control and question. If a cheat imposeth upon some towns and countries, he will be found out by the more piercing inquiries of other places; and it is not easy to name any imposture that hath walked so long in its disguise in the world, without being unmasked and whipped out by some nation or other. If this had been a mere trick, there would have been as much craft in some to discern it as there was in others to contrive it. No man can be imagined so wise in a kingdom, but others may be found as wise as himself: and it is not conceivable, that so many clear-sighted men in all ages should be ignorant of it, and not endeavour to free the world from so great a falsity. It cannot be found that a trick of state should always beguile men of the most piercing insights, as well as the most credulous: that a few crafty men should befool all the wise men in the world, and the world lie in a belief of it and never like to be freed from it.[h] What is the reason the succeeding politicians never knew this stratagem; since their maxims are usually handed to their successors.[i]

This persuasion of the existence of God, owes not itself to any imposture or subtility of men: if it had not been agreeable to common nature and reason, it could not so long have borne sway. The imposed yoke would have been cast off by multitudes; men would not have charged themselves with that which was attended with consequences displeasing to the flesh, and hindered them from a full swing of their rebellious passions; such a shackle would have mouldered of itself, or been broke by the extravagances human nature is inclined unto. The wickedness of men, without question, hath prompted them to endeavour to unmask it, if it were a cosenage, but could never yet be so successful as to free the world from a persuasion, or their own consciences from the tincture of the existence of a Deity. It must be therefore of an ancienter date than the craft of statesmen, and descend into the world with the first appearance of human na-

h Fotherby de Theomastix, p. 64.   i And there is not a Richlieu but leaves his axioms to a Mazarine.

ture. Time, which hath rectified many errors, improves this notion, makes it shock down its roots deeper and spread its branches larger.

It must be a natural truth that shines clear by the detection of those errors that have befooled the world, and the wit of man is never able to name any human author that first insinuated it into the beliefs of men.

Thirdly, Nor was it fear first introduced it. Fear is the consequent of wickedness. As man was not created with any inherent sin, so he was not created with any terrifying fears; the one had been against the holiness of the Creator, the other against his goodness: fear did not make this opinion, but the opinion of the being of a Deity was the cause of this fear, after his sense of angering the Deity by his wickedness. The object of fear is before the act of fear; there could not be an act of fear exercised about the Deity, till it was believed to be existent, and not only so, but offended: for God as existent only, is not the object of fear or love; it is not the existence of a thing that excites any of those affections, but the relation a thing bears to us in particular. God is good, and so the object of love, as well as just, and thereby the object of fear. He was as much called *Love*,[k] and *Mens,* or *Mind,* in regard of his goodness and understanding, by the heathens, as much as by any other name. Neither of those names were proper to insinuate fear; neither was fear the first principle that made the heathens worship a God; they offered sacrifices out of gratitude to some, as well as to other, out of fear; the fear of evils in the world, and the hopes of relief and assistance from their gods, and not a terrifying fear of God, was the principal spring of their worship. When calamities from the hands of men, or judgments by the influences of Heaven were upon them, they implored that which they thought a deity; it was not their fear of him, but a hope in his goodness, and persuasion of remedy from him, for the averting those evils that rendered them adorers of a God: if they had not had pre-existing notions of his being and goodness, they would never have made addresses to him, or so frequently sought to that they only apprehended as a terrifying object.[l] When you hear men calling upon God in a time of affrighting thunder, you cannot imagine that the fear of thunder did first introduce the notion of a God, but implies, that it was before apprehended by them, or stamped upon them, though their fear doth at present actuate that belief, and engage them in a present exercise of piety; and whereas the Scripture saith, "The fear of God is the beginning of wisdom,"[m] or of all religion; it is not understood of a distracted and terrifying fear, but a reverential fear of him, because of his holiness; or a worship of him, a submission to him, and sincere seeking of him.

Well, then, is it not a folly for an atheist to deny that which is the reason and common sentiment of the whole world; to strip himself of humanity, run counter to his own conscience, prefer a private before an universal judgment, give the lie to his own nature and reason, assert things impossible to be proved, nay, impossible to be acted, forge irrationalities for the support of his fancy against the common

---

[k] Ερως.   [l] Gassend. Phys. § 1. lib. iv. c 2. p. 291, 292.   [m] Prov. ix. 10. Psalm. cxi. 10.

persuasion of the world, and against himself, and so much of God as is manifest in him and every man?[n]

Reason II. It is a folly to deny that which all creatures or all things in the world manifest.[o] Let us view this in Scripture, since we acknowledge it, and after consider the arguments from natural reason.

The apostle resolves it (Rom. i. 19, 20), " The invisible things of him from the creation of the world are clearly seen, being understood by the things that are made, even his eternal power and Godhead, so that they are without excuse." They know, or might know, by the things that were made, the eternity and power of God; their sense might take a circuit about every object, and their minds collect the being and something of the perfections of the Deity. The first discourse of the mind upon the sight of a delicate piece of workmanship, is the conclusion of the being of an artificer, and the admiration of his skill and industry. The apostle doth not say, the invisible things of God are *believed*, or they have an opinion of them, but they are *seen*, and *clearly seen*. They are like crystal glasses, which give a clear representation of the existence of a Deity, like that mirror, reported to be in a temple in Arcadia, which represented to the spectator, not his own face, but the image of that deity which he worshipped. The whole world is like a looking-glass, which, whole and entire, represents the image of God, and every broken piece of it, every little shred of a creature doth the like; not only the great ones, elephants and the leviathan, but ants, flies, worms, whose bodies rather than names we know: the greater cattle and the creeping things (Gen. i. 24); not naming there any intermediate creature, to direct us to view him in the smaller letters, as well as the greater characters of the world. His name is " glorious," and his attributes are excellent " in all the earth;"[p] in every creature, as the glory of the sun is in every beam and smaller flash; he is seen in every insect, in every spire of grass. The voice of the Creator is in the most contemptible creature. The apostle adds, that they are so clearly seen, that men are inexcusable if they have not some knowledge of God by them; if they might not certainly know them, they might have some excuse: so that his existence is not only probably, but demonstratively proved from the things of the world.[q]

Especially the heavens declare him, which God " stretches out like a curtain,"[r] or, as some render the word, a " skin," whereby is signified, that heaven is as an open book, which was anciently made of the skins of beasts, that by the knowledge of them we may be taught the knowledge of God. Where Scripture was not revealed, the world served for a witness of a God; whatever arguments the Scripture uses to prove it, are drawn from nature (though, indeed, it doth not so much prove as suppose the existence of a God); but what arguments it uses are from the creatures, and particularly the heavens, which are the public preachers of this doctrine. The breath of God sounds to all the world through those organ-pipes. His being is visible in their existence, his wisdom in their frame, his power in their

---

[n] Rom i. 19.   [o] Jupiter est quodcunque vides, &c.   [p] Psalm viii. 1.
[q] Banes in Aquin. Par. 2. Qu. 2. Artic. 2. p. 78. col. 2.   [r] Psalm civ. 2.

motion, his goodness in their usefulness. They have a voice, and their voice is as intelligible as any common language.[s] And those are so plain heralds of a Deity, that the heathen mistook them for deities, and gave them a particular adoration, which was due to that God they declared. The first idolatry seems to be of those heavenly bodies, which began probably in the time of Nimrod. In Job's time it is certain they admired the glory of the sun, and the brightness of the moon, not without kissing their hands, a sign of adoration.[t] It is evident a man may as well doubt whether there be a sun, when he sees his beams gilding the earth, as doubt whether there be a God, when he sees his works spread in the world.

The things in the world declare the existence of a God. 1. In their production. 2. Harmony. 3. Preservation. 4. Answering their several ends.

First, In their production. The declaration of the existence of God was the chief end for which they were created, that the notion of a supreme and independent Eternal Being might easier incur into the active understanding of man from the objects of sense, dispersed in every corner of the world, that he might pay a homage and devotion to the Lord of all (Isai. xl. 12, 13, 18, 19, &c.), "Have you not understood from the foundation of the earth, it is he that sits upon the circle of the heaven," &c. How could this great heap be brought into being, unless a God had framed it? Every plant, every atom, as well as every star, at the first meeting, whispers this in our ears, "I have a Creator; I am witness to a Deity." Who ever saw statues or pictures but presently thinks of a statuary and limner? Who beholds garments, ships, or houses, but understands there was a weaver, a carpenter, an architect?[u] Who can cast his eyes about the world, but must think of that power that formed it, and that the goodness which appears in the formation of it hath a perfect residence in some being? "Those things that are good must flow from something perfectly good: that which is chief in any kind is the cause of all of that kind. Fire, which is most hot, is the cause of all things which are hot. There is some being, therefore, which is the cause of all that perfection which is in the creature; and this is God." (*Aquin.* 1 *qu.* 2. *Artic.* 3.) All things that are demonstrate something from whence they are. All things have a contracted perfection, and what they have is communicated to them. Perfections are parcelled out among several creatures. Anything that is imperfect cannot exist of itself. We are led, therefore, by them to consider a fountain which bubbles up in all perfection; a hand which distributes those several degrees of being and perfection to what we see. We see that which is imperfect; our minds conclude something perfect to exist before it. Our eye sees the streams, but our understanding riseth to the head; as the eye sees the shadow, but the understanding informs us whether it be the shadow of a man or of a beast.

God hath given us sense to behold the objects in the world, and understanding to reason his existence from them. The understanding cannot conceive a thing to have made itself; that is against all

---

[s] "For their voice goeth to the end of the earth," Psalm xix. 1, 2.   [t] Job xxxi. 26, 27.

[u] Philo. ex Petav. Theolo. Dog. Tom. I. lib. i. c. 1, p. 4, somewhat changed.

reason.   As they are made, they speak out a Maker,[x] and cannot be
a trick of chance, since they are made with such an immense wisdom,
that is too big for the grasp of all human understanding.   Those
that doubt whether the existence of God be an implanted principle,
yet agree that the effects in the world lead to a supreme and universal
cause; and that if we have not the knowledge of it rooted in our
natures, yet we have it by discourse; since, by all masters of reason,
a *processus in infinitum* must be accounted impossible in subordinate
causes.   This will appear in several things.

I. The world and every creature had a beginning.   The Scripture
ascertains this to us.[y]   David, who was not the first man, gives the
praise to God of his being "curiously wrought," &c. (Ps. cxxxix. 14, 15.)
God gave being to men, and plants, and beasts, before they gave
being to one another.   He gives being to them now as the Fountain
of all being, though the several modes of being are from the several
natures of second causes.

· It is true, indeed, we are ascertained that they were made by the
true God; that they were made by his word; that they were made
of nothing; and not only this lower world wherein we live, but,
according to the Jewish division, the world of men, the world of
stars, and the world of spirits and souls.   We do not waver in it, or
doubt of it, as the heathen did in their disputes; we know they are
the workmanship of the true God, of that God we adore, not of false
gods; "by his word," without any instrument or engine, as in earthly
structures; "of things which do not appear," without any pre-existent
matter, as all artificial works of men are framed.   Yet the proof of
the beginning of the world is affirmed with good reason; and if it
had a beginning, it had also some higher cause than itself: every
effect hath a cause.

The world was not eternal, or from eternity.[z]   The matter of the
world cannot be eternal.   Matter cannot subsist without form, nor
put on any form without the action of some cause.   This cause must
be in being before it acted; that which is not cannot act.   The cause
of the world must necessarily exist before any matter was endued
with any form; that, therefore, cannot be eternal before which
another did subsist; if it were from eternity, it would not be subject
to mutation.   If the whole was from eternity, why not also the parts;
what makes the changes so visible, then, if eternity would exempt it
from mutability ?

1. Time cannot be infinite, and, therefore, the world not eternal.
All motion hath its beginning; if it were otherwise, we must say the
number of heavenly revolutions of days and nights, which are past
to this instant, is actually infinite, which cannot be in nature.[a]   If it
were so, it must needs be granted that a part is equal to the whole;
because infinite being equal to infinite, the number of days past, in
all ages to the beginning of one year being infinite (as they would
be, supposing the world had no beginning) would by consequence
be equal to the number of days which shall pass to the end of the

[x] Rom. i. 20.   [y] Gen. i. "By faith we understand that the worlds were framed by
the word of God," &c. Heb. xi. 3.
[z] Daille 20. Serm. Psalm cii. 26. p. 13, 14.   [a] Daille, ut supra.

next; whereas that number of days past is indeed but a part; and so a part would be equal to the whole.

2. Generations of men, animals, and plants, could not be from eternity. If any man say the world was from eternity, then there must be propagations of living creatures in the same manner as are at this day; for without this the world could not consist.[b] What we see now done must have been perpetually done, if it be done by a necessity of nature; but we see nothing now that doth arise but by a mutual propagation from another. If the world were eternal, therefore, it must be so in all eternity. Take any particular species. Suppose a man, if men were from eternity; then there were perpetual generations—some were born into the world, and some died. Now the natural condition of generation is, that a man doth not generate a man, nor a sheep a lamb, as soon as ever itself is brought into the world; but get strength and vigor by degrees, and must arrive to a certain stated age before they can produce the like; for whilst anything is little and below the due age, it cannot increase its kind. Men, therefore, and other creatures, did propagate their kind by the same law, not as soon as ever they were born, but in the interval of some time; and children grew up by degrees in the mother's womb till they were fit to be brought forth. If this be so, then there could not be an eternal succession of propagating; for there is no eternal continuation of time. Time is always to be conceived as having one part before another; but that perpetuity of nativities is always after some time, wherein it could not be for the weakness of age. If no man, then, can conceive a propagation from eternity, there must be then a beginning of generation in time, and, consequently, the creatures were made in time.

"If the world were eternal, it must have been in the same posture as it is now, in a state of generation and corruption; and so corruption must have been as eternal as generation, and then things that do generate and corrupt must have eternally been and eternally not have been: there must be some first way to set generation on work."[c] We must lose ourselves in our conceptions; we cannot conceive a father before a child, as well as we cannot conceive a child before a father: and reason is quite bewildered, and cannot return into a right way of conception, till it conceive one first of every kind: one first man, one first animal, one first plant, from whence others do proceed. The argument is unanswerable, and the wisest atheist (if any atheist can be called wise) cannot unloose the knot. We must come to something that is first in every kind, and this first must have a cause, not of the same kind, but infinite and independent; otherwise men run into inconceivable labyrinths and contradictions.

Man, the noblest creature upon earth, hath a beginning. No man in the world but was some years ago no man. If every man we see had a beginning, then the first man had also a beginning, then the world had a beginning: for the earth, which was made for the use of man, had wanted that end for which it was made. We must pitch upon some one man that was unborn; that first man must either be eternal; that cannot be, for he that hath no beginning hath no end; or must

---

[b] Petar. Theo. Dogmat. Tom. I. lib. i. c. 2. p. 15.   [c] Wolseley, on Atheism, p. 47.

spring out of the earth as plants and trees do;[d] that cannot be; why should not the earth produce men to this day, as it doth plants and trees? He was therefore made; and whatsoever is made hath some cause that made it, which is God. If the world were uncreated, it were then immutable, but every creature upon the earth is in a continual flux, always changing:[e] if things be mutable, they were created; if created, they were made by some author: whatsoever hath a beginning must have a maker; if the world hath a beginning, there was then a time when it was not; it must have some cause to produce it. That which makes is before that which is made, and this is God.

II. Which will appear further in this proposition, No creature can make itself; the world could not make itself.

If every man had a beginning, every man then was once nothing; he could not then make himself, because nothing cannot be the cause of something; 'The Lord he is God; he hath made us, and not we ourselves.' (Ps. c. 3.) Whatsoever begun in time was not; and when it was nothing, it had nothing, and could do nothing; and therefore could never give to itself, nor to any other, to be, or to be able to do: for then it gave what it had not, and did what it could not. Since reason must acknowledge a first of every kind, a first man, &c., it must acknowledge him created and made, not by himself:[f] why have not other men since risen up by themselves, not by chance? why hath not chance produced the like in that long time the world hath stood? If we never knew anything give being to itself, how can we imagine anything ever could? If the chiefest part of this lower world cannot, nor any part of it hath been known to give being to itself, then the whole cannot be supposed to give any being to itself: man did not form himself; his body is not from himself; it would then have the power of moving itself, but that it is not able to live or act without the presence of the soul. Whilst the soul is present, the body moves; when that is absent, the body lies as a senseless log, not having the least action or motion. His soul could not form itself. Can that which cannot form the least mote, the least grain of dust, form itself a nobler substance than any upon the earth? This will be evident to every man's reason, if we consider,

1. Nothing can act before it be. The first man was not, and therefore could not make himself to be. For anything to produce itself is to act; if it acted before it was, it was then something and nothing at the same time; it then had a being before it had a being; it acted when it brought itself into being. How could it act without a being, without it was? So that if it were the cause of itself, it must be before itself as well as after itself; it was before it was; it was as a cause before it was as an effect. Action always supposeth a principle from whence it flows; as nothing hath no existence, so it hath no operation: there must be, therefore, something of real existence to give a being to those things that are, and every cause must be an effect of some other before it be a cause. To be and not to be at the same time, is a manifest contradiction, which would be, if anything made itself. That which makes is always before that

d Petav. ut supra, p. 10.   e Damason.   f Petav. Theo. Dog. Tom. I. lib. i. c. 2. p. 14.

which is made. Who will say the house is before the carpenter, or the picture before the limner? The world as a creator must be before itself as a creature.

2. That which doth not understand itself and order itself could not make itself. If the first man fully understood his own nature, the excellency of his own soul, the manner of its operations, why was not that understanding conveyed to his posterity? Are not many of them found, who understand their own nature, almost as little as a beast understands itself; or a rose understands its own sweetness; or a tulip its own colors? The Scripture, indeed, gives us an account how this came about, viz. by the deplorable rebellion of man, whereby death was brought upon them (a spiritual death, which includes ignorance, as well as an inability to spiritual action.ᵍ) Thus he fell from his honor, and became like the beasts that perish, and not retaining God in his knowledge, retained not himself in his own knowledge.

But what reply can an atheist make to it, who acknowledges no higher cause than nature? If the soul made itself, how comes it to be so muddy, so wanting in its knowledge of itself, and of other things? If the soul made its own understanding, whence did the defect arise? If some first principle was settled by the first man in himself, where was the stop that he did not implant all in his own mind, and, consequently in the minds of all his descendants? Our souls know little of themselves, little of the world, are every day upon new inquiries, have little satisfaction in themselves, meet with many an invincible rub in their way, and when they seem to come to some resolution in some cases, stagger again, and, like a stone rolled up to the top of the hill, quickly find themselves again at the foot. How come they to be so purblind in truth? so short of that which they judge true goodness? How comes it to pass they cannot order their own rebellious affections, and suffer the reins they have to hold over their affections to be taken out of their hands by the unruly fancy and flesh? This no man that denies the being of a God, and the revelation in Scripture, can give an account of. Blessed be God that we have the Scripture, which gives us an account of those things, that all the wit of men could never inform us of; and that when they are discovered and known by revelation, they appear not contrary to reason!

3. If the first man made himself, how came he to limit himself? If he gave himself being, why did he not give himself all the perfections and ornaments of being? Nothing that made itself could sit down contented with a little, but would have had as much power to give itself that which is less, as to give itself being, when it was nothing. The excellences it wanted had not been more difficult to gain than the other which it possessed, as belonging to its nature. If the first man had been independent upon another, and had his perfection from himself, he might have acquired that perfection he wanted as well as have bestowed upon himself that perfection he had; and then there would have been no bounds set to him. He would have been omniscient and immutable. He might have given

ᵍ Gen. ii. 17. Psalm xlix. 8.

himself what he would; if he had had the setting his own bounds, he would have set none at all; for what should restrain him? No man now wants ambition to be what he is not; and if the first man had not been determined by another, but had given himself being, he would not have remained in that determinate being, no more than a toad would remain a toad, if it had power to make itself a man, and that power it would have had, if it had given itself a being. Whatsoever gives itself being, would give itself all degrees of being, and so would have no imperfection, because every imperfection is a want of some degree of being. He that could give himself matter and life, might give himself everything.[h] The giving of life is an act of omnipotence; and what is omnipotent in one thing may be in all. Besides, if the first man had made himself, he would have conveyed himself to all his posterity in the same manner; every man would have had all the perfections of the first man, as every creature hath the perfections of the same kind, from whence it naturally issues; all are desirous to communicate what they can to their posterity. Communicative goodness belongs to every nature. Every plant propagates its kind in the same perfection it hath itself; and the nearer anything comes to a rational nature, the greater affection it hath to that which descends from it; therefore this affection belongs to a rational nature much more. The first man, therefore, if he had had power to give himself being, and, consequently, all perfection, he would have had as much power to convey it down to his posterity; no impediment could have stopped his way; then all souls proceeding from that first man would have been equally intellectual. What should hinder them from inheriting the same perfections? Whence should they have divers qualifications and differences in their understandings? No man then would have been subject to those weaknesses, doubtings, and unsatisfied desires of knowledge and perfection. But being all souls are not alike, it is certain they depend upon some other cause for the communication of that excellency they have. If the perfections of man be so contracted and kept within certain bounds, it is certain that they were not in his own power, and so were not from himself. Whatsoever hath a determinate being must be limited by some superior cause. There is, therefore, some superior power, that hath thus determined the creature by set bounds and distinct measures, and hath assigned to every one its proper nature, that it should not be greater or less than it is; who hath said of every one as of the waves of the sea, "Hitherto shalt thou come, but no further;"[i] and this is God. Man could not have reserved any perfection from his posterity; for since he doth propagate not by choice, but nature, he could no more have kept back any perfection from them, than he could, as he pleased, have given any perfection belonging to his nature to them.

4. That which hath power to give itself being, cannot want power to preserve that being. Preservation is not more difficult than creation. If the first man made himself, why did he not preserve himself? He is not now among the living in the world. How came he

---

[h] Therefore the heathens called God τὸ ὄν, the only Being. Other things were not beings, because they had not all degrees of being.   [i] Job xxxviii. 11.

to be so feeble as to sink into the grave? Why did he not inspire himself with new heat and moisture, and fill his languishing limbs and declining body with new strength? Why did he not chase away diseases and death at the first approach? What creature can find the dust of the first man? All his posterity traverse the stage and retire again; in a short space their age departs, and is removed from them ' as a shepherd's tent,' and is ' cut off with pining sickness.'[k] ' The life of man is as a wind, and like a cloud that is consumed and vanishes away. The eye that sees him shall see him no more; he returns not to his house, neither doth his place know him any more.'[l] The Scripture gives us the reason of this, and lays it upon the score of sin against his Creator, which no man without revelation can give any satisfactory account of. Had the first man made himself, he had been sufficient for himself, able to support himself without the assistance of any creature. He would not have needed animals and plants, and other helps to nourish and refresh him, nor medicines to cure him. He could not be beholden to other things for his support, which he is certain he never made for himself. His own nature would have continued that vigor, which once he had conferred upon himself. He would not have needed the heat and light of the sun; he would have wanted nothing sufficient for himself in himself; he needed not have sought without himself for his own preservation and comfort. What depends upon another is not of itself; and what depends upon things inferior to itself is less of itself. Since nothing can subsist of itself, since we see those things upon which man depends for his nourishment and subsistence, growing and decaying, starting into the world and retiring from it, as well as man himself; some preserving cause must be concluded, upon which all depends.

5. If the first man did produce himself, why did he not produce himself before?

It hath been already proved, that he had a beginning, and could not be from eternity. Why then did he not make himself before? Not because he would not. For having no being, he could have no will; he could neither be willing nor not willing. If he could not then, how could he afterwards? If it were in his own power, he could have done it, he would have done it; if it were not in his own power, then it was in the power of some other cause, and that is God. How came he by that power to produce himself? If the power of producing himself were communicated by another, then man could not be the cause of himself. That is the cause of it which communicated that power to it. But if the power of being was in and from himself and in no other, nor communicated to him, man would always have been in act, and always have existed; no hindrance can be conceived. For that which had the power of being in itself was invincible by anything that should stand in the way of its own being.

We may conclude from hence, the excellency of the Scripture; that it is a word not to be refused credit. It gives us the most rational account of things in the 1st and 2d of Genesis, which nothing in the world else is able to do.

III. No creature could make the world. No creature can create

---

[k] Isaiah xxxviii. 12.   [l] Job. vii. 6-9.

another. If it creates of nothing, it is then omnipotent and so not a creature. If it makes something of matter unfit for that which is produced out of it, then the inquiry will be, Who was the cause of the matter? and so we must arrive to some uncreated being, the cause of all. Whatsoever gives being to any other must be the highest being, and must possess all the perfections of that which it gives being to. What visible creature is there which possesses the perfections of the whole world? If therefore an invisible creature made the world, the same inquiries will return whence that creature had its being? for he could not make himself. If any creature did create the world, he must do it by the strength and virtue of another, which first gave him being, and this is God. For whatsoever hath its existence and virtue of acting from another, is not God. If it hath its virtue from another, it is then a second cause, and so supposeth a first cause. It must have some cause of itself, or be eternally existent. If eternally existent, it is not a second cause, but God; if not eternally existent, we must come to something at length which was the cause of it, or else be bewildered without being able to give an account of anything. We must come at last to an infinite, eternal, independent Being, that was the first cause of this structure and fabric wherein we and all creatures dwell. The Scripture proclaims this aloud, " I am the Lord and there is none else : I form the light, and I create darkness."[m] Man, the noblest creature, cannot of himself make a man, the chiefest part of the world. If our parents only, without a superior power, made our bodies or souls, they would know the frame of them; as he that makes a lock knows the wards of it; he that makes any curious piece of arras, knows how he sets the various colors together, and how many threads went to each division in the web; he that makes a watch, having the idea of the whole work in his mind, knows the motions of it, and the reason of those motions. But both parents and children are equally ignorant of the nature of their souls and bodies, and of the reason of their motions. God only, that had the supreme hand in forming us, in whose " book all our members are written, which in continuance were fashioned,"[n] knows what we all are ignorant of. If man hath in an ordinary course of generation his being chiefly from a higher cause than his parents, the world then certainly had its being from some infinitely wise intelligent Being, which is God. If it were, as some fancy, made by an assembly of atoms, there must be some infinite intelligent cause that made them, some cause that separated them, some cause that mingled them together for the piling up so comely a structure as the world. It is the most absurd thing to think they should meet together by hazard, and rank themselves in that order we see, without a higher and a wise agent. So that no creature could make the world. For supposing any creature was formed before this visible world, and might have a hand in disposing things, yet he must have a cause of himself, and must act by the virtue and strength of another, and this is God.

IV. From hence it follows, that there is a first cause of things, which we call God. There must be something supreme in the order of nature, something which is greater than all, which hath nothing beyond it or above it, otherwise we must run *in infinitum.* We see not a river, but we conclude a fountain; a watch, but we conclude an artificer. As all number begins from unity, so all the multitude of things in the world begins from some unity, oneness as the principle of it. It is natural to arise from a view of those things, to the conception of a nature more perfect than any. As from heat mixed with cold, and light mixed with darkness, men conceive and arise in their understandings to an intense heat and a pure light; and from a corporeal or bodily substance joined with an incorporeal, (as man is an earthly body and a spiritual soul,) we ascend to a conception of a substance purely incorporeal and spiritual: so from a multitude of things in the world, reason leads us to one choice being above all. And since in all natures in the world, we still find a superior nature; the nature of one beast, above the nature of another; the nature of man above the nature of beasts; and some invisible nature, the worker of strange effects in the air and earth, which cannot be ascribed to any visible cause, we must suppose some nature above all those, of unconceivable perfection.

Every skeptic, one that doubts whether there be anything real or no in the world, that counts everything an appearance, must necessarily own a first cause.[o] They cannot reasonably doubt, but that there is some first cause which makes the things appear so to them. They cannot be the cause of their own appearance. For as nothing can have a being from itself, so nothing can appear by itself and its own force. Nothing can be and not be at the same time. But that which is not and yet seems to be; if it be the cause why it seems to be what it is not, it may be said to be and not to be. But certainly such persons must think themselves to exist. If they do not, they cannot think; and if they do exist, they must have some cause of that existence. So that which way soever we turn ourselves, we must in reason own a first cause of the world. Well then might the Psalmist term an atheist a fool, that disowns a God against his own reason. Without owning a God as the first cause of the world, no man can give any tolerable or satisfactory account of the world to his own reason. And this first cause,

1. Must necessarily exist. It is necessary that He by whom all things are, should be before all things, and nothing before him.[p] And if nothing be before him, he comes not from any other; and then he always was, and without beginning. He is from himself; not that he once was not, but because he hath not his existence from another, and therefore of necessity he did exist from all eternity. Nothing can make itself, or bring itself into being; therefore there must be some being which hath no cause, that depends upon no other, never was produced by any other, but was what he is from eternity, and cannot be otherwise; and is not what he is by will, but nature, necessarily existing, and always existing without any capacity or possibility ever not to be.

2. Must be infinitely perfect. Since man knows he is an imperfect being, he must suppose the perfections he wants are seated in some

o Coccei sum. Theol. c. 8. § 33, &c.   p Petav. Theol. Dog. Tom. I. lib. i. c. 2. p. 10, 11.

other being which hath limited him, and upon which he depends. Whatsoever we conceive of excellency or perfection, must be in God. For we can conceive no perfection but what God hath given us a power to conceive. And he that gave us a power to conceive a transcendent perfection above whatever we saw or heard of, hath much more in himself; else he could not give us such a conception.

Secondly, As the production of the world, so the harmony of all the parts of it declare the being and wisdom of a God. Without the acknowledging God, the atheist can give no account of those things. The multitude, elegancy, variety, and beauty of all things are steps whereby to ascend to one fountain and original of them. Is it not a folly to deny the being of a wise agent, who sparkles in the beauty and motions of the heavens, rides upon the wings of the wind, and is writ upon the flowers and fruits of plants? As the cause is known by the effects, so the wisdom of the cause is known by the elegancy of the work, the proportion of the parts to one another. Who can imagine the world could be rashly made, and without consultation, which, in every part of it, is so artificially framed? No work of art springs up of its own accord.[q] The world is framed by an excellent art, and, therefore, made by some skilful artist. As we hear not a melodious instrument, but we conclude there is a musician that touches it, as well as some skilful hand that framed and disposed it for those lessons; and no man that hears the pleasant sound of a lute but will fix his thoughts, not upon the instrument itself, but upon the skill of the artist that made it, and the art of the musician that strikes it, though he should not see the first, when he saw the lute, nor see the other, when he hears the harmony : so a rational creature confines not his thoughts to his sense when he sees the sun in its glory, and the moon walking in its brightness; but riseth up in a contemplation and admiration of that Infinite Spirit that composed, and filled them with such sweetness. This appears,

1. In the linking contrary qualities together. All things are compounded of the elements. Those are endued with contrary qualities, dryness and moisture, heat and cold. These would always be contending with and infesting one another's rights, till the contest ended in the destruction of one or both. Where fire is predominant, it would suck up the water; where water is prevalent, it would quench the fire. The heat would wholly expel the cold, or the cold overpower the heat; yet we see them chained and linked one within another in every body upon the earth, and rendering mutual offices for the benefit of that body wherein they are seated, and all conspiring together in their particular quarrels for the public interest of the body. How could those contraries, that of themselves observe no order, that are always preying upon one another, jointly accord together of themselves, for one common end, if they were not linked in a common band, and reduced to that order by some incomprehensible wisdom and power, which keeps a hand upon them, orders their motions and directs their events, and makes them friendly pass into one another's natures? Confusion had been the result of the discord and diversity of their natures; no composition could have been of

q Philo. Judæ. Petav. Theo. Dog. Tom. I. lib. i. c. 1. p. 9.

those conflicting qualities for the frame of any body, nor any harmony arose from so many jarring strings, if they had not been reduced into concord by one that is supreme Lord over them, and knows how to dispose their varieties and enmities for the public good. If a man should see a large city or country, consisting of great multitudes of men, of different tempers, full of frauds, and factions, and animosities in their natures against one another, yet living together in good order and peace, without oppressing and invading one another, and joining together for the public good, he would presently conclude there were some excellent governor, who tempered them by his wisdom, and preserved the public peace, though he had never yet beheld him with his eye.[r] It is as necessary to conclude a God, who moderates the contrarieties in the world, as to conclude a wise prince who overrules the contrary dispositions in a state, making every one to keep his own bounds and confines. Things that are contrary to one another subsist in an admirable order.

2. In the subserviency of one thing to another. All the members of living creatures are curiously fitted for the service of one another, destined to a particular end, and endued with a virtue to attain that end, and so distinctly placed, that one is no hindrance to the other in its operations.[s] Is not this more admirable than to be the work of chance, which is incapable to settle such an order, and fix particular and general ends, causing an exact correspondency of all the parts with one another, and every part to conspire together for one common end? One thing is fitted for another. The eye is fitted for the sun, and the sun fitted for the eye. Several sorts of food are fitted for several creatures, and those creatures fitted with organs for the partaking that food.

(1.) Subserviency of heavenly bodies. The sun, the heart of the world, is not for itself, but for the good of the world, as the heart of man is for the good of the body.[t] How conveniently is the sun placed, at a distance from the earth, and the upper heavens, to enlighten the stars above, and enliven the earth below! If it were either higher or lower, one part would want its influences. It is not in the higher parts of the heavens; the earth, then, which lives and fructifies by its influence would have been exposed to a perpetual winter and chillness, unable to have produced anything for the sustenance of man or beast. If seated lower, the earth had been parched up, the world made uninhabitable, and long since had been consumed to ashes by the strength of its heat. Consider the motion, as well as the situation of the sun. Had it stood still, one part of the world had been cherished by its beams, and the other left in a desolate widowhood, in a disconsolate darkness. Besides, the earth would have had no shelter from its perpendicular beams striking perpetually, and without any remission, upon it. The same incommodities would have followed upon its fixedness as upon its too great nearness. By a constant day, the beauty of the stars had been obscured, the knowledge of their motions been prevented, and a considerable part of the glorious wisdom of the Creator, in those choice " works of his

[r] Athanasius Petav. Theol. Dog. Tom. I. lib. i. c. 1. p. 4, 5.
[s] Gassend. Physic § 1. lib. iv. c. 2. p. 315.   [t] Lessius.

fingers,"[u] had been veiled from our eyes. It moves in a fixed line,
visits all parts of the earth, scatters in the day its refreshing blessings
in every creek of the earth, and removes the mask from the other
beauties of heaven in the night, which sparkle out to the glory of
the Creator. It spreads its light, warms the earth, cherisheth the
seeds, excites the spirit in the earth, and brings fruit to maturity.
View also the air, the vast extent between heaven and earth, which
serves for a water-course, a cistern for water, to bedew the face of
the sun-burnt earth, to satisfy the desolate ground, and to cause the
" bud of the tender herb to spring forth."[x]   Could chance appoint
the clouds of the air to interpose as fans between the scorching heat
of the sun, and the faint bodies of the creatures?   Can that be the
" father of the rain, or beget the drops of dew?"[y]   Could anything
so blind settle those ordinances of heaven for the preservation of
creatures on the earth?   Can this either bring or stay the bottles of
heaven, when the " dust grows into hardness, and the clouds cleave
fast together?"[z]

(2.) Subserviency of the lower world, the earth, and sea, which
was created to be inhabited, (Isa. xlv. 18.) The sea affords water to
the rivers, the rivers, like so many veins, are spread through the
whole body of the earth, to refresh and enable it to bring forth fruit
for the sustenance of man and beast, (Ps. civ. 10, 11.)   " He sends
the springs into the valleys, which run among the hills; they give
drink to every beast of the field; the wild asses quench their thirst.
He causes the grass to grow for the cattle, and the herb for the service
of man, that he may bring forth food out of the earth." (ver. 14.)
The trees are provided for shades against the extremity of heat, a
refuge for the panting beasts, an " habitation for birds," wherein to
make their nests (ver. 17), and a basket for their provision. How
are the valleys and mountains of the earth disposed for the pleasure
and profit of man! Every year are the fields covered with harvests
for the nourishing the creatures; no part is baren, but beneficial to
man.   The mountains that are not clothed with grass for his food,
are set with stones to make him an habitation; they have their peculiar services of metals and minerals, for the conveniency and comfort, and benefit of man.   Things which are not fit for his food, are
medicines for his cure, under some painful sickness. Where the
earth brings not forth corn, it brings forth roots for the service of
other creatures. Wood abounds more in those countries where the
cold is stronger than in others. Can this be the result of chance, or
not rather of an Infinite Wisdom? Consider the usefulness of the
sea, for the supply of rivers to refresh the earth: " Which go up
by the mountains and down by the valleys into the place God
hath founded for them" (Ps. civ. 8): a store-house for fish, for the
nourishment of other creatures, a shop of medicines for cure, and
pearls for ornament: the band that ties remote nations together, by
giving opportunity of passage to, and commerce with, one another.
How should that natural inclination of the sea to cover the earth,
submit to this subserviency to the creatures? Who hath pounded
in this fluid mass of water in certain limits, and confined it to its

[u] Ps. viii. 3.   [x] Job xxxviii. 25, 27.   [y] Job xxxviii. 28.   [z] Job xxxviii. 37, 38.

own channel, for the accommodation of such creatures, who, by its common law, can only be upon the earth? Naturally the earth was covered with the deep as with a garment; the waters stood above the mountains. "Who set a bound that they might not pass over,"[a] that they return not again to cover the earth? Was it blind chance or an Infinite Power, that "shut up the sea with doors, and made thick darkness a swaddling band for it, and said, Hitherto shall thou come and no farther, and here shall thy proud waves be stayed?"[b] All things are so ordered, that they are not *propter se,* but *propter aliud.* What advantage accrues to the sun by its unwearied rolling about the world? Doth it increase the perfection of its nature by all its circuits? No; but it serves the inferior world, it impregnates things by its heat. Not the most abject thing but hath its end and use. There is a straight connection: the earth could not bring forth fruit without the heavens; the heavens could not water the earth without vapors from it.

(3.) All this subserviency of creatures centres in man. Other creatures are served by those things, as well as ourselves, and they are provided for their nourishment and refreshment, as well as ours;[c] yet, both they, and all creatures meet in man, as lines in their centres. Things that have no life or sense, are made for those that have both life and sense; and those that have life and sense, are made for those that are endued with reason. When the Psalmist admiringly considers the heavens, moon and stars, he intimates man to be the end for which they were created (Ps. viii. 3, 4): "What is man, that thou art mindful of him?" He expresseth more particularly the dominion that man hath "over the beasts of the field, the fowl of the air, and whatsoever passes through the paths of the sea" (ver. 6–8); and concludes from thence, the "excellency of God's name in all the earth." All things in the world, one way or other, centre in an usefulness for man; some to feed him, some to clothe him, some to delight him, others to instruct him, some to exercise his wit, and others his strength. Since man did not make them, he did not also order them for his own use. If they conspire to serve him who never made them, they direct man to acknowledge another, who is the joint Creator both of the lord and the servants under his dominion; and, therefore, as the inferior natures are ordered by an invisible hand for the good of man, so the nature of man is, by the same hand, ordered to acknowledge the existence and the glory of the Creator of him. This visible order man knows he did not constitute; he did not settle those creatures in subserviency to himself; they were placed in that order before he had any acquaintance with them, or existence of himself; which is a question God puts to Job, to consider of (Job xxxviii. 4): "Where wast thou when I laid the foundation of the earth? declare, if thou hast understanding." All is ordered for man's use; the heavens answer to the earth, as a roof to a floor, both composing a delightful habitation for man; vapors ascend from the earth, and the heaven concocts them, and returns them back in welcome showers for the supplying of the earth.[d] The light

---

[a] Psalm civ. 6, 9.   [b] Job xxxviii. 8, 9, 11.
[c] Amirald. de Trinitate, pp. 13, 18.   [d] Jer. x. 13.

of the sun descends to beautify the earth, and employs its heat to midwife its fruits, and this for the good of the community, whereof man is the head; and though all creatures have distinct natures, and must act for particular ends, according to the law of their creation, yet there is a joint combination for the good of the whole, as the common end; just as all the rivers in the world, from what part soever they come, whether north or south, fall into the sea, for the supply of that mass of waters, which loudly proclaims some infinitely wise nature, who made those things in so exact an harmony. " As in a clock, the hammer which strikes the bell leads us to the next wheel, that to another, the little wheel to a greater, whence it derives its motion, this at last to the spring, which acquaints us that there was·some artist that framed them in this subordination to one another for this orderly motion."[e]

(4.) This order or subserviency is regular and uniform; everything is determined to its particular nature.[f] The sun and moon make day and night, months and years, determine the seasons, never are defective in coming back to their station and place; they wander not from their roads, shock not against one another, nor hinder one another in the functions assigned them.   From a small grain or seed, a tree springs, with body, root, bark, leaves, fruit of the same shape, figure, smell, taste; that there should be as many parts in one, as in all of the same kind, and no more; and that in the womb of a sensitive creature should be formed one of the same kind, with all the due members, and no more; and the creature that produceth it knows not how it is formed, or how it is perfected.   If we say this is nature, this nature is an intelligent being; if not, how can it direct all causes to such uniform ends? if it be intelligent, this nature must be the same we call God, " who ordered every herb to yield seed, and every fruit tree to yield fruit after its kind, and also every beast, and every creeping thing after its kind." (Gen. i. 11, 12, 24.)   And everything is determined to its particular season; the sap riseth from the root at its appointed time, enlivening and clothing the branches with a new garment at such a time of the sun's returning, not wholly hindered by any accidental coldness of the weather, it being often colder at its return, than it was at the sun's departure.   All things have their seasons of flourishing, budding, blossoming, bringing forth fruit; they ripen in their seasons, cast their leaves at the same time, throw off their old clothes, and in the spring appear with new garments, but still in the same fashion.   The winds and the rain have their seasons, and seem to be administered by laws for the profit of man.[g]   No satisfactory cause of those things can be ascribed to the earth, the sea, or the air, or stars.   " Can any understand the spreading of his clouds, or the noise of his tabernacle ?" (Job xxxviii 29.) The natural reason of those things cannot be demonstrated, without recourse to an infinite and intelligent being; nothing can be rendered capable of the direction of those things but a God.

This regularity in plants and animals is in all nations.   The heavens have the same motion in all parts of the world; all men have the same law of nature in their mind; all creatures are stamped

---

* Morn. de Verit. c. 1. p. 7.   f Amirant.   g Coccei. sum. Theol. c. 8. § 77.

with the same law of creation. In all parts the same creatures serve for the same use; and though there be different creatures in India and Europe, yet they have the same subordination, the same subserviency to one another, and ultimately to man; which shows that there is a God, and but one God, who tunes all those different strings to the same notes in all places. Is it nature merely conducts these natural causes in due measure to their proper effects, without interfering with one another? Can mere nature be the cause of those musical proportions of time? You may as well conceive a lute to sound its own strings without the hand of an artist; a city well governed without a governor; an army keep its stations without a general, as imagine so exact an order without an orderer. Would any man, when he hears a clock strike, by fit intervals, the hour of the day, imagine this regularity in it without the direction of one that had understanding to manage it? He would not only regard the motion of the clock, but commend the diligence of the clock-keeper.

(5.) This order and subserviency is constant. Children change the customs and manners of their fathers; magistrates change the laws they have received from their ancestors, and enact new ones in their room: but in the world all things consist as they were created at the beginning; the law of nature in the creatures hath met with no change. Who can behold the sun rising in the morning, the moon shining in the night, increasing and decreasing in its due spaces, the stars in their regular motions night after night, for all ages, and yet deny a President over them?[h] And this motion of the heavenly bodies, being contrary to the nature of other creatures, who move in order to rest, must be from some higher cause. But those, ever since the settling in their places, have been perpetually rounding the world. What nature, but one powerful and intelligent, could give that perpetual motion to the sun,[i] which being bigger than the earth a hundred sixty-six times, runs many thousand miles with a mighty swiftness in the space of an hour, with an unwearied diligence performing its daily task, and, as a strong man, rejoicing to run its race, for above five thousand years together, without intermission, but in the time of Joshua?[k] It is not nature's sun, but God's sun, which he " makes to rise upon the just and unjust."[l] So a plant receives its nourishment from the earth, sends forth the juice to every branch, forms a bud which spreads it into a blossom and flower; the leaves of this drop off, and leave a fruit of the same color and taste, every year, which, being ripened by the sun, leaves seeds behind it for the propagation of its like, which contains in the nature of it the same kind of buds, blossoms, fruit, which were before; and being nourished in the womb of the earth, and quickened by the power of the sun, discovers itself at length, in all the progresses and motions which its predecessor did. Thus in all ages, in all places, every year it performs the same task, spins out fruit of the same color, taste, virtue, to refresh the several creatures for which they are provided.

[h] Petav. ex Athanas. Theol. Dog. Tom. I. lib. i. c. 1. § 4.   [i] Whether it be the sun or the earth that moves, it is all one. Whence have either of them this constant and uniform motion?   [k] Josh. x. 13   [l] Matt. v. 45.

This settled state of things comes from that God who laid the "foundations of the earth," that it should "not be removed" forever;[m] and set "ordinances for them" to act by a stated law;[n] according to which they move as if they understood themselves to have made a covenant with their Creator.[o]

3. Add to this union of contrary qualities, and the subserviency of one thing to another, the admirable variety and diversity of things in the world. What variety of metals, living creatures, plants! what variety and distinction in the shape of their leaves, flowers, smell, resulting from them! Who can number up the several sorts of beasts on the earth, birds in the air, fish in the sea? How various are their motions! Some creep, some go, some fly, some swim; and in all this variety each creature hath organs or members, fitted for their peculiar motion. If you consider the multitude of stars, which shine like jewels in the heavens, their different magnitudes, or the variety of colors in the flowers and tapestry of the earth, you could no more conclude they made themselves, or were made by chance, than you can imagine a piece of arras, with a diversity of figures and colors, either wove itself, or were knit together by hazard.

How delicious is the sap of the vine, when turned into wine, above that of a crab! Both have the same womb of earth to conceive them, both agree in the nature of wood and twigs, as channels to convey it into fruit. What is that which makes the one so sweet, the other so sour, or makes that sweet which was a few weeks before unpleasantly sharp? Is it the earth? No: they both have the same soil; the branches may touch each other; the strings of their roots may, under ground, entwine about one another. Is it the sun? both have the same beams. Why is not the taste and color of the one as gratifying as the other? Is it the root? the taste of that is far different from that of the fruit it bears. Why do they not, when they have the same soil, the same sun, and stand near one another, borrow something from one another's natures? No reason can be rendered, but that there is a God of infinite wisdom hath determined this variety, and bound up the nature of each creature within itself. "Everything follows the law of its creation; and it is worthy observation, that the Creator of them hath not given that power to animals, which arise from different species, to propagate the like to themselves; as mules, that arise from different species. No reason can be rendered of this, but the fixed determination of the Creator, that those species which were created by him should not be lost in those mixtures which are contrary to the law of the creation?[p] This cannot possibly be ascribed to that which is commonly called nature, but unto the God of nature, who will not have his creatures exceed their bounds or come short of them.

Now since among those varieties there are some things better than other, yet all are good in their kind, and partake of goodness,[q] there must be something better and more excellent than all those, from whom they derive that goodness, which inheres in their nature and is communicated by them to others: and this excellent Being must

m Psalm civ. 5.   n Job xxxviii. 33.   o Jer. xxxiii. 20.
p Amirald. de Trinitate, p. 21.   q Gen. i. 31.

inherit, in an eminent way in his own nature, the goodness of all those varieties, since they made not themselves, but were made by another. All that goodness which is scattered in those varieties must be infinitely concentered in that nature, which distributed those various perfections to them (Ps. xciv. 9): "He that planted the ear, shall not he hear; he that formed the eye, shall not he see; he that teacheth man knowledge, shall not he know?" The Creator is greater than the creature, and whatsoever is in his effects, is but an impression of some excellency in himself: there is, therefore, some chief fountain of goodness whence all those various goodnesses in the world do flow.

From all this it follows, if there be an order, and harmony, there must be an Orderer: one that "made the earth by his power, established the world by his wisdom, and stretched out the heavens by his discretion" (Jer. x. 12). Order being the effect, cannot be the cause of itself: order is the disposition of things to an end, and is not intelligent, but implies an intelligent Orderer; and, therefore, it is as certain that there is a God, as it is certain there is order in the world. Order is an effect of reason and counsel; this reason and counsel must have its residence in some being before this order was fixed: the things ordered are always distinct from that reason and counsel whereby they are ordered, and also after it, as the effect is after the cause. No man begins a piece of work but he hath the model of it in his own mind: no man builds a house, or makes a watch, but he hath the idea or copy of it in his own head. This beautiful world bespeaks an idea of it, or a model: since there is such a magnificent wisdom in the make of each creature, and the proportion of one creature to another, this model must be before the world, as the pattern is always before the thing that is wrought by it. This, therefore, must be in some intelligent and wise agent, and this is God. Since the reason of those things exceed the reason and all the art of man, who can ascribe them to any inferior cause? Chance it could not be; the motions of chance are not constant, and at set seasons, as the motions of creatures are. That which is by chance is contingent, this is necessary; uniformity can never be the birth of chance. Who can imagine that all the parts of a watch can meet together and put themselves in order and motion by chance? "Nor can it be nature only, which indeed is a disposition of second causes. If nature hath not an understanding, it cannot work such effects. If nature therefore uses counsel to begin a thing, reason to dispose it, art to effect it, virtue to complete it, and power to govern it, why should it be called nature rather than God?"[r] Nothing so sure as that which hath an end to which it tends, hath a cause by which it is ordered to that end. Since therefore all things are ordered in subserviency to the good of man, they are so ordered by Him that made both man and them; and man must acknowledge the wisdom and goodness of his Creator, and act in subserviency to his glory, as other creatures act in subserviency to his good. Sensible objects were not made only to gratify the sense of man, but to hand something to his mind as he is a rational creature: to discover God to

[r] Lactant.

him as an object of love and desire to be enjoyed. If this be not the effect of it, the order of the creature, as to such an one, is in vain, and falls short of its true end.[s]

To conclude this: As when a man comes into a palace, built according to the exactest rule of art, and with an unexceptionable conveniency for the inhabitants, he would acknowledge both the being and skill of the builder; so whosoever shall observe the disposition of all the parts of the world, their connection, comeliness, the variety of seasons, the swarms of different creatures, and the mutual offices they render to one another, cannot conclude less, than that it was contrived by an infinite skill, effected by infinite power, and governed by infinite wisdom. None can imagine a ship to be orderly conducted without a pilot; nor the parts of the world to perform their several functions without a wise guide; considering the members of the body cannot perform theirs, without the active presence of the soul. The atheist, then, is a fool to deny that which every creature in his constitution asserts, and thereby renders himself unable to give a satisfactory account of that constant uniformity in the motions of the creatures.

Thirdly, As the production and harmony, so particular creatures, pursuing and attaining their ends, manifest that there is a God. All particular creatures have natural instincts, which move them for some end. The intending of an end is a property of a rational creature; since the lower creatures cannot challenge that title, they must act by the understanding and direction of another; and since man cannot challenge the honor of inspiring the creatures with such instincts, it must be ascribed to some nature infinitely above any creature in understanding. No creature doth determine itself. Why do the fruits and grain of the earth nourish us, when the earth which instrumentally gives them that fitness, cannot nourish us, but because their several ends are determined by one higher than the world?

1. Several creatures have several natures. How soon will all creatures, as soon as they see the light, move to that whereby they must live, and make use of the natural arms God hath given their kind, for their defence, before they are grown to any maturity to afford them that defence! The Scripture makes the appetite of infants to their milk a foundation of the divine glory, (Ps. viii. 3), "Out of the mouths of babes and sucklings hast thou ordained strength;" that is, matter of praise and acknowledgment of God, in the natural appetite they have to their milk and their relish of it. All creatures have a natural affection to their young ones; all young ones by a natural instinct, move to, and receive the nourishment that is proper for them; some are their own physicians, as well as their own caterers, and naturally discern what preserves them in life, and what restores them when sick. The swallow flies to its celandine, and the toad hastens to its plantain. Can we behold the spider's nets, or silkworm's web, the bee's closets, or the ant's granaries, without acknowledging a higher being than a creature who hath planted that genius in them? The consideration of the nature of several creatures God commended to Job, (chap. xxxix., where he discour-

* Coccei. sum. Theol. c. 8. § 63, 64.

seth to Job of the natural instincts of the goat, the ostrich, horse, and eagle, &c.) to persuade him to the acknowledgment and admiration of God, and humiliation of himself. The spider, as if it understood the art of weaving, fits its web both for its own habitation, and a net to catch its prey. The bee builds a cell which serves for chambers to reside in, and a repository for its provision. Birds are observed to build their nests with a clammy matter without, for the firmer duration of it, and with a soft moss and down within, for the conveniency and warmth of their young. "The stork knows his appointed time," (Jer. viii. 7), and the swallows observe the time of their coming; they go and return according to the seasons of the year; this they gain not by consideration, it descends to them with their nature; they neither gain nor increase it by rational deductions. It is not in vain to speak of these. How little do we improve by meditation those objects which daily offer themselves to our view, full of instructions for us! And our Saviour sends his disciples to spell God in the lilies.[t] It is observed also, that the creatures offensive to man go single; if they went by troops, they would bring destruction upon man and beast; this is the nature of them, for the preservation of others.

2. They know not their end. They have a law in their natures, but have no rational understanding, either of the end to which they are appointed, or the means fit to attain it; they naturally do what they do, and move by no counsel of their own, but by a law impressed by some higher hand upon their natures. What plant knows why it strikes its root into the earth? doth it understand what storms it is to contest with? Or why it shoots up its branches towards heaven? doth it know it needs the droppings of the clouds to preserve itself, and make it fruitful? These are acts of understanding; the root is downward to preserve its own standing, the branches upward to preserve other creatures; this understanding is not in the creature itself, but originally in another. Thunders and tempests know not why they are sent; yet by the direction of a mighty hand, they are instruments of justice upon a wicked world. Rational creatures that act for some end, and know the end they aim at, yet know not the manner of the natural motion of the members to it.[u] When we intend to look upon a thing, we take no counsel about the natural motion of our eyes, we know not all the principles of their operations, or how that dull matter whereof our bodies are composed, is subject to the order of our minds. We are not of counsel with our stomachs about the concoction of our meat, or the distribution of the nourishing juice to the several parts of the body.[x] Neither the mother nor the fœtus sit in council how the formation should be made in the womb. We know no more than a plant knows what stature it is of, and what medicinal virtue its fruit hath for the good of man; yet all those natural operations are perfectly directed to their proper end, by an higher wisdom than any human understanding is able to conceive, since they exceed the ability of an inanimate or fleshly nature, yea, and the wisdom of a man. Do we not often

[t] Matt. vi. 28. [u] Coccei. sum. Theolog. c. 8. § 67, &c.
[x] Peirson on the Creed, p. 35.

see reasonable creatures acting for one end, and perfecting a higher than what they aimed at or could suspect? When Joseph's brethren sold him for a slave, their end was to be rid of an informer;[y] but the action issued in preparing him to be the preserver of them and their families. Cyrus's end was to be a conqueror, but the action ended in being the Jews' deliverer (Prov. xvi. 9). "A man's heart deviseth his way, but the Lord directs his steps."

3. Therefore there is some superior understanding and nature which so acts them. That which acts for an end unknown to itself, depends upon some overruling wisdom that knows that end. Who should direct them in all those ends, but He that bestowed a being upon them for those ends; who knows what is convenient for their life, security and propagation of their natures?[z] An exact knowledge is necessary both of what is agreeable to them, and the means whereby they must attain it, which, since it is not inherent in them, is in that wise God, who puts those instincts into them, and governs them in the exercise of them to such ends. Any man that sees a dart flung, knows it cannot hit the mark without the skill and strength of an archer; or he that sees the hand of a dial pointing to the hours successively, knows that the dial is ignorant of its own end, and is disposed and directed in that motion by another. All creatures ignorant of their own natures, could not universally in the whole kind, and in every climate and country, without any difference in the whole world, tend to a certain end, if some overruling wisdom did not preside over the world and guide them: and if the creatures have a Conductor, they have a Creator; all things are "turned round about by his counsel, that they may do whatsoever he commands them, upon the face of the world in the earth."[a] So that in this respect the folly of atheism appears. Without the owning a God, no account can be given of those actions of creatures, that are an imitation of reason. To say the bees, &c. are rational, is to equal them to man: nay, make them his superiors, since they do more by nature than the wisest man can do by art: it is their own counsel whereby they act, or another's; if it be their own, they are reasonable creatures; if by another's, it is not mere nature that is necessary; then other creatures would not be without the same skill, there would be no difference among them. If nature be restrained by another, it hath a superior; if not, it is a free agent; it is an understanding Being that directs them; and then it is something superior to all creatures in the world; and by this, therefore, we may ascend to the acknowledgment of the necessity of a God.

Fourthly. Add to the production and order of the world and the creatures acting for their end, the preservation of them. Nothing can depend upon itself in its preservation, no more than it could in its being. If the order of the world was not fixed by itself, the preservation of that order cannot be continued by itself. Though the matter of the world after creation cannot return to that nothing whence it was fetched, without the power of God that made it, (because the same power is as requisite to reduce a thing to nothing as to raise a thing from nothing,) yet without the actual exerting of a

[y] Genn. xxxvii.   [z] Lessius de Providen. lib. i. p. 652.   [a] Job xxxvii. 12.

power that made the creatures, they would fall into confusion. Those contesting qualities which are in every part of it, could not have preserved, but would have consumed, and extinguished one another, and reduced the world to that confused chaos, wherein it was before the Spirit moved upon the waters: as contrary parts could not have met together in one form, unless there had been one that had conjoined them; so they could not have kept together after their conjunction unless the same hand had preserved them. Natural contrarieties cannot be reconciled. It is as great power to keep discords knit, as at first to link them. Who would doubt but that an army made up of several nations and humors, would fall into a civil war and sheathe their swords in one another's bowels, if they were not under the management of some wise general; or a ship dash against the rocks without the skill of a pilot? As the body hath neither life nor motion without the active presence of the soul, which distributes to every part the virtue of acting, sets every one in the exercise of its proper function, and resides in every part; so there is some powerful cause which doth the like in the world, that rules and tempers it.[b] There is need of the same power and action to preserve a thing, as there was at first to make it. When we consider that we are preserved, and know that we could not preserve ourselves, we must necessarily run to some first cause which doth preserve us. All works of art depend upon nature, and are preserved while they are kept by the force of nature, as a statue depends upon the matter whereof it is made, whether stone or brass; this nature, therefore, must have some superior by whose influx it is preserved. Since, therefore, we see a stable order in the things of the world, that they conspire together for the good and beauty of the universe; that they depend upon one another; there must be some principle upon which they do depend; something to which the first link of the chain is fastened, which himself depends upon no superior, but wholly rests in his own essence and being. It is the title of God to be the "Preserver of man and beast."[c] The Psalmist elegantly describeth it, (Psalm civ. 24, &c.) "The earth is full of his riches: all wait upon him, that he may give them their meat in due season. When he opens his hand, he fills them with good; when he hides his face they are troubled; if he take away their breath, they die, and return to dust. He sends forth his Spirit, and they are created, and renews the face of the earth. The glory of the Lord shall endure forever; and the Lord shall rejoice in his works." Upon the consideration of all which, the Psalmist (ver. 34) takes a pleasure in the meditation of God as the cause and manager of all those things; which issues into a joy in God, and a praising of him. And why should not the consideration of the power and wisdom of God in the creatures produce the same effect in the hearts of us, if he be our God? Or, as some render it, "My meditation shall be sweet," or acceptable *to* him, whereby I find matter of praise in the things of the world, and offer it to the Creator of it.

Reason III. It is a folly to deny that which a man's own nature witnesseth to him. The whole frame of bodies and souls bears the

---

[b] Gassend. Phys. § 6. lib. iv. c. 2. p. 101.   [c] Psalm xxxvi. 6.

impress of the infinite power and wisdom of the Creator: a body
framed with an admirable architecture, a soul endowed with understanding, will, judgment, memory, imagination. Man is the epitome
of the world, contains in himself the substance of all natures, and the
fulness of the whole universe; not only in regard of the universal-
ness of his knowledge, whereby he comprehends the reasons of many
things; but as all the perfections of the several natures of the world
are gathered and united in man, for the perfection of his own, in a
smaller volume. In his soul he partakes of heaven; in his body of
the earth. There is the life of plants, the sense of beasts, and the
intellectual nature of angels. "The Lord breathed into his nostril
the breath of life, and man,"[d] &c.: חיים, *of lives.* Not one sort of
lives, but several; not only an *animal,* but a *rational* life; a soul of
a nobler extract and nature, than what was given to other creatures.
So that we need not step out of doors, or cast our eyes any further
than ourselves, to behold a God. He shines in the capacity of our
souls, and the vigor of our members. We must fly from ourselves,
and be stripped of our own humanity, before we can put off the
notion of a Deity. He that is ignorant of the existence of God, must
be possessed of so much folly, as to be ignorant of his own make
and frame.

1. In the parts whereof he doth consist, body and soul.

First, Take a prospect of the body. The Psalmist counts it a
matter of praise and admiration (Psalm cxxxix. 15, 16): "I will
praise thee, for I am fearfully and wonderfully made. When I was
made in secret, and curiously wrought in the lowest parts of the
earth, in thy book all my members were written." The scheme of
man and every member was drawn in his book. All the sinews,
veins, arteries, bones, like a piece of embroidery or tapestry, were
wrought by God, as it were, with deliberation; like an artificer, that
draws out the model of what he is to do in writing, and sets it before
him when he begins his work. And, indeed, the fabric of man's
body, as well as his soul, is an argument for a Divinity. The artificial structure of it, the elegancy of every part, the proper situation
of them, their proportion one to another, the fitness for their several
functions, drew from Galen[e] (a heathen, and one that had no raised
sentiments of a Deity) a confession of the admirable wisdom and
power of the Creator, and that none but God could frame it.

1. In the order, fitness, and usefulness of every part. The whole
model of the body is grounded upon reason. Every member hath
its exact proportion, distinct office, regular motion. Every part
hath a particular comeliness, and convenient temperament bestowed
upon it, according to its place in the body. The heart is hot, to enliven the whole; the eye clear, to take in objects to present them to
the soul. Every member is presented for its peculiar service and
action. Some are for sense, some for motion, some for preparing,
and others for dispensing nourishment to the several parts: they
mutually depend upon and serve one another. What small strings
fasten the particular members together, "as the earth, that hangs

---

[d] Gen. ii. 7.

[e] Lib. iii. de Usu. Partium. Petav. Theol. Dog. Tom. I. lib. i. c. 1. p. 6.

upon nothing!"[f] Take but one part away, and you either destroy the whole, or stamp upon it some mark of deformity. All are knit together by an admirable symmetry; all orderly perform their functions, as acting by a settled law; none swerving from their rule, but in case of some predominant humor. And none of them, in so great a multitude of parts, stifled in so little a room, or jostling against one another, to hinder their mutual actions; none can be better disposed. And the greatest wisdom of man could not imagine it, till his eyes present them with the sight and connection of one part and member with another.

(1.) The heart.[g] How strongly it is guarded with ribs like a wall, that it might not be easily hurt! It draws blood from the liver, through a channel made for that purpose; rarefies it, and makes it fit to pass through the arteries and veins, and to carry heat and life to every part of the body: and by a perpetual motion, it sucks in the blood, and spouts it out again; which motion depends not upon the command of the soul, but is pure natural.

(2.) The mouth takes in the meat, the teeth grind it for the stomach, the stomach prepares it, nature strains it through the milky veins, the liver refines it, and mints it into blood, separates the purer from the drossy parts, which go to the heart, circuits through the whole body, running through the veins, like rivers through so many channels of the world, for the watering of the several parts; which are framed of a thin skin for the straining the blood through, for the supply of the members of the body, and framed with several valves or doors, for the thrusting the blood forwards to perform its circular motion.

(3.) The brain, fortified by a strong skull, to hinder outward accidents, a tough membrane or skin, to hinder any oppression by the skull; the seat of sense, that which coins the animal spirits, by purifying and refining those which are sent to it, and seems like a curious piece of needlework.

(4.) The ear, framed with windings and turnings, to keep any thing from entering to offend the brain; so disposed as to admit sounds with the greatest safety and delight; filled with an air within, by the motion whereof the sound is transmitted to the brain:[h] as sounds are made in the air by diffusing themselves, as you see circles made in the water by the flinging in a stone. This is the gate of knowledge, whereby we hear the oracles of God, and the instruction of men for arts. It is by this they are exposed to the mind, and the mind of another man framed in our understandings.

(5.) What a curious workmanship is that of the eye, which is in the body, as the sun in the world; set in the head as in a watch-tower, having the softest nerves for the receiving the greater multitude of spirits necessary for the act of vision! How is it provided with defence, by the variety of coats to secure and accommodate the little humor and part whereby the vision is made! Made of a round figure, and convex, as most commodious to receive the species of objects; shaded by the eyebrows and eyelids; secured by the eyelids, which are its ornament and safety, which refresh it when it is

[f] Job xxvi. 7. [g] Theod. de Providen. Orat. 3. [h] Eccles. xii. 4.

too much dried by heat, hinder too much light from insinuating itself into it to offend it, cleanse it from impurities, by their quick motion preserve it from any invasion, and by contraction confer to the more evident discerning of things. Both the eyes seated in the hollow of the bone for security, yet standing out, that things may be perceived more easily on both sides. And this little member can behold the earth, and in a moment view things as high as heaven.

(6.) The tongue for speech framed like a musical instrument; the teeth serving for variety of sounds; the lungs serving for bellows to blow the organs as it were, to cool the heart, by a continual motion transmitting a pure air to the heart, expelling that which was smoky and superfluous.[i] It is by the tongue that communication of truth hath a passage among men; it opens the sense of the mind; there would be no converse and commerce without it. Speech among all nations hath an elegancy and attractive force, mastering the affections of men. Not to speak of other parts, or of the multitude of spirits that act every part; the quick flight of them where there is a necessity of their presence. Solomon (Eccles. xii.) makes an elegant description of them, in his speech of old age; and Job speaks of this formation of the body (Job x. 9–11), &c. Not the least part of the body is made in vain. The hairs of the head have their use, as well as are an ornament. The whole symmetry of the body is a ravishing object. Every member hath a signature and mark of God and his wisdom. He is visible in the formation of the members, the beauty of the parts, and the vigor of the body. This structure could not be from the body; that only hath a passive power, and cannot act in the absence of the soul. Nor can it be from the soul. How comes it then to be so ignorant of the manner of its formation? The soul knows not the internal parts of its own body, but by information from others, or inspection into other bodies. It knows less of the inward frame of the body than it doth of itself; but he that makes the clock can tell the number and motions of the wheels within, as well as what figures are without.

This short discourse is *useful* to raise our admirations of the wisdom of God, as well as to demonstrate that there is an infinite wise Creator; and the consideration of ourselves every day, and the wisdom of God in our frame, would maintain religion much in the world; since all are so framed that no man can tell any error in the constitution of him. If thus the body of man is fitted for the service of his soul by an infinite God, the body ought to be ordered for the service of this God, and in obedience to him.

2. In the admirable difference of the features of men; which is a great argument that the world was made by a wise Being. This could not be wrought by chance, or be the work of mere nature, since we find never, or very rarely, two persons exactly alike. This distinction is a part of infinite wisdom; otherwise what confusion would be introduced into the world? Without this, parents could not know their children, nor children their parents, nor a brother his sister, nor a subject his magistrate. Without it there had been no comfort of relations, no government, no commerce. Debtors

---

[i] Coccei. sum. Theol. c. 8. § 49.

would not have been known from strangers, nor good men from bad. Propriety could not have been preserved, nor justice executed; the innocent might have been apprehended for the nocent; wickedness could not have been stopped by any law. The faces of men are the same for parts, not for features, a dissimilitude in a likeness. Man, like to all the rest in the world, yet unlike to any, and differenced by some mark from all, which is not to be observed in any other species of creatures. This speaks some wise agent which framed man; since, for the preservation of human society and order in the world, this distinction was necessary.

Secondly, As man's own nature witnesseth a God to him in the structure of his body, so also "in the nature of his soul."[k] We know that we have an understanding in us; a substance we cannot see, but we know it by its operations; as thinking, reasoning, willing, remembering, and as operating about things that are invisible and remote from sense. This must needs be distinct from the body; for that being but dust and earth in its original, hath not the power of reasoning and thinking; for then it would have that power, when the soul were absent, as well as when it is present. Besides, if it had that power of thinking, it could think only of those things which are sensible, and made up of matter, as itself is. This soul hath a greater excellency; it can know itself, rejoice in itself, which other creatures in this world are not capable of. The soul is the greatest glory of this lower world; and, as one saith, "There seems to be no more difference between the soul and an angel, than between a sword in the scabbard and when it is out of the scabbard."[l]

1. Consider the vastness of its capacity. The understanding can conceive the whole world, and paint in itself the invisible pictures of all things. It is capable of apprehending and discoursing of things superior to its own nature. "It is suited to all objects, as the eye to all colors, or the ear to all sounds."[m] How great is the memory, to retain such varieties, such diversities! The will also can accommodate other things to itself. It invents arts for the use of man: prescribes rules for the government of states; ransacks the bowels of nature; makes endless conclusions, and steps in reasoning from one thing to another, for the knowledge of truth. It can contemplate and form notions of things higher than the world.

2. The quickness of its motion. "Nothing is more quick in the whole course of nature. The sun runs through the world in a day; this can do it in a moment. It can, with one flight of fancy, ascend to the battlements of heaven."[n] The mists of the air, that hinder the sight of the eye, cannot hinder the flights of the soul; it can pass in a moment from one end of the world to the other, and think of things a thousand miles distant. It can think of some mean thing in the world; and presently, by one cast, in the twinkling of an eye, mount up as high as heaven. As its desires are not bounded by sensual objects, so neither are the motions of it restrained by them. It will break forth with the greatest vigor, and conceive things infinitely above it; though it be in the body, it acts as if it were ashamed to be cloistered in it. This could not be the result of any

[k] Ibid. c. 8. § 50, 51.   [l] More.   [m] Culverwell.   [n] Theodoret.

material cause. Whoever knew mere matter understand, think, will? and what it hath not, it cannot give. That which is destitute of reason and will, could never confer reason and will. It is not the effect of the body; for the body is fitted with members to be subject to it. It is in part ruled by the activity of the soul, and in part by the counsel of the soul; it is used by the soul, and knows not how it is used.° Nor could it be from the parents, since the souls of the children often transcend those of the parents in vivacity, acuteness and comprehensiveness. One man is stupid, and begets a son with a capacious understanding; one is debauched and beastly in morals, and begets a son who, from his infancy, testifies some virtuous inclinations, which sprout forth in delightful fruit with the ripeness of his age. Whence should this difference arise,—a fool begat the wise man, and a debauched the virtuous man? The wisdom of the one could not descend from the foolish soul of the other; nor the virtues of the son, from the deformed and polluted soul of the parent.ᴾ It lies not in the organs of the body: for if the folly of the parent proceeded not from their souls, but the ill disposition of the organs of their bodies, how comes it to pass that the bodies of the children are better organized beyond the goodness of their immediate cause? We must recur to some invisible hand, that makes the difference, who bestows upon one at his pleasure richer qualities than upon another. You can see nothing in the world endowed with some excellent quality, but you must imagine some bountiful hand did enrich it with that dowry. None can be so foolish as to think that a vessel ever enriched itself with that sprightly liquor wherewith it is filled; or that anything worse than the soul should endow it with that knowledge and activity which sparkles in it. Nature could not produce it. That nature is intelligent, or not; if it be not, then it produceth an effect more excellent than itself, inasmuch as an understanding being surmounts a being that hath no understanding. If the supreme cause of the soul be intelligent, why do we not call it God as well as nature? We must arise from hence to the notion of a God; a spiritual nature cannot proceed but from a spirit higher than itself, and of a transcendent perfection above itself. If we believe we have souls, and understand the state of our own faculties, we must be assured that there was some invisible hand which bestowed those faculties, and the riches of them upon us. A man must be ignorant of himself before he can be ignorant of the existence of God. By considering the nature of our souls, we may as well be assured that there is a God, as that there is a sun, by the shining of the beams in at our windows; and, indeed, the soul is a statue and representation of God, as the landscape of a country or a map represents all the parts of it, but in a far less proportion than the country itself is. The soul fills the body, and God the world; the soul sustains the body, and God the world; the soul sees, but is not seen; God sees all things, but is himself invisible. How base are they

---

° Coccei. sum. Theolog. c. 8. § 51, 52.

ᴾ I do not dispute whether the soul were generated or no. Suppose the substance of it was generated by the parents, yet those more excellent qualities were not the result of them.

then that prostitute their souls, an image of God, to base things un-expressibly below their own nature!

3. I might add, the union of soul and body. Man is a kind of compound of angel and beast, of soul and body; if he were only a soul, he were a kind of angel; if only a body, he were another kind of brute. Now that a body as vile and dull as earth, and a soul that can mount up to heaven, and rove about the world, with so quick a motion, should be linked in so strait an acquaintance; that so noble a being as the soul should be inhabitant in such a tabernacle of clay; must be owned to some infinite power that hath so chained it.

Thirdly, Man witnesseth to a God in the operations and reflections of conscience. (Rom. ii. 15), "Their thoughts are accusing or excu-sing." An inward comfort attends good actions, and an inward tor-ment follows bad ones; for there is in every man's conscience fear of punishment and hope of reward; there is, therefore, a sense of some superior judge, which hath the power both of rewarding and punishing. If man were his supreme rule, what need he fear pun-ishment, since no man would inflict any evil or torment on himself; nor can any man be said to reward himself, for all rewards refer to another, to whom the action is pleasing, and is a conferring some good a man had not before; if an action be done by a subject or servant, with hopes of reward, it cannot be imagined that he expects a reward from himself, but from the prince or person whom he eyes in that action, and for whose sake he doth it.

1. There is a law in the minds of men which is a rule of good and evil. There is a notion of good and evil in the consciences of men, which is evident by those laws which are common in all countries, for the preserving human societies, the encouragement of virtue, and discouragement of vice; what standard should they have for those laws but a common reason? the design of those laws was to keep men within the bounds of goodness for mutual commerce, whence the apostle calls the heathen magistrate a "minister of God for good" (Rom. xiii. 4): and "the Gentiles do by nature the things contained in the law" (Rom. ii. 14).

Man in the first instant of the use of reason, finds natural prin-ciples within himself; directing and choosing them, he finds a dis-tinction between good and evil; how could this be if there were not some rule in him to try and distinguish good and evil? If there was not such a law and rule in man, he could not sin; for where there is no law there is no transgression. If man were a law to himself, and his own will his law, there could be no such thing as evil; whatsoever he willed, would be good and agreeable to the law, and no action could be accounted sinful; the worst act would be as commendable as the best. Everything at man's appointment would be good or evil. If there were no such law, how should men that are naturally inclined to evil disapprove of that which is unlovely, and approve of that good which they practise not? No man but inwardly thinks well of that which is good, while he neglects it; and thinks ill of that which is evil, while he commits it. Those that are vicious, do praise those that practise the contrary virtues. Those that are evil would seem to be good, and those that are blameworth---

yet will rebuke evil in others.   This is really to distinguish between good and evil; whence doth this arise, by what rule do we measure this, but by some innate principle?   And this is universal, the same in one man as in another, the same in one nation as in another; they are born with every man, and inseparable from his nature (Prov. xxvii. 19): as in water, face answers to face, so the heart of man to man.   Common reason supposeth that there is some hand which hath fixed this distinction in man; how could it else be universally impressed?   No law can be without a lawgiver: no sparks but must be kindled, by some other.   Whence should this law then derive its original?   Not from man; he would fain blot it out, and cannot alter it when he pleases.   Natural generation never intended it; it is settled therefore by some higher hand, which, as it imprinted it, so it maintains it against the violence of men, who, were it not for this law, would make the world more than it is, an aceldama and field of blood; for had there not been some supreme good, the measure of all other goodness in the world, we could not have had such a thing as good.   The Scripture gives us an account that this good was distinguished from evil before man fell, they were *objecta scibilia;* good was commanded and evil prohibited, and did not depend upon man.   From this a man may rationally be instructed that there is a God; for he may thus argue: I find myself naturally obliged to do this thing, and avoid that; I have, therefore, a superior that doth oblige me; I find something within me that directs me to such actions, contrary to my sensitive appetite; there must be something above me, therefore, that puts this principle into man's nature; if there were no superior, I should be the supreme judge of good and evil; were I the lord of that law which doth oblige me, I should find no contradiction within myself, between reason and appetite.

2. From the transgression of this law of nature, fears do arise in the consciences of men.   Have we not known or heard of men struck by so deep a dart, that could not be drawn out by the strength of men, or appeased by the pleasure of the world; and men crying out with horror, upon a death-bed, of their past life, when "their fear hath come as a desolation, and destruction as a whirlwind?" (Prov. i. 27): and often in some sharp affliction, the dust hath been blown off from men's consciences, which for a while hath obscured the writing of the law.   If men stand in awe of punishment, there is then some superior to whom they are accountable; if there were no God, there were no punishment to fear.   What reason of any fear, upon the dissolution of the knot betwen the soul and body, if there were not a God to punish, and the soul remained not in being to be punished?   How suddenly will conscience work upon the appearance of an affliction, rouse itself from sleep like an armed man, and fly in a man's face before he is aware of it!   It will "surprise the hypocrites" (Isa. xxxviii. 14): it will bring to mind actions committed long ago, and set them in order before the face, as God's deputy, acting by his authority and omniscience.   As God hath not left himself without a witness among the creatures (Acts xiv. 17), so he hath not left himself without a witness in a man's own breast.

(1.) This operation of conscience hath been universal.   No nation hath been any more exempt from it than from reason; not a man but hath one time or other more or less smarted under the sting of it. All over the world conscience hath shot its darts; it hath torn the hearts of princes in the midst of their pleasures; it hath not flattered them whom most men flatter; nor feared to disturb their rest, whom no man dares to provoke. Judges have trembled on a tribunal, when innocents have rejoiced in their condemnation. The iron bars upon Pharaoh's conscience, were at last broke up, and he acknowledged the justice of God in all that he did, (Exod. ix. 27): "I have sinned, the Lord is righteous, and I and my people are wicked." Had they been like childish frights at the apprehension of bugbears, why hath not reason shaken them off? But, on the contrary, the stronger reason grows, the smarter those lashes are; groundless fears had been short-lived, age and judgment would have worn them off, but they grow sharper with the growth of persons. The Scripture informs us they have been of as ancient a date as the revolt of the first man, (Gen. iii. 10): "I was afraid," saith Adam, "because I was naked;" which was an expectation of the judgment of God. All his posterity inherit his fears, when God expresseth himself in any tokens of his majesty and providence in the world. Every man's conscience testifies that he is unlike what he ought to be, according to that law engraven upon his heart. In some, indeed, conscience may be seared or dimmer; or suppose some men may be devoid of conscience, shall it be denied to be a thing belonging to the nature of man? Some men have not their eyes, yet the power of seeing the light is natural to man, and belongs to the integrity of the body. Who would argue that, because some men are mad, and have lost their reason by a distemper of the brain, that therefore reason hath no reality, but is an imaginary thing? But I think it is a standing truth that every man hath been under the scourge of it, one time or other, in a less or a greater degree; for, since every man is an offender, it cannot be imagined, conscience, which is natural to man, and an active faculty, should always lie idle, without doing this part of its office. The apostle tells us of the thoughts accusing or excusing one another, (or by turns,) according as the actions were. Nor is this truth weakened by the corruptions in the world, whereby many have thought themselves bound in conscience to adhere to a false and superstitious worship and idolatry, as much as any have thought themselves bound to adhere to a worship commanded by God. This very thing infers that all men have a reflecting principle in them; it is no argument against the being of conscience, but only infers that it may err in the application of what it naturally owns. We can no more say, that because some men walk by a false rule, there is no such thing as conscience, than we can say that because men have errors in their minds, therefore they have no such faculty as an understanding; or because men will that which is evil, they have no such faculty as a will in them.

(2.) These operations of conscience are when the wickedness is most secret. These tormenting fears of vengeance have been frequent in men, who have had no reason to fear man, since their wickedness being unknown to any but themselves, they could have no accuser but themselves. They have been in many acts which their companions have justified them in ; persons above the stroke of human laws, yea, such as the people have honored as gods, have been haunted by them. Conscience hath not been frighted by the power of princes, or bribed by the pleasures of courts. David was pursued by his horrors, when he was, by reason of his dignity, above the punishment of the law, or, at least, was not reached by the law ; since, though the murder of Uriah was intended by him, it was not acted by him. Such examples are frequent in human records ; when the crime hath been above any punishment by man, they have had an accuser, judge, and executioner in their own breasts. Can this be originally from a man's self? He who loves and cherishes himself, would fly from anything that disturbs him ; it is a greater power and majesty from whom man cannot hide himself, that holds him in those fetters. What should affect their minds for that which can never bring them shame or punishment in this world, if there were not some supreme judge to whom they were to give an account, whose instrument conscience is? Doth it do this of itself? hath it received an authority from the man himself to sting him? It is some supreme power that doth direct and commission it against our wills.

(3.) These operations of conscience cannot be totally shaken off by man. If there be no God, why do not men silence the clamors of their consciences, and scatter those fears that disturb their rest and pleasures? How inquisitive are men after some remedy against those convulsions! Sometimes they would render the charge insignificant, and sing a rest to themselves, though they " walk in the wickedness of their own hearts."q How often do men attempt to drown it by sensual pleasures, and perhaps overpower it for a time ; but it revives, reinforceth itself, and acts a revenge for its former stop. It holds sin to a man's view, and fixes his eyes upon it, whether he will or no. " The wicked are like a troubled sea, and cannot rest," (Isa. lvii. 20) : they would wallow in sin without control, but this inward principle will not suffer it ; nothing can shelter men from those blows. What is the reason it could never be cried down ? Man is an enemy to his own disquiet ; what man would continue upon the rack, if it were in his power to deliver himself? Why have all human remedies been without success, and not able to extinguish those operations, though all the wickedness of the heart hath been ready to assist and second the attempt ? It hath pursued men notwithstanding all the violence used against it ; and renewed its scourges with more severity, as men deal with their resisting slaves. Man can as little silence those thunders in his soul, as he can the thunders in the heavens ; he must strip himself of his humanity, before he can be stripped of an accusing and affrighting conscience ; it sticks as close to him as his nature ; since man cannot throw out the process it makes against him, it is an evidence that some higher power secures its throne and standing. Who should put this scourge into the hand of conscience, which no man in the world is able to wrest out ?

(4.) We may add, the comfortable reflections of conscience. There are excusing, as well as accusing reflections of conscience, when things are done as works of the " law of nature," (Rom. ii. 15) : as it doth

q Deut. xxix. 19.

not forbear to accuse and torture, when a wickedness, though unknown to others, is committed; so when a man hath done well,
though he be attacked with all the calumnies the wit of man can
forge, yet his conscience justifies the action, and fills him with a
singular contentment.   As there is torture in sinning, so there is
peace and joy in well-doing.   Neither of those it could do, if it did
not understand a Sovereign Judge, who punishes the rebels, and
rewards the well-doer.   Conscience is the foundation of all religion;
and the two pillars upon which it is built, are the being of
God, and the bounty of God to those that "diligently seek him."[r]
This proves the existence of God.   If there were no God, conscience
were useless; the operations of it would have no foundation, if there
were not an eye to take notice, and a hand to punish or reward the
action.   The accusations of conscience evidence the omniscience and
the holiness of God; the terrors of conscience, the justice of God;
the approbations of conscience, the goodness of God.   All the order
in the world owes itself, next to the providence of God, to conscience;
without it the world would be a. Golgotha.   As the creatures witness, there was a first cause that produced them, so this principle in
man evidenceth itself to be set by the same hand, for the good of
that which it had so framed.   There could be no conscience if there
were no God, and man could not be a rational creature, if there
were no conscience.   As there is a rule in us, there must be a judge,
whether our actions be according to the rule.   And since conscience
in our corrupted state is in some particular misled, there must be a
power superior to conscience, to judge how it hath behaved itself in
its deputed office; we must come to some supreme judge, who can
judge conscience itself.   As a man can have no surer evidence that
he is a being, than because he thinks he is a thinking being; so there
is no surer evidence in nature that there is a God, than that every man
hath a natural principle in him, which continually cites him before God,
and puts him in mind of him, and makes him one way or other fear
him, and reflects upon him whether he will or no.   A man hath less
power over his conscience, than over any other faculty; he may choose
whether he will exercise his understanding about, or move his will to
such an object; but he hath no such authority over his conscience: he
cannot limit it, or cause it to cease from acting and reflecting; and
therefore, both that, and the law about which it acts, are settled by
some Supreme Authority in the mind of man, and this is God.

Fourthly. The evidence of a God results from the vastness of desires in man, and the real dissatisfaction he hath in everything below himself.   Man hath a boundless appetite after some sovereign
good; as his understanding is more capacious than anything below,
so is his appetite larger.   This affection of desire exceeds all other
affections.   Love is determined to something known; fear, to something apprehended: but desires approach nearer to infiniteness, and
pursue, not only what we know, or what we have a glimpse of, but
what we find wanting in what we already enjoy.   That which the
desire of man is most naturally carried after is *bonum;* some fully
satisfying good.   We desire knowledge by the sole impulse of reason,

[r] Heb. xi. 6.

but we desire good before the excitement of reason; and the desire is always after good, but not always after knowledge. Now the soul of man finds an imperfection in everything here, and cannot scrape up a perfect satisfaction and felicity. In the highest fruitions of worldly things it is still pursuing something else, which speaks a defect in what it already hath. The world may afford a felicity for our dust, the body, but not for the inhabitant in it; it is too mean for that. Is there any one soul among the sons of men, that can upon a due inquiry say it was at rest and wanted no more, that hath not sometimes had desires after an immaterial good? The soul "follows hard after" such a thing, and hath frequent looks after it (Ps. lxiii. 8). Man desires a stable good, but no sublunary thing is so; and he that doth not desire such a good, wants the rational nature of a man. This is as natural as understanding, will, and conscience. Whence should the soul of man have those desires? how came it to understand that something is still wanting to make its nature more perfect, if there were not in it some notion of a more perfect being which can give it rest? Can such a capacity be supposed to be in it without something in being able to satisfy it? if so, the noblest creature in the world is miserablest, and in a worse condition than any other. Other creatures obtain their ultimate desires, "they are filled with good," (Ps. civ. 28): and shall man only have a vast desire without any possibility of enjoyment? Nothing in man is in vain; he hath objects for his affections, as well as affections for objects; every member of his body hath its end, and doth attain it; every affection of his soul hath an object, and that in this world; and shall there be none for his desire, which comes nearest to infinite of any affection planted in him? This boundless desire had not its original from man himself; nothing would render itself restless; something above the bounds of this world implanted those desires after a higher good, and made him restless in everything else. And since the soul can only rest in that which is infinite, there is something infinite for it to rest in; since nothing in the world, though a man had the whole, can give it a satisfaction, there is something above the world only capable to do it, otherwise the soul would be always without it, and be more in vain than any other creature. There is, therefore, some infinite being that can only give a contentment to the soul, and this is God. And that goodness which implanted such desires in the soul, would not do it to no purpose, and mock it in giving it an infinite desire of satisfaction, without intending it the pleasure of enjoyment, if it doth not by its own folly deprive itself of it. The felicity of human nature must needs exceed that which is allotted to other creatures.

Reason IV. As it is a folly to deny that which all nations in the world have consented to, which the frame of the world evidenceth, which man in his body, soul, operations of conscience, witnesseth to; so it is a folly to deny the being of God, which is witnessed unto by extraordinary occurrences in the world.

1. In extraordinary judgments. When a just revenge follows abominable crimes, especially when the judgment is suited to the sin by a strange concatenation and succession of providences, method-

ized to bring such a particular punishment; when the sin of a nation or person is made legible in the inflicted judgment, which testifies that it cannot be a casual thing. The Scripture gives us an account of the necessity of such judgments, to keep up the reverential thoughts of God in the world (Ps. ix. 16): "The Lord is known by the judgment which he executes; the wicked is snared in the work of his own hand: and jealousy is the name of God, (Exod. xxxiv. 14), "Whose name is jealous." He is distinguished from false gods by the judgments which he sends, as men are by their names. Extraordinary prodigies in many nations have been the heralds of extraordinary judgments, and presages of the particular judgments which afterwards they have felt, of which the Roman histories, and others, are full. That there are such things is undeniable, and that the events have been answerable to the threatening, unless we will throw away all human testimonies, and count all the histories of the world forgeries. Such things are evidences of some invisible power which orders those affairs. And if there be invisible powers, there is also an efficacious cause which moves them; a government certainly there is among them, as well as in the world, and then we must come to some supreme governor which presides over them. Judgments upon notorious offenders have been evident in all ages; the Scripture gives many instances. I shall only mention that of Herod Agrippa, which Josephus mentions.[a] He receives the flattering applause of the people, and thought himself a God; but by the sudden stroke upon him, was forced by his torture to confess another. "I am God," saith he, "in your account, but a higher calls me away; the will of the heavenly Deity is to be endured." The angel of the Lord smote him. The judgment here was suited to the sin; he that would be a god, is eaten up of worms, the vilest creatures. Tully Hostilius, a Roman king, whe counted it the most unroyal thing to be religious, or own any other God but his sword, was consumed himself, and his whole house, by lightning from heaven. Many things are unaccountable unless we have recourse to God. The strange revelations of murderers, that have most secretly committed their crimes; the making good some dreadful imprecations, which some wretches have used to confirm a lie, and immediately have been struck with that judgment they wished; the raising often unexpected persons to be instruments of vengeance on a sinful and perfidious nation; the overturning the deepest and surest counsels of men, when they have had a successful progress, and come to the very point of execution; the whole design of men's preservation hath been beaten in pieces by some unforeseen circumstance, so that judgments have broken in upon them without control, and all their subtleties been outwitted; the strange crossing of some in their estates, though the most wise, industrious, and frugal persons, and that by strange and unexpected ways; and it is observable how often everything contributes to carry on a judgment intended, as if they rationally designed it: all those loudly proclaim a God in the world; if there were no God, there would be no sin; if no sin, there would be no punishment.

[a] Lib. xix. Antiq. Acts xii. 21–23.

2. In miracles. The course of nature is uniform; and when it is put out of its course, it must be by some superior power invisible to the world; and by whatsoever invisible instruments they are wrought, the efficacy of them must depend upon some first cause above nature. (Psalm lxxii. 18): "Blessed be the Lord God of Israel, who only doeth wondrous things," by himself and his sole power. That which cannot be the result of a natural cause, must be the result of something supernatural: what is beyond the reach of nature, is the effect of a power superior to nature; for it is quite against the order of nature, and is the elevation of something to such a pitch, which all nature could not advance it to. Nature cannot go beyond its own limits; if it be determined by another, as hath been formerly proved, it cannot lift itself above itself, without that power that so determined it. Natural agents act necessarily; the sun doth necessarily shine, fire doth necessarily burn: that cannot be the result of nature, which is above the ability of nature; that cannot be the work of nature which is against the order of nature; nature cannot do anything against itself, or invert its own course. We must own that such things have been, or we must accuse all the records of former ages to be a pack of lies; which whosoever doth, destroys the greatest and best part of human knowledge. The miracles mentioned in the Scripture, wrought by our Saviour, are acknowledged by the heathen, by the Jews at this day, though his greatest enemies. There is no dispute whether such things were wrought, "the dead raised," the "blind restored to sight." The heathens have acknowledged the miraculous eclipse of the sun at the passion of Christ, quite against the rule of nature, the moon being then in opposition to the sun; the propagation of Christianity contrary to the methods whereby other religions have been propagated, that in a few years the nations of the world should be sprinkled with this doctrine, and give in a greater catalogue of martyrs courting the devouring flames, than all the religions of the world. To this might be added, the strange hand that was over the Jews, the only people in the world professing the true God, that should so often be befriended by their conquerors, so as to rebuild their temple, though they were looked upon as a people apt to rebel. Dion and Seneca observe, that wherever they were transplanted, they prospered, and gave laws to the victors; so that this proves also the authority of the Scripture, the truth of christian religion, as well as the being of a God, and a superior power over the world. To this might be added, the bridling the tumultuous passions of men for the preservation of human societies, which else would run the world into unconceivable confusions, (Psalm lxv. 7): "Which stilleth the noise of the sea, and the tumults of the people;" as also the miraculous deliverance of a person or nation, when upon the very brink of ruin; the sudden answer of prayer when God hath been sought to, and the turning away a judgment, which in reason could not be expected to be averted, and the raising a sunk people from a ruin which seemed inevitable, by unexpected ways.

3. Accomplishments of prophecies. Those things which are purely contingent, and cannot be known by natural signs and in their causes, as eclipses and changes in nations, which may be discerned

by an observation of the signs of the times; such things that fall not within this compass, if they be foretold and come to pass, are solely from some higher hand, and above the cause of nature. This in Scripture is asserted to be a notice of the true God (Isa. xli. 23): " Show the things that are to come hereafter, that we may know that you are God," and (Isa. xlvi. 10), " I am God declaring the end from the beginning, and from ancient times the things that are not yet done, saying, My counsel shall stand, and I will do all my pleasure." And prophecy was consented to by all the philosophers to be from divine illumination: that power which discovers things future, which all the foresight of men cannot ken and conjecture, is above nature. And to foretell them so certainly as if they did already exist, or had existed long ago, must be the result of a mind infinitely intelligent; because it is the highest way of knowing, and a higher cannot be imagined: and he that knows things future in such a manner, must needs know things present and past. Cyrus was prophesied of by Isaiah (xliv. 28, and xlv. 1) long before he was born; his victories, spoils, all that should happen in Babylon, his bounty to the Jews came to pass, according to that prophecy; and the sight of that prophecy which the Jews shewed him, as other historians report, was that which moved him to be favorable to the Jews.

Alexander's sight of Daniel's prophecy concerning his victories moved him to spare Jerusalem. And are not the four monarchies plainly deciphered in that book, before the fourth rose up in the world? That power which foretells things beyond the reach of the wit of man, and orders all causes to bring about those predictions, must be an infinite power, the same that made the world, sustains it and governs all things in it according to his pleasure, and to bring about his own ends; and this being is God.

Use I. If atheism be a folly, it is then pernicious to the world and to the atheist himself. Wisdom is the band of human societies, the glory of man. Folly is the disturber of families, cities, nations; the disgrace of human nature.

First, It is pernicious to the world.

1. It would root out the foundations of government. It demolisheth all order in nations. The being of a God is the guard of the world: the sense of a God is the foundation of civil order: without this there is no tie upon the consciences of men. What force would there be in oaths for the decisions of controversies, what right could there be in appeals made to one that had no being? A city of atheists would be a heap of confusion; there could be no ground of any commerce, when all the sacred bands of it in the consciences of men were snapt asunder, which are torn to pieces and utterly destroyed by denying the existence of God. What magistrate could be secure in his standing? what private person could be secure in his right? Can that then be a truth that is destructive of all public good? If the atheist's sentiment, that there were no God, were a truth, and the contrary that there were a God, were a falsity, it would then follow, that falsity made men good and serviceable to one another; that error were the foundation of all the beauty, and order, and outward

felicity of the world, the fountain of all good to man.[t] If there were
no God, to believe there is one, would be an error; and to believe
there is none, would be the greatest wisdom, because it would be the
greatest truth. And then as it is the greatest wisdom to fear God,
upon the apprehension of his existence, so it would be the greatest
error to fear him if there were none.[u] It would unquestionably follow, that error is the support of the world, the spring of all human
advantages; and that every part of the world were obliged to a falsity
for being a quiet habitation, which is the most absurd thing to imagine. It is a thing impossible to be tolerated by any prince, without
laying an axe to the root of the government.

2. It would introduce all evil into the world. If you take away
God, you take away conscience, and thereby all measures and rules
of good and evil. And how could any laws be made when the
measure and standard of them were removed? All good laws are
founded upon the dictates of conscience and reason, upon common
sentiments in human nature, which spring from a sense of God; so
that if the foundation be demolished, the whole superstructure must
tumble down: a man might be a thief, a murderer, an adulterer, and
could not in a strict sense be an offender. The worst of actions could
not be evil, if a man were a god to himself, a law to himself. Nothing but evil deserves a censure, and nothing would be evil if there
were no God, the Rector of the world against whom evil is properly
committed. No man can make that morally evil that is not so in
itself: as where there is a faint sense of God, the heart is more
strongly inclined to wickedness; so where there is no sense of God,
the bars are removed, the flood-gates set open for all wickedness to
rush in upon mankind. Religion pinions men from abominable
practices, and restrains them from being slaves to their own passions:
an atheist's arms would be loose to do anything."[x] Nothing so villanous and unjust but would be acted if the natural fear of a Deity
were extinguished. The first consequence issuing from the apprehension of the existence of God, is his government of the world.
If there be no God, then the natural consequence is that there is no
supreme government of the world: such a notion would cashier all
sentiments of good, and be like a Trojan horse, whence all impurity,
tyranny, and all sorts of mischiefs would break out upon mankind:
corruption and abominable works in the text are the fruit of the
fool's persuasion that there is no God. The perverting the ways of
men, oppression and extortion, owe their rise to a forgetfulness of
God (Jer. iii. 21): "They have perverted their way, and they have
forgotten the Lord their God." (Ezek. xxii. 12): "Thou hast greedily gained by extortion, and hast forgotten me, saith the Lord."
The whole earth would be filled with violence, all flesh would corrupt their way, as it was before the deluge, when probably atheism
did abound more than idolatry; and if not a disowning the being,
yet denying the providence of God by the posterity of Cain: those
of the family of Seth only "calling upon the name of the Lord"
(Gen. vi. 11, 12, compared with Gen. iv. 26).

The greatest sense of a Deity in any, hath been attended with the

[t] Lessius de Provid. p. 665.   [u] Psalm cxi. 10.   [x] Lessius de Provid. p. 664.

greatest innocence of life and usefulness to others; and a weaker sense hath been attended with a baser impurity. If there were no God, blasphemy would be praiseworthy; as the reproach of idols is praiseworthy, because we testify that there is no divinity in them.[y] What can be more contemptible than that which hath no being? Sin would be only a false opinion of a violated law, and an offended deity. If such apprehensions prevail, what a wide door is opened to the worst of villanies! If there be no God, no respect is due to him; all the religion in the world is a trifle, and error; and thus the pillars of all human society, and that which hath made commonwealths to flourish, are blown away.

Secondly, It is pernicious to the atheist himself. If he fear no future punishment, he can never expect any future reward: all his hopes must be confined to a swinish and despicable manner of life, without any imaginations of so much as a drachm of reserved happiness. He is in a worse condition than the silliest animal, which hath something to please it in its life: whereas an atheist can have nothing here to give him a full content, no more than any other man in the world, and can have less satisfaction hereafter. He deposeth the noble end of his own being, which was to serve a God and have a satisfaction in him, to seek a God and be rewarded by him; and he that departs from his end, recedes from his own nature. All the content any creature finds, is in performing its end, moving according to its natural instinct; as it is a joy to the sun to run its race.[z] In the same manner it is a satisfaction to every other creature, and its delight to observe the law of its creation. What content can any man have that runs from his end, opposeth his own nature, denies a God by whom and for whom he was created, whose image he bears, which is the glory of his nature, and sinks into the very dregs of brutishness? How elegantly it is described by Bildad,[a] "His own counsel shall cast him down, terrors shall make him afraid on every side, destruction shall be ready at his side, the first-born of death shall devour his strength, his confidence shall be rooted out, and it shall bring him to the king of terrors. Brimstone shall be scattered upon his habitation; he shall be driven from light into darkness, and chased out of the world. They that come after him shall be astonished at his day, as they that went before were affrighted. And this is the place of him that knows not God."[b] If there be a future reckoning (as his own conscience cannot but sometimes inform him of), his condition is desperate, and his misery dreadful and unavoidable. It is not righteous a hell should entertain any else, if it refuse him.

Use II. How lamentable is it, that in our times this folly of atheism should be so rife! That there should be found such monsters in human nature, in the midst of the improvements of reason, and shinings of the gospel, who not only make the Scripture the matter of their jeers, but scoff at the judgments and providences of God in the world, and envy their Creator a being, without whose goodness they had none themselves; who contradict in their carriage what they assert to be their sentiment, when they dreadfully imprecate

[y] Lessius de Provid. p. 665.   [z] Psalm xix. 5.
[a] Job xviii. 7, 8, &c. to the end.   [b] Ver. 24.

damnation to themselves! Whence should that damnation they so rashly wish be poured forth upon them, if there were not a revenging God? Formerly atheism was as rare as prodigious, scarce two or three known in an age; and those that are reported to be so in former ages, are rather thought to be counted so for mocking at the senseless deities the common people adored, and laying open their impurities. A mere natural strength would easily discover that those they adored for gods, could not deserve that title, since their original was known, their uncleanness manifest and acknowledged by their worshippers. And probably it was so; since the Christians were termed ἄθεοι, because they acknowledged not their vain idols.[c]

I question whether there ever was, or can be in the world, an uninterrupted and internal denial of the being of God, or that men (unless we can suppose conscience utterly dead) can arrive to such a degree of impiety; for before they can stifle such sentiments in them (whatsoever they may assert), they must be utter strangers to the common conceptions of reason, and despoil themselves of their own humanity. He that dares to deny a God with his lips, yet sets up something or other as a God in his heart. Is it not lamentable that this sacred truth, consented to by all nations, which is the band of civil societies, the source of all order in the world, should be denied with a bare face, and disputed against in companies, and the glory of a wise Creator ascribed to an unintelligent nature, to blind chance? Are not such worse than heathens? They worshipped many gods, these none; they preserved a notion of God in the world under a disguise of images, these would banish him both from earth and heaven, and demolish the statutes of him in their own consciences; they degraded him, these would destroy him; they coupled creatures with him—(Rom. i. 25), "Who worshipped the creature with the Creator," as it may most properly be rendered—and these would make him worse than the creature, a mere nothing. Earth is hereby become worse than hell. Atheism is a persuasion which finds no footing anywhere else. Hell, that receives such persons, in this point reforms them: they can never deny or doubt of his being, while they feel his strokes. The devil, that rejoices at their wickedness, knows them to be in an error; for he "believes, and trembles at the belief."[d] This is a forerunner of judgment. Boldness in sin is a presage of vengeance, especially when the honor of God is more particularly concerned therein; it tends to the overturning human society, taking off the bridle from the wicked inclinations of men: and God appears not in such visible judgments against sin immediately committed against himself, as in the case of those sins that are destructive to human society. Besides, God, as Governor of the world, will uphold that, without which all his ordinances in the world would be useless. Atheism is point blank against all the glory of God in creation, and against all the glory of God in redemption, and pronounceth at one breath, both the Creator, and all acts of religion and divine institutions, useless and insignificant. Since most have had, one time or other, some risings of doubt, whether there be a God, though few do in expressions deny his being, it may not be unnecessary to propose some things for the further impressing this truth, and guarding themselves against such temptations.

1. It is utterly impossible to demonstrate there is no God. He can choose no medium, but will fall in as a proof for his existence, and a manifestation of his excellency, rather than against it. The pretences of the atheist are so ridiculous, that they are not worth the mentioning. They never saw God, and therefore know not how to believe such a being; they cannot comprehend him. He would not be a God, if he could fall within the narrow model of a human understanding; he would not be infinite, if he were comprehensible, or to be terminated by our sight. How small a thing must that be which is seen by a bodily eye, or grasped by a weak mind! If God were visible or comprehensible, he would be limited. Shall it be a sufficient demonstration from a blind man, that there is no fire in the room, because he sees it not, though he feel the warmth of it? The knowledge of the effect is sufficient to conclude the existence of the cause. Who ever saw his own life? Is it sufficient to deny a man lives, because he beholds not his life, and only knows it by his motion? He never saw his own soul, but knows he hath one by his thinking power. The air renders itself sensible to men in its operations, yet was never seen by the eye. If God should render himself visible, they might question as well as now, whether that which was so visible were God, or some delusion. If he should appear glorious, we can as little behold him in his majestic glory, as an owl can behold the sun in its brightness: we should still but see him in his effects, as we do the sun by his beams. If he should show a new miracle, we should still see him but by his works; so we see him in his creatures, every one of which would be as great a miracle as any can be wrought, to one that had the first prospect of them. To require to see God, is to require that which is impossible (1 Tim. vi. 16): "He dwells in the light which no man can approach unto, whom no man hath seen, nor can see." It is visible that he is, "for he covers himself with light as with a garment" (Psalm civ. 2); it is visible what he is, "for he makes darkness his secret place" (Psalm xviii. 11). Nothing more clear to the eye than light, and nothing more difficult to the understanding than the nature of it: as light is the first object obvious to the eye, so is God the first object obvious to the understanding. The arguments from nature do, with greater strength, evince his existence, than any pretences can manifest there is no God. No man can assure himself by any good reason there is none; for as for the likeness of events to him that is righteous, and him that is wicked; to him that sacrificeth, and to him that sacrificeth not (Eccles. ix. 2): it is an argument for a reserve of judgment in another state, which every man's conscience dictates to him, when the justice of God shall be glorified in another world, as much as his patience is in this.

2. Whosoever doubts of it, makes himself a mark, against which all the creatures fight. All the stars fought against Sisera for Israel: all the stars in heaven, and the dust on earth, fight for God against the atheist. He hath as many arguments against him as there are creatures in the whole compass of heaven and earth. He is most

unreasonable, that denies or doubts of that whose image and shadow
he sees round about him; he may sooner deny the sun that warms
him, the moon that in night walks in her brightness, deny the fruits
he enjoys from the earth, yea, and deny that he doth exist. He must
tear his own conscience, fly from his own thoughts, be changed into
the nature of a stone, which hath neither reason nor sense, before he
can disengage himself from those arguments which evince the being
of a God. He that would make the natural religion professed in the
world a mere romance, must give the lie to the common sense of
mankind; he must be at an irreconcilable enmity with his own reason, resolve to hear nothing that it speaks, if he will not hear what
it speaks in this case, with a greater evidence than it can ascertain
anything else. God hath so settled himself in the reason of man,
that he must vilify the noblest faculty God hath given him, and put
off nature itself, before he can blot out the notion of a God.

3. No question but those that have been so bold as to deny that
there was a God, have sometimes been much afraid they have been
in an error, and have at least suspected there was a God, when some
sudden prodigy hath presented itself to them, and roused their fears;
and whatsoever sentiments they might have in their blinding prosperity, they have had other kind of motions in them in their stormy
afflictions, and, like Jonah's mariners, have been ready to cry to him
for help, whom they disdained to own so much as in being, while
they swam in their pleasures. The thoughts of a Deity cannot be so
extinguished, but they will revive and rush upon a man, at least
under some sharp affliction. Amazing judgments will make them
question their own apprehensions. God sends some messengers to
keep alive the apprehension of him as a Judge, while men resolve
not to own or reverence him as a Governor. A man cannot but
keep a scent of what was born with him; as a vessel that hath been
seasoned first with a strong juice will preserve the scent of it, whatsoever liquors are afterwards put into it.

4. What is it for which such men rack their wits, to form notions
that there is no God? Is it not that they would indulge some vicious
habit, which hath gained the possession of their soul, which they
know "cannot be favored by that holy God," whose notion they
would raze out?[e] Is it not for some brutish affection, as degenera-
tive of human nature, as derogatory to the glory of God; a lust as
unmanly as sinful? The terrors of God are the effects of guilt; and
therefore men would wear out the apprehensions of a Deity, that
they might be brutish without control. They would fain believe
there were no God, that they might not be men, but beasts. How
great a folly is it to take so much pains in vain, for a slavery and
torment; to cast off that which they call a yoke, for that which really
is one! There is more pains and toughness of soul requisite to shake
off the apprehensions of God, than to believe that he is, and cleave
constantly to him. What a madness is it in any to take so much
pains to be less than a man, by razing out the apprehensions of
God, when, with less pains, he may be more than an earthly man, by
cherishing the notions of God, and walking answerably thereunto?

* Psalm xciv. 6, 7.

5. How unreasonable is it for any man to hazard himself at this rate in the denial of a God! The atheist saith he knows not that there is a God; but may he not reasonably think there may be one for aught he knows? and if there be, what a desperate confusion will he be in, when all his bravadoes shall prove false! What can they gain by such an opinion? A freedom, say they, from the burdensome yoke of conscience, a liberty to do what they list, that doth not subject them to divine laws. It is a hard matter to persuade any that they can gain this. They can gain but a sordid pleasure, unworthy the nature of man. But it were well that such would argue thus with themselves: If there be a God, and I fear and obey him, I gain a happy eternity; but if there be no God, I lose nothing but my sordid lusts, by firmly believing there is one. If I be deceived at last, and find a God, can I think to be rewarded by him, for disowning him? Do not I run a desperate hazard to lose his favor, his kingdom, and endless felicity for an endless torment? By confessing a God I venture no loss; but by denying him, I run the most desperate hazard, if there be one. He is not a reasonable creature, that will not put himself upon such a reasonable arguing. What a doleful meeting will there be between the God who is denied, and the atheist that denies him, who shall meet with reproaches on God's part, and terrors on his own! All that he gains is a liberty to defile himself here, and a certainty to be despised hereafter, if he be in an error, as undoubtedly he is.

6. Can any such person say he hath done all that he can to inform himself of the being of God, or of other things which he denies? Or rather they would fain imagine there is none, that they may sleep securely in their lusts, and be free (if they could) from the thunder-claps of conscience. Can such say they have used their utmost endeavors to instruct themselves in this, and can meet with no satisfaction? Were it an abstruse truth it might not be wondered at; but not to meet with satisfaction in this which everything minds us of, and helpeth, is the fruit of an extreme negligence, stupidity, and a willingness to be unsatisfied, and a judicial process of God against them. It is strange any man should be so dark in that upon which depends the conduct of his life, and the expectation of happiness hereafter. I do not know what some of you may think, but I believe these things are not useless to be proposed for ourselves to answer temptations; we know not what wicked temptation in a debauched and skeptic age, meeting with a corrupt heart, may prompt men to; and though there may not be any atheist here present, yet I know there is more than one, who have accidentally met with such, who openly denied a Deity; and if the like occasion happen, these considerations may not be unuseful to apply to their consciences. But I must confess, that since those that live in this sentiment, do not judge themselves worthy of their own care, they are not worthy of the care of others; and a man must have all the charity of the christian religion, which they despise, not to contemn them, and leave them to their own folly. As we are to pity madmen, who sink under an unavoidable distemper, we are as much to abominate them, who wilfully hug this prodigious frenzy.

Use III. If it be the atheist's folly to deny or doubt of the being of God, it is our wisdom to be firmly settled in this truth, that God is. We should never be without our arms in an age wherein atheism appears barefaced without a disguise. You may meet with suggestions to it, though the devil formerly never attempted to demolish this notion in the world, but was willing to keep it up, so the worship due to God might run in his own channel, and was necessitated to preserve it, without which he could not have erected that idolatry, which was his great design in opposition to God; yet since the foundations of that are torn up, and never like to be rebuilt, he may endeavor, as his last refuge, to banish the notion of God out of the world, that he may reign as absolutely without it, as he did before by the mistakes about the divine nature. But we must not lay all upon Satan; the corruption of our own hearts ministers matter to such sparks. It is not said Satan hath suggested to the fool, but "the fool hath said in his heart," there is no God. But let them come from what principle soever, silence them quickly, give them their dismiss; oppose the whole scheme of nature to fight against them, as the stars did against Sisera. Stir up sentiments of conscience to oppose sentiments of corruption. Resolve sooner to believe that yourselves are not, than that God is not; and if you suppose they at any time come from Satan, object to him that you know he believes the contrary to what he suggests. Settle this principle firmly in you, "let us behold Him that is invisible," as Moses did;[f] let us have the sentiments following upon the notion of a God, to be restrained by a fear of him, excited by a love to him, not to violate his laws and offend his goodness. He is not a God careless of our actions, negligent to inflict punishment, and bestow rewards, " he forgets not the labor of our love,"[g] nor the integrity of our ways; he were not a God, if he were not a governor; and punishments and rewards are as essential to government, as a foundation to a building. His being and his government in rewarding, which implies punishment, (for the neglects of him are linked together)[h] are not to be separated in our thoughts of him.

1. Without this truth fixed in us, we can never give him the worship due to his name. When the knowledge of anything is fluctuating and uncertain, our actions about it are careless. We regard not that which we think doth not much concern us. If we do not firmly believe there is a God, we shall pay him no steady worship; and if we believe not the excellency of his nature, we shall offer him but a slight service.[i] The Jews call the knowledge of the being of God the foundation and pillar of wisdom.[k] The whole frame of religion is dissolved without this apprehension, and totters if this apprehension be wavering. Religion in the heart is as water in a weatherglass, which riseth or falls according to the strength or weakness of this belief. How can any man worship that which he believes not to be, or doubts of? Could any man omit the paying a homage to one, whom he did believe to be an omnipotent, wise being, pos-

f Heb. xi. 27.   g Heb. vi. 10.   h Heb. xi. 6.
i Mal. i. 13, 14.   k Maimon. Funda. Legis. cap. 1.

sessing (infinitely above our conceptions) the perfections of all creatures? He must either think there is no such being, or that he is an easy, drowsy, inobservant God, and not such an one as our natural notions of him, if listened to, as well as the Scripture, represents him to be.

2. Without being rooted in this, we cannot order our lives. All our baseness, stupidity, dulness, wanderings, vanity, spring from a wavering and unsettledness in this principle. This gives ground to brutish pleasures, not only to solicit, but conquer us. Abraham expected violence in any place where God was not owned (Gen. xx. 11), "Surely the fear of God is not in this place, and they will slay me for my wife's sake." The natural knowledge of God firmly impressed, would choke that which would stifle our reason and deface our souls. The belief that God is, and what he is, would have a mighty influence to persuade us to a real religion, and serious consideration, and casting about how to be like to him and united with him.

3. Without it we cannot have any comfort of our lives. Who would willingly live in a stormy world, void of a God? If we waver in this principle, to whom should we make our complaints in our afflictions? Where should we meet with supports? How could we satisfy ourselves with the hopes of a future happiness? There is a sweetness in the meditation of his existence, and that he is a Creator.[l] Thoughts of other things have a bitterness mixed with them: houses, lands, children, now are, shortly they will not be; but God is, that made the world: his faithfulness as he is a Creator, is a ground to deposit our souls and concerns in our innocent sufferings.[m] So far as we are weak in the acknowledgment of God, we deprive ourselves of our content in the view of his infinite perfections.

4. Without the rooting of this principle, we cannot have a firm belief of Scripture. The Scripture will be a slight thing to one that hath weak sentiments of God. The belief of a God must necessarily precede the belief of any revelation; the latter cannot take place without the former as a foundation. We must firmly believe the being of a God, wherein our happiness doth consist, before we can believe any means which conduct us to him. Moses begins with the Author of creation, before he treats of the promise of redemption. Paul preached God as a Creator to a university, before he preached Christ as Mediator.[n] What influence can the testimony of God have in his revelation upon one that doth not firmly assent to the truth of his being? All would be in vain that is so often repeated, "Thus saith the Lord," if we do not believe there is a Lord that speaks it. There could be no awe from his sovereignty in his commands, nor any comfortable taste of his goodness in his promises. The more we are strengthened in this principle, the more credit we shall be able to give to divine revelation, to rest in his promise, and to reverence his precept; the authority of all depends upon the being of the Revealer.

To this purpose, since we have handled this discourse by natural arguments,

Psalm civ. 24.   [m] 1 Pet. iv. 19.   [n] Acts xvii. 24.

1. Study God in the creatures as well as in the Scriptures. The primary use of the creatures, is to acknowledge God in them; they were made to be witnesses of himself in his goodness, and heralds of his glory, which glory of God as Creator "shall endure forever" (Psalm civ. 31): that whole psalm is a lecture of creation and providence. The world is a sacred temple; man is introduced to contemplate it, and behold with praise the glory of God in the pieces of his art. As grace doth not destroy nature, so the book of redemption blots not out that of creation. Had he not shown himself in his creatures, he could never have shown himself in his Christ; the order of things required it. God must be read wherever he is legible; the creatures are one book, wherein he hath writ a part of the excellency of his name,° as many artists do in their works and watches. God's glory, like the filings of gold, is too precious to be lost wherever it drops: nothing so vile and base in the world, but carries in it an instruction for man, and drives in further the notion of a God. As he said of his cottage, Enter here, *Sunt hic etiam Dii*, God disdains not this place: so the least creature speaks to man, every shrub in the field, every fly in the air, every limb in a body; Consider me, God disdains not to appear in me; he hath discovered in me his being and a part of his skill, as well as in the highest. The creatures manifest the being of God and part of his perfections. We have indeed a more excellent way, a revelation setting him forth in a more excellent manner, a firmer object of dependence, a brighter object of love, raising our hearts from self-confidence to a confidence in him. Though the appearance of God in the one be clearer than in the other, yet neither is to be neglected. The Scripture directs us to nature to view God; it had been in vain else for the apostle to make use of natural arguments. Nature is not contrary to Scripture, nor Scripture to nature; unless we should think God contrary to himself who is the Author of both.

2. View God in your own experiences of him. There is a taste and sight of his goodness, though no sight of his essence.ᴾ By the taste of his goodness you may know the reality of the fountain, whence it springs and from whence it flows; this surpasseth the greatest capacity of a mere natural understanding. Experience of the sweetness of the ways of Christianity is a mighty preservative against atheism. Many a man knows not how to prove honey to be sweet by his reason, but by his sense; and if all the reason in the world be brought against it, he will not be reasoned out of what he tastes. Have not many found the delightful illapses of God into their souls, often sprinkled with his inward blessings upon their seeking of him; had secret warnings in their approaches to him; and gentle rebukes in their consciences upon their swervings from him? Have not many found sometimes an invisible hand raising them up when they were dejected; some unexpected providence stepping in for their relief; and easily perceived that it could not be a work of chance, nor many times the intention of the instruments he hath used in it? You have often found that

° Psalm viii. 9.   ᴾ Psalm xxxiv. 98.

he is, by finding that he is a rewarder, and can set to your seals that he is what he hath declared himself to be in his word (Isa. xliii. 12): "I have declared, and have saved; therefore you are my witnesses, saith the Lord, that I am God." The secret touches of God upon the heart, and inward converses with him, are a greater evidence of the existence of a supreme and infinitely good Being, than all nature.

Use IV. Is it a folly to deny or doubt of the being of God? It is a folly also not to worship God, when we acknowledge his existence; it is our wisdom then to worship him. As it is not indifferent whether we believe there is a God or no; so it is not indifferent whether we will give honor to that God or no. A worship is his right as he is the Author of our being, and fountain of our happiness. By this only we acknowledge his Deity; though we may profess his being, yet we deny that profession in neglects of worship. To deny him a worship is as great a folly, as to deny his being. He that renounceth all homage to his Creator, envies him the being which he cannot deprive him of. The natural inclination to worship is as universal as the notion of a God; idolatry else had never gained footing in the world. The existence of God was never owned in any nation, but a worship of him was appointed. And many people who have turned their backs upon some other parts of the law of nature, have paid a continual homage to some superior and invisible being. The Jews give a reason why man was created in the evening of the Sabbath, because he should begin his being with the worship of his Maker. As soon as ever he found himself to be a creature, his first solemn act should be a particular respect to his Creator. "To fear God and keep his commandment," is the whole of man,q or is whole man;r he is not a man but a beast, without observance of God. Religion is as requisite as reason to complete a man: he were not reasonable if he were not religious; because by neglecting religion, he neglects the chiefest dictate of reason. Either God framed the world with so much order, elegancy, and variety to no purpose, or this was his end at least, that reasonable creatures should admire him in it, and honor him for it. The notion of God was not stamped upon men, the shadows of God did not appear in the creatures, to be the subject of an idle contemplation, but the motive of a due homage to God. He created the world for his glory, a people for himself, that he might have the honor of his works; that since we live and move in him, and by him, we should live and move to him and for him. It was the condemnation of the heathen world, that when they knew there was a God, they did not give him the glory due to him.s He that denies his being, is an atheist to his essence: he that denies his worship, is an atheist to his honor.

If it be a folly to deny the being of God, it will be our wisdom, then, since we acknowledge his being, often to think of him. Thoughts are the first issue of a creature as reasonable:t He that hath given us the faculty whereby we are able to think, should be the principal object about which the power of it should be exercised. It is a justice to God, the author of our understandings, a justice to

q Eccl. xii. 13.   r Heb.   s Rom. i. 21.   t Prov. iv. 23.

the nature of our understandings, that the noblest faculty should be employed about the most excellent object. Our minds are a beam from God; and, therefore, as the beams of the sun, when they touch the earth, should reflect back upon God. As we seem to deny the being of God not to think of him; we seem also to unsoul our souls in misemploying the activity of them any other way, like flies, to be oftener on dunghills than flowers. It is made the black mark of an ungodly man, or an atheist, that "God is not in all his thoughts' (Psalm x. 4). What comfort can be had in the being of God without thinking of him with reverence and delight? A God forgotten is as good as no God to us.

DISCOURSE II

ON PRACTICAL ATHEISM

PSALM xiv. 1.—The fool hath said in his heart, There is no God. They are corrupt, they have done abominable works, there is none that doeth good.

PRACTICAL atheism is natural to man in his depraved state, and very frequent in the hearts and lives of men.

The fool hath said in his heart, There is no God. He regards him as little as if he had no being. He said in his *heart*, not with his tongue, nor in his head: he never firmly thought it, nor openly asserted it. Shame put a bar to the first, and natural reason to the second; yet, perhaps, he had sometimes some doubts whether there were a God or no. He wished there were not any, and sometimes hoped there were none at all. He could not raze out the notion of a Deity in his mind, but he neglected the fixing the sense of God in his heart, and made it too much his business to deface and blot out those characters of God in his soul, which had been left under the ruins of original nature. Men may have atheistical hearts without atheistical heads. Their reasons may defend the notion of a Deity, while their hearts are empty of affection to the Deity. Job's children may curse God *in their hearts*, though not with their lips.[u]

There is no God. Most understand it of a denial of the providence of God, as I have said in opening the former doctrine. He denies some essential attribute of God, or the exercise of that attribute in the world.[x] He that denies any *essential* attribute, may be said to deny the being of God. Whosoever denies angels or men to have reason and will, denies the human and angelical nature, because understanding and will are essential to both those natures; there could neither be angel nor man without them. No nature can subsist without the perfections essential to that nature, nor God be conceived of without his. The apostle tells us (Eph. ii. 12), that the Gentiles were "without God in the world." So, in some sense, all unbelievers may be termed atheists; for rejecting the Mediator appointed by God, they reject that God who appointed him. But this is beyond the intended scope, natural atheism being the only subject; yet this is deducible from it. That the title of ἄθεοι doth not only belong to those who deny the existence of God, or to those who contemn all sense of a Deity, and would root the conscience and reverence of God out

u Job i. 5.   x So the Chaldee reads לֵית שׁוּלטָנא *Non potestas*, denying the authority of God in the world.

of their souls; but it belongs also to those who give not that worship to God which is due to him, who worship many gods, or who worship one God in a false and superstitious manner, when they have not right conceptions of God, nor intend an adoration of him according to the excellency of his nature. All those that are unconcerned for any particular religion fall under this character : though they own a God in general, yet are willing to acknowledge any God that shall be coined by the powers under whom they live. The Gentiles were without God in the world; without the true notion of God, not without a God of their own framing. This general or practical atheism is natural to men.

1. Not natural by created, but by corrupted nature. It is against nature, as nature came out of the hand of God; but universally natural, as nature hath been sophisticated and infected by the serpent's breath. Inconsideration of God, or misrepresentation of his nature, are as agreeable to corrupt nature, as the disowning the being of a God is contrary to common reason. God is not denied, *naturâ, sed vitiis.*[y]

2. It is universally natural: "The wicked are estranged from the womb (Psalm lviii. 3). They go astray as soon as they be born: their poison is like the poison of a serpent." *The wicked*, (and who by his birth hath a better title?) they go astray from the dictates of God and the rule of their creation as soon as ever they be born. Their poison is like the poison of a serpent, which is radically the same in all of the same species. It is seminally and fundamentally in all men, though there may be a stronger restraint by a divine hand upon some men than upon others. This principle runs through the whole stream of nature. The natural bent of every man's heart is distant from God. When we attempt anything pleasing to God, it is like the climbing up a hill, against nature; when anything is displeasing to him, it is like a current running down the channel in its natural course; when we attempt anything that is an acknowledgment of the holiness of God, we are fain to rush, with arms in our hands, through a multitude of natural passions, and fight the way through the oppositions of our own sensitive appetite. How softly do we naturally sink down into that which sets us at a greater distance from God! There is no active, potent, efficacious sense of a God by nature. "The heart of the sons of men is fully set in them to do evil" (Eccl. viii. 11). *The heart*, in the singular number, as if there were but one common heart beat in all mankind, and bent, as with one pulse, with a joint consent and force to wickedness, without a sense of the authority of God in the earth, as if one heart acted every man in the world. The great apostle cites the text to verify the charge he brought against all mankind.[z] In his interpretation, the Jews, who owned one God, and were dignified with special privileges, as well as the Gentiles that maintained many gods, are within the compass of this character. The apostle leaves out the first part of the text, "The fool hath said in his heart," but takes in the latter part, and the verses following. He charges *all*, because all, every man of them, was under sin—"There is none that seeks God;" and,

y Augustin de Civit. Dei.   z Rom. iii. 9–12.

ver. 19, he adds, "What the law saith, it speaks to those that are under the law," that none should imagine he included only the Gentiles, and exempted the Jews from this description. The leprosy of atheism had infected the whole mass of human nature. No man, among Jews or Gentiles, did naturally seek God; and, therefore, all were void of any spark of the practical sense of the Deity. The effects of this atheism are not in all externally of an equal size; yet, in the fundamentals and radicals of it, there is not a hair's difference between the best and the worst men that ever traversed the world. The distinction is laid either in common grace, bounding and suppressing it; or in special grace, killing and crucifying it. It is in every one either triumphant or militant, reigning or deposed. No man is any more born with sensible acknowledgments of God, than he is born with a clear knowledge of the nature of all the stars in the heavens, or plants upon the earth. None seeks after God.[a] None seek God as his rule, as his end, as his happiness, which is a debt the creature naturally owes to God. He desires no communion with God; he places his happiness in anything inferior to God; he prefers everything before him, glorifies everything above him; he hath no delight to know him; he regards not those paths which lead to him; he loves his own filth better than God's holiness; his actions are tinctured and dyed with self, and are void of that respect which is due from him to God.

The noblest faculty of man, his understanding, wherein the remaining lineaments of the image of God are visible; the highest operation of that faculty, which is wisdom, is, in the judgment of the Spirit of God, devilish, whilst it is earthly and sensual;[b] and the wisdom of the best man is no better by nature; a legion of impure spirits possess it; devilish, as the devil, who, though he believe there is a God, yet acts as if there were none, and wishes he had no superior to prescribe him a law, and inflict that punishment upon him which his crimes have merited. Hence the poison of man by nature is said to be like the poison of a serpent,[c] alluding to that serpentine temptation which first infected mankind, and changed the nature of man into the likeness of that of the devil; so that, notwithstanding the harmony of the world, that presents men not only with the notice of the being of a God, but darts into their minds some remarks of his power and eternity; yet the thoughts and reasonings of man are so corrupt, as may well be called diabolical, and as contrary to the perfection of God, and the original law of their nature, as the actings of the devil are; for since every natural man is a child of the devil, and is acted by the diabolical spirit, he must needs have that nature which his father hath, and the infusion of that venom which the spirit that acts him is possessed with, though the full discovery of it may be restrained by various circumstances (Eph. ii. 2). To conclude: though no man, or at least very few, arrive to a round and positive conclusion in their hearts that there is no God, yet there is no man that naturally hath in his heart any reverence of God. In general, before I come to a particular proof, take some propositions.

[a] Coccei.   [b] James iii. 15.   [c] Psalm lviii. 4.

Prop. I. Actions are a greater discovery of a principle than words. The testimony of works is louder and clearer than that of words; and the frame of men's hearts must be measured rather by what they do than by what they say. There may be a mighty distance between the tongue and the heart, but a course of actions is as little guilty of lying as interest is, according to our common saying. All outward impieties are the branches of an atheism at the root of our nature, as all pestilential sores are expressions of the contagion in the blood; sin is therefore frequently called ungodliness in our English dialect. Men's practices are the best indexes of their principles: the current of a man's life is the counterpart of the frame of his heart. Who can deny an error in the spring or wheels, when he perceives an error in the hand of the dial? Who can deny an atheism in the heart, when so much is visible in the life? The taste of the water discovers what mineral it is strained through. A practical denial of God is worse than a verbal, because deeds have usually more of deliberation than words; words may be the fruit of a passion, but a set of evil actions are the fruit and evidence of a predominant evil principle in the heart. All slighting words of a prince do not argue an habitual treason; but a succession of overt treasonable attempts signify a settled treasonable disposition in the mind. Those, therefore, are more deservedly termed atheists, who acknowledge a God, and walk as if there were none, than those (if there can be any such) that deny a God, and walk as if there were one. A sense of God in the heart would burst out in the life; where there is no reverence of God in the life, it is easily concluded there is less in the heart. What doth not influence a man when it hath the addition of the eyes, and censures of outward spectators, and the care of a reputation (so much the god of the world) to strengthen it and restrain the action, must certainly have less power over the heart when it is single, without any other concurrence. The flames breaking out of a house discover the fire to be much stronger and fiercer within. The apostle judgeth those of the circumcision, who gave heed to Jewish fables, to be deniers of God, though he doth not tax them with any notorious profaneness: (Tit. i. 16), "They profess that they know God, but in works they deny him." He gives them epithets contrary to what they arrogated to themselves.[d] They boasted themselves to be holy; the apostle calls them abominable: they bragged that they fulfilled the law, and observed the traditions of their fathers; the apostle calls them disobedient, or unpersuadable: they boasted that they only had the rule of righteousness, and a sound judgment concerning it; the apostle said they had a reprobate sense, and unfit for any good work; and judges against all their vain-glorious brags, that they had not a reverence of God in their hearts; there was more of the denial of God in their works than there was acknowledgment of God in their words. Those that have neither God in their thoughts, nor in their tongues, nor in their works, cannot properly be said to acknowledge him. Where the honor of God is not practically owned in the lives of men, the being of God is not sensibly acknowledged in the hearts of men. The

[d] Illyric.

principle must be of the same kind with the actions; if the actions be atheistical, the principle of them can be no better.

Prop. II. All sin is founded in a secret atheism. Atheism is the spirit of every sin; all the floods of impieties in the world break in at the gate of a secret atheism, and though several sins may disagree with one another, yet, like Herod and Pilate against Christ, they join hand in hand against the interest of God. Though lusts and pleasures be diverse, yet they are all united in disobedience to him.^e All the wicked inclinations in the heart, and struggling motions, secret repinings, self-applauding confidences in our own wisdom, strength, &c., envy, ambition, revenge, are sparks from this latent fire; the language of every one of these is, I would be a Lord to myself, and would not have a God superior to me. The variety of sins against the first and second table, the neglects of God, and violences against man, are derived from this in the text; first, "The fool hath said in his heart," and then follows a legion of devils. As all virtuous actions spring from an acknowledgment of God, so all vicious actions rise from a lurking denial of him: all licentiousness goes glib down where there is no sense of God. Abraham judged himself not secure from murder, nor his wife from defilement in Gerar, if there were no fear of God there.^f He that makes no conscience of sin has no regard to the honor, and, consequently, none to the being of God. "By the fear of God men depart from evil" (Prov. xvi. 6); by the non-regarding of God men rush into evil. Pharaoh oppressed Israel because he "knew not the Lord." If he did not deny the being of a Deity, yet he had such an unworthy notion of God as was inconsistent with the nature of a Deity; he, a poor creature, thought himself a mate for the Creator. In sins of omission we own not God, in neglecting to perform what he enjoins; in sins of commission we set up some lust in the place of God, and pay to that the homage which is due to our Maker. In both we disown him; in the one by not doing what he commands, in the other by doing what he forbids. We deny his sovereignty when we violate his laws; we disgrace his holiness when we cast our filth before his face; we disparage his wisdom when we set up another rule as the guide of our actions than that law he hath fixed; we slight his sufficiency when we prefer a satisfaction in sin before a happiness in him alone; and his goodness, when we judge it not strong enough to attract us to him. Every sin invades the rights of God, and strips him of one or other of his perfections. It is such a vilifying of God as if he were not God; as if he were not the supreme Creator and Benefactor of the world; as if we had not our being from him; as if the air we breathed in, the food we lived by, were our own by right of supremacy, not of donation. For a subject to slight his sovereign, is to slight his royalty; or a servant his master, is to deny his superiority.

Prop. III. Sin implies that God is unworthy of a being. Every sin is a kind of cursing God in the heart;^g an aim at the destruction of the being of God; not actually, but virtually; not in the intention of every sinner, but in the nature of every sin. That affection which

^e Tit. iii. 3.   ^f Gen. xx. 11.   ^g Job i. 5.

excites a man to break His law, would excite him to annihilate his being if it were in his power. A man in every sin aims to set up his own will as his rule, and his own glory as the end of his actions against the will and glory of God; and could a sinner attain his end, God would be destroyed. God cannot outlive his will and his glory; God cannot have another rule but his own will, nor another end but his own honor. Sin is called a turning the back upon God,[h] a kicking against him,[i] as if he were a slighter person than the meanest beggar. What greater contempt can be shown to the meanest, vilest person, than to turn the back, lift up the heel, and thrust away with indignation? all which actions, though they signify that such a one hath a being, yet they testify also that he is unworthy of a being, that he is an unuseful being in the world, and that it were well the world were rid of him. All sin against knowledge is called a reproach of God.[k] Reproach is a vilifying a man as unworthy to be admitted into company. We naturally judge God unfit to be conversed with. God is the term turned from by a sinner; sin is the term turned to, which implies a greater excellency in the nature of sin than in the nature of God; and as we naturally judge it more worthy to have a being in our affections, so consequently more worthy to have a being in the world, than that infinite nature from whom we derive our beings and our all, and upon whom, with a kind of disdain, we turn our backs. Whosoever thinks the notion of a Deity unfit to be cherished in his mind by warm meditation, implies that he cares not whether he hath a being in the world or no. Now though the light of a Deity shines so clearly in man, and the stings of conscience are so smart, that he cannot absolutely deny the being of a God, yet most men endeavor to smother this knowledge, and make the notion of a God a sapless and useless thing (Rom. i. 28): "They like not to retain God in their knowledge." It is said, "Cain went out from the presence of the Lord" (Gen. iv. 16); that is, from the worship of God. Our refusing or abhorring the presence of a man implies a carelessness whether he continue in the world or no; it is a using him as if he had no being, or as if we were not concerned in it. Hence all men in Adam, under the emblem of the prodigal, are said to go into a far country; not in respect of place, because of God's omnipresence, but in respect of acknowledgment and affection: they mind and love anything but God. And the descriptions of the nations of the world, lying in the ruins of Adam's fall, and the dregs of that revolt, is that they know not God. They forget God, as if there were no such being above them; and, indeed, he that doth the works of the devil, owns the devil to be more worthy of observance, and, consequently, of a being, than God, whose nature he forgets, and whose presence he abhors.

Prop. IV. Every sin in its own nature would render God a foolish and impure being. Many transgressors esteem their acts, which are contrary to the law of God, both wise and good: if so, the law against which they are committed, must be both foolish and impure. What a reflection is there, then, upon the Lawgiver! The moral law is not properly a mere act of God's will considered in itself, or a tyran-

[h] Jer. xxxii. 33.   [i] Deut. xxxii. 15.   [k] Numb. xv. 30. Ezek. xx. 27.

nical edict, like those of whom it may well be said, *stat pro ratione voluntas:* but it commands those things which are good in their own nature, and prohibits those things which are in their own nature evil; and therefore is an act of his wisdom and righteousness; the result of his wise counsel, and an extract of his pure nature; as all the laws of just lawgivers, are not only the acts of their will, but of a will governed by reason and justice, and for the good of the public, whereof they are conservators. If the moral commands of God were only acts of his will, and had not an intrinsic necessity, reason and goodness, God might have commanded the quite contrary, and made a contrary law, whereby that which we now call vice, might have been canonized for virtue: He might then have forbid any worship of him, love to him, fear of his name: He might then have commanded murders, thefts, adulteries. In the first he would have untied the link of duty from the creature, and dissolved the obligations of creatures to him, which is impossible to be conceived; for from the relation of a creature to God, obligations to God, and duties upon those obligations, do necessarily result. It had been against the rule of goodness and justice to have commanded the creature not to love him, and fear and obey him: this had been a command against righteousness, goodness, and intrinsic obligations to gratitude. And should murder, adulteries, rapines have been commanded instead of the contrary, God would have destroyed his own creation; he would have acted against the rule of goodness and order; he had been an unjust tyrannical governor of the world: public society would have been cracked in pieces, and the world become a shambles, a brothel-house, a place below the common sentiments of a mere man. All sin, therefore, being against the law of God, the wisdom and holy rectitude of God's nature is denied in every act of disobedience. And what is the consequence of this, but that God is both foolish and unrighteous in commanding that, which was neither an act of wisdom, as a governor, nor an act of goodness, as a benefactor to his creature? As was said before, presumptuous sins are called reproaches of God (Numb. xv. 30): "The soul that doth aught presumptuously reproacheth the Lord." Reproaches of men are either for natural, moral, or intellectual defects. All reproaches of God must imply a charge, either of unrighteousness or ignorance: if of unrighteousness, it is a denial of his holiness; if of ignorance, it is a blemishing his wisdom. If God's laws were not wise and holy, God would not enjoin them: and if they are so, we deny infinite wisdom and holiness in God by not complying with them. As when a man believes not God when he promises, he makes him a liar (1 John v. 10); so he that obeys not a wise and holy God commanding, makes him guilty either of folly or unrighteousness. Now, suppose you knew an absolute atheist who denied the being of a God, yet had a life free from any notorious spot or defilement; would you in reason count him so bad as the other that owns a God in being, yet lays, by his course of action, such a black imputation of folly and impurity upon the God he professeth to own—an imputation which renders any man a most despicable creature?

Prop. V. Sin in its own nature endeavors to render God the most miserable being. It is nothing but an opposition to the will of God: the will of no creature is so much contradicted as the will of God is by devils and men; and there is nothing under the heavens that the affections of human nature stand more point blank against, than against God. There is a slight of him in all the faculties of man; our souls are as unwilling to know him, as our wills are averse to follow him (Rom. viii. 7): "The carnal mind is enmity against God, it is not subject to the law of God, nor can be subject." It is true, God's will cannot be hindered of its effect, for then God would not be supremely blessed, but unhappy and miserable: all misery ariseth from a want of that which a nature would have, and ought to have: besides, if anything could frustrate God's will, it would be superior to him: God would not be omnipotent, and so would lose the perfection of the Deity, and consequently the Deity itself; for that which did wholly defeat God's will, would be more powerful than he. But sin is a contradiction to the will of God's revelation, to the will of his precept: and therein doth naturally tend to a superiority over God, and would usurp his omnipotence, and deprive him of his blessedness. For if God had not an infinite power to turn the designs of it to his own glory, but the will of sin could prevail, God would be totally deprived of his blessedness. Doth not sin endeavor to subject God to the extravagant and contrary wills of men, and make him more a slave than any creature can be? For the will of no creature, not the meanest and most despicable creature, is so much crossed, as the will of God is by sin (Isa. xliii. 24): "Thou hast made me to serve with thy sins:" thou hast endeavored to make a mere slave of me by sin. Sin endeavors to subject the blessed God to the humor and lust of every person in the world.

Prop. VI. Men sometimes in some circumstances do wish the not being of God. This some think to be the meaning of the text, "The fool hath said in his heart, There is no God," that is, he wishes there were no God. Many tamper with their own hearts to bring them to a persuasion that there is no God: and when they cannot do that, they conjure up wishes that there were none. Men naturally have some conscience of sin, and some notices of justice (Rom. i. 32): "They know the judgment of God," and they know the demerit of sin; "they know the judgment of God, and that they which do such things are worthy of death." What is the consequent of this but fear of punishment; and what is the issue of that fear, but a wishing the Judge either unwilling or unable to vindicate the honor of his violated law? When God is the object of such a wish, it is a virtual undeifying of him: not to be able to punish, is to be impotent; not to be willing to punish, is to be unjust: imperfections inconsistent with the Deity. God cannot be supposed without an infinite power to act, and an infinite righteousness as the rule of acting. Fear of God is natural to all men; not a fear of offending him, but a fear of being punished by him: the wishing the extinction of God has its degree in men, according to the degree of their fears of his just vengeance: and though such a wish be not in its meridian but in the damned in hell, yet it hath its starts and motions in affrighted and awakened consciences on the earth: under this rank of wishers, that there were no God, or that God were destroyed, do fall.

1. Terrified consciences, that are *Magor-missabib*, see nothing but matter of fear round about. As they have lived without the bounds of the law, they are afraid to fall under the stroke of his justice: fear wishes the destruction of that which it apprehends hurtful: it considers him as a God to whom vengeance belongs, as the Judge of all the earth.[1] The less hopes such an one hath of his pardon, the more joy he would have to hear that his judge should be stripped of his life: he would entertain with delight any reasons that might support him in the conceit that there were no God: in his present state such a doctrine would be his security from an account: he would as much rejoice if there were no God to inflame an hell for him, as any guilty malefactor would if there were no judge to order a gibbet for him. Shame may bridle men's words, but the heart will be casting about for some arguments this way, to secure itself: such as are at any time in Spira's case, would be willing to cease to be creatures, that God might cease to be Judge. "The fool hath said in his heart, there is no Elohim, no Judge;" fancying God without any exercise of his judicial authority. And there is not any wicked man under anguish of spirit, but, were it within the reach of his power, would take away the life of God, and rid himself of his fears by destroying his Avenger.

2. Debauched persons are not without such wishes sometimes: an obstinate servant wishes his master's death, from whom he expects correction for his debaucheries. As man stands in his corrupt nature, it is impossible but one time or other most debauched persons at least have some kind of velleities, or imperfect wishes. It is as natural to men to abhor those things which are unsuitable and troublesome, as it is to please themselves in things agreeable to their minds and humors; and since man is so deeply in love with sin, as to count it the most estimable good, he cannot but wish the abolition of that law which checks it, and, consequently, the change of the Lawgiver which enacted it; and in wishing a change in the holy nature of God, he wishes a destruction of God, who could not be God if he ceased to be immutably holy. They do as certainly wish that God had not a holy will to command them, as despairing souls wish that God had not a righteous will to punish them, and to wish conscience extinct for the molestations they receive from it, is to wish the power conscience represents out of the world also. Since the state of sinners is a state of distance from God, and the language of sinners to God is, "Depart from us;"[m] they desire as little the continuance of his being, as they desire the knowledge of his ways; the same reason which moves them to desire God's distance from them, would move them to desire God's not being: since the greatest distance would be most agreeable to them, the destruction of God must be so too; because there is no greater distance from us, than in not being. Men would rather have God not to be, than themselves under control, that sensuality might range at pleasure; he is like a "heifer sliding from the yoke" (Hosea iv. 16). The cursing of God in the heart, feared by Job of his children, intimates a wishing God despoiled of his authority, that their pleasure might not be damped by his law. Besides,

[1] Psalm xciv. 12.   [m] Job xxi. 14.

is there any natural man that sins against actuated knowledge, but either thinks or wishes that God might not see him, that God might not know his actions? And is not this to wish the destruction of God, who could not be God unless he were immense and omniscient?

3. Under this rank fall those who perform external duties only out of a principle of slavish fear. Many men perform those duties that the law enjoins, with the same sentiments that slaves perform their drudgery; and are constrained in their duties by no other considerations but those of the whip and the cudgel. Since, therefore, they do it with reluctancy, and secretly murmur while they seem to obey, they would be willing that both the command were recalled, and the master that commands them were in another world. The spirit of adoption makes men act towards God as a father, a spirit of bondage only eyes him as a judge. Those that look upon their superiors as tyrannical, will not be much concerned in their welfare; and would be more glad to have their nails pared, than be under perpetual fear of them. Many men regard not the Infinite Goodness in the service of him, but consider him as cruel, tyrannical, injurious to their liberty. Adam's posterity are not free from the sentiments of their common father, till they are regenerate. You know what conceit was the hammer whereby the hellish Jael struck the nail into our first parents, which conveyed death, together with the same imagination to all their posterity (Gen. iii. 5): "God knows that in the day you eat thereof, your eyes shall be opened, and you shall be as gods, knowing good and evil." Alas, poor souls! God knew what he did when he forbade you that fruit; he was jealous you should be too happy; it was cruelty in him to deprive you of a food so pleasant and delicious. The apprehension of the severity of God's commands riseth up no less in desires that there were no God over us, than Adam's apprehension of envy in God for the restraint of one tree, moved him to attempt to be equal with God: fear is as powerful to produce the one in his posterity, as pride was to produce the other in the common root. When we apprehend a thing hurtful to us, we desire so much evil to it, as may render it incapable of doing us the hurt we fear. As we wish the preservation of what we love or hope for, so we are naturally apt to wish the not being of that whence we fear some hurt or trouble. We must not understand this as if any man did formally wish the destruction of God, as God. God in himself is an infinite mirror of goodness and ravishing loveliness; he is infinitely good, and so universally good, and nothing but good; and is therefore so agreeable to a creature, as a creature, that it is impossible that the creature, while it bears itself to God as a creature, should be guilty of this, but thirst after him and cherish every motion to him. As no man wishes the destruction of any creature, as a creature, but as it may conduce to something which he counts may be beneficial to himself; so no man doth, nor perhaps can wish the cessation of the being of God, as God; for then he must wish his own being to cease also; but as he considers him clothed with some perfections, which he apprehends as injurious to him, as his holiness in forbidding sin, his justice in punishing sin; and God being judged in those perfections, contrary

to what the revolted creature thinks convenient and good for himself, he may wish God stripped of those perfections, that thereby he may be free from all fear of trouble and grief from him in his fallen state. In wishing God deprived of those, he wishes God deprived of his being; because God cannot retain his deity without a love of righteousness, and hatred of iniquity; and he could not testify his love to the one, or his loathing of the other, without encouraging goodness, and witnessing his anger against iniquity. Let us now appeal to ourselves, and examine our own consciences. Did we never please ourselves sometimes in the thoughts, how happy we should be, how free in our vain pleasures, if there were no God? Have we not desired to be our own lords, without control, subject to no law but our own, and be · guided by no will but that of the flesh? Did we never rage against God under his afflicting hand? Did we never wish God stripped of his holy will to command, and his righteous will to punish? &c.

Thus much for the general. For the proof of this, many considerations will bring in evidence; most may be reduced to these two generals: Man would set himself up, first, as his own rule; secondly, as his own end and happiness.

I. Man would set himself up as his own rule instead of God. This will be evidenced in this method.

1. Man naturally disowns the rule God sets him. 2. He owns any other rule rather than that of God's prescribing. 3. These he doth in order to the setting himself up as his own rule. 4. He makes himself not only his own rule, but he would make himself the rule of God, and give laws to his Creator.

First, Man naturally disowns the rule God sets him. It is all one to deny his royalty, and to deny his being. When we disown his authority, we disown his Godhead. It is the right of God to be the sovereign of his creatures, and it must be a very loose and trivial assent that such men have to God's superiority over them, (and consequently to the excellency of his being, upon which that authority is founded) who are scarce at ease in themselves, but when they are invading his rights, breaking his bands, casting away his cords, and contradicting his will: Every man naturally is a son of Belial, would be without a yoke, and leap over God's enclosures; and in breaking out against his sovereignty, we disown his being, as God, for to be God and sovereign are inseparable; he could not be God, if he were not supreme; nor could he be a Creator without being a Lawgiver. To be God and yet inferior to another, is a contradiction. To make rational creatures without prescribing them a law, is to make them without holiness, wisdom and goodness.

1. There is in man naturally an unwillingness to have any acquaintance with the rule God sets him (Psalm xiv. 2): "None that did understand and seek God." The refusing instruction and casting his Word behind the back is a part of atheism.[n] We are heavy in hearing the instructions either of law or gospel,[o] and slow in the apprehension of what we hear. The people that God had hedged in from the wilderness of the world for his own garden, were foolish

---

[n] Psalm l. 17. [o] Heb. v. 11, 12.

and did not know God; were sottish and had no understanding of him.[p] The law of God is accounted a strange thing;[q] a thing of a different climate, and a far country from the heart of man; wherewith the mind of man had no natural acquaintance, and had no desire to have any; or they regarded it as a sordid thing: what God accounts great and valuable, they account mean and despicable. Men may show a civility to a stranger, but scarce contract an intimacy: there can be no amicable agreement between the holy will of God and the heart of a depraved creature: one is holy, the other unholy; one is universally good, the other stark naught. The purity of the Divine rule renders it nauseous to the impurity of a carnal heart. Water and fire may as well friendly kiss each other and live together without quarrelling and hissing, as the holy will of God and the unregenerate heart of a fallen creature.

The nauseating a holy rule is an evidence of atheism in the heart, as the nauseating wholesome food is of putrefied phlegm in the stomach. It is found more or less in every Christian, in the remainders, though not in a full empire. As there is a law in his mind whereby he delights in the law of God, so there is a law in his members whereby he wars against the law of God (Rom. vii. 22, 23, 25). How predominant is this loathing of the law of God, when corrupt nature is in its full strength, without any principle to control it! There is in the mind of such a one a darkness, whereby it is ignorant of it, and in the will a depravedness, whereby it is repugnant to it. If man were naturally willing and able to have an intimate acquaintance with, and delight in the law of God, it had not been such a signal favor for God to promise to "write the law in the heart." A man may sooner engrave the chronicle of a whole nation, or all the records of God in the Scripture upon the hardest marble with his bare finger, than write one syllable of the law of God in a spiritual manner upon his heart. For,

(1.) Men are negligent in using the means for the knowledge of God's will. All natural men are fools, who know not how to use the price God puts into their hands;[r] they put not a due estimate upon opportunities and means of grace, and account that law folly which is the birth of an infinite and holy wisdom. The knowledge of God which they may glean from creatures, and is more pleasant to the natural gust of men, is not improved to the glory of God, if we will believe the indictment the apostle brings against the Gentiles.[s] And most of those that have dived into the depths of nature, have been more studious of the qualities of the creatures, than of the excellency of the nature, or the discovery of the mind of God in them; who regard only the rising and motions of the star, but follow not with the wise men, its conduct to the King of the Jews. How often do we see men filled with an eager thirst for all other kind of knowledge, that cannot acquiesce in a twilight discovery, but are inquisitive into the causes and reasons of effects, yet are contented with a weak and languishing knowledge of God and his law, and are easily tired with the proposals of them! He now that nauseates the means whereby he may come to know and obey God, has no intention to make the

[p] Jer. iv. 22. [q] Hosea viii. 12. [r] Prov. xvii. 16. [s] Rom. i. 21.

law of God his rule. There is no man that intends seriously an end, but he intends means in order to that end: as when a man intends the preservation or recovery of his health, he will intend means in order to those ends, otherwise he cannot be said to intend his health; so he that is not diligent in using means to know the mind of God, has no sound intention to make the will and law of God his rule. Is not the inquiry after the will of God made a work by the bye, and fain to lacquey after other concerns of an inferior nature, if it hath any place at all in the soul? which is a despising the being of God. The notion of the sovereignty of God bears the same date with the notion of his Godhead; and by the same way that he reveals himself, he reveals his authority over us: whether it be by creatures without, or conscience within. All authority over rational creatures consists in commanding and directing: the duty of rational creatures in compliance with that authority consists in obeying. Where there is therefore a careless neglect of those means which convey the knowledge of God's will and our duty, there is an utter disowning of God as our Sovereign and our rule.

(2.) When any part of the mind and will of God breaks in upon men, they endeavor to shake it off: as a man would a sergeant that comes to arrest him, "they like not to retain God in their knowledge" (Rom. i. 28). "A natural man receives not the things of the Spirit of God;" that is, into his affection; he pusheth them back as men do troublesome and importunate beggars: they have no kindness to bestow upon it: they thrust with both shoulders against the truth of God, when it presseth in upon them; and dash as much contempt upon it as the Pharisees did upon the doctrine our Saviour directed against their covetousness. As men naturally delight to be without God in the world, so they delight to be without any offspring of God in their thoughts. Since the spiritual palate of man is depraved, divine truth is unsavory and ungrateful to us, till our taste and relish is restored by grace: hence men damp and quench the motions of the Spirit to obedience and compliance with the dictates of God; strip them of their life and vigor, and kill them in the womb. How unable are our memories to retain the substance of spiritual truth; but like sand in a glass, put in at one part and runs out at the other! Have not many a secret wish, that the Scripture had never mentioned some truths, or that they were blotted out of the Bible, because they face their consciences, and discourage those boiling lusts they would with eagerness and delight pursue? Methinks that interruption John gives our Saviour when he was upon the reproof of their pride, looks little better than a design to divert him from a discourse so much against the grain, by telling him a story of their prohibiting one to cast out devils, because he followed not them.[t] How glad are men when they can raise a battery against a command of God, and raise some smart objection whereby they may shelter themselves from the strictness of it!

(3.) When men cannot shake off the notices of the will and mind of God, they have no pleasure in the consideration of them; which could not possibly be, if there were a real and fixed design to own

t Mark ix. 33, 38.

the mind and law of God as our rule. Subjects or servants that love
to obey their prince and master, will delight to read and execute
their orders. The devils understand the law of God in their minds,
but they loathe the impressions of it upon their wills: those miserable
spirits are bound in chains of darkness, evil habits in their wills, that
they have not a thought of obeying that law they know. It was an
unclean beast under the law that did not chew the cud: it is a corrupt heart that doth not chew truth by meditation. A natural man
is said not to know God, or the things of God; he may know them
nationally, but he knows them not affectionately. A sensual soul
can have no delight in a spiritual law. To be sensual and not to
have the Spirit are inseparable (Jude 19). Natural men may indeed
meditate upon the law and truth of God, but without delight in it;
if they take any pleasure in it, it is only as it is knowledge, not as it
is a rule; for we delight in nothing that we desire, but upon the
same account that we desire it. Natural men desire to know God
and some part of his will and law, not out of a sense of their practical excellency, but a natural thirst after knowledge: and if they
have a delight, it is in the act of knowing, not in the object known,
not in the duties that stream from that knowledge; they design the
furnishing their understandings, not the quickening their affections,
—like idle boys that strike fire, not to warm themselves by the
heat, but sport themselves with the sparks; whereas a gracious soul
accounts not only his meditation, or the operations of his soul about
God and his will to be sweet, but he hath a joy in the object of that
meditation.[u] Many have the knowledge of God, who have no delight
in him or his will. Owls have eyes to perceive that there is a sun,
but by reason of the weakness of their sight have no pleasure to look
upon a beam of it: so neither can a man by nature love, or delight
in the will of God, because of his natural corruption. That law that
riseth up in men for conviction and instruction, they keep down
under the power of corruption; making their souls not the sanctuary,
but prison of truth (Rom. i. 18). They will keep it down in their
hearts, if they cannot keep it out of their heads, and will not endeavor
to know and taste the spirit of it.

(4.) There is, further, a rising and swelling of the heart against the
will of God. 1st. Internal. God's law cast against a hard heart, is
like a ball thrown against a stone wall, by reason of the resistance
rebounding the further from it; the meeting of a divine truth and
the heart of man, is like the meeting of two tides, the weaker swells
and foams. We have a natural antipathy against a divine rule, and
therefore when it is clapped close to our consciences, there is a snuffing at it, high reasonings against it, corruption breaks out more
strongly: as water poured on lime sets it on fire by an *antiperistasis*,
and the more water is cast upon it, the more furiously it burns; or
as the sunbeams shining upon a dunghill make the steams the thicker,
and the stench the noisomer, neither being the positive cause of the
smoke in the lime, or the stench in the dunghill, but by accident the
causes of the eruption: (Rom. vii. 8), "But sin taking occasion by
the commandment, wrought in me all manner of concupiscence, for

[u] Psalm civ. 34.

without the law sin was dead." Sin was in a languishing posture, as if it were dead, like a lazy garrison in a city, till, upon an alarm from the adversary, it takes arms, and revives its courage; all the sin in the heart gathers together its force to maintain its standing, like the vapors of the night, which unite themselves more closely to resist the beams of the rising sun. Deep conviction often provokes fierce opposition; sometimes disputes against a divine rule end in blasphemies: (Acts xiii. 45), "contradicting and blaspheming" are coupled together. Men naturally desire things that are forbidden, and reject things commanded, from the corruption of nature, which affects an unbounded liberty, and is impatient of returning under that yoke it hath shaken off, and therefore rageth against the bars of the law, as the waves roar against the restraint of a bank. When the understanding is dark, and the mind ignorant, sin lies as dead; "A man scarce knows he hath such motions of concupiscence in him, he finds not the least breath of wind, but a full calm in his soul; but when he is awakened by the law, then the viciousness of nature being sensible of an invasion of its empire, arms itself against the divine law, and the more the command is urged, the more vigorously it bends its strength, and more insolently lifts up itself against it;"[x] he perceives more and more atheistical lusts than before; "all manner of concupiscence," more leprous and contagious than before. When there are any motions to turn to God, a reluctancy is presently perceived; atheistical thoughts bluster in the mind like the wind, they know not whence they come, nor whither they go; so unapt is the heart to any acknowledgment of God as his ruler, and any re-union with him. Hence men are said to resist the Holy Ghost (Acts vii. 51), to fall against it, as the word signifies, as a stone, or any ponderous body falls against that which lies in its way: they would dash to pieces, or grind to powder that very motion which is made for their instruction, and the Spirit too which makes it, and that not from a fit of passion, but an habitual repugnance; "Ye always resist," &c. 2d. External. It is a fruit of atheism in the fourth verse of this psalm, "Who eat up my people as they eat bread." How do the revelations of the mind of God meet with opposition! and the carnal world like dogs bark against the shining of the moon; so much men hate the light, that they spurn at the lanthorns that bear it; and because they cannot endure the treasure, often fling the earthen vessels against the ground wherein it is held. If the entrance of truth render the market worse for Diana's shrines, the whole city will be in an uproar.[y] When Socrates upon natural principles confuted the heathen idolatry, and asserted the unity of God, the whole cry of Athens, a learned university, is against him; and because he opposed the public received religion, though with an undoubted truth, he must end his life by violence. How hath every corner of the world steamed with the blood of those that would maintain the authority of God in the world! The devil's children will follow the steps of their father, and endeavor to bruise the heel of divine truth, that would endeavor to break the head of corrupt lust.

[x] Thes. Salmur. De Spiritu. Servitutis Thes. xix.   [y] Acts xix. 24, 28, 29.

(5.) Men often seem desirous to be acquainted with the will of God, not out of any respect to his will, and to make it their rule, but upon some other consideration.   Truth is scarce received as truth. There is more of hypocrisy than sincerity in the pale of the church, and attendance on the mind of God.   The outward dowry of a religious profession, makes it often more desirable than the beauty. Judas was a follower of Christ for the bag, not out of any affection to the divine revelation.   Men sometime pretend a desire to be acquainted with the will of God, to satisfy their own passions, rather than to conform to God's will; the religion of such is not the judgment of the man, but the passion of the brute.   Many entertain a doctrine for the person's sake, rather than a person for the doctrine's sake, and believe a thing because it comes from a man they esteem, as if his lips were more canonical than Scripture.   The Apostle implies in the commendation he gives the Thessalonians,[z] that some receive the word for human interest, not as it is in truth the word and will of God to command and govern their consciences by its sovereign authority; or else they have the "truth of God" (as St. James speaks of the faith of Christ) "with respect of persons;"[a] and receive it not for the sake of the fountain, but of the channel; so that many times the same truth delivered by another, is disregarded, which, when dropping from the fancy and mouth of a man's own idol, is cried up as an oracle.   This is to make not God, but man the rule; for though we entertain that which materially is the truth of God, yet not formally as his truth, but as conveyed by one we affect; and that we receive a truth and not an error, we owe the obligation to the honesty of the instrument, and not to the strength and clearness of our own judgment.   Wrong considerations may give admittance to an unclean, as well as a clean beast into the ark of the soul. That which is contrary to the mind of God, may be entertained, as well as that which is agreeable.   It is all one to such that have no respect to God, what they have, as it is all one to a sponge to suck up the foulest water or the sweetest wine, when either is applied to it.

(6). Many that entertain the notions of the will and mind of God, admit them with unsettled and wavering affections.   There is a great levity in the heart of man.   The Jews that one day applaud our Saviour with hosannahs as their king, vote his crucifixion the next, and use him as a murderer.   We begin in the Spirit, and end in the flesh.   Our hearts, like lute-strings, are changed with every change of weather, with every appearance of a temptation ; scarce cne motion of God in a thousand prevails with us for a settled abode.   It is a hard task to make a signature of those truths upon our affections, which will with ease pass current with our understandings ; our affections will as soon lose them, as our understandings embrace them. The heart of man is "unstable as water."[b]   Some were willing to rejoice in John's light, which reflected a lustre on their minds ; but not in his heat, which would have conveyed a warmth to their hearts ; and the light was pleasing to them but for a season,[c] while their corruptions lay as if they were dead, not when they were awakened.

     z 1 Thess. ii. 13.   a James ii. 2.   b Gen. xlix. 4. James i. 8.   c John v. 35.

Truth may be admitted one day, and the next day rejected; as Austin saith of a wicked man, he loves the truth shining, but he hates the truth reproving. This is not to make God, but our own humor, our rule and measure.

(7.) Many desire an acquaintance with the law and truth of God, with a design to improve some lust by it; to turn the word of God to be a pander to the breach of his law. This is so far from making God's will our rule, that we make our own vile affections the rule of his law. How many forced interpretations of Scripture have been coined to give content to the lusts of men, and the divine rule forced to bend, and be squared to men's loose and carnal apprehensions! It is a part of the instability or falseness of the heart, to "wrest the Scriptures to their own destruction;"[d] which they could not do, if they did not first wring them to countenance some detestable error or filthy crime. In Paradise the first interpretation made of the first law of God, was point blank against the mind of the Lawgiver, and venomous to the whole race of mankind. Paul himself feared that some might put his doctrine of grace to so ill a use, as to be an altar and sanctuary to shelter their presumption (Rom. vi. 1, 15): "Shall we then continue in sin, that grace may abound?" Poisonous consequences are often drawn from the sweetest truths; as when God's patience is made a topic whence to argue against his providence,[e] or an encouragement to commit evil more greedily; as though because he had not presently a revenging hand, he had not an all-seeing eye: or when the doctrine of justification by faith is made use of to depress a holy life; or God's readiness to receive returning sinners, an encouragement to defer repentance till a death-bed. A liar will hunt for shelter in the reward God gave the midwives that lied to Pharaoh for the preservation of the males of Israel, and Rahab's saving the spies by false intelligence. God knows how to distinguish between grace and corruption, that may lie close together; or between something of moral goodness and moral evil, which may be mixed; we find their fidelity rewarded, which was a moral good; but not their lie approved, which was a moral evil. Nor will Christ's conversing with sinners, be a plea for any to thrust themselves into evil company. Christ conversed with sinners, as a physician with diseased persons, to cure them, not approve them; others with profligate persons, to receive infection from them, not to communicate holiness to them. Satan's children have studied their father's art, who wanted not perverted Scripture to second his temptations against our Saviour.[f] How often do carnal hearts turn divine revelation to carnal ends, as the sea fresh water into salt! As men subject the precepts of God to carnal interests, so they subject the truths of God to carnal fancies. When men will allegorize the word, and make a humorous and crazy fancy the interpreter of divine oracles, and not the Spirit speaking in the word; this is to enthrone our own imaginations as the rule of God's law, and depose his law from being the rule of our reason; this is to rifle truth of its true mind and intent. 'Tis more to rob a man of his reason, the essential constitutive part of man, than of his estate; this is to refuse an intimate acquaintance with his will. We shall

---

[d] 2 Peter iii. 16.   [e] Psalm xciv. 1.   [f] Matt iv. 4-6.

never tell what is the matter of a precept, or the matter of a promise, if we impose a sense upon it contrary to the plain meaning of it; thereby we shall make the law of God to have a distinct sense according to the variety of men's imaginations, and so make every man's fancy a law to himself. Now that this unwillingness to have a spiritual acquaintance with divine truth is a disowning God as our rule, and a setting up self in his stead, is evident; because this unwillingness respects truth.

1st. As it is most spiritual and holy. A fleshly mind is most contrary to a spiritual law, and particularly as it is a searching and discovering law, that would dethrone all other rules in the soul. As men love to be without a holy God in the world, so they love to be without a holy law, the transcript and image of God's holiness in their hearts; and without holy men, the lights kindled by the Father of lights. As the holiness of God, so the holiness of the law most offends a carnal heart (Isa. xxx. 11): "Cause the Holy One of Israel to cease from before us, prophesy to us right things." They could not endure God as a holy one. Herein God places their rebellion, rejecting him as their rule (ver. 9), "Rebellious children, that will not hear the law of the Lord." The more pure and precious any discovery of God is, the more it is disrelished by the world: as spiritual sins are sweetest to a carnal heart, so spiritual truths are most distasteful. The more of the brightness of the sun any beam conveys, the more offensive it is to a distempered eye.

2d. As it doth most relate to, or lead to God. The devil directs his fiercest batteries against those doctrines in the word, and those graces in the heart, which most exalt God, debase man, and bring men to the lowest subjection to their Creator; such is the doctrine and grace of justifying faith. That men hate not knowledge as knowledge, but as it directs them to choose the fear of the Lord, was the determination of the Holy Ghost long ago (Prov. i. 29): "For that they hated knowledge, and did not choose the fear of the Lord." Whatsoever respects God, clears up guilt, witnesses man's revolt to him, rouseth up conscience, and moves to a return to God, a man naturally runs from, as Adam did from God, and seeks a shelter in some weak bushes of error, rather than appear before it. Not that men are unwilling to inquire into and contemplate some divine truths which lie furthest from the heart, and concern not themselves immediately with the rectifying the soul: they may view them with such a pleasure as some might take in beholding the miracles of our Saviour, who could not endure his searching doctrine. The light of speculation may be pleasant, but the light of conviction is grievous; that which galls their consciences, and would affect them with a sense of their duty to God. Is it not easy to perceive, that when a man begins to be serious in the concerns of the honor of God and the duty of his soul, he feels a reluctancy within him, even against the pleas of conscience; which evidenceth that some unworthy principle has got footing in the hearts of men, which fights against the declarations of God without, and the impressions of the law of God within, at the same time when a man's own conscience takes part with it, which is the substance of the apostle's discourse, Rom. vii. 15, 16,

&c. Close discourses of the honor of God, and our duty to him, are irksome when men are upon a merry pin : they are like a damp in a mine, that takes away their breath ; they shuffle them out as soon as they can, and are as unwilling to retain the speech of them in their mouths, as the knowledge of them in their hearts. Gracious speeches, instead of bettering many men, distemper them, as sometimes sweet perfumes affect a weak head with aches.

3d. As it is most contrary to self. Men are unwilling to acquaint themselves with any truth that leads to God, because it leads from self. Every part of the will of God is more or less displeasing, as it sounds harsh against some carnal interest men would set above God, or as a mate with him. Man cannot desire any intimacy with that law which he regards as a bird of prey, to pick out his right eye or gnaw off his right hand, his lust dearer than himself. The reason we have such hard thoughts of God's will is, because we have such high thoughts of ourselves. It is a hard matter to believe or will that which hath no affinity with some principle in the understanding, and no interest in our will and passions : our unwillingness to be acquainted with the will of God ariseth from the disproportion between that and our corrupt hearts ; " We are alienated from the life of God in our minds" (Eph. iv. 18, 19). As we live not like God, so we neither think or will as God ; there is an antipathy in the heart of man against that doctrine which teaches us to deny ourselves and be under the rule of another ; but whatsoever favors the ambition, lusts, and profits of men, is easy entertainable. Many are fond of those sciences which may enrich their understandings, and grate not upon their sensual delights. Many have an admirable dexterity in finding out philosophical reasons, mathematical demonstrations, or raising observations upon the records of history ; and spend much time and many serious and affectionate thoughts in the study of them. In those they have not immediately to do with God, their beloved pleasures are not impaired ; it is a satisfaction to self without the exercise of any hostility against it. But had those sciences been against self, as much as the law and will of God, they had long since been rooted out of the world. Why did the young man turn his back upon the law of Christ ? because of his worldly self. Why did the Pharisees mock at the doctrine of our Saviour, and not at their own traditions ? because of covetous self. Why did the Jews slight the person of our Saviour and put him to death, after the reading so many credentials of his being sent from heaven ? because of ambitious self, that the Romans might not come and take away their kingdom. If the law of God were fitted to the humors of self, it would be readily and cordially observed by all men : self is the measure of a world of seeming religious actions ; while God seems to be the object, and his law the motive, self is the rule and end (Zech. vii. 5): " Did you fast unto me," &c.

2. As men discover their disowning the will of God as a rule by unwillingness to be acquainted with it, so they discover it, by the contempt of it after they cannot avoid the notions and some impressions of it. The rule of God is burthensome to a sinner ; he flies from it as from a frightful bugbear, and unpleasant yoke : sin against

the knowledge of the law is therefore called a going back from the commandment of God's lips (Job xxiii. 12): "A casting God's word behind them,"g as a contemptible thing, fitter to be trodden in the dirt than lodged in the heart; nay it is a casting it off as an abominable thing, for so the word נזה signifies, Hos. viii. 3. "Israel hath cast off the thing that is good;" an utter refusal of God (Jer. xliv. 16): "As for the word which thou hast spoken to us in the name of the Lord, we will not hearken." In the slight of his precepts his essential perfections are slighted. In disowning his will as a rule, we disown all those attributes which flow from his will, as goodness, righteousness, and truth. As an act of the divine understanding is supposed to precede the act of the divine will, so we slight the infinite reason of God. Every law, though it proceeds from the will of the lawgiver, and doth formally consist in an act of the will, yet it doth pre-suppose an act of the understanding. If the commandment be holy, just, and good, as it is (Rom. vii. 12); if it be the image of God's holiness, a transcript of his righteousness, and the efflux of his goodness; then in every breach of it, dirt is cast upon those attributes which shine in it; and a slight of all the regards he hath to his own honor, and all the provisions he makes for his creature. This atheism, or contempt of God, is more taken notice of by God than the matter of the sin itself; as a respect to God in a weak and imperfect obedience is more than the matter of the obedience itself, because it is an acknowledgment of God; so a contempt of God in an act of disobedience, is more than the matter of the disobedience. The creature stands in such an act not only in a posture of distance from God, but defiance of him; it was not the bare act of murder and adultery which Nathan charged upon David, but the atheistical principle which spirited those evil acts. The despising the commandment of the Lord was the venom of them.h It is possible to break a law without contempt; but when men pretend to believe there is a God, and that this is the law of God, it shows a contempt of his majesty:i men naturally account God's laws too strict, his yoke too heavy, and his limits too strait; and he that liveth in a contempt of this law, curseth God in his life. How can they believe there is a God, who despise him as a ruler? How can they believe him to be a guide, that disdain to follow him? To think we firmly believe a God without living conformable to his law, is an idle and vain imagination. The true and sensible notion of a God cannot subsist with disorder and an affected unrighteousness. This contempt is seen,

1. In any presumptuous breach of any part of his law. Such sins are frequently called in Scripture, rebellions, which are a denial of the allegiance we owe to him. By a wilful refusal of his right in one part, we root up the foundation of that rule he doth justly challenge over us; his right is as extensive to command us in one thing, as in another; and if it be disowned in one thing, it is virtually disowned in all, and the whole statute book of God is contemned (James ii. 10, 11: "Whosoever shall keep the whole law and yet offend in one point, is guilty of all." A willing breaking one part, though there be a willing observance of all the other points of it, is a breach

of the whole; because the authority of God, which gives sanction to the whole, is slighted: the obedience to the rest is dissembled: for the love, which is the root of all obedience, is wanting; for "love is the fulfilling the whole law."[k] The rest are obeyed because they cross not carnal desire so much as the other, and so it is an observance of himself, not of God. Besides, the authority of God, which is not prevalent to restrain us from the breach of one point, would be of as little force with us to restrain us from the breach of all the rest, did the allurements of the flesh give us as strong a diversion from the one as from the other; and though the command that is transgressed be the least in the whole law, yet the authority which enjoins it is the same with that which enacts the greatest: and it is not so much the matter of the command, as the authority commanding which lays the obligation.

2. In the natural averseness to the declarations of God's will and mind, which way soever they tend. Since man affected to be as God, he desires to be boundless; he would not have fetters, though they be golden ones, and conduce to his happiness. Though the law of God be a strength to them, yet they will not (Isa. xxx. 15): "In returning shall be your strength, and you would not." They would not have a bridle to restrain them from running into the pit, nor be hedged in by the law, though for their security; as if they thought it too slavish and low-spirited a thing to be guided by the will of another. Hence man is compared to a wild ass, that loves to "snuff up the wind in the wilderness at her pleasure," rather than come under the guidance of God;"[l] from whatsoever quarter of the heavens you pursue her she will run to the other. The Israelites "could not endure what was commanded,"[m] though in regard of the moral part, agreeable to what they found written in their own nature, and to the observance whereof they had the highest obligations of any people under heaven, since God had, by many prodigies, delivered them from a cruel slavery, the memory of which prefaced the Decalogue (Exod. xx. 2), "I am the Lord thy God, which have brought thee out of the land of Egypt, out of the house of bondage." They could not think of the rule of their duty, but they must reflect upon the grand incentive of it in their redemption from Egyptian thraldom; yet this people were cross to God, which way soever he moved. When they were in the brick kilns, they cried for deliverance; when they had heavenly manna, they longed for their onions and garlic. In Num. xiv. 3, they repent of their deliverance from Egypt, and talk of returning again to seek the remedy of their evils in the hands of their cruellest enemies, and would rather put themselves into the irons, whence God had delivered them, than believe one word of the promise of God for giving them a fruitful land; but when Moses tells them God's order, that they should turn back by the way of the Red Sea,[n] and that God had confirmed it by an oath, that they should not see the land of Canaan,[o] they then run cross to this command of God, and, instead of marching towards the Red Sea, which they had wished for before, they will go up to Canaan, as in spite of God and his threatening: "We will go to the place

---

[k] Rom. xiii. 10.   [l] Jer. ii. 24.   [m] Heb. xii. 20.   [n] Ver. 25.   [o] Ver. 28.

which the Lord hath promised" (ver. 40), which Moses calls a transgressing the commandment of the Lord (ver. 41). They would presume to go up, notwithstanding Moses' prohibition, and are smitten
by the Amalekites. When God gives them a precept, with a promise to go up to Canaan, they long for Egypt; when God commands
them to return to the Red Sea, which was nearer to the place they
longed for, they will shift sides, and go up to Canaan;[p] and when
they found they were to traverse the solitudes of the desert, they
took pet against God, and, instead of thanking him for the late victory against the Canaanites, they reproach him for his conduct from
Egypt, and the manna wherewith he nourished them in the wilderness. They would not go to Canaan, the way God had chosen, nor
preserve themselves by the means God had ordained. They would
not be at God's disposal, but complain of the badness of the way,
and the lightness of manna, empty of any necessary juice to sustain
their nature. They murmuringly solicit the will and power of God
to change all that order which he had resolved in his counsel, and
take another, conformable to their vain foolish desires; and they
signified thereby that they would invade his conduct, and that he
should act according to their fancy, which the psalmist calls a
"tempting of God, and limiting the Holy One of Israel" (Psalm
lxxviii. 41). To what point soever the declarations of God stand, the
will of man turns the quite contrary way. Is not the carriage of this
nation the best then in the world? a discovery of the depth of our
natural corruption, how cross man is to God? And that charge God
brings against them, may be brought against all men by nature, that
they despise his judgments, and have a rooted abhorrency of his
statutes in their soul (Lev. xxvi. 43). No sooner had they recovered
from one rebellion, but they revolted to another; so difficult a thing
it is for man's nature to be rendered capable of conforming to the
will of God. The carriage of this people is but a copy of the nature
of mankind, and is "written for our admonition" (1 Cor. x. 11).
From this temper men are said to make "void the law of God;"[q]
to make it of no obligation, an antiquated and moth-eaten record.
And the Pharisees, by setting up their traditions against the will of
God, are said to make his law of "none effect;" to strip it of all its
authority, as the word signifies, (Matt. xv. 6,) *ἠκυρώσατε.*

3. We have the greatest slight of that will of God which is most
for his honor and his greatest pleasure. It is the nature of man, ever
since Adam, to do so (Hos. vi. 6, 7). God desired mercy and not a
sacrifice; the knowledge of himself more than burnt offering; but
they, like men as Adam, have transgressed the covenant, invade
God's rights, and not let him be Lord of one tree. We are more
curious observers of the fringes of the law than of the greater concerns of it. The Jews were diligent in sacrifices and offerings, which
God did not urge upon them as principals, but as types of other
things; but negligent of the faith which was to be established by
him. Holiness, mercy, pity, which concerned the honor of God, as
governor of the world, and were imitations of the holiness and goodness of God, they were strangers to. This is God's complaint (Isa.

---

[p] Num. xxi. 4, 5, and Daillé, Serm. 1 Cor. x. Ser. 9, pp. 234, 235, 40.   [q] Ps. cxix. 126.

i. 11, 12, xvi. 17). We shall find our hearts most averse to the observation of those laws which are eternal, and essential to righteousness; such that he could not but command, as he is a righteous Governor; in the observation of which we come nearest to him, and express his image more clearly; as those laws for an inward and spiritual worship, a supreme affection to him. God, in regard of his righteousness and holiness of his nature, and the excellency of his being, could not command the contrary to these. But this part of his will our hearts most swell against, our corruption doth most snarl at; whereas those laws which are only positive, and have no intrinsic righteousness in them, but depend purely upon the will of the Lawgiver, and may be changed at his pleasure (which the other, that have an intrinsic righteousness in them, cannot), we better comply with, than that part of his will that doth express more the righteousness of his nature;[r] such as the ceremonial part of worship, and the ceremonial law among the Jews. We are more willing to observe order in some outward attendances and glavering devotions, than discard secret affections to evil, crucify inward lusts and delightful thoughts. A "hanging down the head like a bullrush" is not difficult; but the "breaking the heart," like a potter's vessel, to shreds and dust (a sacrifice God delights in, whereby the excellency of God and the vileness of the creature is owned), goes against the grain; to cut off an outward branch is not so hard as to hack at the root. What God most loathes, as most contrary to his will, we most love: no sin did God so severely hate, and no sin were the Jews more inclined unto, than that of idolatry. The heathen had not changed their God, as the Jews had changed their glory (Jer. ii. 11); and all men are naturally tainted with this sin, which is so contrary to the holy and excellent nature of God. By how much the more defect there is of purity in our respects to God, by so much the more respect there is to some idol within or without us, to humor, custom, and interest, &c. Never did any law of God meet with so much opposition as Christianity, which was the design of God from the first promise to the exhibiting the Redeemer, and from thence to the end of the world. All people drew swords at first against it. The Romans prepared yokes for their neighbors, but provided temples for the idols those people worshipped; but Christianity, the choicest design and most delightful part of the will of God, never met with a kind entertainment at first in any place; Rome, that entertained all others, persecuted this with fire and sword, though sealed by greater testimonies from heaven than their own records could report in favor of their idols.

4. In running the greatest hazards, and exposing ourselves to more trouble to cross the will of God, than is necessary to the observance of it. It is a vain charge men bring against the divine precepts, that they are rigorous, severe, difficult; when, besides the contradiction to our Saviour, who tells us his "yoke is easy," and his "burthen light," they thwart their own calm reason and judgment. Is there not more difficulty to be vicious, covetous, violent, cruel, than to be virtuous, charitable, kind? Doth the will of God enjoin that that is

[r] Psalm l, 6, 17, 19.

not conformable to right reason, and secretly delightful in the exercise and issue? And on the contrary, what doth Satan and the world engage us in, that is not full of molestation and hazard? Is it a sweet and comely thing to combat continually against our own consciences, and resist our own light, and commence a perpetual quarrel against ourselves, as we ordinarily do when we sin? They in the Prophet (Micah vi. 6–8) would be at the expense of "thousands of rams, and ten thousand rivers of oil," if they could compass them; yea, would strip themselves of their natural affection to their first-born to expiate the "sin of their soul," rather than to "do justice, love mercy, and walk humbly with God;" things more conducible to the honor of God, the welfare of the world, the security of their souls, and of a more easy practice than the offerings they wished for. Do not men then disown God when they will walk in ways hedged with thorns, wherein they meet with the arrows of conscience, at every turn, in their sides; and slide down to an everlasting punishment, sink under an intolerable slavery, to contradict the will of God? when they will prefer a sensual satisfaction, with a combustion in their consciences, violation of their reasons, gnawing cares and weary travels before the honor of God, the dignity of their natures, the happiness of peace and health, which might be preserved at a cheaper rate, than they are at to destroy them?

5. In the unwillingness and awkwardness of the heart, when it is to pay God a service. Men "do evil with both hands earnestly,"[s] but do good with one hand faintly; no life in the heart, nor any diligence in the hand. What slight and loose thoughts of God doth this unwillingness imply? It is a wrong to his providence, as though we were not under his government, and had no need of his assistance; a wrong to his excellency, as though there were no amiableness in him to make his service desirable; an injury to his goodness and power, as if he were not able or willing to reward the creatures' obedience, or careless not to take notice of it; it is a sign we receive little satisfaction in him, and that there is a great unsuitableness between him and us.

(1.) There is a kind of constraint in the first engagement. We are rather pressed to it than enter ourselves volunteers. What we call service to God is done naturally much against our wills; it is not a delightful food, but a bitter potion; we are rather haled, than run to it. There is a contradiction of sin within us against our service, as there was a contradiction of sinners without our Saviour against his doing the will of God. Our hearts are unwieldy to any spiritual service of God; we are fain to use a violence with them sometimes: Hezekiah, it is said, "walked before the Lord, with a perfect heart" (2 Kings xx. 9); he walked, he made himself to walk: man naturally cares not for a walk with God; if he hath any communion with him, it is with such a dulness and heaviness of spirit as if he wished himself out of his company. Man's nature, being contrary to holiness, hath an aversion to any act of homage to God, because holiness must at least be pretended. In every duty wherein we have a communion with God, holiness is requisite: now as men are against the truth of holiness, because it is unsuitable to them, so they are not friends to those duties which require it, and for some space divert them from the thoughts of their beloved lusts. The word of the Lord is a yoke, prayer a drudgery, obedience a strange element. We are like fish, that "drink up iniquity like water,"[t] and come not to the bank without the force of an angle; no more willing to do service for God, than a fish is of itself to do service for man. It is a constrained act to satisfy conscience, and such are servile, not son-like performances, and spring from bondage more than affection; if conscience, like a task-master, did not scourge them to duty, they would never perform it. Let us appeal to ourselves, whether we are not more unwilling to secret, closet, hearty duty to God, than to join with others in some external service; as if those inward services were a going to the rack, and rather our penance than privilege. How much service hath God in the world from the same principle that vagrants perform their task in Bridewell! How glad are many of evasions to back them in the neglect of the commands of God, of corrupt reasonings from the flesh to waylay an act of obedience, and a multitude of excuses to blunt the edge of the precept! The very service of God shall be a pretence to deprive him of the obedience due to him. Saul will not be ruled by God's will in the destroying the cattle of the Amalekites, but by his own; and will impose upon the will and wisdom of God, judging God mistaken in his command, and that the cattle God thought fittest to be meat to the fowls, were fitter to be sacrifices on the altar.[u] If we do perform any part of his will, is it not for our own ends, to have some deliverance from trouble? (Isa. xxvi. 16): "In trouble have they visited thee; they poured out a prayer when thy chastening was upon them." In affliction, he shall find them kneeling in homage and devotion; in prosperity, he shall feel them kicking with contempt; they can pour out a prayer in distress, and scarce drop one when they are delivered.

(2.) There is a slightness in our service of God. We are loth to come into his presence; and when we do come, we are loth to continue with him. We pay not an homage to him heartily, as to our Lord and Governor; we regard him not as our Master, whose work we ought to do, and whose honor we ought to aim at. 1. In regard of the matter of service. When the torn, the lame, and the sick is offered to God;[x] so thin and lean a sacrifice, that you may have thrown it to the ground with a puff; so some understand the meaning of "you have snuffed at it." Men have naturally such slight thoughts of the majesty and law of God, that they think any service is good enough for him, and conformable to his law. The dullest and deadest time we think fittest to pay God a service in; when sleep is ready to close our eyes, and we are unfit to serve ourselves, we think it a fit time to open our hearts to God. How few morning sacrifices hath God from many persons and families! Men leap out of their beds to their carnal pleasures or worldly employments, without any thought of their Creator and Preserver, or any reflection upon his will as the rule of our daily obedience. And as many reserve the dregs of their lives, their old age, to offer up their souls to

---

[t] Job xv. 16.   [u] 1 Sam. xv. 3, 9, 15, 21.   [x] Mal. i. 13, 14.

God, so they reserve the dregs of the day, their sleeping time, for the offering up their service to him. How many grudge to spend their best time in the serving the will of God, and reserve for him the sickly and rheumatic part of their lives; the remainder of that which the devil and their own lusts have fed upon! Would not any prince or governor judge a present half eaten up by wild beasts, or that which died in a ditch, a contempt of his royalty? A corrupt thing is too base and vile for so great a King as God is, whose name is dreadful.ʸ When by age men are weary of their own bodies, they would present them to God; yet grudgingly, as if a tired body were too good for him, snuffing at the command for service. God calls for our best, and we give him the worst. 2. In respect of frame. We think any frame will serve God's turn, which speaks our slight of God as a Ruler. Man naturally performs duty with an unholy heart, whereby it becomes an abomination to God (Prov. xxviii. 9): "He that turns away his ear from hearing the law, even his prayers shall be an abomination to God." The services which he commands, he hates for their evil frames or corrupt ends (Amos v. 21): "I hate, I despise your feast-days, I will not smell in your solemn assemblies." God requires gracious services, and we give him corrupt ones. We do not rouse up our hearts, as David called upon his lute and harp to awake (Psalm lvii. 8). Our hearts are not given to him; we put him off with bodily exercise. The heart is but ice to what it doth not affect, [1.] There is not that natural vigor in the observance of God, which we have in worldly business. When we see a liveliness in men in other things, change the scene into a motion towards God, how suddenly doth their vigor shrink and their hearts freeze into sluggishness! Many times we serve God as languishingly as if we were afraid he should accept us, and pray as coldly as if we were unwilling he should hear us, and take away that lust by which we are governed, and which conscience forces us to pray against; as if we were afraid God should set up his own throne and government in our hearts. How fleeting are we in divine med- itation, how sleepy in spiritual exercises! but in other exercises ac- tive. The soul doth not awaken itself, and excite those animal and vital spirits, which it will in bodily recreations and sports; much less the powers of the soul: whereby it is evident we prefer the latter before any service to God. Since there is a fulness of animal spirits, why might they not be excited in holy duties as well as in other operations, but that there is a reluctancy in the soul to exer- cise its supremacy in this case, and perform anything becoming a creature in subjection to God as a Ruler? [2.] It is evident also in the distractions we have in his service. How loth are we to serve God fixedly one hour, nay a part of an hour, notwithstanding all the thoughts of his majesty, and the eternity of glory set before our eye! What man is there, since the fall of Adam, that served God one hour without many wanderings and unsuitable thoughts unfit for that service? How ready are our hearts to start out and unite themselves with any worldly objects that please us! [3.] Weariness in it evidenceth it. To be weary of our dulness signifies a desire,

ʸ Mal. i. 14.

to be weary of service signifies a discontent, to be ruled by God. How tired are we in the performance of spiritual duties, when in the vain triflings of time we have a perpetual motion! How will many willingly revel whole nights, when their hearts will flag at the threshold of a religious service! like Dagon,[z] lose both our heads to think, and hands to act, when the ark of God is present. Some in the Prophet wished the new moon and the Sabbath over, that they might sell their corn, and be busied again in their worldly affairs.[a] A slight and weariness of the Sabbath, was a slight of the Lord of the Sabbath, and of that freedom from the yoke and rule of sin, which was signified by it. The design of the sacrifices in the new moon was to signify a rest from the tyranny of sin, and a consecration to the spiritual service of God. Servants that are quickly weary of their work, are weary of the authority of their master that enjoins it. If our hearts had a value for God, it would be with us as with the needle to the loadstone; there would be upon his beck a speedy motion to him, and a fixed union with him. When the judgments and affections of the saints shall be fully refined in glory, they shall be willing to behold the face of God, and be under his government to eternity, without any weariness: as the holy angels have owned God as their sovereign near these six thousand years, without being weary of running on his errands. But, alas, while the flesh clogs us, there will be some relics of unwillingness to hear his injunctions, and weariness in performing them; though men may excuse those things by extrinsic causes, yet God's unerring judgment calls it a weariness of himself (Isaiah xliii. 22): "Thou hast not called upon me, O Jacob, but thou hast been weary of me, O Israel." Of this he taxeth his own people, when he tells them he would have the beasts of the field, the dragons and the owls—the Gentiles, that the Jews counted no better than such—to honor him and acknowledge him their rule in a way of duty (ver. 20, 21.)

6. This contempt is seen in a deserting the rule of God, when our expectations are not answered upon our service. When services are performed from carnal principles, they are soon cast off when carnal ends meet not with desired satisfaction. But when we own ourselves God's servants and God our Master, "our eyes will wait upon him till he have mercy on us."[b] It is one part of the duty we owe to God as our Master in heaven to continue in prayer (Col iv. 1, 2); and by the same reason in all other service, and to watch in the same with thanksgiving: to watch for occasions of praise, to watch with cheerfulness for further manifestations of his will, strength to perform it, success in the performance, that we may from all draw matter of praise. As we are in a posture of obedience to his precepts, so we should be in a posture of waiting for the blessing of it. But naturally we reject the duty we owe to God, if he do not speed the blessing we expect from him. How many do secretly mutter the same as they in Job xxi. 15: "What is the Almighty that we should serve him, and what profit shall we have if we pray to him?" They serve not God out of conscience to his commands, but for some carnal profit; and if God make them to wait for it, they will not

[z] 1 Sam. v. 4.   [a] Amos viii. 5.   [b] Psalm cxxiii. 2.

stay his leisure, but cease soliciting him any longer. Two things are expressed;—that God was not worthy of any homage from them,—" What is the Almighty that we should serve him?" and that the service of him would not bring them in a good revenue or an advantage of that kind they expected. Interest drives many men on to some kind of service, and when they do not find an advance of that, they will acknowledge God no more; but like some beggars, if you give them not upon their asking, and calling you good master, from blessing they will turn to cursing. How often do men do that secretly, practically, if not plainly, which Job's wife advised him to, curse God, and cast off that disguise of integrity they had assumed! (Job ii. 9): " Dost thou still retain thy integrity? curse God·" What a stir, and pulling, and crying is here! Cast off all thoughts of religious service, and be at daggers drawing with that God, who for all thy service of him has made thee so wretched a spectacle to men, and a banquet for worms. The like temper is deciphered in the Jews (Mal. iii. 14), " It is in vain to serve God, and what profit is it that we have kept his ordinances, that we have walked mournfully before the Lord?" What profit is it that we have regarded his statutes, and carried ourselves in a way of subjection to God, as our Sovereign, when we inherit nothing but sorrow, and the idolatrous neighbors swim in all kind of pleasures? as if it were the most miserable thing to acknowledge God? If men have not the benefits they expect, they think God unrighteous in himself, and injurious to them, in not conferring the favor they imagine they have merited; and if they have not that recompense, they will deny God that subjection they owe to him as creatures. Grace moves to God upon a sense of duty; corrupt nature upon a sense of interest. Sincerity is encouraged by gracious returns, but is not melted away by God's delay or refusal. Corrupt nature would have God at its back, and steers a course of duty by hope of some carnal profit, not by a sense of the sovereignty of God.

7. This contempt is seen in breaking promises with God. " One while the conscience of a man makes vows of new obedience, and perhaps binds himself with many an oath; but they prove like Jonah's gourd, withering the next day after their birth. This was Pharaoh's temper: under a storm he would submit to God, and let Israel go; but when the storm is ended, he will not be under God's control, and Israel's slavery shall be increased. The fear of Divine wrath makes many a sinner turn his back upon his sin, and the love of his ruling lust makes him turn his back upon his true Lord. This is from the prevalency of sin, that disputes with God for the sovereignty."[c] When God hath sent a sharp disease, as a messenger to bind men to their beds, and make an interruption of their sinful pleasures, their mouths are full of promises of a new life, in hope to escape the just vengeance of God: the sense of hell, which strikes strongly upon them, makes them full of such pretended resolutions when they howl upon their beds. But if God be pleased in his patience to give them a respite, to take off the chains wherewith he seemed to be binding them for destruction, and recruit their strength,

[c] Reyn.

they are more earnest in their sins than they were in their promises of a reformation, as if they had got the mastery of God, and had out-witted him. How often doth God charge them of not returning to him after a succession of judgments![d] So hard it is, not only to allure, but to scourge men, to an acknowledgment of God as their Ruler!

Consider then, are we not naturally inclined to disobey the known will of God? Can we say, Lord, for thy sake we refrain the thing to which our hearts incline? Do we not allow ourselves to be licentious, earthly, vain, proud, revengeful, though we know it will offend him? Have we not been peevishly cross to his declared will? run counter to him and those laws which express most of the glory of his holiness? Is not this to disown him as our rule? Did we never wish there were no law to bind us, no precept to check our idols? What is this, but to wish that God would depose himself from being our governor, and leave us to our own conduct? or else to wish that he were as unholy as ourselves, as careless of his own laws as we are; that is, that he were no more a God than we, a God as sinful and unrighteous as ourselves? He whose heart riseth against the law of God to unlaw it, riseth against the Author of that law to undeify him. He that casts contempt upon the dearest thing God hath in the world, that which is the image of his holiness, the delight of his soul; that which he hath given a special charge to maintain, and that because it is holy, just, and good, would not stick to rejoice at the destruction of God himself. If God's holiness and righteousness in the beam be despised, much more will an immense goodness and holiness in the fountain be rejected: he that wisheth a beam far from his eyes, because it offends and scorcheth him, can be no friend to the sun, from whence that beam doth issue. How unworthy a crea-ture is man, since he only, a rational creature, is the sole being that withdraws itself from the rule of God in this earth! And how mis-erable a creature is he also, since, departing from the order of God's goodness, he falls into the order of his justice; and while he refuseth God to be the rule of his life, he cannot avoid him being the Judge of his punishment! It is this is the original of all sin, and the foun-tain of all our misery. This is the first thing man disowns, the rule which God sets him.

Secondly, Man naturally owns any other rule rather than that of God's prescribing. The law of God orders one thing, the heart of man desires another. There is not the basest thing in the world, but man would sooner submit to be guided by it, rather than by the holiness of God; and when anything that God commands crosses our own wills, we value it no more than we would the advice of a poor dis-picable beggar. How many are "lovers of pleasure, more than lovers of God!"[e] To make something which contributes to the per-fection of nature, as learning, wisdom, moral virtues, our rule, would be more tolerable; but to pay that homage to a swinish pleasure, which is the right of God, is an inexcusable contempt of him. The greatest excellency in the world is infinitely below God; much more a bestial delight, which is both disgraceful and below the nature of

[d] Amos iv. 6–11   [e] 2 Tim. iii. 4.

man. If we made the vilest creature on earth our idol, it is more excusable than to be the slave of a brutish pleasure. The viler the thing is that doth possess the throne in our heart, the greater contempt it is of him who can only claim a right to it, and is worthy of it. Sin is the first object of man's election, as soon as the faculty whereby he chooses comes to exercise its power; and it is so dear to man, that it is, in the estimate of our Saviour, counted as the right hand, and the right eye, dear, precious, and useful members.

1. The rule of Satan is owned before the rule of God. The natural man would rather be under the guidance of Satan than the yoke of his Creator. Adam chose him to be his governor in Paradise. No sooner had Satan spoke of God in a way of derision (Gen. iii. 1, 5), "Yea, hath God said," but man follows his counsel and approves of the scoff; and the greatest part of his posterity have not been wiser by his fall, but would rather ramble in the devil's wilderness, than to stay in God's fold. It is by the sin of man that the devil is become the god of the world, as if men were the electors of him to the government; sin is an election of him for a lord, and a putting the soul under his government. Those that live according to the course of the world, and are loth to displease it, are under the government of the prince of it. The greatest part of the works done in the world is to enlarge the kingdom of Satan. For how many ages were the laws whereby the greatest part of the world was governed in the affairs of religion, the fruits of his usurpation and policy? When temples were erected to him, priests consecrated to his service; the rites used in most of the worship of the world were either of his own coining, or the misapplying the rites God had ordained to himself, under the notion of a God: whence the apostle calls all idolatrous feasts the table of devils, the cup of devils, sacrifice to devils, fellowship with devils;[f] devils being the real object of the pagan worship, though not formally intended by the worshipper; though in some parts of the Indies, the direct and peculiar worship is to the devil, that he might not hurt them. And though the intention of others was to offer to God, and not the devil, yet since the action was contrary to the will of God, he regards it as a sacrifice to devils. It was not the intention of Jeroboam to establish priests to the devil, when he consecrated them to the service of his calves, for Jehu afterwards calls them "the servants of the Lord" (2 Kings x. 23), "See if there be here none of the servants of the Lord," to distinguish them from the servants of Baal; signifying that the true God was worshipped under those images, and not Baal, nor any of the gods of the heathens; yet the Scripture couples the calves and devils together, and ascribes the worship given to one to be given to the other: "He ordained him priests for the high places, and for the devils, and for the calves which he had made;"[g] so that they were sacrifices to devils, notwithstanding the intention of Jeroboam and his subjects that had set them up and worshipped them, because they were contrary to the mind of God, and agreeable to the doctrine and mind of Satan, though the object of their worship in their own intention were not the devil, but some deified man or some canonized saint.

f 1 Cor. x. 20, 21.   g 2 Chron. xi. 15.

The intention makes not a good action; if so, when men kill the best servants of God with a design to do God service, as our Saviour foretells,[h] the action would not be murder; yet who can call it otherwise, since God is wronged in the persons of his servants? Since most of the worship of the world, which men's corrupt natures incline them to, is false and different from the revealed will of God, it is a practical acknowledgment of the devil, as the governor, by acknowledging and practising those doctrines, which have not the stamp of divine revelation upon them, but were minted by Satan to depress the honor of God in the world. It doth concern men, then, to take good heed, that in their acts of worship they have a divine rule; otherwise it is an owning the devil as the rule: for there is no medium; whatsoever is not from God, is from Satan. But to bring this closer to us, and consider that which is more common among us: men that are in a natural condition, and wedded to their lusts, are under the paternal government of Satan (John viii. 44): "Ye are of your father, the devil, and the lusts of your father you will do." If we divide sin into spiritual and carnal, which division comprehends all, the devil's authority is owned in both; in spiritual, we conform to his example, because those he commits; in carnal, we obey his will, because those he directs: he acts the one, and sets us a copy; he tempts to the other, and gives us a kind of a precept. Thus man by nature being a willing servant of sin, is more desirous to be bound in the devil's iron chain, than in God's silken cords. What greater atheism can there be, than to use God as if he were inferior to the devil? to take the part of his greatest enemy, who drew all others into the faction against him? to pleasure Satan by offending God, and gratify our adversary with the injury of our Creator? For a subject to take arms against his prince with the deadliest enemy both himself and prince hath in the whole world, adds a greater blackness to the rebellion.

2. The more visible rule preferred before God in the world, is man. The opinion of the world is more our rule than the precept of God; and many men's abstinence from sin is not from a sense of the Divine will, no, nor from a principle of reason, but from an affection to some man on whom they depend, or fear of punishment from a superior; the same principle with that in a ravenous beast, who abstains from what he desires, for fear only of a stick or club. Men will walk with the herds, go in fashion with the most, speak and act as the most do. While we conform to the world, we cannot perform a reasonable service to God, nor prove, nor approve practically what the good and acceptable will of God is; the apostle puts them in opposition to one another.[i] This appears,

1. In complying more with the dictates of men, than the will of God. Men draw encouragement from God's forbearance to sin more freely against him; but the fear of punishment for breaking the will of man lays a restraint upon them. The fear of man is a more powerful curb, to restrain men in their duty, than the fear of God; so we may please a friend, a master, a governor, we are regardless whether we please God or no; men-pleasers are more than God-

[h] John xvi. 2.　　　　　　　　　[i] Rom. xii. 1, 2.

pleasers; man is more advanced as a rule, than God, when we submit to human orders, and stagger and dispute against divine. Would not a prince think himself slighted in his authority, if any of his servants should decline his commands, by the order of one of his subjects? And will not God make the same account of us, when we deny or delay our obedience, for fear of one of his creatures? In the fear of man, we as little acknowledge God for our sovereign, as we do for our comforter (Isa. li. 12, 13): "I, even I, am he that comforteth you; who art thou, that thou shouldst be afraid of a man that shall die," &c. "and forgettest the Lord thy maker?" &c. We put a slight upon God, as if he were not able to bear us out in our duty to him, and incapable to balance the strength of an arm of flesh.

2. In observing that which is materially the will of God, not because it is his will, but the injunctions of men. As the word of God may be received, yet not as his word, so the will of God may be performed, yet not as his will; it is materially done, but not formally obeyed. An action, and obedience in that action, are two things; as when man commands the ceasing from all works of the ordinary calling on the Sabbath, it is the same that God enjoins: the cessation, or attendance of his servants on the hearing of the word, are conformable in the matter of it to the will of God; but it is only conformable in the obediential part of the acts to the will of man, when it is done only with respect to a human precept. As God hath a right to enact his laws without consulting his creature in the way of his government, so man is bound to obey those laws, without consulting whether they be agreeable to men's laws or no. If we act the will of God because the will of our superiors concurs with it, we obey not God in that, but man, a human will being the rule of our obedience, and not the divine; this is to vilify God, and make him inferior to man in our esteem, and a valuing the rule of man above that of our Creator. Since God is the highest perfection and infinitely good, whatsoever rule he gives the creature must be good, else it cannot proceed from God. A base thing cannot be the product of an infinite excellency, and an unreasonable thing cannot be the product of an infinite wisdom and goodness; therefore, as the respecting God's will before the will of man is excellent and worthy of a creature, and is an acknowledging the excellency, goodness, and wisdom of God, so the eying the will of man before and above the will of God, is on the contrary, a denial of all those in a lump, and a preferring the wisdom, goodness, and power of man in his law, above all those perfections of God in his. Whatsoever men do that looks like moral virtue or abstinence from vices, not out of obedience to the rule God hath set, but because of custom, necessity, example, or imitation, they may, in the doing of it, be rather said to be apes than Christians.

3. In obeying the will of man when it is contrary to the will of God; as the Israelites willingly "walked after the commandment,"[k] not of God, but of Jeroboam in the case of the calves, and "made the king's heart glad with their lies."[l] They cheered him with their ready obedience to his command for idolatry (which was a lie in itself, and a lie in them) against the commandment of God, and the

k Hos. v. 11.   l Hos. vii. 3.

warnings of the prophets, rather than cheer the heart of God with their obedience to his worship instituted by him; nay, and when God offered them to cure them their wound, their iniquity breaks out afresh; they would neither have him as a lord to rule them, nor a physician to cure them (Hosea vii. 1): "When I would have healed Israel, then the iniquity of Ephraim was discovered." The whole Persian nation shrunk at once from a duty due by the light of nature to the Deity, upon a decree that "neither God or man should be petitioned to for thirty days, but only their king;"ᵐ one only, Daniel, excepted against it, who preferred his homage to God, above obedience to his prince. An adulterous generation is many times made the rule of men's professions, as is implied in those words of our Saviour (Mark viii. 38): "Whosoever shall be ashamed of me and my words in this adulterous and sinful generation:" own him among his disciples, and be ashamed of him among his enemies. Thus men are said to deny God (Tit. i. 16), when they "attend to Jewish fables and the precepts of men rather than the word of God;" when the decrees or canons of fallible men are valued at a higher rate, and preferred before the writings of the Holy Ghost by his apostles. As man naturally disowns the rule God sets him, and owns any other rule than that of God's prescribing, so,

Thirdly, He doth this in order to the setting himself up as his own rule; as though our own wills, and not God's, were the true square and measure of goodness. We make an idol of our own wills, and as much as self is exalted, God is deposed; the more we esteem our own wills, the more we endeavor to annihilate the will of God; account nothing of him, the more we account of ourselves, and endeavor to render ourselves his superiors, by exalting our own wills. No prince but would look upon his authority as invaded, his royalty derided, if a subject should resolve to be a law to himself, in opposition to his known will; true piety is to hate ourselves, deny ourselves, and cleave solely to the service of God. To make ourselves our own rule, and the object of our chiefest love, is atheism. If self-denial be the greatest part of godliness, the great letter in the alphabet of religion; self-love is the great letter in the alphabet of practical atheism. Self is the great antichrist and anti-God in the world, that sets up itself above all that is called God; self-love is the captain of that black band (2 Tim. iii. 2): it sits in the temple of God, and would be adored as God. Self-love begins; but denying the power of godliness, which is the same with denying the ruling power of God, ends the list. It is so far from bending to the righteous will of the Creator, that it would have the eternal will of God stoop to the humor and unrighteous will of a creature; and this is the ground of the contention between the flesh and spirit in the heart of a renewed man; flesh wars for the godhead of self, and spirit fights for the godhead of God; the one would settle the throne of the Creator, and the other maintain a law of covetousness, ambition, envy, lust, in the stead of God. The evidence of this will appear in these propositions:

1. This is natural to man as he is corrupted. What was the venom

ᵐ Dan. vi.

of the sin of Adam, is naturally derived with his nature to all his posterity. It was not the eating a forbidden apple, or the pleasing his palate that Adam aimed at, or was the chief object of his desire, but to live independently on his Creator, and be a God to himself (Gen. iii. 5): "You shall be as gods." That which was the matter of the devil's temptation, was the incentive of man's rebellion; a likeness to God he aspired to in the judgment of God himself, an infallible interpreter of man's thoughts; "Behold, man is become as one of us, to know good and evil," in regard of self-sufficiency and being a rule to himself. The Jews understand the ambition of man to reach no further than an equality with the angelical nature; but Jehovah here understands it in another sense; God had ordered man by this prohibition not to eat of the fruit of the "tree of knowledge of good and evil;" not to attempt the knowledge of good and evil of himself, but to wait upon the dictates of God; not to trust to his own counsels, but to depend wholly upon him for direction and guidance. Certainly he that would not hold off his hand from so small a thing as an apple, when he had his choice of the fruit of the garden, would not have denied himself anything his appetite had desired, when that principle had prevailed upon him; he would not have stuck at a greater matter to pleasure himself with the displeasing of God, when for so small a thing he would incur the anger of his Creator. Thus would he deify his own understanding against the wisdom of God, and his own appetite against the will of God. This desire of equality with God, a learned man[n] thinks the apostle intimates (Phil. ii. 6): "Who being in the form of God, thought it not robbery to be equal with God;" the Son's being in the form of God, and thinking it no robbery to be equal with God, implies that the robbery of sacrilege committed by our first parents, for which the Son of God humbled himself to the death of the cross, was an attempt to be equal with God, and depend no more upon God's directions, but his own conduct; which could be no less than an invasion of the throne of God, and endeavor to put himself into a posture to be his mate. Other sins, adultery, theft, &c. could not be committed by him at that time, but he immediately puts forth his hand to usurp the power of his Maker; this treason is the old Adam in every man. The first Adam contradicted the will of God to set up himself; the second Adam humbled himself, and did nothing but by the command and will of his Father. This principle wherein the venom of the old Adam lies, must be crucified to make way for the throne of the humble and obedient principle of the new Adam, or quickening Spirit; indeed sin in its own nature is nothing else but " a willing according to self, and contrary to the will of God;" lusts are therefore called the wills of the flesh and of the mind.[o] As the precepts of God are God's will, so the violation of these precepts is man's will; and thus man usurps a godhead to himself, by giving that honor to his own will which belongs to God, appropriating the right of rule to himself, and denying it to his Creator. That servant that acts according to his own will, with a neglect of his master's, refuseth the duty of a servant, and invades the right of his master.

ⁿ Dr. Jackson.   ᵒ Eph. ii. 3.

This self-love and desire of independency on God has been the root of all sin in the world. The great controversy between God and man hath been, whether he or they shall be God; whether his reason or theirs, his will or theirs, shall be the guiding principle. As grace is the union of the will of God and the will of the creature, so sin is the opposition of the will of self to the will of God; "Leaning to our own understanding," is opposed as a natural evil to "trusting in the Lord,"[p] a supernatural grace. Men commonly love what is their own, their own inventions, their own fancies; therefore the ways of a wicked man are called the "ways of his own heart,"[q] and the ways of a superstitious man his own devices (Jer. xviii. 11): "We will walk after our own devices;" we will be a law to ourselves; and what the Psalmist saith of the tongue, Our tongues are our own, who shall control us? is as truly the language of men's hearts, Our wills are our own, who shall check us?

2. This is evident in the dissatisfaction of men with their own consciences when they contradict the desires of self. Conscience is nothing but an actuated or reflex knowledge of a superior power and an equitable law; a law impressed, and a power above it impressing it. Conscience is not the lawgiver, but the remembrancer to mind us of that law of nature imprinted upon our souls, and actuate the considerations of the duty and penalty, to apply the rule to our acts, and pass judgment upon matter of fact: it is to give the charge, urge the rule, enjoin the practice of those notions of right, as part of our duty and obedience. But man is as much displeased with the directions of conscience, as he is out of love with the accusations and condemning sentence of this officer of God: we cannot naturally endure any quick and lively practical thoughts of God and his will, and distaste our own consciences for putting us in mind of it: they therefore "like not to retain God in their knowledge,"[r] that is, God in their own consciences; they would blow it out, as it is the candle of the Lord in them to direct them, and their acknowledgments of God, to secure themselves against the practice of its principles: they would stop all the avenues to any beam of light, and would not suffer a sparkle of divine knowledge to flutter in their minds, in order to set up another directing rule suited to the fleshly appetite: and when they cannot stop the light of it from glaring in their faces, they rebel against it, and cannot endure to abide in its paths.[s] He speaks not of those which had the written word, or special revelations; but only a natural light or traditional, handed from Adam: hence are all the endeavors to still it when it begins to speak, by some carnal pleasures, as Saul's evil spirit with a fit of music; or bribe it with some fits of a glavering devotion, when it holds the law of God in its commanding authority before the mind: they would wipe out all the impressions of it when it presses the advancement of God above self, and entertain it with no better compliment than Ahab did Elijah, "Hast thou found me, O my enemy?" If we are like to God in anything of our natural fabric, it is in the superior and more spiritual part of our souls. The resistance of that which is most like to God, and instead of God in us, is a disowning of the Sovereign represented by

[p] Prov. iii. 5. [q] Eccl. xi. 9. [r] Rom. i. 28. [s] Job xxiv. 13.

that officer.   He that would be without conscience, would be without God, whose vicegerent it is, and make the sensitive part, which conscience opposes, his lawgiver.   Thus a man, out of respect to sinful self, quarrels with his natural self, and cannot comport himself in a friendly behavior to his internal implanted principles: he hates to come under the rebukes of them, as much as Adam hated to come into the presence of God, after he turned traitor against him: the bad entertainment God's deputy hath in us, reflects upon that God whose cause it pleads: it is upon no other account that men loathe the upright language of their own reasons in those matters, and wish the eternal silence of their own consciences, but as they maintain the rights of God, and would hinder the idol of self from usurping his godhead and prerogative.   Though this power be part of a man's self, rooted in his nature, as essential to him and inseparable from him as the best part of his being; yet he quarrels with it, as it is God's deputy, and stickling for the honor of God in his soul, and quarrelling with that sinful self he would cherish above God.   We are not displeased with this faculty barely as it exerciseth a self-reflection; but as it is God's vicegerent, and bears the mark of his authority in it.   In some cases this self-reflecting act meets with good entertainment, when it acts not in contradiction to self, but suitable to natural affections.   As suppose a man hath in his passion struck his child, and caused thereby some great mischief to him, the reflection of conscience will not be unwelcome to him; will work some tenderness in him, because it takes the part of self and of natural affection; but in the more spiritual concerns of God it will be rated as a busy-body.

3. Many, if not most actions, materially good in the world, are done more because they are agreeable to self, than as they are honorable to God.   As the word of God may be heard not as his word,[t] but as there may be pleasing notions in it, or discourses against an opinion or party we disaffect; so the will of God may be performed, not as his will, but as it may gratify some selfish consideration, when we will please God so far as it may not displease ourselves, and serve him as our Master, so far as his command may be a servant to our humor; when we consider not who it is that commands, but how short it comes of displeasing that sin which rules in our heart, pick and choose what is least burdensome to the flesh, and distasteful to our lusts.   He that doth the will of God, not out of conscience of that will, but because it is agreeable to himself, casts down the will of God, and sets his own will in the place of it; takes the crown from the head of God, and places it upon the head of self.   If things are done, not because they are commanded by God, but desirable to us, it is a disobedient obedience; a conformity to God's will in regard of the matter, a conformity to our own will in regard of the motive; either as the things done are agreeable to natural and moral self, or sinful self.

(1). As they are agreeable to natural or moral self.   When men will practise some points of religion, and walk in the track of some divine precepts; not because they are divine, but because they are

t 1 Thess. ii. 13.

agreeable to their humor or constitution of nature ; from the sway of a natural bravery, the bias of a secular interest, not from an ingenuous sense of God's authority, or a voluntary submission to his will ; as when a man will avoid excess in drinking, not because it is dishonorable to God, but as it is a blemish to his own reputation, or an impair of the health of his body : doth this deserve the name of an observance of the divine injunction, or rather an obedience to ourselves ? Or when a man will be liberal in the distribution of his charity, not with an eye to God's precept, but in compliance with his own natural compassion, or to pleasure the generosity of his nature : the one is obedience to a man's own preservation; the other an obedience to the interest or impulse of a moral virtue. It is not respect to the rule of God, but the authority of self, and, at the best, is but the performance of the material part of the divine rule, without any concurrence of a spiritual motive or a spiritual manner. That only is a maintaining the rights of God, when we pay an observance to his rule, without examining the agreeableness of it to our secular interest, or consulting with the humor of flesh and blood ; when we will not decline his service, though we find it cross, and hath no affinity with the pleasure of our own nature : such an obedience as Abraham manifested in his readiness to sacrifice his son ; such an obedience as our Saviour demands in cutting off the right hand. When we observe anything of divine order upon the account of its suitableness to our natural sentiments, we shall readily divide from him, when the interest of nature turns its point against the interest of God's honor ; we shall fall off from him according to the change we find in our own humors. And can that be valued as a setting up the rule of God, which must be deposed upon the mutable interest of an inconstant mind ? Esau had no regard to God in delaying the execution of his resolution to shorten his brother's days, though he was awed by the reverence of his father to delay it ; he considered, perhaps, how justly he might lie under the imputation of hastening crazy Isaac's death, by depriving him of a beloved son. But had the old man's head been laid, neither the contrary command of God, nor the nearness of a fraternal relation, could have bound his hands from the act, no more than they did his heart from the resolution (Gen. xxvii. 41) : " Esau hated Jacob because of the blessing wherewith his father blessed him ; and Esau said in his heart, The days of mourning for my father are at hand, then will I slay my brother." So many children, that expect at the death of their parents great inheritances of portions, may be observant of them, not in regard of the rule fixed by God, but to their own hopes, which they would not frustrate by a disobligement. Whence is it that many men abstain from gross sins, but in love to their reputation ? Wickedness may be acted privately, which a man's own credit puts a bar to the open commission of. The preserving his own esteem may divert him from entering into a brothel house, to which he hath set his mind before, against a known precept of his Creator. As Pharaoh parted with the Israelites, so do some men with their blemishing sins ; not out of a sense of God's rule, but the smart of present judgments, or fear of a future wrath. Our security then, and reputation, is set up in the place of God. This also may be, and is in renewed men, who have the law written in their hearts, that is, an habitual disposition to an agreement with the law of God; when what is done is with a respect to this habitual inclination, without eying the divine precept, which is appointed to be their rule. This also is to set up a creature, as renewed self is, instead of the Creator, and that law of his in his word, which ought to be the rule of our actions. Thus it is when men choose a moral life, not so much out of respect to the law of nature, as it is the law of God, but as it is a law become one with their souls and constitutions. There is more of self in this than consideration of God; for if it were the latter, the revealed law of God would, upon the same reason, be received as well as his natural law. From this principle of self, morality comes by some to be advanced above evangelical dictates.

(2.) As they are agreeable to sinful self. Not that the commands of God are suited to bolster up the corruptions of men, no more than the law can be said to excite or revive sin:[u] but it is like a scandal taken, not given; an occasion taken by the tumultuousness of our depraved nature. The Pharisees were devout in long prayers, not from a sense of duty, or a care of God's honor; but to satisfy their ambition, and rake together fuel for their covetousness,[x] that they might have the greater esteem and richer offerings, to free by their prayers the souls of deceased persons from purgatory; an opinion that some think the Jewish synagogue had then entertained,[y] since some of their doctors have defended such a notion. Men may observe some precepts of God to have a better conveniency to break others. Jehu was ordered to cut off the house of Ahab. The service he undertook was in itself acceptable, but corrupt nature misacted that which holiness and righteousness commanded. God appointed it to magnify his justice, and check the idolatry that had been supported by that family; Jehu acted it to satisfy his revenge and ambition: he did it to fulfil his lust, not the will of God who enjoined him: Jehu applauds it as zeal; and God abhors it as murder, and therefore would avenge the blood of Jezreel on the house of Jehu (Hos. i. 4). Such kind of services are not paid to God for his own sake, but to ourselves for our lusts' sake.

4. This is evident in neglecting to take God's direction upon emergent occasions. This follows the text, "None did seek God." When we consult not with him, but trust more to our own will and counsel, we make ourselves our own governors and lords independent upon him; as though we could be our own counsellors, and manage our concerns without his leave and assistance; as though our works were in our own hands, and not in the "hands of God;"[z] that we can by our own strength and sagacity direct them to a successful end without him. If we must "acquaint ourselves with God" before we decree a thing,[a] then to decree a thing without acquainting God with it, is to prefer our purblind wisdom before the infinite wisdom of God: to resolve without consulting God, is to depose

---

[u] Rom. vii. 8, 9.
[x] Matt. xxiii. 14: "You devour widows' houses, and for a pretence make long prayers."
[y] Gerrard *in loc.*   [z] Eccles. ix. 1.   [a] Job xxii. 28.

God and deify self, our own wit and strength. We would rather, like Lot, follow our own humor and stay in Sodom, than observe the angel's order to go out of it.

5. As we account the actions of others to be good or evil, as they suit with, or spurn against our fancies and humors. Virtue is a crime, and vice a virtue, as it is contrary or concurrent with our humors. Little reason have many men to blame the actions of others, but because they are not agreeable to what they affect and desire; we would have all men take directions from us, and move according to our beck, hence that common speech in the world, Such an one is an honest friend. Why? because he is of their humor, and lackeys according to their wills. Thus we make self the measure and square of good and evil in the rest of mankind, and judge of it by our own fancies, and not by the will of God, the proper rule of judgment. Well then, let us consider: Is not this very common? are we not naturally more willing to displease God than displease ourselves, when it comes to a point that we must do one or other? Is not our own counsel of more value with us, than conformity to the will of the Creator? Do not our judgments often run counter to the judgment of God? Have his laws a greater respect from us, than our own humors? Do we scruple the staining his honor when it comes in competition with our own? Are not the lives of most men a pleasing themselves, without a repentance that ever they displeased God? Is not this to undeify God, to deify ourselves, and disown the propriety he hath in us by the right of creation and beneficence? We order our own ways by our own humors, as though we were the authors of our own being, and had given ourselves life and understanding. This is to destroy the order that God hath placed between our wills and his own, and a lifting up of the foot above the head; it is the deformity of the creature. The honor of every rational creature consists in the service of the First Cause of his being; as the welfare of every creature consists in the orders and proportionable motion of its members, according to the law of its creation. He that moves and acts according to a law of his own, offers a manifest wrong to God, the highest wisdom and chiefest good; disturbs the order of the world; nulls the design of the righteousness and holiness of God. The law of God is the rule of that order he would have observed in the world; he that makes another law his rule, thrusts out the order of the Creator, and establishes the disorder of the creature. But this will yet be more evident, in the fourth thing.

Fourthly, Man would make himself the rule of God, and give laws to his Creator. We are willing God should be our benefactor, but not our ruler; we are content to admire his excellency and pay him a worship, provided he will walk by our rule. "This commits a riot upon his nature, To think him to be what we ourselves 'would have him, and wish him to be' (Psalm l. 21), we would amplify his mercy and contract his justice; we would have his power enlarged to supply our wants, and straitened when it goes about to revenge our crimes; we would have him wise to defeat our enemies, but not to disappoint our unworthy projects; we would have him all eye to regard our indigence, and blind not to discern our guilt; we would have him true to his promises, regardless of his precepts, and false to his threatenings; we would new mint the nature of God according to our models, and shape a God according to our own fancies, as he made us at first according to his own image;" instead of obeying him, we would have him obey us; instead of owning and admiring his perfections, we would have him strip himself of his infinite excellency, and clothe himself with a nature agreeable to our own. This is not only to set up self as the law of God, but to make our own imaginations the model of the nature of God.[b] Corrupted man takes a pleasure to accuse or suspect the actions of God: we would not have him act conveniently to his nature; but act what doth gratify us, and abstain from what distastes us. Man is never well but when he is impeaching one or other perfection of God's nature, and undermining his glory, as if all his attributes must stand indicted at the bar of our purblind reason: this weed shoots up in the exercise of grace. Peter intended the refusal of our Saviour's washing his feet, as an act of humility, but Christ understands it to be a prescribing a law to himself, a correcting his love (John xiii. 8, 9). This is evidenced,

1. In the strivings against his law. How many men imply by their lives, that they would have God deposed from his government, and some unrighteous being step into his throne; as if God had or should change his laws of holiness into laws of licentiousness: as if he should abrogate his old eternal precepts, and enact contrary ones in their stead? What is the language of such practices, but that they would be God's lawgivers and not his subjects? that he should deal with them according to their own wills, and not according to his righteousness? that they could make a more holy, wise, and righteous law than the law of God? that their imaginations, and not God's righteousness, should be the rule of his doing good to them? (Jer. ix. 31): "They have forsaken my law, and walked after the imaginations of their own heart." When an act is known to be a sin, and the law that forbids it acknowledged to be the law of God, and after this we persist in that which is contrary to it, we tax his wisdom as if he did not understand what was convenient for us; "we would teach God knowledge;"[c] it is an implicit wish that God had laid aside the holiness of his nature, and framed a law to pleasure our lusts. When God calls for weeping and mourning, and girding with sackcloth upon approaching judgments, then the corrupt heart is for joy and gladness, eating of flesh and drinking of wine, because to-morrow they should die;[d] as if God had mistaken himself when he ordered them so much sorrow, when their lives were so near an end; and had lost his understanding when he ordered such a precept: disobedience is therefore called contention (Rom. ii. 8): "Contentious, and obey not the truth:" contention against God, whose truth it is that they disobey; a dispute with him, which hath more of wisdom in itself, and conveniency for them, his truth of their imaginations. The more the love, goodness, and holiness of God appears in any command, the more are we naturally averse from it, and cast an imputation on him, as if he were foolish, unjust, cruel,

---

[b] Decay of Christian Piety, p. 169, somewhat changed.
[c] Job xxi. 22.   [d] Isa. xxii. 12, 13.

and that we could have advised and directed him better. The goodness of God is eminent to us in appointing a day for his own worship, wherein we might converse with him, and he with us, and our souls be refreshed with spiritual communications from him ; and we rather use it for the ease of our bodies, than the advancement of our souls, as if God were mistaken and injured his creature, when he urged the spiritual part of duty. Every disobedience to the law is an implicit giving law to him, and a charge against him that he might have provided better for his creature.

2. In disapproving the methods of God's government of the world. If the counsels of Heaven roll not about according to their schemes, instead of adoring the unsearchable depths of his judgments, they call him to the bar, and accuse him, because they are not fitted to their narrow vessels, as if a nut-shell could contain an ocean. As corrupt reason esteems the highest truths foolishness, so it counts the most righteous ways unequal. Thus we commence a suit against God, as though he had not acted righteously and wisely, but must give an account of his proceedings at our tribunal. This is to make ourselves God's superiors, and presume to instruct him better in the government of the world; as though God hindered himself and the world, in not making us of his privy council, and not ordering his affairs according to the contrivances of our dim understandings. Is not this manifest in our immoderate complaints of God's dealings with his church, as though there were a coldness in God's affections to his church, and a glowing heat towards it only in us? Hence are those importunate desires for things which are not established by any promise, as though we would overrule and over persuade God to comply with our humor. We have an ambition to be God's tutors and direct him in his counsels: "Who hath been his counsellor?" saith the apostle.[e] Who ought not to be his counsellor? saith corrupt nature. Men will find fault with God in what he suffers to be done according to their own minds, when they feel the bitter fruit of it. When Cain had killed his brother, and his conscience racked him, how saucily and discontentedly doth he answer God! (Gen. iv. 9), "Am I my brother's keeper?" Since thou dost own thyself the rector of the world, thou shouldst have preserved his person from my fury; since thou dost accept his sacrifice before my offering, preservation was due as well as acceptance. If this temper be found on earth, no wonder it is lodged in hell. That deplorable person under the sensible stroke of God's sovereign justice, would oppose his nay to God's will (Luke xvi. 30): " And he said, Nay, father Abraham, but if one went to them from the dead they will repent." He would presume to prescribe more effectual means than Moses and the prophets, to inform men of the danger they incurred by their sensuality. David was displeased, it is said (2 Sam. vi. 8), when the Lord had made a breach upon Uzzah, not with Uzzah, who was the object of his pity, but with God, who was the inflicter of that punishment. When any of our friends have been struck with a rod, against our sentiments and wishes, have not our hearts been apt to swell in complaints against God, as though he disregarded the good-

e Rom. xi. 34.

ness of such a person, did not see with our eyes, and measure him by our esteem of him? as if he should have asked our counsel, before he had resolved, and managed himself according to our will, rather than his own. If he be patient to the wicked, we are apt to tax his holiness, and accuse him as an enemy to his own law. If he inflict severity upon the righteous, we are ready to suspect his goodness, and charge him to be an enemy to his affectionate creature. If he spare the Nimrods of the world, we are ready to ask, "Where is the God of judgment?"[f] If he afflict the pillars of the earth, we are ready to question, where is the God of mercy? It is impossible, since the depraved nature of man, and the various interests and passions in the world, that infinite power and wisdom can act righteously for the good of the universe, but he will shake some corrupt interest or other upon the earth; so various are the inclinations of men, and such a weather-cock judgment hath every man in himself, that the divine method he applauds this day, upon a change of his interest, he will cavil at the next. It is impossible for the just orders of God to please the same person many weeks, scarce many minutes together. God must cease to be God, or to be holy, if he should manage the concerns of the world according to the fancies of men. How unreasonable is it thus to impose laws upon God! Must God revoke his own orders? govern according to the dictates of his creature? Must God, who hath only power and wisdom to sway the sceptre, become the obedient subject of every man's humor, and manage everything to serve the design of a simple creature? This is not to be God, but to set the creature in his throne: though this be not formally done, yet that it is interpretatively and practically done, is every hour's experience.

3. In impatience in our particular concerns. It is ordinary with man to charge God in his complaints in the time of affliction. Therefore it is the commendation the Holy Ghost gives to Job (ch. i. 22), that in all this, that is, in those many waves that rolled over him, he did not charge God foolishly, he never spake nor thought anything unworthy of the majesty and righteousness of God; yet afterwards we find him warping; he nicknames the affliction to be God's oppression of him, and no act of his goodness (x. 3): "Is it good for thee, that thou shouldst oppress?" He seems to charge God with injustice, for punishing him when he was not wicked, for which he appeals to God: "Thou knowest that I am not wicked" (ver. 7), and that God acted not like a Creator (ver. 8). If our projects are disappointed, what fretfulness against God's management are our hearts racked with! How do uncomely passions bubble upon us, interpretatively at least wishing that the arms of his power had been bound, and the eye of his omniscience been hoodwinked, that we might have been left to our own liberty and designs? and this oftentimes when we have more reason to bless him than repine at him. The Israelites murmured more against God in the wilderness, with manna in their mouths, than they did at Pharaoh in the brick-kilns, with their garlic and onions between their teeth. Though we repine at instruments in our afflictions, yet God counts it a reflection upon himself. The Israelites speaking against Moses, was, in God's inter-

f Mal. ii. 17.

pretation, a rebellion against himself:[g] and rebellion is always a desire of imposing laws and conditions upon those against whom the rebellion is raised. The sottish dealings of the vine-dressers in Franconia with the statue of St. Urban, the protector of the vines, upon his own day, is an emblem of our dealing with God : if it be a clear day and portend a prosperous vintage, they honor the statue and drink healths to it; if it be a rainy day, and presage a scantiness, they daub it with dirt in indignation. We cast out our mire and dirt against God when he acts cross to our wishes, and flatter him when the wind of his providence joins itself to the tide of our interest. Men set a high price upon themselves, and are angry God values them not at the same rate, as if their judgment concerning themselves were more piercing than his. This is to disannul God's judgment, and condemn him and count ourselves righteous, as 'tis Job xl. 8. This is the epidemical disease of human nature; they think they deserve caresses instead of rods, and upon crosses are more ready to tear out the heart of God, than reflect humbly upon their own hearts. When we accuse God, we applaud ourselves, and make ourselves his superiors, intimating that we have acted more righteously to him than he to us, which is the highest manner of imposing laws upon him; as that emperor accused the justice of God for snatching him out of the world too soon.[h] What a high piece of practical atheism is this, to desire that infinite wisdom should be guided by our folly, and asperse the righteousness of God rather than blemish our own! Instead of silently submitting to his will and adoring his wisdom, we declaim against him, as an unwise and unjust governor: we would invert his order, make him the steward and ourselves the proprietors of what we are and have : we deny ourselves to be sinners, and our mercies to be forfeited.

4. It is evidenced in envying the gifts and prosperities of others. Envy hath a deep tincture of practical atheism, and is a cause of atheism.[i] We are unwilling to leave God to be the proprietor and do what he will with his own, and as a Creator to do what he pleases with his creatures. We assume a liberty to direct God what portions, when and how, he should bestow upon his creatures. We would not let him choose his own favorites, and pitch upon his own instruments for his glory; as if God should have asked counsel of us how he should dispose of his benefits. We are unwilling to leave to his wisdom the management of his own judgments to the wicked, and the dispensation of his own love to ourselves. This temper is natural: it is as ancient as the first age of the world. Adam envied God a felicity by himself, and would not spare a tree that he had reserved as a mark of his sovereignty. The passion that God had given Cain to employ against his sin, he turns against his Creator. He was wroth with God and with Abel;[k] but envy was at the root, because his brother's sacrifice was accepted and his refused. How could he envy his accepted person, without reflecting upon the

[g] Numb. xvi. 41, compared with xvii. 10.

[h] Cœlum suspiciens vitam, &c. Vita Titi. c. 10.

[i] Because wicked men flourish in the world. Solicitor nullos esse putare Deos.

[k] Gen. iv. 5.

Acceptor of his offering? Good men have not been free from it. Job questions the goodness of God, that he should shine upon the counsel of the wicked (Job x. 3). Jonah had too much of self, in fearing to be counted a false prophet, when he came with absolute denunciations of wrath;[1] and when he could not bring a volley of destroying judgments upon the Ninevites, he would shoot his fury against his Master, envying those poor people the benefit, and God the honor of his mercy; and this after he had been sent into the whale's belly to learn humiliation, which, though he exercised there, yet those two great branches of self-pride and envy were not lopped off from him in the belly of hell; and God was fain to take pains with him, and by a gourd scarce makes him ashamed of his peevishness. Envy is not like to cease till all atheism be cashiered, and that is in heaven. This sin is an imitation of the devil, whose first sin upon earth was envy, as his first sin in heaven was pride. It is a wishing that to ourselves, which the devil asserted as his right, to give the kingdoms of the world to whom he pleased:[m] it is an anger with God, because he hath not given us a patent for government. It utters the same language in disparagement of God, as Absalom did in reflection on his father: If I were king in Israel, justice should be better managed; if I were Lord of the world, there should be more wisdom to discern the merits of men, and more righteousness in distributing to them their several portions. Thus we impose laws upon God, and would have the righteousness of his will submit to the corruptions of ours, and have him lower himself to gratify our minds, rather than fulfil his own. We charge the Author of those gifts with injustice, that he hath not dealt equally; or with ignorance, that he hath mistook his mark. In the same breath that we censure him by our peevishness, we would guide him by our wills. This is an unreasonable part of atheism. If all were in the same state and condition, the order of the world would be impaired. Is God bound to have a care of thee, and neglect all the world besides? "Shall the earth be forsaken for thee?"[n] Joseph had reason to be displeased with his brothers, if they had muttered because he gave Benjamin a double portion, and the rest a single. It was unfit that they, who had deserved no gift at all, should prescribe him rules how to dispense his own doles; much more unworthy it is to deal so with God; yet this is too rife.

5. It is evidenced in corrupt matter or ends of prayer and praise. When we are importunate for those things that we know not whether the righteousness, holiness, and wisdom of God can grant, because he hath not discovered his will in any promise to bestow them, we would then impose such conditions on God, which he never obliged himself to grant; when we pray for things not so much to glorify God, which ought to be the end of prayer, as to gratify ourselves. We acknowledge, indeed, by the act of petitioning, that there is a God; but we would have him ungod himself to be at our beck, and debase himself to serve our turns. When we desire those things which are repugnant to those attributes whereby he doth manage the government of the world; when, by some superficial services, we think we have

gained indulgence to sins, which seems to be the thought of the strumpet, in her paying her vows, to wallow more freely in the mire of her sensual pleasures—" I have peace-offerings with me; this day I have paid my vows, I have made my peace with God, and have entertainment for thee;"° or when men desire God to bless them in the commission of some sin, as when Balak and Balaam offered sacrifices, that they might prosper in the cursing of the Israelites (Numb. xxv. 1, &c.) So for a man to pray to God to save him, while he neglects the means of salvation appointed by God, or to renew him when he slights the word, the only instrument to that purpose; this is to impose laws upon God, contrary to the declared will and wisdom of God, and to desire him to slight his own institutions. When we come into the presence of God with lusts reeking in our hearts, and leap from sin to duty, we would impose the law of our corruption on the holiness of God. While we pray "the will of God may be done," self-love wishes its own will may be performed, as though God should serve our humors, when we will not obey his precepts. And when we make vows under any affliction, what is it often but a secret contrivance to bend and flatter him to our conditions? We will serve him if he will restore us; we think thereby to compound the business with him, and bring him down to our terms.

6. It is evidenced in positive and bold interpretations of the judgments of God in the world. To interpret the judgments of God to the disadvantage of the sufferer, unless it be an unusual judgment, and have a remarkable hand of God in it, and the sin be rendered plainly legible in the affliction, is a presumption of this nature. When men will judge the Galileans, whose blood Pilate mingled with the sacrifices, greater sinners than others, and themselves righteous, because no drops of it were dashed upon them; or when Shimei, being of the house of Saul, shall judge according to his own interest, and desires David's flight upon Absalom's rebellion to be a punishment for invading the rights of Saul's family, and depriving him of the succession in the kingdom,ᴾ as if he had been of God's privy council, when he decreed such acts of justice in the world. Thus we would fasten our own wills as a law or motive upon God, and interpret his acts according to the motions of self. Is it not too ordinary, when God sends an affliction upon those that bear ill-will to us, to judge it to be a righting of our cause, to be a fruit of God's concern for us in revenging our wrongs, as if we "had heard the secrets of God," or, as Eliphaz saith, "had turned over the records of heaven?" (Job xv. 8.) This is a judgment according to self-love, not a divine rule; and imposeth laws upon heaven, implying a secret wish that God would take care only of them, make our concerns his own, not in ways of kindness and justice, but according to our fancies; and this is common in the profane world, in those curses they so readily spit out upon any affront, as if God were bound to draw his arrows and shoot them into the heart of all their offenders at their beck and pleasure.

7. It is evidenced, in mixing rules for the worship of God with those which have been ordered by him. Since men are most prone

° Prov. vii. 14.   ᴾ 2 Sam. xvi. 5.

to live by sense, it is no wonder that a sensible worship, which affects their outward sense with some kind of amazement, is dear to them, and spiritual worship most loathsome.   Pompous rites have been the great engine wherewith the devil hath deceived the souls of men, and wrought them to a nauseating the simplicity of divine worship, as unworthy the majesty and excellency of God.q   Thus the Jews would not understand the glory of the second temple in the presence of the Messiah, because it had not the pompous grandeur of that of Solomon's erecting.   Hence in all ages men have been forward to disfigure God's models, and dress up a brat of their own ; as though God had been defective in providing for his own honor in his institutions, without the assistance of his creature.   This hath always been in the world ; the old world had their imaginations, and the new world hath continued them.   The Israelites in the midst of miracles, and under the memory of a famous deliverance, would erect a calf.   The Pharisees, that sate in Moses' chair, would coin new traditions, and enjoin them to be as current as the law of God.r Papists will be blending the christian appointments with pagan ceremonies, to please the carnal fancies of the common people.   " Altars have been multiplied" under the knowledge of the law of God.s   Interest is made the balance of the conveniency of God's injunctions. Jeroboam fitted a worship to politic ends, and posted up calves to prevent his subjects revolting from his sceptre, which might be occasioned by their resort to Jerusalem, and converse with the body of the people from whom they were separated.t   Men will be putting in their own dictates with God's laws, and are unwilling he should be the sole Governor of the world without their counsel ; they will not suffer him to be Lord of that which is purely and solely his concern.   How often hath the practice of the primitive church, the custom wherein we are bred, the sentiments of our ancestors, been owned as a more authentic rule in matters of worship, than the mind of God delivered in his Word !   It is natural by creation to worship God ; and it is as natural by corruption for man to worship him in a human way, and not in a divine ; is not this to impose laws upon God, to esteem ourselves wiser than he ? to think him negligent of his own service, and that our feeble brains can find out ways to accommodate his honor, better than himself hath done ?   Thus do men for the most part equal their own imaginations to God's oracles : as Solomon built a high place to Moloch and Chemoch, upon the Mount of Olives, to face on the east part Jerusalem and the temple ;u this is not only to impose laws on God, but also to make self the standard of them.

8. It is evidenced, in suiting interpretations of Scripture to their own minds and humors.   Like the Lacedæmonians, that dressed the images of their gods according to the fashion of their own country, we would wring Scripture to serve our own designs, and judge the law of God by the law of sin, and make the serpentine seed in us to be the interpreter of divine oracles : this is like Belshazzar to drink healths out of the sacred vessels.   As God is the author of his law

q 2 Cor. xi. 3.   r Matt. xiii. 6.   s Hos. viii. 12.
t 1 Kings xii. 27.   u 1 Kings xi. 7.

and word, so he is the best interpreter of it; the Scripture having an impress of divine wisdom, holiness, and goodness, must be regarded according to that impress, with a submission and meekness of spirit and reverence of God in it; but when, in our inquiries into the word, we inquire not of God, but consult flesh and blood, the temper of the times wherein we live, or the satisfaction of a party we side withal, and impose glosses upon it according to our own fancies, it is to put laws upon God, and make self the rule of him. He that interprets the law to bolster up some eager appetite against the will of the law-giver, ascribes to himself as great an authority as he that enacted it.

9. In falling off from God after some fair compliances, when his will grateth upon us, and crosseth ours. They will walk with him as far as he pleaseth them, and leave him upon the first distaste, as though God must observe their humors more than they his will. Amos must be suspended from prophesying, because the " land could not bear his words," and his discourses condemned their unworthy practices against God.[x] The young man came not to receive directions from our Saviour, but expected a confirmation of his own rules, rather than an imposition of new.[y] He rather cares for commendations than instructions, and upon the disappointment turns his back; " he was sad," that Christ would not suffer him to be rich, and a Christian together; and leaves him because his command was not suitable to the law of his covetousness. Some truths that are at a further distance from us, we can hear gladly; but when the conscience begins to smart under others, if God will not observe our wills, we will, with Herod, be a law to ourselves.[z] More instances might be observed.—Ingratitude is a setting up self, and an imposing laws on God. It is as much as to say, God did no more than he was obliged to do; as if the mercies we have were an act of duty in God, and not of bounty.—Insatiable desires after wealth: hence are those speeches (James iv. 13), " We will go into such a city, and buy and sell, &c. to get gain;" as though they had the command of God, and God must lacquey after their wills. When our hearts are not contented with any supply of our wants, but are craving an overplus for our lust; when we are unsatisfied in the midst of plenty, and still like the grave, cry, Give, give.—Incorrigibleness under affliction, &c.

II. The second main thing: As man would be a law to himself, so he would be his own end and happiness in opposition to God. Here four things shall be discoursed on. 1. Man would make himself his own end and happiness. 2. He would make anything his end and happiness rather than God. 3. He would make himself the end of all creatures. 4. He would make himself the end of God.

First, Man would make himself his own end and happiness. As God ought to be esteemed the first cause, in point of our dependence on him, so he ought to be our last end, in point of our enjoyment of him. When we therefore trust in ourselves, we refuse him as the first cause; and when we act for ourselves, and expect a blessedness from ourselves, we refuse him as the chiefest good, and last end, which is an undeniable piece of atheism; for man is a creature of a higher rank than others in the world, and was not made as animals,

---

[x] Amos vii. 10. [y] Mark x. 17, 22. [z] Mark vi. 20, 27.

plants, and other works of the divine power, materially to glorify God, but a rational creature, intentionally to honor God by obedience to his rule, dependence on his goodness, and zeal for his glory. It is, therefore, as much a slighting of God, for man, a creature, to set himself up as his own end, as to regard himself as his own law. For the discovery of this, observe that there is a three-fold self-love.

1. Natural, which is common to us by the law of nature with other creatures, inanimate as well as animate, and so closely twisted with the nature of every creature, that it cannot be dissolved but with the dissolution of nature itself. It consisted not with the wisdom and goodness of God to create an unnatural nature, or to command anything unnatural, nor doth he; for when he commands us to sacrifice ourselves, and dearest lives for himself, it is not without a promise of a more noble state of being in exchange for what we lose. This self-love is not only commendable, but necessary, as a rule to measure that duty we owe to our neighbor, whom we cannot love as ourselves, if we do not first love ourselves. God having planted this self-love in our nature, makes this natural principle the measure of our affection to all mankind of the same blood with ourselves.

2. Carnal self-love: when a man loves himself above God, in opposition to God, with a contempt of God; when our thoughts, affections, designs, centre only in our own fleshly interest, and rifle God of his honor, to make a present of it to ourselves: thus the natural self-love, in itself good, becomes criminal by the excess, when it would be superior and not subordinate to God.

3. A gracious self-love: when we love ourselves for higher ends than the nature of a creature, as a creature dictates, viz. in subserviency to the glory of God. This is a reduction of the revolted creature to his true and happy order; a Christian is therefore said to be " created in Christ to good works."[a] As all creatures were created, not only for themselves, but for the honor of God; so the grace of the new creation carries a man to answer this end, and to order all his operations to the honor of God, and his well-pleasing. The first is from nature, the second from sin, the third from grace; the first is implanted by creation, the second the fruit of corruption, and the third is by the powerful operation of grace. This carnal self-love is set up in the stead of God as our last end; like the sea, which all the little and great streams of our actions run to and rest in. And this is, 1. Natural. It sticks as close to us as our souls; it is as natural as sin, the foundation of all the evil in the world. As self-abhorrency is the first stone that is laid in conversion, so an inordinate self-love was the first inlet to all iniquity. As grace is a rising from self to centre in God, so is sin a shrinking from God into the mire of a carnal selfishness; since every creature is nearest to itself and next to God, it cannot fall from God, but must immediately sink into self;[b] and, therefore, all sins are well said to be branches or modifications of this fundamental passion. What is wrath, but a defence and strengthening self against the attempts of some real or imaginary evil? Whence springs envy, but from a self-love, grieved

---

[a] Eph. i. 10.　　　　　[b] More, Dial. 2. § 17. p. 274.

at its own wants in the midst of another's enjoyment, able to supply it? What is impatience, but a regret that self is not provided for at the rate of our wish, and that it hath met with a shock against supposed merit? What is pride, but a sense of self-worth, a desire to have self of a higher elevation than others? What is drunkenness, but a seeking a satisfaction for sensual self in the spoils of reason? No sin is committed as sin, but as it pretends a self-satisfaction. Sin, indeed, may well be termed a man's self, because it is, since the loss of original righteousness, the form that overspreads every part of our souls. The understanding assents to nothing false but under the notion of true, and the will embraceth nothing evil but under the notion of good; but the rule whereby we measure the truth and goodness of proposed objects, is not the unerring Word, but the inclinations of self, the gratifying of which is the aim of our whole lives. Sin and self are all one: what is called a living to sin in one place,[c] is called a living to self in another: "That they that live should not live unto themselves."[d] And upon this account it is that both the Hebrew word, חטא, and the Greek word, ἁμαρτάνειν, used in Scripture to express sin, properly signify to miss the mark, and swerve from that *white* to which all our actions should be directed, viz. the glory of God. When we fell to loving ourselves, we fell from loving God; and, therefore, when the Psalmist saith (Psalm xiv. 2), there were none that sought God, viz. as the last end; he presently adds, "They are all gone aside," viz. from their true mark, and therefore become filthy. 2. Since it is natural, it is also universal.[e] The not seeking God is as universal as our ignorance of him. No man in a state of nature but hath it predominant; no renewed man on this side heaven but hath it partially. The one hath it flourishing, the other hath it struggling. If to aim at the glory of God as the chief end, and not to live to ourselves, be the greatest mark of the restoration of the divine image,[f] and a conformity to Christ, who glorified not himself,[g] but the Father;[h] then every man, wallowing in the mire of corrupt nature, pays a homage to self, as a renewed man is biassed by the honor of God. The Holy Ghost excepts none from this crime (Phil. ii. 21): "All seek their own." It is rare for them to look above or beyond themselves. Whatsoever may be the immediate subject of their thoughts and inquiries, yet the utmost end and stage is their profit, honor, or pleasure. Whatever it be that immediately possesses the mind and will, self sits like a queen, and sways the sceptre, and orders things at that rate, that God is excluded, and can find no room in all his thoughts (Psalm x. 4): "The wicked, through the pride of his countenance, will not seek after God; God is not in all his thoughts." The whole little world of man is so overflowed with a deluge of self, that the dove, the glory of the Creator, can find no place where to set its foot; and if ever it gain the favor of admittance, it is to disguise and be a vassal to some carnal project, as the glory of God was a mask for the murdering his servants. It is from the power of this principle that the difficulty of conversion ariseth: as there is no greater pleasure to a believing

c Rom. vi. d 1 Cor. v. 15. e Psalm xiv. 1.
f 1 Cor. v. 15. g Heb. i. 5. h John xvii. 4.

soul than the giving itself up to God, and no stronger desire in him, than to have a fixed and unchangeable will to serve the designs of his honor; so there is no greater torment to a wicked man, than to part with his carnal ends, and lay down the Dagon of self at the feet of the ark. Self-love and self-opinion in the Pharisees waylaid all the entertainment of truth (John v. 44): "They sought honor one of another, and not the honor which comes from God." It is of so large an extent, and so insinuating nature, that it winds itself into the exercise of moral virtues, mixeth with our charity (Matt. vi. 2), and finds nourishment in the ashes of martyrdom (1 Cor. xiii. 3).

This making ourselves our end will appear in a few things.

1. In frequent self-applauses, and inward overweening reflections. Nothing more ordinary in the natures of men, than a dotage on their own perfections, acquisitions, or actions in the world: "Most think of themselves above what they ought to think (Rom. xii. 3, 4.) Few think of themselves so meanly as they ought to think: this sticks as close to us as our skin; and as humility is the beauty of grace, this is the filthiest soil of nature. Our thoughts run more delightfully upon the track of our own perfections, than the excellency of God; and when we find anything of a seeming worth, that may make us glitter in the eyes of the world, how cheerfully do we grasp and embrace ourselves! When the grosser profanenesses of men have been discarded, and the floods of them dammed up, the head of corruption, whence they sprang, will swell the higher within, in self-applauding speculations of their own reformation, without acknowledgment of their own weaknesses, and desires of divine assistance to make a further progress. "I thank God I am not like this publican;"[i] a self-reflection, with a contempt rather than compassion to his neighbor, is frequent in every Pharisee. The vapors of self-affections, in our clouded understandings, like those in the air in misty mornings, alter the appearance of things, and make them look bigger than they are. This is thought by some to be the sin of the fallen angels, who, reflecting upon their own natural excellency superior to other creatures, would find a blessedness in their own nature, as God did in his, and make themselves the last end of their actions. It is from this principle we are naturally so ready to compare ourselves rather with those that are below us, than with those that are above us; and often think those that are above us inferior to us, and secretly glory that we are become none of the meanest and lowest in natural or moral excellencies. How far were the gracious penmen of the Scripture from this, who, when possessed and directed by the Spirit of God, and filled with a sense of him, instead of applauding themselves, publish upon record their own faults to all the eyes of the world! And if Peter, as some think, dictated the Gospel which Mark wrote as his amanuensis, it is observable that his crime in denying his Master is aggravated in that Gospel in some circumstances, and less spoken of his repentance than in the other evangelists: "When he thought thereon, he wept;"[k] but in the other, "He went out and wept bitterly."[l] This is one part of

---

[i] Luke xviii. 11.   [k] Mark xiv. 72.   [l] Matt. xxvi. 75.   Luke xxii. 62.

atheism and self-idolatry, to magnify ourselves with the forgetfulness, and to the injury of our Creator.

2. In ascribing the glory of what we do or have to ourselves, to our own wisdom, power, virtue, &c. How flaunting is Nebuchadnezzar at the prospect of Babylon, which he had exalted to be the head of so great an empire! (Dan. iv. 30): "Is not this great Babylon that I have built? For," &c. He struts upon the battlements of his palace, as if there were no God but himself in the world, while his eye could not but see the heavens above him to be none of his own framing, attributing his acquisitions to his own arm, and referring them to his own honor, for his own delight; not for the honor of God, as a creature ought, nor for the advantage of his subjects, as the duty of a prince. He regards Babylon as his heaven, and himself as his idol, as if he were all, and God nothing. An example of this we have in the present age. But it is often observed, that God vindicates his own honor, brings the most heroical men to contempt and unfortunate ends, as a punishment of their pride, as he did here (Dan. iv. 31): "While the word was in the king's mouth, there fell a voice from heaven," &c. This was Herod's crime, to suffer others to do it:[m] he had discovered his eloquence actively, and made himself his own end passively, in approving the flatteries of the people, and offered not with one hand to God the glory he received from his people with the other.[n] Samosatenus is reported to put down the hymns which were sung for the glory of God and Christ, and caused songs to be sung in the temple for his own honor. When anything succeeds well, we are ready to attribute it to our own prudence and industry: if we meet with a cross, we fret against the stars and fortune, and second causes, and sometimes against God: as they curse God as well as their king (Isa. viii. 21), not acknowledging any defect in themselves. The Psalmist, by his repetition of, "Not unto us, not unto us, but to thy name give glory" (Psalm cxv. 1), implies the naturality of this temper, and the difficulty to cleanse our hearts from those self-reflections. If it be angelical to refuse an undue glory stolen from God's throne (Rev. xxii. 8, 9), it is diabolical to accept and cherish it. To seek our own glory is not glory (Prov. xxv. 27). It is vile, and the dishonor of a creature, who by the law of his creation is referred to another end. So much as we sacrifice to our own credit, to the dexterity of our hands, or the sagacity of our wit, we detract from God.

3. In desires to have self-pleasing doctrines. When we cannot endure to hear anything that crosses the flesh; though the wise man tells us, it is better to hear the "rebuke of the wise, than the song of fools" (Eccles. vii. 5). If Hanani the seer reprove king Asa for not relying on the Lord, his passion shall be armed for self against the prophet, and arrest him a prisoner (2 Chron. xvi. 10). If Micaiah declare to Ahab the evil that shall befall him, Amon the governor shall receive orders to clap him up in a dungeon. Fire doth not sooner seize upon combustible matter than fury will be kindled, if self be but pinched. This interest of lustful self barred the heart of Herodias against the entertainment of the truth, and caused her

[m] Sanderson's Sermons.   [n] Acts xii. 22, 23.

savagely to dip her hands in the blood of the Baptist, to make him a sacrifice to that inward idol.º

4. In being highly concerned for injuries done to ourselves, and little or not at all concerned for injuries done to God. How will the blood rise in us, when our honor and reputation is invaded, and scarce reflect upon the dishonor God suffers in our sight and hearing! Violent passions will transform us into Boanerges in the one case, and our unconcernedness render us Gallios in the other. We shall extenuate that which concerns God, and aggravate that which concerns ourselves. Nothing but the death of Jonathan, a first-born and a generous son, will satisfy his father Saul, when the authority of his edict was broken by his tasting of honey, though he had recompensed his crime committed in ignorance by the purchase of a gallant victory. But when the authority of God was violated in saving the Amalekites' cattle, against the command of a. greater sovereign than himself, he can daub the business, and excuse it with a design of sacrificing. He was not so earnest in hindering the people from the breach of God's command, as he was in vindicating the honor of his own :ᴾ he could hardly admit of an excuse to salve his own honor; but in the concerns of God's honor, pretend piety, to cloak his avarice. And it is often seen, when the violation of God's authority, and the stain of our own reputation are coupled together, we are more troubled for what disgraces us than for what dishonors God. When Saul had thus transgressed, he is desirous that Samuel would turn again to preserve his own honor before the elders, rather than grieved that he had broken the command of God (ver. 30).

5. In trusting in ourselves. When we consult with our own wit and wisdom, more than inquire of God, and ask leave of him: as the Assyrian (Isa. x. 13), "By the strength of my hands I have done it, and by my wisdom; for I am prudent." When we attempt things in the strength of our own heads, and parts, and trust in our own industry, without application to God for direction, blessing, and success, we affect the privilege of the Deity, and make gods of ourselves. The same language in reality with Ajax in Sophocles: "Others think to overcome with the assistance of the gods, but I hope to gain honor without them." Dependence and trust is an act due from the creature only to God. Hence God aggravates the crime of the Jews in trusting in Egypt (Isa. xxxi. 3), "the Egyptians are men and not gods." Confidence in ourselves is a defection from God (Jer. xvii. 5). And when we depart from and cast off God to depend upon ourselves, which is but an arm of flesh, we choose the arm of flesh for our God; we rob God of that confidence we ought to place in him, and that adoration which is due to him, and build it upon another foundation; not that we are to neglect the reason and parts God hath given us, or spend more time in prayer than in consulting about our own affairs, but to mix our own intentions in business, with ejaculations to heaven, and take God along with us in every motion: but certainly it is an idolizing of self, when we are more diligent in our attendance on our own wit, than fervent in our recourses to God.

6. The power of sinful self, above the efficacy of the notion of God,

º Mark vi. 18, 19, 28.   ᴾ 1 Sam. xv. 21.

is evident in our workings for carnal self against the light of our own consciences. When men of sublime reason, and clear natural wisdom, are voluntary slaves to their own lusts, row against the stream of their own consciences, serve carnal self with a disgraceful and disturbing drudgery, making it their God, sacrificing natural self, all sentiments of virtue, and the quiet of their lives, to the pleasure, honor, and satisfaction of carnal self: this is a prostituting God in his deputy, conscience, to carnal affections, when their eyes are shut against the enlightenings of it, and their ears deaf to its voice, but open to the least breath and whisper of self; a debt that the creature owes supremely to God. Much more might be said, but let us see what atheism lurks in this, and how it entrencheth upon God.

1. It is usurping God's prerogative. It is God's prerogative to be his own end, and act for his own glory; because there is nothing superior to him in excellency and goodness to act for: he had not his being from anything without himself, whereby he should be obliged to act for anything but himself. To make ourselves then our last end, is to corrival God in his being the supreme good, and blessedness to himself: as if we were our own principle, the author of our own being, and were not obliged to a higher power than ourselves, for what we are and have. To direct the lines of all our motions to ourselves, is to imply that they first issued only from ourselves. When we are rivals to God in his chief end, we own or desire to be rivals to him in the principle of his being: this is to set ourselves in the place of God. All things have something without them, and above them as their end; all inferior creatures act for some superior order in the rank of creation; the lesser animals are designed for the greater, and all for man: man, therefore, for something nobler than himself. To make ourselves therefore our own end, is to deny any superior, to whom we are to direct our actions. God alone being the supreme Being, can be his own ultimate end: for if there were anything higher and better than God, the purity and righteousness of his own nature would cause him to act for and toward that as his chiefest mark: this is the highest sacrilege, to alienate the proper good and rights of God, and employ them for our own use; to steal from him his own honor, and put it into our own cabinets; like those birds that ravished the sacrifice from the altar and carried it to their own nests.q When we love only ourselves, and act for no other end but ourselves, we invest ourselves with the dominion which is the right of God, and take the crown from his head. For as the crown belongs to the king, so to love his own will, to will by his own will and for himself, is the property of God; because he hath no other will, no other end above him to be the rule and scope of his actions. When therefore we are by self-love transformed wholly into ourselves, we make ourselves our own foundation, without God and against God; when we mind our own glory and praise, we would have a royal state equal with God, who created all things for himself.r What can man do more for God than he naturally doth for himself, since he doth all those things for himself which he should do for God? We

q Sabunde, Tit. 140.   r Prov. xvi. 4.

own ourselves to be our own creators and benefactors, and fling off all sentiments of gratitude to him.

2. It is a vilifying of God. When we make ourselves our end, it is plain language that God is not our happiness; we postpone God to ourselves, as if he were not an object so excellent and fit for our love as ourselves are (for it is irrational to make that our end, which is not God, and not the chiefest good); it is to deny him to be better than we, to make him not to be so good as ourselves, and so fit to be our chiefest good as ourselves are; that he hath not deserved any such acknowledgment at our hands by all that he hath done for us: we assert ourselves his superiors by such kind of acting, though we are infinitely more inferior to God than any creature can be to us. Man cannot dishonor God more than by referring that to his own glory, which God made for his own praise, upon account whereof he only hath a right to glory and praise, and none else. He thus "changeth the glory of the incorruptible God into a corruptible image;"[s] a perishing fame and reputation, which extends but little beyond the limits of his own habitation; or if it doth, survives but a few years, and perishes at last with the age wherein he lived.

3. It is as much as in us lies a destroying of God. By this temper we destroy that God that made us, because we destroy his intention and his honor. God cannot outlive his will and his glory: because he cannot have any other rule but his own will, or any other end but his own honor. The setting up self as our end puts a nullity upon the true Deity; by paying to ourselves that respect and honor which is due to God, we make the true God as no God. Whosoever makes himself a king of his prince's rights and territories, manifests an intent to throw him out of his government. To choose ourselves as our end is to undeify God, since to be the last end of a rational creature is a right inseparable from the nature of the Deity; and therefore not to set God, but self always before us, is to acknowledge no being but ourselves to be God.

Secondly. The second thing, Man would make anything his end and happiness rather than God. An end is so necessary in all our actions, that he deserves not the name of a rational creature that proposeth not one to himself. This is the distinction between rational creatures and others; they act with a formal intention, whereas other creatures are directed to their end by a natural instinct, and moved by nature to what the others should be moved by reason: when a man, therefore, acts for that end which was not intended him by the law of his creation, nor is suited to the noble faculties of his soul, he acts contrary to God, overturns his order, and merits no better a title than that of an atheist. A man may be said two ways to make a thing his last end and chief good.

1. Formally. When he actually judges this or that thing to be his chiefest good, and orders all things to it. So man doth not formally judge sin to be good, or any object which is the incentive of sin to be his last end: this cannot be while he hath the exercise of his rational faculties.

2. Virtually and implicitly. When he loves anything against the

* Rom. i. 23.

command of God, and prefers in the stream of his actions the enjoyment of that, before the fruition of God, and lays out more strength and expends more time in the gaining that, than answering the true end of his creation: when he acts so as if something below God could make him happy without God, or that God could not make him happy without the addition of something else. Thus the glutton makes a god of his dainties; the ambitious man of his honor; the incontinent man of his lust; and the covetous man of his wealth; and consequently esteems them as his chiefest good, and the most noble end, to which he directs his thoughts: thus he vilifies and lessens the true God, which can make him happy, in a multitude of false gods, that can only render him miserable. He that loves pleasure more than God, says in his heart there is no God but his pleasure. He that loves his belly more than God, says in his heart there is no God but his belly: their happiness is not accounted to lie in that God that made the world, but in the pleasure or profit they make their god. In this, though a created object be the immediate and subordinate term to which we turn, yet principally and ultimately, the affection to it terminates in self. Nothing is naturally entertained by us, but as it affects our sense or mingles with some promise of advantage to us. This is seen,

1. In the fewer thoughts we have of God than of anything else. Did we apprehend God to be our chiefest good and highest end, should we grudge him the pains of a few days' thoughts upon him? Men in their travels are frequently thinking upon their intended stage: but our thoughts run upon new acquisitions to increase our wealth, rear up our families, revenge our injuries, and support our reputation: trifles possess us; but "God is not in all our thoughts;"[t] seldom the sole object of them. We have durable thoughts of transitory things, and flitting thoughts of a durable and eternal good. The covenant of grace engageth the whole heart to God, and bars anything else from engrossing it: but what strangers are God and the souls of most men! Though we have the knowledge of him by creation, yet he is for the most part an unknown God in the relations wherein he stands to us, because a God undelighted in: hence it is, as one observes, that because we observe not the ways of God's wisdom, conceive not of him in his vast perfections, nor are stricken with an admiration of his goodness, that we have fewer good sacred poems, than of any other kind.[u] The wits of men hang the wing when they come to exercise their reasons and fancies about God. Parts and strength are given us, as well as corn and wine to the Israelites, for the service of God; but those are consecrated to some cursed Baal.[x] Like Venus in the Poet, we forsake heaven to follow some Adonis.

2. In the greedy pursuit of the world.[y] When we pursue worldly wealth or worldly reputation with more vehemency than the riches of grace, or the favor of God;—when we have a foolish imagination, that our happiness consists in them, we prefer earth before heaven, broken cisterns which can hold no water, before an ever-springing fountain of glory and bliss; and, as though there were a defect in

[t] Psalm x. 4.   [u] Jackson, Book I. c. 14, p. 48.   [x] Hos. ii. 8.
[y] Quod quisque præ cæteris petit, summum judicat bonum. Boet. lib. iii. p. 24.

God, cannot be content with him as our portion, without an addition of something inferior to him;—when we make it our hopes, and say to the wedge, "Thou art my confidence;" and rejoice more because it is great, and because "our hand hath gotten much, than in the privilege of communion with God and the promise of an everlasting fruition of him;[z] this is so gross, that Job joins it with the idolatry of the sun and moon, which he purgeth himself of (xxxi. 26). And the apostle, when he mentions covetousness or covetous men, passes it not over without the title of idolatry to the vice, and idolater to the person;[a] in that it is a preferring clay and dirt as an end more desirable than the original of all goodness, in regard of affection and dependence.

3. In a strong addictedness to sensual pleasures (Phil. iii. 19). Who make their "belly their god;" subjecting the truths of God to the maintenance of their luxury. In debasing the higher faculties to project for the satisfaction of the sensitive appetite as their chief happiness, whereby many render themselves no better than a rout of sublimated brutes among men, and gross atheists to God. When men's thoughts run also upon inventing new methods to satisfy their bestial appetite, forsaking the pleasures which are to be had in God, which are the delights of angels, for the satisfaction of brutes. This is an open and unquestionable refusal of God for our end, when our rest is in them, as if they were the chief good, and not God.

4. In paying a service, upon any success in the world, to instruments more than to God, their sovereign Author. When "they sacrifice to their net, and burn incense to their drag."[b] Not that the Assyrian did offer a sacrifice to his arms, but ascribed to them what was due only to God, and appropriated the victory to his forces and arms. The prophet alludes to those that worshipped their warlike instruments, whereby they had attained great victories; and those artificers who worshipped the tools by which they had purchased great wealth, in the stead of God; preferring them as the causes of their happiness, before God who governs the world. And are not our affections, upon the receiving of good things, more closely fixed to the instruments of conveyance, than to the chief Benefactor, from whose coffers they are taken? Do we not more delight in them, and hug them with a greater endearedness, as if all our happiness depended on them, and God were no more than a bare spectator? Just as if when a man were warmed by a beam, he should adore that and not admire the sun that darts it out upon him.

5. In paying a respect to man more than God. When in a public attendance on his service, we will not laugh, or be garish, because men see us; but our hearts shall be in a ridiculous posture, playing with feathers and trifling fancies, though God see us; as though our happiness consisted in the pleasing of men, and our misery in a respect to God. There is no fool that saith in his heart, There is no God, but he sets up something in his heart as a god. This is,

1. A debasing of God, (1.) In setting up a creature. It speaks God less amiable than the creature, short of those perfections which some silly, sordid thing, which hath engrossed their affections, is pos-

* Job xxxi. 24, 25.   * Col. iii. 5.   Eph. v. 5.   b Hab. i. 16.

sessed with; as if the cause of all being could be transcended by his creature, and a vile lust could equal, yea, surmount the loveliness of God. It is to say to God, as the rich to the poor (James ii. 3), "Stand thou there, or sit here under my footstool;" it is to sink him below the mire of the world, to order him to come down from his glorious throne, and take his place below a contemptible creature, which, in regard of its infinite distance, is not to be compared with him. It strips God of the love that is due to him by the right of his nature and the greatness of his dignity; and of the trust that is due to him, as the First Cause and the chiefest good, as though he were too feeble and mean to be our blessedness. This is intolerable, to make that which is God's footstool, the earth, to climb up into his throne; to set that in our heart which God hath made even below ourselves and put under our feet; to make that which we trample upon to dispose of the right God hath to our hearts.[c] It is worse than if a queen should fall in love with the little image of the prince in the palace, and slight the beauty of his person; and as if people should adore the footsteps of a king in the dirt, and turn their backs upon his presence. (2.) It doth more debase him to set up a sin, a lust, a carnal affection as our chief end. To steal away the honor due to God, and appropriate it to that which is no work of his hands, to that which is loathsome in his sight, hath disturbed his rest, and wrung out his just breath to kindle a hell for its eternal lodging, a God-dishonoring and a soul-murdering lust, is worse than to prefer Barabbas before Christ. The baser the thing, the worse is the injury to him with whom we would associate it. If it were some generous principle, a thing useful to the world, that we place in an equality with, or a superiority above him, though it were a vile usage, yet it were not altogether so criminal; but to gratify some unworthy appetite with the displeasure of the Creator, something below the rational nature of man, much more infinitely below the excellent majesty of God, is a more unworthy usage of him. To advance one of the most virtuous nobles in a kingdom as a mark of our service and subjection, is not so dishonorable to a despised prince as to take a scabby beggar or a rotten carcase to place in his throne. Creeping things, abominable beasts, the Egyptian idols, cats and crocodiles, were greater abominations, and a greater despite done to God, than the image of jealousy at the gate of the altar.[d] And let not any excuse themselves, that it is but one lust or one creature which is preferred as the end: is not he an idolater that worships the sun or moon, one idol, as well as he that worships the whole host of heaven? The inordinacy of the heart to one lust may imply a stronger contempt of him, than if a legion of lusts did possess the heart. It argues a greater disesteem, when he shall be slighted for a single vanity. The depth of Esau's profaneness in contemning his birth-right, and God in it, is aggravated by his selling it for one morsel of meat,[e] and that none of the daintiest, none of the costliest—a mess of pottage; implying, had he parted with it at a greater rate, it had been more tolerable, and his profaneness more excusable. And it is reckoned as a high aggravation of the corruption of the Israelite judges (Amos

[c] Neremberg de Adorat. p. 30.   [d] Ezek. viii. 5, 6, 10.   [e] Heb. xii. 16.

ii. 6), that they sold the poor for a pair of shoes; that is, that they would betray the cause of the poor for a bribe of no greater value than might purchase them a pair of shoes. To place any one thing as our chief end, though never so light, doth not excuse. He that will not stick to break with God for a trifle, a small pleasure, will leap the hedge upon a greater temptation. Nay, and if wealth, riches, friends, and the best thing in the world, our own lives, be preferred before God, as our chief happiness and end but one moment, it is an infinite wrong, because the infinite goodness and excellency of God is denied; as though the creature or lust we love, or our own life, which we prefer in that short moment before him, had a goodness in itself, superior to, and more desirable than the blessedness in God. And though it should be but one minute, and a man in all the period of his days, both before and after that failure, should actually and intentionally prefer God before all other things; yet he doth him an infinite wrong, because God in every moment is infinitely good, and absolutely desirable, and can never cease to be good, and cannot have the least shadow or change in him and his perfections.

2. It is a denying of God (Job xxxi. 26–28): "If I beheld the sun when it shined, or the moon walking in its brightness, and my heart hath been secretly enticed, or my mouth hath kissed my hand; this also were iniquity to be punished by the judge, for I should have denied the Lord above." This denial of God is not only the act of an open idolater, but the consequent of a secret confidence, and immoderate joy in worldly goods. This denial of God is to be referred to ver. 24, 25. When a man saith to gold, "Thou art my confidence," and rejoices because his wealth is great; he denies that God which is superior to all those, and the proper object of trust. Both idolatries are coupled here together; that which hath wealth and that which hath those glorious creatures in heaven for its object. And though some may think it a light sin, yet the crime being of deeper guilt, a denial of God, deserves a severer punishment, and falls under the sentence of the just Judge of all the earth, under that notion which Job intimates in those words, "This also were an iniquity to be punished by the Judge." The kissing the hand to the sun, moon, or any idol, was an external sign of religious worship among those and other nations. This is far less than an inward hearty confidence, and an affectionate trust. If the motion of the hand be, much more the affection of the heart to an excrementitious creature, or a brutish pleasure, is a denial of God, and a kind of an abjuring of him, since the supreme affection of the soul is undoubtedly and solely the right of the Sovereign Creator, and not to be given in common to others, as the outward gesture may in a way of civil respect. Nothing that is an honor peculiar to God can be given to a creature, without a plain exclusion of God to be God; it being a disowning the rectitude and excellency of his nature. If God should command a creature such a love, and such a confidence in anything inferior to him, he would deny himself his own glory, he would deny himself to be the most excellent being. Can the Romanists be free from this, when they call the cross *spem unicam*, and

say to the Virgin, *In te Domina speravi*, as Bonaventure? &c. Good reason, therefore, have worldlings and sensualists, persons of immoderate fondness to anything in the world, to reflect upon themselves; since though they own the being of God, they are guilty of so great disrespect to him, that cannot be excused from the title of an unworthy atheism; and those that are renewed by the spirit of God, may here see ground of a daily humiliation for the frequent and too common excursions of their souls in creature confidences and affections, whereby they fall under the charge of an act of practical atheism, though they may be free from a habit of it.

Thirdly, Man would make himself the end of all creatures. Man would sit in the seat of God, and set his heart as the heart of God, as the Lord saith of Tyrus (Ezek. xxviii. 2). What is the consequence of this, but to be esteemed the chief good and end of other creatures? a thing that the heart of God cannot but be set upon, it being an inseparable right of the Deity, who must deny himself if he deny this affection of the heart. Since it is the nature of man, derived from his root, to desire to be equal with God, it follows that he desires no creature should be equal with him, but subservient to his ends and his glory. He that would make himself God, would have the honor proper to God. He that thinks himself worthy of his own supreme affection, thinks himself worthy to be the object of the supreme affection of others. Whosoever counts himself the chiefest good and last end, would have the same place in the thoughts of others. Nothing is more natural to man than a desire to have his own judgment the rule and measure of the judgments and opinions of the rest of mankind. He that sets himself in the place of the prince, doth, by that act, challenge all the prerogatives and dues belonging to the prince; and apprehending himself fit to be a king, apprehends himself also worthy of the homage and fealty of the subjects. He that loves himself chiefly, and all other things and persons for himself, would make himself the end of all creatures. It hath not been once or twice only in the world that some vain princes have assumed to themselves the title of gods, and caused divine adorations to be given to them, and altars to smoke with sacrifices for their honor. What hath been practised by one, is by nature seminally in all; we would have all pay an obedience to us, and give to us the esteem that is due to God. This is evident,

1. In pride. When we entertain a high opinion of ourselves, and act for our own reputes, we dispossess God from our own hearts; and while we would have our fame to be in every man's mouth, and be admired in the hearts of men, we would chase God out of the hearts of others, and deny his glory a residence anywhere else, that our glory should reside more in their minds than the glory of God; that their thoughts should be filled with our achievements, more than the works and excellency of God, with our image, and not with the divine. Pride would paramount God in the affections of others, and justle God out of their souls; and by the same reason that man doth thus in the place where he lives, he would do so in the whole world, and press the whole creation from the service of their true Lord, to his own service. Every proud man would be counted by

others as he counts himself, the highest, chiefest piece of goodness, and be adored by others, as much as he adores and admires himself. No proud man, in his self-love, and self-admiration, thinks himself in an error; and if he be worthy of his own admiration, he thinks himself worthy of the highest esteem of others, that they should value him above themselves, and value themselves only for him. What did Nebuchadnezzar intend by setting up a golden image, and commanding all his subjects to worship it, upon the highest penalty he could inflict, but that all should aim only at the pleasing his humor?

2. In using the creatures contrary to the end God has appointed. God created the world and all things in it, as steps whereby men might ascend to a prospect of him, and the acknowledgment of his glory; and we would use them to dishonor God, and gratify ourselves: he appointed them to supply our necessities, and support our rational delights, and we use them to cherish our sinful lusts. We wring groans from the creature in diverting them from their true scope to one of our own fixing, when we use them not in his service, but purely for our own, and turn those things he created for himself, to be instruments of rebellion against him to serve our turns, and hereby endeavor to defeat the ends of God in them, to establish our own ends by them: this is a high dishonor to God, a sacrilegious undermining of his glory,[f] to reduce what God hath made to serve our own glory and our own pleasure; it perverts the whole order of the world, and directs it to another end than what God hath constituted, to another intention contrary to the intention of God; and thus man makes himself a God by his own authority. As all things were made by God, so they are for God; but while we aspire to the end of the creation, we deny and envy God the honor of being Creator; we cannot make ourselves the chief end of the creatures against God's order, but we imply thereby that we were their first principle; for if we lived under a sense of the Creator of them while we enjoy them for our use, we should return the glory to the right owner. This is diabolical; though the devil, for his first affecting an authority in heaven, has been hurled down from the state of an angel of light into that of darkness, vileness, and misery, to be the most accursed creature living, yet he still aspires to mate God, contrary to the knowledge of the impossibility of success in it. Neither the terrors he feels, nor the future torments he doth expect, do a jot abate his ambition to be competitor with his Creator; how often hath he, since his first sin, arrogated to himself the honor of a God from the blind world, and attempted to make the Son of God, by a particular worship, count him as the "chiefest good and benefactor of the world!"[g] Since all men by nature are the devil's children, the serpent's seed, they have something of this venom in their natures, as well as others of his qualities. We see that there may be, and is a prodigious atheism, lurking under the belief of a God; the devil knows there is a God, but acts like an atheist; and so do his children.

Fourthly, Man would make himself the end of God. This necessarily follows upon the former; whosoever makes himself his own law and his own end in the place of God, would make God the sub-

f Sabunde, Tit. 200. p. 352.   g Matt. iv. 9.

ject in making himself the sovereign; he that steps into the throne of a prince, sets the prince at his footstool; and while he assumes the prince's prerogative, demands a subjection from him. The order of the creation has been inverted by the entrance of sin.[h] God implanted an affection in man with a double aspect, the one to pitch upon God, the other to respect ourselves; but with this proviso, that our affection to God should be infinite, in regard of the object, and centre in him as the chiefest happiness and highest end. Our affections to ourselves should be finite, and refer ultimately to God as the original of our being; but sin hath turned man's affections wholly to himself, whereas he should love God first, and himself in order to God; he now loves himself first, and God in order to himself; love to God is lost, and love to self hath usurped the throne. As God by "creation put all things under the feet of man,"[i] reserving the heart for himself, man by corruption hath dispossessed God of his heart, and put him under his own feet. We often intend ourselves when we pretend the honor of God, and make God and religion a stale to some designs we have in hand; our Creator a tool for our own ends. This is evident,

1. In our loving God, because of some self-pleasing benefits distributed by him. There is in men a kind of natural love to God, but it is but a secondary one, because God gives them the good things of this world, spreads their table, fills their cup, stuffs their coffers, and doth them some good turns by unexpected providences; this is not an affection to God for the unbounded excellency of his own nature, but for his beneficence, as he opens his hand for them; an affection to themselves, and those creatures, their gold, their honor, which their hearts are most fixed upon, without a strong spiritual inclination that God should be glorified by them in the use of those mercies. It is rather a disowning of God, than any love to him, because it postpones God to those things they love him for; this would appear to be no love, if God should cease to be their benefactor, and deal with them as a judge; if he should change his outward smiles into afflicting frowns, and not only shut his hand, but strip them of what he sent them. The motive of their love being expired, the affection raised by it must cease for want of fuel to feed it; so that God is beholden to sordid creatures of no value (but as they are his creatures) for most of the love the sons of men pretend to him. The devil spake truth of most men, though not of Job, when he said (Job i. 9): "They love not God for naught;" but while he makes a hedge about them and their families, whilst he blesseth the works of their hands, and increaseth their honor in the land. It is like Peter's sharp reproof of his Master, when he spake of the ill-usage, even to death, he was to meet with at Jerusalem: "This shall not be unto thee." It was as much out of love to himself, as zeal for his Master's interest, knowing his Master could not be in such a storm without some drops lighting upon himself. All the apostasies of men in the world are witnesses to this; they fawn whilst they may have a prosperous profession, but will not bear one chip of the cross for the interest of God; they would partake of his blessings,

[h] Pascal, Pens. § 30, p. 294.　　　　　　　　[i] Psalm viii. 6.

but not endure the prick of a lance for him, as those, that admired the miracles of our Saviour, and shrunk at his sufferings. A time of trial discovers these mercenary souls to be more lovers of themselves than their Maker. This is a pretended love of friendship to God, but a real love to a lust, only to gain by God. A good man's temper is contrary: "Quench hell, burn heaven," said a holy man, "I will love and fear my God."

2. It is evident, in abstinence from some sins, not because they offend God, but because they are against the interest of some other beloved corruption, or a bar to something men hunt after in the world. When temperance is cherished not to honor God, but preserve a crazy carcase; prodigality forsaken, out of a humor of avarice; uncleanness forsaken, not out of a hatred of lust, but love to their money; declining a denial of the interest and truth of God, not out of affection to them, but an ambitious zeal for their own reputation. There is a kind of conversion from sin, when God is not made the term of it (Jer. iv. 1): "If thou wilt return, O Israel, return unto me, saith the Lord."[k] When we forbear sin as dogs do the meat they love: they forbear not out of a hatred of the carrion, but fear of the cudgel; these are as wicked in their abstaining from sin, as others are in their furious committing it. Nothing of the honor of God and the end of his appointments is indeed in all this, but the conveniences self gathers from them. Again, many of the motives the generality of the world uses to their friends and relations to draw them from vices, are drawn from self, and used to prop up natural or sinful self in them. Come, reform yourself, take other courses, you will smut your reputation and be despicable; you will destroy your estate, and commence a beggar; your family will be undone, and you may rot in a prison: not laying close to them the duty they owe to God, the dishonor which accrues to him by their unworthy courses, and the ingratitude to the God of their mercies; not that the other motives are to be laid aside and slighted. Mint and cummin may be tithed, but the weightier concerns are not to be omitted; but this shows that self is the bias, not only of men in their own course, but in their dealings with others; what should be subordinate to the honor of God, and the duty we owe to him, is made superior.

3. It is evident, in performing duties merely for a selfish interest: making ourselves the end of religious actions, paying a homage to that, while we pretend to render it to God (Zech. vii. 5): "Did you at all fast unto me, even unto me?" Things ordained by God may fall in with carnal ends affected by ourselves; and then religion is not kept up by any interest of God in the conscience, but the interest of self in the heart: we then sanctify not the name of God in the duty, but gratify ourselves: God may be the object, self is the end; and a heavenly object is made subservient to a carnal design. Hypocrisy passes a compliment on God, and is called flattery (Psalm lxxviii. 36): "They did flatter him with their lips," &c. They gave him a parcel of good words for their own preservation. Flattery, in the old notion among the heathens, is a vice more peculiar to serve our own turn and purvey for the belly: they knew they could not

[k] Trap, on Gen. p. 148.

subsist without God, and therefore gave him a parcel of good words, that he might spare them, and make provision for them. Israel is an empty vine,[1] a vine, say some, with large branches and few clusters, but brings forth fruit to himself: while they professed love to God with their lips, it was that God should promote their covetous designs, and preserve their wealth and grandeur;[m] in which respect a hypocrite may be well termed a religious atheist, an atheist masked with religion. The chief arguments which prevail with many men to perform some duties and appear religious, are the same that Hamor and Shechem used to the people of their city to submit to circumcision, viz. the engrossing of more wealth (Gen. xxxiv. 21, 22): "If every male among us be circumcised, as they are circumcised, shall not their cattle and their substance, and every beast of theirs, be ours?" This is seen,

(1.) In unwieldiness to religious duties where self is not concerned. With what lively thoughts will many approach to God, when a revenue may be brought in to support their own ends! But when the concerns of God only are in it, the duty is not the delight, but the clog; such feeble devotions, that warm not the soul, unless there be something of self to give strength and heat to them. Jonah was sick of his work, and run from God, because he thought he should get no honor by his message: God's mercy would discredit his prophecy.[n] Thoughts of disadvantage cut the very sinews of service. You may as well persuade a merchant to venture all his estate upon the inconstant waves without hopes of gain, as prevail with a natural man to be serious in duty, without expectation of some warm advantage. "What profit should we have if we pray to him?" is the natural question (Job xxi. 15). "What profit shall I have if I be cleansed from my sin?" (Job xxxv. 3). I shall have more good by my sin than by my service. It is for God that I dance before the ark, saith David, therefore I will be more vile (2 Sam. vi. 22). It is for self that I pray, saith a natural man, therefore I will be more warm and quick. Ordinances of God are observed only as a point of interest, and prayer is often most fervent, when it is least godly, and most selfish; carnal ends and affections will pour out lively expressions. If there be no delight in the means that lead to God, there is no delight in God himself; because love is *appetitus unionis,* a desire of union; and where the object is desirable, the means that brings us to it would be delightful too.

(2.) In calling upon God only in a time of necessity. How officious will men be in affliction, to that God whom they neglect in their prosperity! "When he slew them, then they sought him, and they returned and inquired after God, and they remembered that God was their rock" (Psalm lxxviii. 34). They remembered him under the scourge, and forgot him under his smiles: they visit the throne of grace, knock loud at heaven's gates, and give God no rest for their early and importunate devotions when under distress: but when their desires are answered, and the rod removed, they stand aloof from him, and rest upon their own bottom, as Jer. ii. 31: "We are lords; we will come no more unto thee." When we have need

[1] Hos. x. 1.   [m] Ezek. xxxiii. 31.   [n] Jonah iv. 2.

of him, he shall find us clients at his gate ; and when we have served
our turn, he hears no more of us : like Noah's dove sent out of the
ark, that returned to him when she found no rest on the earth, but
came not back when she found a footing elsewhere. How often do
men apply themselves to God, when they have some business for
him to do for them ! And then too, they are loth to put it solely
into his hand to manage it for his own honor ; but they presume to
be his directors, that he may manage it for their glory. Self spurs
men on to the throne of grace ; they desire to be furnished with
some mercy they want, or to have the clouds of some judgments
which they fear blown over : this is not affection to God, but to ourselves : as the Romans worshipped a quartan ague as a goddess, and
Timorem and Pallorem, fear and paleness, as gods ; not out of any
affection they had to the disease or the passion, but for fear to receive
any hurt by them. Again, when we have gained the mercy we
need, how little do we warm our souls with the consideration of that
God that gave it, or lay out the mercy in his service ! We are importunate to have him our friend in our necessities, and are ungratefully careless of him, and his injuries he suffers by us or others.
When he hath discharged us from the rock where we stuck, we leave
him, as having no more need of him, and able to do well enough
without him ; as if we were petty gods ourselves, and only wanted
a lift from him at first. This is not to glorify God as God, but as
our servant ; not an honoring of God, but a self-seeking : he would
hardly beg at God's door, if he could pleasure himself without him.

(3.) In begging his assistance to our own projects. When we lay
the plot of our own affairs, and then come to God, not for counsel
but blessing, self only shall give us counsel how to act ; but because
we believe there is a God that governs the world, we will desire him
to contribute success. God is not consulted with till the counsel of
self be fixed ; then God must be the executor of our will. Self must
be the principal, and God the instrument to hatch what we have
contrived. It is worse when we beg of God to favor some sinful
aim ; the Psalmist implies this (Psalm lxvi. 18) : " If I regard iniquity in my heart, the Lord will not hear me." Iniquity regarded
as the aim in prayer, renders the prayer successless, and the suppliant an atheist, in debasing God to back his lust by his holy providence. The disciples had determined revenge ; and because they
could not act it without their Master, they would have him be their
second in their vindictive passion (Luke ix. 55) : " Call for fire from
heaven." We scarce seek God till we have modelled the whole contrivance in our own brains, and resolved upon the methods of performance ; as though there were not a fulness of wisdom in God to
guide us in our resolves, as well as power to breathe success upon
them.

(4.) In impatience upon the refusal of our desires. How often do
men's spirits rise against God, when he steps not in with the assistance they want ! If the glory of God swayed more with them than
their private interest, they would let God be judge of his own glory,
and rather magnify his wisdom than complain of his want of goodness. Selfish hearts will charge God with neglect of them, if he be

not as quick in their supplies as they are in their desires; like those in Isa. lviii. 3, "Wherefore have we fasted, say they, and thou seest not? wherefore have we afflicted our souls, and thou takest no knowledge?" When we aim at God's glory in our importunities, we shall fall down in humble submissions when he denies us; whereas self riseth up in bold expostulations, as if God were our servant, and had neglected the service he owed us, not to come at our call. We over-value the satisfactions of self above the honor of God. Besides, if what we desire be a sin, our impatience at a refusal is more intolerable: it is an anger, that God will not lay aside his holiness to serve our corruption.

(5.) In the actual aims men have in their duties. In prayer for temporal things, when we desire health for our own ease, wealth for our own sensuality, strength for our revenge, children for the increase of our family, gifts for our applause; as Simon Magus did the Holy Ghost: or, when some of those ends are aimed at, this is to desire God not to serve himself of us, but to be a servant to our worldly interest, our vain glory, the greatening of our names, &c. In spiritual mercies begged for; when pardon of sin is desired only for our own security from eternal vengeance; sanctification desired only to make us fit for everlasting blessedness; peace of conscience, only that we may lead our lives more comfortably in the world; when we have not actual intentions for the glory of God, or when our thoughts of God's honor are overtopped by the aims of self-advantage: not but that as God hath pressed us to those things by motives drawn from the blessedness derived to ourselves by them, so we may desire them with a respect to ourselves; but this respect must be contained within the due banks, in subordination to the glory of God, not above it, nor in an equal balance with it.[o] That which is nourishing or medicinal in the first or second degree, is in the fourth or fifth degree mere destructive poison. Let us consider it seriously; though a duty be heavenly, doth not some base end smut us in it? [1.] How is it with our confessions of sin? Are they not more to procure our pardon, than to shame ourselves before God, or to be freed from the chains that hinder us from bringing him the glory for which we were created; or more to partake of his benefits, than to honor him in acknowledging the rights of his justice? Do we not bewail sin as it hath ruined us, not as it opposed the holiness of God? Do we not shuffle with God, and confess one sin, while we reserve another; as if we would allure God by declaring our dislike of one, to give us liberty to commit wantonness with another; not to abhor ourselves, but to daub with God. [2.] Is it any better in our private and family worship? Are not such assemblies frequented by some, where some upon whom they have a dependence may eye them, and have a better opinion of them, and affection to them? If God were the sole end of our hearts, would they not be as glowing under the sole eye of God, as our tongues or carriages are seemingly serious under the eye of man? Are not family duties performed by some that their voices may be heard, and their reputation supported among godly neighbors? [3.] Is not the charity of many men tainted with this

° Gurnall, Part III. p. 337.

end—self,[p] as the Pharisees were, while they set the miserable object before them, but not the Lord; bestowing alms not so much upon the necessities of the people, as the friendship we owe them for some particular respects; or casting our bread upon those waters which stream down in the sight of the world, that our doles may be visible to them, and commended by them; or when we think to oblige God to pardon our transgressions, as if we merited it and heaven too at his hands, by bestowing a few pence upon indigent persons? And [4.] Is it not the same with the reproofs of men? Is not heat and anger carried out with full sail when our worldly interest is prejudiced and becalmed in the concerns of God? Do not many masters reprove their servants with more vehemency for the neglect of their trade and business, than the neglect of divine duties; and that upon religious arguments, pretending the honor of God that they may mind their own interest? But when they are negligent in what they owe to God, no noise is made, they pass without rebuke; is not this to make God and religion a stale to their own ends? It is a part of atheism not to regard the injuries done to God, as Tiberius,[q] " Let God's wrongs be looked to or cared for by himself." [5.] Is it not thus in our seeming zeal for religion? as Demetrius and the craftsmen at Ephesus cried up aloud the greatness of Diana of the Ephesians, not out of any true zeal they had for her, but their gain, which was increased by the confluence of her worshippers, and the sale of her own shrines (Acts xix. 24, 28).

4. In making use of the name of God to countenance our sin. When we set up an opinion that is a friend to our lusts, and then dig deep into the Scripture to find crutches to support it, and authorize our practices; when men will thank God for what they have got by unlawful means, fathering the fruit of their cheating craft, and the simplicity of their chapmen upon God; crediting their cozenage by his name, as men do brass money, with a thin plate of silver, and the stamp and image of the prince. The Jews urge the law of God for the crucifying his Son (John xix. 7): "We have a law, and by that law he is to die," and would make him a party in their private revenge. Thus often when we have faltered in some actions, we wipe our mouths, as if we sought God more than our own interest, prostituting the sacred name and honor of God, either to hatch or defend some unworthy lust against his word.[r] Is not all this a high degree of atheism?

1. It is a vilifying God, an abuse of the highest good. Other sins subject the creature and outward things to them, but acting in religious services for self, subjects not only the highest concernments of men's souls, but the Creator himself to the creature, nay, to make God contribute to that which is the pleasure of the devil, a greater slight than to cast the gifts of a prince to a herd of nasty swine. It were more excusable to serve ourselves of God upon the higher accounts, such that materially conduce to his glory; but it is an intolerable wrong to make him and his ordinances caterers for our own bellies, as they did:[s] they sacrificed the נדבות of which the offerer

p Matt. vi. 1.   q Dei injuriæ. Deo curæ.
r Sanderson's Sermons. Part II. p. 158.   s Hosea viii. 13. Vid. Cocc. *in locum.*

might eat, not out of any reference to God, but love to their glut-tony; not to please him, but feast themselves. The belly was truly made the god, when God was served only in order to the belly; as though the blessed God had his being, and his ordinances were en-joined to pleasure their foolish and wanton appetites; as though the work of God were only to patronize unrighteous ends, and be as bad as themselves, and become a pander to their corrupt affections.

2. Because it is a vilifying of God, it is an undeifying or dethron-ing God. It is an acting as if we were the lords, and God our vassal; a setting up those secular ends in the place of God, who ought to be our ultimate end in every action; to whom a glory is as due, as his mercy to us is utterly unmerited by us. He that thinks to cheat and put the fool upon God by his pretences, doth not heartily believe there is such a being. He could not have the notion of a God, without that of omniscience and justice; an eye to see the cheat, and an arm to punish it. The notion of the one would direct him in the manner of his services, and the sense of the other would scare him from the cherishing his unworthy ends. He that serves God with a sole re-spect to himself, is prepared for any idolatry; his religion shall warp with the times and his interest; he shall deny the true God for an idol, when his worldly interest shall advise him to it, and pay the same reverence to the basest image, which he pretends now to pay to God; as the Israelites were as real for idolatry under their basest princes, as they were pretenders to the true religion under those that were pious. Before I come to the use of this, give me leave to evince this practical atheism by two other considerations.

1. Unworthy imaginations of God. "The fool hath said in his heart, There is no God:" that is, he is not such a God as you report him to be; this is meant by their being "corrupt," in the second verse, corrupt being taken for playing the idolaters (Exod. xxxii. 7). We cannot comprehend God; if we could, we should cease to be finite; and because we cannot comprehend him, we erect strange images of him in our fancies and affections. And since guilt came upon us, because we cannot root out the notions of God, we would debase the majesty and nature of God, that we may have some ease in our consciences, and lie down with some comfort in the sparks of our own kindling. This is universal in men by nature. "God is not in all his thoughts;"† not in any of his thoughts, according the excellency of his nature and greatness of his majesty. As the heathen did not glorify God as God, so neither do they conceive of God as God; they are all infected with some one or other ill opinion of him, thinking him not so holy, powerful, just, good, as he is, and as the natural force of the human understanding might arrive to. We join a new notion of God in our vain fancies, and represent him not as he is, but as we would have him to be, fit for our own use, and suited to our own pleasure. We set that active power of imagination on work, and there comes out a god (a calf) whom we own for a notion of God. Adam cast him into so narrow a mould, as to think that himself, who had newly sprouted up by his almighty power, was fit to be his corrival in knowledge, and had vain hopes to grasp as

† Psalm x. 4.

much as infiniteness; if he, in his first declining, begun to have such a conceit, it is no doubt but we have as bad under a mass of corruption. When holy Agur speaks of God, he cries out that he had not "the understanding of a man, nor the knowledge of the holy;"[u] he did not think rationally of God, as man might by his strength at his first creation. There are as many carved images of God as there are minds of men, and as monstrous shapes as those corruptions into which they would transform him. Hence sprang,

1. Idolatry. Vain imaginations first set afloat and kept up this in the world. Vain imaginations of the God "whose glory they changed into the image of corruptible man."[x] They had set up vain images of him in their fancy, before they set up idolatrous representations of him in their temples; the likening him to those idols of wood and stone, and various metals, were the fruit of an idea erected in their own minds. This is a mighty debasing the Divine nature, and rendering him no better than that base and stupid matter they make the visible object of their adoration; equalling him with those base creatures they think worthy to be the representations of him. Yet how far did this crime spread itself in all corners of the world, not only among the more barbarous and ignorant, but the more polished and civilized nations! Judea only, where God had placed the ark of his presence, being free from it, in some intervals of time only after some sweeping judgment. And though they vomited up their idols under some sharp scourge, they licked them up again after the heavens were cleared over their heads: the whole book of Judges makes mention of it. And though an evangelical light hath chased that idolatry away from a great part of the world, yet the principle remaining coins more spiritual idols in the heart, which are brought before God in acts of worship.

2. Hence all superstition received its rise and growth. When we mint a god according to our own complexion, like to us in mutable and various passions, soon angry and soon appeased, it is no wonder that we invent ways of pleasing him after we have offended him, and think to expiate the sin of our souls by some melancholy devotions and self-chastisements. Superstition is nothing else but an unscriptural and unrevealed dread of God.[y] When they imagined him a rigorous and severe master, they cast about for ways to mitigate him whom they thought so hard to be pleased: a very mean thought of him, as if a slight and pompous devotion could as easily bribe and flatter him out of his rigors, as a few good words or baubling rattles could please and quiet little children; and whatsoever pleased us, could please a God infinitely above us. Such narrow conceits had the Philistines, when they thought to still the anger of the God of Israel, whom they thought they possessed in the ark, with the present of a few golden mice.[z] All the superstition this day living in the world is built upon this foundation: so natural it is to man to pull God down to his own imaginations, rather than raise his imaginations up to God. Hence doth arise also the diffidence of his mercy, though they repent; measuring God by the contracted models of their own spirits; as though his nature were as difficult to pardon

---

[u] Prov. xxx. 2, 3.   [x] Rom. i. 21–23.   [y] Δεισιδαιμονία.   [z] 1 Sam. vi. 3, 4.

their offences against him, as they are to remit wrongs done to themselves.

3. Hence springs all presumption, the common disease of the world. All the wickedness in the world, which is nothing else but presuming upon God, rises from the ill interpretations of the goodness of God, breaking out upon them in the works of creation and providence. The corruption of man's nature engendered by those notions of goodness a monstrous birth of vain imaginations; not of themselves primarily, but of God; whence arose all that folly and darkness in their minds and conversations (Rom. i. 20, 21). They glorified him not as God, but, according to themselves, imagined him good that themselves might be bad; fancied him so indulgent, as to neglect his own honor for their sensuality. How doth the unclean person represent him to his own thoughts, but as a goat; the murderer as a tiger; the sensual person as a swine; while they fancy a God indulgent to their crimes without their repentance! As the image on the seal is stamped upon the wax, so the thoughts of the heart are printed upon the actions. God's patience is apprehended to be an approbation of their vices, and from the consideration of his forbearance, they fashion a god that they believe will smile upon their crimes. They imagine a god that plays with them; and though he threatens doth it only to scare, but means not as he speaks. A god they fancy like themselves, that would do as they would do, not be angry for what they count a light offence (Psalm l. 21): " Thou thoughtest I was such a one as thyself;" that God and they were exactly alike as two tallies. " Our wilful misapprehensions of God are the cause of our misbehavior in all his worship. Our slovenly and lazy services tell him to his face what slight thoughts and apprehensions we have of him."[a] Compare these two together. Superstition ariseth from terrifying misapprehensions of God: presumption from self-pleasing thoughts. One represents him only rigorous, and the other careless. One makes us over-officious in serving him by our own rules; and the other over-bold in offending him according to our humors. The want of a true notion of God's justice makes some men slight him; and the want of a true apprehension of his goodness makes others too servile in their approaches to him. One makes us careless of duties, and the other makes us look on them rather as physic than food; an unsupportable penance, than a desirable privilege. In this case hell is the principle of duty performed to heaven. The superstitious man believes God hath scarce mercy to pardon; the presumptuous man believes he hath no such perfection as justice to punish. The one makes him insignificant to what he desires, kindness and goodness; the other renders him insignificant to what he fears, his vindictive justice. What between the idolater, the superstitious, the presumptuous person, God should look like no God in the world. These unworthy imaginations of God are likewise,

2. A vilifying of him. Debasing the Creator to be a creature of their own fancies; putting their own stamp upon him; and fashioning him not according to that beautiful image he impressed upon

[a] Gurnal. Part II. pp. 245, 246.

them by creation; but the defaced image they inherit by their fall, and which is worse, the image of the devil which spread itself over them at their revolt and apostasy. Were it possible to see a picture of God, according to the fancies of men, it would be the most monstrous being, such a God that never was, nor ever can be. We honor God when we have worthy opinions of him suitable to his nature; when we conceive of him as a being of unbounded loveliness and perfection. We detract from him when we ascribe to him such qualities as would be a horrible disgrace to a wise and good man as injustice and impurity. Thus men debase God when they invert his order, and would create him according to their image, as he first created them according to his own; and think him not worthy to be a God, unless he fully answer the mould they would cast him into, and be what is unworthy of his nature. Men do not conceive of God as he would have them; but he must be what they would have him, one of their own shaping.

1. This is worse than idolatry. The grossest idolater commits not a crime so heinous, by changing his glory into the image of creeping things and senseless creatures, as the imagining God to be as one of our sinful selves, and likening him to those filthy images we erect in our fancies. One makes him an earthly God, like an earthly creature; the other fancies him an unjust and impure God, like a wicked creature. One sets up an image of him in the earth, which is his footstool; the other sets up an image of him in the heart, which ought to be his throne.

2. It is worse than absolute atheism, or a denial of God. "*Dignius credimus non esse, quodcunque non ita fuerit, ut esse deberet,*"[b] was the opinion of Tertullian. It is more commendable to think him not to be, than to think him such a one as is inconsistent with his nature. Better to deny his existence, than deny his perfection. No wise man but would rather have his memory rot, than be accounted infamous, and would be more obliged to him that should deny that ever he had a being in the world, than to say he did indeed live, but he was a sot, a debauched person, and a man not to be trusted. When we apprehend God deceitful in his promises, unrighteous in his threatenings, unwilling to pardon upon repentance, or resolved to pardon notwithstanding impenitency : these are things either unworthy of the nature of God, or contrary to that revelation he hath given of himself. Better for a man never to have been born than be forever miserable; so better to be thought no God, than represented impotent or negligent, unjust or deceitful; which are more contrary to the nature of God than hell can be to the greatest criminal. In this sense perhaps the apostle affirms the Gentiles (Eph. ii. 12) to be such as are "without God in the world;" as being more atheists in adoring God under such notions as they commonly did, than if they had acknowledged no God at all.

3. This is evident by our natural desire to be distant from him, and unwillingness to have any acquaintance with him. Sin set us first at a distance from God; and every new act of gross sin estrangeth us more from him, and indisposeth us more for him : it makes us

both afraid and ashamed to be near him. Sensual men were of this frame that Job discourseth of (ch. xxi. 7–9, 14, 15). Where grace reigns, the nearer to God the more vigorous the motion; the nearer anything approaches to us, that is the object of our desires, the more eagerly do we press forward to it: but our blood riseth at the approaches of anything to which we have an aversion. We have naturally a loathing of God's coming to us or our return to him: we seek not after him as our happiness; and when he offers himself, we like it not, but put a disgrace upon him in choosing other things before him. God and we are naturally at as great a distance, as light and darkness, life and death, heaven and hell. The stronger impression of God anything hath, the more we fly from it. The glory of God in reflection upon Moses' face scared the Israelites; they who had desired God to speak to them by Moses, when they saw a signal impression of God upon his countenance, were afraid to come near him, as they were before unwilling to come near to God.[c] Not that the blessed God is in his own nature a frightful object; but our own guilt renders him so to us, and ourselves indisposed to converse with him; as the light of the sun is as irksome to a distempered eye, as it is in its own nature desirable to a sound one. The saints themselves have had so much frailty, that they have cried out, that they were undone, if they had any more than ordinary discoveries of God made unto them; as if they wished him more remote from them. Vileness cannot endure the splendor of majesty, nor guilt the glory of a judge.

We have naturally, 1. No desire of remembrance of him, 2. Or converse with him, 3. Or thorough return to him, 4. Or close imitation of him: as if there were not any such being as God in the world; or as if we wished there were none at all; so feeble and spiritless are our thoughts of the being of a God.

1. No desire for the remembrance of him. How delightful are other things in our minds! How burdensome the memorials of God, from whom we have our being! With what pleasure do we contemplate the nature of creatures, even of flies and toads, while our minds tire in the search of Him, who hath bestowed upon us our knowing and meditating faculties! Though God shows himself to us in every creature, in the meanest weed as well as the highest heavens, and is more apparent in them to our reasons than themselves can be to our sense; yet though we see them, we will not behold God in them: we will view them to please our sense, to improve our reason in their natural perfections; but pass by the consideration of God's perfections so visibly beaming from them. Thus we play the beasts and atheists in the very exercise of reason, and neglect our Creator to gratify our sense, as though the pleasure of that were more desirable than the knowledge of God. The desire of our souls is not towards his name and the remembrance of him,[d] when we set not ourselves in a posture to feast our souls with deep and serious meditations of him; have a thought of him, only by the bye and away, as if we were afraid of too intimate acquaintance with him. Are not the thoughts of God rather our invaders than our guests; seldom invited to reside and take up their home in our hearts? Have we not, when

c Exod. xxxiv. 30.   d Isa. xxvi. 8.

they have broke in upon us, bid them depart from us,[e] and warned them to come no more upon our ground; sent them packing as soon as we could, and were glad when they were gone? And when they have departed, have we not often been afraid they should return again upon us, and therefore looked about for other inmates, things not good, or if good, infinitely below God, to possess the room of our hearts before any thoughts of him should appear again? Have we not often been glad of excuses to shake off present thoughts of him, and when we have wanted real ones, found out pretences to keep God and our hearts at a distance? Is not this a part of atheism, to be so unwilling to employ our faculties about the giver of them, to refuse to exercise them in a way of a grateful remembrance of him; as though they were none of his gift, but our own acquisition; as though the God that truly gave them had no right to them, and he that thinks on us every day in a way of providence, were not worthy to be thought on by us in a way of special remembrance? Do not the best, that love the remembrance of him, and abhor this natural averseness, find, that when they would think of God, many things tempt them and turn them to think elsewhere? Do they not find their apprehensions too feeble, their motions too dull, and the impressions too slight? This natural atheism is spread over human nature.

2. No desire of converse with him. The word "remember" in the command for keeping holy the Sabbath-day, including all the duties of the day, and the choicest of our lives, implies our natural unwillingness to them, and forgetfulness of them. God's pressing this command with more reasons than the rest, manifests that man hath no heart for spiritual duties. No spiritual duty, which sets us immediately face to face with God, but in the attempts of it we find naturally a resistance from some powerful principle; so that every one may subscribe to the speech of the apostle, that "when we would do good, evil is present with them." No reason of this can be rendered, but the natural temper of our souls, and an affecting a distance from God under any consideration: for though our guilt first made the breach, yet this aversion to a converse with him steps up without any actual reflections upon our guilt, which may render God terrible to us as an offended judge. Are we not often also, in our attendance upon him, more pleased with the modes of worship which gratify our fancy, than to have our souls inwardly delighted with the object of worship himself? This is a part of our natural atheism. To cast such duties off by total neglect, or in part, by affecting a coldness in them, is to cast off the fear of the Lord.[f] Not to call upon God, and not to know him, are one and the same thing (Jer. x. 25). Either we think there is no such Being in the world, or that he is so slight a one, that he deserves not the respect he calls for; or so impotent and poor, that he cannot supply what our necessities require.

3. No desire of a thorough return to him. The first man fled from him after his defection, though he had no refuge to fly to but the grace of his Creator. Cain went from his presence, would be a fugi-

tive from God rather than a suppliant to him; when by faith in, and application of the promised Redeemer, he might have escaped the wrath to come for his brother's blood, and mitigated the sorrows he was justly sentenced to bear in the world. Nothing will separate prodigal man from commoning with swine; and make him return to his father, but an empty trough: have we but husks to feed on, we shall never think of a father's presence. It were well if our sores and indigence would drive us to him; but when our strength is devoured, we will not "return to the Lord our God, nor seek him for all this."[g] Not his drawn sword, as a God of judgment, nor his mighty power, as a Lord, nor his open arms, as the Lord their God, could move them to turn their eyes and their hearts towards him. The more he invites us to partake of his grace, the further we run from him to provoke his wrath: the louder God called them by his prophets, the closer they stuck to their Baal.[h] We turn our backs when he stretches out his hand, stop our ears when he lifts up his voice. We fly from him when he courts us, and shelter ourselves in any bush from his merciful hand that would lay hold upon us; nor will we set our faces towards him, till our way be hedged up with thorns, and not a gap left to creep out any by-way.[i] Whosoever is brought to a return, puts the Holy Ghost to the pain of striving; he is not easily brought to a spiritual subjection to God, nor persuaded to a surrender at a summons, but sweetly overpowered by storm, and victoriously drawn into the arms of God. God stands ready, but the heart stands off; grace is full of entreaties, and the soul full of excuses; Divine love offers, and carnal self-love rejects. Nothing so pleases us as when we are farthest from him; as if anything were more amiable, anything more desirable, than himself.

4. No desire of any close imitation of him. When our Saviour was to come as a refiner's fire, to purify the sons of Levi, the cry is, "Who shall abide the day of his coming?" (Mal. iii. 2, 3.) Since we are alienated from the life of God, we desire no more naturally to live the life of God, than a toad, or any other animal, desires to live the life of a man. No heart that knows God but hath a holy ambition to imitate him. No soul that refuseth him for a copy, but is ignorant of his excellency. Of this temper is all mankind naturally. Man in corruption is as loth to be like God in holiness, as Adam, after his creation, was desirous to be like God in knowledge; his posterity are like their father, who soon turned his back upon his original copy. What can be worse than this? Can the denial of his being be a greater injury than this contempt of him; as if he had not goodness to deserve our remembrance, nor amiableness fit for our converse; as if he were not a Lord fit for our subjection, nor had a holiness that deserved our imitation? For the use of this:—

Use I. It serves for information.

1. It gives us occasion to admire the wonderful patience and mercy of God. How many millions of practical atheists breathe every day in his air, and live upon his bounty who deserve to be inhabitants in hell, rather than possessors of the earth! An infinite holiness is offended, an infinite justice is provoked; yet an infinite pa-

g Hos. vii. 10.   h Hos. xi. 2.   i Hos. ii. 6, 7.

uience forbears the punishment, and an infinite goodness relieves our wants: the more we had merited his justice and forfeited his favor, the more is his affection enhanced, which makes his hand so liberal to us.   At the first invasion of his rights, he mitigates the terror of the threatening which was set to defend his law, with the grace of a promise to relieve and recover his rebellious creature.[k]   Who would have looked for anything but tearing thunders, sweeping judgments, to raze up the foundations of the apostate world?   But oh, how great are his bowels to his aspiring competitors!   Have we not experimented his contrivances for our good, though we have refused him for our happiness?   Has he not opened his arms, when we spurned with our feet; held out his alluring mercy, when we have brandished against him a rebellious sword?   Has he not entreated us while we have invaded him, as if he were unwilling to lose us, who are ambitious to destroy ourselves?   Has he yet denied us the care of his providence, while we have denied him the rights of his honor, and would appropriate them to ourselves?   Has the sun forborne shining upon us, though we have shot our arrows against him?   Have not our beings been supported by his goodness, while we have endeavored to climb up to his throne; and his mercies continued to charm us, while we have used them as weapons to injure him?   Our own necessities might excite us to own him as our happiness, but he adds his invitations to the voice of our wants.   Has he not promised a kingdom to those that would strip him or his crown, and proclaimed pardon upon repentance to those that would take away his glory? and hath so twisted together his own end, which is his honor, and man's true end, which is his salvation, that a man cannot truly mind himself and his own salvation, but he must mind God's glory; and cannot be intent upon God's honor, but by the same act he promotes himself and his own happiness? so loth is God to give any just occasion of dissatisfaction to his creature, as well as dishonor to himself.   All those wonders of his mercy are enhanced by the heinousness of our atheism; a multitude of gracious thoughts from him above the multitude of contempts from us.[l]   What rebels in actual arms against their prince, aiming at his life, ever found that favor from him; to have all their necessaries richly afforded them, without which they would starve, and without which they would be unable to manage their attempts, as we have received from God?   Had not God had riches of goodness, forbearance, and long-suffering, and infinite riches too, the despite the world had done him, in refusing him as their rule, happiness, and end, would have emptied him long ago.[m]

2. It brings in a justification of the exercise of his justice.   If it gives us occasion loudly to praise his patience, it also stops our mouths from accusing any acts of his vengeance.   What can be too sharp a recompense for the despising and disgracing so great a Being? The highest contempt merits the greatest anger; and when we will not own him for our happiness, it is equal we should feel the misery of separation from him.   If he that is guilty of treason deserves to lose his life, what punishment can be thought great enough for him that is so disingenuous as to prefer himself before a God so infinitely

k Gen. iii. 15.   l Psalm cvi. 7.   m Rom. ii. 4.

good, and so foolish as to invade the rights of one infinitely powerful? It is no injustice for a creature to be forever left to himself, to see what advantage he can make of that self he was so busily employed to set up in the place of his Creator. The soul of man deserves an infinite punishment for despising an infinite good; and it is not unequitable, that that self which man makes his rule and happiness above God, should become his torment and misery by the righteousness of that God whom he despised.

3. Hence ariseth a necessity of a new state and frame of soul, to alter an atheistical nature. We forget God; think of him with reluctancy; have no respect to God in our course and acts: this cannot be our original state. God, being infinitely good, never let man come out of his hands with this actual unwillingness to acknowledge and serve him; he never intended to dethrone himself for the work of his hands, or that the creature should have any other end than that of his Creator: as the apostle saith, in the case of the Galatians' error (Gal. v. 8), "This persuasion came not of Him that called you;" so this frame comes not from him that created you: how much, therefore, do we need a restoring principle in us! Instead of ordering ourselves according to the will of God, we are desirous to "fulfil the wills of the flesh:"[n] there is a necessity of some other principle in us to make us fulfil the will of God, since we were created for God, not for the flesh. We can no more be voluntarily serviceable to God, while our serpentine nature and devilish habits remain in us, than we can suppose the devil can be willing to glorify God, while the nature he contracted by his fall abides powerfully in him. Our nature and will must be changed, that our actions may regard God as our end, that we may delightfully meditate on him, and draw the motives of our obedience from him. Since this atheism is seated in nature, the change must be in our nature; since our first aspirings to the rights of God were the fruits of the serpent's breath which tainted our nature, there must be a removal of this taint, whereby our natures may be on the side of God against Satan, as they were before on the side of Satan against God. There must be a supernatural principle before we can live a supernatural life, i. e. live to God, since we are naturally alienated from the life of God: the aversion of our natures from God, is as strong as our inclination to evil; we are disgusted with one, and pressed with the other; we have no will, no heart, to come to God in any service. This nature must be broken in pieces and new moulded, before we can make God our rule and our end: while men's "deeds are evil" they cannot comply with God;[o] much less while their natures are evil. Till this be done, all the service a man performs riseth from some "evil imagination of the heart, which is evil, only evil, and that continually;"[p] from wrong notions of God, wrong notions of duty, or corrupt motives. All the pretences of devotion to God are but the adoration of some golden image. Prayers to God for the ends of self, are like those of the devil to our Saviour, when he asked leave to go into the herd of swine: the object was right, Christ; the end was the destruction of the swine, and the satisfaction of their malice to the owners; there

---

[n] Eph. ii. 3.   [o] John iii. 19, 20.   [p] Gen. vi. 5.

is a necessity then that depraved ends should be removed, that that which was God's end in our framing, may be our end in our acting, viz. his glory, which cannot be without a change of nature. We can never honor him supremely whom we do not supremely love; till this be, we cannot glorify God as God, though we do things by his command and order; no more, than when God employed the devil in afflicting Job.q His performance cannot be said to be good, because his end was not the same with God's; he acted out of malice, what God commanded out of sovereignty, and for gracious designs; had God employed an holy angel in his design upon Job, the action had been good in the affliction, because his nature was holy, and therefore his ends holy; but bad in the devil, because his ends were base and unworthy.

4. We may gather from hence, the difficulty of conversion, and mortification to follow thereupon. What is the reason men receive no more impression from the voice of God and the light of his truth, than a dead man in the grave doth from the roaring thunder, or a blind mole from the light of the sun? It is because our atheism is as great as the deadness of the one, or the blindness of the other. The principle in the heart is strong to shut the door both of the thoughts and affections against God. If a friend oblige us, we shall act for him as for ourselves; we are won by entreaties; soft words overcome us; but our hearts are as deaf as the hardest rock at the call of God; neither the joys of heaven proposed by him can allure us, nor the flashed terrors of hell affright us to him, as if we conceived God unable to bestow the one or execute the other: the true reason is, God and self contest for the deity. The law of sin is, God must be at the footstool; the law of God is, sin must be utterly deposed. Now it is difficult to leave a law beloved for a law long ago discarded. The mind of man will hunt after anything; the will of man embrace anything: upon the proposal of mean objects the spirit of man spreads its wings, flies to catch them, becomes one with them: but attempt to bring it under the power of God, the wings flag, the creature looks lifeless, as though there were no spring of motion in it; it is as much crucified to God, as the holy apostle was to the world. The sin of the heart discovers its strength the more God discovers the "holiness of his will."r The love of sin hath been predominant in our nature, has quashed a love to God, if not extinguished it. Hence also is the difficulty of mortification. This is a work tending to the honor of God, the abasing of that inordinately aspiring humor in ourselves. If the nature of man be inclined to sin, as it is, it must needs be bent against anything that opposes it. It is impossible to strike any true blow at any lust till the true sense of God be re-entertained in the soil where it ought to grow. Who can be naturally willing to crucify what is incorporated with him—his flesh? what is dearest to him—himself? Is it an easy thing for man, the competitor with God, to turn his arms against himself, that self should overthrow its own empire, lay aside all its pretensions to, and designs for, a godhead; to hew off its own members, and subdue its own affections? It is the nature of man to "cover his sin,"

q Job i.   r Rom. vii. 9–12.

to hide it in his bosom,[s] not to destroy it; and as unwillingly part with his carnal affections, as the legion of devils were with the man that had been long possessed; and when he is forced and fired from one, he will endeavor to espouse some other lust, as those devils desired to possess swine, when they were chased from their possession of that man.

5. Here we see the reason of unbelief. That which hath most of God in it, meets with most aversion from us; that which hath least of God, finds better and stronger inclinations in us. What is the reason that the heart of man is more unwilling to embrace the gospel, than acknowledge the equity of the law? because there is more of God's nature and perfection evident in the gospel than in the law; besides, there is more reliance on God, and distance from self, commanded in the gospel. The law puts a man upon his own strength, the gospel takes him off from his own bottom; the law acknowledges him to have a power in himself, and to act for his own reward; the gospel strips him of all his proud and towering thoughts,[t] brings him to his due place, the foot of God; orders him to deny himself as his own rule, righteousness, and end, "and henceforth not to live to himself."[u] This is the true reason why men are more against the gospel than against the law; because it doth more deify God, and debase man. Hence it is easier to reduce men to some moral virtue than to faith; to make men blush at their outward vices, but not at the inward impurity of their natures. Hence it is observed, that those that asserted that all happiness did arise from something in a man's self, as the Stoics and Epicureans did, and that a wise man was equal with God, were greater enemies to the truths of the gospel than others (Acts xvii. 18), because it lays the axe to the root of their principal opinion, takes the one from their self-sufficiency, and the other from their self-gratification; it opposeth the brutish principle of the one, which placed happiness in the pleasures of the body, and the more noble principle of the other, which placed happiness in the virtue of the mind; the one was for a sensual, the other for a moral self; both disowned by the doctrine of the gospel.

6. It informs us, consequently, who can be the Author of grace and conversion, and every other good work. No practical atheist ever yet turned to God, but was turned by God; and not to acknowledge it to God is a part of this atheism, since it is a robbing God of the honor of one of his most glorious works. If this practical atheism be natural to man ever since the first taint of nature in Paradise, what can be expected from it, but a resisting of the work of God, and setting up all the forces of nature against the operations of grace, till a day of power dawn and clear up upon the soul?[x] Not all the angels in heaven, or men upon earth, can be imagined to be able to persuade a man to fall out with himself; nothing can turn the tide of nature, but a power above nature. God took away the sanctifying Spirit from man, as a penalty for the first sin; who can regain it but by his will and pleasure? who can restore it, but he that removed it? Since every man hath the same fundamental atheism

---

[s] Job xxxi. 33. "If I cover my transgressions, as Adam."
[t] 2 Cor. x. 5.　　　　[u] 2 Cor. v. 15.　　　　[x] Psalm cx. 3.

in him by nature, and would be a rule to himself and his own end, he is so far from dethroning himself, that all the strength of his corrupted nature is alarmed up to stand to their arms upon any attempt God makes to regain the fort. The will is so strong against God, that it is like many wills twisted together (Eph. ii. 3), " Wills of the flesh ;" we translate it the " desires of the flesh ;" like many threads twisted in a cable, never to be snapped asunder by a human arm ; a power and will above ours, can only untwist so many wills in a knot. Man cannot rise to an acknowledgment of God without God ; hell may as well become heaven, the devil be changed into an angel of light. The devil cannot but desire happiness ; he knows the misery into which he is fallen, he cannot be desirous of that punishment he knows is reserved for him. Why doth he not sanctify God, and glorify his Creator, wherein there is abundantly more pleasure than in his malicious course ? Why doth he not petition to recover his ancient standing ? he will not ; there are chains of darkness upon his faculties ; he will not be otherwise than he is ; his desire to be god of the world sways him against his own interest, and out of love to his malice, he will not sin at a less rate to make a diminution of his punishment. Man, if God utterly refuseth to work upon him, is no better ; and to maintain his atheism would venture a hell. How is it possible for a man to turn himself to that God against whom he hath a quarrel in his nature ; the most rooted and settled habit in him being to set himself in the place of God ? An atheist by nature can no more alter his own temper, and engrave in himself the divine nature, than a rock can carve itself into the statue of a man, or a serpent that is an enemy to man could or would raise itself to the nobility of the human nature. That soul that by nature would strip God of his rights, cannot, without a divine power, be made conformable to him, and acknowledge sincerely and cordially the rights and glory of God.

7. We may here see the reason why there can be no justification by the best and strongest works of nature. Can that which hath atheism at the root justify either the action or person ? What strength can those works have which have neither God's law for their rule, nor his glory for their end ? that are not wrought by any spiritual strength from him, nor tend with any spiritual affection to him ? Can these be a foundation for the most holy God to pronounce a creature righteous ? They will justify his justice in condemning, but cannot sway his justice to an absolution. Every natural man in his works picks and chooses ; he owns the will of God no further than he can wring it to suit the law of his members, and minds not the honor of God, but as it jostles not with his own glory and secular ends. Can he be righteous that prefers his own will and his own honor before the will and honor of the Creator ? However men's actions may be beneficial to others, what reason hath God to esteem them, wherein there is no respect to him, but themselves ; whereby they dethrone him in their thoughts, while they seem to own him in their religious works ? Every day reproves us with something different from the rule ; thousands of wanderings offer themselves to

our eyes: can justification be expected from that which in itself is matter of despair?

8. See here the cause of all the apostasy in the world. Practical atheism was never conquered in such; they are still "alienated from the life of God," and will not live to God, as he lives to himself and his own honor.[y] They loathe his rule, and distaste his glory; are loth to step out of themselves to promote the ends of another; find not the satisfaction in him as they do in themselves; they will be judges of what is good for them and righteous in itself, rather than admit of God to judge for them. When men draw back from truth to error, it is to such opinions which may serve more to foment and cherish their ambition, covetousness, or some beloved lust that disputes with God for precedency, and is designed to be served before him (John xii. 42, 43): "They love the praise of men more than the praise of God." A preferring man before God was the reason they would not confess Christ, and God in him.

9. This shows us the excellency of the gospel and christian religion. It sets man in his due place, and gives to God what the excellency of his nature requires. It lays man in the dust from whence he was taken, and sets God upon that throne where he ought to sit. Man by nature would annihilate God and deify himself; the gospel glorifies God and annihilates man. In our first revolt we would be like him in knowledge; in the means he hath provided for our recovery, he designs to make us like him in grace; the gospel shows ourselves to be an object of humiliation, and God to be a glorious object for our imitation. The light of nature tells us there is a God; the gospel gives us a more magnificent report of him; the light of nature condemns gross atheism, and that of the gospel condemns and conquers spiritual atheism in the hearts of men.

Use II. Of exhortation.

First, Let us labor to be sensible of this atheism in our nature, and be humbled for it. How should we lie in the dust, and go bowing under the humbling thoughts of it all our days! Shall we not be sensible of that whereby we spill the blood of our souls, and give a stab to the heart of our own salvation? Shall we be worse than any creature, not to bewail that which tends to our destruction? He that doth not lament it, cannot challenge the character of a Christian, hath nothing of the divine life and love planted in his soul. Not a man but shall one day be sensible, when the eternal God shall call him out to examination, and charge his conscience to discover every crime, which will then own the authority whereby it acted; when the heart shall be torn open, and the secrets of it brought to public view; and the world and man himself shall see what a viperous brood of corrupt principles and ends nested in his heart. Let us, therefore, be truly sensible of it, till the consideration draw tears from our eyes and sorrow from our souls; let us urge the thoughts of it upon our hearts till the core of that pride be eaten out, and our stubbornness changed into humility; till our heads become waters, and our eyes fountains of tears, and be a spring of prayer to God to change the heart, and mortify the atheism in it; and consider

[y] Eph. iv. 17, 18.

what a sad thing it is to be a practical atheist: and who is not so by nature?

1. Let us be sensible of it in ourselves. Have any of our hearts been a soil wherein the fear and reverence of God hath naturally grown? Have we a desire to know him, or a will to embrace him? Do we delight in his will, and love the remembrance of his name? Are our respects to him, as God, equal to the speculative knowledge we have of his nature? Is the heart, wherein he hath stamped his image, reserved for his residence? Is not the world more affected than the Creator of the world; as though that could contribute to us a greater happiness than the Author of it? Have not creatures as much of our love, fear, trust, nay, more, than God that framed both them and us? Have we not too often relied upon our own strength, and made a calf of our own wisdom, and said of God, as the Israelites of Moses, "As for this Moses we wot not what is become of him?" (Exod. xxxii. 1) and given oftener the glory of our good success to our drag and our net, to our craft and our industry, than to the wisdom and blessing of God? Are we, then, free from this sort of atheism?[z] It is as impossible to have two Gods at one time in one heart, as to have two kings at one time in full power in one kingdom. Have there not been frequent neglects of God? Have we not been deaf whilst he hath knocked at our doors? slept when he hath sounded in our ears, as if there had been no such being as a God in the world? How many strugglings have been against our approaches to him! Hath not folly often been committed, with vain imaginations starting up in the time of religious service, which we would scarce vouchsafe a look to at another time, and in another business, but would have thrust them away with indignation? Had they stept in to interrupt our worldly affairs, they would have been troublesome intruders; but while we are with God they are acceptable guests. How unwilling have our hearts been to fortify themselves with strong and influencing considerations of God, before we addressed to him! Is it not too often that our lifelessness in prayer proceeds from this atheism; a neglect of seeing what arguments and pleas may be drawn from the divine perfections, to second our suit in hand, and quicken our hearts in the service? Whence are those indispositions to any spiritual duty, but because we have not due thoughts of the majesty, holiness, goodness, and excellency of God? Is there any duty which leads to a more particular inquiry after him, or a more clear vision of him, but our hearts have been ready to rise up and call it cursed rather than blessed? Are not our minds bemisted with an ignorance of him, our wills drawn by aversion from him, our affections rising in distaste of him? more willing to know anything than his nature, and more industrious to do anything than his will? Do we not all fall under some one or other of these considerations? Is it not fit, then, that we should have a sense of them? It is to be bewailed by us, that so little of God is in our hearts, when so many evidences of the love of God are in the creatures; that God should be so little our end, who hath been so much our benefactor; that he should be so

---

[z] Lawson's Body of Divinity, pp. 153, 154.

little in our thoughts, who sparkles in everything which presents itself to our eyes.

2. Let us be sensible of it in others. We ought to have a just execration of the too open iniquity in the midst of us; and imitate holy David, whose tears plentifully gushed out, "because men kept not God's law." [a] And is it not a time to exercise this pious lamentation? Hath the wicked atheism of any age been greater, or can you find worse in hell, than we may hear of and behold on earth? How is the excellent Majesty of God adored by the angels in heaven, despised and reproached by men on earth, as if his name were published to be matter of their sport! What a gasping thing is a natural sense of God among men in the world! Is not the law of God, accompanied with such dreadful threatenings and curses, made light of, as if men would place their honor in being above or beyond any sense of that glorious Majesty? How many wallow in pleasures, as if they had been made men only to turn brutes, and their souls given them only for salt, to keep their bodies from putrefying? It is as well a part of atheism not to be sensible of the abuses of God's name and laws by others, as to violate them ourselves: what is the language of a stupid senselessness of them, but that there is no God in the world whose glory is worth a vindication, and deserves our regards? That we may be sensible of the unworthiness of neglecting God as our rule and end, consider,

1. The unreasonableness of it as it concerns God.

1st. It is a high contempt of God. It is an inverting the order of things; a making God the highest to become the lowest; and self the lowest to become the highest: to be guided by every base companion, some idle vanity, some carnal interest, is to acknowledge an excellency abounding in them which is wanting in God; an equity in their orders, and none in God's precepts; a goodness in their promises, and a falsity in God's; as if infinite excellency were a mere vanity, and to act for God were the debasement of our reason; to act for self or some pitiful creature, or sordid lust, were the glory and advancement of it. To prefer any one sin before the honor of God, is as if that sin had been our creator and benefactor, as if it were the original cause of our being and support. Do not men pay as great a homage to that as they do to God? Do not their minds eagerly pursue it? Are not the revolvings of it, in their fancies, as delightful to them as the remembrance of God to a holy soul? Do any obey the commands of God with more readiness than they do the orders of their base affections? Did Peter leap more readily into the sea to meet his Master, than many into the jaws of hell to meet their Dalilahs? How cheerfully did the Israelites part with their ornaments for the sake of an idol, who would not have spared a moiety for the honor of their Deliverer! [b] If to make God our end is the principal duty in nature, then to make ourselves, or anything else, our end, is the greatest vice in the rank of evils.

2d. It is a contempt of God as the most amiable object. God is infinitely excellent and desirable (Zech. ix. 17): "How great is his

---

[a] Psalm cxix. 136.
[b] Exod. xxxii. 3,—" All the people brake off the golden ear-rings."

goodness, and how great is his beauty!" There is nothing in him
but what may ravish our affections; none that knows him but finds
attractives to keep them with him; He hath nothing in him which
can be a proper object of contempt, no defects or shadow of evil;
there is infinite excellency to charm us, and infinite goodness to
allure us,—the Author of our being, the Benefactor of our lives.
Why then should man, which is his image, be so base as to slight
the beautiful Original which stamped it on him? He is the most
lovely object; therefore to be studied, therefore to be honored,
therefore to be followed. In regard of his perfection he hath the
highest right to our thoughts. All other beings were eminently
contained in his essence, and were produced by his infinite power.
The creature hath nothing but what it hath from God. And is it
not unworthy to prefer the copy before the original—to fall in love
with a picture, instead of the beauty it represents? The creature
which we advance to be our rule and end, can no more report to us
the true amiableness of God, than a few colors mixed and suited
together upon a piece of cloth, can the moral and intellectual loveliness of the soul of man. To contemn God one moment is more
base than if all creatures were contemned by us forever; because
the excellency of creatures is, to God, like that of a drop to the sea,
or a spark to the glory of unconceivable millions of suns. As much
as the excellency of God is above our conceptions, so much doth
the debasing of him admit of unexpressible aggravations.

2. Consider the ingratitude in it. That we should resist that God
with our hearts who made us the work of his hands, and count him
as nothing, from whom we derive all the good that we are or have.
There is no contempt of man but steps in here to aggravate our
slighting of God; because there is no relation one man can stand in
to another, wherein God doth not more highly appear to man. If
we abhor the unworthy carriage of a child to a tender father, a servant to an indulgent master, a man to his obliging friend, why do
men daily act that toward God which they cannot speak of without
abhorrency, if acted by another against man? Is God a being less
to be regarded than man, and more worthy of contempt than a creature?—"It would be strange if a benefactor should live in the same
town, in the same house with us, and we never exchange a word
with him; yet this is our case, who have the works of God in our
eyes, the goodness of God in our being, the mercy of God in our
daily food" [c]—yet think so little of him, converse so little with him,
serve everything before him, and prefer everything above him?
Whence have we our mercies but from his hand? Who, besides
him, maintains our breath this moment? Would he call for our
spirits this moment, they must depart from us to attend his command.
There is not a moment wherein our unworthy carriage is not aggravated, because there is not a moment wherein he is not our Guardian, and gives us not tastes of a fresh bounty. And it is no light
aggravation of our crime, that we injure him without whose bounty,
in giving us our being, we had not been capable of casting contempt
upon him: that he that hath the greatest stamp of his image, man,

[c] Reynolds.

should deserve the character of the worst of his rebels: that he who hath only reason by the gift of God to judge of the equity of the laws of God, should swell against them as grievous, and the government of the Lawgiver as burdensome. Can it lessen the crime to use the principle wherein we excel the beasts to the disadvantage of God, who endowed us with that principle above the beasts?

1. It is a debasing of God beyond what the devil doth at present. He is more excusable in his present state of acting, than man is in his present refusing God for his rule and end. He strives against a God that exerciseth upon him a vindictive justice; we debase a God that loads us with his daily mercies. The despairing devils are excluded from any mercy or divine patience; but we are not only under the long-suffering of his patience, but the large expressions of his bounty. He would not be governed by him when he was only his bountiful Creator: we refuse to be guided by him after he hath given us the blessing of creation from his own hand, and the more obliging blessings of redemption by the hand and blood of his Son. It cannot be imagined that the devils and the damned should ever make God their end, since he hath assured them he will not be their happiness; and shut up all his perfections from their experimental notice, but those of his power to preserve them, and his justice to punish them. They have no grant from God of ever having a heart to comply with his will, or ever having the honor to be actively employed for his glory. They have some plea for their present contempt of God, not in regard of his nature, for he is infinitely amiable, excellent and lovely, but in regard of his administration toward them. But what plea can man have for his practical atheism, who lives by his power, is sustained by his bounty, and solicited by his Spirit? What an ungrateful thing is it to put off the nature of man for that of devils, and dishonor God under mercy, as the devils do under his wrathful anger!

2. It is an ungrateful contempt of God, who cannot be injurious to us. He cannot do us wrong, because he cannot be unjust (Gen. xviii. 25): "Shall not the Judge of all the earth do right?" His nature doth as much abhor unrighteousness, as love a communicative goodness: he never commanded anything but what was highly conducible to the happiness of man. Infinite goodness can no more injure man than it can dishonor itself: it lays out itself in additions of kindness, and while we debase him, he continues to benefit us; and is it not an unparalleled ingratitude to turn our backs upon an object so lovely, an object so loving, in the midst of varieties of allurements from him? God did create intellectual creatures, angels and men, that he might communicate more of himself and his own goodness and holiness to man, than creatures of a lower rank were capable of. What do we do, by rejecting him as our rule and end, but cross, as much as in us lies, God's end in our creation, and shut our souls against the communications of those perfections he was so willing to bestow? We use him as if he intended us the greatest wrong, when it is impossible for him to do any to any of his creatures.

3. Consider the misery which will attend such a temper if it con-

tinue predominant. Those that thrust God away as their happiness and end, can expect no other but to be thrust away by him, as to any relief and compassion. A distance from God here can look for nothing, but a remoteness from God hereafter. When the devil, a creature of vast endowments, would advance himself above God, and instruct man to commit the same sin, he is "cursed above all creatures."[d] When we will not acknowledge him a God of all glory, we shall be separated from him as a God of all comfort: "All they that are afar off shall perish" (Psalm lxxiii. 27). This is the spring of all woe. What the Prodigal suffered, was because he would leave his father, and live of himself. Whosoever is ambitious to be his own heaven, will at last find his soul to become its own hell. As it loved all things for itself, so it shall be grieved with all things for itself. As it would be its own god against the right of God, it shall then be its own tormentor by the justice of God.

Secondly, Watch against this atheism, and be daily employed in the mortification of it. In every action we shold make the inquiry, What is the rule I observe? Is it God's will or my own? Whether do my intentions tend to set up God or self? As much as we destroy this, we abate the power of sin: these two things are the head of the serpent in us, which we must be bruising by the power of the cross. Sin is nothing else but a turning from God, and centering in self, and most in the inferior part of self: if we bend our force against those two, self-will and self-ends, we shall intercept atheism at the spring head, take away that which doth constitute and animate all sin : the sparks must vanish if the fire be quenched which affords them fuel. They are but two short things to ask in every undertaking : Is God my rule in regard of his will? Is God my end in regard of his glory? All sin lies in the neglect of these, all grace lies in the practice of them. Without some degree of the mortification of these ; we cannot make profitable and comfortable approaches to God. When we come with idols in our hearts, we shall be answered according to the multitude and the baseness of them too.[e] What expectation of a good look from him can we have, when we come before him with undeifying thoughts of him, a petition in our mouths, and a sword in our hearts, to stab his honor? To this purpose,

1. Be often in the views of the excellencies of God. When we have no intercourse with God by delightful meditations, we begin to be estranged from him, and prepare ourselves to live without God in the world. Strangeness is the mother and nurse of disaffection : we slight men sometimes because we know them not. The very beasts delight in the company of men ; when being tamed and familiar, they become acquainted with their disposition. A daily converse with God would discover so much of loveliness in his nature, so much of sweetness in his ways, that our injurious thoughts of God would wear off, and we should count it our honor to contemn ourselves and magnify him. By this means a slavish fear, which is both a dishonor to God and a torment to the soul,[f] and the root of atheism, will be cast out, and an ingenuous fear of him wrought in the heart. Exercised thoughts on him would issue out in affections to him, which

<hr>

d Gen. iii. 14.   e Ezek. xiv. 4.   f 1 John iv. 18.

would engage our hearts to make him both our rule and our end. This course would stifle any temptations to gross atheism, wherewith good souls are sometimes haunted, by confirming us more in the belief of a God, and discourage any attempts to a deliberate practical atheism. We are not like to espouse any principle which is confuted by the delightful converse we daily have with him. The more we thus enter into the presence chamber of God, the more we cling about him with our affections, the more vigorous and lively will the true notion of God grow up in us, and be able to prevent anything which may dishonor him and debase our souls. Let us therefore consider him as the only happiness; set up the true God in our understandings; possess our hearts with a deep sense of his desirable excellency above all other things. This is the main thing we are to do in order to our great business: all the directions in the world, with the neglect of this, will be insignificant ciphers. The neglect of this is common, and is the basis of all the mischiefs which happen to the souls of men.

2. Prize and study the Scripture. We can have no delight in meditation on him, unless we know him; and we cannot know him but by the means of his own revelation; when the revelation is despised, the revealer will be of little esteem. Men do not throw off God from being their rule, till they throw off Scripture from being their guide; and God must needs be cast off from being an end, when the Scripture is rejected from being a rule. Those that do not care to know his will, that love to be ignorant of his nature, can never be affected to his honor. Let therefore the subtleties of reason veil to the doctrine of faith, and the humor of the will to the command of the word.

3. Take heed of sensual pleasures,' and be very watchful and cautious in the use of those comforts God allows us. Job was afraid, when his "sons feasted, that they should curse God in their hearts."[g] It was not without cause that the apostle Peter joined sobriety with watchfulness and prayer (1 Pet. iv. 7): "The end of all things is at hand; be ye therefore sober, and watch unto prayer."—A moderate use of worldly comforts.—Prayer is the great acknowledgment of God, and too much sensuality is a hindrance of this, and a step to atheism. Belshazzar's lifting himself up against the Lord, and not glorifying of God, is charged upon his sensuality (Dan. v. 23). Nothing is more apt to quench the notions of God, and root out the conscience of him, than an addictedness to sensual pleasures. Therefore take heed of that snare.

4. Take heed of sins against knowledge. The more sins against knowledge are committed, the more careless we are, and the more careless we shall be of God and his honor; we shall more fear his judicial power; and the more we fear that, the more we shall disaffect that God in whose hand vengeance is, and to whom it doth belong. Atheism in conversation proceeds to atheism in affection, and that will endeavor to sink into atheism in opinion and judgment.

The sum of the whole.—And now consider in the whole what has been spoken.

g Job i. 4.

1. Man would set himself up as his own rule. He disowns the rule of God, is unwilling to have any acquaintance with the rule God sets him, negligent in using the means for the knowledge of his will, and endeavors to shake it off when any notices of it break in upon him; when he cannot expel it, he hath no pleasure in the consideration of it, and the heart swells against it. When the notions of the will of God are entertained, it is on some other consideration, or with wavering and unsettled affections. Many times men design to improve some lust by his truth. This unwillingness respects truth as it is most spiritual and holy; as it most relates and leads to God; as it is most contrary to self. He is guilty of contempt of the will of God, which is seen in every presumptuous breach of his law; in the natural aversions to the declaration of his will and mind, which way soever he turns; in slighting that part of his will which is most for his honor; in the awkwardness of the heart when it is to pay God a service. A constraint in the first engagement, slightness in the service, in regard of the matter, in regard of the frame, without a natural vigor. Many distractions, much weariness, in deserting the rule of God, when our expectations are not answered upon our service, in breaking promises with God. Man naturally owns any other rule rather than that of God's prescribing: the rule of Satan; the will of man; in complying more with the dictates of men than the will of God; in observing that which is materially so, not because it is his will, but the injunctions of men; in obeying the will of man when it is contrary to the will of God. This man doth in order to the setting up himself. This is natural to man as he is corrupted. Men are dissatisfied with their own consciences when they contradict the desires of self. Most actions in the world are done, more because they are agreeable to self, than as they are honorable to God; as they are agreeable to natural and moral self, or sinful self. It is evident in neglects of taking God's directions upon emergent occasions; in counting the actions of others to be good or bad, as they suit with, or spurn against our fancies and humors. Man would make himself the rule of God, and give laws to his Creator, in striving against his law; disapproving of his methods of government in the world; in impatience in our particular concerns; envying the gifts and prosperity of others; corrupt matter or ends of prayer or praise; bold interpretations of the judgments of God in the world; mixing rules in the worship of God with those which have been ordained by him; suiting interpretations of Scripture with our own minds and humors; falling off from God after some fair compliances, when his will grates upon us, and crosseth ours.

2. Man would be his own end. This is natural and universal. This is seen in frequent self-applauses and inward overweening reflections; in ascribing the glory of what we do or have to ourselves; in desire of self-pleasing doctrines; in being highly concerned in injuries done to ourselves, and little or not at all concerned for injuries done to God; in trusting in ourselves; in workings for carnal self against the light of our own consciences: this is a usurping God's prerogative, vilifying God, destroying God. Man would make anything his end or happiness rather than God. This appears in the

fewer thoughts we have of him than of anything else; in the greedy pursuit of the world; in the strong addictedness to sensual pleasures; in paying a service, upon any success in the world, to instruments more than to God: this is a debasing God in setting up a creature, but more in setting up a base lust; it is a denying of God. Man would make himself the end of all creatures. In pride; using the creatures contrary to the end God hath appointed: this is to dishonor God, and it is diabolical. Man would make himself the end of God; in loving God, because of some self-pleasing benefits distributed by him; in abstinence from some sins, because they are against the interest of some other beloved corruption; in performing duties merely for a selfish interest, which is evident in unwieldiness in religious duties, where self is not concerned; in calling upon God only in a time of necessity; in begging his assistance to our own projects after we have by our own craft, laid the plot; in impatience upon a refusal of our desires; in selfish aims we have in our duties: this is a vilifying God, a dethroning him; in unworthy imaginations of God, universal in man by nature. Hence spring idolatry, superstition, presumption, the common disease of the world. This is a vilifying God; worse than idolatry, worse than absolute atheism. Natural desires to be distant from him; no desires for the remembrance of him; no desires of converse with him; no desires of a thorough return to him; no desire of any close imitation of him.

DISCOURSE III

ON GOD'S BEING A SPIRIT

John iv. 24.—God is a Spirit: and they that worship him must worship him in spirit and in truth.

The words are part of the dialogue between our Saviour and the Samaritan woman.[h] Christ, intending to return from Judea to Galilee, passed through the country of Samaria, a place inhabited not by Jews, but a mixed company of several nations, and some remainders of the posterity of Israel, who escaped the captivity, and were returned from Assyria; and being weary with his journey, arrived about the sixth hour or noon (according to the Jews' reckoning the time of the day), at a well that Jacob had digged, which was of great account among the inhabitants for the antiquity of it, as well as the usefulness of it, in supplying their necessities: he being thirsty, and having none to furnish him wherewith to draw water, at last comes a woman from the city, whom he desires to give him some water to drink. The woman, perceiving him by his language or habit to be a Jew, wonders at the question, since the hatred the Jews bore the Samaritans was so great, that they would not vouchsafe to have any commerce with them, not only in religious, but civil affairs, and common offices belonging to mankind. Hence our Saviour takes occasion to publish to her the doctrine of the gospel; and excuseth her rude answer by her ignorance of him; and tells her, that if she had asked him a greater matter, even that which concerned her eternal salvation, he would readily have granted it, notwithstanding the rooted hatred between the Jews and Samaritans; and bestowed a water of a greater virtue, the "water of life."[i] The woman is no less astonished at his reply than she was at his first demand. It was strange to hear a man speak of giving living water to one of whom he had begged the water of that spring, and had no vessel to draw any to quench his own thirst. She therefore demands whence he could have this water that he speaks of,[k] since she conceived him not greater than Jacob, who had digged that well and drank of it. Our Saviour, desirous to make a progress in that work he had begun, extols the water he spake of, above this of the well, from its particular virtue fully to refresh those that drank of it, and be as a cooling and comforting fountain within them, of more efficacy than that without.[l] The woman, conceiving a good opinion of our Saviour,

---

[h] Amarant. Paraph. sur Jean.
[k] Ver. 11.

[i] Ver 10; or "living water."
[l] Ver. 13, 14.

desires to partake of this water, to save her pains in coming daily to
the well, not apprehending the spirituality of Christ's discourse to
her:[m] Christ finding her to take some pleasure in his discourse,
partly to bring her to a sense of her sin, before he did communicate
the excellency of his grace, bids her return back to the city and
bring her husband with her to him.[n] She freely acknowledges that
she had no husband; whether having some check of conscience at
present for the unclean life she led, or loth to lose so much time in
the gaining this water so much desired by her:[o] our Saviour takes
an occasion from this to lay open her sin before her, and to make her
sensible of her own wicked life and the prophetic excellency of himself; and tells her she had had five husbands, to whom she had been
false, and by whom she was divorced, and the person she now dwelt
with was not her lawful husband, and in living with him she violated
the rights of marriage, and increased guilt upon her conscience.[p]
The woman being affected with this discourse, and knowing him to
be a stranger that could not be certified of those things but in an
extraordinary way, begins to have a high esteem of him as a prophet.[q]
And upon this opinion she esteems him able to decide a question,
which had been canvassed between them and the Jews, about the
place of worship.[r] Their fathers worshipping in that mountain, and
the Jews affirming Jerusalem to be a place of worship, she pleads
the antiquity of the worship in this place, Abraham having built an
altar there (Gen. xii. 7), and Jacob, upon his return from Syria.
And, surely, had the place been capable of an exception, such persons as they, and so well acquainted with the will of God, would
not have pitched upon that place to celebrate their worship. Antiquity hath, too, too often bewitched the minds of men, and drawn
them from the revealed will of God. Men are more willing to imitate the outward actions of their famous ancestors, than conform
themselves to the revealed will of their Creator. The Samaritans
would imitate the patriarchs in the place of worship, but not in the
faith of the worshippers. Christ answers her, that this question
would quickly be resolved by a new state of the church, which was
near at hand; and neither Jerusalem, which had now the precedency,
nor that mountain, should be of any more value in that concern,
than any other place in the world:[s] but yet, to make her sensible
of her sin and that of her countrymen, tells her, that their worship
in that mountain was not according to the will of God, he having
long after the altars built in this place, fixed Jerusalem as the place
of sacrifices; besides, they had not the knowledge of that God which
ought to be worshipped by them, but the Jews had the "true object
of worship," and the "true manner of worship, according to the declaration God had made of himself to them."[t] But all that service
shall vanish, the veil of the temple shall be rent in twain, and that
carnal worship give place to one more spiritual; shadows shall fly
before substance, and truth advance itself above figures; and the
worship of God shall be with the strength of the Spirit: such a worship, and such worshippers doth the Father seek;[u] for "God is a

m Ver. 15.   n Ver. 16.   o Ver. 17.   p Ver. 18.   q Ver. 19.
r Ver. 20.   s Ver. 21.   t Ver. 22.   u Ver. 23.

Spirit: and those that worship him must worship him in spirit and in truth." The design of our Saviour is to declare, that God is not taken with external worship invented by men, no, nor commanded by himself; and that upon this reason, because he is a spiritual essence, infinitely above gross and corporeal matter, and is not taken with that pomp which is a pleasure to our earthly imaginations.

Πνεῦμα ὁ Θεός. Some translate it just as the words lie: "Spirit is God."[x] But it is not unusual, both in the Old and New Testament languages, to put the predicate before the subject, as Psalm v. 9, "Their throat is an open sepulchre;" in the Hebrew, "A sepulchre open their throat;" so Psalm cxi. 3, "His work is honorable and glorious;" Heb. "Honor and glory is his work;" and there wants not one example in the same evangelist (John i. 1), "And the Word was God;" Greek, "And God was the Word:" in all, the predicate, or what is ascribed, is put before the subject to which it is ascribed. One tells us, and he, a head of a party that hath made a disturbance in the church of God,[y] that this place is not aptly brought to prove God to be a Spirit; and the reason of Christ runs not thus,—God is of a spiritual essence, and therefore must be worshipped with a spiritual worship; for the essence of God is not the foundation of his worship, but his will; for then we were not to worship him with a corporeal worship, because he is not a body; but with an invisible and eternal worship, because he is invisible and eternal. But the nature of God is the foundation of worship; the will of God is the rule of worship; the matter and manner is to be performed according to the will of God. But is the nature of the object of worship to be excluded? No; as the object is, so ought our devotion to be, spiritual as he is spiritual. God, in his commands for worship, respected the discovery of his own nature; in the law, he respected the discovery of his mercy and justice, and therefore commanded a worship by sacrifices; a spiritual worship without those institutions would not have declared those attributes which was God's end to display to the world in Christ; and though the nature of God is to be respected in worship, yet the obligations of the creature are to be considered. God is a Spirit, therefore must have a spiritual worship; the creature hath a body as well as a soul, and both from God; and therefore ought to worship God with the one as well as the other, since one as well as the other is freely bestowed upon him. The spirituality of God was the foundation of the change from the Judaical carnal worship to a more spiritual and evangelical.

God is a Spirit; that is, he hath nothing corporeal, no mixture of matter, not a visible substance, a bodily form.[z] He is a Spirit, not a bare spiritual substance, but an understanding, willing Spirit, holy, wise, good, and just. Before, Christ spake of the Father,[a] the first person in the Trinity; now he speaks of God essentially: the word Father is personal, the word God essential; so that our Saviour would render a reason, not from any one person in the blessed Trinity, but from the Divine nature, why we should worship in spirit, and therefore makes use of the word God, the being a Spirit being common

x Vulgar Lat. Illyrc. Clav.   y Episcop. Institut. lib. iv. c. 3.
z Melancthon.   a Ver. 23.

to the other persons with the Father. This is the reason of the proposition (ver. 23), "*Of a spiritual worship.*" Every nature delights in that which is like it, and distastes that which is most different from it. If God were corporeal, he might be pleased with the victims of beasts, and the beautiful magnificence of temples, and the noise of music; but being a Spirit, he cannot be gratified with carnal things; he demands something better and greater than all those,—that soul which he made, that soul which he hath endowed, a spirit of a frame suitable to his nature. He indeed appointed sacrifices, and a temple, as shadows of those things which were to be most acceptable to him in the Messiah, but they were imposed only "till the time of reformation."[b]

Must worship him; not they may, or it would be more agreeable to God to have such a manner of worship; but they *must.* It is not exclusive of bodily worship; for this were to exclude all public worship in societies, which cannot be performed without reverential postures of the body.[c] The gestures of the body are helps to worship, and declarations of spiritual acts. We can scarcely worship God with our spirits without some tincture upon the outward man; but he excludes all acts merely corporeal, all resting upon an external service and devotion, which was the crime of the Pharisees, and the general persuasion of the Jews as well as heathens, who used the outward ceremonies, not as signs of better things, but as if they did of themselves please God, and render the worshippers accepted with him, without any suitable frame of the inward man.[d] It is as if he had said, Now you must separate yourselves from all carnal modes to which the service of God is now tied, and render a worship chiefly consisting in the affectionate motions of the heart, and accommodated more exactly to the condition of the object, who is a Spirit.

In spirit and truth.[e] The evangelical service now required has the advantage of the former; that was a shadow and figure, this the body and truth.[f] Spirit, say some, is here opposed to the legal ceremonies; truth, to hypocritical services; or, rather truth is opposed to shadows,[g] and an opinion of worth in the outward action; it is principally opposed to external rites, because our Saviour saith (ver. 23): "The hour comes, and now is," &c. Had it been opposed to hypocrisy, Christ had said no new thing; for God always required truth in the inward parts, and all true worshippers had served him with a sincere conscience and single heart. The old patriarchs did worship God in spirit and *truth,* as taken for sincerity; such a worship was always, and is perpetually due to God, because he always was, and eternally will be, a Spirit.[h] And it is said, "The Father seeks such to worship him," not, shall seek; he always sought it; it always was performed to him by one or other in the world: and the prophets had always rebuked them for resting upon their outward solemnities (Isa. lviii. 7, and Micah vi. 8): but a worship without legal rites was proper to an evangelical state and the times of the gospel, God having then exhibited Christ, and brought into the world the substance of those

[b] Heb. ix. 10. [c] Terniti. [d] Amirald, *in loc.* [e] Amirald, *in loc.*
[f] Muscul. [g] Chemnit. [h] Muscul.

shadows, and the end of those institutions; there was no more need to continue them when the true reason of them was ceased. All laws do naturally expire when the true reason upon which they were first framed is changed. Or by spirit may be meant, such a worship as is kindled in the heart by the breath of the Holy Ghost. Since we are dead in sin, a spiritual light and flame in the heart, suitable to the nature of the object of our worship, cannot be raised in us without the operation of a supernatural grace; and though the fathers could not worship God without the Spirit, yet in the gospel-times, there being a fuller effusion of the Spirit, the evangelical state is called, "the administration of the Spirit," and "the newness of the Spirit," in opposition to the legal economy, entitled the "oldness of the letter."[i] The evangelical state is more suited to the nature of God than any other; such a worship God must have, whereby he is acknowledged to be the true sanctifier and quickener of the soul. The nearer God doth approach to us, and the more full his manifestations are, the more spiritual is the worship we return to God. The gospel pares off the rugged parts of the law, and heaven shall remove what is material in the gospel, and change the ordinances of worship into that of a spiritual praise.

In the words there is: 1. A proposition,—"God is a Spirit;" the foundation of all religion. 2. An inference,—"They that worship him," &c.

As God, a worship belongs to him; as a Spirit, a spiritual worship is due to him: in the inference we have, 1. The manner of worship, "in spirit and truth;" 2. The necessity of such a worship, "must."

The proposition declares the nature of God; the inference, the duty of man. The observations lie plain.

Obs. 1. God is a pure spiritual being: "he is a Spirit." 2. The worship due from the creature to God must be agreeable to the nature of God, and purely spiritual. 3. The evangelical state is suited to the nature of God.

I. For the first: "God is a pure spiritual being." It is the observation of one,[k] that the plain assertion of God's being a Spirit is found but once in the whole Bible, and that is in this place; which may well be wondered at, because God is so often described with hands, feet, eyes, and ears, in the form and figure of a man. The spiritual nature of God is deducible from many places; but not anywhere, as I remember, asserted *totidem verbis*, but in this text: some allege that place (2 Cor. iii. 17), "The Lord is that Spirit," for the proof of it; but that seems to have a different sense: in the text, the nature of God is described; in that place, the operations of God in the gospel. "It is not the ministry of Moses, or that old covenant, which communicates to you that Spirit it speaks of; but it is the Lord Jesus, and the doctrine of the gospel delivered by him, whereby this Spirit and liberty is dispensed to you; he opposes here the liberty of the gospel to the servitude of the law;[l] it is from Christ that a divine virtue diffuseth itself by the gospel; it is by him, not by the law, that we partake of that Spirit. The spirituality of God is

i 2 Cor. iii. 8; Rom. vii. 6.   k Episcop. Institut. lib. iv. c. 3.   l Amirald, *in loc.*

as evident as his being.[m]   If we grant that God is, we must necessarily grant that he cannot be corporeal, because a body is of an imperfect nature.   It will appear incredible to any that acknowledge God the first Being and Creator of all things, that he should be a massy, heavy body, and have eyes and ears, feet and hands, as we have.—For the explication of it,

1. Spirit is taken various ways in Scripture.   It signifies sometimes an aërial substance, as Psalm xi. 6; a horrible tempest (Heb. a spirit of tempest); sometimes the breath, which is a thin substance (Gen. vi. 17): "All flesh, wherein is the breath of life" (Heb. spirit of life). A thin substance, though it be material and corporeal, is called spirit; and in the bodies of living creatures, that which is the principle of their actions is called spirits, the animal and vital spirits. And the finer parts extracted from plants and minerals we call spirits, those volatile parts separated from that gross matter wherein they were immersed, because they come nearest to the nature of an incorporeal substance; and from this notion of the word, it is translated to signify those substances that are purely immaterial, as angels and the souls of men.   Angels are called spirits (Psalm civ. 4): "Who makes his angels spirits;"[n] and not only good angels are so called, but evil angels (Mark i. 27); souls of men are called spirits (Eccles. xii.); and the soul of Christ is called so (John xix. 30); whence God is called "the God of the spirits of all flesh" (Numb. xxii. 16).   And spirit is opposed to flesh (Isa. xxxi. 3): "The Egyptians are flesh, and not spirit."   And our Saviour gives us the notion of a spirit to be something above the nature of a body (Luke xxiv. 39), "not having flesh and bones," extended parts, loads of gross matter.   It is also taken for those things which are active and efficacious; because activity is of the nature of a spirit: Caleb had another spirit (Numb. xiv. 24), an active affection.   The vehement motions of sin are called spirit (Hos. iv. 12): "the spirit of whoredoms," in that sense that Prov. xxix. 11, "a fool utters all his mind," all his spirit; he knows not how to restrain the vehement motions of his mind.   So that the notion of a spirit is, that it is a fine, immaterial substance, an active being, that acts itself and other things.   A mere body cannot act itself; as the body of man cannot move without the soul, no more than a ship can move itself without wind and waves. So God is called a Spirit, as being not a body, not having the greatness, figure, thickness, or length of a body, wholly separate from anything of flesh and matter.   We find a principle within us nobler than that of our bodies; and, therefore, we conceive the nature of God, according to that which is more worthy in us, and not according to that which is the vilest part of our natures.   God is a most spiritual Spirit, more spiritual than all angels, all souls.[o]   As he exceeds all in the nature of being, so he exceeds all in the nature of spirit: he hath nothing gross, heavy, material, in his essence.

2. When we say God is a Spirit, it is to be understood by way of negation.   There are two ways of knowing or describing God: by way of affirmation, affirming that of him by way of eminency, which is excellent in the creature, as when we say God is wise, good; the

[m] Suarez. de Deo, vol. i. p. 9, col. 2.   [n] Heb. i. 14.   [o] Gerhard. μονοτρόπως.

other, by way of negation, when we remove from God in our conceptions what is tainted with imperfection in the creature.[p] The first ascribes to him whatsoever is excellent; the other separates from him whatsoever is imperfect. The first is like a limning, which adds one color to another to make a comely picture; the other is like a carving, which pares and cuts away whatsoever is superfluous, to make a complete statue. This way of negation is more easy; we better understand what God is not, than what he is; and most of our knowledge of God is by this way; as when we say God is infinite, immense, immutable, they are negatives; he hath no limits, is confined to no place, admits of no change.[q] When we remove from him what is inconsistent with his being, we do more strongly assert his being, and know more of him when we elevate him above all, and above our own capacity. And when we say God is a Spirit, it is a negation; he is not a body; he consists not of various parts, extended one without and beyond another. He is not a spirit, so as our souls are, to be the form of any body; a spirit, not as angels and souls are, but infinitely higher. We call him so, because, in regard of our weakness, we have not any other term of excellency to express or conceive of him by; we transfer it to God in honor, because spirit is the highest excellency in our nature: yet we must apprehend God above any spirit, since his nature is so great that he cannot be declared by human speech, perceived by human sense, or conceived by human understanding.

II. The second thing, that "God is a Spirit." Some among the heathens imagined God to have a body;[r] some thought him to have a body of air; some a heavenly body; some a human body;[s] and many of them ascribed bodies to their gods, but bodies without blood, without corruption, bodies made up of the finest and thinnest atoms; such bodies, which, if compared with ours, were as no bodies. The Sadducees also, who denied all spirits, and yet acknowledged a God, must conclude him to be a body, and no spirit. Some among Christians have been of that opinion. Tertullian is charged by some, and excused by others; and some monks of Egypt were so fierce for this error, that they attempted to kill one Theophilus, a bishop, for not being of that judgment. But the wiser heathens were of another mind,[t] and esteemed it an unholy thing to have such imaginations of God.[u] And some Christians have thought God only to be free from anything of body, because he is omnipresent, immutable, he is only incorporeal and spiritual; all things else, even the angels, are clothed with bodies, though of a neater matter, and a more active frame than ours; a pure spiritual nature they allowed to no being but God. Scripture and reason meet together to assert the spirituality of God. Had God had the lineaments of a body, the Gentiles had not fallen under that accusation of changing his glory into that of a corruptible man.[x] This is signified by the name God gives himself (Exod. iii. 14): "I am that I am;" a simple, pure, uncompounded

[p] Gamacheus, Tom. I. Q. 3. c. i. p. 42.   [q] Coccei, Sum. Theol. c. 8.
[r] Thes. Sedan. Part II. p. 1000.   [s] Vossius Idolol. lib. ii. c. 1. Forbes, Instrument. lib. i. c. 36.   [t] Οὐκ ὅσιον.
[u] Plutarch, incorporalis ratio divinus spiritus. Seneca.   [x] Rom. i. 23.

being, without any created mixture; as infinitely above the being of creatures as above the conceptions of creatures (Job xxxvii. 23): "Touching the Almighty, we cannot find him out." He is so much a Spirit, that he is the "Father of spirits" (Heb. xii. 9). The Almighty Father is not of a nature inferior to his children. The soul is a spirit; it could not else exert actions without the assistance of the body, as the act of understanding itself, and its own nature, the act of willing, and willing things against the incitements and interest of the body. It could not else conceive of God, angels, and immaterial substances; it could not else be so active, as with one glance to fetch a compass from earth to heaven, and by a sudden motion, to elevate the understanding from an earthly thought, to the thinking of things as high as the highest heavens. If we have this opinion of our souls, which, in the nobleness of their acts, surmount the body, without which the body is but a dull inactive piece of clay, we must needs have a higher conception of God, than to clog him with any matter, though of a finer temper than ours: we must conceive of him by the perfections of our souls, without the vileness of our bodies. If God made man according to his image, we must raise our thoughts of God according to the noblest part of that image, and imagine the exemplar or copy not to come short, but to exceed the thing copied by it. God were not the most excellent substance if he were not a Spirit. Spiritual substances are more excellent than bodily; the soul of man more excellent than other animals; angels more excellent than men. They contain, in their own nature, whatsoever dignity there is in the inferior creatures; God must have, therefore, an excellency above all those, and, therefore, is entirely remote from the conditions of a body. It is a gross conceit, therefore, to think that God is such a spirit as the air is; for that is to be a body as the air is, though it be a thin one; and if God were no more a spirit than that, or than angels, he would not be the most simple being.y Yet some think that the spiritual Deity was represented by the air in the ark of the testament.z It was unlawful to represent him by any image that God had prohibited. Everything about the ark had a particular signification. The gold and other ornaments about it signified something of Christ, but were unfit to represent the nature of God: a thing purely invisible, and falling under nothing of sense, could not represent him to the mind of man. The air in the ark was the fittest; it represented the invisibility of God, air being imperceptible to our eyes. Air diffuseth itself through all parts of the world; it glides through secret passages into all creatures; it fills the space between heaven and earth. There is no place wherein God is not present. To evidence this,

1. If God were not a Spirit, he could not be Creator. All multitude begins in, and is reduced to unity. As above multitude there is an absolute unity, so above mixed creatures there is an absolute simplicity. You cannot conceive number without conceiving the beginning of it in that which was not number, viz. a unit. You cannot conceive any mixture, but you must conceive some simple thing to be the original and basis of it. The works of art done by

<hr />

y Calov. Socin. Proflig. pp. 129, 130.　　　　z Amirald. Sup. Heb. ix. p. 146, &c.

rational creatures have their foundation in something spiritual. Every artificer, watchmaker, carpenter, hath a model in his own mind of the work he designs to frame: the material and outward fabric is squared according to an inward and spiritual idea. A spiritual idea speaks a spiritual faculty as the subject of it. God could not have an idea of that vast number of creatures he brought into being, if he had not had a spiritual nature.[a] The wisdom whereby the world was created could never be the fruit of a corporeal nature; such natures are not capable of understanding and comprehending the things which are within the compass of their nature, much less of producing them; and therefore beasts which have only corporeal faculties move to objects by the force of their sense, and have no knowledge of things as they are comprehended by the understanding of man. All acts of wisdom speak an intelligent and spiritual agent. The effects of wisdom, goodness, power, are so great and admirable, that they bespeak him a more perfect and eminent being than can possibly be beheld under a bodily shape. Can a corporeal substance put "wisdom in the inward parts, and give understanding to the heart?"[b]

2. If God were not a pure Spirit, he could not be one. If God had a body, consisting of distinct members, as ours; or all of one nature, as the water and air are, yet he were then capable of division, and therefore could not be entirely one. Either those parts would be finite or infinite: if finite, they are not parts of God; for to be God and finite is a contradiction; if infinite, then there are as many infinite as distinct members, and therefore as many Deities. Suppose this body had all parts of the same nature, as air and water hath, every little part of air is as much air as the greatest, and every little part of water is as much water as the ocean; so every little part of God would be as much God as the whole; as many particular Deities to make up God, as little atoms to compose a body. What can be more absurd? If God had a body like a human body, and were compounded of body and soul, of substance and quality, he could not be the most perfect unity; he would be made up of distinct parts, and those of a distinct nature, as the members of a human body are. Where there is the greatest unity, there must be the greatest simplicity; but God is one. As he is free from any change, so he is void of any multitude (Deut. vi. 4): "The Lord our God is one Lord."

3. If God had a body as we have, he would not be invisible. Every material thing is not visible: the air is a body yet invisible, but it is sensible; the cooling quality of it is felt by us at every breath, and we know it by our touch, which is the most material sense. Everybody that hath members like to bodies, is visible; but God is invisible.[c] The apostle reckons it amongst his other perfections (1 Tim. i. 17): "Now unto the King eternal, immortal, invisible." He is invisible to our sense, which beholds nothing but material and colored things; and incomprehensible to our understanding, that conceives nothing but what is finite. God is therefore a Spirit incapable of being seen, and infinitely incapable of being un-

---

[a] Amyrant, Morale. Tom. I. p. 282.   [b] Job xxxviii. 36.   [c] Daille, in Tim.

derstood. If he be invisible, he is also spiritual. If he had a body, and hid it from our eyes, he might be said not to be seen, but could not be said to be invisible. When we say a thing is visible, we understand that it hath such qualities which are the objects of sense, though we may never see that which is in its own nature to be seen. God hath no such qualities as fall under the perception of our sense. His works are visible to us, but not his Godhead.[d] The nature of a human body is to be seen and handled; Christ gives us such a description of it (Luke xxiv. 39): "Handle me and see, for a spirit hath not flesh and bones as you see me have;" but man hath been so far from seeing God, "that it is impossible he can see him" (1 Tim. vi. 16). There is such a disproportion between an infinite object and a finite sense and understanding, that it is utterly impossible either to behold or comprehend him. But if God had a body more luminous and glorious than that of the sun, he would be as well visible to us as the sun, though the immensity of that light would dazzle our eyes, and forbid any close inspection into him by the virtue of our sense. We have seen the shape and figure of the sun, but "no man hath ever seen the shape of God."[e] If God had a body, he were visible, though he might not perfectly and fully be seen by us;[f] as we see the heavens, though we see not the extension, latitude, and greatness of them. Though God hath manifested himself in a bodily shape (Gen. xviii. 1), and elsewhere Jehovah appeared to Abraham, yet the substance of God was not seen, no more than the substance of angels was seen in their apparitions to men. A body was formed to be made visible by them, and such actions done in that body, that spake the person that did them to be of a higher eminency than a bare corporeal creature. Sometimes a representation is made to the inward sense and imagination, as to Micaiah,[g] and to Isaiah (vi. 1); but they saw not the essence of God, but some images and figures of him proportioned to their sense or imagination. The essence of God no man ever saw, nor can see. John i. 18. Nor doth it follow that God hath a body,[h] because Jacob is said to "see God face to face" (Gen. xxxii. 30); and Moses had the like privilege (Deut. xxxiv. 10). This only signifies a fuller and clearer manifestation of God by some representations offered to the bodily sense, or rather to the inward spirit. For God tells Moses he could not see his face (Exod. xxxiii. 20); and that none ever saw the similitude of God (Deut. iv. 15). Were God a corporeal substance, he might in some measure be seen by corporeal eyes.

4. If God were not a Spirit, he could not be infinite. All bodies are of a finite nature; everybody is material, and every material thing is terminated. The sun, a vast body, hath a bounded greatness; the heavens, of a mighty bulk, yet have their limits. If God had a body he must consist of parts, those parts would be bounded and limited, and whatsoever is limited is of a finite virtue, and therefore below an infinite nature. Reason therefore tells us, that the most excellent nature, as God is, cannot be of a corporeal condition; because of the limitation and other actions which belong to every

---

[d] Rom. i. 20.   [e] John v. 37.   [f] Goulart. de Dieu, p. 94.

[g] 1 Kings xxii. 19.   [h] Goulart. de Dieu, p. 95, 96.

body. God is infinite, "for the heaven of heavens cannot contain him" (2 Chron. ii. 6). The largest heavens, and those imaginary spaces beyond the world, are no bounds to him. He hath an essence beyond the bounds of the world, and cannot be included in the vastness of the heavens. If God be infinite, then he can have no parts in him; if he had, they must be finite or infinite: finite parts can never make up an infinite being. A vessel of gold, of a pound weight, cannot be made of the quantity of an ounce. Infinite parts they cannot be, because then every part would be equal to the whole, as infinite as the whole, which is contradictory. We see in all things every part is less than the whole bulk that is composed of it; as every member of a man is less than the whole body of man. If all the parts were finite, then God in his essence were finite; and a finite God is not more excellent than a creature: so that if God were not a Spirit, he could not be infinite.

5. If God were not a Spirit, he could not be an independent being. Whatsoever is compounded of many parts depends either essentially or integrally upon those parts; as the essence of a man depends upon the conjunction and union of his two main parts, his soul and body; when they are separated, the essence of a man ceaseth: and the perfection of a man depends upon every member of the body; so that if one be wanting the perfection of the whole is wanting: as if a man hath lost a limb, you call him not a perfect man, because that part is gone upon which his perfection as an entire man did depend. If God therefore had a body, the perfection of the Deity would depend upon every part of that body; and the more parts he were compounded of, the more his dependency would be multiplied according to the number of those parts of the body: for that which is compounded of many parts is more dependent than that which is compounded of fewer. And because God would be a dependent being if he had a body, he could not be the first being; for the compounding parts are in order of nature before that which is compounded by them; as the soul and body are before the man which results from the union of them. If God had parts and bodily members as we have, or any composition, the essence of God would result from those parts, and those parts be supposed to be before God. For that which is a part, is before that whose part it is. As in artificial things you may conceive it: all the parts of a watch or clock are in time before that watch which is made by setting those parts together. In natural things you must suppose the members of a body framed before you can call it a man; so that the parts of this body are before that which is constituted by them. We can conceive no other of God, if he were not a pure, entire, unmixed Spirit. If he had distinct parts, he would depend upon them; those parts would be before him; his essence would be the effect of those distinct parts, and so he would not be absolutely and entirely the first being; but he is so (Isa. xliv. 6): "I am the first, and I am the last." He is the first; nothing is before him. Whereas, if he had bodily parts, and those finite, it would follow, God is made up of those parts which are not God; and that which is not God, is in order of nature before that which is God. So that we see if God were not a Spirit he could not be independent.

6. If God were not a Spirit, he were not immutable and unchangeable. His immutability depends upon his simplicity. He is unchangeable in his essence, because he is a pure and unmixed spiritual Being. Whatsoever is compounded of parts may be divided into those parts, and resolved into those distinct parts which make up and constitute the nature. Whatsoever is compounded is changeable in its own nature, though it should never be changed. Adam, who was constituted of body and soul, had he stood in innocence, had not died; there had been no separation made between his soul and body whereof he was constituted, and his body had not resolved into those principles of dust from whence it was extracted. Yet in his own nature he was dissoluble into those distinct parts whereof he was compounded; and so the glorified saints in heaven, after the resurrection, and the happy meeting of their souls and bodies in a new marriage knot, shall never be dissolved; yet in their own nature they are mutable and dissoluble, and cannot be otherwise, because they are made up of such distinct parts that may be separated in their own nature, unless sustained by the grace of God: they are immutable by will, the will of God, not by nature. God is immutable by nature as well as will: as he hath a necessary existence, so he hath a necessary unchangeableness (Mal. iii. 6), "I, the Lord, change not." He is as unchangeable in his essence as in his veracity and faithfulness: they are perfections belonging to his nature. But if he were not a pure Spirit, he could not be immutable by nature.

7. If God were not a pure Spirit, he could not be omnipresent. He is in heaven above, and the earth below;[i] he fills heaven and earth.[k] The divine essence is at once in heaven and earth; but it is impossible a body can be in two places at one and the same time. Since God is everywhere, he must be spiritual. Had he a body, he could not penetrate all things; he would be circumscribed in place. He could not be everywhere but in parts, not in the whole; one member in one place, and another in another; for to be confined to a particular place, is the property of a body: but, since he is diffused through the whole world, higher than heaven, deeper than hell, longer than the earth, broader than the sea,[l] he hath not any corporeal matter. If he had a body wherewith to fill heaven and earth, there could be no body besides his own: it is the nature of bodies to bound one another, and hinder the extending of one another. Two bodies cannot be in the same place in the same point of earth: one excludes the other; and it will follow hence that we are nothing, no substances, mere illusions; there could be no place for anybody else.[m] If his body were as big as the world, as it must be if with that he filled heaven and earth, there would not be room for him to move a hand or a foot, or extend a finger; for there would be no place remaining for the motion.

8. If God were not a Spirit, he could not be the most perfect being. The more perfect anything is in the rank of creatures, the more spiritual and simple it is, as gold is the more pure and perfect that hath least mixture of other metals. If God were not a Spirit,

---

[i] Deut. iv. 39. [k] Jer. xxiii. 24. [l] Job xi. 8.
[m] Gamacheus, Theol. Tom. I. Quos 3. c. i.

there would be creatures of a more excellent nature than God, as angels and souls, which the Scripture call spirits, in opposition to bodies. There is more of perfection in the first notion of a spirit than in the notion of a body. God cannot be less perfect than his creatures, and contribute an excellency of being to them which he wants himself. If angels and souls possess such an excellency, and God want that excellency, he would be less than his creatures, and the excellency of the effect would exceed the excellency of the cause. But every creature, even the highest creature, is infinitely short of the perfection of God; for whatsoever excellency they have is finite and limited; it is but a spark from the sun—a drop from the ocean; but God is unboundedly perfect, in the highest manner, without any limitation; and therefore above spirits, angels, the highest creatures that were made by him: an infinite sublimity, a pure act, to which nothing can be added, from which nothing can be taken. "In him there is light and no darkness,"[n] spirituality without any matter, perfection without any shadow or taint of imperfection. Light pierceth into all things, preserves its own purity, and admits of no mixture of anything else with it.

Question. It may be said, If God be a Spirit, and it is impossible he can be otherwise than a Spirit, how comes God so often to have such members as we have in our bodies ascribed to him, not only a soul, but particular bodily parts, as heart, arms, hands, eyes, ears, face, and back parts? And how is it that he is never called a Spirit in plain words, but in this text by our Saviour?

Answer. It is true, many parts of the body, and natural affections of the human nature, are reported of God in Scripture. Head,[o] eyes, and eye-lids,[p] apple of the eye, mouth, &c.; our affections also, grief, joy, anger, &c. But it is to be considered,

1. That this is in condescension to our weakness. God being desirous to make himself known to man, whom he created for his glory, humbles, as it were, his own nature to such representations as may suit and assist the capacity of the creature; since by the condition of our nature nothing erects a notion of itself in our understanding, but as it is conducted in by our sense.[q] God hath served himself of those things which are most exposed to our sense, most obvious to our understandings, to give us some acquaintance with his own nature, and those things which otherwise we were not capable of having any notion of. As our souls are linked with our bodies, so our knowledge is linked with our sense; that we can scarce imagine anything, at first, but under a corporeal form and figure, till we come, by great attention to the object, to make, by the help of reason, a separation of the spiritual substance from the corporeal fancy, and consider it in its own nature. We are not able to conceive a spirit, without some kind of resemblance to something below it, nor understand the actions of a spirit, without considering the operations of a human body in its several members. As the glories of another life are signified to us by the pleasures of this; so the nature of God, by a gracious condescension to our capacities, is

---

[n] 1 John i. 5.   [o] Dan. vii. 9.   [p] Psalm xi. 4.
[q] "Loquitur lex secund. ling. filiorum hominum," was the Heathen saying.

signified to us by a likeness to our own. The more familiar the things are to us which God uses to this purpose, the more proper they are to teach us what he intends by them.

2. All such representations are to signify the acts of God, as they bear some likeness to those which we perform by those members he ascribes to himself. So that those members ascribed to him rather note his visible operations to us, than his invisible nature; and signify that God doth some works like to those which men do by the assistance of those organs of their bodies. So the wisdom of God is called his eye, because he knows that with his mind which we see with our eyes.[r] The efficiency of God is called his hand and arm; because as we act with our hands, so doth God with his power. The divine efficacies are signified:—by his eyes and ears, we understand his omniscience; by his face, the manifestation of his favor; by his mouth, the revelation of his will; by his nostrils, the acceptation of our prayers; by his bowels, the tenderness of his compassion; by his heart, the sincerity of his affections; by his hand, the strength of his power; by his feet, the ubiquity of his presence. And in this, he intends instruction and comfort: by his eyes, he signifies his watchfulness over us; by his ears, his readiness to hear the cries of the oppressed;[s] by his arm, his power—an arm to destroy his enemies, and an arm to relieve his people.[t] All those are attributed to God to signify divine actions, which he doth without bodily organs as we do with them.

3. Consider also, that only those members which are the instruments of the noblest actions, and under that consideration, are used by him to represent a notion of him to our minds. Whatsoever is perfect and excellent is ascribed to him, but nothing that savors of imperfection.[u] The heart is ascribed to him, it being the principle of vital actions, to signify the life that he hath in himself; watchful and discerning eyes, not sleepy and lazy ones; a mouth to reveal his will, not to take in food. To eat and sleep are never ascribed to him, nor those parts that belong to the preparing or transmitting nourishment to the several parts of the body, as stomach, liver, reins, nor bowels under that consideration, but as they are significant of compassion; but only those parts are ascribed to him whereby we acquire knowledge, as eyes and ears, the organs of learning and wisdom; or to communicate it to others, as the mouth, lips, tongue, as they are instruments of speaking, not of tasting; or those parts which signify strength and power, or whereby we perform the actions of charity for the relief of others; taste and touch, senses that extend no farther than to corporeal things, and are the grossest of all the senses, are never ascribed to him.

4. It were worth consideration, " whether this describing God by the members of a human body were so much figuratively to be understood, as with respect to the incarnation of our Saviour, who was to assume the human nature, and all the members of a human body?"[x] Asaph, speaking in the person of God (Psalm lxxviii. 1),

[r] Amirald de Trin. pp. 218, 219.   [s] Psalm xxxiv. 15.   [t] Isa. li. 9.
[u] Episcop. institut. lib· iv. § 3. c. 3.
[x] It is Zanchie's observation, Tom. II. De Natura Dei, lib. i. c. 4.   Thes. 9.

"I will open my mouth in parables;" in regard of God it is to be understood figuratively, but in regard of Christ literally, to whom it is applied (Matt. xiii. 34, 35); and that apparition (Isa. vi.) which was the appearance of Jehovah, is applied to Christ (John xii. 40, 41). After the report of the creation, and the forming of man, we read of God's speaking to him, but not of God's appearing to him in any visible shape.[y] A voice might be formed in the air to give man notice of his duty; some way of information he must have what positive laws he was to observe, besides that law which was engraven in his nature, which we call the law of nature; and without a voice the knowledge of the divine will could not be so conveniently communicated to man. Though God was heard in a voice, he was not seen in a shape; but after the fall we several times read of his appearing in such a form; though we read of his speaking before man's committing of sin, yet not of his walking, which is more corporeal, till afterwards.[z] "Though God would not have man believe him to be corporeal, yet he judged it expedient to give some prenotices of that divine incarnation which he had promised."[a]

5. Therefore, we must not conceive of the visible Deity according to the letter of such expressions, but the true intent of them. Though the Scripture speaks of his eyes and arm, yet it denies them to be "arms of flesh."[b] We must not conceive of God according to the letter, but the design of the metaphor. When we hear things described by metaphorical expressions, for the clearing them up to our fancy, we conceive not of them under that garb, but remove the veil by an act of our reason. When Christ is called a sun, a vine, bread, is any so stupid as to conceive him to be a vine with material branches, and clusters, or be of the same nature with a loaf? But the things designed by such metaphors are obvious to the conception of a mean understanding. If we would conceive God to have a body like a man, because he describes himself so, we may conceit him to be like a bird, because he is mentioned with wings;[c] or like a lion, or leopard, because he likens himself to them in the acts of his strength and fury.[d] He is called a rock, a horn, fire, to note his strength and wrath; if any be so stupid as to think God to be really such, they would make him not only a man but worse than a monster. Onkelos, the Chaldee paraphrast upon parts of the Scripture, was so tender of expressing the notion of any corporeity in God, that when he meets with any expressions of that nature, he translates them according to the true intent of them; as when God is said to descend (Gen. xi. 5), which implies a local motion, a motion from one place to another, he translates it, "And God revealed himself."[e] We should conceive of God according to the design of the expressions; when we read of his eyes, we should conceive his omniscience; of his hand, his power; of his sitting, his immutability; of his throne, his majesty; and conceive of him as surmounting, not only the grossness of bodies, but the spiritual excel-

[y] Amyraut, Morale. Tom. I. pp. 293, 294.   [x] Gen. iii. 8.   [a] Amirald.
[b] Job x. 4. 2 Chron. xxxii. 8   [e] Psalm xxxvi. 7.   [d] Hos. xiii. 7, 8.
[e] Maimon. More Nevoc. par. 1. c. 27.

lency of the most dignified creatures; something so perfect, great, spiritual, as nothing can be conceived higher and purer. "Christ," saith one, "is truly *Deus figuratus;* and for his sake, was it more easily permitted to the Jews to think of God in the shape of a man."[f]

Use. If God be a pure spiritual being, then

1. Man is not the image of God, according to his external bodily form and figure. The image of God in man consisted not in what is seen, but in what is not seen; not in the conformation of the members, but rather in the spiritual faculties of the soul; or, most of all, in the holy endowments of those faculties (Eph. iv. 24): "That ye put on the new man, which after God is created in righteousness and true holiness."[g] The image which is restored by redeeming grace, was the image of God by original nature. The image of God cannot be in that part which is common to us with beasts, but rather in that wherein we excel all living creatures, in reason, understanding, and an immortal spirit. God expressly saith, that none "saw a similitude" of him (Deut. iv. 15, 16); which had not been true, if man, in regard of his body, had been the image and similitude of God, for then a figure of God had been seen every day, as often as we saw a man or beheld ourselves. Nor would the apostle's argument stand good (Acts xvii. 29), "That the Godhead is not like to stone graven by art," if we were not the offspring of God, and bore the stamp of his nature in our spirits rather than our bodies.[h] It was a fancy of Eugubinus, that when God set upon the actual creation of man, he took a bodily form for an exemplar of that which he would express in his work, and therefore that the words of Moses[i] are to be understood of the body of man; because there was in man such a shape which God had then assumed. To let alone God's forming himself a body for that work as a groundless fancy, man can in no wise be said to be the image of God, in regard of the substance of his body; but beasts may as well be said to be made in the image of God, whose bodies have the same members as the body of man for the most part, and excel men in the acuteness of the senses and swiftness of their motion, agility of body, greatness of strength, and in some kind of ingenuities also, wherein man hath been a scholar to the brutes, and beholden to their skill. The soul comes nearest the nature of God, as being a spiritual substance; yet considered singly, in regard of its spiritual substance, cannot well be said to be the image of God; a beast, because of its corporeity, may as well be called the image of a man, for there is a greater similitude between man and a brute, in the rank of bodies, than there can be between God and the highest angels in the rank of spirits. If it doth not consist in the substance of the soul, much less can it in any similitude of the body. This image consisted partly in the state of man, as he had dominion over the creatures; partly in the nature of man, as he was an intelligent being, and thereby was capable of having a grant of that dominion; but principally in the conformity of the soul with

---

[f] Mores conjectura Cabalistica, p. 122.
[h] Petav. Theol. Dog. Tom. I. lib. ii. c. 1. p. 104.

[g] Col. iii. 10.
[i] Gen. i. 26.

God, in the frame of his spirit, and the holiness of his actions; not at all in the figure and form of his body, physically, though morally there might be, as there was a rectitude in the body as an instrument to conform to the holy motions of the soul, as the holiness of the soul sparkled in the actions and members of the body. If man were like God because he hath a body, whatsoever hath a body hath some resemblance to God, and may be said to be in part his image; but the truth is, the essence of all creatures cannot be an image of the immense essence of God.

2. If God be a pure Spirit, "it is unreasonable to frame any image or picture of God."[k] Some heathens have been wiser in this than some Christians; Pythagoras forbade his scholars to engrave any shape of him upon a ring, because he was not to be comprehended by sense, but conceived only in our minds: our hands are as unable to fashion him, as our eyes to see him.[l] The ancient Romans worshipped their gods one hundred and seventy years before any material representations of them;[m] and the ancient idolatrous Germans thought it a wicked thing to represent God in a human shape; yet some, and those no Romanists, labor to defend the making images of God in the resemblance of man, because he is so represented in Scripture: "He may be," saith one,[n] "conceived so in our minds, and figured so to our sense." If this were a good reason, why may he not be pictured as a lion, horn, eagle, rock, since he is under such metaphors shadowed to us? The same ground there is for the one as for the other. What though man be a nobler creature, God hath no more the body of a man than that of an eagle; and some perfections in other creatures represent some excellencies in his nature and actions which cannot be figured by a human shape, as strength by the lion, swiftness and readiness by the wings of the bird. But God hath absolutely prohibited the making "any image" whatsoever of him, and that with terrible threatenings (Exod. xx. 5): "I, the Lord, am a jealous God, visiting the iniquities of the fathers upon their children," and Deut. v. 8, 9. After God had given the Israelites the commandment wherein he forbade them to have any other gods before him, he forbids all figuring of him by the hand of man;[o] not only images, but any likeness of him, either by things in heaven, in the earth, or in the water. How often doth he discover his indignation by the prophets, against them that offer to mould him in a creature form! This law was not to serve a particular dispensation, or to endure a particular time, but it was a declaration of his will, invariable in all places and all times; being founded upon the immutable nature of his being, and therefore agreeable to the law of nature, otherwise not chargeable upon the heathens; and therefore when God had declared his nature and his works in a stately and majestic eloquence, he demands of them, "To whom they would liken him, or what likeness they would compare unto him?" (Isa.

---

[k] Iamblic. Protrept. cap. 21. Symb. 24.
[l] Austin de Civitat. Dei, lib. iv. cap. 31. out of Varro.   [m] Tacitus.
[n] Gerhard, *loc.* Comun. Vol. IV. Exegesis de Natura Dei, cap. 8. § 1.
[o] Amyraut. Morale Chrétienne, Tom. I. p. 294.

xl. 18); where they could find anything that would be a lively image and resemblance of his infinite excellency? founding it upon the infiniteness of his nature, which necessarily implies the spirituality of it, God is infinitely above any statue: and those that think to draw God by a stroke of a pencil, or form him by the engravings of art, are more stupid than the statues themselves. To show the unreasonableness of it, consider,

1. It is impossible to fashion any image of God. If our more capacious souls cannot grasp his nature, our weaker sense cannot frame his image; it is more possible, of the two, to comprehend him in our minds, than to frame him in an image to our sense. He inhabits inaccessible light; as it is impossible for the eye of man to see him, it is impossible for the art of man to paint him upon walls, and carve him out of wood. None knows him but himself, none can describe him but himself.[p] Can we draw a figure of our own souls, and express that part of ourselves, wherein we are most like to God? Can we extend this to any bodily figure, and divide it into parts? How can we deal so with the original copy, whence the first draught of our souls was taken, and which is infinitely more spiritual than men or angels? No corporeal thing can represent a spiritual substance; there is no proportion in nature between them. God is a simple, infinite, immense, eternal, invisible, incorruptible being; a statue is a compounded, finite, limited, temporal, visible, and corruptible body. God is a living spirit; but a statue nor sees, nor hears, nor perceives anything. But suppose God had a body, it is impossible to mould an image of it in the true glory of that body; can the statue of an excellent monarch represent the majesty and air of his countenance, though made by the skilfullest workman in the world? If God had a body in some measure suited to his excellency, were it possible for man to make an exact image of him, who cannot picture the light, heat, motion, magnitude, and dazzling property of the sun? The excellency of any corporeal nature of the least creature, the temper, instinct, artifice, are beyond the power of a carving tool; much more is God.

2. To make any corporeal representations of God is unworthy of God. It is a disgrace to his nature. Whosoever thinks a carnal corruptible image to be fit for a representation of God, renders God no better than a carnal and a corporeal being. It is a kind of debasing an angel, who is a spiritual nature, to represent him in a bodily shape, who is as far removed from any fleshliness as heaven from earth; much more to degrade the glory of the divine nature to the lineaments of a man. The whole stock of images is but a lie of God (Jer. x. 8, 14); a doctrine of vanities and falsehood; it represents him in a false garb to the world, and sinks his glory into that of a corruptible creature.[q] It impairs the reverence of God in the minds of men, and by degrees may debase men's apprehensions of God, and be a means to make them believe he is such a one as themselves; and that not being free from the figure, he is not also free from the imperfections of the bodies.[r] Corporeal images of God were the fruits of base imaginations of him; and as they sprung from them, so

[p] Cocceius Sum. Theol. c. 9. p. 47. § 35. [q] Rom. i. 25. [r] Rom. i. 22.

they contribute to a greater corruption of the notions of the divine nature: the heathens begun their first representations of him by the image of a corruptible man, then of birds, till they descended not only to four-footed beasts but creeping things, even serpents, as the apostle seems to intimate in his enumeration (Rom. i. 23): it had been more honorable to have continued in human representations of him, than have sunk so low as beasts and serpents, the baser images; though the first had been infinitely unworthy of him, he being more above a man, though the noblest creature, than man is above a worm, a toad, or the most despicable creeping thing upon the earth. To think we can make an image of God of a piece of marble, or an ingot of gold, is a greater debasing of him, than it would be of a great prince, if you should represent him in the statue of a frog.   When the Israelites represented God by a calf, it is said "they sinned a great sin" (Exod. xxxii. 31): and the sin of Jeroboam, who intended only a representation of God by the calves at Dan and Bethel, is called more emphatically,[s] "the wickedness of your wickedness," the very scum and dregs of wickedness.   As men debased God by this, so God debased men for this; he degraded the Israelites into captivity, under the worst of their enemies, and punished the heathens with spiritual judgments, as uncleanness through the lusts of their own hearts (Rom. i. 24); which is repeated again in other expressions (ver. 26, 27), as a meet recompense for their disgracing the spiritual nature of God.   Had God been like to man, they had not offended in it; but I mention this, to show a probable reason of those base lusts which are in the midst of us, that have scarce been exceeded by any nation, viz., the unworthy and unspiritual conceits of God, which are as much a debasing of him as material images were when they were more rife in the world; and may be as well the cause of spiritual judgments upon men, as the worshipping molten and carved images were the cause of the same upon the heathen.

3. Yet this is natural to man.   Wherein we may see the contrariety of man to God.   Though God be a Spirit, yet there is nothing man is more prone to, than to represent him under a corporeal form. The most famous guides of the heathen world have fashioned him, not only according to the more honorable images of men, but bestialized him in the form of a brute.   The Egyptians, whose country was the school of learning to Greece, were notoriously guilty of this brutishness in worshipping an ox for an image of their God; and the Philistines their Dagon, in a figure composed of the image of a woman and a fish:[t] such representations were ancient in the oriental parts.   The gods of Laban, that he accuseth Jacob of stealing from him, are supposed to be little figures of men.[u]   Such was the Israelites' golden calf; their worship was not terminated on the image, but they worshipped the true God under that representation; they could not be so brutish as to call a calf their deliverer, and give him so great a title ("These be thy gods, O Israel, which brought thee up out of the land of Egypt," Exod. xxxii. 4): or that which they knew belonged to the true God, "the God of Abraham, Isaac,

---

[s] Hos. x. 15.   [t] Daillé, super Cor. i. 10, Ser. III.
[u] Gen xxxi. 30–34.

and Jacob.''ˣ   They knew the calf to be formed of their ear-rings, but they had consecrated it to God as a representation of him; though they chose the form of the Egyptian idol, yet they knew that Apis, Osiris, and Isis, the gods of the Egyptians adored in that figure, had not wrought their redemption from bondage, but would have used their force, had they been possessed of any, to have kept them under the yoke, rather than have freed them from it; the feast also which they celebrated before that image, is called by Aaron the feast of the Lord (Exod. xxxii. 5); a feast to Jehovah, the incommunicable name of the creator of the world; it is therefore evident, that both the priest and the people pretended to serve the true God, not any false divinity of Egypt; that God who had rescued them from Egypt, with a mighty hand, divided the Red Sea before them, destroyed their enemies, conducted them, fed them by miracle, spoken to them from Mount Sinai, and amazed them by his thunderings and lightnings when he instructed them by his law; a God whom they could not so soon forget.   And with this representing God by that image, they are charged by the Psalmist (Psalm cvi. 19, 20), " they made a calf in Horeb, and changed their glory into a similitude of an ox that eateth grass:" they changed their glory, that is, God, the glory of Israel; so that they took this figure for the image of the true God of Israel, their own God; not the God of any other nation in the world.   Jeroboam intended no other by his calves, but symbols of the presence of the true God; instead of the ark and the propitiatory which remained among the Jews.   We see the inclination of our natures in the practice of the Israelites; a people chosen out of the whole world to bear up God's name, and preserve his glory; and in that the images of God were so soon set up in the Christian church; and to this day, the picture of God, in the shape of an old man, is visible in the temple of the Romanists.   It is prone to the nature of man,

4. To represent God by a corporeal image; and to worship him in and by that image, is idolatry.   Though the Israelites did not acknowledge the calf to be God, nor intended a worship to any of the Egyptian deities by it; but worshipped that God in it, who had so lately and miraculously delivered them from a cruel servitude; and could not in natural reason judge him to be clothed with a bodily shape, much less to be like an ox that eateth grass; yet the apostle brings no less a charge against them than that of idolatry (1 Cor. x. 7); he calls them idolaters, who before that calf kept a feast to Jehovah, citing Exod. xxxii. 5.   Suppose we could make such an image of God as might perfectly represent him; yet since God hath prohibited it, shall we be wiser than God?   He hath sufficiently manifested himself in his works without images: He is seen in the creatures, more particularly in the heavens, which declare his glory. His works are more excellent representations of him, as being the works of his own hands, than anything that is the product of the art of man.   His glory sparkles in the heavens, sun, moon, and stars, as being magnificent pieces of his wisdom and power; yet the kissing the hand to the sun or the heavens, as representatives of the

ˣ Gen. iii. 16, 17.

excellency and majesty of God, is idolatry in Scripture account, and a denial of God;[y] a prostituting the glory of God to a creature. Either the worship is terminated on the image itself, and then it is confessed by all to be idolatry, because it is a giving that worship to a creature which is the sole right of God, or not terminated in the image, but in the object represented by it; it is then a foolish thing; we may as well terminate our worship on the true object without, as with an image.[z] An erected statue is no sign or symbol of God's special presence, as the ark, tabernacle, temple were. It is no part of divine institution; has no authority of a command to support it; no cordial of a promise to encourage it; and the image being infinitely distant from, and below the majesty and spirituality of God, cannot constitute one object of worship with him. To put a religious character upon any image formed by the corrupt imagination of man, as a representation of the invisible and spiritual Deity, is to think the Godhead to be like silver and gold, or stone graven by art and man's device.[a]

III. This doctrine will direct us in our conceptions of God, as a pure perfect Spirit, than which nothing can be imagined more perfect, more pure, more spiritual.

1. We cannot have an adequate or suitable conception of God: He dwells in inaccessible light; inaccessible to the acuteness of our fancy, as well as the weakness of our sense. If we could have thoughts of him, as high and excellent as his nature, our conceptions must be as infinite as his nature. All our imaginations of him cannot represent him, because every created species is finite; it cannot therefore represent to us a full and substantial notion of an infinite Being. We cannot speak or think worthily enough of him, who is greater than our words, vaster than our understandings. Whatsoever we speak or think of God, is handed first to us by the notice we have of some perfection in the creature, and explains to us some particular excellency of God, rather than the fulness of his essence. No creature, nor all creatures together, can furnish us with such a magnificent notion of God, as can give us a clear view of him. Yet God in his word is pleased to step below his own excellency, and point us to those excellencies in his works, whereby we may ascend to the knowledge of those excellencies which are in his nature. But the creatures, whence we draw our lessons, being finite, and our understandings being finite, it is utterly impossible to have a notion of God commensurate to the immensity and spirituality of his being. " God is not like to visible creatures, nor is there any proportion between him and the most spiritual."[b] We cannot have a full notion of a spiritual nature, much less can we have of God, who is a Spirit above spirits. No spirit can clearly represent him: the angels, that are great spirits, are bounded in their extent, finite in their being, and of a mutable nature. Yet though we cannot have a suitable conception of God, we must not content ourselves without any conception of him. It is our sin not to endeavor after a true notion of

---

[y] Job xxxi. 26–28. Chin. Predict. Part II. p. 252.
[z] Lawson, Body Divin. p. 161.   [a] Acts xvii. 29.
[b] Amyraut. Morale. Tom. I. p. 289.

him: it is our sin to rest in a mean and low notion of him, when our reason tells us we are capable of having higher: but if we ascend as high as we can, though we shall then come short of a suitable notion of him, this is not our sin, but our weakness. God is infinitely superior to the choicest conceptions, not only of a sinner, but of a creature. If all conceptions of God below the true nature of God were sin, there is not a holy angel in heaven free from sin; because, though they are the most capacious creatures, yet they cannot have such a notion of an infinite Being as is fully suitable to his nature, unless they were infinite as he himself is.

2. But, however, we must by no means conceive of God under a human or corporeal shape. Since we cannot have conceptions honorable enough for his nature, we must take heed we entertain not any which may debase his nature; though we cannot comprehend him as he is, we must be careful not to fancy him to be what he is not. It is a vain thing to conceive him with human lineaments: we must think higher of him than to ascribe to him so mean a shape: we deny his spirituality when we fancy him under such a form. He is spiritual, and between that which is spiritual and that which is corporeal, there is no resemblance.[c] Indeed, Daniel saw God in a human form (Dan. vii. 9): "The Ancient of days did sit, whose garment was white as snow, and the hairs of his head like pure wool:" he is described as coming to judgment; it is not meant of Christ probably, because Christ (ver. 13) is called the Son of Man coming near to the Ancient of days. This is not the proper shape of God, for no man hath seen his shape. It was a vision wherein such representations were made, as were accommodated to the inward sense of Daniel; Daniel saw him in a rapture or ecstacy, wherein outward senses are of no use. God is described, not as he is in himself, of a human form, but in regard of his fitness to judge: "white," notes the purity and simplicity of the Divine nature; "Ancient of days," in regard of his eternity; "white hair," in regard of his prudence and wisdom, which is more eminent in age than youth, and more fit to discern causes and to distinguish between right and wrong. Visions are riddles, and must not be understood in a literal sense. We are to watch against such determinate conceptions of God. Vain imaginations do easily infest us; tinder will not sooner take fire than our natures kindle into wrong notions of the Divine Majesty. We are very apt to fashion a god like ourselves; we must therefore look upon such representations of God, as accommodated to our weakness: and no more think them to be literal descriptions of God, as he is in himself, than we will think the image of the sun in the water, to be the true sun in the heavens. We may, indeed, conceive of Christ as man, who hath in heaven the vestment of our nature, and is *Deus figuratus*, though we cannot conceive the godhead under a human shape.

1. To have such a fancy is to disparage and wrong God. A corporeal fancy of God is as ridiculous in itself, and as injurious to God, as a wooden statue. The caprices of our imagination are often more mysterious than the images which are the works of art; it is as irre-

c Episco. Institut. lib. iv. § 2. c. 10.

ligious to measure God's essence by our line, his perfections by our imperfections, as to measure his thoughts and actings by the weakness and unworthiness of our own. This is to limit an infinite essence, and pull him down to our scanty measures, and render that which is unconceivably above us, equal with us. It is impossible we can conceive God after the manner of a body, but we must bring him down to the proportion of a body, which is to diminish his glory, and stoop him below the dignity of his nature. God is a pure Spirit, he hath nothing of the nature and tincture of a body; whosoever, therefore, conceives of him as having a bodily form, though he fancy the most beautiful and comely body, instead of owning his dignity, detracts from the super-eminent excellency of his nature and blessedness. When men fancy God like themselves in their corporeal nature, they will soon make a progress, and ascribe to him their corrupt nature; and while they clothe him with their bodies, invest him also in the infirmities of them. God is a jealous God, very sensible of any disgrace, and will be as much incensed against an inward idolatry as an outward: that command which forbade corporeal images,[d] would not indulge carnal imaginations; since the nature of God is as much wronged by unworthy images, erected in the fancy, as by statues carved out of stone or metals: one as well as the other is a deserting of our true spouse, and committing adultery; one with a material image, and the other with a carnal notion of God. Since God humbles himself to our apprehensions, we should not debase him in thinking him to be that in his nature, which he makes only a resemblance of himself to us.

2. To have such fancies of God, will obstruct and pollute our worship of him. How is it possible to give him a right worship, of whom we have so debasing a notion? We shall never think a corporeal deity worthy of a dedication of our spirits. The hating instruction, and casting God's word behind the back, is charged upon the imagination they had, that "God was such a one as themselves" (Psalm l. 17, 21). Many of the wiser heathens did not judge their statues to be their gods, or their gods to be like their statues; but suited them to their politic designs; and judged them a good invention to keep people within the bounds of obedience and devotion, by such visible figures of them, which might imprint a reverence and fear of those gods upon them; but these are false measures; a despised and undervalued God is not an object of petition or affection. Who would address seriously to a God he has low apprehensions of? The more raised thoughts we have of him, the viler sense we shall have of ourselves; they would make us humble and self-abhorrent in our supplications to him (Job xlii. 6): "wherefore I abhor myself," &c.

3. Though we must not conceive of God, as of a human or corporeal shape; yet we cannot think of God, without some reflection upon our own being. We cannot conceive him to be an intelligent being, but we must make some comparison between him and our own understanding nature to come to a knowledge of him. Since we are enclosed in bodies, we apprehend nothing but what comes in

d Exod. xx. 4.

by sense, and what we in some sort measure by sensible objects. And in the consideration of those things which we desire to abstract from sense, we are fain to make use of the assistance of sense and visible things: and therefore when we frame the highest notion, there will be some similitude of some corporeal thing in our fancy; and though we would spiritualize our thoughts, and aim at a more abstracted and raised understanding, yet there will be some dregs of matter sticking to our conceptions; yet we still judge by argument and reasoning, what the thing is we think of under those material images. A corporeal image will follow us, as the shadow doth the body.[e] While we are in the body, and surrounded with fleshly matter, we cannot think of things without some help from corporeal representations: something of sense will interpose itself in our purest conceptions of spiritual things;[f] for the faculties which serve for contemplation, are either corporeal, as the sense and fancy, or so allied to them, that nothing passes into them but by the organs of the body; so that there is a natural inclination to figure nothing but under a corporeal notion, till by an attentive application of the mind and reason to the object thought upon, we separate that which is bodily from that which is spiritual, and by degrees ascend to that true notion of that we think upon, and would have a due conception of in our mind. Therefore God tempers the declaration of himself to our weakness, and the condition of our natures. He condescends to our littleness and narrowness, when he declares himself by the similitude of bodily members. As the light of the sun is tempered, and diffuseth itself to our sense through the air and vapors, that our weak eyes may not be too much dazzled with it; without it we could not know or judge of the sun, because we could have no use of our sense, which we must have before we can judge of it in our understanding; so we are not able to conceive of spiritual beings in the purity of their own nature, without such a temperament, and such shadows to usher them into our minds. And therefore we find the Spirit of God accommodates himself to our contracted and teddered capacities, and uses such expressions of God as are suited to us in this state of flesh wherein we are. And therefore because we cannot apprehend God in the simplicity of his own being, and his undivided essence, he draws the representations of himself from several creatures and several actions of those creatures: as sometimes he is said to be angry, to walk, to sit, to fly; not that we should rest in such conceptions of him, but take our rise from this foundation, and such perfections in the creatures, to mount up to a knowledge of God's nature by those several steps, and conceive of him by those divided excellencies, because we cannot conceive of him in the purity of his own essence. We cannot possibly think or speak of God, unless we transfer the names of created perfections to him;[g] yet we are to conceive of them in a higher manner when we apply them to the Divine nature, than when we consider them in the several creatures formally, exceeding those perfections and excellencies which are in the creature, and in a more excellent manner: "as one saith, though

---

[e] Nazianzen.   [f] Amyraut, Morale, Tom. I. p. 180, &c.   [g] Lessius.

we cannot comprehend God without the help of such resemblances, yet we may, without making an image of him; so that inability of ours excuseth those apprehensions of him from any way offending against his Divine nature."h   These are not notions so much suited to the nature of God as the weakness of man. They are helps to our meditations, but ought not to be formal conceptions of him. We may assist ourselves in our apprehensions of him, by considering the subtilty and spirituality of air; and considering the members of a body, without thinking him to be air, or to have any corporeal member.   Our reason tells us, that whatsoever is a body, is limited and bounded; and the notion of infiniteness and bodiliness, cannot agree and consist together: and therefore what is offered by our fancy should be purified by our reason.

4. Therefore we are to elevate and refine all our notions of God, and spiritualize our conceptions of him. Every man is to have a conception of God; therefore he ought to have one of the highest elevation. Since we cannot have a full notion of him, we should endeavor to make it as high and as pure as we can. Though we cannot conceive of God, but some corporeal representations or images in our minds will be conversant with us, as motes in the air when we look upon the heavens, yet our conceptions may and must rise higher. As when we see the draught of the heavens and earth in a globe, or a kingdom in a map, it helps our conceptions, but doth not terminate them: we conceive them to be of a vast extent, far beyond that short description of them. So we should endeavor to refine every representation of God, to rise higher and higher, and have our apprehensions still more purified; separating the perfect from the imperfect, casting away the one, and greatening the other; conceive him to be a Spirit diffused through all, containing all, perceiving all. All the perfections of God are infinitely elevated above the excellencies of the creatures; above whatsoever can be conceived by the clearest and most piercing understanding. The nature of God as a Spirit is infinitely superior to whatsoever we can conceive perfect in the notion of a created spirit. Whatsoever God is, he is infinitely so: he is infinite Wisdom, infinite Goodness, infinite Knowledge, infinite Power, infinite Spirit; infinitely distant from the weakness of creatures, infinitely mounted above the excellencies of creatures: as easy to be known that he is, as impossible to be comprehended what he is. Conceive of him as excellent, without any imperfection; a Spirit without parts; great without quantity; perfect without quality; everywhere without place; powerful without members; understanding without ignorance; wise without reasoning; light without darkness; infinitely more excelling the beauty of all creatures, than the light in the sun, pure and unviolated, exceeds the splendor of the sun dispersed and divided through a cloudy and misty air: and when you have risen to the highest, conceive him yet infinitely above all you can conceive of spirit, and acknowledge the infirmity of your own minds. And whatsoever conception comes into your minds, say, This is not God; God is more than this: if I could conceive

h Towerson on the Commandments, p. 112.

him, he were not God; for God is incomprehensibly above whatsoever I can say, whatsoever I can think and conceive of him.

Inference 1. If God be a Spirit, no corporeal thing can defile him.
Some bring an argument against the omnipresence of God, that it is
a disparagement to the Divine essence to be everywhere, in nasty
cottages as well as beautiful palaces and garnished temples. What
place can defile a spirit? Is light, which approaches to the nature
of spirit, polluted by shining upon a dunghill, or a sunbeam tainted
by darting upon a quagmire? Doth an angel contract any soil, by
stepping into a nasty prison to deliver Peter? What can steam from
the most noisome body to pollute the spiritual nature of God? As
he is "of purer eyes than to behold iniquity,"[i] so he is of a more
spiritual substance than to contract any physical pollution from the
places where he doth diffuse himself. Did our Saviour, who had a
true body, derive any taint from the lepers he touched, the diseases
he cured, or the devils he expelled? God is a pure Spirit; plungeth
himself into no filth; is dashed with no spot by being present with
all bodies. Bodies only receive defilement from bodies.

Inference 2. If God be a Spirit, he is active and communicative. He
is not clogged with heavy and sluggish matter, which is cause of dulness and inactivity. The more subtle, thin, and approaching nearer the
nature of a spirit anything is, the more diffusive it is. Air is a gliding
substance; spreads itself through all regions, pierceth into all bodies; it
fills the space between heaven and earth; there is nothing but partakes
of the virtue of it. Light, which is an emblem of spirit, insinuates itself
into all places, refresheth all things. As spirits are fuller, so they are
more overflowing, more piercing, more operative than bodies. The
Egyptian horses were weak things, because they were "flesh, and not
spirit."[k] The soul being a spirit, conveys more to the body than the
body can to it. What cannot so great a spirit do for us? What cannot so great a spirit work in us? God, being a spirit above all spirits,
can pierce into the centre of all spirits; make his way into the most
secret recesses; stamp what he pleases. It is no more to him to turn
our spirits, than to make a wilderness become waters, and speak a
chaos into a beautiful frame of heaven and earth. He can act our
souls with infinite more ease than our souls can act our bodies; he
can fix in us what motions, frames, inclinations he pleases; he can
come and settle in our hearts with all his treasures. It is an encouragement to confide in him, when we petition him for spiritual
blessings: as he is a spirit, he is possessed with "spiritual blessings."[l]
A spirit delights to bestow things suitable to its nature, as bodies do
to communicate what is agreeable to theirs. As he is a Father of
spirits, we may go to him for the welfare of our spirits; he being a
Spirit, is as able to repair our spirits as he was to create them. As
he is a Spirit, he is indefatigable in acting. The members of the
body tire and flag; but who ever heard of a soul wearied with being
active? who ever heard of a weary angel? In the purest simplicity,
there is the greatest power, the most efficacious goodness, the most
reaching justice to affect the spirit, that can insinuate itself every-

---

[i] Heb. i. 13.   [k] Isa. xxxi. 3.   [l] Eph. i. 3.

where to punish wickedness without weariness, as well as to comfort goodness. God is active, because he is spirit; and if we be like to God, the more spiritual we are, the more active we shall be.

Inference 3. God being a Spirit, is immortal. His being immortal, and being invisible, are joined together.[m] Spirits are in their nature incorruptible; they can only perish by that hand that framed them. Every compounded thing is subject to mutation; but God, being a pure and simple Spirit, is without corruption, without any shadow of change.[n] Where there is composition, there is some kind of repugnancy of one part against the other; and where there is repugnancy, there is a capability of dissolution. God, in regard of his infinite spirituality, hath nothing in his own nature contrary to it; can have nothing in himself which is not himself. The world perishes; friends change and are dissolved; bodies moulder, because they are mutable. God is a Spirit in the highest excellency and glory of spirits; nothing is beyond him; nothing above him; no contrariety within him. This is our comfort, if we devote ourselves to him; this God is our God; this Spirit is our Spirit; this is our all, our immutable, our incorruptible support; a Spirit that cannot die and leave us.

Inference 4. If God be a Spirit, we see how we can only converse with him by our spirits. Bodies and spirits are not suitable to one another: we can only see, know, embrace a spirit with our spirits. He judges not of us by our corporeal actions, nor our external devotions by our masks and disguises: he fixes his eye upon the frame of the heart, bends his ear to the groans of our spirits. He is not pleased with outward pomp. He is not a body; therefore the beauty of temples, delicacy of sacrifices, fumes of incense, are not grateful to him; by those, or any external action, we have no communion with him. A spirit, when broken, is his delightful sacrifice;[o] we must therefore, have our spirits fitted for him, "be renewed in the spirit of our minds,"[p] that we may be in a posture to live with him, and have an intercourse with him. We can never be united to God but in our spirits: bodies unite with bodies, spirits with spirits. The more spiritual anything is, the more closely doth it unite. Air hath the closest union; nothing meets together sooner than that, when the parts are divided by the interposition of a body.

Inference 5. If God be a Spirit, he can only be the true satisfaction of our spirits: spirit can only be filled with spirit: content flows from likeness and suitableness. As we have a resemblance to God in regard of the spiritual nature of our soul, so we can have no satisfaction but in him. Spirit can no more be really satisfied with that which is corporeal, than a beast can delight in the company of an angel. Corporeal things can no more fill a hungry spirit, than pure spirit can feed an hungry body. God, the highest Spirit, can only reach out a full content to our spirits. Man is lord of the creation: nothing below him can be fit for his converse; nothing above him offers itself to his converse but God. We have no correspondence with angels. The influence they have upon us, the protection they

[m] 1 Tim. i. 17.   [n] James i. 17.   [o] Psalm li. 17.   [p] Eph. iv. 23.

afford us, is secret and undiscerned; but God, the highest Spirit, offers himself to us in his Son, in his ordinances, is visible in every creature, presents himself to us in every providence; to him we must seek; in him we must rest. God had no rest from the creation till he had made man; and man can have no rest in the creation till he rests in God. God only is our dwelling place;q our souls should only long for him:r our souls should only wait upon him. The spirit of man never riseth to its original glory, till it be carried up on the wings of faith and love to its original copy. The face of the soul looks most beautiful, when it is turned to the face of God, the Father of spirits; when the derived spirit is fixed upon the original Spirit, drawing from it life and glory. Spirit is only the receptacle of spirit. God, as Spirit, is our principle; we must therefore live upon him. God, as Spirit, hath some resemblance to us as his image; we must, therefore, only satisfy ourselves in him.

Inference 6. If God be a Spirit, we should take most care of that wherein we are like to God. Spirit is nobler than body; we must, therefore, value our spirits above our bodies. The soul, as spirit, partakes more of the divine nature, and deserves more of our choicest cares. If we have any love to this Spirit, we should have a real affection to our own spirits, as bearing a stamp of the spiritual Divinity, the chiefest of all the works of God; as it is said of behemoth (Job xl. 19). That which is most the image of this immense spirit, should be our darling; so David calls his soul (Psalm xxxv. 17). Shall we take care of that wherein we partake not of God, and not delight in the jewel which hath his own signature upon it? God was not only the Framer of spirits, and the End of spirits; but the Copy and Exemplar of spirits. God partakes of no corporeity; he is pure Spirit. But how do we act, as if we were only matter and body! We have but little kindness for this great Spirit as well as our own, if we take no care of his immediate offspring, since he is not only Spirit, but the Father of spirits.s

Inference 7. If God be a Spirit, let us take heed of those sins which are spiritual. Paul distinguisheth between the filth of the flesh, and that of the spirit.t By the one we defile the body; by the other we defile the spirit, which, in regard of its nature, is of kin to the Creator. To wrong one who is near of kin to a prince, is worse than to injure an inferior subject. When we make our spirits, which are most like to God in their nature, and framed according to his image, a stage to act vain imaginations, wicked desires, and unclean affections, we wrong God in the excellency of his work, and reflect upon the nobleness of the pattern; we wrong him in that part where he hath stamped the most signal character of his own spiritual nature; we defile that whereby we have only converse with him as a Spirit, which he hath ordered more immediately to represent him in this nature, than all corporeal things in the world can, and make that Spirit with whom we desire to be joined unfit for such a knot. God's spirituality is the root of his other perfections. We have already heard he could not be infinite, omnipresent, immutable, without it.   Spiritual sins are the greatest root of bitterness within us.   As grace in our spirits renders us more like to a spiritual God, so spiritual sins bring us into a conformity to a degraded devil.[u]   Carnal sins change us from men to brutes, and spiritual sins divest us of the image of God for the image of Satan.   We should by no means make our spirits a dunghill, which bear upon them the character of the spiritual nature of God, and were made for his residence.   Let us, therefore, behave ourselves towards God in all those ways which the spiritual nature of God requires us.

[u] Eph. ii. 2, 3.

DISCOURSE IV

ON SPIRITUAL WORSHIP

JOHN iv. 24.—God is a Spirit: and they that worship him must worship him in spirit and in truth.

HAVING thus despatched the first proposition, "God is a Spirit," it will not be amiss to handle the inference our Saviour makes from that proposition, which is the second observation propounded.

Doct. That the worship due from us to God ought to be spiritual, and spiritually performed. Spirit and truth are understood variously. We are to worship God,

1. Not by legal ceremonies. The evangelical administration being called spirit, in opposition to the legal ordinances as carnal; and truth in opposition to them as typical. As the whole Judaical service is called flesh, so the whole evangelical service is called spirit; or spirit may be opposed to the worship at Jerusalem, as it was carnal; truth, to the worship on the Mount Gerizim, because it was false. They had not the true object of worship, nor the true medium of worship as those at Jerusalem had. Their worship should cease, because it was false; and the Jewish worship should cease, because it was carnal. There is no need of a candle when the sun spreads his beams in the air; no need of those ceremonies when the Sun of righteousness appeared; they only served for candles to instruct and direct men till the time of his coming. The shadows are chased away by displaying the substance, so that they can be of no more use in the worship of God, since the end for which they were instituted is expired; and that discovered to us in the gospel, which the Jews sought for in vain among the baggage and stuff of their ceremonies.

2. With a spiritual and sincere frame. *In spirit, i. e.* with spirit; with the inward operations of all the faculties of our souls, and the cream and flower of them; and the reason is, because there ought to be a worship suitable to the nature of God; and as the worship was to be spiritual, so the exercise of that worship ought to be in a spiritual manner.[x] It shall be a worship "in truth," because the true God shall be adored without those vain imaginations and fantastic resemblances of him,[y] which were common among the blind Gentiles, and contrary to the glorious nature of God, and unworthy ingredients in religious services. It shall be a worship "in spirit," without those carnal rites the degenerate Jews rested on; such a

---

[x] Lingend. Tom. II. p. 777. [y] Taylor's Exemplar, Preface, § 30.

posture of soul which is the life and ornament of every service God looks for at your hands. There must be some proportion between the object adored, and the manner in which we adore it; it must not be a mere corporeal worship, because God is not a body; but it must rise from the centre of our soul, because God is a Spirit. If he were a body, a bodily worship might suit him, images might be fit to represent him; but being a Spirit, our bodily services enter us not into communion with him. Being a spirit, we must banish from our minds all carnal imaginations of him, and separate from our wills all cold and dissembled affections to him. We must not only have a loud voice, but an elevated soul; not only a bended knee, but a broken heart; not only a supplicating tone, but a groaning spirit; not only a ready ear for the word, but a receiving heart; and this shall be of greater value with him, than the most costly outward services offered at Gerizim or Jerusalem. Our Saviour certainly meant not by worshipping in spirit, only the matter of the evangelical service, as opposed to the legal administration, without the manner wherein it was to be performed. It is true, God always sought a worship in spirit; he expected the heart of the worshipper should join with his instituted rights of adoration in every exercise of them; but he expects such a carriage more under the gospel administration, because of the clearer discoveries of his nature made in it, and the greater assistances conveyed by it.

I shall, therefore, 1. Lay down some general propositions. 2. Show what this spiritual worship is. 3. Why we must offer to God a spiritual service. 4. The use.

1. Some general propositions.

Prop I. The right exercise of worship is founded upon, and riseth from, the spirituality of God.[z] The first ground of the worship we render to God, is the infinite excellency of his nature, which is not only one attribute, but results from all; for God, as God, is the object of worship; and the notion of God consists not in thinking him wise, good, just, but all those infinitely beyond any conception; and hence it follows that God is an object infinitely to be loved and honored. His goodness is sometimes spoken of in Scripture as a motive of our homage (Psalm cxxx. 4): "There is forgiveness with thee that thou mayest be feared." Fear, in the Scripture dialect, signifies the "whole worship of God" (Acts x. 35): but in every nation, "he that fears him" is accepted of him.[a] If God should act towards men according to the rigors of his justice due to them for the least of their crimes, there could be no exercise of any affection but that of despair, which could not engender a worship of God, which ought to be joined with love, not with hatred. The beneficence and patience of God, and his readiness to pardon men, is the reason of the honor they return to him; and this is so evident a motive, that generally the idolatrous world ranked those creatures in the number of their gods, which they perceived useful and beneficial to mankind, as the sun and moon, the Egyptians the ox, &c. And the more beneficial anything appeared to mankind, the higher station men gave it in the rank of their deities, and bestowed a more peculiar and solemn wor-

z Ames Medul. lib. ii. c. 4. § 20.   a So 2 Kings xvii. 32, 33.

ship upon it. Men worshipped God to procure and continue his favor, which would not have been acted by them, had they not conceived it a pleasing thing to him to be merciful and gracious. Sometimes his justice is proposed to us as a motive of worship (Heb. xii. 28, 29): "Serve God with reverence and godly fear, for our God is a consuming fire;" which includes his holiness, whereby he doth hate sin, as well as his wrath, whereby he doth punish it. Who but a mad and totally brutish person, or one that was resolved to make war against heaven, could behold the effects of God's anger in the world, consider him in his justice as a " consuming fire," and despise him, and rather be drawn out by that consideration to blasphemy and despair, than to seek all ways to appease him? Now though the infinite power of God, his unspeakable wisdom, his incomprehensible goodness, the holiness of his nature, the vigilance of his providence, the bounty of his hand, signify to man that he should love and honor him, and are the motives of worship; yet the spirituality of his nature is the rule of worship, and directs us to render our duty to him with all the powers of our soul. As his goodness beams out upon us, worship is due in justice to him; and as he is the most excellent nature, veneration is due to him in the highest manner with the choicest affections. So that indeed the spirituality of God comes chiefly into consideration in matter of worship: all his perfections are grounded upon this: he could not be infinite, immutable, omniscient, if he were a corporeal being;[b] we cannot give him a worship unless we judge him worthy, excellent, and deserving a worship at our hands; and we cannot judge him worthy of a worship, unless we have some apprehensions and admirations of his infinite virtues; and we cannot apprehend and admire those perfections, but as we see them as causes shining in their effects. When we see, therefore, the frame of the world to be the work of his power, the order of the world to be the fruit of his wisdom, and the usefulness of the world to be the product of his goodness, we find the motives and reasons of worship; and weighing that this power, wisdom, goodness, infinitely transcend any corporeal nature, we find a rule of worship, that it ought to be offered by us in a manner suitable to such a nature as is infinitely above any bodily being. His being a Spirit declares what he is; his other perfections declare what kind of Spirit he is. All God's perfections suppose him a Spirit; all centre in this; his wisdom doth not suppose him merciful, or his mercy suppose him omniscient; there may be distinct notions of those, but all suppose him to be of a spiritual nature. How cold and frozen will our devotions be, if we consider not his omniscience, whereby he discerns our hearts! How carnal will our services be, if we consider him not as a pure Spirit![c] In our offers to, and transactions with men, we deal not with them as mere animals, but as rational creatures; and we debase their natures if we treat them otherwise; and if we have not raised apprehensions of God's spiritual nature in our treating with him, but allow him only such frames as we think fit enough for men, we debase his spirituality to the littleness of our own being. We must, therefore, possess our souls with

[b] Amirald, Dissert. 6, disp. i. v. 11.   [c] Amyraut, de Relig.

this; we shall else render him no better than a fleshly service. We do not much concern ourselves in those things of which we are either utterly ignorant, or have but slight apprehensions of. That is the first proposition;—The right exercise of worship is grounded upon the spirituality of God.

Prop. II. This spiritual worship of God is manifest by the light of nature, to be due to him. In reference to this, consider,

1. The outward means or matter of that worship which would be acceptable to God, was not known by the light of nature. The law for a worship, and for a spiritual worship by the faculties of our souls was natural, and part of the law of creation; though the determination of the particular acts, whereby God would have this homage testified, was of positive institution, and depended not upon the law of creation. Though Adam in innocence knew God was to be worshipped, yet by nature he did not know by what outward acts he was to pay this respect, or at what time he was more solemnly to be exercised in it than at another: this depended upon the directions God, as the sovereign Governor and Lawgiver, should prescribe. You therefore find the positive institutions of the "tree of the knowledge of good and evil," and the determination of the time of worship (Gen. ii. 3, 17). Had there been any such notion in Adam naturally, as strong as that other, that a worship was due to God, there would have been found some relics of these modes universally consented to by mankind, as well as of the other. But though all nations have by an universal consent concurred in the acknowledgment of the being of God, and his right to adoration, and the obligation of the creature to it; and that there ought to be some public rule and polity in matters of religion (for no nation hath been in the world without a worship, and without external acts and certain ceremonies to signify that worship); yet their modes and rites have been as various as their climates, unless in that common notion of sacrifices, not descending to them by nature, but tradition from Adam; and the various ways of worship have been more provoking than pleasing. Every nation suited the kind of worship to their particular ends and polities they designed to rule by. How God was to be worshipped is more difficult to be discerned by nature with its eyes out than with its eyes clear.[d] The pillars upon which the worship of God stands cannot be discerned without revelation, no more than blind Samson could tell where the pillars of the Philistines' theatre stood, without one to conduct him. What Adam could not see with his sound eyes, we cannot with our dim eyes; he must be told from heaven what worship was fit for the God of heaven. It is not by nature that we can have such a full prospect of God as may content and quiet us; this is the noble effect of Divine revelation; He only knows himself, and can only make himself known to us. It could not be supposed that an infinite God should have no perfections but what were visible in the works of his hands; and that these perfections should not be infinitely greater, than as they were sensible in their present effects: this had been to apprehend God a limited Being, meaner than he is. Now it is impossible to honor God as we ought,

d King, on Jonah, p. 63.

unless we know him as he is; and we could not know him as he is, without divine revelation from himself; for none but God can acquaint us with his own nature: and therefore the nations void of this conduct, heaped up modes of worship from their own imaginations, unworthy of the majesty of God, and below the nature of man. A rational man would scarce have owned such for signs of honor, as the Scripture mentions in the services of Baal and Dagon; much less an infinitely wise and glorious God. And when God had signified his mind to his own people, how unwilling were they to rest satisfied with God's determination, but would be warping to their own inventions, and make gods, and ways of worship to themselves!e as in the matter of the golden calf, as was lately spoken of.

2. Though the outward manner of worship acceptable to God could not be known without revelation, and those revelations might be various; yet the inward manner of worship with our spirits was manifest by nature: and not only manifest by nature to Adam in innocence, but after his fall, and the scales he had brought upon his understanding by that fall. When God gave him his positive institutions before the fall, or whatsoever additions God should have made, had he persisted in that state; or, when he appointed him, after his fall, to testify his acknowledgment of him by sacrifices, there needed no command to him to make those acknowledgments by those outward ways prescribed to him, with the intention and prime affection of his spirit: this nature would instruct him in without revelation; for he could not possibly have any semblance of reason to think that the offering of beasts, or the presenting the first fruits of the increase of the ground, as an acknowledgment of God's sovereignty over him and his bounty to him, was sufficient, without devoting to him that part wherein the image of his Creator did consist: he could not but discern, by a reflection upon his own being, that he was made for God as well as by God: for it is a natural principle of which the apostle speaks (Rom. xi. 36), "For of him, and through him, and to him are all things," &c.: that the whole whereof he did consist was due to God; and that his body, the dreggy and dusty part of his nature, was not fit to be brought alone before God, without that nobler principle, which he had, by creation, linked with it. Nothing in the whole law of nature, as it is informed of religion, was clearer, next to the being of a God, than this manner of worshipping God with the mind and spirit. And as the Gentiles never sunk so low into the mud of idolatry, as to think the images they worshipped were really their gods, but the representations, or habitations of their gods; so they never deserted this principle in the notion of it, that God was to be honored with the best they were, and the best they had: as they never denied the being of a God in the notion, though they did in the practice, so they never rejected this principle in notion, though they did, and now most men do, in the inward observation of it: it was a maxim among them that God was *mens animus*, mind and spirit, and therefore was to be honored with the mind and spirit: that religion did not consist in the ceremonies of the body, but the work of the soul; whence the speech of one of them:

* Amos v. 26.

" Sacrifice to the gods, not so much clothed with purple garments as a pure heart :"[f] and of another : " God regards not the multitude of the sacrifices, but the disposition of the sacrificer."[g] It is not fit we should deny God the cream and the flower, and give him the flotten part and the stalks. And with what reverence and intention of mind they thought their worship was to be performed, is evident by the priests crying out often, *Hoc age*, Mind this, let your spirits be intent upon it. This could not but result,

(1.) From the knowledge of ourselves. It is a natural principle, " God hath made us, and not we ourselves" (Psalm c. 1, 2). Man knows himself to be a rational creature ; as a creature he was to serve his Creator, and as a rational creature with the best part of that rational nature he derived from him. By the same act of reason that he knows himself to be a creature, he knows himself to have a Creator ; that this Creator is more excellent than himself, and that an honor is due from him to the Creator for framing of him ; and, therefore, this honor was to be offered to him by the most excellent part which was framed by him. Man cannot consider himself as a thinking, understanding, being, but he must know that he must give God the honor of his thoughts, and worship him with those faculties whereby he thinks, wills, and acts.[h] He must know his faculties were given him to act, and to act for the glory of that God who gave him his soul, and the faculties of it ; and he could not in reason think they must be only active in his own service, and the service of the creature, and idle and unprofitable in the service of his Creator. With the same powers of our soul, whereby we contemplate God, we must also worship God ; we cannot think of him but with our minds, nor love him but with our will ; and we cannot worship him without the acts of thinking and loving, and therefore cannot worship him without the exercise of our inward faculties : how is it possible then for any man that knows his own nature, to think that extended hands, bended knees, and lifted up eyes, were sufficient acts of worship, without a quickened and active spirit ?

(2.) From the knowledge of God. As there was a knowledge of God by nature, so the same nature did dictate to man, that God was to be glorified as God ; the apostle implies the inference in the charge he brings against them for neglecting it.[i] " We should speak of God as he is," said one ;[k] and the same reason would inform them that they were to act towards God as he is. The excellency of the object required a worship according to the dignity of his nature, which could not be answered but by the most serious inward affection, as well as outward decency ; and a want of this cannot but be judged to be unbecoming the majesty of the Creator of the world, and the excellency of religion. No nation, no person, did ever assert, that the vilest part of man was enough for the most excellent Being, as God is ; that a bodily service could be a sufficient acknowledgment for the greatness of God, or a sufficient return for the bounty of God. Man could not but know that he was to act in religion conformably to the object of religion, and to the excellency of his own

f Menander. Grot. de Veritat Relig. lib. iv. § 12.   g Iamblic.
h Amyraut. Mor. Tom. I. pp. 309, 310.   i Rom. i. 21.   k Bias.

soul :[1] the notion of a God was sufficient to fill the mind of man with admiration and reverence, and the first conclusion from it would be to honor God, and that he have all the affection placed on him that so infinite and spiritual a Being did deserve : the progress then would be, that this excellent Being was to be honored with the motions of the understanding and will, with the purest and most spiritual powers in the nature of man, because he was a spiritual being, and had nothing of matter mingled with him. Such a brutish imagination, to suppose that blood and fumes, beasts and incense, could please a Deity, without a spiritual frame, cannot be supposed to befall any but those that had lost their reason in the rubbish of sense. Mere rational nature could never conclude that so excellent a Spirit would be put off with a mere animal service ; an attendance of matter and body without spirit, when they themselves, of an inferior nature, would be loth to sit down contented with an outside service from those that belong to them; so that this instruction of our Saviour, that God is to be worshipped in spirit and truth, is conformable to the sentiments of nature, and drawn from the most undeniable principles of it. The excellency of God's nature, and the excellent constitution of human faculties, concur naturally to support this persuasion ; this was as natural to be known by men, as the necessity of justice and temperance for the support of human societies and bodies. It is to be feared, that if there be not among us such brutish apprehensions, there are such brutish dealings with God, in our services, against the light of nature ; when we place all our worship of God in outward attendances and drooping countenances, with unbelieving frames and formal devotions ; when prayer is muttered over in private, slightly, as a parrot learns lessons by rote, not understanding what it speaks, or to what end it speaks it ; not glorifying God in thought and spirit, with understanding and will.

Prop. III. Spiritual worship therefore was always required by God, and always offered to him by one or other. Man had a perpetual obligation upon him to such a worship from the nature of God ; and what is founded upon the nature of God is invariable. This and that particular mode of worship may wax old as a garment, and as a vesture may be folded up and changed, as the expression is of the heavens ;[m] but God endures forever ; his spirituality fails not, therefore a worship of him in spirit must run through all ways and rites of worship. God must cease to be Spirit, before any service but that which is spiritual can be accepted by him. The light of nature is the light of God ; the light of nature being unchangeable, what was dictated by that, was alway, and will alway be, required by God. The worship of God being perpetually due from the creature, the worshipping him as God is as perpetually his right. Though the outward expressions of his honor were different, one way in Paradise (for a worship was then due, since a solemn time for that worship was appointed), another under the law, another under the gospel ; the angels also worship God in heaven, and fall down before his throne ; yet, though they differ in rites, they agree in this necessary ingredient, all rites, though of a different shape,

[1] Amyraut, *ib.*   [m] Heb. i. 11, 12.

must be offered to him, not as carcasses, but animated with the affections of the soul. Abel's sacrifice had not been so excellent in God's esteem, without those gracious habits and affections working in his soul.[n] Faith works by love; his heart was on fire as well as his sacrifice. Cain rested upon his present; perhaps thought he had obliged God; he depended upon the outward ceremony, but sought not for the inward purity: it was an offering brought to the Lord;[o] he had the right object, but not the right manner (Gen. iv. 7): "If thou doest well, shalt thou not be accepted?" And in the command afterwards to Abraham, "Walk before me, and be thou perfect," was the direction in all our religious acts and walkings with God. A sincere act of the mind and will, looking above and beyond all symbols, extending the soul to a pitch far above the body, and seeing the day of Christ through the veil of the ceremonies, was required by God: and though Moses, by God's order, had instituted a multitude of carnal ordinances, sacrifices, washings, oblations of sensible things, and recommended to the people the diligent observation of those statutes, by the allurements of promises and denouncing of threatenings; as if there were nothing else to be regarded, and the true workings of grace were to be buried under a heap of ceremonies; yet sometimes he doth point them to the inward worship, and, by the command of God, requires of them the "circumcision of the heart" (Deut. x. 16), the turning to God with "all their heart and all their soul" (Deut. xxx. 10): whereby they might recollect, that it was the engagement of the heart and the worship of the Spirit that was most agreeable to God; and that he took not any pleasure in their observance of ceremonies, without true piety within, and the true purity of their thoughts.

Prop. IV. It is, therefore, as much every man's duty to worship God in spirit, as it is their duty to worship him. Worship is so due to him as God, as that he that denies it disowns his deity; and spiritual worship is so due, that he that waives it denies his spirituality. It is a debt of justice we owe to God, to worship him; and it is as much a debt of justice to worship him according to his nature. Worship is nothing else but a rendering to God the honor that is due to him; and, therefore, the right posture of our spirits in it is as much, or more, due, than the material worship in the modes of his own prescribing: that is, grounded both upon his nature and upon his command; this only upon his command, that is perpetually due; whereas, the channel wherein outward worship runs may be dried up, and the river diverted another way; such a worship wherein the mind thinks of God, feels a sense of God, has a spirit consecrated to God, the heart glowing with affections to God; it is else a mocking God with a feather. A rational nature must worship God with that wherein the glory of God doth most sparkle in him. God is most visible in the frame of the soul, it is there his image glitters; he hath given us a jewel as well as a case, and the jewel as well as the case we must return to him; the spirit is God's gift, and must "return to him;"[p] it must return to him in every service morally, as well as it must return to him at last physically. It is not fit we should serve

n Heb. xi. 4.   o Gen. iv. 5.   p Eccles. xii. 7.

our Maker only with that which is the brute in us, and withhold from him that which doth constitute us reasonable creatures; we must give him our bodies, but a "living sacrifice."q If the spirit be absent from God when the body is before him, we present a dead sacrifice; it is morally dead in the duty, though it be naturally alive in the posture and action. It is not an indifferent thing whether we shall worship God or no; nor is it an indifferent thing whether we shall worship him with our spirits or no; as the excellency of man's knowledge consists in knowing things as they are in truth, so the excellency of the will in willing things as they are in goodness. As it is the excellency of man, to know God as God; so it is no less his excellency, as well as his duty to honor God as God. As the obligation we have to the power of God for our being, binds us to a worship of him; so the obligation we have to his bounty for fashioning us according to his own image, binds us to an exercise of that part wherein his image doth consist. God hath "made all things for himself" (Prov. xvi. 4), that is, for the evidence of his own goodness and wisdom; we are therefore to render him a glory according to the excellency of his nature, discovered in the frame of our own. It is as much our sin not to glorify God as God, as not to attempt the glorifying of him at all; it is our sin not to worship God as God, as well as to omit the testifying any respect at all to him. As the Divine nature is the object of worship, so the Divine perfections are to be honored in worship; we do not honor God if we honor him not as he is; we honor him not as a Spirit, if we think him not worthy of the ardors and ravishing admirations of our spirits. If we think the devotions of the body are sufficient for him, we contract him into the condition of our own being; and not only deny him to be a spiritual nature, but dash out all those perfections which he could not be possessed of were he not a Spirit.

Prop. V. The ceremonial law was abolished to promote the spirituality of divine worship. That service was gross, carnal, calculated for an infant and sensitive church. It consisted in rudiments, the circumcision of the flesh, the blood and smoke of sacrifices, the steams of incense, observation of days, distinction of meats, corporal purifications; every leaf of the law is clogged with some rite to be particularly observed by them. The spirituality of worship lay veiled under a thick cloud, that the people could not behold the glory of the gospel, which lay covered under those shadows (2 Cor. iii. 13): "They could not steadfastly look to the end of that which is abolished:" They understood not the glory and spiritual intent of the law, and therefore came short of that spiritual frame in the worship of God, which was their duty. And therefore in opposition to this administration, the worship of God under the gospel is called by our Saviour in the text, a worship in spirit; more spiritual for the matter, more spiritual for the motives, and more spiritual for the manner and frames of worship.

1. This legal service is called flesh in Scripture, in opposition to the gospel, which is called spirit. The ordinances of the law, though of divine institution, are dignified by the apostle with no better a

q Rom. xii. 1.

title than carnal ordinances,[r] and a carnal command:[s] but the gospel is called the ministration of the Spirit, as being attended with a special and spiritual efficacy on the minds of men.[t] And when the degenerate Galatians, after having tasted of the pure streams of the gospel, turned about to drink of the thicker streams of the law, the apostle tells them, that they begun in the spirit and would now be made perfect in the flesh;[u] they would leave the righteousness of faith for a justification by works. The moral law, which is in its own nature spiritual,[x] in regard of the abuse of it, in expectation of justification by the outward works of it, is called flesh: much more may the ceremonial administration, which was never intended to run parallel with the moral, nor had any foundation in nature as the other had. That whole economy consisted in sensible and material things, which only touched the flesh: it is called the letter and the oldness of the letter;[y] as letters, which are but empty sounds of themselves, but put together and formed into words, signify something to the mind of the hearer or reader: an old letter, a thing of no efficacy upon the spirit, but as a law written upon paper. The gospel hath an efficacious spirit attending it, strongly working upon the mind and will, and moulding the soul into a spiritual frame for God, according to the doctrine of the gospel; the one is old and decays, the other is new and increaseth daily. And as the law itself is called flesh, so the observers of it and resters in it are called Israel after the flesh;[z] and the evangelical worshipper is called a Jew after the spirit (Rom. ii. 29). They were Israel after the flesh as born of Jacob, not Israel after the spirit as born of God; and therefore the apostle calls them Israel and not Israel;[a] Israel after a carnal birth, not Israel after a spiritual; Israel in the circumcision of the flesh, not Israel by a regeneration of the heart.

2. The legal ceremonies were not a fit means to bring the heart into a spiritual frame. They had a spiritual intent; the rock and manna prefigured the salvation and spiritual nourishment by the Redeemer.[b] The sacrifices were to point them to the justice of God in the punishment of sin, and the mercy of God in substituting them in their steads, as types of the Redeemer and the ransom by his blood. The circumcision of the flesh was to instruct them in the circumcision of the heart: they were flesh in regard of their matter, weakness and cloudiness, spiritual in regard of their intent and signification; they did instruct, but not efficaciously work strong spiritual affections in the soul of the worshipper. They were weak and beggarly elements;[c] had neither wealth to enrich nor strength to nourish the soul: they could not perfect the comers to them, or put them into a frame agreeable to the nature of God,[d] nor purge the conscience from those dead and dull dispositions which were by nature in them:[e] being carnal they could not have an efficacy to purify the conscience of the offerer and work spiritual effects: had they continued without the exhibition of Christ, they could never have wrought any change in us or pur-

[r] Heb. ix. 10.	[s] Heb. vii. 16.	[t] 2 Cor. iii 8.	[u] Gal. iii. 3.
[x] Rom. vii. 14.	[y] Rom. vii. 6.	[z] 1 Cor. x. 18.	[a] Rom. ix. 6.
[b] 1 Cor. x. 3, 4.	[c] Gal. iv. 9.	[d] Heb. x. l. ix. 9.	[e] Heb. ix. 14.

chased any favor for us.[f] At the best they were but shadows, and came inexpressibly short of the efficacy of that person and state whose shadows they were. The shadow of a man is too weak to perform what the man himself can do, because it wants the life, spirit, and activity of the substance: the whole pomp and scene was suited more to the sensitive than the intellectual nature; and, like pictures, pleased the fancy of children rather than improved their reason. The Jewish state was a state of childhood,[g] and that administration a pedagogy.[h] The law was a schoolmaster fitted for their weak and childish capacity, and could no more spiritualize the heart, than the teachings in a primer-school can enable the mind, and make it fit for affairs of state; and because they could not better the spirit, they were instituted only for a time, as elements delivered to an infant age, which naturally lives a life of sense rather than a life of reason. It was also a servile state, which doth rather debase than elevate the mind; rather carnalize than spiritualize the heart: besides, it is a sense of mercy that both melts and elevates the heart into a spiritual frame: "There is forgiveness with thee, that thou mayest be feared;"[i] and they had, in that state, but some glimmerings of mercy in the daily bloody intimations of justice. There was no sacrifice for some sins, but a cutting off without the least hints of pardon; and in the yearly remembrance of sin there was as much to shiver them with fear, as to possess them with hopes; and such a state which always held them under the conscience of sin, could not produce a free spirit, which was necessary for a worship of God according to his nature.

3. In their use they rather hindered than furthered a spiritual worship. In their own nature they did not tend to the obstructing a spiritual worship, for then they had been contrary to the nature of religion, and the end of God who appointed them; nor did God cover the evangelical doctrine under the clouds of the legal administration, to hinder the people of Israel from perceiving it, but because they were not yet capable to bear the splendor of it, had it been clearly set before them. The shining of the face of Moses was too dazzling for their weak eyes, and therefore there was a necessity of a veil, not for the things themselves, but the "weakness of their eyes."[k] The carnal affections of that people sunk down into the things themselves; stuck in the outward pomp, and pierced not through the veil to the spiritual intent of them; and by the use of them without rational conceptions, they besotted their minds and became senseless of those spiritual motions required of them. Hence came all their expectations of a carnal Messiah; the veil of ceremonies was so thick, and the film upon their eyes so condensed, that they could not look through the veil to the Spirit of Christ; they beheld not the heavenly Canaan for the beauty of the earthly; nor minded the regeneration of the spirit, while they rested upon the purifications of the flesh; the prevalency of sense and sensitive affections diverted their minds from inquiring into

f Burges' Vind. p. 256. g Gal. v. 2. h Gal. iv. 24.
i Psalm cxxx. 4. k 2 Cor. iii. 13, 14.

the intent of them. Sense and matter are often clogs to the mind, and sensible objects are the same often to spiritual motions. Our souls are never more raised than when they are abstracted from the entanglements of them. A pompous worship, made up of many sensible objects, weakens the spirituality of religion. Those that are most zealous for outward, are usually most cold and indifferent in inward observances; and those that overdo in carnal modes, usually underdo in spiritual affections. This was the Jewish state.[1] The nature of the ceremonies being pompous and earthly by their show and beauty, meeting with their weakness and childish affections, filled their eyes with an outward lustre, allured their minds and detained them from seeking things higher and more spiritual; the kernel of those rights lay concealed in a thick shell; the spiritual glory was little seen, and the spiritual sweetness little tasted. Unless the Scripture be diligently searched, it seems to transfer the worship of God from the true faith and the spiritual motions of the heart, and stake it down to outward observances, and the *opus operatum*. Besides, the voice of the law did only declare sacrifices, and invited the worshippers to them with a promise of the atonement of sin, turning away the wrath of God. It never plainly acquainted them that those things were types and shadows of something future; that they were only outward purifications of the flesh; it never plainly told them, at the time of appointing them, that those sacrifices could not abolish sin, and reconcile them to God. Indeed, we see more of them since their death and dissection, in that one Epistle to the Hebrews, than can be discerned in the five books of Moses. Besides, man naturally affects a carnal life, and therefore affects a carnal worship; he designs the gratifying his sense, and would have a religion of the same nature. Most men have no mind to busy their reasons about the things of sense, and are naturally unwilling to raise them up to those things which are allied to the spiritual nature of God; and therefore the more spiritual any ordinance is, the more averse is the heart of man to it. There is a simplicity of the gospel from which our minds are easily corrupted by things that pleasure the sense, as Eve was by the curiosity of her eyes, and the liquorishness of her palate.[m] From this principle hath sprung all the idolatry in the world. The Jews knew they had a God who had delivered them, but they would have a sensible God to go before them;[n] and the papacy at this day is a witness of the truth of this natural corruption.

4. Upon these accounts, therefore, God never testified himself well pleased with that kind of worship. He was not displeased with them, as they were his own institution, and ordained for the representing (though in an obscure manner) the glorious things of the gospel; nor was he offended with those people's observance of them; for, since he had commanded them, it was their duty to perform them, and their sin to neglect them; but he was displeased with them as they were practised by them, with souls as morally carnal in the practices, as the ceremonies were materially carnal

[1] Illyric de Velam. Mosis, p. 221 &c.   [m] 2 Cor. xi. 3.   [n] Exod. xxxii. 1.

in their substance. It was not their disobedience to observe them; but it was a disobedience, and a contempt of the end of the institution to rest upon them; to be warm in them, and cold in morals; they fed upon the bone and neglected the marrow; pleased themselves with the shell, and sought not for the kernel; they joined not with them the internal worship of God; fear of him, with faith in the promised Seed, which lay veiled under those coverings (Hos. vi. 6); "I desired mercy, and not sacrifice; and the knowledge of God more than burnt-offerings;" and therefore he seems sometimes weary of his own institutions, and calls them not his own, but their sacrifices, their feasts (Isa. i. 11, 14): they were his by appointment, theirs by abuse; the institution was from his goodness and condescension, therefore his; the corruption of them was from the vice of their nature, therefore theirs. He often blamed them for their carnality in them; showed his dislike of placing all their religion in them; gives the sacrificers, on that account, no better a title than that of the princes of Sodom and Gomorrah;[o] and compares the sacrifices themselves to the "cutting off a dog's neck," "swine's blood," and "the murder of a man."[p] And indeed God never valued them, or expressed any delight in them; he despised the feasts of the wicked (Amos v. 21); and had no esteem for the material offerings of the godly (Psalm l. 13): "Will I eat the flesh of bulls, or drink the blood of goats?" which he speaks to his saints and people, before he comes to reprove the wicked; which he begins (ver. 16), "But to the wicked, God said," &c. So slightly he esteems them, that he seems to disown them to be any part of his command, when he brought his people out of the land of Egypt (Jer. vii. 21): "I spake not to your fathers, nor commanded them concerning burnt-offerings and sacrifices." He did not value and regard them, in comparison with that inward frame which he had required by the moral law; that being given before the law of ceremonies, obliged them, in the first place, to an observance of those precepts. They seemed to be below the nature of God, and could not of themselves please him. None could in reason persuade themselves that the death of a beast was a proportionable offering for the sin of a man, or ever was intended for the expiation of transgression. In the same rank are all our bodily services under the gospel; a loud voice without spirit, bended bulrushes without inward affections, are no more delightful to God, than the sacrifices of animals; it is but a change of one brute for another of a higher species; a mere brute for that part of man which hath an agreement with brutes; such a service is a mere animal service, and not spiritual.

5. And therefore God never intended that sort of worship to be durable, and had often mentioned the change of it for one more spiritual. It was not good or evil in itself; whatsoever goodness it had was solely derived to it by institution, and therefore it was mutable. It had no conformity with the spiritual nature of God who was to be worshipped, nor with the rational nature of man who was to worship; and therefore he often speaks of taking away the new

[o] Isai. i. 10.   [p] Isai. lxvi. 3.

moons, and feasts, and sacrifices, and all the ceremonial worship, as
things he took no pleasure in, to have a worship more suited to his
excellent nature; but he never speaks of removing the gospel
administration, and the worship prescribed there, as being more
agreeable to the nature and perfections of God, and displaying them
more illustriously to the world.   The apostle tells us, it was to be
" disannulled because of its weakness;"q a determinate time was
fixed for its duration, till the accomplishment of the truth figured
under that pedagogy.r   Some of the modes of that worship being
only typical, must naturally expire and be insignificant in their
use, upon the finishing of that by the Redeemer, which they
did prefigure: and other parts of it, though God suffered them
so long, because of the weakness of the worshipper, yet because it
became not God to be always worshipped in that manner, he would
reject them, and introduce another more spiritual and elevated.
" Incense and a pure offering" should be offered everywhere unto
his name.s   He often told them he would make a " new covenant
by the Messiah," and the old should be rejected;t that the " former
things should not be remembered, and the things of old no more
considered," when he should do " a new thing in the earth."u   Even
the ark of the covenant, the symbol of his presence, and the glory
of the Lord in that nation, should not any more be remembered and
visited;x that the temple and sacrifices should be rejected, and
others established; that the order of the Aaronical priesthood should
be abolished, and that of Melchizedek set up in the stead of it, in
the person of the Messiah, to endure forever;y that Jerusalem
should be changed; a new heaven and earth created; a worship
more conformable to heaven, more advantageous to earth.   God had
proceeded in the removal of some parts of it, before the time of taking down the whole furniture of this house; the pot of manna was
lost; Urim and Thummim ceased; the glory of the temple was
diminished; and the ignorant people wept at the sight of the one,
without raising their faith and hope in the consideration of the
other, which was promised to be filled with a spiritual glory.   And as
soon as ever the gospel was spread in the world, God thundered out
his judgments upon that place in which he had fixed all those legal
observances; so that the Jews, in the letter and flesh, could never
practise the main part of their worship, since they were expelled
from that place where it was only to be celebrated.   It is one thousand six hundred years since they have been deprived of their altar,
which was the foundation of all the Levitical worship, and have
wandered in the world without a sacrifice, a prince, or priest, an
ephod or teraphim.z   And God fully put an end to it in the command he gave to the apostles, and in them to us, in the presence of
Moses and Elias, to hear his Son only (Matt. xvii. 5): " Behold a
voice out of the cloud, which said, This is my beloved Son, in whom
I am well pleased; hear ye him."   And at the death of our Saviour,
testified it to that whole nation and the world, by the rending in
twain the veil of the temple.   The whole frame of that service,

q Heb. vii. 18.   r Gal. iv. 2.   s Mal. i. 11.   t Pascal. Pen. 142.
u Isai. xliii. 18, 19.   x Jer. iii. 16.   y Psalm cx.   z Hos. iii. 4.

which was carnal, and, by reason of the corruption of man, weakened, is nulled; and a spiritual worship is made known to the world, that we might now serve God in a more spiritual manner, and with more spiritual frames.

Prop. VI. The service and worship the gospel settles is spiritual, and the performance of it more spiritual. Spirituality is the genius of the gospel, as carnality was of the law; the gospel is therefore called spirit; we are abstracted from the employments of sense, and brought nearer to a heavenly state. The Jews had angels' bread poured upon them; we have angels' service prescribed to us, the praises of God, communion with God in spirit, through his Son Jesus Christ, and stronger foundations for spiritual affections. It is called a "reasonable service;"[a] it is suited to a rational nature, though it finds no friendship from the corruption of reason. It prescribes a service fit for the reasonable faculties of the soul, and advanceth them while it employs them. The word reasonable may be translated "word-service,"[b] as well as reasonable service; an evangelical service, in opposition to a law service. All evangelical service is reasonable, and all truly reasonable service is evangelical.

The matter of the worship is spiritual; it consists in love of God, faith in God, recourse to his goodness, meditation on him, and communion with him. It lays aside the ceremonial, spiritualizeth the moral. The commands that concerned our duty to God, as well as those that concerned our duty to our neighbor, were reduced by Christ to their spiritual intention. The motives are spiritual; it is a state of more grace, as well as of more truth,[c] supported by spiritual promises, beaming out in spiritual privileges; heaven comes down in it to earth, to spiritualize earth for heaven. The manner of worship is more spiritual; higher flights of the soul, stronger ardors of affection, sincerer aims at his glory; mists are removed from our minds, clogs from the soul, more of love than fear; faith in Christ kindles the affections, and works by them. The assistances to spiritual worship are greater. The Spirit doth not drop, but is plentifully poured out. It doth not light sometimes upon, but dwells in the heart. Christ suited the gospel to a spiritual heart, and the Spirit changeth the carnal heart to make it fit for a spiritual gospel. He blows upon the garden, and causes the spices to flow forth; and often makes the soul in worship like the chariots of Aminadab, in a quick and nimble motion. Our blessed Lord and Saviour, by his death, discovered to us the nature of God; and after his ascension sent his Spirit to fit us for the worship of God, and converse with him. One spiritual evangelical believing breath is more delightful to God than millions of altars made up of the richest pearls, and smoking with the costliest oblations, because it is spiritual; and a mite of spirit is of more worth than the greatest weight of flesh: one holy angel is more excellent than a whole world of mere bodies.

Prop. VII. Yet the worship of God with our bodies is not to be rejected upon the account that God requires a spiritual worship. Though we must perform the weightier duties of the law, yet we are

---

[a] Rom. xii. 1. [b] Vide Hammond, *in loc.* [c] John i. 17.

not to omit and leave undone the lighter precepts, since both the *magnalia* and *minutula legis*, the greater and the lesser duties of the law, have the stamp of divine authority upon them. As God under the ceremonial law did not command the worship of the body and the observation of outward rites without the engagement of the spirit, so neither doth he command that of the spirit without the peculiar attendance of the body. The Schwelksendians denied bodily worship; and the indecent postures of many in public attendance intimate no great care either of composing their bodies or spirits. A morally discomposed body intimates a tainted heart. Our bodies as well as our spirits are to be presented to God.[d] Our bodies in lieu of the sacrifices of beasts, as in the Judaical institutions; body for the whole man; a living sacrifice, not to be slain, as the beasts were, but living a new life, in a holy posture, with crucified affections. This is the inference the apostle makes of the privileges of justification, adoption, co-heirship with Christ, which he had before discoursed of; privileges conferred upon the person, and not upon a part of man.

1. Bodily worship is due to God. He hath a right to an adoration by our bodies, as they are his by creation; his right is not diminished, but increased, by the blessing of redemption: (1 Cor. vi. 20) "For you are bought with a price; therefore glorify God in your bodies and your spirits, which are God's." The body, as well as the spirit, is redeemed, since our Saviour suffered crucifixion in his body, as well as agonies in his soul. Body is not taken here for the whole man, as it may be in Rom xii.; but for the material part of our nature, it being distinguished from the spirit. If we are to render to God an obedience with our bodies, we are to render him such acts of worship with our bodies as they are capable of. As God is the Father of spirits, so he is the God of all flesh; therefore the flesh he hath framed of the earth, as well as the noble portion he hath breathed into us, cannot be denied him without a palpable injustice. The service of the body we must not deny to God, unless we will deny him to be the author of it, and the exercise of his providential care about it. The mercies of God are renewed every day upon our bodies as well as our souls, and, therefore, they ought to express a fealty to God for his bounty every day. "Both are from God; both should be for God. Man consists of body and soul; the service of man is the service of both. The body is to be sanctified as well as the soul; and, therefore, to be offered to God as well as the soul. Both are to be glorified, both are to glorify. As our Saviour's divinity was manifested in his body, so should our spirituality in ours. To give God the service of the body and not of the soul, is hypocrisy; to give God the service of the spirit and not of the body, is sacrilege; to give him neither, atheism."[e] If the only part of man that is visible were exempted from the service of God, there could be no visible testimonies of piety given upon any occasion. Since not a moiety of man, but the whole is God's creature, he ought to pay a homage with the whole, and not only with a moiety of himself.

<hr/>

d Rom. xii. 1.   e Sherman's Greek in the Temple, pp. 61, 62.

2. Worship in societies is due to God, but this cannot be without some bodily expressions. The law of nature doth as much direct men to combine together in public societies for the acknowledgment of God, as in civil communities for self-preservation and order; and a notice of a society for religion is more ancient than the mention of civil associations for politic government (Gen. iv. 26): "Then began men to call upon the name of the Lord," viz., in the time of Seth. No question but Adam had worshipped God before, as well as Abel, and a family religion had been preserved; but, as mankind increased in distinct families, they knit together in companies to solemnize the worship of God.[f] Hence, as some think, those that incorporated together for such ends, were called the " sons of God ;" sons by profession, though not sons by adoption ; as those of Corinth were saints by profession, though in such a corrupted church they could not be all so by regeneration ; yet saints, as being of a Christian society, and calling upon the name of Christ, that is, worshipping God in Christ, though they might not be all saints in spirit and practice. So Cain and Abel met together to worship (Gen. iv. 3) " at the end of the days," at a set time. God settled a public worship among the Jews, instituted synagogues for their convening together, whence called the "synagogues of God."[g] The Sabbath was instituted to acknowledge God a common benefactor. Public worship keeps up the memorials of God in a world prone to atheism, and a sense of God in a heart prone to forgetfulness. The angels sung in company, not singly, at the birth of Christ,[h] and praised God not only with a simple elevation of their spiritual nature, but audibly, by forming a voice in the air. Affections are more lively, spirits more raised in public than private ; God will credit his own ordinance. Fire increaseth by laying together many coals on one place ; so is devotion inflamed by the union of many hearts, and by a joint presence ; nor can the approach of the last day of judgment, or particular judgments upon a nation, give a writ of ease from such assemblies. (Heb. x. 25): " Not forsaking the assembling ourselves together; but so much the more as you see the day approaching." Whether it be understood of the day of judgment, or the day of the Jewish destruction and the Christian persecution, the apostle uses it as an argument to quicken them to the observance, not to encourage them to a neglect. Since, therefore, natural light informs us, and divine institution commands us, publicly to acknowledge ourselves the servants of God, it implies the service of the body. Such acknowledgments cannot be without visible testimonies, and outward exercises of devotion, as well as inward affections. This promotes God's honor, checks others' profaneness, allures men to the same expressions of duty ; and though there may be hypocrisy and an outward garb without an inward frame, yet better a moiety of worship than none at all ; better acknowledge God's right in one than disown it in both.

3. Jesus Christ, the most spiritual worshipper, worshipped God with his body. He prayed orally, and kneeled, " Father, if it be

---

[f] Stillingfleet's Irenicum, c. 1. § I. p. 23. [g] Psalm lxxiv. 8.
[h] Luke ii. 13.

thy will,"[i] &c.　He blessed with his mouth, "Father, I thank thee."[k] He lifted up his eyes as well as elevated his spirit, when he praised his Father for mercy received, or begged for the blessings his disciples wanted.[l]　The strength of the spirit must have vent at the outward members.　The holy men of God have employed the body in significant expressions of worship; Abraham in falling on his face, Paul in kneeling, employing their tongues, lifting up their hands.　Though Jacob was bed-rid, yet he would not worship God without some devout expression of reverence; it is in one place "leaning upon his staff;"[m] in another, "bowing himself upon his bed's head."[n]　The reason of the diversity is in the Hebrew word, which, without vowels, may be read *mittah*, a bed, or *matteh*, a staff; however, both signify a testimony of adoration by a reverent gesture of the body.　Indeed, in angels and separated souls, a worship is performed purely by the spirit; but while the soul is in conjunction with the body, it can hardly perform a serious act of worship without some tincture upon the outward man and reverential composure of the body.　Fire cannot be in the clothes but it will be felt by the members, nor flames be pent up in the soul without bursting out in the body.　The heart can no more restrain itself from breaking out, than Joseph could inclose his affections without expressing them in tears to his brethren.[o]　"We believe, and therefore speak."[p]

To conclude: God hath appointed some parts of worship which cannot be performed without the body, as sacraments; we have need of them because we are not wholly spiritual and incorporeal creatures.　The religion which consists in externals only is not for an intellectual nature; a worship purely intellectual is too sublime for a nature allied to sense, and depending much upon it.　The christian mode of worship is proportioned to both; it makes the sense to assist the mind, and elevates the spirit above the sense.　Bodily worship helps the spiritual: the members of the body reflect back upon the heart, the voice bars distractions, the tongue sets the heart on fire in good as well as in evil.　It is as much against the light of nature to serve God without external significations, as to serve him only with them without the intention of the mind.　As the invisible God declares himself to men by visible works and signs, so should we declare our invisible frames by visible expressions.　God hath given us a soul and body in conjunction; and we are to serve him in the same manner he hath framed us.

II.　The second thing I am to show is, what spiritual worship is. In general, the whole spirit is to be employed; the name of God is not sanctified but by the engagement of our souls.　Worship is an act of the understanding, applying itself to the knowledge of the excellency of God and actual thoughts of his majesty; recognizing him as the supreme Lord and Governor of the world, which is natural knowledge; beholding the glory of his attributes in the Redeemer, which is evangelical knowledge.　This is the sole act of the spirit of man.　The same reason is for all our worship as for our thanksgiving.　This must be done with understanding: (Psalm

i Luke xxii. 41, 42.　　k Matt. xi. 26.　　l John xi. 41; xii. 1.　　m Heb. xi. 21.
n Gen xlvii. 31.　　　o Gen. xiv. 1, 2.　　p 2 Cor. iv. 13.

xlvii. 7) "Sing ye praise with understanding;" with a knowledge and sense of his greatness, goodness, and wisdom. It is also an act of the will, whereby the soul adores and reverences his majesty, is ravished with his amiableness, embraceth his goodness, enters itself into an intimate communion with this most lovely object, and pitcheth all his affections upon him. We must worship God understandingly; it is not else a reasonable service. The nature of God and the law of God abhor a blind offering; we must worship him heartily, else we offer him a dead sacrifice. A reasonable service is that wherein the mind doth truly act something with God. All spiritual acts must be acts of reason, otherwise they are not human acts, because they want that principle which is constitutive of man, and doth difference him from other creatures. Acts done only by sense are the acts of a brute; acts done by reason are the acts of a man. That which is only an act of sense cannot be an act of religion. The sense, without the conduct of reason, is not the subject of religious acts; for then beasts were capable of religion as well as men. There cannot be religion where there is not reason; and there cannot be the exercise of religion where there is not an exercise of the rational faculties; nothing can be a christian act that is not a human act. Besides, all worship must be for some end; the worship of God must be for God. It is by the exercise of our rational faculties that we only can intend an end. An ignorant and carnal worship is a brutish worship. Particularly,

1. Spiritual worship is a worship from a spiritual nature. Not only physically spiritual, so our souls are in their frame; but morally spiritual, by a renewing principle. The heart must be first cast into the mould of the gospel, before it can perform a worship required by the gospel. Adam living in Paradise might perform a spiritual worship; but Adam fallen from his rectitude could not: we, being heirs of his nature, are heirs of his impotence. Restoration to a spiritual life must precede any act of spiritual worship. As no work can be good, so no worship can be spiritual, till we are created in Christ.[q] Christ is our life.[r] As no natural action can be performed without life in the root or heart, so no spiritual act without Christ in the soul. Our being in Christ is as necessary to every spiritual act as the union of our soul with our body is necessary to natural action. Nothing can exceed the limits of its nature; for then it should exceed itself in acting, and do that which it hath no principle to do. A beast cannot act like a man, without partaking of the nature of a man; nor a man act like an angel, without partaking of the angelical nature. How can we perform spiritual acts without a spiritual principle? Whatsoever worship proceeds from the corrupted nature, cannot deserve the title of spiritual worship, because it springs not from a spiritual habit. If those that are evil cannot speak good things, those that are carnal cannot offer a spiritual service. Poison is the fruit of a viper's nature (Matt. xii. 34): "O generation of vipers, how can you, being evil, speak good things? for out of the abundance of the heart the mouth speaks." As the root is, so is the fruit. If the soul be habitually carnal,

[q] Eph. ii. 10. [r] Col. iii. 4.

the worship cannot be actually spiritual. There may be an intention of spirit, but there is no spiritual principle as a root of that intention. A heart may be sensibly united with a duty, when it is not spiritually united with Christ in it. Carnal motives and carnal ends may fix the mind in an act of worship, as the sense of some pressing affliction may enlarge a man's mind in prayer. Whatsoever is agreeable to the nature of God must have a stamp of Christ upon it; a stamp of his grace in performance, as well as of his mediation in the acceptance. The apostle lived not, but Christ lived in him;[s] the soul worships not, but Christ in him. Not that Christ performs the act of worship, but enables us spiritually to worship, after he enables us spiritually to live. As God counts not any soul living but in Christ, so he counts not any a spiritual worshipper but in Christ. The goodness and fatness of the fruit come from the fatness of the olive wherein we are engrafted. We must find healing in Christ's wings, before God can find spirituality in our services. All worship issuing from a dead nature is but a dead service. A living action cannot be performed, without being knit to a living root.

2. Spiritual worship is done by the influence and with the assistance of the Spirit of God. A heart may be spiritual, when a particular act of worship may not be spiritual. The Spirit may dwell in the heart, when he may suspend his influence on the act. Our worship is then spiritual, when the fire that kindles our affections comes from heaven, as that fire upon the altar wherewith the sacrifices were consumed. God tastes a sweetness in no service, but as it is dressed up by the hand of the Mediator, and hath the air of his own Spirit in it; they are but natural acts, without a supernatural assistance; without an actual influence, we cannot act from spiritual motives, nor for spiritual ends, nor in a spiritual manner. We cannot mortify a lust without the Spirit,[t] nor quicken a service without the Spirit. Whatsoever corruption is killed, is slain by his power; whatsoever duty is spiritualized, is refined by his breath. He quickens our dead bodies in our resurrection;[u] he renews our dead souls in our regeneration; he quickens our carnal services in our adorations; the choicest acts of worship are but infirmities without his auxiliary help.[x] We are logs, unable to move ourselves, till he raise our faculties to a pitch agreeable to God; puts his hand to the duty, and lifts that up and us with it. Never any great act was performed by the apostles to God, or for God; but they are said to be filled with the Holy Ghost. Christ could not have been conceived immaculate as that "holy thing," without the Spirit's overshadowing the Virgin; nor any spiritual act conceived in our heart, without the Spirit's moving upon us, to bring forth a living religion from us. The acts of worship are said to be in the Spirit, "supplication in the Spirit;"[y] not only with the strength and affection of our own spirits, but with the mighty operation of the Holy Ghost, if Jude may be the interpreter;[z] the Holy Ghost exciting us, impelling us, and firing our souls by his divine flame; raising up the affections, and making the

---

| [s] Gal. ii. 20. | [t] Rom. viii. 13. | [u] Rom. viii. 11. |
| [x] Rom. viii. 26. | [y] Eph. vi. 18. | [z] Jude 20. |

soul cry with a holy importunity, Abba, Father. To render our worship spiritual, we should, before every engagement in it, implore the actual presence of the Spirit, without which we are not able to send forth one spiritual breath or groan; but be wind-bound like a ship without a gale, and our worship be no better than carnal. How doth the spouse solicit the Spirit with an "Awake, O north wind, and come, thou south wind,"[a] &c.

3. Spiritual worship is done with sincerity. When the heart stands right to God, and the soul performs what it pretends to perform; when we serve God with our spirits, as the apostle (Rom. i. 9), "God is my witness, whom I serve with my spirit in the gospel of his Son:" this is not meant of the Holy Ghost; for the apostle would never have called the Spirit of God his own spirit; but with my spirit, that is, a sincere frame of heart. A carnal worship, whether under the law or gospel, is, when we are busied about external rites, without an inward compliance of soul. God demands the heart; "My son, give me thy heart;"[b] not give me thy tongue, or thy lips, or thy hands; these may be given without the heart, but the heart can never be bestowed without these as its attendants. A heap of services can be no more welcome to God, without our spirits, than all Jacob's sons could be to Joseph, without the Benjamin he desired to see. God is not taken with the cabinet, but the jewel; he first respected Abel's faith and sincerity, and then his sacrifice; he disrespected Cain's infidelity and hypocrisy, and then his offering. For this cause he rejected the offerings of the Jews, the prayers of the Pharisees, and the alms of Ananias and Sapphira, because their hearts and their duties were at a distance from one another. In all spiritual sacrifices, our spirits are God's portion. Under the law, the reins were to be consumed by the fire on the altar, because the secret intentions of the heart were signified by them (Psalm vii. 9), "The Lord trieth the heart and the reins." It was an ill omen among the heathen, if a victim wanted a heart. The widow's mites, with her heart in them, were more esteemed than the richer offerings without it.[c] Not the quantity of service, but the will in it, is of account with this infinite Spirit. All that was to be brought for the framing of the tabernacle was to be offered "willingly with the heart."[d] The more of will, the more of spirituality and acceptableness to God (Psalm cxix. 108), "Accept the free-will offering of my lips." Sincerity is the salt which seasons every sacrifice. The heart is most like to the object of worship; the heart in the body is the spring of all vital actions; and a spiritual soul is the spring of all spiritual actions. How can we imagine God can delight in the mere service of the body, any more than we can delight in converse with a carcass? Without the heart it is no worship; it is a stage play; an acting a part without being that person really which is acted by us: a hypocrite, in the notion of the word, is a stage-player. We may as well say a man may believe with his body, as worship God only with his body. Faith is a great ingredient in worship; and it is "with the heart man believes unto righteousness."[e] We may be truly said to worship God,

---

[a] Cant. iv. 16.

[c] Moulin. Sermons, Decad. 4. Sermon IV. p. 80.

[b] Prov. xxiii. 26.

[d] Exod. xxv. 7.

[e] Rom. x. 10.

though we want perfection; but we cannot be said to worship him, if we want sincerity; a statue upon a tomb, with eyes and hands lifted up, offers as good and true a service; it wants only a voice, the gestures and postures are the same; nay, the service is better; it is not a mockery; it represents all that it can be framed to; but to worship without our spirits, is a presenting God with a picture, an echo, voice, and nothing else; a compliment; a mere lie; a " compassing him about with lies."[f] Without the heart the tongue is a liar; and the greatest zeal a dissembling with him. To present the spirit, is to present with that which can never naturally die; to present him only the body, is to present him that which is every day crumbling to dust, and will at last lie rotting in the grave; to offer him a few rags, easily torn; a skin for a sacrifice, a thing unworthy the majesty of God; a fixed eye and elevated hands, with a sleepy heart and earthly soul, are pitiful things for an ever-blessed and glorious Spirit: nay, it is so far from being spiritual, that it is blasphemy; to pretend to be a Jew outwardly, without being so inwardly, is, in the judgment of Christ, to blaspheme.[g] And is not the same title to be given with as much reason to those that pretend a worship and perform none? Such a one is not a spiritual worshipper, but a blaspheming devil in Samuel's mantle.

4. Spiritual worship is performed with an unitedness of heart. The heart is not only now and then with God, but "united to fear or worship his name."[h] A spiritual duty must have the engagement of the spirit, and the thoughts tied up to the spiritual object. The union of all the parts of the heart together with the body is the life of the body; and the moral union of our hearts is the life of any duty. A heart quickly flitting from God makes not God his treasure; he slights the worship, and therein affronts the object of worship. All our thoughts ought to be ravished with God; bound up in him as in a bundle of life; but when we start from him to gaze after every feather, and run after every bubble, we disown a full and affecting excellency, and a satisfying sweetness in him. When our thoughts run from God, it is a testimony we have no spiritual affection to God; affection would stake down the thoughts to the object affected; it is but a mouth love, as the prophet praiseth it;[i] but their hearts go "after their covetousness;" covetous objects pipe, and the heart danceth after them; and thoughts of God are shifted off to receive a multitude of other imaginations; the heart and the service staid awhile together, and then took leave of one another. The Psalmist[k] still found his heart with God when he awaked; still with God in spiritual affections and fixed meditations. A carnal heart is seldom with God, either in or out of worship; if God should knock at the heart in any duty, it would be found not at home, but straying abroad. Our worship is spiritual when the door of the heart is shut against all intruders, as our Saviour commands in closet-duties.[l] It was not his meaning to command the shutting the closet-door, and leave the heart-door open for every thought that would be apt to haunt us. Worldly affections are to be laid aside if we would have

f Hos. xi. 12.   g Rev. ii. 9.   h Psalm lxxxvi. 11.
i Ezek. xxxiii. 31.   k Psalm xxxix. 18.   l Matt. vi. 6.

our worship spiritual; this was meant by the Jewish custom of wiping or washing off the dust of their feet before their entrance into the temple, and of not bringing money in their girdles. To be spiritual in worship, is to have our souls gathered and bound up wholly in themselves, and offered to God. Our loins must be girt, as the fashion was in the eastern countries, where they wore long garments, that they might not waver with the wind, and be blown between their legs, to obstruct them in their travel: our faculties must not hang loose about us. He is a carnal worshipper that gives God but a piece of his heart, as well as he that denies him the whole of it; that hath some thoughts pitched upon God in worship, and as many willingly upon the world. David sought God, not with a moiety of his heart, but with his "whole heart;" with his entire frame;[m] he brought not half his heart, and left the other in the possession of another master. It was a good lesson Pythagoras gave his scholars,[n] "Not to make the observance of God a work by the bye." If those guests be invited, or entertained kindly, or if they come unexpected, the spirituality of that worship is lost; the soul kicks down what it wrought before: but if they be brow-beaten by us, and our grief rather than our pleasure, they divert our spiritual intention from the work in hand, but hinder not God's acceptance of it as spiritual, because they are not the acts of our will, but offences to our wills.

5. Spiritual worship is performed with a spiritual activity, and sensibleness of God; with an active understanding to meditate on his excellency, and an active will to embrace him when he drops upon the soul. If we understand the amiableness of God, our affections will be ravished; if we understand the immensity of his goodness, our spirits will be enlarged. We are to act with the highest intention suitable to the greatness of that God with whom we have to do (Psalm cl. 2): "Praise him according to his excellent greatness;" not that we can worship him equally, but in some proportion the frame of the heart is to be suited to the excellency of the object; our spiritual strength is to be put out to the utmost, as creatures that act naturally do. The sun shines, and the fire burns to the utmost of their natural power. This is so necessary, that David, a spiritual worshipper, prays for it before he sets upon acts of adoration (Psalm lxxx. 18): "Quicken us, that we may call upon thy name;" as he was loth to have a drowsy faculty, he was loth to have a drowsy instrument, and would willingly have them as lively as himself (Psalm lvii. 8): "Awake up, my glory; awake, psaltery and harp; I myself will awake early." How would this divine soul screw himself up to God, and be turned into nothing but a holy flame! Our souls must be boiling hot when we serve the Lord.[o] The heart doth no less burn when it spiritually comes to God, than when God doth spiritually approach to it;[p] a Nabal's heart, one as cold as a stone, cannot offer up a spiritual service. Whatsoever is enjoined us as our duty, ought to be performed with the greatest intenseness of our spirit. As it

---

[m] Psalm cxix. 10.
[n] Οὐ γὰρ πάρεργον δεῖ ποεῖσθαι τὸν Θεόν. Iamblic. lib. i. c. 518. p. 87.
[o] Rom. xii. 11, ζέοντες.   [p] Luke xxiv. 32.

is our dnty to pray, so it is our duty to pray with the most fervent importunity. It is our duty to love God, but with the purest and most sublime affections; every command of God requires the whole strength of the creature to be employed in it. That love to God wherein all our duty to God is summed up, is to be with all our strength, with all our might, &c.q Though in the covenant of grace he hath mitigated the severity of the law, and requires not from us such an elevation of our affections as was possible in the state of innocence, yet God requires of us the utmost moral industry to raise our affections to a pitch, at least equal to what they are in other things. What strength of affection we naturally have, ought to be as much and more excited in acts of worship, than upon other occasions and our ordinary works. As there was an inactivity of soul in worship, and a quickness to sin, when sin had the dominion; so when the soul is spiritualized, the temper is changed; there is an inactivity to sin, and an ardor in duty; the more the soul is "dead to sin," the more it is "alive to God,"r and the more lively too in all that concerns God and his honor; for grace being a new strength added to our natural, determines the affections to new objects, and excites them to a greater vigor. And as the hatred of sin is more sharp, the love to everything that destroys the dominion of it is more strong; and acts of worship may be reckoned as the chiefest batteries against the power of this inbred enemy. When the Spirit is in the soul, like the rivers of waters flowing out of the belly, the soul hath the activity of a river, and makes haste to be swallowed up in God, as the streams of the river in the sea. Christ makes his people "kings and priests to God;"s first kings, then priests; gives first a royal temper of heart, that they may offer spiritual sacrifices as priests, kings and priests to God, acting with a magnificent spirit in all their motions to him. We cannot be spiritual priests, till we be spiritual kings. The Spirit appeared in the likeness of fire, and where he resides, communicates, like fire, purity and activity. Dulness is against the light of nature. I do not remember that the heathen ever offered a snail to any of their false deities, nor an ass, but to Priapus, their unclean idol; but the Persians sacrificed to the sun a horse, a swift and generous creature. God provided against those in the law, commanding an ass' firstling, the offspring of a sluggish creature, to be redeemed, or his neck broke, but by no means to be offered to him.t God is a Spirit infinitely active, and therefore frozen and benumbed frames are unsuitable to him; he "rides upon a cherub" and flies; he comes upon the "wings of the wind;" he rides upon a "swift cloud;"u and therefore demands of us not a dull reason, but an active spirit. God is a living God, and therefore must have a lively service. Christ is life, and slothful adorations are not fit to be offered up in the name of life. The worship of God is called wrestling in Scripture; and Paul was a striver in the service of his Master,x "in an agony."y Angels worshipped God spiritually with their wings on; and when God commands them to worship Christ, the next Scripture quoted is, that he makes them

q Lady Falkland's Life, p. 130.   r Rom. vi. 11.   s Rev. i. 6.
t Exod. xiii. 13.   u Isaiah xix. 1.   x Col. i. 29.   y ἀγωνιζόμενος.

"flames of fire."[z] If it be thus, how may we charge ourselves? What Paul said of the sensual widow,[a] that she is "dead while she lives," we may say often of ourselves, we are dead while we worship. Our hearts are in duty as the Jews were in deliverances, as those "in a dream;"[b] by which unexpectedness God showed the greatness of his care and mercy; and we attend him as men in a dream, whereby we discover our negligence and folly. This activity doth not consist in outward acts; the body may be hot, and the heart may be faint, but in an inward stirring, meltings, flights. In the highest raptures the body is most insensible. Strong spiritual affections are abstracted from outward sense.

6. Spiritual worship is performed with acting spiritual habits. When all the living springs of grace are opened, as the fountains of the deep were in the deluge, the soul and all that is within it, all the spiritual impresses of God upon it, erect themselves to "bless his holy name."[c] This is necessary to make a worship spiritual. As natural agents are determined to act suitable to their proper nature, so rational agents are to act conformable to a rational being. When there is a conformity between the act and the nature whence it flows, it is a good act in its kind; if it be rational, it is a good rational act, because suitable to its principle; as a man endowed with reason must act suitable to that endowment, and exercise his reason in his acting; so a Christian endued with grace, must act suitable to that nature, and exercise his grace in his acting. Acts done by a natural inclination are no more human acts than the natural acts of a beast may be said to be human; though they are the acts of a man, as he is the efficient cause of them, yet they are not human acts, because they arise not from that principle of reason which denominates him a man. So acts of worship performed by a bare exercise of reason, are not christian and spiritual acts, because they come not from the principle which constitutes him a Christian; reason is not the principle, for then all rational creatures would be Christians. They ought, therefore, to be acts of a higher principle, exercises of that grace whereby Christians are what they are; not but that rational acts in worship are due to God, for worship is due from us as men, and we are settled in that rank of being by our reason. Grace doth not exclude reason, but ennobles it, and calls it up to another form; but we must not rest in a bare rational worship, but exert that principle whereby we are Christians. To worship God with our reason, is to worship him as men; to worship God with our grace is to worship him as Christians, and so spiritually; but to worship him only with our bodies, is no better than brutes. Our desires of the word are to issue from the regenerate principle (1 Pet. ii. 2): "As new-born babes desire the sincere milk of the word;" it seems to be not a comparison, but a restriction. All worship must have the same spring, and be the exercise of that principle, otherwise we can have no communion with God. Friends that have the same habitual dispositions, have a fundamental fitness for an agreeable converse with one another; but if the temper wherein their likeness consists be languishing, and the string out of tune, there is not an actual fitness;

[z] Heb. i. 7.   [a] 1 Tim. v. 6.   [b] Psalm cxxvi. 1.   [x] Psalm ciii. 1.

and the present indisposition breaks the converse, and renders the company troublesome. Though we may have the habitual graces which compose in us a resemblance to God, yet for want of acting those suitable dispositions, we render ourselves unfit for his converse, and make the worship, which is fundamentally spiritual, to become actually carnal. As the will cannot naturally ,act to any object but by the exercise of its affections, so the heart cannot spiritually act towards God but by the exercise of graces. This is God's music (Eph. v. 19): "Singing and making melody to God in your hearts." Singing and all other acts of worship are outward, but the spiritual melody is "by grace in the heart" (Col. iii. 16): this renders it a spiritual worship; for it is an effect of the fulness of the spirit in the soul, as (ver. 19), "But be filled with the Spirit." The over-flowing of the Spirit in the heart, setting the soul of a believer thus on work to make a spiritual melody to God, shows that something higher than bare reason is put in tune in the heart. Then is the fruit of the garden pleasant to Christ, when the Holy Spirit, "the north and south wind, blow upon the spices," and strike out the fra-grancy of them.[d] Since God is the Author of graces, and bestows them to have a glory from them, they are best employed about him and his service. It is fit he should have the cream of his own gifts. Without the exercise of grace we perform but a work of nature, and offer him a few dry bones without marrow. The whole set of graces must be one way or other exercised. If any treble be want-ing in a lute, there will be great defect in the music. If any one spirital string be dull, the spiritual harmony of worship will be spoiled. And therefore;

1. Faith must be acted in worship; a confidence in God. A natural worship cannot be performed without a natural confidence in the goodness of God; whosoever comes to him, must regard him as a rewarder, and a faithful Creator.[e] A spiritual worship cannot be performed without an evangelical confidence in him as a gracious Redeemer. To think him a tyrant, meditating revenge, damps the soul; to regard him as a gracious king, full of tender bowels, spirits the affections to him. The mercy of God is the proper object of trust (Psalm xxxiii. 18): "The eye of the Lord is upon them that fear him, upon them that hope in his mercy." The worship of God in the Old Testament is most described by fear; in the New Testa-ment by faith. Fear, or the worship of God, and hope in his mercy are linked together; when they go hand in hand, the accepting eye of God is upon us; when we do not trust, we do not worship. Those of Judah had the temple-worship among them, especially in Josiah's time (Zeph. iii. 2), the time of that prophecy; yet it was accounted no worship, because no trust in the worshippers. Interest in God cannot be improved without an exercise of faith. The gospel-worship is prophesied of, to be a confidence in God, as in a husband more than in a lord (Hos. ii. 16): "Thou shalt call me Ishi, and shalt call me no more Baali." "Thou shalt call me;" that is, thou shalt wor-ship me, worship being often comprehended under invocation. More confidence is to be exercised in a husband or father, than in a lord

or master. If a man have not faith, he is without Christ; and though a man be in Christ by the habit of faith, he performs a duty out of Christ without an act of faith: without the habit of faith, our persons are out of Christ; and without the exercise of faith, the duties are out of Christ. As the want of faith in a person is the death of the soul, so the want of faith in a service is the death of the offering. Though a man were at the cost of an ox, yet to kill it without bringing it to the "door of the tabernacle," was not a sacrifice, but a murder (Lev. xvii. 3, 4). The tabernacle was a type of Christ, and a look to him is necessary in every spiritual sacrifice. As there must be faith to make any act an act of obedience, so there must be faith to make any act of worship spiritual. That service is not spiritual that is not vital; and it cannot be vital without the exercise of a vital principle; all spiritual life is "hid in Christ," and drawn from him by faith (Gal. ii. 20). Faith, as it hath relation to Christ, makes every act of worship a living act, and, consequently, a spiritual act. Habitual unbelief cuts us off from the body of Christ (Rom. xi. 20): "Because of unbelief they were broken off;" and a want of actuated belief breaks us off from a present communion with Christ in spirit. As unbelief in us hinders Christ from doing any mighty work, so unbelief in us hinders us from doing any mighty spiritual duty; so that the exercise of faith, and a confidence in God, is necessary to every duty.

2. Love must be acted to render a worship spiritual. Though God commanded love in the Old Testament, yet the manner of giving the law bespoke more of fear than love. The dispensation of the law was with fire, thunder, &c., proper to raise horror, and benumb the spirit; which effect it had upon the Israelites, when they desired that God would speak no more to them. Grace is the genius of the gospel, proper to excite the affection of love. The law was given by the "disposition of angels," with signs to amaze; the gospel was ushered in with the "songs of angels," composed of peace and good-will, calculated to ravish the soul. Instead of the terrible voice of the law, "Do this and live," the comfortable voice of the gospel is, "Grace, grace!" Upon this account the principle of the Old Testament was fear, and the worship often expressed by the fear of God. The principle of the New Testament is love. The Mount Sinai gendereth to bondage (Gal. iv. 44); Mount Sion, from whence the gospel or evangelical law goes forth, gendereth to liberty; and therefore the "spirit of bondage unto fear," as the property of the law, is opposed to the state of adoption, the principle of love, as the property of the gospel (Rom. viii. 15); and therefore the worship of God under the gospel, or New Testament, is oftener expressed by love than fear, as proceeding from higher principles, and acting nobler passions. In this state we are to serve him without fear (Luke i. 74); without a bondage fear; not without a fear of unworthy treating him; with a "fear of his goodness" as it is prophesied of (Hos. ix. 5). Goodness is not the object of terror, but reverence; God, in the law, had more the garb of a judge; in the gospel, of a father; the name of a father is sweeter and bespeaks more of affection. As their services were with a feeling of the thunders of the law in their con-

sciences, so is our worship to be with a sense of gospel grace in our spirits; spiritual worship is that, therefore, which is exercised with a spiritual and heavenly affection, proper to the gospel. The heart should be enlarged according to the liberty the gospel gives of drawing near to God as a father. As he gives us the nobler relation of children, we are to act the nobler qualities of children. Love should act according to its nature, which is desired of union; desire of a moral union by affections, as well as a mystical union by faith; as flame aspires to reach flame, and become one with it. In every act of worship we should endeavor to be united to God, and become one spirit with him. This grace doth spiritualize worship; in that one word, love, God hath wrapt up all the devotion he requires of us; it is the total sum of the first table, "Thou shalt love the Lord thy God:" it is to be acted in everything we do; but in worship our hearts should more solemnly rise up and acknowledge him amiable and lovely, since the law is stripped of its cursing power, and made sweet in the blood of the Redeemer. Love is a thing acceptable of itself, but nothing acceptable without it; the gifts of one man to another are spiritualized by it. We would not value a present without the affection of the donor; every man would lay claim to the love of others, though he would not to their possessions. Love is God's right in every service, and the noblest thing we can bestow upon him in our adorations of him. God's gifts to us are not so estimable without his love; nor our services valuable by him without the exercise of a choice affection. Hezekiah regarded not his deliverance without the love of the Deliverer; "In love to my soul thou hast delivered me" (Isa. xxxviii. 17). So doth God say, In love to my honor thou hast worshipped me: so that love must be acted, to render our worship spiritual.

3. A spiritual sensibleness of our own weakness is necessary to make our worship spiritual. Affections to God cannot be without relentings in ourselves. When the eye is spiritually fixed upon a spiritual God, the heart will mourn that the worship is no more spiritually suitable. The more we act love upon God, as amiable and gracious, the more we should exercise grief in ourselves, as we are vile and offending. Spiritual worship is a melting worship, as well as an elevating worship; it exalts God, and debaseth the creature. The Publican was more spiritual in his humble address to God, when the Pharisee was wholly carnal with his swelling language. A spiritual love in worship will make us grieve that we have given him so little, and could give him no more. It is a part of spiritual duty to bewail our carnality mixed with it; as we receive mercies spiritually, when we receive them with a sense of God's goodness and our own vileness; in the same manner we render a spiritual worship.

4. Spiritual desires for God render the service spiritual; when the soul "follows hard after him" (Psalm lxiii. 8); pursues after God as a God of infinite and communicative goodness, with sighs and groans unutterable. A spiritual soul seems to be transformed into hunger and thirst, and becomes nothing but desire. A carnal worshipper is taken with the beauty and magnificence of the temple; a spiritual worshipper desires to see the glory of God in the sanctuary (Psalm

lxiii. 2), he pants after God: as he came to worship, to find God, he boils up in desires for God, and is loth to go from it without God, "the living God" (Psalm xlii. 2). He would see the Urim and the Thummim; the unusual sparkling of the stones upon the high-priest's breast-plate. That deserves not the title of spiritual worship, when the soul makes no longing inquiries: "Saw you him whom my soul loves?" A spiritual worship is when our desires are chiefly for God in the worship; as David desires to dwell in the house of the Lord; but his desire is not terminated there, but to behold the beauty of the Lord (Psalm xxvii. 4), and taste the ravishing sweetness of his presence. No doubt but Elijah's desires for the enjoyment of God while he was mounting to heaven, were as fiery as the chariot wherein he was carried. Unutterable groans acted in worship are the fruit of the Spirit, and certainly render it a spiritual service (Rom. viii. 26). Strong appetites are agreeable to God, and prepare us to eat the fruit of worship. A spiritual Paul presseth forward to know Christ, and the power of his resurrection; and a spiritual worshipper actually aspires in every duty to know God, and the power of his grace. To desire worship as an end is carnal; to desire it as a means, and act desires in it for communion with God in it, is spiritual, and the fruit of a spiritual life.

5. Thankfulness and admiration are to be exercised in spiritual service. This is a worship of spirits; praise is the adoration of the blessed angels (Isa. vi. 3), and of glorified spirits (Rev. iv. 11): "Thou art worthy, O Lord, to receive glory and honor, and power;" and (Rev. v. 13, 14), they worship him ascribing "Blessing, honor, glory, and power to Him that sits upon the throne, and to the Lamb forever and ever." Other acts of worship are confined to this life, and leave us as soon as we have set our foot in heaven; there, no notes but this of praise are warbled out; the power, wisdom, love, and grace in the dispensation of the gospel, seat themselves in the thoughts and tongues of blessed souls. Can a worship on earth be spiritual, that hath no mixture of an eternal heavenly duty with it? The worship of God in innocence had been chiefly an admiration of him in the works of creation; and should not our evangelical worship be an admiration of him in the works of redemption, which is a restoration to a better state? After the petitioning for pardoning grace (Hos. xiv. 2), there is a rendering the calves or heifers of our lips, alluding to the heifers used in eucharistical sacrifices. The praise of God is the choicest sacrifice and worship under a dispensation of redeeming grace; this is the prime and eternal part of worship under the gospel. The Psalmist (Psalm cxlix. cl.), speaking of the gospel times, spurs on to this kind of worship; "Sing to the Lord a new song; let the children of Zion be joyful in their king; let the saints be joyful in glory, and sing aloud upon their beds; let the high praises of God be in their mouths;" he begins and ends both psalms with "Praise ye the Lord." That cannot be a spiritual and evangelical worship, that hath nothing of the praise of God in the heart. The consideration of God's adorable perfections, discovered in the gospel, will make us come to him with more seriousness; beg blessings of him with more confidence; fly to him with a winged

faith and love, and more spiritually glorify him in our attendances upon him.

6. Spiritual worship is performed with delight. The evangelical worship is prophetically signified by keeping the feast of tabernacles; "They shall go up from year to year, to worship the King, the Lord of Hosts, and to keep the feast of tabernacles" (Zech. xiv. 16): why that feast, when there were other feasts observed by the Jews? That was a feast celebrated with the greatest joy; typical of the gladness which was to be under the exhibition of the Messiah, and a thankful commemoration of the redemption wrought by him. It was to be celebrated five days after the "solemn day of atonement" (Lev. xxiii. 34, compared with ver. 27), wherein there was one of the solemnest types of the sacrifice of the death of Christ. In this feast they commemorated their exchange of Egypt for Canaan; the manna wherewith they were fed; the water out of the rock wherewith they were refreshed; in remembrance of this, they poured water on the ground, pronouncing those words in Isaiah, they shall "draw waters out of the wells of salvation;" which our Saviour refers to himself (John vii. 37), inviting them to him, to drink "upon the last day, the great day of the feast of tabernacles," wherein the solemn ceremony was observed. Since we are freed by the death of the Redeemer from the curses of the law, God requires of us a joy in spiritual privileges. A sad frame in worship gives the lie to all gospel liberty, to the purchase of the Redeemer's death, the triumphs of his resurrection: it is a carriage, as if we were under the influences of the legal fire and lightning, and an entering a protest against the freedom of the gospel. The evangelical worship is a spiritual worship; and praise, joy, and delight are prophesied of, as great ingredients in attendance on gospel ordinances (Isaiah xii. 3–5). What was occasion of terror in the worship of God under the law, is the occasion of delight in the worship of God under the gospel. The justice and holiness of God, so terrible in the law, becomes comfortable under the gospel; since they have feasted themselves on the active and passive obedience of the Redeemer. The approach is to God as gracious, not to God as unpacified; as a son to a father, not as a criminal to a judge. Under the law, God was represented as a judge; remembering their sin in their sacrifices, and representing the punishment they had merited: in the gospel as a father, accepting the atonement, and publishing the reconciliation wrought by the Redeemer. Delight in God is a gospel frame; therefore the more joyful, the more spiritual: "The sabbath is to be a delight;" not only in regard of the day, but in regard to the duties of it (Isa. lviii. 13); in regard of the marvellous work he wrought on it; raising up our blessed Redeemer on that day, whereby a foundation was laid for the rendering our persons and services acceptable to God (Psalm cxviii. 24); "This is the day which the Lord hath made, we will be glad and rejoice in it." A lumpish frame becomes not a day and a duty, that hath so noble and spiritual a mark upon it. The angels, in the first act of worship after the creation, were highly joyful (Job xxxviii. 7): "They shouted for joy," &c. The saints have particularly acted this in their worship. David would not content himself with an approach to the altar, without going to

God as his "exceeding joy" (Psalm xliii. 4). My triumphant joy: when he danced before the ark, he seems to be transformed into delight and pleasure (2 Sam. vi. 14, 16). He had as much delight in worship, as others had in their harvest and vintage. And those that took joyfully the spoiling of their goods, would as joyfully attend upon the communications of God. Where there is a fulness of the Spirit, there is a "waking melody to God in the heart" (Eph. v. 18, 19); and where there is an acting of love (as there is in all spiritual services), the proper fruit of it is joy in a near approach to the object of the soul's affection. Love is *appetitus unionis;* the more love, the more delight in the approachings of God to the soul, or the outgoings of the soul to God. As the object of worship is amiable in a spiritual eye, so the means tending to a communion with this object are delightful in the exercise. Where there is no delight in a duty, there is no delight in the object of the duty; the more of grace, the more of pleasure in the actings of it; as the more of nature there is in any natural agent, the more of pleasure in the act, so the more heavenly the worship, the more spiritual. Delight is the frame and temper of glory. A heart filled up to the brim with joy, is a heart filled up to the brim with the Spirit; joy is the fruit of the Holy Ghost (Gal. v. 22). (1.) Not the joy of God's dispensation flowing from God, but a gracious active joy streaming to God. There is a joy, when the comforts of God are dropped into the soul, as oil upon the wheel; which indeed makes the faculties move with more speed and activity in his service, like the chariots of Aminadab; and a soul may serve God in the strength of this taste, and its delight terminate in the sensible comfort. This is not the joy I mean, but such a joy that hath God for its object, delighting in him as the term, in worship as the way to him; the first is God's dispensation, the other is our duty; the first is an act of God's favor to us, the second a sprout of habitual grace in us. The comforts we have from God may elevate our duties; but the grace we have within doth spiritualize our duties. (2.) Nor is every delight an argument of a spiritual service. All the requisites to worship must be taken in. A man may invent a worship and delight in it; as Micah in the adoration of his idol, when he was glad he had got both an Ephod and a Levite (Judges xvii). As a man may have a contentment in sin, so he may have a contentment in worship; not because it is a worship of God, but the worship of his own invention, agreeable to his own humor and design, as (Isa. lviii. 2) it is said, they "delighted in approaching to God;" but it was for carnal ends. Novelty engenders complacency; but it must be a worship wherein God will delight; and that must be a worship according to his own rule and infinite wisdom, and not our shallow fancies. God requires a cheerfulness in his service, especially under the gospel, where he sits upon a throne of grace; discovers himself in his amiableness, and acts the covenant of grace, and the sweet relation of a father. The priests of old were not to sully themselves with any sorrow, when they were in the exercise of their functions. God put a bar to the natural affections of Aaron and his sons, when Nadab and Abihu had been cut off by a severe hand of God (Lev. x. 6). Every true Christian in a higher order of priesthood, is a person

dedicated to joy and peace, offering himself a lively sacrifice of praise
and thanksgiving; and there is no christian duty, but is to be set off
and seasoned with cheerfulness: he that loves a cheerful giver in acts
of charity, requires no less a cheerful spirit in acts of worship; as this
is an ingredient in worship, so it is the means to make your spirits
intent in worship. When the heart triumphs in the consideration of
divine excellency and goodness, it will be angry at anything that
offers to jog and disturb it.

7. Spiritual worship is to be performed, though with a delight in
God, yet with a deep reverence of God. The gospel, in advancing
the spirituality of worship, takes off the terror, but not the reverence
of God; which is nothing else in its own nature, but a due and high
esteem of the excellency of a thing according to the nature of it;
and, therefore, the gospel presenting us with more illustrious notices
of the glorious nature of God, is so far from indulging any disesteem
of him, that it requires of us a greater reverence suitable to the height
of its discovery, above what could be spelt in the book of creation;
the gospel worship is therefore expressed by trembling (Hos. xi. 10 :)
"They shall walk after the Lord; he shall roar like a lion; when
he shall roar, then the children shall tremble from the West." When
the lion of the tribe of Judah shall lift up his powerful voice in the
gospel, the western Gentiles shall run trembling to walk after the
Lord. God hath alway attended his greatest manifestations with remarkable characters of majesty, to create a reverence in his creature:
he caused the "wind to march before him," to cut the mountain,
when he manifested himself to Elijah (1 Kings xix. 11); "A wind
and a cloud of fire," before that magnificent vision to Ezekiel (chap.
i. 4, 5); "Thunders and lightnings" before the giving the law (Exod.
xix. 18); and a "mighty wind" before the giving the Spirit (Acts
ii.): God requires of us an awe of him in the very act of performance. The angels are pure, and cannot fear him as sinners, but in
"reverence they cover their faces" when they stand before him (Isa.
vi. 2): his power should make us reverence him, as we are creatures;
his justice, as we are sinners; his goodness, as we are restored creatures. "God is clothed with unspeakable majesty; the glory of his
face shines brighter than the lights of heaven in their beauty. Before him the angels tremble, and the heavens melt; we ought not
therefore to come before him with the sacrifice of fools, nor tender a
duty to him, without falling low upon our faces, and bowing the
knees of our hearts in token of reverence."[f] Not a slavish fear, like
that of devils; but a "godly fear," like that of saints (Heb. xii. 28);
joined with a sense of an unmovable kingdom, becometh us; and
this the apostle calls a grace necessary to make our service acceptable, and therefore the grace necessary to make it spiritual, since
nothing finds admission to God, but what is of a spiritual nature.
The consideration of his glorious nature should imprint an awful respect upon our souls to him; his goodness should make his majesty
more adorable to us, as his majesty makes his goodness more admirable
in his condescensions to us. As God is a Spirit, our worship must
be spiritual; and being, as he is, the supreme Spirit, our worship

must be reverential; we must observe the state he takes upon him in his ordinances; "He is in heaven, we upon the earth;" we must not therefore be "hasty to utter anything before God" (Eccles. v. 7). Consider him a Spirit in the highest heavens, and ourselves spirits dwelling in a dreggy earth. Loose and garish frames debase him to our own quality; slight postures of spirit intimate him to be a slight and mean being; our being in covenant with him, must not lower our awful apprehensions of him; as he is the Lord thy God, it is a glorious and fearful name, or wonderful (Deut. xxviii. 58); though he lay by his justice to believers, he doth not lay by his majesty; when we have a confidence in him, because he is the Lord our God, we must have awful thoughts of his majesty, because his name is glorious. God is terrible from his holy places, in regard of the great things he doth for his Israel (Psalm lxviii. 35); we should behave ourselves with that inward honor and respect of him, as if he were present to our bodily eyes; the higher apprehensions we have of his majesty, the greater awe will be upon our hearts in his presence, and the greater spirituality in our acts. We should manage our hearts so, as if we had a view of God in his heavenly glory.

8. Spiritual worship is to be performed with humility in our spirits. This is to follow upon the reverence of God. As we are to have high thoughts of God, that we may not debase him; we must have low thoughts of ourselves, not to vaunt before him. When we have right notions of the Divine Majesty, we shall be as worms in our own thoughts, and creep as worms into his presence; we can never consider him in his glory, but we have a fit opportunity to reflect upon ourselves, and consider how basely we revolted from him, and how graciously we are restored by him. As the gospel affords us greater discoveries of God's nature, and so enhanceth our reverence of him, so it helps us to a fuller understanding of our own vileness and weakness, and therefore is proper to engender humility; the more spiritual and evangelical therefore any service is, the more humble it is. That is a spiritual service that doth most manifest the glory of God; and this cannot be manifested by us, without manifesting our own emptiness and nothingness. The heathens were sensible of the necessity of humility by the light of nature;[g] after the name of God, signified by 'Εἰ inscribed on the temple at Delphos, followed Γνῶθι σεαυτον, whereby was insinuated, that when we have to do with God, who is the only *Ens*, we should behave ourselves with a sense of our own infirmity, and infinite distance from him. As a person, so a duty leavened with pride, hath nothing of sincerity, and therefore nothing of spirituality in it (Hab. ii. 4): "His soul which is lifted up, is not upright in him." The elders that were crowned by God to be kings and priests, to offer spiritual sacrifices, uncrown themselves in their worship of him, and cast down their ornaments at "his feet":[h] the Greek word to worship, προσκυνεῖν, signifies to creep like a dog upon his belly before his master; to lie low. How deep should our sense be of the privilege of God's admitting us to his worship, and affording us such a mercy under our deserts of wrath! How mean should be our thoughts, both of our persons

---

and performances! How patiently should we wait upon God for the success of worship! How did Abraham, the father of the faithful, equal himself to the earth, when he supplicated the God of heaven, and devote himself to him under the title of very "dust and ashes!" (Gen. xviii. 27.) Isaiah did but behold an evangelical apparition of God and the angels worshipping him, and presently reflects upon his "own uncleanness" (Isa. vi. 5). God's presence both requires and causes humility. How lowly is David in his own opinion, after a magnificent duty performed by himself and his people (1 Chron. xxix. 14): "Who am I? and what is my people, that we should be able to offer so willingly?" The more spiritual the soul is in its carriage to God, the more humble it is; and the more gracious God is in his communications to the soul, the lower it lies. God commanded not the fiercer creatures to be offered to him in sacrifices, but lambs and kids, meek and lowly creatures; none that had stings in their tails, or venom in their tongues.[i] The meek lamb was the daily sacrifice; the doves were to be offered by pairs; God would not have honey mixed with any sacrifice (Lev. ii. 11), that breeds choler, and choler pride; but oil he commanded to be used, that supples and mollifies the parts. Swelling pride and boiling passions render our services carnal; they cannot be spiritual, without a humble sweetness and an innocent sincerity; one grain of this transcends the most costly sacrifices: a contrite heart puts a gloss upon worship (Psalm li. 16, 17). The departure of men and angels from God, began in pride; our approaches and return to him must begin in humility; and therefore all those graces, which are bottomed on humility, must be acted in worship, as faith, and a sense of our own indigence. Our blessed Saviour, the most spiritual worshipper, prostrated himself in the garden with the greatest lowliness, and offered himself upon the cross a sacrifice with the greatest humility. Melted souls in worship have the most spiritual conformity to the person of Christ in the state of humiliation, and his design in that state; as worship without it is not suitable to God, so neither is it advantageous for us. A time of worship is a time of God's communication. The vessel must be melted to receive the mould it is designed for; softened wax is fittest to receive a stamp, and a spiritually melted soul fittest to receive a spiritual impression. We cannot perform duty in an evangelical and spiritual strain, without the meltingness and meanness in ourselves which the gospel requires.

9. Spiritual worship is to be performed with holiness. God is a holy Spirit; a likeness to God must attend the worshipping of God as he is; holiness is alway in season; "It becomes his house forever" (Psalm xci. 5). We can never serve the living God till we "have consciences purged from dead works" (Heb. ix. 14). Dead works in our consciences are unsuitable to God, an eternal living Spirit. The more mortified the heart, the more quickened the service. Nothing can please an infinite purity but that which is pure; since God is in his glory, in his ordinances, we must not be in our filthiness. The holiness of his Spirit doth sparkle in his ordinances; the holiness of our spirits ought also to sparkle in our observance of them. The

[i] Caudam aculeatam vel linguam nigram, Alexand. ab Alex. l. 3. c. 12.

holiness of God is most celebrated in the worship of angels;[k] spiritual worship ought to be like angelical; that cannot be with souls totally impure. As there must be perfect holiness to make a worship perfectly spiritual; so there must be some degree of holiness to make it in any measure spiritual. God would have all the utensils of the sanctuary employed about his service to be holy; the inwards of the sacrifice were to be rinsed thrice.[1] The crop and feathers of sacrificed doves were to be hung eastward towards the entrance of the temple, at a distance from the holy of holies, where the presence of God was most eminent (Lev. i. 16). When Aaron was to go into the holy of holies, he was to "sanctify himself" in an extraordinary manner (Lev. xvi. 4). The priests were to be bare-footed in the temple, in the exercise of their office; shoes alway were to be put off upon holy ground: "Look to thy foot when thou goest to the house of God," saith the wise man (Eccles. v. 1). Strip the affections, the feet of the soul, of all the dirt contracted; discard all earthly and base thoughts from the heart. A beast was not to touch the Mount Sinai, without losing his life; nor can we come near the throne with brutish affections, without losing the life and fruit of the worship. An unholy soul degrades himself from a spirit to a brute, and the worship from spiritual to brutish. If any unmortified sin be found in the life, as it was in the comers to the temple, it taints and pollutes the worship (Isa. i. 15). All worship is an acknowledgment of the excellency of God as he is holy; hence it is called, a "sanctifying God's name" (Jer. vii. 9, 10); how can any person sanctify God's name that hath not a holy resemblance to his nature? If he be not holy as he is holy, he cannot worship him according to his excellency in spirit and in truth; no worship is spiritual wherein we have not a communion with God. But what intercourse can there be between a holy God, and an impure creature; between light and darkness? We have no fellowship with him in any service, unless "we walk in the light," in service and out of service, as he is light (1 John i. 7). The heathen thought not their sacrifices agreeable to God without washing their hands; whereby they signified the preparation of their hearts, before they made the oblation: clean hands without a pure heart, signify nothing; the frame of our hearts must answer the purity of the outward symbols (Psalm xxvi. 6): "I will wash my hands in innocence, so will I compass thine altar, O Lord;" he would observe the appointed ceremonies, but not without "cleansing his heart as well as his hands." Vain man is apt to rest upon outward acts and rites of worship; but this must alway be practised; the words are in the present tense, "I wash," "I compass." Purity in worship ought to be our continual care. If we would perform a spiritual service, wherein we would have communion with God, it must be in holiness; if we would walk with Christ, it must be in "white" (Rev. iii. 4), alluding to the white garments the priests put on, when they went to perform their service; as without this we cannot see God in heaven, so neither can we see the beauty of God in his own ordinances.

10. Spiritual worship is performed with spiritual ends, with raised

[k] Isa. vi. 3. Rev. iv. 8.   [1] As the Jewish doctors observe on Lev. i. 9.

aims at the glory of God.   No duty can be spiritual that hath a carnal aim; where God is the sole object, he ought to be the principal
end; in all our actions he is to be our end, as he is the principle of
our being; much more in religious acts, as he is the object of our
worship.   The worship of God in Scripture is expressed by the
"seeking of him" (Heb. xi. 6); him, not ourselves; all is to be
referred to God.   As we are "not to live to ourselves, that being
the sign of a carnal state, so we are not to worship for ourselves"
(Rom. xiv. 7, 8).   As all actions are denominated good from their
end, as well as their object, so upon the same account they are
denominated spiritual.   The end spiritualizeth our natural actions,
much more our religious; then are our faculties devoted to him
when they centre in him.   If the intention be evil, there is nothing
but darkness in the whole service (Luke xi. 34).   The first institution of the Sabbath, the solemn day for worship, was to contemplate
the glory of God in his stupendous works of creation, and render
him a homage for them (Rev. iv. 11): "Thou art worthy, O Lord,
to receive honor, glory, and power; for thou hast created all things,
and for thy pleasure they are and were created."   No worship can
be returned without a glorifying of God; and we cannot actually
glorify him, without direct aims at the promoting his honor.   As
we have immediately to do with God, so we are immediately to mind
the praise of God.   As we are not to content ourselves with habitual
grace, but be rich in the exercise of it in worship, so we are not to
acquiesce in the habitual aims at the glory of God, without the actual
overflowings of our hearts in those aims.   It is natural for man to
worship God for self; self-righteousness is the rooted aim of man in
his worship since his revolt from God, and being sensible it is not to
be found in his natural actions, he seeks for it in his moral and religious.   By the first pride we flung God off from being our sovereign,
and from being our end, since a pharisaical spirit struts it in nature,
not only to do things to be seen of men, but to be admired by God
(Isa. lviii. 3): "Wherefore have we fasted and thou takest no knowledge?"   This is to have God worship them, instead of being worshipped by them.   Cain's carriage after his sacrifice testified some
base end in his worship; he came not to God as a subject to a sovereign, but as if he had been the sovereign, and God the subject; and
when his design is not answered, and his desire not gratified, he
proves more a rebel to God, and a murderer of his brother.   Such
base scents will rise up in our worship from the body of death which
cleaves to us, and mix themselves with our services, as weeds with
the fish in the net.   David, therefore, after his people had offered
willingly to the temple, begs of God that their "hearts might be
prepared to him" (1 Chron. xxix. 18); that their hearts might stand
right to God, without any squinting to self-ends.   Some present
themselves to God, as poor men offer a present to a great person;
not to honor him, but to gain for themselves a reward richer than
their gift.   "What profit is it that we have kept his ordinance?"
&c. (Mal. iii. 14).   Some worship him, intending thereby to make
him amends for the wrong they have done him; wipe off their
scores, and satisfy their debts; as though a spiritual wrong could be

recompensed with a bodily service, and an infinite Spirit be outwitted and appeased by a carnal flattery. Self is the spirit of carnality; to pretend a homage to God, and intend only the advantage of self, is rather to mock him than worship him. When we believe that we ought to be satisfied, rather than God glorified, we set God below ourselves, imagine that he should submit his own honor to our advantage; we make ourselves more glorious than God, as though we were not made for him, but he hath a being only for us; this is to have a very low esteem of the majesty of God. Whatsoever any man aims at in worship above the glory of God, that he forms as an idol to himself instead of God, and sets up a golden image, God counts not this as a worship. The offerings made in the wilderness for forty years together, God esteemed as not offered to him (Amos v. 25): "Have you offered to me sacrifices and offerings in the wilderness forty years, O house of Israel?" They did it not to God, but to themselves; for their own security, and the attainment of the possession of the promised land. A spiritual worshipper performs not worship for some hopes of carnal advantage; he uses ordinances as means to bring God and his soul together, to be more fitted to honor God in the world, in his particular place; when he hath been inflamed and humble in any address or duty, he gives God the glory; his heart suits the doxology at the end of the Lord's Prayer, ascribes the kingdom, power, and glory to God alone, and if any viper of pride starts out upon him, he endeavors presently to shake it off. That which was the first end of our framing, ought to be the chief end of our acting towards God; but when men have the same ends in worship as brutes, the satisfaction of a sensitive part, the service is no more than brutish. The acting for a sensitive end is unworthy the majesty of God to whom we address, and unbecoming a rational creature. The acting for a sensitive end is not a rational, much less can it be a spiritual service; though the act may be good in itself, yet not good in the agent, because he wants a due end. We are, then, spiritual, when we have the same end in our redeemed services, as God had in his redeeming love, viz., his own glory.

11. Spiritual service is offered to God in the name of Christ. Those are only "spiritual sacrifices, that are offered up to God by Jesus Christ" (1 Pet. ii. 5); that are the fruits of the sanctification of the Spirit, and offered in the mediation of the Son: as the altar sanctifies the gift, so doth Christ spiritualize our services for God's acceptation; as the fire upon the altar separated the airy and finer parts of the sacrifice from the terrene and earthly; this is the golden altar upon which the prayers of the saints are offered up "before the throne" (Rev. viii. 3). As all that we have from God streams through his blood, so all that we give to God ascends by virtue of his merits. All the blessings God gave to the Israelites came out of Sion,[m] that is, from the gospel hid under the law; all the duties we present to God are to be presented in Sion, in an evangelical manner; all our worship must be bottomed on Christ. God hath intended that we should "honor the Son, as we honor the Father;" as we honor the Father by offering our service only to him, so we

[m] Psalm cxxxiv. 3. "The Lord bless thee out of Sion."

are to honor the Son by offering it only in his name; in him alone God is well pleased, because in him alone he finds our services spiritual and worthy of acceptation; we must therefore take fast hold of him with our spirits, and the faster we hold him, the more spiritual is our worship.   To do anything in the name of Christ, is not to believe the worship shall be accepted for itself, but to have our eye fixed upon Christ for the acceptance of it, and not to rest upon the work done, as carnal people are apt to do.   The creatures present their acknowledgments to God by man; and man can only present his by Christ.   It was utterly unlawful after the building of the temple, to sacrifice anywhere else; the temple being a type of Christ, it is utterly unlawful for us to present our services in any other name than his.   This is the way to be spiritual.   If we consider God out of Christ, we can have no other notions but those of horror and bondage.   We behold him a Spirit, but environed with justice and wrath for sinners; but the consideration of him in Christ, veils his justice, draws forth his mercy, represents him more a father than a judge.   In Christ the aspect of justice is changed, and by that the temper of the creature; so that in and by this Mediator, we "can have a spiritual boldness, and access to God with confidence" (Eph. iii. 12), whereby the spirit is kept from benumbness and distraction, and our souls quickened and refined.   The thoughts kept upon Christ in a duty of worship quickly elevates the soul, and spiritualizeth the whole service.   Sin makes our services black, and the blood of Christ makes both our persons and services white.

To conclude this head. God is a Spirit infinitely happy, therefore we must approach to him with cheerfulness; he is a Spirit of infinite majesty, therefore we must come before him with reverence; he is a Spirit infinitely high, therefore we must offer up our sacrifices with the deepest humility; he is a Spirit infinitely holy, therefore we must address him with purity; he is a Spirit infinitely glorious, we must therefore acknowledge his excellency in all that we do, and in our measures contribute to his glory, by having the highest aims in his worship; he is a Spirit infinitely provoked by us, therefore we must offer up our worship in the name of a pacifying Mediator and Intercessor.

III. The third general is, Why a spiritual worship is due to God, and to be offered to him.   We must consider the object of worship, and the subject of worship; the worshipper and the worshipped. God is a spiritual Being; man is a reasonable creature.   The nature of God informs us what is fit to be presented to him; our own nature informs us what is fit to be presented by us.

Reason I. The best we have is to be presented to God in worship. For,

1. Since God is the most excellent Being, he is to be served by us with the most excellent thing we have, and with the choicest veneration.   God is so incomprehensibly excellent, that we cannot render him what he deserves: we must render him what we are able to offer: the best of our affections; the flower of our strength; the cream and top of our spirits.   By the same reason that we are bound to give God the best worship, we must offer it to him in the best manner.   We cannot give to God anything too good for so blessed

a Being; God being a "great king," slight services become not his majesty (Mal. i. 13, 14); it is unbecoming the majesty of God, and the reason of a creature, to give him a trivial thing; it is unworthy to bestow the best of our strength on our lust, and the worst and weakest in the service of God. An infinite Spirit should have affections as near to infinite as we can; as he is a Spirit without bounds, so he should have a service without limits; when we have given him all, we cannot serve him according to the excellency of his nature (Josh. xxiv. 19); and shall we give him less than all? His infinite excellency, and our dependence on him as creatures, demands the choicest adoration; our spirits, being the noblest part of our nature, are as due to him as the service of our bodies, which are the vilest; to serve him with the worst only, is to diminish his honor.

2. Under the law, God commanded the best to be offered him. He would have the males, the best of the kind; the fat, the best of the creature;[n] he commanded them to offer him the firstlings of the flock; not the firstlings of the womb, but the firstlings of the year: the Jewish cattle having two breeding-times, in the beginning of the spring and the beginning of September; the latter breed was the weaker, which Jacob knew (Gen. xxx.) when he laid the rods before the cattle when they were strong in the spring, and withheld them when they were feeble in the autumn. One reason (as the Jews say) why God accepted not the offering of Cain was, because he brought the meanest, not the best of the fruit; and therefore, it is said, only that he brought of the "fruit" of the ground (Gen. iv. 3), not the first of the fruit, or the best of the fruit, as Abel, who brought the "firstling" of his flock, and the fat thereof (ver. 4).

3. And this the heathen practised by the light of nature. They for the most part offered males, as being more worthy; and burnt the male, not the female frankincense, as it is divided into those two kinds; they offered the best, when they offered their children to Moloch. Nothing more excellent than man, and nothing dearer to parents than their children, which are part of themselves. When the Israelites would have a golden calf for a representation of God, they would dedicate their jewels, and strip their wives and children of their richest ornaments, to show their devotion. Shall men serve their dumb idols with the best of their substance, and the strength of their souls; and shall the living God have a duller service from us, than idols had from them? God requires no such hard, but delightful worship from us, our spirits.

4. All creatures serve man, by the providential order of God, with the best they have. As we, by God's appointment, receive from creatures the best they can give, ought we not with a free will to render to God the best we can offer? The beasts give us their best fat; the trees their best fruit; the sun its best light; the fountains their best streams; shall God order us the best from creatures, and we put him off with the worst from ourselves?

5. God hath given us the choicest thing he had—a Redeemer that was the power of God, and the wisdom of God; the best he had in

[n] Exod. xxix. 13. The inward fat, not the offal.

heaven, his own Son, and in himself a sacrifice for us, that we might be enabled to present ourselves a sacrifice to him. And Christ offered himself for us, the best he had, and that with the strength of the Deity through the eternal Spirit; and shall we grudge God the best part of ourselves? As God would have a worship from his creature, so it must be with the best part of his creature. If we have "given ourselves to the Lord" (2 Cor. viii. 5), we can worship with no less than ourselves. What is the man without his spirit? If we are to worship God with all that we have received from him, we must worship him with the best part we have received from him; it is but a small glory we can give him with the best, and shall we deprive him of his right by giving him the worst? As what we are is from God, so what we are ought to be for God. Creation is the foundation of worship (Psalm c. 2, 3): "Serve the Lord with gladness; know ye that the Lord he is God; it is he that hath made us." He hath ennobled us with spiritual affections; where is it fittest for us to employ them, but upon him? and at what time, but when we come solemnly to converse with him? Is it justice to deny him the honor of his best gift to us? our souls are more his gift to us, than anything in the world; other things are so given that they are often taken from us, but our spirits are the most durable gift. Rational faculties cannot be removed without a dissolution of nature. Well then, as he is God, he is to be honored with all the propensions and ardor that the infiniteness and excellency of such a Being require, and the incomparable obligations he hath laid upon us in this state deserve at our hands. In all our worship, therefore, our minds ought to be filled with the highest admiration, love, and reverence. Since our end was to glorify God, we answer not our end, and honor him not, unless we give him the choicest we have.[o]

Reason II. We cannot else act towards God according to the nature of rational creatures. Spiritual worship is due to God, because of his nature; and due from us, because of our nature. As we are to adore God, so we are to adore him as men; the nature of a rational creature makes this impression upon him; he cannot view his own nature without having this duty striking upon his mind. As he knows, by inspection into himself, that there was a God that made him; so, that he is made to be in subjection to God, subjection to him in his spirit as well as his body, and ought morally to testify this natural dependence on him. His constitution informs him that he hath a capacity to converse with God; that he cannot converse with him, but by those inward faculties; if it could be managed by his body without his spirit, beasts might as well converse with God as men. It can never be a "reasonable service" (Rom. xii. 1), as it ought to be, unless the reasonable faculties be employed in the management of it; it must be a worship prodigiously lame, without the concurrence of the chiefest part of man with it. As we are to act conformably to the nature of the object, so also to the nature of our own faculties. Our faculties, in the very gift of them to us, were destined to be exercised, about what? What? All other things but the Author of them. It is a conceit cannot enter into the heart

° Amyraut, Mor. Tom. II. p. 311.

of a rational creature, that he should act as such a creature in other things, and as a stone in things relating to the donor of them; as a man, with his mind about him in the affairs of the world; as a beast, without reason in his acts towards God. If a man did not employ his reason in other things, he would be an unprofitable creature in the world: if he do not employ his spiritual faculties in worship, he denies them the proper end and use for which they were given him; it is a practical denial that God hath given him a soul, and that God hath any right to the exercise of it. If there were no worship appointed by God in the world, the natural inclination of man to some kind of religion would be in vain; and if our inward faculties were not employed in the duties of religion they would be in vain; the true end of God in the endowment of us with them would be defeated by us, as much as lies in us, if we did not serve him with that which we have from him solely at his own cost. As no man can with reason conclude, that the rest commanded on the Sabbath and the sanctification of it, was only a rest of the body, that had been performed by the beasts as well as men, but some higher end was aimed at for the rational creature; so no man can think that the command for worship terminated only in the presence of the body; that God should give the command to man as a reasonable creature, and expect no other service from him than that of a brute. God did not require a worship from man for any want he had, or any essential honor that could accrue to him, but that men might testify their gratitude to him, and dependence on him. It is the most horrid ingratitude not to have lively and deep sentiments of gratitude after such obligations, and not to make those due acknowledgments that are proper for a rational creature. Religion is the highest and choicest act of a reasonable creature; no creature under heaven is capable of it that wants reason. As it is a violation of reason not to worship God, so it is no less a violation of reason not to worship him with the heart and spirit; it is a high dishonor to God, and defeats him not only of the service due to him from man, but that which is due to him from all the creatures. Every creature, as it is an effect of God's power and wisdom, doth passively worship God; that is, it doth afford matter of adoration to man that hath reason to collect it, and return it where it is due. Without the exercise of the soul, we can no more hand it to God, than without such an exercise, we can gather it from the creature; so that by this neglect, the creatures are restrained from answering their chief end; they cannot pay any service to God without man; nor can man, without the employment of his rational faculties, render a homage to God, any more than beasts can. This engagement of our inward power stands firm and inviolable, let the modes of worship be what they will, or the changes of them by the sovereign authority of God never so frequent; this could not expire or be changed as long as the nature of man endured. As man had not been capable of a command for worship, unless he had been endued with spiritual faculties; so he is not active in a true practice of worship, unless they be employed by him in it. The constitution of man makes this manner of worship perpetually obligatory, and the oblation can never cease, till man cease to be a creature furnished with such faculties; in our worship, therefore, if we would act like rational creatures, we should extend all the powers of our souls to the utmost pitch, and essay to have apprehensions of God, equal to the excellency of his nature, which, though we may attempt, we can never attain.

Reason III. Without this engagement of our spirits no act is an act of worship. True worship, being an acknowledgment of God and the perfections of his nature, results only from the soul, that being only capable of knowing God and those perfections which are the object and motive of worship. The posture of the body is but to testify the inward temper and affection of the mind; if, therefore, it testifies what it is not, it is a lie, and no worship; the cringes a beast may be taught to make to an altar may as well be called worship, since a man thinks as little of that God he pretends to honor, as the beast doth of the altar to which he bows. Worship is a reverent remembrance of God, and giving some honor to him with the intention of the soul; it cannot justly have the name of worship, that wants the essential part of it; it is an ascribing to God the glory of his nature, an owning subjection and obedience to him as our sovereign Lord; this is as impossible to be performed without the spirit, as that there can be life and motion in a body without a soul; it is a drawing near to God, not in regard of his essential presence, so all things are near to God, but in an acknowledgment of his excellency, which is an act of the spirit; without this, the worst of men in a place of worship are as near to God as the best. The necessity of the conjunction of our soul ariseth from the nature of worship, which being the most serious thing we can be employed in, the highest converse with the highest object requires the choicest temper of spirit in the performance. That cannot be an act of worship, which is not an act of piety and virtue; but there is no act of virtue done by the members of the body, without the concurrence of the powers of the soul. We may as well call the presence of a dead carcass in a place of worship, an act of religion, as the presence of a living body without an intent spirit; the separation of the soul from one is natural, the other moral; that renders the body lifeless, but this renders the act loathsome to God; as the being of the soul gives life to the body, so the operation of the soul gives life to the actions. As he cannot be a man that wants the form of a man, a rational soul; so that cannot be a worship that wants an essential part, the act of the spirit; God will not vouchsafe any acts of man so noble a title without the requisite qualifications (Hos. v. 6): " They shall go with their flocks and their herds to seek the Lord," &c. A multitude of lambs and bullocks for sacrifice, to appease God's anger. God would not give it the title of worship, though instituted by himself, when it wanted the qualities of such a service. " The spirit of whoredom was in the midst of them" (v. 4). In the judgment of our Saviour, it is a " vain worship, when the traditions of men are taught for the doctrines of God" (Matt. xv. 9); and no less vain must it be, when the bodies of men are presented to supply the place of their spirits. As an omission of duty is a contempt of God's sovereign authority, so the omission of the manner of it is a contempt of it, and of his amiable excellency; and that which is a contempt and mockery, can lay no just claim to the title of worship.

Reason IV. There is in worship an approach of God to man. It was instituted to this purpose, that God might give out his blessings to man; and ought not our spirits to be prepared and ready to receive his communications? We are, in such acts, more peculiarly in his presence. In the Israelites hearing the law, it is said, God was to "come among them" (Exod. xix. 10, 11). Then, men are said to stand before the Lord (Deut. x. 8): "God, before whom I stand" (1 Kings, xvii. 1): that is, whom I worship; and therefore when Cain forsook the worship of God settled in his father's family, he is said, "to go out from the presence of the Lord" (Gen. iv. 16). God is essentially present in the world; graciously present in his church. The name of the evangelical city is Jehovah Shammah (Ezek. xlviii. 35), "the Lord is there." God is more graciously present in the evangelical institutions than in the legal; he "loves the gates of Zion more than all the dwellings of Jacob" (Ps. lxxxvii. 2); his evangelical law and worship which was to go forth from Zion, as the other did from Sinai (Mic. iv. 2). God delights to approach to men, and converse with them in the worship instituted in the gospel, more than in all the dwellings of Jacob. If God be graciously present, ought not we to be spiritually present? A lifeless carcass service becomes not so high and delectable a presence as this; it is to thrust him from us, not invite him to us; it is to practise in the ordinances what the prophet predicts concerning men's usage of our Saviour (Isa. liii. 2): "There is no form, no comeliness, nor beauty that we should desire him." A slightness in worship reflects upon the excellency of the object of worship. God and his worship are so linked together, that whosoever thinks the one not worth his inward care, esteems the other not worth his inward affection. How unworthy a slight is it of God, who proffers the opening his treasure; the re-impressing his image; conferring his blessings; admits us into his presence, 'when he hath no need for us; who hath millions of angels to attend him in his court, and celebrate his praise! He that worships not God with his spirit, regards not God's presence in his ordinances, and slights the great end of God in them, and that perfection he may attain by them. We can only expect what God hath promised to give, when we tender to him what he hath commanded us to present. If we put off God with a shell, he will put us off with a husk. How can we expect his heart, when we do not give him ours; or hope for the blessing needful for us, when we render not the glory due to him? It cannot be an advantageous worship without spiritual graces; for those are uniting, and union is the ground of all communion.

Reason V. To have a spiritual worship is God's end in the restoration of the creature, both in redemption by his Son and sanctification by his spirit. A fitness for spiritual offerings was the end of the "coming of Christ" (Mal. iii. 3); he should purge them as gold and silver by fire, a spirit burning up their dross, melting them into a holy compliance with and submission to God. To what purpose? That they may offer to the lord an offering in righteousness; a pure

offering from a purified spirit; he came to "bring us to God" (1 Pet.
iii. 18) in such a garb, as that we might be fit to converse with him.
Can we be thus, without a fixedness of our spirits on him? The
offering of spiritual sacrifices is the end of making any a "spiritual
habitation" and a "holy priesthood" (1 Pet. ii. 5). We can no more
be worshippers of God without a worshipper's nature, than a man
can be a man without human nature. As man was at first created
for the honor and worship of God, so the design of restoring that
image which was defaced by sin tends to the same end. We are
not brought to God by Christ, nor are our services presented to him,
if they be without our spirits; would any man that undertakes to
bring another to a prince, introduce him in a slovenly and sordid
habit, such a garb that he knows hateful to him? or bring the
clothes or skin of a man stuffed with straw, instead of the person?
to come with our skins before God, without our spirits, is contrary to
the design of God in redemption and regeneration. If a carnal worship would have pleased God, a carnal heart would have served his
turn, without the expense of his Spirit in sanctification. He bestows upon man a spiritual nature, that he may return to him a
spiritual service; he enlightens the understanding, that he may have
a rational service; and new moulds the will, that he may have a
voluntary service. As it is the milk of the word wherewith he feeds
us, so it is the service of the word wherewith we must glorify him.
So much as there is of confusedness in our understanding, so much
of starting and levity in our wills, so much of slipperiness and skipping in our affections; so much is abated of the due qualities of the
worship of God, and so much we fall short of the end of redemption and sanctification.

Reason VI. A spiritual worship is to be offered to God, because
no worship but that can be acceptable. We can never be secured of
acceptance without it; he being a Spirit, nothing but the worship in
spirit can be suitable to him: what is unsuitable, cannot be acceptable; there must be something in us, to make our services capable
of being presented by Christ for an actual acceptation. No service
is "acceptable to God by Jesus Christ," but as it is a spiritual sacrifice, and offered by a spiritual heart (1 Pet. ii. 5). The sacrifice is
first spiritual, before it be acceptable to God by Christ; when it is
"an offering in righteousness," it is then, and only then, pleasant to
the Lord (Mal. iii. 3, 4). No prince would accept a gift that is unsuitable to his majesty, and below the condition of the person that
presents it. Would he be pleased with a bottle of water for drink,
from one that hath his cellar full of wine? How unacceptable must
that be that is unsuitable to the Divine Majesty! And what can be
more unsuitable than a withdrawing the operations of our souls from
him, in the oblation of our bodies? We as little glorify God as
God, when we give him only a corporeal worship, as the heathen
did, when they represented him in a corporeal shape (Rom. i. 21);
one as well as the other denies his spiritual nature: this is worse,
for had it been lawful to represent God to the eye, it could not have
been done but by a bodily figure suited to the sense; but since it is
necessary to worship him, it cannot be by a corporeal attendance,

without the operation of the Spirit. A spiritual frame is more pleasing to God than the highest exterior adornments, than the greatest gifts, and the highest prophetic illuminations. "The glory of the second temple" exceeded the glory of the first (Hag. ii. 8, 9). As God accounts the spiritual glory of ordinances most beneficial for us, so our spiritual attendance upon ordinances is most pleasing to him; he that offers the greatest services without it, offers but flesh (Hos. viii. 13): "They sacrifice flesh for the sacrifices of my offerings, but the Lord accepts them not." Spiritual frames are the soul of religious services; all other carriages without them are contemptible to this spirit: we can never lay claim to that promise of God, none shall "seek my face in vain." We affect a vain seeking of him, when we want a due temper of spirit for him; and vain spirits shall have vain returns: it is more contrary to the nature of God's holiness to have communion with such, than it is contrary to the nature of light to have communion with darkness. To make use of this:

Use 1. First it serves for information.

1. If spiritual worship be required by God, how sad is it for them that they are so far from giving God a spiritual worship, that they render him no worship at all! I speak not of the neglect of public, but of private; when men present not a devotion to God from one year's end to the other. The speech of our Saviour, that we must worship God in spirit and truth, implies that a worship is due to him from every one; that is the common impression upon the consciences of all men in the world, if they have not by some constant course in gross sins, hardened their souls, and stifled those natural sentiments. There was never a nation in the world without some kind of religion; and no religion was ever without some modes to testify a devotion; the heathens had their sacrifices and purifications; and the Jews, by God's order, had their rites, whereby they were to express their allegiance to God. Consider,

(1.) Worship is a duty incumbent upon all men. It is a homage mankind owes to God, under the relation wherein he stands obliged to him; it is a prime and immutable justice to own our allegiance to him; it is as unchangeable a truth that God is to be worshipped, as that God is; he is to be worshipped as God, as creator, and therefore by all, since he is the Creator of all, the Lord of all, and "all are his creatures, and all are his subjects. Worship is founded upon creation (Psalm c. 2, 3): it is due to God for himself and his own essential excellency, and therefore due from all; it is due upon the account of man's nature; the human rational nature is the same in all. Whatsoever is due to God upon the account of man's nature, and the natural obligations he hath laid upon man, is due from all men; because they all enjoy the benefits which are proper to their nature. Man in no state was exempted, nor can be exempted from it; in Paradise he had his Sabbath and sacraments; man therefore dissolves the obligation of a reasonable nature, by neglecting the worship of God. Religion is in the first place to be minded. As soon as Noah came out of the ark, he contrived not a habitation for himself, but an altar for the Lord, to acknowledge him the author of his preservation from the deluge (Gen. viii. 20): and whereso-

ever Abraham came, his first business was to erect an altar, and
pay his arrears of gratitude to God, before he ran upon the score
for new mercies (Gen. xii. 7; xiii. 4, 18): he left a testimony of
worship wherever he came.

(2.) Wholly therefore to neglect it, is a high degree of atheism.
He that calls not upon God, "saith in his heart, There is no God;"
and seems to have the sentiments of natural conscience, as to God,
stifled in him (Psalm xiv. 1, 4): it must arise from a conceit that
there is no God, or that we are equal to him, adoration not being
due from persons of an equal state; or that God is unable, or unwilling to take notice of the adoring acts of his creatures: what is
any of these but an undeifying the supreme Majesty? When we
lay aside all thoughts of paying any homage to him, we are in a fair
way opinionatively to deny him, as much as we practically disown
him. Where there is no knowledge of God, that is, no "acknowledgment of God," a gap is opened to all licentiousness (Hos. iv. 1, 2);
and that by degrees brawns the conscience, and razeth out the sense
of God. Those forsake God that "forget his holy mountain" (Isa.
lxv. 11); they do not practically own him as the Creator of their
souls or bodies. It is the sin of Cain, who turning his back upon
worship, is said to " go out from the presence of the Lord" (Gen. iv.
16). Not to worship him with our spirits, is against his law of creation: not to worship him at all, is against his act of creation ; not
to worship him in truth, is hypocrisy; not to worship him at all, is
atheism; whereby we render ourselves worse than the worms in the
earth, or a toad in a ditch.

(3.) To perform a worship to a false God, or to the true God in a
false manner, seems to be less a sin than to live in perpetual neglect
of it. Though it be directed to a false object instead of God, yet it
is under the notion of a God, and so is an acknowledgment of
such a Being as God in the world; whereas the total neglect of any
worship, is a practical denying of the existence of any supreme Majesty. Whosoever constantly omits a public and private worship,
transgresses against an universally received dictate; for all nations
have agreed in the common notion of worshipping God, though they
have disagreed in the several modes and rites whereby they would
testify that adoration. By a worship of God, though superstitious,
a veneration and reverence of such a being is maintained in the
world; whereas by a total neglect of worship, he is virtually disowned and discarded, if not from his existence, yet from his providence and government of the world; all the mercies we breathe in
are denied to flow from him. A foolish worship owns religion,
though it bespatters it; as if a stranger coming into a country mistakes the subject for the prince, and pays that reverence to the subject
which is due to the prince; though he mistakes the object, yet he
owns an authority; or if he pays any respect to the true prince of
that country after the mode of his own, though appearing ridiculous
in the place where he is, he owns the authority of the prince;
whereas the omission of all respect would be a contempt of majesty:
and, therefore, the judgments of God have been more signal upon
the sacrilegious contemners of worship among the heathens, than upon

those that were diligent and devout in their false worship; and they generally owned the blessings received to the preservation of a sense and worship of a Deity among them. Though such a worship be not acceptable to God, and every man is bound to offer to God a devotion agreeable to his own mind; yet it is commendable, not as worship, but as it speaks an acknowledgment of such a being as God, in his power and creation, and his beneficence in his providence. Well, then, omissions of worship are to be avoided. Let no man execute that upon himself which God will pronounce at last as the greatest misery, and bid God depart from him, who will at last be loth to hear God bid him depart from him. Though man hath natural sentiments that God is to be worshipped, yet having an hostility in his nature, he is apt to neglect, or give it him in a slight manner; he therefore sets a particular mark and notice of attention upon the fourth command, "Remember thou keep holy the Sabbath day." Corrupt nature is apt to neglect the worship of God, and flag in it. This command, therefore, which concerns his worship, he fortifies with several reasons. Nor let any neglect worship, because they cannot find their hearts spiritual in it. The further we are from God, the more carnal shall we be. No man can expect heat by a distance from the sunbeams, or other means of warmth. Though God commanded a circumcised heart in the Jewish services, yet he did not warrant a neglect of the outward testimonies of religion he had then appointed. He expected, according to his command, that they should offer the sacrifices, and practise the legal purification he had commanded; he would have them diligently observed, though he had declared that he imposed them only for a time; and our Saviour ordered the practice of those positive rites as long as the law remained unrepealed, as in the case of the leper (Mark xiv. 4). It is an injustice to refuse the offering ourselves to God according to the manner he hath in his wisdom prescribed and required. If spiritual worship be required by God, then,

2. It informs us, that diligence in outward worship is not to be rested in. Men may attend all their days on worship, with a juiceless heart and unquickened frame, and think to compensate the neglect of the manner with abundance of the matter of service.P Outward expressions are but the badges and liveries of service, not the service itself. As the strength of sin lies in the inward frame of the heart, so the strength of worship in the inward complexion and temper of the soul. What do a thousand services avail, without cutting the throat of our carnal affections? What are loud prayers, but as sounding brass and tinkling cymbals, without divine charity? A pharisaical diligence in outward forms, without inward spirit, had no better a title vouchsafed by our Saviour than that of hypocritical. God desires not sacrifices, nor delights in burnt-offerings: shadows are not to be offered instead of substance. God required the heart of man for itself, but commanded outward ceremonies as subservient to inward worship, and goads and spurs unto it. They were never appointed as the substance of religion, but auxiliaries to it. What value had the offering of the human nature of Christ been of, if he

P Daille, Melange des Sermons. Ser. ii.

had not had a divine nature to qualify him to be the Priest? and what is the oblation of our bodies, without a priestly act of the spirit in the presentation of it? Could the Israelites have called themselves worshippers of God according to his order, if they had brought a thousand lambs that had died in a ditch, or been killed at home? They were to be brought living to the altar; the blood shed at the foot of it. A thousand sacrifices killed without had not been so valuable as one brought alive to the place of offering: one sound sacrifice is better than a thousand rotten ones. As God took no pleasure in the blood of beasts without its relation to the Antitype; so he takes no pleasure in the outward rites of worship, without faith in the Redeemer. To offer a body with a sapless spirit, is a sacrilege of the same nature with that of the Israelites when they offered dead beasts. A man without spiritual worship is dead while he worships, though by his diligence in the externals of it, he may, like the angel of the church of Sardis, "have a name to live" (Rev. iii. 1). What security can we expect from a multitude of dead services? What weak shields are they against the holy eye and revenging wrath of God! What man, but one out of his wits, would solicit a dead man to be his advocate or champion? Diligence in outward worship is not to be rested in.

Use II. shall be for examination. Let us try ourselves concerning the manner of our worship. We are now in the end of the world, and the dregs of time; wherein the apostle predicts there may be much of a form, and little of the power of godliness (2 Tim. iii. 1, 5); and, therefore, it stands us in hand to search into ourselves, whether it be not thus with us? whether there be as much reverence in our spirits as there may be devotion in our countenances and outward carriages.

1. How, therefore, are our hearts prepared to worship? Is our diligence greater to put our hearts in an adoring posture, than our bodies in a decent garb? or are we content to have a muddy heart, so we may have a dressed carcass? To have a spirit a cage of unclean birds, while we wipe the filth from the outside of the platter, is no better than a pharisaical devotion, and deserves no better a name than that of a whited sepulchre. Do we take opportunities to excite and quicken our spirits to the performance, and cry aloud with David, "Awake, awake, my glory!" Are not our hearts asleep when Christ knocks? When we hear the voice of God, "Seek my face;" do we answer him with warm resolutions, "Thy face, Lord, we will seek?" (Ps. xxvii. 8.) Do we comply with spiritual motions, and strike whilst the iron is hot? Is there not more of reluctancy than readiness? Is there a quick rising of the soul in reverence to the motion, as Eglon to Ehud; or a sullen hanging the head at the first approach of it? Or if our hearts seem to be engaged and on fire, what are the motives that quicken that fire? Is it only the blast of a natural conscience, fear of hell, desires of heaven, as abstracted from God? or is it an affection to God; an obedient will to please him; longings to enjoy him, as a holy and sanctifying God in his ordinances, as well as a blessed and glorified God in heaven? What do we expect in our approaches from him? that which may make

divine impressions upon us, and more exactly conform us to the Divine nature? or do we design nothing but an empty formality, a rolling eye, and a filling the air with a few words, without any openings of heart to receive the incomes, which, according to the nature of the duty, might be conveyed to us? Can this be a spiritual worship? The soul then closely waits upon him, when its expectation is only from him (Psalm lxii. 6). Are our hearts seasoned with a sense of sin; a sight of our spiritual wants; raised notions of God; glowing affections to him; strong appetite after a spiritual fulness? Do we rouse up our sleepy spirits, and make a covenant with all that is within us to attend upon him? So much as we want of this, so much we come short of a spiritual worship. In Ps. lvii. 7 (" My heart is fixed, O God, my heart is fixed"), David would fix his heart, before he would engage in a praising act of worship. He appeals to God about it, and that with doubling the expression, as being certain of an inward preparedness. Can we make the same appeals in a fixation of spirit?

2. How are our hearts fixed upon him; how do they cleave to him in the duty? Do we resign our spirits to God, and make them an entire holocaust, a whole burnt-offering in his worship? or do we not willingly admit carnal thoughts to mix themselves with spiritual duties, and fasten our minds to the creature, under pretences of directing them to the Creator? Do we not pass a mere compliment upon God, by some superficial act of devotion; while some covetous, envious, ambitious, voluptuous imagination may possess our minds? Do we not invert God's order, and worship a lust instead of God with our spirits, that should not have the least service, either from our souls or bodies, but with a spiritual disdain be sacrificed to the just indignation of God? How often do we fight against his will, while we cry, "Hail, Master!" instead of crucifying our own thoughts, crucifying the Lord of our lives; our outward carriage plausible, and our inward stark naught! Do we not often regard iniquity more than God in our hearts, in a time of worship?—roll some filthy imagination as a sweet morsel under our tongues, and taste more sweetness in that than in God? Do not our spirits smell rank of earth, while we offer to heaven; and have we not hearts full of thick clay, as their " hands were full of blood?" (Isa. i. 15.) When we sacrifice, do we not wrap up our souls in communion with some sordid fancy, when we should entwine our spirits about an amiable God? While we have some fear of him, may we not have a love to something else above him? This is to worship, or swear by the Lord, and by Malcham (Zeph. i. 5). How often doth an apish fancy render a service inwardly ridiculous, under a grave outward posture; skipping to the shop, warehouse, counting-house, in the space of a short prayer! and we are before God as a Babel, a confusion of internal languages; and this in those parts of worship which are, in the right use, most agreeable to God, profitable for ourselves, ruinous to the kingdom of sin and Satan, and means to bring us into a closer communion with the Divine Majesty. Can this be a spiritual worship?

3. How do we act our graces in worship? Though the instru-

ment be strung, if the strings be not wound up, what melody can be the issue? All readiness and alacrity discover a strength of nature; and a readiness in spirituals discovers a spirituality in the heart. As unaffecting thoughts of God are not spiritual thoughts, so unaffecting addresses to God are not spiritual addresses. Well, then, what awakenings, and elevations of faith and love have we? What strong outflowings of our souls to him? What indignation against sin? What admirations of redeeming grace? How low have we brought our corruptions to the footstool of Christ, to be made his conquered enemies? How straitly have we clasped our faith about the cross and throne of Christ, to become his intimate spouse? Do we in hearing hang upon the lips of Christ; in prayer take hold of God, and will not let him go; in confessions rend the caul of our hearts, and indite our souls before him with a deep humility? Do we act more by a soaring love than a drooping fear? So far as our spirits are servile, so far they are legal and carnal; so much as they are free and spontaneous, so much they are evangelical and spiritual. As men under the law are subject to the constraint of "bondage all their life-time" (Heb. ii. 15), in all their worship; so under the gospel they are under a constraint of love (2 Cor. v. 14): how then are believing affections exercised, which are alway accompanied with holy fear; a fear of his goodness that admits us into his presence, and a fear to offend him in our act of worship? So much as we have of forced or feeble affection, so much we have of carnality.

4. How do we find our hearts after worship? By an after carriage we may judge of the spirituality of it.

(1.) How are we as to inward strength? When a worship is spiritually performed, grace is more strengthened, corruption more mortified; the soul, like Samson after his awakening, goes out with a renewed strength; as the inward man is renewed day by day, that is, every day; so it is renewed in every worship. Every shower makes the grass and fruit grow in good ground where the root is good, and the weeds where the ground is naught; the more prepared the heart is to obedience in other duties after worship, the more evidence there is that it hath been spiritual in the exercise of it. It is the end of God in every dispensation, as in that of John Baptist, "to make ready a people prepared for the Lord" (Luke i. 17): when the heart is by worship prepared for fresh acts of obedience, and hath a more exact watchfulness against the encroachments of sin. As carnal men after worship sprout up in spiritual wickedness, so do spiritual worshippers in spiritual graces; spiritual fruits are a sign of a spiritual frame. When men are more prone to sin after duty, it is a sign there was but little communion with God in it; and a greater strength of sin, because such an act is contrary to the end of worship which is the subduing of sin. It is a sign the physic hath wrought well, when the stomach hath a better appetite to its appointed food; and worship hath been well performed, when we have a stronger inclination to other acts well pleasing to God, and a more sensible distaste of those temptations we too much relished before. It is a sign of a good concoction, when there is a greater strength in the vitals of religion, a more eager desire to know God. When Moses had been praying to God, and prevailed with him, he puts up a higher request to "behold his glory" (Exod. xxxiii. 13, 18): when the appetite stands strong to fuller discoveries of God, it is a sign there hath been a spiritual converse with him.

(2.) How is it especially as to humility? The Pharisees' worship was, without dispute, carnal; and we find them not more humble after all their devotions, but overgrown with more weeds of spiritual pride; they performed them as their righteousness. What men dare plead before God in his day, they plead before him in their hearts in their day; but this men will do at the day of judgment: "We have prophesied in thy name," &c. (Matt. vii. 21). They show what tincture their services left upon their spirits; that which excludes them from any acceptation at the last day, excludes them from any estimation of being spiritual in this day. The carnal worshippers charge God with injustice in not rewarding them, and claim an acceptation as a compensation due to them (Isa. lviii. 3): "Wherefore have we afflicted our souls, and thou takest no knowledge?" A spiritual worshipper looks upon his duties with shame, as well as he doth upon his sins with confusion; and implores the mercy of God for the one as well as the other. In Psalm cxliii. 2, the prophet David, after his supplications, begs of God not to enter into judgment with him; and acknowledges any answer that God should give him, as a fruit of his faithfulness to his promise, and not the merit of his worship: "In thy faithfulness answer me," &c. Whatsoever springs from a gracious principle, and is the breath of the Spirit, leaves a man more humble; whereas, that which proceeds from a stock of nature, hath the true blood of nature running in the veins of it; viz., that pride which is naturally derived from Adam. The breathing of the Divine Spirit is, in everything, to conform us to our Redeemer; that being the main work of his office, is his work in every particular christian act influenced by him. Now Jesus Christ, in all his actions, was an exact pattern of all humility. After the institution and celebration of the supper, a special act of worship in the church, though he had a sense of all the authority his Father had given him, yet he "humbles himself to wash his disciples' feet" (John xiii. 2–4); and after his sublime prayer (John xvii.), "He humbles himself to the death, and offers himself" to his murderers, because of his Father's pleasure. (John xviii. 1): "When he had spoken those words, he went over the brook Kedron into the garden." What is the end of God in appointing worship, is the end of a spiritual heart in offering it; not his own exaltation, but God's glory. Glorifying the name of God is the fruit of that evangelical worship the Gentiles were in time to give to God (Ps. lxxxvi. 9): "All nations which thou hast made shall come and worship before thee, O Lord, and shall glorify thy name." Let us examine, then, what debasing ourselves there is in a sense of our own vileness, and distance from so glorious a Spirit. Self-denial is the heart of all gospel grace. Evangelical, spiritual worship cannot be without the ingredient of the main evangelical principle.

(3.) What delight is there after it? What pleasure is there, and what is the object of that pleasure? Is it the communion we have had with God, or a fluency in ourselves? Is it something which hath touched our hearts, or tickled our fancies? As the strength of sin is known by the delightful thoughts of it after the commission; so is the spirituality of duty, by the object of our delightful remembrance after the performance. It was a sign David was spiritual in the worship of God in the tabernacle, when he enjoyed it, because he longed for the spiritual part of it, when he was exiled from it; his desires were not only for liberty to revisit the tabernacle, but to see the "power and glory of God in the sanctuary," as he had seen it before (Ps. lxiii. 2): his desires for it could not have been so ardent, if his reflection upon what had past had not been delightful; nor could his soul be poured out in him, for the want of such opportunities, if the remembrance of the converse he had had with God, had not been accompanied with a delightful relish (Ps. xlii. 4). Let us examine what delight we find in our spirits after worship.

Use III. is of comfort. And it is very comfortable to consider, that the smallest worship with the heart and spirit, flowing from a principle of grace, is more acceptable than the most pompous veneration; yea, if the oblation were as precious as the whole circuit of heaven and earth without it. That God that values a cup of cold water given to any as his disciple, will value a sincere service above a costly sacrifice. God hath his eye upon them that honor his nature; he would not "seek such to worship him," if he did not intend to accept such a worship from them; when we therefore invoke him, and praise him, which are the prime parts of religion, he will receive it as a sweet savor from us, and overlook infirmities mixed with the graces. The great matter of discomfort, and that which makes us question the spirituality of worship, is the many starts of our spirits, and rovings to other things. For answer to which,

1. It is to be confessed that these starts are natural to us. Who is free from them? We bear in our bosoms a nest of turbulent thoughts, which, like busy gnats, will be buzzing about us while we are in our most inward and spiritual converses. Many wild beasts lurk in a man's heart, as in a close and covert wood, and scarce discover themselves but at our solemn worship. No duty so holy, no worship so spiritual, that can wholly privilege us from them; they will jog us in our most weighty employments, that, as God said to Cain, sin lies at the door, and enters in, and makes a riot in our souls. As it is said of wicked men, "they cannot sleep" for multitude of thoughts (Eccles. v. 12); so it may be of many a good man, he cannot worship for multitude of thoughts; there will be starts, and more in our religious than natural employments; it is natural to man. Some therefore think, the bells tied to Aaron's garments, between the pomegranates, were to warn the people, and recall their fugitive minds to the present service, when they heard the sound of them, upon the least motion of the high-priest. The sacrifice of Abraham, the father or the faithful, was not exempt from the fowls

pecking at it (Gen. xv. 11). Zechariah himself was drowsy in the midst of his visions, which being more amazing, might cause a heavenly intentness (Zech. iv. 1): "The angel that talked with me, came again and awaked me, as a man is awaked out of sleep." He had been roused up before, but he was ready to drop down again; his heart was gone, till the angel jogged him. We may complain of such imaginations, as Jeremiah doth of the enemies of the Jews (Lam. iv. 19). Our persecutors are swifter than eagles; they light upon us with as much speed as eagles upon a carcass; they pursue us upon the mountain of divine institutions, and they lay wait for us in the wilderness, in our retired addresses to God. And this will be so while,

(1.) There is natural corruption in us. There are in a godly man two contrary principles, flesh and spirit, which endeavor to hinder one another's acts, and are alway stirring upon the offensive or defensive part (Gal. v. 17). There is a body of death, continually exhaling its noisome vapors: it is a body of death in our worship, as well as in our natures; it snaps our resolutions asunder (Rom. vii. 19); it hinders us in the doing good, and contradicts our wills in the stirring up evil. This corruption being seated in all the faculties, and a constant domestic in them, has the greater opportunity to trouble us, since it is by those faculties that we spiritually transact with God; and it stirs more in the time of religious exercises, though it be in part mortified; as a wounded beast, though tired, will rage and strive to its utmost, when the enemy is about to fetch a blow at it. All duties of worship tend to the wounding of corruption; and it is no wonder to feel the striving of sin to defend itself and offend us, when we have our arms in our hands to mortify it, that the blow may be diverted which is directed against it. The apostles had aspiring thoughts; and being persuaded of an earthly kingdom, expected a grandeur in it; and though we find some appearance of it at other times, as when they were casting out devils, and gave an account of it to their Master, he gives them a kind of a check (Luke x. 20), intimating that there was some kind of evil in their rejoicing upon that account; yet this never swelled so high, as to break out into a quarrel who should be greatest, until they had the most solemn ordinance, the Lord's supper, to quell it (Luke xxii. 24). Our corruption is like lime, which discovers not its fire by any smoke or heat, till you cast water, the enemy of fire, upon it; neither doth our natural corruption rage so much, as when we are using means to quench and destroy it.

(2.) While there is a devil, and we in his precinct. As he accuseth us to God, so he disturbs us in ourselves; he is a bold spirit, and loves to intrude himself when we are conversing with God: we read, that when the angels presented themselves before God, Satan comes among them (Job i. 6). Motions from Satan will thrust themselves in with our most raised and angelical frames; he loves to take off the edge of our spirits from God; he acts but after the old rate; he from the first envied God an obedience from man, and envied man the felicity of communion with God; he is unwilling God should have the honor of worship, and that we should have the fruit of it;

he hath himself lost it, and therefore is unwilling we should enjoy it; and being subtle, he knows how to make impressions upon us suitable to our inbred corruptions, and assault us in the weakest part. He knows all the avenues to get within us (as he did in the temptation of Eve), and being a spirit, he wants not a power to dart them immediately upon our fancy; and being a spirit, and therefore active and nimble, he can shoot those darts faster than our weakness can beat them off. He is diligent also, and watcheth for his prey, and seeks to devour our services as well as our souls, and snatch our best morsels from us. We know he mixed himself with our Saviour's retirements in the wilderness, and endeavored to fly-blow his holy converse with his Father in the preparation to his mediatory work. Satan is God's ape, and imitates the Spirit in the office of a remembrancer; as the Spirit brings good thoughts and divine promises to mind, to quicken our worship, so the devil brings evil things to mind, and endeavors to fasten them in our souls to disturb us; and though all the foolish starts we have in worship are not purely his issue, yet being of kin to him, he claps his hands, and sets them on like so many mastiffs, to tear the service in pieces. And both those distractions, which arise from our own corruption and from Satan, are most rife in worship, when we are under some pressing affliction. This seems to be David's case, Ps. lxxxvi. when in ver. 11 he prays God to unite his heart to fear and worship his name; he seems to be under some affliction, or fear of his enemies: " O free me from those distractions of spirit, and those passions which arise in my soul, upon considering the designs of my enemies against me, and press upon me in my addresses to thee, and attendances on thee." Job also in his affliction complains (Job xvii. 11) that " his purposes were broken off;" he could not make an even thread of thoughts and resolutions; they were frequently snapt asunder, like rotten yarn when one is winding it up. Good men and spiritual worshippers have lain under this trouble. Though they are a sign of weakness of grace, or some obstructions in the acting of strong grace, yet they are not alway evidences of a want of grace; what ariseth from our own corruption, is to be matter of humiliation and resistance; what ariseth from Satan, should edge our minds to a noble conquest of them. If the apostle did comfort himself with his disapproving of what rose from the natural spring of sin within him, with his consent to the law, and dissent from his lust; and charges it not upon himself, but upon the sin that dwelt in him, with which he had broken off the former league, and was resolved never to enter into amity with it; by the same reason we may comfort ourselves, if such thoughts are undelighted in, and alienate not our hearts from the worship of God by all their busy intrusions to interrupt us.

2. These distractions (not allowed) may be occasions, by an holy improvement, to make our hearts more spiritual after worship, though they disturb us in it, by answering those ends for which we may suppose God permits them to invade us. And that is,

First, When they are occasions to humble us,

(1.) For our carriage in the particular worship. There is nothing so dangerous as spiritual pride; it deprived devils and men of the presence of God, and will hinder us of the influence of God. If we had had raised and uninterrupted motions in worship, we should be apt to be lifted up; and the devil stands ready to tempt us to self-confidence. You know how it was with Paul (2 Cor. xii. 1–7); his buffetings were occasions to render him more spiritual than his raptures, because more humble. God suffers those wanderings, starts, and distractions, to prevent our spiritual pride; which is as a worm at the root of spiritual worship, and mind us of the dusty frame of our spirits, how easily they are blown away; as he sends sickness to put us in mind of the shortness of our breath, and the easiness to lose it. God would make us ashamed of ourselves in his presence; that we may own, that what is good in any duty, is merely from his grace and Spirit, and not from ourselves; that with Paul we may cry out, "By grace we are what we are," and by grace we do what we do; we may be hereby made sensible, that God can alway find something in our exactest worship, as a ground of denying us the successful fruit of it. If we cannot stand upon our duties for salvation, what can we bottom upon in ourselves? If therefore they are occasions to make us out of love with any righteousness of our own, to make us break our hearts for them, because we cannot keep them out; if we mourn for them as our sins, and count them our great afflictions, we have attained that brokenness which is a choice ingredient in a spiritual sacrifice. Though we have been disturbed by them, yet we are not robbed of the success; we may behold an answer of our worship in our humiliation, in spite of all of them.

(2.) For the baseness of our nature. These unsteady motions help us to discern that heap of vermin that breeds in our nature. Would any man think he had such an averseness to his Creator and Benefactor; such an unsuitableness to him; such an estrangedness from him, were it not for his inspection into his distracted frame? God suffers this to hang over us as a rod of correction, to discover and fetch out the folly of our hearts. Could we imagine our natures so highly contrary to that God who is so infinitely amiable, so desirable an object; or that there should be so much folly and madness in the heart, as to draw back from God in those services which God hath appointed as pipes through which to communicate his grace, to convey himself, his love and goodness to the creature? If, therefore, we have a deep sense of, and strong reflections upon our base nature, and bewail that mass of averseness which lies there, and that fulness of irreverence towards the God of our mercies, the object of our worship, it is a blessed improvement of our wanderings and diversions. Certainly, if any Israelite had brought a lame and rotten lamb to be sacrificed to God, and afterward had bewailed it, and laid open his heart to God in a sensible and humble confession of it, that repentance had been a better sacrifice, and more acceptable in the sight of God, than if he had brought a sound and a living offering.

Secondly, When they are occasions to make us prize duties of worship. When we argue, as rationally we may, that they are of singular use, since our corrupt hearts and a malicious devil doth chiefly endeavor to hinder us from them, and that we find we have not those gadding thoughts when we are upon worldly business, or upon any sinful design which may dishonor God and wound our souls. This is a sign sin and Satan dislike worship, for he is too subtle a spirit to oppose that which would further his kingdom. As it is an argument the Scripture is the word of God, because the wickedness of the world doth so much oppose it, so it is a ground to believe the profitableness and excellency of worship, because Satan and our own unruly hearts do so much interrupt us in it: if, therefore, we make this use of our cross-steps in worship, to have a greater value for such duties, more affections to them, and desires to be frequent in them, our hearts are growing spiritual under the weights that would depress them to carnality.

Thirdly, When we take a rise from hence, to have heavenly admirations of the graciousness of God, that he should pity and pardon so many slight addresses to him, and give any gracious returns to us. Though men have foolish rangings every day, and in every duty, yet free grace is so tender as not to punish them (Gen. viii. 21): "And the Lord smelt a sweet savor; and the Lord said in his heart, I will not curse the ground for man's sake, for the imagination of man's heart is evil from his youth." It is observable, that this was just after a sacrifice which Noah offered to God (ver. 20): but probably not without infirmities common to human nature, which may be grounded upon the reason God gives, that though he had destroyed the earth before, because of the "evil of man's imaginations" (Gen. vi. 5), he still found evil imaginations; he doth not say in the heart of Cham, or others of Noah's family, but in man's heart, including Noah also, who had both the judgments of God upon the former world, and the mercy of God in his own preservation, before his eyes; yet God saw evil imaginations rooted in the nature of man, and though it were so, yet he would be merciful. If, therefore, we can, after finding our hearts so vagrant in worship, have real frames of thankfulness that God hath spared us, and be heightened in our admirations at God's giving us any fruit of such a distracted worship, we take advantage from them to be raised into an evangelical frame, which consists in the humble acknowledgments of the grace of God. When David takes a review of those tumultuous passions which had ruffled his mind, and possessed him with unbelieving notions of God in the persons of his prophets (Ps. cxvi. 11), how high doth his soul mount in astonishment and thankfulness to God for his mercy! (ver. 12.) Notwithstanding his distrust, God did graciously perform his promise, and answer his desire: then it is, "What shall I render to the Lord?" His heart was more affected for it, because it had been so passionate in former distrusts. It is indeed a ground of wondering at the patience of the Spirit of God, that he should guide our hearts when they are so apt to start out, as it is the patience of a master to guide the hand of his scholar, while he mixes his writing with many blots. It is not one or two infirmities the Spirit helps us in, and helps over, but many (Rom. viii. 26). It is a sign of a spiritual heart, when he can take a rise to bless God for the renewing and blowing up his affections, in the midst of so many incursions from Satan to the contrary, and the readiness of the heart too much to comply with them.

Fourthly, When we take occasion from thence to prize the mediation of Christ. The more distractions jog us, the more need we should see of going out to a Saviour by faith. One part of our Saviour's office is to stand between us and the infirmities of our worship. As he is an advocate, he presents our services, and pleads for them and us (1 John ii. 1), for the sins of our duties, as well as for our other sins. Jesus Christ is an High-priest, appointed by God to take away the "iniquities of our holy things," which was typified by Aaron's plate upon his mitre (Exod. xxviii. 36, 38). Were there no imperfections, were there no creeping up of those frogs into our minds, we should think our worship might merit acceptance with God upon its own account; but if we behold our own weakness, that not a tear, a groan, a sigh, is so pure, but must have Christ to make it entertainable; that there is no worship without those blemishes; and upon this, throw all our services into the arms of Christ for acceptance, and solicit him to put his merits in the front, to make our ciphers appear valuable; it is a spiritual act, the design of God in the gospel being to advance the honor and mediation of his Son. That is a spiritual and evangelical act which answers the evangelical design. The design of Satan, and our own corruption is defeated, when those interruptions make us run swifter, and take faster hold on the High-priest who is to present our worship to God, and our own souls receive comfort thereby. Christ had temptations offered to him by the devil in his wilderness retirement, that, from an experimental knowledge, he might be able more "compassionately to succor us" (Heb. ii. 18); we have such assaults in our retired worship especially, that we may be able more highly to value him and his mediation.

3. Let us not, therefore, be discouraged by those interruptions and starts of our hearts.

(1.) If we find in ourselves a strong resistance of them. The flesh will be lusting; that cannot be hindered; yet if we do not fulfil the lusts of it, rise up at its command, and go about its work, we may be said to walk in the Spirit (Gal. v. 16, 17): we "walk in the Spirit," if we "fulfil not the lusts of the flesh," though there be a lusting of the flesh against the Spirit; so we worship in the Spirit, though there be carnal thoughts arising if we do not fulfil them; though the stirring of them discovers some contrariety in us to God, yet the resistance manifests that there is a principle of contrariety in us to them; that as there is something of flesh that lusts against the spirit, so there is something of spirit in worship which lusts against the flesh: we must take heed of omitting worship, because of such inroads, and lying down in the mire of a total neglect. If our spirits are made more lively and vigorous against them; if those cold vapors which have risen from our hearts make us, like a spring in the midst of the cold earth, more warm, there is, in this case, more reason for us to bless God, than to be discouraged. God looks upon it as the disease, not the wilfulness of our nature; as the weakness of the flesh, not the willingness of the spirit. If we would shut the door upon them, it seems they are unwelcome company; men do not use to lock their doors upon those they love; if they break in and dis-

turb us with their impertinences, we need not be discomforted, unless
we give them a share in our affections, and turn our back upon God
to entertain them; if their presence makes us sad, their flight would
make us joyful.

(2.) If we find ourselves excited to a stricter watch over our
hearts against them; as travellers will be careful when they come to
places where they have been robbed before, that they be not so easily surprised again. We should not only lament when we have had
such foolish imaginations in worship breaking in upon us, but also
bless God that we have had no more, since we have hearts so fruitful of weeds. We should give God the glory when we find our
hearts preserved from these intruders, and not boast of ourselves,
but return him our praise for the watch and guard he kept over us,
to preserve us from such thieves. Let us not be discomforted;
for as the greatness of our sins, upon our turning to God, is no hindrance to our justification, because it doth not depend upon our conversion as the meritorious cause, but upon the infinite value of our
Saviour's satisfaction, which reaches the greatest sins as well as the
least; so the multitude of our bewailed distractions in worship are
not a hindrance to our acceptation, because of the uncontrollable
power of Christ's intercession.

Use IV. is for exhortation. Since spiritual worship is due to God,
and the Father seeks such to worship him, how much should we endeavor to satisfy the desire and order of God, and act conformable
to the law of our creation and the love of redemption! Our
end must be the same in worship which was God's end in creation and redemption; to glorify his name, set forth his perfections,
and be rendered fit, as creatures and redeemed ones, to partake of
that grace which is the fruit of worship. An evangelical dispensation requires a spiritual homage; to neglect, therefore, either the
matter or manner of gospel duties, is to put a slight upon gospel
privileges. The manner of duty is ever of more value than the
matter; the scarlet dye is more precious than the cloth tinctured
with it. God respects more the disposition of the sacrificer than the
multitude of the sacrifices.q The solemn feasts appointed by God
were but dung as managed by the Jews (Mal. ii. 3). The heart
is often welcome without the body, but the body never grateful
without the heart. The inward acts of the spirit require nothing
from without to constitute them good in themselves; but the outward acts of devotion require inward acts to render them savory to
God. As the goodness of outward acts consists not in the acts themselves, so the acceptableness of them results not from the acts themselves, but from the inward frame animating and quickening those
acts, as blood and spirits running through the veins of a duty to
make it a living service in the sight of God. Imperfections in worship hinder not God's acceptation of it, if the heart, spirited by
grace, be there to make it a sweet savor. The stench of burning
flesh and fat in the legal sacrifices might render them noisome to the
outward senses; but God smelt a sweet savor in them, as they

q Μάλλον τὸ δαιμόνιον πρὸς τὸ τῶν φυόντων ἦθος ἢ τῶν θυομένων πλῆθος. Porphyr. de
Abstinentia.

respected Christ. When the heart and spirit are offered up to God, it may be a savory duty, though attended with unsavory imperfections; but a thousand sacrifices without a stamp of faith, a thousand spiritual duties with an habitual carnality, are no better than stench with God. The heart must .be purged, as well as the temple was by our Saviour, of the thieves that would rob God of his due worship. Antiquity had some temples wherein it was a crime to bring any gold; therefore those that came to worship laid their gold aside before they went into the temple. We should lay aside our worldly and trading thoughts before we address to worship (Isa. xxvi. 9): "With my spirit within me will I seek thee early." Let not our minds be gadding abroad, and exiled from God and themselves. It will be thus when the "desire of our soul is to his name, and the remembrance of him" (ver. 8). When he hath given so great and admirable a gift as that of his Son, in whom are all things necessary to salvation, righteousness, peace, and pardon of sin, we should manage the remembrance of his name in worship with the closest unitedness of heart, and the most spiritual affections. The motion of the spirit is the first act in religion; to this we are obliged in every act. The devil requires the spirit of his votaries; should God have a less dedication than the devil?

Motives to back this exhortation.

I. Not to give God our spirit is a great sin. It is a mockery of God, not worship, contempt, not adoration, whatever our outward fervency or protestations may be.[r] Every alienation of our hearts from him is a real scorn put upon him. The acts of the soul are real, and more the acts of the man than the acts of the body; because they are the acts of the choicest part of man, and of that which is the first spring of all bodily motions; it is the λόγος ἐνδιαθετος, the internal speech whereby we must speak with God. To give him, therefore, only an external form of worship without the life of it, is a taking his name in vain. We mock him, when we mind not what we are speaking to him, or what he is speaking to us; when the motions of our hearts are contrary to the motions of our tongues; when we do anything before him slovenly, impudently, or rashly. As in a lutinist it is absurd to sing one tune and play another; so it is a foul thing to tell God one thing with our lips, and think another with our hearts. It is a sin like that the apostle chargeth the heathens with (Rom. i. 28): "They like not to retain God in their knowledge." Their stomachs are sick while they are upon any duty, and never leave working till they have thrown up all the spiritual part of worship, and rid themselves of the thoughts of God, which are as unwelcome and troublesome guests to them. When men behave themselves in the sight of God, as if God were not God, they do not only defame him, but deny him, and violate the unchangeable perfections of the Divine nature.

1. It is against the majesty of God, when we have not awful thoughts of that great Majesty to whom we address; when our souls cleave not to him when we petition him in prayer, or when he gives out his orders to us in his Word. It is a contempt of the majesty of a prince, if, whilst he is speaking to us, we listen not to him with

<hr>
[r] "Non valet protestatio contra factum," is a rule in the civil law.

reverence and attention, but turn our backs on him, to play with one of his hounds, or talk with a beggar; or while we speak to him, to rake in a dunghill. Solomon adviseth us to "keep our foot when we go to the house of God" (Eccles. v. 1). Our affections should be steady, and not slip away again; why? (ver. 2) because "God is in heaven," &c. He is a God of majesty; earthly, dirty frames are unsuitable to the God of heaven; low spirits are unsuitable to the Most High. We would not bring our mean servants or dirty dogs into a prince's presence chamber; yet we bring not only our worldly, but our profane affections into God's presence. We give in this case those services to God which our Governor would think unworthy of him (Mal. i. 8). The more excellent and glorious God is, the greater contempt of him it is to suffer such foolish affections to be competitors with him for our hearts. It is a scorn put upon him to converse with a creature, while we are dealing with him; but a greater to converse in our thoughts and fancies with some sordid lust, which is most hateful to him; and the more aggravation it attracts, in that we are to apprehend him the most glorious object sitting upon his throne in time of worship, and ourselves standing as vile creatures before him, supplicating for our lives, and the conveyance of grace and mercy to our souls; as if a grand mutineer, instead of humbly begging the pardon of his offended prince, should present his petition not only scribbled and blotted, but besmeared with some loathsome excrement. It is unbecoming both the majesty of God, and the worship itself, to present him with a picture instead of a substance, and bring a world of nasty affections in our hearts, and ridiculous toys in our heads before him, and worship with indisposed and heedless souls. He is a great King (Mal. i. 14): therefore address to him with fear and reverence.

2. It is against the life of God. Is a dead worship proportioned to a living God? The separation of heavenly affections from our souls before God, makes them as much a carcass in his sight, as the divorce of the soul makes the body a carcass. When the affections are separated, worship is no longer worship, but a dead offering, a lifeless bulk; for the essence and spirit of worship is departed. Though the soul be present with the body in a way of information, yet it is not present in a way of affection, and this is the worst; for it is not the separation of the soul from informing that doth separate a man from God, but the removal of our affections from him. If a man pretend an application to God, and sleep and snore all the time, without question such a one did not worship. In a careless worship the heart is morally dead while the eyes are open: the heart of the spouse (Cant. v. 2) waked while her eyes slept; and our hearts, on the contrary, sleep while our eyes wake. Our blessed Saviour hath died to purge our consciences from dead works and frames, that we may serve the living God (Heb. ix. 14); to serve God as a God of life. David's soul cried and fainted for God under this consideration (Ps. xlii. 2); but to present our bodies without our spirits, is such a usage of God, that implies he is a dead image, not worthy of any but a dead and heartless service, like one of those idols the Psalmist speaks of (Ps. cxv. 5), that have "eyes, and see not; ears,

and hear not;" no life in it. Though it be not an objective idolatry, because the worship is directed to the true God; yet I may call it a subjective idolatry in regard of the frame, fit only to be presented to some senseless stock. We intimate God to be no better than an idol, and to have no more knowledge of us and insight into us, than an idol can have. If we did believe him to be the living God, we durst not come before him with services so unsuitable to him, and reproaches of him.

3. It is against the infiniteness of God. We should worship God with those boundless affections which bear upon them a shadow or image of his infiniteness; such are the desires of the soul which know no limits, but start out beyond whatsoever enjoyment the heart of man possesses. No creeping creature was to be offered to God in sacrifice, but such as had legs to run, or wings to fly. For us to come before God with a light creeping frame, is to worship him with the lowest finite affections, as though anything, though never so mean or torn, might satisfy an infinite Being; as though a poor shallow creature could give enough to God without giving him the heart, when, indeed, we cannot give him a worship proportionable to his infiniteness, did our hearts swell as large as heaven in our desires for him in every act of our duties.

4. It is against the spirituality of God. God being a Spirit, calls for a worship in spirit; to withhold this from him implies him to be some gross corporeal matter. As a Spirit, he looks for the heart; a wrestling heart in prayer, a trembling heart in the Word (Isa. lxvi. 2). To bring nothing but the body when we come to a spiritual God to beg spiritual benefits, to wait for spiritual communications, which can only be dispensed to us in a spiritual manner, is unsuitable to the spiritual nature of God. A mere carnal service implicitly denies his spirituality, which requires of us higher engagements than mere corporeal ones. Worship should be rational, not an imaginative service, wherein is required the activity of our noblest faculties; and our fancy ought to have no share in it, but in subserviency to the more spiritual part of our soul.

5. It is against the supremacy of God. As God is one and the only Sovereign; so our hearts should be one, cleaving wholly to him, and undivided from him. In pretending to deal with him, we acknowledge his deity and sovereignty; but in withholding our choicest faculties and affections from him, and the starting of our minds to vain objects, we intimate their equality with God, and their right as well as his to our hearts and affections. It is as if a princess should commit adultery with some base scullion while she is before her husband, which would be a plain denial of his sole right to her. It intimates that other things are superior to God; they are true sovereigns that engross our hearts. If a man were addressing himself to a prince, and should in an instant turn his back upon him, upon a beck or nod from some inconsiderable person; is it not an evidence that that person that invited him away hath a greater sovereignty over him than that prince to whom he was applying himself? And do we not discard God's absolute dominion over us, when, at the least beck of a corrupt inclination, we can dispose of our hearts to it, and alienate

them from God? as they, in Ezek. xxxiii. 32, left the service of God for the service of their covetousness, which evidenced that they owned the authority of sin more than the authority of God. This is not to serve God as our Lord and absolute Master, but to make God serve our turn, and submit his sovereignty to the supremacy of some unworthy affection. The creature is preferred before the Creator, when the heart runs most upon it in time of religious worship, and our own carnal interest swallows up the affections that are due to God. It is "an idol set up in the heart" (Ezek. xiv. 4) in his solemn presence, and attracts that devotion to itself which we only owe to our Sovereign Lord; and the more base and contemptible that is to which the spirit is devoted, the more contempt there is of God's dominion. Judas's kiss, with a "Hail Master!" was no act of worship, or an owning his Master's authority, but a designing the satisfaction of his covetousness in the betraying of him.

6. It is against the wisdom of God. God, as a God of order, has put earthly things in subordination to heavenly; and we, by this unworthy carriage, invert this order, and put heavenly things in subordination to earthly; in placing mean and low things in our hearts, and bringing them so placed into God's presence, which his wisdom at the creation put under our feet. A service without spiritual affections is a "sacrifice of fools" (Eccles. v. 1), which have lost their brains and understandings: a foolish spirit is very unsuitable to an infinitely wise God. Well may God say of such a one, as Achish of David, who seemed mad, "Why have you brought this fellow to play the madman in my presence? Shall this fellow come into my house?" (1 Sam. xxi. 15.)

7. It is against the omnisciency of God. To carry it fair without, and impertinently within, is as though God had not an all-seeing eye that could pierce into the heart, and understand every motion of the inward faculties; as though God were easily cheated with an outward fawning service, like an apothecary's box with a gilded title, that may be full of cobwebs within. What is such a carriage, but a design to deceive God, when, with Herod, we pretend to worship Christ, and intend to murder all the motions of Christ in our souls? A heedless spirit, an estrangement of our souls, a giving the reins to them to run out from the presence of God to see every reed shaken with the wind, is to deny him to be the Searcher of hearts, and the Discerner of secret thoughts; as though he could not look through us to the darkness and remoteness of our minds, but were an ignorant God, who might be put off with the worst as well as the best in our flock. If we did really believe there were a God of infinite knowledge, who saw our frames and whether we came dressed with wedding garments suitable to the duties we are about to perform, should we be so garish, and put him off with such trivial stuff, without any reverence of his Majesty?

8. It is against the holiness of God. To alienate our spirits is to offend him while we pretend to worship him; though we may be mighty officious in the external part, yet our base and carnal affections make all our worship but as a heap of dung; and who would not look upon it as an affront to lay dung before a prince's throne?

(Prov. xxi. 27), "The sacrifice of the wicked is an abomination;" how much more when he brings it with a wicked mind? A putrefied carcass under the law had not been so great an affront to the holiness of God, as a frothy unmelted heart, and a wanton fancy, in a time of worship. God is so holy, that if we could offer the worship of angels, and the quintessence of our souls in his service, it would be beneath his infinite purity; how unworthy, then, are they of him, when they are presented not only without the sense of our uncleanness, but sullied with the fumes and exhalations of our corrupt affections, which are as so many plague-spots upon our duties, contrary to the unspotted purity of the Divine nature? Is not this an unworthy conceit of God, and injurious to his infinite holiness?

9. It is against the love and kindness of God. It is a condescension in God to admit a piece of earth to offer up a duty to him, when he hath myriads of angels to attend him in his court, and celebrate his praise. To admit man to be an attendant on him, and a partner with angels, is a high favor. It is not a single mercy, but a heap of mercies, to be admitted into the presence of God (Ps. v. 7): "I will come into thy house in the multitude of thy mercies." When the blessed God is so kind as to give us access to his majesty, do we not undervalue his kindness when we deal uncivilly with him, and deny him the choicest part of ourselves? It is a contempt of his sovereignty, as our spirits are due to him by nature; a contempt of his goodness, as our spirits are due to him by gratitude. How abusive a carriage is it to make use of his mercy to encourage our impudence, that should excite our fear and reverence! How unworthy would it be for an indigent debtor to bring to his indulgent creditor an empty purse instead of payment! When God holds out his golden sceptre to encourage our approaches to him, stands ready to give us the pardon of sin and full felicity, the best things he hath, is it a fit requital of his kindness to give him a formal outside only, a shadow of religion; to have the heart overswayed with other thoughts and affections, as if all his proffers were so contemptible as to deserve only a slight at our hands? It is a contempt of the love and kindness of God.

10. It is against the sufficiency and fulness of God. When we give God our bodies, and the creature our spirits, it intimates a conceit that there is more content to be had in the creature than in God blessed forever; that the waters in the cistern are sweeter than those in the fountain. Is not this a practical giving God the lie, and denying those promises wherein he hath declared the satisfaction he can give to the spirit, as he is the God of the spirits of all flesh? If we did imagine the excellency and loveliness of God were worthy to be the ultimate object of our affections, the heart would attend more closely upon him, and be terminated in him; did we believe God to be all-sufficient, full of grace and goodness, a tender Father, not willing to forsake his own, willing, as well as able, to supply their wants, the heart would not so lamely attend upon him, and would not upon every impertinency be diverted from him. There is much of a wrong notion of God, and a predominancy of the world above him in the heart, when we can more savorly relish the thoughts of

low inferior things than heavenly, and let our spirits upon every trifling occasion be fugitive from him; it is a testimony that we make not God our chiefest good. If apprehensions of his excellency did possess our souls, they would be fastened on him, glued to him; we should not listen to that rabble of foolish thoughts that steal our hearts so often from him. Were our breathings after God as strong as the pantings of the hart after the water-brooks, we should be like that creature, not diverted in our course by every puddle. Were God the predominant satisfactory object in our eye, he would carry our whole soul along with him. When our spirits readily retreat from God in worship upon every giddy motion, it is a kind of repentance that ever we did come near him, and implies that there is a fuller satisfaction, and more attractive excellency in that which doth so easily divert us, than in that God to whose worship we did pretend to address ourselves. It is as if, when we are petitioning a prince, we should immediately turn about, and make request to one of his guard, as though so mean a person were more able to give us the boon we want than the sovereign is.

II. Consideration by way of motive. To have our spirits off from God in worship is a bad sign: it was not so in innocence. The heart of Adam could cleave to God: the law of God was engraven upon him, he could apply himself to the fulfilling of it without any twinkling. There was no folly and vanity in his mind, no independency in his thoughts, no duty was his burden; for there was in him a proneness to, and a delight in, all the duties of worship. It is the fall hath distempered us; and the more unwieldiness there is in our spirits, the more carnal our affections are in worship, the more evidence there is of the strength of that revolted state.

1. It argues much corruption in the heart. As by the eructations of the stomach, we may judge of the windiness and foulness of it; so, by the inordinate motions of our minds and hearts, we may judge of the weakness of its complexion. A strength of sin is evidenced by the eruptions and ebullitions of it in worship, when they are more sudden, numerous, and vigorous than the motions of grace. When the heart is apt, like tinder, to catch fire from Satan, it is a sign of much combustible matter suitable to his temptation. Were not corruption strong, the soul could not turn so easily from God when it is in his presence, and hath an advantageous opportunity to create a fear and awe of God in it. Such base fruit could not sprout up so suddenly, were there not much sap and juice in the root of sin. What communion with a living root can be evidenced without exercises of an inward life? That spirit, which is a well of living waters in a gracious heart, will be especially springing up when it is before God.

2. It shows much affection to earthly things, and little to heavenly. There must needs be an inordinate affection to earthly things, when, upon every slight solicitation, we can part with God, and turn the back upon a service glorious for him and advantageous for ourselves, to wed our hearts to some idle fancy that signifies nothing. How can we be said to entertain God in our affections, when we give him not the precedency in our understandings, but let every

trifle jostle the sense of God out of our minds? Were our hearts fully determined to spiritual things, such vanities could not seat themselves in our understandings, and divide our spirits from God. Were our hearts balanced with a love to God, the world could never steal our hearts so much from his worship, but his worship would draw our hearts to it. It shows a base neutrality in the greatest concernments; a halting between God and Baal; a contrariety between affection and conscience, when natural conscience presses a man to duties of worship, and his other affections pull him back, draw him to carnal objects, and make him slight that whereby he may honor God. God argues the profaneness of the Jews' hearts from the wickedness they brought into his house, and acted there (Jer. xxiii. 11): "Yea, in my house," that is, my worship, "I found their wickedness," saith the Lord. Carnality in worship is a kind of an idolatrous frame; when the heart is renewed, idols are cast to the moles and the bats (Isa. ii. 20).

3. It shows much hypocrisy to have our spirits off from God. The mouth speaks, and the carriage pretends what the heart doth not think; there is a dissent of the heart from the pretence of the body. Instability is a sure sign of hypocrisy. Double thoughts argue a double heart. The wicked are compared to chaff (Ps. i. 4), for the uncertain and various motions of their minds, by the least wind of fancy. The least motion of a carnal object diverts the spirit from God, as the scent of carrion doth the raven from the flight it was set upon. The people of God are called God's spouse, and God calls himself their husband; whereby is noted the most intimate union of the soul with God; and that there ought to be the highest love and affection to him, and faithfulness in his worship; but when the heart doth start from him in worship, it is a sign of the unsteadfastness of it with God, and a disrelish of any communion with him; it is, as God complains of the Israelites, a going a whoring after our own imaginations. As grace respects God as the object of worship, so it looks most upon God in approaching to him. Where there is a likeness and love, there is a desire of converse and intimacy; if there be no spiritual entwining about God in our worship, it is a sign there is no likeness to him, no true sense of him, no renewed image of God in us; every living image will move strongly to join itself with its original copy, and be glad, with Jacob, to sit steadily in those chariots that shall convey him to his beloved Joseph.

III. Consider the danger of a carnal worship.

1. We lose the comfort of worship. The soul is a great gainer when it offers a spiritual worship, and as great a loser when it is unfaithful with God. Treachery and perfidiousness hinder commerce among men; so doth hypocrisy in its own nature communion with God. God never promised anything to the carcass, but to the spirit of worship. God hath no obligation upon him, by any word of his, to reward us with himself, when we perform it not to himself; when we give an outside worship, we have only the outside of an ordinance; we can expect no kernel, when we give God only the shell: he that only licks the outside of the glass, can never be refreshed

with the rich cordial enclosed within. A cold and lazy formality will make God to withdraw the light of his countenance, and not shine with any delightful communications upon our souls; but if we come before him with a liveliness of affections, and steadiness of heart, he will draw the veil, and cause his glory to display itself before us. An humble praying Christian, and a warm, affectionate Christian in worship, will soon find a God who is delighted with such frames, and cannot long withhold himself from the soul. When our hearts are inflamed with love to him in worship, it is a preparation to some act of love on his part, whereby he intends further to gratify us. When John was in the Spirit on the Lord's day, that is, in spiritual employment, and meditation, and other duties, he had that great revelation of what should happen to the church in all ages (Rev. i. 10); his being in the Spirit, intimates his ordinary course on that day, and not any extraordinary act in him, though it was followed with an extraordinary discovery of God to him; when he was thus engaged, "he heard a voice behind him." God doth not require of us spirituality in worship to advantage himself, but that we might be prepared to be advantaged by him. If we have a clear and well-disposed eye, it is not a benefit to the sun, but fits us to receive benefits from his beams. Worship is an act that perfects our own souls; they are then most widened by spiritual frames, to receive the influence of divine blessings, as an eye most opened receives the fruit of the sun's light better than the eye that is shut. The communications of God are more or less, according as our spiritual frames are more or less in our worship; God will not give his blessings to unsuitable hearts. What a nasty vessel is a carnal heart for a spiritual communication! The chief end of every duty enjoined by God, is to have communion with him; and therefore it is called a drawing near to God; it is impossible, therefore, that the outward part of any duty can answer the end of God in his institution. It is not a bodily appearance or gesture whereby men can have communion with God, but by the impressions of the heart, and reflections of the heart upon God; without this, all the rich streams of grace will run beside us, and the growth of the soul be hindered and impaired. A "diligent hand makes rich," saith the wise man; a diligent heart in spiritual worship, brings in rich incomes to the humble and spiritual soul.

2. It renders the worship not only unacceptable, but abominable to God. It makes our gold to become dross, it soils our duties, and bespots our souls. A carnal and unsteady frame shows an indifferency of spirit at best; and lukewarmness is as ungrateful to God, as heavy and nauseous meat is to the stomach; he "spews them out of his mouth" (Rev. iii. 16). As our gracious God doth overlook infirmities where intentions are good, and endeavors serious and strong; so he loathes the services where the frames are stark naught (Ps. lxvi. 118): "If I regard iniquity in my heart, the Lord will not hear my prayer." Lukewarm and indifferent services stink in the nostrils of God. The heart seems to loathe God when it starts from him upon every occasion, when it is unwilling to employ itself about, and stick close to him: and can God be pleased with such a frame? The

more of the heart and spirit is in any service, the more real goodness there is in it, and the more savory it is to God; the less of the heart and spirit, the less of goodness, and the more nauseous to God, who loves righteousness and "truth in the inward parts" (Ps. li. 6). And therefore infinite goodness and holiness cannot but hate worship presented to him with deceitful, carnal, and flitting affections; they must be more nauseous to God, than a putrefied carcass can be to man; they are the profanings of that which should be the habitation of the Spirit; they make the spirit, the seat of duty, a filthy dunghill; and are as loathsome to God, as money-changers in the temple were to our Saviour. We see the evil of carnal frames, and the necessity and benefit of spiritual frames: for further help in this last, let us practise these following directions:

1. Keep up spiritual frames out of worship. To avoid low affections, we must keep our hearts as much as we can in a settled elevation. If we admit unworthy dispositions at one time, we shall not easily be rid of them in another;[s] as he that would not be bitten with gnats in the night, must keep his windows shut in the day: when they are once entered, it is not easy to expel them; in which respect, one adviseth to be such out of worship as we would be in worship. If we mix spiritual affections with our worldly employments, worldly affections will not mingle themselves so easily with our heavenly engagements. If our hearts be spiritual in our outward calling, they will scarce be carnal in our religious service. If "we walk in the Spirit, we shall not fulfil the lusts of the flesh" (Gal. v. 16). A spiritual walk in the day will hinder carnal lustings in worship. The fire was to be kept alive upon the altar, when sacrifices were not offered, from morning till night, from night till morning, as well as in the very time of sacrifice. A spiritual life and vigor out of worship would render it at its season sweet and easy, and preserve a spontaneity and preparedness to it, and make it both natural and pleasant to us. Anything that doth unhinge and discompose our spirits, is inconsistent with religious services, which are to be performed with the greatest sedateness and gravity. All irregular passions disturb the serenity of the spirit, and open the door for Satan: saith the apostle (Eph. iv. 26, 27), "Let not the sun go down upon your wrath; neither give place to the devil." Where wrath breaks the lock, the devil will quickly be over the threshold; and though they be allayed, yet they leave the heart sometime after, like the sea rolling and swelling after the storm is ceased. Mixture with ill company leaves a tincture upon us in worship. Ephraim's allying himself with the Gentiles, bred an indifference in religion (Hos. vii. 8): "Ephraim hath mixed himself with the people; Ephraim is a cake not turned:" it will make our hearts, and consequently our services, half dough, as well as half baked; these and the like, make the Holy Spirit withdraw himself, and then the soul is like a windbound vessel, and can make no way. When the sun departs from us, it carries its beams away with it; then "doth darkness spread itself over the earth, and the beasts of the forests creep out" (Ps. civ. 20). When the Spirit withdraws awhile from a good man, it carries

[s] Fitzherbert, Pol. in Relig. Part II. c. 19, § 12.

away (though not habitual, yet) much of the exciting and assisting grace; and then carnal dispositions perk up themselves from the bosom of natural corruption. To be spiritual in worship, we must bar the door at other times against that which is contrary to it; as he that would not be infected with a contagious disease, carries some preservative about with him, and inures himself to good scents. To this end, be much in secret ejaculations to God; these are the purest flights of the soul, that have more of fervor and less of carnality; they preserve a liveliness in the spirit, and make it more fit to perform solemn stated worship with greater freedom and activity; a constant use of this would make our whole lives, lives of worship. As frequent sinful acts strengthen habits of sin, so frequent religious acts strengthen habits of grace.

2. Excite and exercise particularly a love to God, and dependence on him. Love is a commanding affection, a uniting grace; it draws all the faculties of the soul to one centre. The soul that loves God, when it hath to do with him, is bound to the beloved object; it can mind nothing else during such impressions. When the affection is set to the worship of God, everything the soul hath will be bestowed upon it; as David's disposition was to the temple (1 Chron. xxix. 3). Carnal frames, like the fowls, will be lighting upon the sacrifice, but not when it is inflamed; though the scent of the flesh invite them, yet the heat of the fire drives them to their distance. A flaming love will singe the flies that endeavor to interrupt and disturb us. The happiness of heaven consists in a full attraction of the soul to God, by his glorious influence upon it; there will be such a diffusion of his goodness throughout the souls of the blessed, as will unite the affections perfectly to him; these affections which are scattered here, will be there gathered into one flame, moving to him, and centering in him: therefore, the more of a heavenly frame possesses our affections here, the more settled and uniform will our hearts be in all their motions to God, and operations about him. Excite a dependence on him: (Prov. xvi. 3) "Commit thy works to the Lord, and thy thoughts shall be established." Let us go out in God's strength, and not in our own; vain is the help of man in anything, and vain is the help of the heart. It is through God only we can do valiantly in spiritual concerns as well as temporal; the want of this makes but slight impressions upon the spirit.

3. Nourish right conceptions of the majesty of God in your minds. Let us consider that we are drawing to God, the most amiable object, the best of beings, worthy of infinite honor, and highly meriting the highest affections we can give; a God that made the world by a word, that upholds the great frame of heaven and earth; a Majesty above the conceptions of angels; who uses not his power to strike us to our deserved punishment, but his love and bounty to allure us; a God that gave all the creatures to serve us, and can, in a trice, make them as much our enemies as he hath now made them our servants. Let us view him in his greatness, and in his goodness, that our hearts may have a true value of the worship of so great a majesty, and count it the most worthy employment with all diligence to attend upon him. When we have a fear of God, it will make our worship

serious; when we have a joy in God, it will make our worship durable. Our affections will be raised when we represent God in the most reverential, endearing, and obliging circumstances. We honor the majesty of God, when we consider him with due reverence according to the greatness and perfection of his works, and in this reverence of his majesty doth worship chiefly consist. Low thoughts of God will make low frames in us before him. If we thought God an infinite glorious Spirit, how would our hearts be lower than our knees in his presence! How humbly, how believingly pleading is the Psalmist, when he considers God to be without comparison in the heavens; to whom none of the sons of the mighty can be likened; when there was none like to him in strength and faithfulness round about (Ps. lxxxix 6–8). We should have also deep impressions of the omniscience of God, and remember we have to deal with a God that searcheth the heart and trieth the reins, to whom the most secret temper is as visible as the loudest words are audible; that though man judges by outward expressions, God judges by inward affections. As the law of God regulates the inward frames of the heart, so the eye of God pitches upon the inward intentions of the soul. If God were visibly present with us, should we not approach to him with strong affections, summon our spirits to attend upon him, behave ourselves modestly before him? Let us consider he is as really present with us, as if he were visible to us; let us, therefore, preserve a strong sense of the presence of God. No man, but one out of his wits, when he were in the presence of a prince, and making a speech to him, would break off at every period, and run after the catching of butterflies. Remember in all worship you are before the Lord, to whom all things are open and naked.

4. Let us take heed of inordinate desires after the world. As the world steals away a man's heart from the word, so it doth from all other worship; "It chokes the word" (Matt. xiii. 27); it stifles all the spiritual breathings after God in every duty; the edge of the soul is blunted by it, and made too dull for such sublime exercises. The apostle's rule in prayer, when he joins "sobriety with watching unto prayer" (1 Pet. iv. 7), is of concern in all worship, sobriety in the pursuit and use of all worldly things. A man drunk with worldly fumes cannot watch, cannot be heavenly, affectionate, spiritual in service. There is a magnetic force in the earth to hinder our flights to heaven. Birds, when they take their first flights from the earth, have more flutterings of their wings, than when they are mounted further in the air, and got more without the sphere of the earth's attractiveness: the motion of their wings is more steady, that you can perceive them stir; they move like a ship with a full gale. The world is a clog upon the soul, and a bar to spiritual frames; it is as hard to elevate the heart to God in the midst of a hurry of worldly affairs, as it is difficult to meditate when we are near a great noise of waters falling from a precipice, or in the midst of a volley of muskets. Thick clayey affections bemire the heart, and make it unfit for such high flights it is to take in worship; therefore, get your hearts clear from worldly thoughts and desires, if you would be more spiritual in worship.

5. Let us be deeply sensible of our present wants, and the supplies we may meet with in worship. Cold affections to the things we would have will grow cooler; weakness of desire for the communications in worship, will freeze our hearts at the time of worship, and make way for vain and foolish diversions. A beggar that is ready to perish, and knows he is next door to ruin, will not slightly and dully beg an alms, and will not be diverted from his importunity by every slight call, or the moving of an atom in the air. Is it pardon we would have? let us apprehend the blackness of sin, with the aggravations of it as it respects God; let us be deeply sensible of the want of pardon and worth of mercy, and get your affections into such a frame as a condemned man would do; let us consider, that as we are now at the throne of God's grace, we shall shortly be at the bar of God's justice; and if the soul should be forlorn there, how fixedly and earnestly would it plead for mercy! Let us endeavor to stir up the same affections now, which we have seen some dying men have, and which we suppose despairing souls would have done at God's tribunal. We must be sensible that the life or death of our souls depends upon worship.[t] Would we not be ashamed to be ridiculous in our carriage while we are eating; and shall we not be ashamed to be cold or garish before God, when the salvation of our souls, as well as the honor of God, is concerned? If we did see the heaps of sins, the eternity of punishment due to them; if we did see an angry and offended Judge; if we did see the riches of mercy, the glorious outgoings of God in the sanctuary, the blessed doles he gives out to men when they spiritually attend upon him, both the one and the other would make us perform our duties humbly, sincerely, earnestly, and affectionately, and wait upon him with our whole souls, to have misery averted, and mercy bestowed. Let our sense of this be encouraged by the consideration of our Saviour presenting his merits; with what affection doth he present his merits, his blood shed upon the cross, now in heaven? And shall our hearts be cold and frozen, flitting and unsteady, when his affections are so much concerned? Christ doth not present any man's case and duties without a sense of his wants; and shall we have none of our own? Let me add this; let us affect our hearts with a sense of what supplies we have met with in former worship; the delightful remembrance of what converse we have had with God in former worship would spiritualize our hearts for the present worship. Had Peter had a view of Christ's glory in the mount fresh in his thoughts, he would not so easily have turned his back upon his Master, nor would the Israelites have been at leisure for their idolatry, had they preserved the sense of the majesty of God discovered in his late thunders from Mount Sinai.

6. If anything intrudes that may choke the worship, cast it speedily out. We cannot hinder Satan and our own corruption from presenting coolers to us, but we may hinder the success of them; we cannot hinder the gnats from buzzing about us when we are in our business, but we may prevent them from settling upon us. A man that is running on a considerable errand, will shun all unnecessary discourse, that may make him forget or loiter in his business. What

t Guliel. Paris. Rhetor. Divin. c. 26, p. 350, col. 1.

though there may be something offered that is good in itself, yet if it hath a tendency to despoil God of his honor, and ourselves of the spiritual intentness in worship, send it away. Those that weed a field of corn, examine not the nature and particular virtues of the weeds, but consider only how they choke the corn, to which the native juice of the soil is designed. Consider what you are about; and if anything interpose that may divert you, or cool your affections in your present worship, cast it out.

7. As to private worship, let us lay hold of the most melting opportunities and frames. When we find our hearts in a more than ordinary spiritual frame, let us look upon it as a call from God to attend him; such impressions and notions are God's voice, inviting us into communion with him in some particular act of worship, and promising us some success in it. When the Psalmist had a secret motion to "seek God's face" (Ps. xxvii. 8), and complied with it, the issue is the encouragement of his heart, which breaks out into an exhortation to others to be of good courage, and wait on the Lord (v. 13, 14): "Wait on the Lord, be of good courage, and he shall strengthen thy heart; wait, I say, on the Lord." One blow will do more on the iron when it is hot, than a hundred when it is cold; melted metals may be stamped with any impression; but, once hardened, will with difficulty be brought into the figure we intend.[u]

8. Let us examine ourselves at the end of every act of worship, and chide ourselves for any carnality we perceive in them. Let us take a review of them, and examine the reason, why art thou so low and carnal, O my soul? as David did of his disquietedness (Ps. xlii. 5): "Why art thou cast down, O my soul, and why art thou disquieted within me?" If any unworthy frames have surprised us in worship, let us seek them out after worship; call them to the bar; make an exact scrutiny into the causes of them, that we may prevent their incursions another time; let our pulses beat quick by way of anger and indignation against them; this would be a repairing what hath been amiss; otherwise they may grow, and clog an afterworship more than they did a former. Daily examination is an antidote against the temptations of the following day, and constant examination of ourselves after duty is a preservative against vain encroachments in following duties; and upon the finding them out, let us apply the blood of Christ by faith for our cure, and draw strength from the death of Christ for the conquest of them, and let us also be humbled for them. God lifts up the humble; when we are humbled for our carnal frames in one duty, we shall find ourselves by the grace of God more elevated in the next.

<hr>

[u] Reynolds.

DISCOURSE V

ON THE ETERNITY OF GOD

Psalm xc. 2.—Before the mountains were brought forth, or ever thou hadst formed the earth and the world, even from everlasting to everlasting, thou art God.

THE title of this psalm is a prayer; the author, Moses. Some think not only this, but the ten following psalms, were composed by him. The title wherewith he is dignified is, "The man of God," as also in Deut. xxxiii. 1. One inspired by him to be his interpreter, and deliver his oracles; one particularly directed by him;[x] one who as a servant did diligently employ himself in his master's business, and acted for the glory of God;[y] he was the minister of the Old Testament, and the prophet of the New.[z]

There are two parts of this psalm. 1. A complaint of the frailty of man's life in general (v. 3–6); and then a particular complaint of the condition of the church (v. 8–10). 2. A prayer (v. 12). But before he speaks of the shortness of human life, he fortifies them by the consideration of the refuge they had, and should find in God (v. 1): "Lord, thou hast been our dwelling-place in all generations. We have had no settled abode in the earth, since the time of Abraham's being called out from Ur of the Chaldees. We have had Canaan in a promise, we have it not yet in possession; we have been exposed to the cruelties of an oppressing enemy, and the incommodities of a desert wilderness; we have wanted the fruits of the earth, but not the dews of heaven. "Thou hast been our dwelling-place in all generations." Abraham was under thy conduct; Isaac and Jacob under thy care; their posterity was multiplied by thee, and that under their oppressions. Thou hast been our shield against dangers, our security in the times of trouble; when we were pursued to the Red Sea, it was not a creature delivered us; and when we feared the pinching of our bowels in the desert, it was no creature rained manna upon us. Thou hast been our dwelling-place; thou hast kept open house for us, sheltered us against storms, and preserved us from mischief, as a house doth an inhabitant from wind and weather; and that not in one or two, but in all generations. Some think an allusion is here made to the ark, to which they were to have recourse in all emergencies. Our refuge and defence hath not been from created things; not from the ark, but from the God of the ark. Observe,

1. God is a perpetual refuge and security to his people. His providence is not confined to one generation; it is not one age

only that tastes of his bounty and compassion. His eye never yet slept, nor hath he suffered the little ship of his church to be swallowed up, though it hath been tossed upon the waves; he hath always been a haven to preserve us, a house to secure us; he hath always had compassions to pity us, and power to protect us; he hath had a face to shine, when the world hath had an angry countenance to frown.[a] He brought Enoch home by an extraordinary translation from a brutish world; and when he was resolved to reckon with men for their brutish lives, he lodged Noah, the phœnix of the world, in an ark, and kept him alive as a spark in the midst of many waters, whereby to rekindle a church in the world; in all generations he is a dwelling-place to secure his people here, or entertain them above. His providence is not wearied, nor his care fainting; he never wanted will to relieve us, "for he hath been our refuge," nor ever can want power to support us, "for he is a God from everlasting to everlasting." The church never wanted a pilot to steer her, and a rock to shelter her, and dash in pieces the waves which threaten her.

2. How worthy is it to remember former benefits, when we come to beg for new. Never were the records of God's mercies so exactly revised, as when his people have stood in need of new editions of his power. How necessary are our wants to stir us up to pay the rent of thankfulness in arrear! He renders himself doubly unworthy of the mercies he wants, that doth not gratefully acknowledge the mercies he hath received. God scarce promised any deliverance to the Israelites, and they, in their distress, scarce prayed for any deliverance; but that from Egypt was mentioned on both sides, by God to encourage them, and by them to acknowledge their confidence in him. The greater our dangers, the more we should call to mind God's former kindness. We are not only thankfully to acknowledge the mercies bestowed upon our persons, or in our age, but those of former times. "Thou hast been our dwelling-place in all generations." Moses was not living in the former generations, yet he appropriates the former mercies to the present age. Mercies, as well as generations, proceed out of the loins of those that have gone before. All mankind are but one Adam; the whole church but one body. In the second verse he backs his former consideration. 1. By the greatness of his power in forming the world. 2. By the boundlessness of his duration: "From everlasting to everlasting." As thou hast been our dwelling-place, and expended upon us the strength of thy power and riches of thy love, so we have no reason to doubt the continuance on thy part, if we be not wanting on our parts; for the vast mountains and fruitful earth are the works of thy hands, and there is less power requisite for our relief, than there was for their creation; and though so much strength hath been upon various occasions manifested, yet thy arm is not weakened, for "from everlasting to everlasting thou art God."[b] Thou hast always been God, and no time can be assigned as the beginning of thy being.[c] The mountains are not of so long a standing as thyself; they are

[a] Theodoret *in loc.*   [b] אל, strong.   [c] Amyrald *in loc.*

the effects of thy power, and therefore cannot be equal to thy duration; since they are the effects, they suppose the precedency of their cause. If we would look back, we can reach no further than the beginning of the creation, and account the years from the first foundation of the world; but after that we must lose ourselves in the abyss of eternity; we have no cue to guide our thoughts; we can see no bounds in thy eternity. But as for man, he traverseth the world a few days, and by thy order pronounced concerning all men, returns to the dust, and moulders into the grave. By mountains, some understand angels, as being creatures of a more elevated nature; by earth, they understand human nature, the earth being the habitation of men. There is no need to divert in this place from the letter to such a sense. The description seems to be poetical, and amounts to this: he neither began with the beginning of time, nor will expire with the end of it; he did not begin when he made himself known to our fathers, but his being did precede the creation of the world, before any created being was formed, and any time settled.[d] "Before the mountains were brought forth," or before they were begotten or born; the word being used in those senses in Scripture; before they stood up higher than the rest of the earthly mass God had created. It seems that mountains were not casually cast up by the force of the deluge softening the ground, and driving several parcels of it together, to grow up into a massy body, as the sea doth the sand in several places; but they were at first formed by God. The eternity of God is here described,

1. In his priority: "Before the world."
2. In the extension of his duration: "From everlasting to everlasting thou art God." He was before the world, yet he neither began nor ends; he is not a temporary, but an eternal God; it takes in both parts of eternity, what was before the creation of the world, and what is after; though the eternity of God be one permanent state, without succession, yet the spirit of God, suiting himself to the weakness of our conception, divides it into two parts; one past before the foundation of the world, another to come after the destruction of the world; as he did exist before all ages, and as he will exist after all ages. Many truths lie couched in the verse.

1. The world hath a beginning of being: it was not from eternity, it was once nothing; had it been of a very long duration, some records would have remained of some memorable actions done of a longer date than any extant. 2. The world owes its being to the creating power of God: "Thou hast formed it" out of nothing into being; Thou, that is, God; it could not spring into being of itself; it was nothing; it must have a former. 3. God was in being before the world: the cause must be before the effect; that word which gives being, must be before that which receives being. 4. This Being was from eternity: "From everlasting." 5. This Being shall endure to eternity: "To everlasting." 6. There is but one God, one eternal: "From everlasting to everlasting, thou art

d. Ἄναρχος καὶ ἀτελεύτητος, Theodoret *in loc.*

God." None else but one hath the property of eternity; the gods of the heathen cannot lay claim to it.

Doct. God is of an eternal duration. The eternity of God is the foundation of the stability of the covenant, the great comfort of a Christian. The design of God in Scripture is, to set forth his dealing with men in the way of a covenant. The priority of God before all things begins the Bible: "In the beginning God created" (Gen. i. 1). His covenant can have no foundation, but in his duration before and after the world:[e] and Moses here mentions his eternity, not only with respect to the essence of God, but to his federal providence; as he is the dwelling-place of his people in all generations. The duration of God forever is more spoken of in Scripture than his eternity, *à parte ante*, though that is the foundation of all the comfort we can take from his immortality: if he had a beginning, he might have an end, and so all our happiness, hope and being would expire with him; but the Scripture sometimes takes notice of his being without beginning, as well as without end: "Thou art from everlasting" (Ps. xciii. 2); "Blessed be God from everlasting to everlasting" (Ps. xli. 13); "I was set up from everlasting" (Prov. viii. 23): if his wisdom were from everlasting, himself was from everlasting: whether we understand it of Christ the Son of God, or of the essential wisdom of God, it is all one to the present purpose. The wisdom of God supposeth the essence of God, as habits in creatures suppose the being of some power or faculty as their subject. The wisdom of God supposeth mind and understanding, essence and substance. The notion of eternity is difficult; as Austin said of time,[f] if no man will ask me the question, what time is, I know well enough what it is; but if any ask me what it is, I know not how to explain it; so may I say of eternity; it is easy in the word pronounced, but hardly understood, and more hardly expressed; it is better expressed by negative than positive words. Though we cannot comprehend eternity, yet we may comprehend that there is an eternity; as, though we cannot comprehend the essence of God what he is, yet we may comprehend that he is; we may understand the notion of his existence, though we cannot understand the infiniteness of his nature; yet we may better understand eternity than infiniteness; we can better conceive a time with the addition of numberless days and years, than imagine a Being without bounds; whence the apostle joins his eternity with his power; "His eternal power and Godhead" (Rom. i. 20); because, next to the power of God, apprehended in the creature, we come necessarily by reasoning, to acknowledge the eternity of God. He that hath an incomprehensible power must needs have an eternity of nature; his power is most sensible in the creatures to the eye of man, and his eternity easily from thence deducible by the reason of man. Eternity is a perpetual duration, which hath neither beginning nor end; time hath both. Those things we say are in time that have beginning, grow up by degrees, have succession of parts; eternity is contrary to time, and is therefore a permanent and immutable state; a perfect possession

e Calv. *in loc.* f Confes. lib. ii. Confes. 14.

of life without any variation; it comprehends in itself all years, all ages, all periods of ages; it never begins; it endures after every duration of time, and never ceaseth; it doth as much outrun time, as it went before the beginning of it: time supposeth something before it; but there can be nothing before eternity; it were not then eternity. Time hath a continual succession; the former time passeth away and another succeeds: the last year is not this year, nor this year the next. We must conceive of eternity contrary to the notion of time; as the nature of time consists in the succession of parts, so the nature of eternity in an infinite immutable duration. Eternity and time differ as the sea and rivers; the sea never changes place, and is always one water; but the rivers glide along, and are swallowed up in the sea; so is time by eternity.ᵍ A thing is said to be eternal, or everlasting rather, in Scripture,

1. When it is of a long duration, though it will have an end; when it hath no measures of time determined to it; so circumcision is said to be in the flesh for an "everlasting covenant" (Gen. xvii. 13); not purely everlasting, but so long as that administration of the covenant should endure. And so when a servant would not leave his master, but would have his ear bored, it is said, he should be a servant "forever" (Deut. xv. 17); i. e. till the jubilee, which was every fiftieth year: so the meat-offering they were to offer is said to be "perpetual" (Lev. vi. 20); Canaan is said to be given to Abraham for an "everlasting" possession (Gen. xvii. 8); when as the Jews are expelled from Canaan, which is given a prey to the barbarous nations. Indeed circumcision was not everlasting; yet the substance of the covenant whereof this was a sign, viz. that God would be the God of believers, endures forever; and that circumcision of the heart, which was signified by circumcision of the flesh, shall remain forever in the kingdom of glory: it was not so much the lasting of the sign, as of the thing signified by it, and the covenant sealed by it: the sign had its abolition; so that the apostle is so peremptory in it, that he asserts, that if any went about to establish it, he excluded himself from a participation of Christ (Gal. v. 2). The sacrifices were to be perpetual, in regard to the thing signified by them; viz. the death of Christ, which was to endure in the efficacy of it: and the passover was to be "forever" (Exod. xii. 24), in regard of the redemption signified by it, which was to be of everlasting remembrance. Canaan was to be an everlasting possession, in regard of the glory of heaven typified, to be forever conferred upon the spiritual seed of Abraham.

2. When a thing hath no end, though it hath a beginning. So angels and souls are everlasting; though their being shall never cease, yet there was a time when their being began; they were nothing before they were something, though they shall never be nothing again, but shall live in endless happiness or misery. But that properly is eternal that hath neither beginning nor end; and thus eternity is a property of God.

In this doctrine I shall show, I. How God is eternal, or in what respects eternity is his property. II. That he is eternal, and must

ᵍ Moulin. Cod. 1, Ser. 2, p. 52.

needs be so. III. That eternity is only proper to God, and not common to him with any creature. IV. The use.

I. How God is eternal, or in what respects he is so. Eternity is a negative attribute, and is a denying of God any measures of time, as immensity is a denying of him any bounds of place. As immensity is the diffusion of his essence, so eternity is the duration of his essence; and when we say God is eternal, we exclude from him all possibility of beginning and ending, all flux and change. As the essence of God cannot be bounded by any place, so it is not to be limited by any time: as it is his immensity to be everywhere, so it is his eternity to be alway. As created things are said to be somewhere in regard of place, and to be present, past, or future, in regard of time; so the Creator in regard of place is everywhere, in regard of time is *semper*.[h] His duration is as endless as his essence is boundless: he always was and always will be, and will no more have an end than he had a beginning; and this is an excellency belonging to the Supreme Being.[i] As his essence comprehends all beings, and exceeds them, and his immensity surmounts all places; so his eternity comprehends all times, all durations, and infinitely excels them.[k]

1. God is without beginning. " In the beginning" God created the world (Gen. i. 1). God was then before the beginning of it; and what point can be set wherein God began, if he were before the beginning of created things? God was without beginning, though all other things had time and beginning from him. As unity is before all numbers, so is God before all his creatures. Abraham called upon the name of the everlasting God (Gen. xxi. 33) the eternal God.[l]—It is opposed to the heathen gods, which were but of yesterday, new coined, and so new; but the eternal God was before the world was made. In that sense it is to be understood; " The mystery which was kept secret since the world began, but now is made manifest, and by the scriptures of the prophets, according to the command of the everlasting God, made known to all nations for the obedience of faith" (Rom. xvi. 26). The gospel is not preached by the command of a new and temporary god, but of that God that was before all ages: though the manifestation of it be in time, yet the purpose and resolve of it was from eternity. If there were decrees before the foundation of the world, there was a Decreer before the foundation of the world. Before the foundation of the world he loved Christ as a Mediator; a fore-ordination of him was before the foundation of the world (John xvii. 24); a choice of men, and therefore a Chooser before the foundation of the world (Eph. i. 4); a grace given in Christ before the world began (2 Tim. i. 9), and therefore a Donor of that grace. From those places, saith Crellius, it appears that God was before the foundation of the world, but they do not assert an absolute eternity; but to be before all creatures is equivalent to his being from eternity.[m] Time began with the foundation of the world; but God being before time, could have no beginning in time. Before the beginning of the creation, and the beginning of

[h] Gassend.   [i] Crellius de Deo. c. 18. p. 41.   [k] Lingend Tom. II. p. 496.
[l] אֵל עֹדְלָם.   [m] Coccei Sum. p. 48. Theol. Gerhard Exeges. c. 86. 4. p. 266.

time, there could be nothing but eternity; nothing but what was uncreated, that is, nothing but what was without beginning. To be in time is to have a beginning; to be before all time is never to have a beginning, but always to be; for as between the Creator and creatures there is no medium, so between time and eternity there is no medium. It is as easily deduced that he that was before all creatures is eternal, as he that made all creatures is God. If he had a beginning, he must have it from another, or from himself; if from another, that from whom he received his being would be better than he, so more a God than he. He cannot be God that is not supreme; he cannot be supreme that owes his being to the power of another. He would not be said only to have immortality as he is (1 Tim. vi. 16), if he had it dependent upon another; nor could he have a beginning from himself; if he had given beginning to himself, then he was once nothing; there was a time when he was not; if he was not, how could he be the Cause of himself? It is impossible for any to give a beginning and being to itself: if it acts it must exist, and so exist before it existed. A thing would exist as a cause before it existed as an effect. He that is not, cannot be the cause that he is; if, therefore, God doth exist, and hath not his being from another, he must exist from eternity. Therefore, when we say God is of and from himself, we mean not that God gave being to himself; but it is negatively to be understood that he hath no cause of existence without himself. Whatsoever number of millions of millions of years we can imagine before the creation of the world, yet God was infinitely before those; he is therefore called the "Ancient of Days" (Dan. vii. 9), as being before all days and time, and eminently containing in himself all times and ages. Though, indeed, God cannot properly be called ancient, that will testify that he is decaying, and shortly will not be; no more than he can be called young, which would signify that he was not long before. All created things are new and fresh; but no creature can find out any beginning of God: it is impossible there should be any beginning of him.

2. God is without end. He always was, always is, and always will be what he is. He remains always the same in being; so far from any change, that no shadow of it can touch him (James i. 17). He will continue in being as long as he hath already enjoyed it; and if we could add never so many millions of years together, we are still as far from an end as from a beginning; for "the Lord shall endure forever" (Ps. ix. 7). As it is impossible he should not be, being from all eternity, so it is impossible that he should not be to all eternity. The Scripture is most plentiful in testimonies of this eternity of God, à parte post, or after the creation of the world: he is said to "live forever" (Rev. iv. 9, 10). The earth shall perish, but God shall "endure forever," and his "years shall have no end" (Ps. cii. 27). Plants and animals grow up from small beginnings, arrive to their full growth, and decline again, and have always remarkable alterations in their nature; but there is no declination in God by all the revolutions of time. Hence some think the incorruptibility of the Deity was signified by the shittim, or cedar wood, whereof the ark was made, it being of an incorruptible nature (Exod. xxv. 10).

That which had no beginning of duration can never have an end, or any interruptions in it. Since God never depended upon any, what should make him cease to be what eternally he hath been, or put a stop to the continuance of his perfections? He cannot will his own destruction; that is against universal nature in all things to cease from being, if they can preserve themselves. He cannot desert his own being, because he cannot but love himself as the best and chiefest good. The reason that anything decays is either its own native weakness, or a superior power of something contrary to it. There is no weakness in the nature of God that can introduce any corruption, because he is infinitely simple without any mixture; nor can he be overpowered by anything else; a weaker cannot hurt him, and a stronger than he there cannot be; nor can he be outwitted or circumvented, because of his infinite wisdom.[n] As he received his being from none, so he cannot be deprived of it by any: as he doth necessarily exist, so he doth necessarily always exist. This, indeed, is the property of God; nothing so proper to him as always to be. Whatsoever perfections any being hath, if it be not eternal, it is not divine. God only is immortal;[o] he only is so by a necessity of nature. Angels, souls, and bodies too, after the resurrection, shall be immortal, not by nature, but grant; they are subject to return to nothing, if that word that raised them from nothing should speak them into nothing again. It is as easy with God to strip them of it, as to invest them with it; nay, it is impossible but that they should perish, if God should withdraw his power from preserving them, which he exerted in creating them; but God is immovably fixed in his own being; that as none gave him his life, so none can deprive him of his life, or the least particle of it. Not a jot of the happiness and life which God infinitely possesses can be lost; it will be as durable to everlasting, as it hath been possessed from everlasting.

3. There is no succession in God. God is without succession or change. It is a part of eternity; "from everlasting to everlasting he is God," i. e. the same. God doth not only always remain in being, but he always remains the same in that being: "thou art the same" (Ps. cii. 27). The being of creatures is successive; the being of God is permanent, and remains entire with all its perfections unchanged in an infinite duration. Indeed, the first notion of eternity is to be without beginning and end, which notes to us the duration of a being in regard of its existence; but to have no succession, nothing first or last, notes rather the perfection of a being in regard of its essence. The creatures are in a perpetual flux; something is acquired or something lost every day. A man is the same in regard of existence when he is a man, as he was when he was a child; but there is a new succession of quantities and qualities in him. Every day he acquires something till he comes to his maturity; every day he loseth something till he comes to his period. A man is not the same at night that he was in the morning; something is expired, and something is added; every day there is a change in his age, a change in his substance, a change in his accidents. But God hath his whole being in one and the same point, or moment of eternity.

[n] Crellius de Deo, c. 18, p. 41.   [o] 1 Tim. vi. 16. Daille, in loc.

He receives nothing as an addition to what he was before; he loseth nothing of what he was before; he is always the same excellency and perfection in the same infiniteness as ever. His years do not fail (Heb. i. 12), his years do not come and go as others do; there is not this day, to-morrow, or yesterday, with him. As nothing is past or future with him in regard of knowledge, but all things are present, so nothing is past or future in regard of his essence. He is not in his essence this day what he was not before, or will be the next day and year what he is not now. All his perfections are most perfect in him every moment; before all ages, after all ages.[p] As he hath his whole essence undivided in every place, as well as in an immense space, so he hath all his being in one moment of time, as well as in infinite intervals of time. Some illustrate the difference between eternity and time by the similitude of a tree, or a rock standing upon the side of a river, or shore of the sea; the tree stands always the same and unmoved, while the waters of the river glide along at the foot. The flux is in the river, but the tree acquires nothing but a diverse respect and relation of presence to the various parts of the river as they flow. The waters of the river press on, and push forward one another, and what the river had this minute, it hath not the same the next.[q] So are all sublunary things in a continual flux. And though the angels have no substantial change, yet they have an accidental; for the actions of the angels this day are not the same individual actions which they performed yesterday: but in God there is no change; he always remains the same. Of a creature, it may be said he was, or he is, or he shall be; of God it cannot be said but only he is.[r] He is what he always was, and he is what he always will be; whereas a creature is what he was not, and will be what he is not now. As it may be said of the flame of a candle, it is a flame: but it is not the same individual flame as was before, nor is it the same that will be presently after; there is a continual dissolution of it into air, and a continual supply for the generation of more. While it continues it may be said there is a flame; yet not entirely one, but in a succession of parts. So of a man it may be said, he is in a succession of parts; but he is not the same that he was, and will not be the same that he is. But God is the same, without any succession of parts and of time; of him it may be said, " He is." He is no more now than he was, and he shall be no more hereafter than he is. God possesses a firm and absolute being, always constant to himself.[s] He sees all things sliding under him in a continual variation; he beholds the revolutions in the world without any change of his most glorious and immovable nature. All other things pass from one state to another; from their original, to their eclipse and destruction; but God possesses his being in one indivisible point, having neither beginning, end, nor middle.

(1.) There is no succession in the knowledge of God. The variety of successions and changes in the world make not succession, or new

p Lessius de Perfect. Divin. lib. iv. c. 1.
q Gamacheus in Aquin. Part I. Qu. 10. c. 1.
r Gassend. Tom. I. Physic. § 1. lib. ii. c. 7. p. 223.
s Daille,.Melange de Sermon, p. 252.

objects in the Divine mind; for all things are present to him from eternity in regard of his knowledge, though they are not actually present in the world, in regard of their existence. He doth not know one thing now, and another anon; he sees all things at once; "Known unto God are all things from the beginning of the world" (Acts xv. 18); but in their true order of succession, as they lie in the eternal council of God, to be brought forth in time. Though there be a succession and order of things as they are wrought, there is yet no succession in God in regard of his knowledge of them. God knows the things that shall be wrought, and the order of them in their being brought upon the stage of the world; yet both the things and the order he knows by one act. Though all things be present with God, yet they are present to him in the order of their appearance in the world, and not so present with him as if they should be wrought at once. The death of Christ was to precede his resurrection in order of time; there is a succession in this; both at once are known by God; yet the act of his knowledge is not exercised about Christ as dying and rising at the same time; so that there is succession in things when there is no succession in God's knowledge of them. Since God knows time, he knows all things as they are in time; he doth not know all things to be at once, though he knows at once what is, has been, and will be. All things are past, present, and to come, in regard of their existence; but there is not past, present, and to come, in regard of God's knowledge of them,[t] because he sees and knows not by any other, but by himself; he is his own light by which he sees, his own glass wherein he sees; beholding himself, he beholds all things.

(2.) There is no succession in the decrees of God. He doth not decree this now, which he decreed not before; for as his works were known from the beginning of the world, so his works were decreed from the beginning of the world; as they are known at once, so they are decreed at once; there is a succession in the execution of them; first grace, then glory; but the purpose of God for the bestowing of both, was in one and the same moment of eternity. "He chose us in him before the foundation of the world, that we should be holy" (Eph. i. 4): The choice of Christ, and the choice of some in him to be holy and to be happy, were before the foundation of the world. It is by the eternal counsel of God all things appear in time; they appear in their order according to the counsel and will of God from eternity. The redemption of the world is after the creation of the world; but the decree whereby the world was created, and whereby it was redeemed, was from eternity.

(3.) God is his own eternity. He is not eternal by grant, and the disposal of any other, but by nature and essence.[u] The eternity of God is nothing else but the duration of God; and the duration of God is nothing else but his existence enduring.[x] If eternity were anything distinct from God, and not of the essence of God, then there would be something which was not God, necessary to perfect God. As immortality is the great perfection of a rational creature, so eternity is the choice perfection of God, yea, the gloss and lustre of all

<hr>

[t] Parsiensis.   [u] Calov. Socinian.   [x] Existentia durans.

others. Every perfection would be imperfect, if it were not always a perfection. God is essentially whatsoever he is, and there is nothing in God but his essence. Duration or continuance in being in creatures, differs from their being; for they might exist but for one instant, in which case they may be said to have being, but not duration, because all duration includes *prius et posterius.* All creatures may cease from being if it be the pleasure of God; they are not, therefore, durable by their essence, and therefore are not their own duration, no more than they are their own existence. And though some creatures, as angels, and souls, may be called everlasting, as a perpetual life is communicated to them by God; yet they can never be called their own eternity, because such a duration is not simply necessary, nor essential to them, but accidental, depending upon the pleasure of another; there is nothing in their nature that can hinder them from losing it, if God, from whom they received it, should design to take it away; but as God is his own necessity of existing, so he is his own duration in existing; as he doth necessarily exist by himself, so he will always necessarily exist by himself.[y]

(4.) Hence all the perfections of God are eternal. In regard of the Divine eternity, all things in God are eternal; his power, mercy, wisdom, justice, knowledge. God himself were not eternal if any of his perfections, which are essential to him, were not eternal also; he had not else been a perfect God from all eternity, and so his whole self had not been eternal. If anything belonging to the nature of a thing be wanting, it cannot be said to be that thing which it ought to be. If anything requisite to the nature of God had been wanting one moment, he could not have been said to be an eternal God.

II. God is eternal. The Spirit of God in Scripture condescends to our capacities in signifying the eternity of God by days and years, which are terms belonging to time, whereby we measure it (Ps. cii. 27). But we must no more conceive that God is bounded or measured by time, and hath succession of days, because of those expressions, than we can conclude him to have a body, because members are ascribed to him in Scripture, to help our conceptions of his glorious nature and operations. Though years are ascribed to him, yet they are such as cannot be numbered, cannot be finished, since there is no proportion between the duration of God, and the years of men. "The number of his years cannot be searched out, for he makes small the drops of water; they pour down rain according to the vapor thereof" (Job xxxvi. 26, 27). The numbers of the drops of rain which have fallen in all parts of the earth since the creation of the world, if subtracted from the number of the years of God, would be found a small quantity, a mere nothing, to the years of God. As all the nations in the world compared with God, are but as the "drop of a bucket, worse than nothing, than vanity" (Isa. xl. 15); so all the ages of the world, if compared with God, amount not to so much as the one hundred thousandth part of a minute; the minutes from the creation may be numbered, but the years of the duration of God being infinite, are without measure. As one day is to the life of man, so are a thousand years to the life of God. The Holy Ghost ex-

y Gassend.

presseth himself to the capacity of man, to give us some notion of an infinite duration, by a resemblance suited to the capacity of man.[z] If a thousand years be but as a day to the life of God, then as a year is to the life of man, so are three hundred and sixty-five thousand years to the life of God; and as seventy years are to the life of man, so are twenty-five millions four hundred and fifty thousand years to the life of God. Yet still, since there is no proportion between time and eternity, we must dart our thoughts beyond all those; for years and days measure only the duration of created things, and of those only that are material and corporeal, subject to the motion of the heavens, which makes days and years.[a] Sometimes this eternity is expressed by parts, as looking backward and forward; by the differences of time, "past, present, and to come" (Rev. i. 8), "which was, and is, and is to come" (Rev. iv. 8).[b] Though this might be spoken of anything in being, though but for an hour, it was the last minute, it is now, and it will be the next minute; yet the Holy Ghost would declare something proper to God, as including all parts of time; he always was, is now, and always shall be. It might always be said of him, he was, and it may always be said of him, he will be; there is no time when he began, no time when he shall cease. It cannot be said of a creature he always was, he always is what he was, and he always will be what he is; but God always is what he was, and always will be what he is; so that it is a very significant expression of the eternity of God, as can be suited to our capacities.

1. His eternity is evident, by the name God gives himself (Exod. iii. 14): " And God said unto Moses, I am that I am; thus shalt thou say to the children of Israel, 'I Am hath sent me unto you.'" This is the name whereby he is distinguished from all creatures; I Am, is his proper name. This description being in the present tense, shows that his essence knows no past, nor future; if it were *he was*, it would intimate he were not now what he once was; if it were *he will be*, it would intimate he were not yet what he will be; but *I Am;* I am the only being, the root of all beings; he is therefore, at the greatest distance from not being, and that is eternal. So that *is* signifies his eternity, as well as his perfection and immutability. As *I Am* speaks the want of no blessedness, so it speaks the want of no duration; and therefore the French, wherever they find this word Jehovah, in the Scripture, which we translate Lord, and Lord eternal, render it the Eternal,—I am always and immutably the same. The eternity of God is opposed to the volubility of time, which is extended into past, present and to come. Our time is but a small drop, as a sand to all the atoms and small particles of which the world is made; but God is an unbounded sea of being. "I Am that I Am;" *i. e.* an infinite life; I have not that now, which I had not formerly; I shall not afterwards have that which I have not now; I am that in every moment which I was, and will be in all moments of time; nothing can be added to me, nothing can be detracted from me; there is nothing superior to him, which can detract from him; nothing desi-

---

[z] Ps. xc. 4. Amyrald, Trin. p. 44.

[a] Daille, Vent. Sermons, Serm. I. sur 102 Ps. 27, p. 21.

[b] Crellius weakens this argument, De Deo, c. 18, p. 42.

rable that can be added to him.   Now if there were any beginning
and end of God, any succession in him, he could not be "I Am;"[c]
for in regard of what was past, he would not be; in regard of what
was to come, he is not yet; and upon this account a heathen argues
well;[d] of all creatures it may be said they were, or they will be; but
of God it cannot be said anything else but *est*, God is, because he fills
an eternal duration.   A creature cannot be said to be, if it be not yet,
nor if it be not now, but hath been.[e]   God only can be called "I
Am;" all creatures have more of not being, than being; for every
creature was nothing from eternity, before it was made something in
time; and if it be incorruptible in its whole nature, it will be nothing
to eternity after it hath been something in time; and if it be not corruptible in its nature, as the angels, or in every part of its nature, as
man in regard of his soul; yet it hath not properly a being, because
it is dependent upon the pleasure of God to continue it, or deprive it
of it; and while it is, it is mutable, and all mutability is a mixture
of not being.   If God therefore be properly "I Am," *i. e.* being, it
follows that he always was; for if he were not always, he must, as
was argued before, be produced by some other, or by himself; by
another he could not; then he had not been God, but a creature; nor
by himself, for then as producing, he must be before himself, as produced; he had been before he was.   And he always will be; for being
"I Am," having all being in himself, and the fountain of all being to
everything else, how can he ever have his name changed to I am not.

    2. God hath life in himself (John v. 26): "The Father hath life
in himself;" he is the "living God;" therefore "steadfast forever"
(Dan. vi. 26).   He hath life by his essence, not by participation.   He
is a sun to give light and life to all creatures, but receives not light
or life from anything; and therefore he hath an unlimited life, not
a drop of life, but a fountain; not a spark of a limited life, but a
life transcending all bounds.   He hath life in himself; all creatures
have their life in him and from him.   He that hath life in himself
doth necessarily exist, and could never be made to exist; for then
he had not life in himself, but in that which made him to exist, and
gave him life.   What doth necessarily exist therefore, exists from
eternity; what hath being of itself could never be produced in time,
could not want being one moment, because it hath being from its essence, without influence of any efficient cause.   When God pronounced his name, "I Am that I Am," angels and men were in
being; the world had been created above two thousand four hundred
years; Moses, to whom he then speaks, was in being; yet God only
is, because he only hath the fountain of being in himself; but all
that they were was a rivulet from him.   He hath from nothing else,
that he doth subsist; everything else hath its subsistence from him
as their root, as the beam from the sun, as the rivers and fountains
from the sea.[f]   All life is seated in God, as in its proper throne, in
its most perfect purity.   God is life; it is in him originally, radically, therefore eternally.   He is a pure act, nothing but vigor and act;
he hath by his nature that life which others have by his grant;

---

c Thes. Salmur. p. 1. p 145, Thes. 14.   d Plutarch de El, I. p. 392.
f Perer. in Exo. 3. Disput. 13.   f Petav. Theol. Dogm. Tom. I. lib. i. c. 6, § 6, 7.

whence the Apostle saith (1 Tim. vi. 16) not only that he is immortal, but he hath immortality in a full possession; fee simple, not depending upon the will of another, but containing all things within
himself. He that hath life in himself, and is from himself, cannot but
be. He always was, because he received his being from no other,
and none can take away that being which was not given by another.
If there were any space before he did exist, then there was something which made him to exist; life would not then be in him, but
in that which produced him into being; he could not then be God,
but that other which gave him being would be God.ᵍ And to say
God sprung into being by chance, when we see nothing in the world
that is brought forth by chance, but hath some cause of its existence,
would be vain; for since God is a being, chance, which is nothing,
could not bring forth something; and by the same reason, that he
sprung up by chance, he might totally vanish by chance. What a
strange notion of a God would this be! such a God that had no life
in himself but from chance! Since he hath life in himself, and that
there was no cause of his existence, he can have no cause of his
limitation, and can no more be determined to a time, than he can to
a place. What hath life in itself, hath life without bounds, and can
never desert it, nor be deprived of it; so that he lives necessarily,
and it is absolutely impossible that he should not live; whereas all
other things "live, and move, and have their being in him" (Acts
xvii. 28); and as they live by his will, so they can return to nothing
at his word.

3. If God were not eternal, he were not immutable in his nature.
It is contrary to the nature of immutability to be without eternity;
for whatsoever begins, is changed in its passing from not being to
being. It began to be what it was not; and if it ends, it ceaseth to
be what it was; it cannot therefore be said to be God, if there were
neither beginning or ending, or succession in it (Mal. iii. 6): "I am
the Lord, I change not;" (Job xxxvii. 23): "Touching the Almighty, we cannot find him out." God argues here, saith Calvin,
from his unchangeable nature as Jehovah, to his immutability in his
purpose. Had he not been eternal, there had been the greatest
change from nothing to something. A change of essence is greater
than a change of purpose. God is a sun glittering always in the
same glory; no growing up in youth; no passing on to age. If he
were not without succession, standing in one point of eternity, there
would be a change from past to present, from present to future. The
eternity of God is a shield against all kind of mutability. If anything sprang up in the essence of God that was not there before,
he could not be said to be either an eternal, or an unchanged substance.

4. God could not be an infinitely perfect Being, if he were not
eternal. A finite duration is inconsistent with infinite perfection.
Whatsoever is contracted within the limits of time, cannot swallow
up all perfections in itself. God hath an unsearchable perfection.
"Canst thou by searching find out God? canst thou find out the Almighty unto perfection?" (Job xi. 7.) He cannot be found out: he

ᵍ Amyrald de Trinit. p. 48.

is infinite, because he is incomprehensible. Incomprehensibility ariseth from an infinite perfection, which cannot be fathomed by the short line of man's understanding. His essence in regard of its diffusion, and in regard of its duration, is incomprehensible, as well as his action : if God, therefore, had beginning, he could not be infinite; if not infinite, he did not possess the highest perfection ; because a perfection might be conceived beyond it. If his being could fail, he were not perfect; can that deserve the name of the highest perfection, which is capable of corruption and dissolution ? To be finite and limited, is the greatest imperfection, for it consists in a denial of being. He could not be the most blessed Being if he were not always so, and should not forever remain so ; and whatsoever perfections he had, would be soured by the thoughts, that in time they would cease, and so could not be pure affections, because not permanent ; but "He is blessed from everlasting to everlasting" (Ps. xli. 13). Had he a beginning, he could not have all perfection without limitation ; he would have been limited by that which gave him beginning ; that which gave him being would be God, and not himself, and so more perfect than he : but since God is the most sovereign perfection, than which nothing can be imagined perfecter by the most capacious understanding, He is certainly " eternal ;" being infinite, nothing can be added to him, nothing detracted from him.

5. God could not be omnipotent, almighty, if he were not eternal. The title of almighty agrees not with a nature that had a beginning; whatsoever hath a beginning was once nothing ; and when it was nothing, could act nothing : where there is no being there is no power. Neither doth the title of almighty agree with a perishing nature : he can do nothing to purpose, that cannot preserve himself against the outward force and violence of enemies, or against the inward causes of corruption and dissolution. No account is to be made of man, because "his breath is in his nostrils" (Isa. ii. 22); could a better account be made of God, if he were of the like condition ? He could not properly be almighty, that were not always mighty ; if he be omnipotent, nothing can impair him ; he that hath all power, can have no hurt. If he doth whatsoever he pleaseth, nothing can make him miserable, since misery consists in those things which happen against our will.[h] The almightiness and eternity of God are linked together : " I am Alpha and Omega, the beginning and ending, saith the Lord, which was, and which is, and which is to come, the Almighty" (Rev. i. 8) : almighty because eternal, and eternal because almighty.

6. God would not be the first cause of all if he were not eternal; but he is the first and the last ; the first cause of all things, the last end of all things :[i] that which is the first cannot begin to be ; it were not then the first ; it cannot cease to be : whatsoever is dissolved, is dissolved into that whereof it doth consist, which was before it, and then it was not the first. The world might not have been ; it was once nothing ; it must have some cause to call it out of nothing : nothing hath no power to make itself something ; there

ʰ Voet. Natural. Theol. p. 310.   ⁱ Rev. i. 8. Ficin. de Immort. lib. ii. c. 5.

is a superior cause, by whose will and power it comes into being, and so gives all the creatures their distinct forms.[k] This power cannot but be eternal; it must be before the world; the founder must be before the foundation; and his existence must be from eternity; or we must say nothing did exist from eternity:[l] and if there were no being from eternity, there could not now be any being in time. What we see, and what we are, must arise from itself or some other; it cannot from itself: if anything made itself, it had a power to make itself; it then had an active power before it had a being; it was something in regard of power, and was nothing in regard of existence at the same time. Suppose it had a power to produce itself, this power must be conferred upon it by another; and so the power of producing itself, was not from itself, but from another; but if the power of being was from itself, why did it not produce itself before? why was it one moment out of being?[m] If there be any existence of things, it is necessary that that which was the "first cause," should "exist from eternity." Whatsoever was the immediate cause of the world, yet the first and chief cause wherein we must rest, must have nothing before it; if it had anything before it, it were not the first; he therefore that is the first cause, must be without beginning; nothing must be before him; if he had a beginning from some other, he could not be the first principle and author of all things; if he be the first cause of all things, he must give himself a beginning, or be from eternity: he could not give himself a beginning; whatsoever begins in time was nothing before, and when it was nothing, it could do nothing; it could not give itself anything, for then it gave what it had not, and did what it could not. If he made himself in time, why did he not make himself before? what hindered him? It was either because he could not, or because he would not; if he could not, he always wanted power, and always would, unless it were bestowed upon him, and then he could not be said to be from himself. If he would not make himself before, then he might have made himself when he would: how had he the power of willing and nilling without a being? Nothing cannot will or nill; nothing hath no faculties; so that it is necessary to grant some eternal being, or run into inextricable labyrinths and mazes. If we deny some eternal being, we must deny all being; our own being, the being of everything about us; unconceivable absurdities will arise. So, then, if God were the cause of all things, he did exist before all things, and that from eternity.

III. Eternity is only proper to God, and not communicable. It is as great a madness to ascribe eternity to the creature, as to deprive the Lord of the creature of eternity.[n] It is so proper to God, that when the apostle would prove the deity of Christ, he proves it by his immutability and eternity, as well as his creating power: "Thou art the same, and thy years shall not fail (Heb. i. 10–12). The argument had not strength, if eternity belonged essentially to any but God; and therefore he is said only to have "immortality" (1 Tim. vi. 16): all other things receive their being from him, and can be de-

---

[k] Coccei Sum. Theol. c. 8. [l] Crellius de Deo, c. 18. p. 43.
[m] Petav. Theol. Dogmat. Tom. I. lib. i. c. 10, 11. [n] Bapt.

prived of their being by him: all things depend on him; he of none: all other things are like clothes, which would consume if God preserved them not. Immortality is appropriated to God, *i. e.* an independent immortality. Angels and souls have an immortality, but by donation from God, not by their own essence; dependent upon their Creator, not necessary in their own nature: God might have annihilated them after he had created them; so that their duration cannot properly be called an eternity, it being extrinsical to them, and dependent upon the will of their Creator, by whom they may be extinguished; it is not an absolute and necessary, but a precarious immortality. Whatsoever is not God, is temporary; whatsoever is eternal, is God. It is a contradiction to say a creature can be eternal; as nothing eternal is created, so nothing created is eternal. What is distinct from the nature of God cannot be eternal, eternity being the essence of God. Every creature, in the notion of a creature, speaks a dependence on some cause, and therefore cannot be eternal. As it is repugnant to the nature of God not to be eternal, so it is repugnant to the nature of a creature to be eternal; for then a creature would be equal to the Creator, and the Creator, or the Cause, would not be before the creature, or effect.º It would be all one to admit many gods, as many eternals; and all one to say, God can be created, as to say a creature can be uncreated, which is to be eternal.

1. Creation is a producing something from nothing. What was once nothing, cannot therefore be eternal; not being was eternal; therefore its being could not be eternal, for it should be then before it was, and would be something when it was nothing. It is the nature of a creature to be nothing before it was created; what was nothing before it was, cannot be equal with God in an eternity of duration.

2. There is no creature but is mutable, therefore not eternal. As it had a change from nothing to something, so it may be changed from being to not being. If the creature were not mutable, it would be most perfect, and so would not be a creature, but God; for God only is most perfect. It is as much the essence of a creature to be mutable, as it is the essence of God to be immutable. Mutability and eternity are utterly inconsistent.

3. No creature is infinite, therefore not eternal: to be infinite in duration is all one as to be infinite in essence. It is as reasonable to conceive a creature immense, filling all places at once, as eternal, extended to all ages; because neither can be without infiniteness, which is the property of the Deity.ᴾ A creature may as well be without bounds of place, as limitations of time.

4. No effect of an intellectual free agent can be equal in duration to its cause. The productions of natural agents are as ancient often as themselves; the sun produceth a beam as old in time as itself; but who ever heard of a piece of wise workmanship as old as the wise artificer? God produced a creature, not necessarily and naturally, as the sun doth a beam, but freely, as an intelligent agent. The sun was not necessary; it might be or not be, according to the

º Lessius de Perfect. lib. iv. c. 2.   ᴾ Ibid.

pleasure of God. A free act of the will is necessary to precede in order of time, as the cause of such effects as are purely voluntary.q Those causes that act as soon as they exist act naturally, necessarily, not freely, and cannot cease from acting. But suppose a creature might have existed by the will of God from eternity; yet, as some think, it could not be said absolutely, and in its own nature to be eternal, because eternity was not of the essence of it. The creature could not be its own duration; for though it were from eternity, it might not have been from eternity, because its existence depended upon the free will of God, who might have chose whether he would have created it or no. God only is eternal; "the first and the last, the beginning and the end;" who, as he subsisted before any creature had a being, so he will eternally subsist if all creatures were reduced to nothing.

IV. *Use* 1. Information. If God be of an eternal duration, then "Christ is God." Eternity is the property of God, but it is ascribed to Christ: "He is before all things" (Col. i. 17), *i. e.* all created things; he is therefore no creature, and if no creature, eternal. "All things were created by him," both in heaven and in earth, angels, as well as men, whether they be thrones or dominions (ver. 16). If all things were his creatures, then he is no creature; if he were, all things were not created by him, or he must create himself. He hath no difference of time; for he is "the same yesterday, to-day, and forever:"r the same, with the name of God, "I Am," which signifies his eternity. He is no more to-day than he was yesterday, nor will be any other to-morrow than he is to-day; and therefore Melchizedec, whose descent, birth, and death, father and mother, beginning and end of days, are not upon record, was a type of the existence of Christ without difference of time; "Having neither beginning of days nor end of life, but made like the Son of God" (Heb. vii. 3). The suppression of his birth and death was intended by the Holy Ghost as a type of the excellency of Christ's person in regard of his eternity, and the duration of his charge in regard of his priesthood. As there was an appearance of an eternity in the suppression of the race of Melchisedec, so there is a true eternity in the Son of God. How could the eternity of the Son of God be expressed by any resemblance so well, as by such a suppression of the beginning and end of this great person, different from the custom of the Spirit of God in the Old Testament, who often records the generations and ends of holy men; and why might not this, which was a kind of a shadow of eternity, be a representation of the true eternity of Christ, as well as the restoration of Isaac to his father without death, is said to be a figure of the resurrection of Christ after a real death?s Melchisedec is only mentioned once (without any record of his extraction) in his appearance to Abraham after his victory, as if he came from heaven only for that action, and instantly disappeared again, as if he had been an eternal person. And Christ himself hints his own eternity: "I came forth from the Father, and am come into

q Crellius de Deo, c. 18. p. 43.
r Heb. xiii. 8. Rev. i. 8. "He which is, and which was, and which is to come."
s Mestræzat. *in loc.*

the world; again I leave the world, and go to the Father" (John xvi. 28). He goes to the Father as he came from the Father; he goes to the Father "for everlasting," so he came from the Father "from everlasting;" there is the same duration in coming forth from the Father, as in returning to the Father. But more plainly: he speaks of a glory that he "had with the Father before the world was" (John xvii. 5), when there was no creature in being. This is an actual glory, and not only in decree; for a decreed glory believers had, and why may not every one of them say the same words, "Father, glorify me with that glory which I had with thee before the world was," if it were only a glory in decree? Nay, it may be said of every man, he was before the world was, because he was so in decree. Christ speaks of something peculiar to him, a glory in actual possession before the world was: "Glorify me, embrace, honor me as thy Son, whereas I have now been, in the eyes of the world, handled disgracefully as a servant." If it were only in decree, why is not the like expression used of others in Scripture as well as of Christ? Why did he not use the same words for his disciples that were then with him, who had a glory in decree? His eternity is also mentioned in the Old Testament: "The Lord possessed me in the beginning of his way, before his works of old" (Prov. viii. 22). If he were the work of God, he existed before himself, if he existed before all the works of God. It is so not properly meant of the essential wisdom of God, since the discourse runs in the name of a person; and several passages there are which belong not so much to the essential wisdom of God, as ver. 13: "The evil way and the froward mouth do I hate," which belongs rather to the holiness of God, than to the essential wisdom of God; besides, it is distinguished from Jehovah, as possessed by him, "and rejoicing before him." Yet plainer: "Out of thee," *i. e.* Bethlehem, "shall he come forth to be Ruler in Israel, whose goings forth have been from of old, from everlasting," מימי עולם "from the ways of eternity" (Mic. v. 2). There are two goings forth of Christ described, one from Bethlehem, in the days of his incarnation, and another from eternity. The Holy Ghost adds, after his prediction of his incarnation, his going out from everlasting, that none should doubt of his deity. If this going out from everlasting were only in the purpose of God, it might be said of David, and of every creature; and in Isa. ix. 6 he is particularly called the "everlasting," or "eternal Father;" not the Father in the Trinity, but a Father to us; yet "eternal," the "Father of eternity." As he is the "mighty God," so he is "the everlasting Father." Can such a title be ascribed to any whose being depends upon the will of another, and may be dashed out at the pleasure of a superior? As the eternity of God is the ground of all religion, so the eternity of Christ is the ground of the Christian religion. Could our sins be perfectly expiated had he not an eternal divinity to answer for the offences committed against an eternal God? Temporary sufferings had been of little validity, without an infiniteness and eternity in his person to add weight to his passion.

2. If God be eternal, he knows all things as present. All things are present to him in his eternity; for this is the notion of eter-

nity, to be without succession.[t] If eternity be one indivisible point, and is not diffused into preceding and succeeding parts, then that which is known in it or by it is perceived without any succession, for knowledge is as the substance of the person knowing; if that hath various actions and distinct from itself, then it understands things in differences of time as time presents them to view. But, since God's being depends not upon the revolutions of time, so neither does his knowledge; it exceeds all motions of years and days, comprehends infinite spaces of past and future. God considers all things in his eternity in one simple knowledge, as if they were now acted before him: "Known unto God are all his works from the beginning of the world;" $\dot{\alpha}\pi'$ $\alpha\dot{\iota}\tilde{\omega}\nu o\varsigma$, à seculo, "from eternity" (Acts xv. 18). God's knowledge is co-eternal with him; if he knows that in time which he did not not know from eternity, he would not be eternally perfect, since knowledge is the perfection of an intelligent nature.

3. How bold and foolish is it for a mortal creature to censure the counsels and actions of an eternal God, or be too curious in his inquisitions! It is by the consideration of the unsearchable number of the years of God that Elihu checks too bold inquiries: "who hath enjoined him his way, or who can say, Thou hast wrought iniquity? Behold, God is great, and we know him not; neither can the number of his years be searched out."[u] Eternity sets God above our inquiries and censures. Infants of a day old are not able to understand the acts of wise and gray heads: shall we, that are of so short a being and understanding as yesterday, presume to measure the motions of eternity by our scanty intellects? We that cannot foresee an unexpected accident which falls in to blast a well-laid design, and run a ship many leagues back from the intended harbor; we cannot understand the reason of things we see done in time, the motions of the sea, the generation of rain, the nature of light, the sympathies and antipathies of the creatures; and shall we dare to censure the actions of an eternal God, so infinitely beyond our reach? The counsels of a boundless being are not to be scanned by the brain of a silly worm, that hath breathed but a few minutes in the world. Since eternity cannot be comprehended in time, it is not to be judged by a creature of time: "Let us remember to magnify his works which we behold," because he is eternal, which is the exhortation of Elihu, backed by this doctrine of God's eternity (Job xxxvi. 24), and not accuse any work of him who is the "Ancient of Days," or presume to direct him of whose eternity we come infinitely short. Whenever, therefore, any unworthy notion of the counsels and works of God is suggested to us by Satan, or our own corrupt hearts, let us look backward to God's eternal and our own short duration, and silence ourselves with the same question wherewith God put a stop to the reasoning of Job—"Where wast thou when I laid the foundations of the earth?" (Job xxxviii. 4), and reprove ourselves for our curiosity, since we are of so short a standing, and were nothing when the eternal God laid the first stone of the world.

4. What a folly and boldness is there in sin, since an eternal God

[t] Petav.   [u] Job xxxvi. 26, compared with ver. 23.

is offended thereby! All sin is aggravated by God's eternity. The blackness of the heathen idolatry was in changing the glory of the incorruptible God (Rom. i. 23); erecting resemblances of him contrary to his immortal nature; as if the eternal God, whose life is as unlimited as eternity, were like those creatures whose beings are measured by the short ell of time, which are of a corruptible nature, and daily passing on to corruption; they could not really deprive God of his glory and immortality, but they did in estimation. There is in the nature of every sin a tendency to reduce God to a not being. He that thinks unworthily of God, or acts unworthily towards him, doth (as much as in him lies) sully and destroy these two perfections of his, immutability and eternity. It is a carriage, as if he were as contemptible as a creature that were but of yesterday, and shall not remain in being to-morrow. He that would put an end to God's glory by darkening it, would put an end to God's life by destroying it. He that should love a beast with as great an affection as he loves a man, contemns a rational nature; and he that loves a perishing thing with the same affection he should love an everlasting God, contemns his eternity; he debaseth the duration of God below that of the world. The low valuation of God speaks him in his esteem no better than withering grass, or a gourd, which lasts for a night; and the creature which possesses his affection, to be a good that lasts forever. How foolish, then, is every sin that tends to destroy a being that cannot destroy or desert himself; a Being, without whose eternity the sinner himself could not have had the capacity of a being to affront him! How base is that which would not let the works of God remain in their established posture! How much more base is not enduring the fountain and glory of all beings, that would not only put an end to the beauty of the world, but the eternity of God!

5. How dreadful is it to lie under the stroke of an eternal God! His eternity is as great a terror to him that hates him, as it is a comfort to him that loves him; because he is the "living God, an everlasting king, the nations shall not be able to abide his indignation" (Jer. x. 10). Though God be least in their thoughts, and is made light of in the world, yet the thoughts of God's eternity, when he comes to judge the world, shall make the slighters of him tremble. That the Judge and punisher lives forever, is the greatest grievance to a soul in misery, and adds an inconceivable weight to it, above what the infiniteness of God's executive power could do without that duration. His eternity makes the punishment more dreadful than his power; his power makes it sharp, but his eternity renders it perpetual; ever to endure, is the sting at the end of every lash. And how sad is it to think that God lays his eternity to pawn for the punishment of obstinate sinners, and engageth it by an oath, that he will "whet his glittering sword," that his "hand shall take hold of judgment," that he will "render vengeance to his enemies, and a reward to them that hate him;" a reward proportioned to the greatness of their offences, and the glory of an eternal God! "I lift up my hand to heaven, and say, I live forever;" (Deut. xxxii. 40, 41): *i. e.*, as surely as I live forever, I will whet my glittering sword.

As none can convey good with a perpetuity, so none can convey evil with such a lastingness as God. It is a great loss to lose a ship richly fraught in the bottom of the sea, never to be cast upon the shore; but how much greater is it to lose eternally a sovereign God, which we were capable of eternally enjoying, and undergo an evil as durable as that God we slighted, and were in a possibility of avoiding! The miseries of men after this life are not eased, but sharpened, by the life and eternity of God.

Use 2. Of comfort. What foundation of comfort can we have in any of God's attributes, were it not for his infiniteness and eternity, though he be "merciful, good, wise, faithful?" What support could there be, if they were perfections belonging to a corruptible God? What hopes of a resurrection to happiness can we have, or of the duration of it, if that God that promised it were not immortal to continue it, as well as powerful to effect it? His power were not Almighty, if his duration were not eternal.

1. If God be eternal, his covenant will be so. It is founded upon the eternity of God; the oath whereby he confirms it, is by his life. Since there is none greater than himself, he swears by himself (Heb. vi. 13), or by his own life, which he engageth together with his eternity for the full performance; so that if he lives forever, the covenant shall not be disannulled; it is an "immutable counsel" (ver. 16, 17). The immutability of his counsel follows the immutability of his nature. Immutability and eternity go hand in hand together. The promise of eternal life is as ancient as God himself in regard of the purpose of the promise, or in regard of the promise made to Christ for us. " Eternal life which God promised before the world began." (Tit. i. 2): As it hath an ante-eternity, so it hath a post-eternity; therefore the gospel, which is the new covenant published, is termed the "everlasting gospel" (Rev. xiv. 6), which can no more be altered and perish, than God can change and vanish into nothing; he can as little morally deny his truth, as he can naturally desert his life. The covenant is there represented in a green color, to note its perpetual verdure; the rainbow, the emblem of the covenant "about the throne, was like to an emerald" (Rev. iv. 3), a stone of a green color, whereas the natural rainbow hath many colors; this but one, to signify its eternity.

2. If God be eternal, he being our God in covenant, is an eternal good and possession. " This God is our God forever and ever" (Ps. xlviii. 14): " He is a dwelling-place in all generations." We shall traverse the world awhile, and then arrive at the blessings Jacob wished for Joseph, "the blessings of the everlasting hills" (Gen. xlix. 26). If an estate of a thousand pound per annum render a man's life comfortable for a short term, how much more may the soul be swallowed up with joy in the enjoyment of the Creator, whose years never fail, who lives forever to be enjoyed, and can keep us in life forever to enjoy him! Death, indeed, will seize upon us by God's irreversible order, but the immortal Creator will make him disgorge his morsel, and land us in a glorious immortality; our souls at their dissolution, and our bodies at the resurrection, after which they shall remain forever, and employ the extent of that boundless

eternity, in the fruition of the sovereign and eternal God; for it is impossible that the believer, who is united to the immortal God that is from everlasting to everlasting, can ever perish; for being in conjunction with him who is an ever-flowing fountain of life, he cannot suffer him to remain in the jaws of death. While God is eternal, and always the same, it is not possible that those that partake of his spiritual life, should not also partake of his eternal. It is from the consideration of the endlessness of the years of God that the church comforts herself that "her children shall continue, and their seed be established forever" (Ps. cii. 27, 28). And from the eternity of God Habakkuk (chap. i. 12) concludes the eternity of believers, "Art not thou from everlasting, O Lord, my God, my Holy One? we shall not die, O Lord." After they are retired from this world, they shall live forever with God, without any change by the multitude of those imaginable years and ages that shall run forever. It is that God that hath neither beginning nor end, that is our God; who hath not only immortality in himself, but immortality to give out to others. As he hath "abundance of spirit" to quicken them (Mal. ii. 15), so he hath abundance of immortality to continue them. It is only in the consideration of this a man can with wisdom say, "Soul, take thy ease; thou hast goods laid up for many years" (Luke xii. 19, 20): to say it of any other possession is the greatest folly in the judgment of our Saviour. "Mortality shall be swallowed up of immortality;" "rivers of pleasure" shall be "for evermore." Death is a word never spoken there by any; never heard by any in that possession of eternity; it is forever put out as one of Christ's conquered enemies. The happiness depends upon the presence of God, with whom believers shall be forever present. Happiness cannot perish as long as God lives; he is the first and the last; the first of all delights, nothing before him; the last of all pleasures, nothing beyond him; a paradise of delights in every point, without a flaming sword.

3. The enjoyment of God will be as fresh and glorious after many ages, as it was at first. God is eternal, and eternity knows no change; there will then be the fullest possession without any decay in the object enjoyed. There can be nothing past, nothing future; time neither adds to it, nor detracts from it; that infinite fulness of perfection which flourisheth in him now, will flourish eternally, without any discoloring of it in the least, by those innumerable ages that shall run to eternity, much less any despoiling him of them: "He is the same in his endless duration" (Ps. cii. 27). As God is, so will the eternity of him be, without succession, without division; the fulness of joy will be always present; without past to be thought of with regret for being gone; without future to be expected with tormenting desires. When we enjoy God, we enjoy him in his eternity without any flux; an entire possession of all together, without the passing away of pleasures that may be wished to return, or expectation of future joys which might be desired to hasten. Time is fluid, but eternity is stable; and after many ages, the joys will be as savory and satisfying as if they had been but that moment first tasted by our hungry appetites. When the glory of the Lord shall rise upon you, it shall be so far from ever setting, that after millions

of years are expired, as numerous as the sands on the sea-shore, the sun, in the light of whose countenance you shall live, shall be as bright as at the first appearance; he will be so far from ceasing to flow, that he will flow as strong, as full, as at the first communication of himself in glory to the creature. God, therefore, as sitting upon his throne of grace, and acting according to his covenant, is like a jasper-stone, which is of a green color, a color always delightful (Rev. iv. 3); because God is always vigorous and flourishing; a pure act of life, sparkling new and fresh rays of life and light to the creature, flourishing with a perpetual spring, and contenting the most capacious desire; forming your interest, pleasure, and satisfaction; with an infinite variety, without any change or succession; he will have variety to increase delights, and eternity to perpetuate them; this will be the fruit of the enjoyment of an infinite and eternal God: he is not a cistern, but a fountain, wherein water is always living, and never putrefies.

4. If God be eternal, here is a strong ground of comfort against all the distresses of the church, and the threats of the church's enemies. God's abiding forever is the plea Jeremy makes for his return to his forsaken church: "Thou, O Lord, remainest forever; thy throne from generation to generation" (Lam. v. 19, 20). The church is weak; created things are easily cut off; what prop is there, but that God that lives forever? What, though Jerusalem lost its bulwarks, the temple were defaced, the land wasted; yet the God of Jerusalem sits upon an eternal throne, and from everlasting to everlasting there is no diminution of his power. The prophet intimates in this complaint, that it is not agreeable to God's eternity to forget his people, to whom he hath from eternity borne good-will. In the greatest confusions, the church's eyes are to be fixed upon the eternity of God's throne, where he sits as governor of the world. No creature can take any comfort in this perfection, but the church; other creatures depend upon God, but the church is united to him. The first discovery of the name "I am," which signifies the divine eternity, as well as immutability, was for the comfort of the "oppressed Israelites in Egypt" (Exod. iii. 14, 15): it was then published from the secret place of the Almighty, as the only strong cordial to refresh them: it hath not yet, it shall not ever lose its virtue in any of the miseries that have, or shall successively befall the church. It is a comfort as durable as the God whose name it is; he is still "I Am;" and the same to the church, as he was then to his Israel. His spiritual Israel have a greater right to the glories of it, than the carnal Israel could have. No oppression can be greater than theirs; what was a comfort suited to that distress, hath the same suitableness to every other oppression. It was not a temporary name, but a name forever; his "memorial to all generations" (ver. 15), and reacheth to the church of the Gentiles with whom he treats as the God of Abraham; ratifying that covenant by the Messiah, which he made with Abraham, the father of the faithful. The church's enemies are not to be feared; they may spring as the grass, but soon after do wither by their own inward principles of decay, or are cut down by the hand of God (Ps. xcii. 7–9). They may be instruments of the

anger of God, but " they shall be scattered as the workers of iniquity by the hand of the Lord, that is high for evermore" (ver. 8), and is engaged by his promise, to preserve a church in the world. They may threaten, but their breath may vanish as soon as their threatenings are pronounced ; for they carry their breath in no surer a place than their own nostrils, upon which the eternal God can put his hand, and sink them with all their rage. Do the prophets and instructers of the church " live forever" (Zech. i. 5) ? No : shall, then, the adversaries and disturbers of the church live forever ? They shall vanish as a shadow ; their being depends upon the eternal God of the faithful, and the everlasting Judge of the wicked. He that inhabits eternity is above them that inhabit mortality ; and must, whether they will or no, " say to corruption, Thou art my father, and to the worm, Thou art my mother, and my sister" (Job xvii. 14.) When they will act with a confidence, as if they were living gods, he will not be mated ; but evidence himself to be a living God above them. Why, then, should mortal men be feared in their frowns, when an immortal God hath promised protection in his word, and lives forever to perform it ?

5. Hence follows another comfort; since God is eternal, he hath as much power as will to be as good as his word. His promises are established upon his eternity ; and his perfection is a main ground of trust; " Trust in the Lord forever: for in the Lord Jehovah is everlasting strength" (Isa. xxvi. 4). בְּיָהּ יְהוָֹה צוּר צוּל עָם   His name is doubled ; that name, Jah and Jehovah, which was always the strength of his people ; and not a single one, but the strength or rock of eternities : not a failing, but an eternal truth and power ; that as his strength is eternal, so our trust in him should imitate his eternity in its perpetuity ; and therefore in the despondency of his people, as if God had forgot his promises, and made no account of them, or his word, and were weary of doing good, he calls them to reflect on what they had heard of his eternity, which is attended with immutability, who hath an infiniteness of power to perform his will, and an infiniteness of understanding to judge of the right seasons of it. His wisdom, will, truth, have always been, and will to eternity be the same (Isa. xl. 27, 28). He wants not life, any more than love, forever to help us ; since his word is past, he will never fail us ; since his life continues, he can never be out of a capacity to relieve us ; and, therefore, whenever we foolishly charge him by our distrustful thoughts, we forget his love, which made the promise, and his eternal life, which can accomplish it. As his word is the bottom of our trust, and his truth is the assurance of his sincerity, so his eternity is the assurance of his ability to perform: " His word stands forever" (ver 8). A man may be my friend this day, and be in another world to-morrow ; and though he be never so sincere in his word, yet death snaps his life asunder, and forbids the execution. But as God cannot die, so he cannot lie ; because he is the eternity of Israel: " The strength of Israel will not lie, nor repent," נצח perpetuity, or eternity of Israel (1 Sam. xv. 29). Eternity implies immutability ; we could have no ground for our hopes, if we knew him not to be longer lived than ourselves. The Psalmist beats

off our hands from trust in men, "because their breath goes forth, they return to their earth, and in that day their thoughts perish" (Ps. cxlvi. 3, 4). And if the God of Jacob were like them, what happiness could we have in making him our help? As his sovereignty in giving precepts had not been a strong ground of obedience, without considering him as an eternal lawgiver, who could maintain his rights; so his kindness in making the promises had not been a strong ground of confidence, without considering him as an eternal promiser, whose thoughts and whose life can never perish.[x] And this may be one reason why the Holy Ghost mentions so often the post-eternity of God, and so little his ante-eternity; because that is the strongest foundation of our faith and hope, which respects chiefly that which is future, and not that which is past; yet, indeed, no assurance of his after-eternity can be had, if his ante-eternity be not certain. If he had a beginning, he may have an end; and if he had a change in his nature, he might have in his counsels; but since all the resolves of God are as himself is, eternal, and all the promises of God are the fruits of his counsel, therefore they cannot be changed; if he should change them for the better, he would not have been eternally wise, to know what was best; if for the worse, he had not been eternally good or just. Men may break their promises, because they are made without foresight; but God, that inhabits eternity, foreknows all things that shall be done under the sun, as if they had been then acting before him; and nothing can intervene, or work a change in his resolves; because the least circumstances were eternally foreseen by him. Though there may be variations, and changes to our sight, the wind may tack about, and every hour new and cross accidents happen; yet the eternal God, who is eternally true to his word, sits at the helm, and the winds and the waves obey him. And though he should defer his promise a thousand years, yet he is "not slack" (2 Pet. iii. 8, 9); for he defers it but a day to his eternity: and who would not with comfort stay a day in expectation of a considerable advantage?

Use 3. For exhortation. 1. To something which concerns us in ourselves; 2. To something which concerns us with respect to God.

1. To something which concerns us in ourselves.

(1.) Let us be deeply affected with our sins long since committed. Though they are past with us, they are, in regard of God's eternity, present with him; there is no succession in eternity, as there is in time. All things are before God at once; our sins are before him, as if committed this moment, though committed long ago. As he is what he is in regard of duration, so he knows what he knows in regard of knowledge. As he is not more than he was, nor shall not be any more than he is, so he always knew what he knows, and shall not cease to know what he now knows. As himself, so his knowledge, is one indivisible point of eternity. He knows nothing but what he did know from eternity; he shall know no more for the future than he now knows. Our sins being present with him in his eternity, should be present with us in our regard of remembrance of them, and sorrow for them. What though many years are lapsed, much time run out,

[x] Crellius de Deo, c. 18, p. 44, 45.

and our iniquities almost blotted out of our memory; yet since a thousand years are, in God's sight, and in regard of his eternity, but as a day—" A thousand years in thy sight are but as yesterday, when it is past, and as a watch in the night" (Ps. xc. 4)—they are before him. For suppose a man were as old as the world, above five thousand six hundred years; the sins committed five thousand years ago, are, according to that rule, but as if they were committed five days ago; so that sixty-two years are but as an hour and a half; and the sins committed forty years since as if they were committed but this present hour. But if we will go further, and consider them but as a watch of the night, about three hours (for the night, consisting of twelve hours, was divided into set watches), then a thousand years are but as three hours in the sight of God; and then sins committed sixty years ago are but as if they were committed within this five minutes. Let none of us set light by the iniquities committed many years ago, and imagine that length of time can wipe out their guilt. No: let us consider them in relation to God's eternity, and excite an inward remorse, as if they had been but the birth of this moment.

(2.) Let the consideration of God's eternity abate our pride. This is the design of the verses following the text: the eternity of God being so sufficient to make us understand our own nothingness, which ought to be one great end of man, especially as fallen. The eternity of God should make us as much disesteem ourselves, as the excellency of God made Job abhor himself (Job xlii. 5, 6). His excellency should humble us under a sense of our vanity, and his eternity under a sense of the shortness of our duration. If man compares himself with other creatures, he may be too sensible of his greatness; but if he compares himself with God, he cannot but be sensible of his baseness.

1st. In regard of our impotence to comprehend this eternity of God. How little do we know, how little can we know, of God's eternity! We cannot fully conceive it, much less express it; we have but a brutish understanding in all those things, as Agur said of himself (Prov. xxx. 7). What is infinite and eternal, cannot be comprehended by finite and temporary creatures; if it could, it would not be infinite and eternal;y for to know a thing, is to know the extent and cause of it. It is repugnant to eternity to be known, because it hath no limits, no causes; the most soaring understanding cannot have a proportionable understanding of it. What disproportion is there between a drop of water and the sea in their greatness and motion; yet by a drop we may arrive to a knowledge of the nature of the sea, which is a mass of drops joined together; but the longest duration of times cannot make us know what eternity is, because there is no proportion between time and eternity. The years of God are as numberless as his thoughts (Ps. xl. 5), and our minds as far from reckoning the one as the other. If our understandings are too gross to comprehend the majesty of his infinite works, they are much more too short to comprehend the infiniteness of his eternity.

2d. In regard of the vast disproportion of our duration to this duration of God.

[1.] We have more of nothing than being. We were nothing from an unbegun eternity, and we might have been nothing to an endless eternity, had not God called us into being; and if he please we may be nothing by as short an annihilating word, as we were something by a creating word. As it is the prerogative of God to be, "I am that I am;" so it is the property of a creature to be, "I am not what I am;" I am not by myself what I am, but by the indulgence of another. I was nothing formerly; I may be nothing again, unless he that is "I Am" make me to subsist what I now am. Nothing is as much the title of the creature as being is the title of God. Nothing is so holy as God, because nothing hath being as God: "There is none holy as the Lord, for there is none besides thee" (1 Sam. ii. 2). Man's life is an image, a dream, which are next to nothing; and if compared with God, worse than nothing; a nullity as well as a vanity, because "with God only is the fountain of life" (Ps. xxxvi. 9). The creature is but a drop of life from him, dependent on him: a drop of water is a nothing if compared with the vast conflux of waters and numberless drops in the ocean. How unworthy is it for dust and ashes, kneaded together in time, to strut against the Father of eternity! Much more unworthy for that which is nothing, worse than nothing, to quarrel with that which is only being, and equal himself with Him that inhabits eternity.

[2.] What being we have had a beginning. After an unaccountable eternity was run out, in the very dregs of time, a few years ago we were created, and made of the basest and vilest dross of the world, the slime and dust of the earth; made of that wherewith birds build their nests; made of that which creeping things make their habitation, and beasts trample upon. How monstrous is pride in such a creature, to aspire, as if he were the Father of eternity, and as eternal as God, and so his own eternity!

[3.] What being we have is but of a short duration in regard of our life in this world. Our life is in a constant change and flux; we remain not the same an entire day; youth quickly succeeds childhood, and age as speedily treads upon the heels of youth; there is a continual defluxion of minutes, as there is of sands in a glass. He is as a watch wound up at the beginning of his life, and from that time is running down, till he comes to the bottom; some part of our lives is cut off every day, every minute. Life is but a moment: what is past cannot be recalled, what is future cannot be ensured. If we enjoy this moment, we have lost that which is past, and shall presently lose this by the next that is to come. The short duration of men is set out in Scripture by such creatures as soon disappear: a worm (Job xxv. 6), that can scarce outlive a winter; grass, that withers by the summer sun. Life is a "flower," soon withering (Job xiv. 2); a "vapor," soon vanishing (James iv. 14); a "smoke," soon disappearing (Ps. cii. 3). The strongest man is but compacted dust; the fabric must moulder; the highest mountain falls and comes to naught. Time gives place to eternity; we live now, and die to-morrow. Not a man since the world began ever lived a day in God's sight; for no man ever lived a thousand years. The longest day of any man's life never amounted to twenty-four hours in the account of divine eternity: a life of so many hundred years, with the addition "he died," makes up the greatest part of the history of the patriarchs (Gen. v.); and since the life of man hath been curtailed, if any be in the world eighty years, he scarce properly lives sixty of them, since the fourth part of time is at least consumed in sleep. A greater difference there is between the duration of God and that of a creature, than between the life of one for a minute, and the life of one that should live as many years as the whole globe of heaven and earth, if changed into papers, could contain figures. And this life, though but of a short duration according to the period God hath determined, is easily cut off; the treasure of life is deposited in a brittle vessel. A small stone hitting against Nebuchadnezzar's statue will tumble it down into a poor and nasty grave; a grape-stone, the bone of a fish, a small fly in the throat, a moist damp, are enough to destroy an earthly eternity, and reduce it to nothing. What a nothing, then, is our shortness, if compared with God's eternity; our frailty, with God's duration! How humble, then, should perishing creatures be before an eternal God, with whom "our days are as a hand's breadth, and our age as nothing!" (Ps. xxxix. 5.) The angels, that have been of as long a duration as heaven and earth, tremble before him; the heavens melt at his presence; and shall we, that are but of yesterday, approach a divine eternity with unhumbled souls, and offer the calves of our lips with the pride of devils, and stand upon our terms with him, without falling upon our faces, with a sense that we are but dust and ashes, and creatures of time? How easy is it to reason out man's humility! but how hard is it to reason man into it!

(3.) Let the consideration of God's eternity take off our love and confidence from the world, and the things thereof. The eternity of God reproaches a pursuit of the world, as preferring a momentary pleasure before an everlasting God; as though a temporal world could be a better supply than a God whose years never fail. Alas! what is this earth men are so greedy of, and will get, though by blood and sweat? What is this whole earth, if we had the entire possession of it, if compared with the vast heavens, the seat of angels and blessed spirits? It is but as an atom to the greatest mountain, or as a drop of dew to the immense ocean. How foolish is it to prefer a drop before the sea, or an atom before the world! The earth is but a point to the sun; the sun with its whole orb, but a little part of the heavens if compared with the whole fabric. If a man had the possession of all those, there could be no comparison between those that have had a beginning, and shall have an end, and God who is without either of them. Yet how many are there that make nothing of the divine eternity, and imagine an eternity of nothing!

[1.] The world hath been but of a short standing. It is not yet six thousand years since the foundations of it were laid, and therefore it cannot have a boundless excellency, as that God, who hath been from everlasting, doth possess. If Adam had lived to this day, and been as absolute lord of his posterity, as he was of the other creatures, had it been a competent object to take up his heart? had he not been a madman, to have preferred this little created pleasure before an everlasting uncreated God? a thing that had a dependent beginning, before that which had an independent eternity?

[2.] The beauties of the world are transitory and perishing. The whole world is nothing else but a fluid thing; the fashion of it is a pageantry, "passing away" (1 Cor. vii. 31): though the glories of it might be conceived greater than they are, yet they are not consistent, but transient; there cannot be an entire enjoyment of them, because they grow up and expire every moment, and slip away between our fingers while we are using them. Have we not heard of God's dispersing the greatest empires like "chaff before a whirlwind," or as "smoke out of a chimney" (Hos. xiii. 3), which, though it appears as a compacted cloud, as if it would choke the sun, is quickly scattered into several parts of the air, and becomes invisible? Nettles have often been heirs to stately palaces, as God threatens Israel (Hos. ix. 6). We cannot promise ourselves over night anything the next day. A kingdom with the glory of a throne may be cut off in a morning (Hos. x. 15). The new wine may be taken from the mouth when the vintage is ripe; the devouring locust may snatch away both the hopes of that and the harvest (Joel i. 15); they are, therefore, things which are not, and nothing cannot be a fit object for confidence or affection; "Wilt thou set thy eyes upon that which is not? for riches certainly make themselves wings" (Prov. xxiii. 5). They are not properly beings, because they are not stable, but flitting. They are not, because they may not be the next moment to us what they are this: they are but cisterns, not springs, and broken cisterns, not sound and stable; no solidity in their substance, nor stability in their duration. What a foolish thing is it then, to prefer a transient felicity, a mere nullity, before an eternal God! What a senseless thing would it be in a man to prefer the map of a kingdom, which the hand of a child can tear in pieces, before the kingdom shadowed by it! How much more inexcusable is it to value things, that are so far from being eternal, that they are not so much as dusky resemblances of an eternity. Were the things of the world more glorious than they are, yet they are but as a counterfeit sun in a cloud, which comes short of the true sun in the heavens, both in glory and duration; and to esteem them before God, is inconceivably baser, than if a man should value a party-colored bubble in the air, before a durable rock of diamonds. The comforts of this world are as candles, that will end in a snuff; whereas the felicity that flows from an eternal God, is like the sun, that shines more and more to a perfect day.

[3.] They cannot therefore be fit for a soul, which was made to have an interest in God's eternity. The soul being of a perpetual nature, was made for the fruition of an eternal good; without such a good it can never be perfect. Perfection, that noble thing, riseth not from anything in this world, nor is a title due to a soul while in this world; it is then they are said to be made perfect, when they arrive at that entire conjunction with the eternal God in another life (Heb. xii. 23). The soul cannot be ennobled by an acquaintance with these things, or established by a dependence on them; they cannot confer what a rational nature should desire, or supply it with what it wants. The soul hath a resemblance to God in a post-eternity; why should it be drawn aside by the blandishments of earthly things, to neglect its true establishment, and lackey after the body, which is but the shadow of the soul, and was made to follow it and serve it? But while it busieth itself altogether in the concerns of a perishing body, and seeks satisfaction in things that glide away, it becomes rather a body than soul, descends below its nature, reproacheth that God who hath imprinted upon it an image of his own eternity, and loseth the comfort of the everlastingness of its Creator. How shall the whole world, if our lives were as durable as that, be a happy eternity to us, who have souls that shall survive all the delights of it, which must fry in those flames that shall fire the whole frame of nature at the general conflagration of the world? (2 Pet. iii. 10.)

[4.] Therefore let us provide for a happy interest in the eternity of God. Man is made for an eternal state. The soul hath such a perfection in its nature, that it is fit for eternity, and cannot display all its operations but in eternity. To an eternity it must go, and live as long as God himself lives. Things of a short duration are not proportioned to a soul made for an eternal continuance; to see that it be a comfortable eternity, is worth all our care. Man is a forecasting creature, and considers not only the present, but the future too, in his provisions for his family; and shall he disgrace his nature in casting off all consideration of a future eternity? Get possession, therefore, of the eternal God. "A portion in this life" is the lot of those who shall be forever miserable (Ps. xvii. 14). But God, "an everlasting portion," is the lot of them that are designed for happiness. "God is my portion forever" (Ps. lxxiii. 26). "Time is short" (1 Cor. vii. 29). The whole time for which God designed this building of the world, is of a little compass; it is a stage erected for rational creatures to act their parts upon for a few thousand years; the greatest part of which time is run out; and then shall time, like a rivulet, fall into the sea of eternity, from whence it sprung. As time is but a slip of eternity, so it will end in eternity; our advantages consist in the present instant; what is past never promised a return, and cannot be fetched back by all our vows. What is future, we cannot promise ourselves to enjoy; we may be snatched away before it comes. Every minute that passeth, speaks the fewer remaining, till the time of death; and as we are every hour further from our beginning, we are nearer our end. The child born this day grows up, to grow nothing at last. In all ages there is "but a step between us and death," as David said of himself (1 Sam. xx. 3). The little time that remains for the devil till the day of judgment, envenoms his wrath; he rageth, because "his time is short" (Rev. xii. 12). The little time that remains between this moment and our death, should quicken our diligence to inherit the endless and unchangeable eternity of God.

[5.] Often meditate on the eternity of God. The holiness, power, and eternity of God, are the fundamental articles of all religion, upon which the whole body of it leans; his holiness for conformity to him, his power and eternity for the support of faith and hope. The strong and incessant cries of the four beasts, representing that christian church, are "Holy, holy, holy, Lord God Almighty, which was, and is, and is to come" (Rev. iv. 8). Though his power is intimated, yet the chiefest are his holiness, three times expressed; and his eternity which is repeated, "who lives forever and ever" (ver. 9). This ought to be the constant practice in the church of the Gentiles, which this book chiefly respects; the meditation of his converting grace manifested to Paul, ravished the apostle's heart; but not without the triumphant consideration of his immortality and eternity, which are the principal parts of the doxology: "Now unto the King eternal, immortal, invisible, the only wise God, be honor and glory forever and ever" (1 Tim. i. 15–17). It could be no great transport to the spirit, to consider him glorious without considering him immortal. The unconfinedness of his perfections in regard of time, presents the soul with matter of the greatest complacency. The happiness of our souls depends upon his other attributes, but the perpetuity of it upon his eternity. Is it a comfort to view his immense wisdom; his overflowing goodness; his tender mercy; his unerring truth? What comfort were there in any of those, if it were a wisdom that could be baffled; a goodness that could be damped; a mercy that can expire; and a truth that can perish with the subject of it? Without eternity, what were all his other perfections, but as glorious, yet withering flowers; a great, but a decaying beauty? By a frequent meditation of God's eternity, we should become more sensible of our own vanity and the world's triflingness; how nothing should ourselves; how nothing would all other things appear in our eyes! how coldly should we desire them! how feebly should we place any trust in them! Should we not think ourselves worthy of contempt to dote upon a perishing glory, to expect support from an arm of flesh, when there is an eternal beauty to ravish us, an eternal arm to protect us? Asaph, when he considered God "a portion forever," thought nothing of the glories of the earth, or the beauties of the created heavens, worth his appetite or complacency, but "God" (Ps. lxxiii. 25, 26). Besides, an elevated frame of heart at the consideration of God's eternity, would batter down the strongholds and engines of any temptation: a slight temptation will not know where to find and catch hold of a soul high and hid in a meditation of it; and if it doth, there will not be wanting from hence preservatives to resist and conquer it. What transitory pleasures will not the thoughts of God's eternity stifle? When this work busieth a soul, it is too great to suffer it to descend, to listen to a sleeveless errand from hell or the world. The wanton allurements of the flesh will be put off with indignation. The proffers of the world will be ridiculous when they are cast into the balance with the eternity of God, which sticking in our thoughts, we shall not be so easy a prey for the fowler's gin.   Let us, therefore, often meditate upon this, but not in a bare speculation, without engaging our affections, and making every notion of the divine eternity end in a suitable impression upon our hearts.   This would be much like the disciples gazing upon the heavens at the ascension of their Master, while they forgot the practice of his orders (Acts i. 11).   We may else find something of the nature of God, and lose ourselves, not only in eternity, but to eternity.

2. And hence the second part of the exhortation is, to something which concerns us with a respect to God.

(1.) If God be eternal, how worthy is he of our choicest affections, and strongest desires of communion with him!   Is not everything to be valued according to the greatness of its being!   How, then, should we love him, who is not only lovely in his nature, but eternally lovely; having from everlasting all those perfections centered in himself, which appear in time!   If everything be lovely, by how much more it partakes of the nature of God, who is the chief good; how much more infinitely lovely is God, who is superior to all other goods, and eternally so!   Not a God of a few minutes, months, years, or millions of years; not of the dregs of time or the top of time, but of eternity; above time, inconceivably immense beyond time.   The loving him infinitely, perpetually, is an act of homage due to him for his eternal excellency; we may give him the one, since our souls are immortal, though we cannot the other, because they are finite.   Since he incloseth in himself all the excellencies of heaven and earth forever, he should have an affection, not only of time in this world, but of eternity in future; and if we did not owe him a love for what we are by him, we owe him a love for what he is in himself; and more for what he is, than for what he is to us.   He is more worthy of our affections because he is the eternal God, than because he is our Creator; because he is more excellent in his nature, than in his transient actions; the beams of his goodness to us, are to direct our thoughts and affections to him; but his own eternal excellency ought to be the ground and foundation of our affections to him.   And truly, since nothing but God is eternal, nothing but God is worth the loving; and we do but a just right to our love, to pitch it upon that which can always possess us and be possessed by us; upon an object that cannot deceive our affection, and put it out of countenance by a dissolution.   And if our happiness consists in being like to God, we should imitate him in loving him as he loves himself, and as long as he loves himself; God cannot do more to himself than love himself; he can make no addition to his essence, nor diminution from it.   What should we do less to an eternal Being, than to bestow affections upon him, like his own to himself; since we can find nothing so durable as himself, for which we should love it?

(2.) He only is worthy of our best service.   The Ancient of Days is to be served before all that are younger than himself; our best obedience is due to him as a God of unconfined excellency; everything that is excellent deserves a veneration suitable to its excellency.   As God is infinite, he hath right to a boundless service; as he is eternal, he hath right to a perpetual service: as service is a debt of justice upon the account of the excellency of his nature, so a perpetual service is as much a debt of justice upon the account of his eternity. If God be infinite and eternal, he merits an honor and comportment from his creatures, suited to the unlimited perfection of his nature, and the duration of his being. How worthy is the Psalmist's resolution! "I will sing unto the Lord as long as I live; I will sing praise to my God while I have any being" (Ps. civ. 33). It is the use he makes of the endless duration of the glory of God; and will extend to all other service as well as praise. To serve other things, or to serve ourselves, is too vast a service upon that which is nothing. In devoting ourselves to God, we serve him that is, that was, so as that he never began; is to come, so as that he never shall end; by whom all things are what they are; who hath both eternal knowledge to remember our service, and eternal goodness to reward it.

DISCOURSE VI

ON THE IMMUTABILITY OF GOD

Psalm cii. 26, 27.—They shall perish, but thou shalt endure: yea, all of them shall wax old as a garment; as a vesture shalt thou change them, and they shall be changed: But thou art the same, and thy years shall have no end.

This Psalm contains a complaint of a people pressed with a great calamity; some think of the Jewish church in Babylon; others think the Psalmist doth here personate mankind lying under a state of corruption, because he wishes for the coming of the Messiah, to accomplish that redemption promised by God, and needed by them. Indeed the title of the Psalm is "A prayer of the afflicted when he is overwhelmed, and pours out his complaint before the Lord;" whether afflicted with the sense of corruption, or with the sense of oppression. And the redemption by the Messiah, which the ancient church looked upon as the fountain of their deliverance from a sinful or a servile bondage, is in this psalm spoken of. A set time appointed for the discovery of his mercy to Sion (ver. 13); an appearance in glory to build up Sion (ver. 16); the loosing of the prisoner by redemption, and them that are appointed to death (ver. 20); the calling of the Gentiles (ver. 22); and the latter part of the psalm, wherein are the verses I have read, are applied to Christ (Heb. i.) Whatsoever the design of the psalm might be, many things are intermingled that concern the kingdom of the Messiah, and redemption by Christ.

Some make three parts of the psalm. 1. A petition plainly delivered (ver. 1, 2): "Hear my prayer, O Lord, and let my cry come unto thee," &c. 2. The petition strongly and argumentatively enforced and pleaded (ver. 3), from the misery of the petitioner in himself, and his reproach from his enemies. 3. An acting of faith in the expectation of an answer in the general redemption promised (ver. 12, 13): "But thou, O Lord, shalt endure forever; thou shalt arise and have mercy upon Sion; the heathen shall fear thy name." The first part is the petition pleaded; the second part is the petition answered, in an assurance that there should in time be a full deliverance.[z] The design of the penman is to confirm the church in the truth of the divine promises; that though the foundations of the world should be ripped up, and the heavens clatter together, and the whole fabric of them be unpinned and fall to pieces, the firmest parts of it dissolved; yet the church should con-

z Pareus.

tinue in its stability, because it stands not upon the changeableness of creatures, but is built upon the immutable rock of the truth of God, which is as little subject to change, as his essence.

They shall perish, thou shalt change them. As he had before ascribed to God the "foundation of heaven and earth" (ver. 25), so he ascribes to God here the destruction of them. Both the beginning and end of the world are here ascertained. There is nothing, indeed, from the present appearance of things, that can demonstrate the cessation of the world. The heaven and earth stand firm; the motions of the heavenly bodies are the same, their beauty is not decayed; individuals corrupt, but the species and kinds remain. The successions of the year observe their due order; but the sin of man renders the change of the present appearance of the world necessary to accomplish the design of God for the glory of his elect. The heavens do not naturally perish, as some fancied an old age of the world, wherein it must necessarily decay as the bodies of animals do; or that the parts of the heavens are broken off by their rubbing one against another in their motion, and falling to the earth, are the seeds of those things that grow among us.[a]

The earth and heavens. He names here the most stable parts of the world, and the most beautiful parts of the creation; those that are freest from corruptibility and change, to illustrate thereby the immutability of God; that though the heavens and earth have a prerogative of fixedness above other parts of the world, and the creatures that reside below, the heavens remain the same as they were created, and the centre of the earth retains its fixedness, and are as beautiful and fresh in their age as they were in their youth many years ago, notwithstanding the change of the elements, fire and water being often turned into air, so that there may remain but little of that air which was first created by reason of the continual transmutation; yet this firmness of the earth and heavens is not to be regarded in comparison of the unmovableness and fixedness of the being of God; as their beauty comes short of the glory of his being, so doth their firmness come short of his stability. Some, by heavens and earth, understand the creatures which reside in the earth, and those which are in the air, which is called heaven often in Scripture; but the ruin and fall of these being seen every day, had been no fit illustration of the unchangeableness of God.

They shall perish, they shall be changed. 1. They *may* perish, say some; they have it not from themselves that they do not perish, but from thee, who didst endue them with an incorruptible nature; they shall perish if thou speakest the word; thou canst with as much ease destroy them, as thou didst create them. But the Psalmist speaks not of their possibility, but the certainty of their perishing. 2. They *shall* perish in their qualities and motion, not in their substance, say others. They shall cease from that motion which is designed properly for the generation and corruption of things in the earth; but in regard of their substance and beauty they shall remain. As when the strings or wheels of a clock or watch are taken off, the material parts remain, though the motion of it, and the use for discovering

the time of the day, ceaseth.[b] To perish, doth not signify alway a
falling into nothing, an annihilation, by which both the matter and
the form are destroyed, but a ceasing of the present appearance of
them; a ceasing to be what they now are; as a man is said to perish
when he dies, whereas the better part of man doth not cease to be.
The figure of the body moulders away, and the matter of it returns
to dust; but the soul being immortal ceaseth not to act, when the
body, by reason of the absence of the soul, is incapable of acting.
So the heavens shall perish; the appearance they now have shall
vanish, and a more glorious and incorruptible frame be erected by
the power and goodness of God. The dissolution of heaven and
earth is meant by the word *perish;* the raising a new frame is signified by the word *changed:* as if the Spirit of God would prevent any
wrong meaning of the word *perish,* by alleviating the sense of that,
by another which signifies only a mutation and change; as when we
change a habit and garment, we quit the old to receive the new.

As a garment, as a vesture. Thou shalt change them, ἑλίξεις,[c] thou
shalt fold them up. The heavens are compared to a curtain (Ps.
civ. 2), and shall in due time be folded up as clothes and curtains
are. As a garment encompasseth the whole body, so do the heavens
encircle the earth.[d] Some say, as a garment is folded up to be laid
aside, that when there is need it may be taken again for use; so shalt
thou fold up the heavens like a garment, that when they are repaired,
thou mayest again stretch them out about the earth; thou shalt fold
them up, so that what did appear shall not now appear. It may be
illustrated by the metaphor of a scroll or book, which the Spirit of
God useth (Isa. xxxiv. 4; Rev. vi. 14): "The heavens departed as a
scroll when it is rolled together." When a book is rolled up or
shut, nothing can be read in it till it be opened again; so the face
of the heavens, wherein the stars are as letters declaring the glory
of God, shall be shut or rolled together, so that nothing shall appear,
till by its renovation it be opened again: as a garment it shall be
changed, not to be used in the same fashion, and for the same use
again. It seems, indeed, to be for the worse; an old garment is not
changed but into rags, to be put to other uses, and afterwards thrown
upon the dunghill; but similitudes are not to be pressed too far; and
this will not agree with the new heavens and new earth, physically
so, as well as metaphorically so. It is not likely the heavens will be
put to a worse use than God designed them for in creation; however,
a change as a garment, speaks not a total corruption, but an alteration of qualities; as a garment not to be used in the same fashion as
before. We may observe, that it is probable the world shall not be
annihilated, but refined. It shall lose its present form and fashion;
but not its foundation: indeed, as God raised it from nothing, so he
can reduce it into nothing; yet it doth not appear that God will annihilate it, and utterly destroy both the matter and form of it; part
shall be consumed, and part purified (2 Pet. iii. 12, 13): "The
heavens shall be on fire and dissolved; nevertheless, we, according
to his promise, look for a new heaven and a new earth." They shall
be melted down as gold by the artificer, to be refined from its dross,

---

[b] Coccei. *in loc.*   [c] Septuag.   [d] Estius in Heb. i.

and wrought into a more beautiful fashion, that they may serve the design of God for those that shall reside therein; a new world wherein righteousness shall dwell: the apostle opposing it thereby to the old world wherein wickedness did reside. The heavens are to be purged, as the vessels that held the sin-offering were to be purified by the fire of the sanctuary. God, indeed, will take down this scaffold, which he hath built to publish his glory. As every individual hath a certain term of its duration, so an end is appointed for the universal nature of heaven and earth (Isa. li. 6): "The heavens shall vanish like smoke" which disappears. As smoke is resolved and attenuated into air, not annihilated, so shall the world assume a new face, and have a greater clearness and splendor; as the bodies of men, dissolved into dust, shall have more glorious qualities at their resurrection; as a vessel of gold is melted down to remove the batterings in it, and receive a more comely form by the skill of the workman.

1. The world was not destroyed by the deluge: it was rather washed by water, than consumed; so it shall be rather refined by the last fire, than lie under an irrecoverable ruin.

2. It is not likely God would liken the everlastingness of his covenant, and the perpetuity of his spiritual Israel, to the duration of the ordinances of the heavens (as he doth in Jer. xxxi. 35, 36), if they were wholly to depart from before him. Though that place may only tend to an assurance of a church in the world, while the world endures; yet it would be but small comfort, if the happiness of believers should endure no longer than the heavens and earth, if they were to have a total period.

3. Besides, the bodies of the saints must have place for their support to move in, and glorious objects suited to those glorious senses which shall be restored to them; not in any carnal way, which our Saviour rejects, when he saith, There is no eating, or drinking, or marrying, &c. in the other world; but whereby they may glorify God; though how or in what manner their senses shall be used, would be rashness to determine; only something is necessary for the corporeal state of men, that there may be an employment for their senses as well as their souls.

4. Again, How could the creature, the world, or any part of it, be said to be delivered from the bondage of corruption, into the glorious liberty of the sons of God, if the whole frame of heaven and earth were to be annihilated (Rom. viii. 21)? The apostle saith also, that the creature waits with an "earnest expectation for this manifestation of the sons of God" (ver. 19); which would have no foundation if the whole frame should be reduced to nothing. What joyful expectation can there be in any of a total ruin? How should the creature be capable of partaking in this glorious liberty of the sons of God?[e] As the world for the sin of man lost its first dignity, and was cursed after the fall, and the beauty bestowed upon it by creation defaced; so it shall recover that ancient glory, when he shall be fully restored by the resurrection to that dignity he lost by his first sin. As man shall be freed from his corruptibility to receive

[e] Hyper. in Heb. 1.

that glory which is prepared for him, so shall the creatures be freed
from that imperfection or corruptibility, those stains and spots upon
the face of them, to receive a new glory suited to their nature, and
answerable to the design of God, when the glorious liberty of the
saints shall be accomplished.[f] As when a prince's nuptials are sol-
emnized, the whole country echoes with joy ; so the inanimate creatures, when the time of the marriage of the Lamb is come, shall
have a delight and pleasure from that renovation. The apostle sets
forth the whole world as a person groaning ; and the Scripture is
frequent in such metaphors ; as when the creatures are said to wait
upon God, and to be troubled, the hills are said to leap and the
mountains to rejoice (Ps. civ. 27–29) ; the creature is said to groan,
as the heavens are said to declare the glory of God, passively,
naturally, not rationally. It is not likely angels are here meant,
though they cannot but desire it ; since they are affected with the
dishonor and reproach God hath in the world, they cannot but long
for the restoration of his honor in the restoration of the creature to
its true end : and, indeed, the angels are employed to serve man in
this sinful state, and cannot but in holiness wish the creature freed
from his corruption. Nor is it meant of the new creatures, which
have the first fruits of the Spirit ; those he brings in afterwards,
groaning and waiting for the adoption (ver. 23) ; where he distinguisheth the rational creature from the creature he had spoken of
before. If he had meant the believing creature by that creature
that desired the liberty of the sons of God, what need had there
been of that additional distinction, and not only they, but we also
who have the first fruits of the Spirit, groan within ourselves ?
Whereby it seems he means some creatures below rational creatures,
since neither angels nor blessed souls can be said to travail in pain,
with that distress as a woman in travail hath, as the word signifies,
who perform the work joyfully which God sets them upon.[g] If the
creatures be subject to vanity by the sin of man, they shall also
partake of a happiness by the restoration of man. The earth hath
borne thorns and thistles, and venomous beasts ; the air hath had
its tempests and infectious qualities ; the water hath caused its floods
and deluges. The creature hath been abused to luxury and intem-
perance ; and been tyrannized over by man, contrary to the end of
its creation. It is convenient that some time should be allotted for the
creature's attaining its true end, and that it may partake of the
peace of man, as it hath done of the fruits of his sin ; otherwise it
would seem, that sin had prevailed more than grace, and would have
had more power to deface, than grace to restore things into their due
order.

5. Again, Upon what account should the Psalmist exhort the
heavens to rejoice, and the earth to be glad, when God "comes to
judge the world with righteousness" (Ps. xcvi. 11–13), if they should
be annihilated and sunk forever into nothing ? "It would seem,"
saith Daille, "to be an impertinent figure, if the Judge of the world
brought to them a total destruction ; an entire ruin could not be
matter of triumph to creatures, who naturally have that instinct or

inclination put into them by their Creator, to preserve themselves, and to effect their own preservation."

6. Again, the Lord is to rejoice in his works (Ps. civ. 31): "The glory of the Lord shall endure forever; the Lord shall rejoice in his works;" not hath, but shall rejoice in his works: in the works of creation, which the Psalmist had enumerated, and which is the whole scope of the Psalm: and he intimates that it is part of the glory of the Lord which endures forever; that is, his manifestative glory, to rejoice in his works: the glory of the Lord must be understood with reference to the creation he had spoken of before. How short was that joy God had in his works after he had sent them beautified out of his hand! How soon did he repent, not only that he had made man, but was grieved at the heart also, that he made the other creatures which man's sin had disordered! (Gen. vi. 7.) What joy can God have in them, since the curse upon the entrance of sin into the world remains upon them? If they are to be annihilated upon the full restoration of his holiness, what time will God have to rejoice·in the other works of creation? It is the joy of God to see all his works in due order; every one pointing to their true end; marching together in their excellency, according to his first intendment in their creation. Did God create the world to perform its end only for one day; scarce so much, if Adam fell the very first day of his creation? What would have been their end, if Adam had been confirmed in a state of happiness as the angels were? 'tis likely will be answered and performed upon the complete restoration of man to that happy state from whence he fell. What artificer compiles a work by his skill, but to rejoice in it? And shall God have no joy from the works of his hands? Since God can only rejoice in goodness, the creatures must have that goodness restored to them which God pronounced them to have at the first creation, and which he ordained them for, before he can again rejoice in his works. The goodness of the creatures is the glory and joy of God.

Inference 1. We may infer from hence, what a base and vile thing sin is, which lays the foundation of the world's change. Sin brings it to a decrepit age; sin overturned the whole work of God (Gen. iii. 17); so that to render it useful to its proper end, there is a necessity of a kind of a new creating it. This causes God to fire the earth for a purification of it from that infection and contagion brought upon it by the apostasy and corruption of man. It hath served sinful man, and therefore must undergo a purging flame, to be fit to serve the holy and righteous Creator. As sin is so riveted in the body of man, that there is need of a change by death to raze it out; so hath the curse for sin got so deep into the·bowels of the world, that there is need of a change by fire to refine it for its master's use. Let us look upon sin with no other notion than as the object of God's hatred, the cause of his grief in the creatures, and the spring of the pain and ruin of the world.

2. How foolish a thing is it to set our hearts upon that which shall perish, and be no more what it is now! The heavens and the earth, the solidest and firmest parts of the creation, shall not continue in the posture they are; they must perish and undergo a refining

change. How feeble and weak are the other parts of the creation, the little creatures walking upon and fluttering about the world, that are perishing and dying every day; and we scarce see them clothed with life and beauty this day, but they wither and are despoiled of all the next; and are such frail things fit objects for our everlasting spirits and affections? Though the daily employment of the heavens is the declaration of the glory of God (Ps. xix. 1), yet neither this, nor their harmony, order, beauty, amazing greatness and glory of them, shall preserve them from a dissolution and melting at the presence of the Lord. Though they have remained in the same posture from the creation till this day, and are of so great antiquity, yet they must bow down to a change before the will and word of their Creator; and shall we rest upon that which shall vanish like smoke? Shall we take any creature for our support like ice, that will crack under our feet, and must, by the order of their Lord Creator, deceive our hopes? Perishing things can be no support to the soul; if we would have rest, we must run to God and rest in God. How contemptible should that be to us, whose fashion shall pass away, which shall not endure long in its present form and appearance; contemptible as a rest, not contemptible as the work of God; contemptible as an end, not contemptible as a means to attain our end! If these must be changed, how unworthy are other things to be the centre of our souls, that change in our very using of them, and slide away in our very enjoyment of them!

Thou art the same. The essence of God, with all the perfections of his nature, are pronounced the same, without any variation from eternity to eternity; so that the text doth not only assert the eternal duration of God, but his immutability in that duration. His eternity is signified in that expression, "Thou shalt endure;" his immutability in this, "Thou art the same." To endure, argues indeed his immutability as well as eternity; for what endures, is not changed, and what is changed, doth not endure;[h] but "Thou art the same"[i] doth more fully signify it. He could not be the same if he could be changed into any other thing than what he is; the Psalmist therefore puts not thou hast been, or shalt be, but thou art the same, without any alteration. "Thou art the same;" that is, the same God; the same in essence and nature; the same in will and purpose. Thou dost change all other things as thou pleasest, but thou art immutable in every respect, and receivest no shadow of change, though never so light and small. The Psalmist here alludes to the name Jehovah, I Am;[k] and doth not only ascribe immutability to God, but exclude everything else from partaking in that perfection. All things else are tottering; God sees all other things in continual motion under his feet, like water passing away and no more seen; while he remains fixed and immovable; his wisdom and power, his knowledge and will, are always the same. His essence can receive no alteration, neither by itself, nor by any external cause; whereas other things either naturally decline to destruction, pass from one term to another, till they come to their period; or shall at the last

[h] Estius in Heb. i. [i] Chrysostom, אתה הוא.
[k] Ἀλλοιώσεως κρέιττων above all change. Theodor.

day be wrapped up, after God hath completed his will in them and by them, as a man doth a garment he intends to repair and transform to another use. So that in the text, God, as immutable, is opposed to all creatures as perishing and changeable.

Doctrine. God is unchangeable in his essence, nature, and perfections. Immutability and eternity are linked together; and, indeed, true eternity is true immutability; whence eternity is defined the possession of an immutable life. Yet immutability differs from eternity in our conception; immutability respects the essence or existence of a thing; eternity respects the duration of a being in that state, or rather, immutability is the state itself;[1] eternity is the measure of that state. A thing is said to be changed, when it is otherwise now in regard of nature, state, will, or any quality than it was before; when either something is added to it, or taken from it; when it either loses or acquires. But now it is the essential property of God, not to have any accession to, or diminution of, his essence or attributes, but to remain entirely the same. He wants nothing; he loses nothing; but doth uniformly exist by himself, without any new nature, new thoughts, new will, new purpose, or new place. This unchangeableness of God was anciently represented by the figure of a cube, a piece of metal or wood framed four-square, when every side is exactly of the same equality; cast it which way you will, it will always be in the same posture, because it is equal to itself in all its dimensions.[m] He was therefore said to be the centre of all things, and other things the circumference; the centre is never moved, while the circumference is; it remains immovable in the midst of the circle; "There is no variableness nor shadow of turning with him" (James i. 17). The moon hath her spots, so hath the sun; there is a mixture of light and darkness; it hath its changes; sometimes it is in the increase, sometimes in the wane; it is always either gaining or losing, and by the turnings and motions, either of the heavenly bodies or of the earth, it is in its eclipse, by the interposition of the earth between that and the sun. The sun also hath its diurnal and annual motion; it riseth and sets, and puts on a different face; it doth not always shine with the noon-day light; it is sometimes veiled with clouds and vapors; it is always going from one tropic to another, whereby it makes various shadows on the earth, and produceth the various seasons of the year; it is not always in our hemisphere, nor doth it always shine with an equal force and brightness in it. Such shadows and variations have no place in the eternal Father of Lights; he hath not the least spot or diminution of brightness; nothing can cloud him or eclipse him.

For the better understanding this perfection of God, I shall premise three things.

1. The immutability of God is a perfection. Immutability considered in itself, without relation to other things, is not a perfection. It is the greatest misery and imperfection of the evil angels, that they are immutable in malice against God; but as God is infinite in essence, infinitely good, wise, holy; so it is a perfection necessary to his nature, that he should be immutably all this, all excellency,

---

[1] Gamacheus.   [m] Amyrant sur Heb. ix. p. 153.

goodness, wisdom, immutably all that he is; without this he would
be an imperfect Being. Are not the angels in heaven, who are confirmed in a holy and happy state, more perfect than when they were
in a possibility of committing evil and becoming miserable? Are
not the saints in heaven, whose wills by grace do unalterably cleave
to God and goodness, more perfect than if they were as Adam in
Paradise, capable of losing their felicity, as well as preserving it?
We count a rock, in regard of its stability, more excellent than the
dust of the ground, or a feather that is tossed about with every
wind; is it not also the perfection of the body to have a constant
tenor of health, and the glory of a man not to warp aside from what
is just and right, by the persuasions of any temptations?

2. Immutability is a glory belonging to all the attributes of God.
It is not a single perfection of the Divine nature, nor is it limited to
particular objects thus and thus disposed. Mercy and justice have
their distinct objects and distinct acts; mercy is conversant about a
penitent, justice conversant about an obstinate sinner. In our notion
and conception of the Divine perfections, his perfections are different: the wisdom of God is not his power, nor his power his holiness, but immutability is the centre wherein they all unite. There
is not one perfection but may be said to be and truly is, immutable;
none of them will appear so glorious without this beam, this sun of
immutability, which renders them highly excellent without the least
shadow of imperfection. How cloudy would his blessedness be if it
were changeable! How dim his wisdom, if it might be obscured!
How feeble his power, if it were capable to be sickly and languish!
How would mercy lose much of its lustre, if it could change into
wrath; and justice much of its dread, if it could be turned into
mercy, while the object of justice remains unfit for mercy, and one
that hath need of mercy continues only fit for the Divine fury! But
unchangeableness is a thread that runs through the whole web; it is
the enamel of all the rest; none of them without it could look with
a triumphant aspect. His power is unchangeable: "In the Lord
Jehovah is everlasting strength" (Isa. xxvi. 4). His mercy and his
holiness endure forever: he never could, nor ever can, look upon
iniquity (Hab. i. 13). He is a rock in the righteousness of his ways,
the truth of his word, the holiness of his proceedings, and the rectitude of his nature. All are expressed Deut xxxii. 4: "He is a rock,
his work is perfect, for all his ways are judgment; a God of truth,
and without iniquity; just and right is he." All that we consider
in God is unchangeable; for his essence and his properties are the
same, and, therefore, what is necessarily belonging to the essence of
God, belongs also to every perfection of the nature of God; none of
them can receive any addition or diminution. From the unchangeableness of his nature, the apostle (James i. 17) infers the unchangeableness of his holiness, and himself (in Mal. iii. 6) the unchangeableness of his counsel.

3. Unchangeableness doth necessarily pertain to the nature of God.
It is of the same necessity with the rectitude of his nature; he can no
more be changeable in his essence than he can be unrighteous in his
actions. God is a necessary Being; he is necessarily what he is, and,

therefore, is unchangeably what he is. Mutability belongs to contingency. If any perfection of his nature could be separated from him, he would cease to be God. What did not possess the whole nature of God, could not have the essence of God; it is reciprocated with the nature of God. Whatsoever is immutable by nature is God; whatsoever is God is immutable by nature. Some creatures are immutable by his grace and power. God is holy, happy, wise, good, by his essence; angels and men are made holy, wise, happy, strong, and good, by qualities and graces.[n] The holiness, happiness, and wisdom of saints and angels, as they had a beginning, so they are capable of increase and diminution, and of an end also; for their standing is not from themselves, or from the nature of created strength, holiness, or wisdom, which in themselves are apt to fail, and finally to decay; but from the stability and confirmation they have by the gift and grace of God. The heaven and earth shall be changed; and after that renewal and reparation they shall not be changed. Our bodies after the resurrection shall not be changed, but forever be "made conformable to the glorious body of Christ" (Phil. iii. 21); but this is by the powerful grace of God: so that, indeed, those things may be said afterwards rather to be unchanged than unchangeable, because they are not so by nature, but by sovereign dispensation. As creatures have not necessary beings, so they have not necessary immutability. Necessity of being, and, therefore, immutability of being, belongs by nature only to God; otherwise, if there were any change in God, he would be sometimes what he was not, and would cease to be what he was, which is against the nature, and, indeed, against the natural notion of a Deity. Let us see then,

I. In what regards God is immutable. II. Prove that God is immutable. III. That this is proper to God, and incommunicable to any creature. IV. Some propositions to clear the unchangeableness of God from anything that seems contrary to it. V. The use.

I. In what respects God is unchangeable.

1. God is unchangeable in his essence. He is unalterably fixed in his being, so that not a particle of it can be lost from it, not a mite added to it. If a man continue in being as long as Methuselah, nine hundred and sixty-nine years; yet there is not a day, nay, an hour, wherein there is not some alteration in his substance. Though no substantial part is wanting, yet there is an addition to him by his food, a diminution of something by his labor; he is always making some acquisition, or suffering some loss: but in God there can be no alteration, by the accession of anything to make his substance greater or better, or by diminution to make it less or worse. He who hath not being from another, cannot but be always what he is: God is the first Being, an independent Being; he was not produced of himself, or of any other, but by nature always hath been, and, therefore, cannot by himself, or by any other, be changed from what he is in his own nature. That which is not may as well assume to itself a being, as he who hath and is all being, have the least change from what he is. Again, because he is a Spirit, he is not subject to those mutations which are found in corporeal and bodily natures; because he is an

[n] Archbold, Serm.

absolutely simple Spirit, not having the least particle of composition; he is not capable of those changes which may be in created spirits.

(1.) If his essence were mutable, God would not truly be; it could not be truly said by himself, "I Am that I Am" (Exod. iii. 14), if he were such a thing or Being at this time, and a different Being at another time. Whatsoever is changed properly is not, because it doth not remain to be what it was; that which is changed was something, is something, and will be something. A being remains to that thing which is changed; yet though it may be said such a thing is, yet it may be also said such a thing is not, because it is not what it was in its first being; it is not now what it was, it is now what it was not; it is another thing than it was, it was another thing than it is; it will be another thing than what it is or was. It is, indeed, a being, but a different being from what it was before. But if God were changed, it could not be said of him that he is, but it might also be said of him that he is not; or if he were changeable, or could be changed, it might be said of him he is, but he will not be what he is; or he may not be what he is, but there will be or may be some difference in his being, and so God would not be "I Am that I Am;" for though he would not cease utterly to be, yet he would cease to be what he was before.

(2.) Again: if his essence were mutable, he could not be perfectly blessed, and fully rejoice in himself. If he changed for the better, he could not have an infinite pleasure in what he was before the change, because he was not infinitely blessed; and the pleasure of that state could not be of a higher kind than the state itself, or, at least, the apprehension of a happiness in it. If he changed for the worse, he could not have a pleasure in it after the change; for according to the diminution of his state would be the decrease of his pleasure. His pleasure could not be infinite before the change, if he changed for the better; it could not be infinite after the change, if he changed for the worse. If he changed for the better, he would not have had an infinite goodness of being before; and not having an infinite goodness of being, he would have a finite goodness of being; for there is no medium between finite and infinite. Then, though the change were for the better, yet, being finite before, something would be still wanting to make him infinitely blessed; because being finite, he could not change to that which is infinite; for finite and infinite are extremes so distant, that they can never pass into one another; that is, that that which is finite should become infinite, or that which is infinite should become finite; so that supposing him mutable, his essence in no state of change could furnish him with an infinite peace and blessedness.

(3.) Again: if God's essence be changed, he either increaseth or diminisheth.[o] Whatsoever is changed, doth either gain by receiving something larger and greater than it had in itself before, or gains nothing by being changed. If the former, then it receives more than itself, more than it had in itself before. The Divine nature cannot be increased; for whatsoever receives anything than what it had in itself before, must necessarily receive it from another, because

                    o Hugo Victorin. in Petavio.

nothing can give to itself that which it hath not. But God cannot receive from another what he hath not already, because whatsoever other things possess is derived from him, and, therefore, contained in him, as the fountain contains the virtue in itself which it conveys to the streams; so that God cannot gain anything. If a thing that is changed gain nothing by that change, it loseth something of what it had before in itself; and this loss must be by itself or some other. God cannot receive any loss from anything in himself; he cannot will his own diminution, that is repugnant to every nature. He may as well will his own destruction as his own decrease: every decrease is a partial destruction. But it is impossible for God to die any kind of death, to have any resemblance of death, for he is immortal, and "only hath immortality" (1 Tim. vi. 16), therefore impossible to be diminished in any particle of his essence; nor can he be diminished by anything in his own nature, because his infinite simplicity admits of nothing distinct from himself, or contrary to himself. All decreases come from something contrary to the nature of that thing which doth decrease. Whatsoever is made less than itself, was not truly *unum*, one and simple, because that which divides itself in separation was not the same in conjunction. Nor can he be diminished by any other without himself; because nothing is superior to God, nothing stronger than God which can oppress him. But whatsoever is changed is weaker than that which changeth it, and sinks under a power it cannot successfully resist; weakness belongs not to the Deity.[P] Nor, lastly, can God change from a state wherein he is, to another state equal to the former, as men in some cases may do; for in passing from one state to another equal to it, something must be parted with which he had before, that some other thing may accrue to him as a recompense for that loss, to make him equal to what he was. This recompense then he had not before, though he had something equal to it. And in this case it could not be said by God "I Am that I Am," but I am equal to what I was; for in this case there would be a diminution and increase which, as was showed, cannot be in God.

(4.) Again: God is of himself, from no other.[q] Natures, which are made by God, may increase, because they began to be; they may decrease, because they were made of nothing, and so tend to nothing; the condition of their original leads them to defect, and the power of their Creator brings them to increase. But God hath no original, he hath no defect, because he was not made of nothing: he hath no increase, because he had no beginning. He was before all things, and, therefore, depends upon no other thing which, by its own change, can bring any change upon him. That which is from itself cannot be changed, because it hath nothing before it, nothing more excellent than itself; but that which is from another as its first cause and chief good, may be changed by that which was its efficient cause and last end.[r]

2. God is immutable in regard of knowledge. God hath known from all eternity all that which he can know, so that nothing is hid from him. He knows not at present any more than he hath known

p *Ibid.*   q Austin. Fulgen in Petavio.   r Petav. Tom. I. p. 173.

from eternity : and that which he knows now he always knows : " All things are open and naked before him" (Heb. iv. 13). A man is said to be changed in regard of knowledge, when he knows that now which he did not know before, or knows that to be false now which he thought true before, or has something for the object of his understanding now, which he had not before. But,

(1.) This would be repugnant to the wisdom and omniscience which belongs to the notions of a Deity. That cannot be God that is not infinitely wise ; that cannot be infinitely wise that is either ignorant of, or mistaken in, his apprehension of any one thing. If God be changed in knowledge, it must be for want of wisdom ; all change of this nature in creatures implies this defect preceding or accompanying it. Such a thought of God would have been unworthy of him that is " only wise," that hath no mate for wisdom (1 Tim. i. 17); none wise beside himself. If he knew that thing this day which he knew not before, he would not be an "only wise" Being ; for a being that did know everything at once might be conceived, and so a wiser being be apprehended by the mind of man. If God understood a thing at one time which he did not at another, he would be changed from ignorance to knowledge ; as if he could not do that this day which he could do to-morrow, he would be changed from impotence to power. He could not be always omniscient, because there might be yet something still to come which he yet knows not, though he may know all things that are past. What way soever you suppose a change, you must suppose a present or a past ignorance ; if he be changed in his knowledge for the perfection of his understanding, he was ignorant before ; if his understanding be impaired by the change, he is ignorant after it.

(2.) If God were changeable in his knowledge, it would make him unfit to be an object of trust to any rational creature. His revelations would want the due ground for entertainment, if his understanding were changeable ; for that might be revealed as truth now which might prove false hereafter, and that as false now which hereafter might prove true ; and so God would be an unfit object of obedience in regard of his precepts, and an unfit object of confidence in regard of his promises. For if he be changeable in knowledge he is defective in knowledge, and might promise that now which he would know afterwards was unfit to be promised, and, therefore, unfit to be performed. It would make him an incompetent object of dread, in regard of his threatenings ; for he might threaten that now which he might know hereafter were not fit or just to be inflicted. A changeable mind and understanding cannot make a due and right judgment of things to be done, and things to be avoided ; no wise man would judge it reasonable to trust a weak and flitting person. God must needs be unchangeable in his knowledge ; but, as the schoolmen say, that, as the sun always shines, so God always knows ; as the sun never ceaseth to shine, so God never ceaseth to know. Nothing can be hid from the vast compass of his understanding, no more than anything can shelter itself without the verge of his power. This farther appears in that,

1st. God knows by his own essence. He doth not know, as we

do, by habits, qualities, species, whereby we may be mistaken at one time and rectified at another. He hath not an understanding distinct from his essence as we have, but being the most simple Being, his understanding is his essence; and as from the infiniteness of his essence we conclude the infiniteness of his understanding, so from the unchangeableness of his essence, we may justly conclude the unchangeableness of his knowledge. Since, therefore, God is without all composition, and his understanding is not distinct from his essence, what he knows, he knows by his essence, and there can then be no more mutability in his knowledge than there can be in his essence; and if there were any in that, he could not be God, because he would have the property of a creature. If his understanding then be his essence, his knowledge is as necessary, as unchangeable as his essence. As his essence eminently contains all perfections in itself, so his understanding comprehends all things past, present, and future, in itself. If his understanding and his essence were not one and the same, he were not simple, but compounded: if compounded, he would consist of parts; if he consisted of parts, he would not be an independent Being, and so would not be God.

2d. God knows all things by one intuitive act. As there is no succession in his being, so that he is one thing now and another thing hereafter; so there is no succession in his knowledge. He knows things that are successive, before their existence and succession, by one single act of intuition; by one cast of his eye all things future are present to him in regard of his eternity and omnipresence; so that though there is a change and variation in the things known, yet his knowledge of them and their several changes in nature is invariable and unalterable. As imagine a creature that could see with his eye at one glance the whole compass of the heavens, by sending out beams from his eye without receiving any species from them, he would see the whole heavens uniformly, this part now in the east, then in the west, without any change in his eye, for he sees every part and every motion together; and though that great body varies and whirls about, and is in continual agitation, his eye remains steadfast, suffers no change, beholds all their motions at once and by one glance. God knows all things from eternity, and, therefore, perpetually knows them;[s] the reason is because the Divine knowledge is infinite,[t] and therefore, comprehends all knowable truths at once. An eternal knowledge comprehends in itself all time, and beholds past and present in the same manner, and, therefore, his knowledge is immutable: by one simple knowledge he considers the infinite spaces of past and future.

3d. God's knowledge and will is the cause of all things and their successions.[u] There can be no pretence of any changeableness of knowledge in God; but in this case, before things come to pass, he knows that they will come to pass; after they are come to pass, he knows that they are past, and slide away. This would be something if the succession of things were the cause of the Divine knowledge, as it is of our knowledge; but on the contrary, the

[s] Suarez. Vol. I. p. 137.   [t] Psalm cxlv. 5. "His understanding is infinite."
[u] Austin. Bradwardine.

Divine knowledge and will is the cause of the succession of them:
God doth not know creatures because they are; but they are because
he knows them: "All his works were known to him from the beginning of the world" (Acts xv. 18). All his works were not known
to him, if the events of all those works were not also known to
him; if they were not known to him, how should he make them? he
could not do anything ignorantly. He made them then after he
knew them, and did not know them after he made them. His knowledge of them made a change in them; their existence made no change
in his knowledge. He knew them when they were to be created, in
the same manner that he knew them after they were created; before
they were brought into act, as well as after they were brought into
act; before they were made, they were, and were not; they were in
the knowledge of God, when they were not in their own nature;
God did not receive his knowledge from their existence, but his
knowledge and will acted upon them to bring them into being.

4th. Therefore the distinction of past and future makes no change
in the knowledge of God. When a thing is past, God hath no
more distinct knowledge of it after it is past, than he had when it
was to come; all things were all in their circumstances of past, present, and to come ; seen by his understanding, as they were determined by his will.[x] Besides, to know a day to be past or future,
is only to know the state of that day in itself, and to know its relation to that which follows, and that which went before. This day
wherein we are, if we consider it in the state wherein it was yesterday, it was to come, it was future; but if we consider it in that
state wherein it will be to-morrow, we understand it as past. This
in man cannot be said to be a different knowledge of the thing
itself, but only of the circumstance attending a thing, and the different relation of it. As I see the sun this day, I know it was up
yesterday, I know it will be up to-morrow ; my knowledge of the sun
is the same; if there be any change, it is in the sun, not in my
knowledge; only I apply my knowledge to such particular circumstances. How much more must the knowledge of those things in
God be unchangeable, who knows all those states, conditions, and
circumstances, most perfectly from eternity ; wherein there is no
succession, no past or future, and therefore will know them forever! He always beholds the same thing; he sees, indeed, succession in things, and he sees a thing to be past which before was future.
As from eternity he saw Adam as existing in such a time; in the
first time he saw that he would be, in the following time he saw
that he had been; but this he knew from eternity; this he knew in
the same manner; though there was a variation in Adam, yet there
was no variation in God's knowledge of him, in all his states; though
Adam was not present to himself, yet in all his states he was present to God's eternity.

5th. Consider, that the knowledge of God, in regard of the manner of it, as well as the objects, is incomprehensible to a finite creature. So that though we cannot arrive to a full understanding of
the manner of God's knowledge, yet we must conceive so of it, as to

[x] Gamch. p. 1. Acquin. Qu. 9. c. i. p. 73.

remove all imperfection from him in it. And since it is an imperfection to be changeable, we must remove that from God; the knowledge of God about things past, present and future, must be inconceivably above ours: "His understanding is infinite" (Ps. cxlvii. 5). There is no number of it; it can no more be calculated or drawn into an account by us, than infinite spaces, which have no bounds and limits, can be measured by us. We can no more arrive, even in heaven, to a comprehensive understanding of the manner of his knowledge, than of the infinite glory of his essence; we may as well comprehend one as the other. This we must conclude, that God being not a body, doth not see one thing with eyes, and another thing with mind, as we do; but being a spirit, he sees and knows only with mind, and his mind is himself, and is as unchangeable as himself; and therefore as he is not now another thing than what he was, so he knows not anything now in another manner than as he knew it from eternity; he sees all things in the glass of his own essence; as, therefore, the glass doth not vary, so neither doth his vision.

3. God is unchangeable in regard of his will and purpose. A change in his purpose is, when a man determines to do that now which before he determined not to do, or to do the contrary; when a man hates that thing which he loved, or begins to love that which he before hated; when the will is changed, a man begins to will that which he willed not before, and ceaseth to will that which he willed before. But whatsoever God hath decreed, is immutable; whatsoever God hath promised, shall be accomplished: "The word that goes forth of his mouth shall not return to him void, but it shall accomplish that which he pleaseth" (Isa. lv. 11); whatsoever "he purposeth, he will do" (Isa. xlvi. 11; Numb. xxiii. 19); his decrees are therefore called "mountains of brass" (Zech. vi. 1): brass, as having substance and solidity; mountains, as being immovable, not only by any creature, but by himself; because they stand upon the basis of infallible wisdom, and are supported by uncontrollable power. From this immutability of his will, published to man, there could be no release from the severity of the law, without satisfaction made by the death of a Mediator, since it was the unalterable will of God, that death should be the wages of sin; and from this immutable will it was, that the length of time, from the first promise of the Redeemer to his mission, and the daily provocations of men, altered not his purpose for the accomplishment of it in the fulness of that time he had resolved upon; nor did the wickedness of former ages hinder the addition of several promises as buttresses to the first. To make this out, consider,

(1.) The will of God is the same with his essence. If God had a will distinct from his essence, he would not be the most simple Being. God hath not a faculty of will distinct from himself; as his understanding is nothing else but *Deus intelligens*, God understanding; so his will is nothing else but *Deus volens*, God willing; being, therefore, the essence of God; though it is considered, according to our weakness, as a faculty, it is as his understanding and wisdom, eternal and immutable; and can no more be changed than his essence. The immutability of the Divine counsel depends upon that of his essence; he is the Lord Jehovah, therefore he is true to his word (Mal. iii. 6; Isa. xliii. 13): "Yea, before the day I am he, and there is none that can deliver out of my hand." He is the same, immutable in his essence, therefore irresistible in his power.

(2.) There is a concurrence of God's will and understanding in everything. As his knowledge is eternal, so is his purpose. Things created had not been known to be, had not God resolved them to be the act of his will; the existence of anything supposeth an act of his will. Again, as God knows all things by one simple vision of his understanding, so he wills all things by one act of volition; therefore the purpose of God in the Scripture is not expressed by counsels in the plural number, but counsel; showing that all the purposes of God are not various, but as one will, branching itself out into many acts towards the creature; but all knit in one root, all links of one chain. Whatsoever is eternal is immutable; as his knowledge is eternal, and therefore immutable, so is his will; he wills or nills nothing to be in time, but what he willed and nilled from eternity; if he willed in time that to be that he willed not from eternity, then he would know that in time which he knew not from eternity; for God knows nothing future, but as his will orders it to be future, and in time to be brought into being.

(3.) There can be no reason for any change in the will of God. When men change in their minds, it must be for want of foresight; because they could not foresee all the rubs and bars which might suddenly offer themselves; which if they had foreseen, they would not have taken such measures: hence men often will that which they afterwards wish they had not willed when they come to understand it clearer, and see that to be injurious to them which they thought to be good for them; or else the change proceeds from a natural instability without any just cause, and an easiness to be drawn into that which is unrighteous; or else it proceeds from a want of power, when men take new counsels, because they are invincibly hindered from executing the old. But none of those can be in God.

1st. It cannot be for want of foresight. What can be wanting to an infinite understanding? How can any unknown event defeat his purpose, since nothing happens in the world but what he wills to effect, or wills to permit; and therefore all future events are present with him? Besides, it doth not consist with God's wisdom to resolve anything, but upon the highest reason; and what is the highest and infinite reason, cannot but be unalterable in itself; for there can be no reason and wisdom higher than the highest. All God's purposes are not bare acts of will, but acts of counsel. "He works all things according to the counsel of his own will" (Eph. i. 11): and he doth not say so much that his will, as that "his counsel shall stand" (Isa. xlvi. 10). It stands, because it is counsel; and the immutability of a promise is called the "immutability of his counsel" (Heb. vi. 17), as being introduced and settled by the most perfect wisdom, and therefore to be carried on to a full and complete execution; his purpose, then, cannot be changed for want of foresight; for this would be a charge of weakness.

2d. Nor can it proceed from a natural instability of his will, or an easiness to be drawn to that which is unrighteous. If his will should not adhere to his counsel, it is because it is not fit to be followed, or because it will not follow it; if not fit to be followed, it is a reflection upon his wisdom; if it be established, and he will not follow it, there is a contrariety in God, as there is in a fallen creature, will against wisdom. That cannot be in God which he hates in a creature, viz. the disorder of faculties, and being out of their due place. The righteousness of God is like a " great mountain" (Ps. xxxvi. 6). The rectitude of his nature is as immovable in itself, as all the mountains in the world are by the strength of man. " He is not as a man, that he should repent or lie" (Numb. xxiii. 19); who often changes, out of a perversity of will, as well as want of wisdom to foresee, or want of ability to perform. His eternal purpose must either be righteous or unrighteous; if righteous and holy, he would become unholy by the change; if not righteous nor holy, then he was unrighteous before the change; which way soever it falls, it would reflect upon the righteousness of God, which is a blasphemous imagination.y If God did change his purpose, it must be either for the better,—then the counsel of God was bad before; or for the worse,—then he was not wise and good before.

3d. Nor can it be for want of strength. Who hath power to control him? Not all the combined devices and endeavors of men can make the counsel of God to totter (Prov. xix. 21): " There are many devices in a man's heart; nevertheless the counsel of the Lord, that shall stand ;" that, and that only shall stand. Man hath a power to devise and imagine, but no power to effect and execute of himself. God wants no more power to effect what he will, than he wants understanding to know what is fit. Well, then, since God wanted not wisdom to frame his decrees, nor holiness to regulate them, nor power to effect them, what should make him change them? since there can be no reason superior to his, no event unforeseen by him, no holiness comparable to his, no unrighteousness found in him, no power equal to his, to put a rub in his way.

4th. Though the will of God be immutable, yet it is not to be understood so, as that the things themselves so willed are immutable. Nor will the immutability of the things willed by him, follow upon the unchangeableness of his will in willing them; though God be firm in willing them, yet he doth not will that they should alway be. God did not perpetually will the doing those things which he once decreed to be done; he decreed that Christ should suffer, but he did not decree that Christ should alway suffer; so he willed the Mosaical rites for a time, but he did not will that they should alway continue; he willed that they should endure only for a time; and when the time came for their ceasing, God had been mutable if he had not put an end to them, because his will had fixed such a period. So that the changing of those things which he had once appointed to be practised, is so far from charging God with changeableness, that God would be mutable if he did not take them away; since he decreed as well their abolition at such a time, as their continuance till such a

y Maxim. Pyrius dissert. 3, 30.

time; so that the removal of them was pursuant to his unchangeable will and decree. If God had decreed that such laws should alway continue, and afterwards changed that decree, and resolved the abrogation of them, then indeed God had been mutable; he had rescinded one decree by another; he had then seen an error in his first resolve, and there must be some weakness in the reason and wisdom whereon it was grounded.[z] But it was not so here; for the change of those laws is so far from slurring God with any mutability, that the very change of them is no other than the issue of his eternal decree; for from eternity he purposed in himself to change this or that dispensation, though he did decree to bring such a dispensation into the world. The decree itself was eternal and immutable, but the thing decreed was temporary and mutable. As a decree from eternity doth not make the thing decreed to be eternal, so neither doth the immutability of the decree render the thing so decreed to be immutable: as for example, God decreed from all eternity to create the world; the eternity of this decree did not make the world to be in being and actually created from eternity; so God decreed immutably that the world so created should continue for such a time; the decree is immutable if the world perish at that time, and would not be immutable if the world did endure beyond that time that God hath fixed for the duration of it: as when a prince orders a man's remaining in prison for so many days; if he be prevailed with to give him a delivery before those days, or to continue him in custody for the same crime after those days, his order is changed; but if he orders the delivery of him just at that time, till which he had before decreed that he should continue in prison, the purpose and order of the prince remains firm, and the change in the state of the prisoner is the fruit of that firm and fixed resolution: so that we must distinguish between the person decreeing, the decree itself, and the thing decreed. The person decreeing, viz., God, is in himself immutable, and the decree is immutable; but the thing decreed may be mutable; and if it were not changed according to the first purpose, it would argue the decree itself to be changed; for while a man wills that this may be done now, and another thing done afterwards, the same will remains; and though there be a change in the effects, there is no change in the will.

5th. The immutability of God's will doth not infringe the liberty of it. The liberty of God's will consists with the necessity of continuing his purpose. God is necessarily good, immutably good; yet he is freely so, and would not be otherwise than what he is. God was free in his first purpose; and purposing this or that by an infallible and unerring wisdom, it would be a weakness to change the purpose. But, indeed, the liberty of God's will doth not seem so much to consist in an indifferency to this or that, as in an independency on anything without himself: his will was free, because it did not depend upon the objects about which his will was conversant. To be immutably good is no point of imperfection, but the height of perfection.

4. As God is unchangeable in regard of essence, knowledge, pur-

* Turrentin de Satisfac. p. 266.

pose, so he is unchangeable in regard of place. He cannot be changed in time, because he is eternity; so he cannot be changed in place, because he hath ubiquity: he is eternal, therefore cannot be changed in time; he is omnipresent, therefore cannot be changed in place: he doth not begin to be in one place wherein he was not before, or cease to be in a place wherein he was before. He that fills every place in heaven and earth, cannot change place; he cannot leave one to possess another, that is equally, in regard of his essence, in all: "He fills heaven and earth" (Jer. xxiii. 24). The heavens that are not subject to those changes to which sublunary bodies are subject, that are not diminished in quantity or quality; yet they are alway changing place in regard of their motion; no part of them doth alway continue in the same point: but God hath no change of his nature, because he is most inward in everything; he is substantially in all spaces, real and imaginary; there is no part of the world which he doth not fill; no place can be imagined wherein he doth not exist. Suppose a million of worlds above and about this, encircling one another; his essence would be in every part and point of those worlds; because it is indivisible, it cannot be divided; nor can it be contained within those created limits of millions of worlds, when the most soaring and best coining fancy hath run through all creatures to the highest sphere of the heavens, and imagined one world after another, till it can fancy no more: none of these, nor all of these, can contain God; for the "heaven of heavens cannot contain him" (1 Kings viii. 27); "He is higher than heaven, deeper than hell" (Job xi. 8), and possesses infinite imaginary spaces beyond created limits. He who hath no cause of being, can have no limits of being;[a] and though by creation he began to be in the world, yet he did not begin to be where the world is, but was in the same imaginary space from all eternity; for he was alway in himself by his own eternal *ubi*. Therefore observe, that when God is said to draw near to us when we draw near to him (James iv. 8), it is not by local motion or change of place, but by special and spiritual influences, by exciting and supporting grace. As we ordinarily say, the sun is come into the house when yet it remains in its place and order in the heavens, because the beams pierce through the windows and enlighten the room, so when God is said to come down or descend (Gen. xi. 5; Exod. xxxiv. 5), it is not by a change of place, but a change of outward acts, when he puts forth himself in ways of fresh mercy or new judgments, in the effluxes of his love or the flames of his wrath. When good men feel the warm beams of his grace refreshing them, or wicked men feel the hot coals of his anger scorching them. God's drawing near to us is not so much his coming to us, but his drawing us to him;[b] as when watermen pull a rope that is in one end fastened to the shore, and the other end to the vessel; the shore is immovable, yet it seems to the eye to come to them, but they really move to the shore. God is an immovable rock; we are floating and uncertain creatures; while he seems to approach to us, he doth really make us to approach to him; he comes not to us by

[a] Gamacheus ut supra.

[b] The ancients, as Dionysius, expressed it by this similitude.

any change of place himself, but draws us to him by a change of
mind, will, and affections in us.

II. The second thing propounded, is the reasons to prove God
immutable. The heathens acknowledged God to be so: Plato[c] and
the Pythagoreans called God, or the stable good principle, αὐτὸν,
idem: the evil principle, ἕτερον, another thing, changeable; one thing
one time, and another thing another time[d] (Dan. vi. 26): "He is the
living God, and steadfast forever."

1. The name Jehovah signifies this attribute (Exod. iii. 14): "I
am that I am; I am hath sent me to you." It signifies his immutability as well as eternity. I am, signifies his eternity; that, or the
same that I am, his immutability:[e] as it respects the essence of God,
it signifies his unchangeable being from eternity to eternity; as it
respects the creature, it signifies his constancy in his counsels and
promises, which spring from no other cause but the unchangeableness of his nature.[f] The reason why men stand not to their covenant, is because they are not always the same; I am, that is, I am
the same, before the creation of the world, and since the creation of
the world; before the entrance of sin, and since the entrance of sin;
before their going into Egypt, and while they remain in Egypt.
The very name Jehovah[g] bears, according to the grammatical order,
a mark of God's unchangeableness; it never hath anything added to
it, nor anything taken from it; it hath no plural number, no affixes
—a custom peculiar to the eastern languages; it never changes its
letters as other words do. That only is a true being which hath not
only an eternal existence, but stability in it: that is not truly a
being, that never remains in the same state.[h] All things that are
changed cease to be what they were, and begin to be what they were
not, and therefore cannot have the title truly applied to them, they
are; they are, indeed, but like a river in a continual flux, that no
man ever sees the same; let his eye be fixed upon one place of it,
the water he sees, slides away, and that which he saw not succeeds
in its place; let him take his eye off but for the least moment, and
fix it there again, and he sees not the same that he saw before. All
sensible things are in a perpetual stream; that which is sometimes
this and sometimes that, is not, because it is not always the same;
whatsoever is changed, is something now which it was not alway;
but of God it is said, I am, which could not be if he were changeable; for it may be said of him, he is not, as well as he is, because
he is not what he was; if we say not of him, he was, nor he will be,
but only he is, whence should any change arrive? He must invincibly remain the same, of whose nature, perfections, knowledge and
will, it cannot be said it was, as if it were not now in him; or it shall
be, as if it were not yet in him; but he is, because he doth not only
exist, but doth alway exist the same. I am, that is, I receive from
no other what I am in myself; he depends upon no other in his

c Plato calls God οὐσίαν ἀεὶ ἐχομένον, lib. i. de Be.
d Stabilisque manens dat cuncta moveri. Boet. Consolat. lib. iii.   e Trap. on Exod.
f Amyrald, de Trinitat. p. 433.   g Spanhe. Synta. Part. I. p. 39.
h Petav. Theol. Dogmat. Tom. I. c. 6. § 6–8.

essence, knowledge, purposes, and therefore hath no changing power over him.

2. If God were changeable, he could not be the most perfect Being. God is the most perfect Being, and possesses in himself infinite and essential goodness (Matt. v. 48): "Your heavenly Father is perfect." If he could change from that perfection, he were not the highest exemplar and copy for us to write after. If God doth change, it must be either to a greater perfection than he had before, or to a less, *mutatio perfectiva vel amissiva;* if he changes to acquire a perfection he had not, then he was not before the most excellent Being; necessarily, he was not what he might be; there was a defect in him, and a privation of that which is better than what he had and was; and then he was not alway the best, and so was not alway God; and being not alway God, could never be God; for to begin to be God is against the notion of God; not to a less perfection than he had; that were to change to imperfection, and to lose a perfection which he possessed before, and cease to be the best Being; for he would lose some good which he had, and acquire some evil which he was free from before. So that the sovereign perfection of God is an invincible bar to any change in him; for which way soever you cast it for a change, his supreme excellency is impaired and nulled by it: for in all change there is something from which a thing is changed, and something to which it is changed; so that on the one part there is a loss of what it had, and on the other part there is an acquisition of what it had not. If to the better, he was not perfect, and so was not God; if to the worse, he will not be perfect, and so be no longer God after that change. If God be changed, his change must be voluntary or necessary; if voluntary, he then intends the change for the better, and chose it to acquire a perfection by it; the will must be carried out to anything under the notion of some goodness in that which it desires. Since good is the object of the desire and will of the creature, evil cannot be the object of the desire and will of the Creator. And if he should be changed for the worse, when he did really intend the better, it would speak a defect of wisdom, and a mistake of that for good which was evil and imperfect in itself; and if it be for the better, it must be a motion or change for something without himself; that which he desireth is not possessed by himself, but by some other. There is, then, some good without him and above him, which is the end in this change; for nothing acts but for some end, and that end is within itself or without itself; if the end for which God changes be without himself, then there is something better than himself: besides, if he were voluntarily changed for the better, why did he not change before? If it were for want of power, he had the imperfection of weakness; if for want of knowledge of what was the best good, he had the imperfection of wisdom, he was ignorant of his own happiness; if he had both wisdom to know it, and power to effect it, it must be for want of will; he then wanted that love to himself and his own glory, which is necessary in the Supreme Being. Voluntarily he could not be changed for the worse, he could not be such an enemy

to his own glory; there is nothing but would hinder its own imperfection and becoming worse. Necessarily he could not be changed,
for that necessity must arise from himself, and then the difficulties
spoken of before will recur, or it must arise from another; he cannot be bettered by another, because nothing hath any good but
what it hath received from the hands of his bounty, and that
without loss to himself, nor made worse; if anything made him
worse, it would be sin, but that cannot touch his essence or obscure
his glory, but in the design and nature of the sin itself (Job xxxv.
6, 7): "If thou sinnest, what dost thou against him? or if thy
transgressions be multiplied, what dost thou unto him? if thou be
righteous, what givest thou him; or what receives he at thy hand?"
He hath no addition by the service of man, no more than the sun
hath of light by a multitude of torches kindled on the earth; nor
any more impair by the sins of men, than the light of the sun
hath by men's shooting arrows against it.

3. God were not the most simple being if he were not immutable.[i]
There is in everything that is mutable a composition either essential or accidental; and in all changes, something of the thing
changed remains, and something of it ceaseth and is done away;
as for example, in an accidental change, if a white wall be made
black, it loses its white color; but the wall itself, which was the
subject of that color, remains and loses nothing of its substance:
likewise in a substantial change, as when wood is burnt, the substantial part of wood is lost, the earthly part is changed into ashes,
the airy part ascends in smoke, the watery part is changed into
air by the fire: there is not an annihilation of it, but a resolution
of it into those parts whereof it was compounded; and this change
doth evidence that it was compounded of several parts distinct
from one another. If there were any change in God, it is by separating something from him, or adding something to him; if by
separating something from him, then he was compounded of something distinct from himself; for if it were not distinct from himself
it could not be separated from him without loss of his being; if by
adding anything to him, then it is a compounding of him, either
substantially or accidentally. Mutability is absolutely inconsistent
with simplicity, whether the change come from an internal or external principle. If a change be wrought by something without, it
supposeth either contrary or various parts in the thing so changed,
whereof it doth consist; if it be wrought by anything within, it supposeth that the thing so changed doth consist of one part that doth
change it, and another part that is changed, and so it would not be
a simple being. If God could be changed by anything within himself, all in God would not be God; his essence would depend upon
some parts, whereof some would be superior to others; if one part
were able to change or destroy another, that which doth change
would be God, that which is changed would not be God; so God
would be made up of a Deity and a non-Deity, and part of God
would depend upon God; part would be dependent, and part would
be independent; part would be mutable, part immutable: so that

[i] Gamach. in prim. part. Aquin. qu. 9. c. 1. part. 72.

mutability is against the notion of God's independency as well as his simplicity. God is the most simple being; for that which is first in nature, having nothing beyond it, cannot by any means be thought to be compounded; for whatsoever is so, depends upon the parts whereof it is compounded, and so is not the first being: now God being infinitely simple, hath nothing in himself which is not himself, and therefore cannot will any change in himself, he being his own essence and existence.[k]

4. God were not eternal if he were mutable. In all change there is something that perishes, either substantially or accidentally. All change is a kind of death, or imitation of death; that which was dies, and begins to be what it was not. The soul of man, though it ceaseth not to be and exist, yet when it ceaseth to be in quality what it was, is said to die. Adam died when he changed from integrity to corruption, though both his soul and body were in being (Gen. ii. 17); and the soul of a regenerate man is said to "die to sin," when it is changed from sin to grace (Rom. vi. 11). In all change there is a resemblance of death; so the notion of mutability is against the eternity of God. If anything be acquired by a change, then that which is acquired was not from eternity, and so he was not wholly eternal; if anything be lost which was from eternity, he is not wholly everlasting; if he did decrease by the change, something in him which had no beginning would have an end; if he did increase by that change, something in him would have a beginning that might have no end. What is changed doth not remain, and what doth not remain is not eternal.[l] Though God alway remains in regard of existence, he would be immortal, and live alway; yet if he should suffer any change, he could not properly be eternal, because he would not alway be the same, and would not in every part be eternal; for all change is finished in time, one moment preceding, another moment following; but that which is before time cannot be changed by time. God cannot be eternally what he was; that is, he cannot have a true eternity, if he had a new knowledge, a new purpose, a new essence; if he were sometimes this and sometimes that, sometimes know this and sometimes know that, sometimes purpose this and afterwards hath a new purpose; he would be partly temporary and partly eternal, not truly and universally eternal. He that hath anything of newness, hath not properly and truly an entire eternity. Again, by the same reason that God could in the least cease to be what he was, he might also cease wholly to be; and no reason can be rendered why God might not cease wholly to be, as well as cease to be entirely and uniformly what he was. All changeableness implies a corruptibility.

5. If God were changeable, he were not infinite and almighty. All change ends in addition or diminution; if anything be added, he was not infinite before, if anything be diminished, he is not infinite after. All change implies bounds and limits to that which is changed; but God is infinite; "His greatness is unsearchable:"[m] we can add number to number without any end, and can conceive

---

[k] Ficinus Zachar. mitylen in Peta. Tom. I. p. 169.
[l] Austin in Pet. Tom. I. p. 201.   [m] Ps. cxlv. 3, אֵין חֵקֶר no end, no term.

an infinite number; yet the greatness of God is beyond all our conceptions. But if there could be any change in his greatness for the better, it would not be unsearchable before that change; if for the worse, it would not be unsearchable after that change. Whatsoever hath limits and is changeable, is conceivable and searchable; but God is not only not known, but impossible in his own nature to be known and searched out, and, therefore, impossible to have any diminution in his nature. All that which is changed arrives to something which it was not before, or ceaseth in part to be what it was before. He would not also be almighty. What is omnipotent cannot be made worse; for to be made worse, is in part to be corrupted. If he be made better, he was not almighty before; something of power was wanting to him. If there should be any change, it must proceed from himself or from another; if from himself, it would be an inability to preserve himself in the perfection of his nature; if from another, he would be inferior in strength, knowledge, and power, to that which changes him, either in his nature, knowledge, or will; in both an inability; an inability in him to continue the same, or an inability in him to resist the power of another.

6. The world could not be ordered and governed but by some Principle or Being which were immutable. Principles are alway more fixed and stable than things which proceed from those principles; and this is true both in morals and naturals. Principles in conscience, whereby men are governed, remain firmly engraven in their minds. The root lies firmly in the earth, while branches are shaken with the wind. The heavens, the cause of generation, are more firm and stable than those things which are wrought by their influence. All things in the world are moved by some power and virtue which is stable; and unless it were so, no order would be observed in motion, no motion could be regularly continued. He could not be a full satisfaction to the infinite desire of the souls of his people. Nothing can truly satisfy the soul of man but rest; and nothing can give it rest but that which is perfect and immutably perfect; for else it would be subject to those agitations and variations which the being it depends upon is subject to. The principle of all things must be immutable,[n] which is described by some by a unity, the principle of number, wherein there is a resemblance of God's unchangeableness. A unit is not variable; it continues in its own nature immutably a unit. It never varies from itself; it cannot be changed from itself; but is, as it were, so omnipotent towards others, that it changes all numbers. If you add any number, it is the beginning of that number, but the unit is not increased by it; a new number ariseth from that addition, but the unit still remains the same, and adds value to other figures, but receives none from them.

III. The third thing to speak to is, that immutability is proper to God, and incommunicable to any creature. Mutability is natural to every creature as a creature, and immutability is the sole perfection of God. He only is infinite wisdom, able to foreknow future events; he only is infinitely powerful, able to call forth all means to effect; so that wanting neither wisdom to contrive, nor strength to execute,

[n] Fotherby Atheomastix, p. 308. Gerhard loc. com.

he cannot alter his counsel.   None being above him, nothing in him contrary to him, and being defective in no blessedness and perfection, he cannot vary in his essence and nature.   Had not immutability as well as eternity been a property solely pertaining to the Divine nature, as well as creative power and eternal duration, the apostle's argument to prove Christ to be God from this perpetual sameness, had come short of any convincing strength.   These words of the text he applies to Christ (Heb. i. 10–12): "They shall be changed, but thou art the same."   There had been no strength in the reason, if immutability by nature did belong to any creature.

The changeableness of all creatures is evident:

1. Of corporeal creatures it is evident to sense.   All plants and animals, as they have their duration bounded in certain limits; so while they do exist, they proceed from their rise to their fall.   They pass through many sensible alterations, from one degree of growth to another, from buds to blossoms, from blossoms to flowers and fruits.   They come to their pitch that nature had set them, and return back to the state from whence they sprung; there is not a day but they make some acquisition, or suffer some loss.   They die and spring up every day; nothing in them more certain than their inconstancy: "The creature is subject to vanity" (Rom. viii. 20).   The heavenly bodies are changing their place; the sun every day is running his race, and stays not in the same point; and though they are not changed in their essence, yet they are in their place.   Some, indeed, say there is a continual generation of light in the sun, as there is a loss of light by the casting out its beams, as in a fountain there is a flowing out of the streams, and a continual generation of supply.   And though these heavenly bodies have kept their standing and motion from the time of their creation, yet both the sun's standing still in Joshua's time, and its going back in Hezekiah's time, show that they are changeable at the pleasure of God.   But in man the change is perpetually visible; every day there is a change from ignorance to knowledge, from one will to another, from passion to passion, sometimes sad and sometimes cheerful, sometimes craving this, and presently nauseating it; his body changes from health to sickness, or from weakness to strength; some alteration there is either in body or mind.   Man, who is the noblest creature, the subordinate end of the creation of other things, cannot assure himself of a consistency and fixedness in anything the short space of a day, no, not of a minute.   All his months are months of vanity (Job vii. 3); whence the Psalmist calls man at the "best estate altogether vanity," a mere heap of vanity (Ps. xxxv.)   As he contains in his nature the nature of all creatures, so he inherits in his nature the vanity of all creatures.   A little world, the centre of the world and of the vanity of the world; yea, "lighter than vanity" (Ps. lxii. 9), more movable than a feather; tossed between passion and passion, daily changing his end, and changing the means; an image of nothing.

2. Spiritual natures, as angels.   They change not in their being, but that is from the indulgence of God.   They change not in their goodness, but that is not from their nature, but divine grace in their

confirmation; but they change in their knowledge; they know more by Christ than they did by creation (1 Tim. iii. 16). They have an addition of knowledge every day, by the providential dispensations of God to his church (Eph. iii. 10); and the increase of their astonishment and love is according to the increase of their knowledge and insight. They cannot have a new discovery without new admirations of what is discovered to them : there is a change in their joy when there is a change in a sinner (Luke xv. 10). They were changed in their essence, when they were made such glorious spirits of nothing; some of them were changed in their will, when of holy they became impure. The good angels were changed in their understandings, when the glories of God in Christ were presented to their view ; and all can be changed in their essence again ; and as they were made of nothing, so by the power of God may be reduced to nothing again. So glorified souls shall have an unchanged operation about God, for they shall behold his face without any grief or fear of loss, without vagrant thoughts; but they can never be unchangeable in their nature, because they can never pass from finite to infinite.

No creature can be unchangeable in its nature:—1. Because every creature rose from nothing. As they rose from nothing, so they tend to nothing, unless they are preserved by God. The notion of a creature speaks changeableness; because to be a creature is to be made something of nothing, and, therefore, creation is a change of nothing into something. The being of a creature begins from change, and, therefore, the essence of a creature is subject to change. God only is uncreated, and, therefore, unchangeable. If he were made he could not be immutable ; for the very making is a change of not being into being. All creatures were made good, as they were the fruits of God's goodness and power ; but must needs be mutable, because they were the extracts of nothing. 2. Because every creature depends purely upon the will of God. They depend not upon themselves, but upon another for their being. As they received their being from the word of his mouth and the arm of his power, so by the same word they can be cancelled into nothing, and return into as little significancy as when they were nothing. He that created them by a word, can by a word destroy them: if God should "take away their breath, they die, and return into their dust" (Ps. civ. 29). As it was in the power of the Creator that things might be, before they actually were, so it is in the power of the Creator that things after they are may cease to be what they are ; and they are, in their own nature, as reducible to nothing as they were producible by the power of God from nothing; for there needs no more than an act of God's will to null them, as there needed only an act of God's will to make them. Creatures are all subject to a higher cause: they are all reputed as nothing. "He doth according to his will in the armies of heaven, and among the inhabitants of the earth, and none can stay his hand, or say unto him, What dost thou ?" (Dan. iv. 35.) But God is unchangeable, because he is the highest good ; none above him, all below him ; all dependent on him ; himself upon none. 3. No creature is absolutely perfect. No creature can be so perfect, or can ever be, but something by the infinite power of God may be added to it; for whatsoever is finite may receive greater additions, and, therefore, a change. No creature you can imagine, but in your thoughts you may fancy him capable of greater perfections than you know he hath, or than really he hath. The perfections of all creatures are searchable; the perfection of God is only unsearchable (Job xi. 6), and, therefore, he only immutable. God only is always the same. Time makes no addition to him, nor diminisheth anything of him. His nature and essence, his wisdom and will, have always been the same from eternity, and shall be the same to eternity, without any variation.

IV. The fourth thing propounded is, Some propositions to clear this unchangeableness of God from anything that seems contrary to it.

Prop. I. There was no change in God when he began to create the world in time. The creation was a real change, but the change was not subjectively in God, but in the creature; the creature began to be what it was not before. Creation is considered as active or passive.[o] Active creation is the will and power of God to create. This is from eternity, because God willed from eternity to create in time; this never had beginning, for God never began in time to understand anything, to will anything, or to be able to do anything; but he alway understood and alway willed those things which he determined from eternity to produce in time. The decree of God may be taken for the act decreeing, that is eternal and the same, or for the object decreed, that is in time; so that there may be a change in the object, but not in the will whereby the object doth exist.

1. There was no change in God by the act of creation, because there was no new will in him. There was no new act of his will which was not before. The creation began in time, but the will of creating was from eternity. The work was new, but the decree whence that new work sprung was as ancient as the Ancient of Days. When the time of creating came, God was not made *ex nolente volens*, as we are; for whatsoever God willed to be now done, he willed from eternity to be done; but he willed also that it should not be done till such an instant of time, and that it should not exist before such a time. If God had willed the creation of the world only at that time when the world was produced, and not before, then, indeed, God had been changeable. But though God spake that word which he had not spoke before, whereby the world was brought into act; yet he did not will that will he willed not before. God did not create by a new counsel or new will, but by that which was from eternity (Eph. i. 9). All things are wrought according to that "purpose in himself," and according to " the counsel of his will" (ver. 11); and as the holiness of the elect is the fruit of his eternal will " before the foundation of the world" (ver. 4), so, likewise, is the existence of things, and of those persons whom he did elect. As when an artificer frames a house or a temple according to that model he had in his mind some years before, there is no change

o Gamach. in Part I. Aquin. Q. 9. c. i. p. 72.

in the model in his mind; the artificer is the same, though the work is produced by him some time after he had framed that copy of it in his own mind, but there is a change of the thing produced by him according to that model. Or, when a rich man intends, four or five years hence, if he lives, to build a hospital, is there any change in will, when, after the expiration of that time, he builds and endows it? Though it be after his will, yet it is the fruit of his precedent will. So God, from all eternity, did will and command that the creatures should exist in such a part of time; and, by his eternal will, all things, whether past, present, or to come, did, do, and shall exist, at that point of time which that will did appoint for them: not, as though God had a new will when things stood up in being, but only that which was prepared in his immutable counsel and will from eternity, doth then appear. There can be no instant fixed from eternity, wherein it can be said, God did not will the creation of the world; for had the will of God for the shortest moment been undetermined to the creation of the world, and afterwards resolved upon it, there had been a moral change in God from not willing to willing; but this there was not, for God executes nothing in time which he had not ordained from eternity, and appointed all the means and circumstances whereby it should be brought about. As the determination of our Saviour to suffer was not a new will, but an eternal counsel, and wrought no change in God (Acts ii. 23).

2. There is no change in God by the act of creation, because there was no new power in God. Had God had a will at the time of creation which he had not before, there had been a moral change in him; so had there been in him a power only to create then and not before, there had been a physical change in him from weakness to ability. There can be no more new power in God, than there can be a new will in God; for his will is his power, and what he willeth to effect, that he doth effect: as he was unchangeably holy, so he was unchangeably almighty, "which was, and is, and is to come" (Rev. iv. 8); which was almighty, and is almighty, and ever will be almighty. The work therefore makes no change in God, but there is a change in the thing wrought by that power of God. Suppose you had a seal engraven upon some metal a hundred years old, or as old as the creation, and you should this day, so many ages after the engraving of it, make an impression of that seal upon wax; would you say the engravement upon the seal were changed, because it produced that stamp upon the wax now which it did not before? No, the change is purely in the wax, which receives a new figure or form by the impression; not in the seal, that was capable of imprinting the same long before. God was the same from eternity as he was when he made a signature of himself upon the creatures by creation, and is no more changed by stamping them into several forms, than the seal is changed by making impression upon the wax. As when a house is enlightened by the sun, or that which was cold is heated by it, there is a change in the house from darkness to light, from coldness to heat; but is there any change in the light and heat of the sun? There is a change in the thing enlightened or warmed by that light and heat which remains fixed and constant in the sun, which was as

capable in itself to produce the same effects before, as at that instant when it works them; so when God is the author of a new work, he is not changed, because he works it by an eternal will and an eternal power.

3. Nor is there any new relation acquired by God by the creation of the world. There was a new relation acquired by the creature, as, when a man sins, he hath another relation to God than he had before,—he hath relation to God, as a criminal to a Judge; but there is no change in God, but in the malefactor. The being of men makes no more change in God than the sins of men. As a tree is now on our right hand, and by our turning about it is on our left hand, sometimes before us, sometimes behind us, according to our motion near it or about it, and the turning of the body; there is no change in the tree, which remains firm and fixed in the earth, but the change is wholly in the posture of the body, whereby the tree may be said to be before us or behind us, or on the right hand or on the left hand.ᵖ God gained no new relation of Lord or Creator by the creation; for though he had created nothing to rule over, yet he had the power to create and rule, though he did not create and rule: as a man may be called a skilful writer, though he does not write, because he is able to do it when he pleases; or a man skilful in physic is called a physician, though he doth not practise that skill, or discover his art in the distribution of medicines, because he may do it when he pleases; it depends upon his own will to show his art when he has a mind to it. So the name Creator and Lord belongs to God from eternity, because he could create and rule, though he did not create and rule. But, howsoever, if there were any such change of relation, that God may be called Creator and Lord after the creation and not before, it is not a change in essence, nor in knowledge, nor in will; God gains no perfection nor diminution by it; his knowledge is not increased by it; he is no more by it than he was, and will be, if all those things ceased; and therefore Austin illustrates it by this similitude:—as a piece of money when it is given as the price of a thing, or deposited only as a pledge for the security of a thing borrowed; the coin is the same, and is not changed, though the relation it had as a pledge and as a price be different from one another: so that suppose any new relation be added, yet there is nothing happens to the nature of God which may infer any change.

Prop. II. There was no change in the Divine nature of the Son, when he assumed human nature. There was an union of the two natures, but no change of the Deity into the humanity, or of the humanity into the Deity: both preserved their peculiar properties. The humanity was changed by a communication of excellent gifts from the divine nature, not by being brought into an equality with it, for that was impossible that a creature should become equal to the Creator. He took the "form of a servant," but he lost not the form of God; he despoiled not himself of the perfections of the Deity. He was indeed emptied, "and became of no reputation" (Phil. ii. 7); but he did not cease to be God, though he was reputed to be only a man,

ᵖ Petav. Theol. Dogmat. Tom. I.

and a very mean one too. The glory of his divinity was not extinguished nor diminished, though it was obscured and darkened, under the veil of our infirmities; but there was no more change in the hiding of it, than there is in the body of the sun when it is shadowed by the interposition of a cloud. His blood while it was pouring out from his veins was the "blood of God" (Acts xx. 28); and, therefore, when he was bowing the head of his humanity upon the cross, he had the nature and perfections of God; for had he ceased to be God, he had been a mere creature, and his sufferings would have been of as little value and satisfaction as the sufferings of a creature. He could not have been a sufficient Mediator, had he ceased to be God: and he had ceased to be God, had he lost any one perfection proper to the divine nature; and losing none, he lost not this of unchangeableness, which is none of the meanest belonging to the Deity. Why by his union with the human nature should he lose this, any more than he lost his omniscience, which he discovered by his knowledge of the thoughts of men; or his mercy, which he manifested to the height in the time of his suffering? That is truly a change, when a thing ceaseth to be what it was before: this was not in Christ; he assumed our nature without laying aside his own. When the soul is united to the body, doth it lose any of those perfections that are proper to its nature? Is there any change either in the substance or qualities of it? No; but it makes a change in the body, and of a dull lump it makes it a living mass, conveys vigor and strength to it, and, by its power, quickens it to sense and motion.[q] So did the divine nature and human remain entire; there was no change of the one into the other, as Christ by a miracle changed water into wine, or men by art change sand or ashes into glass: and when he prays "for the glory he had with God before the world was" (John xvii. 5), he prays that a glory he had in his Deity might shine forth in his person as Mediator, and be evidenced in that height and splendor suitable to his dignity, which had been so lately darkened by his abasement; that as he had appeared to be the Son of Man in the infirmity of the flesh, he might appear to be the Son of God in the glory of his person, that he might appear to be the Son of God and the Son of Man in one person.[r] Again, there could be no change in this union; for, in a real change, something is acquired which was not possessed before, neither formally nor eminently: but the divinity had from eternity, before the incarnation, all the perfections of the human nature eminently in a nobler manner than they are in themselves, and therefore could not be changed by a real union.[s]

Prop. III. Repentance and other affections ascribed to God in Scripture, argue no change in God. We often read of God's repenting, repenting of the good he promised (Jer. xviii. 10), and of the evil he threatened (Exod. xxxii. 14; John iii. 10), or of the work he hath wrought (Gen. vi. 6). We must observe, therefore, that,

1. Repentance is not properly in God. He is a pure Spirit, and is not capable of those passions which are signs of weakness and im-

[q] Zanch. de Immutab. Dei.

[r] Goulart de Immutab. de Dieu.

[s] Gamach. in Part I. Aquin. Qu. 9. c. i.

potence, or subject to those regrets we are subject to. Where there is a proper repentance there is a want of foresight, an ignorance of what would succeed, or a defect in the examination of the occurrences which might fall within consideration. All repentance of a fact is grounded upon a mistake in the event which was not foreseen, or upon an after knowledge of the evil of the thing which was acted by the person repenting. But God is so wise that he cannot err, so holy he cannot do evil; and his certain prescience, or foreknowledge, secures him against any unexpected events. God doth not act but upon clear and infallible reason; and a change upon passion is accounted by all so great a weakness in man, that none can entertain so unworthy a conceit of God. Where he is said to repent (Gen. vi. 6), he is also said to grieve; now no proper grief can be imagined to be in God. As repentance is inconsistent with infallible foresight, so is grief no less inconsistent with undefiled blessedness. God is "blessed forever" (Rom. ix. 8), and therefore nothing can befall him that can stain that blessedness. His blessedness would be impaired and interrupted while he is repenting, though he did soon rectify that which is the cause of his repentance. "God is of one mind, and who can turn him? what his soul desires that he doth" (Job xxiii. 13).

2. But God accommodates himself in the Scripture to our weak capacity. God hath no more of a proper repentance, than he hath of a real body; though he, in accommodation to our weakness, ascribes to himself the members of our bodies to set out to our understanding the greatness of his perfections, we must not conclude him a body like us; so, because he is said to have anger and repentance, we must not conclude him to have passions like us. When we cannot fully comprehend him as he is, he clothes himself with our nature in his expressions that we may apprehend him as we are able, and by an inspection into ourselves, learn something of the nature of God; yet those human ways of speaking ought to be understood in a manner agreeable to the infinite excellency and majesty of God, and are only designed to mark out something in God which hath a resemblance with something in us; as we cannot speak to God as gods, but as men, so we cannot understand him speaking to us as a God, unless he condescend to speak to us like a man. God therefore frames his language to our dulness, not to his own state, and informs us by our own phrases, what he would have us learn of his nature, as nurses talk broken language to young children. In all such expressions, therefore, we must ascribe the perfection we conceive in them to God, and lay the imperfection at the door of the creature.

3. Therefore, repentance in God is only a change of his outward conduct, according to his infallible foresight and immutable will. He changes the way of his providential proceeding according to the carriage of the creature, without changing his will, which is the rule of his providence. When God speaks of his repenting "that he had made man" (Gen. vi. 6), it is only his changing his conduct from a way of kindness to a way of severity, and is a word suited to our capacities to signify his detestation of sin, and his resolution to pun-

ish it, after man had made himself quite another thing, than God had made him; "it repents me," that is, I am purposed to destroy the world, as he that repents of his work throws it away;[t] as if a potter cast away the vessel he had framed, it were a testimony that he repented that ever he took pains about it, so the destruction of them seems to be a repentance in God that ever he made them; it is a change of events, not of counsels. Repentance in us is a grief for a former fact, and a changing of our course in it; grief is not in God, but his repentance is a willing a thing should not be as it was, which will was fixed from eternity; for God, foreseeing man would fall, and decreeing to permit it, he could not be said to repent in time of what he did not repent from eternity; and therefore, if there were no repentance in God from eternity, there could be none in time.[u] But God is said to repent when he changes the disposition of affairs without himself; as men, when they repent, alter the course of their actions, so God alters things, *extra se*, or without himself, but changes nothing of his own purpose within himself. It rather notes the action he is about to do, than anything in his own nature, or any change in his eternal purpose. God's repenting of his kindness is nothing but an inflicting of punishment, which the creature by the change of his carriage hath merited: as his repenting of the evil threatened is the withholding the punishment denounced, when the creature hath humbly submitted to his authority, and acknowledged his crime. Or else we may understand those expressions of joy, and grief, and repentance, to signify thus much, that the things declared to be the objects of joy, and grief, and repentance, are of that nature, that if God were capable of our passions, he would discover himself in such cases as we do; as when the prophets mention the joys and applaudings of heaven, earth, and the sea, they only signify that the things they speak of are so good, that if the heavens and the sea had natures capable of joy, they would express it upon that occasion in such a manner as we do; so would God have joy at the obedience of men, and grief at the unworthy carriage of men, and repent of his kindness when men abuse it, and repent of his punishment when men reform under his rod, were the majesty of his nature capable of such affections.[x]

Prop. IV. The not fulfilling of some predictions in Scripture, which seem to imply a changeableness of the Divine will, do not argue any change in it. As when he reprieved Hezekiah from death, after a message sent by the prophet Isaiah, that he should die (2 Kings xx. 1–5; Isa. xxxviii. 1–5), and when he made an arrest of that judgment he had threatened by Jonah against Nineveh (Jon. iii. 4–10). There is not, indeed, the same reason of promises and threatenings altogether; for in promising, the obligation lies upon God, and the right to demand is in the party that performs the condition of the promise: but in threatenings, the obligation lies upon the sinner, and God's right to punish is declared thereby; so that though God doth not punish, his will is not changed, because his will was to declare the demerit of sin, and his right to punish

---

[t] Mercer *in loc.*.   [u] Petavius Theol. Dogmat.
[x] Daille, in Sermon on 2 Pet. iii. 9. p. 30.

upon the commission of it; though he may not punish according to the strict letter of the threatening the person sinning, but relax his own law for the honor of his attributes, and transfer the punishment from the offender to a person substituted in his room: this was the case in the first threatening against man, and the substituting a Surety in the place of the malefactor. But the answer to these cases is this, that where we find predictions in Scripture declared, and yet not executed, we must consider them, not as absolute but conditional, or as the civil law calls it, an interlocutory sentence.[y] God declared what would follow by natural causes, or by the demerit of man, not what he would absolutely himself do: and in many of those predictions, though the condition be not expressed, yet it is to be understood; so the promises of God are to be understood, with the condition of perseverance in well doing; and threatenings, with a clause of revocation annexed to them, provided that men repent: and this God lays down as a general case, alway to be remembered as a rule for the interpreting his threatenings against a nation, and the same reason will hold in threatenings against a particular person. (Jer. xviii. 7–10) "At what instant I shall speak concerning a nation, and concerning a kingdom, to pluck up, and to pull down, and destroy it; if that nation, against whom I have pronounced, turn from their evil, I will repent of the evil that I thought to do unto them;" and so when he speaks of planting a nation, if they do evil, he will repent of the good, &c. It is a universal rule by which all particular cases of this nature are to be tried; so that when man's repentance arrives, God remains firm in his first will, always equal to himself; and it is not he that changes, but man. For since the interposition of the Mediator, with an eye to whom God governed the world after the fall, the right of punishing was taken off if men repented, and mercy was to flow out, if by a conversion men returned to their duty (Ezek. xviii. 20, 21). This, I say, is grounded upon God's entertaining the Mediator; for the covenant of works discovered no such thing as repentance or pardon. Now these general rules are to be the interpreters of particular cases: so that predictions of good are not to be counted absolute, if men return to evil; nor predictions of evil, if men be thereby reduced to a repentance of their crimes. So Nineveh shall be destroyed, that is, according to the general rule, unless the inhabitants repent, which they did; they manifested a belief of the threatening, and gave glory to God by giving credit to the prophet: and they had a notion of this rule God lays down in the other prophets; for they had an apprehension that, upon their humbling themselves, they might escape the threatened vengeance, and stop the shooting those arrows that were ready in the bow.[z] Though Jonah proclaimed destruction without declaring any hopes of an arrest of judgment, yet their natural notion of God afforded some natural hopes of relief if they did their duty, and spurned not against the prophet's message; and therefore, saith one, God did not always express this condition, because it was needless; his own rule revealed in Scripture was sufficient to some; and the natural notion all men had of God's goodness upon their repentance, made it not absolutely necessary to declare it. And besides, saith he, it is bootless; the expressing it can do but little good; secure ones will repent never the sooner, but rather presume upon their hopes of God's forbearance, and linger out their repentance till it be too late. And to work men to repentance, whom he hath purposed to spare, he threatens them with terrible judgments; which by how much the more terrible and peremptory they are, are likely to be more effectual for that end God in his purpose designs them; viz. to humble them under a sense of their demerit, and an acknowledgment of his right-eous justice; and, therefore, though they be absolutely denounced, yet they are to be conditionally interpreted with a reservation of repentance. As for that answer which one gives, that by forty days was not meant forty natural days, but forty prophetical days, that is years, a day for a year; and that the city was destroyed forty years after by the Medes; the expression of God's repenting upon their humiliation puts a bar to that interpretation; God repented, that is, he did not bring the punishment upon them according to those days the prophet had expressed; and, therefore, forty natural days are to be understood; and if it were meant forty years, and they were destroyed at the end of that term, how could God be said to repent, since according to that, the punishment threatened was, according to the time fixed, brought upon them? and the destruction of it forty years after will not be easily evinced, if Jonah lived in the time of Jeroboam, the second king of Israel, as he did (2 Kings xiv. 25); and Nineveh was destroyed in the time of Josiah, king of Judah. But the other answer is plain. God did not fulfil what he had threatened, because they reformed what they had committed: when the threatening was made, they were a fit object for justice; but when they repented, they were a fit object for a merciful respite. To threaten when sins are high, is a part of God's justice; not to execute when sins are revoked by repentance, is a part of God's goodness. And in the case of Hezekiah (2 Kings xx. 1, 5), Isaiah comes with a message from God, that he should " set his house in order," for he shall die; that is, the disease was mortal, and no out-ward applications could in their own nature resist the distemper: " Behold, I will add to thy days fifteen years; I will heal thee" (Isa. xxxviii. 1, 5). It seems to me to be one entire message, because the latter part of it was so suddenly after the other committed to Isaiah, to be delivered to Hezekiah; for he was not gone out of the king's house, before he was ordered to return with the news of his health, by an extraordinary indulgence of God against the power of nature and force of the disease, " Behold, I will add to thy life;" noting it as an extraordinary thing; he was in the second court of the king's house when this word came to him (2 Kings xx. 4); the king's house having three courts, so that he was not gone above half-way out of the palace. God might send this message of death, to prevent the pride Hezekiah might swell with for his deliverance from Senna-cherib: as Paul had a messenger of Satan to buffet him to prevent his lifting up (2 Cor. xii. 7); and this good man was subject to this sin, as we find afterwards in the case of the Babylonish ambassadors; and God delayed this other part of the message to humble him, and draw out his prayer: and as soon as ever he found Hezekiah in this temper, he sent Isaiah with a comfortable message of recovery ; so that the will of God was to signify to him the mortality of his distemper, and afterwards to relieve him by a message of an extraordinary recovery.

Prop. V. God is not changed, when of loving to any creatures he becomes angry with them, or of angry he becomes appeased. The change in these cases is in the creature; according to the alteration in the creature, it stands in a various relation to God : an innocent creature is the object of his kindness, an offending creature is the object of his anger; there is a change in the dispensations of God, as there is a change in the creature making himself capable of such dispensations. God always acts according to the immutable nature of his holiness, and can no more change in his affections to good and evil, than he can in his essence. When the devils, now fallen, stood as glorious angels, they were the objects of God's love, because holy ; when they fell, they were the objects of God's hatred, because impure ; the same reason which made him love them while they were pure, made him hate them when they were criminal. The reason of his various dispensations to them was the same in both, as considered in God, his immutable holiness ; but as respecting the creature, different; the nature of the creature was changed, but the Divine holy nature of God remained the same : " With the pure thou wilt show thyself pure, and with the froward, thou wilt show thyself froward" (Ps. xviii. 26) : he is a refreshing light to those that obey him, and a consuming fire to those that resist him. Though the same angels were not always loved, yet the same reason that moved him to love them, moved him to hate them. It had argued a change in God if he had loved them alway, in whatsoever posture they were towards him ; it could not be counted love, but a weakness and impotent fondness ; the change is in the object, not in the affection of God ; for the object loved before is not beloved now, because that which was the motive of love, is not now in it ; so that the creature having a different state from what it had, falls under a different affection or dispensation. It had been a mutable affection in God to love that which was not worthy of love with the same love wherewith he loved that which had the greatest resemblance to himself ; had God loved the fallen angels in that state and for that state, he had hated himself, because he had loved that which was contrary to himself and the image of his own holiness, which made them appear before, good in his sight. The will of God is unchangeably set to love righteousness and hate iniquity, and from this hatred to punish it ; and if a righteous creature contracts the wrath of God, or a sinful creature hath the communications of God's love, it must be by a change in themselves. Is the sun changed when it hardens one thing and softens another, according to the disposition of the several subjects ? Or when the sun makes a flower more fragrant, and a dead carcass more noisome ? There are divers effects, but the reason of that diversity is not in the sun, but in the subject ; the sun is the same, and produceth those different effects by the same quality of heat ; so if an unholy soul approach to God, God looks angrily upon him ; if a holy soul come before him, the same immutable perfection in God draws out his kindness towards him : as some think, the sun would rather refresh than scorch us, if our bodies were of the same nature and substance with that luminary. As the will of God for creating the world was no new, but an eternal will, though it manifested itself in time, so the will of God for the punishment of sin, or the reconciliation of the sinner, was no new will : though his wrath in time break out in the effects of it upon sinners, and his love flows out in the effects of it upon penitents. Christ by his death reconciling God to man, did not alter the will of God, but did what was consonant to his eternal will ; he came not to change his will, but to execute his will : " Lo, I come to do thy will, O God" (Heb. x. 7). And the grace of God in Christ was not a new grace, but an old grace in a new appearance ; " the grace of God hath appeared" (Tit. i. 11).

Prop. VI. A change of laws by God argues no change in God, when God abrogates some laws which he had settled in the church, and enacts others. I spake of this something the last day ; I shall only add this : God commanded one thing to the Jews, when the church was in an infant state ; and removed those laws, when the church came to some growth. The elements of the world were suited to the state of children (Gal. iv. 3). A mother feeds not the infant with the same diet as she doth when it is grown up. Our Saviour acquainted not his disciples with some things at one time which he did at another, because they were not able to bear them : where was the change ; in Christ's will, or in their growth from a state of weakness to that of strength ? A physician prescribes not the same thing to a person in health, as he doth to one conflicting with a distemper ; nor the same thing in the beginning as he doth in the state or declination of the disease. The physician's will and skill are the same, but the capacity and necessity of the patient for this or that medicine, or method of proceeding, are not the same. When God changed the ceremonial law, there was no change in the Divine will, but an execution of his will ; for when God commanded the observance of the law he intended not the perpetuity of it ; nay, in the prophets he declares the cessation of it ; he decreed to command it, but he decreed to command it only for such a time ; so that the abrogation of it was no less an execution of his decree, than the establishment of it for a season was ; the commanding of it was pursuant to his decree for the appointing of it, and the nulling of it was pursuant to his decree of continuing it only for such a season ; so that in all this there was no change in the will of God. The counsel of God stands sure ; what changes soever there are in the world, are not in God or his will, but in the events of things, and the different relations of things to God : it is in the creature, not in the Creator. The sun alway remains of the same hue, and is not discolored in itself, because it shines green through a green glass, and blue through a blue glass ; the different colors come from the glass, not from the sun ; the change is alway in the disposition of the creature, and not in the nature of God or his will.

V. *Use* 1. For information.

1. If God be unchangeable in his nature, and immutability be a

property of God, then Christ hath a Divine nature. This in the Psalm is applied to Christ in the Hebrews (Heb. i. 11), where he joins the citation out of this Psalm with that out of Ps. xlv. 6, 7, "Thy throne, O God, is forever and ever; thou hast loved righteousness and hated iniquity; therefore God, even thy God, hath anointed thee with the oil of gladness above thy fellows; and thou, Lord, in the beginning hast laid the foundation of the earth," &c. As the first must necessarily be meant of Christ the Mediator, and therein he is distinguished from God, as one anointed by him; so the other must be meant of Christ, whereby he is made one with God in regard of the creation and dissolution of the world, in regard of eternity and immutability. Both the testimonies are linked together by the copulative *and*, "and thou, Lord;" declaring thereby that they are both to be understood of the same person, the Son of God. The design of the chapter is to prove Christ to be God; and such things are spoken of him as could not belong to any creature; no, not to the most excellent of the angels. The same person that is said to be anointed above his fellows, and is said to lay the foundation of the earth and heavens, is said to be the same; that is, the same in himself; the prerogative of sameness belongs to that person as well as creation of heaven and earth. The Socinians say it is spoken of God, and that God shall destroy the heavens by Christ; if so, Christ is not a mere creature, not created when he was incarnate; for the same person that shall change the world did create the world; if God shall change the world by him, God also created the world by him; he was then before the world was; for how could God create the world by one that was not; that was not in being till after the creation of the world? The heavens shall be changed, but the person who is to change the heavens is said to be the same, or unchangeable in the creation as well as the dissolution of the world. This sameness refers to the whole sentence. The Psalm wherein the text is, and whence this in the Hebrews is cited, is properly meant of Christ, and redemption by him, and the completing of it at the last day, and not of the Babylonish captivity;[a] that captivity was not so deplorable as the state of the Psalmist describes; Daniel and his companions flourished in that captivity; it could not reasonably be said of them, that their days were consumed like smoke, their hearts withered like grass; that they forgot to "eat their bread" (ver. 3, 4). Besides, he complains of "shortness of life" (ver. 11); but none had any more reason to complain of that in the time of the captivity, than before and after it, than at any other time: their deliverance would contribute nothing to the natural length of their lives. Besides, when Sion should be built, the heathen should "fear the name of the Lord" (that is, worship God), and "all the kings of the earth his glory" (ver. 15). The rearing the second temple after the deliverance, did not proselyte the nations; nor did the kings of the earth worship the glory of God; nor did God appear in such glory at the erecting the second temple. The second temple was less glorious than the first, for it wanted some of the ornaments which were the glory of the first; but it is

[a] Placeus de Deitate Christi.

said of this state, that when the Lord should build up Sion, he should " appear in his glory" (ver. 16); his proper glory, and extraordinary glory. Now that God who shall appear in glory, and build up Sion, is the Son of God, the Redeemer of the world; he builds up the church, he causes the nations to fear the Lord, and the kings of the earth his glory; he broke down the partition wall, and opened a door for the entrance of the Gentiles; he struck the chains from off the prisoners, and loosed those that were appointed to death by the curse of the law (ver. 20): and to this person is ascribed the creation of the world; and he is pronounced to remain the same in the midst of an infinite number of changes in inferior things. And it is likely the Psalmist considers not only the beginning of redemption, but the completing of it at the second coming of Christ; for he complains of those evils which shall be removed by his second coming, viz., the shortness of life, persecutions and reproaches wherewith the church is afflicted in this world; and comforts not himself with those attributes which are directly opposed to sin, as the mercy of God, the covenant of God, but with those that are opposed to mortality and calamities, as the unchangeableness and eternity of God; and from thence infers a perpetual establishment of believers. " The children of thy servants shall continue, and their seed shall be established before thee" (ver. 28): so that the Psalm itself seems to aim in the whole discourse at Christ, and asserts his divinity, which the apostle, as an interpreter, doth fully evidence; applying it to him, and manifesting his deity by his immutability as well as eternity.[b] While all other things lose their forms, and pass through multitudes of variations, he constantly remains the same, and shall be the same, when all the empires of the world shall slide away, and a period be put to the present motions of the creation: and as there was no change made in his being by the creation of things, so neither shall there be by the final alteration of things; he shall see them finish, as he saw them rise up into being, and be the same after their reign, as he was before their original; he is the first and the last (Rev. i. 17).

2. Here is ground and encouragement for worship. An atheist will make another use of this; if God be immutable, why should we worship him, why should we pray to him? good will come if he wills it; evil cannot be averted by all our supplications, if he hath ordained it to fall upon us. But certainly since unchangeableness is knowing, and willing goodness is a perfection, an adoration and admiration is due to God, upon the account of this excellence. If he be God, he is to be reverenced, and the more highly reverenced, because he cannot but be God. Again, what comfort could it be to pray to a God, that like the chameleon changed colors every day, every moment? What encouragement could there be to lift up our eyes to one that were of one mind this day and of another mind tomorrow? Who would put up a petition to an earthly prince that were so mutable, as to grant a petition one day and deny it another, and change his own act? But if a prince promise this or that thing upon such or such a condition, and you know his promise to be as unchangeable as the laws of the Medes and Persians, would any man

[b] Daille, Melang. des Sermons, Part II. § 1. p. 8–10, &c.

reason thus? because it is unchangeable we will not seek to him, we will not perform the condition, upon which the fruit of the proclamation is to be enjoyed. Who would not count such an inference ridiculous? What blessings hath not God promised upon the condition of seeking him? Were he of an unrighteous nature, or changeable in his mind, this would be a bar to our seeking him, and frustrate our hopes; but since it is otherwise, is not this excellency of his nature the highest encouragement, to ask of him the blessings he hath promised, and a beam from heaven to fire our zeal in asking? If you desire things against his will, which he hath declared he will not grant, prayer then would be an act of disobedience and injury to him, as well as an act of folly in itself; his unchangeableness then might stifle such desires: but if we ask according to his will, and according to our reasonable wants, what ground have we to make such a ridiculous argument? He hath willed everything that may be for our good, if we perform the condition he hath required; and hath put it upon record, that we may know it and regulate our desires and supplications according to it. If we will not seek him, his immutability cannot be a bar, but our own folly is the cause; and by our neglect we despoil him of this perfection as to us, and either imply that he is not sincere, and means not as he speaks; or that he is as changeable as the wind, sometimes this thing, sometimes that, and not at all to be confided in. If we ask according to his revealed will, the unchangeableness of his nature will assure us of the grant; and what a presumption would it be in a creature dependent upon his sovereign, to ask that which he knows he has declared his will against; since there is no good we can want, but he hath promised to give, upon our sincere and ardent desire for it? God hath decreed to give this or that to man, but conditionally, and by the means of inquiring after him, and asking for it: "Ask, and you shall receive" (Ezek. xxxvi. 37; Matt. vii. 7): as much as to say, You shall not receive unless you ask. When the highest promises are made, God expects they should be put in suit; our Saviour joins the promise and the petition together; the promise to encourage the petition, and the petition to enjoy the promise: he doth not say perhaps it shall be given, but it shall, that is, it certainly shall; your heavenly Father is unchangeably willing to give you those things. We must depend upon his immutability for the thing, and submit to his wisdom for the time. Prayer is an acknowledgment of our dependence upon God; which dependence could have no firm foundation without unchangeableness. Prayer doth not desire any change in God, but is offered to God that he would confer those things which he hath immutably willed to communicate; but he willed them not without prayer as the means of bestowing them. The light of the sun is ordered for our comfort, for the discovery of visible things, for the ripening the fruits of the earth; but withal it is required that we use our faculty of seeing, that we employ our industry in sowing and planting, and expose our fruits to the view of the sun, that they may receive the influence of it. If a man shuts his eyes, and complains that the sun is changed into darkness, it would be ridiculous; the sun is not changed, but we alter ourselves; nor is God changed in not giving us the blessings he hath promised, because he hath promised in the way of a due address to him, and opening our souls to receive his influence, and to this, his immutability is the greatest encouragement.

3. This shows how contrary man is to God in regard of his inconstancy. What an infinite distance is there between the immutable God, and mutable man, and how should we bewail this flittingness in our nature! There is a mutability in us as creatures, and a creature cannot but be mutable by nature, otherwise it were not a creature but God. The establishment of any creature is from grace and gift; naturally we tend to nothing, as we come from nothing. This creature-mutability is not our sin, yet it should cause us to lie down under a sense of our own nothingness, in the presence of the Creator. The angels as creatures, though not corrupt, cover their faces before him: and the arguments God uses to humble Job, though a fallen creature, are not from his corruption: for I do not remember that he taxed him with that; but from the greatness of his majesty and excellency of his nature declared in his works (Job xxxviii.–xli.); and, therefore, men that have no sense of God and humility before him, forget that they are creatures as well as corrupt ones. How great is the distance between God and us, in regard of our inconstancy in good, which is not natural to us by creation: for the mind and affections were regular, and by the great artificer were pointed to God as the object of knowledge and love. We have the same faculties of understanding, will, and affection, as Adam had in innocence; but not with the same light, the same bias, and the same ballast. Man, by his fall, wounded his head and heart; the wound in his head made him unstable in the truth, and that in his heart unsteadfast in his affections: he changed himself from the image of God to that of the devil, from innocence to corruption, and from an ability to be steadfast to a perpetual inconstancy; " his silver became dross, and his wine was mixed with water" (Isa. i. 22). He changed,

(1.) To inconstancy in truth, opposed to the immutability of knowledge in God. How are our minds floating between ignorance and knowledge! Truth in us is like those ephemera, creatures of a day's continuance,—springs up in the morning, and expires at night. How soon doth that fly away from us which we have had, not only some weak flashes of, but which we have learned and have had some relish of! The devil stood not in the truth (John viii. 44), and therefore manages his engines to make us as unstable as himself: our minds reel, and corrupt reasonings oversway us; like sponges we suck up water, and a light compression makes us spout it out again. Truths are not engraven upon our hearts, but writ as in dust, defaced by the next puff of wind, "carried about with every wind of doctrine" (Eph. iv. 14); like a ship without a pilot and sails, at the courtesy of the next storm, or like clouds that are tenants to the wind and sun, moved by the wind and melted by the sun. The Galatians were no sooner called into the grace of God, but they were removed from it (Gal. i. 6); some have been reported to have *menstruam fidem*, kept an opinion for a month; and many are like him that believed the soul's immortality no longer than he had Plato's book of that subject in his hand:[c] one likens such to children; they play with truths as children do with babies, one while embrace them, and a little after throw them into the dirt. How soon do we forget what the truth is delivered to us, and what it represented us to be (James i. 23, 24). Is it not a thing to be bewailed, that man should be such a weathercock, turned about with every breath of wind, and shifting aspects as the wind shifts points?

(2.) Inconstancy in will, and affections opposed to the immutability of will in God. We waver between God and Baal; and while we are not only resolving, but upon motion a little way, look back with a hankering after Sodom; sometimes lifted up with heavenly intentions, and presently cast down with earthly cares, like a ship that by an advancing wave seems to aspire to heaven, and the next fall of the waves makes it sink down to the depths. We change purposes oftener than fashions, and our resolutions are like letters in water, whereof no mark remains; we will be as John to-day to love Christ, and as Judas to-morrow to betray him, and, by an unworthy levity, pass into the camp of the enemies of God; resolved to be as holy as angels in the morning, when the evening beholds us as impure as devils. How often do we hate what before we loved, and shun what before we longed for! and our resolutions are like vessels of crystal, which break at the first knock, are dashed in pieces by the next temptation. Saul resolved not to persecute David any more, but you soon find him upon his old game. Pharaoh more than once promised, and probably resolved, to let Israel go, but at the end of the storm his purposes vanish (Exod. viii. 27, 32). When an affliction pincheth men, they intend to change their course, and the next news of ease changes their intentions; like a bow not fully bent in their inclinations, they cannot reach the mark, but live many years between resolutions of obedience and affections to rebellion (Ps. lxxviii. 17): and what promises men make to God are often the fruit of their passion, their fear, not of their will. The Israelites were startled at the terrors wherewith the law was delivered, and promised obedience (Exod. xx. 19), but a month after forgot them, and make a golden calf, and in the sight of Sinai call for, and dance before, their gods (Exod. xxxii.); never people more unconstant. Peter, who vowed an allegiance to his Master, and a courage to stick to him, forswears him almost with the same breath. Those that cry out with a zeal, "The Lord he is God," shortly after return to the service of their idols (1 Kings xviii. 39). That which seems to be our pleasure this day, is our vexation to-morrow; a fear of a judgment puts us into a religious pang, and a love to our lusts reduceth us to a rebellious inclination; as soon as the danger is over, the saint is forgotten: salvation and damnation present themselves to us, touch us, and engender some weak wishes, which are dissolved by the next allurements of a carnal interest. No hold can be taken of our promises, no credit is to be given to our resolutions.

(3.) Inconstancy in practice. How much beginning in the Spirit, and ending in the flesh; one day in the sanctuary, another in the stews; clear in the morning as the sun, and clouded before noon;

[c] Sedgwick Christ's Counsel, p. 230.

in heaven by an excellency of gifts, in hell by a course of profaneness; like a flower, which some mention, that changes its color three times a day, one part white, then purple, then yellow! The spirit lusts against the flesh, and the flesh quickly triumphs over the spirit. In a good man how often is there a spiritual lethargy; though he doth not openly defame God, yet he doth not always glorify him; he doth not forsake the truth, but he doth not always make the attainment of it, and settlement in it his business. This levity discovers itself in religious duty, "when I would do good, evil is present with me" (Rom. vii. 21). Never more present, than when we have a mind to do good, and never more present than when we have a mind to do the best and greatest good. How hard is it to make our thoughts and affections keep their stand! place them upon a good object, and they will be frisking from it, as a bird from one bough, one fruit, to another: we vary postures according to the various objects we meet with. The course of the world is a very airy thing, suited to the uncertain notions of that "prince of the power of the air," which works in it (Eph. ii. 2). This ought to be bewailed by us. Though we may stand fast in the truth, though we may spin our resolutions into a firm web, though the spirit may triumph over the flesh in our practice, yet we ought to bewail it, because inconstancy is our nature, and what fixedness we have in good is from grace. What we find practised by most men is natural to all;[d] "as face answers to face in a glass, so doth heart to heart" (Prov. xxvii. 19); a face in the glass is not more like a natural face, whose image it is, than one man's heart is naturally like another.

1st. It is natural to those out of the church. Nebuchadnezzar is so affected with Daniel's prophetic spirit, that he would have none accounted the true God, but the "God of Daniel" (Dan. ii. 47). How soon doth this notion slip from him, and an image must be set up for all to worship, upon pain of a most cruel, painful death! Daniel's God is quite forgotten. The miraculous deliverance of the three children, for not worshipping his image, makes him settle a decree to secure the honor of God from the reproach of his subjects (Dan. iii. 29); yet, a little while after, you have him strutting in his palace, as if there were no God but himself.

2d. It is natural to those in the Church. The Israelites were the only church God had in the world, and a notable example of inconstancy. After the miracles of Egypt, they murmured against God, when they saw Pharaoh marching with an army at their heels. They desired food, and soon nauseated the manna they were before fond of. When they came into Canaan, they sometimes worshipped God, and sometimes idols, not only the idols of one nation, but of all their neighbors. In which regard God calls this, his heritage; "a speckled bird" (Jer. xii. 9); a peacock, saith Hierom, inconstant, made up of varieties of idolatrous colors and ceremonies. This levity of spirit is the root of all mischief; it scatters our thoughts in the service of God; it is the cause of all revolts and apostasies from him; it makes us unfit to receive the communications of God: whatsoever we hear is like words writ in sand, ruffled out by the

d Lawrence, of Faith, p. 262.

next gale; whatsoever is put into us is like precious liquor in a palsy hand, soon spilt: it breeds distrust of God when we have an uncertain judgment of him, we are not like to confide in him; an uncertain judgment will be followed with a distrustful heart. In fine, where it is prevalent, it is a certain sign of ungodliness. To be driven with the wind like chaff, and to be ungodly, is all one in the judgment of the Holy Ghost (Ps. i. 4); the ungodly are "like the chaff which the wind drives away," which signifies not their destruction, but their disposition, for their destruction is inferred from it (ver. 5), "therefore the ungodly shall not stand in judgment." How contrary is this to the unchangeable God, who is alway the same, and would have us the same, in our religious promises and resolutions for good!

4. If God be immutable, it is sad news to those that are resolved in wickedness, or careless of returning to that duty he requires. Sinners must not expect that God will alter his will, make a breach upon his nature, and violate his own word to gratify their lusts. No, it is not reasonable God should dishonor himself to secure them, and cease to be God, that they may continue to be wicked, by changing his own nature, that they may be unchanged in their vanity. God is the same; goodness is as amiable in his sight, and sin as abominable in his eyes now, as it was at the beginning of the world. Being the same God, he is the same enemy to the wicked as the same friend to the righteous. He is the same in knowledge, and cannot forget sinful acts. He is the same in will, and cannot approve of unrighteous practices. Goodness cannot but be alway the object of his love, and wickedness cannot but be alway the object of his hatred: and as his aversion to sin is alway the same, so as he hath been in his judgments upon sinners, the same he will be still; for the same perfection of immutability belongs to his justice for the punishment of sin, as to his holiness for his disaffection to sin. Though the covenant of works was changeable by the crime of man violating it, yet it was unchangeable in regard of God's justice vindicating it, which is inflexible in the punishment of the breaches of his law. The law had a preceptive part, and a minatory part: when man changed the observation of the precept, the righteous nature of God could not null the execution of the threatening; he could not, upon the account of this perfection, neglect his just word, and countenance the unrighteous transgression. Though there were no more rational creatures in being but Adam and Eve, yet God subjected them to that death he had assured them of: and from this immutability of his will, ariseth the necessity of the suffering of the Son of God for the relief of the apostate creature. His will in the second covenant is as unchangeable as that in the first, only repentance is settled as the condition of the second, which was not indulged in the first; and without repentance, the sinner must irrevocably perish, or God must change his nature: there must be a change in man; there can be none in God; his bow is bent, his arrows are ready, if the wicked do not turn (Ps. vii. 11). There is not an atheist, an hypocrite, a profane person, that ever was upon the earth, but God's soul abhorred him as such, and the like he will

abhor forever; while any therefore continue so, they may sooner
expect the heavens should roll as they please, the sun stand still at
their order, the stars change their course at their beck, than that God
should change his nature, which is opposite to profaneness and
vanity; "Who hath hardened himself against him, and hath prospered?" (Job ix. 4.)

Use 2. Of comfort. The immutability of a good God is a strong
ground of consolation. Subjects wish a good prince to live forever, as
being loth to change him, but care not how soon they are rid of an oppressor. This unchangeableness of God's will shows him as ready to
accept any that come to him as ever he was; so that we may with confidence make our address to him, since he cannot change his affections
to goodness. The fear of change in a friend hinders a full reliance
upon him; an assurance of stability encourages hope and confidence.
This attribute is the strongest prop for faith in all our addresses; it
is not a single perfection, but the glory of all those that belong to
his nature; for he is unchangeable in his love (Jer. xxxi. 3), in his
truth (Ps. cxvii. 2). The more solemn revelation of himself in this
name, Jehovah, which signifies chiefly his eternity and immutability,
was to support the Israelites' faith in expectation of a deliverance
from Egypt, that he had not retracted his purpose, and his promise
made to Abraham for giving Canaan to his posterity (Exod. iii. 14–
17). Herein is the basis and strength of all his promises; therefore,
saith the Psalmist, "Those that know thy name, will put their trust
in thee" (Ps. ix. 10): those that are spiritually acquainted with thy
name, Jehovah, and have a true sense of it upon their hearts, will
put their trust in thee. His goodness could not be distrusted, if his
unchangeableness were well apprehended and considered. All distrust would fly before it, as darkness before the sun; it only gets
advantage of us when we are not well grounded in his name; and
if ever we trusted God, we have the same reason to trust him forever:
(Isa. xxvi. 4) "Trust in the Lord forever, for in the Lord Jehovah
is everlasting strength;" or, as it is in the Hebrew, "a Rock of Ages,"
that is, perpetually unchangeable. We find the traces of God's immutability in the creatures. He has, by his peremptory decree, set
bounds to the sea: "Hitherto shalt thou come, but no further, and
here shall thy proud waves be stayed" (Job xxxviii. 11). Do we fear
the sea overflowing us in this island? No, because of his fixed decree. And is not his promise in his Word as unchangeable as his
word concerning inanimate things, as good a ground to rest upon?

1. The covenant stands unchangeable. Mutable creatures break
their leagues and covenants, and snap them asunder like Samson's
cords, when they are not accommodated to their interests. But an
unchangeable God keeps his: "The mountains shall depart, and the
hills be removed, but my kindness shall not depart from thee, nor
shall the covenant of my peace be removed (Isa. liv. 10). The
heaven and earth shall sooner fall asunder, and the strongest and
firmest parts of the creation crumble to dust, sooner than one iota of
my covenant shall fail. It depends upon the unchangeableness of
his will and the unchangeableness of his word, and, therefore, is
called "the immutability of his counsel" (Heb. vi. 17). It is the

fruit of the everlasting purpose of God; whence the apostle links purpose and grace together (2 Tim. i. 9). A covenant with a nation may be changeable, because it may not be built upon the eternal purpose of God, "to put his fear in the heart;" but with respect to the creature's obedience. Thus God chose Jerusalem as the place wherein he would " dwell forever" (Ps. cxxxii. 14), yet he threatens to depart from them when they had broken covenant with him; "and the glory of the Lord went up from the midst of the city to the mountain on the east side" (Ezek. xi. 33). The covenant of grace doth not run, "I will be your God if you will be my people;" but "I will be their God, and they shall be my people" (Hos. ii. 19, &c.) "I will betroth thee to me forever; I will say, Thou art my people, and they shall say, Thou art my God." His everlasting purpose is, to write his laws in the hearts of the elect. He puts a condition to his covenant of grace, the condition of faith, and he resolves to work that condition in the hearts of the elect; and, therefore, believers have two immutable pillars for their support, stronger than those erected by Solomon at the porch of the temple (1 Kings vii. 21), called Jakin and Boaz, to note the firmness of that building dedicated to God; these are election, or the standing counsel of God, and the covenant of grace. He will not revoke the covenant, and blot the names of his elect out of the book of life.

2. Perseverance is ascertained. It consists not with the majesty of God to call a person effectually to himself to-day, to make him fit for his eternal love, to give him faith, and take away that faith to-morrow. His effectual call is the fruit of his eternal election, and that counsel hath no other foundation but his constant and unchangeable will; a foundation that stands sure, and, therefore, called the foundation of God, and not of the creature ; " the foundation of God stands sure, the Lord knows who are his" (2 Tim. ii. 19). It is not founded upon our own natural strength ; it may be then subject to change, as all the products of nature are. The fallen angels had created grace in their innocency, but lost it by their fall. Were this the foundation of the creature, it might soon be shaken; since man, after his revolt, can ascribe nothing constant to himself, but his own inconstancy. But the foundation is not in the infirmity of nature, but the strength of grace, and of the grace of God, who is immutable, who wants not virtue to be able, nor kindness to be willing, to preserve his own foundation.[e] To what purpose doth our Saviour tell his disciples their names "were written in heaven" (Luke x. 20), but to mark the infallible certainty of their salvation by an opposition to those things which perish, and have their "names written in the earth" (Jer. xvii. 23); or upon the sand, where they may be defaced? And why should Christ order his disciples to rejoice that their names were written in heaven, if God were changeable to blot them out again? or why should the apostle assure us, that though God had rejected the greatest part of the Jews, he had not, therefore, rejected his people elected according to his purpose and immutable counsel; because there are none of the elect of God but will come to salvation? For, saith he, the "election hath obtained it" (Rom. xi. 7); that is,

[e] Turretin. Ser. p. 322.

all those that are of the election have obtained it, and the others are hardened. Where the seal of sanctification is stamped, it is a testimony of God's election, and that foundation shall stand sure: "The foundation of the Lord stands sure, having this seal, the Lord knows who are his;" that is the foundation, the "naming the name of Christ," or believing in Christ, and "departing from iniquity," is the seal.[f] As it is impossible when God calls those things that are not, but that they should spring up into being and appear before him; so it is impossible but that the seed of God, by his eternal purpose, should be brought to a spiritual life, and that calling cannot be retracted; for that "gift and calling is without repentance" (Rom. xi. 29). And when repentance is removed from God in regard of some works, the immutability of those works is declared; and the reason of that immutability is their pure dependence on the eternal favor and unchangeable grace of God "purposed in himself" (Eph. i. 9, 11), and not upon the mutability of the creature. Hence their happiness is not as patents among men, *quam diu bene se gesserint,* so long as they behave themselves well; but they have a promise that they shall behave themselves so as never wholly to depart from God (Jer. xxxii. 40): "I will make an everlasting covenant with them, that I will not turn away from them to do them good, but I will put my fear in their hearts, that they shall not depart from me." God will not turn from them, to do them good, and promiseth that they shall not turn from him forever, or forsake him. And the bottom of it is the everlasting covenant, and, therefore, believing and sealing for security are linked together (Eph. i. 13). And when God doth inwardly teach us his law, he puts in a will not to depart from it: (Ps. cxix. 102) "I have not departed from thy judgments;" what is the reason? "For thou hast taught me."

3. By this eternal happiness is insured. This is the inference made from the eternity and unchangeableness of God in the verse following the text (ver. 28): "The children of thy servants shall continue, and their seed shall be established before thee." This is the sole conclusion drawn from those perfections of God solemnly asserted before. The children which the prophets and apostles have begotten to thee, shall be totally delivered from the relics of their apostasy, and the punishment due to them, and rendered partakers of immortality with thee, as sons to dwell in their Father's house forever. The Spirit begins a spiritual life here, to fit for an immutable life in glory hereafter, where believers shall be placed upon a throne that cannot be shaken, and possess a crown that shall not be taken off their heads forever.

Use 3. Of exhortation. 1. Let a sense of the changeableness and uncertainty of all other things beside God, be upon us. There are as many changes as there are figures in the world. The whole fashion of the world is a transient thing; every man may say as Job, "Changes and war are against me" (Job x. 17). Lot chose the plain of Sodom, because it was the richer soil. He was but a little time there before he was taken prisoner, and his substance made the spoil of his enemies. That is again restored; but a while after, fire from

f Cocceius.

heaven devours his wealth, though his person was secured from the judgment by a special Providence. We burn with a desire to settle ourselves, but mistake the way, and build castles in the air, which vanish like bubbles of soap in water. And, therefore,

(1.) Let not our thoughts dwell much upon them. Do but consider those souls that are in the possession of an unchangeable God, that behold his never-fading glory! Would it not be a kind of hell to them to have their thoughts starting out to these things, or find any desire in themselves to the changeable trifles of the earth? Nay, have we not reason to think that they cover their faces with shame, that ever they should have such a weakness of spirit when they were here below, as to spend more thoughts upon them than were necessary for this present life; much more that they should at any time value and court them above an unchangeable good? Do they not disdain themselves that they should ever debase the immutable perfections of God, as to have neglecting thoughts of him at any time, for the entertainment of such a mean and inconstant rival?

(2.) Much less should we trust in them, or rejoice in them. The best things are mutable, and things of such a nature are not fit objects of confidence. Trust not in riches, they have their wanes as well as increases; they rise sometimes like a torrent, and flow in upon men, but resemble also a torrent in as sudden a fall and departure, and leave nothing but slime behind them. Trust not in honor; all the honor and applause in the world is no better than an inheritance of wind, which the pilot is not sure of, but shifts from one corner to another, and stands not perpetually in the same point of the heavens. How, in a few ages did the house of David, a great monarch, and a man after God's own heart, descend to a mean condition, and all the glory of that house shut up in the stock of a carpenter? David's sheep-hook was turned into a sceptre, and the sceptre by the same hand of Providence turned into a hatchet in Joseph his descendant. Rejoice not immoderately in wisdom; that, and learning languish with age. A wound in the head may impair that which is the glory of man. If an organ be out of frame, folly may succeed, and all a man's prudence be wound up in an irrecoverable dotage. Nebuchadnezzar was no fool, yet, by a sudden hand of God, he became not only a fool or a madman, but a kind of brute. Rejoice not in strength; that decays, and a mighty man may live to see his strong arm withered, and a grasshopper to become a burthen (Eccles. xii. 5): "The strong men shall bow themselves, and the grinders shall cease because they are few" (ver. 3): nor rejoice in children; they are like birds upon a tree, that make a little chirping music, and presently fall into the fowler's net. Little did Job expect such sad news as the loss of all his progeny at a blow, when the messenger knocked at his gate; and such changes happen oftentimes when our expectations of comfort, and a contentment in them, are at the highest. How often doth a string crack when the musician hath wound it up to a just height for a tune, and all his pains and delight marred in a moment! Nay, all these things change while we are using them, like ice that melts between our fingers, and flowers that wither while we are smelling to them.   The apostle gave them a good title when he called them " uncertain riches," and thought it a strong argument to dissuade them from trusting in them (1 Tim. vi. 17).   The wealth of the merchant depends upon the winds and waves, and the revenue of the husbandman upon the clouds ; and since they depend upon those things which are used to express the most changeableness, they can be no fit object for trust. Besides, God sometimes kindles a fire under all a man's glory, which doth insensibly consume it (Isa. x. 16) ; and while we have them, the fear of losing them renders us not very happy in the fruition of them ; we can scarce tell whether they are contentments or no, because sorrow follows them so close at the heels.   It is not an unnecessary exhortation for good men ; the best men have been apt to place too much trust in them.   David thought himself immutable in his prosperity, and such thoughts could not be without some immoderate outlets of the heart to them, and confidences in them; and Job promised himself to die in his nest, and " multiply his days as the sand," without any interruption (Job xxix. 18, 19, &c.); but he was mistaken and disappointed.   Let me add this : trust not in men, who are as inconstant as anything else, and often change their most ardent affections into implacable hatred ; and though their affections may not be changed, the power to help you may.   Haman's friends, that depended on him one day, were crest-fallen the next, when their patron was to exchange his chariot of state for an ignominious gallows.

(3.) Prefer an immutable God before mutable creatures.   Is it not a horrible thing to see what we are, and what we possess, daily crumbling to dust, and in a continual flux from us, and not seek out something that is permanent, and always abide the same, for our portion ?   In God, or Wisdom, which is Christ, there is substance (Prov. viii. 21), in which respect he is opposed to all the things in the world, that are but shadows, that are shorter or longer, according to the motion of the sun ; mutable also, by every little body that intervenes.   God is subject to no decay within, to no force without ; nothing in his own nature can change him from what he is, and there is no power above can hinder him from being what he will to the soul.   He is an ocean of all perfection : he wants nothing without himself to render him blessed, which may allure him to a change. His creatures can want nothing out of him to make them happy, whereby they may be enticed to prefer anything before him.   If we enjoy other things, it is by God's donation, who can as well withdraw them as bestow them ; and it is but a reasonable, as well as a necessary thing, to endeavor the enjoyment of the immutable Benefactor, rather than his revocable gifts.   If the creatures had a sufficient virtue in themselves to ravish our thoughts and engross our souls; yet when we take a prospect of a fixed and unchangeable Being, what beauty, what strength have any of those things to vie with him ?   How can they bear up and maintain their interest against a lively thought and sense of God?   All the glory of them would fly before him like that of the stars before the sun.   They were once nothing, they may be nothing again ; as their own nature brought them not out of nothing, so their nature secures them not from being reduced to nothing. What an unhappiness is it to have our affections set upon that which retains something of its *non esse* with its *esse*, its not being with its being; that lives indeed, but in a continual flux, and may lose that pleasurableness to-morrow which charms us to-day?

2. This doctrine will teach us patience under such providences as declare his unchangeable will. The rectitude of our wills consists in conformity to the Divine, as discovered in his words, and manifested in his providence, which are the effluxes of his immutable will. The time of trial is appointed by his immutable will (Dan. xi. 35); it is not in the power of the sufferer's will to shorten it, nor in the power of the enemies' will to lengthen it. Whatsoever doth happen hath been decreed by God (Eccles. vi. 10), " That which hath been is named already ;" therefore to murmur or be discontented is to contend with God, who is mightier than we, to maintain his own purposes. God doth act all things conveniently for that immutable end intended by himself, and according to the reason of his own will, in the true point of time most proper for it and for us, not too soon or too slow, because he is unchangeable in knowledge and wisdom. God doth not act anything barely by an immutable will, but by an immutable wisdom, and an unchangeable rule of goodness; and, therefore, we should not only acquiesce in what he works, but have a complacency in it; and by having our wills thus knitting themselves with the immutable will of God, we attain some degree of likeness to him in his own unchangeableness. When, therefore, God hath manifested his will in opening his decree to the world by his work of providence, we must cease all disputes against it, and, with Aaron hold our peace, though the affliction be very smart (Rev. x. 3). "All flesh must be silent before God" (Zech. ii. 13); for whatsoever is his counsel shall stand, and cannot be recalled. All struggling against it is like a brittle glass contending with a rock ; for " if he cut off and shut up, or gather together, then who can hinder him ?" (Job xi. 10.) Nothing can help us, if he hath determined to afflict us, as nothing can hurt us, if he hath determined to secure us. The more clearly God hath evidenced this or that to be his will, the more sinful is our struggling against it. Pharaoh's sin was the greater in keeping Israel, by how much the more God's miracles had been demonstrations of his settled will to deliver them. Let nothing snatch our hearts to a contradiction to him, but let us fear and give glory to him, when the hour of judgment which he hath appointed is come (Rev. xiv. 7); that is, comply with the unchangeable will of his precept, the more he declares the immutable will of his providence. We must not think God must disgrace his nature and change his proceedings for us ; better the creature should suffer, than God be impaired in any of his perfections. If God changed his purpose he would change his nature. Patience is the way to perform the immutable will of God, and a means to attain a gracious immutability for ourselves by receiving the promise (Heb. x. 36), "Ye have need of patience, that after ye have done the will of God, ye might receive the promise."

3. This doctrine will teach us to imitate God in this perfection, by striving to be immovable in goodness. God never goes back from himself; he finds nothing better than himself for which he should change; and can we find anything better than God, to allure our hearts to a change from him? The sun never declines from the ecliptic line, nor should we from the paths of holiness. A steadfast obedience is encouraged by an unchangeable God to reward it (1 Cor. xv. 58): "Be steadfast and immovable, always abounding in the work of the Lord, knowing that your labor shall not be in vain in the Lord." Unsteadfastness is the note of a hypocrite (Ps. lxxviii. 37): steadfastness in that which is good is the mark of a saint; it is the character of a righteous person to "keep the truth" (Isa. xxvi. 2). And it is as positively said that "he that abides not in the doctrine of Christ hath not God" (2 John, 9); but he that doth, "hath both the Father and the Son." So much of uncertainty, so much of nature, so much of firmness in duty, so much of grace. We can never honor God unless we finish his work; as Christ did not glorify God but in finishing the work God gave him to do (John xvii. 4). The nearer the world comes to an end, the more is God's immutability seen in his promises and predictions, and the more must our unchangeableness be seen in our obedience (Heb. x. 23, 25): "Let us hold fast the profession of our faith without wavering, and so much the more as you see the day approaching." The christian Jews were to be the more tenacious of their faith, the nearer they saw the day approaching, the day of Jerusalem's destruction prophesied of by Daniel (Dan. ix. 26), which accomplishment must be a great argument to establish the christian Jews in the profession of Christ to be the Messiah, because the destruction of the city was not to be before the cutting off the Messiah. Let us be, therefore, constant in our profession and service of God, and not suffer ourselves to be driven from him by the ill usage, or flattered from him by the caresses of the world.

(1.) It is reasonable. If God be unchangeable in doing us good, it is reason we should be unchangeable in doing him service. If he assure us that he is our God, our "I Am," he would also that we should be his people; his we are. If he declare himself constant in his promises, he expects we should be so in our obedience. As a spouse, we should be unchangeably faithful to him as a Husband; as subjects, have an unchangeable allegiance to him as our Prince. He would not have us faithful to him for an hour or a day, but "to the death" (Rev. ii. 10); and it is reason we should be his, and if we be his children, imitate him in his constancy of his holy purposes.

(2.) It is our glory and interest. To be a reed shaken with every wind is no commendation among men, and it is less a ground of praise with God. It was Job's glory that he held fast his integrity (Job i. 22): "In all this Job sinned not;" in all this,—which whole cities and kingdoms would have thought ground enough of high exclamations against God, and also against the temptation of his wife,—he retained his integrity (Job ii. 9): "Dost thou still retain thy integrity?" The devil, who by God's permission stripped him of his goods and health, yet could not strip him of his grace. As a traveller, when the wind and snow beats in his face, wraps his cloak more closely about him to preserve that and himself. Better we had never made profession, than afterwards to abandon it; such a withering profession serves for no other use than to aggravate the crime, if any of us fly like a coward, or revolt like a traitor; what profit will it be to a soldier, if he hath withstood many assaults, and turn his back at last? If we would have God crown us with an immutable glory, we must crown our beginnings with a happy perseverance (Rev. ii. 10): "Be faithful to the death, and I will give thee a crown of life;" not as though this were the cause to merit it, but a necessary condition to possess it: constancy in good is accompanied with an immutability of glory.

(3.) By an unchangeable disposition to good, we should begin the happiness of heaven upon earth. This is the perfection of blessed spirits, those that are nearest to God as angels and glorified souls, they are immutable; not, indeed, by nature, but by grace; yet not only by a necessity of grace, but a liberty of will: grace will not let them change; and that grace doth animate their wills that they would not change; an immutable God fills their understandings and affections, and gives satisfaction to their desires. The saints when they were below, tried other things, and found them deficient; but now they are so fully satisfied with the beatific vision, that if Satan should have an entrance among the angels and sons of God, it is not likely he should have any influence upon them; he could not present to their understandings anything that could either at the first glance, or upon a deliberate view, be preferable to what they enjoy and are fixed in. Well, then, let us be immovable in the knowledge and love of God. It is the delight of God to see his creatures resemble him in what they are able. Let not our affections to him be as Jonah's gourd, growing up in one night and withering the next. Let us not only fight a good fight, but do so till we have finished our course, and imitate God in an unchangeableness of holy purposes; and to that purpose, examine ourselves daily what fixedness we have arrived unto; and to prevent any temptation to a revolt, let us often possess our minds with thoughts of the immutability of God's nature and will, which, like fire under water, will keep a good matter boiling up in us, and make it both retain and increase its heat.

(4.) Let this doctrine teach us to have recourse to God, and aim at a near conjunction with him. When our spirits begin to flag, and a cold aguish temper is drawing upon us, let us go to him who can only fix our hearts, and furnish us with a ballast to render them steadfast. As he is only immutable in his nature, so he is the only principle of immutability, as well as being in the creature. Without his grace, we shall be as changeable in our appearances as the chameleon, and in our turnings as the wind. When Peter trusted in himself, he changed to the worse; it was his Master's recourse to God for him that preserved in him a reducing principle, which changed him again for the better, and fixed him in it (Luke xxii. 32). It will be our interest to be in conjunction with him, that moves not about with the heavens, nor is turned by the force of nature, nor changed by the accidents in the world; but sits in the heavens, moving all things by his powerful arm, according to his infinite skill. While we have him for our God, we have his immutability as well as any other perfection of his nature for our advantage; the nearer we come to him, the more stability we shall have in ourselves; the further from him, the more liable to change. The line that is nearest to the place where it is first fixed, is least subject to motion; the further it is stretched from it, the weaker it is, and more liable to be shaken. Let us also affect those things which are nearest to him in this perfection; the righteousness of Christ that shall never wear out, and the graces of the Spirit that shall never burn out; by this means, what God is infinitely by nature, we shall come to be finitely immutable by grace, as much as the capacity of a creature can contain.

DISCOURSE VII

ON GOD'S OMNIPRESENCE

JEREMIAH xxiii. 24.—Can any hide himself in secret places, that I shall not see him?
saith the Lord. Do not I fill heaven and earth? saith the Lord.

THE occasion of this discourse begins ver. 16, where God admonisheth the people, not to hearken to the words of the false prophets
which spake a vision of their own heart, and not out of the mouth
of the Lord. They made the people vain by their insinuations of
peace, when God had proclaimed war and calamity; and uttered the
dreams of their fancies, and not the visions of the Lord; and so
turned the people from the expectation of the evil day which God
had threatened (ver. 17): "They say still unto them that despise me,
The Lord hath said, Ye shall have peace: and they say unto every
one that walks after the imagination of his own heart, No evil shall
come upon you." And they invalidate the prophecies of those whom
God had sent, ver. 18: "Who hath stood in the counsel of the Lord,
and hath perceived and heard his word? who hath marked his word,
and heard it?" Who hath stood in the counsel of the Lord? Are
they acquainted with the secrets of God more than we? Who have
the word of the Lord, if we have not? Or, it may be a continuation
of God's admonition: believe not those prophets; for who of them
have been acquainted with the secrets of God? or by what means
should they learn his counsel? No; assure yourselves "a whirlwind
of the Lord is gone forth in fury, even a grievous whirlwind; it shall
fall grievously upon the head of the wicked" (ver. 19). A whirlwind
shall come from Babylon; it is just at the door, and shall not be
blown over; it shall fall with a witness upon the wicked people and
the deceiving prophets, and sweep them together into captivity. For
(ver. 20), "The anger of the Lord shall not return, until he have executed, and till he have performed the thoughts of his heart." My
fury shall not be a childish fury, that quickly languisheth, but shall
accomplish whatsoever I threaten; and burn so hot, as not to be
cool, till I have satisfied my vengeance; "in the latter days ye shall
consider it perfectly" (ver. 20), when the storm shall beat upon you,
you shall then know that the calamities shall answer the words you
have heard. When the conqueror shall waste your grounds, demolish
your houses, and manacle your hands, then shall you consider it, and
have the wishes of fools, that you had had your eyes in your heads
before; you shall then know the falseness of your guides, and the

truth of my prophets, and discern who stood in the counsel of the
Lord, and subscribe to the messages I have sent you.

Some understand this not only of the Babylonish captivity, but
refer it to the time of Christ, and the false doctrine of men's own
righteousness in opposition to the righteousness of God; understanding this verse to be partly a threatening of wrath, which shall
end in an advantage to the Jews, who shall in the latter time consider the falseness of their notions about a legal righteousness, and
so make it a promise; they shall then know the intent of the Scripture, and in the latter days, the latter end of the world, when time
shall be near the rolling up, they shall reflect upon themselves;
they shall "look upon Him whom they have pierced;" and till
these latter days, they shall be hardened, and believe nothing of
evangelical truths. Now God denieth that he sent those prophets
(ver. 21): "I have not sent these prophets, yet they ran; I have
not spoken to them, yet they prophesied." They have intruded
themselves without a commission from me, whatsoever their brags
are. The reason to prove it is (ver. 22), "If they had stood in my
counsel," if they had been instructed, and inspired by me, "they
would have caused my people to hear my words;" they would have
regulated themselves according to my word, "and have turned them
from their evil way;" i. e. endeavored to shake down their false confidences of peace, and make them sensible of their false notions of
me, and my ways. Now because those false prophets could not be
so impudent as to boast that they prophesied in the name of God,
when they had not commission from him, unless they had some secret sentiment, that they and their intentions were hid from the
knowledge and eye of God; he adds (ver. 33), "Am I a God at
hand, and not a God afar off? Can any hide himself in secret places,
that I shall not see him?" Have I not the power of seeing and
knowing what they do, what they design, what they think? Why
should I not have such a power, since I fill heaven and earth by my
essence? "Am I a God at hand, and not a God afar off? He excludes here the doctrine of those that excluded the providence of
God from extending itself to the inferior things of the earth; which
error was ancient, as ancient as the time of Job, as appears by their
opinion, that God's eyes were hood-winked and muffled by the thickness of the clouds, and could not pierce through their dark and dense
body (Job xxii. 14): "Thick clouds are a covering to him, that he
seeth not."

Some refer it to time.[g] Do you imagine me a God new framed
like your idols, beginning a little time ago, and not existing before
the foundation of the world; yea, from eternity? a God afar off,
further than your acutest understandings can reach? I am of a
longer standing, and you ought to know my majesty. But it rather
refers to place than time. Do you think I do not behold everything
in the earth, as well as in heaven? Am I locked up within the walls
of my palace, and cannot peep out to behold the things done in the
world? or that am I so linked to pleasure in the place of my glory,
as earthly kings are in their courts, that I have no mind or leisure

[g] Munster, Vatablus, Castalio Oecolamp.

to take notice of the carriages of men upon earth? God doth not say, He was afar off, but only gives an account of the inward thoughts of their minds, or at least of the language expressed by their actions. The interrogation carries in it a strong affirmation, and assures us more of God's care, and the folly of men in not considering it. " Am I a God at hand, and not a God afar off? Can any hide himself in secret places ?" (Heb.) In hiddenesses, in the deepest cells. What! are you besotted by your base lusts, that you think me a God careless, ignorant, blind, that I can see nothing, but as a purblind man, what is very near my eye? Are you so out of your wits, that you imagine you can deceive me? Do not all your behaviors speak such a sentiment to lie secret in your heart, though not formed into a full conception, yet testified by your actions? No, you are much mistaken ; it is impossible but that I should see and know all things, since I am present with all things, and am not at a greater distance from the things on earth than from the things in heaven; for I fill all that vast fabric which is divided into those two parts of heaven and earth ; and he that hath such an infinite essence, cannot be distant, cannot be ignorant ; nothing can be far from his eyes, since everything is so near to his essence. So that it is an elegant expression of the omniscience of God, and a strong argument for it. He asserts, first, the universality of his knowledge ; but lest they should mistake, and confine his presence only to heaven, he adds, That he " fills heaven and earth." I do not see things so, as if I were in one place, and the things seen in another, as it is with man ; but whatsoever I see, I see not without myself, because every corner of heaven and earth is filled by me. He that fills all, must needs see and know all. And indeed, men that question the knowledge of God, would be more convinced by the doctrine of his immediate presence with them. And this seems to be the design and manner of arguing in this place. Nothing is remote from my knowledge, because nothing is distant from my presence.

I fill heaven and earth : he doth not say, "I am in heaven and earth," but I *fill* heaven and earth ;" *i. e.* say some, with my knowledge, others, with my authority or my power.[h] But,

1. The word *filling* cannot properly be referred to the act of understanding and will. A presence by knowledge is to be granted, but to say such a presence fills a place is an improper speech : knowledge is not enough to constitute a presence. A man at London knows there is such a city as Paris, and knows many things in it ; can he be concluded, therefore, to be present in Paris, or fill any place there, or be present with the things he knows there? If I know anything to be distant from me, how can it be present with me? For by knowing it to be distant, I know it not to be present. Besides, filling heaven and earth is distinguished here from knowing or seeing : his presence is rendered as an argument to prove his knowledge. Now a proposition, and the proof of that proposition, are distinct, and not the same. It cannot be imagined that God should prove *idem per idem,* as we say ; for what would be the import of the speech then ? I know all things, I see all things, because

h Tum perspicacia, tum efficacia, Grot.

I know and see all things.[i] The Holy Ghost here accommodates himself to the capacity of men ; because we know that a man sees and knows that which is done, where he is corporally present; so he proves that God knows all things that are done in the most secret caverns of the heart, because he is everywhere in heaven and earth, as light is everywhere in the air, and air everywhere in the world. Hence the schools use the term *repletive* for the presence of God.

2. Nor by filling of heaven and earth is meant his authority and power. It would be improperly said of a king, that in regard of the government of his kingdom, is everywhere by his authority, that he fills all the cities and countries of his dominions. " I, do not I fill ?"[k] That " I " notes the essence of God, as distinguished according to our capacity, from the perfections pertaining to his essence, and is in reason better referred to the substance of God, than to those things we conceive as attributes in him. Besides, were it meant only of his authority or power, the argument would not run well. I see all things, because my authority and power fills heaven and earth. Power doth not always rightly infer knowledge, no, not in a rational agent. Many things in a kingdom are done by the authority of the king, that never arrive to the knowledge of the king. Many things in us are done by the power of our souls, which yet we have not a distinct knowledge of in our understandings. There are many motions in sleep, by the virtue of the soul informing the body, that we have not so much as a simple knowledge of in our minds. Knowledge is not rightly inferred from power, or power from knowledge. By filling heaven and earth is meant, therefore, a filling it with his essence. No place can be imagined that is deprived of the presence of God; and therefore when the Scripture anywhere speaks of the presence of God, it joins heaven and earth together : He so fills them, that there is no place without him. We do not say a vessel is full so long as there is any space to contain more. Not a part of heaven, nor a part of earth, but the whole heaven, the whole earth, at one and the same time. If he were only in one part of heaven, or one part of earth ; nay, if there were any part of heaven, or any part of earth void of him, he could not be said to fill them. " I fill heaven and earth," not a part of me fills one place, and another part of me fills another, but I, God, fill heaven and earth ; I am whole God filling the heaven, and whole God, filling the earth. I fill heaven, and yet fill earth; I fill earth, and yet fill heaven, and fill heaven and earth at one and the same time. " God fills his own works," a heathen philosopher saith.[l]

I. Here is then a description of God's presence. 1. By power, " Am I not a God afar off?" a God in the extension of his arm. 2. By knowledge, " Shall I not see them ?" 3. By essence ; as an undeniable ground for inferring the two former : " I fill heaven and earth."

Doctrine. God is essentially everywhere present in heaven and earth. If God be, he must be somewhere ; that which is nowhere, is nothing. Since God is, he is in the world ; not in one part of it ; for

i Suarez.   k Amirald. de Trinitate, p. 57.
l Seneca de Benefic. lib. 4. c. 8. Ipse opus suum implet.

then he were circumscribed by it: if in the world, and only there, though it be a great space, he were also limited. Some therefore said, "God was everywhere, and nowhere."[m] Nowhere, *i. e.* not bounded by any place, nor receiving from any place anything for his preservation or sustainment. He is everywhere, because no creature, either body or spirit, can exclude the presence of his essence; for he is not only near, but in everything (Acts xvii. 28): "In him we live, and move, and have our being." Not absent from anything, but so present with them, that they live and move in him, and move more in God, than in the air or earth wherein they are; nearer to us than our flesh to our bones, than the air to our breath; he cannot be far from them that live, and have every motion in him. The apostle doth not say, By him, but in him, to show the inwardness of his presence. As eternity is the perfection whereby he hath neither beginning nor end, immutability is the perfection whereby he hath neither increase nor diminution, so immensity or omnipresence is that whereby he hath neither bounds nor limitation. As he is in all time, yet so as to be above time; so is he in all places, yet so as to be above limitation by any place. It was a good expression of a heathen to illustrate this, "That God is a sphere or circle, whose centre is everywhere, and circumference nowhere." His meaning was, that the essence of God was indivisible; *i. e.* could not be divided. It cannot be said, here and there the lines of it terminate; it is like a line drawn out in infinite spaces, that no point can be conceived where its length and breadth ends. The sea is a vast mass of waters; yet to that it is said, "Hitherto shalt thou go, and no further." But it cannot be said of God's essence, hitherto it reaches, and no further; here it is, and there it is not. It is plain, that God is thus immense, because he is infinite; we have reason and Scripture to assent to it, though we cannot conceive it. We know that God is eternal, though eternity is too great to be measured by the short line of a created understanding. We cannot conceive the vastness and glory of the heavens, much less that which is so great, as to fill heaven and earth, yea (1 Kings viii. 27), "not to be contained in the heaven of Heavens." Things are said to be present, or in a place,

1. Circumscriptive, as circumscribed. This belongs to things that have quantity, as bodies that are encompassed by that place wherein they are; and a body fills but one particular space wherein it is, and the space is commensurate to every part of it, and every member hath a distinct place. The hand is not in the same particular space that the foot or head is.

2. Definitive, which belongs to angels and spirits, which are said to be in a point, yet so as that they cannot be said to be in another at the same time.

3. *Repletive*, filling all places. This belongs only to God: as he is not measured by time, so he is not limited by place. A body or spirit, because finite, fills but one space; God, because infinite, fills all, yet so as not to be contained in them, as wine and water is in a vessel. He is from the height of the heavens to the bottom of the deeps, in

[m] Chrysostom.

every point of the world, and in the whole circle of it, yet not limited by it, but beyond it. Now this hath been acknowledged by the wisest in the world. Some indeed had other notions of God. The more ignorant sort of the Jews confined him to the temple.[n] And God intimates, that they had such a thought when he asserts his presence in heaven and earth, in opposition to the temple they built as his house, and the place of his rest.[o] And the idolaters among them, thought their gods might be at a distance from them, which Elias intimates in the scoff he puts upon them (1 Kings xviii. 17), "Cry aloud, for he is a god," meaning Baal; "either he is talking, or he is pursuing, or he is in a journey;" and they followed his advice, and cried louder (ver. 28), whereby it is evident, they looked not on it as a mock, but as a truth. And the Syrians called the God of Israel the God of the hills, as though his presence were fixed there, and not in the valleys (1 Kings xx. 23); and their own gods in the valleys, and not in the mountains; they fancied every god to have a particular dominion and presence in one place and not in another, and bounded the territories of their gods as they did those of their princes.[p] And some thought him tied to and shut up in their temples and groves wherein they worshipped him.[q] Some of them thought God to be confined to heaven, and therefore sacrificed upon the highest mountains, that the steam might ascend nearer heaven, and their praises be heard better in those places which were nearest to the habitation of God. But the wiser Jews acknowledged it, and therefore called God place,[r] whereby they denoted his immensity; he was not contained in any place; every part of the world subsists by Him: he was a place to himself, greater than anything made by Him. And the wiser heathens acknowledged it also. One calls God a mind passing through the universal nature of things;[s] another, that He was an infinite and immense air;[t] another, that it is as natural to think God is everywhere, as to think that God is: hence they called God the soul of the world; that as the soul is in every part of the body to quicken it, so is God in every part of the world to support it. And there are some resemblances of this in the world, though no creature can fully resemble God in any one perfection; for then it would not be a creature, but God. But air and light are some resemblances of it: air is in all the spaces of the world, in the pores of all bodies, in the bowels of the earth, and extends itself from the lowest earth to the highest regions; and the heavens themselves are probably nothing else but a refined kind of air; and light diffuseth itself through the whole air, and every part of it is truly light, as every part of the air is truly air; and though they seem to be mingled together, yet they are distinct things, and not of the same essence; so is the essence of God in the whole world, not by diffusion as air or light, not mixed with any creature, but remaining distinct from the essence of any created being. Now, when this hath been owned by men instructed only in the school of nature, it is a greater

---

[n] Hierom. on Isa. lxvi. 1.

[p] Med. Diatrib. Vol. I. pp. 71, 72.

[r] מקום Grot. upon Matt. v. 16. Mares. contra Volk. lib. i. cap. 27. p. 494.

[s] Vide Minut. Fel. p. 20.

[o] Hammond on Matt. vi. 7.

[q] Dought Analec. excurs. 61, 113.

[t] Plotin. Enead. 6. lib. 5. cap. 4.

shame to any acquainted with the Scripture to deny. For the understanding of this, there shall be some propositions premised in general.

Prop. I. This is negatively to be understood. Our knowledge of God is most by withdrawing from him, or denying to him in our conceptions any weaknesses or imperfections in the creature. As the infiniteness of God is a denial of limitation of being, so immensity or omnipresence is a denial of limitation of place: and when we say, God is *totus* in every place, we must understand it thus; that he is not everywhere by parts, as bodies are, as air and light are; He is everywhere, *i. e.* his nature hath no bounds; he is not tied to any place, as the creature is, who, when he is present in one place, is absent from another. As no place can be without God, so no place can compass and contain him.

Prop. II. There is an influential omnipresence of God.

1. Universal with all creatures. He is present with all things by his authority, because all things are subject to him: by his power, because all things are sustained by him: by his knowledge, because all things are naked before him. He is present in the world, as a king is in all parts of his kingdom regally present: providentially present with all, since his care extends to the meanest of his creatures. His power reacheth all, and his knowledge pierceth all. As everything in the world was created by God, so everything in the world is preserved by God; and since preservation is not wholly distinct from creation, it is necessary God should be present with everything while he preserves it, as well as present with it when he created it. "Thou preservest man and beast" (Ps. xxxvi. 6). "He upholds all things by the word of his power" (Heb. i. 3). There is a virtue sustaining every creature, that it may not fall back into that nothing from whence it was elevated by the power of God. All those natural virtues we call the principles of operation, are fountains springing from his goodness and power; all things are acted and managed by him, as well as preserved by him; and in this sense God is present with all creatures; for whatsoever acts another, is present with that which it acts, by sending forth some virtue and influence whereby it acts: if free agents do not only live, but move in him and by him (Acts xvii. 28), much more are the motions of other natural agents by a virtue communicated to them, and upheld in them in the time of their acting. This virtual presence of God is evident to our sense, a presence we feel; his essential presence is evident in our reason. This influential presence may be compared to that of the sun, which though at so great a distance from the earth, is present in the air and earth by its light, and within the earth by its influence in concocting those metals which are in the bowels of it, without being substantially either of them. God is thus so intimate with every creature, that there is not the least particle of any creature, but the marks of his power and goodness are seen in it, and his goodness doth attend them, and is more swift in its effluxes than the breakings out of light from the sun, which yet are more swift than can be declared; but to say he is in the world only by his virtue, is to acknowledge only the effects of his power and wisdom in the world,

that his eye sees all, his arm supports all, his goodness nourisheth all, but himself and his essence at a distance from them ;[u] and so the soul of man according to its measure would have in some kind a more excellent manner of presence in the body, than God according to the infiniteness of his Being with his creatures; for that doth not only communicate life to the body, but is actually present with it, and spreads its whole essence through the body and every member of it. All grant, that God is efficaciously in every creek of the world; but some say he is only substantially in heaven.

2. Limited to such subjects that are capacitated for this or that kind of presence. Yet it is an omnipresence, because it is a presence in all the subjects capacitated for it; thus there is a special providential presence of God with some in assisting them when he sets them on work as his instruments for some special service in the world. As with Cyrus (Isa. xlv. 2), "I will go before thee ;" and with Nebuchadnezzar and Alexander, whom he protected and directed to execute his counsels in the world ; such a presence Judas and others[x] that shall not enjoy his glorious presence, had in the working of miracles in the world. Besides,[y] as there is an effective presence of God with all creatures, because he produced them and preserves them, so there is an objective presence of God with rational creatures, because he offers himself to them to be known and loved by them. He is near to wicked men in the offers of his grace, "Call ye upon him while he is near" (Isa. lv. 6); besides, there is a gracious presence of God with his people in whom he dwells and makes his abode, as in a temple consecrated to him by the graces of the Spirit. "We will come" (John xiv. 23), i. e. the Father and the Son, and make our abode with him. He is present with all by the presence of his Divinity, but only in his saints by a presence of a gracious efficacy ; he walks in the midst of the golden candlesticks, and hath dignified the congregation of his people with the title of Jehovah Shammah, "the Lord is there" (Ezek. xlviii. 35): " in Salem is his tabernacle, and his dwelling-place in Sion" (Ps. lxxvi. 2). As he filled the tabernacle, so he doth the church with the signs of his presence ; this is not the presence wherewith he fills heaven and earth. His Spirit is not bestowed upon all to reside in their hearts, enlighten their minds, and bedew them with refreshing comforts. When the Apostle speaks of God being " above all and through all" (Eph. iv. 6), above all in his majesty, through all in his providence ; he doth not appropriate that as he doth what follows, " and in you all ;" in you all by a special grace ; as God was specially present with Christ by the grace of union, so he is specially present with his people by the grace of regeneration. So there are several manifestations of his presence ; he hath a presence of glory in heaven, whereby he comforts the saints ; a presence of wrath in hell, whereby he torments the damned ; in heaven he is a God spreading his beams of light ; in hell, a God distributing his strokes of justice ; by the one he fills heaven ; by the other he fills hell ; by his providence and essence he fills both heaven and earth.

● Zanch.   ✗ Matt. vii. 22. " In thy name we have done many wonderful works."
ʸ Cajetan in Aquin. Par. i. Qu. 8. Art. 3.

Prop. III. There is an essential presence of God in the world. He is not only everywhere by his power upholding the creatures, by his wisdom understanding them, but by his essence containing them. That anything is essentially present anywhere, it hath from God; God is therefore much more present everywhere, for he cannot give that which he hath not.

1. He is essentially present in all places.[z] It is as reasonable to think the essence of God to be everywhere as to be always. Immensity is as rational as eternity. That indivisible essence which reaches through all times may as well reach through all places. It is more excellent to be always than to be everywhere; for to be always in duration is intrinsical; to be everywhere is intrinsic. If the greater belongs to God, why not the less? As all times are a moment to his eternity, so all places are as a point to his essence. As he is larger than all time, so he is vaster than all place. The nations of the world are to him "as the dust of the balance" or "drop of a bucket" (Isa. xl. 15). "The nations are accounted as the small dust." The essence of God may well be thought to be present everywhere with that which is no more than a grain of dust to him, and in all those isles, which, if put together, "are a very little thing" in his hand. Therefore, saith a learned Jew,[a] if a man were set in the highest heavens he would not be nearer to the essence of God than if he were in the centre of the earth. Why may not the presence of God in the world be as noble as that of the soul in the body, which is generally granted to be essentially in every part of the body of man, which is but a little world, and animates every member by its actual presence, though it exerts not the same operation in every part?[b] The world is less to the Creator than the body to the soul, and needs more the presence of God than the body needs the presence of the soul. That glorious body of the sun visits every part of the habitable earth in twenty-four hours by its beams, which reaches the troughs of the lowest valleys as well as the pinnacles of the highest mountains; must we not acknowledge in the Creator of this sun an infinite greater proportion of presence? Is it not as easy, with the essence of God, to overspread the whole body of heaven and earth as it is for the sun to pierce and diffuse itself through the whole air, between it and the earth, and send up its light also as far to the regions above? Do we not see something like it in sounds and voices? Is not the same sound of a trumpet, or any other musical instrument, at the first breaking out of a blast, in several places within such a compass at the same time? Doth not every ear that hears it receive alike the whole sound of it? And fragrant odors, scented in several places at the same time, in the same manner; and the organ proper for smelling takes in the same in every person within the compass of it. How far is the noise of thunder heard alike to every ear in places something distant from one another! And do we daily find such a manner of presence in those things of so low a concern, and not imagine a kind of presence of God greater than all those? Is the sound of thunder, the voice of God as it is called, everywhere in such a compass? and shall not the essence of

[z] Ficin.   [a] Maimonid.   [b] Ficin.

an infinite God be much more everywhere ?   Those that would confine the essence of God only to heaven, and exclude it from the
earth, run into great inconveniences.   It may be demanded whether
he be in one part of the heavens or in the whole vast body of them.
If in one part of them, his essence is bounded ; if he moves from that
part he is mutable, for he changes a place wherein he was, for another
wherein he was not.   If he be always fixed in one part of the
heavens, such a notion would render him little better than a living
statue.[c]   If he be in the whole heaven, why cannot his essence possess a greater space than the whole heavens, which are so vast ?
How comes he to be confined within the compass of that, since the
whole heaven compasseth the earth ?   If he be in the whole heaven
he is in places farther distant one from another than any part of the
earth can be from the heavens ; since the earth is like a centre in
the midst of a circle, it must be nearer to every part of the circle
than some parts of the circle can be to one another.   If, therefore,
his essence possesses the whole heavens, no reason can be rendered
why he doth not also possess the earth, since also the earth is but a
little point in comparison of the vastness of the heavens: if, therefore, he be in every part of the heavens, why not in every part of
the earth ?   The Scripture is plain (Ps. cxxxix. 7–9), " Whither shall
I go from thy Spirit? or whither shall I fly from thy presence ?   If
I ascend up to heaven, thou art there ; if I make my bed in hell, behold thou art there ; if I take the wings of the morning, and dwell
in the uttermost parts of the sea, even there shall thy hand lead me,
and thy right hand shall uphold me."   If he be in heaven, earth,
hell, sea, he fills all places with his presence.   His presence is here
asserted in places the most distant from one another.   All the places
then between heaven and earth are possessed by his presence.   It is
not meant of his knowledge, for that the Psalmist had spoken of before (ver. 2, 3), " Thou understandest my thoughts afar off ; thou
art acquainted with all my ways :" besides, " thou art there ;" not
thy wisdom or knowledge, but thou, thy essence, not only thy virtue.
For, having before spoken of his omniscience, he proves that such
knowledge could not be in God, unless he were present in his essence
in all places, so as to be excluded from none.   He fills the depths of
hell, the extension of the earth, and the heights of the heavens.
When the Scripture mentions the power of God only, it expresseth
it by hand or arm ; but when it mentions the Spirit of God, and
doth not intend the Third Person in the Trinity, it signifies the
nature and essence of God.   And so here, when he saith, " Whither
shall I go from thy Spirit ?" he adds, exegetically, " Whither shall
I fly from thy presence ?" or (Heb.) " face :" and the face of God in
Scripture signifies the essence of God (Exod. xxxiii. 20, 23) ; " Thou
canst not see my face," and " My face shall not be seen."   The effects
of his power, wisdom, and providence are seen, which are his back
parts, but not his face.   The effects of his power and wisdom are
seen in the world, but his essence is invisible ; and this the Psalmist
elegantly expresseth, Had I wings endued with as much quickness
as the first dawnings of the morning light, or the first darts of any

          c Hornbeck Soun. Part I. p. 303.

sunbeam that spreads itself through the hemisphere, and passeth many miles in as short a space as I can think a thought, I should find thy presence in all places before me, and could not fly out of the infinite compass of thy essence.

2. " He is essentially present with all creatures." If he be in all places, it follows that he is with all creatures in those places; as he is in heaven, so he is with all angels; as he is in hell, so he is with all devils: as he is in the earth and sea, he is with all creatures inhabiting those elements; as his essential presence was the ground of the first being of things by creation, so it is the ground of the continued being of things by conservation; as his essential presence was the original, so it is the support of the existence of all the creatures. What are all those magnificent expressions of his creative virtue, but testimonies of his essential presence at the laying the foundation of the world (Isa. xl. 12), " when he measured the waters in the hollow of his hand, meted out heaven with the span, and comprehended the dust of the earth in a measure, and weighed the mountains in scales, and the hills in a balance?" He sets forth the power and majesty of God in the creation and preservation of things, and every expression testifies his presence with them. The waters that were upon the face of the earth at first were no more than a drop in the palm of a man's hand, which in every part is touched by his hand; and thus he is equally present with the blackest devils, as well as the brightest angels; with the lowest dust, as well as with the most sparkling sun. He is equally present with the damned and the blessed, as he is an infinite Being, but not in regard of his goodness and grace. He is equally present with the good and the bad, with the scoffing Athenians, as well as the believing apostles, in regard of his essence, but not in regard of the breathing of his divine virtues upon them to make them like himself (Acts xvii. 27). " He is not far from every one of us; for in him we live, and move, and have our being." The apostle includes all; he tells them they should seek the Lord; the Lord that they were to seek, is God essentially considered. We are, indeed, to seek the perfections of God, that glitter in his works, but to the end that they should direct us to the seeking of God himself in his own nature and essence;[d] and, therefore, what follows, " In him we live," is to be understood, not of his power and goodness, perfections of his nature, distinguished according to our manner of conception from his essence, but of the essential presence of God with his creatures. If he had meant it of his efficacy in preserving us, it had not been any proof of his nearness to us. Who would go about to prove the body or substance of the sun to be near us because it doth warm and enlighten us, when our sense evidenceth the distance of it? We live in the beams of the sun, but we cannot be said to live in the sun, which is so far distant from us. The expression seems to be more emphatical than to intend any less than his essential presence; but we live in him not only as the efficient cause of our life, but as the foundation sustaining our lives and motions, as if he were like air, diffused round about us; and we move in him, as Austin saith, as a sponge in the

<hr>

d Amyrald. de Trinit.

sea, not containing him, but being contained by him. He compass-eth all, is encompassed by none; he fills all, is comprehended by none. The Creator contains the world, the world contains not the Creator; as the hollow of the hand contains the water, the water in the hollow of the hand contains not the hand; and therefore some have chose to say, rather, that the world is in God, it lives and moves in him, than that God is in the world. If all things thus live and move in him, then he is present with everything that hath life and motion; and as long as the devils and damned have life, and motion, and being, so long is he with them; for whatsoever lives and moves, lives and moves in him. This essential presence is,

(1) Without any mixture. I fill heaven and earth; not, I am mixed with heaven and earth: his essence is not mixed with the creatures; it remains entire in itself. The sponge retains the nature of a sponge, though encompassed by the sea, and moving in it; and the sea still retains its own nature. God is most simple; his essence therefore is not mixed with anything. The light of the sun is present with the air, but not mixed with it; it remains light, and the air remains air; the light of the sun is diffused through all the hemis-phere, it pierceth all transparent bodies, it seems to mix itself with all things, yet remains unmixed and undivided; the light remains light, and the air remains air; the air is not light, though it be en-lightened. Or, take this similitude: When many candles are lighted up in a room, the light is all together, yet not mixed with one an-other; every candle hath a particular light belonging to it, which may be separated in a moment, by removing one candle from another; but if they were mixed, they could not be separated, at least so easily. God is not formally one with the world, or with any creature in the world by his presence in it; nor can any creature in the world, no, not the soul of man, or an angel, come to be essentially one with God, though God be essentially present with it.

(2.) The essential presence is without any division of himself. "I fill heaven and earth," not part in heaven, and part in earth; I fill one as well as the other: one part of his essence is not in one place, and another part of his essence in another place, he would then be changeable; for that part of his essence which were now in this place, he might alter it to another, and place that part of his essence which were in another place to this; but he is undivided everywhere. As his eternity is one indivisible point, though in our conception we divide it into past, present, and to come, so the whole world is as a point to him, in regard of place, as before was said; it is as a small dust, and grain of dust: it is impossible that one part of his essence can be separated from another, for he is not a body, to have one part separable from another. The light of the sun cannot be cut into parts, it cannot be shut into any place and kept there, it is entire in every place. Shall not God, who gives the light that power, be much more present himself? Whatsoever hath parts is finite, but God is infinite, therefore hath no parts of his essence. Besides, if there were such a division of his being, he would not be the most simple and uncompounded being, but would be made up of various parts; he would not be a Spirit, for parts are evidences of composition; and it could not be said that God is here or there, but only a part of God here, and a part of God there. But he fills heaven and earth; he is as much a God in the earth beneath as in heaven above (Deut. iv. 39); entirely in all places, not by scraps and fragments of his essence.

(3.) This essential presence is not by multiplication. For that which is infinite cannot multiply itself, or make itself more or greater than it was.

(4.) This essential presence is not by extension or diffusion, as a piece of gold may be beaten out to cover a large compass of ground; no, if God should create millions of worlds he would be in them all, not by stretching out his being, but by the infiniteness of his being; not by a new growth of his being, but by the same essence he had from eternity: upon the same reasons mentioned before, his simplicity and indivisibility.

(5.) But totally. There is no space, not the least, wherein God is not wholly, according to his essence, and wherein his whole substance doth not exist; not a part of heaven can be designed wherein the Creator is not wholly; as he is in one part of heaven, he is in every part of heaven. Some kind of resemblance we may have from the water of the sea, which fills the great space of the world, and is diffused through all; yet the essence of water is in every drop of water in the sea, as much as the whole; and the same quality of water, though it comes short in quantity; and why shall we not allow God a nobler way of presence without diffusion, as is in that? or take this resemblance; since God likens himself to light in the Scripture, " he covereth himself with light."[e] A crystal globe hung up in the air hath light all about it, all within it, every part is pierced by it, wherever you see the crystal you see the light; the light in one part of the crystal cannot be distinguished from the light in the other part; and the whole essence of light is in every part; and shall not God be as much present with his creatures, as one creature can be with another?[f] God is totally everywhere by his own simple substance.

Prop. IV. God is present beyond the world. He is within and above all places, though places should be infinite in number; as he was before and beyond all time, so he is above and beyond all place; being from eternity before any real time, he must also be without as well as within any real space; if God were only confined to the world, he would be no more infinite in his essence than the world is in quantity; as a moment cannot be conceived from eternity, wherein God was not in being, so a space cannot be conceived in the mind of man, wherein God is not present; he is not contained in the world nor in the heavens (1 Kings viii. 27). " But will God indeed dwell on the earth? Behold, the heaven of heavens cannot contain thee." Solomon wonders that God should appoint a temple to be erected to him upon the earth, when he is not contained in the vast circuit of the heavens; his essence is not straitened in the limits of any created work; he is not contained in the heavens, *i. e.* in the manner that he is there; but he is there in his essence, and therefore cannot be con-

---

• Ps. civ. 2. John i. 5. " God is light, and in him is no darkness at all. ᶠ Bernard.

tained there in his essence. If it should be meant only of his power and providence, it would conclude also for his essence; if his power and providence were infinite, his essence must be so too; for the infiniteness of his essence is the ground of the infiniteness of his power. It can never enter into any thought, that a finite essence can have an infinite power, and that an infinite power can be without an infinite essence; it cannot be meant of his providence, as if Solomon should say, the heaven of heavens cannot contain thy providence; for naming the heaven of heavens, that which encircles and bounds the other parts of the world, he could not suppose a providence to be exercised where there was no object to exercise it about; as no creature is mentioned to be beyond the uttermost heaven, which he calls here the heaven of heavens: besides, to understand it of his providence, doth not consist with Solomon's admiration : he wonders that God, that hath so immense an essence, should dwell in a temple made with hands ; he could not so much wonder at his providence in those things that immediately concern his worship. Solomon plainly asserts this of God, That he was so far from being bounded within the rich wall of the temple, which with so much cost he had framed for the glory of his name, that the richer palace of the heaven of heavens could not contain him; it is true, it could not contain his power and wisdom, because his wisdom could contrive other kind of worlds, and his power erect them. But doth the meaning of that wise king reach no farther than this ? Will the power and wisdom of God reside on the earth ? He was too wise to ask such a question, since every object that his eyes met with in the world resolved him, that the wisdom and power of God dwelt upon the earth, and glittered in everything he had created ; and reason would assure him that the power that had framed this world, was able to frame any more; but Solomon, considering the immensity of God's essence, wonders that God should order a house to be built for him, as if he wanted roofs and coverings, and habitation, as bodily creatures do. Will God indeed dwell in a temple, who hath an essence so immense as not to be contained in the heaven of heavens? It is not the heaven of heavens that can contain him, his substance. Here he asserts the immensity of his essence, and his presence not only in the heaven, but beyond the heavens ; he that is not contained in the heavens, as a man is in a chamber, is without, and above, and beyond the heavens; it is not said, they do not contain him, but it is impossible they should contain him ; they cannot contain him. It is impossible, then, but that he should be above them ; he that is without the compass of the world, is not bounded by the limits of the world, as his power is not limited by the things he hath made, but can create innumerable worlds, so can his essence be in innumerable spaces; for as he hath power enough to make more worlds, so he hath essence enough to fill them, and therefore cannot be confined to what he hath already created ; innumerable worlds cannot be a sufficient place to contain God ; he can only be a sufficient place to himself ;[g] He that was before the world, and place, and all things, was to himself a world, a place, and everything :[h] He is really out

     [g] Petar.   [h] Maccor. loc. commun. cap. 19, p. 153.

of the world in himself, as he was in himself before the creation of the world: as because God was before the foundation of the world, we conclude his eternity; so because he is without the bounds of the world, we conclude his immensity, and from thence his omnipresence. The world cannot be said to contain him, since it was created by him; it cannot contain him now, who was contained by nothing before the world was: as there was no place to contain him before the world was, there can be no place to contain him since the world was. God might create more worlds, circular and round as this, and those could not be so contiguous, but some spaces would be left between; as, take three round balls, lay them as close as you can to one another, there will be some spaces between; none would say but God would be in these spaces, as well as in the world he had created, though there were nothing real and positive in those spaces: why should we then exclude God from those imaginary spaces without the world? God might also create many worlds, and separate them by distances, that they might not touch one another, but be at a great distance from one another; and would not God fill them as well as he doth this? if so, he must also fill the spaces between them; for if he were in all those worlds, and not in the spaces between those worlds, his essence would be divided; there would be gaps in it, his essence would be cut into parts, and the distance between every part of his essence, would be as great as the space between each world. The essence of God may be conceived then well enough to be in all those infinite spaces where he can erect new worlds.

I shall give one place more to prove both these propositions, viz. that God is essentially in every part of the world, and essentially above ours without the world (Isa. lxvi. 1): "The heaven is my throne, and the earth is my footstool." He is essentially in every part of the world; he is in heaven and earth at the same time, as a man is upon his throne and his footstool. God describes himself in a human shape, accommodated to our capacity; as if he had his head in heaven, and his feet on earth. Doth not his essence then, fill all intermediate spaces between heaven and earth? As when the head of a man is in the upper part of a room, and his feet upon the floor, his body fills up the space between the head and his feet: this is meant of the essence of God; it is a similitude drawn from kings sitting upon the throne, and not their power and authority, but the feet of their persons are supported by the footstool; so here it is not meant only of the perfections of God, but the essence of God. Besides, God seems to tax them with an erroneous conceit they had, as though his essence were in the temple, and not in any part of the world; therefore God makes an opposition between heaven and earth, and the temple: "Where is the house that you built unto me? and where is the place of my rest?" Had he understood it only of his providence, it had not been anything against their mistake; for they granted his providence to be not only in the temple, but in all parts of the world. "Where is the house that you build to me;" to Me, not to my power or providence, but think to include Me within those walls. Again, it shows God to be above the heavens, if the heavens be his throne; he sits upon them, and is above them, as kings are above the thrones on which they sit. So it cannot be meant of his providence, because no creature being without the sphere of the heavens, there is nothing of the power and the providence of God visible there, for there is nothing for him to employ his providence about; for providence supposeth a creature in actual being; it must be therefore meant of his essence, which is above the world and in the world. And the like proof you may see (Job. xi. 7, 8), "It is as high as heaven, what canst thou do? deeper than hell, what canst thou know? the measure thereof is longer than the earth, and broader than the sea." Where he intends the unsearchableness of God's wisdom, but proves it by the infiniteness of his essence, (Heb.) "he is the height of the heavens," he is the top of all the heavens; so that, when you have begun at the lowest part, and traced him through all the creatures, you will find his essence filling all the creatures, to be at the top of the world, and infinitely beyond it.

Prop. V. This is the property of God, incommunicable to any creature. As no creature can be eternal and immutable, so no creature can be immense, because it cannot be infinite; nothing can be of an infinite nature, and therefore nothing of an immense presence but God. It cannot be communicated to the human nature of Christ, though in union with the Divine;[i] some indeed argue, that Christ in regard of his human nature is everywhere, because he sits at the right hand of God, and the right hand of God is everywhere. His sitting at the right hand of God signifies his exaltation, and cannot with any reason, be extended to such a kind of arguing. "The hearts of kings are in the hand of God;" are the hearts of kings everywhere, because God's hand is everywhere? The souls of the righteous are in the hand of God; is the soul, therefore, of every righteous man everywhere in the world? The right hand of God is from eternity; is the humanity of Christ, therefore, from eternity, because it sits at the right hand of God? The right hand of God made the world; did the humanity of Christ, therefore, make heaven and earth? the humanity of Christ must then be confounded with his divinity; be the same with it, not united to it. All creatures are distinct from their Creator, and cannot inherit the properties essential to his nature, as eternity, immensity, immutability, omnipresence, omniscience; no angel, no soul, no creature can be in all places at once; before they can be so they must be immense, and so must cease to be creatures, and commence God; this is impossible.

II. Reasons to prove God's essential presence. *Reason* I. Because he is infinite. As he is infinite, he is everywhere; as he is simple, his whole essence is everywhere: for, in regard of his infiniteness, he hath no bounds; in regard of his simplicity, he hath no parts: and, therefore, those that deny God's omnipresence, though they pretend to own him infinite, must really conceive him finite.

1. God is infinite in his perfections. None can set bounds to terminate the greatness and excellency of God (Ps. cxlv. 3): "His greatness is unsearchable," Sept. οὐκ ἔστι πέρας, there is no end, no limitation. What hath no end is infinite; his power is infinite (Job

[i] Rivet. Ps. cx. p. 301, col. 2.

v. 9): "which doth great things and unsearchable;"—no end of those things he is able to do. His wisdom infinite (Ps. cxlvii. 5); he understands all things past, present, and to come; what is already made, what is possible to be made. His duration infinite (Job xxxvi. 26): "The number of his years cannot be searched out," ἀπέραντος. To make a finite thing of nothing is an argument of an infinite virtue. Infinite power can only extract something out of the barren womb of nothing; but all things were drawn forth by the word of God, the heavens, and all the host of them; the sun, moon, stars, the rich embellishments of the world, appeared in being "at the breath of his mouth" (Ps. xxxiii. 6). The author, therefore, must be infinite; and since nothing is the cause of God, or of any perfection in him,— since he derives not his being, or the least spark of his glorious nature, from anything without him,—he cannot be limited in any part of his nature by anything without him; and, indeed, the infiniteness of his power and his other perfections is asserted by the prophet, when he tells us that "the nations are as a drop of a bucket, or the dust of the balance, and less than nothing and vanity" (Isa. xl. 15, 17), they are all so in regard of his power, wisdom, &c. Conceive what a little thing a grain of dust or sand is to all the dust that may be made by the rubbish of a house: what a little thing the heap of the rubbish of a house is to the vast heap of the rubbish of a whole city, such an one as London; how little that, also, would be to the dust of a whole empire; how inconsiderable that, also, to the dust of one quarter of the world, Europe or Asia; how much less that, still, to the dust of the whole world! The whole world is composed of an unconceivable number of atoms, and the sea of an unconceivable number of drops; now what a little grain of dust is in comparison to the dust of the whole world—a drop of water from the sea, to all the drops remaining in the sea—that is the whole world to God. Conceive it still less, a mere nothing, yet is it all less than this in comparison of God; there can be nothing more magnificently expressive of the infiniteness of God to a human conception, than this expression of God himself in the prophet. In the perfection of a creature, something still may be thought greater to be added to it; but God containing all perfections in himself formally, if they be mere perfections, and eminently, if they be but perfections in the creature, mixed with imperfection, nothing can be thought greater, and therefore every one of them is infinite.

2. If his perfections be infinite, his essence must be so. How God can have infinite perfections, and a finite essence, is unconceivable by a human or angelical understanding; an infinite power, an infinite wisdom, an infinite duration, must needs speak an infinite essence; since the infiniteness of his attributes is grounded upon the infiniteness of his essence: to own infinite perfections in a finite subject is contradictory. The manner of acting by his power, and knowing by his wisdom, cannot exceed the manner of being by his essence. His perfections flow from his essence, and the principle must be of the same rank with what flows from it; and, if we conceive his essence to be the cause of his perfections, it is utterly impossible that an infinite effect should arise from a finite cause: but, indeed, his

perfections are his essence; for though we conceive the essence of
God as the subject, and the attributes of God as faculties and qualities
in that subject, according to our weak model, who cannot conceive
of an infinite God without some manner of likeness to ourselves—
who find understanding, and will, and power in us distinct from our
substance; yet truly and really there is no distinction between his
essence and attributes; one is inseparable from the other. His power
and wisdom are his essence; and therefore to maintain God infinite
in the one, and finite in the other, is to make a monstrous god, and
have an unreasonable notion of the Deity; for there would be the
greatest disproportion in his nature, since there is no greater disproportion can possibly be between one thing and another than there
is between finite and infinite. God must not only then be compounded, but have parts of the greatest distance from one another
in nature; but God, being the most simple being without the least
composition, both must be equally infinite: if, then, his essence be
not infinite, his power and wisdom cannot be infinite, which is both
against scripture and reason. Again, how should his essence be
finite, and his perfections be infinite, since nothing out of himself
gave them either the one or the other?[k] Again, either the essence
can be infinite, or it cannot; if it cannot, there must be some cause
of that impossibility; that can be nothing without him, because
nothing without him can be as powerful as himself, much less too
powerful for him; nothing within him can be an enemy to his highest perfection; since he is necessarily what he is, he must be necessarily the most perfect being, and therefore necessarily infinite, since
to be something infinitely is a greater perfection than to be something finitely:[l] if he can be infinite he is infinite, otherwise he could
be greater than he is, and so more blessed and more perfect than he
is, which is impossible: for being the most perfect Being, to whom
nothing can be added, he must needs be infinite.

3. If, therefore, God have an infinite essence, he hath an infinite
presence. An infinite essence cannot be contained in a finite place,
as those things which are finite have a bounded space wherein they
are; so that which is infinite hath an unbounded space; for, as finite-
ness speaks limitedness, so infiniteness speaks unboundedness; and
if we grant to God an infinite duration, there is no difficulty in acknowledging an infinite presence: indeed, the infiniteness of God is
a property belonging to him in regard of time and place; he is
bounded by no place, and limited to no time. Again, infinite essence
may as well be everywhere, as infinite power reaches everything;
it may as well be present with every being, as infinite power in its
working may be present with nothing to bring it into being. Where
God works by his power, he is present in his essence; because his
power and his essence cannot be separated; and therefore his power,
wisdom, goodness, cannot be anywhere where his essence is not:
his essence cannot be severed from his power, nor his power from
his essence; for the power of God is nothing but God acting, and
the wisdom of God nothing but God knowing. As the power of God

k Amyrald de Trinitat. p. 89.
l Deus est actus parvus et nullam habet potentiam passivam.

is always, so is his essence—as the power of God is everywhere, so is his essence: whatsoever God is, he is alway, and everywhere. To confine him to a place, is to measure his essence; as to confine his actions, is to limit his power; his essence being no less infinite than his power and his wisdom, can be no more bounded than his power and wisdom; but they are not separable from his essence, yea, they are his essence. If God did not fill the whole world, he would be determined to some place, and excluded from others; and so his substance would have bounds and limits, and then something might be conceived greater than God; for we may conceive that a creature may be made by God of so vast a greatness as to fill the whole world, for the power of God is able to make a body that should take up the whole space between heaven and earth, and reach to every corner of it. But nothing can be conceived by any creature greater than God; he exceeds all things, and is exceeded by none. God, therefore, cannot be included in heaven, nor included in the earth; cannot be contained in either of them; for, if we should imagine them vaster than they are, yet still they would be finite; and if his essence were contained in them, it could be no more infinite than the world which contains it, as water is not of a larger compass than the vessel which contains it. If the essence of God were limited, either in the heavens or earth, it must needs be finite, as the heaven and earth are; but there is no proportion between finite and infinite; God, therefore, cannot be contained in them. If there were an infinite body, that must be everywhere; certainly, then, an infinite Spirit must be everywhere; unless we will account him finite, we can render no reason why he should not be in one creature as well as in another. If he be in heaven, which is his creature, why can he not be in the earth, which is as well his creature as the heavens?

Reason II. Because of the continual operation of God in the world. This was one reason which made the heathen believe that there was an infinite Spirit in the vast body of the world, acting in everything, and producing those admirable motions which we see everywhere in nature: that cause which acts in the most perfect manner, is also in the most perfect manner present with its effects.

God preserves all, and therefore is in all; the apostle thought it a good induction (Acts xvii. 27), "He is not far from us, for in him we live." *For* being as much as *because*, shows, that from his operation he concluded his real presence with all: it is not, His virtue is not far from every one of us, but He, his substance, himself; for, none that acknowledge a God will deny the absence of the virtue of God from any part of the world. He works in everything, everything lives and works in him; therefore he is present with all:[m] or rather, if things live, they are in God, who gives them life. If things live, God is in them, and gives them life; if things move, God is in them, and gives them motion; if things have any being, God is in them, and gives them being; if God withdraws himself, they presently lose their being, and therefore some have compared the creature to the impression of a seal upon the water, that cannot be preserved but by the presence of the seal. As his presence was actual

[m] Pont.

with what he created, so his presence is actual with what he preserves, since creation and preservation do so little differ; if God creates things by his essential presence, by the same he supports them; if his substance cannot be disjoined from his preserving power, his power and wisdom cannot be separated from his essence; where there are the marks of the one, there is the presence of the other; for it is by his essence that he is powerful and wise; no man can distinguish the one from the other in a simple being; God doth not preserve and act things by a virtue diffused from him. It may be demanded whether that virtue be distinct from God; if it be not, it is then the essence of God; if it be distinct it is a creature, and then it may be asked, how that virtue which preserves other things, is preserved itself; it must be ultimately resolved into the essence of God, or else there must be a running *in infinitum:* or else,[n] is that virtue of God a substance, or not? Is it endued with understanding, or not? If it hath understanding, how doth it differ from God? If it wants understanding, can any imagine that the support of the world, the guidance of all creatures, the wonders of nature, can be wrought, preserved, managed by a virtue that hath nothing of understanding in it? If it be not a substance, it can much less be able to produce such excellent operations as the preserving all the kinds of things in the world, and ordering them to perform such excellent ends; this virtue is, therefore, God himself—the infinite power and wisdom of God; and therefore, wheresoever the effects of these are seen in the world, God is essentially present: some creatures, indeed, act at a distance by a virtue diffused. But such a manner of acting comes from a limitedness of nature, that such a nature cannot be everywhere present and extend its substance to all parts. To act by a virtue, speaks the subject finite, and it is a part of indigence: kings act in their kindoms by ministers and messengers, because they cannot act otherwise; but God being infinitely perfect, works all things in all immediately (1 Cor. xii. 6). Illumination, sanctification, grace, &c., are the immediate works of God in the heart, and immediate agents are present with what they do: it is an argument of the greater perfection of a being, to know things immediately, which are done in several places, than to know them at the second hand by instruments; it is no less a perfection to be everywhere, rather than to be tied to one place of action, and to act in other places by instruments, for want of a power to act immediately itself. God, indeed, acts by means and second causes in his providential dispensations in the world, but this is not out of any defect of power to work all immediately himself; but he thereby accommodates his way of acting to the nature of the creature, and the order of things which he hath settled in the world. And when he works by means, he acts with those means, in those means, sustains their faculties and virtues in them, concurs with them by his power; so that God's acting by means doth rather strengthen his essential presence than weaken it, since there is a necessary dependence of the creatures upon the Creator in their being and acting; and what they are, they are by the power of God; what they act, they act in the power of God, concurring

* Amyrald de Trinitat, p. 106, 107.

with them; they have their motion in him as well as their being; and where the power of God is, his essence is, because they are inseparable; and so this omnipresence ariseth from the simplicity of the nature of God; the more vast anything is, the less confined. All that will acknowledge God so great, as to be able to work all things by his will, without an essential presence, cannot imagine him upon the same reason, so little as to be contained in, and bounded by any place.

Reason III. Because of his supreme perfection. No perfection is wanting to God; but an unbounded essence is a perfection; a limited one is an imperfection. Though it be a perfection in a man to be wise, yet it is an imperfection that his wisdom cannot rule all the things that concern him; though it be a perfection to be present in a place where his affairs lie, yet is it an imperfection that he cannot be present everywhere in the midst of all his concerns; if any man could be so, it would be universally owned as a prime perfection in him above others: is that which would be a perfection in man to be denied to God?[o] as that which hath life is more perfect than that which hath not life; and that which hath sense is more perfect than that which hath only life as the plants have; and what hath reason, is more perfect than that which hath only life and sense, as the beasts have; so what is everywhere, is more perfect than that which is bounded in some narrow confines: if a power of motion be more excellent than to be bed-rid, and swiftness in a creature be a more excellent endowment than to be slow and snail-like, then to be everywhere without motion, is inconceivably a greater excellency than to be everywhere successively by motion. God sets forth his readiness to help his people and punish his enemies, or his omnipresence, by swiftness, or "flying upon the wings of the wind" (Ps. xviii. 10): the wind is in every part of the air, where it blows; it cannot be said that it is in this or that point of the air where you feel it, so as to exclude it from another part of the air where you are not; it seems to possess all at once. If the Divine essence had any bounds of place, it would be imperfect, as well as if it had bounds of time; where anything hath limitation, it hath some defect in being; and therefore if God were confined or concluded, he would be as good as nothing in regard of infiniteness. Whence should this restraint arise? there is no power above him to restrain him to a certain space; if so, then he would not be God, but that power which restrained him would be God: not from his own nature, for the being everywhere implies no contradiction to his nature; if his own nature determined him to a certain place, then if he removed from that place, he would act against his nature; to conceive any such thing of God is highly absurd. It cannot be thought God should voluntarily impose any such restraint or confinement upon himself; this would be to deny himself a perfection he might have; if God have not this perfection, it is either because it is inconsistent with his nature; or, because he cannot have it; or, because he will not. The former cannot be; for if he hath impressed upon air and light a resemblance of his excellency, to diffuse themselves and fill so vast a space, is such an excel-

[o] Amyrald de Trinitat, p. 74, 75.

lency inconsistent with the Creator more than the creature? whatsoever perfection the creature hath, is eminently in God. "Understand, O ye brutish among the people: and ye fools, when will you be wise? He that planted the ear, shall he not hear? he that formed the eye, shall he not see? he that teacheth man knowledge, shall not he know?" (Ps. xciv. 8, 9.) By the same reason he that hath given such a power to those creatures, air and light, shall not he be much more filling all spaces of the world? It is so clear a rule, that the Psalmist fixes a folly and brutishness upon those that deny it; it is not therefore inconsistent with his nature, it were not then a perfection but an imperfection; but whatsoever is an excellency in creatures, cannot in a way of eminency be an imperfection in God; if it be then a perfection, and God want it, it is because he cannot have it; where, then, is his power? How can he be then the fountain of his own Being? If he will not, where is his love to his own nature and glory? since no creature would deny that to itself which it can have, and is an excellency to it; God, therefore, hath not only a power or fitness to be everywhere, but he is actually everywhere.

Reason IV. Because of his immutability. If God did not fill all the spaces of heaven and earth, but only possess one, yet it must be acknowledged that God hath a power to move himself to another. It were absurd to fix God in a part of the heavens, like a star in an orb, without a power of motion to another place. If he be therefore essentially in heaven, may he not be upon the earth if he please, and transfer his substance from one place to another? to say he cannot, is to deny him a perfection which he hath bestowed upon his creatures; the angels, his messengers, are sometimes in heaven, sometimes on the earth; the eagles, meaner creatures, are sometimes in the air out of sight, sometimes upon the earth. If he doth move, therefore, and recede from one place and settle in another, doth he not declare himself mutable by changing places?—by being where he was not before, and in not being where he was before? He would not fill heaven and earth at once, but successively; no man can be said to fill a room, that moves from one part of a room to another; if therefore any in their imaginations stake God to the heavens, they render him less than his creatures; if they allow him a power of motion from one place to another, they conceive him changeable; and in either of them they own him no greater than a finite and limited Being; limited to heaven, if they fix him there; limited to that space to which they imagine him to move.

Reason V. Because of his omnipotency. The Almightiness of God is a notion settled in the minds of all,—that God can do whatsoever he pleases, everything that is not against the purity of his nature, and doth not imply a contradiction in itself; he can therefore create millions of worlds greater than this; and millions of heavens greater than this heaven he hath already created; if so, he is then in inconceivable spaces beyond this world, for his essence is not less narrower than his power; and his power is not to be thought of a further extent than his essence; he cannot be excluded therefore from those vast spaces where his power may fix those worlds if he please; if so, it is no wonder that he should fill this world: and there is no reason to exclude God from the narrow space of this world, that is not contained in infinite spaces beyond the world. God is wheresoever he hath a power to act; but he hath a power to act everywhere in the world, everywhere out of the world; he is therefore everywhere in the world, everywhere out of the world. Before this world was made, he had a power to make it in the space where now it stands; was he not then unlimitedly where the world now is, before the world received a being by his powerful word? Why should he not then be in every part of the world now? Can it be thought that God who was immense before, should, after he had created the world, contract himself to the limits of one of his creatures, and tie himself to a particular place of his own creation, and be less after his creation than he was before? This might also be prosecuted by an argument from his eternity. What is eternal in duration, is immense in essence; the same reason which renders him eternal, renders him immense; that which proves him to be always, will prove him to be everywhere.

III. The third thing is, Propositions for the further clearing this doctrine from any exceptions.

1. This truth is not weakened by the expressions in Scripture, where God is said to dwell in heaven and in the temple.

(1.) He is indeed said to sit in heaven (Ps. ii. 4), and to dwell on high (Ps. cxiii. 5), but he is nowhere said to dwell only in the heavens, as confined to them. It is the court of his majestical presence, but not the prison of his essence: for when we are told that "the heaven is his throne," we are told with the same breath that the "earth is his footstool" (Isa. lxvi. 1). He dwells on high, in regard of the excellency of his nature, but he is in all places, in regard of the diffusion of his presence. The soul is essentially in all parts of the body, but it doth not exert the same operations in all; the more noble discoveries of it are in the head and heart. In the head where it exerciseth the chiefest senses for the enriching the understanding; in the heart, where it vitally resides, and communicates life and motion to the rest of the body. It doth not understand with the foot or toe, though it be in all parts of the body it informs; and so God may be said to dwell in heaven, in regard of the more excellent and majestic representations of himself, both to the creatures that inhabit the place, as angels and blessed spirits, and also in those marks of his greatness which he hath planted before, those spiritual natures which have a nobler stamp of God upon them, and those excellent bodies, as sun and stars, which, as so many tapers, light us to behold his glory (Ps. xix. 1), and astonish the minds of men when they gaze upon them. It is his court, where he hath the most solemn worship from his creatures, all his courtiers attending there with a pure love and glowing zeal. He reigns there in a special manner, without any opposition to his government; it is, therefore, called his "holy dwelling place" (2 Chron. iii. 27). The earth hath not that title, since sin cast a stain and a ruining curse upon it. The earth is not his throne, because his government is opposed: but heaven is none of Satan's precinct, and the rule of God is uncontradicted by the inhabitants of it. It is from thence also he hath given the greatest discoveries of himself; thence he sends the angels his messengers, his Son upon Redemption, his Spirit for sanctification. From heaven his gifts drop down upon our heads, and his grace upon our hearts (James iii. 17). From thence the chiefest blessings of earth descend. The motions of the heavens fatten the earth; and the heavenly bodies are but stewards to the earthly comforts for man by their influence. Heaven is the richest, vastest, most steadfast, and majestic part of the visible creation. It is there where he will at last manifest himself to his people in a full conjunction of grace and glory, and be forever open to his people in uninterrupted expressions of goodness, and discoveries of his presence, as a reward of their labor and service; and in these respects it may peculiarly be called his throne. And this doth no more hinder his essential presence in all parts of the earth, than it doth his gracious presence in all the hearts of his people. God is in heaven, in regard of the manifestation of his glory; in hell, by the expressions of his justice; in the earth, by the discoveries of his wisdom, power, patience, and compassion; in his people, by the monuments of his grace; and in all, in regard of his substance.

(2.) He is said also to dwell in the ark and temple. It is called (Ps. xxvi. 8) "the habitation of his house, and the place where his honor dwells;" and to dwell in Jerusalem as in his holy mountain, "The mountain of the Lord of Hosts" (Zech. viii. 3), in regard of publishing his oracles, answering their prayers, manifesting more of his goodness to the Israelites, than to any other nation in the world; erecting his true worship among them, which was not settled in any part of the world besides: and his worship is principally intended in that psalm. The ark is the place where his honor dwells. The worship of God is called the glory of God; "They changed the glory of God into an image made like to corruptible man" (Rom. i. 23), i. e., they changed the worship of God into idolatry; and to that also doth the place in Zechariah refer. Now, because he is said to dwell in heaven, is he essentially only there? Is he not as essentially in the temple and ark as he is in heaven, since there are as high expressions of his habitation there as of his dwelling in heaven? If he dwell only in heaven, how came he to dwell in the temple? both are asserted in Scripture, one as much as the other. If his dwelling in heaven did not hinder his dwelling in the ark, it could as little hinder the presence of his essence on the earth. To dwell in heaven, and in one part of the earth at the same time, is all one as to dwell in all parts of heaven, and all parts of earth. If he were in heaven, and in the ark and temple, it was the same essence in both, though not the same kind of manifestation of himself. If by his dwelling in heaven he meant his whole essence, why is it not also to be meant by his dwelling in the ark? It was not, sure, part of his essence that was in heaven, and part of his essence that was on earth; his essence would then be divided; and can it be imagined that he should be in heaven and the ark at the same time, and not in the spaces between? Could his essence be split into fragments, and a gap made in it, that two distant spaces should be filled by him, and all between be empty of him, so that God's being said to dwell in heaven, and in the temple, is so far from impairing the truth of this doctrine, that it more confirms and evidences it.

2. Nor do the expressions of God's coming to us, or departing from us, impair this doctrine of his omnipresence. God is said to hide his face from his people (Ps. x. 1); to be far from the wicked; and the Gentiles are said to be afar off, viz. from God (Prov. xv. 29; Eph. ii. 17), and upon the manifestation of Christ made near. These must not be understood of any distance or nearness of his essence, for that is equally near to all persons and things; but of some other special way and manifestation of his presence. Thus, God is said to be in believers by love, as they are in him (1 John iv. 15); "He that abides in love, abides in God, and God in him." He that loves, is in the thing beloved; and when two love one another, they are in one another. God is in a righteous man by a special grace, and far from the wicked in regard of such special works; and God is said to be in a place by a special manifestation, as when he was in the bush (Exod. iii.), or manifesting his glory upon Mount Sinai (Exod. xxiv. 16); "The glory of the Lord abode about Mount Sinai." God is said to hide his face when he withdraws his comforting presence, disturbs the repose of our hearts, flasheth terror into our consciences, when he puts men under the smart of the cross; as though he had ordered his mercy utterly to depart from them; or when he doth withdraw his special assisting providence from us in our affairs; so he departed from Saul, when he withdrew his direction and protection from him in the concerns of his government (1 Sam. xvi. 14); "The Spirit of the Lord departed from Saul," *i. e.* the spirit of government. God may be far from us in one respect, and near to us in another; far from us in regard of comfort, yet near to us in regard of support, when his essential presence continues the same: this is a necessary consequent upon the infiniteness of God, the other is an act of the will of God; so he was said to forsake Christ, in regard of his obscuring his glory from his human nature, and inflicting his wrath, though he was near to him in regard of his grace, and preserved him from contracting any spot in his sufferings. We do not say the sun is departed out of the heavens when it is bemisted; it remains in the same part of the heavens, passes on its course, though its beams do not reach us by reason of the bar between us and it. The soul is in every part of the body, in regard of its substance, and constantly in it, though it doth not act so sprightly and vigorously at one time as at another in one and the same member, and discover itself so sensibly in its operations; so all the various effects of God towards the sons of men, are but divers operations of one and the same essence. He is far from us, or near to us, as he is a judge or a benefactor. When he comes to punish, it notes not the approach of his essence, but the stroke of his justice; when he comes to benefit, it is not by a new access of his essence, but an efflux of his grace: he departs from us when he leaves us to the frowns of his justice; he comes to us when he encircles us in the arms of his mercy; but he was equally present with us in both dispensations, in regard of his essence. And, likewise, God is said to come down (Gen. xi. 5, "And the Lord came down to see the city"), when he doth some signal and wonderful

works which attract the minds of men to the acknowledgment of a Supreme Power and Providence in the world, who judged God absent and careless before.

3. Nor is the essential presence of God with all creatures any disparagement to him. Since it was no disparagement to create the heaven and the earth, it is no disparagement to him to fill them; if he were essentially present with them when he created them, it is no dishonor to him to be essentially present with them to support them; if it were his glory to create them by his essence, when they were nothing, can it be his disgrace to be present by his essence, since they are something, and something good, and very good in his eye (Gen. i. 31)? God saw every thing, and behold it was very good, or mighty good; all ordered to declare his goodness wisdom, power, and to make him adorable to man, and therefore took complacency in them. There is a harmony in all things, a combination in them for those glorious ends for which God created them; and is it a disgrace for God to be present with his own harmonious composition? Is it not a musician's glory to touch with his fingers the treble, the least and tenderest string, as well as the strongest and greatest bass? Hath not everything some stamp of God's own being upon it, since he eminently contains in himself the perfections of all his works? Whatsoever hath being, hath a footstep of God upon it, who is all being; everything in the earth is his footstool, having a mark of his foot upon it; all declare the being of God, because they had their being from God; and will God account it any disparagement to him to be present with that which confirms his being, and the glorious perfections of his nature, to his intelligent creatures? The meanest things are not without their virtues, which may boast God's being the Creator of them, and rank them in the midst of his works of wisdom as well as power. Doth God debase himself to be present by his essence, with the things he hath made, more than he doth to know them by his essence? Is not the least thing known by him? How? not by a faculty or act distinct from his essence, but by his essence itself. How is anything disgraceful to the essential presence of God, that is not disgraceful to his knowledge by his essence? Besides, would God make anything that should be an invincible reason to him to part with his own infiniteness, by a contraction of his own essence into a less compass than before? it was immense before, it had no bounds; and would God make a world that he would be ashamed to be present with, and continue it to the diminution and lessening of himself, rather than annihilate it to avoid the disparagement? This were to impeach the wisdom of God, and cast a blemish upon his infinite understanding, that he knows not the consequences of his work, or is well contented to be impaired in the immensity of his own essence by it. No man thinks it a dishonor to light, a most excellent creature, to be present with a toad or serpent; and though there be an infinite disproportion between light, a creature, and the Father of lights, the Creator: yet God, being a Spirit, knows how to be with bodies as if they were not bodies;[p] and being

jealous of his own honor, would not, could not do any thing that might impair it.

4. Nor will it follow, That because God is essentially everywhere, that everything is God. God is not everywhere by any conjunction, composition or mixture with anything on earth. When light is in every part of a crystal globe, and encircles it close on every side, do they become one? No; the crystal remains what it is, and the light retains its own nature; God is not in us as a part of us, but as an efficient and preserving cause; it is not by his essential presence, but his efficacious presence, that he brings any person into a like-ness to his own nature; God is so in his essence with things, as to be distinct from them, as a cause from the effect; as a Creator differ-ent from the creature, preserving their nature, not communicating his own; his essence touches all, is in conjunction with none; finite and infinite cannot be joined; he is not far from us, therefore near to us; so near that we live and move in him (Acts xvii. 28). Nothing is God because it moves in him, any more than a fish in the sea, is the sea, or a part of the sea, because it moves in it. Doth a man that holds a thing in the hollow of his hand, transform it by that action, and make it like his hand?q The soul and body are more straitly united, than the essence of God is, by his presence, with any creature. The soul is in the body as a form in matter, and from their union doth arise a man; yet in this near conjunction, both body and soul remain distinct; the soul is not the body, nor the body the soul; they both have distinct natures and essences; the body can never be changed into a soul, nor the soul into a body; no more can God into the creature, or the creature into God. Fire is in heated iron in every part of it, so that it seems to be nothing but fire; yet is not fire and iron the same thing. But such a kind of arguing against God's omnipresence, that if God were essentially present, everything would be God, would exclude him from heaven as well as from earth. By the same reason, since they acknowledge God essentially in heaven, the heaven where he is should be changed into the nature of God; and by arguing against his presence in earth, upon this ground they run such an inconvenience, that they must own him to be nowhere, and that which is nowhere is nothing. Doth the earth become God, because God is essentially there, any more than the heavens, where God is acknowledged by all to be essentially present? Again, if where God is essentially, that must be God; then if they place God in a point of the heavens, not only that point must be God, but all the world; because if that point be God, because God is there, then the point touched by that point must be God, and so consequently as far as there are any points, touched by one another. We live and move in God, so we live and move in the air; we are no more God by that, than we are mere air because we breathe in it, and it enters into all the pores of our body; nay, where there was a straiter union of the divine nature to the human in our Saviour, yet the nature of both was distinct, and the humanity was not changed into the divinity, nor the divinity into the humanity.

5. Nor doth it follow, that because God is everywhere, therefore

q Amyrald de Trinit. pp. 99, 100.

a creature may be worshipped without idolatry. Some of the heathens who acknowledged God's omnipresence, abused it to the countenancing idolatry; because God was resident in everything, they thought everything might be worshipped; and some have used it as an argument against this doctrine; the best doctrines may by men's corruption be drawn out into unreasonable and pernicious conclusions. Have you not met with any, that from the doctrine of God's free mercy, and our Saviour's satisfactory death, have drawn poison to feed their lusts, and consume their souls?—a poison composed by their own corruption, and not offered by those truths. The Apostle intimates to us, that some did, or at least were ready to be more lavish in sinning, because God was abundant in grace;[r] " Shall we continue in sin, that grace may abound?" when he prevents an objection that he thought might be made by some : but as to this case, since though God be present in everything, yet everything retains its nature distinct from the nature of God; therefore it is not to have a worship due to the excellency of God. As long as anything remains a creature, it is only to have the respect from us, which is due to it in the rank of creatures. When a prince is present with his guard, or if he should go arm in arm with a peasant, is, therefore, the veneration and honor due to the prince to be paid to the peasant, or any of his guard? Would the presence of the prince excuse it, or would it not rather aggravate it? He acknowledged such a person equal to me, by giving him my rights, even in my sight. Though God dwelt in the temple, would not the Israelites have been accounted guilty of idolatry had they worshipped the images of the cherubims, or the ark, or the altar, as objects of worship, which were erected only as means for his service? Is there not as much reason to think God was as essentially present in the temple as in heaven, since the same expressions are used of the one and the other? The sanctuary is called the glorious high throne (Jer. xvii. 13); and he is said to dwell between the cherubims (Ps. lxxx. 1), *i. e.* the two cherubims that were at the two ends of the mercy seat, appointed by God as the two sides of his throne in the sanctuary (Exod. xxv. 18), where he was to dwell (ver. 8), and meet, and commune, with his people (ver. 22). Could this excuse Manasseh's idolatry in bringing in a carved image into the house of God (1 Chron. xxxiii. 7)? had it been a good answer to the charge, God is present here, and therefore everything may be worshipped as God? If he be only essentially in heaven, would it not be idolatry to direct a worship to the heavens, or any part of it as a due object, because of the presence of God there? Though we look up to the heavens, where we pray and worship God, yet heaven is not the object of worship; the soul abstracts God from the creature.

6. Nor is God defiled by being present with those creatures which seem filthy to us. Nothing is filthy in the eye of God as his creature; he could never else have pronounced all good; whatsoever is filthy to us, yet, as it is a creature, it owes itself to the power of God: his essence is no more defiled by being present with it, than his

---

[r] Rom. vi. 1, 2, 15. " Shall we sin, because we are not under the law. but under grace?"

power by producing it: no creature is foul in itself, though it may seem so to us. Doth not an infant lie in a womb of filthiness and rottenness? yet is not the power of God present with it, in working it curiously in the lower parts of the earth? Are his eyes defiled by seeing the substance when it is yet imperfect? or his hand defiled by writing every member in his book (Ps. cxxxix. 15, 16)? Have not the vilest and most noisome things excellent medicinal virtues? How are they endued with them? How are those qualities preserved in them? by anything without God, or no? Every artificer looks with pleasure upon the work he hath wrought with art and skill. Can his essence be defiled by being present with them, any more than it was in giving them such virtues, and preserving them in them? God measures the heavens and the earth with his hand; is his hand defiled by the evil influences of the planets, or the corporeal impurities of the earth? Nothing can be filthy in the eye of God but sin, since everything else owes its being to him. What may appear deformed and unworthy to us, is not so to the Creator; he sees beauty where we see deformity; finds goodness where we behold what is nauseous to us. All creatures being the effects of his power, may be the objects of his presence. Can any place be more foul than hell, if you take it either for the hell of the damned, or for the grave where there is rottenness? yet there he is (Ps. cxxxix. 8). When Satan appeared before God, and God spake with him (Job i. 7), could God contract any impurity by being present where that filthy spirit was, more impure than any corporeal, noisome, and defiling thing can be? No; God is purity to himself in the midst of noisomeness; a heaven to himself in the midst of hell. Whoever heard of a sunbeam stained by shining upon a quagmire, any more than sweetened by breaking into a perfumed room?[s] Though the light shines upon pure and impure things, yet it mixes not itself with either of them; so though God be present with devils and wicked men, yet without any mixture; he is present with their essence to sustain it and support it; not in their defection, wherein lies their defilement, and which is not a physical, but a moral evil; bodily filth can never touch an incorporeal substance. Spirits are not present with us in the same manner that one body is present with another; bodies can by a touch only, defile bodies. Is the glory of an angel stained by being in a coal-mine? or could the angel that came into the lion's den to deliver Daniel, be any more disturbed by the stench of the place, than he could be scratched by the paws, or torn by the teeth, of the beasts (Dan. vi. 22)? Their spiritual nature secures them against any infection when they are ministering spirits to persecuted believers in their nasty prisons (Acts xii. 7). The soul is straitly united with the body, but it is not made white or black by the whiteness or blackness of its habitation. Is it infected by the corporeal impurities of the body, while it continually dwells in a sea of filthy pollution? If the body be cast into a common shore, is the soul defiled by it? Can a diseased body derive a contagion to the spirit that animates it? Is it not often the purer by grace, the more the body is infected by nature? Hezekiah's spirit was scarce ever more fer-

* Shelford on the Attributes, p. 170.

vent with God, than when the sore, which some think to be a plague sore, was upon him (Isa. xxxviii. 3). How can any corporeal filth impair the purity of the divine essence? It may as well be said, that God is not present in battles and fights for his people (Joshua xxiii. 10), because he would not be disturbed by the noise of cannons, and clashing of swords, as that he is not present in the world because of the ill scents. Let us therefore conclude this with the expresssion of a learned man of our own :[t] " To deny the omnipresence of God, because of ill scented places, is to measure God rather by the nicety of sense, than by the sagacity of reason."

IV. *Use.* First, of information.

1. Christ hath a divine nature. As eternity and immutability, two incommunicable properties of the divine nature, are ascribed to Christ, so also is this of omnipresence or immensity (John iii. 13 :) " No man hath ascended up to heaven, but he that came down from heaven, even the Son of Man which is in heaven." Not which was, but which is. He comes from heaven by incarnation, and remains in heaven by his divinity. He was, while he spake to Nicodemus, locally on earth, in regard of his humanity; but in heaven according to his deity, as well as upon earth in the union of his divine and human nature. He descended upon earth, but he left not heaven; he was in the world before he came in the flesh (John i. 10): "He was in the world, and the world was made by him." He was in the world, as the "light that enlightens every man that comes into the world." In the world as God, before he was in the world as man. He was then in the world as man, while he discoursed with Nicodemus; yet so, that he was also in heaven as God. No creature but is bounded in place, either circumscribed as body, or determined as spirit to be in one space, so as not to be in another at the same time; to leave a place where they were, and possess a place where they were not. But Christ is so on earth, that at the same time he is in heaven; he is therefore infinite. To be in heaven and earth at the same moment of time, is a property solely belonging to the Deity, wherein no creature can be a partner with him. He was in the world before he came to the world, and "the world was made by him" (John i. 10). His coming was not as the coming of angels, that leave heaven, and begin to be on earth, where they were not before; but such a presence as can be ascribed only to God, who fills heaven and earth. Again, if all things were made by him, then he was present with all things which were made; for where there is a presence of power, there is also a presence of essence, and therefore he is still present; for the right and power of conservation follows the power of creation. And, according to this divine nature, he promiseth his presence with his church (Matt. xviii. 20): " There am I in the midst of them:" and (Matt. xxviii. 20), "I am with you alway, even to the end of the world," *i. e.* by his divinity : for he had before told them (Matt. xxvi. 11), that they were not to have him alway with them, *i. e.* according to his humanity; but in his Divine nature he is present with, and walks in the midst of, the golden candlesticks. If we understand it of a presence by his Spirit in the midst of

[t] Dr. More.

the church, doth it invalidate his essential presence? No; he is no less than the Spirit whom he sends; and therefore as little confined as the Spirit is, who dwells in every believer: and this may also be inferred from John x. 30: "My father and I are one;" not one by consent, though that be included, but one in power: for he speaks not of their consent, but of their joint power in keeping his people. Where there is a unity of essence, there is a unity of presence.

2. Here is a confirmation of the spiritual nature of God. If he were an infinite body, he could not fill heaven and earth, but with the exclusion of all creatures. Two bodies cannot be in the same space; they may be near one another, but not in any of the same points together. A body bounded he hath not, for that would destroy his immensity; he could not then fill heaven and earth, because a body cannot be at one and the same time in two different spaces; but God doth not fill heaven at one time, and the earth at another, but both at the same time. Besides a limited body cannot be said to fill the whole earth, but one particular space in the earth at a time. A body may fill the earth with its virtue, as the sun, but not with its substance. Nothing can be everywhere with a corporeal weight and mass; but God being infinite, is not tied to any part of the world, but penetrates all, and equally acts by his infinite power in all.

3. Here is an argument for providence. His presence is mentioned in the text, in order to his government of the affairs of the world. Is he everywhere, to be unconcerned with everything? Before the world had a being, God was present with himself; since the world hath a being, he is present with his creatures, to exercise his wisdom in the ordering, as he did his power in the production of them. As the knowledge of God is not a bare contemplation of a thing, so his presence is not a bare inspection into a thing. Were it an idle careless presence, it were a presence to no purpose, which cannot be imagined of God. Infinite power. goodness, and wisdom, being everywhere present with his essence, are never without their exercise. He never manifests any of his perfections, but the manifestation is full of some indulgence and benefit to his creatures. It cannot be supposed God should neglect those things, wherewith he is constantly present in a way of efficiency and operation. He is not everywhere without acting everywhere. "Wherever his essence is, there is a power and virtue worthy of God everywhere dispensed."[u] He governs by his presence what he made by his power; and is present as an agent with all his works. His power and essence are together, to preserve them while he pleases, as his power and his essence were together, to create them when he saw good to do it. Every creature hath a stamp of God, and his presence is necessary to keep the impression standing upon the creature. As all things are his works, they are the objects of his cares; and the wisdom he employed in framing them will not suffer him to be careless of them. His presence with them engageth him in honor not to be a negligent Governor.

[u] Cyril.

His immensity fits him for government; and where there is a fitness, there is an exercise of government, where there are objects for the exercise of it. He is worthy to have the universal rule of the world; he can be present in all places of his empire; there is nothing can be done by any of his subjects, but in his sight. As his eternity renders him King alway, so his immensity renders him King everywhere. If he were only present in heaven, it might occasion a suspicion that he minded only the things of heaven, and had no concern for things below that vast body; but if he be present here, his presence hath a tendency to the government of those things with which he is present. We are all in him as fish in the sea; and he bears all creatures in the womb of his providence, and the arms of his goodness. It is most certain that his presence with his people is far from being an idle one; for when he promises to be with them, he adds some special cordial, as, "I will be with thee, and bless thee" (Gen. xxvi. 3.) "I am with thee, and I will strengthen thee" (Jer. xv. 20.) "I will help thee, I will uphold thee" (Isa. xli. 10, 14.) Infinite goodness will never countenance a negligent presence.

4. The omniscience of God is inferred from hence. If God be present everywhere, he must needs know what is done everywhere. It is for this end he proclaims himself a God filling heaven and earth, in the text, "Can any hide himself in secret places that I shall not see him, saith the Lord? I have heard what the prophets say, that prophesy lies in my name: if I fill heaven and earth, the most secret thing cannot be hid from my sight." An intelligent being cannot be everywhere present, and more intimate in everything, than it can be in itself; but he must know what is done without, what is thought within. Nothing can be obscure to Him who is in every part of the world, in every part of his creatures. Not a thought can start up but in his sight, who is present in the souls and minds of everything. How easy is it with him, to whose essence the world is but a point, to know and observe everything done in this world, as any of us can know what is done in one point of place where we are present! If light were an understanding being, it would behold and know everything done where it diffuseth itself. God is light (as light in a crystal glass all within it, all without it), and is not ignorant of what is done within and without; no ignorance can be fastened upon him who hath an universal presence. Hence, by the way, we may take notice of the wonderful patience of God, who bears with so many provocations; not from a principal of ignorance, for he bears with sins that are committed near him in his sight, sins that he sees, and cannot but see.

5. Hence may be inferred the incomprehensibility of God. He that fills heaven and earth cannot be contained in anything; he fills the understandings of men, the understandings of angels, but is comprehended by neither; it is a rashness to think to find out any bounds of God; there is no measuring of an infinite Being; if it were to be measured it were not infinite; but because it is infinite, it is not to be measured. God sits above the cherubims

(Ezek. x. 1), above the fulness, above the brightness, not only of a human, but a created understanding. Nothing is more present than God, yet nothing more hid; he is light, and yet obscurity;[x] his perfections are visible, yet unsearchable; we know there is an infinite God, but it surpasseth the compass of our minds; we know there is no number so great, but another may be added to it; but no man can put it in practice, without losing himself in a maze of figures. What is the reason we comprehend not many, nay, most things in the world? partly from the excellency of the object, and partly from the imperfection of our understandings. How can we then comprehend God, who exceeds all, and is exceeded by none; contains all, and is contained by none; is above our understanding, as well as above our sense? as considered in himself infinite; as considered in comparison with our understandings, incomprehensible; who can, with his eye, measure the breadth, length and depth of the sea, and at one cast, view every dimension of the heavens? God is greater, and we cannot know him (Job xxxvi. 26); he fills the understanding as he fills heaven and earth; yet is above the understanding as he is above heaven and earth. He is known by faith, enjoyed by love, but comprehended by no mind. God is not contained in that one syllable, God; by it we apprehend an excellent and unlimited nature; himself only understands himself, and can unveil himself.

6. How wonderful is God, and how nothing are creatures! "Ascribe the greatness to our God" (Deut. xxxiii. 3); he is admirable in the consideration of his power, in the extent of his understanding, and no less wonderful in the immensity of his essence: that, as Austin saith, he is in the world, yet not confined to it; he is out of the world, yet not debarred from it; he is above the world, yet not elevated by it; he is below the world, yet not depressed by it; he is above all, equalled by none; he is in all, not because he needs them, but they stand in need of him; this, as well as eternity, makes a vast disproportion between God and the creature: the creature is bounded by a little space, and no space is so great as to bound the Creator. By this we may take a prospect of our own nothingness: as in the consideration of God's holiness we are minded of our own impurity; and in the thoughts of his wisdom have a view of our own folly; and in the meditation of his power, have a sense of our weakness; so his immensity should make us, according to our own nature, appear little in our own eyes. What little, little, little things are we to God! less than an atom in the beams of the sun; poor drops to a God that fills heaven and earth, and yet dare we to strut against him, and dash ourselves against a rock? If the consideration of ourselves in comparison with others, be apt to puff us up, the consideration of ourselves in comparison with God, will be sufficient to pull us down. If we consider him in the greatness of his essence, there is but little more proportion between him and us, than between being and not being, than between a drop and the ocean. How should we never think of God without a holy admiration of his greatness,

[x] Κρυφιότης, Dionysius called God.

and a deep sense of our own littleness! and as the angels cover their faces before him, with what awe should creeping worms come into his sight! and since God fills heaven and earth with his presence, we should fill heaven and earth with his glory; for this end he created angels to praise him in heaven, and men to worship him on earth, that the places he fills with his presence may be filled with his praise: we should be swallowed up in admiration of the immensity of God, as men are at the first sight of the sea, when they behold a mass of waters, without beholding the bounds and immense depth of it.

7. How much is this attribute of God forgotten or contemned! We pretend to believe him to be present everywhere, and yet many live as if he were present nowhere.

(1.) It is commonly forgotten, or not believed. All the extravagances of men may be traced to the forgetfulness of this attribute as their spring. The first speech Adam spake in paradise after his fall, testified his unbelief of this (Gen. iii. 10); "I heard thy voice in the garden, and I hid myself;" his ear understood the voice of God, but his mind did not conclude the presence of God; he thought the trees could shelter him from Him whose eye was present in the minutest parts of the earth; he that thought after his sin, that he could hide himself from the presence of his justice, thought before that he could hide himself from the presence of his knowledge; and being deceived in the one, he would try what would be the fruit of the other. In both he forgets, if not denies, this attribute; either corrupt notions of God, or a slight belief of what in general men assent unto, gives birth to every sin. In all transgressions there is something of atheism; either denying the being of God, or a dash upon some perfection of God;—a not believing his holiness to hate it, his truth that threatens, his justice to punish it, and his presence to observe it. Though God be not afar off in his essence, he is "afar off in the apprehension of the sinner."[y] There is no wicked man, but if he be an atheist, he is a heretic; and to gratify his lust, will fancy himself to be out of the presence of his Judge. His reason tells him, God is present with him, his lust presseth him to embrace the season of sensual pleasure; he will forsake his reason, and prove a heretic, that he may be an undisturbed sinner; and sins doubly, both in the error of his mind, and the vileness of his practice; he will conceit God with those in Job, "veiled with thick clouds" (Job xxii. 14), and not able to pierce into the lower world, as if his presence and cares were confined to celestial things, and the earth were too low a sphere for his essence to reach, at least with any credit. It is forgotten by good men, when they fear too much the designs of their enemies; "Fear not, for I am with thee" (Isa. xliii. 5). If the presence of God be enough to strengthen against fear, then the prevailing of fear issues from our forgetfulness of it.

(2.) This attribute of God's omnipresence is for the most part contemned. When men will commit that in the presence of God which they would be afraid or ashamed to do before the eye of man, men do not practice that modesty before God as before men. He that would restrain his tongue out of fear of men's eye, will not restrain either tongue or hands out of fear of God's. What is the language of this, but that God is not present with us, or his presence ought to be of less regard with us, and influence upon us, than that of a creature?[z] Ask the thief why he dares to steal? will he not answer, "No eye sees him?" Ask the adulterer why he strips himself of his chastity, and invades the rights of another? will he not answer (Job xxiv. 15), "No eye sees me?" He disguiseth himself to be unseen by man, but slights the all-seeing eye of God. If only a man know them, they are in terror of the shadow of death; they are planet-struck, but stand unshaken at the presence of God (Job xxiv. 17). Is not this to account God as limited as man—as ignorant, as absenting, as if God were something less than those things which restrain us? 'Tis a debasing God below a creature. If we can forbear sin from an awe of the presence of man, to whom we are equal in regard of nature, or from the presence of a very mean man, to whom we are superior in regard of condition, and not forbear it because we are within the ken of God, we respect him not only as our inferior, but inferior to the meanest man or child of his creation, in whose sight we would not commit the like action: it is to represent him as a sleepy, negligent, or careless God; as though anything might be concealed from him, before whom the least fibres of the heart are anatomised and open, who sees as plainly midnight as noon-day sins (Heb. iv. 13). Now this is a high aggravation of sin: to break a king's laws, in his sight, is more bold than to violate them behind his back; as it was Haman's offence when he lay upon Esther's bed, to force the queen before the king's face. The least iniquity receives a high tincture from this; and no sin can be little that is an affront in the face of God, and casting the filth of the creature before the eyes of his holiness: as if a wife should commit adultery before her husband's face, or a slave dishonor his master, and disobey his commands in his presence. And hath it not often been thus with us? have we not been disloyal to God in his sight, before his eyes, those pure eyes that cannot behold iniquity without anger and grief? (Isa. lxv. 12), "Ye did evil before my eyes." Nathan chargeth this home upon David (2 Sam. xii. 9), "Thou hast despised the commandment of the Lord, to do evil in his sight;" and David, in his repentance, reflects upon himself for it (Ps. li. 4); "Against thee, thee only, have I sinned, and done this evil in thy sight." I observed not thy presence, I neglected thee while thy eye was upon me. And this consideration should sting our hearts in all our confessions of our crimes. Men will be afraid of the presence of others, whatsoever they think in their heart. How unworthily do we deal with God, in not giving him so much as an eye-service, which we do man!

8. How terrible should the thoughts of this attribute be to sinners! How foolish is it, to imagine any hiding-place from the incomprehensible God, who fills and contains all things, and is present in every point of the world![a] When men have shut the door, and

---

[z] Drexel, Nicet. lib. ii. cap. 10.

[a] Quo fugis Encelade quas cunque accesseris oras, sub Jove semper eris.

made all darkness within, to meditate or commit a crime, they cannot in the most intricate recesses be sheltered from the presence of God. If they could separate themselves from their own shadows, they could not avoid his company, or be obscured from his sight.[b] Hypocrites cannot disguise their sentiments from him; he is in the most secret nook of their hearts. No thought is hid, no lust is secret, but the eye of God beholds this, and that, and the other. He is present with our heart when we imagine, with our hands when we act. We may exclude the sun from peeping into our solitudes, but not the eyes of God from beholding our actions. "The eyes of the Lord are in every place, beholding the evil and good" (Prov. xv. 3). He lies in the depths of our souls, and sees afar off our designs before we have conceived them. He is in the greatest darkness, as well as the clearest light; in the closest thought of the mind, as well as the openest expressions. Nothing can be hid from him, no, not in the darkest cells or thickest walls. "He compasseth our path wherever we are (Ps. cxxxix. 3), and "is acquainted with all our ways." He is as much present with wicked men to observe their sins, as he is to detest them. Where he is present in his essence, he is present in his attributes: his holiness to hate, and his justice to punish, if he please to speak the word. It is strange men should not be mindful of this, when their very sins themselves might put them in mind of his presence. Whence hast thou the power to act? who preserves thy being, whereby thou art capable of committing that evil? Is it not his essential presence that sustains us, and his arm that supports us? and where can any man fly from his presence? Not the vast regions of heaven could shelter a sinning angel from his eye: how was Adam ferreted out of his hiding-places in paradise? Nor can we find the depths of the sea a sufficient covering to us. If we were with Jonah, closeted up in the belly of a whale; if we had the "wings of the morning," as quick a motion as the light at the dawning of the day, that doth in an instant surprise and overpower the regions of darkness, and could pass to the utmost parts of the earth or hell, there we should find him, there his eye would be upon us, there would his hand lay hold of us, and lead us as a conqueror triumphing over a captive (Ps. cxxxix. 8—10). Nay, if we could leap out of the compass of heaven and earth, we should find as little reserves from him: he is without the world in those infinite spaces which the mind of man can imagine. In regard of his immensity, nothing in being can be distant from him, wheresoever it is.

Second, *Use* is for comfort. That God is present everywhere, is as much a comfort to a good man, as it is a terror to a wicked one, He is everywhere for his people, not only by a necessary perfection of his nature, but an immense diffusion of his goodness. He is in all creatures as their preserver: in the damned, as their terror; in his people, as their protector. He fills hell with his severity, heaven with his glory, his people with his grace. He is with his people as light in darkness, a fountain in a garden, as manna in the ark. God is in the world as a spring of preservation; in the church as his

[b] Ps. cxxxix. 12. "The darkness and light are both alike to him."

cabinet, his spring of grace and consolation. A man is present sometimes in his field, but more delightfully in his garden. A vine yard, as it hath more of cost, so more of care, and a watchful presence of the owner (Isa. xxvii. 3); "I, the Lord, do keep it," viz. his vineyard; "I will water it every moment, lest any hurt it; I will keep it night and day." As there is a presence of essence, which is natural, so there is a presence of grace, which is federal: a presence by covenant; "I will not leave thee, I will be with thee." This latter depends upon the former; for, take away the immensity of God, and you leave no foundation for his universal gracious presence with his people in all their emergencies, in all their hearts. And, therefore, where he is present in his essence, he cannot be absent in his grace, from them that fear him. It is from his filling heaven and earth he proves his knowledge of the designs of the false prophets; and from the same topic may as well be inferred the employment of his power and grace for his people.

1. The omnipresence of God is a comfort in all violent temptations. No fiery dart can be so present with us, as God is present both with that and the marksman. The most raging devils cannot be so near us, as God is to us and them. He is present with his people to relieve them, and present with the devil to manage him to his own holy purposes: so he was with Job, defeating his enemies, and bringing him triumphantly out of those pressing trials. This presence is such a terror, that whatsoever the devil can despoil us of, he must leave this untouched. He might scratch the apostle with a thorn (2 Cor. xii. 7, 9), but he could not rifle him of the presence of divine grace, which God promised him. He must prevail so far as to make God cease to be God, before he can make him to be distant from us; and while this cannot be, the devils and men can no more hinder the emanations of God to the soul, than a child can cut off the rays of the sun from embellishing the earth. It is no mean support for a good man, at any time, buffeted by a messenger of Satan, to think God stands near him, and behold how ill he is used. It would be a satisfaction to a king's favorite, in the midst of the violence some enemies might use to him upon a surprise, to understand that the king who loves him stands behind a curtain, and through a hole sees the injuries he suffers: and were the devil as considering as he is malicious, he could not but be in great fear at God's being in the generation of the righteous, as his serpentine seed is (Prov. iii. 6): "They were in great fear, for God is in the generation of the righteous."

2. The omnipresence of God is a comfort in sharp afflictions. Good men have a comfort in this presence in their nasty prisons, oppressing tribunals; in the overflowing waters or scorching flames he is still with them (Isa. xliii. 2); and many times by his presence keeps the bush from consuming, when it seems to be all in a flame. In afflictions God shows himself most present, when friends are most absent: "When my father and mother forsake me, then the Lord shall take me up" (Ps. xxvii. 10), then God will stoop and gather me into his protection; or, (Heb.) "shall gather me," alluding to those tribes that were to bring up the rear in the Israelites' march, to take care that

none were left behind, and exposed to famine or wild beasts, by reason of some disease that disenabled them to keep pace with their brethren.   He that is the sanctuary of his people in all calamities, is more present with them to support them, than their adversaries can be present with them to afflict them (Psal. xlvi. 2), a present help in the time of trouble; He is present with all things for this end; though his presence be a necessary presence in regard of the immensity of his nature, yet the end of this presence in regard that it is for the good of his people, is a voluntary presence.   It is for the good of man he is present in the lower world, and principally for the good of his people, for whose sake he keeps up the world (2 Chron. xvi. 9). "His eyes run to and fro throughout the whole earth, to show himself strong in the behalf of them whose heart is perfect towards him." If he doth not deliver good men from afflictions, he will be so present as to manage them in them, as that his glory shall issue from them, and their grace be brightened by them.[c]   What a man was Paul when he was lodged in a prison, or dragged to the courts of judicature, when he was torn with rods, or laden with chains! then did he show the greatest miracles, made the judge tremble upon the bench, and brake the heart, though not the prison, of the jailor; so powerful is the presence of God in the pressures of his people.   This presence outweighs all other comforts, and is more valuable to a Christian than barns of corn, or cellars of wine can be to a covetous man (Ps. iv. 7): it was this presence was David's cordial in the mutinying of his soldiers (1 Sam. xxx. 6).   What a comfort is this in exile, or a forced desertion of our habitations!   Good men may be banished from their country, but never from the presence of their Protector; ye cannot say of any corner of the earth, or of any dungeon in a prison, God is not here; if you were cast out of your country a thousand miles off, you are not out of God's precinct; his arm is there to cherish the good, as well as to drag out the wicked; it is the same God, the same presence in every country, as well as the same sun, moon, and stars; and were not God everywhere, yet he could not be meaner than his creature the sun in the firmament, which visits every part of the habitable world in twenty-four hours.

3. The omnipresence of God is a comfort in all duties of worship. He is present to observe, and present to accept our petitions, and answer our suits.   Good men have not only the essential presence, which is common to all, but his gracious presence; not only the presence that flows from his nature, but that which flows from his promise; his essential presence makes no difference between this and that man in regard of spirituals, without this in conjunction with it; his nature is the cause of the presence of his essence; his will engaged by his truth is the cause of the presence of his grace.   He promised to meet the Israelites in the place where he should set his name, and in all places where he doth record it (Exod. xx. 4).   "In all places where I record my name, I will come unto thee, and I will bless thee;" in every place where I shall manifest the special presence of my divinity.   In all places, hands may be lifted up, without doubting of his ability to hear; he dwells in the contrite hearts, wherever

[c] Chrysostome.

it is most in the exercise of contrition; which is usually in times of special worship (Isa. lvii. 15), and that to revive and refresh them. Habitation notes a special presence, though he dwell in the highest heavens in the sparklings of his glory, he dwells also in the lowest hearts in the beams of his grace; as none can expel him from his dwelling in heaven, so none can reject him from his residence in the heart. The tabernacle had his peculiar presence fixed to it (Levit. xxvi. 11); his soul should not abhor them, as they are washed by Christ, though they are loathsome by sin: in a greater dispensation there cannot be a less presence, since the church under the New Testament is called the temple of the Lord, wherein he will both dwell and walk (2 Cor. vi. 6); or, I will indwell in them; as if he should say, I will dwell in and in them; I will dwell in them by grace, and walk in them by exciting their graces; he will be more intimate with them than their own souls, and converse with them as the living God, *i. e.* as a God that hath life in himself, and life to convey to them in their converse with him; and show his spiritual glory among them in a greater measure than in the temple, since that was but a heap of stones, and the figure of the Christian church the mystical body of his Son. His presence is not less in the substance than it was in the shadow; this presence of God in his ordinances, is the glory of a church, as the presence of a king is the glory of a court, the defence of it, too, as a wall of fire (Zech. ii. 5); alluding to the fire travellers in a wilderness made to fright away wild beasts. It is not the meanness of the place of worship can exclude him; the second temple was not so magnificent as the first of Solomon's erecting, and the Jews seemed to despond of so glorious a presence of God in the second, as they had in the first, because they thought it not so good for the entertainment of Him that inhabits eternity; but God comforts them against this conceit again and again (Hag. ii. 3, 4): " be strong, be strong, be strong, I am with you;" the meanness of the place shall not hinder the grandeur of my presence, no matter what the room is, so it be the presence-chamber of the king, wherein he will favor our suits; he can everywhere slide into our souls with a perpetual sweetness, since he is everywhere, and so, intimate with every one that fears him. If we should see God on earth in his amiableness, as Moses did, should we not be encouraged by his presence, to present our requests to him, to echo out our praises of him? and have we not as great a ground now to do it, since he is as really present with us, as if he were visible to us? he is in the same room with us, as near to us as our souls to our bodies, not a word but he hears, not a motion but he sees, not a breath but he perceives; he is through all, he is in all.

4. The omnipresence of God is a comfort in all special services. God never puts any upon a hard task, but he makes promises to encourage them and assist them, and the matter of the promise is that of his presence; so he did assure the prophets of old when he set them difficult tasks, and strengthened Moses against the face of Pharaoh, by assuring him " he would be with his mouth" (Exod. iv. 12); and when Christ put his apostles upon a contest with the whole world, to preach a gospel that would be foolishness to the Greeks,

and a stumbling block to the Jews, he gives them a cordial only composed of his presence (Matt. xxviii. 20), I will be with you; it is this presence scatters by its light the darkness of our spirits; it is this that is the cause of what is done for his glory in the world; it is this that mingles itself with all that is done for his honor; it is this from whence springs all the assistance of his creatures, marked out for special purposes.

5. This presence is not without the special presence of all his attributes. Where his essence is, his perfections are, because they are one with his essence; yea, they are his essence, though they have their several degrees of manifestation. As in the covenant, he makes over himself, not a part of himself, but his whole deity; so in promising of his presence, he means not a part of it, but the whole, the presence of all the excellencies of his nature to be manifested for our good. It is not a piece of God is here and another parcel there, but God in his whole essence and perfections; in his wisdom to guide us, his power to protect and support us, his mercy to pity us, his fulness to refresh us, and his goodness to relieve us: he is ready to sparkle out in this or that perfection, as the necessities of his people require, and his own wisdom directs for his own honor; so that being not far from us in an excellency of his nature, we can quickly have recourse to him upon any emergency; so that if we are miserable, we have the presence of his goodness; if we want direction, we have the presence of his wisdom; if we are weak, we have the presence of his power; and should we not rejoice in it, as a man doth in the presence of a powerful, wealthy, and compassionate friend?

Third, *Use.* Of Exhortation.

1. Let us be much in the actual thoughts of this truth. How should we enrich our understandings with the knowledge of the excellency of God, whereof this is none of the least; nor hath less of honey in its bowels, though it be more terrible to the wicked than the presence of a lion; it is this that makes all other excellencies of the divine nature sweet. What would grace, wisdom, power, signify at a distance from us? Let us frame in our minds a strong idea of it; it is this makes so great a difference between the actions of one man and another; one maintains actual thoughts of it, another doth not: though all believe it as a perfection pertaining to the infiniteness of his essence. David, or rather a greater than David, had God always before him; there was no time, no occasion, wherein he did not stir up some lively thoughts of him (Ps. xvi. 8). Let us have right notions of it; imagine not God as a great King, sitting only in his majesty in heaven; acting all by his servants and ministers. This, saith one,[d] is a childish and unworthy conceit of God, and may in time bring such a conceiver by degrees to deny his providence; the denial of this perfection is an axe at the root of religion; if it be not deeply imprinted in the mind, personal religion grows faint and feeble. Who would fear that God that is not imagined to be a witness of his actions? Who would worship a God at a distance both from the worship and the worshipper?[e] Let us believe this truth,

---

[d] Musculus.   [e] Drexel.

but not with an idle faith, as if we did not believe it. Let us know, that as wheresoever the fish moves, it is in the water; wheresoever the bird moves, it is in the air; so wheresoever we move, we are in God. As there is not a moment but we are under his mercy, so there is not a moment that we are out of his presence. Let us therefore look upon nothing, without thinking who stands by, without reflecting upon him in whom it lives, moves and hath its being. When you view a man, you fix your eyes upon his body, but your mind upon that invisible part that acts every member by life and motion, and makes them fit for your converse. Let us not bound our thoughts to the creatures we see, but pierce through the creature to that boundless God we do not see: we have continual remembrances of his presence; the light, whereby we see, and the air, whereby we live, give us perpetual notices of it, and some weak resemblance; why should we forget it? yea, what a shame is our unmindfulness of it, when every cast of our eye, every motion of our lungs, jogs us to remember it? Light is in every part of the air, in every part of the world, yet not mixed with any, both remain entire in their own substance. Let us not be worse than some of the heathens, who pressed this notion upon themselves for the spiriting their actions with virtue, that all places were full of God. This was the means Basil used to prescribe, upon a question asked him, How shall we do to be serious? mind God's presence. How shall we avoid distractions in service? think of God's presence. How shall we resist temptation? oppose to them the presence of God.[f]

(1.) This will be a shield against all temptations. God is present, is enough to blunt the weapons of hell; this will secure us from a ready compliance with any base and vile attractives, and curb that headstrong principle in our nature, that would join hands with them; the thoughts of this would, like the powerful presence of God with the Israelites, take off the wheels from the chariots of our sensitive appetites, and make them perhaps move slower, at least, towards a temptation. How did Peter fling off the temptation which had worsted him, upon a look from Christ! The actuated faith of this would stifle the darts of Satan, and fire us with an anger against his solicitations, as strong as the fire that inflames the darts. Moses' sight of Him that was invisible, strengthened him against the costly pleasures and luxuries of a prince's court (Heb. xi. 27). We are utterly senseless of a Deity, if we are not moved with this item from our consciences, God is present. Had our first parents actually considered the nearness of God to them, when they were tempted to eat of the forbidden fruit, they had not probably been so easily overcome by the temptation. What soldier would be so base as to revolt under the eye of a tender and obliging general? or what man so negligent of himself, as to rob a house in the sight of a judge? Let us consider that God is as near to observe us, as the devil to solicit us, yea, nearer; the devil stands by us, but God is in us; we may have a thought the devil knows not, but not a thought but God is actually present with, as our souls are with the thoughts they think; nor can any creature attract our heart, if our minds were fixed on that invisible presence

[f] Omnia diis plena.

that contributes to that excellency, and sustains it, and considered that no creature could be so present with us as the Creator is.

(2.) It will be a spur to holy actions. What man would do an unworthy action, or speak an unhandsome word, in the presence of his prince? The eye of the general inflames the spirit of a soldier. Why did David keep God's testimonies (Ps. cxix. 168)? because he considered that all his ways were before him; because he was persuaded his ways were present with God; God's precepts should be present with him. The same was the cause of Job's integrity (Job xxxi. 4): "Doth he not see my ways?" To have God in our eye is the way to be sincere (Gen. xvii. 1); "walk before me" as in my sight, "and be thou perfect." Communion with God consists chiefly in an ordering our ways as in the presence of him that is invisible. This would make us spiritual, raised and watchful in all our passions, if we considered that God is present with us in our shops, in our chambers, in our walks, and in our meetings, as present with us as with the angels in heaven; who, though they have a presence of glory above us, yet have not a greater measure of his essential presence than we have. What an awe had Jacob upon him when he considered God was present in Bethel (Gen. xxviii. 16, 17)! If God should appear visibly to us when we were alone, should we not be reverend and serious before him? God is everywhere about us, he doth encompass us with his presence. Should not God's seeing us have the same influence upon us as our seeing God? He is not more essentially present if he should so manifest himself to us, than when he doth not. Who would appear besmeared in the presence of a great person? or not be ashamed to be found in his chamber in a nasty posture by some visitant? Would not a man blush to be catched about some mean action, though it were not an immoral crime? If this truth were impressed upon our spirits, we should more blush to have our souls daubed with some loathsome lust; swarms of sin, like Egyptian lice and frogs, creeping about our heart in his sight. If the most sensual man be ashamed to do a dishonest action in the sight of a grave and holy man, one of great reputation for wisdom and integrity, how much more should we lift up ourselves in the ways of God, who is infinite and immense, is everywhere, and infinitely superior to man, and more to be regarded! We could not seriously think of his presence but there would pass some intercourse between us; we should be putting up some petition upon the sense of our indigence, or sending up our praises to him upon the sense of his bounty. The actual thoughts of the presence of God is the life and spirit of all religion; we could not have sluggish spirits and a careless watch if we considered that his eye is upon us all the day.

(3.) It will quell distractions in worship. The actual thoughts of this would establish our thoughts, and pull them back when they begin to rove: the mind could not boldly give God the slip if it had lively thoughts of it; the consideration of this would blow off all the froth that lies on the top of our spirits. An eye, taken up with the presence of one object, is not at leisure to be filled with another: he that looks intently upon the sun, shall have nothing for a while but the sun in his eye. Oppose to every intruding thought the idea of the Divine omnipresence, and put it to silence by the awe of his Majesty. When the master is present, scholars mind their books, keep their places, and run not over the forms to play with one another; the master's eye keeps an idle servant to his work, that otherwise would be gazing at every straw, and prating to every passenger. How soon would the remembrance of this dash all extravagant fancies out of countenance, just as the news of the approach of a prince would make the courtiers bustle up themselves, huddle up their vain sports, and prepare themselves for a reverent behavior in his sight! We should not dare to give God a piece of our heart when we apprehended him present with the whole: we should not dare to mock one that we knew were more inwards with us than we are with ourselves, and that beheld every motion of our mind, as well as action of our body.

2. Let us endeavor for the more special and influential presence of God. Let the essential presence of God be the ground of our awe, and his gracious influential presence the object of our desire. The heathen thought themselves secure if they had their little petty household gods with them in their journeys: such seem to be the images Rachel stole from her father (Gen. xxxi. 19) to company her travel with their blessings: she might not at that time have cast off all respect to those idols, in the acknowledgment of which she had been educated from her infancy; and they seem to be kept by her till God called Jacob to Bethel, after the rape of Dinah (Gen. xxxv. 4), when Jacob called for the strange gods, and hid them under the oak. The gracious presence of God we should look after, in our actions, as travellers, that have a charge of money or jewels, desire to keep themselves in company that may protect them from highwaymen that would rifle them. Since we have the concerns of the eternal happiness of our souls upon our hands, we should endeavor to have God's merciful and powerful presence with us in all our ways (Ps. xiv. 5); "In all thy ways acknowledge him, and he shall direct thy paths:" acknowledge him before any action, by imploring; acknowledge him after, by rendering him the glory; acknowledge his presence before worship, in worship, after worship: it is this presence makes a kind of heaven upon earth; causeth affliction to put off the nature of misery. How much will the presence of the sun outshine the stars of lesser comforts, and fully answer the want of them! The ark of God going before us, can only make all things successful. It was this led the Israelites over Jordan, and settled them in Canaan. Without this we signify nothing: though we live without this, we cannot be distinguished forever from devils; his essential presence they have; and if we have no more, we shall be no better. It is the enlivening fructifying presence of the sun that revives the languishing earth; and this only can repair our ruined soul. Let it be, therefore, our desire, that as he fills heaven and earth by his essence, he may fill our understandings and wills by his grace, that we may have another kind of presence with us than animals have in their brutish state, or devils in their chains: his essential presence maintains our beings, but his gracious presence confers and continues a happiness.

DISCOURSE VIII

ON GOD'S KNOWLEDGE

Ps cxlvii. 5.—Great is our Lord, and of great power ; his understanding is infinite.

It is uncertain who was the author of this psalm, and when it was penned; some think after the return from the Babylonish captivity. It is a psalm of praise, and is made up of matter of praise from the beginning to the end: God's benefits to the church, his providence over his creatures, and the essential excellency of his nature.

The psalmist doubles his exhortation to praise God (ver. 1), "Praise ye the Lord, sing praise to our God;" to praise him from his dominion as "Lord," from his grace and mercy as "our God;" from the excellency of the duty itself, "it is good, it is comely :" some read it comely, some lovely, or desirable, from the various derivations of the word. Nothing doth so much delight a gracious soul, as an opportunity of celebrating the perfections and goodness of the Creator. The highest duties a creature can render to the Creator are pleasant and delightful in themselves; "it is comely." Praise is a duty that affects the whole soul. The praise of God is a decent thing ; the excellency of God's nature deserves it, and the benefits of God's grace requires it. It is comely when done as it ought to be, with the heart as well as with the voice ; a sinner sings ill, though his voice be good ; the soul in it is to be elevated above earthly things. The first matter of praise is God's erecting and preserving his church (ver. 2) : "The Lord doth build up Jerusalem, he gathers together the outcasts of Israel." The walls of demolished Jerusalem are now re-edified ; God hath brought back the captivity of Jacob, and reduced his people from their Babylonish exile, and those that were dispersed into strange regions, he hath restored to their habitations. Or, it may be prophetic of the calling of the Gentiles, and the gathering the outcasts of the spiritual Israel, that were before as without God in the world, and strangers to the covenant of promise. Let God be praised, but especially for building up his church, and gathering the Gentiles, before counted as outcasts (Isa. xi. 12) ; he gathers them in this world to the faith, and hereafter to glory.

Obs. 1. From the two first verses, observe: 1. All people are under God's care ; but he has a particular regard to his church. This is the signet on his hand, as a bracelet upon his arm ; this is his garden which he delights to dress ; if he prunes it, it is to purge it;

if he digs about his vine, and wounds the branches, it is to make it beautiful with new clusters, and restore it to a fruitful vigor. 2. All great deliverances are to be ascribed to God, as the principal Author, whosoever are the instruments. The Lord doth build up Jerusalem, he gathers together the outcasts of Israel. This great deliverance from Babylon is not to be ascribed to Cyrus or Darius, or the rest of our favorers; it is the Lord that doth it; we had his promise for it, we have now his performance. Let us not ascribe that which is the effect of his truth, only to the good will of men; it is God's act, not by might, nor by power, nor by weapons of war, or strength of horses, but by the Spirit of the Lord. He sent prophets to comfort us while we were exiles; and now he hath stretched out his own arm to work our deliverance according to his word; blind man looks so much upon instruments, that he hardly takes notice of God, either in afflictions or mercies, and this is the cause that robs God of so much prayer and praise in the world. (ver. 3.) "He heals the broken in heart, and bi ds up their wounds." He hath now restored those who had no hope but in his word; he hath dealt with them as a tender and skilful chirurgeon; he hath applied his curing plasters, and dropped in his sovereign balsams; he hath now furnished our fainting hearts with refreshing cordials, and comforted our wounds with strengthening ligatures. How gracious is God, that restores liberty to the captives, and righteousness to the penitent! Man's misery is the fittest opportunity for God to make his mercy illustrious in itself, and most welcome to the patient. He proceeds (ver. 4), wonder not that God calls together the outcasts, and singles them out from every corner for a return; why can he not do this, as well as tell the number of the stars, and call them all by their names? There are none of his people so despicable in the eye of man, but they are known and regarded by God; though they are clouded in the world, yet they are the stars of the world; and shall God number the inanimate stars in the heavens, and make no account of his living stars on the earth? No, wherever they are dispersed, he will not forget them; however they are afflicted, he will not despise them; the stars are so numerous, that they are innumerable by man; some are visible and known by men; others lie more hid and undiscovered in a confused light, as those in the milky way; man cannot see one of them distinctly. God knows all his people. As he can do what is above the power of man to perform, so he understands what is above the skill of man to discover; shall man measure God by his scantiness? Proud man must not equal himself to God, nor cut God as short as his own line. He tells the number of the stars, and calls them all by their names. He hath them all in his list, as generals the names of their soldiers in their muster-roll, for they are his host, which he marshals in the heavens, as in Isaiah xl. 26, where you have the like expression; he knows them more distinctly than man can know anything, and so distinctly, as to call "them all by their names." He knows their names, that is, their natural offices, influences the different degrees of heat and light, their order and motion; and all of them, the least glimmering star, as well as the most glaring planet: this, man cannot do; "Tell the

stars if thou be able to number them" (Gen. xv. 5), saith God to
Abraham, whom Josephus represents as a great astronomer : " Yea,
they cannot be numbered" (Jer. xxxiii. 22) ; and the uncertainty of
the opinions of men, evidenceth their ignorance of their number ;
some reckoning 1022 ; others 1025 ; others 1098 ; others 7000, beside those that by reason of their mixture of light with one another,
cannot be distinctly discerned, and others perhaps so high, as
not to be reached by the eye of man. To impose names on things,
and names according to their natures, is both an argument of power
and dominion, and of wisdom and understanding : from the imposition of names upon the creatures by Adam, the knowledge of
Adam is generally concluded ; and it was also a fruit of that dominion God allowed him over the creatures. Now he that numbers
and names the stars that seem to lie confused among one another,
as well as those that appear to us in an unclouded night, may
well be supposed accurately to know his people, though lurking
in secret caverns, and know those that are fit to be instruments
of their deliverance ; the one is as easy to him as the other; and
the number of the one as distinctly known by him as the multitude of the other. "For great is our Lord, and of great power;
his understanding is infinite" (ver. 5). He wants not knowledge
to know the objects, nor power to effect his will concerning them.
Of great power, רבכוח. Much power, plenteous in power; so the
word רב, is rendered (Ps. v. 15), רבחרד, a multitude of power, as
well as a multitude of mercy ; a power that exceeds all created
power and understanding. His understanding is infinite. You may
not imagine, how he can call all the stars by name, the multitude of
the visible being so great, and the multitude of the invisible being
greater; but you must know, that as God is Almighty, so he is omniscient ; and as there is no end of his power, so no account can
exactly be given of his understanding ; his understanding is infinite,
אירמםפו. No number or account of it ; and so the same words are
rendered, "a nation strong, and without number" (Joel i. 6): no end
of his understanding : (Syriac) no measure, no bounds. His essence
is infinite, and so is his power and understanding ; and so vast is his
knowledge, that we can no more comprehend it, than we can
measure spaces that are without limits, or tell the minutes or hours
of eternity. Who, then, can fathom that whereof there is no number, but which exceeds all, so that there is no searching of it
out? He knows universals, he knows particulars : we must not
take understanding here, as noting a faculty, but the use of the
understanding in the knowledge of things, and the judgment,
תגונח, in the consideration of them, and so it is often used. In
the verse there is a description of God. 1. In his essence, "great
is our Lord." 2. In his power of "great power." 3. In his
knowledge, "his understanding is infinite:" his understanding is
his eye, and his power is his arm. Of his infinite understanding I
am to discourse.

Doctrine. God hath an infinite knowledge and understanding. All
knowledge. Omnipresence, which before we spake of, respects his
essence ; omniscience respects his understanding, according to our

manner of conception. This is clear in Scripture; hence God is called a God of knowledge (Sam. ii. 3), "the Lord is a God of knowledge," (*Heb.*) knowledges, in the plural number, of all kind of knowledge; it is spoken there to quell man's pride in his own reason and parts; what is the knowledge of man but a spark to the whole element of fire, a grain of dust, and worse than nothing, in comparison of the knowledge of God, as his essence is in comparison of the essence of God? All kind of knowledge. He knows what angels know, what man knows, and infinitely more; he knows himself, his own operations, all his creatures, the notions and thoughts of them; he is understanding above understanding, mind above mind, the mind of minds, the light of lights; this the Greek word, Θεὸς, signifies in the etymology of it, of Θεῖσθαι, to *see*, to contemplate; and δαίμων of δαίω, *scio*. The names of God signify a nature, viewing and piercing all things; and the attribution of our senses to God in Scripture, as hearing and seeing, which are the senses whereby knowledge enters into us, signifies God's knowledge.

1. The notion of God's knowledge of all things lies above the ruins of nature; it was not obliterated by the fall of man. It was necessary offending man was to know that he had a Creator whom he had injured, that he had a Judge to try and punish him; since God thought fit to keep up the world, it had been kept up to no purpose, had not this notion been continued alive in the minds of men; there would not have been any practice of his laws, no bar to the worst of crimes. If men had thought they had to deal with an ignorant Deity, there could be no practice of religion. Who would lift up his eyes, or spread his hands towards heaven, if he imagined his devotion were directed to a God as blind as the heathens imagined fortune? To what boot would it be for them to make heaven and earth resound with their cries, if they had not thought God had an eye to see them, and an ear to hear them? And indeed the very notion of a God at the first blush, speaks him a Being endued with understanding; no man can imagine a Creator void of one of the noblest perfections belonging to those creatures, that are the flower and cream of his works.

2. Therefore all nations acknowledge this, as well as the existence and being of God. No nation but had their temples, particular ceremonies of worship, and presented their sacrifices, which they could not have been so vain as to do, without an acknowledgment of this attribute. This notion of God's knowledge owed not its rise to tradition, but to natural implantation; it was born and grew up with every rational creature. Though the several nations and men of the world agreed not in one kind of deity, or in their sentiments of his nature or other perfections, some judging him clothed with a fine and pure body, others judging him an uncompounded spirit, some fixing him to a seat in the heavens, others owning his universal presence in all parts of the world; yet they all agreed in the universality of his knowledge, and their own consciences reflecting their crimes, unknown to any but themselves, would keep this notion in some vigor, whether they would or no. Now this being implanted in the minds of all men by nature, cannot be false, for nature im-

prints not in the minds of all men an assent to a falsity.   Nature
would not pervert the reason and minds of men.   Universal notions
of God are from original, not lapsed nature, and preserved in mankind in order to a restoration from a lapsed state.   The heathens
did acknowledge this: in all the solemn covenants, selemnized with
oaths and the invocation of the name of God, this attribute was supposed.[a]   They confessed knowledge to be peculiar to the Deity;
scientia deorum vita, saith Cicero.   Some called him *Νοῦς, mens,* mind,
pure understanding, without any note, *'Επόπιης,* the inspector of all.
As they called him life, because he was the author of life, so they
called him *intellectus,* because he was the author of all knowledge
and understanding in his creatures; and one being asked, whether any
man could be hid from God? no, saith he, not so much as thinking.[b]
Some call him the eye of the world; and the Egyptians represented
God by an eye on the top of a sceptre, because God is all eye, and
can be ignorant of nothing.

And the same nation made eyes and ears of the most excellent
metals, consecrating them to God, and hanging them up in the midst
of their temples, in signification of God's seeing and hearing all
things; hence they called God light, as well as the Scripture, because
all things are visible to him.

For the better understanding of this, we will enquire, I. What
kind of knowledge or understanding there is in God.   II. What
God knows.   III. How God knows things.   IV. The proof that
God knows all things.   V. The use of all to ourselves.

I. What kind of understanding or knowledge there is in God.
The knowledge of God in Scripture hath various names, according
to the various relations or objects of it: in respect of present things,
it is called knowledge or sight; in respect of things past, remembrance; in respect of things future, or to come, it is called foreknowledge, or prescience (1 Pet. i. 2); in regard of the universality
of the objects, it is called omniscience; in regard to the simple understanding of things, it is called knowledge; in regard of acting and
modelling the ways of acting, it is called wisdom and prudence
(Eph. i. 8).   He must have knowledge, otherwise he could not be
wise; wisdom is the flower of knowledge, and knowledge is the root
of wisdom.   As to what this knowledge is, if we know what knowledge is in man, we may apprehend what it is in God, removing all
imperfection from it, and ascribing to him the most eminent way of
understanding; because we cannot comprehend God, but as he is
pleased to condescend to us in his own ways of discovery, that is,
under some way of similitude to his perfectest creatures, therefore
we have a notion of God by his understanding and will; understanding, whereby he conceives and apprehends things; will, whereby he
extends himself in acting according to his wisdom, and whereby he
doth approve or disapprove; yet we must not measure his understanding by our own, or think it to be of so gross a temper as a
created mind; that he hath eyes of flesh, or sees or knows as man

---

[a] Agamemnon, (Homer Il. 3. v. 8.) making a Covenant with Priam, invocates the Sun,
'Ἥλιος ὅς πάντ' ἐφορᾷς καὶ πάντ' ἐπακούεις.
[b] Gamach in 1 Pa. Aqui. Q. 14. cap. 1 p. 119.   Clem. Alexander Strom. lib. 6.

sees (Job x. 4). We can no more measure his knowledge by ours than we can measure his essence by our essence. As he hath an incomprehensible essence, to which ours is but as a drop of a bucket, so he hath an incomprehensible knowledge, to which ours is but as a grain of dust, or mere darkness: his thoughts are above our thoughts, as the heavens are above the earth. The knowledge of God is variously divided by the schools, and acknowledged by all divines.

1. A knowledge *visionis et simplicis intelligentiæ;* the one we may call a sight, the other an understanding; the one refers to sense, the other to the mind. (1.) A knowledge of vision or sight. Thus God knows himself and all things that really were, are, or shall be in time; all those things which he hath decreed to be, though they are not yet actually sprung up in the world, but lie couchant in their causes. (2.) A knowledge of intelligence or simple understanding. The object of this is not things that are in being, or that shall by any decree of God ever be existent in the world, but such things as are possible to be wrought by the power of God, though they shall never in the least peep up into being, but lie forever wrapt up in darkness and nothing.[c] This also is a necessary knowledge to be allowed to God, because the object of this knowledge is necessary. The possibility of more creatures than ever were or shall be, is a conclusion that hath a necessary truth in it; as it is necessary that the power of God can produce more creatures, though it be not necessary that it should produce more creatures, so it is necessary that whatsoever the power of God can work, is possible to be. And as God knows this possibility, so he knows all the objects that are thus possible; and herein doth much consist the infiniteness of his knowledge, as shall be shown presently. These two kinds of knowledge differ; that of vision, is of things which God hath decreed to be, though they are not yet; that of intelligence is of things which never shall be; yet they may be, or are possible to be, if God please to will and order their being; one respects things that shall be, the other, things that may be, and are not repugnant to the nature of God to be. The knowledge of vision follows the act of God's will, and supposeth an act of God's will before, decreeing things to be. (If we could suppose any first or second in God's decree, we might say God knew them as possible before he decreed them; he knew them as future, because he decreed them.) For without the will of God decreeing a thing to come to pass, God cannot know that it will infallibly come to pass. But the knowledge of intelligence stands without any act of his will, in order to the being of those things he knows; he knows possible things only in his power; he knows other things both in his power as able to effect them, and in his will, as determining the being of them; such knowledge we must grant to be in God, for there is such a kind of knowledge in man; for man doth not only know and see what is before his eyes in this world, but he may have a conception of many more worlds, and many more creatures, which he knows are possible to the power of God.

2. There is a speculative and practical knowledge in God. (1.) A

[c] Suarez de Deo, lib. 3. cap. 4. p. 130.

speculative knowledge is, when the truth of a thing is known without a respect to any working or practical operation.   The knowledge of things possible is in God only speculative,[d] and some say God's knowledge of himself is only speculative, because there is nothing for God to work in himself: and though he knows himself, yet this knowledge of himself doth not terminate there, but flowers into a love of himself, and delight in himself; yet this love of himself, and delight in himself, is not enough to make it a practical knowledge, because it is natural, and naturally and necessarily flows from the knowledge of himself and his own goodness: he cannot but love himself, and delight in himself, upon the knowledge of himself. But that which is properly practice, is where there is a dominion over the action, and it is wrought not naturally and necessarily, but in a way of freedom and counsel.   As when we see a beautiful flower or other thing, there ariseth a delight in the mind ; this no man will call practice, because it is a natural affection of the will, arising from the virtue of the object, without any consideration of the understanding in a practical manner by counselling, commanding, &c.   (2.) A practical knowledge: which tends to operation and practice, and is the principle of working about things that are known ; as the knowledge an artificer hath in an art or mystery.   This knowledge is in God: the knowledge he hath of the things he hath decreed, is such a kind of knowledge ; for it terminates in the act of creation, which is not a natural and necessary act, as the loving himself, and delighting in himself is, but wholly free: for it was at his liberty whether he would create them or no; this is called discretion (Jer. x. 12): "He hath stretched out the heavens by his discretion."   Such also is his knowledge of the things he hath created, and which are in being, for it terminates in the government of them for his own glorious ends.   It is by this knowledge "the depths are broken up, and the clouds drop down their dew" (Prov. iii. 20).   This is a knowledge whereby he knows the essence, qualities, and properties of what he creates and governs in order to his own glory, and the common good of the world over which he resides; so that speculative knowledge is God's knowledge of himself and things possible ; practical knowledge is his knowledge of his creatures and things governable ; yet in some sort this practical knowledge is not only of things that are made, but of things which are possible, which God might make, though he will not: for as he knows that they can be created, so he knows how they are to be created, and how to be governed, though he never will create them.   This is a practical knowledge: for it is not requisite to constitute a knowledge practical, actually to act, but that the knowledge in itself be referable to action.[e]

3. There is a knowledge of approbation, as well as apprehension. This the Scripture often mentions.   Words of understanding are used to signify the acts of affection.   This knowledge adds to the simple act of the understanding, the complacency and pleasure of the will, and is improperly knowledge, because it belongs to the will, and not to the understanding ; only it is radically in the understanding, because affection implies knowledge : men cannot approve of

    [d] Suarez de Deo, lib. 3. cap. 4. p. 138.   [e] Ibid. p. 140.

that which they are ignorant of. Thus knowledge is taken (Amos iii. 2), "You only have I known of all the families of the earth; and (2 Tim. ii. 19), "The Lord knows who are his," that is, he loves them; he doth not only know them, but acknowledges them for his own. It notes, not only an exact understanding, but a special care of them; and so is that to be understood (Gen. i.), "God saw every thing that he had made, and behold it was very good:" that is, he saw it with an eye of approbation, as well as apprehension. This is grounded upon God's knowledge of vision, his sight of his creatures; for God doth not love or delight in anything but what is actually in being, or what he hath decreed to bring into being. On the contrary, also, when God doth not approve, he is said not to know (Matt. xxv. 12), "I know you not," and (Matt. vii. 23), "I never knew you;" he doth not approve of their works. It is not an ignorance of understanding, but an ignorance of will; for while he saith he never knew them, he testifies that he did know them, in rendering the reason of his disapproving them, because he knows all their works: so he knows them, and doth not know them in a different manner: he knows them so as to understand them, but he doth not know them so as to love them. We must, then, ascribe an universal knowledge to God. If we deny him a speculative knowledge, or knowledge of intelligence, we destroy his Deity, we make him ignorant of his own power: if we deny him practical knowledge, we deny ourselves to be his creatures; for, as his creatures, we are the fruits of this, his discretion, discovered in creation: if we deny his knowledge of vision, we deny his governing dominion. How can he exercise a sovereign and uncontrollable dominion, that is ignorant of the nature and qualities of the things he is to govern? If he had not knowledge he could make no revelation; he that knows not cannot dictate; we could then have no Scripture. To deny God knowledge, is to dash out the Scripture, and demolish the Deity. God is described in Zech. iii. 9, "with seven eyes," to show his perfect knowledge of all things, all occurrences in the world; and the cherubims, or whatsoever is meant by the wings, are described to be full of eyes, both "before and behind" (Ezek. i. 18), round about them; much more is God all eye, all ear, all understanding. The sun is a natural image of God; if the sun had an eye, it would see; if it had an understanding, it would know all visible things; it would see what it shines upon, and understand what it influenceth, in the most obscure bowels of the earth. Doth God excel his creature, the sun, in excellency and beauty, and not in light and understanding? certainly more than the sun excels an atom or grain of dust. We may yet make some representation of this knowledge of God by a lower thing, a picture, which seems to look upon every one, though there be never so great a multitude in the room where it hangs; no man can cast his eye upon it, but it seems to behold him in particular, and so exactly, as if there were none but him upon whom the eye of it were fixed; and every man finds the same cast of it: shall art frame a thing of that nature, and shall not the God of art and all knowledge, be much more in reality than that is in imagination? Shall not God have a far greater capacity to behold everything in the world, which is infinitely less to him than a wide room to a picture?

II. The second thing, What God knows; how far his understanding reaches.

1. God knows himself, and only knows himself. This is the first and original knowledge, wherein he excels all creatures. No man doth exactly know himself; much less doth he understand the full nature of a spirit; much less still the nature and perfections of God; for what proportion can there be between a finite faculty and an infinite object? Herein consists the infiniteness of God's knowledge, that he knows his own essence, that he knows that which is unknowable to any else. It doth not so much consist in knowing the creatures, which he hath made, as in knowing himself, who was never made. It is not so much infinite, because he knows all things which are in the world, or that shall be; or things that he can make, because the number of them is finite; but because he hath a perfect and comprehensive knowledge of his own infinite perfections.[f] Though it be said that angels "see his face" (Matt. xviii. 10), that sight notes rather their immediate attendance, than their exact knowledge; they see some signs of his presence and majesty, more illustrious and express than ever appeared to man in this life; but the essence of God is invisible to them, hid from them in the secret place of eternity; none knows God but himself (1 Cor. ii. 11): "What man knows the things of a man save the spirit of a man? so the things of God knows no man but the Spirit of God; the Spirit of God searches the deep things of God;" searcheth, that is, exactly knows, thoroughly understands, as those who have their eyes in every chink and crevice, to see what lies hid there; the word search notes not an inquiry, but an exact knowledge, such as men have of things upon a diligent scrutiny: as when God is said to search the heart and the reins, it doth not signify a precedent ignorance, but an exact knowledge of the most intimate corners of the hearts of men. As the conceptions of men are unknown to any but themselves, so the depths of the divine essence, perfections, and decrees, are unknown to any but to God himself; he only knows what he is, and what he knows, what he can do, and what he hath decreed to do. For first, if God did not know himself, he would not be perfect. It is the perfection of a creature to know itself, much more a perfection belonging to God. If God did not comprehend himself, he would want an infinite perfection, and so would cease to be God, in being defective in that which intellectual creatures in some measure possess. As God is the most perfect being, so he must have the most perfect understanding: if he did not understand himself, he would be under the greatest ignorance, because he would be ignorant of the most excellent object. Ignorance is the imperfection of the understanding; and ignorance of one's self is a greater imperfection than ignorance of things without. If God should know all things without himself, and not know himself, he would not have the most perfect knowledge, because he would not have the knowledge of the best

f Moulin.

of objects. Secondly, Without the knowledge of himself, he could not be blessed. Nothing can have any complacency in itself, without knowledge of itself. Nothing can in a rational manner enjoy itself, without understanding itself. The blessedness of God consists not in the knowledge of anything without him, but in the knowledge of himself and his own excellency, as the principle of all things; if, therefore, he did not perfectly know himself and his own happiness, he could not enjoy a happiness; for to be, and not to know to be, is as if a thing were not. "He is God, blessed forever" (Rom. ix. 5.), and therefore forever had a knowledge of himself. Thirdly, Without the knowledge of himself, he could create nothing. For he would be ignorant of his own power, and his own ability; and he that doth not know how far his power extends, could not act: if he did not know himself, he could know nothing; and he that knows nothing, can do nothing; he could not know an effect to be possible to him, unless he knew his own power as a cause. Fourthly, Without the knowledge of himself, he could govern nothing. He could not, without the knowledge of his own holiness and righteousness, prescribe laws to men, nor without a knowledge of his own nature order himself a manner of worship suitable to it. All worship must be congruous to the dignity and nature of the object worshipped: he must therefore know his own authority, whereby worship was to be enacted; his own excellency, to which worship was to be suited; his own glory, to which worship was to be directed. If he did not know himself, he did not know what to punish, because he would not know what was contrary to himself: not knowing himself, he would not know what was a contempt of him, and what an adoration of him; what was worthy of God, and what was unworthy of him. In fine, he could not know other things, unless he knew himself; unless he knew his own power, he could not know how he created things; unless he knew his own wisdom, he could not know the beauty of his works; unless he knew his own glory, he could not know the end of his works; unless he knew his own holiness, he could not know what was evil; and unless he knew his own justice, he could not know how to punish the crimes of his offending creatures. And, therefore,

(1.) God knows himself, because his knowledge, with his will, is the cause of all other things that can fall under his cognizance: he knows himself first, before he can know any other thing; that is, first according to our conceptions; for, indeed, God knows himself and all other things at once; he is the first truth, and therefore is the first object of his own understanding. There is nothing more excellent than himself, and therefore nothing more known to him than himself. As he is all knowledge, so he hath in himself the most excellent object of knowledge. To understand, is properly to know one's self. No object is so intelligible to God as God is to himself, nor so intimately and immediately joined with his understanding as himself; for his understanding is his essence, himself.

(2.) He knows himself by his own essence. He knows not himself and his own power by the effect, because he knows himself

from eternity, before there was a world, or any effect of his power
extant. It is not a knowledge by the cause, for God hath no cause;
nor a knowledge of himself by any species, or anything from without: if it were anything from without himself, that must be created
or uncreated; if uncreated it would be God; and so we must either
own many Gods, or own ' it to be his essence, and so not distinct
from himself: if created, then his knowledge of himself would depend upon a creature: he could not, then, know himself from eternity, but in time, because nothing can be created from eternity, but
in time. God knows not himself by any faculty, for there is no
composition in God; he is not made up of parts, but is a simple being; some, therefore, have called God, not *intellectus*, understanding,
because that savors of a faculty, but *intellectio*, intellection: God is
all act in the knowledge of himself and his knowledge of other
things.

(3.) God, therefore, knows himself perfectly, comprehensively.
Nothing in his own nature is concealed from him; he reflects upon
everything that he is.[g] There is a positive comprehension, so God
doth not comprehend himself; for what is comprehended hath
bounds, and what is comprehended by itself is finite to itself; and
there is a negative comprehension—God so comprehends himself;
nothing in his own nature is obscure to him, unknown by him; for
there is as great a perfection in the understanding of God to know,
as there is in the divine nature to be known. The understanding
of God, and the nature of God, are both infinite, and so equal to
one another: his understanding is equal to himself; he knows himself so well, that nothing can be known by him more perfectly
than himself is known to himself. He knows himself in the highest manner, because nothing is so proportioned to the understanding of God as himself. He knows his own essence, goodness,
power; all his perfections, decrees, intentions, acts, the infinite
capacity of his own understanding, so that nothing of himself is in
the dark to himself: and, in this respect, some use this expression,
that the infiniteness of God is in a manner finite to himself, because
it is comprehended by himself. Thus God transcends all creatures;
thus his understanding is truly infinite, because nothing but himself is an infinite object for it: what angels may understand of
themselves perfectly I know not, but no creature in the world understands himself. Man understands not fully the excellency and
parts of his own nature; upon God's knowledge of himself depends
the comfort of his people, and the terror of the wicked: this is
also a clear argument for his knowledge of all other things without himself; he that knows himself, must needs know all other
things less than himself, and which were made by himself; when
the knowledge of his own immensity and infiniteness is not an
object too difficult for him, the knowledge of a finite and limited
creature, in all his actions, thoughts, circumstances, cannot be too
hard for him: since he knows himself, who is infinite, he cannot but know whatsoever is finite. This is the foundation of all
his other knowledge; the knowledge of everything present, past,

g Magalaneus.

and to come, is far less than the knowledge of himself. He is more incomprehensible in his own nature, than all things created, or that can be created, put together can be. If he, then, have a perfect comprehensive knowledge of his own nature, any knowledge of all other things is less than the knowledge of himself; this ought to be well considered by us, as the fountain whence all his other knowledge flows.

2. Therefore God knows all other things, whether they be possible, past, present, or future ; whether they be things that he can do, but will never do, or whether they be things that he hath done, but are not now ; things that are now in being, or things that are not now existing, that lie in the womb of their proper and immediate causes.[h] If his understanding be infinite, he then knows all things whatsoever that can be known, else his understanding would have bounds, and what hath limits is not infinite, but finite. If he be ignorant of any one thing that is knowable, that is a bound to him, it comes with an exception, a *but*, God knows all things *but* this; a bar is then set to his knowledge. If there were anything, any particular circumstance in the whole creation or non-creation, and possible to be known by him, and yet were unknown to him, he could not be said to be omniscient ; as he would not be Almighty if any one thing, that implied not a repugnancy to his nature, did transcend his power.

First, All things possible. No question but God knows what he could create, as well as what he hath created ; what he would not create, as well as what he resolved to create ; he knew what he would not do before he willed to do it ; this is the next thing which declares the infiniteness of his understanding ; for, as his power is infinite, and can create innumerable worlds and creatures, so is his knowedge infinite, in knowing innumerable things possible to his power. Possibles are infinite ; that is, there is no end of what God can do, and therefore no end of what God doth know ; otherwise his power would be more infinite than his knowledge: if he knew only what is created, there would be an end of his understanding, because all creatures may be numbered, but possible things cannot be reckoned up by any creature. There is the same reason of this in eternity ; when never so many numbers of years are run out, there is still more to come, there still wants an end; and when millions of worlds are created, there is no more an end of God's power than of eternity. Thus there is no end of his understanding ; that is, his knowledge is not terminated by anything. This the Scripture gives us some account of: God knows things that are not, "for he calls things that are not as if they were" (Rom. iv. 17); he calls things that are not, as if they were in being; what he calls is not unknown to him: if he knows things that are not, he knows things that may never be ; as he knows things that shall be, because he wills them, so he knows things that might be, because he is able to effect them: he knew that the inhabitants of Keilah would betray David to Saul if he remained in that place (1 Sam. xxiii. 11); he knew what they would do upon that occasion, though it was never done ; as he knew what was in

[h] Petar. Theol. Dogm. lib. p. 257.

their power and in their wills, so he must needs know what is within the compass of his own power ; as he can permit more than he doth permit so he knows what he can permit, and what, upon that permission, would be done by his creatures; so God knew the possibility of the Tyrians' repentance, if they had had the same means, heard the same truths, and beheld the same miracles which were offered to the ears, and presented to the eyes of the Jews (Matt. xi. 21). This must needs be so, because,

1. Man knows things that are possible to him, though he will never effect them. A carpenter knows a house in the model he hath of it in his head, though he never build a house according to that model. A watch-maker hath the frame of a watch in his mind, which he will never work with his instruments ; man knows what he could do, though he never intends to do it.[i] As the understanding of man hath a virtue, that where it sees one man it may imagine thousands of men of the same shape, stature, form, parts ; yea, taller, more vigorous, sprightly, intelligent, than the man he sees ; because it is possible such a number may be. Shall not the understanding of God much more know what he is able to effect, since the understanding of man can know what he is never able to produce, yet may be produced by God, viz. that he who produced this man which I see, can produce a thousand exactly like him ? If the Divine understanding did not know infinite things, but were confined to a certain number, it may be demanded whether God can understand anything farther than that number, or whether he cannot ? If he can, then he doth actually understand all those things which he hath a power to understand; otherwise there would be an increase of God's knowledge, if it were actually now, and not before, and so he would be more perfect than he was before ; if he cannot understand them, then he cannot understand what a human mind can understand ; for our understandings can multiply numbers *in infinitum ;* and there is no number so great, but a man can still add to it : we must suppose the divine understanding more excellent in knowledge. God knows all that a man can imagine, though it never were, nor never shall be ; he must needs know whatsoever is in the power of man to imagine or think, because God concurs to the support of the faculty in that imagination ; and though it may be replied, an atheist may imagine that there is no God, a man may imagine that God can lie, or that he can be destroyed ; doth God know therefore that he is not? or that he can lie, or cease to be ? No, he knows he cannot ; his knowledge extends to things possible, not to things impossible to himself ; he knows it as imaginable by man, not as possible in itself ; because it is utterly impossible, and repugnant to the nature of God,[k] since he eminently contains in himself all things possible, past, present, and to come ; he cannot know himself without knowing them.

2. God knowing his own power, knows whatsoever is in his power to effect. If he knows not all things possible, he could not know the extent of his own power, and so would not know himself, as a cause sufficient for more things than he hath created. How can he

i Ficin de Immort. lib. 2. cap. 10.   k Gamach.

comprehend himself, who comprehends not all effluxes of things possible that may come from him, and be wrought by him? How can he know himself as a cause, if he know not the objects and works which he is able to produce?[1] Since the power of God extends to numberless things, his knowledge also extends to numberless objects; as if a unit is, could see the numbers it could produce, it would see infinite numbers: for a unit, as it were, all number. God knowing the fruitfulness of his own virtue, knows a numberless multitude of things which he can do, more than have been done, or shall be done by him; he therefore knows innumerable worlds, innumerable angels, with higher perfections, than any of them which he hath created have: so that if the world should last many millions of years, God knows that he can every day create another world more capacious than this; and having created an inconceivable number, he knows he could still create more: so that he beholds infinite worlds, infinite numbers of men, and other creatures in himself, infinite kinds of things, infinite species, and individuals under those kinds, even as many as he can create, if his will did order and determine it; for not being ignorant of his own power, he cannot be ignorant of the effects wherein it may display and discover itself. A comprehensive knowledge of his own power doth necessarily include the objects of that power; so he knows whatsoever he could effect, and whatsoever he could permit, if he pleased to do it. If God could not understand more than he hath created, he could not create more than he hath created: for it cannot be conceived how he can create anything that he is ignorant of; what he doth not know, he cannot do: he must know also the extent of his own goodness, and how far anything is capable to partake of it: so much therefore, as any detract from the knowledge of God, they detract from his power.

3. It is further evident that God knows all possible things, because he knew those things which he has created, before they were created, when they were yet in a possibility. If God knew things before they were created, he knew them when they were in a possibility, and not in actual reality. It is absurd to imagine that his understanding did lackey after the creatures, and draw knowledge from them after they were created. It is absurd to think that God did create, before he knew what he could or would create. If he knew those things he did create when they were possible, he must know all things which he can create, and therefore all things that are possible. To conclude this, we must consider that this knowledge is of another kind than his knowledge of things that are or shall be. He sees possible things as possible, not as things that ever are or shall be. If he saw them as existing or future, and they shall never be, this knowledge would be false, there would be a deceit in it, which cannot be. He knows those things not in themselves, because they are not, nor in their causes, because they shall never be: he knows them in his own power, not in his will: he understands them as able to produce them, not as willing to effect them. Things possible he knows only in his power; things future he knows both in his power and his

[1] Ficin de Immort. lib. 2. cap. 10.

will, as he is both able and determined in his own good pleasure to give being to them. Those that shall never come to pass, he knows only in himself as a sufficient cause; those things that shall come into being, he knows in himself as the efficient cause, and also in their immediate second causes. This should teach us to spend our thoughts in the admiration of the excellency of God, and the divine knowledge; his understanding is infinite.

Secondly, God knows all things past. This is an argument used by God himself to elevate his excellency above all the commonly adored idols (Isa. xli. 22): "Let them show the former things, what they be, that we may consider them, and know the latter end of them." He knows them as if they were now present, and not past: for indeed in his eternity there is nothing past or future to his knowledge. This is called remembrance, in Scripture, as when God remembered Rachel's prayer for a child (Gen. xxx. 22), and he is said to put tears into his bottle, and write them in his book of accompts, which signifies the exact and unerring knowledge in God of the minute circumstances past in the world; and this knowledge is called a book of remembrance (Mal. iii. 16), signifying the perpetual presence of things past, before him. There are two elegant expressions, signifying the certainty and perpetuity of God's knowledge of sins past (Job xiv. 17), "My transgression is sealed up in a bag, and thou sewest up mine iniquity;" a metaphor, taken from men that put up in a bag the money they would charily keep, tie the bag, sew up the holes, and bind it hard, that nothing may fall out; or a vessel, wherein they reserve liquors, and daub it with pitch and glutinous stuff, that nothing may leak out, but be safely kept till the time of use; or else, as some think, from the bags attornies carry with them, full of writings, when they are to manage a cause against a person. Thus we find God often in Scripture calling to men's minds their past actions, upbraiding them with their ingratitude, wherein he testifies his remembrance of his own past benefits and their crimes. His knowledge in this regard hath something of infinity in it, since though the sins of all men that have been in the world are finite in regard of number, yet when the sins of one man in thoughts, words, and deeds, are numberless in his own account, and perhaps in the count of any creature, the sins of all the vast numbers of men that have been, or shall be, are much more numberless, it cannot be less than infinite knowledge that can make a collection of them, and take a survey of them all at once. If past things had not been known by God, how could Moses have been acquainted with the original of things? How could he have declared the former transactions, wherein all histories are silent but the Scripture? How could he know the cause of man's present misery so many ages after, wherewith all philosophy was unacquainted? How could he have writ the order of the creation, the particulars of the sin of Adam, the circumstances of Cain's murder, the private speech of Lamech to his wives, if God had not revealed them? And how could a revelation be made, if things past were forgotten by him? Do we not remember many things done among men, as well as by ourselves, and reserve the forms of divers things in our minds, which rise as occasions are presented to draw them forth? And shall not God much more, who hath no cloud of darkness upon his understanding? A man that makes a curious picture, hath the form of it in his mind before he made it; and if the fire burn it, the form of it in his mind is not destroyed by the fire, but retained in it. God's memory is no less perfect than his understanding. If he did not know things past, he could not be a righteous Governor, or exercise any judicial act in a righteous manner; he could not dispense rewards and punishments, according to his promises and threatenings, if things that were past could be forgotten by him; he could not require that which is past (Eccles. iii. 15), if he did not remember that which is past. And though God be said to forget in Scripture, and not to know his people, and his people pray to him to remember them, as if he had forgotten them (Ps. cxix. 49), this is improperly ascribed to God.[m] As God is said to repent, when he changes things according to his counsel beyond the expectation of men, so he is said to forget, when he defers the making good his promise to the godly, or his threatenings to the wicked; this is not a defect of memory belonging to his mind, but an act of his will. When he is said to remember his covenant, it is to will grace according to his covenant; when he is said to forget his covenant, it is to intercept the influences of it, whereby to punish the sin of his people; and when he is said not to know his people, it is not an absolute forgetfulness of them, but withdrawing from them the testimonies of his kindness, and clouding the signs of his favor; so God in pardon is said to forget sin, not that he ceaseth to know it, but ceaseth to punish it. It is not to be meant of a simple forgetfulness, or a lapse of his memory, but of a judicial forgetfulness; so when his people in Scripture pray, Lord, remember thy word unto thy servant, no more is to be understood but, Lord, fulfil thy word and promise to thy servant.

Thirdly, He knows things present (Heb. iv. 13): "All things are naked and opened unto the eyes of him with whom we have to do;" this is grounded upon the knowledge of himself; it is not so difficult to know all creatures exactly, as to know himself, because they are finite, but himself is infinite; he knows his own power, and therefore everything through which his omnipotence is diffused, all the acts and objects of it; not the least thing that is the birth of his power, can be concealed from him; he knows his own goodness, and therefore every object upon which the warm beams of his goodness strike; he therefore knows distinctly the properties of every creature, because every property in them is a ray of his goodness; he is not only the efficient, but the exemplary cause; therefore as he knows all that his power hath wrought, as he is the efficient, so he knows them in himself as the pattern; as a carpenter can give an account of every part and passage in a house he hath built, by consulting the model in his own mind, whereby he built it. "He looked upon all things after he had made them, and pronounced them good" (Gen. i. 3), full of a natural goodness he had endowed them with: he did not ignorantly pronounce them so, and call them good,

m Bradward.

whether he knew them or not; and therefore he knows them in particular, as he knew them all in their first presence. Is there any reason he should be ignorant of everything now present in the world, or that anything that derives an existence from him as a free cause, should be concealed from him? If he did not know things present in their particularities, many things would be known by man, yea, by beasts, which the infinite God were ignorant of; and if he did not know all things present, but only some, it is possible for the most blessed God to be deceived and be miserable: ignorance is a calamity to the understanding: he could not prescribe laws to his creatures, unless he knew their natures to which those laws were to be suited: no, not natural ordinances to the sun, moon, and heavenly bodies, and inanimate creatures, unless he knew the vigor and virtue in them, to execute those ordinances; for to prescribe laws above the nature of things, is inconsistent with the wisdom of government; he must know how far they were able to obey; whether the laws were suited to their ability: and for his rational creatures, whether the punishments annexed to the law were proper, and suited to the transgression of the creature.

1. He knows all creatures from the highest to the lowest, the least as well as the greatest. He knows the ravens and their young ones (Job xxxviii. 41); the drops of rain and dew which he hath begotten (Job xxxviii. 29); every bird in the air, as well as any man doth what he hath in a cage at home (Ps. l. 11): " I know all the fowls in the mountains, and the wild beasts in the field;" which some read creeping things   The clouds are numbered in his wisdom (Job xxxviii. 37); every worm in the earth, every drop of rain that falls upon the ground, the flakes of snow, and the knots of hail, the sands upon the sea-shore, the hairs upon the head; it is no more absurd to imagine that God knows them, than that God made them; they are all the effects of his power, as well as the stars which he calls by their names, as well as the most glorious angel and blessed spirit; he knows them as well as if there were none but them in particular for him to know; the least things were framed by his art as well as the greatest; the least things partake of his goodness as well as the greatest; he knows his own arts, and his own goodness, and therefore all the stamps and impressions of them upon all his creatures; he knows the immediate causes of the least, and therefore the effects of those causes. Since his knowledge is infinite, it must extend to those things which are at the greatest distance from him, to those which approach nearest to not being; since he did not want power to create, he cannot want understanding to know everything he hath created, the dispositions, qualities, and virtues of the minutest creature. Nor is the understanding of God embased, and suffers a diminution by the knowledge of the vilest and most inconsiderable things. Is it not an imperfection to be ignorant of the nature of anything? and can God have such a defect in his most perfect understanding? Is the understanding of man of an impurer alloy by knowing the nature of the rankest poisons? by understanding a fly, or a small insect? or by considering the deformity of a toad? Is it not generally counted a note of a dignified mind to be able to discourse of the

nature of them? Was Solomon, who knew all from the cedar to the hyssop, debased by so rich a present of wisdom from his Creator? Is any glass defiled by presenting a deformed image? Is there anything more vile than the "imaginations, which are only evil, and continually?" Doth not the mind of man descend to the mud of the earth, play the adulterer or idolater with mean objects, suck in the most unclean things? yet God knows these in all their circumstances, in every appearance, inside and outside. Is there anything viler than some thoughts of men? than some actions of men? their unclean beds and gluttonous vomiting, and Luciferian pride? yet do not these fall under the eye of God, in all their nakedness? The Second Person's taking human nature, though it obscured, yet it did not disparage the Deity, or bring any disgrace to it. Is gold the worse for being formed into the image of a fly? doth it not still retain the nobleness of the metal? When men are despised for descending to the knowledge of mean and vile things, it is because they neglect the knowledge of the greater, and sin in their inquiries after lesser things, with a neglect of that which concerns more the honor of God and the happiness of themselves; to be ambitious of such a knowledge, and careless of that of more concern, is criminal and contemptible. But God knows the greatest as well as the least; mean things are not known by him to exclude the knowledge of the greater; nor are vile things governed by him to exclude the order of the better. The deformity of objects known by God doth not deform him, nor defile him; he doth not view them without himself, but within himself, wherein all things in their ideas are beautiful and comely: our knowledge of a deformed thing is not a deforming of our understanding, but is beautiful in the knowledge, though it be not in the object; nor is there any fear that the understanding of God should become material by knowing material things, any more than our understandings lose their spirituality by knowing the nature of bodies; it is to be observed, therefore, that only those senses of men, as seeing, hearing, smelling, which have those qualities for their objects that come nearest the nature of spiritual things, as light, sounds, fragrant odors, are ascribed to God in Scripture; not touching or tasting, which are senses that are not exercised without a more immediate commerce with gross matter; and the reason may be, because we should have no gross thoughts of God, as if he were a body, and made of matter, like the things he knows.

2. As he knows all creatures, so God knows all the actions of creatures. He counts in particular all the ways of men. "Doth he not see all my ways, and count all my steps" (Job xxxi. 4)? He "tells" their "wanderings," as if one by one (Ps. lvi. 8). His eyes are upon all the ways of man, and he sees all his goings" (Job xxxiv. 21); a metaphor taken from men, when they look wistly, with fixed eyes upon a thing, to view it in every circumstance, whence it comes, whether it goes, to observe every little motion of it. God's eye is not a wandering, but a fixed eye; and the ways of man are not only "before his eyes," but he doth exactly "ponder them" (Prov. v. 21); as one that will not be ignorant of the least mite in them, but weigh and examine them by the standard of his law; he may as well know

the motions of our members, as the hairs of our heads; the smallest actions before they be, whether civil, natural, or religious, fall under his cognizance; what meaner than a man carrying a pitcher, yet our Saviour foretels it (Luke xxii. 10); God knows not only what men do, but what they would have done, had he not restrained them; what Abimelech would have done to Sarah, had not God put a bar in his way (Gen. xx. 6); what a man that is taken away in his youth would have done, had he lived to a riper age; yea, he knows the most secret words as well as actions; the words spoken by the king of Israel in his bed-chamber, were revealed to Elisha (2 Kings vi. 12); and indeed, how can any action of man be concealed from God? Can we view the various actions of a heap of ants, or a hive of bees in a glass, without turning our eyes; and shall not God behold the actions of all men in the world, which are less than bees or ants in his sight, and more visible to him than an ant-hill or bee-hive can be to the acutest eye of man?

3. As God knows all the actions of creatures, so he knows all the thoughts of creatures. The thoughts are the most closeted acts of man, hid from men and angels, unless disclosed by some outward expressions; but God descends into the depths and abysses of the soul, discerns the most inward contrivances; nothing is impenetrable to him; the sun doth not so much enlighten the earth, as God understands the heart; all things are as visible to him, as flies and motes enclosed in a body of transparent crystal; this man naturally allows to God. Men often speak to God by the motions of their minds and secret ejaculations, which they would not do, if it were not naturally implanted in them, that God knows all their inward motions; the Scripture is plain and positive in this, " He tries the heart and the reins" (Ps. vii. 9), as men, by the use of fire, discern the drossy and purer parts of metals. The secret intentions and aims, the most lurking affections seated in the reins; he knows that which no man, no angel, is able to know, which a man himself knows not, nor makes any particular reflection upon; yea, " he weighs the Spirit" (Prov. xvi. 2); he exactly numbers all the devices and inclinations of men, as men do every piece of coin they tell out of a heap. " He discerns the thoughts and intents of the heart" (Heb. iv. 12); all that is in the mind, all that is in the affections, every stirring and purpose; so that not one thought can be withheld from him" (Job xlii. 2); yea, " Hell and destruction are before him, much more then the hearts of the children of men" (Prov. xv. 11); he works all things in the bowels of the earth, and brings forth all things out of that treasure, say some; but more naturally, God knows the whole state of the dead, all the receptacles and graves of their bodies, all the bodies of men consumed by the earth, or devoured by living creatures; things that seem to be out of all being; he knows the thoughts of the devils and damned creatures, whom he hath cast out of his care forever into the arms of his justice, never more to cast a delightful glance towards them; not a secret in any soul in hell (which he hath no need to know, because he shall not judge them by any of the thoughts they now have, since they were condemned to punishment) is hid from him; much more is he acquainted with the

thoughts of living men, the counsels of whose hearts are yet to be manifested, in order to their trial and censure; yea, he knows them before they spring up into actual being (Ps. cxxxix. 2): "Thou understandest my thoughts afar off;" my thoughts, that is, every thought; though innumerable thoughts pass through me in a day, and that in the source and fountain, when it is yet in the womb, before it is our thought; if he knows them before their existence, before they can be properly called ours, much more doth he know them when they actually spring up in us: he knows the tendency of them; where the bird will light when it is in flight; he knows them exactly, he is therefore called a "discerner" or criticiser "of the heart" (Heb. iv. 12), as a critic discerns every letter, point, and stop; he is more intimate with us than our souls with our bodies, and hath more the possession of us than we have of ourselves; he knows them by an inspection into the heart, not by the mediation of second causes, by the looks or gestures of men, as men may discern the thoughts of one another. (1.) God discerns all good motions of the mind and will. These he puts into men, and needs must God know his own act; he knew the son of "Jeroboam to have some good thing in him towards the Lord God of Israel" (1 Kings xiv. 13); and the integrity of David and Hezekiah; the freest motions of the will and affections to him: "Lord, thou knowest that I love thee," saith Peter (John xxi. 17). Love can be no more restrained, than the will itself can; a man may make another to grieve and desire, but none can force another to love. (2.) God discerns all the evil motions of the mind and will; "Every imagination of the heart" (Gen. vi. 5); the vanity of "men's thoughts" (Ps. xciv. 11); their inward darkness, and deceitful disguises. No wonder that God, who fashioned the heart, should understand the motions of it (Ps. xxxiii. 13, 15): "He looks from heaven and beholds all the children of men; he fashioneth their hearts alike, and considers all their works." Doth any man make a watch, and yet be ignorant of its motion? Did God fling away the key to this secret cabinet, when he framed it, and put off the power of unlocking it when he pleased? He did not surely frame it in such a posture as that anything in it should be hid from his eye; he did not fashion it to be privileged from his government; which would follow if he were ignorant of what was minted and coined in it. He could not be a Judge to punish men, if the inward frames and principles of men's actions were concealed from him; an outward action may glitter to an outward eye, yet the secret spring be a desire of applause, and not the fear and love of God. If the inward frames of the heart did lie covered from him in the secret recesses of the heart; those plausible acts, which in regard of their principles, would merit a punishment, would meet with a reward; and God should bestow happiness where he had denounced misery. As without the knowledge of what is just, he could not be a wise Lawgiver, so without the knowledge of what is inwardly committed, he could not be a righteous Judge: acts that are rotten in the spring, might be judged good by the fair color and appearance. This is the glory of God at the last day, "to manifest the secrets of all hearts" (1 Cor. iv. 5); and the prophet Jeremiah links the power of judging and the prerogative of trying the hearts together (Jer. xi. 20): "But thou, O Lord of hosts, that judgest righteously, that triest the reins and the heart;" and (Jer. xvii. 10): "I, the Lord, search, the heart, I try the reins;" to what end? even to "give every man according to his way, and according to the fruit of his doings." And, indeed, his binding up the whole law with that command of not coveting, evidenceth that he will judge men by the inward affections and frames of their hearts. Again, God sustains the mind of man in every act of thinking; in him we have not only the principle of life, but every motion, the motion of our minds as well as of our members: "In him we live and move," &c. (Acts xvii. 28). Since he supports the vigor of the faculty in every act, can he be ignorant of those acts which spring from the faculty, to which he doth at that instant communicate power and ability? Now this knowledge of the thoughts of men is,

1st. An incommunicable property, belonging only to the Divine understanding. Creatures, indeed, may know the thoughts of others by divine revelation, but not by themselves; no creature hath a key immediately to open the minds of men, and see all that lodgeth there; no creature can fathom the heart by the line of created knowledge.[n] Devils may have a conjectural knowledge, and may guess at them, by the acquaintance they have with the disposition and constitution of men, and the images they behold in their fancies; and by some marks which an inward imagination may stamp upon the brain, blood, animal spirits, face, &c. But the knowing the thoughts merely as thought, without any impression by it, is a royalty God appropriates to himself, as the main secret of his government, and a perfection declarative of his Deity, as much as any else (Jer. xvii. 9, 10): "The heart of man is desperately wicked, who can know it?" yes, there is one, and but one, "I, the Lord, search the heart, I try the reins." "Man looks on the outward appearance, but the Lord looks upon the heart" (1 Sam. xvi. 7); where God is distinguished by this perfection from all men whatsoever, others may know by revelation, as Elisha did what was in Gehazi's heart (2 Kings, v. 26). But God knows a man more than any man knows himself; what person upon earth understands the windings and turnings of his own heart, what reserves it will have, what contrivances, what inclinations? all which God knows exactly.

2d. God acquires no new knowledge of the thoughts and hearts by the discovery of them in the actions. He would then be but equal in this part of knowledge to his creature; no man or angel but may thus arrive to the knowledge of them; God were then excluded from an absolute dominion over the prime work of his lower creation; he would have made a creature superior in this respect to himself, upon whose will to discover, his knowledge of their inward intentions should depend; and therefore when God is said to search the heart, we must not understand it as if God were ignorant before, and was fain to make an exact scrutiny and inquiry, before he attained what he desired to know; but God condescends to our capacity in the expression of his own knowledge, signifying that his knowledge is as complete as any man's knowledge can be of the designs of others, after he hath sifted them by a strict and thorough examination, and wrung out a discovery of their intentions; that he knows them as perfectly as if he had put them upon the rack, and and forced them to make a discovery of their secret plottings. Nor must we understand that in Gen. xxii 12, where God saith, after Abraham had stretched out his hand to sacrifice his son, "Now I know that thou fearest God," as though God was ignorant of Abraham's gracious disposition to him; did Abraham's drawing his knife furnish God with a new knowledge? no, God knew Abraham's pious inclinations before (Gen. xviii. 19): "I know him, that he will command his children after him," &c. Knowledge is sometimes taken for approbation; then the sense will be, Now I approve this fact as a testimony of thy fear of me, since thy affection to thy Isaac is extinguished by the more powerful flame of affection to my will and command; I now accept thee, and count thee a meet subject of my choicest benefits: or, Now I know, that is, I have made known and manifested the faith of Abraham to himself and to the world: thus Paul uses the word know (1 Cor. ii. 2): "I have determined to know nothing;" that is, to declare and teach nothing, to make known nothing but Christ crucified: or else, Now I know, that is, I have an evidence and experiment in this noble fact, that thou fearest me. God often condescends to our capacity in speaking of himself after the manner of men, as if he had (as men do) known the inward affections of others by their outward actions.

4. God knows all the evils and sins of creatures. (1.) God knows all sin. This follows upon the other. If he knows all the actions and thoughts of creatures, he knows also all the sinfulness in those acts and thoughts. This Zophar infers from God's punishing men (Job xi. 11); for he knows vain man, he sees his wickedness also; he knows every man, and sees the wickedness of every man; he looks down from heaven, and beholds not only the filthy persons, but what is filthy in them (Psal. xiv. 2, 3), all nations in the world, and every man of every nation; none of their iniquity is hid from his eyes; he searches Jerusalem with candles (Jer. xvi. 17). God follows sinners step by step, with his eye, and will not leave searching out till he hath taken them; a metaphor taken from one that searches all chinks with a candle, that nothing can be hid from him. He knows it distinctly in all the parts of it, how an adulterer rises out of his bed to commit uncleanness, what contrivances he had, what steps he took, every circumstance in the whole progress; not only evil in the bulk, but every one of the blacker spots upon it, which may most aggravate it. If he did not know evil, how could he permit it, order it, punish it, or pardon it? Doth he permit he knows not what? order to his own holy ends what he is ignorant of? punish or pardon that which he is uncertain whether it be a crime or no? "Cleanse me," saith David, "from my secret faults" (Ps. xix. 12), secret in regard of others, secret in regard of himself; how could God cleanse him from that whereof he was ignorant? He knows sins before they are committed, much more when they are in act; he foreknew the idolatry and apostacy of the Jews;

what gods they would serve, in what measure they would provoke him, and violate his covenant (Deut. xxxi. 20, 21); he knew Judas' sin long before Judas' actual existence, foretelling it in the Psalms; and Christ predicts it before he acted it. He sees sins future in his own permitting will; he sees sins present in his own supporting act. As he knows things possible to himself, because he knows his own power, so he knows things practicable by the creature, because he knows the power and principles of the creature.° This sentiment of God is naturally written in the fears of sinners, upon lightning, thunder, or some prodigious operation of God in the world; what is the language of them, but that he sees their deeds, hears their words, knows the inward sinfulness of their hearts; that he doth not only behold them as a mere spectator, but considers them as a just judge. And the poets say, that the sins of men leaped into heaven, and were writ in parchments of Jupiter,ᴾ *scelus in terram geritur, in cœlo scribitur:* sin is acted on earth, and recorded in heaven. God indeed doth not behold evil with the approving eye; he knows it not with a practical knowledge to be the author of it, but with a speculative knowledge, so as to understand the sinfulness of it; or a knowledge *simplicis intelligentiœ,* of simple intelligence, as he permits them, not positively wills them; he knows them not with a knowledge of assent to them, but dissent from them. Evil pertains to a dissenting act of the mind, and an aversive act of the will; and what though evil formerly taken, hath no distinct conception, because it is a privation; a defect hath no being, and all knowledge is by the apprehension of some being; would not this lie as strongly against our own knowledge of sin? Sin is a privation of the rectitude due to an act; and who doubts man's knowledge of sin? by his knowing the act, he knows the deficiency of the act; the subject of evil hath a being, and so hath a conception in the mind; that which hath no being cannot be known by itself, or in itself; but will it follow that it cannot be known by its contrary? as we know darkness to be a privation of light, and folly to be a privation of wisdom. God knows good all by himself, because he is the sovereign good; is it strange then, that he should know all evil, since all evil is in some natural good. (2.) The manner of God's knowing evil is not so easily known. And indeed, as we cannot comprehend the essence of God, though it is easily intelligible that there is such a Being, so we can as little comprehend the manner of God's knowledge, though we cannot but conclude him to be an intelligent Being, a pure understanding, knowing all things. As God hath a higher manner of being than his creatures, so he hath another and higher manner of knowing; and we can as little comprehend the manner of his knowing, as we can the manner of his being. But as to the manner, doth not God know his own law? and shall he not know how much any action comes short of his rule? he cannot know his own rule without knowing all the deviations from it. He knows his own holiness, and shall he not see how any action is contrary to the holiness of his own

---

° Fotherby Atheoma, p. 132.   ᴾ 'Εν Διὸς ἐλτ Cross. Anthol. Dec. 1. cap. 395. p. 101.

nature? Doth not God know everything that is true? and is it not true that this or that is evil? and shall God be ignorant of any truth? How doth God know that he cannot lie, but by knowing his own veracity? How doth God know that he cannot die, but by knowing his own immutability? and by knowing those, he knows what a lie is, he knows what death is; so if sin never had been, if no creature had ever been, God would have known what sin was, because he knows his own holiness; because he knew what law was fit to be appointed to his creatures if he should create them, and that that law might be transgressed by them. God knows all good, all goodness in himself; he therefore hath a foundation in himself to know all that comes short of that goodness, that is opposite to that holiness: as if light were capable of understanding, it would know darkness only by knowing itself; by knowing itself, it would know what is contrary to itself. God knows all created goodness which he hath planted in the creature; he knows then all defects from this goodness, what perfection an act is deprived of; what is opposite to that goodness, and that is evil. As we know sickness by health, discord by harmony, blindness by sight, because it is a privation of sight, whosoever knows one contrary knows the other; God knows unrighteousness by the idea which he hath of righteousness, and sees an act deprived of that rectitude and goodness which ought to be in it; he knows evil because he knows the causes whence evil proceeds.[q] A painter knows a picture of his own framing, and if any one dashes any base color upon it, shall not he also know that? God by his hand painted all creatures, impressed upon man the fair stamp and color of his own image; the devil defiles it; man daubs it. Doth not God, that knows his own work, know how this piece is become different from his work? Doth not God, that knows his creatures' goodness, which himself was the fountain of, know the change of this goodness? Yea, he knew before, that the devil would sow tares where he had sown wheat; and therefore that controversy of some in the schools, whether God knew evil by its opposition to created or uncreated goodness, is needless. We may say God knows sin as it is opposite to created goodness, yet he knows it radically by his own goodness, because he knows the goodness he hath communicated to the creature by his own essential goodness in himself. To conclude this head: The knowledge of sin doth not bespot the holiness of God's nature; for the bare knowledge of a crime doth not infect the mind of man with the filth and pollution of that crime, for then every man that knows an act of murder committed by another, would, by that bare knowledge, be tainted with his sin; yea, and a judge that condemns a malefactor, may as well condemn himself if this were so: the knowledge of sins infects not the understandings that knows them, but only the will that approves them. It is no discredit to us to know evil, in order to pass a right judgment upon it; so neither can it be to God.

Fourthly, God knows all future things, all things to come. The differences of time cannot hinder a knowledge of all things by him, who is before time, above time, that is not measured by hours, or

[q] Cusan, p. 246.

days, or years; if God did not know them, the hindrance must be in himself, or in the things themselves, because they are things to come: not in himself; if it did, it must arise from some impotency in his own nature, and so we render him weak; or from an unwillingness to know, and so we render him lazy, and an enemy to his own perfection; for, simply considered, the knowledge of more things is a greater perfection than the knowledge of a few; and if the knowledge of a thing includes something of perfection, the ignorance of a thing includes something of imperfection. The knowledge of future things is a greater perfection than not to know them, and is accounted among men a great part of wisdom, which they call foresight; it is then surely a greater perfection in God to know future things, than to be ignorant of them. And would God rather have something of imperfection than be possessor of all perfection? Nor doth the hindrance lie in the things themselves, because their futurition depends upon his will; for as nothing can actually be without his will, giving it existence, so nothing can be future without his will, designing the futurity of it. Certainly if God knows all things possible, which he will not do, he must know all things future, which he is not only able, but resolved to do, or resolved to permit. God's perfect knowledge of himself, that is, of his own infinite power and concluding will, necessarily includes a foreknowledge of what he is able to do, and what he will do. Again, if God doth not know future things, there was a time when God was ignorant of most things in the world; for before the deluge he was more ignorant than after; the more things were done in the world, the more knowledge did accrue to God, and so the more perfection; then the understanding of God was not perfect from eternity, but in time; nay, is not perfect yet, if he be ignorant of those things which are still to come to pass; he must tarry for a perfection he wants, till those futurities come to be in act, till those things which are to come, cease to be future, and begin to be present. Either God knows them, or desires to know them; if he desires to know them and doth not, there is something wanting to him; all desire speaks an absence of the object desired, and a sentiment of want in the person desiring: if he doth not desire to know them, nay, if he doth not actually know them, it destroys all providence, all his government of affairs; for his providence hath a concatenation of means with a prospect of something that is future: as in Joseph's case, who was put into the pit, and sold to the Egyptians in order to his future advancement, and the preservation both of his father and his envious brethren. If God did not know all the future inclinations and actions of men, something might have been done by the will of Potiphar, or by the free-will of Pharoah, whereby Joseph might have been cut short of his advancement, and so God have been interrupted in the track and method of his designed providences. He that hath decreed to govern man for that end he hath designed him, knows all the means before, whereby he will govern him, and therefore hath a distinct and certain knowledge of all things; for a confused knowledge is an imperfection in government; it is in this the infiniteness of his understanding is more seen than in knowing things past or present; his eyes are a flame of fire (Rev. i. 14), in regard of the penetrating virtue of them into things impenetrable by any else. To make it further appear that God knows all things future, consider,

1. Everything which is the object of God's knowledge without himself was once only future. There was a moment when nothing was in being but himself: he knew nothing actually past, because nothing was past; nothing actually present, because nothing had any existence but himself; therefore only what was future. And why not everything that is future now, as well as only what was future and to come to pass just at the beginning of the creation? God indeed knows everything as present, but the things themselves known by him were not present, but future; the whole creation was once future, or else it was from eternity; if it begun in time, it was once future in itself, else it could never have begun to be. Did not God know what would be created by him, before it was created by him?[r] Did he create he knew not what, and knew not before, what he should create? Was he ignorant before he acted, and in his acting, what his operation would tend to? or did he not know the nature of things, and the ends of them, till he had produced them and saw them in being? Creatures, then, did not arise from his knowledge, but his knowledge from them; he did not then will that his creatures should be, for he had then willed what he knew not, and knew not what he willed; they, therefore, must be known before they were made, and not known because they were made; he knew them to make them, and he did not make them to know them; By the same reason that he knew what creatures should be before they were, he knows still what creatures shall be before they are;[s] for all things that are, were in God, not really in their own nature, but in him as a cause; so the earth and heavens were in him, as a model is in the mind of a workman, which is in his mind and soul, before it be brought forth into outward act.

2. The predictions of future things evidence this. There is not a prophecy of any thing to come, but is a spark of his foreknowledge, and bears witness to the truth of this assertion, in the punctual accomplishment of it; this is a thing challenged by God as his own peculiar, wherein he surmounts all the idols that man's inventions have godded in the world (Isa. xli. 21, 22): Let them bring them forth (speaking of the idols) and show us what shall happen, or declare us things to come: show the things that are to come hereafter, that we may know that you are gods. Such a fore-knowledge of things to come, is here ascribed to God by God himself, as a distinction of him from all false gods; such a knowledge, that if any could prove that they were possessors of, he would acknowledge them gods as well as himself: "that we may know that you are gods." He puts his Deity to stand or fall upon this account, and this should be the point which should decide the controversy, whether he or the heathen idols were the true God; the dispute is managed by this medium,— He that knows things to come, is God; I know things to come, ergo, I am God; the idols know not things to come, therefore they are not gods; God submits the being of his Deity to this trial. If God know

---

[r] Petavius changed.   [s] Bradward, lib. 3 cap. 14.

things to come no more than the heathen idols, which were either
devils or men, he would be, in his own account, no more a God than
devils or men, no more a God than the pagan idols he doth scoff at
for this defect. If the heathen idols were to be stripped of their
deity for want of this foreknowledge of things to come, would not
the true God also fall from the same excellency if he were defective
in knowledge? He would, in his own judgment, no more deserve
the title and character of a God than they. How could he reproach
them for that, if it were wanting in himself? It cannot be understood of future things in their causes, when the effects necessarily
arise from such causes, as light from the sun, and heat from the fire:
many of these men know; more of them angels and devils know:
if God, therefore, had not a higher and farther knowledge than this,
he would not by this be proved to be God any more than angels and
devils, who know necessary effects in their causes. The devils, indeed, did predict some things in the heathen oracles; but God is
differenced from them here by the infiniteness of his knowledge, in
being able to predict things to come that they knew not, or things
in their particularities, things that depended on the liberty of man's
will, which the devils could lay no claim to a certain knowledge of.
Were it only a conjectural knowledge that is here meant, the devils
might answer, they can conjecture, and so their deity was as good as
God's; for, though God might know more things, and conjecture nearer
to what would be, yet still it would be but conjectural, and therefore
not a higher kind of knowledge than what the devils might challenge.
How much, then, is God beholden to the Socinians for denying the
knowledge of all future things to him, upon which here he puts the trial
of his Deity? God asserts his knowledge of things to come, as a manifest evidence of his Godhead; those that deny, therefore, the argument
that proves it, deny the conclusion too; for this will necessarily follow,
that if he be God, because he knows future things then he that doth not
know future things is not God; and if God knows not future things
but only by conjecture, then there is no God, because a certain knowledge, so as infallibly to predict things to come, is an inseparable perfection of the Deity: it was, therefore, well said of Austin, that it
was as high a madness to deny God to be, as to deny him the foreknowledge of things to come. The whole prophetic part of Scripture
declares this perfection of God; every prophet's candle was lighted
at this torch; they could not have this foreknowledge of themselves;
why might not many other men have the same insight, if it were
nature? It must be from some superior Agent; and all nations
owned prophecy as a beam from God, a fruit of Divine illumination.[t] Prophecy must be totally expunged if this be denied; for the
subjects of prophecy are things future, and no man is properly a
prophet but in prediction. Now prediction is nothing but foretelling, and things foretold are not yet come, and the foretelling of them
supposeth them not to be yet, but that they shall be in time; several
such predictions we have in Scripture, the event whereof hath been
certain. The years of famine in Egypt foretold that he would order
second causes for bringing that judgment upon them; the captivity

t Pacuvius said, Siqui quæ eventura sunt provident, æqui parent, Gell. lib. 14. c. 1.

of his people in Babylon, the calling of the Gentiles, the rejection of the Jews. Daniel's revelation of Nebuchadnezzar's dream; that prince refers to God as the revealer of secrets (Dan. ii. 47). By the same reason that he knows one thing future by himself, and by the infiniteness of his knowledge before any causes of them appear, he doth know all things future.

3. Some future things are known by men; and we must allow God a greater knowledge than any creature. Future things in their causes may be known by angels and men, (as I said before); whosoever knows necessary causes, and the efficacy of them, may foretell the effects; and when he sees the meeting and concurrence of several causes together, he may presage what the consequent effect will be of such a concurrence : so physicians foretel the progress of a disease, the increase or diminution of it by natural signs; and astronomers foretel eclipses by their observation of the motion of heavenly bodies, many years before they happen;[u] can they be hid from God, with whom are the reasons of all things?[x] An expert gardener, by knowing the root in the depth of winter, can tell what flowers and what fruit it will bear, and the month when they will peep out their heads; and shall not God much more, that knows the principles of all his creatures, and is exactly privy to all their natures and qualities, know what they will be, and what operations shall be from those principles? Now, if God did know things only in their causes, his knowledge would not be more excellent than the knowledge of angels and men, though he might know more than they of the things that will come to pass, from every cause singly, and from the concurrence of many. Now, as God is more excellent in being than his creature, so he is more excellent in the objects of his knowledge, and the manner of his knowledge; well, then, shall a certain knowledge of something future, and a conjectural knowledge of many things, be found among men? and shall a determinate and infallible knowledge of things to come be found nowhere, in no being? If the conjecture of future things savours of ignorance, and God knows them only by conjecture, there is, then, no such thing in being as a perfect intelligent Being, and so no God.

4. God knows his own decree and will, and therefore must needs know all future things. If anything be future, or to come to pass, it must be from itself or from God : not from itself, then it would be independent and absolute : if it hath its futurity from God, then God must know what he hath decreed to come to pass; those things that are future, in necessary causes, God must know, because he willed them to be causes of such effects; he, therefore, knows them, because he knows what he willed. The knowledge of God cannot arise from the things themselves, for then the knowledge of God would have a cause without him; and knowledge, which is an eminent perfection, would be conferred upon him by his creatures. But as God sees things possible in the glass of his own power, so he sees things future in the glass of his own will; in his effecting will, if he hath decreed to produce them; in his permitting will, as he hath decreed to suffer them and dispose of them; nothing can pass out of the rank of

[u] Cusanus. [x] Fuller's Pisgah, 1. 2. p. 281.

things merely possible into the order of things future, before some
act of God's will hath passed for its futurition.[y]   It is not from the
infiniteness of his own nature, simply considered, that God knows
things to be future;[z] for as things are not future because God is infinite (for then all possible things should be future), so neither is any
thing known to be future only because God is infinite, but because
God hath decreed it; his declaration of things to come, is founded
upon his appointment of things to come.[a]   In Isaiah xliv. 7, it is
said, "And who, as I, shall call and declare it, since I appointed the
ancient people, and the things that are coming?"[b]   Nothing is created or ordered in the world but what God decreed to be created and
ordered.   God knows his own decree, and therefore all things which
he hath decreed to exist in time; not the minutest part of the world
could have existed without his will, not an action can be done without his will; as life, the principle, so motion, the fruit of that life, is
by and from God; as he decreed life to this or that thing, so he decreed motion as the effect of life, and decreed to exert his power in
concurring with them, for producing effects natural from such causes;
for without such a concourse they could not have acted anything, or
produced anything; and therefore as for natural things, which we
call necessary causes, God foreseeing them all particularly in his own
decree, foresaw also all effects which must necessarily flow from them,
because such causes cannot but act when they are furnished with all
things necessary for action: he knows his own decrees, and therefore
necessarily knows what he hath decreed, or else we must say things
come to pass whether God will or no, or that he wills he knows not
what; but this cannot be, for "known unto God are all his works,
from the beginning of the world" (Acts xv. 18).   Now this necessarily flows from that principle first laid down, that God knows himself, since nothing is future without God's will; if God did not know
future things, he would not know his own will; for as things possible could not be known by him, unless he knew the fulness of his
own power, so things future could not be known by his understanding, unless he knew the resolves of his own will.   Thus the knowledge of God differs from the knowledge of men;[c] God's knowledge
of his works precedes his works; man's knowledge of God's works
follows his works, just as an artificer's knowledge of a watch, instrument, or engine, which he would make, is before his making of it;
he knows the motion of it, and the reason of those motions before it
is made, because he knows what he hath determined to work; he
knows not those motions from the consideration of them after they
were made, as the spectator doth, who, by viewing the instrument
after it is made, gains a knowledge from the sight and the consideration of it, till he understands the reason of the whole; so we know
things from the consideration of them after we see them in being,
and therefore we know not future things: but God's knowledge doth
not arise from things because they are, but because he wills them to
be; and therefore he knows everything that shall be, because it

[y] Chequell.   [z] Coccei sum. Theol. p. 50.   [a] Ibid.
[b] Gamaul in Aquin, Part I. Q. 14. cap. 3. p. 124.
[c] Maimonid.   More Nevoch, Part 3. cap. 21. pp. 393, 394.

cannot be without his will, as the Creator and maintainer of all things; knowing his own substance, he knows all his works.

5. If God did not know all future things, he would be mutable in his knowledge. If he did not know all things that ever were or are to be, there would be upon the appearance of every new object, an addition of light to his understanding, and therefore such a change in him as every new knowledge causes in the mind of a man, or as the sun works in the world upon its rising every morning, scattering the darkness that was upon the face of the earth; if he did not know them before they came, he would gain a knowledge by them when they came to pass, which he had not before they were effected; his knowledge would be new according to the newness of the objects, and multiplied according to the multitude of the objects. If God did know things to come as perfectly as he knew things present and past, but knew those certainly, and the others doubtfully and conjecturally, he would suffer some change, and acquire some perfection in his knowledge, when those future things should cease to be future, and become present; for he would know it more perfectly when it were present, than he did when it was future, and so there would be a change from imperfection to a perfection; but God is every way immutable. Besides, that perfection would not arise from the nature of God, but from the existence and presence of the thing; but who will affirm that God acquires any perfection of knowledge from his creatures, any more than he doth of being? he would not then have that knowledge, and consequently that perfection from eternity, as he had when he created the world, and will not have a full perfection of the knowledge of his creature till the end of the world, nor of immortal souls, which will certainly act as well as live to eternity; and so God never was, nor ever will be, perfect in knowledge; for when you have conceived millions of years, wherein angels and souls live and act, there is still more coming than you can conceive, wherein they will act. And if God be always changing to eternity, from ignorance to knowledge, as those acts come to be exerted by his creatures, he will not be perfect in knowledge, no, not to eternity, but will always be changing from one degree of knowledge to another; a very unworthy conceit to entertain of the most blessed, perfect, and infinite God! Hence, then, it follows, that

(1.) God foreknows all his creatures. All kinds which he determined to make; all particulars that should spring out of every species; the time when they should come forth of the womb; the manner how; "In thy Book all my members were written" (Ps. cxxxix. 16). Members is not in the *Heb.* whence some refer all, to all living creatures whatsoever, and all the parts of them which God did foresee; he knew the number of creatures with all their parts; they were written in the book of his foreknowledge; the duration of them, how long they shall remain in being, and act upon the stage; he knows their strength, the links of one cause with another, and what will follow in all their circumstances, and the series and combinations of effects with their causes. The duration of everything is foreknown, because determined (Job. xiv. 5); "seeing his days

are determined, the number of his months are with thee; thou hast
appointed his bounds, that he cannot pass;" bounds are fixed, beyond which none shall reach; he speaks of days and months, not
of years, to give us notice of God's particular foreknowledge of
everything, of every day, month, year, hour of a man's life.

(2.) All the acts of his creatures are foreknown by him. All
natural acts, because he knows their causes; voluntary acts I shall
speak of afterwards.

(3.) This foreknowledge was certain. For it is an unworthy notion of God to ascribe to him a conjectural knowledge; if there
were only a conjectural knowledge, he could but conjecturally foretel anything; and then it is possible the events of things might be
contrary to his predictions. It would appear then that God were
deceived and mistaken, and then there could be no rule of trying
things, whether there were from God or no; for the rule God sets
down to discern his words from the words of false prophets, is the
event and certain accomplishment of what is predicted (Deut. xviii.
21) to that question, "How shall we know whether God hath
spoken or no?" he answers, that "if the thing doth not come to
pass, the Lord hath not spoken." If his knowledge of future things
were not certain, there were no stability in this rule, it would fall
to the ground: we never yet find God deceived in any prediction,
but the event did answer his forerevelation; his foreknowledge,
therefore, is certain and infallible. We cannot make God uncertain
in his knowledge, but we must conceive him fluctuating and wavering in his will; but if his will be not yea and nay, but yea, his
knowledge is certain, because he doth certainly will and resolve.

(4.) This foreknowledge was from eternity. Seeing he knows
things possible in his power, and things future in his will; if his
power and resolves were from eternity, his knowledge must be so
too, or else we must make him ignorant of his own power, and ignorant of his own will from eternity; and consequently not from
eternity blessed and perfect. His knowledge of possible things must
run parallel with his power, and his knowledge of future things run
parallel with his will. If he willed from eternity, he knew from
eternity what he willed; but that he did will from eternity, we must
grant, unless we would render him changeable, and conceive him to
be made in time of not willing, willing. The knowledge God hath
in time, was always one and the same, because his understanding is
his proper essence, and of an immutable nature.[d] And indeed the
actual existence of a thing is not simply necessary to its being perfectly known; we may see a thing that is past out of being, when it
doth actually exist; and a carpenter may know the house he is to
build, before it be built, by the model of it in his own mind; much
more we may conceive the same of God whose decrees were before
the foundation of the world;[e] and to be before time was, and to be
from eternity, hath no difference. As God in his being exceeds all
beginning of time, so doth his knowledge all motions of time.

(5.) God foreknows all things as present with him from eternity.
As he knows mutable things with an immutable and firm knowledge,

d Gamach. in Aquin. Part I. Q. 14. cap. 3. p. 124.   • Eph. i. 5. and in other places.

so he knows future things with a present knowledge ;[f] not that the things which are produced in time, were actually and really present with him in their own beings from eternity ; for then they could not be produced in time ; had they a real existence, then they would not be creatures, but God ; and had they actual being, then they could not be future, for future speaks a thing to come that is not yet. If things had been actually present with him, and yet future, they had been made before they were made, and had a being before they had a being ; but they were all present to his knowledge as if they were in actual being, because the reason of all things that were to be made, was present with him. The reason of the will of God that they shall be, was equally eternal with him, wherein he saw what, and when, and how he would create things, how he would govern them, to what ends he would direct them.[g] Thus all things are present to God's knowledge, though in their own nature they may be past or future, not in *esse reali,* but in *esse intelligibili,* objectively, not actually present ;[h] for as the unchangeableness and infiniteness of God's knowledge of changeable and finite things, doth not make the things he knows immutable and infinite, so neither doth the eternity of his knowledge make them actually present with him from eternity ; but all things are present to his understanding, because he hath at once a view of all successions of times ; and his knowledge of future things is as perfect as of present things, or what is past ; it is not a certain knowledge of present things, and an uncertain knowledge of future, but his knowledge of one is as certain and unerring as his knowledge of the other ;[i] as a man that beholds a circle with several lines from the centre, beholds the lines as they are joined in the centre, beholds them also as they are distant and severed from one another, beholds them in their extent and in their point all at once, though they may have a great distance from one another. He saw from the beginning of time to the last minute of it, all things coming out of their causes, marching in their order according to his own appointment ; as a man may see a multitude of ants, some creeping one way, some another, employed in several businesses for their winter provision. The eye of God at once runs through the whole circle of time ; as the eye of man upon a tower sees all the passengers at once, though some be past, some under the tower, some coming at a farther distance. "God," saith Job, "looks to the end of the earth, and sees under the whole heaven" (Job xxviii. 24) ; the knowledge of God is expressed by sight in Scripture, and futurity to God is the same thing as distance to us; we can with a perspective-glass make things that are afar off appear as if they were near ; and the sun, so many thousand miles distant from us, to appear as if it were at the end of the glass : why, then, should future things be at so great a distance from God's knowledge, when things so far from us may be made to approach so near to us ? God considers all things in his own simple knowledge, as if they were now acted ; and therefore some have chosen to call the knowledge of things to come, not prescience, or foreknowledge, but knowledge;

[f] Gerhard Exeges, ch. 8. de Deo sect. 13. p. 303. [g] Bradward, lib. 3. cap. 14.
[h] Hornbeck. [i] Pugio Fidei, Part I. ch. 19.

because God sees all things in one instant, *scientiâ nunquam deficientis instantiœ*.[k] Upon this account, things that are to come, are set down in Scripture as present, and sometimes as past (Isa. ix. 6): "Unto us a child is born," though not yet born; so of the sufferings of Christ (Isa. liii. 4, &c.): "He hath borne our griefs, he was wounded for our transgressions, he was taken from prison," &c., not shall be; and (Ps. xxii. 18): "they part my garments among them," as if it were present; all to express the certainty of God's foreknowledge, as if things were actually present before him.

(6.) This is proper to God, and incommunicable to any creature. Nothing but what is eternal can know all things that are to come. Suppose a creature might know things that are to come, after he is in being, he cannot know things simply as future, because there were things future before he was in being. The devils know not men's hearts, therefore cannot foretel their actions with any certainty; they may indeed have a knowledge of some things to come, but it is only conjectural, and often mistaken; as the devil was in his predictions among the heathen, and in his presage of "Job's cursing God to his face" upon his pressing calamities (Job i. 11). Sometimes, indeed, they have a certain knowledge of something future by the revelation of God, when he uses them as instruments of his vengeance, or for the trial of his people, as in the case of Job, when he gave him a commission to strip him of his goods; or, as the angels have, when he uses them as instruments of the deliverance of his people.

(7.) Though this be certain, that God foreknows all things and actions, yet the manner of his knowing all things before they come, is not so easily resolved. We must not, therefore, deny this perfection in God, because we understand not the manner how he hath the knowledge of all things. It were unworthy for us to own no more of God than we can perfectly conceive of him; we should then own no more of him than that he doth exist. "Canst thou," saith Job, "by searching, find out God? canst thou find out the Almighty unto perfection?" (Job xi. 7). Do we not see things unknown to inferior creatures, to be known to ourselves? Irrational creatures do not apprehend the nature of a man, nor what we conceived of them when we look upon them; nor do we know what they fancy of us when they look wistly upon us; for ought as I know, we understand as little the manner of their imaginations, as they do of ours; and shall we ascribe a darkness in God as to future things, because we are ignorant of them, and of the manner how he should know them?[1] shall we doubt whether God doth certainly know those things which we only conjecture? As our power is not the measure of the power of God, so neither is our knowledge the judge of the knowledge of God, no better nor so well as an irrational nature can be the judge of our reason. Do we perfectly know the manner how we know? shall we therefore deny that we know anything? We know we have such a faculty which we call understanding, but doth any man certainly know what it is? and became he doth not, shall he deny that which is plain and evident to him?

[k] Boet. consolat lib. 5. pros. 6   [1] Ficinus in Procl. cap. 91.

Because we cannot ascertain ourselves of the causes of the ebbing and flowing of the sea, of the manner how minerals are engendered in the earth, shall we therefore deny that which our eyes convince us of? And this will be a preparation to the last thing.

Fifthly, God knows all future contingencies, that is, God knows all things that shall accidentally happen, or, as we say, by chance; and he knows all the free motions of men's wills that shall be to the end of the world. If all things be open to him (Heb. iv. 13), then all contingencies are, for they are in the number of things; and as, according to Christ's speech, those things that are impossible to man, are possible to God, so those things which are unknown to man, are known to God; because of the infinite fulness and perfection of the divine understanding. Let us see what a contingent is. That is contingent which we commonly call accidental, as when a tile falls suddenly upon a man's head as he is walking in the street; or when one letting off a musket at random shoots another he did not intend to hit; such was that arrow whereby Ahab was killed, shot by a soldier at a venture (1 Kings xxii. 39); this some call a mixed contingent, made up partly of necessity, and partly of accident; it is necessary the bullet, when sent out of the gun, or arrow out of the bow, should fly and light somewhere; but it is an accident that it hits this or that man, that was never intended by the archer. Other things, as voluntary actions, are purely contingents, and have nothing of necessity in them; all free actions that depend upon the will of man, whether to do, or not to do, are of this nature, because they depend not upon a necessary cause, as burning doth upon the fire, moistening upon water, or as descent or falling down is necessary to a heavy body; for those cannot in their own nature do otherwise; but the other actions depend upon a free agent, able to turn to this or that point, and determine himself as he pleases. Now we must know, that what is accidental in regard of the creature, is not so in regard of God; the manner of Ahab's death was accidental, in regard of the hand by which he was slain, but not in regard of God who foretold his death, and foreknew the shot, and directed the arrow; God was not uncertain before of the manner of his fall, nor hovered over the battle to watch for an opportunity to accomplish his own prediction; what may be or not be, in regard of us, is certain in regard of God; to imagine that what is accidental to us, is so to God, is to measure God by our short line. How many events following upon the results of princes in their counsels, seem to persons, ignorant of those counsels, to be a haphazard, yet were not contingencies to the prince and his assistants, but foreseen by him as certainly to issue so as they do, which they knew before would be the fruit of such causes and instruments they would knit together! That may be necessary in regard of God's foreknowledge, which is merely accidental in regard of the natural disposition of the immediate causes which do actually produce it; contingent in its own nature, and in regard of us, but fixed in the knowledge of God. One illustrates it by this similitude;[m] a master sends two servants to one and the same place, two several ways, unknown to one an-

m Zanch.

other; they meet at the place which their master had appointed them; their meeting is accidental to them, one knows not of the other, but it was foreseen by the master that they should so meet; and that in regard of them it would seem a mere accident, till they came to explain the business to one another; both the necessity of their meeting, in regard of their master's order, and the accidentalness of it in regard of themselves, were in both their circumstances foreknown by the master that employed them. For the clearing of this, take it in this method.

1. It is an unworthy conceit of God in any to exclude him from the knowledge of these things.

(1.) It will be a strange contracting of him to allow him no greater a knowledge than we have ourselves. Contingencies are known to us when they come into act, and pass from futurity to reality; and when they are present to us, we can order our affairs accordingly; shall we allow God no greater a measure of knowledge than we have, and make him as blind as ourselves, not to see things of that nature before they come to pass? Shall God know them no more? Shall we imagine God knows no otherwise than we know? and that he doth, like us, stand gazing with admiration at events? man can conjecture many things; is it fit to ascribe the same uncertainty to God, as though he, as well as we, could have no assurance till the issue appear in the view of all? If God doth not certainly foreknow them, he doth but conjecture them; but a conjectural knowledge is by no means to be fastened on God; for that is not knowledge, but guess, and destroys a Deity by making him subject to mistake; for he that only guesseth, may guess wrong; so that this is to make God like ourselves, and strip him of an universally acknowledged perfection of omniscience. A conjectural knowledge, saith one,[n] is as unworthy of God as the creature is unworthy of omniscience. It is certain man hath a liberty to act many things this or that way as he pleases; to walk to this or that quarter, to speak or not to speak; to do this or that thing, or not to do it; which way a man will certainly determine himself, is unknown before to any creature, yea, often at the present to himself, for he may be in suspense; but shall we imagine this future determination of himself is concealed from God? Those that deny God's foreknowledge in such cases, must either say, that God hath an opinion that a man will resolve rather this way than that; but then if a man by his liberty determine himself contrary to the opinion of God, is not God then deceived? and what rational creature can own him for a God that can be deceived in anything? or else they must say that God is at uncertainty, and suspends his opinion without determining it any way; then he cannot know free acts till they are done; he would then depend upon the creature for his information; his knowledge would be every instant increased, as things, he knew not before, came into act; and since there are every minute an innumerable multitude of various imaginations in the minds of men, there would be every minute an accession of new knowledge to God which he had not before; besides, this knowledge would be mutable according to the wavering and weathercock resolutions of men, one while standing to this point, another while to that, if he depended upon the creature's determination for his knowledge.

(2.) If the free acts of men were unknown before to God, no man can see how there can be any government of the world by him. Such contingencies may happen, and such resolves of men's free-wills unknown to God, as may perplex his affairs, and put him upon new counsels and methods for attaining those ends which he settled at the first creation of things; if things happen which God knows not of before, this must be the consequence; where there is no foresight, there is no providence; things may happen so sudden, if God be ignorant of them, that they may give a check to his intentions and scheme of government, and put him upon changing the whole model of it. How often doth a small intervening circumstance, unforeseen by man, dash in pieces a long meditated and well-formed design! To govern necessary causes, as sun and stars, whose effects are natural and constant in themselves, is easy to be imagined; but how to govern the world that consists of so many men of free-will, able to determine themselves to this or that, and which have no constancy in themselves, as the sun and stars have, cannot be imagined; unless we will allow in God as great a certainty of foreknowledge of the designs and actions of men, as there is inconstancy in their resolves. God must be altering the methods of his government every day, every hour, every minute, according to the determinations of men, which are so various and changeable in the whole compass of the world in the space of one minute; he must wait to see what the counsels of men will be, before he could settle his own methods of government; and so must govern the world according to their mutability, and not according to any certainty in himself. But his counsel is stable in the midst of multitudes of free devices in the heart of man (Prov. xix. 21), and knowing them all before, orders them to be subservient to his own stable counsel. If he cannot know what to-morrow will bring forth in the mind of a man, how can he certainly settle his own determination of governing him? His decrees and resolves must be temporal, and arise *pro re nata*, and he must alway be in counsel what he should do upon every change of men's minds. This is an unworthy conceit of the infinite majesty of heaven, to make his government depend upon the resolves of men, rather than their resolves upon the design of God.

2. It is therefore certain, that God doth foreknow the free and voluntary acts of man. How could he else order his people to ask of him things to come, in order to their deliverance, such things as depended upon the will of man, if he foreknew not the motions of their will (Isa. xlv. 11)?

(1.) Actions good or indifferent depending upon the liberty of man's will as much as any whatsoever. Several of these he hath foretold; not only a person to build up Jerusalem was predicted by him, but the name of that person, Cyrus (Isa. xliv. 28). What is more contingent, or is more the effect of the liberty of man's will, than the names of their children? Was not the destruction of the Babylonish empire foretold, which Cyrus undertook, not by any compulsion, but by a free inclination and resolve of his own will? And was not the dismission of the Jews into their own country a voluntary act in that conqueror? If you consider the liberty of man's will, might not Cyrus as well have continued their yoke, as have struck off their chains, and kept them captive, as well as dismissed them? Had it not been for his own interest, rather to have strengthened the fetters of so turbulent a people, who being tenacious of their religion and laws different from that professed by the whole world, were like to make disturbances more when they were linked in a body in their own country, than when they were transplanted and scattered into the several parts of his empire? It was in the power of Cyrus (take him as a man) to choose one or the other; his interest invited him to continue their captivity, rather than grant their deliverance; yet God knew that he would willingly do this rather than the other; he knew this which depended upon the will of Cyrus; and why may not an infinite God foreknow the free acts of all men, as well as of one? If the liberty of Cyrus' will was no hindrance to God's certain and infallible foreknowledge of it, how can the contingency of any other thing be a hindrance to him? for there is the same reason of one and all; and his government extends to every village, every family, every person, as well as to kingdoms and nations. So God foretold, by his prophet, not only the destruction of Jeroboam's altar, but the name of the person that should be the instrument of it (1 Kings xiii. 2), and this about 300 years before Josiah's birth. It is a wonder that none of the pious kings of Judah, in detestation of idolatry, and hopes to recover again the kingdom of Israel, had in all that space named one of their sons by that name of Josiah, in hopes that that prophecy should be accomplished by him; that Manasseh only should do this, who was the greatest imitator of Jeroboam's idolatry among all the Jewish kings, and indeed went beyond them; and had no mind to destroy in another kingdom what he propagated in his own. What is freer than the imposition of a name? yet this he foreknew, and this Josiah was Manasseh's son (2 Kings xxi. 26). Was there anything more voluntary than for Pharaoh to honor the butler by restoring him to his place, and punish the baker by hanging him on a gibbet? yet this was foretold (Gen. xl. 8). And were not all the voluntary acts of men, which were the means of Joseph's advancement, foreknown by God, as well as his exaltation, which was the end he aimed at by those means? Many of these may be reckoned up. Can all the free acts of man surmount the infinite capacity of the Divine understanding? If God singles out one voluntary action in man as contingent as any, and lying among a vast number of other designs and resolutions, both antecedent and subsequent, why should he not know the whole mass of men's thoughts and actions, and pierce into all that the liberty of man's will can effect? why should he not know every grain, as well as one that lies in the midst of many of the same kind? And since the Scripture gives so large an account of contingents, predicted by God, no man can certainly prove that anything is unforeknown to him. It is as reasonable to think he knows every contingent, as that he knows some that lie as much hid from the eye of any creature, since there is no more difficulty to an infinite nnderstanding to know all, than to know some.[o] Indeed, if we deny God's foreknowledge of the voluntary actions of men, we must strike ourselves off from the belief of scripture predictions that yet remain unaccomplished, and will be brought about by the voluntary engagements of men, as the ruin of antichrist, &c. If God foreknows not the secret motions of man's will, how can he foretel them? if we strip him of this perfection of prescience, why should we believe a word of scripture predictions? all the credit of the word of God is torn up by the roots. If God were uncertain of such events, how can we reconcile God's declaration of them to his truth; and his demanding our belief of them to his goodness? Were it good and righteous in God to urge us to the belief of that he were uncertain of himself, how could he be true in predicting things he were not sure of? or good, in requiring credit to be given to that which might be false? This would necessarily follow, if God did not foreknow the motions of men's wills, whereby many of his predictions were fulfilled, and some remain yet to be accomplished.

(2.) God foreknows the voluntary sinful motions of men's wills. First, God had foretold several of them. Were not all the minute sinful circumstances about the death of our blessed Redeemer, as the piercing him, giving him gall to drink, foretold, as well as the not breaking his bones, and parting his garments? What were those but the free actions of men, which they did willingly without any constraint? and those foretold by David, Isaiah, and other prophets; some above a thousand, some eight hundred, and some more, some fewer years before they came to pass; and the events punctually answered the prophesies. Many sinful acts of men, which depended upon their free will, have been foretold. The Egyptians' voluntary oppressing Israel (Gen. xv. 13); Pharaoh's hardening his heart against the voice of Moses (Exod. iii. 19); that Isaiah's message would be in vain to the people (Isa. vi. 9); that the Israelites would be rebellious after Moses' death, and turn idolaters (Deut. xxxi. 16); Judas' betraying of our Saviour, a voluntary action (John vi. *ult.*); he was not forced to do what he did, for he had some kind of repentance for it; and not violence, but voluntariness falls under repentance. Second, His truth had depended upon this foresight. Let us consider that in Gen. xv. 16, "But in the fourth generation they shall come hither again;" that is, the posterity of Abraham shall come into Canaan, for the iniquity of the Amorites is not yet full.[p] God makes a promise to Abraham, of giving his posterity the land of Canaan, not presently, but in the fourth generation; if the truth of God be infallible in the performance of his promise, his understanding is as infallible in the foresight of the Amorites' sin; the fullness of their iniquity was to precede the Israelites' possession. Did the truth of God depend upon an uncertainty? did he make the promise hand over head (as we say)? How could he, with any wisdom and truth,

---

[o] The Stoics, that thought their souls to be some particle of God, Ἀποσπάσματα, pieces pulled off from him, did conclude from thence that he knew all the motions of their souls as his own mover, as things coherent with him. Arrian Epictet. lib. 1. cap. 14. p. 60. [p] Vid. Rivet. *in loc.* exerci. 86. p. 329

assure Israel of the possession of the land in the fourth generation, if he had not been sure that the Amorites would fill up the measure of their iniquities by that time? If Abraham had been a Socinian, to deny God's knowledge of the free acts of men, had he not a fine excuse for unbelief? What would his reply have been to God? Alas, Lord, this is not a promise to be relied upon, the Amorites' iniquity depends upon the acts of their free will, and such thou canst have no knowledge of; thou canst see no more than a likelihood of their iniquity being full, and therefore there is but a likelihood of thy performing thy promise, and not a certainty! Would not this be judged not only a saucy, but a blasphemous answer? And upon these principles the truth of the most faithful God had been dashed to uncertainty and a peradventure. Third, God provided a remedy for man's sin, and therefore foresaw the entrance of it into the world by the fall of Adam. He had a decree before the foundation of the world, to manifest his wisdom in the gospel by Jesus Christ, an "eternal purpose in Jesus Christ" (Eph. iii. 11), and a decree of election past before the foundation of the world;—a separation of some to redemption, and forgiveness of sin in the blood of Christ, in whom they were from eternity chosen, as well as in time accepted in Christ (Eph. i. 4, 6, 7), which is called a "purpose in himself" (ver, 9); had not sin entered, there had been no occasion for the death of the Son of God, it being everywhere in Scripture laid upon that score;—a decree for the shedding of blood, supposed a decree for the permission of sin, and a certain foreknowledge of God, that it would be committed by man. An uncertainty of foreknowledge, and a fixedness of purpose, are not consistent in a wise man, much less in the only wise God. God's purpose to manifest his wisdom to men and angels in this way might have been defeated, had God had only a conjectural foreknowledge of the fall of man; and all those solemn purposes of displaying his perfections in those methods had been to no purpose; [q] the provision of a remedy supposed a certainty of the disease. If a sparrow fall not to the ground without the will of God, how much less could such a deplorable ruin fall upon mankind, without God's will permitting it, and his knowledge foreseeing it? It is not hard to conceive how God might foreknow it?[r] he indeed decreed to create man in an excellent state; the goodness of God could not but furnish him with a power to stand; yet in his wisdom he might foresee that the devil would be envious to man's happiness, and would, out of envy, attempt his subversion. As God knew of what temper the faculties were he had endued man with, and how far they were able to endure the assaults of a temptation, so he also foreknew the grand subtelties of Satan, how he would lay his mine, and to what point he would drive his temptation; how he would propose and manage it, and direct his battery against the sensitive appetite, and assault the weakest part of the fort; might he not foresee that the efficacy of the temptation would exceed the measure of the resistance; cannot God know how far the malice of Satan would extend, what shots he would, according to his nature, use, how high he would charge his temptation without his powerful restraint,

[q] Mare'. cont. Volkel. lib 1. cap. 24. p. 343.   [r] Amyrald. de Prædestin. cap. 6.

as well as an engineer judge how many shots of a cannon will make
a breach in a town, and how many casks of powder will blow up a
fortress, who never yet built the one, nor founded the other? We
may easily conclude God could not be deceived in the judgment of
the issue and event, since he knew how far he would let Satan loose,
how far he would permit man to act; and since he dives to the bottom of the nature of all things, he foresaw that Adam was endued
with an ability to stand; as he foresaw that Benhadad might naturally recover of his disease; but he foresaw also that Adam would
sink under the allurements of the temptation, as he foresaw that
Hazael would let Benhadad live (2 Kings viii. 10). Now since the
whole race of mankind lies in corruption, and is subject to the
power of the devil (1 John iii. 18), may not God, that knows that
corruption in every man's nature, and the force of every man's
spirit, and what every particular nature will incline him to upon
such objects proposed to him, and what the reasons of the temptation will be, know also the issues? is there any difficulty in
God's foreknowing this, since man knowing the nature of one
he is well acquainted with, can conclude what sentiments he will
have, and how he will behave himself upon presenting this or
that object to him? If a man that understands the disposition of his child or servant, knows before what he will do upon
such an occasion, may not God much more, who knows the inclinations of all his creatures, and from eternity run with his eyes over
all the works he intended? Our wills are in the number of causes;
and since God knows our wills, as causes, better than we do ourselves, why should he be ignorant of the effects? God determines
to give grace to such a man, not to give it to another, but leave him
to himself, and suffer such temptations to assault him; now God
knowing the corruption of man in the whole mass, and in every part
of it, is it not easy for him to foreknow what the future actions of the
will will be, when the tinder and fire meet together, and how such
a man will determine himself, both as to the substance and manner
of the action? Is it not easy for him to know how a corrupted
temper and a temptation will suit? God is exactly privy to all the
gall in the hearts of men, and what principles they will have, before
they have a being. He "knows their thoughts afar off" (Ps. cxxxix.
2), as far off as eternity, as some explain the words, and thoughts
are as voluntary as anything; he knows the power and inclinations
of men in the order of second causes; he understands the corruption of men, as well as "the poison of dragons, and the venom of
asps;" this is "laid up in store with him, and sealed among his treasures" (Deut. xxxii. 33, 34): among the treasures of his foreknowledge, say some. What was the cruelty of Hazael, but a free act?
yet God knew the frame of his heart, and what acts of murder and
oppression would spring from that bitter fountain, before Hazael had
conceived them in himself (2 Kings viii. 12), as a man that knows
the minerals through which the waters pass, may know what relish they
will have before they appear above the earth, so our Saviour knew how
Peter would deny him; he knew what quantity of powder would
serve for such a battery, in what measure he would let loose Satan,

how far he would leave the reins in Peter's hands, and then the issue might easily be known ; and so in every act of man, God knows in his own will what measure of grace he will give, to determine the will to good, and what measure of grace he will withdraw from such a person, or not give to him ; and, consequently, how far such a person will fall or not. God knows the inclinations of the creature ; he knows his own permissions, what degrees of grace he will either allow him, or keep from him, according to which will be the degree of his sin. This may in some measure help our conceptions in this, though, as was said before, the manner of God's foreknowledge is not so easily explicable.

(3.) God's foreknowledge of man's voluntary actions doth not necessitate the will of man. The foreknowledge of God is not deceived, nor the liberty of man's will diminished. I shall not trouble you with any school distinctions, but be as plain as I can, laying down several propositions in this case.

Prop. I. It is certain all necessity doth not take away liberty, indeed a compulsive necessity takes away liberty, but a necessity of immutability removes not liberty from God ; why should, then, a necessity of infallibility in God remove liberty from the creature? God did necessarily create the world, because he decreed it ; yet freely, because his will from eternity stood to it, he freely decreed it and freely created it, as the apostle saith in regard of God's decrees, " Who hath been his counsellor" (Rom. xi. 34)? so in regard of his actions I may say, Who hath been his compeller? he freely decreed, and he freely created. Jesus Christ necessarily took our flesh, because he had covenanted with God so to do, yet he acted freely and voluntarily according to that covenant, otherwise his death had not been efficacious for us. A good man doth naturally, necessarily, love his children, yet voluntarily : it is part of the happiness of the blessed to love God unchangeably, yet freely, for it would not be their happiness if it were done by compulsion. What is done by force cannot be called felicity, because there is no delight or complacency in it ; and, though the blessed love God freely, yet, if there were a possibility of change, it would not be their happiness, their blessedness would be damped by their fear of falling from this love, and consequently from their nearness to God, in whom their happiness consists : God foreknows that they will love him forever, but are they therefore compelled forever to love him? If there were such a kind of constraint, heaven would be rendered burdensome to them, and so no heaven. Again, God's foreknowledge of what he will do, doth not necessitate him to do : he foreknew that he would create a world, yet he freely created a world. God's foreknowledge doth not necessitate himself ; why should it necessitate us more than himself? We may instance in ourselves : when we will a thing, we necessarily use our faculty of will ; and when we freely will any thing, it is necessary that we freely will ; but this necessity doth not exclude, but include, liberty ; or, more plainly, when a man writes or speaks, whilst he writes or speaks, those actions are necessary, because to speak and be silent, to write and not to write, at the same time, are impossible ; yet our writing or speaking doth not take away the power not to write or to be silent at that time if a man would be so; for he might have chose whether he would have spoke or writ. So there is a necessity of such actions of man, which God foresees; that is, a necessity of infallibility, because God cannot be deceived, but not a coactive necessity, as if they were compelled by God to act thus or thus.

Prop. II. No man can say in any of his voluntary actions that he ever found any force upon him. When any of us have done anything according to our wills, can we say we could not have done the contrary to it? were we determined to it in our own intrinsic nature, or did we not determine ourselves? did we not act either according to our reason, or according to outward allurements? did we find anything without us, or within us, that did force our wills to the embracing this or that? Whatever action you do, you do it because you judge it fit to be done, or because you will do it. What, though God foresaw that you would do so, and that you would do this or that, did you feel any force upon you? did you not act according to your nature? God foresees that you will eat or walk at such a time; do you find anything that moves you to eat, but your own appetite? or to walk, but your own reason and will? If prescience had imposed any necessity upon man, should we not probably have found some kind of plea from it in the mouth of Adam? he knew as much as any man ever since knew of the nature of God, as discoverable in creation; he could not in innocence fancy an ignorant God, a God that knew nothing of future things; he could not be so ignorant of his own action, but he must have perceived a force upon his will, had there been any; had he thought that God's prescience imposed any necessity upon him, he would not have omitted the plea, especially when he was so daring as to charge the providence of God in the gift of the woman to him, to be the cause of his crime (Gen. iii. 12.) How come his posterity to invent new charges against God, which their father Adam never thought of, who had more knowledge than all of them? He could find no cause of his sin but the liberty of his own will; he charges it, not upon any necessity from the devil, or any necessity from God; nor doth he allege the gift of the woman as a necessary cause of his sin, but an occasion of it, by giving the fruit to him. Judas knew that our Saviour did foreknow his treachery, for he had told him of it in the hearing of his disciples (John xiii. 21—26), yet he never charged the necessity of his crime upon the foreknowledge of his Master; if Judas had not done it freely, he had had no reason to repent of it; his repentance justifies Christ from imposing any necessity upon him by that foreknowledge. No man acts anything, but he can give an account of the motives of his action; he cannot father it upon a blind necessity; the will cannot be compelled, for then it would cease to be the will: God doth not root up the foundations of nature, or change the order of it, and make men unable to act like men, that is, as free agents. God foreknows the actions of irrational creatures; this concludes no violence upon their nature, for we find their actions to be according to their nature, and spontaneous.

Prop. III. God's foreknowledge is not, simply considered, the cause of anything. It puts nothing into things, but only beholds them as present, and arising from their proper causes. The knowledge of God is not the principle of things, or the cause of their existence, but directive of the action; nothing is because God knows it, but because God wills it, either positively or permissively; God knows all things possible; yet, because God knows them they are not brought into actual existence, but remain still only as things possible; knowledge only apprehends a thing, but acts nothing; it is the rule of acting, but not the cause of acting; the will is the immediate principle, and the power the immediate cause; to know a thing is not to do a thing, for then we may be said to do everything that we know : but every man knows those things which he never did, nor never will do; knowledge in itself is an apprehension of a thing, and is not the cause of it. A spectator of a thing is not the cause of that thing which he sees, that is, he is not the cause of it, as he beholds it. We see a man write, we know before that he will write at such a time; but this foreknowledge is not the cause of his writing. We see a man walk, but our vision of him brings no necessity of walking upon him; he was free to walk or not to walk.[s] We foreknow that death will seize upon all men, we foreknow that the seasons of the year will succeed one another, yet is not our foreknowledge the cause of this succession of spring after winter, or of the death of all men, or any man? We see one man fighting with another; our sight is not the cause of that contest, but some quarrel among themselves, exciting their own passions. As the knowledge of present things imposeth no necessity upon them while they are acting, and present, so the knowledge of future things imposeth no necessity upon them while they are coming. We are certain there will be men in the world to-morrow, and that the sea will ebb and flow; but is this knowledge of ours the cause that those things will be so? I know that the sun will rise to-morrow, it is true that it shall rise; but it is not true that my foreknowledge makes it to rise. If a physician prognosticates, upon seeing the intemperances and debaucheries of men, that they will fall into such a distemper, is his prognostication any cause of their disease, or of the sharpness of any symptoms attending it? The prophet foretold the cruelty of Hazael before he committed it; but who will say that the prophet was the cause of his commission of that evil? And thus the foreknowledge of God takes not away the liberty of man's will, no more than a foreknowledge that we have of any man's actions takes away his liberty. We may upon our knowledge of the temper of a man, certainly foreknow, that if he falls into such company, and get among his cups, he will be drunk; but is this foreknowledge the cause that he is drunk? No; the cause is the liberty of his own will, and not resisting the temptation. God purposes to leave such a man to himself and his own ways; and man being so left, God foreknows what will be done by him according to that corrupt nature which is in him; though the decree of God of leaving a

[s] Rawley of the World, lib. i. cap. 1, sec. 12.

man to the liberty of his own will be certain, yet the liberty of man's will as thus left, is the cause of all the extravagances he doth commit. Suppose Adam had stood, would not God certainly have foreseen that he would have stood? yet it would have been concluded that Adam had stood, not by any necessity of God's foreknowledge, but by the liberty of his own will. Why should then the foreknowledge of God add more necessity to his falling than to his standing? And though it be said sometimes in Scripture, that such a thing was done "that the Scripture might be fulfilled," as John xii. 38, "that the saying of Esais might be fulfilled, Lord, who hath believed our report?" the word *that* doth not infer that the prediction of the prophet was the cause of the Jews' belief, but infers this, that the prediction was manifested to be true by their unbelief, and the event answered the prediction; this prediction was not the cause of their sin, but their foreseen sin was the cause of this prediction; and so the particle that is taken (Ps. li. 6), "Against thee, thee only have I sinned, that thou mightest be justified," &c.; the justifying God was not the end and intent of the sin, but the event of it upon his acknowledgment.[t]

Prop. IV. God foreknows things, because they will come to pass; but things are not future, because God knows them. Foreknowledge presupposeth the object which is foreknown; a thing that is to come to pass is the object of the Divine knowledge, but not the cause of the act of divine knowledge; and though the foreknowledge of God doth in eternity precede the actual presence of a thing which is foreseen as future, yet the future thing, in regard of its futurity, is as eternal as the foreknowledge of God: as the voice is uttered before it be heard, and a thing is visible before it be seen, and a thing knowable before it be known. But how comes it to be knowable to God? it must be answered, either in the power of God as a thing possible, or in the will of God as a thing future; he first willed, and then knew what he willed; he knew what he willed to effect, and he knew what he willed to permit; as he willed the death of Christ by a determinate counsel, and willed the permission of the Jew's sin, and the ordering of the malice of their nature to that end (Acts ii. 22). God decrees to make a rational creature, and to govern him by a law; God decrees not to hinder this rational creature from transgressing his law; and God foresees that what he would not hinder, would come to pass. Man did not sin because God foresaw him; but God foresaw him to sin, because man would sin. If Adam and other men would have acted otherwise, God would have foreknown that they would have acted well; God foresaw our actions because they would so come to pass by the motion of our free-will, which he would permit, which he would concur with, which he would order to his own holy and glorious ends, for the manifestation of the perfection of his nature. If I see a man lie in a sink, no necessity is inferred upon him from my sight to lie in that filthy place, but there is a necessity inferred by him that lies there, that I should see him in that condition if I pass by, and cast my eye that way.

Prop. V. God did not only foreknow our actions, but the manner

[t] Rivet, in Isa. liii. 1. p. 16.

of our actions. That is, he did not only know that we would do such actions, but that we would do them freely; he foresaw that the will would freely determine itself to this or that; the knowledge of God takes not away the nature of things; though God knows possible things, yet they remain in the nature of possibility; and though God knows contingent things, yet they remain in the nature of contingencies; and though God knows free agents, yet they remain in the nature of liberty. God did not foreknow the actions of man, as necessary, but as free; so that liberty is rather established by this foreknowledge, than removed. God did not foreknow that Adam had not a power to stand, or that any man hath not a power to omit such a sinful action, but that he would not omit it. Man hath a power to do otherwise than that which God foreknows he will do. Adam was not determined by any inward necessity to fall, nor any man by any inward necessity to commit this or that particular sin; but God foresaw that he would fall, and fall freely; for he saw the whole circle of means and causes whereby such and such actions should be produced, and can be no more ignorant of the motions of our wills, and the manner of them, than an artificer can be ignorant of the motions of his watch, and how far the spring will let down the string in the space of an hour; he sees all causes leading to such events in their whole order, and how the free-will of man will comply with this, or refuse that; he changes not the manner of the creature's operation, whatsoever it be.

Prop. VI. But what if the foreknowledge of God, and the liberty of the will, cannot be fully reconciled by man? shall we therefore deny a perfection in God to support a liberty in ourselves? Shall we rather fasten ignorance upon God, and accuse him of blindness, to maintain our liberty? That God doth foreknow everything, and yet that there is liberty in the rational creature, are both certain; but how fully to reconcile them, may surmount the understanding of man. Some truths the disciples were not capable of bearing in the days of Christ; and several truths our understandings cannot reach as long as the world doth last; yet, in the mean time, we must, on the one hand, take heed of conceiving God ignorant, and on the other hand, of imagining the creature necessitated; the one will render God imperfect, and the other will seem to render him unjust, in punishing man for that sin which he could not avoid, but was brought into by a fatal necessity. God is sufficient to render a reason of his own proceedings, and clear up all at the day of judgment; it is a part of man's curiosity, since the fall, to be prying into God's secrets, things too high for him; whereby he singes his own wings, and con founds his own understanding. It is a cursed affectation that runs in the blood of Adam's posterity, to know as God, though our first father smarted and ruined his posterity in that attempt; the ways and knowledge of God are as much above our thoughts and conceptions as the heavens are above the earth (Isa. lv. 9),[u] and so sublime, that we cannot comprehend them in their true and just greatness; his designs are so mysterious, and the ways of his conduct so profound, that it is not possible to dive into them. The force of our

[u] Daille, Melang. Part II. pp. 712, 725.

understandings is below his infinite wisdom, and therefore we should adore him with an humble astonishment, and cry out with the apostle (Rom. xi. 33): "O the depth of the riches of the wisdom and knowledge of God! how unsearchable are his judgments, and his ways past finding out!" Whenever we meet with depths that we cannot fathom, let us remember that he is God, and we his creatures; and not be guilty of so great extravagance, as to think that a subject can pierce into all the secrets of a prince, or a work understand all the operations of the artificer. Let us only resolve not to fasten anything on God that is unworthy of the perfection of his nature, and dishonorable to the glory of his majesty; nor imagine that we can ever step out of the rank of creatures to the glory of the Deity, to understand fully everything in his nature. So much for the second general, what God knows.

III. The third is, how God knows all things. As it is necessary we should conceive God to be an understanding being, else he could not be God, so we must conceive his understanding to be infinitely more pure and perfect than ours in the act of it, else we liken him to ourselves, and debase him as low as his footstool.[x] As among creatures there are degrees of being and perfection, plants above earth and sand, because they have a power of growth, beasts above plants, because to their power of growth there is an addition of excellency of sense, rational creatures above beasts, because to sense there is added the dignity of reason. The understanding of man is more noble than all the vegetative power of plants, or the sensative power of beasts: God therefore must be infinitely more excellent in his understanding, and therefore in the manner of it. As man differs from a beast in regard of his knowledge, so doth God also from man, in regard of his knowledge. As God therefore is in being and perfection, infinitely more above a man than a man is above a beast, the manner of his knowledge must be infinitely more above a man's knowledge, than the knowledge of a man is above that of a beast; our understanding can clasp an object in a moment that is at a great distance from our sense; our eye, by one elevated motion, can view the heavens; the manner of God's understanding must be unconceivably above our glimmerings; as the manner of his being is infinitely more perfect than all beings, so must the manner of his understanding be infinitely more perfect than all created understandings.[y] Indeed, the manner of God's knowledge can no more be known by us than his essence can be known by us; and the same incapacity in man, which renders him unable to comprehend the being of God, renders him as unable to comprehend the manner of God's understanding. As there is a vast distance between the essence of God and our beings, so there is between the thoughts of God and our thoughts; the heavens are not so much higher than the earth, as the thoughts of God are above the thoughts of men, yea, and of the highest angel (Isa. lv. 8, 9), yet though we know not the manner of God's knowledge, we know that he knows; as though we know not the infiniteness of God, yet we know that he is infinite. It is God's

[x] Maxim. Tyrius. Dissert. 1. pp. 9, 10.
[y] Maimonides More Nevochim. Part III. c. 20. pp. 291—293.

sole prerogative to know himself, what he is; and it is equally his prerogative to know how he knows; the manner of God's knowledge therefore must be considered by us as free from those imperfections our knowledge is encumbered with. In general, God doth necessarily know all things; he is necessarily omnipresent, because of the immensity of his essence; so he is necessarily omniscient, because of the infiniteness of his understanding. It is no more at the liberty of his will, whether he will know all things, than whether he will be able to create all things; it is no more at the liberty of his will, whether he will be omniscient, than whether he will be holy; he can as little be ignorant, as he can be impure; he knows not all things, because he will know them, but because it is essential to his nature to know them. In particular,

Prop. I. God knows by his own essence; that is, he sees the nature of things in the ideas of his own mind, and the events of things in the decrees of his own will; he knows them not by viewing the things, but by viewing himself; his own essence is the mirror and book, wherein he beholds all things that he doth ordain, dispose and execute; and so he knows all things in their first and original cause; which is no other than his own essence willing, and his own essence executing what he wills; he knows them in his power, as the physical principle; in his will, as the moral principle of things, as some speak. He borrows not the knowledge of creatures from the creatures, nor depends upon them for means of understanding, as we poor worms do, who are beholden to the objects abroad to assist us with images of things, and to our senses to convey them into our minds; God would then acquire a perfection from those things which are below himself, and an excellency from those things which are vile; his knowledge would not precede the being of the creatures, but the creatures would be before the act of his knowledge. If he understood by images drawn from the creatures, as we do, there would be something in God which is not God, viz. the images of things drawn from outward objects: God would then depend upon creatures for that which is more noble than a bare being; for to be understanding, is more excellent than barely to be. Besides, if God's knowledge of his creatures were derived from the creatures by the impression of anything upon him, as there is upon us, he could not know from eternity, because from eternity there was no actual existence of anything but himself; and therefore there could not be any images shot out from anything, because there was not anything in being but God; as there is no principle of being to anything but by his essence, so there is no principle of the knowledge of anything by himself but his essence; if the knowledge of God were distinct from his essence, his knowledge were not eternal, because there is nothing eternal but his essence. His understanding is not a faculty in him as it is in us, but the same with his essence, because of the simplicity of his nature; God is not made up of various parts, one distinct from another, as we are, and therefore doth not understand by a part of himself, but by himself; so that to be, and to understand, is the same with God; his essence is not one thing, and the power whereby he understands another; he would then be compounded, and not be the most simple being. This is also necessary for the perfection of God; for the more perfect and noble the way and manner of knowing is, the more perfect and noble is the knowledge. The perfection of knowledge depends upon the excellency of the medium whereby we know. As a knowledge by reason, is a more noble way of knowing than knowledge by sense; so it is more excellent for God to know by his essence, than by anything without him, anything mixed with him; the first would render him dependent, and the other would demolish his simplicity. Again, the natures of all things are contained in God, not formally; for then the nature of the creatures would be God; but eminently, "He that planted the ear, shall he not hear? he that formed the eye, shall he not see?" (Ps. xciv. 9.) He hath in himself eminently the beauty, perfection, life and vigor of all creatures; he created nothing contrary to himself, but everything with some footsteps of himself in them; he could not have pronounced them good, as he did, had there been anything in them contrary to his own goodness; and therefore as his essence primarily represents itself, so it represents the creatures, and makes them known to him. As the essence of God is eminently all things, so by understanding his essence, he eminently understands all things.[z] And therefore he hath not one knowledge of himself, and another knowledge of the creatures; but by knowing himself as the original and exemplary cause of all things, he cannot be ignorant of any creature which he is the cause of; so that he knows all things, not by an understanding of them, but by an understanding of himself; by understanding his own power as the efficient of them, his own will as the orderer of them, his own goodness as the adorner and beautifier of them, his own wisdom as the disposer of them, and his own holiness, to which many of their actions are contrary. As he sees all things possible in his own power, because he is able to produce them; so he sees all things future in his own will, decreeing to effect them, if they be good, or decreeing to permit them if they be evil.[a] In this class he sees what he will give being to, and what he will suffer to fall into a deficiency, without looking out of himself, or borrowing knowledge from his creatures; he knows all things in himself. And thus his knowledge is more noble, and of a higher elevation than ours, or the knowledge of any creature can be; he knows all things by one comprehension of the causes in himself.

Prop. II. God knows all things by one act of intuition. This the schools call an intuitive knowledge. This follows upon the other; for if he know by his own essence, he knows all things by one act, there would be otherwise a division in his essence, a first and a last, a nearness and a distance. As what he made, he made by one word; so what he sees, he pierceth into by one glance from eternity to eternity: as he wills all things by one act of his will, so he knows all things by one act of his understanding: he knows not some things discursively from other things, nor knows one thing successively after another. As by one act he imparts essence to things; so by one act he knows the nature of things.

1. He doth not know by discourse, as we do;—that is, by deducing

---

[z] Dionys.   [a] Kendall against Goodwin of Foreknowledge.

one thing from another, and from common notions drawing out other rational conclusions and arguing one thing from another, and springing up various consequences from some principle assented to. But God stands in no need of reasonings; the making inferences and abstracting things, would be stains in the infinite perfection of God; here would be a mixture of knowledge and ignorance; while he knew the principle, he would not know the consequence and conclusion, till he had actually deduced it; one thing would be known after another, and so he would have an ignorance, and then a knowledge; and there would be different conceptions in God, and knowledge would be multiplied according to the multitude of objects; as it is in human understandings. But God knows all things before they did exist, and never was ignorant of them (Acts xv. 18): "Known unto God are all his works from the beginning of the world." He therefore knows them all at once; the knowledge of one thing was not before another, nor depended upon another, as it doth in the way of human reasoning.[b] Though, indeed, some make a virtual discourse in God; that is, though God hath a simple knowledge, yet it doth virtually contain a discourse by the flowing of one knowledge from another; as from the knowledge of his own power, he knows what things are possible to be made by him; and from the knowledge of himself, he passes to the knowledge of the creatures; but this is only according to our conception, and because of our weakness they are apprehended as two distinct acts in God, one of which is the reason of another; as we say that one attribute is the reason of another; as his mercy may be said to be the reason of his patience; and his omnipresence to be the reason of the knowledge of present things done in the world. God, indeed, by one simple act, knows himself and the creatures; but when that act whereby he knows himself, is conceived by us to pass to the knowledge of the creatures, we must not understand it to be a new act, distinct from the other; but the same act upon different terms or objects; such an order is in our understandings and conceptions, not in God's.

2. Nor doth he know successively as we do: that is, not by drops, one thing after another. This follows from the former; a knowledge of all things without discourse, is a knowledge without succession.[c] The knowledge of one thing is not in God before another, one act of knowledge doth not beget another; in regard of the objects, one thing is before another, one year before another, one generation of men before another, one is the cause, the other is the effect; in the creatures there is such a succession, and God knows there will be such a succession; but there is no such order in God's knowledge, for he knows all those successions by one glance, without any succession of knowledge in himself. Man, in his view of things, must turn sometimes his body, sometimes only his eyes, he cannot see all the contents of a letter at once; and though he beholds all the lines in the page of a book at once, and a whole country in a map, yet to know what is contained in them, he must turn his eye from word to word, and line to line, and so spin out one thing after another by

b Suarez. Vol. I. de Deo, lib. 3. cap. 2. pp. 133, 134.
c Gamach in Aquin Q. 14. cap. 1. p. 113.

several acts and motions. We behold a great part of the sea at once,[d] but not all the dimensions of it; for to know the length of the sea, we move our eyes one way; to see the breadth of it, we turn our eyes another way; to behold the depth of it, we have another motion of them. And when we cast our eyes up to heaven, we seem to receive in an instant, the whole extent of the hemisphere; yet there is but one object the eye can attentively pitch upon, and we cannot distinctly view what we see in a lump, without various motions of our eyes, which is not done without succession of time.[e] And certainly the understanding of angels is bounded, according to the measure of their beings; so that it cannot extend itself at one time, to a quantity of objects, to make a distinct application of them, but the objects must present themselves one by one; but God is all eye, all understanding; as there is no succession in his essence, so there is none in his knowledge; his understanding in the nature and in the act, is infinite, as it is in the text. He therefore sees, eternally and universally, all things by one act, without any motion, much less various motions; the various changes of things, in their substance, qualities, places, and relations, withdraw not anything from his eye, nor bring any new thing to his knowledge; he doth not upon consideration of present things turn his mind from past; or when he beholds future things turn his mind from present; but he sees them not one after another, but all at once and all together; the whole circle of his own counsels, and all the various lines drawn forth from the centre of his will, to the circumference of his creatures; just as if a man were able in one moment to read a whole library; or, as if you should imagine a transparent crystal globe, hung up in the midst of a room, and so framed as to take in the images of all things in the room, the fret-work in the ceiling, the inlaid parts of the floor and the particular parts of the tapestry about it, the eye of a man would behold all the beauty of the room at once in it. As the sun by one light and heat frames sensible things, so God by one simple act knows all things; as he knows mutable things by an immutable knowledge, bodily things by a spiritual knowledge, so he knows many things by one knowledge (Heb. iv. 13): "All things are open and naked to him," more than any one thing can be to us; and therefore he views all things at once, as well as we can behold and contemplate one thing alone. As he is the Father of lights, a God of infinite understanding, there is no variableness in his mind, nor any shadow of turning of his eye, as there is of ours, to behold various things (James i. 17); his knowledge being eternal, includes all times; there is nothing past or future with him, and therefore he beholds all things by one and the same manner of knowledge, and comprehends all knowable things by one act, and in one moment. This must needs be so,

(1.) Because of the eminency of God. God is above all, and therefore cannot but see the motions of all. He that sits in a theatre, or at the top of a place, sees all things, all persons; by one aspect he comprehends the whole circle of the place; whereas, he that sits below, when he looks before, he cannot see things behind; God

---

[d] Epiphanius.   [e] Amyrant, Morale Chréti. Tom. III. p. 137.

being above all, about all, in all, sees at once the motions of all. The whole world, in the eye of God, is less than a point that divides one sentence from another in a book; as a cypher, a "grain of dust" (Isa. xl. 15); so little a thing can be seen by man at once; and all things being as little in the eye of God, are seen at once by him. As all time is but a moment to his eternity, so all things are but as a point to the immensity of his knowledge, which he can behold with more ease than we can move or turn our eye.

(2.) Because all the perfections of knowing are united in God.[f] As particular senses are divided in man,—by one he sees, by another he smells, yet all those are united in one common sense, and this common sense comprehends all,—so the various and distinct ways of knowledge in the creatures are all eminently united in God. A man when he sees a grain of wheat, understands at once all things that can in time proceed from that seed; so God, by beholding his own virtue and power, beholds all things which shall in time be unfolded by him. We have a shadow of this way of knowledge in our own understanding; the sense only perceives a thing present, and one object only proper and suitable to it; as the eye sees color, the ear hears sounds; we see this and that man, one time this, another minute that; but the understanding abstracts a notion of the common nature of man, and frames a conception of that nature wherein all men agree; and so in a manner beholds and understands all men at once, by understanding the common nature of man, which is a degree of knowledge above the sense and fancy; we may then conceive an infinite vaster perfection in the understanding of God. As to know, is simply better than not to know at all; so to know by one act comprehensive, is a greater perfection than to know by divided acts, by succession to receive information, and to have an increase or decrease of knowledge; to be like a bucket, always descending into the well, and fetching water from thence. It is a man's weakness that he is fixed on one object only at a time; it is God's perfection that he can behold all at once, and is fixed upon one no more than upon another.

Prop. III. God knows all things independently. This is essential to an infinite understanding. He receives not his knowledge from anything without him; he hath no tutor to instruct him, or book to inform him: "Who hath been his counsellor?" saith the prophet (Isa. xl. 13); he hath no need of the counsels of others, nor of the instructions of others. This follows upon the first and second propositions; if he knows things by his essence, then, as his essence is independent from the creatures, so is his knowledge; he borrows not any images from the creature; hath no species or pictures of things in his understanding, as we have; no beams from the creature strike upon him to enlighten him, but beams from him upon the world; the earth sends not light to the sun, but the sun to the earth. Our knowledge, indeed, depends upon the object, but all created objects depend upon God's knowledge and will; we could not know creatures unless they were; but creatures could not be unless God knew them. As nothing that he wills is the cause of his will, so

---

[f] Cusan. p. 646.

nothing that he knows is the cause of his knowledge; he did not make things to know them, but he knows them to make them: who will imagine that the mark of the foot in the dust is the cause that the foot stands in this or that particular place? If his knowledge did depend upon the things, then the existence of things did precede God's knowledge of them: to say that they are the cause of God's knowledge, is to say that God was not the cause of their being; and if he did create them, it was effected by a blind and ignorant power; he created he knew not what, till he had produced it. If he be beholden for his knowledge to the creatures he hath made, he had then no knowledge of them before he made them. If his knowledge were dependent upon them, it could not be eternal, but must have a beginning when the creatures had a beginning, and be of no longer a date than since the nature of things was in actual existence; for whatsoever is a cause of knowledge, doth precede the knowledge it causes, either in order of time, or order of nature: temporal things, therefore, cannot be the cause of that knowledge which is eternal. His works could not be foreknown to him, if his knowledge commenced with the existence of his works (Acts xv. 18): if he knew them before he made them, he could not derive a knowledge from them after they were made. He made all things in wisdom (Ps. civ. 24). How can this be imagined, if the things known where the cause of his knowledge, and so before his knowledge, and therefore before his action? ᵍ God would not then be the first in the order of knowing agents, because he would not act by knowledge, but act before he knew, and know after he had acted; and so the creature which he made would be before the act of his understanding, whereby he knew what he made. Again, since knowledge is a perfection, if God's knowledge of the creatures depended upon the creatures, he would derive an excellency from them, they would derive no excellency from any idea in the Divine mind; he would not be infinitely perfect in himself; if his perfection in knowledge were gained from anything without himself and below himself, he would not be sufficient of himself, but be under an indigence, which wanted a supply from the things he had made, and could not be eternally perfect till he had created and seen the effects of his own power, goodness, and wisdom, to render him more wise and knowing in time than he was from eternity. Who can fancy such a God as this without destroying the Deity he pretends to adore? for if his understanding be perfected by something without him, why may not his essence be perfected by something without him; that, as he was made knowing by something without him, he might be made God by something without him? How could his understanding be infinite if it depended upon a finite object, as upon a cause? Is the majesty of God to be debased to a mendicant condition, to seek for a supply from things inferior to himself? Is it to be imagined that a fool, a toad, a fly, should be assistant to the knowledge of God? that the most noble being should be perfected by things so vile; that the Supreme Cause of all things should receive any addition of knowledge, and be determined in his understanding, by the notiou

ᵍ Bradward, lib. 1. cap. 15.

of things so mean? To conclude this particular, all things depend upon his knowledge, his knowledge depends upon nothing, but is as independent as himself and his own essence.

Prop. IV. God knows all things distinctly. His understanding is infinite in regard of clearness; "God is light, and in him is no darkness at all" (John i. 5); he sees not through a mist or cloud; there is no blemish in his understanding, no mote or beam in his eye, to render any thing obscure to him. Man discerns the surface and outside of things; little or nothing of the essence of things; we see the noblest thing but "as in a glass darkly" (1 Cor. xiii. 12); the too great nearness, as well as the too great distance of a thing, hinders our sight; the smallness of a mote escapes our eye, and so our knowledge; also the weakness of our understanding is troubled with the multitude of things, and cannot know many things but confusedly: but God knows the forms and essence of things, every circumstance; nothing is so deep, but he sees to the bottom; he sees the mass, and sees the motes of beings; his understanding being infinite, is not offended with a multitude of things, or distracted with the variety of them; he discerns every thing infinitely more clearly and perfectly than Adam or Solomon could any one thing in the circle of their knowledge; what knowledge they had, was from him; he hath, therefore, infinitely a more perfect knowledge than they were capable in their natures to receive a communication of. All things are open to him (Heb. iv. 13); the least fibre, in its nakedness and distinct frame, is transparent to him, as, by the help of glasses, the mouth, feet, hands, of a small insect, are visible to a man, which seem to the eye, without that assistance, one entire piece, not diversified into parts. All the causes, qualities, natures, properties of things, are open to him; "he brings out the host of heaven by number, and calleth them by names" (Isa. xl. 26); he numbers the hairs of our heads: what more distinct than number? Thus God beholds things in every unity, which makes up the heap; he knows, and none else can, every thing in its true and intimate causes, in its original and intermediate causes; in himself, as the cause of every particular of their being, every property in their being. Knowledge by the causes is the most noble and perfect knowledge, and most suited to the infinite excellency of the Divine Being; he created all things, and ordered them to a universal and particular end; he, therefore, knows the essential properties of every thing, every activity of their nature, all their fitness for those distinct ends, to which he orders them, and for which he governs and disposeth them, and understands their darkest and most hidden qualities infinitely clearer than any eye can behold the clear beams of the sun. He knows all things as he made them; he made them distinctly, and therefore knows them distinctly, and that every individual; therefore God is said (Gen. i. 31) to see every thing that he had made; he took a review of every particular creature he had made, and upon his view pronounced it good. To pronounce that good, which was not exactly known in every creek, in every mite of its nature, had not consisted with his veracity; for every one that speaks truth ignorantly, that knows not that he speaks truth, is a liar in speaking that which is true. God knows every act of his own will, whether it be positive or permissive, and therefore every effect of his will. We must needs ascribe to God a perfect knowledge; but a confused knowledge cannot challenge that title. To know things only in a heap is unworthy of the Divine perfection; for if God knows his own ends in the creation of things, he knows distinctly the means whereby he will bring them to those ends for which he hath appointed them: no wise man intends an end, without a knowledge of the means conducing to that end; an ignorance, then, of any thing in the world, which falls under the nature of a means to a Divine end (and there is nothing in the world but doth), would be inconsistent with the perfection of God; it would ascribe to him a blind providence in the world. As there can be nothing imperfect in his being and essence, so there can be nothing imperfect in his understanding and knowledge, and therefore not a confused knowledge, which is an imperfection. "Darkness and light are both alike to him" (Ps. cxxxix. 12); he sees distinctly into the one, as well as the other; what is darkness to us, is not so to him.

Prop. V. God knows all things infallibly. His understanding is infinite in regard of certainty; every tittle of what he knows is as far from failing as what he speaks; our Saviour affirms the one (Matt. v. 18), and there is the same reason of the certainty of one as well as the other; his essence is the measure of his knowledge; whence it is as impossible that God should be mistaken in the knowledge of the least thing in the world, as it is that he should be mistaken in his own essence; for, knowing himself comprehensively, he must know all others things infallibly; since he is essentially omniscient, he is no more capable of error in his understanding than of imperfection in his essence; his counsels are as unerring as his essence is perfect, and his knowledge as infallible as his essence is free from defect. Again, since God knows all things with a knowledge of vision, because he wills them, his knowledge must be as infallible as his purpose; now his purpose will certainly be effected; "what he hath thought shall come to pass, and what he hath purposed shall stand" (Isa. xiv. 24); "his counsel shall stand, and he will do all his pleasure" (Isa. xlvi. 10). There may be interruptions of nature, the foundation of it may be out of course, but there can be no bar upon the Author of nature; he hath an infinite power to carry on and perfect the resolves of his own will; he can effect what he pleases by a word. Speech is one of the least motions; yet when God said, "let there be light, there was light" arising from darkness. No reason can be given why God knows a thing to be, but because he infallibly wills it to be. Again,[h] the schools make this difference between the knowledge of the good and bad angels, that the good are never deceived; for that is repugnant to their blessed state; for deceit is an evil and an imperfection inconsistent with that perfect blessedness the good angels are possessed of; and would it not much more be a stain upon the blessedness of that God, that is blessed forever, to be subject to deceit? His knowledge therefore is not an opinion, for an opinion is uncertain; a man knows not

[h] Saurez. Vol. II. p. 228.

what to think, but leans to one part of the question proposed, rather than to the other. If things did not come to pass therefore as God knows them, his knowledge would be imperfect; and since he knows by his essence, his essence also would be imperfect, if God were exposed to any deceit in his knowledge; he knows by himself, who is the highest truth; and therefore it is impossible he should err in his understanding.

Prop. VI. God knows immutably. His understanding else could not be infinite; everything and every act that is mutable, is finite, it hath its bounds; for there is a term from which it changeth, and a term to which it changes.[i] There is a change in the understanding, when we gain the knowledge of a thing, which was unknown to us before; or when we actually consider a thing which we did not know before, though we had the principles of the knowledge of it; or, when we know that distinctly, which we before knew confusedly. None of these can be ascribed to God without a manifest disparagement of his infiniteness. Our knowledge indeed is alway arriving to us or flowing from us; we pass from one degree to another; from worse to better, or from better to worse; but God loses nothing by the ages that are run, nor will gain anything by the ages that are to come. If there were a variation in the knowledge of God, by the daily and hourly changes in the world, he would grow wiser than he was, he was not then perfectly wise before. A change in the objects known, infers not any change in the understanding exercised about them ; the wheel moves round, the spokes that are lowest are presently highest, and presently return to be low again ; but the eye that beholds them changes not with the motions of the wheels. God's knowledge admits no more of increase or decrease, than his essence doth ; since God knows by his essence, and the essence of God is God himself, his knowledge must be void of any change. The knowledge of possible things, arising from the knowledge of his own power, cannot be changed unless his power be changed, and God become weak and impotent; the knowledge of future things cannot be changed, because that knowledge ariseth from his will, which is irreversible, "the counsel of the Lord that shall stand" (Prov. xix. 21); so that if God can never decay into weakness, and never turn to inconstancy, there can be no variation of his knowledge. He knows what he can do, and he knows what he will do; and both these being immutable, his knowledge must, consequently, be so too. It was not necessary that this or that creature should be, and therefore it was not necessary that God should know this or that creature with a knowledge of vision; but after the will of God had determined the existence of this or that creature, his knowledge being then determined to this or that object, did necessarily continue unchangeable. God, therefore, knows no more now than he did before; and at the end of the world, he shall know no more than he doth now; and from eternity, he knows no less than he doth now, and shall do to eternity. Though things pass into being and out of being, the knowledge of God doth not vary with them, for he knows them as well before they were, as when

i Tileni Syntagina, Part I. Disp. 13. Thes. 14.

they are, and knows them as well when they are past, as when they are present.

Prop. VII. God knows all things perpetually, *i. e.* in act. Since he knows by his essence, he always knows, because his essence never ceaseth, but is a pure act; so that he doth not know only in habit, but in act. Men that have the knowledge of some art or science, have it always in habit, though when they are asleep they have it not in act: a musician hath the habit of music, but doth not so much as think of it when his senses are bound up. But God is an unsleepy eye;[k] he never slumbers nor sleeps; he never slumbers, in regard of his providence, and therefore never slumbers in regard of his knowledge. He knows not himself, nor any other creature more perfectly at one time than at another; he is perpetually in the act of knowing, as the sun is in the act of shining; the sun never ceased to shine in one or other part of the world, since it was first fixed in the heavens; nor God to be in the act of knowledge, since he was God; and therefore since he always was, and always will be God, he always was and always will be in the act of knowledge; always knowing his own essence, he must alway actually know what hath been gone and ceased from being, and what shall come and arise into being; as a watchmaker knows what watch he intends to make, and after he hath made it, though it be broken to pieces, or consumed by the fire, he still knows it, because he knows the copy of it in his own mind. Some, therefore, in regard of this perpetual act of the Divine knowledge, have called God not *intellectus*, but the intellection of intellections; we have no proper English word to express the act of the understanding; as his power is co-eternal with him, so is his knowledge; all times past, present, and to come, are embraced in the bosom of his understanding; he fixed all things in their seasons, that nothing new comes to him, nothing old passes from him.[l] What is done in a thousand years, is actually present with his knowledge, as what is done in one day, or in one watch in the night, is with ours; since a "thousand years are no more to God than a day," or a "watch in the night" is to us (Ps. xc. 4). God is in the highest degree of being, and therefore in the highest degree of understanding. Knowledge is one of the most perfect acts in any creature. God therefore hath all actual, as well as essential and habitual knowledge; his understanding is infinite.

IV. The fourth general is, Reasons to prove this.

Reason 1. God must know what any creature knows, and more than any creature knows. There is nothing done in the world but is known by some creature or other; every action is at least known by the person that acts, and therefore known by the Creator, who cannot be exceeded by any of the creatures, or all of them together; and every creature is known by him, since every creature is made by him.[m] And as God works all things by an infinite power, so he knows all things by an infinite understanding. First, the perfection of God requires this.[n] All perfections that include no essential defect, are formally in God; but knowledge includes no essential de-

---

[k] Plato, ἀκοίμητος ὀφθαλμός.   [l] Damianus.   [m] Gerhard.
[n] Gamach in Aquin. Part 1. Q. 14, cap. 1. pp. 118, 119.

fect in itself, therefore it is in God. Knowledge in itself is desirable, and an excellency; ignorance is a defect; it is impossible that the least grain of defect can be found in the most perfect Being. Since God is wise, he must be knowing; for wisdom must have knowledge for the basis of it. A creature can no more be wise without knowledge, than he can be active without strength. Now God is "only wise" (Rom. xvi. 27); and, therefore, only knowing in the highest degree of knowledge, incomprehensibly beyond all degrees of knowledge, because infinite. Again, the more spiritual anything is, the more understanding it is. The dull body understands nothing; sense perceives, but the understanding faculty is seated in the soul, which is of a spiritual nature, which knows things that are present, remembers things that are past, foresees many things to come. What is the property of a spiritual nature, must be, in a most eminent manner, in the supreme spirit of the world; that is, in the highest degree of spirituality, and most remote from any matter. Again, nothing can enjoy other things, but by some kind of understanding them; God hath the highest enjoyment of himself, of all things he hath created, of all the glory that accrues to him by them; nothing of perfection and blessedness can be wanting to him. Felicity doth not consist with ignorance, and all imperfect knowledge is a degree of ignorance: God, therefore, doth perfectly know himself, and all things from whence he designs any glory to himself. The most noble manner of acting must be ascribed to God, as being the most noble and excellent Being; to act by knowledge is the most excellent manner of acting; God hath, therefore, not only knowledge, but the most excellent manner of knowledge; for as it is better to know than to be ignorant, so it is better to know in the most excellent manner, than to have a mean and low kind of knowledge; his knowledge, therefore, must be every way as perfect as his essence, infinite as well as that. An infinite nature must have an infinite knowledge: a God ignorant of anything cannot be counted infinite, for he is not infinite to whom any degree of perfection is wanting.

Reason 2. All the knowledge in any creature is from God. And you must allow God a greater and more perfect knowledge than any creature hath, yea, than all creatures have. All the drops of knowledge any creature hath, come from God; and all the knowledge in every creature, that ever was, is, or shall be, in the whole mass, was derived from him. If all those several drops in particular creatures, were collected into one spirit, into one creature, it would be an unconceivable knowledge, yet still lower than what the Author of all that knowledge hath; for God cannot give more knowledge than he hath himself; nor is the creature capable of receiving so much knowledge as God hath. As the creature is incapable of receiving so much power as God hath, for then it would be almighty, so it is incapable of receiving so much knowledge as God hath, for then it would be God. Nothing can be made by God equal to him in anything; if anything could be made as knowing as God, it would be eternal as God, it would be the cause of all things as God. The knowledge that we poor worms have, is an argument God uses for the asserting the greatness of his own knowledge (Ps. xciv. 10): "He that teaches man knowledge, shall not he know?" Man hath here knowledge ascribed to him; the author of this knowledge is God; he furnished him with it, and therefore doth in a higher manner possess it, and much more than can fall under the comprehension of any creature; as the sun enlightens all things, but hath more light in itself than it darts upon the earth or the heavens: and shall not God eminently contain all that knowledge he imparts to the creatures, and infinitely more exact and comprehensive?

Reason 3. The accusations of conscience evidence God's knowledge of all actions of his creatures. Doth not conscience check for the most secret sins, to which none are privy but a man's self, the whole world beside being ignorant of his crime? Do not the fears of another Judge gall the heart? If a judgment above him be feared, an understanding above him discerning their secrets is confessed by those fears; whence can those horrors arise, if there be not a superior that understands and records the crime? What perfection of the Divine Being can this relate unto, but omniscience? What other attribute is to be feared, if God were defective in this? The condemnation of us by our own hearts, when none in the world can condemn us, renders it legible, that there is One "greater than our hearts" in respect of knowledge, who "knoweth all things" (1 John iii. 20). Conscience would be a vain principle, and stingless without this; it would be an easy matter to silence all its accusations, and mockingly laugh in the face of its severest frowns. What need any trouble themselves, if none knows their crimes but themselves? Concealed sins, gnawing the conscience, are arguments of God's omniscience of all present and past actions.

Reason 4. God is the first cause of everything, every creature is his production. Since all creatures, from the highest angel to the lowest worm, exist by the power of God, if God understands his own power and excellency, nothing can be hid from him, that was brought forth by that power, as well as nothing can be unknown to him, that that power is able to produce. "If God knows nothing besides himself, he may then believe there is nothing besides himself; we shall then fancy a God miserably mistaken: if he knows nothing besides himself, then things were not created by him, or not understandingly and voluntarily created, but dropped from him before he was aware.º To think that the First Cause of all should be ignorant of those things he is the cause of, is to make him not a voluntary, but natural agent, and therefore necessary; and then that the creature came from him as light from the sun, and moisture from the water; this would be an absurd opinion of the world's creation; if God be a voluntary agent, as he is, he must be an intelligent agent. The faculty of will is not in any creature, without that of understanding also. If God be an intelligent agent, his knowledge must extend as far as his operation, and every object of his operation, unless we imagine God hath lost his memory, in that long tract of time since the first creation of them. An artificer cannot be ignorant of his own work: if God knows himself, he knows himself to be a

---

º Bradwardin, p. 6.

cause; how can he know himself to be a cause, unless he know the effects he is the cause of? One relation implies another; a man cannot know himself to be a father, unless he hath a child, because it is a name of relation, and in the notion of it refers to another. The name of cause is a name of relation, and implies an effect; if God therefore know himself in all his perfections, as the cause of things, he must know all his acts, what his wisdom contrived, what his counsel determined, and what his power effected. The knowledge of God is to be supposed in a free determination of himself; and that knowledge must be perfect, both of the object, act, and all the circumstances of it. How can his will freely produce anything that was not first known in his understanding? From this the prophet argues the understanding of God, and the unsearchableness of it, because he is the " Creator of the ends of the earth" (Isa. xl. 28), and the same reason David gives of God's knowledge of him, and of everything he did, and that afar off, because he was formed by him (Ps. cxxxix. 2, 15, 16). As the perfect making of things only belongs to God : so doth the perfect knowledge of things ; it is as absurd to think, that God should be ignorant of what he hath given being to ; that he should not know all the creatures and their qualities, the plants and their virtues ; as that a man should not know the letters that are formed by him in writing. Everything bears in itself the mark of God's perfection ; and shall not God know the representation of his own virtue?

Reason 5. Without this knowledge, God could no more be the Governor, than he could be the Creator of the world. Knowledge is the basis of providence ; to know things, is before the government of things ; a practical knowledge cannot be without a theoretical knowledge. Nothing could be directed to its proper end, without the knowledge of the nature of it, and its suitableness to answer that end for which it is intended. As everything, even the minutest, falls under the conduct of God, so everything falls under the knowledge of God. A blind coachman is not able to hold the reins of his horses, and direct them in right paths : since the providence of God is about particulars, his knowledge must be about particulars ; he could not else govern them in particular ; nor could all things be said to depend upon him in their being and operations. Providence depends upon the knowledge of God, and the exercise of it upon the goodness of God ; it cannot be without understanding and will ; understanding, to know what is convenient, and will to perform it. When our Saviour therefore speaks of providence, he intimates these two in a special manner, " Your heavenly Father knows that you have need of these things" (Matt. vi. 32), and goodness, in Luke xi. 13. The reason of providence is so joined with omniscience, that they cannot be separated. What a kind of God would he be that were ignorant of those things that were governed by him ! The ascribing this perfection to him, asserts his providence ; for it is as easy for one that knows all things, to look over the whole world, if writ with monosyllables, in every little particular of it ; as it is with a man to take a view of one letter in an alphabet. Again, if God were not omniscient, how could he reward the good, and punish the evil? the

works of men are either rewardable or punishable ; not only according to their outward circumstances, but inward principles and ends,
and the degrees of venom lurking in the heart.ᴾ The exact discerning of these, without a possibility to be deceived, is necessary to pass
a right and infallible judgment upon them, and proportion the censure and punishment to the crime : without such a knowledge and
discerning, men would not have their due ; nay, a judgment just for the
matter, would be unjust in the manner, because unjustly past, without an understanding of the merit of the cause. It is necessary
therefore that the Supreme Judge of the world should not be thought
to be blindfold, when he distributes his rewards and punishments,
and muffle his face when he passes his sentence. It is necessary to
ascribe to him the knowledge of men's thoughts and intentions ; the
secret wills and aims ; the hidden works of darkness in every man's
conscience, because every man's work is to be measured by the will
and inward frame. It is necessary that he should perpetually retain
all those things in the indelible and plain records of his memory,
that there may not be any work without a just proportion of what
is due to it. This is the glory of God, to discover the secrets of all
hearts at last, as 1 Cor. iv. 5, " The Lord shall bring to light the
hidden things of darkness, and will make manifest the counsels of
all hearts, and then shall every man have praise of God." This
knowledge fits him to be a judge ; the reason why the ungodly shall
not stand in judgment, is because God knows their ways, which is
implied in his knowing the way of the righteous (Ps. i. 5, 6). I now
proceed to the use.

Use I. is of information or instruction. If God hath all knowledge ; then,

Instruct 1. Jesus Christ is not a mere creature. The two titles of
wonderful Counsellor, and mighty God, are given him in conjunction
(Isa. ix. 6), not only the Angel of the covenant, as he is called
(Malach. iii. 1), or the executor of his counsels, but a counsellor, in
conjunction with him in counsel as well as power : this title is superior to any title given to any of the prophets in regard of their predictions ; and therefore I should take it rather as the note of his
perfect understanding, than of his perfect teaching and discovering ;
as Calvin doth. He is not only the revealer of what he knows, so
were the prophets according to their measures ; but the counsellor
of what he revealed, having a perfect understanding of all the counsels of God, as being interested in them, as the mighty God. He
calls himself by the peculiar title of God, and declares that he will
manifest himself by this prerogative to all the churches (Rev. ii. 23) :
" And all the churches shall know that I am he which searches the
reins and hearts," the most hidden operations of the minds of men,
that lie locked up from the view of all the world besides. And this
was no new thing to Him, after his ascension ; for the same perfection he had in the time of his earthly flesh (Luke vi. 8), he knew
their thoughts ; his eyes are therefore compared (Cant. v. 12) to
doves' eyes, which are clear and quick ; and to a flame of fire (Rev.
i. 14), not only heat to consume his enemies, but light to discern

ᴾ Sabund. Tit. 84. much changed.

their contrivances against the church; he pierceth by his knowledge, into all parts, as fire pierceth into the closest particle of iron, and separates between the most united parts of metals; and some tell us, he is called a Roe, from the perspicacity of his sight, as well as from the swiftness of his motion.

1. He hath a perfect knowledge of the Father; he knows the Father, and none else knows the Father; angels know God, men know God, but Christ in a peculiar manner knows the Father; no man knows the Son but the Father; neither knows any man the Father, save the Son (Matt. xi. 27); he knows so, as that he learns not from any other; he doth perfectly comprehend him, which is beyond the reach of any creature, with the addition of all the divine virtue; not because of any incapacity in God to reveal, but the incapacity of the creature to receive; finite is incapable of being made infinite, and therefore incapable of comprehending infinite; so that Christ cannot be *Deus factus*, made of a creature a God, to comprehend God; for then of finite he would become infinite, which is a contradiction. As the Spirit is God, because he searches the deep things of God (1 Cor. ii. 10), that is comprehends them,[q] as the spirit of a man doth the things of a man (now the spirit of man understands what it thinks, and what it wills), so the Spirit of God understands what is in the understanding of God, and what is in the will of God. He hath an absolute knowledge ascribed to him, and such as could not be ascribed to anything but a divinity: now if the Spirit knows the deep things of God, and takes from Christ what he shows to us of him (John xvi. 15), he cannot be ignorant of those things himself; he must know the depths of God, that affords us that Spirit, that is not ignorant of any of the counsels of the Father's will; since he comprehends the Father, and the Father him, he is in himself infinite; for God whose essence is infinite, is infinitely knowable; but no created understanding can infinitely know God. The infiniteness of the object hinders it from being understood by anything that is not infinite. Though a creature should understand all the works of God, yet it cannot be therefore said to understand God himself: as though I may understand all the volitions and motions of my soul, yet it doth not follow that therefore I understand the whole nature and substance of my soul; or if a man understood all the effects of the sun, that therefore he understands fully the nature of the sun. But Christ knows the Father, he lay in the bosom of the Father, was in the greatest intimacy with him (John i. 18), and from this intimacy with him, he saw him and knew him; so he knows God as much as he is knowable; and therefore knows him perfectly as the Father knows himself by a comprehensive vision; this is the knowledge of God wherein properly the infiniteness of his understanding appears: and our Saviour uses such expressions which manifest his knowledge to be above all created knowledge, and such a manner of knowledge of the Father, as the Father hath of him.

2. Christ knows all creatures. That knowledge which comprehends God, comprehends all created things as they are in God; it is a knowledge that sinks to the depths of his will, and therefore extends

to all the acts of his will in creation and providence; by knowing the Father he knows all things that are contained in the virtue, power, and will of God; "whatsoever the Father doth, that the Son doth" (John v. 19.) As the Father therefore knows all things he is the cause of, so doth the Son know all things he is the worker of; as the perfect making of all things belongs to both, so doth the perfect knowledge of all things belong to both; where the action is the same, the knowledge is the same. Now the Father did not create one thing and Christ another; "but all things were created by him, and for him, all things both in heaven and earth" (Col. i. 16): as he knows himself as the cause of all things, and the end of all things, he cannot be ignorant of all things that were effected by him, and are referred to him; he knows all creatures in God, as he knows the essence of God, and knows all creatures in themselves, as he knows his own acts and the fruits of his power; those things must be in his knowledge that were in his power; all the treasures of the wisdom and knowledge of God are hid in him (Col. ii. 3). Now it is not the wisdom of God to know in part, and be in part ignorant. He cannot be ignorant of anything, since there is nothing but what was made by him (John i. 3), and since it is less to know than create; for we know many things which we cannot make.[r] If he be the Creator, he cannot but be the discerner of what he made; this is a part of wisdom belonging to an artificer, to know the nature and quality of what he makes. Since he cannot be ignorant of what he furnished with being, and with various endowments, he must know them not only universally, but particularly.

3. Christ knows the heart and affections of men. Peter scruples not to ascribe to him this knowledge, among the knowledge of all other things (John xxi. 17). "Lord thou knowest all things, thou knowest that I love thee." From Christ's knowledge of all things, he concludes his knowledge of the inward frames and dispositions of men. To search the heart is the sole prerogative of God (1 Kings viii. 39), for thou, even thou only knowest the hearts of all the children of men: shall we take *only* here with a limitation, as some that are no friends to the Deity of Christ would, and say, God only knows the hearts of men from himself, and by his own infinite virtue? Why may we not take *only* in other places with a limitation, and make nonsense of it, as Ps. lxxxvi. 10, "Thou art God alone." Is it to be understood that God is God alone from himself, but other gods may be made by him, and so there may be numberless infinites? As God is God alone, so that none can be God but himself; so he alone knows all the hearts of all the children of men, and none but he can know them; this knowledge is from his nature. The reason why God knows the hearts of men, is rendered in the Scripture double, because he created them, and because he is present everywhere (Ps. xxxiii. 13, 15),[s] these two are by the confession of Christians and Pagans universally received as the proper characters of divinity, whereby the Deity is distinguished from all creatures. Now when Christ ascribes this to himself, and that with such an emphasis, that nothing greater than that could be urged, as he doth (Rev. ii. 23), we must conclude that he is of the same essence with

r Petav. Theol. Dogmat. Tom. I. p. 467.   s Placæus de Deitate Christi.

God, one with him in his nature, as well as one with him in his attributes. God only knows the hearts of the children of men; there is the unity of God: Christ searches the hearts and reins; there is a distinction of persons in a oneness of essence; he knows the hearts of all men, not only of those that were with him in the time of the flesh, that have been, and shall be, since his ascension; but of those that lived and died before his coming; because he is to be the Judge of all that lived before his humiliation on earth, as well as after his exaltation in heaven. It pertains to him, as a Judge, to know distinctly the merits of the cause of which he is to judge; and this excellency of searching the hearts is mentioned by himself with relation to his judicial proceeding, "I will give to every one of you according to your works." And though a creature may know what is in a man's heart, if it be revealed to him, yet such a knowledge is a knowledge only by report, not by inspection; yet this latter is ascribed to Christ (John ii. 24, 25): "he knew all men, and needed not that any should testify of man, for he knew what was in man:" he looked into their hearts. The Evangelist, to allay the amazement of men at his relation of our Saviour's knowledge of the inward falsity of those that made a splendid profession of him, doth not say the Father revealed it to him, but intimates it to be an unseparable property of his nature. No covering was so thick as to bound his eye; no pretence so glittering as to impose upon his understanding. Those that made a profession of him, and could not be discerned by the eye of man from his faithfulest attendants, were in their inside known to him plainer than their outside was to others; and, therefore, he committed not himself to them, though they seemed to be persuaded to a real belief in his name, because of the power of his miracles, and were touched with an admiration of him, as some great prophet, and, perhaps, declared him to be the Messiah (ver. 23.)

4. He had a foreknowledge of the particular inclinations of men, before those distinct inclinations were in actual being in them. This is plainly asserted, John vi. 64: "But there are some of you that believe not; for Jesus knew from the beginning who they were that believed not, and who should betray him." When Christ assured them, from the knowledge of the hearts of his followers, that some of them were void of that faith they professed, the Evangelist, to stop their amazement that Christ should have such a power and virtue, adds, that he " knew from the beginning;" that he had not only a present knowledge, but a foreknowledge, of every one's inclination; he knew, not only now and then what was in the hearts of his disciples, but from the beginning, of any one's giving up their names to him; he knew whether it were a pretence or sincere; he knew who should betray him; and there was no man's inward affection but was foreseen by him.[t] " From the beginning," whether we understand it from the beginning of the world, as when Christ saith, concerning divorces, " From the beginning it was not so," that is, from the beginning of the world, from the beginning of the law of nature; or, from the beginning of their attending him, as it is taken, Luke i. 2; he had a certain prescience of the inward dispo-

---

[t] Ἐξ ἀρχῆς.

sitions of men's hearts, and their succeeding sentiments; he foreknew the treacherous heart of Judas in the midst of his splendid profession, and discerned his resolution in the root, and his thought in the confused chaos of his natural corruption; he knew how it would spring up before it did spring up, before Judas had any distinct and formal conception of it himself, or before there was any actual preparation to a resolve. Peter's denial was not unknown to him, when Peter had a present resolution, and no question spake it in the present sincerity of his soul, "never to forsake him;" he foreknew what would be the result of that poison which lurked in Peter's nature, before Peter himself imagined anything of it; he discerned Peter's apostatizing heart, when Peter resolved the contrary: our Saviour's prediction was accomplished, and Peter's valiant resolution languished into cowardice. Shall we then conclude our blessed Saviour a creature, who perfectly and only knew the Father, who knew all creatures; who had all the treasures of wisdom and knowledge who knew the inward motions of men's hearts by his own virtue, and had, not only a present knowledge, but a prescience of them?

Instruct. 2. The second instruction from this position, That God hath an infinite knowledge and understanding. Then there is a providence exercised by God in the world, and that about everything. As providence infers omniscience as the guide of it, so omniscience infers providence as the end of it. What exercise would there be of this attribute, but in the government of the world? To this, this infinite perfection refers (Jer. xvii. 10), "I the Lord search the heart, I try the reins, to give every man according to his ways, and according to the fruit of his doings." He searches the heart to reward, he rewards every man according to the rewardableness of his actions; his government, therefore, extends to every man in the world; there is no heart but he searches, therefore no heart but he governs; to what purpose, else, would be this knowledge of all his creatures? for a mere contemplation of them? No. What pleasure can that be to God, who knows himself, who is infinitely more excellent than all his creatures? Doth he know them to neglect all care of them? this must be either out of sloth; but how incompatible is laziness to a pure and infinite activity! or out of majesty; but it is no less for the glory of his majesty to conduct them, than it was for the glory of his power to erect them into being. He that counts nothing unworthy of his arms to make, nothing unworthy of his understanding to know, why should he count anything unworthy of his wisdom to govern? If he knows them to neglect them, it must be because he hath no will to it, or no goodness for it; either of these would be a stain upon God; to want goodness is to be evil, and to want will is to be negligent and scornful, which are inconsistent with an infinite, active goodness. Doth a father neglect providing for the wants of the family which he knows? or a physician, the cure of that disease he understands? God is omniscient, he therefore sees all things; he is good, he doth not therefore neglect anything, but conducts it to the end he appointed it. There is nothing so little that can escape his knowledge, and therefore nothing so little but falls under his providence; nothing so sublime as to be above his understanding, and therefore nothing can be without the compass of his conduct; nothing can escape his eye, and therefore nothing can escape his care; nothing is known to him in vain, as nothing was made by him in vain; there must be acknowledged, therefore, some end of this knowledge of all his creatures.

Instruct. 3. Hence, then, will follow the certainty of a day of judgment. To what purpose can we imagine this attribute of omniscience, so often declared and urged in Scripture to our consideration, but in order to a government of our practice, and a future trial? Every perfection of the Divine nature hath sent out brighter rays in the world than this of his infinite knowledge. His power hath been seen in the being of the world, and his wisdom in the order and harmony of the creatures; his grace and mercy hath been plentifully poured out in his mission of a Redeemer, and his justice hath been elevated by the dying groans of the Son of God upon the cross. But hath his omniscience yet met with a glory proportionable to that of his other perfections? All the attributes of God that have appeared in some beautiful glimmerings in the world, wait for a more full manifestation in glory, as the creatures do for the "manifestation of the sons of God" (Rom. viii. 19); but especially this, since it hath been less evidenced than others, and as much, or more, abused than any; it expects, therefore, a public righting in the eye of the world. There have been, indeed, some few sparks of this perfection sensibly struck out now and then in the world in some horrors of conscience, which have made men become their own accusers of unknown crimes, in bringing out hidden wickedness to a public view by various providences. This hath also been the design of sprinklings of judgments upon several generations, as (Ps. xc. 8), "We are consumed by thy anger, and by thy wrath we are troubled; thou hast set our iniquities before thee, and our secret sins in the light of thy countenance." The word צלומנו signifies youth, as well as secret, *i. e.*, sins committed long ago, and that with secrecy. By this he hath manifested that secret sins are not hid from his eye. Though inward terrors and outward judgments have been let loose to worry men into a belief of this, yet the corruptions of men would still keep a contrary notion in their minds, that "God hath forgotten, that he hides his face from transgression, and will not regard their impiety" (Ps. x. 11). There must, therefore, be a time of trial for the public demonstration of this excellency, that it may receive its due honor, by a full testimony that no secrecy can be a shelter from it. As his justice, which consists in giving every one his due, could not be glorified, unless men were called to an account for their actions, so neither would his omniscience appear in its illustrious colors, without such a manfestation of the secret motions of men's hearts, and of villanies done under lock and key, when none were conscious to them, but the committers of them. Now the last judgment is the time appointed for the "opening of the books" (Dan. vii. 10). The book of God's records, and conscience the counterpart, were never fully opened and read before, only now and then some pages turned to, in particular judgments; and out of those "books shall men be judged according to their works"

(Rev. xx. 12). Then shall the defaced sins be brought, with all their circumstances, to every man's memory; the counsels of men's hearts fled far from their present remembrance, all the habitual knowledge they had of their own actions, shall, by God's knowledge of them, be excited to an actual review; and their works not only made manifest to themselves, but notorious to the world: all the words, thoughts, deeds of men, shall be brought forth into the light of their own minds by the infinite light of God's understanding reflecting on them. His knowledge renders him an unerring witness, as well as his justice " a swift witness" (Mal. iii. 5); a swift witness, because he shall, without any circuit, or length of speech, convince their consciences, by an inward illumination of them, to take notice of the blackness and deformity of their hearts and works. In all judgments God is somewhat known to be the searcher of hearts; the time of judgment is the time of his remembrance (Hos. viii. 13): " Now will he remember their iniquity, and visit their sins;" but the great instant, or now, of the full glorifying it, is the grand day of account. This attribute must have a time for its full discovery; and no time can be fit for it but a time of a general reckoning. Justice cannot be exercised without omniscience; for as justice is a giving to every one his due, so there must be knowledge to discern what is due to every man; the searching the heart is in order to the rewarding the works.

Instruct 4. This perfection in God gives us ground to believe a resurrection. Who can think this too hard for his power, since not the least atom of the dust of our bodies can escape his knowledge? An infinite understanding comprehends every mite of a departed carcase; this will not appear impossible, nor irrational, to any, upon a serious consideration, of this excellency in God. The body is perished, the matter of it hath been since clothed with different forms and figures; part of it hath been made the body of a worm, part of it returned to the dust that hath been blown away by the wind; part of it hath been concocted in the bodies of canibals, fish, ravenous beasts; the spirits have evaporated into air, part of the blood melted into water; what, then, is the matter of the body annihilated? is that wholly perished? no; the foundation remains, though it hath put on a variety of forms; the body of Abel, the first man that died, nor the body of Adam, are not, to this day, reduced to nothing; indeed, the quantity and the quality of those bodies have been lost by various changes they have past through since their dissolution; but the matter, or substance of them, remains entire, and is not capable to be destroyed by all those transforming alterations, in so long a revolution of time. The body of a man in his infancy and his old age, if it were Methuselah's, is the same in the foundation in those multitude of years; though the quantity of it be altered, the quality different; though the color and other things be changed in it, the matter of this body remains the same among all the alterations after death. And can it be so mixed with other natures and creatures, as that it is past finding out by an infinite understanding? Can any particle of this matter escape the eye of Him that makes and beholds all those various alterations, and where every mite of the substance of those bodies is particularly lodged, so as that he cannot compact it together again for a habitation of that soul, that many a year before fled from it?[u] Since the knowledge of God is infinite, and his providence extensive over the least as well as the greatest parts of the world, he must needs know the least as well as the greatest of his creatures in their beginning, progress, and dissolution; all the forms through which the bodies of all creatures roll, the particular instants of time, and the particular place when and where those changes are made, they are all present with him; and, therefore, when the revolution of time allotted by him for the reunion of souls and deceased bodies is come, it cannot be doubted but, out of the treasures of his knowledge, he can call forth every part of the matter of the bodies of men, from the first to the last man that expired, and strip it of all those forms and figures which it shall then have, to compact it to be a lodging for that soul which before it entertained; and though the bodies of men have been devoured by wild beasts in the earth, and fish in the sea, and been lodged in the stomachs of barbarous men-eaters, the matter is not lost. There is but little of the food we take that is turned into the substance of our own bodies; that which is not proper for nourishment, which is the greatest part, is separated, and concocted, and rejected; whatsoever objections are made, are answered by this attribute. Nothing hinders a God of infinite knowledge from discerning every particle of the matter, wheresoever it is disposed; and since he hath an eye to discern, and a hand to recollect and unite, what difficulty is there in believing this article of the christian faith? he that questions this revealed truth of the resurrection of the body, must question God's omniscience as well as his omnipotence and power.

Instruct. 5. What semblance of reason is there to expect a justification in the sight of God by anything in ourselves? Is there any action done by any of us, but upon a scrutiny we may find flaws and deficiency in it? What then? shall not this perfection of God discern them? the motes that escape our eyes cannot escape his (1 John iii. 20): "God is greater than our hearts, and knows all things;" so that it is in vain for any man to flatter himself with the rectitude of any work, or enter into any debate with him who can bring a thousand articles against us, out of his own infinite records, unknown to us, and unanswerable by us. If conscience, a representative or counterpart of God's omniscience in our own bosoms, find nothing done by us, but in a copy short of the original, and beholds, if not blurs, yet imperfections in the best actions, God must much more discern them; we never knew a copy equally exact with the original. If our own conscience be as a thousand witnesses, the knowledge of God is as millions of witnesses against us; if our corruption be so great, and our holiness so low, in our own eyes, how much greater must the one, and how much meaner must the other, appear in the eyes of God? God hath an unerring eye to see, as well as an unspotted holiness to hate, and an unbribable justice to punish; he wants no more understanding to know the shortness of our actions,

[u] Daille, Serm. 15. pp. 21–24.

than he doth holiness to enact, and power to execute, his laws; nay, suppose we could recollect many actions, wherein there were no spot visible to us, the consideration of this attribute should scare us from resting upon any or all of them, since it is the Lord that, by a piercing eye, sees and judges according to the heart, and not according to appearance. The least crookedness of a stick, not sensible to an acute eye, yet will appear when laid to the line; and the impurity of a counterfeit metal be manifest when applied to the touchstone; so will the best action of any mere man in the world, when it comes to be measured in God's knowledge by the straight line of his law. Let every man, therefore, as Paul, though he should know nothing by himself, think not himself therefore justified; since it is the Lord, who is of an infinite understanding, that judgeth (1 Cor. iv. 4). A man may be justified in his own sight, "but not any living man can be justified in the sight of God" (Ps. cxliii. 2); in his sight, whose eye pierceth into our unknown secrets and frames: it was, therefore, well answered of a good man upon his death bed, being asked "What he was afraid of?" "I have labored," saith he, "with all my strength to observe the commands of God; but since I am a man, I am ignorant whether my works are acceptable to God, since God judges in one manner, and I in another manner." Let the consideration therefore of this attribute, make us join with Job in his resolution (Job ix. 21): "Though we were perfect, yet would we not know our own souls." I would not stand up to plead any of my virtues before God. Let us, therefore, look after another righteousness, wherein the exact eye of the Divine omniscience, we are sure, can discern no stain or crookedness.

Instruct. 6. What honorable and adoring thoughts ought we to have of God for this perfection! Do we not honor a man that is able to predict? do we not think it a great part of wisdom? Have not all nations regarded such a faculty as a character and a mark of divinity? There is something more ravishing in the knowledge of future things, both to the person that knows them, and the person that hears them, than there is in any other kind of knowledge; whence the greatest prophets have been accounted in the greatest veneration, and men have thought it a way to glory, to divine and predict. Hence it was that the devils and pagan oracles gained so much credit; upon this foundation were they established, and the enemies of mankind owned for a true God;—I say, from the prediction of future things, though their oracles were often ambiguous, many times false; yet those poor heathens framed many ingenious excuses to free their adored gods from the charge of falsity and imposture: and shall we not adore the true God, the God of Israel, the God blessed for ever, for this incommunicable property, whereby he flies above the wings of the wind, the understandings of men and cherubims?[x] Consider how great it is to know the thoughts and intentions, and works of one man, from the beginning to the end of his life; to foreknow all these before the being of this man, when he was lodged afar off in the loins of his ancestors, yea, of Adam; how much greater is it to foreknow and know the thoughts and

[x] Sabund. Theol. Natural. Tit. 84. somewhat changed.

works of three or four men, of a whole village or neighborhood! It is greater still to know the imaginations and actions of such a multitude of men as are contained in London, Paris, or Constantinople; how much greater still to know the intentions and practices, the clandestine contrivances of so many millions that have, do, or shall swarm in all quarters of the world, every person of them having millions of thoughts, desires, designs, affections, and actions! Let this attribute, then, make the blessed God honorable in our eyes, and adorable in all our affections; especially since it is an excellency which hath so lately discovered itself, in bringing to light the hidden things of darkness, in opening, and in part confounding, the wicked devices of bloody men. Especially let us adore God for it, and admire it in God, since it is so necessary a perfection, that without it the goodness of God had been impotent, and could not have relieved us; for what help can a distressed person expect from a man of the sweetest disposition and the strongest arm, if the eyes which should discover the danger, and direct the defence and rescue, were closed up by blindness and darkness? Adore God for this wonderful perfection.

Instruct. 7. In the consideration of this excellent attribute, what low thoughts should we have of our own knowledge, and how humble ought we to be before God! There is nothing man is more apt to be proud of than his knowledge; it is a perfection he glories in; but if our own knowledge of the little outside and barks of things puffs us up, the consideration of the infiniteness of God's knowledge should abate the tumor: as our beings are nothing in regard to the infiniteness of his essence, so our knowledge is nothing in regard of the vastness of his understanding. We have a spark of being, but nothing to the heat of the sun; we have a drop of knowledge, but nothing to the Divine ocean. What a vain thing is it for a shallow brook to boast of its streams before a sea, whose depths are unfathomable! As it is a vanity to brag of our strength, when we remember the power of God, and of our prudence, when we glance upon the wisdom of God, so it is no less a vanity to boast of our knowledge, when we think of the understanding and knowledge of God. How hard is it for us to know anything![y] Too much noise deafens us, and too much light dazzles us; too much distance alienates the object from us, and too much nearness bars up our sight from beholding it. When we think ourselves to be near the knowledge of a thing, as a ship to the haven, a puff of wind blows us away, and the object which we desired to know eternally flies from us; we burn with a desire of knowledge, and yet are oppressed with the darkness of ignorance; we spend our days more in dark Egypt, than in enlightened Goshen. In what narrow bounds is all the knowledge of the most intelligent persons included![z] How few understand the exact harmony of their own bodies, the nature of the life they have in common with other animals! Who understands the nature of his own faculties, how he knows, and how he wills; how the understanding proposeth, and how the will embraceth; how his spiritual soul is united to his material body; what the nature is of the operation of

y Pascall, p. 170.   z Amyrant, de Prædest. pp. 116, 117. somewhat changed.

our spirits? Nay, who understands the nature of his own body, the offices of his senses, the motion of his members, how they come to obey the command of the will, and a thousand other things? What a vain, weak, and ignorant thing is man, when compared with God! yet there is not a greater pride to be found among devils, than among ignorant men, with a little, very little, flashy knowledge. Ignorant man is as proud as if he knew as God. As the consideration of God's omniscience should render him honorable in our eyes, so it should render us vile in our own. God, because of his knowledge, is so far from disdaining his creatures, that his omniscience is a minister to his goodness. No knowledge that we are possessed of should make us swell with too high a conceit of ourselves, and a disdain of others. We have infinitely more of ignorance than knowledge. Let us therefore remember, in all our thoughts of God, that he is God, and we are men; and therefore ought to be humble, as becomes men, and ignorant and foolish men, to be; as weak creatures should lie low before an Almighty God, and impure creatures before a holy God, false creatures before a faithful God, finite creatures before an infinite God, so should ignorant creatures before an all-knowing God. All God's attributes teach admiring thoughts of God, and low thoughts of ourselves.

Instruct. 8. It may inform us how much this attribute is injured in the world. The first error after Adam's eating the forbidden fruit was the denial of this, as well as the omnipresence of God, (Gen. iii. 10,) "I heard thy voice in the garden, and I hid myself;" as if the thickness of the trees could screen him from the eye of his Creator. And after Cain's murder, this is the first perfection he affronts, (Gen. iv. 9), "Where is Abel, thy brother?" saith God. How roundly doth he answer, "I know not!" as if God were as weak as man, to be put off with a lie. Man doth as naturally hate this perfection as much as he cannot naturally but acknowledge it; he wishes God stripped of this eminency, that he might be incapable to be an inspector of his crimes, and a searcher of the closets of his heart. In wishing him deprived of this, there is a hatred of God himself; for it is a loathing an essential property of God, without which he would be a pitiful Governor of the world. What a kind of God should that be, of a sinner's wishing, that had wanted eyes to see a crime, and righteousness to punish it! The want of the consideration of this attribute, is the cause of all sin in the world (Hos. vii. 2), "They consider not in their hearts that I remember all their wickedness;" they speak not to their hearts, or make any reflection upon the infiniteness of my knowledge; it is a high contempt of God, as if he were an idol, a senseless stock or stone; in all evil practices this is denied. We know God sees all things, yet we live and walk as if he knew nothing. We call him omniscient, and live as if he were ignorant; we say he is all eye, yet act as if he were wholly blind.

In particular, this attribute is injured, by invading the peculiar rights of it, by presuming on it, and by a practical denial of it. First, By invading the peculiar rights of it. 1. By invocation of creatures. Praying to saints, by the Romanists, is a disparagement to this divine excellency; he that knows all things, is only fit to have the petitions of men presented to him; prayer supposeth an omniscient Being, as the object of it; no other being but God ought to have that honor acknowledged to it; no understanding but his is infinite; no other presence but his is everywhere; to implore any deceased creature for a supply of our wants, is to own in them a property of the Deity, and make them deities that were but men; and increase their glory by a diminution of God's honor, in ascribing that perfection to creatures which belongs only to God. Alas! they are so far from understanding the desires of our souls, that they know not the words of our lips: it is against reason to address our supplications to them that neither understand us nor discern us (Isa. lxiii. 16), "Abraham is ignorant of us, and Israel acknowledges us not." The Jews never called upon Abraham, though the covenant was made with him for the whole seed; not one departed saint for the whole four thousand years, between the creation of the world, and the coming of Christ, was ever prayed to by the Israelites, or ever imagined to have a share in God's omniscience: so that to pray to St. Peter, St. Paul, much less to St. Roch, St. Swithin, St. Martin, St. Francis, &c. is such a superstition, that hath no footing in the Scripture. To desire the prayers of the living, with whom we have a communion, who can understand and grant our desires, is founded upon a mutual charity; but to implore persons that are absent, at a great distance from us, with whom we have not, nor know how to have, any commerce, supposeth them, in their departure, to have put off humanity, and commenced gods, and endued with some part of the Divinity to understand our petitions; we are, indeed, to cherish their memories, consider their examples, imitate their graces, and observe their doctrines; we are to follow them as saints, but not elevate them as gods, in ascribing to them such a knowledge, which is the only necessary right of their and our common Creator.[a] As the invocation of saints mingles them with Christ, in the exercise of his office, so it sets them equal with God in the throne of his omniscience, as if they had as much credit with God as Christ, by way of mediation, and as much knowledge of men's affairs as God himself. Omniscience is peculiar to God, and incommunicable to any creature; it is the foundation of all religion, and therefore one of the choicest acts of it; viz. prayer and invocation. To direct our vows and petitions to any one else, is to invade the peculiarity of this perfection in God, and to rank some creatures in a partnership with him in it.

2. This attribute is injured by curiosity of knowledge; especially of future things, which God hath not discovered in natural causes, or supernatural revelation. It is a common error of men's spirits to aspire to know what God would have hidden, and to pry into Divine secrets; and many men are more willing to remain without the knowledge of those things which may, with a little industry, be attained, than be divested of the curiosity of inquiring into those things which are above their reach; it is hence that some have laid aside the study of the common remedies of nature to find out the

---

[a] Daille, Melang. Part II., pp. 560, 561.

philosopher's stone, which scarce any ever yet attempted but sunk in the enterprise.[b] From this inclination to know the most abstruse and difficult things, it is that the horrors of magic and vanities of astrology have sprung, whereby men have thought to find, in a commerce with devils and the jurisdiction of the stars, the events of their lives, and the disposal of states and kingdoms. Hence, also, arose those multitudes of ways of divination, invented among the heathen, and practised too commonly in these ages of the world. This is an invasion of God's prerogative, to whom secret things belong (Deut. xxix. 29); "Secret things belong unto the Lord our God, but revealed things belong to us and our children." It is an intolerable boldness to attempt to fathom those, the knowledge whereof God hath reserved to himself, and to search that which God will have to surpass our understandings, whereby we more truly envy God a knowledge superior to our own, than we, in Adam, imagined that he envied us. Ambition is the greatest cause of this; ambition to be accounted some great thing among men, by reason of a knowledge estranged from the common mass of mankind, but more especially that soaring pride to be equal with God, which lurks in our nature ever since the fall of our first parents: this is not yet laid aside by men, though it was the first thing that embroiled the world with the wrath of God. Some think a curiosity of knowledge was the cause of the fall of devils; I am sure it was the fall of Adam, and is yet the crime of his posterity; had he been contented to know what God had furnished him with, neither he nor his posterity had smarted under the venom of the serpent's breath. All curious and bold inquiries into things not revealed are an attempt upon the throne of God, and are both sinful and pernicious, like to glaring upon the sun, where, instead of a greater acuteness, we meet with blindness, and too dearly buy our ignorance in attempting a superfluous knowledge. As God's knowledge is destined to the government of the world, so should ours be to the advantage of the world, and not degenerate into vain speculations.

3. This attribute is injured by swearing by creatures. To swear by the name of God, in a righteous cause,[c] when we are lawfully called to it by a superior power, or for the necessary decision of some controversy, for the ends of charity and justice, is an act of religion, and a part of worship, founded upon, and directed to, the honor of this attribute; by it we acknowledge the glory of his infallible knowledge of all things; but to swear by false gods, or by any creature, is blasphemous; it sets the creature in the place of God, and invests it in that which is the peculiar honor of the Divinity; for when any swear truly, they intend the invocation of an infallible Witness, and the bringing an undoubted testimony for what they do assert: while, any, therefore, swear by a creature, or a false god, they profess that that creature, or that which they esteem to be a god, is an infallible witness, which to be is only the right of God; they attribute to the creature that which is the property of God alone, to know the heart, and to be a witness whether they speak true or no: and this was accounted, by all nations, the true design

[b] Amyrant. Moral. Tom. III. p. 75, &c.   [c] Cajetan, Sum. p. 190.

of an oath. As to swear falsely is a plain denial of the all-knowledge of God, so to swear by any creature is to set the creature upon the throne of God, in ascribing that perfection to the creature which sovereignly belongs to the Creator; for it is not in the power of any to witness to the truth of the heart, but of him that is the searcher of hearts.

4. We sin against this attribute by censuring the hearts of others. An open crime, indeed, falls under our cognizance, and therefore under our judgment; for whatsoever falls under the authority of man to be punished, falls under the judgment of man to be censured, as an act contrary to the law of God; yet, when a censure is built upon the evil of the act which is obvious to the view, if we take a step farther to judge the heart and state, we leave the revealed rule of the law, and ambitiously erect a tribunal equal with God's, and usurp a judicial power, pertaining only to the Supreme Governor of the world, and consequently pretend to be possessed of the perfection of omniscience, which is necessary to render him capable of the exercise of that sovereign authority: for it is in respect of his dominion that God hath the supreme right to judge; and in respect of his knowledge that he hath an incommunicable capacity to judge. In an action that is doubtful, the good or evil whereof depends only upon God's determination, and wherein much of the judgment depends upon the discerning the intention of the agent, we cannot judge any man without a manifest invasion of God's peculiar right: such actions are to be tried by God's knowledge, not by our surmises; God only is the master in such cases, to whom a person stands or falls (Rom. xiv. 4). 'Till the true principle and ends of an action be known by the confession of the party acting it, a true judgment of it is not in our power. Principles and ends lie deep and hid from us; and it is intolerable pride to pretend to have a joint key with God to open that cabinet which he hath reserved to himself. Besides the violation of the rule of charity in misconstruing actions which may be great and generous in their root and principle, we invade God's right, as if our ungrounded imaginations and conjectures were in joint commission with this sovereign perfection; and thereby we become usurping judges of evil thoughts (James ii. 4). It is, therefore, a boldness worthy to be punished by the judge, to assume to ourselves the capacity and authority of him who is the only Judge: for as the execution of the Divine law, for the inward violation of it, belongs only to God, so is the right of judging a prerogative belonging only to his omniscience; his right is, therefore, invaded, if we pretend to a knowledge of it. This humor of men the apostle checks, when he saith (1 Cor. iv. 5), " He that judgeth me is the Lord; therefore judge nothing before the time, until the Lord come, who will manifest the counsels of all hearts." It is not the time yet for God to erect the tribunal for the trial of men's hearts, and the principles of their actions; he hath reserved the glorious discovery of this attribute for another season: we must not, therefore, presume to judge of the counsels of men's hearts till God hath revealed them by opening the treasures of his own knowledge; much less are we to judge any man's final condition. Manasseh may sacrifice to devils,

and unconverted Paul tear the church in pieces; but God had mercy on them, and called them. The actions may be censured, not the state, for we know not whom God may call. In censuring men, we may doubly imitate the devil, in a false accusation of the brethren, as well as in an ambitious usurpation of the rights of God.

Secondly, This perfection is injured by presuming upon it, or making an ill use of it. As in the neglect of prayer for the supply of men's wants, because God knows them already, so that that which is an encouragement to prayer, they make the reason of restraining it before God. Prayer is not to administer knowledge to God, but to acknowledge this admirable perfection of the Divine nature. If God did not know, there were indeed no use of prayer; it would be as vain a thing to send up our prayers to heaven, as to implore the senseless statue, or picture of a prince, for a protection. We pray because God knows: for though he knows our wants with a knowledge of vision, yet he will not know them with a knowledge of supply, till he be sought unto (Matt. vi. 32, 33; vii. 11.) All the excellencies of God are ground of adoration; and this excellency is the ground of that part of worship we call prayer. If God be to be worshipped, he is to be called upon: invocations of his name in our necessities is a chief act of worship; whence the temple, the place of solemn worship, was not called the house of sacrifice, but the house of prayer. Prayer was not appointed for God's information, as if he were ignorant, but for the expression of our desires; not to furnish him with a knowledge of what we want, but to manifest to him, by some rational sign convenient to our nature, our sense of that want, which he knows by himself. So that prayer is not designed to acquaint God with our wants, but to express the desire of a remedy of our wants. God knows our wants, but hath not made promises barely to our wants, but to our asking, that his omniscience in hearing, as well as his sufficiency in supplying, may have a sensible honor in our acknowledgments and receipts. It is therefore an ill use of this excellency of God to neglect prayer to him as needless, because he knows already.

Thirdly. This perfection of God is wronged by a practical denial of it. It is the language of every sin, and so God takes it when he comes to reckon with men for their impieties. Upon this he charges the greatness of the iniquity of Israel, the overflowing of blood in the land, and the perverseness of the city: "They say, the Lord hath forsaken the earth, and the Lord sees not" (Ezek. ix. 9): they deny his eyes to see, and his resolution to punish.

1. It will appear, in forbearing sin from a sense of man's knowledge, not of God's. Open impieties are refrained because of the eye of man, but secret sins are not checked because of the eye of God. Wickedness is committed in darkness, that is restrained in light, as if darkness were as great a clog to God's eyes as it is to ours; as though his eyes were muffled with the curtains of the night (Job xxii. 14.) This, it is likely, was at the root of Jonah's flight; he might have some secret thought that his Master's eye could not follow him, as though the close hatches of a ship could secure him from the knowledge of God, as well as the sides of a ship

could from the dashing of the waves. What lies most upon the conscience when it is graciously wounded, is least regarded or contemned when it is basely inclined. David's heart smote him not only for his sin in the gross, but as particularly cirumstantiated by the commission of it in the sight of God (Ps. li. 4) : " Against thee, thee only have I sinned, and done this evil in thy sight." None knew the reason of Uriah's death but myself, and because others knew it not, I neglected any regard to this Divine eye. When Jacob's sons used their brother Joseph so barbarously, they took care to hide it from their father, but cast away all thoughts of God, from whom it could not be concealed. Doth not the presence of a child bridle a man from the act of a longed-for sin, when the eye of God is of no force to restrain him, as if God's knowledge were of less value than the sight of a little boy or girl, as if a child only could see, and God were blind? He that will forbear an unworthy action for fear of an informer, will not forbear it for God ; as if God's omniscience were not as full an intelligencer to him, as man can be an informer to a magistrate. As we acknowledge the power of men seeing us when we are ashamed to commit a filthy action in their view, so we discover the power of God seeing us, when we regard not what we do before the light of his eyes. Secret sins are more against God than open : open sins are against the law ; secret sins are against the law, and this prime perfection of his nature. The majesty of God is not only violated, but the omniscience of God disowned, who is the only witness ; we must, in all of them, either imagine him to be without eyes to behold us, or without an arm of justice to punish us. And often it is, I believe, in such cases, that if any thoughts of God's knowledge strike upon men, they quickly damp them, lest they should begin to know what they fear, and fear that they might not eat their pleasant sinful morsels.

2. It appears in partial confessions of sin before God. As by a free, full, and ingenious confession, we offer a due glory to this attribute, so by a feigned and curtailed confession, we deny him the honor of it : for, though by any confession we in part own him to be a Sovereign and Judge, yet by a half and pared acknowledgment, we own him to be no more than a humane and ignorant one. Achan's full confession gave God the glory of his omniscience, manifested in the discovery of his secret crime. " And Joshua said unto Achan, My son, give, I pray thee, glory to the Lord God of Israel, and make confession unto him" (Joshua vii. 19.) And so (Ps. l. 23) : " Whoso offereth praise glorifieth me," or confession, as the word signifieth, in which sense I would rather take it, referring to this attribute, which God seems to tax sinners with the denial of (ver. 21), telling them that he would open the records of their sins before them, and indict them particularly for every one. If, therefore, you would glorify this attribute, which shall one day break open your consciences, offer to me a sincere confession. When David speaks of the happiness of a pardoned man, he adds, " in whose spirit there is no guile,"[d] not meaning a sincerity in general, but an ingenuity in confessing. To excuse, or extenuate sin, is to deny God the

d Ps. xxxii. 1, 2, Camero. p. 89, col. 1.

knowledge of the depths of our deceitful hearts: when we will mince it rather than aggravate it; lay it upon the inducements of others, when it was the free act of our own wills, study shifts to deceive our Judge; this is to speak lies of him, as the expression is (Hos. vii. 13), as though he were a God easy to be cheated, and knew no more than we were willing to declare. What did Saul's transferring his sin from himself to the people (1 Sam. xv. 15), but charge God with a defect in this attribute? When man could not be like God, in his knowledge, he would fancy a God like to him in his ignorance, and imagine a possibility of hiding himself from his knowledge. And all men tread, more or less, in their father's steps, and are fruitful to devise distinctions to disguise errors in doctrine, and excuses to palliate errors in practice: this crime Job removes from himself, when he speaks of several acts of his sincerity (Job xxxi. 33): "If I covered my transgressions as Adam, by hiding my iniquity in my bosom:" I hid not any of my sins in my own conscience, but acknowledged God a witness to them, and gave him the glory of his knowledge by a free confession. I did not conceal it from God as Adam did, or as men ordinarily do; as if God could understand no more of their secret crimes than they will let him, and had no more sense of their faults than they would furnish him with. As the first rise of confession is the owning of this attribute (for the justice of God would not scare men, nor the holiness of God awe them, without a sense of his knowledge of their iniquities), so to drop out some fragments of confession, discover some sins, and conceal others, is a plain denial of the extensiveness of the Divine knowledge.

3. It is discovered by putting God off with an outside worship. Men are often flatterers of God, and think to bend him by formal glavering devotions, without the concurrence of their hearts; as though he could not pierce into the darkness of the mind, but did as little know us as one man knows another. There are such things as feigned lips (Ps. xvii. 1), a contradiction between the heart and the tongue, a clamor in the voice, and scoffing in the soul; a crying out to God, thou art my Father, the guide of my youth, and yet speaking and doing evil to the utmost of our power (Jer. iii. 4, 5). As if God could be imposed upon by fawning pretences; and like old Isaac, take Jacob for Esau, and be cozened by the smell of his garments: as if he could not discern the negro heart under an angel's garb. Thus Ephraim, the ten tribes, apostatized from the true religion, would go with their flocks and their herds to seek the Lord (Hos. v. 6), would sacrifice multitudes of sheep and heifers, which was the main outside of the Jewish religion; only with their flocks and their herds, not with their hearts, with those inward qualifications of deep humiliation and repentance for sin; as though outside appearances limited God's observation, whereas God had told them before (ver. 3), that he "knew Ephraim, and Israel was not hid from him." Thus to do is to put a cheat upon God, and think to blind his all-seeing eye, and therefore it is called deceit (Ps. lxxviii. 36). They did flatter him with their mouths. The word פתה signifies to deceive, as well as to flatter; not that they, or any else, can deceive

God, but it implies an endeavor to deceive him, by a few dissembling words and gestures, or an imagination that God was satisfied with bare professions, and would not concern himself in a further inquisition. This is an unworthy conceit of God, to fancy that we can satisfy for inward sins, and avert approaching judgments, by external offerings, by a loud voice with a false heart, as if God (like children) would be pleased with the glittering of an empty shell, or the rattling of stones, the chinkling of money, a mere voice and crying, without inward frames and intentions of service.

4. In cherishing multitudes of evil thoughts. No man but would blush for shame, if the base, impure, slovenly thoughts, either in or out of duties of worship, were visible to the understanding of man; how diligent would he be to curb his luxuriant and unworthy fancies, as well as bite in his words! but when we give the reins to the motions of our hearts, and suffer them to run at random without a curb, it is an evidence we are not concerned for their falling under the notice of the eye of God; and it argues a very weak belief of this perfection, or scarce any belief at all. Who can think any man's heart, possessed with a sense of this infinite excellency, that suffers his mind, in his meditations on God, to wander into every sty, and be picking up stones upon a dunghill? What doth it intimate, but that those thoughts are as invisible, or unaudible to God, as they are to men without the garments of words?[e] When a man thinks of obscene things, his own natural notions, if revived, would tell him that God discerns what he thinks, that the depths of his heart are open to him: and the voice of those notions are—deface those vain imaginations out of your minds. But what is done? Men cast away rational light, muster up conceits that God sees them not, knows them not, and so sink into the puddle of their sordid imaginations, as though they remained in darkness to God. I might further instance. *In omissions of prayer*, which arise sometimes from a flat atheism: who will call upon a God, that believes no such Being? or from partial atheism, either a denial of God's sufficiency to help, or of his omniscience to know, as if God were like the statue of Jupiter in Crete, framed without ears. *In the hypocritical pretences of men, to exempt them from the service God calls them to.* When men pretend one thing and intend another: this lurks in the veins sometimes of the best men; sometimes it ariseth from the fear of man; when men are more afraid of the power of man, than of dissembling with the Almighty, it will pretend a virtue to cover a secret wile, and choose the tongue of the crafty as the expression in Job (ch. xv. 5). The case is plain in Moses, who, when ordered to undertake an eminent service, pretends a want of eloquence, and an ungrateful "slowness of speech" (Exod. iv. 10). This generous soul, that before was not afraid to discover himself in the midst of Egypt for his countrymen, answers sneakingly to God, and would veil his carnal fear with a pretence of insufficiency and humility; "Who am I, that I should go unto Pharaoh (Exod. iii. 11)? He could not well allege an inability to go to Pharaoh, since he had had an education in the Egyptian learning, which rendered him capable to ap-

pear at court. God at last uncaseth him, and shews it all to be a dissimulation, and whatsoever was the pretence, fear lay at the bottom. He was afraid of his life upon his appearance before Pharaoh, from whose face he had fled upon the slaying the Egyptians; which God intimates to him (Exod. iv. 19), "Go, and return into Egypt, for all the men are dead which sought thy life." What doth this carriage speak, but as if God's eye were not upon our inward parts, as though we could lock him out of our hearts, that cannot be shut out from any creek of the hearts of men and angels?

Use II. is of comfort. It is a ground of great comfort under the present dispensation wherein we are; we have heard the doctrinal part, and God hath given us the experimental part of it in his special providence this day, upon the stage of the world.[f] And, blessed be God, that he hath given us a ground of comfort, without going out of our ordinary course to fetch it, whereby it seems to be peculiarly of God's ordering for us.

1. It is a comfort in all the clandestine contrivances of men against the church. His eyes pierce as far as the depths of hell. Not one of his church's adversaries lies in a mist; all are as plain as the stars which he numbers: "Mine adversaries are all before thee" (Ps. lxix. 19), more exactly known to thee than I can recount them. It is a prophecy of Christ, wherein Christ is brought in speaking to God of his own and the church's enemies: he comforts himself with this, that God hath his eye upon every particular person among his adversaries: he knows where they repose themselves, when they go out to consult, and when they come in with their resolves. He discerns all the rage that spirits their hearts, in what corner it lurks, how it acts; all the disorders, motions of it, and every object of that rage; he cannot be deceived by the closest and subtlest person. Thus God speaks concerning Sennacherib and his host against Jerusalem (Isa. xxxvii. 28, 29). After he had spoke of the forming of his church, and the weakness of it, he adds, "But I know thy abode, and thy going out, and thy coming in, and thy rage against me. Because thy rage against me, and thy tumult, is come up into mine ears, therefore will I put my hook in thy nose, and my bridle in thy lips, and I will turn thee back," &c. He knows all the methods of the counsels, the stages they had laid, the manner of the execution of their designs, all the ways whither they turned themselves, and would use them no better than men do devouring fish and untamed beasts, with a hook in the nose, and a bridle in the mouth. Those statesmen (in Isa. xxix. 15) thought their contrivances too deep for God to fathom, and too close for God to frustrate; "they seek deep to hide their counsels from the Lord; surely your turning of things upside down shall be esteemed as the potter's clay," of no more force and understanding than a potter's vessel, which understands not its own form wrought by the artificer, nor the use it is put to by the buyer and possessor; or shall be esteemed as a potter's vessel, that can be as easily flung back into the mass from whence it was taken, as preserved in the figure it is now endued with. No secret designer is shrouded from God's sight, or

[f] Nov. 1678, when the Popish Plot was discovered:

can be sheltered from God's arm; he understands the venom of
their hearts better than we can feel it, and discovers their inward
fury more plainly than we can see the sting or teeth of a viper when
they are opened for mischief; and to what purpose doth God know
and see them, but in order to deliver his people from them in his
own due time? "I know their sorrow, and am come down to deliver
them (Exod. iii. 7, 8). The walls of Jerusalem are continually before him; he knows, therefore, all that would undermine and demolish them; none can hurt Zion by any ignorance or inadvertency
in God. It is observable, that our Saviour, assuming to himself a
different title in every epistle to the seven churches, doth particularly ascribe to himself this of knowledge and wrath in that to
Thyatira, an emblem or description of the Romish state (Rev. ii.
18): " And unto the angel of the church of Thyatira write, These
things, saith the Son of God, who hath his eyes like a flame of fire,
and his feet like fine brass." His eyes, like a flame of fire, are of a
piercing nature, insinuating themselves into all the pores and parts
of the body they encounter with, and his feet like brass, to crush
them with, is explained (ver. 23), "I will kill her children with
death, and all the churches shall know that I am he which searches
the reins and the heart, and I will give to every one of you according to your works." He knows every design of the Romish party,
designed by that church of Thyatira.[g] Jezebel, there, signifies a
whorish church; such a church as shall act as Jezebel, Ahab's wife,
who was not only a worshipper of idols, but propagated idolatry in
Israel, slew the prophets, persecuted Elijah, murdered Naboth, the
name whereof signifies prophecy, seized upon his possession. And
if it be said that (ver. 19) this church was commended for her works,
faith, patience, it is true Rome did at first strongly profess Christianity, and maintained the interest of it, but afterwards fell into the
practice of Jezebel, and committed spiritual adultery: and is she to
be owned for a wife, that now plays the harlot, because she was
honest and modest at her first marriage? And though she shall be
destroyed, yet not speedily (ver. 22); "I will cast her into a bed,"
seems to intimate the destruction of Jezebel, not to be at once and
speedily, but in a lingering way, and by degrees, as sickness consumes a body.[h]

2. This perfection of God fits him to be a special object of trust.
If he were forgetful, what comfort could we have in any promise?
How could we depend upon him, if he were ignorant of our state?
His compassion to pity us, his readiness to relieve us, his power to
protect and assist us, would be insignificant, without his omniscience
to inform his goodness, and direct the arm of his power. This perfection is, as it were, God's office of intelligence: as you go to your
memorandum-book to know what you are to do, so doth God to his
omniscience; this perfection is God's eye, to acquaint him with the
necessities of his church, and directs all his other attributes in their
exercise for and about his people. You may depend upon his mercy

---

[g] For the evidence of it I refer you to Dr. More's Exposition of the Seven Churches,
worthy every learned and understanding man's reading, and of every sober Romanist.
[h] Coc. in loc.

that hath promised, and upon his truth to perform; upon his sufficiency to supply you, and his goodness to relieve you, and his righteousness to reward you; because he hath an infinite understanding to know you and your wants, you and your services. And without this knowledge of his, no comfort could be drawn from any other perfection; none of them could be a sure nail to hang our hopes and confidence upon. This is that the church alway celebrated (Ps. cv. 7): "He hath remembered his covenant forever, and the word which he hath commanded to a thousand generations;" and (ver. 42), "He remembered his holy promise;" "And he remembered for them his covenant" (Ps. cvi. 45). He remembers and understands his covenant, therefore his promise to perform it, and therefore our wants to supply them.

3. And the rather, because God knows the persons of all his own. He hath in his infinite understanding, the exact number of all the individual persons that belong to him (2 Tim. ii. 19): "The Lord knows them that are his." He knows all things, because he hath created them; and he knows his people because he hath not only made them, but also chose them; he could no more choose he knew not what, than he could create he knew not what; and he knows them under a double title; of creation as creatures, in the common mass of creation; as new creatures by a particular act of separation. He cannot be ignorant of them in time, whom he foreknew from eternity; his knowledge in time is the same he had from eternity; he foreknew them that he intended to give the grace of faith unto; and he knows them after they believe, because he knows his own act, in bestowing grace upon them, and his own mark and seal wherewith he hath stamped them. No doubt but he that "calls the stars of heaven by their names" (Ps. clxvii, 4), knows the number of those living stars that sparkle in the firmament of his church. He cannot be ignorant of their persons, when he numbers the hairs of their heads, and hath registered their names in the book of life. As he only had an infinite mercy to make the choice, so he only hath an infinite understanding to comprehend their persons. We only know the elect of God by a moral assurance in the judgment of charity, when the conversation of men is according to the doctrine of God. We have not an infallible knowledge of them, we may be often mistaken; Judas, a devil, may be judged by man for a saint, till he be stripped of his disguise. God only hath an infallible knowledge of them, he knows his own records, and the counterparts in the hearts of his people; none can counterfeit his seal, nor can any rase it out. When the church is either scattered like dust by persecution, or overgrown with superstition and idolatry, that there is scarce any grain of true religion appearing, as in the time of Elijah, who complained that he was left alone, as if the church had been rooted out of that corner of the world (1 Kings xix. 14, 18); yet God knew that he had a number fed in a cave, and had reserved seven thousand men that had preserved the purity of his worship, and not bowed their knee to Baal.[i] Christ knew his sheep, as well as he is known of them; yea, better than they can know him (John x. 14). History acquaints us, that Cyrus had so

i Turretin's Sermons, p. 362.

vast a memory, that he knew the name of every particular soldier
in his army, which consisted of divers nations; shall it be too hard
for an infinite understanding to know every one of that host that
march under his banners? may he not as well know them, as know
the number, qualities, influences, of those stars which lie concealed
from our eye, as well as those that are visible to our sense? Yes,
he knows them, as a general to employ them, as a shepherd to preserve them; he knows them in the world to guard them, and he
knows them when they are out of the world to gather them, and cull
out their bodies, though wrapped up in a cloud of the putrified carcases
of the wicked. As he knew them from all eternity to elect them,
so he knows them in time to clothe their persons with righteousness,
to protect their persons in calamity, according to his good pleasure,
and at last to raise and reward them according to his promise.

4. We may take comfort from hence, that our sincerity cannot be
unknown to an infinite understanding. Not a way of the righteous
is concealed from him, and, therefore, " they shall stand in judgment
before him" (Ps. i. 6): "The Lord knows the way of the righteous;"
he knows them to observe them, and he knows them to reward
them. How comfortable is it to appeal to this attribute of God for
our integrity, with Hezekiah (2 Kings xx. 3)! "Remember, Lord,
how I have walked before thee in truth, and with a perfect heart."
Christ himself is brought in in this prophetical psalm, drawing out
the comfort of this attribute (Ps. xl. 9): " I have not restrained my
lips, O Lord, thou knowest;" meaning his faithfulness in declaring
the righteousness of God. Job follows the same steps, "Also now
behold, my record is in heaven, and my witness is on high" (Job xvi.
19); my innocence hath the testimony of men, but my greatest support is in the records of God. Also now, or, besides the testimony
of my own heart, I have another witness in heaven, that knows the
heart, and can only judge of the principles of my actions, and clear
me from the scorns of my friends and the accusations of men, with
a justification of my innocence; he repeats it twice, to take the
greater comfort in it. God knows that we do that in the simplicity
of our hearts, which may be judged by men to be done for unworthy
and sordid ends: he knows not only the outward action, but the
inward affection, and praises that which men often dispraise, and
writes down that with an *Euge!* "Well done, good and faithful servant," which men daub with their severest censures (Rom. ii. 29).
How refreshing is it to consider, that God never mistakes the appearance for reality, nor is led by the judgment of man! He sits in
heaven, and laughs at their follies and censures. If God had no
sounder and no more piercing a judgment than man, woe be to the
sincerest souls that are often judged hypocrites by some. What a
happiness is it for integrity to have a judge of infinite understanding,
who will one day wipe off the dirt of worldly reproaches! Again,
God knows the least dram of grace and righteousness in the hearts
of his people, though but as a smoking flax, or the least bruise of a
saving conviction (Matt. xii. 20), and knows it so as to cherish it;
he knows that work he hath begun, and never hath his eye off from
it to abandon it.

5. The consideration of this excellent perfection in God may comfort us in our secret prayers, sighs, and works. If God were not of infinite understanding to pierce into the heart, what comfort hath a poor creature that hath a scantiness of expressions but a heart in a flame? If God did not understand the heart, faith and prayer, which are eternal works, would be in vain. How could he give that mercy our hearts plead for if he were ignorant of our inward affections? Hypocrites might scale heaven by lofty expressions, and a sincere soul come short of the happiness he is prepared for, for want of flourishing gifts. Prayer is an eternal work; words are but the garment of prayer; meditation is the body, and affection the soul and life of prayer; "Give ear to my words, O Lord, consider my meditation" (Ps. v. 1). Prayer is a rational act; an act of the mind, not the act of a parrot: prayer is an act of the heart, though the speaking prayer is the work of the tongue; now God gives ear to the words, but he considers the meditation of the frame of the heart. Consideration is a more exact notice than hearing; the act only of the ear. Were not God of an infinite understanding, and omniscient, he might take fine clothes, a heap of garments, for the man himself, and be put off by glittering words, without a spiritual frame. What matter of rejoicing is it that we call not upon a deaf and ignorant idol, but on one that listens to our secret petitions, to give them a dispatch, that knows our desires afar off, and from the infiniteness of his mercy, joined with his omniscience, stands ready to give us a return? Hath he not a book of remembrance for them that fear him, and for their sighs and ejaculations to him, as well as their discourses of him, (Mal. iii. 16); and not only what prayers they utter, but what gracious and holy thoughts they have of him that thought upon his name? Though millions of supplications be put up at the same time, yet they have all a distinct file (as I may say) in an infinite understanding, which perceives and comprehends them all. As he observes millions of sins committed at the same time, by a vast number of persons, to record them in order to punishment, so he distinctly discerns an infinite number of cries, at the same moment, to register them in order to an answer. A sigh cannot escape an infinite understanding, though crowded among a mighty multitude of cries from others, or covered with many unwelcome distractions in ourselves, no more than a believing touch from the woman that had the bloody issue could be concealed from Christ, and be undiscerned from the press of the thronging multitudes: our groans are as audible and intelligible to him as our words, and he knows what is the mind of his own Spirit, though expressed in no plainer language than sobs and heavings (Rom. viii. 27). Thus David cheers up himself under the neglects of his friends (Ps. xxxviii. 9); ". Lord, my desire is before thee, and my groaning is not hid from thee." Not a groan of a panting spirit shall be lost, till God hath lost his knowledge; not a petition forgotten while God hath a record, nor a tear dried while God hath a bottle to reserve it in (Ps. lvi. 8). Our secret works are also known and observed by him; not only our outward labor, but our inward love in it (Heb. vi. 10). If, with Isaac, we go privately into the field to meditate, or secretly " cast

our bread upon the waters," he keeps his eye upon us to reward us, and returns the fruit into our own bosoms (Matt. vi. 4, 6); yea, though it be but a cup of cold water, from an inward spring of love, given to a disciple, "He sees your works, and your labor, and faith, and patience" in working them (Rev. ii. 2); all the marks of your industry, and strength of your intentions, and will be as exact at last, in order to a due praise, as to open sins, in order to a just recompense (1 Cor. iv. 5).

6. The consideration of this excellent attribute affords comfort in the afflictions of good men. He knows their pressures, as well as hears their cries (Exod. iii. 7). His knowledge comes not by information from us; but his compassionate listening to our cries springs from his own inspection into our sorrows; he is affected with them, before we make any discovery of them; he is not ignorant of the best season, when they may be usefully inflicted, and when they may be profitaby removed. The tribulation and poverty of his church is not unknown to him (Rev. ii. 8, 9); "I know thy works and tribulation," &c. He knows their works, and what tribulation they meet with for him; he sees their extremities, when they are toiling against the wind and tide of the world (Mark vi. 48); yea, the natural exigencies of the multitude are not neglected by him; he discerns to take care of them. Our Saviour considered the three days' fasting of his followers, and miraculously provides a dish for them in the wilderness. No good man is ever out of God's mind, and therefore never out of his compassionate care: his eye pierceth into their dungeons, and pities their miseries. Joseph may forget his brethren, and the disciples not know Christ, when he walks upon the midnight waves and turbulent sea,[k] but a lion's den cannot obscure a Daniel from his sight, nor the depths of the whale's belly bury Jonah from the Divine understanding: he discerns Peter in his chains, and Stephen under the stones of martyrdom; he knows Lazarus under his tattered rags, and Abel wallowing in his blood; his eye and knowledge goes along with his people, when they are transplanted into foreign countries, and sold for slaves into the islands of the Grecians, "for he will raise them out of the place" (Joel iii. 6, 7). He would defeat the hopes of the persecutors, and applaud the patience of his people. He knows his people in the tabernacle of life, and in the valley of the shadow of death (Ps. xxiii). He knows all penal evils, because he commissions and directs them. He knows the instruments, because they are his sword (Ps. xvii. 13); and he knows his gracious sufferer because he hath his mark. He discerns Job in his anguish, and the devil in his malice. By the direction of this attribute he orders calamities, and rescues from them. "Thou hast seen it, for thou beholdest mischief and spite" (Ps. x. 14). That is the comfort of the psalmist, and the comfort of every believer, and the ground of committing themselves to God under all the injustice of men.

7. It is a comfort in all our infirmities. As he knows our sins to charge them, so he knows the weakness of our nature to pity us. As his infinite understanding may scare us, because he knows our

[k] Barlow's Man's Refuge, pp. 29, 30.

transgressions, so it may relieve us, because he knows our natural mutability in our first creation; " he knows our frame, he remembers that we are dust" (Ps. ciii. 14). 'Tis the reason of the precedent verses why he removes our transgression from us, why he is so backward in punishing, so patient in waiting, so forward in pitying; Why? He doth not only remember our sins, but remember our frame of forming; what brittle, though clear glasses we were by creation, how easy to be cracked! He remembers our impotent and weak condition by corruption; what a sink we have of vain imaginations that remain in us after regeneration; he doth not only consider that we were made according to his image, and therefore able to stand, but that we were made of dust and weak matter, and had a sensitive soul, like that of beasts, as well as an intellectual nature, like that of angels, and therefore liable to follow the dictates of it, without exact care and watchfulness. If he remembered only the first, there would be no issue but indignation; but the consideration of the latter moves his compassion. How miserable should we be for want of this perfection in the Divine nature, whereby God remembers and reflects upon his past act in our first frame, and the mindfulness of our condition excites the motion of his bowels to us! Had he lost the knowledge how he first framed us, did he not still remember the mutability of our nature, as we were formed and stamped in his mint, how much more wretched would our condition be than it is! If his remembrance of our original be one ground of his pity, the sense of his omniscience should be a ground of our comfort in the stirring of our infirmities: he remembers we were but dust when he made us, and yet remembers we are but dust while he preserves and forbears us.

8. It is some comfort in the fears of some lurking corruption in our hearts. We know by this whither to address ourselves for the search and discovery of it: perhaps some blessings we want are retarded; some calamities we understand not the particular cause of, are inflicted; some petitions we have put up, hang too long for an answer; and the chariot wheels of Divine goodness move slow, and are long in coming. Let us beg the aid of this attribute to open to us the remoras, to discover what base affection there is that retards the mercies we want, or attracts the affliction we feel, or bars the door against the return of our supplications. What our dim sight cannot discover, the clear eye of God can make visible to us (Job x. 2): "Show me wherefore thou contendest with me." As in want of pardon, we particularly plead his mercy, and in our desires for the performance of his promise, we argue with him from his faithfulness, so in the fear of any insincerity or hidden corruption we should implore his omniscience: for as God is a God in covenant, our God, our God in the whole of his nature, so the perfections of his nature are employed in their several stations, as assistances of his creatures. This was David's practice and comfort, after that large meditation, on the omniscience and omnipresence of God, he turns his thoughts of it into petitions for the employment of it in the concerns of his soul, and begs a mercy suitable to the glory of this perfection (Ps. cxxxix. 23): "Search me, O God, and try my heart,

try me, and know my thoughts;" dive to the bottom (ver. 24), "and see if there be any wicked way in me, and lead me in the way everlasting." His desire is not barely that God should know him, for it would be senseless to beg of God that he should have mercy, or faithfulness, or power, or knowledge in his nature; but he desires the exercise of this attribute, in the discovery of himself to himself, in order to his sight of any wicked way, and humiliation for it, and reformation of it, in order to his conduct to everlasting life. As we may appeal to this perfection to judge us when the sincerity of our actions is censured by others, so we may implore it to search us when our sincerity is questioned by ourselves, that our minds may be enlightened by a beam from his knowledge, and the little thieves may be pulled out of their dens in our hearts by the hand of his power. In particular, it is our comfort that we can, and our necessity that we must address particularly to this, when we engage solemnly in a work of self-examination; that we may have a clearer eye to direct us than our own, that we may not mistake brass for gold, or counterfeit graces for true; that nothing that is filthy and fit to be cast out, may escape our sight, and preserve its station. And we need not question the laying at the door of this neglect (viz. not calling in this attribute to our aid, whose proper office it is, as I may so say, to search and inquire) all the mistakes, ill success, and fruitlessness of our endeavors in self-examination, because we would engage in it in the pitiful strength of our own dimness, and not in the light of God's countenance, and the assistance of his eye, which can discern what we cannot see, and discover that to us which we cannot manifest to ourselves. It is a comfort to a learner of an art to have a skilful eye to overlook his work, and inform him of the defects. Beg the help of the eye of God in all your searches and self-examinations.

9. The consideration of this attribute is comfortable in our assurances of, and reflections upon, the pardon of sin, or seeking of it. As God punishes men for sin according to his knowledge of them, which is greater than the knowledge their own consciences have of them, so he pardons according to his knowledge: he pardons not only according to our knowledge, but according to his own; he is greater than any man's heart, to condemn for that which a man is at present ignorant of; and greater than our hearts, to pardon that which is not at present visible to us; he knows that which the most watchful conscience cannot take a survey of: if God had not an infinite understanding of us, how could we have a perfect and full pardon from him? It would not stand with his honor to pardon he knew not what. He knows what crimes we have to be pardoned, when we know not all of them ourselves, that stand in need of a gracious remission; his omniscience beholds every sin to charge it upon our Saviour. If he knows our sins that are black, he knows every mite of Christ's righteousness which is pure, and the utmost extent of his merits, as well as the demerit of our iniquities. As he knows the filth of our sin, he also knows the covering of our Saviour: he knows the value of the Redeemer's sufferings, and exactly understands every plea in the intercession of our Ad-

vocate. Though God knows our sins *oculo indice*, yet he doth not see them *oculo judice*, with a judicial eye : his omniscience stirs not up his justice to revenge, but his mercy to pity. His infinite understanding of what Christ hath done, directs him to disarm his justice, and sound an alarm to his bowels. As he understands better than we what we have committed, so he understands better than we what our Saviour hath merited ; and his eye directs his hand in the blotting out guilt, and applying the remedy.

Use III. shall be to sinners, to humble them, and put them upon serious consideration. This attribute speaks terrible things to a profligate sinner. Basil thinks that the ripping open the sins of the damned to their faces by this perfection of God, is more terrible than their other torments in hell. God knows the persons of wicked men, not one is exempted from his eye ; he sees all the actions of men, as well as he knows their persons (Job. xi. 11): "He knows vain men, he sees wickedness also" (Job xxxiv. 21): "His eye is upon all their goings." He hears the most private whispers (Ps. cxxxix. 4), the scope, manner, circumstance of speaking, he knows it altogether: he understands all our thoughts, the first bubblings of that bitter spring (Ps. cxxxix. 2) ; the quickest glances of the fancy, the closest musings of the mind, and the abortive wouldings or wishes of the will, the language of the heart, as well as the language of the tongue ; not a foolish thought, or an idle word, not a wanton glance, or a dishonest action, not a negligent service, or a distracting fancy, but is more visible to him, than the filth of a dunghill can be to any man by the help of a sun beam. How much better would it be for desperate sinners to have their crimes known to all the angels in heaven, and men upon earth, and devils in hell, than that they should be known to their Sovereign, whose laws they have violated, and to their Judge, whose righteousness obligeth him to revenge the injury !

1. Consider what a poor refuge is secrecy to a sinner. Not the mists of a foggy day, nor the obscurity of the darkest night, not the closest curtains, nor the deepest dungeon, can hide any sin from the eye of God. Adam is known in his thickets, and Jonah in his cabin. Achan's wedge of gold is discerned by him, though buried in the earth, and hooded with a tent. Shall Sarah be unseen by him, when she mockingly laughs behind the door? Shall Gehazi tell a lie, and comfort himself with an imagination of his master's ignorance, as long as God knows it? Whatsoever works men do, are not hid from God, whether done in the darkness or daylight, in the midnight darkness, or the noon-day sun : he is all eye to see, and he hath a great wrath to punish. The wheels of Ezekiel are full of eyes : a piercing eye to behold the sinner, and a swift wheel of wrath to overtake him. God is light, and of all things light is most difficultly kept out. The secretest sins are set in the light of his countenance (Ps. xc. 8), as legible to him, as if written with a sun-beam ; more visible to him than the greatest print to the sharpest eye. The fornications of the Samaritan woman, perhaps known only to her own conscience, were manifest to Christ (John iv. 16.) There is nothing so secretly done, but there is an infallible witness to prepare

a charge. Though God be invisible to us, we must not imagine we are so to him; it is a vanity, therefore, to think that we can conceal ourselves from God, by concealing the notions of God from our sense and practice. If men be as close from the eyes of all men, as from those of the sun, yea, if they could separate themselves from their own shadow, they could not draw themselves from God's understanding: how, then, can darkness shelter us, or crafty artifices defend us? With what shame will sinners be filled, when God, who hath traced their steps, and writ their sins in a book, shall make a repetition of their ways, and unveil the web of their wickedness!

2. What a dreadful consideration is this to the juggling hypocrite, that masks himself with an appearance of piety? An infinite understanding judges not according to veils and shadows, but according to truth; "He judges not according to appearance" (1 Sam. xvi. 7). The outward comeliness of a work imposeth not on him, his knowledge, and therefore his estimations are quite of another nature than those of men. By this perfection God looks through the veil, and beholds the litter of abominations in the secrets of the soul; the true quality and principle of every work, and judges of them as they are, and not as they appear. Disguised pretexts cannot deceive him; the disguises are known afar off, before they are weaved; he pierceth into the depths of the most abstruse wills; all secret ends are dissected before him; every action is naked in its outside, and open in its inside; all are as clear to him as if their bodies were of crystal; so that if there be any secret reserves, he will certainly reprove us (Job xiii. 10). We are often deceived; we may take wolves for sheep, and hypocrites for believers; for the eyes of men are no better than flesh, and dive no further than appearance; but an infinite understanding, that fathoms the secret depths of the heart, is too knowing to let a dream pass for a truth, or mistake a shadow for a body. Though we call God Father all our days, speak the language of angels, or be endowed with the gifts of miracles, he can discern whether we have his mark upon us; he can espy the treason of Judas in a kiss; Herod's intent of murdering under a specious pretence of worship; a Pharisee's fraud under a broad phylactery; a ravenous wolf under the softness of a sheep's skin; and the devil in Samuel's mantle, or when he would shroud himself among the sons of God (Job i. 6, 7). All the rooms of the heart, and every atom of dust in the least chink of it, is clear to his eye; he can strip sin from the fairest excuses, pierce into the heart with more ease than the sun can through the thinnest cloud or vapor; and look through all Ephraim's ingenuous inventions to excuse his idolatry (Hos. v. 3). Hypocrisy, then, is a senseless thing, since it cannot escape unmasking, by an infinite understanding. As all our force cannot stop his arm, when he is resolved to punish, so all our sophistry cannot blind his understanding, when he comes to judge. Woe to the hypocrite, for God sees him; all his juggling is open and naked to infinite understanding.

3. Is it not also a senseless thing to be careless of sins committed long ago? The old sins forgotten by men, stick fast in an infinite

understanding: time cannot rase out that which hath been known from eternity. Why should they be forgotten many years after they were acted, since they were foreknown in an eternity before they were committed, or the criminal capable to practise them? Amalek must pay their arrears of their ancient unkindness to Israel in the time of Saul, though the generation that committed them were rotten in their graves (1 Sam. xv. 2). Old sins are written in a book, which lies always before God; and not only our own sins, but the sins of our fathers, to be requited upon their posterity.[1] What a vanity is it then to be regardless of the sins of an age that went before us! because they are in some measure out of our knowledge, are they therefore blotted out of God's remembrance? Sins are bound up with him, as men do bonds, till they resolve to sue for the debt; the iniquity of Ephraim is bound up (Hos. xiii. 12). As his foreknowledge extends to all acts that shall be done, so his remembrance extends to all acts that have been done. We may as well say, God foreknows nothing that shall be done to the end of the world, as that he forgets anything that hath been done from the beginning of the world. The former ages of the world are no further distant from him than the latter. God hath a calendar (as it were) or an account book of men's sins ever since the beginning of the world, what they did in their childhood, what in their youth, what in their manhood, and what in their old age: he hath them in store among his treasures (Deut. xxxii. 34): he hath neither lost his understanding to know them, nor his resolution to revenge them: as it follows, "to me vengeance belongs" (ver. 35). He intends to enrich his justice with a glorious manifestation, by rendering a due recompense. And it is to be observed, that God doth not only necessarily remember them, but sometimes binds himself by an oath to do it (Amos viii. 7); "The Lord hath sworn by the excellency of Jacob, Surely I will never forget any of their works." Or, in the Hebrew, "If I ever forget any of their works;" that is, let me not be accounted a God forever, if I do forget; let me lose my godhead, if I lose my remembrance. It is not less a misery to the wicked, than it is a comfort to the godly, that their record is in heaven.

4. Let it be observed, that this infinite understanding doth exactly know the sins of men; he knows so as to consider. He doth not only know them, but intently behold them (Ps. xi. 4): "His eyelids try the children of men," a metaphor taken from men that contract the eyelids, when they would wistly and accurately behold a thing; it is not a transient and careless look (Ps. x. 14): "Thou hast seen it;" thou hast intently beheld it, as the word properly signifies: he beholds and knows the actions of every particular man, as if there were none but he in the world; and doth not only know, but ponder (Prov. v. 21), and consider their works (Ps. xxxiii. 15); he is not a bare spectator, but a diligent observer (1 Sam. ii. 3); "By him actions are weighed:" to see what degree of good or evil there is in them, what there is to blemish them, what to advantage them, what the quality and quantity of every action is. Consideration takes in every

---

[1] Isai. lxv. 6. "Behold it is written."

circumstance of the considered object: notice is taken of the place where, the minute when, the mercy against which it is committed; the number of them is exact in God's book: "They have tempted me now these ten times (Numb. xiv. 22), against the demonstrations of my glory in Egypt and the wilderness. The whole guilt in every circumstance is spread before him: his knowledge of men's sins is not confused; such an imperfection an infinite understanding cannot be subject to: it is exact, for iniquity is marked before him (Jer. ii. 22).

5. God knows men's miscarriage so as to judge. This use his omniscience is put to, to maintain his sovereign authority in the exercise of his justice. His notice of the sins of men is in order to a just retribution (Ps. x. 14): "Thou hast seen mischief to requite it with thy hand." The eye of his knowledge directs the hand of his justice; and no sinful action that falls under his cognizance, but will fall under his revenge; they can as little escape his censure as they can his knowledge: he is a witness in his omniscience, that he may be a judge in his righteousness; he knows the hearts of the wicked, so as to hate their works, and testify his abhorrency of that which is of high value with men (Luke xvi. 15). Sin is not preserved in his understanding, or written down in his book to be moth-eaten as an old manuscript, but to be opened one day, and copied out in the consciences of men: he writes them to publish them, and sets them in the light of his countenance, to bring them to the light of their consciences. What a terrible consideration is it, to think that the sins of a day are upon record in an infallible understanding, much more the sins of a week; what a number, then, do the sins of a month, a year, ten or forty years, arise to! How many actions against charity, against sincerity! what an infinite number is there of them, all bound up in the court rolls of God's omniscience, in order to a trial, to be brought out before the eyes of men! Who can seriously consider all those bonds, reserved in the cabinet of God's knowledge, to be sued out against the sinner in due time, without an inexpressible horror?

Use IV. is of exhortation. Let us have a sense of God's knowledge upon our hearts. All wickedness hath a spring from a want of due consideration and sense of it. David concludes it so (Ps. lxxxvi. 14), "the proud rose against him, and violent men sought after his soul, because they did not set God before them." They think God doth not know, and therefore care not what, nor how they act. When the fear of this attribute is removed, a door is opened to all impiety. What is there so villanous, but the minds of men will attempt to act? What reverence of a Deity can be left, when the sense of his infinite understanding is extinguished? What faith could there be in judgments in witnesses? How would the foundations of human society be overturned; the pillars upon which commerce stands, be utterly broken and dissolved! What society can be preserved, if this be not truly believed, and faithfully stuck to! But how easily would oaths be swallowed and quickly violated, if the sense of this perfection were rooted out of the minds of men! What fear could they have of calling to witness a Being they imagine blind and ignorant? Men secretly imagine, that God knows not, or soon forgets, and then make bold to sin against him (Ezek. viii. 12). How much does it therefore concern us to cherish and keep alive the sense of this? "If God writes us upon the palms of his hands," as the expression is, to remember us, let us engrave him upon the tables of our hearts to remember him. It would be a good motto to write upon our minds, God knows all, he is of infinite understanding.

1. This would give check to much iniquity. Can a man's conscience easily and delightfully swallow that which he is sensible falls under the cognizance of God, when it is hateful to the eyes of his holiness, and renders the actor odious to him? "Doth he not see my ways, and count all my steps," saith Job (xxxi. 4)? To what end doth he fix this consideration? To keep him from wanton glances; temptations have no encouragement to come near him, that is constantly armed with the thoughts that his sin is booked in God's omniscience. If any impudent devil hath the face to tempt us, we should not have the impudence to join issue with him under the sense of an infinite understanding. How fruitless would his wiles be against this consideration! How easily would his snares be cracked by one sensible thought of this! This doth Solomon prescribe to allay the heat of carnal imaginations (Prov. v. 20, 21). It were a useful question to ask, at the appearance of every temptation, at the entrance upon every action, as the church did in temptations to idolatry (Ps. xliv. 21): "Shall not God search this out, for he knows the secrets of the heart?" His understanding comprehends us more than our consciences can our acts, or our understanding our thoughts. Who durst speak treason against a prince, if he were sure he heard him, or that it would come to his knowledge? A sense of God's knowledge of wickedness in the first motion, and inward contrivance, would bar the accomplishment and execution. The consideration of God's infinite understanding would cry *stand* to the first glances of the heart to sin.

2. It would make us watchful over our hearts and thoughts. Should we harbor any unworthy thoughts in our cabinet, if our heads and hearts were possessed with this useful truth, that God knows everything which comes into our minds (Ezek. xi. 5)? We should as much blush at the rising of impure thoughts before the understanding of God, as at the discovery of unworthy actions to the knowledge of men, if we lived under a sense, that not a thought of all those millions, which flutter about our minds, can be concealed from him. How watchful and careful should we be of our hearts and thoughts!

3. It would be a good preparation to every duty. This consideration should be the preface to every service; the Divine understanding knows how I now act. This would engage us to serious intention, and quell wandering and distracting fancies. Who would come before God, with a careless and ignorant soul, under a sense of his infinite understanding, and prerogative of searching the heart? "O thou that sittest in heaven!" was a consideration the psalmist had at the beginning of his prayer (Ps. cxxiii. 1): whereby he testifies not only an apprehension of the majesty and power of God, but of his

omniscience; as one sitting above, beholds all that is below; would
we offer to God such raw and undigested petitions? would there be
so much flatness in our services? should our hearts so often give us
the slip? would any hang down their heads like a bulrush, by an
affected or counterfeit humility, while the heart is filled with pride,
if we did actuate faith in this attribute? No; our prayers would be
more sound, our devotions more vigorous, our hearts more close, our
spirits like the chariots of Aminadab, more swift in their motions:
everything would be done by us with all our might, which would
be very feeble and faint, if we conceived God to be of a finite understanding like ourselves. Let us therefore, before every duty, not
draw, but open the curtains between God and our souls, and think
that we are going before him that sees us, before him that knows us
(Gen. xvi. 12). And the stronger impressions of the Divine knowledge are upon our minds, the better would our preparation be for,
and the more active our frames in every service: and certainly we
may judge of the suitableness of our preparations, by the strength
of such impressions upon us.

4. This would tend to make us sincere in our whole course. This
prescription David gave to Solomon, to maintain a soundness and
health of spirit in his walk before God (1 Chron. xxviii. 9): "And
thou, Solomon, my son, know the God of thy fathers, and serve him
with a perfect heart, for the Lord understands all the imaginations
of the thoughts." Josephus gives this reason for Abel's holiness,
that he believed God was ignorant of nothing.[m] As the doctrine
of omniscience is the foundation of all religion, so the impression of
it would promote the practice of all religion. When all our ways
are imagined by us to be before the Lord, we shall then keep his
precepts (Ps. cxix. 168). And we can never be perfect or sincere
till we " walk before God" (Gen. xvii. 1); as under the eye of God's
knowledge. What we speak, what we think, what we act, is in his
sight; he knows every place where we are, everything that we do,
as well as Christ knew Nathaniel under the fig-tree. As he is too
powerful to be vanquished, so he is too understanding to be deceived; the sense of this would make us walk with as much care, as if
the understanding of all men did comprehend us and our actions.

5. The consideration of this attribute would make us humble.
How dejected would a person be if he were sure all the angels in
heaven and men upon earth, did perfectly know his crimes, with all
their aggravations! But what is created knowledge to an infinite
and just censuring understanding! When we consider that he
knows our actions, whereof there are multitudes, and our thoughts,
whereof there are millions; that he views all the blessings bestowed
upon us; all the injuries we have returned to him; that he exactly
knows his own bounty, and our ingratitude; all the idolatry, blasphemy, and secret enmity in every man's heart against him; all tyrannical oppressions, hidden lusts, omissions of necessary duties,
violations of plain precepts, every foolish imagination, with all the
circumstances of them, and that perfectly in their full anatomy, every
mite of unworthiness and wickedness in every circumstance; and

[m] Antiquit. lib. i. cap. 3.

add to this his knowledge, the wonders of his patience, which are miraculous upon the score of his omniscience, that he is not as quick in his revenge as he is in his understanding, but is so far from inflicting punishment, that he continues his former benefits, arms not his justice against us, but solicits our repentance, and waits to be gracious with all this knowledge of our crimes; should not the consideration of this melt our hearts into humiliation before him, and make us earnest in begging pardon and forgiveness of him? Again, do we not all find a worm in our best fruit, a flaw in our soundest duties? Shall any of us vaunt, as if God beheld only the gold, and not any dross; as if he knew one thing only, and not another? If we knew something by ourselves to cheer us, do we not also know something, yea, many things, to condemn us, and therefore to humble us? Let the sense of God's infinite knowledge, therefore, be an incentive and argument for more humiliation in us. If we know enough to render ourselves vile in our own eyes, how much more doth God know to render us vile in his!

6. The consideration of this excellent perfection should make us to acquiesce in God, and rely upon him in every strait. In public, in private; he knows all cases, and he knows all remedies; he knows the seasons of bringing them, and he knows the seasons of removing them, for his own glory. What is contingent in respect of us, and of our foreknowledge, and in respect of second causes, is not so in regard of God's, who hath the knowledge of the futurition of all things; he knows all causes in themselves, and, therefore, knows what every cause will produce, what will be the event of every counsel and of every action. How should we commit ourselves to this God of infinite understanding, who knows all things, and foreknows everything; that cannot be forced through ignorance to take new counsel, or be surprised with anything that can happen to us! This use the Psalmist makes of it (Ps. x. 14): "Thou hast seen it, the poor committeth himself unto thee." Though "some trust in chariots and horses" (Ps. xx. 7), some in counsels and counsellors, some in their arms and courage, and some in mere vanity and nothing; yet, let us remember the name and nature of the Lord our God, his divine perfections, of which this of his infinite understanding and omniscience is none of the least, but so necessary, that without it he could not be God, and the whole world would be a mere chaos and confusion.

DISCOURSE IX

ON THE WISDOM OF GOD

Rom. xvi. 27.—To God only wise be glory, through Jesus Christ, for ever. Amen.

This chapter being the last of this Epistle, is chiefly made up of charitable and friendly salutations and commendations of particular persons, according to the earliness and strength of their several graces, and their labor of love for the interest of God and his people. In verse 17, he warns them not to be drawn aside from the gospel doctrine, which had been taught them, by the plausible pretences and insinuations which the corrupters of the doctrine and rule of Christ never want from the suggestions of their carnal wisdom. The brats of soul-destroying errors may walk about the world in a garb and disguise of good words and fair speeches, as it is in the 18th verse; by "good words and fair speeches deceive the hearts of the simple." And for their encouragement to a constancy in the gospel doctrine, he assures them, that all those that would dispossess them of truth, to possess them with vanity, are but Satan's instruments, and will fall under the same captivity and yoke with their principal (ver 18); "The God of peace shall bruise Satan under your feet shortly." Whence, observe,

1. All corrupters of divine truth, and troublers of the church's peace, are no better than devils. Our Saviour thought the name, Satan, a title merited by Peter, when he breathed out an advice, as an axe at the root of the gospel, the death of Christ, the foundation of all gospel truth; and the apostle concludes them under the same character, which hinder the superstructure, and would mix their chaff with his wheat (Matt. xvi. 23), "Get thee behind me, Satan." It is not, Get thee behind me, Simon, or, Get thee behind me, Peter; but "Get thee behind me, Satan; thou art an offence to me." Thou dost oppose thyself to the wisdom, and grace, and authority of God, to the redemption of man, and to the good of the world. As the Holy Ghost is the Spirit of truth, so is Satan the spirit of falsehood: as the Holy Ghost inspires believers with truth, so doth the devil corrupt unbelievers with error. Let us cleave to the truth of the gospel, that we may not be counted by God as part of the corporation of fallen angels, and not be barely reckoned as enemies of God, but in league with the greatest enemy to his glory in the world.

2. The Reconciler of the world will be the Subduer of Satan. The God of peace sent the Prince of peace to be the restorer of his rights, and the hammer to beat in pieces the usurper of them. As a

God of truth, he will make good his promise; as a God of peace, he will perfect the design his wisdom hath laid, and begun to act. In the subduing Satan, he will be the conqueror of his instruments: he saith not, God shall bruise your troublers and heretics, but Satan: the fall of a general proves the rout of the army. Since God, as a God of peace, hath delivered his own, he will perfect the victory, and make them cease from bruising the heel of his spiritual seed.

3. Divine evangelical truth shall be victorious. No weapon formed against it shall prosper: the head of the wicked shall fall as low as the feet of the godly. The devil never yet blustered in the world, but he met at last with a disappointment: his fall hath been like lightning, sudden, certain, vanishing.

4. Faith must look back as far as the foundation promise. "The God of peace shall bruise," &c. The apostle seems to allude to the first promise (Gen. ii. 15),—a promise that hath vigor to nourish the church in all ages of the world: it is the standing cordial; out of the womb of this promise all the rest have taken their birth. The promises of the Old Testament were designed for those under the New, and the full performance of them is to be expected, and will be enjoyed by them. It is a mighty strengthening to faith, to trace the footsteps of God's truth and wisdom, from the threatening against the serpent in Eden, to the bruise he received in Calvary, and the triumph over him upon Mount Olivet.

5. We are to confide in the promise of God, but leave the season of its accomplishment to his wisdom. He will "bruise Satan under your feet," therefore do not doubt it; and shortly, therefore, wait for it. Shortly it will be done, that is, quickly, when you think it may be a great way off; or shortly, that is, seasonably, when Satan's rage is hottest. God is the best judge of the seasons of distributing his own mercies, and darting out his own glory: it is enough to encourage our waiting, that it will be, and that it will be shortly; but we must not measure God's shortly by our minutes.

The apostle after this, concludes with a comfortable prayer, that since they were liable to many temptations to turn their backs upon the doctrine which they had learned; yet he desires God, who had brought them to the knowledge of his truth, would confirm them in the belief of it, since it was the gospel of Christ, his dear Son, and a mystery he had been chary of and kept in his own cabinet, and now brought forth to the world in pursuance of the ancient prophesies, and now had published to all nations for that end that it might be obeyed; and concludes with a doxology, a voice of praise, to Him, who was only wise to effect his own purposes (ver. 25, 26, 27), "Now to him that is of power to establish you according to my gospel, and the preaching of Jesus Christ, according to the revelation of the mystery, which was kept secret since the world began, but now is made manifest, and by the Scriptures of the prophets, according to the commandment of the everlasting God, made known to all nations for the obedience of faith." This doxology is interlaced with many comforts for the Romans. He explains the causes of this glory to God, power, and wisdom; power to establish the Romans in grace, which includes his will. This he proves from a

divine testimony, viz., the gospel; the gospel committed to him, and
preached by him, which he commends, by calling it the preaching
of Christ; and describes it, for the instruction and comfort of the
church from the adjuncts, the obscurity of it under the Old Testament, and the clearness of it under the New. It was hid from the
former ages, and kept in silence; not simply and absolutely, but
comparatively and in part; because in the Old Testament, the doctrine of salvation by Christ was confined to the limits of Judea,
preached only to the inhabitants of that country : to them he gave
" his statutes and his judgments, and dealt not so magnificently with
any nation" (Ps. cxlvii. 19, 20); but now he causes it to spring with
greater majesty out of those narrow bounds, and spread its wings
about the world. This manifestation of the gospel he declares, 1.
from the subject, All nations. 2. From the principal efficient cause
of it, The commandment and order of God. 3. The instrumental
cause, The prophetic Scriptures. 4. From the end of it, The obedience of faith.[n]

Observ. 1. The glorious attributes of God bear a comfortable respect to believers. Power and wisdom are here mentioned as two
props of their faith; his power here includes his goodness. Power
to help, without will to assist, is a dry chip. The apostle mentions
not God's power simply and absolutely considered, for that of itself
is no more comfort to men, then it is to devils; but, as considered in
the gospel covenant, his power, as well as his other perfections, are
ingredients in that cordial of God's being our God. We should
never think of the excellencies of the Divine nature, without considering the duties they demand, and gathering the honey they present.

Observ. 2. The stability of a gracious soul depends upon the wisdom as well as the power of God. It would be a disrepute to the
Almightiness of God if that should be totally vanquished which was
introduced by his mighty arm, and rooted in the soul by an irresistible grace. It would speak a want of strength to maintain it, or a
change of resolution, and so would be no honor to the wisdom of
his first design. It is no part of the wisdom of an artificer, to
let a work wherein he determined to shew the greatness of his
skill, be dashed in pieces, when he hath power to preserve it. God
designed every gracious soul for a piece of his workmanship (Eph.
ii. 10). What, to have the skill of his grace defeated? If any
soul which he hath graciously conquered should be wrested from
him, what could be thought but that his power is enfeebled? If
deserted by him, what could be imagined, but that he repented of
his labor, and altered his counsel, as if rashly undertaken? These
Romans were rugged pieces, and lay in a filthy quarry, when God
came first to smooth them; for so the apostle represents them with
the rest of the heathen (Rom. i. 19); and would he throw them away,
or leave them to the power of his enemy, after all his pains he had
taken with them to fit them for his building? Did he not foresee
the designs of Satan against them, what stratagems he would use to
defeat his purposes and strip him of the honor of his work; and
would God so gratify his enemy, and disgrace his own wisdom? The

[n] Gomarus, *in loc.*

deserting of what hath been acted is a real repentance, and argues an imprudence in the first resolve and attempt. The gospel is called the manifold wisdom of God (Eph. iii. 10); the fruit of it, in the heart of any person, which is a main design of it, hath a title to the same character; and shall this grace, which is the product of this gospel, and therefore the birth of manifold wisdom, be suppressed? It is at God's hand we must seek our fixedness and establishment, and act faith upon these two attributes of God. Power is no ground to expect stability, without wisdom interesting the agent in it, and finding out and applying the means for it. Wisdom is naked without power to act, and power is useless without wisdom to direct. They are these two excellencies of the Deity the apostle here pitches the hope and faith of the converted Romans upon for their stability.

Observ. 3. Perseverance of believers in grace is a gospel doctrine. " According to my gospel," my gospel ministerially, according to that gospel doctrine I have taught you in this epistle (for, as the prophets were comments upon the law, so are the epistles upon the gospel), this very doctrine he had discoursed of (Rom. viii. 38, 39), where he tells them, that neither death nor life, the terrors of a cruel death, or the allurements of an honorable and pleasant life, nor principalities and powers, with all their subtelty and strength, nor the things we have before us, nor the promises of a future felicity, by either angels in heaven or devils in hell, not the highest angel, nor the deepest devil, is able to separate us, us Romans, "from the love of God which is in Christ Jesus." So that, according to my gospel, may be according to that declaration of the gospel, which I have made in this epistle, which doth not only promise the first creating grace, but the perfecting and crowning grace; for not only the being of grace, but the health, liveness, and perpetuity of grace is the fruit of the new covenant (Jer. xxxii. 40.)

Observ. 4. That the gospel is the sole means of a Christian's establishment; " According to my gospel," that is, by my gospel. The gospel is the instrumental cause of our spiritual life; it is the cause also of the continuance of it; it is the seed whereby we were born, and the milk whereby we are nourished (1 Pet. i. 23); it is the " power of God to salvation" (1 Pet. ii. 2), and therefore to all the degrees of it (John xvii. 17); "Sanctify them by thy truth," or through thy truth; by or through his truth he sanctifies us, and by the same truth he establisheth us. The first sanctification, and the progress of it, the first lineaments, and the last colors, are wrought by the gospel. The gospel, therefore, ought to be known, studied, and considered by us. It is the charter of our inheritance, and the security for our standing. The law acquaints us with our duty, but contributes nothing to our strength and settlement.

Observ. 5. The gospel is nothing else but the revelation of Christ (ver. 25); "According to my gospel and the preaching of Jesus Christ;" the discovery of the mystery of redemption and salvation in and by him. It is *genitivus objecti,* that preaching wherein Christ is declared and set out, with the benefits accruing by him. This is the privilege, the wisdom of God reserved for the latter times, which the Old Testament church had only under a veil.

Observ. 6. It is a part of the excellency of the gospel that it had the Son of God for its publisher: "The preaching of Jesus Christ." It was first preached to Adam, in Paradise, by God; and afterwards published by Christ in person, to the inhabitants of Judea. It was not the invention of man, but copied from the bosom of the Father by him that lay in his bosom. The gospel we have, is the same which our Saviour himself preached when he was in the world: he preached it not to the Romans, but the same gospel he preached is transmitted to the Romans. It, therefore, commands our respect; whoever slights it, it is as much as if he slighted Jesus Christ himself, were he in person to sound it from his own lips. The validity of a proclamation is derived from the authority of the prince that dictates it and orders it; yet the greater the person that publisheth it, the more dishonor is cast upon the authority of the prince that enjoins it, if it be contemned. The everlasting God ordained it, and the eternal Son published it.

Observ. 7. The gospel was of an eternal resolution, though of a temporary revelation (ver. 25); "According to the revelation of the mystery, which was kept secret since the world began." It is an everlasting gospel; it was a promise "before the world began" (Titus i. 2.) It was not a new invention, but only kept secret among the arcana, in the breast of the Almighty. It was hidden from angels, for the depths of it are not yet fully made known to them; their desire to look into it, speaks yet a deficiency in their knowledge of it (1 Peter, i. 12.) It was published in paradise, but in such words as Adam did not fully understand: it was both discovered and clouded in the smoke of sacrifices: it was wrapped up in a veil under the law, but not opened till the death of the Redeemer: it was then plainly said to the cities of Judah, "Behold! your God comes!" The whole transaction of it between the Father and the Son, which is the spirit of the gospel, was from eternity; the creation of the world was in order to the manifestation of it. Let us not, then, regard the gospel as a novelty; the consideration of it, as one of God's cabinet rarities, should enhance our estimation of it. No traditions of men, no inventions of vain wits, that pretend to be wiser than God, should have the same credit with that which bears date from eternity.

Observ. 8. That divine truth is mysterious; "According to the revelation of the mystery, Christ manifested in the flesh." The whole scheme of godliness is a mystery. No man or angel could imagine how two natures so distant as the Divine and human should be united; how the same person should be criminal and righteous; how a just God should have a satisfaction, and sinful man a justification; how the sin should be punished, and the sinner saved. None could imagine such a way of justification as the apostle in this epistle declares: it was a mystery when hid under the shadows of the law, and a mystery to the prophets when it sounded from their mouths; they searched it, without being able to comprehend it (1 Peter, i. 10, 11.) If it be a mystery, it is humbly to be submitted to: mysteries surmount human reason. The study of the gospel must not be with a yawning and careless frame. Trades, you call mysteries, are not learned sleeping and nodding: diligence is required; we must be disciples at God's feet. As it had God for the author, so we must have God for the teacher of it; the contrivance was his, and the illumination of our minds must be from him. As God only manifested the gospel, so he can only open our eyes to see the mysteries of Christ in it. In verse 26 we may observe,

1. The Scriptures of the Old Testament verify the substance of the New, and the New doth evidence the authority of the Old, by the Scriptures of the prophets made known. The Old Testament credits the New, and the New illustrates the Old. The New Testament is a comment upon the prophetic part of the Old. The Old shews the promises and predictions of God, and the New shews the performance. What was foretold in the Old, is fulfilled in the New; the predictions are cleared by the events. The predictions of the Old are divine, because they are above the reason of man to foreknow; none but an infinite knowledge could foretel them, because none but an infinite wisdom could order all things for the accomplishment of them. The Christian religion hath, then, the surest foundation, since the Scriptures of the prophets, wherein it is foretold, are of undoubted antiquity, and owned by the Jews and many heathens, which are and were the great enemies of Christ. The Old Testament is therefore to be read for the strengthening of our faith. Our blessed Saviour himself draws the streams of his doctrine from the Old Testament: he clears up the promise of eternal life, and the doctrine of the resurrection, from the words of the covenant, "I am the God of Abraham," &c. (Matt. xxii. 32.) And our apostle clears up the doctrine of justification by faith from God's covenant with Abraham (Rom. iv.) It must be read, and it must be read as it is writ: it was writ to a gospel end, it must be studied with a gospel spirit. The Old Testament was writ to give credit to the New, when it should be manifested in the world. It must be read by us to give strength to our faith, and establish us in the doctrine of Christianity. How many view it as a bare story, an almanack out of date, and regard it as a dry bone, without sucking from it the evangelical marrow! Christ is, in Genesis, Abraham's seed; in David's psalms and the prophets, the Messiah and Redeemer of the world.

2. Observe, 'The antiquity of the gospel is made manifest by the Scriptures of the prophets. It was of as ancient a date as any prophecy: the first prophecy was nothing else but a gospel charter; it was not made at the incarnation of Christ, but made manifest. It then rose up to its meridian lustre, and sprung out of the clouds, wherewith it was before obscured. The gospel was preached to the ancients by the prophets, as well as to the Gentiles by the apostles (Heb. iv. 2); "Unto us was the gospel preached, as well as unto them." To them first, to us after; to them indeed more cloudy, to us more clear; but they as well as we, were evangelized, as the word signifies. The covenant of grace was the same in the writings of the prophets, and the declarations of the evangelists and apostles. Though by our Saviour's incarnation, the gospel light was clearer, and by his ascension, the effusions of the Spirit

fuller and stronger; yet the believers under the Old Testament, saw Christ in the swaddling bands of legal ceremonies, and the lattice of prophetical writings; they could not else offer one sacrifice, or read one prophecy with a faith of the right stamp. Abraham's justifying faith had Christ for its object, though it was not so explicit as ours, because the manifestation was not so clear as ours.

3. All truth is to be drawn from Scripture. The apostle refers them here to the gospel and the prophets: the Scripture is the source of divine knowledge; not the traditions of men, nor reason separate from Scripture. Whosoever brings another doctrine, coins another Christ; nothing is to be added to what is written, nothing detracted from it. He doth not send us for truth, to the puddles of human inventions, to the enthusiasms of our brain; not to the See of Rome, no, nor to the instructions of angels; but the writings of the prophets, as they clear up the declarations of the apostles. The church of Rome is not made here the standard of truth: but the Scriptures of the prophets are to be the touch-stone to the Romans, for the trial of the truth of the gospel.

4. How great is the goodness of God! The borders of grace are enlarged to the Gentiles, and not hid under the skirts of the Jews. He that was so long the God of the Jews, is now also manifest to be the God of the Gentiles: the gospel is now made known to all nations, according to the commandment of the everlasting God. Not only in a way of common providence, but special grace; in calling them to the knowledge of himself, and a justification of them by faith, he hath brought strangers to him, to the adoption of children, and lodged them under the wings of the covenant, that were before alienated from him through the universal corruption of nature. Now he hath manifested himself a God of truth, mindful of his promise in blessing all nations in the seed of Abraham. The fury of devils, and the violence of men could not hinder the propagation of the gospel: its light hath been dispersed as far as that of the sun; and that grace that founded in the Gentile's ears, hath bent many of their hearts to the obedience of it.

5. Observe that libertinism and licentiousness find no encouragement in the gospel. It was made known to all nations for the obedience of faith. The goodness of God is published, that our enmity to him may be parted with. Christ's righteousness is not offered to us to be put on, that we may roll more warmly in our lusts. The doctrine of grace commands us to give up ourselves to Christ, to be accepted through him, and to be ruled by him. Obedience is due to God, as a sovereign lord in his law; and it is due out of gratitude, as he is a God of grace in the gospel. The discovery of a further perfection in God weakens not the right of another, nor the obligation of the duty the former attribute claims at our hands. The gospel frees us from the curse, but not from the duty and service: " We are delivered from the hands of our enemies, that we might serve God in holiness and righteousness" (Luke i. 74.) " This is the will of God" in the gospel, " even our sanctification." When a prince strikes off a malefactor's chains, though he deliver him from the punishment of his crime, he frees him not from the duty of

a subject: his pardon adds a greater obligation than his protection did before, while he was loyal. Christ's righteousness gives
us a title to heaven; but there must be a holiness to give us a fitness for heaven.

6. Observe, that evangelical obedience, or the obedience of Faith,
is only acceptable to God. Obedience of faith; *genitivus speciei*,
noting the kind of obedience God requires; an obedience springing
from faith, animated and influenced by faith. Not obedience of
faith, as though faith were the rule, and the law were abrogated;
but to the law as a rule, and from faith as a principle. There is
no true obedience before faith (Heb. xi. 6.) "Without faith it is
impossible to please God;" and therefore without faith impossible
to obey him. A good work cannot proceed from a defiled mind
and conscience; and without faith every man's mind is darkened,
and his conscience polluted (Tit. i. 15.) Faith is the band of union
to Christ, and obedience is the fruit of union; we cannot bring
forth fruit without being branches (John xv. 4, 5), and we cannot
be branches without believing. Legitimate fruit follows upon marriage to Christ, not before it (Rom. vii. 4.) "That you should be
married to another, even to him that is raised from the dead, that
you should bring forth fruit unto God." All fruit before marriage
is bastard, and bastards were excluded from the sanctuary. Our
persons must be first accepted in Christ, before our services can be
acceptable; those works are not acceptable where the person is not
pardoned. Good works flow from a pure heart; but the heart cannot be pure before faith. All the good works reckoned up in the elev-
enth chapter of the Hebrews were from this spring; those heroes
first believed and then obeyed. By faith Abel was righteous before
God, without it his sacrifice had been no better than Cain's: by
faith Enoch pleased God, and had a divine testimony to his obedience before his translation; by faith Abraham offered up Isaac,
without which he had been no better than a murderer. All obedience hath its root in faith, and is not done in our own strength,
but in the strength and virtue of another, of Christ, whom God
hath set forth as our head and root.

7. Observe, faith and obedience are distinct, though inseparable:
"The obedience of faith." Faith, indeed, is obedience to a gospel
command, which enjoins us to believe; but it is not all our obedience. Justification and sanctification are distinct acts of God;
justification respects the person, sanctification the nature; justification is first in order of nature, and sanctification follows: they are
distinct, but inseparable; every justified person hath a sanctified nature, and every sanctified nature supposeth a justified person. So
faith and obedience are distinct: faith as the principle, obedience as
the product; faith as the cause, obedience as the effect; the cause
and the effect are not the same. By faith we own Christ as our
Lord: by obedience we regulate ourselves according to his command. The acceptance of the relation to him as a subject, precedes
the performance of our duty: by faith we receive his law, and by
obedience we fulfil it. Faith makes us God's children (Gal. iii. 26).
Obedience manifests us to be Christ's disciples (John xv. 8). Faith is

the touchstone of obedience; the touchstone, and that which is tried by it, are not the same. But though they are distinct, yet they are inseparable. Faith and obedience are joined together; obedience follows faith at the heels. Faith purifies the heart, and a pure heart cannot be without pure actions. Faith unites us to Christ, whereby we partake of his life; and a living branch cannot be without fruit in its season, and "much fruit" (John xv. 5), and that naturally from a "newness of spirit" (Rom. vii. 9); not constrained by the rigors of the law, but drawn forth from a sweetness of love; for faith works by love. The love of God is the strong motive, and love to God is the quickening principle; as there can be no obedience without faith, so no faith without obedience. After all this, the apostle ends with the celebration of the wisdom of God; "To God only wise, be glory, through Jesus Christ forever." The rich discovery of the gospel cannot be thought of, by a gracious soul, without a return of praise to God, and admiration of his singular wisdom.

Wise God. His power before, and his wisdom here, are mentioned in conjunction (in which his goodness is included, as interested in his establishing power) as the ground of all the glory and praise God hath from his creatures.

Only wise. As Christ saith (Matt. xix. 17), "None is good, but God;" so the apostle saith, None wise, but God. As all creatures are unclean in regard of his purity, so they are all fools in regard of his wisdom; yea, the glorious angels themselves (Job iv. 18). Wisdom is the royalty of God; the proper dialect of all his ways and works. No creature can lay claim to it; he is so wise, that he is wisdom itself.

Be glory, through Jesus Christ. As God is only known in and by Christ, so he must be only worshipped and celebrated in and through Christ. In him we must pray to him, and in him we must praise him. As all mercies flow from God through Christ to us, so all our duties are to be presented to God through Christ. In the Greek, *verbatim,* it runs thus: "To the alone wise God, through Jesus Christ, to him be glory forever." But we must not understand it, as if God were wise by Jesus Christ, but that thanks is to be given to God through Christ; because in and by Christ God hath revealed his wisdom to the world. The Greek hath a repetition of the article ᾧ, and expressed in the translation, "To him be glory." Beza expungeth this article, but without reason, for ᾧ is as much as αὐτῷ, "to him;" and joining this, "the only wise God" with ver. 25, "to him that is of power to establish you;" reading it thus, "To him that is of power to establish you, the only wise God," leaving the rest in a parenthesis, it runs smoothly, "to him be glory, through Jesus Christ," And Crellius, the Socinian, observes, that this article ᾧ, which some leave out, might be industriously inserted by the apostle, to shew that the glory we ascribe to God is also given to Christ. We may observe, that neither in this place, nor any where in Scripture, is the Virgin Mary, or any of the saints, associated with God or Christ in the glory ascribed to them.

In the words there is, 1. An appropriation of wisdom to God, and a remotion of it from all creatures; "only wise God." 2. A glorifying him for it. The point I shall insist upon is, That wisdom is a transcendant excellency of the Divine nature. We have before spoken of the knowledge of God, and the infiniteness of it; the next attribute is the wisdom of God. Most confound the knowledge and wisdom of God together; but there is a manifest distinction between them in our conception. I shall handle it thus: I. Shew what wisdom is. Then lay down, II. Some propositions about the wisdom of God. And shew, III. That God is wise, and only wise. IV. Wherein his wisdom appears. V. The Use.

I. What wisdom is. Wisdom, among the Greeks, first signified an eminent perfection in any art or mystery; so a good statuary, engraver, or limner, was called wise, as having an excellent knowledge in his particular art. But afterwards the title of wise was appropriated to those that devoted themselves to the contemplation of the highest things that served for a foundation to speculative sciences.[o] But ordinarily we count a man a wise man, when he conducts his affairs with discretion, and governs his passions with moderation, and carries himself with a due proportion and harmony in all his concerns. But in particular, wisdom consists,

1. In acting for a right end. The chiefest part of prudence is in fixing a right end, and in choosing fit means, and directing them to that scope; to shoot at random is a mark of folly. As he is the wisest man that hath the noblest end and fittest means, so God is infinitely wise; as he is the most excellent being, so he hath the most excellent end. As there is none more excellent than himself, nothing can be his end but himself; as he is the cause of all, so he is the end of all; and he puts a true bias into all the means he useth to hit the mark he aims at: "Of him, and through him, and to him, are all things" (Rom. xi. 36).

2. Wisdom consists in observing all circumstances for action. He is counted a wise man that lays hold of the fittest opportunities to bring his designs about, that hath the fullest foresight of all the little intrigues which may happen in a business he is to manage, and times every part of his action in an exact harmony with the proper minutes of it. God hath all the circumstances of things in one entire image before him; he hath a prospect of every little creek in any design. He sees what second causes will act, and when they will act this or that; yea, he determines them to such and such acts; so that it is impossible he should be mistaken, or miss of the due season of bringing about his own purposes. As he hath more goodness than to deceive any, so he hath more understanding than to be mistaken in any thing. Hence the time of the incarnation of our blessed Saviour is called the fulness of time, the proper season for his coming. Every circumstance about Christ was timed according to the predictions of God; even so little a thing as not parting his garment, and the giving him gall and vinegar to drink; and all the blessings he showers down upon his people, according to the covenant of grace, are said to come "in his season" (Ezek. xxxiv. 25, 26).

[o] Amyraut. Moral. Tom. III. p. 123.

3. Wisdom consists in willing and acting according to the right reason, according to a right judgment of things. We can never count a wilful man a wise man; but him only that acts according to a right rule, when right counsels are taken and vigorously executed. The resolves and ways of God are not mere will, but will guided by the reason and counsel of his own infinite understanding (Eph. i. 11); "Who works all things according to the counsel of his own will." The motions of the Divine will are not rash, but follow the proposals of the Divine mind; he chooses that which is fittest to be done, so that all his works are graceful, and all his ways have a comeliness and decorum in them. Hence all his ways are said to be "judgment" (Deut. xxxii. 4), not mere will. Hence it appears, that wisdom and knowledge are two distinct perfections. Knowledge hath its seat in the speculative understanding, wisdom in the practical. Wisdom and knowledge are evidently distinguished as two several gifts of the Spirit in man (1 Cor. xii. 8); "To one is given, by the Spirit, the word of wisdom; to another, the word of knowledge, by the same Spirit." Knowledge is an understanding of general rules, and wisdom is a drawing conclusions from those rules in order to particular cases. A man may have the knowledge of the whole Scripture, and have all learning in the treasury of his memory, and yet be destitute of skill to make use of them upon particular occasions, and untie those knotty questions which may be proposed to him, by a ready application of those rules. Again, knowledge and wisdom may be distinguished, in our conception, as two distinct perfections in God: the knowledge of God is his understanding of all things; his wisdom is the skilful resolving and acting of all things. And the apostle, in his admiration of him, owns them as distinct; " O the depths of the riches, both of the wisdom and knowledge of God" (Rom. xi. 33)! Knowledge is the foundation of wisdom, and antecedent to it; wisdom the superstructure upon knowledge: men may have knowledge without wisdom, but not wisdom without knowledge; according to our common proverb, " The greatest clerks are not the wisest men." All practical knowledge is founded in speculation, either *secundum rem*, as in a man; or, *secundum rationem*, as in God. They agree in this, that they are both acts of the understanding; but knowledge is the apprehension of a thing, and wisdom is the appointing and ordering of things. Wisdom is the splendor and lustre of knowledge shining forth in operations, and is an act both of understanding and will; understanding in counselling and contriving, will in resolving and executing: counsel and will are linked together (Eph. i. 11).

II. The second thing is to lay down some propositions in general, concerning the wisdom of God.

First, There is an essential and a personal wisdom of God. The essential wisdom, is the essence of God; the personal wisdom is the Son of God. Christ is called Wisdom by himself (Luke vii. 35). The wisdom of God by the apostle (1 Cor. i. 24). The wisdom I speak of belongs to the nature of God, and is considered a necessary perfection. The personal wisdom is called so, because he opens to us the secrets of God. If the Son were that wisdom whereby the

Father is wise, the Son would be also the essence whereby the Father is God. If the Son were the wisdom of the Father, whereby he is essentially wise, the Son would be the essence of the Father, and the Father would have his essence from the Son, since the wisdom of God is the essence of God; and so the Son would be the Father, if the wisdom and power of the Father were originally in the Son.

Secondly, Therefore the wisdom of God is the same with the essence of God. Wisdom in God is not a habit added to his essence, as it is in man, but it is his essence. It is like the splendor of the sun, the same with the sun itself; or like the brightness of crystal, which is not communicated to it by anything else, as the brightness of a mountain is by the beam of the sun, but it is one with the crystal itself. It is not a habit superadded to the Divine essence; that would be repugnant to the simplicity of God, and speak him compounded of divers principles; it would be contrary to the eternity of his perfections: if he be eternally wise, his wisdom is his essence; for there is nothing eternal but the essence of God. As the sun melts some things, and hardens others; blackens some things, and whitens others, and produceth contrary qualities in different subjects, yet it is but one and the same quality in the sun, which is the cause of those contrary operations; so the perfections of God seem to be diverse in our conceptions, yet they are but one and the same in God.[p] The wisdom of God, is God acting prudently; as the power of God, is God acting powerfully; and the justice of God, is God acting righteously; and therefore it is more truly said, that God is wisdom, justice, truth, power, than that he is wise, just, true, &c. as if he were compounded of substance and qualities. All the operations of God proceed from one simple essence; as all the operations of the mind of man, though various, proceed from one faculty of understanding.

Thirdly, Wisdom is the property of God alone: He is "only wise." It is an honor peculiar to him. Upon the account that no man deserved the title of wise, but that it was a royalty belonging to God,[q] Pythagoras would not be called Σόφος, a title given to their learned men, but Φιλόσοφος. The name philosopher arose out of a respect to this transcendent perfection of God.

1. God is "only wise" *necessarily*. As he is necessarily God, so he is necessarily wise; for the notion of wisdom is inseparable from the notion of a Deity. When we say, God is a Spirit, is true, righteous, wise; we understand that he is transcendently these, by an intrinsic and absolute necessity, by virtue of his own essence, without the efficiency of any other, or any efficiency in and by himself. God doth not make himself wise, no more than he makes himself God. As he is a necessary Being in regard of his life, so he is necessarily wise in regard of his understanding. Synesius saith, that God is essentiated, οὐσιοῦσθαι, by his understanding. He places the substance of God in understanding and wisdom: wisdom is the first vital operation of God. He can no more be unwise than he can be untrue; for folly in the mind is much the same with falsity in speech. Wisdom among men is gained by age and experience, furthered by instructions and exercise; but the wisdom of

<hr/>

[p] Maimon. Mor. Part I. cap. 53.   [q] Laert. lib. i. Proem.

God is his nature. As the sun cannot be without light, while it re-mains a sun, and as eternity cannot be without immortality, so neither can God be without wisdom As he only hath immortality (1 Tim. vi. 16), not arbitrarily, but necessarily; so he only hath wis-dom: not because he will be wise, but because he cannot but be wise. He cannot but contrive counsels, and exert operations, be-coming the greatness and majesty of his nature.

2. Therefore "only wise" *originally.* God is αὐδίδακτος αὐτόσοφος. Men acquire wisdom by the loss of their fairest years; but his wis-dom is the perfection of the Divine nature, not the birth of study, or the growth of experience, but as necessary, as eternal, as his es-sence. He goes not out of himself to search wisdom: he needs no more the brains of creatures in the contrivance of his purposes, than he doth their arm in the execution of them. He needs no counsel, he receives no counsel from any (Rom. xi. 34): "Who hath been his counsellor?" and (Isa. xl. 14) "With whom took he counsel, and who instructed him, or taught him, in the path of judgment, and taught him knowledge, and showed to him the path of understand-ing?" He is the only Fountain of wisdom to others; angels and men have what wisdom they have, by communication from him. All created wisdom is a spark of the Divine light, like that of the stars borrowed from the sun. He that borrows wisdom from another, and doth not originally possess it in his own nature, cannot properly be called wise. As God is the only Being, in regard that all other beings are derived from him, so he is only wise, because all other wisdom flows from him. He is the spring of wisdom to all; none the original of wisdom to him.

3. Therefore "only wise" *perfectly.* There is no cloud upon his understanding. He hath a distinct and certain knowledge of all things that can fall under action; as he hath a perfect knowl-edge without ignorance, so he hath a beautiful wisdom without mole or wart. Men are wise, yet have not an understanding so vast as to grasp all things, nor a perspicacity so clear, as to pene-trate into the depths of all being. Angels have more delightful and lively sparks of wisdom, yet so imperfect, that in regard of the wisdom of God they are charged with folly (Job iv. 18). Their wisdom as well as their holiness is veiled in the presence of God. It vanisheth, as the glowing of a fire doth before the beauty of the sun, or as the light of a candle in the midst of a sunshine contracts itself, and none of its rays are seen, but in the body of the flame. The angels are not perfectly wise, because they are not perfectly knowing: the gospel, the great discovery of God's wisdom, was hid from them for ages.

4. Therefore "only wise" *universally.* Wisdom in one man is of one sort, in another of another sort; one is a wise tradesman, another a wise statesman, and another a wise philosopher: one is wise in the business of the world, another is wise in divine con-cerns. One hath not so much of plenty of one sort, but he may have a scantiness in another; one may be wise for invention, and foolish in execution; an artificer may have skill to frame an engine, and not skill to use it. The ground that is fit for olives may not be fit

for vines; that will bear one sort of grain and not another. But God hath an universal wisdom, because his nature is wise; it is not limited, but hovers over everything, shines in every being. His executions are as wise as his contrivances: he is wise in his resolves, and wise in his ways: wise in all the varieties of his works of creation, government, redemption. As his will wills all things, and his power effects all things, so his wisdom is the universal director of the motions of his will, and the executions of his power: as his righteousness is the measure of the matter of his actions, so his wisdom is the rule that directs the manner of his actions. The absolute power of God is not an unruly power: his wisdom orders all things, so that nothing is done but what is fit and convenient, and agreeable to so excellent a Being: as he cannot do an unjust thing because of his righteousnesness, so he cannot do an unwise act, because of his infinite wisdom. Though God be not necessitated to any operation without himself, as to the creation of anything, yet supposing he will act, his wisdom necessitates him to do that which is congruous, as his righteousness necessitates him to do that which is just: so that though the will of God be the principle, yet his wisdom is the rule of his actions. We must, in our conceiving of the order, suppose wisdom antecedent to will: none that acknowledges a God can have such an impious thought as to affix temerity and rashness to any of his proceedings. All his decrees are drawn out of the infinite treasury of wisdom in himself.[r] He resolves nothing about any of his creatures without reason; but the reason of his purposes is in himself, and springs from himself, and not from the creatures: there is not one thing that he wills but "he wills by counsel, and works by counsel" (Eph. i. 11). Counsel writ down every line, every letter, in his eternal Book; and all the orders are drawn out from thence by his wisdom and will: what was illustrious in the contrivance, glitters in the execution. His understanding and will are infinite; what is therefore the act of his will, is the result of his understanding, and therefore rational. His understanding and will join hands; there is no contest in God, will against mind, and mind against will; they are one in God, one in his resolves, and one in all his works.

5. Therefore he is "only wise" *perpetually*. As the wisdom of man is got by ripeness of age, so it is lost by decay of years; it is got by instruction, and lost by dotage. The perfectest minds, when in the wane, have been darkened with folly: Nebuchadnezzar, that was wise for a man, became as foolish as a brute. But the Ancient of Days is an unchangeable possessor of prudence; his wisdom is a mirror of brightness, without a defacing spot. It was "possessed by him in the beginning of his ways, before his works of old" (Prov. viii. 22), and he can never be dispossessed of it in the end of his works. It is inseparable from him: the being of his Godhead may as soon cease as the beauty of his mind; "with him is wisdom" (Job xii. 13); it is inseparable from him; therefore, as durable as his essence. It is a wisdom infinite, and therefore without increase or decrease in itself. The experience of so many ages in the govern-

---

[r] Polhill against Sherlock, p. 377.

ment of the world hath added nothing to the immensity of it, as the shining of the sun since the creation of the world hath added nothing to the light of that glorious body. As ignorance never darkens his knowledge, so folly never disgraces his prudence. God infatuates men, but neither men nor devils can infatuate God; he is unerringly wise; his counsel doth not vary and flatter; it is not one day one counsel, and another day another, but it stands like an immovable rock, or a mountain of brass. " The counsel of the Lord stands forever, and the thoughts of his heart to all generations" (Ps. xxxiii. 11).

6. He is only wise *incomprehensibly.* " His thoughts are deep" (Ps. xcii. 5); " His judgments unsearchable, his ways past finding out" (Rom. xi. 33): depths that cannot be fathomed; a splendor more dazzling to our dim minds than the light of the sun to our weak eyes. The wisdom of one man may be comprehended by another, and over-comprehended ; and often men are understood by others to be wiser in their actions than they understand themselves to be ; and the wisdom of one angel may be measured by another angel of the same perfection. But as the essence, so the wisdom of God is incomprehensible to any creature; God is only comprehended by God. The secrets of wisdom in God are double to the expressions of it in his works (Job xi. 6, 7): " Canst thou, by searching, find out God?" There is an unfathomable depth in all his decrees, in all his works; we cannot comprehend the reason of his works, much less that of his decrees, much less that in his nature; because his wisdom, being infinite as well as his power, can no more act to the highest pitch than his power. As his power is not terminated by what he hath wrought, but he could give further testimonies of it, so neither is his wisdom, but he could furnish us with infinite expressions and pieces of his skill. As in regard of his immensity he is not bounded by the limits of place ; in regard of his eternity, not measured by the minutes of time ; in regard of his power, not terminated with this or that number of objects ; so, in regard of his wisdom, he is not confined to this or that particular mode of working ; so that in regard of the reason of his actions, as well as the glory and majesty of his nature, he dwells in unapproachable light (1 Tim. vi. 16) ; and whatsoever we understand of his wisdom in creation and providence, is infinitely less than what is in himself and his own unbounded nature. Many things in Scripture are declared chiefly to be the acts of the Divine will, yet we must not think that they were acts of mere will without wisdom, but they are represented so to us, because we are not capable of understanding the infinite reason of its acts : his sovereignty is more intelligible to us than his wisdom. We can better know the commands of a superior, and the laws of a prince, than understand the reason that gave birth to those laws. We may know the orders of the Divine will, as they are published, but not the sublime reason of his will. Though election be an act of God's sovereignty, and he hath no cause from without to determine him, yet his infinite wisdom stood not silent while mere dominion acted. Whatsoever God doth, he doth wisely, as well as sovereignly ; though that wisdom which lies in the secret places of the Divine Being be as incomprehensible to us as the effects of his

sovereignty and power in the world are visible, God can give a reason of his proceeding, and that drawn from himself, though we understand it not. The causes of things visible lie hid from us. Doth any man know how to distinguish the seminal virtue of a small seed from the body of it, and in what nook and corner that lies, and what that is that spreads itself in so fair a plant, and so many flowers? Can we comprehend the justice of God's proceedings in the prosperity of the wicked, and the afflictions of the godly? Yet as we must conclude them the fruits of an unerring righteousness, so we must conclude all his actions the fruits of an unspotted wisdom, though the concatenation of all his counsels is not intelligible to us; for he is as essentially and necessarily wise, as he is essentially and necessarily good and righteous. God is not only so wise that nothing more wise can be conceived, but he is more wise than can be imagined; something greater in all his perfections than can be comprehended by any creature. It is a foolish thing, therefore, to question that which we cannot comprehend; we should adore it instead of disputing against it; and take it for granted, that God would not order anything, were it not agreeable to the sovereignty of his wisdom, as well as that of his will. Though the reason of man proceed from the wisdom of God, yet there is more difference between the reason of man, and the wisdom of God, than between the light of the sun, and the feeble shining of the glow-worm; yet we presume to censure the ways of God, as if our purblind reason had a reach above him.

7. God is "only wise" *infallibly*. The wisest men meet with rubs in the way, that make them fall short of what they aim at; they often design, and fail; then begin again; and yet all their counsels end in smoke, and none of them arrive at perfection. If the wisest angels lay a plot, they may be disappointed; for though they are higher and wiser than man, yet there is One higher and wiser than they, that can check their projects. God always compasseth his end, never fails of anything he designs and aims at; all his undertakings are counsel and will; as nothing can resist the efficacy of his will, so nothing can countermine the skill of his counsel: "There is no wisdom, nor understanding, nor counsel against the Lord" (Prov. xxi. 30). He compasseth his ends by those actions of men and devils, wherein they think to cross him; they shoot at their own mark, and hit his. Lucifer's plot, by divine wisdom, fulfilled God's purpose against Lucifer's mind. The counsel of redemption by Christ, the end of the creation of the world, rode into the world upon the back of the serpent's temptation. God never mistakes the means, nor can there be any disappointments to make him vary his counsels, and pitch upon other means than what before he had ordained. His "word that goeth forth of his mouth shall not return to him void, but it shall accomplish that which he pleases, and it shall prosper in the thing whereto he sent it" (Isa. lv. 11). What is said of his word, is true of his counsel; it shall prosper in the thing for which it is appointed; it cannot be defeated by all the legions of men and devils; for "as he thinks, so shall it come to pass; and as he hath purposed, so shall it stand; the Lord hath purposed, and who shall

disannul it" (Isa. xiv. 24, 27)? The wisdom of the creature is a drop from the wisdom of God, and is like a drop to the ocean, and a shadow to the sun; and, therefore, is not able to meet the wisdom of God, which is infinite and boundless. No wisdom is exempted from mistakes, but the Divine: he is wise in all his resolves, and never "calls back his words" and purposes (Isa. xxxi. 2).

III. The third general is to prove that God is wise. This is ascribed to God in Scripture (Dan. ii. 20); "Wisdom and might are his;" wisdom to contrive, and power to effect. Where should wisdom dwell, but in the head of a Deity? and where should power triumph, but in the arm of Omnipotency?[s] All that God doth, he doth artificially, skilfully; whence he is called the "Builder of the heavens" (Heb. xi. 10), Τεχνιης an artifical and curious builder, a builder by art: and that word (Prov. viii. 30) meant of Christ; "Then I was by him as one brought up with him;" some render it, Then I was the curious artificer; and the same word, is translated, a cunning workman (Cant. vii. 5). For this cause, counsel is ascribed to God;[t] not properly, for counsel implies something of ignorance, or irresolution, antecedent to the consultation, and a posture of will afterwards, which was not before. Counsel is, properly, a laborious deliberation, and a reasoning of things; an invention of means for the attainment of the end, after a discussing and reasoning of all the doubts which arise, *pro re natâ*, about the matter in counsel. But God hath no need to deliberate in himself what are the best means to accomplish his ends: he is never ignorant or undetermined what course he should take, as men are before they consult. But it is an expression, in condescension to our capacity, to signify that God doth nothing but with reason and understanding, with the highest prudence and for the most glorious ends, as men do after consultation and the weighing of every foreseen circumstance. Though he acts all things sovereignly by his will, yet he acts all things wisely by his understanding; and there is not a decree of his will but he can render a satisfactory reason for, in the face of men and angels. As he is the cause of all things, so he hath the highest wisdom for the ordering of all things. If wisdom among men be the knowledge of divine and human things, God must be infinitely wise, since knowledge is most radiant in him; he knows what angels and men do. and infinitely more; what is known by them obscurely, is known by him clearly; what is known by man after it is done, was known by God before it was wrought. By his wisdom, as much as by anything, he infinitely differs from all his creatures, as by wisdom man differs from a brute. We cannot frame a notion of God, without conceiving him infinitely wise. We should render him very inconsiderable, to imagine him furnished with an infinite knowledge, and not have an infinite wisdom to make use of that knowledge, or to fancy him with a mighty power destitute of prudence. Knowledge without prudence, is an eye without motion; and power without discretion, is an arm without a head; a hand to act, without

---

[s] Culverwell, Light of Nature, p. 30.
[t] Isa. xlvi. 10. Jer xxxii. 19. "Great in counsel." Job xii. 13. "He hath counsel and understanding."

understanding to contrive and model; a strength to act, without reason to know how to act: it would be a miserable notion of a God, to fancy him with a brutish and unguided power. The heathens, therefore, had, and could not but have, this natural notion of God. Plato, therefore, calls him *Mens;*[u] and Cleanthes used to call God Reason; and Socrates thought the title of Σοφός too magnificent to be attributed to anything else but God alone.

Arguments to prove that God is wise.—*Reason* 1. God could not be infinitely perfect without wisdom. A rational nature is better than an irrational nature. A man is not a perfect man without reason; how can God without it be an infinitely perfect God? Wisdom is the most eminent of all virtues; all the other perfections of God without this, would be as a body without an eye, a soul without understanding. A Christian's graces want their lustre, when they are destitute of the guidance of wisdom: mercy is a feebleness, and justice a cruelty; patience a timorousness, and courage a madness, without the conduct of wisdom; so the patience of God would be cowardice, his power an oppression, his justice a tyranny, without wisdom as the spring and holiness as the rule. No attribute of God could shine with a due lustre and brightness without it. Power is a great perfection, but wisdom a greater.[x] Wisdom may be without much power, as in bees and ants; but power is a tyrannical thing without wisdom and righteousness. The pilot is more valuable because of his skill, than the galley slave because of his strength; and the conduct of a general more estimable than the might of a private soldier. Generals are chosen more by their skill to guide, than their strength to act; what a clod is a man without prudence; what a nothing would God be without it! This is the salt that gives relish to all other perfections in a creature; this is the jewel in the ring of all the excellencies of the Divine nature, and holiness is the splendor of that jewel. Now God being the first Being, possesses whatsoever is most noble in any being. If therefore wisdom, which is the most noble perfection in any creature, were wanting to God, he would be deficient in that which is the highest excellency. God being the living God, as he is frequently termed in Scripture, he hath therefore the most perfect manner of living, and that must be a pure and intellectual life; being essentially living, he is essentially in the highest degree of living. As he hath an infinite life above all creatures, so he hath an infinite intellectual life, and therefore an infinite wisdom; whence some have called God, not *sapientem,* but *super sapientem,*[y] not only wise, but above all wisdom.

Reason 2. Without infinite wisdom he could not govern the world. Without wisdom in forming the matter, which was made by Divine power, the world could have been no other than a chaos; and without wisdom in government, it could have been no other than a heap of confusion; without wisdom the world could not have been created in the posture it is. Creation supposeth a determination of the will putting power upon acting; the determination of the will supposeth

---

[u] Eugub. per Philosoph. lib. i. cap. 5.
[x] Licet magnum sit posse, majus tamen est sapere.
[y] Suarez, Vol. I. lib. i. cap. 3. p. 10.

the counsel of the understanding, determining the will: no work, but supposeth understanding as well as will in a rational agent. As without skill things could not be created, so without it things cannot be governed. Reason is a necessary perfection to him that presides over all things: without knowledge there could not be in God a foundation for government, and without wisdom there could not be an exercise of government; and without the most excellent wisdom, he could not be the most excellent governor. He could not be an universal governor, without a universal wisdom; nor the sole governor without an unimitable wisdom; nor an independent governor without an original and independent wisdom; nor a perpetual governor wihout an incorruptible wisdom. He would not be the Lord of the world in all points, without skill to order the affairs of it. Power and wisdom are foundations of all authority and government; wisdom to know how to rule and command; power to make those commands obeyed: no regular order could issue out without the first, nor could any order be enforced without the second. A feeble wisdom, and a brutish power, seldom or never produce any good effect. Magistracy without wisdom, would be a frantic power, a rash conduct; like a strong arm when the eye is out, it strikes it knows not what, and leads it knows not whither. Wisdom without power, would be like a great body without feet,[z] like the knowledge of a pilot that hath lost his arm, who, though he knows the rule of navigation, and what course to follow in his voyage, yet cannot manage the helm: but when those two, wisdom and power, are linked together, there ariseth from both a fitness for government. There is wisdom to propose an end, and both wisdom and power employ means that conduct to that end. And therefore when God demonstrates to Job his right of government, and the unreasonableness of Job's quarrelling with his proceedings, he chiefly urgeth upon him the consideration of those two excellencies of his nature, power and wisdom, which are expressed in his works (chap. xxxviii.—xli) A prince without wisdom, is but a title without a capacity to perform the office; no man without it is fit for government; nor could God without wisdom exercise a just dominion in the world. He hath, therefore, the highest wisdom, since he is the universal governor. That wisdom which is able to govern a family, may not be able to govern a city; and that wisdom which governs a city, may not be able to govern a nation or kingdom, much less a world. The bounds of God's government being greater than any, his wisdom for government must needs surmount the wisdom of all. And though the creatures be not in number actually infinite, yet they cannot be well governed, but by One endowed with infinite discretion.[a] Providential government can be no more without infinite wisdom, than infinite wisdom can be without Providence.

Reason 3. The creatures working for an end, without their own knowledge, demonstrate the wisdom of God that guides them. All things in the world work for some end; the ends are unknown to them, though many of their ends are visible to us. As there was some prime cause, which by his power inspired them with their sev-

z Amiraut. Moral.   a Amyrald. Desart. Theol. p. 111.

eral instincts; so there must be some supreme wisdom, which moves and guides them to their end. As their being manifests his power that endowed them, so the acting according to the rules of their nature, which they themselves understand not, manifests his wisdom in directing them. Everything that acts for an end, must know that end, or be directed by another to attain that end. The arrow doth not know who shoots it, or to what end it is shot, or what mark is aimed at; but the archer that puts it in, and darts it out of the bow, knows. A watch hath a regular motion, but neither the spring, nor the wheels that move, know the end of their motion; no man will judge a wisdom to be in the watch, but in the artificer that disposed the wheels and spring, by a joint combination to produce such a motion for such an end. Doth either the sun that enlivens the earth, or the earth that travels with the plant, know what plant it produceth in such a soil, what temper it should be of, what fruit it should bear, and of what color? What plant knows its own medicinal qualities, its own beautiful flowers, and for what use they are ordained? When it strikes up its head from the earth, doth it know what proportion of them there will be? yet it produceth all these things in a state of ignorance. The sun warms the earth, concocts the humors, excites the virtue of it, and cherishes the seeds which are cast into her lap, yet all unknown to the sun or the earth. Since, therefore, that nature, that is the immediate cause of those things doth not understand its own quality, nor operation, nor the end of its action, that which thus directs them must be conceived to have an infinite wisdom. When things act by a rule they know not, and move for an end they understand not, and yet work harmoniously together for an end, that all of them, we are sure, are ignorant of, it mounts up our minds to acknowledge the wisdom of that Supreme Cause that hath ranged all these inferior causes in their order, and imprinted upon them the laws of their motions. according to the ideas in his own mind, who orders the rule by which they act, and the end for which they act, and directs every motion according to their several natures, and therefore possessed with infinite wisdom in his own nature.

Reason 4. God is the fountain of all wisdom in the creatures, and, therefore, is infinitely wise himself. As he hath a fulness of being in himself, because the streams of being are derived to other things from him, so he hath a fulness of wisdom, because he is the spring of wisdom to angels and men. That being must be infinitely wise from whence all other wisdom derives its original; for nothing can be in the effect, which is not eminently in the cause; the cause is alway more perfect than the effect. If, therefore, the creatures are wise, the Creator must be much more wise. If the Creator were destitute of wisdom, the creature would be much more perfect than the Creator. If you consider the wisdom of the spider in her web, which is both her house and net; the artifice of the bee in her comb, which is both her chamber and granary; the provision of the pismire in her repositories for corn,—the wisdom of the Creator is illustrated by them: whatsoever excellency you see in any creature, is an image of some excellency in God. The skill of the artificer is visible in the fruits of his art; a workman transcribes his spirit in the work of his hands. But the wisdom of rational creatures, as men, doth more illustrate it; all arts among men are the rays of Divine wisdom shining upon them, and, by a common gift of the Spirit, enlightening their minds to curious inventions, as (Prov. viii. 12): " I, wisdom, find out the knowledge of witty inventions;" that is, I give a faculty to men to find them out; without my wisdom all things would be buried in darkness and ignorance: whatsoever wisdom there is in the world, it is but a shadow of the wisdom of God, a small rivulet derived from him, a spark leaping out from uncreated wisdom (Isa. liv. 16): " He created the smith that bloweth the coals in the fire, and makes the instruments." The skill to use those weapons in warlike enterprises is from him: " I have created the waster to destroy;" it is not meant of creating their persons, but communicating to them their art; he speaks it there to expel fear from the church of all warlike preparations against them; he had given men the skill to form and use weapons, and could as well strip them of it, and defeat their purposes. The art of husbandry is a fruit of divine teaching (Isa. xxviii. 24, 25). If those lower kinds of knowledge, that are common to all nations, and easily learned by all, are discoveries of Divine wisdom, much more the nobler sciences, intellectual and political wisdom (Dan. ii. 21): " He gives wisdom to the wise, and knowledge to them that know understanding;" speaking of the more abstruse parts of knowledge, " The inspiration of the Almighty gives understanding" (Job xxxii. 8). Hence the wisdom which Solomon expressed in the harlot's case (1 Kings iii. 28), was, in the judgment of all Israel, the wisdom of God; that is, a fruit of Divine wisdom, a beam communicated to him from God. Every man's soul is endowed, more or less, with those noble qualities; the soul of every man exceeds that of a brute; if the streams be so excellent, the fountain must be fuller and clearer. The first Spirit must infinitely more possess what other spirits derive from him by creation; were the wisdom of all the angels in heaven, and men on earth, collected in one spirit, it must be infinitely less than what is in the spring; for no creature can be equal to the Creator. As the highest creature already made, or that we can conceive may be made by infinite power, would be infinitely below God in the notion of a creature, so it would be infinitely below God in the notion of wise.

IV. The fourth thing is, wherein the wisdom of God appears. It appears, 1st, In creation. 2dly, In government. 3dly, In redemption.

First, In creation. As in a musical instrument there is first the skill of the workman in the frame, then the skill of the musician in stringing it proper for such musical notes as he will express upon it, and after that the tempering of the strings, by various stops, to a delightful harmony, so is the wisdom of God seen in framing the world, then in tuning it, and afterwards in the motion of the several creatures. The fabric of the world is called the wisdom of God (1 Cor. i. 21): " After that, in the wisdom of God, the world by wisdom knew not God;" i. e., by the creation the world knew not God. The framing cause is there put for the effect and the work framed; because the Divine wisdom stepped forth in the creatures, to a public appearance, as if it had presented itself in a visible shape to man, giving instructions in and by the creatures, to know and adore him. What we translate (Gen. i. 1) "In the beginning God created the heaven and the earth," the Targum expresseth, "In wisdom God created the heaven and the earth." Both bear a stamp of this perfection on them;[b] and when the apostle tells the Romans (Rom. i. 20) "The invisible things of God were clearly understood by the things that are made," the word he uses is ποιήμασι not ἔργοις; this signifies a work of labor, but ποίημα a work of skill, or a poem. The whole creation is a poem, every species a stanza, and every individual creature a verse in it. The creation presents us with a prospect of the wisdom of God, as a poem doth the reader with the wit and fancy of the composer: "By wisdom he created the earth" (Prov. iii. 19), "and stretched out the heavens by discretion" (Jer. x. 12). There is not anything so mean, so small, but glitters with a beam of Divine skill; and the consideration of them would justly make every man subscribe to that of the psalmist, "O Lord, how manifold are thy works! in wisdom hast thou made them all" (Ps. civ. 24). All, the least as well as the greatest, and the meanest as well as the noblest; even those creatures which seem ugly and deformed to us, as toads, &c., because they fall short of those perfections which are the dowry of other animals: in these there is a footstep of Divine wisdom, since they were not produced by him at random, but determined to some particular end, and designed to some usefulness, as parts of the world in their several natures and stations. God could never have had a satisfaction in the review of his works, and pronounced them good or comely, as he did (Gen. i. 31), had they not been agreeable to that eternal original copy in his own mind. It is said he was refreshed, *viz.* with that review (Exod. xxxi. 17), which could not have been, if his piercing eye had found any defect in any thing which had sprung out of his hand, or an unsuitableness to that end for which he created them. He seems to do as a man that hath made a curious and polite work, with exact care to peer about every part and line, if he could perceive any imperfection in it, to rectify the mistake: but no defect was found by the infinitely wise God upon this second examination. This wisdom of the creation appears, 1. In the variety. 2. In the beauty. 3. The fitness of every creature for its use. 4. The subordination of one creature to another, and the joint concurrence of all to one common end.

1. In the variety (Ps. civ. 24): "O Lord, how manifold are thy works!" How great a variety is there of animals and plants, with a great variety of forms, shapes, figurations, colors, various smells, virtues, and qualities! and this rarity is produced from one and the same matter, as beasts and plants from the earth (Gen. i. 11, 24): "Let the earth bring forth living creatures; and the earth brought forth grass, and the herb yielding seed after his kind:" such diversity of fowl and fish from the water (Gen. i. 20): "Let the waters bring forth abundantly the moving creature that hath life, and fowl that may fly;" such a beautiful and active variety from so dull a matter

[b] Omne opus naturæ est opus intelligentiæ.

as the earth ; so solid a variety from so fluid a matter as the water ; so noble a piece as the body of man, with such variety of members fit to entertain a more·excellent soul as a guest, from so mean a matter as the dust of the ground (Gen. ii. 7). This extraction of such variety of forms out of one single and dull matter, is the chemistry of Divine wisdom. It is a greater skill to frame noble bodies of vile matter, as varieties of precious vessels of clay and earth, than of a nobler matter, as gold and silver. Again, all those varieties propagate their kind in every particular and quality of their nature, and uniformly bring forth exact copies according to the first pattern God made of the kind (Gen. i. 11, 12, 24). Consider, also, how the same piece of ground is garnished with plants and flowers of several virtues, fruits, colors, scents, without our being able to perceive any variety in the earth that breeds them, and not so great a difference in the roots that bear them. Add to this the diversities of birds of different colors, shapes, notes, consisting of various parts, wings like oars, to cut the air, and tails as the rudder of a ship, to guide their motion. How various, also, are the endowments of the creatures! some have vegetation, and the power of growth ; others have the addition of sense, and others the excellency of reason ; something wherein all agree, and something wherein all differ ; variety in unity, and unity in variety : the wisdom of the workman had not been so conspicuous had there been only one degree of goodness : the greatest skill is seen in the greatest variety. The comeliness of the body is visible in the variety of members, and their usefulness to one another. What an inform thing had man been had he been all ear, or all eye ! If God had made all the stars to be suns, it would have been a demonstration of his power, but, perhaps, less of his wisdom : no creatures, with the natures they now have, could have continued in being under so much heat : there was no less wisdom went to the frame of the least, than to the greatest creature. It speaks more art in a limner to paint a landscape exactly, than to draw the sun, though the sun be a more glorious body. I might instance also, in the different characters and features imprinted upon the countenances of men and women, the differences of voices and statures, whereby they are distinguished from one another : these are the foundations of order and of human society, and administration of justice. What confusion would have been, if a grown-up son could not be known from his father, the magistrate from the subject, the creditor from the debtor, the innocent from the criminal! The laws God hath given to mankind could not have been put in execution : this variety speaks the wisdom of God.

2. The wisdom of the creation appears in the beauty, and order, and situation of the several creatures (Eccles. iii. 11): "He hath made everything beautiful in his time." As their being was a fruit of Divine power, so their order is a fruit of Divine wisdom. All creatures are as members in the great body of the world, proportioned to one another, and contributing to the beauty of the whole ; so that if the particular forms of everything, the union of all for the composition of the world, and the laws which are established in the order of nature for its conservation, be considered, it would ravish us

with an admiration of God.[c] All the creatures are so many pictures or statues, exactly framed by line (Ps. xix. 4): "Their line is gone through all the earth;" their "line," a measuring line, or a carpenter's rule, whereby he proportions several pieces to be exactly linked and coupled together. "Their line," that is, their harmonious proportion, and the instruction from it, is gone forth through all the earth. Upon the account of this harmony, some of the ancient heathens framed the images of their gods with musical instruments in their hands, signifying that God wrought all things in a due proportion.[d] The heavens speak this wisdom in their order. The revolutions of the sun and moon determine the seasons of the year, and make day and night in orderly succession. The stars beautify the heavens, and influence the earth, and keep their courses (Judges v. 20). They keep their stations without interfering with one another; and though they have rolled about for so many ages, they observe their distinct laws, and in the variety of their motions have not disturbed one another's functions. The sun is set as the heart in the midst of this great body, to afford warmth to all: and had it been set lower, it had long since turned the earth into flame and ashes: had it been placed higher, the earth would have wanted the nourishment and refreshment necessary for it. Too much nearness had ruined the earth by parching heat, and too great a distance had destroyed the earth by starving it with cold.[e] The sun hath also its appointed motion; had it been fixed without motion, half of the earth had been unprofitable; there had been a perpetual darkness in a moiety of it; nothing had been produced for nourishment, and so it had been rendered uninhabitable: but now, by its motion, it visits all the climates of the world, runs its circuit, so that "nothing is hid from the heat thereof", (Ps. xix. 6). It imparts its virtue to every corner of the world in its daily and yearly visits. Had it been fixed, the fruits of the earth under it had been parched and destroyed before their maturity; but all those inconveniences are provided against by the perpetual motion of the sun. This motion is orderly; it makes its daily course from east to west, its yearly motion from north to south: it goes to the north, till it comes to the point God hath set it, and then turns back to the south, and gains some point every day: it never riseth nor sets in the same place one day, where it did the day before. The world is never without its light; some see it rising the same moment we see it setting.[f] The earth also speaks the Divine wisdom; it is the pavement of the world, as the heaven is the ceiling of fretwork. It is placed lowermost, as being the heaviest body, and fit to receive the weightiest matter, and provided as an habitation proper for those creatures which derive the matter of their bodies from it, and partake of its earthly nature; and garnished with other creatures for the profit or pleasure of man.[g] The sea also speaks the same Divine wisdom. "He strengthened the fountains of the deep, and gave the sea a decree that it should not pass his

[c] Amyraut. Moral, Vol. I. p. 257

[d] Mountag. against Selden, p. 281. Plutarch calls God ἁρμονικὸς καὶ μουσικὸς ; he saith nothing was made without music.

[e] Charlton, Light of Nature, p. 57.

[f] Daille, Mel. Part I. p. 483.

[g] Amyraut. Predestin. p. 9.

command" (Prov. viii. 28, 29). He hath given it certain bounds that it should not overflow the earth (Job xxviii. 11). It contains itself in the situation wherein God hath placed it, and doth not transgress its bounds. What if some part of a country, a little spot, hath been overflowed by it, and groaned under its waves? yet for the main, it retains the same channels wherein it was at first lodged. All creatures are clothed with an outward beauty, and endowed with an inward harmony; there is an agreement in all parts of this great body; every one is beautiful and orderly; but the beauty of the world results from all of them disposed and linked together.

3. This wisdom is seen in the fitness of everything for its end, and the usefulness of it. Divine wisdom is more illustrious in the fitness and usefulness of this great variety, than in the composure of their distinct parts: as the artificer's skill is more eminent in fitting the wheels, and setting them in order for their due motion, than in the external fabric of the materials which compose the clock. After the most diligent inspection, there can be found nothing in the creation unprofitable; nothing but is capable of some service, either for the support of our bodies, recreation of our senses, or moral instruction of our minds: not the least creature but is formed, and shaped, and furnished with members and parts, in a due proportion for its end and service in the world; nothing is superfluous, nothing defective. The earth is fitted in its parts;[h] the valleys are appointed for granaries, the mountains to shadow them from the scorching heat of the sun; the rivers, like veins, carry refreshment to every member of this body; plants and trees thrive on the face of the earth, and metals are engendered in the bowels of it, for materials for building, and other uses for the service of man. "There he causes the grass to grow for the cattle and herb for the service of man, that he may bring forth food out of the earth" (Ps. civ. 14). The sea is fitted for use; it is a fish pond for the nourishment of man; a boundary for the dividing of lands and several dominions: it joins together nations far distant: a great vessel for commerce (Ps. civ. 26), "there go the ships." It affords vapors to the clouds, wherewith to water the earth, which the sun draws up, separating the finer from the salter parts, that the earth may be fruitful without being burdened with barrenness by the salt. The sea hath also its salt, its ebbs, and floods; the one as brine, the other as motion, to preserve it from putrefaction, that it may not be contagious to the rest of the world. Showers are appointed to refresh the bodies of living creatures, to open the womb of the earth, and "water the ground to make it fruitful" (Ps. civ. 3). The clouds, therefore, are called the chariots of God; he rides in them in the manifestation of his goodness and wisdom. Winds are fitted to purify the air, to preserve it from putrefaction, to carry the clouds to several parts, to refresh the parched earth, and assist her fruits: and also to serve for the commerce of one nation with another by navigation.[i] God, in his wisdom and goodness, "walks upon the wings of the wind" (Ps. civ. 3). Rivers[k] are appointed to bathe the ground, and render it fresh and lively;

---

h Amyraut. sur diverses Text. p. 127,   i Lessius.
k Daille, Melan. Part II, pp. 472, 473,

they fortify cities, are the limits of countries, serve for commerce; they are the watering-pots of the earth, and the vessels for drink for the living creatures that dwell upon the earth. God cut those channels for the wild asses, the beasts of the desert, which are his creatures as well as the rest (Ps. civ. 10, 12, 13). Trees are appointed for the habitations of birds, shadows for the earth, nourishment for the creatures, materials for building, and fuel for the relief of man against cold. The seasons of the year have their use; the winter makes the juice retire into the earth, fortifies plants, and fixes their roots: it moistens the earth that was dried before by the heat of summer. and cleanseth and prepares it for a new fruitfulness. The spring calls out the sap in new leaves and fruit. The summer consumes the superfluous moisture, and produceth nourishment for the inhabtants of the world.[1] The day and night have also their usefulness: the day gives life to labor, and is a guide to motion and action (Ps. civ. 24), " The sun ariseth, man goeth forth to his labor until the evening." It warms the air, and quickens nature; without day the world would be a chaos, an unseen beauty. The night indeed casts a veil upon the bravery of the earth, but it draws the curtains from that of heaven ; though it darkens below, it makes us see the beauty of the world above, and discovers to us a glorious part of the creation of God, the tapestry of heaven, and the motions of the stars, hid from us by the eminent light of the day. It procures a truce from labor, and refresheth the bodies of creatures, by recruiting the spirits which are scattered by watching. It prevents the ruin of life, by a reparation of what was wasted in the day. It takes from us the sight of flowers and plants, but it washeth their face with dews for a new appearance next morning. The length of the day and night is not without a mark of wisdom; were they of a greater length, as the length of a week or month, the one would too much dry, and the other too much moisten ; and for want of action, the members would be stupified. The perpetual succession of day and night is an evidence of the Divine wisdom in tempering the travel and rest of creatures. Hence, the psalmist tells us (Ps. lxxxiv. 16, 17), " The day is thine, and the night is thine; thou hast prepared the light of the sun, and made summer and winter ;" i. e. they are of God's framing, not without a wise counsel and end. Hence, let us ascend to the bodies of living creatures, and we shall find every member fitted for use. What a curiosity is there in every member! Every one fitted to a particular use in their situation, form, temper, and mutual agreement for the good of the whole : the eye to direct; the ear to receive directions from others; the hands to act; the feet to move. Every creature hath members fitted for that element wherein it resides; and in the body, some parts are appointed to change the food into blood, others to refine it, and others to distribute and convey it to several parts for the maintenance of the whole : the heart to mint vital spirits for preserving life, and the brain to coin animal spirits for life and motion ; the lungs to serve for the cooling the heart, which else would be parched as the ground in summer. The motion of the members of the body by one act of the will, and also without the will by a

[1] Daille, Melan. II. p. 477, &c.

natural instinct, is an admirable evidence of Divine skill in the structure of the body; so that well might the psalmist cry out (Ps. cxxxix. 14), "I am fearfully and wonderfully made!" But how much more of this Divine perfection is seen in the soul! A nature, furnished with a faculty of understanding to judge of things, to gather in things that are distant, and to reason and draw conclusions from one thing to another, with a memory to treasure up things that are past, with a will to apply itself so readily to what the mind judges fit and comely, and fly so speedily from what it judges ill and hurtful. The whole world is a stage; every creature in it hath a part to act, and a nature suited to that part and end it is designed for; and all concur in a joint language to publish the glory of Divine wisdom; they have a voice to proclaim the "glory of God" (Ps. xix. 1, 3). And it is not the least part of God's skill, in framing the creatures so, that upon man's obedience, they are the channels of his goodness; and upon man's disobedience, they can, in their natures, be the ministers of his justice for the punishing of offending creatures.

4. This wisdom is apparent in the linking of all these useful parts together, so that one is subordinate to the other for a common end. All parts are exactly suited to one another, and every part to the whole, though they are of different natures, as lines distant in themselves, yet they meet in one common centre, the good and the preservation of the universe; they are all jointed together, as the word translated *framed* (Heb. xi. 2) signifies; knit by fit hands and ligaments to contribute mutual beauty, strength, and assistance to one another; like so many links of a chain coupled together, that though there be a distance in place, there is a unity in regard of connection and end, there is a consent in the whole (Hos. ii. 21, 22). "The heavens hear the earth; and the earth hears the corn, and the wine, and the oil." The heavens communicate their qualities to the earth, and the earth conveys them to the fruits she bears.[m] The air distributes light, wind and rain to the earth; the earth and the sea render to the air exhalations and vapors, and altogether charitably give to the plants and animals that which is necessary for their nourishment and refreshment. The influences of the heavens animate the earth; and the earth affords matter, in part, for the influences it receives from the regions above. Living creatures are maintained by nourishment; nourishment is conveyed to them by the fruits of the earth; the fruits of the earth are produced by means of rain and heat; matter for rain and dew is raised by the heat of the sun; and the sun by its motion distributes heat and quickening virtue to all parts of the earth. So colors are made for the pleasure of the eye, sounds for the delight of the ear; light is formed, whereby the eye may see the one, and air to convey the species of colors to the eye, and sound to the ear; all things are like the wheels of a watch compacted: and though many of the creatures be endowed with contrary qualities, yet they are joined in a marriage-knot for the public security, and subserviency to the preservation and order of the universe; as the variety of strings upon an instrument, sending forth various and distinct sounds, are tempered together, for the framing excellent and

[m] Daille Sermon XV. p. 170.

delightful airs. In this universal conspiring of the creatures together to one end, is the wisdom of the Creator apparent; in tuning so many contraries as the elements are, and preserving them in their order, which if once broken, the whole frame of nature would crack, and fall in pieces; all are so interwoven and inlaid together, by the Divine workmanship, as to make up one entire beauty in the whole fabric: as every part in the body of man hath a distinct comeliness, yet there is besides, the beauty of the whole, that results from the union of divers parts exactly fashioned to one another, and linked together.

By the way, *Use.* How much may we see of the perfection of God in everything that presents itself to our eyes! And how should we be convinced of our unworthy neglect of ascending to him with reverend and admiring thoughts, upon the prospect of the creatures! What dull scholars are we, when every creature is our teacher, every part of the creature a lively instruction! Those things that we tread under our feet, if used by us according to the full design of their creation, would afford rich matter, not only for our heads, but our hearts. As grace doth not destroy nature, but elevate it, so neither should the fresher and fuller discoveries of Divine wisdom in redemption deface all our thoughts of his wisdom in creation. Though the greater light of the sun obscures the lesser sparkling of the stars, yet it gives way in the night to the discovery of them, that God may be seen, known, and considered, in all his works of wonder, and miracles of nature. No part of Scripture is more spiritual than the Psalms; none filled with clearer discoveries of Christ in the Old Testament; yet how often do the penmen consider the creation of God, and find their meditations on him to be sweet, as considered in his works (Ps. civ. 34)! " My meditation of him shall be sweet." When? why, after a short history of the goodness and wisdom of God in the frame of the world, and the species of the creatures.

Secondly. The wisdom of God appears in his government of his creatures. The regular motion of the creatures speaks for this perfection, as well as the exact composition of them. If the exquisiteness of the frame conducts us to the skill of the Contriver, the exactness of their order, according to his will and law, speaks no less the wisdom of the Governor. It cannot be thought that a rash and irrational power presides over a world so well disposed: the disposition of things hath no less characters of skill, than the creation of them. No man can hear an excellent lesson upon a lute, but must presently reflect upon the art of the person that touches it. The prudence of man appears in wrapping up the concerns of a kingdom in his mind, for the well-ordering of it; and shall not the wisdom of God shine forth, as he is the director of the world? I shall omit his government of inanimate creatures, and confine the discourse to his government of man, as rational, as sinful, as restored.

1st. In his government of man as a rational creature.

1. In the law he gives to man. Wisdom framed it, though will enacted it. The will of God is the rule of righteousness to us, but the wisdom of God is the foundation of that rule of righteousness which he prescribes us. The composure of a musician is the rule

of singing to his scholars; yet the consent and harmony in that composure derives not itself from his will, but from his understanding; he would not be a musician if his composures were contrary to the rules of true harmony: so the laws of men are composed by wisdom, though they are enforced by will and authority.[n] The moral law, which was the law of nature, the law imprinted upon Adam, is so framed as to secure the rights of God as supreme, and the rights of men in their distinctions of superiority and equality: it is therefore called "holy and good" (Rom. vii. 12); holy, as it prescribes our duty to God in his worship; good, as it regulates the offices of human life, and preserves the common interest of mankind.

(1.) It is suited to the nature of man. As God hath given a law of nature, a fixed order to inanimate creatures, so he hath given a law of reason to rational creatures: other creatures are not capable of a law differencing good and evil, because they are destitute of faculties and capacities to make distinction between them. It had not been agreeable to the wisdom of God to propose any moral law to them, who had neither understanding to discern, nor will to choose. It is therefore to be observed, that whilst Christ exhorted others to the embracing his doctrine, yet he exhorted not little children, though he took them in his arms, because, though they had faculties, yet they were not come to such a maturity as to be capable of a rational instruction. But there was a necessity for some command for the government of man; since God had made him a rational creature, it was not agreeable to his wisdom to govern him as a brute, but as a rational creature, capable of knowing his precepts, and voluntarily walking in them; and without a law, he had not been capable of any exercise of his reason in services respecting God. He therefore gives him a law, with a covenant annexed to it, whereby man is obliged to obedience, and secured of a reward. This was enforced with severe penalties, death, with all the horrors attending it, to deter him from transgression (Gen. ii. 17); wherein is implied a promise of continuance of life, and all its felicities, to allure him to a mindfulness of his obligation. So perfect a hedge did Divine wisdom set about him, to keep him within the bounds of that obedience, which was both his debt and security, that wheresoever he looked, he saw either something to invite him, or something to drive him to the payment of his duty, and perseverance in it. Thus the law was exactly framed to the nature of man; man had twisted in him a desire of happiness; the promise was suited to cherish this natural desire. He had also the passion of fear; the proper object of this was any thing destructive to his being, nature, and felicity; this the threatening met with. In the whole it was accommodated to man as rational; precepts to the law in his mind, promises to the natural appetite, threatenings to the most prevailing affection, and to the implanted desires of preserving both his being and happiness in that being. These were rational motives, fitted to the nature of Adam, which was above the life God had given plants, and the sense he had given animals. The command given man in innocence was suited to his strength and power. God gave him not

[n] Castellio, Dialog. l. 4, p. 46.

any command but what he had ability to observe: and since we want not power to forbear an apple in our corrupted and impotent state, he wanted not strength in his state of integrity. The wisdom of God commanded nothing but what was very easy to be observed by him, and inferior to his natural ability. It had been both unjust and unwise to have commanded him to fly up to the sun, when he had not wings; or stop the course of the sea, when he had not strength.

(2.) It is suited to the happiness and benefit of man. God's laws are not an act of mere authority respecting his own glory, but of wisdom and goodness respecting man's benefit. They are perfective of man's nature, conferring a wisdom upon him, "rejoicing his heart, enlightening his eyes" (Ps. xix. 7, 8), affording him both a knowledge of God and of himself. To be without a law, is for men to be as beasts, without justice and without religion: other things are for the good of the body, but the laws of God for the good of the soul; the more perfect the law, the greater the benefit. The laws given to the Jews were the honor and excellency of that nation (Deut. i. 8); "What nation is there so great, that hath statutes and judgments so righteous?" They were made statesmen in the judicial law, ecclesiastics in the ceremonial, honest men in the second table, and divine in the first. All his laws are suited to the true satisfaction of man, and the good of human society. Had God framed a law only for one nation, there would have been the characters of a particular wisdom; but now an universal wisdom appears, in accommodating his law, not only to this or that particular society or corporation of men, but to the benefit of all mankind, in the variety of climates and countries wherein they live; everything that is disturbing to human society is provided against; nothing is enjoined but what is sweet, rational, and useful: it orders us not to attempt anything against the life of our neighbor, the honor of his bed, propriety in his goods, and the clearness of his reputation; and, if well observed, would alter the face of the world, and make it look with another hue. The world would be altered from a brutish to a human world; it would change lions and wolves, men of lion-like and wolfish disposition, into reason and sweetness. And because the whole law is summed up in love, it obligeth us to endeavor the preservation of one another's beings, the favoring of one another's interests, and increasing the goods, as much as justice will permit, and keeping up one another's credits, because love, which is the soul of the law, is not shown by a cessation from action, but signifies an ardor, upon all occasions, in doing good. I say, were this law well observed, the world would be another thing than it is: it would become a religious fraternity; the voice of enmity, and the noise of groans and cursings, would not be heard in our streets; peace would be in all borders; plenty of charity in the midst of cities and countries; joy and singing would sound in all habitations. Man's advantage was designed in God's laws, and doth naturally result from the observance of them. God so ordered them, by his wisdom, that the obedience of man should draw forth his goodness, and prevent those smarting judgments which were necessary to reduce the creature to order that would not voluntarily continue in the order God had appointed. The laws of men are often unjust, oppressive, cruel, sometimes against the law of nature; but an universal wisdom and righteousness glitters in the Divine law; there is nothing in it but is worthy of God, and useful for the creature; so that we may well say, with Job, "Who teaches like God" (Job xxxvi. 22)? or as some render it, "Who is a lawgiver like God? Who can say to him, Thou hast wrought iniquity or folly among men? His precepts were framed for the preservation of man in that rectitude wherein he was created, in that likeness to God wherein he was first made, that there might be a correspondence between the integrity of the creature and the goodness of his Creator, by the obedience of man; that man might exercise his faculties in operation worthy of him, and beneficial to the world.

(3.) The wisdom of God is seen in suiting his laws to the consciences as well as the interests of all mankind (Rom. ii. 14); "The Gentiles do, by nature, the things contained in the law;" so great an affinity there is between the wise law and the reason of man. There is a natural beauty emerging from them, and darting upon the reasons and consciences of men, which dictates to them that this law is worthy to be observed in itself. The two main principles of the law, the love and worship of God, and doing as we would be done by, have an indelible impression in the consciences of all men, in regard of the principle, though they are not suitably expressed in the practice. Were there no law outwardly published, yet every man's conscience would dictate to him that God was to be acknowledged, worshipped, loved, as naturally as his reason would acquaint him that there was such a being as God. This suitableness of them to the consciences of men is manifest, in that the laws of the best governed nations among the heathen have had an agreement with them. Nothing can be more exactly composed, according to the rules of right and exact reason, than this; no man but approves of something in it, yea, of the whole, when he exerciseth that dim reason which he hath. Suppose any man, not an absolute atheist, he cannot but acknowledge the reasonableness of worshipping God. Grant him to be a spirit, and it will presently appear absurd to represent him by any corporeal image, and derogate from his excellency by so mean a resemblance; with the same easiness he will grant a reverence due to the name of God; that we must not serve our turn of him, by calling him to witness to a lie in a solemn oath; that as worship is due to him, so is some stated time a circumstance necessary to the performance of that worship. And as to the second table, will any man, in his right reason, quarrel with that command that engageth his inferiors to honor him, that secures his being from a violent murder, and his goods from unjust rapine? and though, by the fury of his lusts, he break the laws of wedlock himself, yet he cannot but approve of that law, as it prohibits every man from doing him the like injury and disgrace. The suitableness of the law to the consciences of men is further evidenced by those furious reflections, and strong alarms of conscience, upon a transgression of it, and that in all parts of the world, more or less, in all men; so exactly hath Divine wisdom fitted the law to the reason and consciences of men, as one tally to another: indeed, without such an agreement, no man's conscience could have any ground for a hue and cry; nor need any man be startled with the records of it. This manifests the wisdom of God in framing his laws so that the reasons and consciences of all men do, one time or other, subscribe to it. What governor in the world is able to make any law distinct from this revealed by God, that shall reach all places, all persons, all hearts? We may add to this the extent of his commands, in ordering goodness at the root, not only in action, but affection; not only in the motion of the members, but the disposition of the soul; which suiting a law to the inward frame of man, is quite out of the compass of the wisdom of any creature.

(4.) His wisdom is seen in the encouragements he gives for the studying and observing his will (Ps. xix. 11); "In keeping thy commandments there is great reward." The variety of them; there is not any particular genius in man but may find something suitable to win upon him in the revealed will of God. There is a strain of reason to satisfy the rational; of eloquence, to gratify the fanciful; of interest, to allure the selfish; of terror, to startle the obstinate. As a skilful angler stores himself with baits, according to the appetites of the sorts of fish he intends to catch, so in the word of God there are varieties of baits, according to the varieties of the inclinations of men; threatenings to work upon fear; promises to work upon love; examples of holy men set out for imitation; and those plainly; neither his threatenings nor his promises are dark, as the heathen oracles; but peremptory, as becomes a sovereign lawgiver; and plain, as was necessary for the understanding of a creature. As he deals graciously with men in exhorting and encouraging them, so he deals wisely herein, by taking away all excuse from them if they ruin the interest of their souls, by denying obedience to their Sovereign. Again, the rewards God proposeth are accommodated, not to the brutish parts of man, his carnal sense and fleshly appetite, but to the capacity of a spiritual soul, which admits only of spiritual gratifications; and cannot, in its own nature, without a sordid subjection to the humors of the body, be moved by sensual proposals. God backs his precepts with that which the nature of man longed for, and with spiritual delights, which can only satisfy a rational appetite; and thereby did as well gratify the noblest desires in man, as oblige him to the noblest service and work.[o] Indeed, virtue and holiness being perfectly amiable, ought chiefly to affect our understandings, and by them draw our wills to the esteem and pursuit of them. But since the desire of happiness is inseparable from the nature of man, as impossible to be disjoined as an inclination to descend to be severed from heavy bodies, or an instinct to ascend from light and airy substances; God serves himself of the inclination of our natures to happiness, to enjender in us an esteem and affection to the holiness he doth require. He proposeth the enjoyment of a supernatural good and everlasting glory, as a bait to that insatiable

[o] Amyraut.

longing our natures have for happiness, to receive the impression of holiness into our souls. And, besides, he doth proportion rewards according the degrees of men's industry, labor, and zeal for him; and weighs out a recompense, not only suited to, but above the service. He that improves five talents, is to be ruler over five cities; that is, a greater proportion of honor and glory than another (Luke xix. 17, 18); as a wise father excites the affection of his children to things worthy of praise, by varieties of recompenses according to their several actions. And it was the wisdom of the steward, in the judgment of our Saviour, to give every one the "portion that belonged to him" (Luke xii. 42). There is no part of the word wherein we meet not with the will and wisdom of God, varieties of duties, and varieties of encouragement, mingled together.

(5.) The wisdom of God is seen in fitting the revelations of his will to aftertimes, and for the preventing of the foreseen corruptions of men. The whole revelation of the mind of God is stored with wisdom in the words, connexion, sense; it looks backwards to past, and forwards to ages to come : a hidden wisdom lies in the bowels of it, like gold in a mine. The Old Testament was so composed, as to fortify the New, when God should bring it to light. The foundations of the gospel were laid in the law : the predictions of the Prophets, and figures of the law, were so wisely framed, and laid down in such clear expressions, as to be proofs of the authority of the New Testament, and convictions of Jesus' being the Messiah (Luke xxiv. 14). Things concerning Christ were written in Moses, the Prophets, and Psalms; and do, to this day, stare the Jews so in the face, that they are fain to invent absurd and nonsensical interpretations to excuse their unbelief, and continue themselves in their obstinate blindness. And in pursuance of the efficacy of those predictions, it was a part of the wisdom of God to bring forth the translation of the Old Testament, (by the means of Ptolomy, king of Egypt, some hundreds of years before the coming of Christ) into the Greek language, the tongue then most known in the world; and why? to prepare the Gentiles, by the reading of it, for that gracious call he intended them, and for the entertainment of the gospel, which some few years after was to be published among them; that, by reading the predictions so long before made, they might more readily receive the accomplishment of them in their due time. The Scripture is written in such a manner, as to obviate errors foreseen by God to enter into the church. It may be wondered, why the universal particle should be inserted by Christ, in the giving the cup in the supper, which was not in the distributing the bread (Matt. xxvi. 27): "Drink ye all of it;" not at the distributing the bread, "Eat you all of it;" and Mark, in his relation, tells us, "They all drank of it" (Mark xi. 23). The church of Rome hath been the occasion of discovering to us the wisdom of our Saviour, in inserting that particle *all*, since they were so bold to exclude the communicants from the cup by a trick of concomitancy. Christ foresaw the error, and therefore put in a little word to obviate a great invasion : and the Spirit of God hath particularly left upon record that particle, as we may reasonably suppose to such a purpose. And so, in the description of the " blessed Virgin" (Luke i. 27), there is nothing of her holiness mentioned, which is with much diligence recorded of Elizabeth (ver. 6) : " Righteous, walking in all the commandments of God, blameless ;" probably to prevent the superstition which God foresaw would arise in the world. And we do not find more under-valuing speeches uttered by Christ to any of his disciples, in the ex-ercise of his office, than to her, except to Peter. As when she ac-quainted him with the want of wine at the marriage in Cana, she re-ceives a slighting answer : " Woman, what have I to do with thee" (John ii. 4) ? And when one was admiring the blessedness of her that bare him, he turns the discourse another way, to pronounce a blessedness rather belonging to them that " hear the word of God, and keep it" (Luke xi. 27, 28) ; in a mighty wisdom to antidote his people against any conceit of the prevalency of the Virgin over him in heaven, in the exercise of his mediatory office.

2. As his wisdom appears in his government by his laws, so it ap-pears in the various inclinations and conditions of men. As there is a distinction of several creatures, and several qualities in them, for the common good of the world, so among men there are several in-clinations and several abilities, as donatives from God, for the com-mon advantage of human society ; as several channels cut out from the same river run several ways, and refresh several soils, one man is qualified for one employment, another marked out by God for a different work, yet all of them fruitful to bring in a revenue of glory to God, and a harvest of profit to the rest of mankind. How unuse-ful would the body be, if it had but " one member" (1 Cor. xii. 19) ! How unprovided would a house be, if it had not vessels of dishonor as well as of honor ! The corporation of mankind would be as much a chaos, as the matter of the heavens and the earth was, before it was distinguished by several forms breathed into it at the creation. Some are inspired with a particular genius for one art, some for another ; every man hath a distinct talent. If all were husband-men, where would be the instruments to plough and reap ? If all were artificers, where would they have corn to nourish themselves ? All men are like vessels, and parts in the body, designed for distinct offices and functions for the good of the whole, and mutually return an advantage to one another. As the variety of gifts in the church is a fruit of the wisdom of God, for the preservation and increase of the church, so the variety of inclinations and employments in the world is a fruit of the wisdom of God, for the preservation and sub-sistence of the world by mutual commerce. What the apostle large-ly discourseth of the former, in 1 Cor. xii. may be applied to the other. The various conditions of men is also a fruit of Divine wis-dom. Some are rich, and some poor ; the rich have as much need of the poor, as the poor have of the rich ; if the poor depend upon the rich for their livelihood, the rich depend upon the poor for their conveniences. Many arts would not be learned by men, if poverty did not oblige them to it ; and many would faint in the learning of them, if they were not thereunto encouraged by the rich. The poor labor for the rich, as the earth sends vapors into the vaster and fuller air ; and the rich return advantages again to the poor, as the clouds

do the vapors in rain upon the earth. As meat would not afford a nourishing juice without bread, and bread without other food would immoderately fill the stomach, and not be well digested, so the rich would be unprofitable in the commonwealth without the poor, and the poor would be burdensome to a commonwealth without the rich. The poor could not be easily governed without the rich, nor the rich sufficiently and conveniently provided for without the poor. If all were rich, there would be no objects for the exercise of a noble part of charity : if all were poor, there were no matter for the exercise of it. Thus the Divine wisdom planted various inclinations, and diversified the conditions of men for the public advantages of the world.

2dly. God's wisdom appears, in the government of men, as fallen and sinful ; or, in the government of sin. After the law of God was broke, and sin invaded and conquered the world, divine wisdom had another scene to act in, and other methods of government were necessary. The wisdom of God is then seen in ordering those jarring discords, drawing good out of evil, and honour to himself out of that which in its own nature tended to the supplanting of his glory. God being a sovereign good, would not suffer so great an evil to enter, but to serve himself of it for some greater end, for all his thoughts are full of goodness and wisdom. Now, though the permission of sin be an act of his sovereignty, and the punishment of sin be an act of his justice, yet the ordination of sin to good, is an act of his wisdom, whereby he doth dispose the evil, overrules the malice, and orders the events of it to his own purposes. Sin in itself is a disorder, and therefore God doth not permit sin for itself; for in its own nature it hath nothing of amiableness, but he wills it for some righteous end, which belongs to the manifestation of his glory, which is his aim in all the acts of his will ; he wills it not as sin, but as his wisdom can order it to some greater good than was before in the world, and make it contribute to the beauty of the order he intends. As a dark shadow is not delightful and pleasant in itself, nor is drawn by a painter for any amiableness there is in the shadow itself, but as it serves to set forth that beauty which is the main design of his art, so the glorious effects which arise from the entrance of sin into the world, are not from the creatures evil, but the depths of divine wisdom. Particularly,

1. God's wisdom is seen in the bounding of sin ; as it is said of the wrath of man, it shall praise him, and the remainder of wrath God doth restrain (Ps. lxxvi. 10). He sets limits to the boiling corruption of the heart, as he doth to the boisterous waves of the sea ; " Hitherto shalt thou go, and no further." As God is the rector of the world, he doth so restrain sin, so temper and direct it, as that human society is preserved, which else would be overflown with a deluge of wickedness, and ruin would be brought upon all communities. The world would be a shambles, a brothel-house, if God, by his wisdom and goodness, did not set bars to that wickedness which is in the hearts of men : the whole earth would be as bad as hell. Since the heart of man is a hell of corruption, by that the souls of all men would be excited to the acting the worst villanies ; since

"every thought of the heart of man is only evil, and that continually" (Gen. vi. 5). If the wisdom of God did not stop these floodgates of evil in the hearts of men, it would overflow the world, and frustrate all the gracious designs he carries on among the sons of men. Were it not for this wisdom, every house would be filled with violence, as well as every nature is with sin. What harm would not strong and furious beasts do, did not the skill of man tame and bridle them? How often hath Divine wisdom restrained the viciousness of human nature, and let it run, not to that point they designed, but to the end he purposed! Laban's fury, and Esau's enmity against Jacob, were pent in within bounds for Jacob's safety, and their hearts overruled from an intended destruction of the good man, to a perfect amity (Gen. xxxi. 29, and xxxii.)

2. God's wisdom is seen in the bringing glory to himself out of sin.

(1.) Out of sin itself. God erects the trophies of honor upon that which is a natural means to hinder and deface it. His glorious attributes are drawn out to our view, upon the occasion of sin, which otherwise had lain hid in his own Being. Sin is altogether black and abominable; but by the admirable wisdom of God, he hath drawn out of the dreadful darkness of sin the saving beams of his mercy, and displayed his grace in the incarnation and passion of his Son for the atonement of sin. Thus he permitted Adam's fall, and wisely ordered it, for a fuller discovery of his own nature, and a higher elevation of man's good, that "as sin reigned to death, so might grace reign through righteousness to eternal life, by Jesus Christ" (Rom. v. 21). The unbounded goodness of God could not have appeared without it. His goodness in rewarding innocent obedience would have been manifested; but not his mercy, in pardoning rebellious crimes. An innocent creature is the object of the rewards of grace, as the standing angels are under the beams of grace; but not under the beams of mercy, because they were never sinful, and, consequently, never miserable. Without sin the creature had not been miserable: had man remained innocent, he had not been the subject of punishment; and without the creature's misery, God's mercy in sending his Son to save his enemies, could not have appeared. The abundance of sin is a passive occasion for God to manifest the abundance of his grace. The power of God in the changing the heart of a rebellious creature, had not appeared, had not sin infected our nature. We had not clearly known the vindictive justice of God, had no crime been committed; for that is the proper object of Divine wrath. The goodness of God could never have permitted justice to exercise itself upon an innocent creature, that was not guilty either personally or by imputation (Ps. xi. 7), "The righteous Lord loveth righteousness, his countenance doth uphold the upright." Wisdom is illustrious hereby. God suffered man to fall into a mortal disease, to shew the virtue of his own restoratives to cure sin, which in itself is incurable by the art of any creature. And otherwise this perfection, whereby God draws good out of evil, had been utterly useless, and would have been destitute of an object wherein to discover itself. Again, wisdom, in ordering a rebellious head-strong world to its own ends, is greater than the ordering an innocent world, exactly observant of his precepts, and complying with the end of the creation. Now, without the entrance of sin, this wisdom had wanted a stage to act upon. Thus God raised the honor of this wisdom, while man ruined the integrity of his nature; and made use of the creature's breach of his divine law, to establish the honor of it in a more signal and stable manner, by the active and passive obedience of the Son of his bosom. Nothing serves God so much, as an occasion of glorifying himself, as the entrance of sin into the world; by this occasion God communicates to us the knowledge of those perfections of his nature, which had else been folded up from us in an eternal night; his justice had lain in the dark, as having nothing to punish; his mercy had been obscure, as having none to pardon; a great part of his wisdom had been silent, as having no such object to order.

(2.) His wisdom appears, in making use of sinful instruments. He uses the malice and enmity of the devil to bring about his own purposes, and makes the sworn enemy of his honor contribute to the illustrating of it against his will. This great craftsmaster he took in his own net, and defeated the devil by the devil's malice; by turning the contrivances he had hatched and accomplished against man, against himself. He used him as a tempter, to grapple with our Saviour in the wilderness, whereby to make him fit to succor us; and as the god of this world, to conspire the wicked Jews to crucify him, whereby to render him actually the Redeemer of the world, and so make him an ignorant instrument of that divine glory he designed to ruin. It is more skill to make a curious piece of workmanship with ill-conditioned tools, than with instruments naturally fitted for the work: it is no such great wonder for a limner to draw an exact piece with a fit pencil and suitable colors, as to begin and perfect a beautiful work with a straw and water, things improper for such a design.[p] This wisdom of God is more admirable and astonishing than if a man were able to rear a vast palace by fire, whose nature is to consume combustible matter not to erect a building. To make things serviceable contrary to their own nature, is a wisdom peculiar to the Creator of Nature. God's making use of devils, for the glory of his name, and the good of his people, is a more amazing piece of wisdom than his goodness in employing the blessed angels in his work. To promise, that the world, (which includes the god of the world), and death, and things present, let them be as evil as they will, should be ours, that is, for our good, and for his glory, is an act of goodness; but to make them serviceable to the honor of Christ, and the good of his people, is a wisdom that may well raise our highest admirations: they are for believers, as they are for the glory of Christ, and as Christ is for the glory of God (1 Cor. iii. 22). To chain up Satan wholly, and frustrate his wiles, would be an argument of Divine goodness; but to suffer him to run his risk, and then improve all his contrivances for his own glorious and gracious ends and purposes, manifests, besides his power and goodness, his wisdom also. He uses the sins of evil instruments for the glory of his justice (Isa. x. 5–7). Thus he served

p Moulin's Serm. decad. 10. p. 231, 232.

himself of the ambition and covetousness of the Assyrians, Chaldeans, and Romans, for the correction of his people, and punishment of his rebels, just as the Roman magistrates used the fury of lions and other wild beasts, in their theatres, for the punishment of criminals: the lions acted their natural temper in tearing those that were exposed to them for a prey; but the intent of the magistrates was to punish their crimes. The magistate inspired not the lions with their rage, that they had from their natures; but served themselves of that natural rage to execute justice.

(3.) God's wisdom is seen in bringing good to the creature out of sin. He hath ordered sin to such an end as man never dreamt of, the devil never imagined, and sin in its own nature could never attain. Sin in its own nature tends to no good, but that of punishment, whereby the creature is brought into order. It hath no relation to the creatures good in itself, but to the creature's mischief: but God, by an act of infinite wisdom, brings good out of it to the creature, as well as glory to his name, contrary to the nature of the crime, the intention of the criminal, and the design of the tempter. God willed sin, that is, he willed to permit it, that he might communicate himself to the creature in the most excellent manner. He willed the permission of sin, as an occasion to bring forth the mystery of the incarnation and passion of our Saviour; as he permitted the sin of Joseph's brethren, that he might use their evil to a good end. He never, because of his holiness, wills sin as an end; but in regard of his wisdom he wills to permit it as a means and occasion; and thus, to draw good out of those things which are in their own nature most contrary to good, is the highest pitch of wisdom.

[1.] The redemption of man in so excellent a way, was drawn from the occasion of sin. The greatest blessing that ever the world was blessed with, was ushered in by contraieties, by the lust and irregular affection of man; the first promise of the Redeemer by the fall of Adam (Gen. iii. 15), and the bruising the heel of that promised Seed, by the blackest tragedy acted by wicked rebels, the treachery of Judas, and the rage of the Jews; the highest good hath been brought forth by the greatest wickedness. As God out of the chaos of rude and indigested matter framed the first creation; so from the sins of men, and malice of Satan, he hath erected the everlasting scheme of honor in a new creation of all things by Jesus Christ. The devil inspired man, to content his own fury in the death of Christ; and God ordered it to accomplish his own design of redemption in the passion of the Redeemer; the devil had his diabolical ends, and God overpowers his actions to serve his own divine ends. The person that betrayed him was admitted to be a spectator of the most private actions of our Saviour, that his innocence might be justified; to shew, that he was not afraid to have his enemies judges of his most retired privacies. While they all thought to do their own wills, Divine wisdom orders them to do God's will (Acts ii. 23): "Him, being delivered by the determinate counsel and foreknowledge of God, you have taken, and by wicked hands have crucified and slain." And wherein the crucifiers of

Christ sinned, in shedding the richest blood, upon their repentance they found the expiation of their crimes, and the discovery of a superabundant mercy. Nothing but the blood was aimed at by them: the best blood was shed by them; but infinite Wisdom makes the cross the scene of his own righteousness, and the womb of man's recovery. By the occasion of man's lapsed state, there was a way open to raise man to a more excellent condition than that whereinto he was put by creation: and the depriving man of the happiness of an earthly paradise, in a way of justice, was an occasion of advancing him to a heavenly felicity, in a way of grace. The violation of the old covenant occasionally introduced a better: the loss of the first integrity ushered in a more stable righteousness, an everlasting righteousness (Dan. ix. 24). And the falling of the first head was succeeded by one whose standing could not but be eternal. The fall of the devil was ordered by infinite Wisdom, for the good of that body from which he fell. It is supposed by some, that the devil was the chief angel in heaven, the head of all the rest; and that he falling, the angels were left as a body without a head; and after he had politically beheaded the angels, he endeavored to destroy man, and rout him out of paradise; but God takes the opportunity to set up his Son, as the head of angels and men. And thus whilst the devil endeavored to spoil the corporation of angels, and make them a body contrary to God, God makes angels and men one body under one head, for his service. The angels in losing a defectible head, attained a more excellent and glorious Head in another nature, which they had not before; though of a lower nature in his humanity, yet of a more glorious nature in his divinity: from whence many suppose they derive their confirming grace, and the stability of their standing. "All things in heaven and earth are gathered together in Christ" (Eph i. 10), ἀνακεφαλαιώσασθαι, all united in him, and reduced under one head: that though our Saviour be not properly their Redeemer, for redemption supposeth captivity, yet in some sense he is their Head and Mediator: so that now the inhabitants of heaven and earth are but one family (Eph. iii. 15.) And the innumerable company of angels are parts of that heavenly and triumphant Jerusalem, and that general assembly, whereof Jesus Christ is Mediator (Heb. xii. 22, 29.)

[2.] The good of a nation often, by the skill of Divine wisdom, is promoted by the sins of some men. The patriarchs' selling Joseph to the Midianites (Gen. xxxvii. 28), was without question a sin, and a breach of natural affection; yet, by God's wise ordination, it proved the safety of the whole church of God in the world, as well as the Egyptian nation (Gen. xlv. 5, 8; l. 20.) The Jews' unbelief was a step whereby the Gentiles arose to the knowledge of the gospel; as the setting of the sun in one place is the rising of it in another (Matt. xxii. 9.) He uses the corruptions of men instrumentally to propogate his gospel: he built up the true church by the preaching of some out of envy (Phil. i. 15), as he blessed Israel out of the mouth of a false prophet (Numb. xxiii.) How often have the heresies of men been the occasion of clearing up the truth of God, and fixing the more lively impressions of it on the hearts of believers! Neither Judah nor Tamar, in their lust, dreamt of a stock for the Redeemer; yet God gave a son from that unlawful bed, whereof "Christ came according to the flesh" (Gen. xxxviii. 29, compared with Matt. i. 3.) Jonah's sin was probably the first and remote occasion of the Ninevites giving credit to his prophecy; his sin was the cause of his punishment, and his being flung into the sea might facilitate the reception of his message, and excite the Ninevites' repentance, whereby a cloud of severe judgment was blown away from them. It is thought by some, that when Jonah passed through the streets of Nineveh, with his proclamation of destruction, he might be known by some of the mariners of that ship, from whence he was cast overboard into the sea, and might, after their voyage, be occasionally in that city, the metropolis of the nation, and the place of some of their births; and might acquaint the people, that this was the same person they had cast into the sea, by his own consent, for his acknowledged running from the presence of the Lord: for that he had told them (Jonah i. 10); and the mariner's prayer (ver. 14) evidenced it; whereupon they might conclude his message worthy of belief, since they knew from such evidences, that he had sunk into the bowels of the waters, and now saw him safe in their streets, by a deliverence unknown to them; and that therefore that power that delivered him, could easily verify his word in the threatened judgment. Had Jonah gone at first, without committing that sin, and receiving that punishment, his message had not been judged a divine prediction, but a fruit of some enthusiastic madness; his sin upon this account was the first occasion of averting a judgment from so great a city.

[3.] The good of the sinner himself is sometimes promoted by Divine wisdom ordering the sin. As God had not permitted sin to enter upon the world, unless to bring glory to himself by it; so he would not let sin remain in the little world of a believer's heart, if he did not intend to order it for his good. What is done by man, to his damage and disparagement, is directed by Divine wisdom to his advantage; not that it is the intent of the sin, or the sinner; but it is the event of the sin, by the ordination of Divine wisdom and grace. As without the wisdom of God permitting sin to enter into the world, some attributes of God had not been experimentally known, so some graces could not have been exercised; for where had there been an object for that noble zeal, in vindicating the glory of God, had it not been invaded by an enemy? The intenseness of love to him could not have been so strong, had we not an enemy to hate for his sake. Where had there been any place for that noble part of charity in holy admonitions and compassion to the souls of our neighbors, and endeavors to reduce them out of a destructive, to a happy path? Humility would not have had so many grounds for its growth and exercise, and holy sorrow had no fuel. And as without the appearance of sin there had been no exercise of the patience of God, so without afflictions, the fruits of sin, there had been no ground for the exercise of the patience of a christian, one of the noblest parts of valor. Now sin being evil, and such as cannot but be evil, hath no respect in itself to any good, and cannot work a gracious end, or anything profitable to the creature; nay it is a hindrance to any good, and, therefore, what good comes from it, is accidental; occasioned, indeed, by sin, but efficiently caused by the over-ruling wisdom of God, taking occasion thereby to display itself and the Divine goodness.

1. The sins and corruptions remaining in the heart of man, God orders for good; and there are good effects by the direction of his wisdom and grace, as the soul respects God.

(1.) God often brings forth a sensibleness of the necessity of dependence on him. The nurse often lets the child slip, that it may the better know who supports it, and may not be too venturous and confident of its own strength. Peter would trust in habitual grace, and God suffers him to fall, that he might trust more in assisting grace (Matt. xxvi. 35): "Though I should die with thee, yet I will not deny thee." God leaves sometimes the brightest souls in eclipse, to manifest that their holiness, and the preservation of it, depend upon the darting out his beams upon them. As the falls of men are the effects of their coldness and remissness in acts of faith and repentance, so the fruit of these falls is often a running to him for refuge, and a deeper sensibleness where their security lies. It makes us lower our swelling sails, and come under the lee and protection of Divine grace. When the pleasures of sin answer not the expectations of a revolted creature, he reflects upon his former state, and sticks more close to God, when before God had little of his company (Hos. ii. 7): "I will return to my first husband, for then it was better with me than now." As God makes the sins of men sometimes an occasion of their conversion, so he sometimes makes them an occasion of a further conversion. Onesimus run from Philemon, and was met with by Paul, who proved an instrument of his conversion (Philem. 10.): "My son, Onesimus, whom I have begotten in my bonds." His flight from his master was the occasion of his regeneration by Paul, a prisoner. The falls of believers God orders to their further stability; he that is fallen for want of using his staff, will lean more upon it to preserve himself from the like disaster. God, by permitting the lapses of men, doth often make them despair of their own strength to subdue their enemies, and rely upon the strength of Christ, wherein God hath laid up power for us, and so becomes stronger in that strength which God hath ordained for them. We are very apt to trust in ourselves, and have confidence in our own worth and strength; and God lets loose corruptions to abate this swelling humor. This was the reason of the apostle Paul's "thorn in the flesh" (2 Cor. xii. 7); whether it were a temptation, or corruption, or sickness, that he might be sensible of his own inability, and where the sufficiency of grace for him was placed. He that is in danger of drowning, and hath the waves come over his head, will, with all the might he hath, lay hold upon anything near him, which is capable to save him. God lets his people sometimes sink into such a condition, that they may lay the faster hold on him who is near to all that call upon him.

(2.) God hereby raiseth higher estimations of the value and virtue of the blood of Christ. As the great reason why God permitted sin to enter into the world, was to honor himself in the Redeemer, so the continuance of sin, and the conquests it sometimes makes in renewed men, are to honor the infinite value and virtue of the Redeemer's merit, which God, from the beginning, intended to magnify: the value of it, in taking off so much successive guilt; and the virtue of it, in washing away so much daily filth. The wisdom of God hereby keeps up the credit of imputed righteousness, and manifests the immense treasure of the Redeemer's merit to pay such daily debts. Were we perfectly sanctified, we should stand upon our own bottom, and imagine no need of the continual and repeated imputation of the righteousness of Christ for our justification: we should confide in inherent righteousness, and slight imputed. If God should take off all remainders of sin, as well as the guilt of it, we should be apt to forget that we are fallen creatures, and that we had a Redeemer; but the relics of sin in us mind us of the necessity of some higher strength to set us right: they mind us both of our own misery, and the Redeemer's perpetual benefit. God, by this, keeps up the dignity and honor of our Saviour's blood to the height, and therefore sometimes lets us see, to our own cost, what filth yet remains in us for the employment of that blood, which we should else but little think of, and less admire. Our gratitude is so small to God as well as man, that the first obligations are soon forgot if we stand not in need of fresh ones successively to second them; we should lose our thankful remembrance of the first virtue of Christ's blood in washing us, if our infirmities did not mind us of fresh reiterations and applications of it. Our Saviour's office of advocacy was erected especially for sins committed after a justified and renewed state (1 John ii. 1). We should scarce remember we had an Advocate, and scarce make use of him without some sensible necessity; but our remainders of sin discover our impotency, and an impossibility for us either to expiate our sin, or conform to the law, which necessitates us to have recourse to that person whom God hath appointed to make up the breaches between God and us. So the apostle wraps up himself in the covenant of grace and his interest in Christ, after his conflict with sin (Rom. vii. *ult.*), " I thank God, through Jesus Christ." Now, after such a body of death, a principle within me that sends up daily steams, yet as long as I serve God with my mind, as long as I keep the main condition of the covenant, " there is no condemnation" (Rom. viii. 1): Christ takes my part, procures my acceptance, and holds the band of salvation firm in his hands. The brightness of Christ's grace is set off by the darkness of our sin. We should not understand the sovereignty of his medicines, if there were no relics of sin for him to exercise his skill upon: the physician's art is most experimented, and therefore most valued in relapses, as dangerous as the former disease. As the wisdom of God brought our Saviour into temptation, that he might have compassion to us, so it permits us to be overcome by temptation, that we might have due valuations of him.

(3.) God hereby often engageth the soul to a greater industry for his glory. The highest persecutors, when they have become converts have been the greatest champions for that cause they both hated and oppressed. The apostle Paul is such an instance of this, that it needs no enlargement. By how much they have failed of answering the end of their creation in glorifying God, by so much the more they summon up all their force for such an end, after their conversion; to restore as much as they can of that glory to God, which they, by their sin, had robbed him of. Their sins, by the order of Divine wisdom, prove whetstones to sharpen the edge of their spirits for God. Paul never remembered his persecuting fury, but he doubled his industry for the service of God, which before he trampled under his feet. The further we go back, the greater leap many times we take forward. Our Saviour, after his resurrection, put Peter upon the exercise of that love to him, which had so lately shrunk his head out of suffering (John xxi. 15-17); and no doubt, but the consideration of his base denial, together with a reflection upon a gracious pardon, engaged his ingenuous soul to stronger and fiercer flames of affection. A believer's courage for God is more sharpened oftentimes by the shame of his fall: he endeavors to repair the faults of his ingratitude and his disingenuity by larger and stronger steps of obedience; as a man in a fight, having been foiled by his enemy, reassumes new courage by his fall, and is many times obliged to his foil, both for his spirit and his victory. A gracious heart will, upon the very motions to sin, double its vigor, as well as by good ones: it is usually more quickened, both in its motion to God and for God, by the temptations and motions to sin which run upon it. This is another good the wisdom of God brings forth from sin.

(4.) Again, humility towards God is another good Divine wisdom brings forth from the occasion of sin. By this God beats down all good opinion of ourselves. Hezekiah was more humbled by his fall into pride, than by all the distress he had been in by Sennacherib's army (2 Chron. xxxii. 26). Peter's confidence before his fall, gave way to an humble modesty after it; you see his confidence (Mark xiv. 24). "Though all should be offended in thee, yet will not I;" and you have the mark of his modesty (John xxi. 17). It is not then, Lord, I will love thee to the death, I will not start from thee; but, "Lord, thou knowest that I love thee:" I cannot assure myself of anything after this miscarriage; but, Lord, thou knowest there is a principle of love in me to thy name. He was ashamed, that himself who appeared such a pillar, should bend as meanly as a shrub to a temptation. The reflection upon sin lays a man as low as hell in his humiliation, as the commission of sin did in the merit. When David comes to exercise repentance for his sin, he begins it from the well-head of sin (Ps. li. 5), his original corruption, and draws down the streams of it to the last commission; perhaps he did not so seriously humble himself for the sin of his nature all his days, so much as at that time; at least, we have not such evidences of it. And Hezekiah humbled himself for the pride of his heart; not only for the pride of his act (2 Chron. xxxii. 26), but for the pride in the heart, which was the spring of that pride in act, in showing his treasures to the Babylonish ambassadors. God lets sin continue in the hearts of the best in this world, and sometimes gives the reins to Satan, and a man's own corruption, to keep up a sense of the ancient sale we made of ourselves to both.

2. In regard of ourselves. Herein is the wonder of Divine wisdom, that God many times makes a sin, which meritoriously fits us for hell, a providential occasion to fit us for heaven; when it is an occasion of a more humble faith and believing humility, and an occasion of a thorough sanctification and growth in grace, which prepares us for a state of glory.

(1.) He makes use of one sin's breaking out to discover more; and so brings us to a self-abhorrency and indignation against sin, the first step towards heaven. Perhaps David, before his gross fall, thought he had no hypocrisy in him. We often find him appealing to God for his integrity, and desiring God to try him, if any guile could be found in his heart, as if he could find none himself; but his lapse into that great wickedness makes him discern much falseness in his soul, when he desires God to renew a right spirit within him, and speaks of truth in the inward parts (Ps. li. 6, 10). The stirring of corruption makes all the mud at the bottom appear, which oefore a soul did not suspect. No man would think there were so great a cloud of smoke contained in a little stick of wood, were it not for the powerful operation of the fire, that both discovers and separates it. Job, that cursed the day of his birth, and uttered many impatient expressions against God upon the account of his own integrity; upon his recovery from his affliction, and God's close application of himself, was wrought to a greater abhorrency of himself than ever we read he was exercised in before (Job xlii. 6). The hostile acts of sin increase the soul's hatred of it; and the deeper our humiliations are for it, the stronger impressions of abhorrency are made upon us.

(2.) He often orders it, to make conscience more tender, and the soul more watchful. He that finds by his calamity his enemy to have more strength against him than he suspected, will double his guards, and quicken his diligence against him. A being overtaken by some sin, is, by the wisdom of God, disposed to make us more fearful of cherishing any occasion to inflame it, and watchful against every motion and start of it. By a fall, the soul hath more experience of the deceitfulness of the heart; and by observing its methods, is rendered better able to watch against them. It is our ignorance of the devices of Satan, and our own hearts, that makes us obnoxious to their surprises. A fall into one sin is often a prevention of more which lay in wait for us; as the fall of a small body into an ambush prevents the design of the enemy upon a greater: as God suffers heresies in the church, to try our faith, so he suffers sins to remain, and sometimes to break out, to try our watchfulness. This advantage he brings from them, to steel our resolutions against the same sins, and quicken our circumspection for the future against new surprises by a temptation. David's sin was ever before him (Ps. li. 3), and made his conscience cry, Blood, blood! upon every occasion: he refused the water of the well of Bethlehem (2 Sam. xxiii. 16, 17), because it was gained with the hazard of lives: he could endure nothing that had the taste of blood in it. Our fear of a thing depends much upon a trial of it : a child will not fear too near approaches to the fire till he feels the smart of it. Mortification doth not wholly suppress the motions of sin, though it doth the resolutions to commit it; but that there will be a proneness in the relics of it, to entice a man into those faults, which, upon sight of their blemishes, cost him so many tears; as great sicknesses, after the cure, are more watched, and the body humored, that a man might not fall from the craziness they have left in him, which he is apt to do if relapses are not provided against. A man becomes more careful of anything that may contribute to the resurrection of an expired disease.

(3.) God makes it an occasion of the mortification of that sin which was the matter of the fall. The liveliness of one sin, in a renewed man, many times is the occasion of the death of it. A wild beast, while kept close in a den, is secure in its life, but when it breaks out to rapine, it makes the master resolve to prevent any further mischief by the death of it. The impetuous stirring of a humor, in a disease, is sometimes critical, and a prognostic of the strength of nature against it, whereby the disease loses its strength, by its struggling, and makes room for health to take place by degrees. One sin is used by God for the destruction both of itself and others, as the flesh of a scorpion cures the biting of it. It sometimes, by wounding us, loseth its sting, and, like the bee, renders itself incapable of a second revenge. Peter, after his gross denial, never denied his Master afterwards. The sin that lay undiscovered, is, by a fall, become visible, and so more obvious to a mortifying stroke. The soul lays the faster hold on Christ and the promise, and goes out against that enemy, in the name of that Lord of Hosts, of which he was too negligent before ; and, therefore, as he proves more strong, so more successful : he hath more strength, because he hath less confidence in himself, and more in God, the prime strength of his soul. As it was with Christ, so it is with us; while the devil was bruising his heel, he was bruising his head ; and while the devil is bruising our heel, the God of peace and wisdom is sometimes bruising his head, both in us and for us, so that the strugglings of sin are often as the faint groans or bitings of a beast that is ready to expire. It is just with a man, sometimes, as with a running fountain that hath mud at the bottom, when it is stirred the mud tinctures and defiles it all over ; yet some of that mud hath a vent with the streams which run from it, so that, when it is re-settled at the bottom, it is not so much in quantity as it was before. God, by his wisdom, weakens the sin by permitting it to stir and defile.

(4.) Sometimes Divine wisdom makes it an occasion to promote a sanctification in all parts of the soul. As the working of one illhumor in the body is an occasion of cashiering, not only that, but the rest, by a sound purge ; as a man, that is a little cold, doth not think of the fire, but if he slips with one foot into an icy puddle, he hastens to the fire, whereby not only that part, but all the rest receive a warmth and strength upon that occasion ; or, as if a person fall into the mire, his clothes are washed, and by that means cleansed, not only from the filth at present contracted, but from the former spots that were before unregarded. God, by his wisdom, brings secret sins to a discovery, and thereby cleanseth the soul of them. David's fall might be ordered as an answer to his former petition (Ps. xix. 12): "Cleanse thou me from my secret sins;" and as he did earnestly pray after his fall, so no doubt but he endeavored a thorough sanctification (Ps. li. 7); "Purge me, wash me;" and that he meant not only a sanctification from that single sin, but from all, root and branch, is evident by that complaint of the flaw in his nature (ver. 5): the dross and chaff which lies in the heart is hereby discovered, and an opportunity administered of throwing it out, and searching all the corners of the heart to discover where it lay. As God sometimes takes occasion from one sin to reckon with men, in a way of justice, for others, so he sometimes takes occasion, from the commission of one sin, to bring out all the actions against the sinner, to make him, in a way of gracious wisdom, set more cordially upon the work of sanctification. A great fall sometimes hath been the occasion of a man's conversion. The fall of mankind occasioned a more blessed restoration; and the falls of particular believers ofttimes occasion a more extensive sanctification. Thus the only wise God makes poisons in nature to become medicines in a way of grace and wisdom.

(5.) Hereby the growth in grace is furthered. It is a wonder of Divine wisdom, to subtract sometimes grace from a person, and let him fall into sin, thereby to occasion the increase of habitual grace in him, and to augment it by those ways that seemed to depress it. By making sins an occasion of a more vigorous acting, the contrary grace, the wisdom of God, makes our corruptions, in their own nature destructive, to become profitable to us. Grace often breaks out more strongly afterwards, as the sun doth with its heat, after it hath been masked and interrupted with a mist: they often, through the mighty working of the Spirit, make us more humble, and "humility fits us to receive more grace from God" (James iv. 6). How doth faith, that sunk under the waves, lift up its head again, and carry the soul out with a greater liveliness! What ardors of love, what floods of repenting tears, what severity of revenge, what horrors at the remembrance of the sin, what tremblings at the appearance of a second temptation! so that grace seems to be awakened to a new and more vigorous life (2 Cor. vii. 11). The broken joint is many times stronger in the rupture than it was before. The luxuriancy of the branches of corruption is an occasion of purging, and purging is with a design to make grace more fruitful (John xv. 2); "He purgeth it, that it may bring forth more fruit." Thus Divine wisdom doth both sharpen and brighten us by the dust of sin, and ripen and mellow the fruits of grace by the dung of corruption. Grace grows the stronger by opposition, as the fire burns hottest and clearest when it is most surrounded by a cold air; and our natural heat reassumes a new strength by the coldness of the winter. The foil under a diamond, though an imperfection in itself, increaseth the beauty and lustre of the stone. The enmity of man was a commendation of the grace of God: it occasioned the breaking out of the grace of God upon us; and is an occasion, by the wisdom and grace of God, of the increase of grace many times in us. How should the consideration of God's incomprehensible wisdom, in the management of evil, swallow us up in admiration! who brings forth such beauty, such eminent discoveries of himself, such excellent good to the creature, out of the bowels of the greatest contrarieties, making dark shadows serve to display and beautify, to our apprehensions, the Divine glory! If evil were not in the world, men would not know what good is; they would not behold the lustre of Divine wisdom, as without night we could not understand the beauty of the day. Though God is not the author of sin, because of his holiness, yet he is the administrator of sin by his wisdom, and accomplisheth his own purposes, by the iniquities of his enemies, and the lapses and infirmities of his friends. Thus much for the second, the government of man in his lapsed state, and the government of sin, wherein the wisdom of God doth wonderfully appear.

3dly. The wisdom of God appears in the government of man in his conversion and return to him. If there be a counsel in framing the lowest creature, and in the minutest passages of providence, there must needs be a higher wisdom in the government of the creature to a supernatural end, and framing the soul to be a monument of his glory. The wisdom of God is seen with more admirations, and in more varieties, by the angels, in the church than in the creation (Eph. iii. 10); that is, in forming a church out of the rubbish of the world, out of contrarieties and contradictions to him, which is greater than the framing a celestial and elementary world out of a rude chaos. The most glorious bodies in the world, even those of the sun, moon, and stars, have not such stamps of Divine skill upon them as the soul of man; nor is there so much of wisdom in the fabric and faculties of that, as in the reduction of a blind, wilful, rebellious soul, to its own happiness, and God's glory (Eph. i. 11. 12); "He worketh all things according to the counsel of his own will, that we should be for the praise of his glory." If all things, then this, which is none of the least of his works; to the praise of the glory of his goodness in his work, and to the praise of the rule of his work, his counsel, in both the act of his will, and the act of his wisdom. The restoring of the beauty of the soul, and its fitness for its true end, speaks no less wisdom than the first draught of it in creation: and the application of redemption, and bringing forth the fruits of it, is as well an act of his prudence, as the contrivance was of his counsel. Divine wisdom appears,

1. In the subjects of conversion. His goodness reigns in the very dust, and he erects the walls and ornaments of his temple from the clay and mud of the world. He passes over the wise, and noble, and mighty, that may pretend some grounds of boasting in their own natural or acquired endowments; and pitches upon the most contemptible materials, wherewith to build a spiritual tabernacle for himself (1 Cor. i. 26, 27), "the foolish, and weak things of the world;" those that are naturally most unfit for it, and most refractory to it. Herein lies the skill of an architect, to render the most knotty,

crooked, and inform pieces, by his art, subservient to his main pur
pose and design. Thus God hath ordered, from the beginning of
the world, contrary tempers, various humors, diverse nations, as
stones of several natures, to be a building for himself, fitly framed
together, and to be his own family (1 Cor. iii. 9). Who will question
the skill that alters a black jet into a clear crystal, a glow-worm into
a star, a lion into a lamb, and a swine into a dove? The more intricate and knotty any business is, the more eminent is any man's
ability and prudence, in untying the knots and bringing it to a good
issue. The more desperate the disease, the more admirable is the
physician's skill in the cure. He pitches upon men for his service,
who have natural dispositions to serve him in such ways as he disposeth of them, after their conversion : so Paul was naturally a conscientious man ; what he did against Christ was from the dictates of
an erroneous conscience, soaked in the Pharisaical interpretations of
the Jewish law : he had a strain of zeal to prosecute what his depraved reason and conscience did inform him in. God pitches upon
this man, and works him in the fire for his service. He alters not
his natural disposition, to make him of a constitution and temper
contrary to what he was before; but directs it to another object,
claps in another bias into the bowl, and makes his ill-governed dispositions move in a new way of his own appointment, and guides
that natural heat to the service of that interest which he was before
ambitious to extirpate ; as a high-mettled horse, when left to himself, creates both disturbance and danger, but under the conduct of
a wise rider, moves regularly ; not by a change of his natural fierceness, but a skilful management of the beast to the rider's purpose.

2. In the means of conversion. The prudence of man consists in
the timing the executions of his counsels ; and no less doth the wisdom of God consist in this. As he is a God of judgment or wisdom,
he waits to introduce his grace into the soul in the fittest season.
This attribute, Paul, in the story of his own conversion, puts a particular remark upon, which he doth not upon any other; in that
catalogue he reckons up (1 Tim. i. 17), "Now, unto the King eternal,
immortal, invisible, the only wise God, be honor and glory, for ever
and ever. Amen." A most solemn doxology, wherein wisdom sits
upon the throne above all the rest, with a special Amen to the glory
of it, which refers to the timing of his mercy so to Paul, as made
most for the glory of his grace, and the encouragement of others
from him as the pattern. God took him at a time when he was upon
the brink of hell ; when he was ready to devour the new-born infant church at Damascus ; when he was armed with all the authority
from without, and fired with all the zeal from within, for the prosecution of his design : then God seizeth upon him, and runs him in a
channel for his own honor, and his creatures' happiness. It is ob-
servableq how God set his eye upon Paul all along in his furious
course, and lets him have the reins, without putting out his hand to
bridle him ; yet no motion he could take, but the eye of God runs
along with him : he suffered him to kick against the pricks of miracles, and the convincing discourse of Stephen at his martyrdom.

q Which I have upon another occasion noted.

There were many that voted for Stephen's death, as the witnesses that flung the stones first at him; but they are not named, only Saul, who testified his approbation as well as the rest, and that by watching the witnesses' clothes while they were about that bloody work (Acts vii. 58); "the witnesses laid their clothes at a young man's feet, named Saul." Again, though multitudes were consenting to his death, yet (Acts viii. 1) Saul only is mentioned. God's eye is upon him, yet he would not at that time stop his fury. He goes on further, and makes "havoc of the church" (Acts viii. 3.) He had surely many more complices, but none are named (as if none regarded with any design of grace) but Saul: yet God would not reach out his hand to change him, but eyes him, waiting for a fitter opportunity, which in his wisdom he did foresee. And, therefore (Acts ix. 1) the Spirit of God adds a *yet;* "Saul yet breathing out threatenings." It was not God's time yet, but it would be shortly. But, when Saul was putting in execution his design against the church of Damascus, when the devil was at the top of his hopes, and Saul in the height of his fury, and the Christians sunk into the depth of their fears, the wisdom of God lays hold of the opportunity, and by Paul's conversion at this season, defeats the devil, disappoints the high priests, shields his people, discharges their fears, by pulling Saul out of the devil's hands, and forming Satan's instruments to a holy activity against him.

3. The wisdom of God appears in the manner of conversion. So great a change God makes, not by a destruction, but with a preservation of, and suitableness to nature. As the devil tempts us, not by offering violence to our natures, but by proposing things convenient to our corrupt natures, so doth God solicit us to a return by proposals suited to our faculties. As he doth in nature convey nourishment to men, by means of the fruits of the earth, and produceth the fruits of the earth by the influences of heaven; the influences of heaven do not force the earth, but excite that natural virtue and strength which is in it. So God produceth grace in the soul by the means of the word, fitted to the capacity of man, as man, and proportioned to his rational faculties, as rational. It would be contrary to the wisdom of God to move man like a stone, to invert the order and privilege of that nature which he settled in creation; for then God would in vain have given man understanding and will: because, without moving man according to those faculties, they would remain unprofitable and unuseful in man.[r] God doth not reduce us to himself, as logs, by a mere force, or as slaves forced by a cudgel, to go forth to that place, and do that work which they have no stomach to : but he doth accommodate himself to those foundations he hath laid in our nature, and guides us in a way agreeable thereunto, by an action as sweet as powerful; clearing our understandings of dark principles, whereby we may see his truth, our own misery, and the seat of our happiness; and bending our wills according to this light, to desire and move conveniently to this end of our calling; efficaciously, yet agreeably; powerfully, yet without imposing on our natural faculties; sweetly, without violence, in ordering the

means; but effectually, without failing, in accomplishing the end.[s] And therefore the Scripture calleth it, teaching (John vi. 45), alluring (Hos. ii. 15), calling us to seek the Lord (Ps. xxvii. 8). Teaching is an act of wisdom; alluring, an act of love; calling, an act of authority: but none of them argue a violent constraint. The principle that moves the will is supernatural; but the will, as a natural faculty, concurs in the act or motion. God doth not act in this in a way of absolute power, without an infinite wisdom, suiting himself to the nature of the things he acts upon: he doth not change the physical nature, though he doth the moral. As in the government of the world, he doth not make heavy things ascend, nor light things descend, ordinarily, but guides their motions according to their natural qualities: so God doth not strain the faculties beyond their due pitch. He lets the nature of the faculty remain, but changes the principle in it: the understanding remains understanding, and the will remains will. But where there was before folly in the understanding, he puts in a spirit of wisdom; and where there was before a stoutness in the will, he forms it to a pliableness to his offers. He hath a key to fit every ward in the lock, and opens the will without injuring the nature of the will. He doth not change the soul by an alteration of the faculties, but by an alteration of something in them: not by an inroad upon them, or by mere power, or a blind instinct, but by proposing to the understanding something to be known, and informing it of the reasonableness of his precepts, and the innate goodness and excellency of his offers, and by inclining the will to love and embrace what is proposed. And things are proposed under those notions, which usually move our wills and affections. We are moved by things as they are good, pleasant, profitable; we entertain things as they make for us, and detest things as they are contrary to us. Nothing affects us but under such qualities, and God suits his encouragements to these natural affections which are in us: his power and wisdom go hand in hand together; his power to act what his wisdom orders, and his wisdom to conduct what his power executes. He brings men to him in ways suited to their natural dispositions. The stubborn he tears like a lion, the gentle he wins like a turtle, by sweetness; he hath a hammer to break the stout, and a cord of love to draw the more pliable tempers: he works upon the more rational in a way of gospel reason; upon the more ingenuous in a way of kindness, and draws them by the cords of love. The wise men were led to Christ by a star, and means suited to the knowledge and study that those eastern nations used, which was much in astronomy: he worketh upon others by miracles accommodated to every one's sense, and so proportions the means according to the nature of the subjects he works upon.

4. The wisdom of God is apparent in his discipline and penal evils. The wisdom of human governments is seen in the matter of their laws, and in the penalties of their laws, and in the proportion of the punishment to the offence, and in the good that redounds from the punishment either to the offender, or to the community. The wisdom of God is seen in the penalty of death upon the transgression

[s] Sanderson, Part II. p. 205.

of his law; both in that it was the greatest evil that man might fear, and so was a convenient means to keep him in his due bound, and also in the proportion of it to the transgression. Nothing less could be in a wise justice inflicted upon an offender for a crime against the highest Being and the Supreme Excellency: but this hath been spoken of before in the wisdom of his laws. I shall only mention some few; it would be too tedious to run into all.

(1.) His wisdom appears in judgments, in the suiting them to the qualities of persons, and nature of sins. He deviseth evil (Jer. xviii. 11); his judgments are fruits of counsel. "He also is wise, and will bring evil" (Isa. xxxi. 2),—evil suitable to the person offending, and evil suitable to the offence committed: as the husbandman doth his threshing instruments to the grain: he hath a rod for the cummin, a tenderer seed, and a flail for the harder; so hath God greater judgments for the obdurate sinner, and lighter for those that have something of tenderness in their wickedness (Isa. xxviii. 27, 29): "Because he is wonderful in counsel and excellent in working;" so some understand the place, " With the froward, he will show himself froward." He proportions punishment to the sin, and writes the cause of the judgment in the forehead of the judgment itself. Sodom burned in lust, and was consumed by fire from heaven. The Jews sold Christ for thirty pence; and at the taking of Jerusalem, thirty of them were sold for a penny. So Adonibezek cut off the thumbs and great toes of others, and he is served in the same kind (Judges i. 7). The Babel builders designed an indissoluble union, and God brings upon them an unintelligible confusion. And in Exod. ix. 9, the ashes of the furnace where the Israelites burnt the Egyptian bricks, sprinkled towards heaven, brought boils upon the Egyptian bodies, that they might feel in their own, what pain they had caused in the Israelites' flesh; and find, by the smart of the inflamed scab, what they had made the Israelites endure. The waters of the river Nilus are turned into blood, wherein they had stifled the breath of the Israelites' infants: and at last the prince, and the flower of their nobility, are drowned in the Red Sea. It is part of the wisdom of justice to proportion punishment to the crime, and the degrees of wrath to the degrees of malice in the sin. Afflictions also are wisely proportioned: God, as a wise physician, considers the nature of the humor and strength of the patient, and suits his medicines both to the one and the other (1 Cor. x. 13).

(2.) In the seasons of punishments and afflictions. He stays till sin be ripe, that his justice may appear more equitable, and the offender more inexcusable (Dan. ix. 14); he watches upon the evil to bring it upon men; to bring it in the just season and order for his righteous and gracious purpose; his righteous purpose on the enemies, and his gracious purpose on his people. Jerusalem's calamity came upon them, when the city was full of people at the solemnity of the passover, that he might mow down his enemies at once, and time their destruction to such a moment wherein they had timed the crucifixion of his Son. He watched over the clouds of his judgments, and kept them from pouring down, till his people, the Christians, were provided for, and had departed out of the city to the chambers and retiring places God had provided for them. He made not Jerusalem the shambles of his enemies, till he had made Pella, and other places, the arks of his friends. As Pliny tells us, "The providence of God holds the sea in a calm for fifteen days, that the halcyons, little birds that frequent the shore, may build their nests, and hatch up their young." The judgment upon Sodom was suspended for some hours, till Lot was secured. God suffered not the church to be invaded by violent persecutions, till she was established in the faith: he would not expose her to so great combats, while she was weak and feeble, but gave her time to fortify herself, to be rendered more capable of bearing up under them.[t] He stifled all the motions of passion the idolaters might have for their superstition, till religion was in such a condition, as rather to be increased and purified, than extinguished by opposition. Paul was secured from Nero's chains, and the nets of his enemies, till he had broke off the chain of the devil from many cities of the Gentiles, and catched them by the net of the gospel out of the sea of the world. Thus the wisdom of God is seen in the seasons of judgments and afflictions.

(3.) It is apparent in the gracious issue of afflictions and penal evils. It is a part of wisdom to bring good out of evil of punishment, as well as to bring good out of sin. The church never was so like to heaven, as when it was most persecuted by hell: the storms often cleansed it and the lance often made it more healthful. Job's integrity had not been so clear, nor his patience so illustrious, had not the devil been permitted to afflict him. God, by his wisdom, outwits Satan; when he by his temptations intends to pollute us and buffet us, God orders it to purify us; he often brings the clearest light out of the thickest darkness, makes poisons to become medicines. Death itself, the greatest punishment in this life, and the entrance into hell in its own nature, he hath by his wise contrivance, made to his people the gate of heaven, and the passage into immortality.[u] Penal evils in a nation often end in a public advantage: troubles and wars among a people are many times not destroying, but medicinal, and cure them of that degeneracy, luxury, and effeminateness, they contracted by a long peace.

(4.) This wisdom is evident in the various ends which God brings about by afflictions. The attainment of various ends by one and the same means, is the fruit of the agent's prudence. By the same affliction, the wise God corrects sometimes for some base affection, excites some sleepy grace, drives out some lurking corruption, refines the soul, and ruins the lust; discovers the greatness of a crime, the vanity of the creature, and the sufficiency in himself. The Jews bind Paul, and by the judge he is sent to Rome; while his mouth is stopped in Judea, it is opened in one of the greatest cities of the world, and his enemies unwittingly contribute to the increase of the knowledge of Christ by those chains, in that city (Acts xxviii. 31) that triumphed over the earth. And his afflictive bonds added courage and resolution to others (Phil. i. 14): "Many waxing confident by my bonds;" which could not in their own nature produce such an effect, but by the order and contrivance of Divine wisdom:

[t] Daille sur 1 Cor. x. p. 390.   [u] Turretin, Serm. p. 53.

in their own nature, they would rather make them disgust the doctrine he suffered for, and cool their zeal in the propagating of it, for fear of the same disgrace and hardship they saw him suffer.[x] But the wisdom of God changed the nature of these fetters, and conducted them to the glory of his name, the encouragement of others, the increase of the gospel, and the comfort of the apostle himself (Phil. i. 12, 13, 18). The sufferings of Paul at Rome confirmed the Philippians, a people at a distance from thence, in the doctrine they had already received at his hands. Thus God makes sufferings sometimes, which appear like judgments, to be like the viper on Paul's hand (Acts xxviii. 6), a means to clear up innocence, and procure favor to the doctrine among those barbarians. How often hath he multiplied the church by death and massacres, and increased it by those means used to annihilate it!

(5.) The Divine wisdom is apparent in the deliverances he affords to other parts of the world, as well as to his church. There are delicate composures, curious threads in his webs, and he works them like an artificer: a goodness wrought for them, curiously wrought (Ps. xxxi. 19), [1.] In making the creatures subservient in their natural order to his gracious ends and purposes. He orders things in such a manner, as not to be necessitated to put forth an extraordinary power in things, which some part of the creation might accomplish. Miraculous productions would speak his power; but the ordering the natural course of things, to occasion such effects they were never intended for, is one part of the glory of his wisdom. And that his wisdom may be seen in the course of nature, he conducts the motions of creatures, and acts them in their own strength; and doth that by various windings and turnings of them, which he might do in an instant by his power, in a supernatural way. Indeed, sometimes he hath made invasions on nature, and suspended the order of their natural laws for a season, to show himself the absolute Lord and Governor of nature: yet if frequent alterations of this nature were made, they would impede the knowledge of the nature of things, and be some bar to the discovery and glory of his wisdom, which is best seen by moving the wheels of inferior creatures in an exact regularity to his own ends. He might, when his little church in Jacob's family was like to starve in Canaan, have, for their preservation, turned the stones of the country into bread; but he sends them down to Egypt to procure corn, that a way might be opened for their removal into that country; the truth of his prediction in their captivity accomplished, and a way made after the declaration of his great name, Jehovah, both in the fidelity of his word and the greatness of his power, in their deliverance from that furnace of affliction. He might have struck Goliath, the captain of the Philistine's army, with a thunderbolt from heaven, when he blasphemed his name, and scared his people; but he useth the natural strength of a stone, and the artificial motion of a sling, by the arm of David, to confront the giant, and thereby to free Judea from the ravage of a potent enemy. He might have delivered the Jews from Babylon by as strange miracles as he used in their deliverance from Egypt: he might have plagued their enemies, gathered his people into a body, and protected them by the bulwark of a cloud and a pillar of fire, against the assaults of their enemies. But he uses the differences between the Persians and those of Babylon, to accomplish his ends. How sometimes hath the veering about of the wind on a sudden been the loss of a navy, when it hath been put upon the point of victory, and driven back the destruction upon those which intended it for others! and the accidental stumbling, or the natural fierceness of a horse, flung down a general in the midst of a battle, where he hath lost his life by the throng, and his death hath brought a defeat to his army, and deliverance to the other party, that were upon the brink of ruin! Thus doth the wisdom of God link things together according to natural order, to work out his intended preservation of a people. [2.] In the season of deliverance. The timing of affairs is a part of the wisdom of man, and an eminent part of the wisdom of God. It is in due season he sends the former and the latter rain, when the earth is in the greatest indigence, and when his influences may most contribute to the bringing forth and ripening the fruit. The dumb creatures have their meat from him in due season (Ps. civ. 27): and in his due season have his darling people their deliverance. When Paul was upon his journey to Damascus with a persecuting commission, he is struck down for the security of the church in that city. The nature of the lion is changed in due season, for the preservation of the lambs from worrying. The Israelites are miraculously rescued from Egypt, when their wits were at a loss, when their danger to human understanding was unavoidable; when earth and sea refused protection, then the wisdom and power of heaven stepped in to effect that which was past the skill of the conductors of that multitude. And when the lives of the Jews lay at the stake, and their necks were upon the block at the mercy of their enemies' swords by an order from Shushan, not only a reprieve, but a triumph, arrives to the Jews, by the wisdom of God guiding the affair, whereby of persons designed to execution, they are made conquerors, and have opportunity to exercise their revenge instead of their patience, proving triumphers where they expected to be sufferers (Esth. viii. 9). How strangely doth God, by secret ways, bow the hearts of men and the nature of things to the execution of that which he designs, notwithstanding all the resistance of that which would traverse the security of his people! How often doth he trap the wicked in the work of their own hands, make their confidence to become their ruin, and ensnare them in those nets they wrought and laid for others (Ps. ix. 16)! "The wicked is snared in the work of his own hands. He scatters the proud in the imagination of their hearts" (Luke i. 51), in the height of their hopes, when their designs have been laid so deep in the foundation, and knit and cemented so close in their superstructure, that no human power or wisdom could rase them down: he hath then disappointed their projects, and befooled their craft. How often hath he kept back the fire, when it hath been ready to devour; broke the arrows when they have been prepared in the bow; turned the spear into the bowels of the bearers, and wounded them at the very instant they were ready to wound

others!   [3.] In suiting instruments to his purpose.   He either finds
them fit, or makes them on a sudden fit for his gracious ends.   If he
hath a tabernacle to build, he will fit a Bezaleel and an Aholiab with
the spirit of wisdom and understanding in all cunning workmanship
(Exod. xxxi. 3, 6).   If he finds them crooked pieces, he can, like a
wise architect, make them straight beams for the rearing his house,
and for the honor of his name.   He sometimes picks out men according to their natural tempers, and employs them in his work.   Jehu,
a man of a furious temper, and ambitious spirit, is called out for the
destruction of Ahab's house.   Moses, a man furnished with all Egyptian wisdom, fitted by a generous education, prepared also by the
affliction he met with in his flight, and one who had had the benefit
of conversation with Jethro, a man of more than an ordinary wisdom
and goodness, as appears by his prudent and religious counsel; this
man is called out to be the head and captain of an oppressed people,
and to rescue them from their bondage, and settle the first national
church in the world.   So Elijah, a high-spirited man, of a hot and
angry temper, one that slighted the frowns, and undervalued the
favor of princes, is set up to stem the torrent of Israelitish idolatry.
So Luther, a man of the same temper, is drawn out by the same
wisdom to encounter the corruptions in the church, against such opposition, which a milder temper would have sunk under.   The earth,
in Rev. xii. 16, is made an instrument to help the woman: when the
grandees of that age transferred the imperial power upon Constan-
tine, who became afterwards a protecting and nursing father to the
church, an end which many of his favorers never designed, nor ever
dreamt of: but God, by his infinite wisdom, made these several designs, like several arrows shot at rovers, meet in one mark to which
he directed them, viz., in bringing forth an instrument to render
peace to the world and security and increase to his church.

   III. The wisdom of God doth wonderfully appear in redemption.
His wisdom in creature ravisheth the eye and understanding; his
wisdom in government doth no less affect a curious observer of the
links and concatenation of the means; but his wisdom in redemption mounts the mind to a greater astonishment.   The works of
creation are the footsteps of his wisdom; the work of redemption
is the face of his wisdom.   A man is better known by the features
of his face, than by the prints of his feet.   We, with "open face,"
or a revealed face, "beholding the glory of the Lord" (2 Cor. iii.
18).   Face, there, refers to God, not to us; the glory of God's wisdom is now open, and no longer covered and veiled by the shadows
of the law.   As we behold the light glorious as scattered in the air
before the appearance of the sun, but more gloriously in the face of
the sun when it begins its race in our horizon.   All the wisdom of
God in creation, and government in his variety of laws, was like the
light the three first days of the creation, dispersed about the world;
but the fourth day it was more glorious, when all gathered into the
body of the sun (Gen. i. 4, 16).   So the light of Divine wisdom and
glory was scattered about the world, and so more obscure, till the
fourth divine day of the world, about the four thousandth year, it
was gathered into one body, the Sun of Righteousness, and so shone

out more gloriously to men and angels. All things are weaker the thinner they are extended, but stronger the more they are united and compacted in one body and appearance. In Christ, in the dispensation by him, as well as his person, were "hid all the treasures of wisdom and knowledge" (Coloss. ii. 3). Some doles of wisdom were given out in creation, but the treasures of it opened in redemption, the highest degrees of it that ever God did exert in the world. Christ is therefore called the "wisdom of God," as well as the "power of God" (1 Cor. i. 24); and the gospel is called the "wisdom of God." Christ is the wisdom of God principally, and the gospel instrumentally, as it is the power of God instrumentally to subdue the heart to himself. This is wrapped up in the appointing Christ as Redeemer, and opened to us in the revelation of it by the gospel.

1. It is a hidden wisdom. In this regard God is said, in the text, to be only wise: and it is said to be a "hidden wisdom" (1 Tim. i. 17), and "wisdom in a mystery" (1 Cor. ii. 7), incomprehensible to the ordinary capacity of an angel, more than the obstruse qualities of the creatures are to the understanding of man. No wisdom of men or angels is able to search the veins of this mine, to tell all the threads of this web, or to understand all the lustre of it; they are as far from an ability fully to comprehend it, as they were at first to contrive it. That wisdom that invented it can only comprehend it. In the uncreated understanding only there is a clearness of light without any shadow of darkness. We come as short of full apprehensions of it, as a child doth of the counsel of the wisest prince. It is so hidden from us, that, without revelation, we could not have the least imagination of it; and though it be revealed to us, yet, without the help of an infiniteness of understanding, we cannot fully fathom it: it is such a tractate of divine wisdom, that the angels never before had seen the edition of it, till it was published to the world (Eph. iii. 10): "to the intent that now unto principalities and powers in heavenly places might be known by the church the manifold wisdom of God." Now made known to them, not before; and now made known to them "in the heavenly places." They had not the knowledge of all heavenly mysteries, though they had the possession of heavenly glory: they knew the prophecies of it in the word, but attained not a clear interpretation of those prophecies till the things that were prophesied of came upon the stage.

2. Manifold wisdom: so it is called. As manifold as mysterious: variety in the mystery, and mystery in every part of the variety. It was not one single act, but a variety of counsels met in it; a conjunction of excellent ends and excellent means. The glory of God, the salvation of man, the defeat of the apostate angels, the discovery of the blessed Trinity in their nature, operations, their combined and distinct acts and expressions of goodness. The means are the conjunction of two natures, infinitely distinct from one another; the union of eternity and time, of mortality and immortality: death is made the way to life, and shame the path to glory. The weakness of the cross is the reparation of man, and the creature is made wise by the "foolishness of preaching;" fallen man grows rich by

the poverty of the Redeemer, and man is filled by the emptiness of God; the heir of hell made a son of God, by God's taking upon him the "form of a servant;" the son of man advanced to the highest degree of honor, by the Son of God becoming of "no reputation." It is called (Eph. i. 8) "abundance of wisdom and prudence." Wisdom, in the eternal counsel, contriving a way; prudence, in the temporary revelation, ordering all affairs and occurrences in the world for the attaining the end of his counsel. Wisdom refers to the mystery; prudence, to the manifestation of it in fit ways and convenient seasons. Wisdom, to the contrivance and order; prudence, to the execution and accomplishment. In all things God acted as became him, as a wise and just Governor of the world (Heb. ii. 10). Whether the wisdom of God might not have found out some other way, or whether he were, in regard of the necessity and naturalness of his justice, limited to this, is not the question; but that it is the best and wisest way for the manifestation of his glory, is out of question.

This wisdom will appear in the different interests reconciled by it: in the subject, the second person in the Trinity, wherein they were reconciled: in the two natures, wherein he accomplished it; whereby God is made known to man in his glory, sin eternally condemned, and the repenting and believing sinner eternally rescued: the honor and righteousness of the law vindicated both in the precept and penalty: the devil's empire overthrown by the same nature he had overturned, and the subtilty of hell defeated by that nature he had spoiled: the creature engaged in the very act to the highest obedience and humility, that, as God appears as a God upon his throne, the creature might appear in the lowest posture of a creature, in the depths of resignation and dependence: the publication of this made in the gospel, by ways congruous to the wisdom which appeared in the execution of his counsel, and the conditions of enjoying the fruit of it, most wise and reasonable.

1. The greatest different interests are reconciled, justice in punishing, and mercy in pardoning. For man had broken the law, and plunged himself into a gulf of misery: the sword of vengeance was unsheathed by justice, for the punishment of the criminal; the bowels of compassion were stirred by mercy, for the rescue of the miserable. Justice severely beholds the sin, and mercy compassionately reflects upon the misery. Two different claims are entered by those concerned attributes: justice votes for destruction, and mercy votes for salvation. Justice would draw the sword, and drench it in the blood of the offender; mercy would stop the sword, and turn it from the breast of the sinner. Justice would edge it, and mercy would blunt it. The arguments are strong on both sides.

(1.) Justice pleads. I arraign, before thy tribunal, a rebel, who was the glorious work of thy hands, the centre of thy rich goodness, and a counterpart of thy own image; he is indeed miserable, whereby to excite thy compassion; but he is not miserable, without being criminal. Thou didst create him in a state, and with ability to be otherwise: the riches of thy bounty aggravate the blackness of his crime. He is a rebel, not by necessity, but will. What constraint was there upon him to listen to the counsels of the enemy of God? What force could there be upon him, since it is without the compass of any creature to work upon, or constrain the will? Nothing of ignorance can excuse him; the law was not ambiguously expressed, but in plain words, both as to precept and penalty; it was writ in his nature in legible characters: had he received any disgust from thee after his creation, it would not excuse his apostasy, since, as a Sovereign, thou wert not obliged to thy creature. Thou hadst provided all things richly for him; he was crowned with glory and honor: thy infinite power had bestowed upon him an habitation richly furnished, and varieties of servants to attend him. Whatever he viewed without, and whatever he viewed within himself, were several marks of thy Divine bounty, to engage him to obedience: had there been some reason of any disgust, it could not have balanced that kindness which had so much reason to oblige him: however, he had received no courtesy from the fallen angel, to oblige him to turn into his camp. Was it not enough, that one of thy creatures would have stripped thee of the glory of heaven, but this also must deprive thee of thy glory upon earth, which was due from him to thee as his Creator? Can he charge the difficulty of the command? No: it was rather below, than above his strength. He might rather complain that it was no higher, whereby his obedience and gratitude might have a larger scope, and a more spacious field to move in than a precept so light; so easy, as to abstain from one fruit in the garden. What excuse can he have, that would prefer the liquorishness of his sense before the dictates of his reason, and the obligations of his creation? The law thou didst set him was righteous and reasonable; and shall righteousness and reason be rejected by the supreme and infallible reason, because the rebellious creature hath trampled upon it? What! must God abrogate his holy law, because the creature hath slighted it? What reflection will this be upon the wisdom that enacted it, and upon the equity of the command and sanction of it? Either man must suffer, or the holy law be expunged, and forever out of date. And is it not better man should eternally smart under his crime, than any dishonorable reflections of unrighteousness be cast upon the law, and of folly, and want of foresight upon the Lawgiver? Not to punish, would be to approve the devil's lie, and justify the creature's revolt. It would be a condemnation of thy own law as unrighteous, and a sentencing thy own wisdom as imprudent. Better man should forever bear the punishment of his offence, than God bear the dishonor of his attributes: better man should be miserable than God should be unrighteous, unwise, false, and tamely bear the denial of his sovereignty. But what advantage would it be to gratify mercy by pardoning the malefactor? Besides the irreparable dishonor to the law, the falsifying thy veracity in not executing the denounced threatenings, he would receive encouragement by such a grace to spurn more at thy sovereignty, and oppose thy holiness by running on in a course of sin with hopes of impunity. If the creature be restored, it cannot be expected that he that hath fared so well, after the breach of it, should be very careful of a future observance: his easy readmission would abet him in the repetition of his offence, and thou shalt soon find him cast off all moral dependence on thee. Shall he be restored without any condition, or covenant? He is a creature not to be governed without a law, and a law is not to be enacted without a penalty. What future regard will he have to thy precept, or what fear will he have of thy threatening, if his crime be so lightly past over? Is it the stability of thy word? What reason will he have to give credit to that, which he hath found already disregarded by thyself? Thy truth in future threatenings will be of no force with him, who hath experienced thy laying it aside in the former. It is necessary, therefore, that the rebellious creature should be punished for the preservation of the honor of the law, and the honor of the Lawgiver, with all those perfections that are united in the composure of it.

(2.) Mercy doth not want a plea. It is true, indeed, the sin of man wants not its aggravations: he hath slighted thy goodness, and accepted thy enemy as his counsellor; but it was not a pure act of his own, as the devil's revolt was: he had a tempter, and the devil had none: he had, I acknowledge, an understanding to know thy will, and a power to obey it; yet he was mutable, and had a capacity to fall. It was no difficult task that was set him, nor a hard yoke that was laid upon him; yet he had a brutish part, as well as a rational, and sense as well as soul; whereas the fallen angel was a pure intellectual spirit. Did God create the world to suffer an eternal dishonor, in letting himself be outwitted by Satan, and his work wrested out of his hands? Shall the work of eternal counsel presently sink into irreparable destruction, and the honor of an almighty and wise work be lost in the ruin of the creature? This would seem contrary to the nature of thy goodness, to make man only to render him miserable: to design him in his creation for the service of the devil, and not for the service of his Creator. What else could be the issue, if the chief work of thy hand, defaced presently after the erecting, should forever remain in this marred condition? What can be expected upon the continuance of his misery, but a perpetual hatred, and enmity of thy creature against thee? Did God in creation design his being hated, or his being loved by his creature? Shall God make a holy law, and have no obedience to that law from that creature whom it was made to govern? Shall the curious workmanship of God, and the excellent engravings of the law of nature in his heart, be so soon defaced, and remain in that blotted condition forever? This fall thou couldst not but in the treasures of thy infinite knowledge foresee. Why hadst thou goodness then to create him in an integrity, if thou wouldst not have mercy to pity him in misery? Shall thy enemy forever trample upon the honor of thy work, and triumph over the glory of God, and applaud himself in the success of his subtilty? Shall thy creature only passively glorify thee as an avenger, and not actively as a compassionater? Am not I a perfection of thy nature as well as justice? Shall justice engross all, and I never come into view? It is resolved already, that the fallen angels shall be no subjects for me to exercise myself upon;

and I have now less reason than before to plead for them: they fell with a full consent of will, without any motion from another; and not content with their own apostasy they envy thee, and thy glory upon earth, as well as in heaven, and have drawn into their party the best part of the creation below. Shall Satan plunge the whole creation in the same irreparable ruin with himself? If the creature be restored, will he contract a boldness in sin by impurity? Hast thou not a grace to render him ingenuous in obedience, as well as a compassion to recover him from misery? What will hinder, but that such a grace, which hath established the standing angels, may establish this recovered creature? If I am utterly excluded from exercising myself on men, as I have been from devils, a whole species is lost; nay, I can never expect to appear upon the stage: if thou wilt quite ruin him by justice, and create another world, and another man, if he stand, thy bounty will be eminent, yet there is no room for mercy to act, unless by the commission of sin, he exposeth himself to misery; and if sin enter into another world, I have little hopes to be heard then, if I am rejected now. Worlds will be perpetually created by goodness, wisdom, and power; sin entering into these worlds, will be perpetually punished by justice; and mercy, which is a perfection of thy nature, will forever be commanded silence, and lie wrapt up in an eternal darkness. Take occasion now, therefore, to expose me to the knowledge of thy creature, since without misery, mercy can never set foot into the world. Mercy pleads, if man be ruined, the creation is in vain; justice pleads, if man be not sentenced, the law is in vain; truth backs justice, and grace abets mercy. What shall be done in this seeming contradiction? Mercy is not manifested, if man be not pardoned; justice will complain, if man be not punished.

(3.) An expedient is found out, by the wisdom of God, to answer these demands, and adjust the differences between them. The wisdom of God answers, I will satisfy your pleas. The pleas of justice shall be satisfied in punishing, and the pleas of mercy shall be received in pardoning. Justice shall not complain for want of punishment, nor mercy for want of compassion. I will have an infinite sacrifice to content justice; and the virtue and fruit of that sacrifice shall delight mercy. Here shall justice have punishment to accept, and mercy shall have pardon to bestow. The rights of both are preserved, and the demands of both amicably accorded in punishment and pardon, by transferring the punishment of our crimes upon a surety, exacting a recompense from his blood by justice, and conferring life and salvation upon us by mercy without the expense of one drop of our own. Thus is justice satisfied in its severities, and mercy in its indulgences. The riches of grace are twisted with the terrors of wrath. The bowels of mercy are wound about the flaming sword of justice, and the sword of justice protects and secures the bowels of mercy. Thus is God righteous without being cruel, and merciful without being unjust; his righteousness inviolable, and the world recoverable. Thus is a resplendent mercy brought forth in the midst of all the curses, confusions, and wrath threatened to the offender. This is the admirable temperament found out by the wis-

dom of God: his justice is honored in the sufferings of man's surety;
and his mercy is honored in the application of the propitiation to the
offender (Rom. iii. 24, 25): "Being justified freely by his grace,
through the redemption that is in Jesus Christ: whom God hath set
forth to be a propitiation through faith in his blood, to declare his
righteousness for the remission of sins that are past, through the forbearance of God." Had we in our persons been sacrifices to justice,
mercy had forever been unknown; had we been solely fostered by
mercy, justice had forever been secluded; had we, being guilty,
been absolved, mercy might have rejoiced, and justice might have
complained; had we been solely punished, justice would have
triumphed, and mercy grieved. But by this medium of redemption,
neither hath ground of complaint; justice hath nothing to charge,
when the punishment is inflicted; mercy hath whereof to boast when
the surety is accepted. The debt of the sinner is transferred upon
the surety, that the merit of the surety may be conferred upon the
sinner; so that God now deals with our sins in a way of consuming
justice, and with our persons in a way of relieving mercy. It is
highly better, and more glorious, than if the claim of one had been
granted, with the exclusion of the demand of the other; it had then
been either an unrighteous mercy, or a merciless justice; it is now a
righteous mercy, and a merciful justice.

2. The wisdom of God appears in the subject or person wherein
these were accorded; the Second Person is the blessed Trinity.
There was a congruity in the Son's undertaking and effecting it
rather than any other person, according to the order of the persons,
and the several functions of the persons, as represented in Scripture.
The Father, after creation, is the lawgiver, and presents man with
the image of his own holiness and the way to his creatures' happiness; but after the fall, man was too impotent to perform the law,
and too polluted to enjoy a felicity. Redemption was then necessary; not that it was necessary for God to redeem man, but it was
necessary for man's happiness that he should be recovered. To this
the Second Person is appointed, that by communion with him, man
might derive a happiness, and be brought again to God. But since
man was blind in his understanding, and an enemy in his will to
God, there must be the exerting of a virtue to enlighten his mind,
and bend his will to understand, and accept of this redemption; and
this work is assigned to the Third Person, the Holy Ghost.

(1.) It was not congruous that the Father should assume human
nature, and suffer in it for the redemption of man. He was first in
order; he was the lawgiver, and therefore to be the judge. As
lawgiver, it was not convenient he should stand in the stead of the
law-breaker; and as judge, it was as little convenient he should be
reputed a malefactor. That he who had made a law against sin denounced a penalty upon the commission of sin, and whose part it
was actually to punish the sinner, should become sin for the wilful
transgressor of his law. He being the rector, how could he be an
advocate and intercessor to himself? How could he be the judge
and the sacrifice? a judge, and yet a mediator to himself? If he
had been the sacrifice, there must be some person to examine the va-

lidity of it, and pronounce the sentence of acceptance. Was it agreeable that the Son should sit upon a throne of judgment, and the Father stand at the bar, and be responsible to the Son? That the Son should be in the place of a governor, and the Father in the place of the criminal? That the Father should be bruised (Isa. liii. 10) by the Son, as the Son was by the Father (Zech. xiii. 70)? that the Son should awaken a sword against the Father, as the Father did against the Son? That the Father should be sent by the Son, as the Son was by the Father (Gal. iv. 4)? The order of the persons in the blessed Trinity had been inverted and disturbed. Had the Father been sent, he had not been first in order; the sender is before the person sent: as the Father begets, and the son is begotten (John i. 14), so the Father sends, and the son is sent. He whose orders is to send, cannot properly send himself.

(2.) Nor was it congruous that the Spirit should be sent upon this affair. If the Holy Ghost had been sent to redeem us, and the Son to apply that redemption to us, the order of the Persons had also been inverted; the Spirit, then, who was third in order, had been second in operation. The Son would then have received of the Spirit, as the Spirit doth now of Christ, "and shew it unto us" (John i. 15). As the Spirit proceeded from the Father and the Son, so the proper function and operation of it was in order after the operations of the Father and the Son. Had the Spirit been sent to redeem us, and the Son sent by the Father, and the Spirit to apply that redemption to us, the Son in his acts had proceeded from the Father and the Spirit; the Spirit, as sender, had been in order before the Son; whereas, the Spirit is called "the Spirit of Christ," as sent by Christ from the "Father" (Gal. iv. 6; John xv. 27). But as the order of the works, so the order of the Persons is preserved in their several operations. Creation, and a law to govern the creature, precedes redemption. Nothing, or that which hath no being, is not capable of a redeemed being. Redemption supposeth the existence and the misery of a person redeemed. As creation precedes redemption, so redemption precedes the application of it. As redemption supposeth the being of the creature, so application of redemption supposeth the efficacy of redemption. According to the order of these works, is the order of the operations of the Three Persons. Creation belongs to the Father, the first person; redemption, the second work, is the function of the Son, the second person; application, the third work, is the office of the Holy Ghost, the third person. The Father orders it, the Son acts it, the Holy Ghost applies it. He purifies our souls to understand, believe, and love these mysteries. He forms Christ in the womb of the soul, as he did the body of Christ in the womb of the Virgin. As the Spirit of God moved upon the waters, to garnish and adorn the world, after the matter of it was formed (Gen. i. 2), so he moves upon the heart, to supple it to a compliance with Christ, and draws the lineaments of the new creation in the soul, after the foundation is laid. The Son pays the price that was due from us to God, and the Spirit is the earnest of the promises of life and glory purchased by the merit of that

death.ʸ It is to be observed, that the, Father, under the dispensation
of the law, proposed the commands, with the promises and threatenings, to the understandings of men ; and Christ, under the dispensation of grace, when he was upon the earth, proposeth the gospel as
the means of salvation, exhorts to faith as the condition of salvation ; but it was neither the functions of the one or the other to display such an efficacy in the understanding and will to make men
believe and obey ; and, therefore, there were such few conversions
in the time of Christ, by his miracles. But this work was reserved
for the fuller and brighter appearance of the Spirit, whose office it
was to convince the world of the necessity of a Redeemer, because
of their lost condition ; of the person of the Redeemer, the Son of
God ; of the sufficiency and efficacy of redemption, because of his
righteousness and acceptation by the Father. The wisdom of God
is seen in preparing and presenting the objects, and then in making
impression of them upon the subject he intends. And thus is the
order of the Three Persons preserved.

(3.) The Second Person had the greatest congruity in this work.
He by whom God created the world was most conveniently employed in restoring the defaced world (John i. 4): who more fit to recover it from its lapsed state than he that had erected it in its primitive state (Heb. i. 2)? He was the light of men in creation, and
therefore it was most reasonable he should be the light of men in
redemption. Who fitter to reform the Divine image than he that
first formed it? Who fitter to speak for us to God than he who was
the Word (John i. 1)? Who could better intercede with the Father
than he who was the only begotten and beloved Son? Who so fit
to redeem the forfeited inheritance as the Heir of all things? Who
fitter and better to prevail for us to have the right of children than
he that possessed it by nature? We fell from being the sons of
God, and who fitter to introduce us into an adopted state than the
Son of God? Herein was an expression of the richer grace, because
the first sin was immediately against the wisdom of God, by an ambitious affectation of a wisdom equal to God, that that person, who
was the wisdom of God, should be made a sacrifice for the expiation
of the sin against wisdom.

3. The wisdom of God is seen in the two natures of Christ,
whereby this redemption was accomplished. The union of the
two natures was the foundation of the union of God and the fallen
creature.

1st. The union itself is admirable: " The Word is made flesh"
(John i. 14), one " equal with God in the form of a servant" (Phil.
ii. 7). When the apostle speaks of "God manifested in the flesh,"
he speaks " the wisdom of God in a mystery" (1 Tim. iii. 16); that
which is incomprehensible to the angels, which they never imagined
before it was revealed, which perhaps they never knew till they beheld it. I am sure, under the law, the figures of the cherubims were
placed in the sanctuary, with their " faces looking towards the propitiatory," in a perpetual posture of contemplation and admiration
(Exod. xxxvii. 9), to which the apostle alludes (1 Pet. i. 12). Mys-

terious is the wisdom of God to unite finite and infinite, almightiness and weakness, immortality and mortality, immutability, with a thing subject to change; to have a nature from eternity, and yet a nature subject to the revolutions of time; a nature to make a law, and a nature to be subjected to the law; to be God blessed forever, in the bosom of his Father, and an infant exposed to calamities from the womb of his mother: terms seeming most distant from union, most uncapable of conjunction, to shake hands together, to be most intimately conjoined; glory and vileness, fulness and emptiness, heaven and earth; the creature with the Creator; he that made all things, in one person with a nature that is made; Immanuel, God, and man in one; that which is most spiritual to partake of that which is carnal flesh and blood (Heb. ii. 14); one with the Father in his Godhead, one with us in his manhood; the Godhead to be in him in the fullest perfection, and the manhood in the greatest purity; the creature one with the Creator, and the Creator one with the creature. Thus is the incomprehensible wisdom of God declared in the "Word being made flesh."

2d. In the manner of this union. A union of two natures, yet no natural union. It transcends all the unions visible among creatures:[z] it is not like the union of stones in a building, or two pieces of timber fastened together, which touch one another only in their superficies and outside, without any intimacy with one another. By such a kind of union God would not be a man: the Word could not so be made flesh. Nor is it a union of parts to the whole, as the members and the body; the members are parts, the body is the whole; for the whole results from the parts, and depends upon the parts: but Christ, being God, is independent upon anything. The parts are in order of nature before the whole, but nothing can be in order of nature before God. Nor is it as the union of two liquors, as when wine and water are mixed together, for they are so incorporated as not to be distinguished from one another; no man can tell which particle is wine, and which is water. But the properties of the Divine nature are distinguishable from the properties of the human. Nor is it as the union of the soul and body, so as that the Deity is the form of the humanity, as the soul is the form of the body: for as the soul is but a part of the man, so the Divinity would be then but a part of the humanity; and as a form, or the soul, is in a state of imperfection, without that which it is to inform, so the Divinity of Christ would have been imperfect till it had assumed the humanity, and so the perfection of an eternal Deity would have depended on a creature of time. This union of two natures in Christ is incomprehensible: and it is a mystery we cannot arrive to the top of, how the Divine nature, which is the same with that of the Father and the Holy Ghost, should be united to the human nature, without its being said that the Father and the Holy Ghost were united to the flesh; but the Scripture doth not encourage any such notion; it speaks only of the Word, the person of the Word being made flesh, and in his being made flesh, distinguisheth him from the Father, as "the

[z] Savana Triump. Crucis, lib. iii. cap. 7. p. 211.

only begotten of the Father" (John i. 14).   The person of the Son
was the term of this union.
   (1.) This union doth not confound the properties of the Deity and
those of the humanity.   They remain distinct and entire in each
other.   The Deity is not changed into flesh, nor the flesh transformed into God: they are distinct, and yet united; they are conjoined,
and yet unmixed: the dues of either nature are preserved.   It is impossible that the majesty of the Divinity can receive an alteration.
It is as impossible that the meanness of the humanity can receive
the impressions of the Deity, so as to be changed into it, and a creature be metamorphosed into the Creator, and temporary flesh become
eternal, and finite mount up into infinity : as the soul and body are
united, and make one person, yet the soul is not changed into the
perfections of the body, nor the body into the perfections of the soul.
There is a change made in the humanity, by being advanced to a
more excellent union, but not in the Deity, as a change is made in
the air, when it is enlightened by the sun, not in the sun, which
communicates that brightness to the air.   Athanasius makes the
burning bush to be a type of Christ's incarnation (Exod. iii. 2): the
fire signifying the Divine nature, and the bush the human.   The
bush is a branch springing up from the earth, and the fire descends
from heaven ; as the bush was united to the fire, yet was not hurt
by the flame, nor converted into fire, there remained a difference
between the bush and the fire, yet the properties of the fire shined
in the bush, so that the whole bush seemed to be on fire.   So in the
incarnation of Christ, the human nature is not swallowed up by the
Divine, nor changed into it, nor confounded with it, but so united,
that the properties of both remain firm : two are so become one, that
they remain two still : one person in two natures, containing the
glorious perfections of the Divine, and the weaknesses of the human.
The "fulness of the Deity dwells bodily in Christ" (Col. ii. 9).
   (2.) The Divine nature is united to every part of the humanity.
The whole Divinity to the whole humanity ; so that no part but may
be said to be the member of God, as well as the blood is said to be
the "blood of God" (Acts xx. 28).   By the same reason, it may be
said, the hand of God, the eye of God, the arm of God.   As God is
infinitely present everywhere, so as to be excluded from no place, so
is the Deity hypostatically everywhere in the humanity, not excluded from any part of it ; as the light of the sun in every part of the
air ; as a sparkling splendor in every part of the diamond.   Therefore, it is concluded, by all that acknowledge the Deity of Christ,
that when his soul was separated from the body, the Deity remained
united both to soul and body, as light doth in every part of a broken
crystal.
   (3.) Therefore, perpetually united (Col. ii. 9).   The "fulness of the
Godhead dwells in him bodily."   It dwells in him, not lodges in
him, as a traveller in an inn: it resides in him as a fixed habitation.
As God describes the perpetuity of his presence in the ark by his
habitation or dwelling in it (Exod. xxix. 44), so doth the apostle the
inseparable duration of the Deity in the humanity, and the indissoluble union of the humanity with the Deity.   It was united on earth ;

it remains united in heaven. It was not an image or an apparition, as the tongues wherein the Spirit came upon the apostles, were a temporary representation, not a thing united perpetually to the person of the Holy Ghost.

(4.) It was a personal union. It was not an union of persons, though it was a personal union; so Davenant expounds (Col. ii. 9), Christ did not take the person of man, but the nature of man into subsistence with himself. The body and soul of Christ were not united in themselves, had no subsistence in themselves, till they were united to the person of the Son of God. If the person of a man were united to him, the human nature would have been the nature of the person so united to him, and not the nature of the Son of God (Heb. ii. 14, 16), " Forasmuch then as the children are partakers of flesh and blood, he also himself likewise took part of the same; that through death he might destroy him that had the power of death, that is, the devil. For verily he took not on him the nature of angels; but he took on him the seed of Abraham." He took flesh and blood to be his own nature, perpetually to subsist in the person of the Λόγος, which must be by a personal union, or no way: the Deity united to the humanity, and both natures to be one person. This is the mysterious and manifold wisdom of God.

3d. The end of this union.

(1.) He was hereby fitted to be a Mediator. He hath something like to man, and something like to God. If he were in all things only like to man, he would be at a distance from God: if he were in all things only like to God, he would be at a distance from man. He is a true Mediator between mortal sinners and the immortal righteous One. He was near to us by the infirmities of our nature, and near to God by the perfections of the Divine; as near to God in his nature, as to us in ours; as near to us in our nature, as he is to God in the Divine. Nothing that belongs to the Deity, but he possesses; nothing that belongs to the human nature, but he is clothed with. He had both the nature which had offended, and that nature which was offended: a nature to please God, and a nature to pleasure us: a nature, whereby he experimentally knew the excellency of God, which was injured, and understood the glory due to him, and consequently the greatness of the offence, which was to be measured by the dignity of his person: and a nature whereby he might be sensible of the miseries contracted by, and endure the calamities due to the offender, that he might both have compassion on him, and make due satisfaction for him. He had two distinct natures capable of the affections and sentiments of the two persons he was to accord; he was a just judge of the rights of the one, and the demerit of the other.[a] He could not have this full and perfect understanding if he did not possess the perfections of the one, and the qualities of the other; the one fitted him for "things appertaining to God" (Heb. v. 1), and the other furnished him with a sense of the "infirmities of man" (Heb. iv. 15).

(2.) He was hereby fitted for the working out the happiness of man. A Divine nature to communicate to man, and a human na-

ᵃ Gomb. de Relig. p. 42.

ture to carry up to God. [1.] He had a nature whereby to suffer for us, and a nature whereby to be meritorious in those sufferings. A nature to make him capable to bear the penalty, and a nature to make his sufferings sufficient for all that embraced him. A nature, capable to be exposed to the flames of Divine wrath, and another nature, incapable to be crushed by the weight, or consumed by the heat of it: a human nature to suffer, and stand a sacrifice in the stead of man; a Divine nature to sanctify these sufferings, and fill the nostrils of God with a sweet savor, and thereby atone his wrath: the one to bear the stroke due to us, and the other to add merit to his sufferings for us. Had he not been man, he could not have filled our place in suffering; and could he otherwise have suffered, his sufferings had not been applicable to us; and had he not been God, his sufferings had not been meritoriously and fruitfully applicable. Had not his blood been the blood of God, it had been of as little advantage as the blood of an ordinary man, or the blood of the legal sacrifices (Heb. ix. 12). Nothing less than God could have satisfied God for the injury done by man. Nothing less than God could have countervailed the torments due to the offending creature. Nothing less than God could have rescued us out of the hands of the jailor, too powerful for us. [2.] He had, therefore, a nature to be compassionate to us, and victorious for us. A nature sensibly to compassionate us, and another nature, to render those compassions effectual for our relief; he had the compassions of our nature to pity us, and the patience of the Divine nature to bear with us. He hath the affections of a man to us, and the power of a God for us: a nature to disarm the devil for us, and another nature to be insensible of the working of the devil in us, and against us. If he had been only God, he would not have had an experimental sense of our misery; and if he had been only man, he could not have vanquished our enemies; had he been only God, he could not have died; and had he been only man, he could not have conquered death. [3.] A nature efficaciously to instruct us. As man, he was to instruct us sensibly; as God, he was to instruct us infallibly. A nature, whereby he might converse with us, and a nature, whereby he might influence us in those converses. A human mouth to minister instruction to man, and a Divine power to imprint it with efficacy. [4.] A nature to be a pattern to us. A pattern of grace as man, as Adam was to have been to his posterity:[b] a Divine nature shining in the human, the image of the invisible God in the glass of our flesh, that he might be a perfect copy for our imitation (Col. i. 15), "The image of the invisible God, and the first-born of every creature" in conjunction. The virtues of the Deity are sweetened and tempered by the union with the humanity, as the beams of the son are by shining through a colored glass, which condescends more to the weakness of our eye. Thus the perfections of the invisible God, breaking through the first-born of every creature, glittering in Christ's created state, became more sensible for contemplation by our mind, and more imitiable for conformity in our practice. [5.] A nature to be a ground of confidence in our approach to God. A nature wherein we may behold him, and wherein we may approach

[b] Amyraut. Morals. Tom. V. pp. 468, 469.

to him. A nature for our comfort, and a nature for our confidence. Had he been only man, he had been too feeble to assure us ; and had he been only God, he had been too high to attract us : but now we are allured by his human nature, and assured by his Divine, in our drawing near to heaven. Communion with God was desired by us, but our guilt stifled our hopes, and the infinite excellency of the Divine nature would have damped our hopes of speeding; but since these two natures, so far distant, are met in a marriage-knot, we have a ground of hope, nay, an earnest, that the Creator and believing creature shall meet and converse together. And since our sins are expatiated by the death of the human nature in conjunction with the Divine, our guilt, upon believing, shall not hinder us from this comfortable approach. Had he been only man, he could not have assured us an approach to God : had he been only God, his justice would not have admitted us to approach to him ; he had been too terrible for guilty persons, and too holy for polluted persons to come near to him : but by being made man, his justice is tempered, and by his being God and man, his mercy is ensured. A human nature he had, one with us, that we might be related to God, as one with him. [6.] A nature to derive all good to us. Had he not been man, we had had no share or part in him : a satisfaction by him had not been imputed to us. If he were not God, he could not communicate to us divine graces and eternal happiness ; he could not have had power to convey so great a good to us, had he been only man ; and he could not have done it, according to the rule of inflexible righteousness, had he been only God. As man, he is the way of conveyance ; as God, he is the spring of conveyance. From this grace of union, and the grace of unction, we find rivers of waters flowing to make glad the city of God. Believers are his branches, and draw sap from him, as he is their root in his human nature, and have an endless duration of it from his Divine. Had he not been man, he had not been in a state to obey the law ; had he not been God as well as man, his obedience could not have been valuable to be imputed to us. How should this mystery be studied by us, which would afford us both admiration and content! Admiration, in the incomprehensibleness of it; contentment, in the fitness of the Mediator. By this wisdom of God we receive the props of our faith, and the fruits of joy and peace. Wisdom consists in choosing fit means, and conducting them in such a method, as may reach with good success the variety of marks which are aimed at. Thus hath the wisdom of God set forth a Mediator, suited to our wants, fitted for our supplies, and ordered so the whole affair by the union of these two natures in the person of the Redeemer, that there could be no disappointment, by all the bustle hell and hellish instruments could raise against it.

4. The wisdom of God is seen in this way of redemption, in vindicating the honor and righteousness of the law, both as to precept and penalty. The first and irreversible design of the law was obedience. The penalty of the law had only entrance upon transgression. Obedience was the design, and the penalty was added to enforce the observance of the precept (Gen. ii. 17): "Thou shalt not eat;" there is the precept: "In the day thou eatest thereof thou shalt die;"

there is the penalty. Obedience was our debt to the law, as creatures; punishment was due from the law to us, as sinners: we are bound to endure the penalty for our first transgression, but the penalty did not cancel the bond of future obedience; the penalty had not been incurred without transgressing the precept; yet the precept was not abrogated by enduring the penalty. Since man so soon revolted, and by this revolt fell under the threatening, the justice of the law had been honored by man's sufferings, but the holiness and equity of the law had been honored by man's obedience. The wisdom of God finds out a medium to satisfy both: the justice of the law is preserved in the execution of the penalty; and the holiness of the law is honored in the observance of the precept. The life of our Saviour is a conformity to the precept, and his death is a conformity to the penalty; the precepts are exactly performed, and the curse punctually executed, by a voluntary observing the one, and a voluntary undergoing the other. It is obeyed, as if it had not been transgressed, and executed as if it had not been obeyed. It became the wisdom, justice, and holiness of God, as the Rector of the world, to exact it (Heb. ii. 10), and it became the holiness of the Mediator to "fulfil all the righteousness of the law" (Rom. viii. 3; Matt. iii. 15). And thus the honor of the law was vindicated in all the parts of it. The transgression of the law was condemned in the flesh of the Redeemer, and the righteousness of the law was fulfilled in his person: and both these acts of obedience, being counted as one righteousness, and imputed to the believing sinner, render him a subject to the law, both in its perceptive and minatory part. By Adam's sinful acting we were made sinners, and by Christ's righteous acting we are made righteous (Rom. v. 19): "As by one man's disobedience many were made sinners, so by the obedience of one shall many be made righteous." The law was obeyed by him, that the righteousness of it might be fulfilled in us (Rom. viii. 4). It is not fulfilled in us, or in our actions, by inherency, but fulfilled in us by imputation of that righteousness which was exactly fulfilled by another. As he died for us, and rose again for us, so he lived for us. The commands of the law were as well observed for us, as the threatenings of the law were endured for us. This justification of a sinner, with the preservation of the holiness of the law in truth, in the inward parts, in sincerity of intention, as well as conformity in action, is the wisdom of God, the gospel wisdom which David desires to know (Ps. li. 6): "Thou desirest truth in the inward parts, and in the hidden part thou shalt make me to know wisdom;" or, as some render it, "the hidden things of wisdom." Not an inherent wisdom in the acknowledgments of his sin, which he had confessed before, but the wisdom of God in providing a medicine, so as to keep up the holiness of the law in the observance of it in truth, and the averting the judgment due to the sinner. In and by this way methodized by the wisdom of God, all doubts and troubles are discharged. Naturally, if we take a view of the law to behold its holiness and justice, and then of our hearts, to see the contrariety in them to the command, and the pollution repugnant to its holiness; and after this, cast our eyes upward, and beholding a flaming sword, edged with curses and wrath;

is there any matter, but that of terror, afforded by any of these? But when we behold, in the life of Christ, a conformity to the mandatory part of the law, and in the cross of Christ, a sustaining the minatory part of the law, this wisdom of God gives a well-grounded and rational dismiss to all the horrors that can seize upon us.

5. The wisdom of God in redemption is visible in manifesting two contrary affections at the same time, and in one act: the greatest hatred of sin, and the greatest love to the sinner. In this way he punishes the sin without ruining the sinner, and repairs the ruins of the sinner without indulging the sin. Here is eternal love and eternal hatred; a condemning the sin to what it merited, and an advancing the sinner to what he could not expect. Herein is the choicest love and the deepest hatred manifested: an implacableness against the sin, and a placableness to the sinner. His hatred of sin hath been discovered in other ways: in punishing the devil without remedy; sentencing man to an expulsion from paradise, though seduced by another; in accursing the serpent, an irrational creature, though but a misguided instrument. The whole tenor of his threatenings declare his loathing of sin, and the sprinklings of his judgments in the world, and the horrible expectations of terrified consciences confirm it. But what are all these testimonies to the highest evidence that can possibly be given in the sheathing the sword of his wrath in the heart of his Son? If a father should order his son to take a mean garb below his dignity, order him to be dragged to prison, seem to throw off all affection of a father for the severity of a judge, condemn his son to a horrible death, be a spectator of his bleeding condition, withhold his hand from assuaging his misery, regard it rather with joy than sorrow, give him a bitter cup to drink, and stand by to see him drink it off to the bottom, dregs and all, and flash frowns in his face all the while; and this not for any fault of his own, but the rebellion of some subjects he undertook for, and that the offenders might have a pardon sealed by the blood of the son, the sufferer: all this would evidence his detestation of the rebellion, and his affection to the rebels; his hatred to their crime, and his love to their welfare. This did God do. He "delivered Christ up for our offences" (Rom. viii. 32); the Father gave him the cup (John xviii. 18); the Lord bruised him with pleasure (Isa. liii. 10), and that for sin. He transferred upon the shoulders of his Son the pain we had merited, that the criminal might be restored to the place he had forfeited. He hates the sin so as to condemn it forever, and wrap it up in the curse he had threatened; and loves the sinner, believing and repenting, so as to mount him to an expectation of a happiness exceeding the first estate, both in glory and perpetuity. Instead of an earthly paradise, lays the foundation of an heavenly mansion, brings forth a weight of glory from a weight of misery, separates the comfortable light of the sun from the scorching heat we had deserved at his hands. Thus hath God's hatred of sin been manifested. He is at eternal defiance with sin, yet nearer in alliance with the sinner than he was before the revolt; as if man's miserable fall had endeared him to the Judge. This is the wisdom

and prudence of "grace wherein God hath abounded" (Eph. i. 9): a wisdom in twisting the happy restoration of the broken amity, with an everlasting curse upon that which made the breach, both upon sin the cause, and upon Satan the seducer to it. Thus is hatred and love, in their highest glory, manifested together : hatred to sin, in the death of Christ, more than if the torments of hell had been undergone by the sinner ; and love to the sinner, more than if he had, by an absolute and simple bounty, bestowed upon him the possession of heaven ; because the gift of his Son, for such an end, is a greater token of his boundless affections, than a re-instating man in paradise. Thus is the wisdom of God seen in redemption, consuming the sin, and recovering the sinner.

6. The wisdom of God is evident in overturning the devil's empire by the nature he had vanquished, and by ways quite contrary to what that malicious spirit could imagine. The devil, indeed, read his own doom in the first promise, and found his ruin resolved upon, by the means of the "Seed of the woman;" but by what seed was not so easily known to him.[c] And the methods whereby it was to be brought about was a mystery kept secret from the malicious devils, since it was not discovered to the obedient angels. He might know, from Isa. liii., that the Redeemer was assured to divide the spoil with the strong, and rescue a part of the lost creation out of his hands ; and that this was to be effected by making his soul an offering for sin : but could he imagine which way his soul was to be made such an offering? He shrewdly suspected Christ, just after his inauguration into his office by baptism, to be the Son of God : but did he ever dream that the Messiah, by dying as a reputed malefactor, should be a sacrifice for the expiation of the sin the devil had introduced by his subtilty? Did he ever imagine a cross should dispossess him of his crown, and that dying groans should wrest the victory out of his hands? He was conquered by that nature he had cast headlong into ruin : a woman, by his subtilty, was the occasion of our death ; and a woman, by the conduct of the only wise God, brings forth the Author of our life, and the Conqueror of our enemies. The flesh of the old Adam had infected us, and the flesh of the new Adam cures us (1 Cor. xv. 21): "By man came death ; by man also came the resurrection from the dead." We are killed by the old Adam, and raised by the new ; as among the Israelites, a fiery serpent gave the wound, and a brazen serpent administers the cure. The nature that was deceived bruiseth the deceiver, and raiseth up the foundations of his kingdom. Satan is defeated by the counsels he took to secure his possession, and loses the victory by the same means whereby he thought to preserve it. His tempting the Jews to the sin of crucifying the Son of God, had a contrary success to his tempting Adam to eat of the tree. The first death he brought upon Adam, ruined us, and the death he brought by his instruments upon the second Adam, restored us. By a tree, if one may so say, he had triumphed over the world, and by the fruit of a tree, one hanging upon a tree, he is discharged of his

And indeed the Heathen oracles, managed by the devils, declared that they were not long to hold their sceptre in the world, but the Hebrew child should vanquish them.

power over us (Heb. ii. 14): "Through death he destroyed Him that had the power of death." And thus the devil ruins his own kingdom while he thinks to confirm and enlarge it; and is defeated by his own policy, whereby he thought to continue the world under his chains, and deprive the Creator of the world of his purposed honor. What deeper counsel could he resolve upon for his own security, than to be instrumental in the death of him, who was God, the terror of the devil himself, and to bring the Redeemer of the world to expire with disgrace in the sight of a multitude of men? Thus did the wisdom of God shine forth in restoring us by methods seemingly repugnant to the end he aimed at, and above the suspicion of a subtle devil, whom he intended to baffle. Could he imagine that we should be healed by stripes, quickened by death, purified by blood, crowned by a cross, advanced to the highest honor by the lowest humility, comforted by sorrows, glorified by disgrace, absolved by condemnation, and made rich by poverty? That the sweetest honey should at once spring out of the belly of a dead lion, the lion of the tribe of Judah, and out of the bosom of the living God? How wonderful is this wisdom of God! that the Seed of the woman, born of a mean virgin, brought forth in a stable, spending his days in affliction, misery, and poverty, without any pomp and splendor, passing some time in a carpenter's shop, with carpenter's tools (Mark vi. 6), and afterwards exposed to a horrible and disgraceful death, should, by this way, pull down the gates of hell, subvert the kingdom of the devil, and be the hammer to break in pieces that power, which he had so long exercised over the world! Thus became he the author of our life, by being bound for a while in the chains of death, and arrived to a principality over the most malicious powers, by being a prisoner for us, and the anvil of their rage and fury.

7. The wisdom of God appears, in giving us this way the surest ground of comfort, and the strongest incentive to obedience. The rebel is reconciled, and the rebellion shamed; God is propitiated, and the sinner sanctified, by the same blood. What can more contribute to our comfort and confidence, than God's richest gift to us? What can more enflame our love to him, than our recovery from death by the oblation of his Son to misery and death for us? It doth as much engage our duty as secure our happiness. It presents God glorious and gracious, and therefore every way fit to be trusted in regard of the interest of his own glory in it, and in regard of the effusions of his grace by it. It renders the creature obliged in the highest manner, and so awakens his industry to the strictest and noblest obedience. Nothing so effectual as a crucified Christ to wean us from sin, and stifle all motions of despair; a means, in regard of the justice signalized in it, to make man to hate the sin which had ruined him; and a means, in regard of the love expressed to make him delight in that law he had violated (2 Cor. v. 14, 15). The love of Christ, and therefore the love of God expressed in it, constrains us no longer to live to ourselves.

(1.) It is a ground of the highest comfort and confidence in God.

Since he hath given such an evidence of his impartial truth to his threatening for the honor of his justice, we need not question but he will be as punctual to his promise for the honor of his mercy. It is a ground of confidence in God, since he hath redeemed us in such a way as glorifies the steadiness of his veracity, as well as the severity of his justice; we may well trust him for the performance of his promise, since we have experience of the execution of his threatening; his merciful truth will as much engage him to accomplish the one, as his just truth did to inflict the other. The goodness which shone forth in weaker rays in the creation, breaks out with stronger beams in redemption. And the mercy which before the appearance of Christ was manifested in some small rivulets, diffuseth itself like a boundless ocean. That God, that was our Creator, is our Redeemer, the repairer of our breaches, and the restorer of our paths to dwell in. And the plenteous redemption from all iniquity, manifested in the incarnation and passion of the Son of God, is much more a ground of hope in the Lord than it was in past ages, when it could not be said, " The Lord hath, but the Lord shall, redeem Israel from all his iniquities" (Ps. cxxx. 8). It is a full warrant to cast ourselves into his arms.

(2.) An incentive to obedience.

[1.] The commands of the gospel require the obedience of the creature. There is not one precept in the gospel which interferes with any rule in the law, but strengthens it, and represents it in its true exactness: the heat to scorch us is allayed, but the light to direct us is not extinguished. Not the least allowance to any sin is granted; not the least affection to any sin is indulged. The law is tempered by the gospel, but not nulled and cast out of doors by it: it enacts that none but those that are sanctified, shall be glorified; that there must be grace here, if we expect glory hereafter; that we must not presume to expect an admittance to the vision of God's face unless our souls be clothed with a robe of holiness (Heb. xii. 14). It requires an obedience to the whole law in our intention and purpose, and an endeavor to observe it in our actions; it promotes the honor of God, and ordains a universal charity among men; it reveals the whole counsel of God, and furnisheth men with the holiest laws.

[2.] It presents to us the exactest pattern for our obedience. The redeeming person is not only a propitiation for the sin, but a pattern to the sinner (1 Pet. ii. 21). The conscience of man, after the fall of Adam, approved of the reason of the law, but by the corruption of nature man had no strength to perform the law. The possibility of keeping the law, by human nature, is evidenced by the appearance and life of the Redeemer, and an assurance given that it shall be advanced to such a state as to be able to observe it: we aspire to it in this life, and have hopes to attain it in a future; and, while we are here, the actor of our redemption is the copy for our imitation. The pattern to imitate is greater than the law to be ruled by. What a lustre did his virtues cast about the world! How attractive are his graces! With what high examples for all duties has he furnished us out of the copy of his life!

[3.] It presents us with the strongest motives to obedience (Tit. ii.

11, 12): " The grace of God teaches us to deny ungodlinsss." What chains bind us faster and closer than love? Here is love to our nature in his incarnation; love to us, though enemies, in his death and passion; encouragements to obedience by the proffers of pardon for former rebellions. By the disobedience of man, God introduceth his redeeming grace, and engageth his creature to more ingenuous and excellent returns than his innocent state could oblige him to. In his created state he had goodness to move him, he hath the same goodness now to oblige him as a creature, and a greater love and mercy to oblige him as a repaired creature; and the terror of justice is taken off, which might envenom his heart as a criminal. In his revolted state he had misery to discourage him; in his redeemed state he hath love to attract him. Without such a way, black despair had seized upon the creature exposed to a remediless misery, and God would have had no returns of love from the best of his earthly works; but if any sparks of ingenuity be left, they will be excited by the efficacy of this argument. The willingness of God to receive returning sinners, is manifested in the highest degree; and the willingness of a sinner to return to him in duty hath the strongest engagements. He hath done as much to encourage our obedience, as to illustrate his glory. We cannot conceive what could be done greater for the salvation of our souls, and consequently what could have been done, more to enforce our observance. We have a Redeemer, as man, to copy it to us, and as God, to perfect us in it. It would make the heart of any to tremble to wound him that hath provided such a salve for our sores, and to make grace a warrant for rebellion —motives capable to form rocks into a flexibleness. Thus is the wisdom of God seen in giving us a ground to the surest confidence, and furnishing us with incentives to the greatest obedience, by the horrors of wrath, death and sufferings of our Saviour.

8. The wisdom of God is apparent in the condition he hath settled for the enjoying the fruits of redemption: and this is faith, a wise and reasonable condition and the concomitants of it—

(1.) In that it is suited to man's lapsed state and God's glory. Innocence is not required here; that had been a condition impossible in its own nature after the fall. The rejecting of mercy is now only condemning, where mercy is proposed. Had the condition of perfection in works been required, it had rather been a condemnation than redemption. Works are not demanded, whereby the creature might ascribe anything to himself, but a condition, which continues in man a sense of his apostasy, abates all aspiring pride, and makes the reward of grace, not of debt; a condition, whereby mercy is owned, and the creature emptied; flesh silenced in the dust, and God set upon his throne of grace and authority; the creature brought to the lowest debasement, and Divine glory raised to the highest pitch. The creature is brought to acknowledge mercy, and seal to justice; to own the holiness of God, in the hatred of sin; the justice of God, in the punishment of sin; and the mercy of God, in the pardoning of sin: a condition that despoils nature of all its pretended excellency; beats down the glory of man at the foot of God (1 Cor. i. 29, 31). It subjects the reason and will of man to the wisdom and authority of God; it brings the creature to an unreserved submission and entire resignation. God is made the sovereign cause of all; the creature continued in his emptiness, and reduced to a greater dependence upon God than by a creation; depending upon him for a constant influx, for an entire happiness: a condition that renders God glorious in the creature, and the fallen creature happy in God; God glorious in his condescension to man, and man happy in his emptiness before God. Faith is made the condition of man's recovery, that "the lofty looks of man might be humbled, and the haughtiness of man be pulled down" (Isa. ii. 11); that every towering imagination might be levelled (2 Cor. x. 5). Man must have all from without doors; he must not live upon himself, but upon another's allowance. He must stand to the provision of God, and be a perpetual suitor at his gates.

(2.) A condition opposite to that which was the cause of the fall. We fell from God by an unbelief of the threatening; he recovers us by a belief of the promise; by unbelief we laid the foundation of God's dishonor; by faith, therefore, God exalts the glory of his free grace. We lost ourselves by a desire of self-dependence, and our return is ordered by way of self-emptiness. It is reasonable we should be restored in a way contrary to that whereby we fell; we sinned by a refusal of cleaving to God; it is a part of Divine wisdom to restore us in a denial of our own righteousness and strength.[d] Man having sinned by pride, the wisdom of God humbles him (saith one) at the very root of the tree of knowledge, and makes him deny his own understanding, and submit to faith, or else, forever to lose his desired felicity.

(3.) It is a condition suited to the common sentiment and custom of the world. There is more of belief than reason in the world. All instructors and masters in sciences and arts, require, first a belief in their disciples, and a resignation of their understandings and wills to them. And it is the wisdom of God to require that of man, which his own reason makes him submit to another which is his fellow-creature. He, therefore, that quarrels with the condition of faith, must quarrel with all the world, since belief is the beginning of all knowledge;[e] yea, and most of the knowledge in the world, may rather come under the title of belief, than of knowledge; for what we think we know this day, we may find from others such arguments as may stagger our knowledge, and make us doubt of that we thought ourselves certain of before: nay, sometimes we change our opinions ourselves without any instructor, and see a reason to entertain an opinion quite contrary to what we had before. And if we found a general judgment of others to vote against what we think we know, it would make us give the less credit to ourselves and our own sentiments. All knowledge in the world is only a belief, depending upon the testimony or arguings of others; for, indeed, it may be said of all men, as in Job (viii. 9), "We are but of yesterday, and know nothing." Since, therefore, belief is so universal a thing in the world, the wisdom of God requires that of us which every man must count reasonable, or render himself utterly ignorant of anything. It is a condition that is common to all religions. All

[d] Laud against Fisher, p. 5.   [e] Bradward, p. 28.

religions are founded upon a belief: unless men did believe future things, they would not hope nor fear. A belief and resignation was required in all the idolatries in the world; so that God requires nothing but what a universal custom of the world gives its suffrage to the reasonableness of: indeed, justifying faith is not suited to the sentiments of men; but that faith which must precede justifying, a belief of the doctrine, though not comprehended by reason, is common to the custom of the world.[f] It is no less madness not to submit our reason to faith, than not to regulate our fancies by reason.

(4.) This condition of faith and repentance is suited to the conscience of men. The law of nature teaches us, that we are bound to believe every revelation from God, when it is made known to us: and not only to assent to it as true, but embrace it as good. This nature dictates, that we are as much obliged to believe God, because of his truth, as to love him, because of his goodness. Every man's reason tells him, he cannot obey a precept, nor depend upon a promise, unless he believes both the one and the other. No man's conscience but will inform him, upon hearing the revelation of God concerning his excellent contrivance of redemption, and the way to enjoy it, that it is very reasonable he should strip off all affections to sin, lie down in sorrow, and bewail what he hath done amiss against so tender a God. Can you expect that any man that promises you a great honor or a rich donative, should demand less of you than to trust his word, bear an affection to him, and return him kindness? Can any less be expected by a prince than obedience from a pardoned subject, and a redeemed captive? If you have injured any man in his body, estate, reputation, would you not count it a reasonable condition for the partaking of his clemency and forgiveness, to express a hearty sorrow for it, and a resolution not to fall into the like crime again? Such are the conditions of the gospel, suited to the consciences of men.

(5.) The wisdom of God appears, in that this condition was only likely to attain the end. There are but two common heads appointed by God,—Adam and Christ: by one we are made a living soul, by the other a quickening spirit: by the one we are made sinners, by the other we are made righteous. Adam fell as a head, and all his members, his whole issue and posterity, fell with him, because they proceeded from him by natural generation. But since the second Adam cannot be our head by natural generation, there must be some other way of engrafting us in him, and uniting us to him as our Head, which must be moral and spiritual; this cannot rationally be conceived to be by any other way than what is suitable to a reasonable creature, and, therefore, must be by an act of the will, consent and acceptance, and owning the terms settled for an admission to that union. And this is that we properly call faith, and, therefore, called a receiving of him (John i. 12).

[1.] Now this condition of enjoying the fruits of redemption could not be a bare knowledge; for that is but only an act of the understanding, and doth not in itself include the act of the will, and so would have united only one faculty to him, not the whole soul: but

[f] Janeway, p. 88.

faith is an act both of the understanding and will too ; and principally of the will, which doth presuppose an act of the understanding :
for there cannot be a persuasion in the will, without a proposition
from the understanding. The understanding must be convinced of
the truth and goodness of a thing, before the will can be persuaded
to make any motion towards it ; and, therefore, all the promises, invitations, and proffers, are suited to the understanding and will ; to
the understanding in regard of knowledge, to the will in regard of
appetite ; to the understanding as true, to the will as good; to the
understanding as practical, and influencing the will.

[2.] Nor could it be an entire obedience. That, as was said before,
would have made the creature have some matter of boasting, and
this was not suitable to the condition he was sunk into by the fall.
Besides, man's nature being corrupted, was rendered incapable to
obey, and unable to have one thought of a due obedience (2 Cor. iii.
5).   When man turned from God, and upon that was turned out of
paradise, his return was impossible by any strength of his own ; his
nature was as much corrupted as his re-entrance into paradise was
prohibited.   That covenant, whereby he stood in the garden, required a perfection of action and intention in the observance of all
the commands of God : but his fall had cracked his ability to recover
happiness by the terms and condition of an entire obedience ; yet
man being a person governable by a law, and capable of happiness
by a covenant, if God would restore him, and enter into a covenant
with him, we must suppose it to have some condition, as all covenants have.   That condition could not be works, because man's
nature was polluted.   Indeed, had God reduced man's body to the
dust, and his soul to nothing, and framed another man, he might
have governed him by a covenant of works : but that had not been
the same man that had revolted, and upon his revolt was stained and
disabled.   But suppose God had, by any transcendent grace, wholly
purified him from the stain of his former transgression, and restored
to him the strength and ability he had lost, might he not as easily
have rebelled again ?   And so the condition would never have been
accomplished, the covenant never have been performed, and happiness never have been enjoyed.   There must be some other condition
then in the covenant God would make for man's security.   Now
faith is the most proper for receiving the promise of pardon of sin :
belief of those promises is the first natural reflection that a malefactor
can make upon a pardon offered him, and acceptance of it is the first
consequent from that belief.   Hence is faith entitled a persuasion of,
and embracing the promises (Heb. xi. 13), and a receiving the atonement (Rom. v. 11).   Thus the wisdom of God is apparent in annexing such a condition to the covenant, whereby man is restored, as
answers the end of God for his glory, the state, conscience, and
necessity of man, and had the greatest congruity to his recovery.

9. This wisdom of God is manifest in the manner of the publishing and propagating this doctrine of redemption.

(1.) In the gradual discoveries of it. Flashing a great light in the
face of a sudden is amazing ; should the sun glare in our eye in all
its brightness on a sudden, after we have been in a thick darkness,

it would blind us, instead of comforting us: so great a work as this must have several digestions. God first reveals of what seed the Redeeming Person should be, "the Seed of the woman" (Gen. iii. 15); then of what nation (Gen. xxvi. 4); then of what tribe (Gen. xlix. 12),—of the tribe of Judah ; then of what family,—the family of David ; then what works he was to do, what sufferings to undergo. The first predictions of our Saviour were obscure. Adam could not well see the redemption in the promise for the punishment of death which succeeded in the threatening ; the promise exercised his faith, and the obscurity and bodily death, his humility. The promise made to Abraham was clearer than the revelations made before, yet he could not tell how to reconcile his redemption with his exile. God supported his faith by the promise, and exercised his humility by making him a pilgrim, and keeping him in a perpetual dependence upon him in all his motions. The declarations to Moses are brighter than those to Abraham : the delineations of Christ by David, in the Psalms, more illustrious than the former : and all those exceeded by the revelations made to the prophet Isaiah, and the other prophets, according as the age did approach wherein the Redeemer was to enter into his office. God wrapped up this gospel in a multitude of types and ceremonies fitted to the infant state of the church (Gal. iv. 3). An infant state is usually affected with sensible things ; yet all those ceremonies were fitted to that great end of the gospel, which he would bring forth in time to the world. And the wisdom of God in them would be amazing, if we could understand the analogy between every ceremony in the law and the thing signified by it: as it cannot but affect a diligent reader to observe that little account of them we have by the apostle Paul, sprinkled in his epistles, and more largely in that to the Hebrews. As the political laws of the Jews flowed from the depth of the moral law, so their ceremonial did from the depth of evangelical counsels, and all of them had a special relation to the honor of God, and the debasing the creature. Though God formed the mass and matter of the world at the first creation at once, yet his wisdom took six days time for the disposing and adorning it. The more illustrious truths of God are not to be comprehended on a sudden by the weakness of men. Christ did not declare all truths to his disciples in the time of his life, because they were not able at that present to bear them (John xvi. 12) : "Ye cannot bear them now;" some were reserved for his resurrection, others for the coming of the Spirit, and the full discovery of all kept back for another world. This doctrine God figured out in the law, oracled by the prophets, and unveiled by Christ and his apostles.

(2.) The wisdom of God appeared in using all proper means to render the belief of it easy.

[1.] The most minute things that were to be transacted were predicted in the ancient foregoing age, long before the coming of the Redeemer. The vinegar and gall offered to him upon the cross, the parting his garments, the not breaking of his bones, the piercing of his hands and feet, the betraying of him, the slighting of him by the multitude, all were exactly painted and represented in variety of figures. There was light enough to good men not to mistake him, and yet not so plain as to hinder bad men from being serviceable to the counsels of God in the crucifying of him when he came.

[2.] The translation of the Old Testament from the private language of the Jews, into the most public language of the world; that translation which we call Septuagint, from Hebrew into Greek,. some years before the coming of Christ, that tongue being most diffused at that time, by reason of the Macedonian empire, raised by Alexander, and the university of Athens, to which other nations resorted for learning and education. This was a preparation for the sons of Japhet to "dwell in the tents of Shem." By this was the entertainment of the gospel facilitated; when they compared the prophesies of the Old Testament with the declarations of the New, and found things so long predicted before they were transacted in the public view.

[3.] By ordering concurrent testimonies, as to matter of fact, that the matter of fact was not deniable. That there was such a person as Christ, that his miracles were stupendous, that his doctrine did not incline to sedition, that he affected not worldly applause, that he did suffer at Jerusalem, was acknowledged by all; not a man among the greatest enemies of Christians was found that denied the matter of fact. And this great truth, that Christ is the Messiah and Redeemer, hath been with universal consent owned by all the professors of Christianity throughout the world: whatever bickerings there have been among them about some particular doctrines, they all centred in that truth of Christ's being the Redeemer. The first publication of this doctrine was sealed by a thousand miracles, and so illustrious, that he was an utter stranger to the world that was ignorant of them.

[4.] In keeping up some principles and opinions in the world to facilitate the belief of this, or render men inexcusable for rejecting of it. The incarnation of the son of God could not be so strange to the world, if we consider the general belief of the appearances[g] of their gods among them; that the Epicureans and others, that denied any such appearances, were counted atheists.[h] And Pythagoras was esteemed to be one, not of the inferior genii and lunar demons, but one of the higher gods, who appeared in a human body, for the curing and rectifying mortal life;[i] and himself tells Abaris, the Scythian, that he was ἀνθρωπόμορφος, that he "took the flesh of man," that men might not be astonished at him, and in a fright fly from his instructions. It was not therefore accounted an irrational thing among them, that God should be incarnate: but, indeed, the great stumbling-block was a crucified God. But had they known the holy and righteous nature of God, the malice of sin, the universal corruption of human nature, the first threatening, and the necessity of vindicating the honor of the law, and clearing the justice of God, the notion of his crucifixion would not have appeared so incredible, since they believed the possibility of an incarnation.

Another principle was that universal one of sacrifices for expiation, and rendering God propitious to man, and was practised among

g Ἐπιφάνειαι.   h Dionys. Halicar, Antiq. l. 2, p. 128.
i Iamblych. Vit. Pythag., lib. i. cap. 6, p. 44, and lib. ii. c. 19, p. 94.

all nations. I remember not any wherein this custom did not prevail; for it did even among those people where the Jews, as being no trading nation, had not any commerce; and also in America, found out in these latter ages. It was not a law of nature; no man can find any such thing written in his own heart, but a tradition from Adam. Now that among the loss of so many other doctrines that were handed down from Adam to his immediate posterity, as, in particular, that of the "Seed of the woman," which one would think a necessary appendix to that of sacrificing, this latter should be preserved as a fragment of an ancient tradition, seems to be an act of Divine wisdom, to prepare men for the entertainment of the doctrine of the great Sacrifice for the expiation of the sin of the world. And as the apostle forms his argument from the Jewish sacrifices, in the epistle to the Hebrews, for the convincing them of the end of the death of Christ, so did the ancient fathers make use of this practice of the heathen to convince them of the same doctrine.

[5.] The wisdom of God appeared in the time and circumstances of the first solemn publication of the gospel by the apostles at Jerusalem. The relation you may read in Acts ii. 1—12. The Spirit was given to the apostles on the day of Pentecost; a time wherein there were multitudes of Jews from all nations, not only near, but remote, that heard the great things of God spoken in the several languages of those nations where their habitations were fixed, and that by twelve illiterate men, that two or three hours before knew no language but that of their native country. It was the custom of the Jews, that dwelt among other nations, at a distance from Jerusalem, to assemble together at Jerusalem at the feast of Pentecost: and God pitched upon this season, that there might be witnesses of this miracle in many parts of the world: there were some of every nation under heaven (ver 5); that is, of that known part of the world, so saith the text. Fourteen several nations are mentioned; and proselytes as well as Jews by birth. They are called " devout men," men of conscience, whose testimony would carry weight with it among their neighbors at their return, because of their reputation by their religious carriage. Again, this was not heard and seen by some of them at one time, and some at another, by some one hour, by others the next successively,[k] but altogether, in a solemn assembly, that the testimony of so many witnesses at a time, might be more valid, and the truth of the doctrine appear more illustrious and undeniable. And it must needs be astonishing to them, to hear that person magnified in so miraculous a manner, who had so lately been condemned by their countrymen as a malefactor. Wisdom consists in the timing of things. And in this circumstance doth the wisdom of God appear, in furnishing the apostles with the Spirit at such a time, and bringing forth such a miracle, as the gift of tongues, on a sudden, that every nation might hear in their own language the wonder of redemption, and as witnesses at their returns into their own countries, report it to others; that the credit they had, in their several places, might facilitate the belief and entertainment of the gospel, when the apostles, or others, should arrive to those several charges and dio-

[k] Faucheur. *in loc.* pp. 294, 295.

ceses appointed for them to preach the gospel in. Had this miracle been wrought in the presence only of the inhabitants of Judea, that understood only their own language, or one or two of the neighboring tongues, it had been counted by them rather a madness than a miracle. Or had they understood all the tongues which they spoke, the news of it had spread no further than the limits of their own habitations, and had been confined within the narrow bounds of the land of Judea. But now it is carried to several remote nations, where any of those auditors then assembled had their residence. As God chose the time of the Passover for the death of Christ, that there might be the greatest number of the inhabitants of the country, as witnesses of the matter of fact, the innocence and sufferings of Christ, so he chose the time of Pentecost for the first publishing the value and end of this blood to the world. Thus the evangelical law was given in a confluence of people from all parts and nations, because it was a covenant with all nations: and the variety of languages spoken by a company of poor Galileans, bred up at the lake of Tiberias, and in poor corners of Canaan, without the instructions of men for so great a skill, might well evidence to the hearers, that God that brought the confusion of languages first at Babel, did only work that cure of them, and combine all together at Jerusalem.

(3.) The wisdom of God is seen in the instruments he employed in the publishing the gospel. He did not employ philosophers, but fishermen ; used not acquired arts, but infused wisdom and courage. This treasure was put into, and preserved in earthen vessels, that the wisdom, as well as the power of God, might be magnified. The weaker the means are which attain the end, the greater is the skill of the conductor of them. Wise princes choose men of most credit, interest, wisdom, and ability, to be ministers of their affairs, and ambassadors to others. But what were these that God chose for so great a work, as the publishing a new doctrine to the world? What was their quality but mean, what was their authority without interest? What was their ability, without eminent parts for so great a work, but what Divine grace in a special manner endowed them with? Nay, what was their disposition to it? as dull and unwieldy. Witness the frequent rebukes for their slow-heartedness, from their Master, when he conversed in the flesh with them. And one of the greatest of them, so fond of the Jewish ceremonies and Pharisaical principles, wherein he had been more than ordinarily principled, that he hated the Christian religion to extirpation, and the professors of it to death; by those ways which were out of the road of human wisdom, and would be accounted the greatest absurdity to be practised by men that have a repute for discretion, did God advance his wisdom (1 Cor. i. 25): "The foolishness of God is wiser than man." By this means it was indisputably evidenced to unbiassed minds, that the doctrine was divine. It could not rationally be imagined, that instruments destitute of all human advantages, should be able to vanquish the world, confound Judaism, overturn heathenism, chase away the devils, strip them of their temples, alienate the minds of men from their several religions, which had been rooted in them by education, and established by a long succession. It could not, I say, reasonably be imagined to be without a supernatural assistance, an heavenly and efficacious working: whereas, had God taken a course agreeable to the prudence of man, and used those that had been furnished with learning, tipped with eloquence, and armed with human authority, the doctrines would have been thought to have been of a human invention, and to be some subtle contrivance for some unworthy and ambitious end: the nothingness and weakness of the instruments manifest them to be conducted by a Divine power, and declare the doctrine itself to be from heaven. When we see such feeble instruments proclaiming a doctrine repugnant to flesh and blood, sounding forth a crucified Christ to be believed in, and trusted on, and declaiming against the religion and worship under which the Roman empire had long flourished; exhorting them to the contempt of the world, preparation for afflictions, denying themselves, and their own honors, by the hopes of an unseen reward, things so repugnant to flesh and blood; and these instruments concurring in the same story, with an admirable harmony in all parts, and sealing this doctrine with their blood; can we upon all this, ascribe this doctrine to a human contrivance, or fix any lower author of it than the wisdom of heaven? It is the wisdom of God that carries on his own designs in methods most suitable to his own greatness, and different from the customs and modes of men, that less of humanity, and more of divinity might appear.

(4.) The wisdom of God appears in the ways and manner, as well as in the instruments of its propagation, by ways seemingly contrary. You know how God had sent the Jews into captivity in Babylon, and though he struck off their chains, and restored them to their country, yet many of them had no mind to leave a country wherein they had been born and bred. The distance from the place of the original of their ancestors, and their affection to the country wherein they were born, might have occasioned their embracing the idolatrous worship of the place. Afterwards the persecutions of Antiochus scattered many of the Jews for their security into other nations; yet a great part, and perhaps the greatest, preserved their religion, and by that were obliged to come every year to Jerusalem to offer, and so were present at the effusion of the Spirit on the day of Pentecost, and were witnesses of the miraculous effects of it. Had they not been dispersed by persecution, had they not resided in several countries, and been acquainted with their languages, the gospel had not so easily been diffused into several countries of the world. The first persecutions also raised against the church, propagated the gospel; the scattering of the disciples enflamed their courage, and dispersed the doctrine (Acts viii. 3), according to the prophecy of Daniel (xii. 4): "Many should run to and fro, and knowledge should be increased." The flights and hurryings of men should enlarge the territories of the gospel. There was not a tribunal, but the primitive Christians were cited to; not a horrible punishment, but was inflicted upon them. Treated they were, as the dregs and offals of mankind, as the common enemies of the world; yet the flames of the martyrs brightened the doctrine, and the captivity of its professors made way for the throne of its empire. The imprisonment of the ark was the downfall of Dagon. Religion grew stronger by sufferings, and Christianity taller by injuries. What can this be ascribed to, but the conduct of a wisdom superior to that of men and devils, defeating the methods of human and hellish policy; thereby making the "wisdom of this world foolishness with God" (1 Cor. iii. 19)?

V. The *Use*, 1. Of Information. If wisdom be an excellency of the Divine nature; then,

1. Christ's Deity may hence be asserted. Wisdom is the emphatical title of Christ in Scripture (Prov. viii. 12, 13, 31), where wisdom is brought in speaking as a distinct person; ascribing counsel, and understanding, and the knowledge of witty inventions to itself. He is called also the power of God, and the wisdom of God (1 Cor. i. 24). And the ancients generally understood that place (Col. ii. 3), " In him are hid all the treasures of wisdom and knowledge," as an assertion of the Godhead of Christ, in regard of the infiniteness of his knowledge; referring wisdom to his knowledge of divine things; and knowledge to his understanding of all human things. But the natural sense of the place seems to be this, that all wisdom and knowledge is displayed by Christ in the gospel; and the words, *ἐν αὐτῷ*, refer either to Christ, or the mystery of God spoken of, (ver. 2). But the Deity of Christ, in regard of infinite wisdom, may be deduced from his creation of things, and his government of things; both which are ascribed to him in Scripture. The first ascribed to him (John i. 3): "All things were made by him;" and (ver. 27), " Without him was not any thing made, that was made." The second (John v. 22): " The Father hath committed all judgment to the Son;" and both put together (Col. ii. 16, 17). Now since he hath the government of the world, he hath the perfections necessary to so great a work. As the creation of the world, which is ascribed to him, requires an infinite power, so the government of the world requires an infinite wisdom. That he hath the knowledge of the hearts of men, was proved in handling the omniscience of God. That knowledge would be to little purpose without wisdom to order the motions of men's hearts, and conduct all the qualities and actions of creatures, to such an end as is answerable to a wise government; we cannot think so great an employment can be without an ability necessary for it. The government of men and angels is a great part of the glory of God; and if God should entrust the greatest part of his glory in hands unfit for so great a trust, it would be an argument of weakness in God, as it is in men, to pitch upon unfit instruments for particular charges; since God hath therefore committed to him his greatest glory, the conduct of all things for the highest end, he hath a wisdom requisite for so great an end, which can be no less than infinite. If then Christ were a finite person, he would not be capable of an infinite communication; he could not be a subject wherein infinite wisdom could be lodged; for the terms finite and infinite are so distant, that they cannot commence one another; finite can never be changed into infinite, no more than infinite can into finite.

(2.) Hence we may assert the right and fitness of God for the government of the world, as he is the wisest Being. Among men, those who are excellent in judgment, are accounted fittest to preside over, and give orders to others; the wisest in a city are most capable to govern a city; or at least, though ignorant men may bear the title, yet the advice of the soundest and skilfullest heads should prevail in all public affairs: we see in nature, that the eye guides the body, and the mind directs the eye. Power and wisdom are the two arms of authority; wisdom knows the end, and directs the means; power executes the means designed for such an end.[1] The more splendid and strong those are in any, the more authority results from thence, for the conduct of others that are of an inferior orb; now God being infinitely excellent in both, his ability and right to the management of the world cannot be suspected; the whole world is but one commonwealth, whereof God is the monarch. Did the government of the world depend upon the election of men and angels, where could they pitch, or where would they find perfections capable of so great a work, but in the Supreme Wisdom? His wisdom hath already been apparent in those laws, whereby he formed the world into a civil society, and the Israelites into a commonwealth. The one suited to the consciences and reasons of all his subjects, and the other suited to the genius of that particular nation, drawn out of the righteousness of the moral law, and applicable to all cases that might arise among them in their government; so that Moses asserts, that the wisdom apparent in their laws enacted by God, as their chief magistrate, would render them famous among other nations, in regard of their wisdom, as well as their righteousness (Deut. iv. 6, 7, 9). Also, this perfection doth evidence, that God doth actually govern the world. It would not be a commendable thing for a man to make a curious piece of clock-work, and take no care for the orderly motion of it. Would God display so much of his skill in framing the heaven and earth, and none in actual guidance of them to their particular and universal ends? Did he lay the foundation in order, and fit every stone in the building, make all things in weight and measure, to let them afterwards run at hap-hazard? Would he bring forth his power to view in the creation, and let a more glorious perfection lie idle, when it had so large a field to move in? Infinite wisdom is inconsistent with inactivity. All prudence doth illustrate itself in untying the hardest knots, and disposing the most difficult affairs to a happy and successful issue. All those various arts and inventions among men which lend their assisting hand to one another, and those various employments their several geniuses lead them to, whereby they support one another's welfare, are beams and instincts of Divine wisdom in the government of the world. He that "made all things in wisdom" (Ps. civ. 24), would not leave his works to act and move only according to their own folly, and idly behold them jumble together, and run counter to that end he designed them for; we must not fancy Divine wisdom to be destitute of activity.

3. Here we may see a ground of God's patience. The most impotent persons are the most impatient, when unforeseen emergencies

[1] Amyraut, Moral. Tom. I. pp. 258, 259.

arise; or at events expected by them, when their feeble prudence was not a sufficient match to contest with them, or prevent them. But the wiser any man is, the more he bears with those things which seem to cross his intentions, because he knows he grasps the whole affair, and is sure of attaining the end he proposeth to himself; yet, as a finite wisdom can have but a finite patience, so an infinite wisdom possesses an infinite patience. The wise God intends to bring glory to himself, and good to some of his creatures, out of the greatest evils that can happen in the world, he beholds no exorbitant afflictions and monstrous actions, but what he can dispose to a good and glorious end, even to "work together for good to them that love God" (Rom. viii. 28); and, therefore, doth not presently fall foul upon the actors, till he hath wrought out that temporary glory to himself, and good to his people which he designs. The times of ignorance God winked at, till he had brought his Son into the world, and manifested his wisdom in redemption, and when this was done he presseth men to a "speedy repentance" (Acts xvii. 30); that, as he forbore punishing their crimes, in order to the displaying his wisdom in the designed redemption; so when he had effected it, they must forbear any longer abusing his patience.

4. Hence appears the immutability of God in his decrees. He is not destitute of a power and strength to change his own purposes, but his infinite perfection of wisdom is a bar to his laying aside his eternal resolves and forming new ones (Isa. xlvi. 10); he resolves the end from the beginning, and his counsel stands; stands immovable, because it is his counsel. It is an impotent counsel, that is subject to a daily thwarting itself. Inconstant persons are accounted, by men, destitute of a due measure of prudence. If God change his mind it is either for the better or the worse; if for the better, he was not wise in his former purpose; if for the worse, he is not wise in his present resolve. No alteration can be without a reflection of weakness upon the former or present determination. God must either cease to be as wise as he was before, or begin to be wiser than he was before the change, which to think or imagine is to deny a Deity. If any man change his resolution, he is apprehensive of a flaw in his former purpose, and finds an inconvenience in it, which moves him to such a change, which must be either for want of foresight in himself, or want of a due consideration of the object of his counsel, neither of which can be imagined of God without a denial of the Deity. No, there are no blots and blemishes in his purposes and promises. Repentance, indeed, is an act of wisdom in the creature, but it presupposeth folly in his former actions, which is inconsistent with infinite perfection. Men are often too rash in promising; and, therefore, what they promise in haste, they perform at leisure, or not at all: they consider not before they vow, and make after-inquiries, whether they had best stand to it. The only wise God needs not any after-game: as he is sovereignly wise, he sees no cause of reversing anything, and wants not expedients for his own purpose; and as he is infinitely powerful, he hath no superior to hinder him from executing his will, and making his people enjoy the effects of his wisdom. If he had a recollection of thoughts, as man hath, and

and saw a necessity to mend them, he were not infinitely wise in his first decrees: as in creation he looked back upon the several pieces of that goodly frame he had erected, and saw them so exact that he did not take up his pencil again to mend any particle of the first draught, so his promises are made with such infinite wisdom and judgment, that what he writes is irreversible and forever, as the decrees of the Medes and Persians. All the words of God are eternal because they are the births of righteousness and judgment (Hos. ii. 19); "I will betroth thee to me forever, in righteousness and judgment." He is not of a wavering and flitting discretion: if he threatens, he wisely considers what he threatens; if he promises, he wisely considers what he promises; and therefore is immutable in both.

5. Hence it follows that God is a fit object for our trust and confidence: for God being infinitely wise, when he promises anything, he sees everything which may hinder, and everything which may promote the execution of it, so that he cannot discover anything afterwards that may move him to take up after-thoughts: he hath more wisdom than to promise anything hand over head, or anything which he knows he cannot accomplish. Though God, as true, be the object of our trust, yet God, as wise, is the foundation of our trust. We trust him in his promise; the promise was made by mercy, and it is performed by truth; but wisdom conducts all means to the accomplishment of it. There are many men, whose honesty we can confide in, but whose discretion we are diffident of: but there is no defect, either of the one or the other, which may scare us from a depending upon God in our concerns. The words of man's wisdom the apostle entitles "enticing" (1 Cor. ii. 4), in opposition to the words of God's wisdom, which are firm, stable, and undeniable demonstrations. As the power of God is an encouragement of trust, because he is able to effect, so the wisdom of God comes into the rank of those attributes which support our faith. To put a confidence in him, we must be persuaded, not only that he is ignorant of nothing in the world, but that he is wise to manage the whole course of nature, and dispose of all his creatures, for the bringing his purposes and his promises to their designed perfection.

6. Hence appears the necessity of a public review of the management of the world, and of a day of judgment. As a day of judgment may be inferred from many attributes of God, as his sovereignty, justice, omniscience, &c., so, among the rest, from this of wisdom. How much of this perfection will lie unveiled and obscure, if the sins of men be not brought to view, whereby the ordering the unrighteous actions of men, by his directing and over-ruling hand of providence, in subserviency to his own purposes and his people's good, may appear in all its glory! Without such a public review, this part of wisdom will not be clearly visible; how those actions, which had a vile foundation in the hearts and designs of men, and were formed there to gratify some base lust, ambition, and covetousness, &c. were, by a secret wisdom presiding over them, conducted to amazing ends. It is a part of Divine wisdom to right itself, and convince men of the reasonableness of its laws, and the unreasonableness of their contra-

dictions to it. The execution of the sentence is an act of justice, but the conviction of the reasonableness of the sentence is an act of wisdom, clearing up the righteousness of the proceeding; and this precedes, and the other follows (Jude 15); "To convince all that are ungodly of all their ungodly deeds." That wisdom which contrived satisfaction, as well as that justice which required it, is concerned in righting the law which was enacted by it. The wisdom of a sovereign Lawgiver is engaged not to see his law vilified and trampled on, and exposed to the lusts and affronts of men, without being concerned in vindicating the honor of it. It would appear a folly to enact and publish it, if there were not a resolution to right and execute it. The wisdom of God can no more associate iniquity and happiness together, than the justice of God can separate iniquity from punishment. It would be defective, if it did always tamely bear the insolences of offenders, without a time of remark of their crimes, and a justification of the precept, rebelliously spurned at. He would be unwise, if he were unjust; unrighteousness hath no better a title in Scripture than that of folly. It is no part of Wisdom to give birth to those laws which he will always behold ineffectual, and neither vindicate his law by a due execution of the penalty, nor right his own authority, contemned in the violation of his law, by a just revenge : besides, what wisdom would it be for the Sovereign Judge to lodge such a spokesman for himself as conscience in the soul of man, if it should be alway found speaking, and at length be found false in all that it speaks? There is, therefore, an apparent prospect of the day of account, from the consideration of this perfection of the Divine nature.

7. Hence we have a ground for a mighty reverence and veneration of the Divine Majesty. Who can contemplate the sparklings of this perfection in the variety of the works of his hands, and the exact government of all his creatures, without a raised admiration of the excellency of his Being, and a falling flat before him, in a posture of reverence to so great a Being? Can we behold so great a mass of matter, digested into several forms, so exact a harmony and temperament in all the creatures, the proportions of numbers and measures, and one creature answering the ends and designs of another, the distinct beauties of all, the perpetual motion of all things without checking one another; the variety of the nature of things, and all acting according to their nature with an admirable agreement, and all together, like different strings upon an instrument, emitting divers sounds, but all reduced to order in one delightful lesson;—I say, can we behold all this without admiring and adoring the Divine wisdom, which appears in all? And from the consideration of this, let us pass to the consideration of his wisdom in redemption, in reconciling divided interests, untying hard knots, drawing one contrary out of another ; and we must needs acknowledge that the wisdom of all the men on earth, and angels in heaven, is worse than nothing and vanity in comparison of this vast Ocean. And as we have a greater esteem for those that invent some excellent artificial engines, what reverence ought we to have for him that hath stamped an unimitable wisdom upon all his works! Nature orders

us to give honor to our superiors in knowledge, and confide in their counsels; but none ought to be reverenced as much as God, since none equals him in wisdom.

8. If God be infinitely wise, it shows us the necessity of our address to him, and invocation of his Name. We are subject to mistakes, and often overseen; we are not able rightly to counsel ourselves. In some cases, all creatures are too short-sighted to apprehend them, and too ignorant to give advice proper for them, and to contrive remedies for their ease; but with the Lord there is counsel (Jer. xxxii. 19), "He is great in counsel, and mighty in working;" great in counsel to advise us, mighty in working to assist us. We know not how to effect a design, or prevent an expected evil. We have an infinite Wisdom to go to, that is every way skilful to manage any business we desire, to avert any evil we fear, to accomplish anything we commit into his hands. When we know not what to resolve, he hath a counsel to "guide us" (Ps. lxxiii. 24). He is not more powerful to effect what is needful, than wise to direct what is fitting. All men stand in need of the help of God, as one man stands in need of the assistance of other men, and will not do anything without advice; and he that takes advice, deserves the title of a wise man, as well as he that gives advice. But no man needs so much the advice of another man, as all men need the counsel and assistance of God: neither is any man's wit and wisdom so far inferior to the prudence and ability of an angel, as the wisdom of the wisest man and the most sharp-sighted angel, is inferior to the infinite wisdom of God. We see, therefore, that it is best for us to go to the fountain, and not content ourselves with the streams; to beg advice from a wisdom that is infinite and infallible, rather than from that which is finite and fallible.

Use 2. If wisdom be the perfection of the Divine Majesty, how prodigious is the contempt of it in the world? In general, all sin strikes at this attribute, and is in one part or other a degrading of it: the first sin directed its venom against this. As the devils endeavored to equal their Creator in power, so man endeavored to equal him in wisdom: both indeed scorned to be ruled by his order; but man evidently exalted himself against the wisdom of God, and aspired to be a sharer with him in his infinite knowledge; would not let him be the only wise God, but cherished an ambition to be his partner. Just as if a beam were able to imagine it might be as bright as the sun; or a spark fancy it could be as full fraught with heat as the whole element of fire. Man would not submit to the infinite wisdom of God in the prohibition of one single fruit in the garden, when by the right of his sovereign authority, he might have granted him only the use of one. All presumptuous sins are of this nature; they are, therefore, called reproaches of God (Num. xv. 30), "the soul that doth ought presumptuously, reproacheth the Lord." All reproaches are either for natural, moral, or intellectual defects. All reproaches of God must imply either a weakness or unrighteousness in God: if unrighteousness, his holiness is denied; if weakness, his wisdom is blemished. In general, all sin strikes at this perfection two ways.

1. As it defaceth the wise workmanship of God. Every sin is a deforming and blemishing our own souls, which, as they are the prime creatures in the lower world, so they have greater characters of Divine wisdom in the fabric of them: but this image of God is ruined and broken by sin. Though the spoiling of it be a scorn of his holiness, it is also an affront to his wisdom ; for though his power was the cause of the production of so fair a piece, yet his wisdom was the guide of his power, and his holiness the pattern whereby he wrought it. His power effected it, and his holiness was exemplified in it ; but his wisdom contrived it. If a man had a curious clock or watch, which had cost him many years pains and the strength of his skill to frame it ; for another, after he had seen and considered it, to trample upon it, and crush it in pieces, would argue a contempt of the artificer's skill. God hath shown infinite art in the creation of man ; but sin unbeautifies man, and ravisheth his excellency. It cuts and slasheth the image of God stamped by divine wisdom, as though it were an object only of scorn and contempt. The sinner in every sin acts, as if he intended to put himself in a better posture, and in a fairer dress, than the wisdom of God hath put him in by creation.

2. In the slighting his laws. The laws of God are highly rational ; they are drawn from the depths of the Divine understanding, wherein there is no unclearness, and no defect. As his understanding apprehends all things in their true reason, so his will enjoins all things for worthy and wise ends. His laws are contrived by his wisdom for the happiness of man, whose happiness, and the methods to it, he understands better than men or angels can do. His laws being the orders of the wisest understanding, every breach of his law is a flying in the face of his wisdom. All human laws, though they are enforced by sovereign authority, yet they are, or ought to be, in the composing of them, founded upon reason, and should be particular applications of the law of nature to this or that particular emergency. The laws of God, then, who is *summa ratio*, are the birth of the truest reason ; though the reason of every one of them may not be so clear to us. Every law, though it consists in an act of the will, yet doth pre-suppose an act of the understanding. The act of the Divine understanding in framing the law, must be supposed to precede the act of his will in commanding the observance of that law. So every sin against the law, is not only against the will of God commanding, but the reason of God contriving, and a cleaving to our own reason, rather than the understanding or mind of God: as if God had mistaken in making his law, and we had more understanding to frame a better, and more conducing to our happiness: as if God were not wise enough to govern us, and prescribe what we should do, and what we should avoid ; as if he designed not our welfare but our misfortune. Whereas, the precepts of God are not tyrannical edicts, or acts of mere will, but the fruits of counsel ; and, therefore, every breach of them is a real declamation against his discretion and judgment, and preferring our own imaginations, or the suggestions of the devil, as our rule, before the results of Divine counsel. While we acknowledge

him wise in our opinion, we speak him foolish by our practice; when, instead of being guided by him, we will guide ourselves. No man will question, but it is a controlling Divine wisdom, to make alterations in his precepts; dogmatically, either to add some of their own, or expunge any of his: and is it not a crime of the like reflection to alter them practically? When we will observe one part of the law, and not another part; but pick and choose where we please ourselves, as our humors and carnal interest prompt us; it is to charge that part of the law with folly, which we refuse to conform unto. The more cunning any man is in sin, the more his sin is against Divine wisdom, as if he thought to outwit God. He that receives the promises of God, and the " testimony of Christ, sets to his seal, that God is true" (John iii. 33). By the like strength of argument, it will undeniably follow, that he that refuseth obedience to his precepts, sets to his seal that God is foolish. Were they not rational, God would not enjoin them; and if they are rational, we are enemies to infinite wisdom, by not complying with them. If infinite prudence hath made the law, why is not every part of it observed; if it were not made with the best wisdom, why is any part of it observed? If the defacing of his image be any sin, as being a defaming his wisdom in creation, the breaking his law is no less a sin, as being a disgracing his wisdom in his administration. 'Tis upon this account, likely, that the Scripture so often counts sinners fools, since it is certainly inexcusable folly to contradict undeniable and infallible Wisdom; yet this is done in the least sin: and as he that breaks one tittle of the law, is deservedly accounted guilty of the breach of the whole (James ii. 10), so he that despiseth the least stamp of wisdom in the minutest part of the law, is deservedly counted as a contemner of it, in the frame of the whole statute-book. But, in particular, the wisdom of God is affronted and invaded.

(1.) By introducing new rules and modes of worship, different from Divine institutions. Is not this a manifest reflection on this perfection of God, as though he had not been wise enough to provide for his own honor, and model his own service, but stood in need of our directions, and the *caprichios* of our brains? Some have observed, that it is a greater sin in worship to do that we should not, than to omit what we should perform.[m] The one seems to be out of weakness, because of the high exactness of the law; and the other out of impudence, accusing the wisdom of God of imperfection, and controlling it in its institutions. At best, it seems to be an imputation of human bashfulness to the Supreme Sovereign; as if he had been ashamed to prescribe all that was necessary to his own honor, but had left something to the ingenuity and gratitude of men. Man has, ever since the foolish conceit of his old ancestor Adam, presumed he could be as wise as God; and if he who was created upright entertained such conceits, much more doth man now, under a mass of corruption, so capable to foment them. This hath been the continual practice of men; not so much to reject what once they had received as Divine, but add something of their own inventions to it. The

m Strong, of The Will.

heathens renounced not the sacrificing of beasts for the expiation of their offences (which the old world had received by tradition from Adam, and the new world, after the deluge, from Noah). But they had blended that tradition with rites of their own, and offered creatures unclean in themselves, and not fit to be offered to an infinitely pure Being; for the distinction of clean and unclean was as ancient as Noah (Gen. viii. 20), yea, before (Gen. vii. 2). So the Jews did not discard what they had received from God, as circumcision, the Passover, and sacrifices; but they would mix a heap of heathenish rites with the ceremonies of Divine ordination, and practise things which he had not commanded, as well as things which he had enjoined them. And, therefore, it is observable, that when God taxeth them with sin, he doth not say, they brought in those things which he had forbidden into his worship; but those things which he had not commanded, and had given no order for, to intimate, that they were not to move a step without his rule (Jer. vii. 31): "They have built the high palaces of Tophet, which I commanded them not, neither came it into my heart;" and (Levit. x. 1); Nadab's and Abihu's strange fire was not commanded; so charging them with impudence and rashness in adding something of their own, after he had revealed to them the manner of his service, as if they were as wise as God. So loth is man to acknowledge the supremacy of Divine understanding, and be sensible of his own ignorance. So after the divulging of the gospel, the corruptors of religion did not fling off, but preserved the institutions of God, but painted and patched them up with pagan ceremonies; imposed their own dreams with as much force as the revelations of God. Thus hath the papacy turned the simplicity of the gospel into pagan pomp, and religion into politics; and revived the ceremonial law, and raked some limbs of it out of the grave, after the wisdom of God had rung her knell, and honorably interred her; and sheltered the heathenish superstitions in christian temples, after the power of the gospel had chased the devils, with all their trumpery, from their ancient habitations. Whence should this proceed, but from a partial atheism, and a mean deceit of the Divine wisdom? As though God had not understanding enough to prescribe the form of his own worship; and not wisdom enough to support it, without the crutches of human prudence. Human prudence is too low to parallel Divine wisdom; it is an incompetent judge of what is fit for an infinite Majesty. It is sufficiently seen in the ridiculous and senseless rights among the heathens; and the cruel and devilish ones fetched from them by the Jews. What work will human wisdom make with divine worship, when it will presume to be the director of it, as a mate with the wisdom of God! Whence will it take its measures, but from sense, humor and fancy? as though what is grateful and comely to a depraved reason, were as beautiful to an unspotted and Infinite Mind. Do not such tell the world, that they were of God's cabinet council, since they will take upon them to judge, as well as God, what is well-pleasing to him? Where will it have the humility to stop, if it hath the presumption to add any one thing to revealed modes of worship? How did God tax the Israelites with making idols "according to their own understanding"

(Hos. xiii. 2)! imagining their own understandings to be of a finer make, and a perfecter mould than their Creator's; and that they had fetched more light from the chaos of their own brains, than God had from eternity in his own nature. How slight will the excuse be, God hath not forbidden this, or that, when God shall silence men with the question, Where, or when did I command this, or that? There was no addition to be made under the law to the meanest instrument God had appointed in his service. The sacred perfume was not to have one ingredient more put into it, than what God had prescribed in the composition; nor was any man upon pain of death to imitate it; nor would God endure that sacrifices should be consumed with any other fire than that which came down from heaven. So tender is God of any invasions of his wisdom and authority. In all things of this nature, whatsoever voluntary humility and respect to God they may be disguised with, there is a swelling of the fleshly mind against infinite understanding, which the apostle nauseates (Col. ii. 18). Such mixtures have not been blessed by God: as God never prospered the mixtures of several kinds of creatures, to form and multiply a new species, as being a dissatisfaction with his wisdom as Creator; so he doth not prosper mixtures in worship, as being a conspiracy against his wisdom as a Lawgiver. The destruction of the Jews was judged by some of their doctors to be, for preferring human traditions before the written word; which they ground on (Isaiah xxix. 33): "Their fear for me was taught by the precepts of men." The injunctions of men were the rule of their worship, and not the prescripts of my law.[n] To conclude, such as make alterations in religion, different from the first institution, are intolerable busy bodies, that will not let God alone with his own affairs. Vain man would be wiser than his Maker, and be dabbling in that which is His sole prerogative.

2. In neglecting means instituted by God. When men have risings of heart against God's ordinances, "they reject the counsel of the Lord against themselves," or, in themselves (Luke vii. 30), $\dot{\eta}\theta\acute{\epsilon}\tau\eta\sigma\alpha\nu$. They disannulled the wisdom of God, the spring of his ordinances. All neglects are disregards of Divine prescriptions, as impertinent and unavailable to that end for which they were appointed, as not being suited to the common dictates of reason; sometimes out of a voluntary humility, such as Peter's was, when he denied Christ's condescension to wash his feet (John xiii. 8), and thereby judged of the comeliness of his Master's intention and action. Such as continually neglect the great institution of the Lord's supper, out of a sense of unworthiness, are in the same rank with Peter, and do, as well as he, fall under the blame and reproof of Christ. Men would be saved, and use the means, but either means of their own appointment, or not at all the means of God's ordering.[o] They would have God's wisdom and will condescend to theirs, and not theirs conformed to God's; as if our blind judgments were fittest to make the election of the paths to happiness. Like Naaman, who, when he was ordered

---

[n] Vaisin. The Talmud takes notice, that the court of Bethany was wasted three years before Jerusalem, because they preferred their own words before the words of the Law.
[o] Pont. Medit. Part III. p. 366.

by the prophet, for the cure of his leprosy, to "wash seven times in Jordan," would be the prophet's director, and have him touch him with his hand; as if a patient, sick of a desperate disease, should prescribe to his skilful physician what remedies he should order for his cure, and make his own infirm reason, or his gust and palate, the rule, rather than the physician's skill. Men's inquiries are, "Who will show us any good?" They rather fasten upon any means than that which God hath ordained.[p] We invert the order Divine wisdom hath established, when we would have God save us in our own way, not in his. It is the same thing as if we would have God nourish us without bread, and cure our disease without medicines, and increase our wealth without our industry, and cherish our souls without his word and ordinances. It is to demand of him an alteration of his methods, and a separation of that which he hath by his eternal judgment joined together. Therefore for a man to pray to God to save him when he will not use the means he hath appointed for salvation, when he slights the word, which is the instrument of salvation, is a contempt of the wisdom of Divine institutions. Also in omissions of prayer. When we consult not with God upon emergent occasions, we trust more to our own wisdom than God's, and imply that we stand not in need of his conduct, but have ability to direct ourselves, and accomplish our ends without his guidance. Not seeking God is, by the prophet, taxed to be a reflection upon this perfection of God (Isa. xxxi. 1, 2): "They look not to the Holy One of Israel, neither seek the Lord" &c. And the like charge he brings against them (Hos. viii. 9): "They are gone up to Assyria, a wild ass alone by himself, not consulting God."

3. In censuring God's revelations and actions, if they be not according to our schemes: when we will not submit to his plain will without penetrating into the unrevealed reason of it, nor adore his counsels without controlling them, as if we could correct both law and gospel, and frame a better method of redemption than that of God's contriving. Thus men slighted the wisdom of God in the gospel, because it did not agree with that philosophical wisdom and reason they had sucked in by education from their masters (1 Cor. i. 21, 22), contrary to their practice in their superstitious worship, where the oracles they thought divine were entertained with reverence, not with dispute, and though ambiguous, were not counted ridiculous by the worshipper. How foolish is man in this wherein he would be accounted wise! Adam, in innocence, was unfit to control the doctrine of God when the eye of his reason was clear; and much more are we, since the depravation of our natures. The revelations of God tower above reason in its purity, much more above reason in its mud and earthiness. The rays of Divine wisdom are too bright for our human understandings, much more for our sinful understandings. It is base to set up reason, a finite principle, against an infinite wisdom; much baser to set up a depraved and purblind reason against an all-seeing and holy wisdom. If we would have a reason for all that God speaks, and all that God acts, our wisdom must become infinite as his, or his wisdom become finite as

[p] Durant de Tent, pp. 403, 404.

ours. All the censures of God's revelations arise from some prejudicate opinions, or traditional maxims, that have enthroned themselves in our minds, which are made the standard whereby to judge the things of God, and receive or reject them as they agree with, or dissent from, those principles (Col. ii. 8). Hence it was that the philosophers, in the primitive times, were the greatest enemies to the gospel: and the contempt of Divine wisdom, in making reason the supreme judge of Divine revelation, was the fruitful mother of the heresies in all ages springing up in the church, and especially of that Socinianism, that daily insinuates itself into the minds of men. This is a wrong to the wisdom of God. He that censures the words or actions of another, implies that he is, in his censure, wiser than the person censured by him. It is as insupportable to determine the truth of God's plain dictates by our reason, as it is to measure the suitableness or unsuitableness of his actions by the humor of our will. We may sooner think to span the sun, or grasp a star, or see a gnat swallow a Leviathan, than fully understand the debates of eternity. To this we may refer too curious inquiries into Divine methods, and "intruding into those things which are not revealed" (Col. ii. 18). It is to affect a wisdom equal with God, and an ambition to be of his cabinet council. We are not content to be creatures, that is, to be every way below God; below him in wisdom, as well as power.

4. In prescribing God's method of acting. When we pray for a thing without a due submission to God's will; as if we were his counsellors, yea his tutors, and not his subjects, and God were bound to follow our humors, and be swayed according to the judgment of our ignorance; when we would have such a mercy which God thinks not fit to give, or have it in this method, which God designs to convey through another channel. Thus would we have the only wise God take his measures from our passions; such a controlling of God was Jonah's anger about a gourd (chap. iv. 1): "It displeased Jonah exceedingly, and he was very angry." We would direct Him how to dispose of us; as though he, that had infinite wisdom to contrive and rear the excellent fabric of the world, had not wisdom enough, without our discretions, to place us in a sphere proper for his own ends, and the use he intends us in the universe. All the speeches of men (would I had been in such an office, had such a charge; would I had such a mercy, in such a method, or by such instruments,) are entrenchments upon God's wise disposal of affairs. This imposing upon God is a hellish disposition, and in hell we find it. The rich man in hell, that pretends some charity for his brethren on earth, would direct God a way to prevent their ruin, by sending one from the dead to school them, as a more effectual means than "Moses and the prophets" (Luke xvi. 29, 30). It is a temper also to be found on earth; what else was the language of Saul's saving the Amalekites' cattle against the plain command of God (1 Sam. xv. 15)? As if God in his fury had overshot himself and overlooked his altar, in depriving it of so great a booty for its service; as if it were an unwise thing in God, to lose the prey of so many stately cattle, that might make the altar smoke with their entrails, and serve to expiate the sins of the people; and therefore he would rectify that which he

thought to be an oversight in God, and so magnifies his own prudence and discretion above the Divine. We will not let God act as he thinks fit, but will be directing him, and "teaching him knowledge" (Job. xxi. 22.) As if God were a statue, an idol, that had eyes and saw not, hands, but acted not; and could be turned as an image may be, to what quarter of the heaven we please ourselves. The wisdom of God is unbiassed; he orders nothing but what is fittest for his end, and we would have our shallow brains the bias of God's acting. And will not God resent such an indignity, as a reflection upon his wisdom as well as authority, when we intimate that we have better heads than he, and that he comes short of us in understanding?

5. In murmuring and impatience. One demands a reason, why he hath this or that cross? Why he hath been deprived of such a comfort, lost such a venture, languisheth under such a sickness, is tormented with such pains, oppressed by tyrannical neighbors, is unsuccessful in such designs? In these, and such like, the wisdom of God is questioned and defamed. All impatience is a suspicion, if not a condemnation of the prudence of God's methods, and would make human feebleness and folly the rule of God's dealing with his creatures. This is a presuming to instruct God, and a reproving him for unreasonableness in his proceedings, when his dealings with us do not exactly answer our fancies and wishes; as if God, who made the world in wisdom, wanted skill for the management of his creatures in it (Job xl. 2): "Shall he that contends with the Almighty, instruct him? he that reproveth God, let him answer it." We that are not wise enough to know ourselves, and what is needful for us; presume to have wit enough to guide God in his dealing with us. The wisdom of God rendered Job more useful to the world by his afflictions, in making him a pattern of patience, than if he had continued him in a confluence of all worldly comforts, wherein he had been beneficial only in communicating his morsels to his poor neighbors. All murmuring is a fastening error upon unerring Wisdom.

6. In pride and haughtiness of spirit. No proud man, but sets his heart "as the heart of God" (Ezek. xxviii. 2, 3). The wisdom of God hath given to men divers offices, set them in divers places; some have more honorable charges, some meaner. Not to give that respect their offices and places call for, is to quarrel with the wisdom of God, and overturn the rank and order wherein he hath placed things. It is unfit we should affront God in the disposal of his creatures, and intimate to him by our carriage, that he had done more wisely in placing another, and that he hath done foolishly in placing this or that man in such a charge. Sometimes men are unworthy the place they fill; they may be set there in judgment to themselves and others: but the wisdom of God in his management of things, is to be honored and regarded. It is an infringing the wisdom of God, when we have a vain opinion of ourselves, and are blind to others. When we think ourselves monarchs, and treat others as worms or flies in comparison of us. He who would reduce all things to his own honor, perverts the order of the world, and would constitute another

order than what the wisdom of God hath established; and move them to an end contrary to the intention of God, and charges God with want of discretion and skill.

7. Distrust of God's promise is an impeachment of his wisdom. A secret reviling of it, as if he had not taken due consideration before he past his word; or a suspicion of his power, as if he could not accomplish his word. We trust the physician's skill with our bodies, and the lawyer's counsel with our estates; but are loath to rely upon God for the concerns of our lives. If he be wise to dispose of us, why do we distrust him? If we distrust him, why do we embrace an opinion of wisdom? Unbelief also is a contradiction to the wisdom of God in the gospel, &c., but that I have already handled in a discourse of the nature of unbelief.

Use 3. Of comfort. God hath an infinite wisdom, to conduct us in our affairs, rectify us in our mistakes, and assist us in our straits. It is an inestimable privilege to have a God in covenant with us; so wise, to communicate all good, to prevent all evil; who hath infinite ways to bring to pass his gracious intentions towards us. "How unsearchable are his judgments, and his ways past finding out" (Rom. xi. 33)! His judgments or decrees are incomprehensibly wise, and the ways of effecting them are as wise as his resolves effected by them. We can as little search into his methods of acting, as we can into his wisdom of resolving; both his judgments and ways are unsearchable.

1. Comfort in all straits and afflictions. There is a wisdom in inflicting them, and a wisdom in removing them. He is wise to suit his medicines to the humor of our disease, though he doth not to the humor of our wills: he cannot mistake the nature of our distemper, or the virtue of his own physic. Like a skilful physician, he sometimes prescribes bitter potions, und sometimes cheering cordials, according to the strength of the malady, and necessity of the patient, to reduce him to health. As nothing comes from him, but what is for our good, so nothing is acted by him in a rash and temerarious way. His wisdom is as infinite as his goodness; and as exact in managing, as his goodness is plentiful in streaming out to us. He understands our griefs, weighs our necessities, and no remedies are beyond the reach of his contrivance. When our feeble wits are bewildered in a maze, and at the end of their line for a rescue, the remedies unknown to us are not unknown to God. When we know not how to prevent a danger, the wise God hath a thousand blocks to lay in the way; when we know not how to free ourselves from an oppressive evil, he hath a thousand ways of relief. He knows how to time our crosses, and his own blessings. The heart of a wise God, as well as the heart of a wise man, discerns both time and judgment (Eccles. viii. 5). There is as much judgment in sending them, as judgment in removing them. How comfortable is it to think, that our distresses, as well as our deliverances, are the fruits of infinite wisdom! Nothing is done by him too soon or too slow; but in the true point of time, with all its due circumstances, most conveniently for his glory and our good. How wise is God to bring the glory of our salvation out of the depths of a seeming ruin.

and make the evils of affliction subservient to the good of the afflicted.

2. In temptations, his wisdom is no less employed in permitting them, than in bringing them to a good issue. His wisdom in leading our Saviour to be tempted of the devil, was to fit him for our succor; and his wisdom in suffering us to be tempted, is to fit us for his own service, and our salvation. He makes a thorn in the flesh to be an occasion of a refreshing grace to the spirit, and brings forth cordial grapes from those pricking brambles, and magnifies his grace by his wisdom, from the deepest subtilties of hell. Let Satan's intentions be what they will, he can be for him at every turn, to outwit him in his stratagems, to baffle him in his enterprises; to make him instrumental for our good, where he designs nothing but our hurt. The Lord hath his methods of deliverance from him (2 Pet. ii. 9). "The Lord knows how to deliver the godly out of temptation."

3. In denials, or delays of answers of prayer. He is gracious to hear; but he is wise to answer in an acceptable time, and succor us in a day proper for our salvation (2 Cor. vi. 2). We have partial affections to ourselves, ignorance is natural to us (Rom. viii. 26). We ask we know not what, because we ask out of ignorance. God grants what he knows, what is fit for him to do, and fit for us to receive; and the exact season wherein it is fittest for him to bestow a mercy. As God would have us bring forth our fruit in season, so he will send forth his mercies in season. He is wise to suit his remedy to our condition, to time it so, as that we shall have an evident prospect of his wisdom in it; that more of Divine skill, and less of human, may appear in the issue. He is ready at our call; but he will not answer, till he see the season fit to reach out his hand. He is wise to prove our faith, to humble us under the sense of our own unworthiness, to wet our affections, to set a better estimate on the blessings prayed for, and that he may double the blessing, as we do our devotion: but when his wisdom sees us fit to receive his goodness, he grants what we stand in need of. He is wise to choose the fittest time, and faithful to give the best covenant mercy.

4. In all evils threatened to the church by her enemies. He hath knowledge to foresee them, and wisdom to disappoint them (Job. v. 13); "He taketh the wise in their own craftiness, and the counsel of the froward is carried headlong." The church hath the wisdom of God, to enter the lists with the policy of hell. He defeated the serpent in the first net he laid, and brought a glorious salvation out of hell's rubbish, and is yet as skilful to disappoint the after-game of the surpentine brood. The policy of hell, and the subtilty of the world, are no better than folly with God (1 Cor. iii. 19). All creatures are fools, as creatures, in comparison with the Creator. The angels he chargeth with folly, much more us sinners. Depraved understandings are not fit mates for a pure and unblemished mind. Pharaoh, with his wisdom, finds a grave in the sea; and Ahitophel's plots are finished in his own murder. He breaks the enemies by his power, and orders them by his skill to be a feast to his people (Ps. lxxiv. 14); "Thou breakest the head of the leviathan, and gav-

est him to be meat to the people in the wilderness." The spoils of the Egyptians' carcasses, cast upon the shore, served the Israelites' necessities (or were as meat to them); as being a deliverance the church might feed upon in all ages, in a wilderness condition, to maintain their faith, the vital principle of the soul. There is a wisdom superior to the subtilties of men, which laughs at their follies, and "hath them in derision" (Ps. ii. 4). "There is no wisdom or counsel against the Lord" (Prov. xxi. 30). You never question the wisdom of an artist to use his file, when he takes it into his hand. Wicked instruments are God's axes and files; let him alone, he hath skill enough to manage them: God hath too much affection to destroy his people, and wisdom enough to beautify them by the worst tools he uses. He can make all things conspire to a perfect harmony for his own ends, and his people's good, when they see no way to escape a danger feared, or attain a blessing wanted.

Use 4. For Exhortation. 1. Meditate on the wisdom of God in creation and government. How little do we think of God when we behold his works! Our sense dwells upon the surface of plants and animals, beholds the variety of their colors, and the progress in their motion; our reason studies the qualities of them; our spirits seldom take a flight to the Divine wisdom which framed them. Our senses engross our minds from God, that we scarce have a thought free to bestow upon the Maker of them, but only on the by. The constancy of seeing things that are common stifles our admiration of God, due upon the sight of them. How seldom do we raise our souls as far as heaven, in our views of the order of the world, the revolutions of the seasons, the nature of the creatures that are common among us, and the mutual assistance they give to each other! Since God hath manifested himself in them, to neglect the consideration of them is to neglect the manifestation of God, and the way whereby he hath transmitted something of his perfections to our understanding. It renders men inexcusably guilty of not glorifying of God (Rom. i. 19, 20). We can never neglect the meditation of the creatures, without a blemish cast upon the Creator's wisdom. As every river can conduct us to the sea, so every creature points us to an ocean of infinite wisdom. Not the minutest of them, but rich tracts of this may be observed in them, and a due sense of God result from them. They are exposed to our view, that something of God may be lodged in our minds; that, as our bodies extract their quintessence for our nourishment, so our minds may extract a quintessence for the Maker's praise. Though God is principally to be praised, in and for Christ, yet, as grace doth not rase out the law of nature, so the operations of grace put not the dictates of nature to silence, nor suspend the homage due to God upon our inspection of his works. God hath given full testimonies of this perfection in the heavenly bodies, dispersing their light, and distributing their influences to every part of the world; in framing men into societies, giving them various dispositions for the preservation of governments; making some wise for counsel, others martial for action; changing old empires, and raising new. Which way soever we cast our eyes, we shall find frequent occasions to cry out, "O the depth of the riches, both of the wisdom and knowledge of God" (Rom. xi. 33)! To this purpose, we must not only look upon the bulk and outside of his works, but consider from what principles they were raised, in what order disposed, and the exact symmetry and proportion of their parts. When a man comes into a city or temple, and only considers the surface of the buildings, they will amaze his sense, but not better his understanding, unless he considers the methods of the work, and the art whereby it was erected.

(1.) This was an end for which they were created. God did not make the world for man's use only, but chiefly for his own glory; for man's use to enjoy his creatures, and for his own glory to be acknowledged in his creatures, that we may consider his art in framing them, and his skill in disposing them, and not only gaze upon the glass without considering the image it represents, and acquainting ourselves whose image it is. The creatures were not made for themselves, but for the service of the Creator, and the service of man. Man was not made for himself, but for the service of the Lord that created him. He is to consider the beauty of the creation, that he may thereby glorify the Creator. He knows in part their excellency; the creatures themselves do not. If, therefore, man be idle and unobservant of them, he deprives God of the glory of his wisdom, which he should have by his creatures. The inferior creatures themselves cannot observe it. If man regard it not, what becomes of it? his glory can only be handed to him by man. The other creatures cannot be active instruments of his glory, because they know not themselves, and therefore cannot render him an active praise. Man is, therefore, bound to praise God for himself, and for all his creatures, because he only knows himself, and the perfections of the creatures, and the Author both of himself and them. God created such variety, to make a report of himself to us; we are to receive the report, and to reflect it back to him. To what purpose did he make so many things, not necessary, for the support and pleasure of our lives, but that we should behold him in them, as well as in the other? We cannot behold the wisdom of God in his own essence, and eternal ideas, but by the reflection of it in the creatures: as we cannot steadily behold the sun with our eye, but either through a glass, or by reflection of the image of it in the water. God would have us meditate on his perfections; he therefore chose the same day wherein he reviewed his work and rested from it, to be celebrated by man for the contemplation of him (Gen. ii. 2, 3), that we should follow his example, and rejoice, as himself did, in the frequent reviews of his wisdom and goodness in them. In vain would the creatures afford matter for this study, if they were wholly neglected. God offers something to our consideration in every creature. Shall the beams of God shine round about us, and strike our eyes, and not affect our minds? Shall we be like ignorant children, that view the pictures, or point to the letters in a book, without any sense and meaning? How shall God have the homage due to him from his works, if man hath no care to observe them? The 148th Psalm is an exhortation to this. The view of them should often extract from us a wonder of the like nature of that of David's (Ps. civ. 24): "O Lord, how wonderful are thy works, in wisdom hast thou made them all!" The world was not created to be forgotten, nor man created to be unobservant of it.

(2.) If we observe not the wisdom of God in the views of the creatures, we do no more than brutes. To look upon the works of God in the world, is no higher an act than mere animals perform. The glories of heaven, and beauties of the earth, are visible to the sense of beasts and birds. A brute beholds the motion of a man, as it may see the wheels of a clock, but understands not the inward springs of motion; the end for which we move, or the soul that acts us in our motion; much less that Invisible Power which presides over the creatures, and conducts their motion. If a man do no more than this, he goes not a step beyond a brutish nature, and may very well acknowledge himself with Asaph, a foolish and ignorant beast before God (Ps. lxxiii. 22). The world is viewed by beasts, but the Author of it to be contemplated by man. Since we are in a higher rank than beasts, we owe a greater debt than beasts; not only to enjoy the creatures, as they do, but behold God in the creatures, which they cannot do. The contemplation of the reason of God in his works, is a noble and suitable employment for a rational creature: we have not only sense to perceive them, but souls to mind them. The soul is not to be without its operation: where the operation of sense ends, the work of the soul ought to begin. We travel over them by our senses, as brutes; but we must pierce further by our understandings, as men, and perceive and praise Him that lies invisible in his visible manufactures. Our senses are given us as servants to the soul, and our souls bestowed upon us for the knowledge and praise of their and our common Creator.

(3.) This would be a means to increase our humility. We should then flag our wings, and vail our sails, and acknowledge our own wisdom to be as a drop to the ocean, and a shadow to the sun. We should have mean thoughts of the nothingness of our reason, when we consider the sublimity of the Divine wisdom. Who can seriously consider the sparks of infinite skill in the creature, without falling down at the feet of the Divine Majesty, and acknowledge himself a dark and foolish creature (Ps. viii. 4, 5)? When the Psalmist considered the heavens, the moon, and stars, and God's ordination and disposal of them, the use that results from it is, "What is man, that thou art mindful of him?" We should no more think to mate him in prudence, or set up the spark of our reason to vie with the sun. Our reason would more willingly submit to the revelation, when the characters of Divine wisdom are stamped upon it, when we find his wisdom in creation incomprehensible to us.

(4.) It would help us in our acknowledgments of God, for his goodness to us. When we behold the wisdom of God in creatures below us, and how ignorant they are of what they possess, it will cause us to reflect upon the deeper impressions of wisdom in the frame of our own bodies and souls, an excellency far superior to theirs; this would make us admire the magnificence of his wisdom and goodness, sound forth his praise for advancing us in dignity above other works of his hands, and stamping on us, by infinite art, a nobler image of himself. And by such a comparison of ourselves with the creatures below us, we should be induced to act excellently, according to the nature of our souls; not brutishly, according to the nature of the creatures God hath put under our feet.

(5.) By the contemplation of the creatures, we may receive some assistance in clearing our knowledge in the wisdom of redemption. Though they cannot of themselves inform us of it, yet since God hath revealed his redeeming grace, they can illustrate some particulars of it to us. Hence the Scripture makes use of the creatures, to set forth things of a higher orb to us: our Saviour is called a Sun, a Vine, and a Lion; the Spirit likened to a dove, fire, and water. The union of Christ and his church, is set forth by the marriage union of Adam and Eve. God hath placed in corporeal things the images of spiritual, and wrapped up in his creating wisdom the representations of his redeeming grace: whence some call the creatures, natural types of what was to be transacted in a new formation of the world, and allusions to what God intended in and by Christ.

(6.) The meditation of God's wisdom in the creatures is, in part, a beginning of heaven upon earth. No doubt but there will be a perfect opening of the model of Divine wisdom. Heaven is for clearing what is now obscure, and a full discovering of what seems at present intricate (Ps. xxxvi. 9.): ' In his light shall we see light: all the light in creation, government, and redemption. The wisdom of God in the new heavens, and the new earth, would be to little purpose, if that also were not to be regarded by the inhabitants of them. As the saints are to be restored to the state of Adam, and higher; so they are to be restored to the employment of Adam, and higher: but his employment was, to behold God in the creatures. The world was so soon depraved, that God had but little joy in, and man but little knowledge of his works. And since the wisdom of God in creation is so little seen by our ignorance here, would not God lose much of the glory of it, if the glorified souls should lose the understanding of it above? When their darkness shall be expelled, and their advantages improved; when the eye that Adam lost shall be fully restored, and with a greater clearness; when the creature shall be restored to its true end, and reason to its true perfection (Rom. viii. 21, 22); when the fountains of the depths of nature and government shall be opened, knowledge shall increase, and according to the increase of our knowledge, shall the admiration of Divine wisdom increase also. The wisdom of God in creation was not surely intended to lie wholly unobserved in the greatest part of it; but since there was so little time for the full observation of it, there will be a time wherein the wisdom of God shall enjoy a resurrection, and be fully contemplated by his understanding and glorified creature.

Exhort. 2. Study and admire the wisdom of God in redemption. This is the duty of all Christians. We are not called to understand the great depth of philosophy; we are not called to a skill in the intricacies of civil government, or understand all the methods of physic; but we are called to be Christians, that is, studiers of Divine evangelical wisdom. There are first principles to be learned; but not those principles to be rested in without a further progress (Heb. vi. 1): " Therefore, leaving the principles of the doctrine of Christ, let us go on to perfection." Duties must be practised, but knowledge is not to be neglected. The study of Gospel mysteries, the harmony of Divine truths, the sparkling of Divine wisdom, in their mutual combination to the great ends of God's glory and man's salvation, is an incentive to duty, a spur to worship, and particularly to the greatest and highest part of worship, that part which shall remain in heaven; the admiration and praise of God, and delight in him. If we acquaint not ourselves with the impressions of the glory of Divine wisdom in it, we shall not much regard it as worthy our observance in regard of that duty. The gospel is a mystery; and, as a mystery, hath something great and magnificent in it worthy of our daily inspection; we shall find fresh springs of new wonders, which we shall be invited to adore with a religious astonishment. It will both raise and satisfy our longings. Who can come to the depths of " God manifested in the flesh?" How amazing is it, and unworthy of a slight thought, that the death of the Son of God should purchase the happy immortality of a sinful creature, and the glory of a rebel be wrought by the ignominy of so great a person! that our Mediator should have a nature whereby to covenant with his Father, and a nature whereby to be a Surety for the creature! How admirable is it, that the fallen creature should receive an advantage by the forfeiture of his happiness! How mysterious is it, that the Son of God should bow down to death upon a cross for the satisfaction of justice; and rise triumphantly out of the grave, as a declaration, that justice was contented and satisfied! that he should be exalted to heaven to intercede for us; and at last return into the world to receive us, and invest us with a glory forever with himself! Are these things worthy of a careless regard, or a blockish amazement? What understanding can pierce into the depths of the divine doctrine of the incarnation and birth of Christ; the indissoluble union of the two natures? What capacity is able to measure the miracles of that wisdom, found in the whole draught and scheme of the gospel? Doth it not merit, then, to be the object of our daily meditation? How comes it to pass, then, that we are so little curious to concern our thoughts in those wonders, that we scarce taste or sip of these delicacies? that we busy ourselves in trifles, and consider what we shall eat, and in what fashion we shall be dressed; please ourselves with the ingeniousness of a lace or feather; admire a moth-eaten manuscript, or some half-worn piece of antiquity, and think our time ill-spent in the contemplating and celebrating that wherein God hath busied himself, and eternity is designed for the perpetual expressions of? How inquisitive are the blessed angels! with what vigor do they renew their daily contemplations of it, and receive a fresh contentment from it; still learning, and still inquiring (1 Pet. i. 12)! Their eye is never off the mercy-seat; they strive to see the bottom of it, and employ all the understanding they have to conceive the wonders of it. Shall the angels be ravished with it, and bend themselves down to study it, who have but little interest in it in comparison of us, for whom it was both contrived and dispensed;—and shall not our pains be greater for this hidden treasure? Is not that worthy the study of a rational creature, that is worthy the study of the angelical? There must indeed be pains; it is expressed by "digging" (Prov. ii. 4). A lazy arm will not sink to the depth of a mine. The neglect of meditating on it is inexcusable, since it hath the title and character of the wisdom of God. The ancient prophets searched into it, when it was folded up in shadows, when they saw only the fringes of Wisdom's garment (1 Pet. i. 10); and shall not we, since the sun hath mounted up in our horizon, and sensibly scattered the light of the knowledge of this and the other perfections of God? As the Jewish sabbath was appointed to celebrate the perfections of God, discovered in creation, so is the Christian sabbath appointed to meditate on, and bless God, for the discovery of his perfections in redemption. Let us, therefore, receive it according to its worth: let it be our only rule to walk by. It is worthy to be valued above all other counsels; and we should never think of it without the doxology of the apostle, "To the only wise God be glory through Jesus Christ, for ever!" that our speculations may end in affectionate admirations, and thanksgivings, for that which is so full of wonders. What a little prospect should we have had of God, and the happiness of man, had not his wisdom and goodness revealed these things to us! The gospel is a marvellous light, and should not be regarded with a stupid ignorance, and pursued with a duller practice.

Exhort. 3. Let none of us be proud of, or trust in our own wisdom. Man, by affecting wisdom out of the way of God, got a crack in his head, which hath continued five thousand years and upwards, and ever since our own wisdom and "knowledge hath perverted us" (Isa. xlvii. 10). To be guided by this, is to be under the conduct of a blind leader, and follow a traitor and enemy to God and ourselves. Man's prudence often proves hurtful to him : he often accomplisheth his ruin, while he designs his establishment; and finds his fall, where he thought to settle his fortune : such bad eyes hath human wisdom often in its own affairs. Those that have been heightened with a conceit of their own cunning, have at last proved the greatest fools. God delights to make "foolish the wisdom of this world" (1 Cor. i. 20). Thus God writ folly upon the crafty brains of Ahithophel, and simplicity upon the subtle projects of Herod against our Saviour; and the devil, the prince of carnal wisdom, was befooled into a furthering our redemption by his own projects to hinder it. Carnal policy, against the prescripts of Divine wisdom, never prospers : it is like an *ignis fatuus*, which leads men out of the way of duty, and out of the way of security, and perverts them into the mire and dangerous precipices. When Jeroboam would coin a religion to serve his interest of state, he tore up the foundations both of his kingdom and family. The way the Jews took to prevent a fresh invasion of the Romans, by the crucifying Christ, brought the judgment more swift upon them (John xi. 48). There is no man ruined here, or damned hereafter, but by his own wisdom and will. (Prov. iii. 5, 7), "The fear of the Lord, and departure from evil, are inconsistent with an overweening conceit of our own wisdom;" and leaning to our own understanding, is inconsistent with a trusting in the Lord with all our hearts. It is as much a deifying ourselves, to trust to our own wit, as it is a deifying the creature to affect or confide in it, superior to God or equally with him. The true way to wisdom is to be sensible of our own folly (1 Cor. iii. 18), "If any man be wise, let him become a fool." He that distrusts his own guidance, will more securely and successfully follow the counsel of another in whom he confides. The more water, or any other liquor, is poured out of a vessel, the more air enters. The more we distrust our own wisdom, the more capable we are of the conduct of God's. Had Jehoshaphat relied upon his own policy, he might have found a defeat when he met with a deliverance; but he disowned his own skill and strength in telling God, "We know not what to do, but our eyes are upon thee" (2 Chron. xx. 12). Let us, therefore, with Agur, disesteem our own understanding to esteem Divine. Human prudence is like a spider's web, easily blown away, and swept down by the besom of some unexpected revolution. God, by his infinite wisdom, can cross the wisdom of man, and make a man's own prudence hang in his own light. (Isa. xxix. 14), "The understanding of their prudent men shall be hid."

Exhort. 4. Seek to God for wisdom. The wisdom we have by nature, is like the weeds the earth brings forth without tillage. Our wisdom since the fall, is the wisdom of the serpent, without the innocency of the dove: it flows from self-love, runs into self-interest. It is the wisdom of the flesh, and a prudence to manage means for the contending our lusts. Our best wisdom is imperfect, a mere nothing and vanity, in comparison of the Divine, as our beings are in comparison of his essence. We must go to God for a holy and innocent wisdom, and fill our cisterns from a pure fountain. The wisdom that was the glory of Solomon, was the donation of the Most High. (James i. 5), "If any man want wisdom, let him ask of God, that giveth to all men liberally, and upbraideth not; and it shall be given him." The faculty of understanding is from God by nature; but a heavenly light to direct the understanding is from God by grace. Children have an understanding, but stand in need of wise masters to rectify it, and form judicious notions in it. "There is a spirit in man, but the inspiration of the Almighty gives him understanding" (Job xxxii. 8). We must beg of God, wisdom. The gospel is the wisdom of God; the concerns of it great and mysterious, not to be known without a "new understanding" (1 John v. 20). A new understanding is not to be had but from the Creator of the first. The Spirit of God is the "searcher of the deep things of God;" the revealer of them to us, and the enlightener of our minds to apprehend them; and, therefore, called a "Spirit of wisdom and revelation" (Eph. i. 17). Christ is made wisdom to us, as well as righteousness; not only by imputation, but effusion.q Seek to God, therefore, for that wisdom which is like the sun, and not that worldly wisdom which is like a shadow: for that wisdom whose effects are not so outwardly glorious, but inwardly sweet, seek it from him, and seek it in

q Seaman's Sermon before the Parliament.

his word, that is, the transcript of Divine wisdom; "through his precepts understanding is to be had" (Ps. cxix. 104). As the wisdom of men appears in their laws, so doth the wisdom of God in his statutes. By this means we arrive to a heavenly sagacity. If these be rejected, what wisdom can there be in us? a dream and conceit only (Jer. viii): "They have rejected the word of the Lord, and what wisdom is in them?" Who knows how to order any concerns as he ought, or any one faculty of his soul? Therefore, desire God's direction in outward concerns, in personal, family, in private and public. He hath not only a wisdom for our salvation, but for our outward direction. He doth not only guide us in the one, and leave Satan to manage us in the other. Those that go with Saul to a witch of Endor, go to hell for craft, and prefer the wisdom of the hostile serpent before the holy counsel of a faithful Creator. If you want health in your body, you advise with a physician; if direction for your estate, you resort to a lawyer; if passage for a voyage, you address to a pilot; why not much more yourselves, your all, to a wise God? As Pliny said, concerning a wise man, "O, Sir, how many Catos are there in that wise person!" how much more wisdom than men or angels possess, is infinitely centered in the wise God!

Exhort. 5. Submit to the wisdom of God in all cases. What else was inculcated in the first precept, forbidding man to eat of the fruit of the "tree of knowledge of good and evil," but that he should take heed of the swelling of his mind against the wisdom of God? It is a wisdom incomprehensible to flesh and blood; we should adore it in our minds, and resign up ourselves to it in our practice. How unreasonable are repinings against God, whereby a creature's ignorance indicts and judges a Creator's prudence! Were God weak in wisdom, and only mighty in power, we might suspect his conduct. Power without wisdom and goodness is an unruly and ruinous thing in the world. But God being infinite in one, as well as the other, we have no reason to be jealous of him, and repine against his methods; why should we quarrel with him that we are not as high, or as wealthy as others; that we have not presently the mercy we want? If he be wise, we ought to stay his time, and wait his leisure, because "he is a God of judgment" (Isa. xxx. 18). Presume not to shorten the time which his discretion hath fixed; it is a folly to think to do it. By impatience we cannot hasten relief; we alienate him from us by debasing him to stand at our bar, disturb ourselves, lose the comfort of our lives, and the sweetness of his mercy. Submission to God we are in no case exempted from, because there is no case wherein God doth not direct all the acts of his will by counsel. Whatsoever is drawn by a straight rule must be right and straight; the rule that is right in itself, is the measure of the straightness of everything else; whatsoever is wrought in the world by God, must be wise, good, righteous; because God is essentially wisdom, goodness, and righteousness.

(1.) Submit to God, in his revelations. 1. Measure them not by reason: the truths of the gospel must be received with a self-emptiness and annihilation of the creature. If our reason seems to lift up itself against revelation, because it finds no testimony for it in its own light, consider how crazy it is in natural and obvious things, and therefore sure it is not strong enough to enter into the depths of Divine wisdom: the wisdom of God in the gospel is too great an ocean to be contained or laved out by a cockleshell. It were not infinite, if it were not beyond our finite reach; our reason must as well stoop to his wisdom, as our wills to his sovereignty. How great a vanity is it for a glow-worm to boast that it is as full of light as the sun in the firmament! for reason to leave its proper sphere, is to fall into confusion, and thicken its own darkness. We should settle ourselves in the belief of the Scripture, and confirm ourselves by a meditation on those many undeniable arguments for its Divine authority,—the fulfilling of its predictions, the antiquity of the writing, the holiness of the precepts, the heavenliness of the doctrine, the glorious effects it hath produced, and doth yet produce, different from human methods of success; and submit our reason to the voice of so high a majesty. 2. Not to be too curiously inquisitive into what is not revealed. There is something hid in whatsoever is revealed. We know the Son of God was begotten from eternity, but how he was begotten, we are ignorant. We know there is a union of the Divine nature with the human, and that the fulness of the Godhead dwells in him bodily; but the manner of its inhabitation we are in a great part ignorant of. We know that God hath chosen some and refused others, and that he did it with counsel; but the reason why he chose this man and not that, we know not; we can refer it to nothing but God's sovereign pleasure. It is revealed that there will be a day wherein God shall judge the world; but the particular time is not revealed. We know that God created the world in time; but why he did not create the world millions of years before, we are ignorant of, and our reasons would be bewildered in their too much curiosity. If we ask why he did not create it before, we may as well ask why he did create it then? And may not the same question be asked, if the world had been created millions of years before it was? That he created it in six days, and not in an instant, is revealed; but why he did not do it in a moment, since we are sure he was able to do it, is not revealed. Are the reasons of a wise man's proceedings hid from us? and shall we presume to dive into the reason of the proceedings of an only wise God, which he hath judged not expedient to discover to us? Some sparks of his wisdom he hath caused to issue out, to exercise and delight our minds; others he keeps within the centre of his own breast; we must not go about to unlock his cabinet. As we cannot reach to the utmost lines of his power, so we cannot grasp the intimate reasons of his wisdom. We must still remember, that which is finite can never be able to comprehend the reasons, motives, and methods of that which is infinite. It doth not become us to be resty, because God hath not admitted us into the debates of eternity. We are as little to be curious at what God hath hid, as to be careless of what God hath manifested. Too great an inquisitiveness beyond our line, is as much a provoking arrogance, as a blockish negligence of what is revealed, is a slighting ingratitude.

(2.) Submit to God in his precepts and methods. Since they are the results of infinite wisdom, disputes against them are not tolerable; what orders are given out by infallible Wisdom are to be entertained with respect and reverence, though the reason of them be not visible to our purblind minds. Shall God have less respect from us than earthly princes, whose laws we observe without being able to pierce into the exact reason of them all? Since we know he hath not a will without an understanding, our observance of him must be without repining; we must not think to mend our Creator's laws, and presume to judge and condemn his righteous statutes. If the flesh rise up in opposition, we must cross its motions, and silence its murmurings; his will should be an acceptable will to us, because it is a wise will in itself. God hath no need to impose upon us and deceive us; he hath just and righteous ways to attain his glory and his creatures's good. To deceive us, would be to dishonor himself, and contradict his own nature. He cannot impose false injurious precepts, or unavailable to his subjects' happiness; not false, because of his truth; not injurious, because of his goodness; not vain, because of his wisdom. Submit, therefore, to him in his precepts, and in his methods too. The honor of his wisdom, and the interest of our happiness, call for it. Had Noah disputed with God about building an ark, and listened to the scoffs of the senseless world, he had perished under the same fate, and lost the honor of a preacher and worker of righteousness. Had not the Israelites been their own enemies, if they had been permitted to be their own guides, and returned to the Egyptian bondage and furnaces, instead of a liberty and earthly felicity in Canaan? Had our Saviour gratified the Jews by descending from the cross, and freeing himself from the power of his adversaries, he might have had that faith from them which they promised him; but it had been a faith to no purpose, because without ground; they might have believed him to be the Son of God, but he could not have been the Saviour of the world. His death, the great ground and object of faith, had been unaccomplished; they had believed a God pardoning without a consent to his justice, and such a faith could not have rescued them from falling into eternal misery. The precepts and methods of Divine wisdom must be submitted to.

(3.) Submit to God in all crosses and revolutions. Infinite Wisdom cannot err in any of his paths, or step the least hair's breadth from the way of righteousness: there is the understanding of God in every motion; an eye in every wheel, the wheel that goes over us and crusheth us. We are led by fancy more than reason: we know no more what we ask, or what is fit for us, than the mother of Zebedee's children did, when she petitioned Christ for her sons' advancement, when he came into his temporal kingdom (Matt. xx. 22): the things we desire might pleasure our fancy or appetite, but impair our health: one man complains for want of children, but knows not whether they may prove comforts or crosses: another for want of health, but knows not whether the health of his body may not prove the disease of his soul. We might lose in heavenly things, if we possess in earthly things what we long for. God, in regard of his infinite wisdom, is fitter to carve out a condition than we ourselves; our shallow reason and self-love, would wish for those things that are injurious to God, to ourselves, to the world; but God always chooses what is best for his glory, and what is best for his creatures, either in regard to themselves, or as they stand in relation to him, or to others, as parts of the world. We are in danger from our self-love, in no danger in complying with God's wisdom: when Rachel would die, if she had no children, she had children, but death with one of them (Gen. xxx. 1). Good men may conclude, that whatsoever is done by God in them, or with them, is best and fittest for them; because by the covenant which makes over God to them, as their God, the conduct of his wisdom is assured to them as well as any other attribute: and, therefore, as God in every transaction appears as their God, so he appears as their wise Director, and by this wisdom he extracts good out of evil, makes the affliction which destroys our outward comforts consume our inward defilements; and the waves which threatened to swallow up the vessel, to cast it upon the shore: and when he hath occasion to manifest his anger against his people, his wisdom directs his wrath. In judgment he hath " a work to do upon Zion;" and when that work is done, he punishes the fruit of the " stout heart of the king of Assyria" (Isa. x. 12); as in the answers of prayer he doth give oftentimes " above what we ask or think" (Eph. iii. 20), so in outward concerns he doth above what we can expect, or by our short-sightedness, conclude will be done. Let us, therefore, in all things, frame our minds to the Divine Wisdom, and say with the Psalmist (Ps. xlvii. 4): " The Lord shall choose our inheritance and condition for us."

Exhort. 6. Censure not God in any of his ways. Can we understand the full scope of Divine wisdom in creation, which is perfected before our eyes? Can we, by a rational knowledge, walk over the whole surface of the earth, and wade through the sea? Can we understand the nature of the heavens? Are all, or most, or the thousandth part of the particles of Divine skill, known by us, yea, or any of them thoroughly known? How can we, then, understand his deeper methods in things that are but of yesterday, that we have not had a time to view? We should not be too quick, or too rash, in our judgments of him: the best that we attain to, is but feeble conjectures at the designs of God. As there is something hid in whatsoever is revealed in his word, so there is something inaccessible to us in his works, as well as in his nature and Majesty. In our Saviour's act in washing his disciples' feet, he checked Peter's contradiction (John xiii. 7): " What I do, thou knowest not now, but thou shalt know hereafter." God were not infinitely wise if the reason of all his acts were obvious to our shallowness. He is no profound statesman, whose inward intention can be sounded by vulgar heads at the first act he starts in his designed method. The wise God is, in this, like wise men, that have not breasts like glasses of crystal, to discover all that they intend. There are " secrets of wisdom above our reach" (Job xi. 6); nay, when we see all his acts, we cannot see all the draughts of his skill in them. An unskilful hearer of a musical lesson may receive the melody with his ear, and understand not the rarities of the composition as it was wrought by the musician's mind. Under the Old Testament there was more of Divine power, and less of his wisdom apparent in his acts: as his laws, so his acts, were more fitted to their sense. Under the New Testament there is more of wisdom, and less of power; as his laws, so his acts, are more fitted to a spiritual mind; wisdom is less discernible than power. Our wisdom, therefore, in this case, as it doth other things, consists in silence and expectation of the end and event of a work. We owe that honor to God that we do to men wiser than ourselves, to imagine he hath reason to do what he doth, though our shallowness cannot comprehend it. We must suffer God to be wiser than ourselves, and acknowledge that there is something sovereign in his ways not to be measured by the feeble reed of our weak understandings. And, therefore, we should acquiesce in his proceedings; take heed we be not found slanderers of God, but be adorers instead of censurers; and lift up our heads in admiration of him and his ways, instead of citing him to answer it at our bar. Many things in the first appearance may seem to be rash and unjust, which, in the issue, appear comely and regular. If it had been plainly spoke before that the Son of God should die, that a most holy person should be crucified, it would have seemed cruel to expose a son to misery; unjust to inflict punishment upon one that was no criminal; to join together exact goodness and physical evil; that the sovereign should die for the malefactor, and the observer of the law for the violators of it. But when the whole design is unravelled, what an admirable connexion is there of justice and mercy, love and wisdom, which before would have appeared absurd to the muddied reason of man! We see the gardener pulling up some delightful flowers by the roots, digging up the earth, overwhelming it with dung; an ignorant person would imagine him wild, out of his wits, and charge him with spoiling his garden: but when the spring is arrived, the spectator will acknowledge his skill in his former operations. The truth is, the whole design and methods of God are not to be judged by us in this world; the full declaration of the whole contexture is reserved for the other world, to make up a part of good men's happiness in the amazing views of Divine wisdom, as well as the other perfections of his nature. We can no more perfectly understand his wisdom than we can his mercy and justice, till we see the last lines of all drawn, and the full expressions of them; we should therefore be sober and modest in the consideration of God's ways; "his judgments are unsearchable, and his ways past finding out." The riches of his wisdom are past our counting, his depths not to be fathomed, yet they are depths of righteousness and equity; though the full manifestation of that equity, the grounds and methods of his proceedings are unknown to us. As we are too short fully to know God, so we are too ignorant fully to comprehend the acts of God: since he is a God of judgment, we should wait till we see the issue of his works (Isa. xxx. 18). And in the meantime, with the apostle in the text, give him the glory of all, in the same expressions, "To the only wise God be glory, through Jesus Christ for ever. Amen."

THE EXISTENCE
AND ATTRIBUTES OF GOD

STEPHEN CHARNOCK

TWO VOLUMES IN ONE

Volume 2

CONTENTS OF VOL. II

DISCOURSE X

ON THE POWER OF GOD

Job xxvi. 14.—Lo! these are parts of his ways: but how little a portion is heard of him? but the thunder of his power who can understand?

BILDAD had, in the foregoing chapter, entertained Job with a discourse of the dominion and power of God, and the purity of his righteousness, whence he argues an impossibility of the justification of man in his presence, who is no better than a worm. Job, in this chapter, acknowledges the greatness of God's power, and descants more largely upon it than Bildad had done; but doth preface it with a kind of ironical speech, as if he had not acted a friendly part, or spake little to the purpose, or the matter in hand: the subject of Job's discourse was the worldly happiness of the wicked, and the calamities of the godly: and Bildad reads him a lecture, of the extent of God's dominion, the number of his armies, and the unspotted rectitude of his nature, in comparison of which the purest creatures are foul and crooked. Job, therefore, from ver. 1—4, taxeth him in a kind of scoffing manner, that he had not touched the point, but rambled from the subject in hand, and had not applied a salve proper to this sore (ver. 2): "How hast thou helped him that is without power? how savest thou the arm of him that hath no strength?" &c.; your discourse is so impertinent, that it will neither strengthen a weak person, nor instruct a simple one.[r] But since Bildad would take up the argument of God's power, and discourse so short of it, Job would show that he wanted not his instructions in that kind, and that he had more distinct conceptions of it than his antagonist had uttered: and therefore from ver. 5 to the end of the chapter, he doth magnificently treat of the power of God in several branches. And (ver. 5) he begins with the lowest. "Dead things are formed from under the waters, and the inhabitants thereof:" You read me a lecture of the power of God in the heavenly host: indeed it is visible there, yet of a larger extent; and monuments of it are found in the lower parts. What do you think of those dead things under the earth and waters, of the corn that dies, and by the moistening influences of the clouds, springs up again with a numerous progeny and increase for the nourishment of man? What do you think of those varieties of metals and minerals conceived in the bowels of the earth; those pearls and riches in the depths of the waters, midwifed by this power of God? Add to these those more prodigious creatures in the

[r] Munster.

sea, the inhabitants of the waters, with their vastness and variety,
which are all the births of God's power; both in their first creation
by his mighty voice, and their propagation by his cherishing providence. Stop not here, but consider also that his power extends to
hell; either the graves the repositories of all the crumbled dust that
hath yet been in the world (for so hell is sometimes taken in Scripture: ver. 6, "Hell is naked before him, and destruction hath no
covering.") The several lodgings of deceased men are known to
him: no screen can obscure them from his sight, nor their dissolution be any bar to his power, when the time is come to compact
those mouldered bodies to entertain again their departed souls, either
for weal or woe. The grave, or hell, the place of punishment, is
naked before him; as distinctly discerned by him, as a naked body
in all its lineaments by us, or a dissected body is in all its parts by a
skilful eye.

Destruction hath no covering; none can free himself from the
power of his hand. Every person in the bowels of hell; every person punished there is known to him, and feels the power of his
wrath. From the lower parts of the world he ascends to the consideration of the power of God in the creation of heaven and earth;
"He stretches out the north over the empty places" (ver. 7). The
north, or the north pole, over the air, which, by the Greeks, was
called void or empty, because of the tenuity and thinness of that
element; and he mentions here the north, or north pole, for the
whole heaven, because it is more known and apparent than the
southern pole. "And hangs the earth upon nothing:" the massy
and weighty earth hangs like a thick globe in the midst of a thin
air, that there is as much air on the one side of it, as on the other.
The heavens have no prop to sustain them in their height, and the
earth hath no basis to support it in its place. The heavens are as if
you saw a curtain stretched smooth in the air without any hand to
hold it; and the earth is as if you saw a ball hanging in the air without any solid body to under-prop it, or any line to hinder it from
falling; both standing monuments of the omnipotence of God. He
then takes notice of his daily power in the clouds; "He binds up
the waters in his thick clouds, and the cloud is not rent under them"
(ver. 8). He compacts the waters together in clouds, and keeps them
by his power in the air against the force of their natural gravity and
heaviness, till they are fit to flow down upon the earth, and perform
his pleasure in the places for which he designs them. "The cloud
is not rent under them;" the thin air is not split asunder by the
weight of the waters contained in the cloud above it. He causes
them to distil by drops, and strains them, as it were, through a
thin lawn, for the refreshment of the earth; and suffers them not
to fall in the whole lump, with a violent torrent, to waste the
industry of man, and bring famine upon the world, by destroying the fruits of the earth. What a wonder it would be to see
but one entire drop of water hang itself but one inch above the
ground, unless it be a bubble which is preserved by the air enclosed within it! What a wonder would it be to see a gallon
of water contained in a thin cobweb as strongly as in a vessel

of brass! Greater is the wonder of Divine power in those thin bottles of heaven, as they are called (Job xxxviii. 37); and therefore called his clouds here, as being daily instances of his omnipotence: that the air should sustain those rolling vessels, as it should seem, weightier than itself; that the force of this mass of waters should not break so thin a prison, and hasten to its proper place, which is below the air: that they should be daily confined against their natural inclination, and held by so slight a chain ; that there should be such a gradual and successive falling of them, as if the air were pierced with holes like a gardener's watering-pot, and not fall in one entire body to drown or drench some parts of the earth. These are hourly miracles of Divine power, as little regarded as clearly visible. He proceeds (ver. 9), "He holds back the face of his throne, and spreads the clouds upon it." The clouds are designed as curtains to cover the heavens, as well as vessels to water the earth (Ps. cxlvii. 8). As a tapestry curtain between the heavens, the throne of God (Isa. lxvi. 1), and the earth his footstool: the heavens are called his throne, because his power doth most shine forth there, and magnificently declare the glory of God ; and the clouds are as a screen between the scorching heat of the sun, and the tender plants of the earth, and the weak bodies of men. From hence he descends to the sea, and considers the Divine power apparent in the bounding of it (ver. 10); "He hath compassed the waters with bounds, till the day and night come to an end." This is several times mentioned in Scripture as a signal mark of Divine strength (Job xxxviii. 8; Prov. viii. 27). He hath measured a place for the sea, and struck the limits of it as with a compass, that it might not mount above the surface of the land, and ruin the ends of the earth's creation; and this, while day and night have their mutual turns, till he shall make an end of time by removing the measures of it. The bounds of the tumultuous sea are, in many places, as weak as the bottles of the upper waters; the one is contained in thin air, and the other restrained by weak sands, in many places, as well as by stubborn rocks in others; that, though it swells, foams, roars, and the waves, encouraged and egged on by strong winds, come like mountains against the shore; they overflow it not, but humble themselves when they come near to those sands, which are set as their lists and limits, and retire back to the womb that brought them forth, as if they were ashamed and repented of their proud invasion: or else it may be meant of the tides of the sea, and the stated time God hath set it for its ebbing and flowing, till night and day come to an end ;[s] both that the fluid waters should contain themselves within due bounds, and keep their perpetually orderly motion, are amazing arguments of Divine power. He passes on to the consideration of the commotions in the air and earth, raised and stilled by the power of God ; "The pillars of heaven tremble, and are astonished at his reproof." By pillars of heaven are not meant angels, as some think, but either the air, called the pillars of heaven in regard of place, as it continues and knits together the parts of the world, as pillars do the upper and nether parts of a building: as the lowest parts of the earth are

[s] Coccei *in loc.*

called the foundations of the earth, so the lowest parts of the heaven may be called the pillars of heaven :[t] or else by that phrase may be meant mountains, which seem, at a distance, to touch the sky, as pillars do the top of a structure ; and so it may be spoken, according to vulgar capacity, which imagines the heavens to be sustained by the two extreme parts of the earth, as a convex body, or to be arched by pillars ; whence the Scripture, according to common apprehensions, mentions the ends of the earth, and the utmost parts of the heavens, though they have properly no end, as being round. The power of God is seen in those commotions in the air and earth, by thunders, lightnings, storms, earthquakes, which rack the air, and make the mountains and hills tremble as servants before a frowning and rebuking master. And as he makes motions in the earth and air, so is his power seen in their influences upon the sea ; " He judges the sea with his power, and by his understanding he smites through the proud" (ver. 12). At the creation he put the waters into several channels, and caused the dry land to appear barefaced for a habitation for man and beasts ; or rather, he splits the sea by storms, as though he would make the bottom of the deep visible, and rakes up the sands to the surface of the waters, and marshals the waves into mountains and valleys. After that, " he smites through the proud," that is, humbles the proud waves, and, by allaying the storm, reduceth them to their former level : the power of God is visible, as well in rebuking, as in awakening the winds ; he makes them sensible of his voice, and, according to his pleasure, exasperates or calms them. The " striking through the proud" here, is not, probably, meant of the destruction of the Egyptian army, for some guess that Job died that year,[u] or about the time of the Israelites coming out of Egypt ; so that this discourse here, being in the time of his affliction, could not point at that which was done after his restoration to his temporal prosperity. And now, at last, he sums up the power of God, in the chiefest of his works above, and the greatest wonder of his works below (ver. 13) ; " By his Spirit he hath garnished the heavens ; his hand hath formed the crooked serpent," &c. The greater and lesser lights, sun, moon, and stars, the ornaments and furniture of heaven ; and the whale, a prodigious monument of God's power, often mentioned in Scripture to this purpose, and, in particular, in this book of Job (ch. xli.) ; and called by the same name of crooked serpent (Isa. xxvii. 1), where it is applied, by way of metaphor, to the king of Assyria or Egypt, or all oppressors of the church. Various interpretations there are of this crooked serpent : some understanding that constellation in heaven which astronomers call the dragon ; some that combination of weaker stars, which they call the galaxia, which winds about the heavens : but it is most probable that Job, drawing near to a conclusion of his discourse, joins the two greatest testimonies of God's power in the world, the highest heavens, and the lowest leviathan, which is here called a bar serpent,[x] in regard of his strength and hardness, as mighty men are called bars in Scripture (Jer. li. 30) ; " Her bars are broken things." And in regard of this power of God

[t] Coccei.   [u] Drusius *in loc.*   [x] As the word signifies in the Hebrew.

in the creation of this creature, it is particularly mentioned in the catalogue of God's works (Gen. i. 21); "And God created great whales;" all the other creatures being put into one sum, and not particularly expressed. And now he makes use of this lecture in the text, "Lo, these are parts of his ways; but how little a portion is heard of him? but the thunder of his power who can understand?" This is but a small landscape of some of his works of power; the outsides and extremities of it; more glorious things are within his palaces: though those things argue a stupendous power of the Creator, in his works of creation and providence, yet they are nothing to what may be declared of his power. And what may be declared, is nothing to what may be conceived; and what may be conceived, is nothing to what is above the conceptions of any creature. These are but little crumbs and fragments of that Infinite Power, which is, in his nature, like a drop in comparison of the mighty ocean; a hiss or whisper in comparison of a mighty voice of thunder.ʸ This, which I have spoken, is but like a spark to the fiery region, a few lines, by the by, a drop of speech.

The thunder of his power. Some understand it of thunder literally, for material thunder in the air: "The thunder of his power," that is, according to the Hebrew dialect, "his powerful thunder." This is not the sense; the nature of thunder in the air doth not so much exceed the capacity of human understanding; it is, therefore, rather to be understood metaphorically, "the thunder of his power," that is, the greatness and immensity of his power, manifested in the magnificent miracles of nature, in the consideration whereof men are astonished, as if they had heard an unusual clap of thunder. So thunder is used (Job xxxix. 25), "The thunder of the captains;" that is, strength and force of the captains of an army: and (ver. 19), God, speaking to Job of a horse, saith, "Hast thou clothed his neck with thunder?" that is, strength: and thunder being a mark of the power of God, some of the heathen have called God by the name of a Thunderer.ᶻ As thunder pierceth the lowest places, and alters the state of things, so doth the power of God penetrate into all things whatsoever; the thunder of his power, that is, the greatness of his power; as "the strength of salvation" (Ps. xx. 6), that is, a mighty salvation.

Who can understand? Who is able to count all the monuments of his power? How doth this little, which I have spoken of, exceed the capacity of our understanding, and is rather the matter of our astonishment, than the object of our comprehensive knowledge. The power of the greatest potentate, or the mightiest creature, is but of small extent: none but have their limits; it may be understood how far they can act, in what sphere their activity is bounded: but when I have spoken all of Divine power that I can, when you have thought all that you can think of it, your souls will prompt you to

---

ʸ Oecolamp.

ᶻ The ancient Gauls worshipped him under the name of Taranis. The Greeks called Jupiter Βροντᾶος, and Thor; whence our Thursday is derived, signifieth Thunderer, a title the Germans gave their God. And Toran, in the British language, signifies thunder. Voss. Idolo. lib. ii. cap. 33. Camb. Britan. p. 17.

conceive something more beyond what I have spoken, and what you have thought. His power shines in everything, and is beyond everything. There is infinitely more power lodged in his nature, not expressed to the world. The understanding of men and angels, centred in one creature, would fall short of the perception of the infiniteness of it. All that can be comprehended of it, are but little fringes of it, a small portion. No man ever discoursed, or can, of God's power, according to the magnificence of it. No creature can conceive it; God himself only comprehends it; God himself is only able to express it. Man's power being limited, his line is too short to measure the incomprehensible omnipotence of God. "The thunder of his power who can understand?" that is, none can. The text is a lofty declaration of the Divine power, with a particular note of attention, *Lo!* I. In the expressions of it, in the works of creation and providence, *Lo, these are his ways;* ways and works excelling any created strength, referring to the little summary of them he had made before. II. In the insufficiency of these ways to measure his power, *But how little a portion is heard of him.* III. In the incomprehensibleness of it, *The thunder of his power, who can understand?* *Doctrine.* Infinite and incomprehensible power pertains to the nature of God, and is expressed, in part, in his works; or, though there be a mighty expression of Divine power in his works, yet an incomprehensible power pertains to his nature. "The thunder of his power, who can understand?"

His power glitters in all his works, as well as his wisdom (Ps. lxii. 11): "Twice have I heard this, that power belongs unto God." In the law and in the prophets, say some; but why power twice, and not mercy, which he speaks of in the following verse? he had heard of power twice, from the voice of creation, and from the voice of government. Mercy was heard in government after man's fall, not creation; innocent man was an object of God's goodness, not of his mercy, till he made himself miserable; power was expressed in both; or, twice have I heard that power belongs to God, that is, it is a certain and undoubted truth, that power is essential to the Divine nature. It is true, mercy is essential, justice is essential; but power more apparently essential, because no acts of mercy, or justice, or wisdom, can be exercised by him without power; the repetition of a thing confirms the certainty of it. Some observe, that God is called Almighty seventy times in Scripture.[d] Though his power be evident in all his works, yet he hath a power beyond the expression of it in his works, which, as it is the glory of his nature, so it is the comfort of a believer. To which purpose the apostle expresseth it by an excellent paraphrasis for the honor of the Divine nature (Eph. iii. 20): "Now unto him that is able to do exceeding abundantly above all that we can ask or think, unto him be glory in the churches." We have reason to acknowledge him Almighty, who hath a power of acting above our power of understanding. Who could have imagined such a powerful operation in the propagation of the gospel, and the conversion of the Gentiles, which the apostle seems to hint at in that place? His power is expressed by "horns in his hands" (Hab.

---

[d] Lessius, de Perfect. Divin. lib. v. cap. 1.

iii. 4); because all the works of his hands are wrought with Almighty strength. Power is also used as a name of God (Mark. xiv. 62): "The Son of Man sitting on the right hand of power," that is, at the right hand of God; God and power are so inseparable, that they are reciprocated. As his essence is immense, not to be confined in place; as it is eternal, not to be measured by time; so it is Almighty, not to be limited in regard of action.

1. It is ingenuously illustrated by some by a unit;[b] all numbers depend upon it; it makes numbers by addition, multiplies them unexpressibly; when one unit is removed from a number, how vastly doth it diminish it! It gives perfection to all other numbers, it receives perfection from none. If you add a unit before 100, how doth it multiply it to 1,100! If you set a unit before 20,000,000, it presently makes the number swell up to 120,000,000; and so powerful is a unit, by adding it to numbers, that it will infinitely enlarge them to such a vastness, that shall transcend the capacity of the best arithmetician to count them. By such a meditation as this, you may have some prospect of the power of that God who is only unity; the beginning of all things, as a unit is the beginning of all numbers; and can perform as many things really, as a unit can numerically; that is, can do as much in the making of creatures, as a unit can do in the multiplying of numbers. The omnipotence of God was scarce denied by any heathen that did not deny the being of a God; and that was Pliny, and that upon weak arguments.

2. Indeed we cannot have a conception of God, if we conceive him not most powerful, as well as most wise; he is not a God that cannot do what he will, and perform all his pleasure. If we imagine him restrained in his power, we imagine him limited in his essence; as he hath an infinite knowledge to know what is possible, he cannot be without an infinite power to do what is possible; as he hath a will to resolve what he sees good, so he cannot want a power to effect what he sees good to decree; as the essence of a creature cannot be conceived without that activity that belongs to his nature; as when you conceive fire, you cannot conceive it without a power of burning and warming; and when you conceive water, you cannot conceive it without a power of moistening and cleansing: so you cannot conceive an infinite essence without an infinite power of activity; and therefore a heathen could say, "If you know God, you know he can do all things;" and therefore, saith Austin, "Give me not only a Christian, but a Jew; not only a Jew, but a heathen, that will deny God to be Almighty." A Jew, a heathen, may deny Christ to be omnipotent, but no heathen will deny God to be omnipotent, and no devil will deny either to be so: God cannot be conceived without some power, for then he must be conceived without action. Whose, then, are those products and effects of power, which are visible to us in the world? to whom do they belong? who is the Father of them? God cannot be conceived without a power suitable to his nature and essence. If we imagine him to be of an infinite essence, we must imagine him to be of an infinite power and strength.

[b] Fotherby, Atheomastic, pp. 306, 307.

In particular, I shall show—I. The nature of God's power. II. Reasons to prove that God must needs be powerful. III. How his power appears in creation, in government, in redemption. IV. The Use.

I. What this power is; or the nature of it.

1. Power sometimes signifies authority: and a man is said to be mighty and powerful in regard of his dominion, and the right he hath to command multitudes of other persons to take his part; but power taken for strength, and power taken for authority, are distinct things, and may be separated from one another. Power may be without authority; as in successful invasions, that have no just foundation. Authority may be without power; as in a just prince, expelled by an unjust rebellion, the authority resides in him, though he be overpowered, and is destitute of strength to support and exercise that authority. The power of God is not to be understood of his authority and dominion, but his strength to act; and the word in the text properly signifies strength.[c]

2. This power is divided ordinarily into absolute and ordinate. Absolute, is that power whereby God is able to do that which he will not do, but is possible to be done; ordinate, is that power whereby God doth that which he hath decreed to do, that is, which he hath ordained or appointed to be exercised;[d] which are not distinct powers, but one and the same power. His ordinate power is a part of his absolute; for if he had not a power to do every thing that he could will, he might not have the power to do everything that he doth will. The object of his absolute power is all things possible; such things that imply not a contradiction, such that are not repugnant in their own nature to be done, and such as are not contrary to the nature and perfections of God to be done. Those things that are repugnant in their own nature to be done are several, as to make a thing which is past not to be past. As, for example, the world is created; God could have chose whether he would create the world, and after it is created he hath power to dissolve it; but after it was created, and when it is dissolved, it will be eternally true, that the world was created, and that it was dissolved; for it is impossible, that that which was once true, should ever be false: if it be true that the world was created, it will forever be true that it was created, and cannot be otherwise. And also, if it be once true that God hath decreed, it is impossible in its own nature to be true that God hath not decreed. Some things are repugnant to the nature and perfections of God; as it is impossible for his nature to die and perish; impossible for him, in regard of truth, to lie and deceive. But of this hereafter; only at present to understand the object of God's absolute power to be things possible, that is, possible in nature; not by any strength in themselves, or of themselves; for nothing hath no strength, and everything is nothing before it comes into being;[e] so God, by his absolute power, might have prevented the sin of the fallen angels, and so have preserved them in their first habitation. He might, by his absolute power, have restrained the devil from tempting of Eve, or restrained her and Adam from swal-

c גבורתו Sept. σθενος.   d Scaliger, Publ. Exercit. 365, § 8.
e Estius in Sent. lib. i. dist, 43. § 2.

lowing the bait, and joining hands with the temptation. By his absolute power, God might have given the reins to Peter to betray his Master, as well as to deny him; and employed Judas in the sam glorious and successful service, wherein he employed Paul. By his absolute power, he might have created the world millions of years before he did create it, and can reduce it into its empty nothing this moment. This the Baptist affirms, when he tells us, "That God is able of these stones (meaning the stones in the wilderness, and not the people which came out to him out of Judea, which were children of Abraham) to raise up children to Abraham" (Matt. iii. 9); that is, there is a possibility of such a thing there is no contradiction in it, but that God is able to do it if he please. But now the object of his ordinate power, is all things ordained by him to be done, all things decreed by him; and because of the Divine ordination of things, this power is called ordinate; and what is thus ordained by him he cannot but do, because of his unchangeableness. Both those powers are expressed (Matt. xxvi. 53, 54), "My Father can send twelve legions of angels," there is his absolute power; " but how then shall the Scriptures be fulfilled, that thus it must be ?" there is his ordinate power. As his power is free from any act of his will, it is called absolute; as it is joined with an act of his will, it is called ordinate. His absolute power is necessary, and belongs to his nature; his ordinate power is free, and belongs to his will;—a power guided by his will,—not, as I said before, that they are two distinct powers, both belonging to his nature, but the latter is the same with the former, only it is guided by his will and wisdom.

3. It follows, then, that the power of God is that ability and strength, whereby he can bring to pass whatsoever he please; whatsoever his infinite wisdom can direct, and whatsoever the infinite purity of his will can resolve. Power, in the primary notion of it, doth not signify an act, but an ability to bring a thing into act; it is power, as able to act before it doth actually produce a thing: as God had an ability to create before he did create, he had power before he acted that power without. Power notes the principle of the action, and, therefore, is greater than the act itself. Power exercised and diffused, in bringing forth and nursing in its particular objects without, is inconceivably less than that strength which is infinite in himself, the same with his essence, and is indeed himself: by his power exercised he doth whatsoever he actually wills; but by the power in his nature, he is able to do whatsoever he is able to will. The will of creatures may be, and is more extensive than their power; and their power more contracted and shortened than their will: but, as the prophet saith, "His counsel shall stand, and he will do all his pleasure" (Isa. xlvi. 10). His power is as great as his will, that is, whatsoever can fall within the verge of his will, falls within the compass of his power. Though he will never actually will this or that, yet supposing he should will it, he is able to perform it: so that you must, in your notion of Divine power, enlarge it further than to think God can only do what he hath resolved to do; but that he hath as infinite a capacity of power to act, as he hath an infinite capacity of will to resolve. Besides, this power is of that

nature, that he can do whatsoever he pleases without difficulty, without resistance; it cannot be checked, restrained, frustrated.[f] As he can do all things possible in regard of the object, he can do all things easily in regard of the manner of acting: what in human artificers is knowledge, labor, industry, that in God is his will; his will works without labor; his works stand forth as he wills them. Hands and arms are ascribed to him for our conceptions, because our power of acting is distinct from our will; but God's power of acting is not really distinct from his will; it is sufficient to the existence of a thing that God wills it to exist; he can act what he will only by his will, without any instruments. He needs no matter to work upon, because he can make something from nothing; all matter owes itself to his creative power: he needs no time to work in, for he can make time when he pleases to begin to work: he needs no copy to work by; himself is his own pattern and copy in his works. All created agents want matter to work upon, instruments to work with, copies to work by; time to bring either the births of their minds, or the works of their hands, to perfection: but the power of God needs none of these things, but is of a vast and incomprehensible nature, beyond all these. As nothing can be done without the compass of it, so itself is without the compass of every created understanding.

4. This power is of a distinct conception from the wisdom and will of God. They are not really distinct, but according to our conceptions. We cannot discourse of Divine things, without observing some proportion of them with human, ascribing unto God the perfections, sifted from the imperfections of our nature. In us there are three orders—of understanding, will, power; and, accordingly, three acts, counsel, resolution, execution; which, though they are distinct in us, are not really distinct in God. In our conceptions, the apprehension of a thing belongs to the understanding of God; determination, to the will of God; direction, to the wisdom of God; execution, to the power of God. The knowledge of God regards a thing as possible, and as it may be done; the wisdom of God regards a thing as fit, and convenient to be done; the will of God resolves that it shall be done; the power of God is the application of his will to effect what it hath resolved. Wisdom is a fixing the being of things, the measures and perfections of their several beings; power is a conferring those perfections and beings upon them. His power is his ability to act, and his wisdom is the director of his action: his will orders, his wisdom guides, and his power effects. His will as the spring, and his power as the worker, are expressed (Ps. cxv. 3). "He hath done whatsoever he pleased. He commanded, and they were created" (Ps. cxl. 5); and all three expressed (Eph. i. 11), "Who works all things according to the counsel of his own will:" so that the power of God is a perfection, as it were, subordinate to his understanding and will, to execute the results of his wisdom, and the orders of his will; to his wisdom as directing, because he works skilfully; to his will as moving and applying, because he works voluntarily and freely. The exercise of his power depends upon his will: his will is the supreme cause of everything

[f] Cra. Syntag. lib. iii. cap. 17. p. 611.

that stands up in time, and all things receive a being as he wills them. His power is but will perpetually working, and diffusing itself in the season his will hath fixed from eternity ; it is his eternal will in perpetual and successive springs and streams in the creatures; it is nothing else but the constant efficacy of his omnipotent will. This must be understood of his ordinate power ; but his absolute power is larger than his resolving will : for though the Scripture tells us, " He hath done whatsoever he will," yet it tells us not, that he hath done whatsoever he could : he can do things that he will never do. Again, his power is distinguished from his will in regard of the exercise of it, which is after the act of his will : his will was conversant about objects, when his power was not exercised about them. Creatures were the objects of his will from eternity, but they were not from eternity the effects of his power. His purpose to create was from eternity, but the execution of his purpose was in time. Now this execution of his will we call his ordinate power : his wisdom and his will are supposed antecedent to his power, as the counsel and resolve ; as the cause precedes the performance of the purpose as the effect. Some [g] distinguish his power from his understanding and will, in regard that his understanding and will are larger than his absolute power ; for God understands sins, and wills to permit them, but he cannot himself do any evil or unjust action, nor have a power of doing it. But this is not to distinguish that Divine power, but impotence ; for to be unable to do evil is the perfection of power ; and to be able to do things unjust and evil, is a weakness, imperfection, and inability. Man indeed wills many things that he is not able to perform, and understands many things that he is not able to effect ; he understands much of the creatures, something of sun, moon, and stars ; he can conceive many suns, many moons, yet is not able to create the least atom : but there is nothing that belongs to power but God understands, and is able to effect. To sum this up, the will of God is the root of all, the wisdom of God is the copy of all, and the power of God is the framer of all.

5. The power of God gives activity to all the other perfections of his nature, and is of a larger extent and efficacy, in regard of its objects, than some perfections of his nature. I put them both together.

(1.) It contributes life and activity to all the other perfections of his nature. How vain would be his eternal counsels, if power did not step in to execute them ! His mercy would be a feeble pity, if he were destitute of power to relieve; and his justice a slighted scarecrow, without power to punish; his promises an empty sound, without power to accomplish them. As holiness is the beauty, so power is the life of all his attributes in their exercise ; and as holiness, so power, is an adjunct belonging to all, a term that may be given to all. God hath a powerful wisdom to attain his ends without interruption : he hath a powerful mercy to remove our misery ; a powerful justice to lay all misery upon offenders : he hath a powerful truth to perform his promises ; an infinite power to bestow rewards, and inflict penalties. It is to this purpose power is first put

[g] Gamacheus.

in the two things which the Psalmist had heard (Ps. lxii. 11, 12). "Twice have I heard," or two things have I heard; first power, then mercy and justice, included in that expression, "Thou renderest to every man according to his work:" in every perfection of God he heard of power. This is the arm, the hand of the Deity, which all his other attributes lay hold on, when they would appear in their glory; this hands them to the world: by this they act, in this they triumph. Power framed every stage for their appearance in creation, providence, redemption.

(2.) It is of a larger extent, in regard of its objects, than some other attributes. Power doth not alway suppose an object, but constitutes an object. It supposeth an object in the act of preservation, but it makes an object in the act of creation; but mercy supposeth an object miserable, yet doth not make it so. Justice supposeth an object criminal, but doth not constitute it so: mercy supposeth him miserable, to relieve him; justice supposeth him criminal, to punish him: but power supposeth not a thing in real existence, but as possible; or rather, it is from power that any thing hath a possibility, if there be no repugnancy in the nature of the thing. Again, power extends further than either mercy or justice. Mercy hath particular objects, which justice shall not at last be willing to punish; and justice hath particular objects, which mercy at last shall not be willing to refresh: but power doth, and alway will, extend to the objects of both mercy and justice. A creature, as a creature, is neither the object of mercy nor justice, nor of rewarding goodness: a creature, as innocent, is the object of rewarding goodness; a creature, as miserable, is the object of compassionate mercy; a creature, as criminal, is the object of revenging justice: but all of them the objects of power, in conjunction with those attributes of goodness, mercy, and justice, to which they belong. All the objects that mercy, and justice, and truth, and wisdom, exercise themselves about, hath a possibility and an actual being from this perfection of Divine power. It is power first frames a creature in a capacity of nature for mercy or justice, though it doth not give an immediate qualification for the exercise of either. Power makes man a rational creature, and so confers upon him a nature mutable, which may be miserable by its own fault, and punishable by God's justice; or pitiable by God's compassion, and relievable by God's mercy: but it doth not make him sinful, whereby he becomes miserable and punishable. Again, power runs through all the degrees of the states of a creature. As a thing is possible, or may be made, it is the object of absolute power; as it is factibile, or ordered to be made, it is the object of ordinate power: as a thing is actually made, and brought into being, it is the object of preserving power. So that power doth stretch out its arms to all the works of God, in all their circumstances, and at all times. When mercy ceaseth to relieve a creature, when justice ceaseth to punish a creature, power ceaseth not to preserve a creature. The blessed in heaven, that are out of the reach of punishing justice, are forever maintained by power in that blessed condition: the damned in hell, that are cast out of the bosom of entreating mercy, are forever sustained in those remediless torments by the Arm of Power.

6. This power is originally and essentially in the nature of God, and not distinct from his essence. It is originally and essentially in God. The strength and power of great kings is originally in their people, and managed and ordered by the authority of the prince for the common good. Though a prince hath authority in his person to command, yet he hath not sufficient strength in his person, without the assistance of others, to make his commands to be obeyed. He hath not a single strength in his own person to conquer countries and kingdoms, and increase the number of his subjects: he must make use of the arms of his own subjects, to overrun other places, and yoke them under his dominion: but the power of all things that ever were, are, or shall be, is originally and essentially in God. It is not derived from any thing without him, as the power of the greatest potentates in the world is: therefore (Ps. lxii. 11) it is said, "Power belongs unto God," that is, solely and to none else. He hath a power to make his subjects, and as many as he pleases; to create worlds, to enjoin precepts, to execute penalties, without calling in the strength of his creatures to his aid. The strength that the subjects of a mortal prince have, is not derived to them from the prince, though the exercise of it for this or that end, is ordered and directed by the authority of the prince: but what strength soever any thing hath to act as a means, it hath from the power of God as Creator, as well as whatsoever authority it hath to act is from God, as a Rector and Governor of the world. God hath a strength to act without means, and no means can act any thing without his power and strength communicated to them. As the clouds, in ver. 8, before the text, are called God's clouds, "his clouds:" so all the strength of creatures may be called, and truly is, God's strength and power in them: a drop of power shot down from heaven, originally only in God. Creatures have but a little mite of power; somewhat communicated to them, somewhat kept and reserved from them, of what they are capable to possess. They have limited natures, and therefore a limited sphere of activity. Clothes can warm us, but not feed us; bread can nourish us, but not clothe us. One plant hath a medicinal quality against one disease, another against another; but God is the possessor of universal power, the common exchequer of this mighty treasure. He acts by creatures, as not needing their power, but deriving power to them: what he acts by them, he could act himself without them: and what they act as from themselves, is derived to them from him through invisible channels. And hence it will follow, that because power is essentially in God, more operations of God are possible than are exerted. And as power is essentially in God, so it is not distinct from his essence. It belongs to God in regard of the inconceivable excellency and activity of his essence.[h] And omnipotent is nothing but the Divine essence efficacious *ad extra*. It is his essence as operative, and the immediate principle of operation: as the power of enlightening in the sun, and the power of heating in the fire, are not things distinct

[h] Ratione summæ actualitatis essentiæ. Suarez, Vol, I. pp. 150, 151.

from the nature of them; but the nature of the sun bringing forth light, and the nature of the fire bringeth forth heat. The power of acting is the same with the substance of God, though the action from that power be terminated in the creature. If the power of God were distinct from his essence, he were then compounded of substance and power, and would not be the most simple being. As when the understanding is informed in several parts of knowledge, it is skilled in the government of cities and countries, it knows this or that art: it learns mathematics, philosophy; this, or that science. The understanding hath a power to do this; but this power, whereby it learns those excellent things, and brings forth excellent births, is not a thing distinct from the understanding itself; we may rather call it the understanding powerful, than the power of the understanding; and so we may rather say, God powerful, than say, the power of God; because his power is not distinct from his essence. From both these, it will follow, that this omnipotence is incommunicable to any creature; no creature can inherit it, because it is a contradiction for any creature to have the essence of God. This omnipotence is a peculiar right of God, wherein no creature can share with him. To be omnipotent is to be essentially God. And for a creature to be omnipotent, is for a creature to be its own Creator. It being therefore the same with the essence of the Godhead, it cannot be communicated to the humanity of Christ, as the Lutherans say it is, without the communication of the essence of the Godhead; for then the humanity of Christ would not be humanity, but Deity. If omnipotence were communicated to the humanity of Christ, the essence of God were also communicated to his humanity, and then eternity would be communicated. His humanity then was not given him in time; his humanity would be uncompounded, that is, his body would be no body, his soul no soul. Omnipotence is essentially in God; it is not distinct from the essence of God, it is his essence, omnipotent, able to do all things.

7. Hence it follows, that this power is infinite (Eph. i. 19); "What is the exceeding greatness of his power," &c. "according to the working of his mighty power." God were not omnipotent, unless his power were infinite; for a finite power is a limited power, and a limited power cannot effect everything that is possible. Nothing can be too difficult for the Divine power to effect; he hath a fullness of power, an exceeding strength, above all human capacities; it is a "mighty power" (Eph. i. 19), "able to do above all that we can ask or think" (Eph. iii. 20): that which he acts, is above the power of any creature to act. Infinite power consists in the bringing things forth from nothing. No creature can imitate God in this prerogative of power. Man indeed can carve various forms, and erect various pieces of art, but from pre-existent matter. Every artificer hath the matter brought to his hand, he only brings it forth in a new figure. Chemists separate one thing from another, but create nothing, but sever those things which were before compacted and crudled together: but when God speaks a powerful word, nothing begins to be something: things stand forth from the womb of nothing, and obey his mighty command, and take what forms he

is pleased to give them. The creating one thing, though never so small and minute, as the least fly, cannot be but by an infinite power; much less can the producing of such variety we see in the world. His power is infinite, in regard it cannot be resisted by anything that he hath made ; nor can it be confined by anything he can will to make. " His greatness is unsearchable" (Ps. cxlv. 3). It is a greatness, not of quantity, but quality. The greatness of his power hath no end : it is a vanity to imagine any limits can be affixed to it, or that any creature can say, " Hitherto it can go, and no further." It is above all conception, all inquisition of any created understanding. No creature ever had, nor ever can have, that strength of wit and understanding, to conceive the extent of his power, and how magnificently he can work.

First, His essence is infinite. As in a finite subject there is a finite virtue, so in an infinite subject there must be an infinite virtue. Where the essence is limited, the power is so :[i] where the essence is unlimited, the power knows no bounds.[k] Among creatures, the more excellency of being and form anything hath, the more activity, vigor, and power it hath, to work according to its nature. The sun hath a mighty power to warm, enlighten, and fructify, above what the stars have ; because it hath a vaster body, more intense degrees of light, heat, and vigor. Now, if you conceive the sun made much greater than it is, it would proportionably have greater degrees of power to heat and enlighten than it hath now : and were it possible to have an infinite heat and light, it would infinitely heat and enlighten other things ; for everything is able to act according to the measures of its being: therefore, since the essence of God is unquestionably infinite, his power of acting must be so also. His power (as was said before) is one and the same with his essence: and though the knowledge of God extends to more objects than his power, because he knows all evils of sin, which because of his holiness he cannot commit, yet it is as infinite as his knowledge, because it is as much one with his essence, as his knowledge and wisdom is : for as the wisdom or knowledge of God is nothing but the essence of God, *knowing*, so the power of God is nothing but the essence of God, *able*.

The objects of Divine power are innumerable. The objects of Divine power are not essentially infinite ; and therefore we must not measure the infiniteness of Divine power by an ability to make an infinite being ; because there is an incapacity in any created thing to be infinite ; for to be a creature and to be infinite ; to be infinite and yet made, is a contradiction. To be infinite, and to be God, is one and the same thing. Nothing can be infinite but God ; nothing but God is infinite. But the power of God is infinite, because it can produce infinite effects, or innumerable things, such as surpass the arithmetic of a creature ; nor yet doth the infiniteness consist simply in producing innumerable effects ; for that a finite cause can produce. Fire can, by its finite and limited heat, burn numberless combustible things and parcels ; and the understanding of man hath an infinite number of thoughts and acts of intellection,

[i] Operationes sequuntur essentiam.   [k] Aquin. Part 1 Qu. 25. Articæ.

and thoughts different from one another. Who can number the imaginations of his fancy, and thoughts of his mind, the space of one month or year? much less of forty or an hundred years; yet all these thoughts are about things that are in being, or have a foundation in things that are in being. But the infiniteness of God's power consists in an ability to produce infinite effects, formally distinct, and diverse from one another; such as never had being, such as the mind of man cannot conceive: "Able to do above what we can think" (Eph. iii. 20). And whatsoever God hath made, or is able to make, he is able to make in an infinite manner, by calling them to stand forth from nothing. To produce innumerable effects of distinct natures, and from so distant a term as nothing, is an argument of infinite power. Now, that the objects of Divine power are innumerable, appears, because God can do infinitely more than he hath done, or will do. Nothing that God hath done can enfeeble or dull his power; there still resides in him an ability beyond all the settled contrivances of his understanding and resolves of his will, which no effects which he hath wrought can drain and put to a stand. As he can raise stones to be children to Abraham (Matt. iii. 9); so with the same mighty word, whereby he made one world, he can make infinite numbers of worlds to be the monuments of his glory. After the prophet Jeremiah (ch. xxxii. 17), had spoke of God's power in creation, he adds, "And there is nothing too hard for thee." For one world that he hath made, he can create millions: for one star which he hath beautified the heavens with, he could have garnished it with a thousand, and multiplied, if he had pleased, every one of those into millions, "for he can call things that are not" (Rom. iv. 17); not some things, but all things possible. The barren womb of nothing can no more resist his power now to educe a world from it, than it could at first: no doubt, but for one angel which he hath made, he could make many worlds of angels. He that made one with so much ease, as by a word, cannot want power to make many more, till he wants a word. The word that was not too weak to make one, cannot be too weak to make multitudes. If from one man he hath, in a way of nature, multiplied so many in all ages of the world, and covered with them the whole face of the earth; he could, in a supernatural way, by one word, multiply as many more. "It is the breath of the Almighty that gives life" (Job. xxxiii. 4). He can create infinite species and kinds of creatures more than he hath created, more variety of forms: for since there is no searching of his greatness, there is no conceiving the numberless possible effects of his power. The understanding of man can conceive numberless things possible to be, more than have been or shall be. And shall we imagine, that a finite understanding of a creature hath a greater omnipotency to conceive things possible, than God hath to produce things possible? When the understanding of man is tired in its conceptions, it must still be concluded, that the power of God extends, not only to what can be conceived, but infinitely beyond the measures of a finite faculty. "Touching the Almighty, we cannot find him out; he is excellent in power and in judgment" (Job xxxvi. 23). For the understanding of man, in its conceptions of more kind of creatures, is limited to those creatures which are : it cannot, in its own imagination, conceive anything but what hath some foundation in and from something already in being. It may frame a new kind of creature, made up of a lion, a horse, an ox ; but all those parts whereof its conception is made, have distinct beings in the world, though not in that composition as his mind mixes and joins them ; but no question but God can create creatures that have no resemblance with any kind of creatures yet in being. It is certain that if God only knows those things which he hath done, and will do, and not all things possible to be done by him, his knowledge were finite ; so if he could do no more than what he hath done, his power would be finite.

(1.) Creatures have a power to act about more objects than they do. The understanding of man can frame from one principle of truth, many conclusions and inferences more than it doth. Why cannot, then, the power of God frame from one first matter, an infinite number of creatures more than have been created? The Almightiness of God in producing real effects, is not inferior to the understanding of man in drawing out real truths. An artificer that makes a watch, supposing his life and health, can make many more of a different form and motion ; and a limner can draw many draughts, and frame many pictures with a new variety of colors, according to the richness of his fancy. If these can do so, that require a pre-existent matter framed to their hands, God can much more, who can raise beautiful structures from nothing. As long as men have matter, they can diversify the matter, and make new figures from it ; so long as there is nothing, God can produce out of that nothing whatsoever he pleases. We see the same in inanimate creatures. A spark of fire hath a vast power in it : it will kindle other things, increase and enlarge itself ; nothing can be exempt from the active force of it. It will alter, by consuming or refining, whatsoever you offer to it. It will reach all, and refuse none ; and by the efficacious power of it, all those new figures which we see in metals, are brought forth ; when you have exposed to it a multitude of things, still add more, it will exert the same strength ; yea, the vigor is increased rather than diminished. The more it catcheth, the more fiercely and irresistibly it will act ; you cannot suppose an end of its operation, or a decrease of its strength, as long as you can conceive its duration and continuance : this must be but a weak shadow of that infinite power which is in God. Take another instance, in the sun : it hath power every year to produce flowers and plants from the earth ; and is as able to produce them now, as it was at the first lighting it and rearing it in that sphere wherein it moves. And if there were no kind of flowers and plants now created, the sun hath a power residing in it, ever since its first creation, to afford the same warmth to them for the nourishing and bringing them forth. Whatsoever you can conceive the sun to be able to do in regard of plants, that can God do in regard of worlds ; produce more worlds than the sun doth plants every year, without weariness, without languishment. The sun is able to influence more things than it doth, and produce numberless effects; but it doth not do so much as it is able to do, because it wants matter to work upon. God, therefore, who wants no matter, can do much more than he doth; he can either act by second causes if there were more, or make more second causes if he pleased.

(2.) God is the most free agent. Every free agent can do more than he will do. Man being a free creature, can do more than ordinarily he doth will to do. God is most free, as being the spring of liberty in other creatures; he acts not by a necessity of nature, as the waves of the sea, or the motions of the wind; and, therefore, is not determined to those things which he hath already called forth into the world. If God be infinitely wise in contrivance, he could contrive more than he hath, and therefore, can effect more than he hath effected. He doth not act to the extent of his power upon all occasions. It is according to his will that he works (Eph. i.). It is not according to his work that he wills; his work is an evidence of his will, but not the rule of his will. His power is not the rule of his will, but his will is the disposer of his power, according to the light of his infinite wisdom, and other attributes that direct his will; and therefore his power is not to be measured by his actual will. No doubt, but he could in a moment have produced that world which he took six days' time to frame; he could have drowned the old world at once, without prolonging the time till the revolution of forty days; he was not limited to such a term of time by any weakness, but by the determination of his own will. God doth not do the hundred thousandth part of what he is able to do, but what is convenient to do, according to the end which he hath proposed to himself. Jesus Christ, as man, could have asked legions of angels; and God, as a sovereign, could have sent them (Matt. xxvi. 53). God could raise the dead every day if he pleased, but he doth not: he could heal every diseased person in a moment, but he doth not. As God can will more than he doth actually will, so he can do more than he hath actually done; he can do whatsoever he can will; he can will more worlds, and therefore can create more worlds. If God hath not ability to do more than he will do, he then can do no more than what he actually hath done; and then it will follow, that he is not a free, but a natural and necessary agent, which cannot be supposed of God.

Second. This power is infinite in regard of action. As he can produce numberless objects above what he hath produced, so he could produce them more magnificently than he hath made them. As he never works to the extent of his power in regard of things, so neither in regard of the manner of acting; for he never acts so but he could act in a higher and perfecter manner.

(1.) His power is infinite in regard of the independency of action: he wants no instrument to act. When there was nothing but God, there was no cause of action but God; when there was nothing in being but God, there could be no instrumental cause of the being of anything. God can perfect his action without dependence on any thing;[1] and to be simply independent, is to be simply infinite. In

[1] Suarez, Vol. I, de Deo. p. 151.

this respect it is a power incommunicable to any creature, though you conceive a creature in higher degrees of perfection than it is. A creature cannot cease to be dependent, but it must cease to be a creature; to be a creature and independent, are terms repugnant to one another.

(2.) But the infiniteness of Divine power consists in an ability to give higher degrees of perfection to everything which he hath made. As his power is infinite extensive, in regard of the multitude of objects he can bring into being, so it is infinite intensive, in regard of the manner of operation, and the endowments he can bestow upon them.[m] Some things, indeed, God doth so perfect, that higher degrees of perfection cannot be imagined to be added to them.[n] As the humanity of Christ cannot be united more gloriously than to the person of the Son of God, a greater degree of perfection cannot be conferred upon it. Nor can the souls of the blessed have a nobler object of vision and fruition than God himself, the infinite Being: no higher than the enjoyment of himself can be conferred upon a creature, *respectu termini*. This is not want of power; he cannot be greater, because he is greatest; not better, because he is best; nothing can be more than infinite. But as to the things which God hath made in the world, he could have given them other manner of being than they have. A human understanding may improve a thought or conclusion; strengthen it with more and more force of reason; and adorn it with richer and richer elegancy of language: why, then, may not the Divine providence produce a world more perfect and excellent than this? He that makes a plain vessel, can embellish it more, engrave more figures upon it, according to the capacity of the subject: and cannot God do so much more with his works? Could not God have made this world of a larger quantity, and the sun of a greater bulk and proportionable strength, to influence a bigger world? so that this world would have been to another that God might have made, as a ball or a mount, this sun as a star to another sun that he might have kindled. He could have made every star a sun, every spire of grass a star, every grain of dust a flower, every soul an angel. And though the angels be perfect creatures, and inexpressibly more glorious than a visible creature, yet who can imagine God so confined, that he cannot create a more excellent kind, and endow those which he hath made with excellency of a higher rank than he invested them with at the first moment of their creation? Without question God might have given the meaner creatures more excellent endowments, put them into another order of nature for their own good and more diffusive usefulness in the world. What is made use of by the prophet (Mal. ii. 15) in another case, may be used in this: "Yet had he a residue of Spirit." The capacity of every creature might have been enlarged by God; for no work of his in the world doth equal his power, as nothing that he hath framed doth equal his wisdom. The same matter which is the matter of the body of a beast, is the matter of a plant and flower; is the matter of the body of a man; and so was capable of a higher form and higher perfections, than God hath been pleased

[m] Becan. Sum. Theol. p. 82.   [n] Ibid. p. 84.

to bestow upon it. And he had power to bestow that perfection on one part of matter which he denied to it, and bestowed on another part. If God cannot make things in a greater perfection, there must be some limitation of him: he cannot be limited by another, because nothing is superior to God. If limited by himself, that limition is not from a want of power, but a want of will. He can, by his own power, raise stones to be children to Abraham (Matt. iii. 9): he could alter the nature of the stones, form them into human bodies, dignify them with rational souls, inspire those souls with such graces that may render them the children of Abraham. But for the more fully understanding the nature of this power, we may observe,

[1.] That though God can make everything with a higher degree of perfection, yet still within the limits of a finite being. No creature can be made infinite, because no creature can be made God. No creature can be so improved as to equal the goodness and perfection of God;[o] yet there is no creature but we may conceive a possibility of its being made more perfect in that rank of a creature than it is: as we may imagine a flower or plant to have greater beauty and richer qualities imparted to it by Divine power, without rearing it so high as to the dignity of a rational or sensitive creature. Whatsoever perfections may be added by God to a creature, are still finite perfections; and a multitude of finite excellences can never amount to the value and honor of infinite: as if you add one number to another as high as you can, as much as a large piece of paper can contain, you can never make the numbers really infinite, though they may be infinite in regard of the inability of any human understanding to count them. The finite condition of the creature suffers it not to be capable of an infinite perfection. God is so great, so excellent, that it is his perfection not to have any equal; the defect is in the creature, which cannot be elevated to such a pitch; as you can never make a gallon measure to hold the quantity of a butt, or a butt the quantity of a river, or a river the fulness of the sea.

[2.] Though God hath a power to furnish every creature with greater and nobler perfections than he hath bestowed upon it, yet he hath framed all things in the perfectest manner, and most convenient to that end for which he intended them. Everything is endowed with the best nature and quality suitable to God's end in creation, though not in the best manner for itself.[p] In regard of the universal end, there cannot be a better; for God himself is the end of all things, who is the Supreme Goodness. Nothing can be better than God, who could not be God if he were not superlatively best, or *optimus;* and he hath ordered all things for the declaration of his goodness or justice, according to the behaviors of his creatures. Man doth not consider what strength or power he can put forth in the means he useth to attain such an end, but the suitableness of them to his main design, and so fits and marshals them to his grand purpose. Had God only created things that are most excellent, he had created only angels and men; how, then, would his wisdom have

---

[o] Gamach in Aquin. Tom. I. Qu. 25.

[p] Best, *ex parte facientis et modi:* but not *ex parte rei.* Esti. in Senten. lib. i. distin. 44. § 2.

been conspicuous in other works in the subordination and subserviency of them to one another? God therefore determined his power by his wisdom: and though his absolute power could have made every creature better, yet his ordinate power, which in every step was regulated by his wisdom, made everything best for his designed intention.[q] A musician hath a power to wind up a string on a lute to a higher and more perfect note in itself, but in wisdom he will not do it, because the intended melody would be disturbed thereby if it were not suited to the other strings on the instrument; a discord would mar and taint the harmony which the lutenist designed. God, in creation, observed the proportions of nature: he can make a spider as strong as a lion; but according to the order of nature which he hath settled, it is not convenient that a creature of so small a compass should be as strong as one of a greater bulk. The absolute power of God could have prepared a body for Christ as glorious as that he had after his resurrection; but that had not been agreeable to the end designed in his humiliation: and, therefore, God acted most perfectly by his ordinate power, in giving him a body that wore the livery of our infirmities. God's power is alway regulated by his wisdom and will; and though it produceth not what is most perfect in itself, yet what is most perfect and decent in relation to the end he fixed. And so in his providence, though he could rack the whole frame of nature to bring about his ends in a more miraculous way and astonishment to mortals, yet his power is usually and ordinarily confined by his will to act in concurrence with the nature of the creatures, and direct them according to the laws of their being, to such ends which he aims at in their conduct, without violencing their nature.

[3.] Though God hath an absolute power to make more worlds, and infinite numbers of other creatures, and to render every creature a higher mark of his power, yet in regard of his decree to the contrary, he cannot do it. He hath a physical power, but after his resolve to the contrary, not a moral power: the exercise of his power is subordinate to his decree, but not the essence of his power. The decree of God takes not away any power from God, because the power of God is his own essence, and incapable of change; and is as great physically and essentially after his decree, as it was before; only his will hath put in a bar to the demonstration of all that power which he is able to exercise.[r] As a prince that can raise 100,000 men for an invasion, raises only 20 or 30,000; he here, by his order, limits his power, but doth not divest himself of his authority and power to raise the whole number of the forces of his dominions if he pleases: the power of God hath more objects than his decree hath; but since it is his perfection to be immutable, and not to change his decree, he cannot morally put forth his power upon all those objects, which, as it is essentially in him, he hath ability to do. God hath decreed to save those that believe in Christ, and to judge unbelievers to everlasting perdition: he cannot morally damn the first, or save the latter; yet he hath not divested himself of his absolute power to

[q] Aquin. Part I, Qu, 25, art. 6.

[r] Gamach in Aquin. Tom. I. Qu. 25.

save all or damn all.[s] Or suppose God hath decreed not to create more worlds than this we are now in, doth his decree weaken his strength to create more if he pleased? His not creating more is not a want of strength, but a want of will: it is an act of liberty, not an act of impotency. As when a man solemnly resolves not to walk in such a way, or come at such a place, his resolution deprives him not of his natural strength to walk thither, but fortifies his will against using his strength in any such motion to that place. The will of God hath set bounds to the exercise of his power, but doth not infringe that absolute power which still resides in his nature: he is girded about with more power than he puts forth (Ps. lxv. 6).

[4.] As the power of God is infinite in regard of his essence, in regard of the objects, in regard of action, so, fourthly, in regard of duration. The apostle calls it "an eternal power" (Rom. i. 20). His eternal power is collected and concluded from the things that are made: they must needs be the products of some Being which contains truly in itself all power, who wrought them without engines, without instruments; and, therefore, this power must be infinite, and possessed of an unalterable virtue of acting. If it be eternal, it must be infinite, and hath neither beginning nor end; what is eternal hath no bounds. If it be eternal, and not limited by time, it must be infinite, and not to be restrained by any finite object: his power never begun to be, nor ever ceaseth to be; it cannot languish; men are fain to unbend themselves, and must have some time to recruit their tired spirits: but the power of God is perpetually vigorous, without any interrupting qualm (Isa. xl. 28): "Hast thou not known, hast thou not heard, that the everlasting God, the Lord, the Creator of the ends of the earth, fainteth not, neither is weary?" That might which suffered no diminution from eternity, but hatched so great a world by brooding upon nothing, will not suffer any dimness or decrease to eternity. This power being the same with his essence, is as durable as his essence, and resides for ever in his nature.

8. The eighth consideration, for the right understanding of this attribute, the impossibility of God's doing some things, is no infringing of his almightiness, but rather a strengthening of it. It is granted that some things God cannot do; or, rather, as Aquinas and others, it is better to say, such things cannot be done, than to say that God cannot do them; to remove all kind of imputation or reflection of weakness on God,[t] and because the reason of the impossibility of those things is in the nature of the things themselves.

1. Some things are impossible in their own nature. Such are all those things which imply a contradiction; as for a thing to be, and not to be at the same time; for the sun to shine, and not to shine at the same moment of time; for a creature to act, and not to act at the same instant: one of those parts must be false; for if it be true that the sun shines this moment, it must be false to say it doth not shine. So it is impossible that a rational creature can be without reason: 'Tis a contradiction to be a rational creature, and yet want that which is essential to a rational creature. So it is impossible that the will of man can be compelled, because liberty is the essence of the

[s] Crell. de Deo. cap. 22.   [t] Robins. Observ. p. 14.

will; while it is will it cannot be constrained; and if it be constrained, it ceaseth to be will. God cannot at one time act as the author of the will and the destroyer of the will.[u] It is impossible that vice and virtue, light and darkness, life and death, should be the same thing. Those things admit not of a conception in any understanding. Some things are impossible to be done, because of the incapability of the subject; as for a creature to be made infinite, independent, to preserve itself without the Divine concourse and assistance. So a brute cannot be taken into communion with God, and to everlasting spiritual blessedness, because the nature of a brute is incapable of such an elevation: a rational creature only can understand and relish spiritual delights, and is capable to enjoy God, and have communion with him. Indeed, God may change the nature of a brute, and bestow such faculties of understanding and will upon it, as to render it capable of such a blessedness; but then it is no more a brute, but a rational creature: but, while it remains a brute, the excellency of the nature of God doth not admit of communion with such a subject; so that this is not for want of power in God, but because of a deficiency in the creature: to suppose that God could make a contradiction true, is to make himself false, and to do just nothing.

2. Some things are impossible to the nature and being of God. As to die, implies a flat repugnance to the nature of God; to be able to die, is to be able to be cashiered out of being. If God were able to deprive himself of life, he might then cease to be: he were not then a necessary, but an uncertain, contingent being, and could not be said only to have immortality, as he is (1 Tim. vi. 16). He cannot die who is life itself, and necessarily existent; he cannot grow old or decay, because he cannot be measured by time: and this is no part of weakness, but the perfection of power. His power is that whereby he remains forever fixed in his own everlasting being. That cannot be reckoned as necessary to the omnipotence of God which all mankind count a part of weakness in themselves: God is omnipotent, because he is not impotent; and if he could die, he would be impotent, not omnipotent: death is the feebleness of nature. It is undoubtedly the greatest impotence to cease to be: who would count it a part of omnipotency to disenable himself, and sink into nothing and not being? The impossibility for God to die is not a fit article to impeach his omnipotence; this would be a strange way of arguing: a thing is not powerful, because it is not feeble, and cannot cease to be powerful, for death is a cessation of all power. God is almighty in doing what he will, not in suffering what he will not.[x] To die is not an active, but a passive power; a defect of a power: God is of too noble a nature to perish. Some things are impossible to that eminency of nature which he hath above all creatures; as to walk, sleep, feed, these are imperfections belonging to bodies and compounded natures. If he could walk, he were not everywhere present: motion speaks succession. If he could increase, he would not have been perfect before.

3. Some things are impossible to the glorious perfections of God. God cannot do anything unbecoming his holiness and goodness;

[u] Magalano. de Scientia Dei, Part II. c. 6, §. 3.   [x] Augus.

any thing unworthy of himself, and against the perfections of his nature. God can do whatsoever he can will. As he doth actually do whatsoever he doth actually will, so it is possible for him to do whatsoever it is possible for him to will. He doth whatsoever he will, and can do whatsoever he can will; but he cannot do what he cannot will: he cannot will any unrighteous thing, and therefore cannot do any unrighteous thing. God cannot love sin, this is contrary to his holiness; he cannot violate his word, this is a denial of his truth; he cannot punish an innocent, this is contrary to his goodness; he cannot cherish an impenitent sinner, this is an injury to his justice; he cannot forget what is done in the world, this is a disgrace to his omniscience; he cannot deceive his creature, this is contrary to his faithfulness: none of these things can be done by him, because of the perfection of his nature. Would it not be an imperfection in God to absolve the guilty, and condemn the innocent? Is it congruous to the righteous and holy nature of God, to command murder and adultery; to command men not to worship him, but to be base and unthankful? These things would be against the rules of righteousness; as, when we say of a good man, he cannot rob or fight a duel, we do not mean that he wants a courage for such an act, or that he hath not a natural strength and knowledge to manage his weapon as well as another, but he hath a righteous principle strong in him which will not suffer him to do it; his will is settled against it: no power can pass into act unless applied by the will; but the will of God cannot will anything but what is worthy of him, and decent for his goodness.

(1.) The Scripture saith it is impossible for God to lie (Heb. vi. 18); and God cannot deny himself because of his faithfulness (2 Tim. ii. 13). As he cannot die, because he is life itself; as he cannot deceive, because he is goodness itself; as he cannot do an unwise action, because he is wisdom itself, so he cannot speak a false word, because he is truth itself. If he should speak anything as true, and not know it, where is his infinite knowledge and comprehensiveness of understanding? If he should speak anything as true, which he knows to be false, where is his infinite righteousness? If he should deceive any creature, there is an end of his perfection of fidelity and veracity. If he should be deceived himself, there is an end of his omniscience; we must then fancy him to be a deceitful God, an ignorant God, that is, no God at all. If he should lie, he would be God and no God; God upon supposition, and no God, because not the first truth.ʸ All unrighteousness is weakness, not power; it is a defection from right reason, a deviation from moral principles, and the rule of perfect action, and ariseth from a defect of goodness and power: it is a weakness, and not omnipotence, to lose goodness: God is light; it is the perfection of light not to become darkness, and a want of power in light, if it should become darkness:ᶻ his power is infinitely strong, so is his wisdom infinitely clear, and his will infinitely pure: would it not be a part of weakness to have a disorder in himself, and these perfections shock one against another? Since all perfections are in God, in the most sov-

ʸ Becan. sum. Theolog. p. 83.   ᶻ Maximus Tyrius.

ereign height of perfection, nothing can be done by the infiniteness of one against the infiniteness of the other. He would then be unstable in his own perfections, and depart from the infinite rectitude of his own will, if he should do an evil action. Again,[a] what is an argument of greater strength, than to be utterly ignorant of infirmity? God is omnipotent because he cannot do evil, and would not be omnipotent if he could; those things would be marks of weakness, and not characters of majesty. Would you count a sweet fountain impotent because it cannot send forth bitter streams? or the sun weak, because it cannot diffuse darkness as well as light in the air? There is an inability arising from weakness, and an ability arising from perfection: it is the perfection of angels and blessed spirits, that they cannot sin; and it would be the imperfection of God, if he could do evil.

(2.) Hence it follows, that it is impossible that a thing past should not be past. If we ascribe a power to God, to make a thing that is past not to be past, we do not truly ascribe power to him, but a weakness; for it is to make God to lie, as though God might not have created man, yet, after he had created Adam, though he should presently have reduced Adam to his first nothing, yet it would be forever true that Adam was created, and it would forever be false that Adam never was created: so, though God may prevent sin, yet when sin hath been committed, it will alway be true that sin was committed; it will never be true to say such a creature that did sin, did not sin; his sin cannot be recalled: though God, by pardon, take off the guilt of Peter's denying our Saviour, yet it will be eternally true that Peter did deny him. It is repugnant to the righteousness and truth of God to make that which was once true to become false, and not true; that is, to make a truth to become a lie, and a lie to become a truth. This is well argued from Heb. vi. 18: "It is impossible for God to lie." The apostle argues, that what God had promised and sworn will come to pass, and cannot but come to pass.[b] Now, if God could make a thing past not to be past, this consequence would not be good, for then he might make himself not to have promised, not to have sworn, after he hath promised and sworn; and so, if there were a power to undo that which is past, there would be no foundation for faith, no certainty of revelation. It cannot be asserted, that God hath created the world; that God hath sent his Son to die; that God hath accepted his death for man. These might not be true, if it were possible, that that which hath been done, might be said never to have been done: so that what any may imagine to be a want of power in God, is the highest perfection of God, and the greatest security to a believing creature that hath to do with God.

4. Some things are impossible to be done, because of God's ordination. Some things are impossible, not in their own nature, but in regard of the determined will of God: so God might have destroyed the world after Adam's fall, but it was impossible; not that God wanted power to do it, but because he did not only decree from eternity to create the world, but did also decree to redeem the world

---

[a] Ambrose. [b] Becan. sum. Theol. p. 84. Crel. de Deo, cap. 22.

by Jesus Christ, and erected the world in order to the manifestation of his "glory in Christ" (Eph. i. 4, 5). The choice of some in Christ was "before the foundation of the world." Supposing that there was no hindrance in the justice of God to pardon the sin of Adam after his fall, and to execute no punishment on him, yet in regard of God's threatening, that in the day he eat of the forbidden fruit he should die, it was impossible: so, though it was possible that the cup should pass from our blessed Saviour, that is, possible in its own nature, yet it was not possible in regard of the determination of God's will, since he had both decreed and published his will to redeem man by the passion and blood of his Son. These things God, by his absolute power, might have done; but upon the account of his decree, they were impossible, because it is repugnant to the nature of God to be mutable: it is to deny his own wisdom which contrived them, and his own will which resolved them, not to do that which he had decreed to do. This would be a diffidence in his wisdom, and a change of his will. The impossibility of them is no result of a want of power, no mark of an imperfection, of feebleness and impotence; but the perfection of immutability and unchangeableness. Thus have I endeavored to give you a right notion of this excellent attribute of the power of God, in as plain terms as I could, which may serve us for a matter of meditation, admiration, fear of him, trust in him, which are the proper uses we should make of this doctrine of Divine power. The want of a right understanding of this doctrine of the Divine power hath caused many to run into mighty absurdities; I have, therefore, taken the more pains to explain it.

II. The second thing I proposed, is the reasons to prove God to be omnipotent. The Scripture describes God by this attribute of power (Ps. cxv. 3): "He hath done whatsoever he pleased." It sometimes sets forth his power in a way of derision of those that seem to doubt of it. When Sarah doubted of his ability to give her a child in her old age (Gen. xviii. 14), "Is anything too hard for the Lord?" They deserve to be scoffed, that will despoil God of his strength, and measure him by their shallow models. And when Moses uttered something of unbelief of this attribute, as if God were not able to feed 600,000 Israelites, besides women and children, which he aggravates by a kind of imperious scoff; "Shall the flocks and the herds be slain for them to suffice them? Or, shall all the fish of the sea be gathered together for them?" &c. (Numb. xi. 22). God takes him up short (ver. 23): "Is the Lord's hand waxed short?" What! can any weakness seize upon my hand? Can I draw out of my own treasures what is needful for a supply? The hand of God is not at one time strong, and another time feeble. Hence it is that we read of the hand and arm of God, an outstretched arm; because the strength of a man is exerted by his hand and arm; the power of God is called the arm of his power, and the right hand of his strength. Sometimes, according to the different manifestation of it, it is expressed by finger, when a less power is evidenced; by hand, when something greater; by arm, when more mighty than the former. Since God is eternal, without limits of time, he is also Almighty, without limits of strength. As he cannot be said to be more in being now than he was before, so he is neither more nor less in strength than he was before: as he cannot cease to be so, so he cannot cease to be powerful, because he is eternal. His eternity and power are linked together as equally demonstrable (Rom. i. 20); God is called the God of gods *El Elohim* (Dan. xi. 36); the Mighty of mighties, whence all mighty persons have their activity and vigor: he is called the Lord of Hosts, as being the Creator and Conductor of the heavenly militia.

Reason 1. The power that is in creatures demonstrates a greater and an unconceivable power in God. Nothing in the world is without a power of activity according to its nature: no creature but can act something. The sun warms and enlightens everything: it sends its influences upon the earth, into the bowels of the earth, into the depths of the sea: all generations owe themselves to its instrumental virtue. How powerful is a small seed to rise into a mighty tree with a lofty top, and extensive branches, and send forth other seeds, which can still multiply into numberless plants! How wonderful is the power of the Creator, who hath endowed so small a creature as a seed, with so fruitful an activity! Yet this is but the virtue of a limited nature. God is both the producing and preserving cause of all the virtue in any creature, in every creature. The power of every creature belongs to him as the Fountain, and is truly his power in the creature. As he is the first Being, he is the original of all being ; as he is the first Good, he is the spring of all goodness; as he is the first Truth, he is the source of all truth ; so, as he is the first Power, he is the fountain of all power.

1. He, therefore, that communicates to the creature what power it hath, contains eminently much more power in himself. (Ps. xciv. 10), " He that teaches man knowledge, shall not he know ?" So he that gives created beings power, shall not he be powerful ? The first Being must have as much power as he hath given to others: he could not transfer that upon another, which he did not transcendently possess himself. The sole cause of created power cannot be destitute of any power in himself. We see that the power of one creature transcends the power of another. Beasts can do the things that plants cannot do ; besides the power of growth, they have a power of sense and progressive motion. Men can do more than beasts; they have rational souls to measure the earth and heavens, and to be repositories of multitudes of things, notions, and conclusions. We may well imagine angels to be far superior to man : the power of the Creator must far surmount the power of the creature, and must needs be infinite: for if it be limited, it is limited by himself or by some other ; if by some other, he is no longer a Creator, but a creature ; for that which limits him in his nature, did communicate that nature to him ; not by himself, for he would not deny himself any necessary perfection : we must still conclude a reserve of power in him, that he that made these can make many more of the same kind.

2. All the power which is distinct in the creatures, must be united in God. One creature hath a strength to do this, another to do that; every creature is as a cistern filled with a particular and limited

power, according to the capacity of its nature, from this fountain; all are distinct streams from God. But the strength of every creature, though distinct in the rank of creatures, is united in God the centre, whence those lines were drawn, the fountain whence those streams were derived. If the power of one creature be admirable, as the power of an angel, which the Psalmist saith (Ps. ciii. 20), " excelleth in strength;" how much greater must the power of a legion of angels be! How inconceivably superior the power of all those numbers of spiritual natures, which are the excellent works of God! Now, if all this particular power, which is in every angel distinct, were compacted in one angel, how would it exceed our understanding, and be above our power to form a distinct conception of it! What is thus divided in every angel, must be thought united in the Creator of angels, and far more excellent in him. Everything is in a more noble manner in the fountain, than in the streams which distil and descend from it. He that is the Original of all those distinct powers, must be the seat of all power without distinction: in him is the union of all without division; what is in them as a quality, is in him as his essence. Again, if all the powers of several creatures, with all their principal qualities and vigors, both of beasts, plants, and rational creatures, were united in one subject; as if one lion had the strength of all the lions that ever were; or, if one elephant had the strength of all the elephants that ever were; nay, if one bee had all the power of motion and stinging that all bees ever had, it would have a vast strength; but if the strength of all those thus gathered into one of every kind should be lodged in one sole creature, one man, would it not be a strength too big for our conception? Or, suppose one cannon had all the force of all the cannons that ever were in the world, what a battery would it make, and, as it were, shake the whole frame of heaven and earth! All this strength must be much more incomprehensible in God; all is united in him. If it were in one individual created nature, it would still be but a finite power in a finite nature: but in God it is infinite and immense.

Reason 2. If there were not an incomprehensible power in God, he would not be infinitely perfect. God is the first Being; it can only be said of him, *Est*, he is. All other things are nothing to him; " less than nothing and vanity" (Isa. xl. 17), and " reputed as nothing" (Dan. iv. 35). All the inhabitants of the earth, with all their wit and strength, are counted as if they were not; just in comparison with Him and his being, as a little mote in the sun-beams: God, therefore, is a pure Being. Any kind of weakness whatsoever is a defect, a degree of not being; so far as anything wants this or that power, it may be said not to be. Were there anything of weakness in God, any want of strength which belonged to the perfection of a nature, it might be said of God, He is not this or that, he wants this or that perfection of Being, and so he would not be a pure Being, there would be something of not being in him. But God being the first Being, the only original Being, he is infinitely distant from not being, and therefore infinitely distant from anything of weakness. Again, if God can know whatsoever is possible to be done by him, and cannot do it, there would be something more in his knowledge than in his power.[c] What would then follow? That the essence of God would be in some regard greater than itself, and less than itself, because his knowledge and his power are his essence; his power as much his essence as his knowledge: and therefore, in regard of his knowledge, his essence would be greater; in regard of his power, his essence would be less; which is a thing impossible to be conceived in a most perfect Being. We must understand this of those things which are properly and in their own nature subjected to the Divine knowledge; for otherwise God knows more than he can do, for he knows sin, but he cannot act it, because sin belongs not to power but weakness; and sin comes under the knowledge of God, not in itself and its own nature, but as it is a defect from God, and contrary to good, which is the proper object of Divine knowledge. He knows it also not as possible to be done by himself, but as possible to be done by the creature. Again, if God were not omnipotent, we might imagine something more perfect than God :[d] for if we bar God from any one thing which in its own nature is possible, we may imagine a being that can do that thing, one that is able to effect it; and so imagine an agent greater than God, a being able to do more than God is able to do, and consequently a being more perfect than God : but no being more perfect than God can be imagined by any creature. Nothing can be called most perfect, if anything of activity be wanting to it. Active power follows the perfection of a thing, and all things are counted more noble by how much more of efficacy and virtue they possess. We count those the best and most perfect plants, that have the greatest medicinal virtue in them, and power of working upon the body for the cure of distempers. God is perfect of himself, and therefore most powerful of himself. If his perfection in wisdom and goodness be unsearchable, his power, which belongs to perfection, and without which all the other excellencies of his nature were insignificant, and could not show themselves, (as was before evidenced,) must be unsearchable also. It is by the title of Almighty he is denominated, when declared to be unsearchable to perfection (Job xi. 7): "Canst thou by searching find out God, canst thou find out the Almighty to perfection?" This would be limited and searched out, if he were destitute of an active ability to do whatsoever he pleased to do, whatsoever was possible to be done. As he hath not a perfect liberty of will, if he could not will what he pleased; so he would not have a perfect activity, if he could not do what he willed.

Reason 3. The simplicity of God manifests it. Every substance, the more spiritual it is, the more powerful it is. All perfections are more united in a simple, than in a compounded being. Angels, being spirits, are more powerful than bodies. Where there is the greatest simplicity, there is the greatest unity; and where there is the greatest unity, there is the greatest power. Where there is a composition of a faculty and a member, the member or organ may be weakened and rendered unable to act, though the power doth still reside in the faculty. As a man, when his arm or hand is cut off or broke, he hath the faculty of motion still; but he hath lost

c Victorin. in Petar. Tom. I. p. 333.   d Ibid. p. 233.

that instrument that part whereby he did manifest and put forth that motion : but God being a pure spiritual nature, hath no members, no organs to be defaced or impaired.   All impediments of actions arise either from the nature of the thing that acts, or from something without it.   There can be no hindrance to God to do whatsoever he pleases; not in himself, because he is the most simple being, hath no contrariety in himself, is not composed of divers things; and it cannot be from anything without himself, because nothing is equal to him, much less superior.   He is the greatest, the Supreme : all things were made by him, depend upon him, nothing can disappoint his intentions.

Reason 4. The miracles that have been in the world evidence the power of God.   Extraordinary productions have awakened men from their stupidity, to the acknowledgment of the immensity of Divine power.   Miracles are such effects as have been wrought without the assistance and co-operation of natural causes, yea, contrary and besides the ordinary course of nature, above the reach of any created power.   Miracles have been ; and saith Bradwardine,[e] to deny that ever such things were, is uncivil: it is inhuman to deny all the histories of Jews and Christians; whosoever denies miracles, must deny all possibility of miracles, and so must imagine himself fully skilled in the extent of Divine power.   How was the sun suspended from its motion for some hours (Josh. x. 13) ; " the dead raised from the grave ;" those reduced from the brink of it, that had been brought near to it by prevailing diseases; and this by a word speaking?   How were the famished lions bridled from exercising their rage upon Daniel, exposed to them for a prey (Dan. vi. 22)? the activity of the fire curbed for the preservation of the three children (Dan. iii. 15)? which proves a Deity more powerful than all creatures.   No power upon earth can hinder the operation of the fire upon combustible matter, when they are united, unless by quenching the fire, or removing the matter : but no created power can restrain the fire, so long as it remains so, from acting according to its nature.   This was done by God in the case of the three children, and that of the burning bush (Exod. iii. 2).   It was as much miraculous that the bush should not consume, as it was natural that it should burn by the efficacy of the fire upon it.   No element is so obstinate and deaf, but it hears and obeys his voice, and performs his orders, though contrary to its own nature : all the violence or the creature is suspended as soon as it receives his command.   He that gave the original to nature, can take away the necessity of nature ;[f] he presides over creatures, but is not confined to those laws he hath prescribed to creatures.   He framed nature, and can turn the channels of nature according to his own pleasure.   Men dig into the bowels of nature, search into all the treasures of it, to find medicines to cure a disease, and after all their attempts it may prove labor in vain : but God, by one act of his will, one word of his mouth, overturns the victory of death, and rescues from the most desperate diseases.[g]   All the miracles which were wrought by the apostles, either speaking some words or touching with the hand,

• Lib. i. cap. l. p. 38.   f Damianus, in Petar.   g Fauch. in Acts. Vol. II. § 56.

were not effected by any virtue inherent in their words or in their touches; for such virtue inherent in any created finite subject would be created and finite itself, and consequently were incapable to produce effects which required an infinite virtue, as miracles do which are above the power of nature. So when our Saviour wrought miracles, it was not by any quality resident in his human nature, but by the sole power of his Divinity. The flesh could only do what was proper to the flesh; but the Deity did what was proper to the Deity. " God alone doth wonders" (Ps. cxxxvi. 4): excluding every other cause from producing those things. He only doth those things which are above the power of nature, and cannot be wrought by any natural causes whatsoever. He doth not hereby put his omnipotence to any stress: it is as easy with him to turn nature out of its settled course, as it was to place it in that station it holds, and appoint it that course it runs. All the works of nature are indeed miracles and testimonies of the power of God producing them, and sustaining them: but works above the power of nature, being novelties and unusual, strike men with a greater admiration upon their appearance, because they are not the products of nature, but the convulsions of it. I might also add as an argument, the power of the mind of man to conceive more than hath been wrought by God in the world. And God can work whatsoever perfection the mind of man can conceive: otherwise the reaches of a created imagination and fancy would be more extensive than the power of God. His power, therefore, is far greater than the conception of any intellectual creature; else the creature would be of a greater capacity to conceive than God is to effect. The creature would have a power of conception above God's power of activity; and consequently a creature, in some respect greater than himself. Now whatsoever a creature can conceive possible to be done, is but finite in its own nature; and if God could not produce what being a created understanding can conceive possible to be done, he would be less than infinite in power, nay, he could not go to the extent of what is finite. But I have touched this before; that God can create more than he hath created, and in a more perfect way of being, as considered simply in themselves.

III. The third general thing is to declare, how the power of God appears in Creation, in Government, in Redemption.

First, In Creation. With what majestic lines doth God set for his power, in the giving being and endowments to all the creatures in the world (Job xxxviii.)! All that is in heaven and earth is his, and shows the greatness of his power, glory, victory, and majesty (1 Chron. xxix. 11). The heaven being so magnificent a piece of work, is called emphatically, " the firmament of his power" (Ps. cl. 1); his power being more conspicuous and unavailed in that glorious arch of the world. Indeed, " God exalts by his power" (Job xxxvi. 22), that is, exalts himself by his power in all the works of his hands; in the smallest shrub, as well as the most glorious sun. All his works of nature are truly miracles, though we consider them not, being blinded with too frequent and customary a sight of them; yet, in the neglect of all the rest, the view of the heavens doth more affect us with astonishment at the might of God's arm: these declare his glory, and "the firmament showeth his handy work" (Ps. xix. 1). And the Psalmist peculiarly calls them his heavens, and the work of his fingers (Ps. viii. 3): these were immediately created by God, whereas many other things in the world were brought into being by the power of God, yet by the means of the influence of the heavens.

1. His power is the first thing evident in the story of the creation. "In the beginning God created the heavens and the earth" (Gen. i. 1). There is no appearance of anything in this declaratory preface, but of power: the characters of wisdom march after in the distinct formation of things, and animating them with suitable qualities for an universal good. By heaven and earth, is meant the whole mass of the creatures: by heaven, all the airy region, with all the host of it; by the earth, is meant, all that which makes the entire inferior globe.[h] The Jews observe, that in the first of Genesis, in the whole chapter, unto the finishing the work in six days, God is called אלהים, which is a name of Power, and that thirty-two times in that chapter; but after the finishing the six days' work, he is called האלהים, which, according to their notion, is a name of goodness and kindness: his power is first visible in framing the world, before his goodness is visible in the sustaining and preserving it. It was by this name of Power and Almighty that he was known in the first ages of the world, not by his name, Jehovah (Exod. vi. 3): "And I appeared unto Abraham, Isaac, and Jacob, by the name of God Almighty; but by my name Jehovah was I not known to them." Not but that they were acquainted with the name, but did not experience the intent of the name, which signified his truth in the performance of his promises; they knew him by that name as promising, but they knew him not by that name, as performing. He would be known by his name Jehovah, true to his word, when he was about to effect the deliverance from Egypt; a type of the eternal redemption, wherein the truth of God, in performing of his first promise, is gloriously magnified. And hence it is that God is called Almighty more in the book of Job than in all the Scripture besides, I think about thirty-two times, and Jehovah but once, which is Job xii. 9, unless in Job xxxviii. when God is introduced speaking himself; which is an argument of Job's living before the deliverance from Egypt, when God was known more by his works of creation than by the performance of his promises, before the name Jehovah was formally published. Indeed, this attribute of his eternal power, is the first thing visible and intelligible upon the first glance of the eye upon the creatures (Rom. i. 20). Bring a man out of the cave where he hath been nursed, without seeing anything out of the confines of it, and let him lift up his eyes to the heavens, and take a prospect of that glorious body, the sun, then cast them down to the earth, and behold the surface of it, with its green clothing; the first notion which will start up in his mind from that spring of wonders, is that of power, which he will at first adore with a religious astonishment. The wisdom of God in them is not so presently apparent, till after a more

<hr />

[h] Mercer. p. 7, col. 1, 2.

exquisite consideration of his works and knowledge of the properties of their natures, the conveniency of their situations, and the usefulness of their functions, and the order wherein they are linked
together for the good of the universe.

2. By this creative power God is often distinguished from all the
idols and false gods in the world. And by this title he sets forth
himself when he would act any great and wonderful work in the
world (Ps. cxxxv. 5, 6): "He is great above all gods," for "he hath
done whatsoever he pleased in heaven and in earth." Upon this is
founded all the worship he challengeth in the world, as his peculiar,
glory (Rev. iv. 11): "Thou art worthy, O Lord, to receive glory,
honor, and power, for thou hast created all things." And (Rev. x. 6)
"I have made the earth, and created man upon it." "I, even my
hands, have stretched out the heavens, and all their host have I
commanded" (Isa. xlv. 12). What is the issue (ver. 16)? "They
shall be ashamed and confounded, all of them, that are makers of
idols." And the weakness of idols is expressed by this title. "The
gods that have not made the heavens and the earth" (Jer. x. 11).
"The portion of Jacob is not like them, for he is the former of all
things" (ver. 16). What is not that God able to do, that hath created
so great a world? How doth the power of God appear in creation?

1st. In making the world of nothing. When we say, the world
was made of nothing, we mean, that there was no matter existent for
God to work upon, but what he raised himself in the first act of
creation. In this regard, the power of God in creation surmounts
his power in providence. Creation supposeth nothing, providence
supposeth something in being. Creation intimates a creature making,
providence speaks a thing already made, and capable of government,
and in government. God uses second causes to bring about his
purposes.

1. The world was made of nothing. The earth which is described
as the first matter, without any form or ornament, without any distinction or figures, was of God's forming in the bulk, before he did
adorn it with his pencil (Gen. i. 1, 2). God, in the beginning, creating the heaven and the earth, includes two things: First. That
those were created in the beginning of time, and before all other
things. Secondly. That God begun the creation of the world from
those things.[i] Therefore before the heavens and the earth there was
nothing absolutely created, and therefore no matter in being before
an act of creation passed upon it. It could not be eternal, because
nothing can be eternal but God; it must therefore have a beginning.
If it had a beginning from itself, then it was before it was. If it
acted in the making itself before it was made, then it had a being
before it had a being; for that which is nothing, can act nothing:
the action of anything supposeth the existence of the thing which
acts. It being made, it was not before it was made; for to be made
is to be brought into being. It was made, then, by another, and
that Maker is God. It is necessary that the First Original of things
was from nothing: when we see one thing to arise from another, we
must suppose an original of the first of each kind; as, when we see

a tree spring up from a seed, we know that seed came out of the bowels of another tree; it had a parent, it had a master; we must come to some first, or else we run into an endless maze: we must come to some first tree, some first seed that had no cause of the same kind, no matter of it, but was mere nothing. Creation doth suppose a production from nothing; because, if you suppose a thing without any real or actual existence, it is not capable of any other production than from nothing: nothing must be supposed before the world, or we must suppose it eternal, and that is to deny it to be a creature, and make it God.[k] The creation of spiritual substances, such as angels and souls, evince this; those things that are purely spiritual, and consist not of matter, cannot pretend to any original from matter, and therefore they rose up from nothing. If spiritual things arose from nothing, much more may corporeal, because they are of a lower nature than spiritual; and he that can create a higher nature of nothing, can create an inferior nature of nothing. As bodily things are more imperfect than spiritual, so their creation may be supposed easier than that of spiritual. There was as little need of any matter to be wrought to his hands, to contrive into this visible fabric, as there was to erect such an excellent order as the glorious cherubims.

2. This creation of things from nothing speaks an infinite power. The distance between nothing and being hath been alway counted so great, that nothing but an Infinite Power can make such distances meet together, either for nothing to pass into being, or being to return to nothing. To have a thing arise from nothing, was so difficult a text to those that were ignorant of the Scripture, that they knew not how to fathom it, and therefore laid it down as a certain rule, that of nothing, nothing is made; which is true of a created power, but not of an uncreated and Almighty Power. A greater distance cannot be imagined than that which is between nothing and something; that which hath no being, and that which hath; and a greater power cannot be imagined than that which brings something out of nothing. We know not how to conceive a nothing, and afterwards a being from that nothing; but we must remain swallowed up in admiration of the Cause that gives it being, and acknowledge it to be without any bounds and measures of greatness and power.[l] The further anything is from being, the more immense must that power be which brings it into being: it is not conceivable that the power of all the angels in one can give being to the smallest spire of grass. To imagine, therefore, so small a thing as a bee, a fly, a grain of corn, or an atom of dust, to be made of nothing, would stupefy any creature in the consideration of it, much more to behold the heavens, with all the troop of stars; the earth, with all its embroidery; and the sea, with all her inhabitants of fish; and man, the noblest creature of all, to arise out of the womb of mere emptiness. Indeed, God had not acted as an almighty Creator, if he had stood in need of any materials but of his own framing: it had been as much as his Deity was worth, if he had not had all within the compass of his own power that was necessary to operation; if he must have been

k Suarez, Vol. III. p. 6.   l Amyrald Morale. Tom. I. p. 252.

beholden to something without himself, and above himself, for matter to work upon : had there been such a necessity, we could not have imagined him to be omnipotent, and, consequently, not God.

3. In this the power of God exceeds the power of all natural and rational agents. Nature, or the order of second causes, hath a vast power ; the sun generates flies and other insects, but of some matter, the slime of the earth or a dunghill ; the sun and the earth bring forth harvests of corn, but from seed first sown in the earth ; fruits are brought forth, but from the sap of the plant ; were there no seed or plants in the earth, the power of the earth would be idle, and the influence of the sun insignificant ; whatsoever strength either of them had in their nature, must be useless without matter to work upon. All the united strength of nature cannot produce the least thing out of nothing ; it may multiply and increase things, by the powerful blessing God gave it at the first erecting of the world, but it cannot create. The word which signifies *creation*, used in Gen. i. 1, is not ascribed to any second cause, but only to God ; a word, in that sense, as incommunicable to anything else as the action it signifies. Rational creatures can produce admirable pieces of art from small things, yet still out of matter created to their hands. Excellent garments may be woven, but from the entrails of a small silkworm. Delightful and medicinal spirits and essences may be extracted, by ingenious chemists, but out of the bodies of plants and minerals. No picture can be drawn without colors ; no statue engraven without stone ; no building erected without timber, stones, and other materials : nor can any man raise a thought without some matter framed to his hands, or cast into him. Matter is, by nature, formed to the hands of all artificers ; they bestow a new figure upon it, by the help of instruments, and the product of their own wit and skill, but they create not the least particle of matter ; when they want it, they must be supplied or else stand still, as well as nature, for none of them, or all together, can make the least mite or atom : and when they have wrought all that they can, they will not want some to find a flaw and defect in their work. God, as a Creator, hath the only prerogative to draw what he pleases from nothing, without any defect, without any imperfection : he can raise what matter he please ; ennoble it with what form he pleases. Of nothing, nothing can be made, by any created agent : but the omnipotent Architect of the world is not under the same necessity, nor is limited to the same rule, and tied by so short a tedder as created nature, or an ingenious, yet feeble artificer.

2d. It appears, in raising such variety of creatures from this barren womb of nothing, or from the matter which he first commanded to appear out of nothing. Had there been any pre-existent matter, yet the bringing forth such varieties and diversities of excellent creatures, some with life, some with sense, and others with reason superadded to the rest, and those out of indisposed and undigested matter, would argue an infinite power resident in the first Author of this variegated fabric. From this matter he formed that glorious sun, which every day displays its glory, scatters its beams, clears the air, ripens our fruits, and maintains the propagation of creatures in the world. From this matter he lighted those torches which he set in the heaven to qualify the darkness of the night : from this he compacted those bodies of light, which, though they seem to us as little sparks, as if they were the glow-worms of heaven, yet some of them exceed in greatness this globe of the earth on which we live : and the highest of them hath so quick a motion, that some tell us they run, in the space of every hour, 42,000,000 of leagues. From the same matter he drew the earth on which we walk ; from thence he extracted the flowers to adorn it, the hills to secure the valleys, and the rocks to fortify it against the inundations of the sea ; and on this dull and sluggish element he bestowed so great a fruitfulness, to maintain, feed, and multiply so many seeds of different kinds, and conferred upon those little bodies of seeds a power to multiply their kinds, in conjunction with the fruitfulness of the earth, to many thousands. From this rude matter, the slime or dust of the earth, he kneaded the body of man, and wrought so curious a fabric, fit to entertain a soul of a heavenly extraction, formed by the breath of God (Gen. ii. 7). He brought light out of thick darkness, and living creatures, fish and fowl, out of inanimate waters (Gen. i. 20), and gave a power of spontaneous motion to things arising from that matter which had no living motion. To convert one thing into another, is an evidence of infinite power, as well as creating things of nothing ; for the distance between life and not life is next to that which is between being and not being. God first forms matter out of nothing, and then draws upon, and from this indisposed chaos, many excellent portraitures. Neither earth nor sea were capable of producing living creatures without an infinite power working upon it, and bringing into it such variety and multitude of forms ; and this is called, by some, mediate creation, as the producing the chaos, which was without form and void, is called immediate creation. Is not the power of the potter admirable in forming, out of tempered clay, such varieties of neat and curious vessels, that, after they are fashioned and past the furnace, look as if they were not of any kin to the matter they are formed of ? and is it not the same with the glass-maker, that, from a little melted jelly of sand and ashes, or the dust of flint, can blow up so pure a body as glass, and in such varieties of shapes ? and is not the power of God more admirable, because infinite in speaking out so beautiful a world out of nothing, and such varieties of living creatures from matter utterly indisposed, in its own nature, for such forms ?

3d. And this conducts to a third thing, wherein the power of God appears, in that he did all this with the greatest ease and facility.

1. Without instruments. As God made the world without the advice, so without the assistance, of any other : " He stretched forth the heavens alone, and spread abroad the earth by himself " (Isa. xliv. 24). He had no engine, but his word ; no pattern or model, but himself. What need can he have of instruments, that is able to create what instruments he pleases ? Where there is no resistance in the object, where no need of preparation or instrumental advantage in the agent ; there the actual determination of the will is sufficient to a production. What instrument need

we to the thinking of a thought, or an act of our will? Men, indeed, cannot act anything without tools; the best artificer must be beholden to something else for his noblest works of art. The carpenter cannot work without his rule, and axe, and saw, and other instruments; the watch-maker cannot act without his file and pliers; but in creation, there is nothing necessary to God's bringing forth a world, but a simple act of his will, which is both the principal cause, and instrumental. He had no scaffolds to rear it, no engines to polish it, no hammers or mattocks to clod and work it together. It is a miserable error to measure the actions of an Infinite Cause by the imperfect model of a finite, since, by his own "power and out-stretched arm, he made the heaven and the earth" (Jer. xxxii. 17). What excellency would God have in his work above others, if he needed instruments, as feeble men do?[m] Every artificer is counted more admirable, that can frame curious works with the less matter, fewer tools, and assistances. God uses instruments in his works of providence, not for necessity, but for the display of his wisdom in the management of them; yet those instruments were originally framed by him without instruments. Indeed, some of the Jews thought the angels were the instruments of God in creating man, and that those words, "Let us make man in our own image" (Gen. i. 26), were spoken to angels. But certainly the Scripture, which denies God any counsellor in the model of creation (Isa. xl. 12—14), doth not join any instrument with him in the operation, which is everywhere ascribed to himself "without created assistance" (Isa. xlv. 18). It was not to angels God spake in that affair; if so, man was made after the image of angels, if they were companions with God in that work; but it is everywhere said, that "Man was made after the image of God" (Gen. i. 27). Again, the image wherein man was created, was that of dominion over the lower creatures, as appears ver. 26, which we find not conferred upon angels; and it is not likely that Moses should introduce the angels, as God's privy counsel, of whose creation he had not mentioned one syllable. "Let us make man," rather signifies the Trinity, and not spoken in a royal style, as some think. Which of the Jewish kings wrote in the style, *We?* That was the custom of later times; and we must not measure the language of Scripture by the style of Europe, of a far later date than the penning the history of the creation. If angels were his counsellors in the creation of the material world, what instrument had he in the creation of angels? If his own wisdom were the director, and his own will the producer of the one; why should we not think, that he acted by his sole power in the other? It is concluded by most, that the power of creation cannot be derived to any creature, it being a work of omnipotency; the drawing something out from nothing, cannot be communicated without a communication of the Deity itself. The educing things from nothing exceeds the capacity of any creature, and the creature is of too feeble a nature to be elevated to so high a degree. It is very unreasonable to think, that God needed any such aid. If an instrument were necessary for God to create the world, then he could not do it without that instrument: if he could not, he were not then all-sufficient in himself, if he depended upon anything without himself, for the production or consummation of his works. And it might be inquired, how that instrument came into being; if it begun to be, and there was a time when it was not, it must have its being from the power of God; and then, why could not God as well create all things without an instrment, as create that instrument without an instrument? For there was no more power necessary to a producing the whole without instruments, than to produce one creature without an instrument. No creature can, in its own nature, be an instrument of creation. If any such instrument were used by God, it must be elevated in a miraculous and supernatural way; and what is so an instrument, is, in effect, no instrument; for it works nothing by its own nature, but from an elevation by a superior nature, and beyond its own nature. All that power in the instrument is truly the power of God, and not the power of the instrument; and, therefore, what God doth by an instrument, he could do as well without. If you should see one apply straw to iron, for the cutting of it, and effect it, you would not call the straw an instrument in that action, because there was nothing in the nature of the straw to do it. It was done wholly by some other force, which might have done it as well without the straw as with it. The narrative of the creation in Genesis, removes any instrument from God. The plants which are preserved and propagated by the influence of the sun, were created the day before the sun, viz. on the "third day," whereas, the light was collected into the body of the sun on the "fourth day" (Gen. i. 11, 16); to show, that though the plants do instrumentally owe their yearly beauty and preservation to the sun, yet they did not in any manner owe their creation to the instrumental heat and vigor of it.

2. God created the world by a word, by a simple act of his will. The whole creation is wrought by a word; "God said, Let there be light;" and "God said, Let there be a firmament."[n] Not that we should understand it of a sensible word, but understand it of a powerful order of his own will, which is expressed by the Psalmist in the nature of a command (Ps. xxxiii 9): "He spake, and it was done; he commanded, and it stood fast;" and (Ps. cxlviii, 5), "He commanded, and they were created." At the same instant that he willed them to stand forth, they did stand forth. The efficacious command of the Creator was the original of all things: the insensibility of nothing obeyed the act of his will. Creation is therefore entitled a calling (Rom. iv. 17): "He calls those things which are not, as if they were." To create is no more with God, than to call; and what he calls, presents itself before him in the same posture that he calls it. He did with more ease make a world, than we can form a thought. It is the same ease to him to create worlds, as to decree them; there needs no more than a resolve to have things wrought at such a time, and they will be, according to his pleasure. This will is his power; "Let there be light," is the precept of his will;

<hr>

[n] Gen. i. 3, 5, &c. throughout the whole chapter.

and "there was light," is the effect of his precept. By a word, was the matter of the heavens and the earth framed; by a word, things separate themselves from the rude mass into their proper forms; by a word, light associates itself into one body, and forms a sun; by a word, are the heavens, as it were, bespangled with stars, and the earth dressed with flowers; by a word, is the world both ceiled and floored : one act of his will, formed the world, and perfected its beauty. All the variety and several exploits of his power were not caused by distinct words or acts of power. God uttered not distinct words for distinct species; as, let there be an elephant, and let there be a lion ; but as he produced those various creatures out of one matter, so by one word. By one single command, those varieties of creatures, with their clothing, ornaments, distinct notes, qualities, functions, were brought forth (Gen. i. 11): by one word, all the seeds of the earth, with their various virtues: by one word, all the fish of the sea, and fowls of the air, in their distinct natures, instincts, colors (Gen. i. 20): by one word, all the beasts of the field, with their varieties (Gen. i. 24). Heaven and earth, spiritual and corporeal creatures, mortal and immortal, the greater and the less, visible and invisible, were formed with the same ease :[o] a word made the least, and a word made the greatest. It is as little difficulty to him to produce the highest angel, as the lighest atom. It is enough for the existence of the stateliest cherubim, for God only to will his being. It was enough for the forming and fixing the sun, to will the compacting of light into one body. The creation of the soul of man is expressed by inspiration (Gen. ii. 7); to show, that it is as easy with God to create a rational soul, as for man to breathe.[p] Breathing is natural to man, by a communication of God's goodness; and the creation of the soul is as easy to God, by virtue of his Almighty word. As there was no proportion between nothing and being, so there was as little proportion between a word and such glorious effects. A mere voice, coming from an Omnipotent will, was capable to produce such varieties, which angels and men have seen in all ages of the world, and this without weariness. What labor is there in willing? what pain could there be in speaking a word ? (Isa. xl. 28), "The Creator of the ends of the earth is not weary." And though he be said to rest after the creation, it is to be meant a rest from work, not a repose from weariness. So great is the power of God, that without any matter, without any instruments, he could create many worlds, and with the same ease as he made this.

4th. I might add also, the appearance of this power in the instantaneous production of things. The ending of his word was not only the beginning, but the perfection of every thing he spake into being; not several words to several parts and members, but one word, one breath of his mouth, one act of his will, to the whole species of the creatures, and to every member in each individual. Heaven and earth were created in a moment; six days went to their disposal; and that comely order we observe in the world was the work of a week : the matter was formed as soon as God had spoken the word; and in every part of the creation, as soon as God spake the word,

---

[o] Augus. [p] Theodoret.

"Let it be so" (Gen. i.), the answer immediately is, "It was so;" which notes the present standing up of the creature according to the act of his will: and, therefore,q one observes, that "Let there be light, and there was light;" in the Hebrew are the same words, without any alteration of letter or point, only the conjunctive particle added, יהי אור ויהי אור, "Let there be light, and let there be light," to show, that the same instant of the speaking the Divine word, was the appearance of the creature: so great was the authority of his will.

SECONDLY, We are to show God's power in the GOVERNMENT of the world. As God decreed from eternity the creation of things in time, so he decreed from eternity the particular ends of creatures, and their operation respecting those ends. Now, as there was need of his power to execute his decree of creation, there is also need of his power to execute his decree about the manner of government.r All government is an act of the understanding, will, and power. Prudence to design belongs to the understanding; the election of the means belongs to the will; and the accomplishment of the whole is an act of power. It is a hard matter to determine which is most necessary: wisdom stands in as much need of power to perfect, as power doth of wisdom, to model and draw out a scheme; though wisdom directs, power must effect. Wisdom and power are distinct things among men: a poor man in a cottage may have more prudence to advise, than a privy counsellor; and a prince more power to act, than wisdom to conduct. A pilot may direct though he be lame, and cannot climb the masts, and spread the sails: but God is wanting in nothing; neither in wisdom to design, nor in will to determine, nor in power to accomplish. His wisdom is not feeble, nor his power foolish: a feeble wisdom could not act what it would, and a foolish power would act more than it should. The power expressed in his government is shadowed forth in the living creatures, which are God's instruments in it. It is said, "Every one of them had four faces" (Ezek. i. 10); that of a man to signify wisdom; of a lion, eagle, the strongest among birds, to signify their courage and strength to perform their offices. This power is evident in the *natural, moral, gracious* government. There is a natural providence, which consists in the preservation of all things, propogation of them by corruptions and generations, and in a co-operation with them in their motions to attain their ends. Moral government is of the hearts and actions of men. Gracious government, as respecting the Church.

First, His power is evident in *natural* government.

1. In preservation. God is the great Father of the world, to nourish it as well as create it.s Man and beast would perish if there were not herbs for their food; and herbs would wither and perish, if the earth were not watered with fruitful showers. This some of the heathens acknowledged, in their worshipping God under the image of an ox, a useful creature, by reason of its strength, to which we owe so much of our food in corn. Hence, God is styled the "Preserver of man and beast" (Ps. xxxvi. 6). Hence, the Jews called God,t *Place;* because he is the subsistence of all things. By

---

q Peirs. p. 111.
 Daille, in 1 Cor. x. p. 102.

r Suarez, Vol. I. lib. iii. cap. 10.
t מקום.

the same word whereby he gave being to things, he gives to them continuance and duration in being so much a term of time. As they were "created by his word," they are supported by his word (Heb. i. 3). The same powerful fiat, "Let the earth bring forth grass" (Gen. i. 11), when the plants peeped upon man out of nothing, is expressed every spring, when they begin to lift up their heads from their naked roots and winter graves. The resurrection of light every morning, the reviving the pleasure of all things to the eye; the watering the valleys from the mountain springs; the curbing the natural appetite of the waters from covering the earth; every draught that the beasts drink, every lodging the fowls have, every bit of food for the sustenance of man and beast, is ascribed to the "opening of his hand," the diffusing of his power (Ps. civ. 27, &c.), as much as the first creation of things, and endowing them with their particular nature: whence the plants, which are so serviceable, are called "the trees of the Lord" (ver. 16), of Jehovah, that hath only being and power in himself. The whole Psalm is but the description of his preserving, as the first of Genesis is of his creating power. It is by this power angels have so many thousand years remained in the power of understanding and willing. By this power things distant in their natures have been joined together; a spiritual soul and a dusty body knit in a marriage knot. By this power the heavenly bodies have for so many ages rolled in their spheres, and the tumultuous elements have persisted in their order: by this hath the matter of the world been to this day continued, and as capable of entertaining forms as it was at the first creation. What an amazing sight would it be to see a man hold a pillar of the Exchange upon one of his fingers? What is this to the power of God, "who holds the waters in the hollow of his hand, metes out the heaven with a span, and weighs the mountains in scales, and the hills in a balance" (Isa. xl. 12)? The preserving the earth from the violence of the sea is a plain instance of this power.[u] How is that raging element kept pent within those lists where he first lodged it; continues its course in its channel without overflowing the earth, and dashing in pieces the lower part of the creation? The natural situation of the water is to be above the earth, because it is lighter; and to be immediately under the air, because it is heavier than that thinner element. Who restrains this natural quality of it, but that God that first formed it? The word of command at first, "Hitherto shalt thou go, and no further," keeps those waters linked together in their den, that they may not ravage the earth, but be useful to the inhabitants of it. And when once it finds a gap to enter, what power of earth can hinder its passage? How fruitless sometimes is all the art of man to send it to its proper channel, when once it hath spread its mighty waves over some countries, and trampled part of the inhabited earth under its feet? It hath triumphed in its victory, and withstood all the power of man to conquer its force. It is only the power of God that doth bridle it from spreading itself over the whole earth. And that his power might be more manifest, he hath set but a weak and small bank against it. Though he hath bounded it in some places by

[u] Daille Melange, Part II. p. 457.

mighty rocks, which lift up their heads above it, yet in most places by feeble sand. How often is it seen in every stormy motion, when the waves boil high and roll furiously, as if they would swallow up all the neighboring houses upon the shore; when they come to touch those sandy limits, they bow their heads, fall flat, and sink into the lap whence they were raised, and seem to foam with anger that they can march no further, but must split themselves at so weak an obstacle! Can the sand be thought to be the cause of this? The weakness of it gives no footing to such a thought. Who can apprehend, that an enraged army should retire upon the opposition of a straw in an infant's hand? Is it the nature of the water? Its retirement is against the natural quality of it; pour but a little upon the ground, and you always see it spread itself. No cause can be rendered in nature; it is a standing monument of the power of God in the preservation of the world, and ought to be more taken notice of by us in this island, surrounded with it, than by some other countries in the world.

(1.) We find nothing hath power to preserve itself. Doth not every creature upon earth require the assistance of some other for its maintenance? "Can the rush grow up without mire? can the flag grow up without water" (Job viii. 11)? Can man or beast maintain itself without grain from the bowels of the earth? Would not every man tumble into the grave, without the aid of other creatures to nourish him? Whence do these creatures receive that virtue of supplying him nourishment, but from the sun and earth? and whence do they derive that virtue, but from the Creator of all things? And should he but slack his hand, how soon would they and all their qualities perish, and the links of the world fall in pieces, and dash one another into their first chaos and confusion! All creatures indeed have an appetite to preserve themselves; they have some knowledge of the outward means for their preservation; so have irrational animals a natural instinct, as well as men have some skill to avoid things that are hurtful, and apply things that are helpful. But what thing in the world can preserve itself by an inward influx into its own being? All things want such a power without God's *fiat*, "Let it be so:" nothing but is destitute of such a power for its own preservation, as much as it is of a power for its own creation. Were there any true power for such a work, what need of so many external helps from things of an inferior nature to that which is preserved by them? No created thing hath a power to preserve any decayed being. Who can lay claim to such a virtue, as to recall a withering flower to its former beauty, to raise the head of a drooping plant, or put life into a gasping worm when it is expiring; or put impaired vitals into their former posture? Not a man upon earth, nor an angel in heaven, can pretend to such a virtue; they may be spectators, but not assisters, and are, in this case, physicians of no value.

(2.) It is, therefore, the same Power preserves things which at first created them. The creature doth as much depend upon God, in the first instant of its being, for its preservation, as it did, when it was nothing, for its production and creation into being: as the continuance of a thought of our mind depends upon the power of our mind,

as well as the first framing of that thought.[x]   There is a little difference between creating and preserving power, as there is between the
power of mine eye to begin an act of vision and continue that act of
vision, as to cast my eye upon an object and continue it upon that
object: as the first act is caused by the eye, so the duration of the act
is preserved by the eye; shut the eye, and the act of vision perishes;
divert the eye from that object, and that act of vision is exchanged
for another.   And, therefore, the preservation of things is commonly
called a continual creation: and certainly it is no less, if we understand it of a preservation by an inward influence into the being of
things.   It is one and the same action invariably continued, and
obtaining its force every moment; the same action whereby he
created them of nothing, and which every moment hath a virtue to
produce a thing out of nothing, if it were not yet extant in the
world: it remains the same without any diminution throughout the
whole time wherein anything doth remain in the world.[y]   For all
things would return to nothing, if God did not keep them up in the
elevation and state to which he at first raised them by his creative
power (Acts xvii. 28): " In him we live, and move, and have our
being."   By him, or by the same Power whence we derived our
being, are our lives maintained: as it was his Almighty Power
whereby we were, after we had been nothing, so it is the same power
whereby we now are, after he hath made us something.   Certainly
all things have no less a dependence on God than light upon the
sun, which vanisheth and hides its head upon the withdrawing of the
sun.   And should God suspend that powerful Word, whereby he
erected the frame of the world, it would sink down to what it was,
before he commanded it to stand up.   There needs no new act of
power to reduce things to nothing, but the cessation of that Omnipotent influx.   When the appointed time set them for their being
comes to a period, they faint and bend down their heads to their
dissolution; they return to their elements, and perish (Ps. civ. 29):
" Thou hidest thy face, and they are troubled: thou takest away
their breath, they die, and return to their dust.   That which was
nothing cannot remain on this side nothing, but by the same Power
that first called it out of nothing.   As when God withdrew his concurring power from the fire, its quality ceased to act upon the three
children: so if he withdraws his sustaining power from the creature,
its nature will cease to be.

2. It appears in propagation.   That powerful word (Gen. i. 22,
23), " Increase and multiply," pronounced at the first creation, hath
spread itself over every part of the world; every animal in the
world, in the formation of every one of them.   From two of a kind,
how great a number of individuals and single creatures have been
multiplied, to cover the face of the earth in their continued successions!   What a world of plants spring up from the womb of a dry
earth, moistened by the influence of a cloud, and hatched by the
beams of the sun!   How admirable an instance of his propagating
power is it, that from a little seed a massy root should strike into
the bowels of the earth, a tall body and thick branches, with leaves

[x] Lessius de Perfect. Divin. p. 69.   [y] Lessius de Snm. Bon. pp. 580—582.

and flowers of various colors, should break through the surface of the earth, and mount up towards heaven, when in the seed you neither smell the scent, nor see any firmness of a tree, nor behold any of those colors which you view in the flowers that the ears produce! A power not to be imitated by any creature. How astonishing is it, that a small seed, whereof many will not amount to the weight of a grain, should spread itself into leaves, bark, fruit of a vast weight, and multiply itself into millions of seeds! What power is that, that from one man and woman hath multiplied families, and from families, stocked the world with people! Consider the living creatures, as formed in the womb of their several kinds; every one is a wonder of power. The Psalmist instanceth in the forming and propagation of man (Ps. cxxxix. 14): "I am fearfully and wonderfully made; marvellous are thy works." The forming of the parts distinctly in the womb, the bringing forth into the world every particular member, is a roll of wonders, of power. That so fine a structure as the body of man should be polished in "the lower parts of the earth," as he calls the womb (ver. 15), in so short a time, with members of a various form and usefulness, each laboring in their several functions! Can any man give an exact account of the manner "how the bones do grow in the womb" (Eccles. xi. 5)? It is unknown to the father, and no less hid from the mother, and the wisest men cannot search out the depth of it. It is one of the secret works of an Omnipotent Power, secret in the manner, though open in the effect. So that we must ascribe it to God, as Job doth, "Thine hands have made me and fashioned me together round about" (Job x. 8). Thy hands which formed heaven, have formed every part, every member, and wrought me like a mighty workman. The heavens are said to be the "work of God's hands," and man is here said to be no less. The forming and propagation of man from that earthy matter, is no less a wonder of power than the structure of the world from a rude and indisposed matter. A heathen philosopher descants elegantly upon it: "Dost thou understand (my son) the forming of man in the womb; who erected that noble fabric? who carved the eyes, the crystal windows of light, and the conductors of the body; who bored the nostrils and ears, those loopholes of scents and sounds; who stretched out and knit the sinews and ligaments for the fastening of every member; who cast the hollow veins, the channels of blood; set and strengthened the bones, the pillars and rafters of the body; who digged the pores, the sinks to expel the filth; who made the heart, the repository of the soul, and formed the lungs like a pipe? What mother, what father, wrought these things? No, none but the Almighty God, who made all things according to his pleasure; it is He who propagates this noble piece from a pile of dust. Who is born by his own advice; who gives stature, features, sense, wit, strength, speech, but God?"[z] It is no less a wonder, that a little infant can live so long in a dark sink, in the midst of filth, without breathing; and the eduction of it out of the womb is no less a wonder than the forming, increase, nourishment of it in that cell. A wonder, that the life of the infant

[z] Trismegist, in Serm. Greek, in the Temple, p. 57.

is not the death of the mother, or the life of the mother the death of the infant. This little creature when it springs up from such small beginnings by the power of God, grows up to be one of the lords of the world, to have a dominion over the creatures, and propagates its kind in the same manner : all this is unaccountable without having recourse to the power of God in the government of the creatures. And to add to this wonder, consider also what multitudes of formations and births there are at one time all over the world, in every of which the finger of God is at work ; and it will speak an unwearied power. It is admirable in one man, more in a town of men, still more in a greater and larger kingdom, a vaster world ; there is a birth for every hour in this city, were but 168 born in a week, though the weekly bills mention more : what is this city to three kingdoms ? what three kingdoms to a populous world ? Eleven thousand and eighty will make one for every minute in the week ; what is this to the weekly propagation in all the nations of the universe, besides the generation of all the living creatures in that space, which are the works of God's fingers as well as man ? What will be the result of this, but the notion of an unconceivable, unwearied Almightiness, always active, always operating?

3. It appears in the motions of all creatures. " All things live and move in him" (Acts xvii. 28) ; by the same power that creatures have their beings, they have their motions : they have not only a being by his powerful command, but they have their minutely motion by his powerful concurrence. Nothing can act without the almighty influx of God, no more than it can exist without the creative word of God. It is true indeed, the ordering of all motions to his holy ends, is an act of wisdom ; but the motion itself, whereby those ends are attained, is a work of his power.

(1). God, as the first cause, hath an influence into the motions of all second causes. As all the wheels in a clock are moved in their different motions by the force and strength of the principal and primary wheel; if there be any defect in that, or if that stand still, all the rest languish and stand idle the same moment. All creatures are his instruments, his engines, and have no spirit, but what he gives, and what he assists. Whatsoever nature works, God works in nature ; nature is the instrument, God is the supporter, director, mover of nature ; that which the prophet saith in another case, may be the language of universal nature : " Lord, thou hast wrought all our work in us" (Isa. xxvi. 12). They are works subjectively, efficiently, as second causes ; God's works originally, concurrently. The sun moved not in the valley of Ajalon for the space of many hours, in the time of Joshua (Josh. x. 13) ; nor did the fire exercise its consuming quality upon the three children, in Nebuchadnezzar's furnace (Dan. iii. 25) : he withdrew not his supporting power from their being, for then they had vanished, but his influencing power from their qualities, whereby their motion ceased, till he returned his influential concurrence to them ; which evidenceth, that without a perpetual derivation of Divine power, the sun could not run one stride or inch of its race, nor the fire devour one grain of light chaff, or an inch of straw. Nothing without his sustaining power can continue in being; nothing without his co-working power can exercise one mite of those qualities it is possessed of. All creatures are wound up by him, and his hand is constantly upon them, to keep them in perpetual motion.

(2). Consider the variety of motions in a single creature. How many motions are there in the vital parts of a man, or in any other animal, which a man knows not, and is unable to number! The renewed motion of the lungs, the systoles and diastoles of the heart; the contractions and dilations of the heart, whereby it spouts out and takes in blood; the power of concoction in the stomach; the motion of the blood in the veins, &c., all which were not only settled by the powerful hand of God, but are upheld by the same, preserved and influenced in every distinct motion by that power that stamped them with that nature. To every one of those there is not only the sustaining power of God holding up their natures, but the motive power of God concurring to every motion; for if we move in him as well as we live in him, then every particle of our motion is exercised by his concurring power, as well as every moment of our life supported by his preserving power. What an infinite variety of motions is there in the whole world in universal nature, to all which God concurs, all which he conducts, even the motions of the meanest as well as the greatest creatures, which demonstrate the indefatigable power of the governor! It is an Infinite Power which doth act in so many varieties, whereby the souls forms every thought, the tongue speaks every word, the body exerts every action. What an Infinite Power is that which presides over the birth of all things, concurs with the motion of the sap in the tree, rivers on the earth, clouds in the air, every drop of rain, fleece of snow, crack of thunder! Not the least motion in the world, but is under an actual influence of this Almighty Mover. And lest any should scruple the concurrence of God to so many varieties of the creature's motion, as a thing utterly inconceivable, let them consider the sun, a natural image and shadow of the perfections of God; doth not the power of that finite creature extend itself to various objects at the same moment of time? How many insects doth it animate, as flies, &c., at the same moment throughout the world! How many several plants doth it erect at its appearance in the spring, whose roots lay mourning in the earth all the foregoing winter! What multitudes of spires of grass, and nobler flowers, doth it midwife in the same hour! It warms the air, melts the blood, cherishes living creatures of various kinds, in distinct places, without tiring: and shall the God of this sun be less than his creature?

(3.) And since I speak of the sun, consider the power of God in the motion of it. The vastness of the sun is computed to be, at the least, 166 times bigger than the earth, and its distance from the earth, some tell us, to be about 4,000,000 of miles;[a] whence it follows, that it is whirled about the world with that swiftness, that in the space of an hour it runs 1,000,000 of miles, which is as much as if it should move round about the surface of the earth fifty times in one hour; which vastness exceeds the swiftness of a bullet shot out

[a] A Lapide, in 1 cap. Gen. xvi. Lessius, de Perfect. Divin. pp. 90, 91.

of a cannon, which is computed to fly not above three miles in a minute :[b] so that the sun runs further in one hour's space, than a bullet can in 5,000, if it were kept in motion ; so that if it were near the earth, the swiftness of its motion would shatter the whole frame of the world, and dash it in pieces ; so that the Psalmist may well say, " It runs a race like a strong man" (Ps. xix. 5). What an incomprehensible Power is that which hath communicated such a strength and swiftness to the sun, and doth daily influence its motion ; especially since after all those years of its motion, wherein one would think it should have spent itself, we behold it every day as vigorous as Adam did in Paradise, without limping, without shattering itself, or losing any thing of its natural spirits in its unwearied motion. How great must that power be, which hath kept this great body so entire, and thus swiftly moves it every day ! Is it not now an argument of omnipotency, to keep all the strings of nature in tune ; to wind them up to a due pitch for the harmony he intended by them ; to keep things that are contrary from that confusion they would naturally fall into ; to prevent those jarrings which would naturally result from their various and snarling qualities ; to preserve every being in its true nature ; to propagate every kind of creature ; order all the operations, even the meanest of them, when there are such innumerable varieties ? But let us consider, that this power or preserving things in their station and motion, and the renewing of them, is more stupendous than that which we commonly call miraculous. We call those miracles, which are wrought out of the track of nature, and contrary to the usual stream and current of it ; which men wonder at, because they seldom see them, and hear of them as things rarely brought forth in the world ; when the truth is, there is more of power expressed in the ordinary station and motion of natural causes than in those extraordinary exertings of power. Is not more power signalized in that whirling motion of the sun every hour for so many ages, than in the suspending of its motion one day, as it was in the days of Joshua ? That fire should continually ravage and consume, and greedily swallow up every thing that is offered to it, seems to be the effect of as admirable a power, as the stopping of its appetite a few moments, as in the case of the three children. Is not the rising of some small seeds from the ground, with a multiplication of their numerous posterity, an effect of as great a power, as our Saviour's feeding many thousands with a few loaves, by a secret augmentation of them ?[c] Is not the chemical producing so pleasant and delicious a fruit as the grape, from a dry earth, insipid rain, and a sour vine, as admirable a token of Divine power, as our Saviour's turning water into wine ? Is not the cure of diseases by the application of a simple inconsiderable weed, or a slight infusion, as wonderful in itself, as the cure of it by a powerful weed ? What if it be naturally designed to heal ; what is that nature, who gave that nature, who maintains that nature, who conducts it, co-operates with it ? Doth it work of itself, and by its own strength ? why not then equally in all, in one as well as another ?

[b] Lessius, de Providen, p. 633. Voss. de Idol. lib. ii. cap. 2.
[c] Faucher sur Act. Vol. II. p. 47.

Miracles, indeed, affect more, because they testify the immediate operation of God, without the concurrence of second causes; not that there is more of the power of God shining in them than in the other.

Secondly, This power is evident in *moral* government.

1. In the restraint of the malicious nature of the devil. Since Satan hath the power of an angel, and the malice of a devil, what safety would there be for our persons from destruction, what security for our goods from rifling, by this invisible, potent, and envious spirit, if his power were not restrained, and his malice curbed, by One more mighty than himself? How much doth he envy God the glory of his creation; and man, the use and benefit of it! How desirous would he be, in regard of his passion, how able in regard of his strength and subtlety, to overthrow or infect all worship, but what was directed to himself; to manage all things according to his lusts, turn all things topsy-turvy, plague the world, burn cities, houses, plunder us of the supports of nature, waste kingdoms, &c.; if he were not held in a chain, as a ravenous lion, or a furious wild horse, by the Creator and Governor of the world! What remedy could be used by man against the activity of this unseen and swift spirit? The world could not subsist under his malice; he would practise the same things upon all as he did upon Job, when he had got leave from his Governor; turn the swords of men into one another's bowels; send fire from heaven upon the fruits of the earth and the cattle intended for the use of man; raise winds, to shake and tear our houses upon our heads; daub our bodies with scalbs and boils, and let all the humors in our blood loose upon us. He that envied Adam a paradise, doth envy us the pleasure of enjoying its out-works. If we were not destroyed by him, we should live in a continued vexation by spectrums and apparitions, affrighting sounds and noise, as some think the Egyptians did in that three days' darkness: he would be alway winnowing us, as he desired to winnow Peter (Luke xxii. 31). But God over-masters his strength, that he cannot move a hair's breadth beyond his tedder; not only is he unable to touch an upright Job, but to lay his fingers upon one of the unbelieving Gadarenes forbidden and filthy swine without special license (Matt. viii. 31). When he is cast out of one place, he walks "through dry places seeking rest" (Luke xi. 24), new objects for his malicious designs,—but finding none, till God lets loose the reins upon him for a new employment. Though Satan's power be great, yet God suffers him not to tempt as much as his diabolical appetite would, but as much as Divine wisdom thinks fit; and the Divine power tempers the other's active malice, and gives the creature victory, where the enemy intended spoil and captivity. How much stronger is God, than all the legions of hell; as he that holds a "strong man" (Luke xi. 22) from effecting his purpose, testifies more ability than his adversary! How doth he lock him up for a "thousand years" (Rev. xx. 3) in a pound, which he cannot leap over! and this restraint is wrought partly by blinding the devil in his designs, partly by denying him concourse to his motion; as he hindered the active quality of the fire upon the three children, by withdrawing

his power, which was necessary to the motion of it; and his power is as necessary for the motion of the devil, as for that of any other creature: sometimes he makes him to confess him against his own interest, as Apollo's oracle confessed.[d]   And though when the devil was cast out of the possessed person, he publicly owned Christ to be the "Holy one of God" (Mark i. 24), to render him suspected by the people of having commerce with the unclean spirits; yet this he could not do without the leave and permission of God, that the power of Christ, in stopping his mouth and imposing silence upon him, might be evidenced; and that it reaches to the gates of hell, as well as to the quieting of winds and waves. This is a part of the strength, as well as the wisdom of God, that "the deceived and the deceiver are his" (Job xii. 16): wisdom to defeat, and power to over-rule his most malicious designs, to his own glory.

2. In the restraint of the natural corruption of men. Since the *impetus* of original corruption runs in the blood, conveyed down from Adam to the veins of all his posterity, and universally diffused in all mankind; what wreck and havoc would it make in the world, if it were not suppressed by this Divine power which presides over the hearts of men !   Man is so wretched by nature, that nothing but what is vile and pernicious can drop from him.   Man " drinks iniquity like water," being, by nature, "abominable and filthy" (Job xv. 16). He greedily swallows all matter for iniquity, everything suitable to the mire and poison in his nature, and would sprout it out with all fierceness and insolence. God himself gives us the description of man's nature (Gen. vi. 5), that he hath not one good imagination at any time; and the apostle from the Psalmist dilates and comments upon it (Rom. iii. 10, &c.) "There is none righteous; no, not one; their mouth is full of cursing and bitterness, their feet are swift to shed blood," &c. This corruption is equal in all, natural in all; it is not more poisonous or more fierce in one man, than in another. The róot of all men is the same; all the branches therefore do equally possess the villanous nature of the root. No child of Adam can, by natural descent, be better than Adam, or have less of baseness, and vileness, and venom, than Adam. How fruitful would this loathsome lake be in all kind of streams ! What unbridled licentiousness and headstrong fury would triumph in the world, if the power of God did not interpose itself to lock down the flood-gates of it ! What rooting up of human society would there be ! how would the world be drenched in blood, the number of malefactors be greater than that of apprehenders and punishers ! How would the prints of natural laws be rased out of the heart, if God should leave human nature to itself! Who can read the first chapter of Romans, (verses 24 to 29), without acknowledging this truth ? where there is a catalogue of those villanies which followed upon God's pulling up the sluices, and letting the malignity of their inward corruption have its natural course! If God did not hold back the fury of man, his garden would be overrun, his vine rooted up; the inclinations of men would hurry them to the worst of wickedness. How great is that Power that curbs, bridles, or changes

[d] Cæteros deos cereos esse, &c. Grot. Verit. Rel. lib. 4,

as many headstrong horses at once, and every minute, as there are
sons of Adam upon the earth? The "floods lift up their waves;
the Lord on high is mightier than the noise of many waters, yea,
than the mighty waves of the sea" (Ps. xciii. 3, 4); that doth hush
and pen in the turbulent passions of men.

3. In the ordering and framing the hearts of men to his own ends.
That must be an Omnipotent hand that grasps and contains the hearts
of all men; the heart of the meanest person, as well as of the most
towering angel, and turns them as he pleases, and makes them sometime ignorantly, sometime knowingly, concur to the accomplishment
of his own purposes! When the hearts of men are so numerous,
their thoughts so various and different from one another, yet he hath
a key to those millions of hearts, and with infinite power, guided by
as infinite wisdom, he draws them into what channels he pleases, for
the gaining his own ends. Though the Jews had imbrued their
hands in the blood of our Saviour, and their rage was yet reeking-
hot against his followers, God bridled their fury in the church's infancy, till it had got some strength, and cast a terror upon them by
the wonders wrought by the apostles (Acts ii. 43): "And fear came
upon every soul, and many wonders and signs were done by the
apostles." Was there not the same reason in the nature of the works
our Saviour wrought, to point them to the finger of God, and calm
their rage? Yet did not the power of God work upon their passions
in those miracles, nor stop the impetuousness of the corruption resident in their hearts. Yet now those who had the boldness to attack
the Son of God and nail him to the cross, are frighted at the appearance of twelve unarmed apostles; as the sea seems to be afraid when
it approacheth the bounds of the feeble sand. How did God bend
the hearts of the Egyptians to the Israelites, and turn them to that
point, as to lend their most costly vessels, their precious jewels, and
rich garments, to supply those whom they had just before tyrani-
cally loaded with their chains (Exod. iii. 21, 22)! When a great
part of an army came upon Jehoshaphat, to dispatch him into another
world, how doth God, in a trice, touch their hearts, and move them,
by a secret instinct, at once to depart from him (1 Chron. xviii. 31)!
as if you should see a numerous sight of birds in a moment turn
wing another way, by a sudden and joint consent. When he gave
Saul a kingdom, he gave him a spirit fit for government, "and gave
him another heart" (1 Sam. x. 9); and brought the people to submit
to his yoke, who, a little before, wandered about the land upon no
nobler employment than the seeking of asses. It is no small remark
of the power of God, to make a number of strong and discontented
persons, and desirous enough of liberty, to bend their necks under
the yoke of government, and submit to the authority of one, and
that of their own nature, often weaker and unwiser than the most of
them, and many times an oppressor and invader of their rights.
Upon this account David calls God "his fortress, tower, shield" (Ps.
cxliv. 2); all terms of strength in subduing the people under him.
It is the mighty hand of God that links princes and people together
in the bands of government. The same hand that assuageth the
waves of the sea, suppresseth the tumults of the people.

Thirdly, It appears in his *gracious* and judicial government.

1. In his gracious government. In the deliverance of his church: he is the "strength of Israel" (1 Sam. xv. 29), and hath protected his little flock in the midst of wolves; and maintained their standing, when the strongest kingdoms have sunk, and the best jointed states have been broken in pieces; when judgments have ravaged countries, and torn up the mighty, as a tempestuous wind hath often done the tallest trees, which seemed to threaten heaven with their tops, and dare the storm with the depth of their roots, when yet the vine and rose-bushes have stood firm, and been seen in their beauty next morning. The state of the church hath outlived the most flourishing monarchies, when there hath been a mighty knot of adversaries against her; when the bulls of Bashan have pushed her, and the whole tribe of the dragon have sharpened their weapons, and edged their malice; when the voice was strong, and the hopes high to rase her foundation even with the ground; when hell hath roared; when the wit of the world hath contrived, and the strength of the world hath attempted her ruin; when decrees have been passed against her, and the powers of the world armed for the execution of them; when her friends have drooped and skulked in corners; when there was no eye to pity, and no hand to assist, help hath come from heaven; her enemies have been defeated; kings have brought gifts to her, and reared her; tears have been wiped off her cheeks, and her very enemies, by an unseen power, have been forced to court her whom before they would have devoured quick. The devil and his armies have sneaked into their den, and the church hath triumphed when she hath been upon the brink of the grave. Thus did God send a mighty angel to be the executioner of Sennacherib's army, and the protector of Jerusalem, who run his sword into the hearts of eighty thousand (2 Kings xix. 35), when they were ready to swallow up his beloved city. When the knife was at the throats of the Jews, in Shushan (Esther viii.), by a powerful hand it was turned into the hearts of their enemies. With what an outstretched arm were the Israelites freed from the Egyptian yoke (Deut. iv. 34)! When Pharaoh had mustered a great army to pursue them, assisted with six hundred chariots of war, the Red Sea obstructed their passage before, and an enraged enemy trod on their rear; when the fearful Israelites despaired of deliverance, and the insolent Egyptian assured himself of his revenge, God stretches out his irresistible arm to defeat the enemy, and assist his people; he strikes down the wolves, and preserves the flock. God restrained the Egyptian enmity against the Israelites till they were at the brink of the Red Sea, and then lets them follow their humor, and pursue the fugitives, that his power might more gloriously shine forth in the deliverance of the one, and the destruction of the other. God might have brought Israel out of Egypt in the time of those kings that had remembered the good service of Joseph to their country, but he leaves them till the reign of a cruel tyrant, suffers them to be slaves, that they might by his sole power, be conquerors, which had had no appearance had there been a willing dismission of them at the first summons (Exod. ix. 16); "In very deed for this cause have I raised thee up, for to

shew my power, and that my name might be declared throughout all the earth. I have permitted thee to rise up against my people, and keep them in captivity, that thou mightest be an occasion for the manifestation of my power in their rescue ; and whilst thou art obstinate to enslave them, I will stretch out my arm to deliver them, and make my name famous among the Gentiles, in the wreck of thee and thy host in the Red Sea. The deliverance of the church hath not been in one age, or in one part of the world, but God hath signalized his power in all kingdoms where she hath had a footing : as he hath guided her in all places by one rule, animated her by one spirit, so he hath protected her by the same arm of power. When the Roman emperors bandied all their force against her, for about three hundred years, they were further from effecting her ruin at the end than when they first attempted it ; the church grew under their sword, and was hatched under the wings of the Roman eagle, which were spread to destroy her. The ark was elevated by the deluge, and the waters the devil poured out to drown her did but slime the earth for a new increase of her. She hath sometimes been beaten down, and, like Lazarus, hath seemed to be in the grave for some days, that the power of God might be more visible in her sudden resurrection, and lifting up her head above the throne of her persecutors.

2. In his judicial proceedings. The deluge was no small testimony of his power, in opening the cisterns of heaven, and pulling up the sluices of the sea. He doth but call for the waters of the sea, and they "pour themselves upon the face of the earth" (Amos ix. 6.) In forty days' time the waters overtopped the highest mountains fifteen cubits (Gen. vii. 17—20) ; and by the same power he afterwards reduced the sea to its proper channel, as a roaring lion into his den. A shower of fire from heaven, upon Sodom, and the cities of the plain, was a signal display of his power, either in creating it on the sudden, for the execution of his righteous sentence, or sending down the element of fire, contrary to its nature, which affects ascent, for the punishment of rebels against the light of nature. How often hath he ruined the most flourishing monarchies, led princes away spoiled, and overthrown the mighty, which Job makes an argument of his strength (Job xii. 13, 14). Troops of unknown people, the Goths and Vandals, broke the Romans, a warlike people, and hurled down all before them. They could not have had the thought to succeed in such an attempt, unless God had given them strength and motion for the executing his judicial vengeance upon the people of his wrath. How did he evidence his power, by daubing the throne of Pharaoh, and his chamber of presence, as well as the houses of his subjects, with the slime of frogs (Exod. viii. 3) ; turning their waters into blood, and their dust into biting lice (Exod. vii. 20) ; raising his militia of locusts against them ; causing a three days' darkness without stopping the motion of the sun ; taking off their first-born, the excellency of their strength, in a night, by the stroke of the angel's sword ! He takes off the chariot wheels of Pharaoh, and presents him with a destruction where he expected a victory ; brings those waves over the heads of him and his host, which stood

firm as marble walls for the safety of his people; the sea is made to swallow them up, that durst not, by the order of their Governor, touch the Israelites: it only sprinkled the one as a type of baptism, and drowned the other as an image of hell. Thus he made it both a deliverer and a revenger, the instrument of an offensive and defensive war (Isa. xl. 23, 24); "He brings princes to nothing, and makes the judges of the earth as vanity." Great monarchs have, by his power, been hurled from their thrones and their sceptres, like Venice-glasses, broken before their faces, and they been advanced that have had the least hopes of grandeur. He hath plucked up cedars by the roots, lopped off the branches, and set a shrub to grow up in the place; dissolved rocks, and established bubbles (Luke i. 52): "He hath showed strength with his arm; he hath scattered the proud in the imagination of their hearts; he hath put down the mighty from their seat, and exalted them of low degree."—And these things he doth magnify his power in:—

(1.) By ordering the nature of creatures as he pleases. By restraining their force, or guiding their motions. The restraint of the destructive qualities of the creatures argues as great a power as the change of their natures, yea, and a greater. The qualities of creatures may be changed by art and composition, as in the preparing of medicines; but what but a Divine Power could restrain the operation of the fire from the three children, while it retained its heat and burning quality in Nebuchadnezzar's furnace? The operation was curbed while its nature was preserved. All creatures are called his host, because he marshals and ranks them as an army to serve his purposes. The whole scheme of nature is ready to favor men when God orders it, and ready to punish men when God commissions it. He gave the Red Sea but a check, and it obeyed his voice (Ps. cvi. 9): "He rebuked the Red Sea also, and it was dried up;" the motion of it ceased, and the waters of it were ranged as defensive walls, to secure the march of his people: and at the motion of the hand of Moses, the servant of the Lord, the sea recovered its violence, and the walls that were framed came tumbling down upon the Egyptian's heads (Exod. xiv. 27). The Creator of nature is not led by the necessity of nature: he that settled the order of nature, can change or restrain the order of nature according to his sovereign pleasure. The most necessary and useful creatures he can use as instruments of his vengeance: water is necessary to cleanse, and by that he can deface a world; fire is necessary to warm, and by that he can burn a Sodom: from the water he formed the fowl (Gen. i. 21), and by that he dissolves them in the deluge; fire or heat is necessary to the generation of creatures, and by that he ruins the cities of the plain. He orders all as he pleases, to perform every tittle and punctilio of his purpose. The sea observed him so exactly, that it drowned not one Israelite, nor saved one Egyptian (Ps. cvi. 11). There was not one of them left. And to perfect the Israelites' deliverance, he followed them with testimonies of his power above the strength of nature. When they wanted drink, he orders Moses to strike a rock, and the rock spouts a river, and a channel is formed for it to attend them in their journey. When they wanted bread, he dressed manna for them in the heavens, and sent it to their tables in the desert. When he would declare his strength, he calls to the heavens to pour down righteousness, and to the earth to bring forth salvation (Isa. xlv. 8). Though God had created righteousness or deliverance for the Jews in Babylon, yet he calls to the heavens and the earth to be assistant to the design of Cyrus, whom he had raised for that purpose, as he speaks in the beginning of the chapter (verses 1—4). As God created man for a supernatural end, and all creatures for man as their immediate end, so he makes them, according to opportunities, subservient to that supernatural end of man, for which he created him. He that spans the heavens with his fist, can shoot all creatures like an arrow, to hit what mark he pleases. He that spread the heavens and the earth by a word, and can by a word fold them up more easily than a man can a garment (Heb. i. 12), can order the streams of nature; cannot he work without nature as well as with it, beyond nature, contrary to nature, that can, as it were, fillip nature with his finger into that nothing whence he drew it; who can cast down the sun from his throne, clap the distinguished parts of the world together, and make them march in the same order to their confusion, as they did in their creation: who can jumble the whole frame together, and, by a word, dissolve the pillars of the world, and make the fabric lie in a ruinous heap?

(2.) In effecting his purposes by small means: in making use of the meanest creatures. As the power of God is seen in the creation of the smallest creatures, and assembling so many perfections in the little body of an insect, as an ant, or spider, so his power is not less magnified in the use he makes of them. As he magnifies his wisdom, by using ignorant instruments, so he exalts his power, by employing weak instruments in his service: the meanness and imperfection of the matter sets off the excellency of the workman; so the weakness of the instrument is no foil to the power of the principal Agent. When God hath effected things by means in the Scripture, he hath usually brought about his purposes by weak instruments. Moses, a fugitive from Egypt, and Aaron a captive in it, are the instruments of the Israelites' deliverance. By the motion of Moses' rod, he works wonders in the court of Pharaoh, and summons up his judgments against him. He brought down Pharaoh's stomach for a while, by a squadron of lice and locusts, wherein Divine power was more seen, than if Moses had brought him to his own articles by a multitude of warlike troops. The fall of the walls of Jericho by the sound of rams' horns, was a more glorious character of God's power, than if Joshua had battered it down with a hundred of warlike engines (Josh vi. 20). Thus the great army of the Midianites, which lay as grasshoppers upon the ground, were routed by Gideon in the head of three hundred men; and Goliath, a giant, laid level with the ground by David, a stripling, by the force of a sling: a thousand Philistines dispatched out of the world by the jaw-bone of an ass in the hand of Samson. He can master a stout nation by an army of locusts, and render the teeth of those little insects as destructive as the teeth, yea, the strongest teeth, the cheek-teeth, of a great lion (Joel i. 6, 7). The thunderbolt, which produces sometimes dreadful effects, is compacted of little atoms which fly in the air, small vapors drawn up by the sun, and mixed with other sulphurous matter and petrifying juice. Nothing is so weak, but his strength can make victorious; nothing so small, but by his power he can accomplish his great ends by it; nothing so vile, but his might can conduct to his glory; and no nation so mighty, but he can waste and enfeeble by the meanest creatures. God is great in power in the greatest things, and not little in the smallest; his power in the minutest creatures which he uses for his service, surmounts the force of our understanding.

THIRDLY. The power of God appears in REDEMPTION. As our Saviour is called the Wisdom of God, so he is called the Power of God (1 Cor. i. 24). The arm of Power was lifted up as high as the designs of Wisdom were laid deep: as this way of redemption could not be contrived but by an Infinite Wisdom, so it could not be accomplished but by an Infinite Power. None but God could shape such a design, and none but God could effect it. The Divine Power in temporal deliverances, and freedom from the slavery of human oppressors, vails to that which glitters in redemption; whereby the devil is defeated in his designs, stripped of his spoils, and yoked in his strength. The power of God in creation requires not those degrees of admiration, as in redemption. In creation, the world was erected from nothing; as there was nothing to act, so there was nothing to oppose; no victorious devil was in that to be subdued; no thundering law to be silenced; no death to be conquered; no transgression to be pardoned and rooted out; no hell to be shut; no ignominious death upon the cross to be suffered. It had been, in the nature of the thing, an easier thing to Divine Power to have created a new world than repaired a broken, and purified a polluted one. This is the most admirable work that ever God brought forth in the world, greater than all the marks of his power in the first creation.

And this will appear, I. In the Person redeeming. II. In the publication and propagation of the doctrine of redemption. III. In the application of redemption.

I. In the Person redeeming. *First*, In his conception.

1. He was conceived by the Holy Ghost in the womb of the Virgin (Luke i. 35): "The Holy Ghost shall come upon thee, and the power of the Highest shall overshadow thee:" which act is expressed to be the effect of the infinite power of God; and it expresses the supernatural manner of the forming the humanity of our Saviour, and signifies not the Divine nature of Christ infusing itself into the womb of the virgin; for the angel refers it to the manner of the operation of the Holy Ghost in the producing the human nature of Christ, and not to the nature assuming that humanity into union with itself. The Holy Ghost, or the Third Person in the Trinity, overshadowed the virgin, and by a creative act framed the humanity of Christ, and united it to the Divinity. It is, therefore, expressed by a word of the same import with that used in Gen. i. 2, "The Spirit moved upon the face of the waters," which signifies (as it were) a brooding upon the chaos, shadowing it with his wings, as hens sit upon their eggs, to form them and hatch them

into animals; or else it is an allusion to the "cloud which covered the tent of the congregation, when the glory of the Lord filled the tabernacle" (Exod. xl. 34). It was not such a creative act as we call immediate, which is a production out of nothing; but a mediate creation, such as God's bringing things into form out of the first matter, which had nothing but an obediential or passive disposition to whatsoever stamp the powerful wisdom of God should imprint upon it. So the substance of the Virgin had no active, but only a passive disposition to this work: the matter of the body was earthy, the substance of the virgin; the forming of it was heavenly, the Holy Ghost working upon that matter. And therefore when it is said, that "she was found with child of the Holy Ghost" (Matt. i. 18), it is to be understood of the efficacy of the Holy Ghost, not of the substance of the Holy Ghost. The matter was natural, but the manner of conceiving was in a supernatural way, above the methods of nature. In reference to the active principle the Redeemer is called in the prophecy (Isa. iv. 2), "The branch of the Lord," in regard of the Divine hand that planted him: in respect to the passive principle, the fruit of the earth, in regard of the womb that bare him; and therefore said to be "made of a woman" (Gal. iv. 4). That part of the flesh of the virgin whereof the human nature of Christ was made, was refined and purified from corruption by the overshadowing of the Holy Ghost, as a skilful workman separates the dross from the gold: our Saviour is therefore called, "that holy thing" (Luke i. 35), though born of the virgin: he was necessarily some way to descend from Adam. God, indeed, might have created his body out of nothing, or have formed it (as he did Adam's) out of the dust of the ground: but had he been thus extraordinarily formed, and not propagated from Adam, though he had been a man like one of us, yet he would not have been of kin to us, because it would not have been a nature derived from Adam, the common parent of us all. It was therefore necessary to an affinity with us, not only that he should have the same human nature, but that it should flow from the same principle, and be propagated to him.[e] But now, by this way of producing the humanity of Christ of the substance of the virgin, he was in Adam (say some) corporally, but not seminally; of the substance of Adam, or a daughter of Adam, but not of the seed of Adam: and so he is of the same nature that had sinned, and so what he did and suffered may be imputed to us; which, had he been created as Adam, could not be claimed in a legal and judicial way.

2. It was not convenient he should be born in the common order of nature, of father and mother: for whosoever is so born is polluted. "A clean thing cannot be brought out of an unclean" (Job xiv. 4). And our Saviour had been incapable of being a redeemer, had he been tainted with the least spot of our nature, but would have stood in need of redemption himself. Besides, it had been inconsistent with the holiness of the Divine nature, to have assumed a tainted and defiled body. He that was the fountain of blessedness to all nations, was not to be subject to the curse of the law for himself; which he would have been, had he been conceived in an ordinary

e Amyrald. in Symbol. p. 103, &c.

way. He that was to overturn the devil's empire, was not to be any way captive under the devil's power, as a creature under the curse; nor could he be able to break the serpent's head, had he been tainted with the serpent's breath. Again, supposing that Almighty God by his divine power had so ordered the matter, and so perfectly sanctified an earthly father and mother from all original spot, that the human nature might have been transmitted immaculate to him, as well as the Holy Ghost did purge that part of the flesh of the virgin of which the body of Christ was made, yet it was not convenient that that person, that was God blessed for ever as well as man, partaking of our nature, should have a conception in the same manner as ours, but different, and in some measure conformable to the infinite dignity of his person: which could not have been, had not a supernatural power and a Divine person been concerned as an active principle in it; besides, such a birth had not been agreeable to the first promise, which calls him "the Seed of the woman" (Gen. i. 15), not of the man; and so the veracity of God had suffered some detriment: the Seed of the woman only is set in opposition to the seed of the serpent.

3. By this manner of conception the holiness of his nature is secured, and his fitness for his office is atsured to us. It is now a pure and unpolluted humanity that is the temple and tabernacle of the Divinity: the fulness of the Godhead dwells in him bodily, and dwells in him holily. His humanity is supernaturalized and elevated by the activity of the Holy Ghost, hatching the flesh of the virgin into man, as the chaos into a world. Though we read of some sanctified from the womb, it was not a pure and perfect holiness; it was like the light of fire mixed with smoke, an infused holiness accompanied with a natural taint: but the holiness of the Redeemer by this conception, is like the light of the sun, pure, and without spot. The Spirit of holiness supplying the place of a father in the way of creation. His fitness for his office is also assured to us; for being born of the virgin, one of our nature, but conceived by the Spirit of a Divine person, the guilt of our sins may be imputed to him because of our nature, without the stain of sin inherent in him; because of his supernatural conception he is capable, as one of kin to us, to bear our curse without being touched by our taint. By this means our sinful nature is assumed without sin in that nature which was assumed by him: "flesh he hath, but not sinful flesh" (Rom. viii. 3). Real flesh, but not really sinful, only by way of imputation. Nothing but the power of God is evident in this whole work: by ordinary laws and the course of nature a virgin could not bear a son: nothing but a supernatural and almighty grace could intervene to make so holy and perfect a conjunction. The generation of others, in an ordinary way, is by male and female: but the virgin is overshadowed by the Spirit and power of the Highest.[f] Man only is the product of natural generation; this which is born of the virgin is the holy thing, the Son of God. In other generations, a rational soul is only united to a material body: but in this, the Divine nature is united with the human in one person by an indissoluble union.

[f] Amyrant. sur Timole, p. 292.

The *Second* act of power in the person redeeming, is the union of the two natures, the Divine and human. The designing indeed of this was an act of wisdom; but the accomplishing it was an act of power.

1. There is in this redeeming person a union of two natures. He is God and man in one person (Heb. i. 8, 9). " Thy throne, O God, is for ever and ever: God, even thy God, hath anointed thee with the oil of gladness," &c. The Son is called God, having a throne for ever and ever, and the unction speaks him man: the Godhead cannot be anointed, nor hath any fellows. Humanity and Divinity are ascribed to him (Rom. i. 3, 4). " He was of the seed of David according to the flesh, and declared to be the Son of God, by his resurrection from the dead." The Divinity and humanity are both prophetically joined (Zech. xii. 10), " I will pour out my Spirit;" the pouring forth the Spirit is an act only of Divine grace and power. " And they shall look upon me whom they have pierced;" the same person pours forth the Spirit as God, and is pierced as man. " The Word was made flesh" (John i. 14). Word from eternity was made flesh in time; Word and flesh in one person; a great God, and a little infant.

2. The terms of this union were infinitely distant. What greater distance can there be than between the Deity and humanity, between the Creator and a creature ? Can you imagine the distance between eternity and time, Infinite Power and miserable infirmity, an immortal spirit and dying flesh, the highest Being and nothing ? yet these are espoused. A God of unmixed blessedness is linked personally with a man of perpetual sorrows : life incapable to die, joined to a body in that economy incapable to live without dying first; infinite purity, and a reputed sinner; eternal blessedness with a cursed nature, Almightiness and weakness, omniscience and ignorance, immutability and changeableness, incomprehensibleness and comprehensibility; that which cannot be comprehended, and that which can be comprehended; that which is entirely independent, and that which is totally dependent; the Creator forming all things, and the creature made, met together to a personal union; " The word made flesh".(John i. 14), the eternal Son, the " Seed of Abraham" (Heb. ii. 16). What more miraculous, than for God to become man, and man to become God? That a person possessed of all the perfections of the Godhead, should inherit all the imperfections of the manhood in one person, sin only excepted : a holiness incapable of sinning to be made sin ; God blessed forever, taking the properties of human nature, and human nature admitted to a union with the properties of the Creator : the fulness of the Deity, and the emptiness of man united together (Col. ii. 9) ; not by a shining of the Deity upon the humanity, as the light of the sun upon the earth, but by an inhabitation or indwelling of the Deity in the humanity. Was there not need of an Infinite Power to bring together terms so far asunder, to elevate the humanity to be capable of, and disposed for, a conjunction with the Deity ? If a clod of earth should be advanced to, and united with the body of the sun, such an advance would evidence itself to be a work of Almighty power : the clod hath nothing in its

own nature to render it so glorious, no power to climb up to so high a dignity : how little would such a union be, to that we are speaking of! Nothing less than an Incomprehensible Power could effect what an Incomprehensible Wisdom did project in this affair.

3. Especially since the union is so strait. It is not such a union as is between a man and his house he dwells in, whence he goes out and to which he returns, without any alteration of himself or his house ; nor such a union as is between a man and his garment, which both communicate and receive warmth from one another ; nor such as is between an artificer and his instrument wherewith he works ; nor such a union as one friend hath with another : all these are distant things, not one in nature, but have distinct substances. Two friends, though united by love, are distinct persons ; a man and his clothes, an artificer and his instruments, have distinct subsistencies ; but the humanity of Christ hath no subsistence, but in the person of Christ. The straitness of this union is expressed, and may be somewhat conceived, by the union of fire with iron ; "fire pierceth through all the parts of iron, it unites itself with every particle, bestows a light, heat, purity, upon all of it ; you cannot distinguish the iron from the fire, or the fire from the iron, yet they are distinct natures ; so the Deity is united to the whole humanity, seasons it, and bestows an excellency upon it, yet the natures still remain distinct. And as during that union of fire with iron, the iron is incapable of rust or blackness, so is the humanity incapable of sin : and as the operation of fire is attributed to the red-hot iron (as the iron may be said to heat, burn, and the fire may be said to cut and pierce), yet the imperfections of the iron do not affect the fire ; so in this mystery, those things which belong to the Divinity are ascribed to the humanity, and those things which belong to the humanity, are ascribed to the Divinity, in regard of the person in whom those natures are united : yet the imperfections of the humanity do not hurt the Divinity."[g] The Divinity of Christ is as really united with the humanity, as the soul with the body ; the person was one, though the natures were two ; so united, that the sufferings of the human nature were the sufferings of that person, and the dignity of the Divine was imputed to the human, by reason of that unity of both in one person ; hence the blood of the human nature is said to be the "blood of God" (Acts xx. 28). All things ascribed to the Son of God, may be ascribed to this man ; and the things ascribed to this man, may be ascribed to the Son of God, as this man is the Son of God, eternal, Almighty ; and it may be said, " God suffered, was crucified," &c., for the person of Christ is but one, most simple ; the person suffered, that was God and Man united, making one person.[h]

4. And though the union be so strait, yet without confusion of the natures, or change of them into one another. The two natures of Christ are not mixed, as liquors that incorporate with one another when they are poured into a vessel ; the Divine nature is not turned into the human, nor the human into the Divine ; one nature doth not swallow up another, and make a third nature distinct from each

[g] Lessius de Perf. Divin. lib. xii. cap. 4. p. 104.   [h] Lessius, pp. 103, 104.

of them.[i] The Deity is not turned into the humanity, as air (which is next to a spirit) may be thickened and turned into water, and water may be rarified into air by the power of heat boiling it. The Deity cannot be changed, because the nature of it is to be unchangeable; it would not be Deity, if it were mortal and capable of suffering. The humanity is not changed into the Deity, for then Christ could not have been a sufferer; if the humanity had been swallowed up into the Deity, it had lost its own distinct nature, and put on the nature of the Deity, and, consequently, been incapable of suffering; finite can never, by any mixture, be changed into infinite, nor infinite into finite. This union, in. this regard, may be resembled to the union of light and air, which are strictly joined; for the light passes through all parts of the air, but they are not confounded, but remain in their distinct essences as before the union, without the least confusion with one another. The Divine nature remains as it was before the union, entire in itself; only the Divine person assumes another nature to himself.[k] The human nature remains, as it would have done, had it existed separately from the Λόγος, except that then it would have had a proper subsistence by itself, which now it borrows from its union with the Λόγος, or, word; but that doth not belong to the constitution of its nature. Now let us consider, what a wonder of power is all this: the knitting a noble soul to a body of clay, was not so great an exploit of Almightiness, as the espousing infinite and finite together. Man is further distant from God, than man from nothing. What a wonder is it, that two natures infinitely distant, should be more intimately united than anything in the world; and yet without any confusion! that the same person should have both a glory and a grief; an infinite joy in the Deity, and an inexpressible sorrow in the humanity! That a God upon a throne should be an infant in a cradle; the thundering Creator be a weeping babe and a suffering man, are such expressions of mighty power, as well as condescending love, that they astonish men upon earth, and angels in heaven.

Thirdly, Power was evident in the progress of his life; in the miracles he wrought. How often did he expel malicious and powerful devils from their habitations; hurl them from their thrones, and make them fall from heaven like lightning! How many wonders were wrought by his bare word, or a single touch! Sight restored to the blind, and hearing to the deaf; palsy members restored to the exercise of their functions; a dismiss given to many deplorable maladies; impure leprosies chased from the persons they had infected, and bodies beginning to putrefy raised from the grave. But the mightiest argument of power was his patience; that He who was, in his Divine nature, elevated above the world, should so long continue upon a dunghill, endure the contradiction of sinners against himself, be patiently subject to the reproaches and indignities of men, without displaying that justice which was essential to the Deity; and, in especial manner, daily merited by their provoking crimes. The patience of man under great affronts, is a greater argument of power, than the brawniness of his arm; a strength employ-

i Lessius pp. 103, 104. Amyrald. Irenic. p. 284.   k Amyrald. Irenic. p. 282.

ed in the revenge of every injury, signifies a greater infirmity in the soul, than there can be ability in the body.

Fourthly, Divine power was apparent in his resurrection. The unlocking the belly of the whale for the deliverance of Jonas; the rescue of Daniel from the den of lions; and the restraining the fire from burning the three children, were signal declarations of his power, and types of the resurrection of our Saviour. But what are those to that which was represented by them? That was a power over natural causes, a curbing of beasts, and restraining of elements; but in the resurrection of Christ, God exercised a power over him-self, and quenched the flames of his own wrath, hotter than millions of Nebuchadnezzar's furnaces; unlocked the prison doors, wherein the curses of the law had lodged our Saviour, stronger than the belly and ribs of a leviathan. In the rescue of Daniel and Jonas, God overpowered beasts; and in this tore up the strength of the old ser-pent, and plucked the sceptre from the hand of the enemy of man-kind. The work of resurrection, indeed, considered in itself, re-quires the efficacy of an Almighty power; neither man nor angel can create new dispositions in a dead body, to render it capable of lodging a spiritual soul; nor can they restore a dislodged soul, by their own power, to such a body. The restoring a dead body to life requires an infinite power, as well as the creation of the world; but there was in the resurrection of Christ, something more difficult than this; while he lay in the grave he was under the curse of the law, under the execution of that dreadful sentence, "Thou shalt die the death." His resurrection was not only the re-tying the marriage knot between his soul and body, or the rolling the stone from the grave; but a taking off an infinite weight, the sin of mankind, which lay upon him. So vast a weight could not be removed without the strength of an Almighty arm. It is, therefore, not to an ordinary operation, but an operation with power (Rom. i. 4), and such a power wherein the glory of the Father did appear (Rom. vi. 4); "Raised up from the dead by the glory of the Father," that is, the glorious power of God. As the Eternal generation is stupendous, so is his resurrection, which is called, a new begetting of him (Acts xiii. 33). It is a wonder of power, that the Divine and human nature should be joined; and no less wonder that his person should surmount and rise up from the curse of God, under which he lay. The apostle, therefore, adds one expression to another, and heaps up a variety, signifying thereby that one was not enough to represent it (Eph. i. 19); "Exceeding greatness of power, and working of mighty power, which he wrought in Christ when he raised him from the dead." It was an hyperbole of power, the excellency of the mightiness of his strength: the loftiness of the expressions seems to come short of the apprehension he had of it in his soul.

II. This power appears in the publication and propagation of the doctrine of redemption. The Divine power will appear, if you con-sider, 1. The nature of the doctrine. 2. The instruments employed in it. 3. The means they used to propagate it. 4. The success they had.

1. The nature of the doctrine. (1.) It was contary to the common

received reason of the world. The philosphers, the masters of
knowledge among the Gentiles, had maxims of a different stamp
from it. Though they agreed in the being of a God, yet their notions of his nature were confused and embroiled with many errors;
the unity of God was not commonly assented unto; they had multiplied deities according to the fancies they had received from some
of a more elevated wit and refined brain than others. Though they
had some notion of mediators, yet they placed in those seats their
public benefactors, men that had been useful to the world, or their
particular countries, in imparting to them some profitable invention.
To discard those, was to charge themselves with ingratitude to them,
from whom they had received signal benefits, and to whose mediation, conduct, or protection, they ascribed all the success they had
been blessed with in their several provinces, and to charge themselves with folly for rendering an honor and worship to them so
long. Could the doctrine of a crucified Mediator, whom they had
never seen, that had conquered no country for them, never enlarged
their territories, brought to light no new profitable invention for the
increase of their earthly welfare, as the rest had done, be thought
sufficient to balance so many of their reputed heroes? How ignorant were they in the foundations of the true religion! The belief
of a Providence was staggering; nor had they a true prospect of the
nature of virtue and vice; yet they had a fond opinion of the
strength of their own reason, and the maxims that had been handed
down to them by their predecessors, which Paul (1 Tim. vi. 20) entitles, a " science falsely so called," either meant of the philosophers
or the Gnostics. They presumed that they were able to measure all
things by their own reason; whence, when the apostle came to
preach the doctrine of the Gospel at Athens, the great school of
reason in that age, they gave him no better a title than that of a
babbler (Acts xvii. 18), and openly mocked him (ver. 32); a seed
gatherer,[1] one that hath no more brain or sense than a fellow that
gathers up seeds that are spilled in a market, or one that hath a vain
and empty sound, without sense or reason, like a foolish mounte-
bank; so slightly did those rationalists of the world think of the
wisdom of heaven. That the Son of God should veil himself in a
mortal body, and suffer a disgraceful death in it, were things above
the ken of reason. Besides, the world had a general disesteem of
the religion of the Jews, and were prejudiced against anything that
came from them; whence the Romans, that used to incorporate the
gods of other conquered nations in their capital, never moved to
have the God of Israel worshipped among them. Again, they might
argue against it with much fleshly reason: here is a crucified God,
preached by a company of mean and ignorant persons, what reason
can we have to entertain this doctrine, since the Jews, who, as they
tell us, had the prophecies of him, did not acknowledge him? Surely, had there been such predictions, they would not have crucified,
but crowned their King, and expected from him the conquest of the
earth under their power. What reason have we to entertain him,
whom his own nation, among whom he lived, with whom he con-

[1] Σπερμολόγος.

versed so unanimously, by the vote of the rulers as well as the rout, rejected? It was impossible to conquer minds possessed with so many errors, and applauding themselves in their own reason, and to render them capable of receiving revealed truths without the influence of a Divine power.

(2.) It was contrary to the customs of the world. The strength of custom in most men, surmounts the strength of reason, and men commonly are so wedded to it, that they will be sooner divorced from anything than the modes and patterns received from their ancestors. The endeavoring to change customs of an ancient standing, hath begotten tumults and furious mutinies among nations, though the change would have been much for their advantage. This doctrine struck at the root of the religion of the world, and the ceremonies, wherein they had been educated from their infancy, delivered to them from their ancestors, confirmed by the customary observance of many ages, rooted in their minds and established by their laws (Acts xviii. 13); "This fellow persuadeth us to worship God contrary to the law;" against customs, to which they ascribed the happiness of their states, and the prosperity of their people, and would put, in the place of this religion they would abolish, a new one instituted by a man, whom the Jews had condemned, and put to death upon a cross, as an impostor, blasphemer, and seditious person. It was a doctrine that would change the customs of the Jews, who were intrusted with the oracles of God. It would bury forever their ceremonial rites, delivered to them by Moses, from that God, who had, with a mighty hand, brought them out of Egypt, consecrated their law with thunders and lightnings from Mount Sinai, at the time of its publication, backed it with severe sanctions, confirmed it by many miracles, both in the wilderness and their Canaan, and had continued it for so many hundred years. They could not but remember how they had been ravaged by other nations, and judgments sent upon them when they neglected and slighted it; and with what great success they were followed when they valued and observed it; and how they had abhorred the Author of this new religion, who had spoken slightly of their traditions, till they put him to death with infamy. Was it an easy matter to divorce them from that worship, upon which were entailed, as they imagined, their peace, plenty, and glory, things of the dearest regard with mankind? The Jews were no less devoted to their ceremonial traditions than the heathen were to their vain superstitions. This doctrine of the gospel was of that nature, that the state of religion, all over the earth, must be overturned by it; the wisdom of the Greeks must vail to it, the idolatry of the people must stoop to it, and the profane customs of men must moulder under the weight of it. Was it an easy matter for the pride of nature to deny a customary wisdom, to entertain a new doctrine against the authority of their ancestors, to inscribe folly upon that which hath made them admired by the rest of the world? Nothing can be of greater esteem with men, than the credit of their lawgivers and founders, the religion of their fathers, and prosperity of themselves: hence the minds of men were sharpened against it. The Greeks, the wisest nation, slighted it as foolish; the Jews, the religious nation, stumbled at it, as contrary to the received interpretations of ancient prophecies and carnal conceits of an earthly glory. The dimmest eye may behold the difficulty to change custom, a second nature: it is as hard as to change a wolf into a lamb, to level a mountain, stop the course of the sun, or change the inhabitants of Africa into the color of Europe. Custom dips men in as durable a dye as nature. The difficulties of carrying it on against the Divine religion of the Jew, and rooted custom of the Gentiles, were unconquerable by any but an Almighty power. And in this the power of God hath appeared wonderfully.

(3.) It was contrary to the sensuality of the world, and the lusts of the flesh. How much the Gentiles were overgrown with base and unworthy lusts at the time of the publication of the gospel, needs no other memento than the apostle's discourse (Rom. i). As there was no error but prevailed upon their minds, so there was no brutish affection but was wedded to their hearts. The doctrine proposed to them was not easy; it flattered not the sense, but checked the stream of nature. It thundered down those three great engines whereby the devil had subdued the world to himself: "the lust of the flesh, the lust of the eye, and the pride of life:" not only the most sordid affections of the flesh, but the more refined gratifications of the mind: it stripped nature both of devil and man; of what was commonly esteemed great and virtuous. That which was the root of their fame, and the satisfaction of their ambition, was struck at by this axe of the gospel. The first article of it ordered them to deny themselves, not to presume upon their own worth; to lay their understandings and wills at the foot of the cross, and resign them up to one newly crucified at Jerusalem: honors and wealth were to be despised, flesh to be tamed, the cross to be borne, enemies to be loved, revenge not to be satisfied, blood to be spilled, and torments to be endured for the honor of One they never saw, nor ever before heard of; who was preached with the circumstances of a shameful death, enough to affright them from the entertainment: and the report of a resurrection and glorious ascension were things never heard of by them before, and unknown in the world, that would not easily enter into the belief of men: the cross, disgrace, self-denial, were only discoursed of in order to the attainment of an invisible world, and an unseen reward, which none of their predecessors ever returned to acquaint them with; a patient death, contrary to the pride of nature, was published as the way to happiness and a blessed immortality: the dearest lusts were to be pierced to death for the honor of this new Lord. Other religions brought wealth and honor; this struck them off from such expectations, and presented them with no promise of anything in this life, but a prospect of misery; except those inward consolations to which before they had been utter strangers, and had never experimented. It made them to depend not upon themselves, but upon the sole grace of God. It decried all natural, all moral idolatry, things as dear to men as the apple of their eyes. It despoiled them of whatsoever the mind, will, and affections of men, naturally lay claim to, and glory in. It pulled self up by the roots, unmanned carnal man, and debased the principle of honor and self-satisfaction, which the world counted at that time noble and brave. In a word, it took them off from themselves, to act like creatures of God's framing; to know no more than he would admit them, and do no more than he did command them. How difficult must it needs be to reduce men, that placed all their happiness in the pleasures of this life, from their pompous idolatry and brutish affections, to this mortifying religion! What might the world say? Here is a doctrine will render us a company of puling animals: farewell generosity, bravery, sense of honor, courage in enlarging the bounds of our country, for an ardent charity to the bitterest of our enemies. Here is a religion will rust our swords, canker our arms, dispirit what we have hitherto called virtue, and annihilate what hath been esteemed worthy and comely among mankind. Must we change conquest for suffering, the increase of our reputation for self-denial, the natural sentiment of self-preservation for affecting a dreadful death? How impossible was it that a crucified Lord, and a crucifying doctrine should be received in the world without the mighty operation of a divine power upon the hearts of men! And in this also the almighty power of God did notably shine forth.

2. Divine power appeared in the instruments employed for the publishing and propagating the gospel; who were (1.) Mean and worthless in themselves: not noble and dignified with an earthly grandeur, but of a low condition, meanly bred: so far from any splendid estates, that they possessed nothing but their nets; without any credit and reputation in the world; without comeliness and strength; as unfit to subdue the world by preaching, as an army of hares were to conquer it by war: not learned doctors, bred up at the feet of the famous Rabbins at Jerusalem, whom Paul calls "the princes of the world" (1 Cor. ii. 8); nor nursed up in the school of Athens, under the philosophers and orators of the time: not the wise men of Greece, but the fishermen of Galilee; naturally skilled in no language but their own, and no more exact in that than those of the same condition in any other nation: ignorant of everything but the language of their lakes, and their fishing trade; except Paul, called some time after the rest to that employment: and after the descent of the Spirit, they were ignorant and unlearned in everything but the doctrine they were commanded to publish; for the council, before whom they were summoned, proved them to be so, which increased their wonder at them (Acts iv. 13). Had it been published by a voice from heaven, that twelve poor men, taken out of boats and creeks, without any help of learning, should conquer the world to the cross, it might have been thought an illusion against all the reason of men; yet we know it was undertaken and accomplished by them. They published this doctrine in Jerusalem, and quickly spread it over the greatest part of the world. Folly outwitted wisdom, and weakness overpowered strength. The conquest of the east by Alexander was not so admirable as the enterprise of these poor men. He attempted his conquest with the hands of a warlike nation, though, indeed, but a small number of thirty thou-

sand against multitudes, many hundred thousands of the enemies; yet an effeminate enemy; a people inured to slaughter and victory attacked great numbers, but enfeebled by luxury and voluptuousness. Besides, he was bred up to such enterprises, had a learned education under the best philosopher, and a military education under the best commander, and a natural courage to animate him. These instruments had no such advantage from nature; the heavenly treasure was placed in those earthen vessels, as Gideon's lamps in empty pitchers (Judges vii. 16), that the excellency, or hyperbole, of the power, might be of God (2 Cor. iv. 7), and the strength of his arm be displayed in the infirmity of the instruments. They were destitute of earthly wisdom, and therefore despised by the Jews, and derided by the Gentiles; the publishers were accounted madmen, and the embracers fools. Had they been men of known natural endowments, the power of God had been veiled under the gifts of the creature.

(2.) Therefore a Divine power suddenly spirited them, and fitted them for so great a work. Instead of ignorance, they had the knowledge of the tongues; and they that were scarce well skilled in their own dialect, were instructed on the sudden to speak the most flourishing languages in the world, and discourse to the people of several nations the great things of God (Acts ii. 11). Though they were not enriched with any worldly wealth, and possessed nothing, yet they were so sustained that they wanted nothing in any place where they came; a table was spread for them in the midst of their bitterest enemies. Their fearfulness was changed into courage, and they that a few days before skulked in corners for fear of the Jews (John xx. 19), speak boldly in the name of that Jesus, whom they had seen put to death by the power of the rulers and the fury of the people: they reproach them with the murder of their Master, and outbrave that great people in the midst of their temple, with the glory of that person they had so lately crucified (Acts ii 23; iii. 13). Peter, that was not long before qualmed at the presence of a maid, was not daunted at the presence of the council, that had their hands yet reeking with the blood of his Master; but being filled with the Holy Ghost, seems to dare the power of the priests and Jewish governors, and is as confident in the council chamber, as he had been cowardly in the high-priest's hall (Acts iv. 9), &c., the efficacy of grace triumphing over the fearfulness of nature. Whence should this ardor and zeal, to propagate a doctrine that had already borne the scars of the peoples' fury be, but from a mighty Power, which changed those hares into lions, and stripped them of their natural cowardice to clothe them with a Divine courage; making them in a moment both wise and magnanimous, alienating them from any consultations with flesh and blood? As soon as ever the Holy Ghost came upon them as a mighty rushing wind, they move up and down for the interest of God; as fish, after a great clap of thunder, are roused, and move more nimbly on the top of the water; therefore, that which did so fit them for this undertaking, is called by the title of "power from on high" (Luke xxiv. 49).

3. The Divine power appears in the means whereby it was propagated.

(1.) By means different from the methods of the world. Not by force of arms, as some religions have taken root in the world. Mahomet's horse hath trampled upon the heads of men, to imprint an Alcoran in their brains, and robbed men of their goods to plant their religion. But the apostles bore not this doctrine through the world upon the points of their swords; they presented a bodily death where they would bestow an immortal life. They employed not troops of men in a warlike posture, which had been possible for them after the gospel was once spread; they had no ambition to subdue men unto themselve, but to God; they coveted not the possessions of others; designed not to enrich themselves; invaded not the rights of princes, nor the liberties and properties of the people: they rifled them not of their estates, nor scared them into this religion by a fear of losing their worldly happiness. The arguments they used would naturally drive them from an entertainment of this doctrine, rather than allure them to be proselytes to it: their design was to change their hearts, not their government; to wean them from the love of the world, to a love of a Redeemer; to remove that which would ruin their souls. It was not to enslave them, but ransom them; they had a warfare, but not with carnal weapons, but such as were "mighty through God for the pulling down strongholds" (2 Cor. x. 4); they used no weapons but the doctrine they preached. Others that have not gained conquests by the edge of the sword and the stratagems of war, have extended their opinions to others by the strength of human reason, and the insinuations of eloquence. But the apostles had as little flourish in their tongues, as edge upon their swords: their preaching was "not with the enticing words of man's wisdom" (1 Cor. ii. 4); their presence was mean, and their discourses without varnish; their doctrine was plain, a "crucified Christ;" a doctrine unlaced, ungarnished, untoothsome to the world; but they had the demonstration of the Spirit, and a mighty power for their companion in the work. The doctrine they preached, viz. the death, resurrection and ascension of Christ, are called the powers, not of this world, but "of the world to come" (Heb. vi. 5). No less than a supernatural power could conduct them in this attempt, with such weak methods in human appearance.

(2.) Against all the force, power, and wit of the world. The division in the eastern empire, and the feeble and consuming state of the western, contributed to Mahomet's success.[m] But never was Rome in a more flourishing condition: learning, eloquence, wisdom, strength, were at the highest pitch. Never was there a more diligent watch against any innovations; never was that state governed by more severe and suspicious princes, than at the time when Tiberius and Nero held the reins. No time seemed to be more unfit for the entrance of a new doctrine than that age, wherein it begun to be first published; never did any religion meet with that opposition from men. Idolatry hath been often settled without any contest; but this hath suffered the same fate with the institutor of it, and endured the contradictions of sinners against itself: and those that published it, were not only without any worldly prop, but exposed

[m] Daille. Serm. XV. p. 57.

themselves to the hatred and fury, to the racks and tortures, of the strongest powers on earth. It never set foot in any place, but the country was in an uproar (Acts xix. 28); swords were drawn to destroy it; laws made to suppress it; prisons provided for the professors of it; fires kindled to consume them, and executioners had a perpetual employment to stifle the progress of it. Rome, in its conquest of countries, changed not the religion, rites, and modes of their worship: they altered their civil government, but left them to the liberty of their religion, and many times joined with them in the worship of their peculiar gods; and sometime imitated them at Rome, instead of abolishing them in the cities they had subdued. But all their councils were assembled, and their force was bandied "against the Lord, and against his Christ;" and that city that kindly received all manner of superstitions, hated this doctrine with an irreconcileable hatred. It met with reproaches from the wise, and fury from the potentates; it was derided by the one as the greatest folly, and persecuted by the other as contrary to God and mankind; the one were afraid to lose their esteems by the doctrine, and the other to lose their authority by a sedition they thought a change of religion would introduce. The Romans, that had been conquerors of the earth, feared intestine commotions, and the falling asunder the links of their empire: scarce any of their first emperors, but had their swords dyed red in the blood of the Christians. The flesh with all its lusts, the world with all its flatteries the statesmen with all their craft, and the mighty with all their strength, joined together to extirpate it: though many members were taken off by the fires, yet the church not only lived, but flourished, in the furnace. Converts were made by the death of martyrs; and the flames which consumed their bodies, were the occasion of firing men's hearts with a zeal for the profession of it. Instead of being extinguished, the doctrine shone more bright, and multiplied under the sickles that were employed to cut it down. God ordered every circumstance so, both in the persons that published it, the means whereby, and the time when, that nothing but his power might appear in it, without anything to dim and darken it.

4. The Divine power was conspicuous in the great success it had under all these difficulties. Multitudes were prophesied of to embrace it; whence the prophet Isaiah, after the prophecy of the death of Christ (Isa. liii.), calls upon the church to enlarge her tents, and "lengthen out her cords" to receive those multitudes of children that should call her mother (Isa. liv. 2, 3); for she should "break forth on the right hand and on the left, and her seed should inherit the Gentiles!" the idolaters and persecutors should list their names in the muster-roll of the church. Presently, after the descent of the Holy Ghost from heaven upon the apostles, you find the hearts of three thousand melted by a plain declaration of this doctrine; who were a little before so far from having a favorable thought of it, that some of them at least, if not all, had expressed their rage against it, in voting for the condemning and crucifying the Author of it (Acts ii. 41, 42): but in a moment they were so altered, that they breathe out affections instead of fury; neither the

respect they had to their rulers, nor the honor they bore to their priests; not the derisions of the people, nor the threatening of punishment, could stop them from owning it in the face of multitudes of discouragements. How wonderful is it that they should so soon, and by such small means, pay a reverence to the servants, who had none for the Master! that they should hear them with patience, without the same clamor against them as against Christ, " Crucify them, crucify them!" but, that their hearts should so suddenly be inflamed with devotion to him dead, whom they so much abhorred when living. It had gained footing not in a corner of the world, but in the most famous cities; in Jerusalem, where Christ had been crucified; in Antioch, where the name of Christians first began ; in Corinth, a place of ingenious arts; and Ephesus, the seat of a noted idol. In less than twenty years, there was never a province of the Roman empire, and scarce any part of the known world, but was stored with the professors of it. Rome, that was the metropolis of the idolatrous world, had multitudes of them sprinkled in every corner, whose "faith was spoken of throughout the world" (Rom. i. 8). The court of Nero, that monster of mankind, and the cruelest and sordidest tyrant that ever breathed, was not empty of sincere votaries to it; there were "saints in Cæsar's house" while Paul was under Nero's chain (Phil. iv.): and it maintained its standing, and and flourished in spite of all the force of hell, two hundred and fifty years before any sovereign prince espoused it. The potentates of the earth had conquered the lands of men, and subdued their bodies; these vanquished hearts and wills, and brought the most beloved thoughts under the yoke of Christ: so much did this doctrine overmaster the consciences of its followers, that they rejoiced more at their yoke, than others at their liberty; and counted it more a glory to die for the honor of it, than to live in the profession of it. Thus did our Saviour reign and gather subjects in the midst of his enemies; in which respect, in the first discovery of the gospel, he is described as "a mighty Conqueror" (Rev. vi. 2), and still conquering in the greatness of his strength. How great a testimony of his power is it, that from so small a cloud should rise so glorious a sun, that should chase before it the darkness and power of hell; triumph over the idolatry, superstition, and profaneness of the world! This plain doctrine vanquished the obstinacy of the Jews, baffled the understanding of the Greeks, humbled the pride of the grandees, threw the devil not only out of bodies, but hearts; tore up the foundation of his empire, and planted the cross, where the devil had for many ages before established his standard. How much more than a human force is illustrious in this whole conduct! Nothing in any age of the world can parallel it: it being so much against the methods of nature, the disposition of the world, and (considering the resistance against it) seems to surmount even the works of creation. Never were there, in any profession, such multitudes, not of bedlams, but men of sobriety, acuteness, and wisdom, that exposed themselves to the fury of the flames, and challenged death in the most terrifying shapes for the honor of this doctrine. To conclude, this should be often meditated upon to form our understandings to a full assent to the gospel, and the truth of it; the want of which consideration of power, and the customariness of an education in the outward profession of it, is the ground of all the profaneness under it, and apostasy from it; the disesteem of the truth it declares, and the neglect of the duties it enjoins. The more we have a prospect and sense of the impressions of Divine power in it, the more we shall have a reverence of the Divine precepts.

III. The third thing is, the power of God appears in the application of redemption, as well as in the Person redeeming, and the publication and propagation of the doctrine of redemption: 1. In the planting grace. 2. In the pardon of sin. 3. In the preserving grace.

First, In the planting grace. There is no expression which the Spirit of God hath thought fit in Scripture to resemble this work to, but argues the exerting of a Divine power for the effecting of it. When it is expressed by light, it is as much as the power of God in the creating the sun; when by regeneration, it is as much as the power of God in forming an infant, and fashioning all the parts of a man; when it is called resurrection, it is as much as the rearing of a body again out of putrified matter; when it is called creation, it is as much as erecting a comely world out of mere nothing, or an inform and uncomely mass. As we could not contrive the death of Christ for our redemption, so we cannot form our souls to the acceptation of it; the infinite efficacy of grace is as necessary for the one, as the infinite wisdom of God was for laying the platform of the other. It is by his power we have whatsoever pertains to godliness as well as life (2 Pet. i. 3); he puts his fingers upon the handle of the lock, and turns the heart to what point he pleases; the action whereby he performs this, is expressed by a word of force; " He hath snatched us from the power of darkness:"[n] the action whereby it is performed manifests it. In reference to this power, it is called creation, which is a production from nothing; and conversion is a production from something more incapable of that state, than mere nothing is of being. There is greater distance between the terms of sin and righteousness, corruption and grace, than between the terms of nothing and being; the greater the distance is, the more power is required to the producing any thing. As in miracles, the miracle is the greater, where the change is the greater; and the change is the greater, where the distance is the greater. As it was a more signal mark of power to change a dead man to life, than to change a sick man to health; so that the change here being from a term of a greater distance, is more powerful than the creation of heaven and earth. Therefore, whereas creation is said to be wrought by his hands, and the heavens by his fingers, or his word; conversion is said to be wrought by his arm (Isa. liii. 1). In creation, we had an earthly; by conversion, a heavenly state: in creation, nothing is changed into something; in conversion, hell is transformed into heaven, which is more than the turning nothing into a glorious angel. In that thanksgiving of our Saviour, for the revelation of the knowledge of himself to babes, the simple of the world, he gives

[n] Colos. i. 19.   ἐρρύσατο.

the title to his Father, of "Lord of heaven and earth" (Matt. xi. 5); intimating it to be an act of his creative and preserving power; that power whereby he formed heaven and earth, hath preserved the standing, and governed the motions of all creatures from the beginning of the world. It is resembled to the most magnificent act of divine power that God ever put forth, viz. that "in the resurrection of our Saviour" (Eph. i. 19); wherein there was more than an ordinary impression of might. It is not so small a power as that whereby we speak with tongues, or whereby Christ opened the mouths of the dumb, and the ears of the deaf, or unloosed the cords of death from a person. It is not that power whereby our Saviour wrought those stupendous miracles when he was in the world: but that power which wrought a miracle that amazed the most knowing angels, as well as ignorant man; the taking off the weight of the sin of the world from our Saviour, and advancing him in his human nature to rule over the angelic host, making him head of principalities and powers; as much as to say, as great as all that power which is displayed in our redemption, from the first foundation to the last line in the superstructure. It is, therefore, often set forth with an emphasis, as "Excellency of power" (2 Cor. iv. 7), and "Glorious power" (2 Pet. i. 3): "to glory and virtue," we translate it, but it is δια δοξης, through glory and virtue, that is, by a glorious virtue or strength.

The instrument whereby it is wrought, is dignified with the title of power. The gospel which God useth in this great affair is called "The power of God to salvation" (Rom. i. 16), and the "Rod of his strength" (Ps. cx. 2); and the day of the gospel's appearance in the heart is emphatically called, "The day of power" (ver. 3); wherein he brings down strong-holds and towering imaginations. And, therefore, the angel Gabriel, which name signifies the power of God, was always sent upon those messages which concerned the gospel, as to Daniel, Zacharias, Mary.[o] The gospel is the power of God in a way of instrumentality, but the almightiness of God is the principal in a way of efficiency. The gospel is the sceptre of Christ; but the power of Christ is the mover of that sceptre. The gospel is not as a bare word spoken, and proposing the thing; but as backed with a higher efficacy of grace; as the sword doth instrumentally cut, but the arm that wields it gives the blow, and makes it successful in the stroke. But this gospel is the power of God, because he edgeth this by his own power, to surmount all resistance, and vanquish the greatest malice of that man he designs to work upon. The power of God is conspicuous,

1, In turning the heart of man against the strength of the inclinations of nature. In the forming of man of the dust of the ground; as the matter contributed nothing to the action whereby God formed it, so it had no principle of resistance contrary to the design of God; but in converting the heart, there is not only wanting a principle of assistance from him in this work, but the whole strength of corrupt nature is alarmed to combat against the power of his grace. When the gospel is presented, the understanding is not only ignorant of it, but the will perverse against it; the one doth not relish, and the

<hr>

° Grotius in Luke i. 19.

other doth not esteem, the excellency of the object. The carnal wisdom in the mind contrives against it, and the rebellious will puts the orders in execution against the counsel of God, which requires the invincible power of God to enlighten the dark mind, to know what it slights; and the fierce will, to embrace what it loathes. The stream of nature cannot be turned, but by a power above nature; it is not all the created power in heaven and earth can change a swine into a man, or a venemous toad into an holy and illustrious angel. Yet this work is not so great, in some respect, as the stilling the fierceness of nature, the silencing the swelling waves in the heart, and the casting out those brutish affections which are born and grow up with us. There would be no, or far less, resistance in a mere animal, to be changed into a creature of a higher rank, than there is in a natural man to be turned into a serious Christian. There is in every natural man a stoutness of heart, a stiff neck, unwillingness to good, forwardness to evil; Infinite Power quells this stoutness, demolisheth these strongholds, turns this wild ass in her course, and routs those armies of turbulent nature against the grace of God. To stop the floods of the sea is not such an act of power, as to turn the tide of the heart. This power hath been employed upon every convert in the world; what would you say, then, if you knew all the channels in which it hath run since the days of Adam? If the alteration of one rocky heart into a pool of water be a wonder of power, what then is the calming and sweetening by his word those 144,000 of the tribes of Israel, and that numberless multitude of all nations and people that shall stand "before the throne" (Rev. vii. 9), which were all naturally so many raging seas? Not one converted soul from Adam to the last that shall be in the end of the world, but is a trophy of the Divine conquest. None were pure volunteers, nor listed themselves in his service, till he put forth his strong arm to draw them to him. No man's understanding, but was chained with darkness, and fond of it; no man but had corruption in his will, which was dearer to him than anything else which could be proposed for his true happiness. These things are most evident in Scripture and experience.

2. As it is wrought against the inclinations of nature, so against a multitude of corrupt habits rooted in the souls of men. A distemper in its first invasion may more easily be cured, than when it becomes chronical and inveterate. The strength of a disease, or the complication of many, magnifies the power of the physician, and efficacy of the medicine that tames and expels it. What power is that which hath made men stoop, when natural habits have been grown giants by custom; when the putrefaction of nature hath engendered a multitude of worms; when the ulcers are many and deplorable; when many cords, wherewith God would have bound the sinner, have been broken, and (like Sampson) the wicked heart hath gloried in its strength, and grown more proud, that it hath stood like a strong fort against those batteries, under which others have fallen flat; every proud thought, every evil habit captivated, serves for matter of triumph to the "power of God" (2 Cor. x. 5). What resistance will a multitude of them make, when one of them is enough

to hold the faculty under its dominion, and intercept its operations? So many customary habits, so many old natures, so many different strengths added to nature, every one of them standing as a barricado against the way of grace; all the errors the understanding is possessed with, think the gospel folly; all the vices the will is filled with, count it the fetter and band. Nothing so contrary to man, as to be thought a fool; nothing so contrary to man, as to enter into slavery. It is no easy matter to plant the cross of Christ upon a heart guided by many principles against the truth of it, and biased by a world of wickedness against the holiness of it. Nature renders a man too feeble and indisposed, and custom renders a man more weak and unwilling to change his hue (Jer. xiii. 23). To dispossess man then of his self-esteem and self-excellency; to make room for God in the heart, where there was none but for sin, as dear to him as himself; to hurl down the pride of nature; to make stout imaginations stoop to the cross; to makes desires of self-advancement sink into a zeal for the glorifying of God, and an overruling design for his honor, is not to be ascribed to any but an outstretched arm wielding the sword of the Spirit. To have a heart full of the fear of God, that was just before filled with a contempt of him; to have a sense of his power, an eye to his glory, admiring thoughts of his wisdom, a faith in his truth, that had lower thoughts of him and all his perfections, than he had of a creature; to have a hatred of his habitual lusts, that had brought him in much sensitive pleasure; to loath them as much as he loved them; to cherish the duties he hated; to live by faith in, and obedience to, the Redeemer, who was before so heartily under the conduct of Satan and self; to chase the acts of sin from his members, and the pleasing thoughts of sin from his mind; to make a stout wretch willingly fall down, crawl upon the ground, and adore that Saviour whom before he out-dared, is a triumphant act of Infinite Power that can subdue all things to itself, and break those multitudes of locks and bolts that were upon us.

3. Against a multitude of temptations and interests. The temptations rich men have in this world are so numerous and strong, that the entrance of one of them into the kingdom of heaven, that is, the entertainment of the gospel, is made by our Saviour an impossible thing with men, and procurable only by the power of God (Luke xviii. 24—26). The Divine strength only can separate the world from the heart, and the heart from the world. There must be an incomprehensible power to chase away the devil, that had so long, so strong a footing in the affections; to render the soil he had sown with so many tares and weeds, capable of good grain; to make spirits, that had found the sweetness of worldly prosperity, wrapt up all their happiness in it, and not only bent down, but—as it were—buried in earth and mud, to be loosened from those beloved cords, to disrelish the earth for a crucified Christ; I say, this must be the effect of an almighty power.

4. The manner of conversion shews no less the power of God. There is not only an irresistible force used in it, but an agreeable sweetness. The power is so efficacious, that nothing can vanquish it; and so sweet, that none did ever complain of it. The Almighty

virtue displays itself invincibly, yet without constraint; compelling
the will without offering violence to it, and making it cease to be
will: not forcing it, but changing it: not dragging it, but drawing
it; making it will where before it nilled; removing the corrupt nature of the will, without invading the created nature and rights of
the faculty; not working in us against the physical nature of the
will, but working it "to will" (Phil. ii. 13). This work is therefore
called creation, resurrection, to shew its irresistible power; it is called
illumination, persuasion, drawing, to shew the suitableness of its efficacy to the nature of the human faculties: it is a drawing with
cords, which testifies an invincible strength; but, with cords of love,
which testifies a delightful conquest. It is hard to determine
whether it be more powerful than sweet, or more sweet than powerful. It is no mean part of the power of God to twist together victory and pleasure; to give a blow as delightful as strong, as pleasing
to the sufferer, as it is sharp to the sinner.

Secondly, The power of God, in the application of redemption, is
evident in the pardoning a sinner.

1. In the pardon itself. The power of God is made the ground of
his patience; or the reason why he is patient, is, because he would
"shew his power" (Rom. ix. 22). It is a part of magnanimity to pass
by injuries: as weaker stomachs cannot concoct the tougher food, so
weak minds cannot digest the harder injuries: he that passes over a
wrong is superior to his adversary that does it. When God speaks
of his own name as merciful, he speaks first of himself as powerful
(Exod. xxxiv. 6), "The Lord, The Lord God," that is, The Lord,
the strong Lord, Jehovah, the strong Jehovah. Let the power of
my Lord be great, saith Moses, when he prays for the forgiveness of
the people:ᴾ the word *jigdal* is written with a great *jod*, or a *jod*
above the other letters. The power of God in pardoning is advanced
beyond an ordinary strain, beyond the creative strength. In the
creation, he had power over the creatures; in this, power over himself: in creation, not himself, but the creatures were the object of his
power; in that, no attribute of his nature could article against his
design. In the pardon of a sinner, after many overtures made to
him and refused by him, God exerciseth a power over himself; for
the sinner hath dishonored God, provoked his justice, abused his
goodness, done injury to all those attributes which are necessary to
his relief: it was not so in creation, nothing was incapable of dis-
obliging God from bringing it into being. The dust, which was the
matter of Adam's body, needed only the extrinsic power of God to
form it into a man, and inspire it with a living soul: it had not rendered itself obnoxious to Divine justice, nor was capable to excite
any disputes between his perfections. But after the entrance of sin,
and the merit of death, thereby there was a resistance in justice to
the free remission of man: God was to exercise a power over himself, to answer his justice, and pardon the sinner; as well as a power
over the creature, to reduce the run away and rebel. Unless we
have recourse to the infiniteness of God's power, the infiniteness of
our guilt will weigh us down: we must consider not only that we

ᴾ Numb. xiv. 17. ὑψωθήτω, be exalted.   Sept.   Strength, &c.

have a mighty guilt to press us, but a mighty God to relieve us. In the same act of his being our righteousness, he is our strength: "In the Lord have I righteousness and strength" (Isa. xlv. 24).

2. In the sense of pardon. When the soul hath been wounded with the sense of sin, and its iniquities have stared it in the face, the raising the soul from a despairing condition, and lifting it above those waters which terrified it, to cast the light of comfort, as well as the light of grace, into a heart covered with more than an Egyptian darkness, is an act of his infinite and creating power (Isa. lvii. 19); "I create the fruit of the lips; Peace." Men may wear out their lips with numbering up the promises of grace and arguments of peace, but all will signify no more, without a creative power, than if all men and angels should call to that white upon the wall to shine as splendidly as the sun. God only can create Jerusalem, and every child of Jerusalem a rejoicing (Isa. xlv. 18). A man is no more able to apply to himself any word of comfort, under the sense of sin, than he is able to convert himself, and turn the proposals of the word into gracious affections in his heart. To restore the joy of salvation, is, in David's judgment, an act of sovereign power, equal to that of creating a clean heart (Ps. li. 10, 12). Alas! it is a state like to that of death; as infinite power can only raise from natural death, so from a spiritual death; also from a comfortless death: "In his favor there is life;" in the want of his favor there is death. The power of God hath so placed light in the sun, that all creatures in the world, all the torches upon earth, kindled together, cannot make it day, if that doth not rise; so all the angels in heaven, and men upon earth, are not competent chirurgeons for a wounded spirit. The cure of our spiritual ulcers, and the pouring in balm, is an act of sovereign creative power: it is more visible in silencing a tempestuous conscience than the power of our Saviour was in the stilling the stormy winds and the roaring waves. As none but infinite power can remove the guilt of sin, so none but infinite power can remove the despairing sense of it.

Thirdly, This power is evident in the preserving grace. As the providence of God is a manifestation of his power in a continued creation, so the preservation of grace is a manifestation of his power in a continued regeneration. To keep a nation under the yoke, is an act of the same power that subdued it. It is this that strengthens men in suffering against the fury of hell (Col. i. 13); it is this that keeps them from falling against the force of hell—the Father's hand (John x. 29). His strength abates and moderates the violence of temptations; his staff sustains his people under them; his might defeats the power of Satan, and bruiseth him under a believer's feet. The counter-workings of indwelling corruption, the reluctances of the flesh against the breathings of the spirit, the fallacy of the senses, and the rovings of the mind, have ability quickly to stifle and extinguish grace, if it were not maintained by that powerful blast that first imbreathed it. No less power is seen in perfecting it, than was in planting it (2 Pet. i 3); no less in fulfilling the work of faith, than in engrafting the word of faith (2 Thess. i. 11). The apostle well understood the necessity and efficacy of it in the preservation of faith,

as well as in the first infusion, when he expresses himself in those
terms of a greatness or hyperbole of power, "His mighty power,"
or the power of his might (Eph. i. 19). The salvation he bestows,
and the strength whereby he effects it, are joined together in the prophet's song (Isa. xii. 2): "The Lord is my strength and my salvation." And indeed, God doth more magnify his power in continuing a believer in the world, a weak and half-rigged vessel, in the
midst of so many sands wheron it might split, so many rocks whereon
it might dash, so many corruptions within, and so many temptations
without, than if he did immediately transport him into heaven, and
clothe him with a perfect sanctified nature.—To conclude, what is
there, then, in the world which is destitute of notices of Divine
power? Every creature affords us the lesson ; all acts of Divine government are the marks of it. Look into the word, and the manner of
its propagation instructs us in it; your changed natures, your pardoned guilt, your shining comfort, your quelled corruptions, the
standing of your staggering graces, are sufficient to preserve a sense,
and to prevent a forgetfulness, of this great attribute, so necessary for
your support, and conducing so much to your comfort.

Use I. Of information and instruction.

Instruct. 1. If incomprehensible and infinite power belongs to the
nature of God, then Jesus Christ hath a divine nature, because the
acts of power proper to God are ascribed to him. This perfection
of omnipotence doth unquestionably pertain to the Deity, and is an
incommunicable property, and the same with the essence of God : he,
therefore, to whom this attribute is ascribed, is essentially God. This
is challenged by Christ, in conjunction with eternity (Rev. i. 8); "I
am Alpha and Omega, the beginning and the ending, saith the Lord,
which is, and which was, and which is to come, the Almighty."
This the Lord Christ speaks of himself. He who was equal with
God, proclaims himself by the essential title of the Godhead, part of
which he repeats again (ver. 11), and this is the person which "walks
in the midst of the seven golden candlesticks," the person that "was
dead and now lives" (ver. 17, 18), which cannot possibly be meant
of the Father, the First Person, who can never come under the denomination of having been dead. Being, therefore, adorned with
the same title, he hath the same Deity; and though his omnipotence
be only positively asserted (ver. 8), yet, his eternity being asserted
(ver. 11, 17), it inferreth his immense power; for he that is eternal,
without limits of time, must needs be conceived powerful, without
any dash of infirmity. Again, when he is said to be a child born,
and a son given, in the same breath he is called the Mighty God
(Isa. ix. 6). It is introduced as a ground of comfort to the church,
to preserve their hopes in the accomplishment of the promises made
to them before. They should not imagine him to have only the
infirmity of a man, though he was veiled in the appearance of a man.
No, they should look through the disguise of his flesh, to the might
of his Godhead. The attribute of mighty is added to the title of
God, because the consideration of power is most capable to sustain
the drooping church in such a condition, and to prop up her hopes.
It is upon this account he saith of himself, " Whatsoever things the

Father doth, those also doth the Son likewise" (John v. 19). In the creation of heaven, earth, sea, and the preservation of all creatures, the Son works with the same will, wisdom, virtue, power, as the Father works: not as two may concur in an action in a different manner, as an agent and an instrument, a carpenter and his tools, but in the same manner of operation, ὁμοίως, which we translate likeness, which doth not express so well the emphasis of the word. There is no diversity of action between us; what the Father doth, that I do by the same power, with the same easiness in every respect; there is the same creative, productive, conservative power in both of us; and that not in one work that is done, *ad extra*, but in all, in whatsoever the Father doth. In the same manner, not by a delegated, but natural and essential power, by one undivided operation and manner of working.

1st. The creation, which is a work of Omnipotence, is more than once ascribed to him. This he doth own himself; the creation of the earth, and of man upon it; the stretching out the heavens by his hands, and the forming of "all the hosts of them by his command" (Isa. xlv. 12). He is not only the Creator of Israel, the church (ver. 12), but of the whole world, and every creature on the face of the earth, and in the glories of the heavens; which is repeated also ver. 18, where, in this act of creation, he is called God himself, and speaks of himself in the term Jehovah; and swears by himself (ver. 23). What doth he swear? "That unto me every knee shall bow, and every tongue shall swear." Is this Christ? Yes, if the apostle may be believed, who applies it to him (Rom. xiv. 11) to prove the appearance of all men before the judgment-seat of Christ, whom the prophet calls (ver. 15) "a God that hides himself;" and so he was a hidden God when obscured in our fleshly infirmities. He was in conjunction with the Father when the sea received his decree, and the foundations of the earth were appointed; not as a spectator, but as an artificer, for so the word in Prov. viii. 30, signifies, " as one brought up with him;" it signifies also, "a cunning workman" (Cant. vii. 1). He was the east, or the sun, from whence sprang all the light of life and being to the creature; so the word קֶדֶם (ver. 22), which is translated, " before his works of old," is rendered by some, and signifies the east as well as before: but if it notes only his existence before, it is enough to prove his Deity. The Scripture doth not only allow him an existence before the world, but exalts him as the cause of the world: a thing may precede another that is not the cause of that which follows; a precedency in age doth not entitle one brother, or thing, the cause of another: but our Saviour is not only ancienter than the world, but is the Creator of the world (Heb. i. 10, 11). " Who laid the foundations of the earth, and the heavens are the work of his hands." So great an eulogy cannot be given to one destitute of omnipotence; since the distance between being and not being is so vast a gulf that cannot be surmounded and stepped over, but by an Infinite Power: he is the first and the last, that called the " generations from the beginning" (Isa. xli. 4), and had an almighty voice to call them out of nothing. In which regard he is called the " everlasting Father" (Isa. ix. 6), as being the efficient of creation; as God is called the Father of the rain, or as father is taken for the inventor of an art; as Jubal, the first framer and inventor of music, is called "the father of such as handle the harp" (Gen. iv. 21). And that Person is said to "make the sea, and form the dry land by his hands" (Ps. xcv. 5, 6) against whom we are exhorted not to harden our hearts, which is applied to Christ by the apostle (Heb. iii. 8); in ver. 6, he is called " a great King," and a great God our Maker." The places wherein the creation is attributed to Christ, those that are the antagonists of his Deity, would evade by understanding them of the new, or evangelical, not of the first, old material creation : but what appearance is there for such a sense? Consider,

(1.) That of Heb. i. 10, 11, it is spoken of that earth and heavens which were in the beginning of time; it is that earth shall perish, that heaven that shall be folded up, that creation that shall grow old towards a decay; that is, only the visible and material creation : the spiritual shall endure forever; it grows not old to decay, but grows up to a perfection; it sprouts up to its happiness, not to its detriment. The same Person creates that shall destroy, and the same world is created by him that shall be destroyed by him, as well as it subsisted by virtue of his omnipotency.

(2.) Can that also (Heb. i. 2), " By whom also he made the worlds," speaking of Christ, bear the same plea? It was the same Person by whom "God spake to us in these last times," the same Person which he hath constituted " Heir of all things, by whom also he made the worlds:" and the particle *also*, intimates it to be a distinct act from his speaking or prophetical office, whereby he restored and new created the world, as well as the rightful foundation God had to make him "Heir of all things." It refers likewise, not to the time of Christ's speaking upon earth, but to something past, and something different from the publication of the gospel: it is not " doth make," which had been more likely if the apostle had meant only the new creation; but " hath made,"q referring to time long since past, something done before his appearance upon earth as a Prophet: " By whom also he made the worlds," or ages, all things subjected to, or measured by time; which must be meant according to the Jewish phrase of this material visible world: so they entitle God in their Liturgy, the " Lord of Ages," that is, the Lord of the world, and all ages and revolutions of the world, from the creation to the last period of time. If anything were in being before this frame of heaven and earth, and within the compass of time, it received being and duration from the Son of God. The apostle would give an argument to prove the equity of making him Heir of all things as Mediator, because he was the framer of all things as God. He may well be the Heir or Lord of angels as well as men, who created angels as well as men: all things were justly under his power as Mediator, since they derived their existence from him as Creator.

(3.) But what evasion can there be for that (Col. i. 16)? " By him were all things created that are in heaven and that are in earth, whether they be thrones, or dominions, or principalities, or powers,

q ἐποίσεν.

all things were created by him and for him." He is said to be the
Creator of material and visible things, as well as spiritual and invisible; of things in heaven, which needed no restoration, as well as
things on earth, which were polluted by sin, and stood in need of a
new creation. How could the angels belong to the new creation,
who had never put off the honor and purity of the first? Since they
never divested themselves of their original integrity, they could not
be reinvested with that which they never lost. Besides, suppose the
holy angels be one way or other reduced as parts of the new creation, as being under the mediatory government of our Saviour, as
their Head, and in regard of their confirmation by him in that happy
state. In what manner shall the devils be ranked among new creatures? They are called principalities and powers as well as the
angels, and may come under the title of things invisible: that they
are called principalities and powers is plain (Eph. vi. 12): "For we
wrestle not against flesh and blood, but against principalities and
powers, and the rulers of the darkness of this world; against spiritual
wickedness in high places." Good angels are not there meant, for
what war have believers with them, or they with believers? They
are the guardians of them, since Christ hath taken away the enmity
between our Lord and theirs, in whose quarrel they were engaged
against us: and since the apostle, speaking of "all things created by
him," expresseth it so, that it cannot be conceived he should except
anything; how come the finally impenitent and unbelievers, which
are things in earth, and visible, to be listed here in the roll of new
creatures? None of these can be called new creatures, because they
are subjected to the government of Christ; no more than the earth
and sea, and the animals in it, are made new creatures, because they
are all under the dominion of Christ and his providential government. Again, the apostle manifestly makes the creation he here
speaks of, to be the material, and not the new creation; for that he
speaks of afterwards as a distinct act of our Lord Jesus, under the
title of Reconciliation (Col. i. 20, 21), which was the restoration of
the world, and the satisfying for that curse that lay upon it. His
intent is here to show that not an angel in heaven, nor a creature
upon earth, but was placed in their several degrees of excellency by
the power of the Son of God, who, after that act of creation, and the
entrance of sin, was the "reconciler" of the world through the blood
of his cross.

(4.) There is another place as clear (John i. 3): "All things were
made by him, and without him was nothing made that was made."
The creation is here ascribed to him; affirmatively, "All things
were made by him;" negatively, there was nothing made without
him: and the words are emphatical, οὐδὲ ἕν, not one thing; except-
ing nothing; including invisible things, as well as things conspicuous to sense only, mentioned in the story of the creation (Gen. i.);
not only the entire mass, but the distinct parcels, the smallest worm
and the highest angel, owe their original to him. And if not *one*
thing, then the matter was not created to his hands; and his work
consisted not only in the forming things from that matter: if that
one thing of matter were excepted, a chief thing were excepted; if

not one thing were excepted, then he created something of nothing, because spirits, as angels and souls, are not made of any pre-existing or fore-created matter. How could the evangelist phrase it more extensively and comprehensively? This is a character of Omnipotency; to create the world, and everything in it, of nothing, requires an infinite virtue and power. If all things were created by Him, they were not created by him as man, because himself, as man, was not in being before the creation; if all things were made by him, then himself was not made, himself was not created; and to be existent without being made, without being created, is to be unboundedly omnipotent. And if we understand it of the new creation, as they do that will not allow him an existence in his Deity before his humanity, it cannot be true of that; for how could he regenerate Abraham, make Simeon and Anna new creatures, who "waited for the salvation of Israel," and form John Baptist, and fill him with the Holy Ghost, even from the womb (Luke i. 15), who belonged to the new creation, and was to prepare the way, if Christ had not a being before him? The evangelist alludes to, and explains the history of the creation, in the beginning, and acquaints us what was meant by God, said so often, *viz.* the eternal Word, and describes him in his creative power, manifested in the framing the world, before he describes him in his incarnation, when he came to lay the foundation of the restoration of the world (John i. 14), "The Word was made flesh;" this Word who was "with God, who was God, who made all things," and gave being to the most glorious angels and the meanest creature without exception; this Word, in time, "was made flesh."

(5.) The creation of things mentioned in these Scriptures cannot be attributed to him as an instrument. As if when it is said, "God created all things by him, and by him made the worlds," we were to understand the Father to be the agent, and the Son to be a tool in his Father's hand, as an axe in the hand of a carpenter, or a file in the hand of a smith, or a servant acting by command as the organ of his master. The preposition *per,* or δια, doth not always signify an instrumental cause: when it is said, that the apostle gave the Thessalonians a command "by Jesus Christ" (1 Thess. iv. 2), was Christ the instrument, and not the Lord of that command the apostle gave? The immediate operation of Christ dwelling in the apostles, was that whereby they gave the commands to their disciples. When we are called "by God" (1 Cor. i. 9), is he the instrumental, or principal cause of our effectual vocation? And can the will of God be the instrument of putting Paul into the apostleship, or the sovereign cause of investing him with that dignity, when he calls himself an "Apostle by the will of God" (Eph. i. 3)? And when all things are said to be through God, as well as of him, must he be counted the instrumental cause of his own creation, counsels, and judgments (Rom. xi. 36)? When we "mortify the deeds of the body through the Spirit (Rom. viii. 13), or keep the "treasure of the word by the Holy Ghost" (2 Tim. i. 14), is the Holy Ghost of no more dignity in such acts than an instrument? Nor doth the gaining a thing by a person make him a mere instrument or inferior; as when a man gains his right in a way of justice against his adversary by the magistrate, is the judge inferior to the suppliant? If the Word were an instrument in creation, it must be a created or uncreated instrument: if created, it could not be true what the Evangelist saith, that "all things were made by him,' since himself, the principal thing, could not be made by himself: if uncreated, he was God, and so acted by a Divine omnipotency, which surmounts an instrumental cause. But, indeed, an instrument is impossible in creation, since it is wrought only by an act of the Divine will. Do we need any organ to an act of volition? The efficacious will of the Creator is the cause of the original of the body of the world, with its particular members and exact harmony. It was formed "by a word, and established by a command" (Ps. xxxiii. 9); the beauty of the creation stood up at the precept of his will. Nor was the Son a partial cause; as when many are said to build a house, one works one part, and another frames another part: God created all things by the immediate operation of the Son, in the unity of essence, goodness, power, wisdom; not an extrinsic, but a connatural instrument. As the sun doth illustrate all things by his light, and quickens all things by his heat, so God created the worlds by Christ, as he was the "brightness or splendor of his glory, the exact image of his person;" which follows the declaration of his making the worlds by him (Heb. i. 3, 4), to show, that he acted not as an instrument, but one in essential conjunction with him, as light and brightness with the sun. But suppose he did make the world as a kind of instrument, he was then before the world, not bounded by time; and eternity cannot well be conceived belonging to a Being without omnipotency. He is the End, as well as the Author, of the creatures (Col. i. 16); not only the principle which gave them being, but the sea, into whose glory they run and dissolve themselves, which consists not with the meanness of an instrument.

2d. As creation, so preservation, is ascribed to Him (Col. i. 17). "By him all things consist." As he preceded all things in his eternity, so he establishes all things by his omnipotency, and fixes them in their several centres, that they sink not into that nothing from whence he fetched them. By him they flourish in their several beings, and observe the laws and orders he first appointed: that power of his which extracted them from insensible nothing, upholds them in their several beings with the same facility as he spake being into them, even "by the word of his power" (Heb. i. 3), and by one creative continued voice, called all generations, from the beginning to the period of the world (Isa. xli. 4), and causes them to flourish in their several seasons. It is "by him kings reign, and princes decree justice," and all things are confined within the limits of government. All which are acts of an Infinite Power.

3d. Resurrection is also ascribed to Him. The body crumbled to dust, and that dust blown to several quarters of the world, cannot be gathered in its distinct parts, and new formed for the entertainment of the soul, without the strength of an infinite arm. This he will do, and more; change the vileness of an earthly body into the glory of an heavenly one; a dusty flesh into a spiritual body, which is an argument of a power invincible, to which all things cannot but stoop;

for it is by such an operation, which testifies an ability " to subdue all things to himself" (Phil. iii. 21), especially when he works it with the same ease as he did the creation, by the power of his voice. (John v. 28), " All that are in the graves shall hear his voice, and shall come forth:" speaking them into a restored life from insensible dust, as he did into being from an empty nothing. The greatest acts of power are owned to belong to creation, preservation, resurrection. Omnipotence, therefore, is his right; and, therefore, a Deity cannot be denied to him that inherits a perfection essential to none but God, and impossible to be entrusted in, or managed by the hands of any creatures. And this is no mean comfort to those that believe in him: he is, in regard of his power, " the horn of salvation;" so Zacharias sings of him (Luke i. 69). Nor could there be any more mighty found out upon whom God could have " laid our help" (Ps. lxxxix. 19). No reason, therefore, to doubt his ability to save to the utmost, who hath the power of creation, preservation, and resurrection in his hands. His promises must be accomplished, since nothing can resist him: he hath power to fulfil his word, and bring all things to a final issue, because he is Almighty: by his outstretched arm in the deliverance of his Israel from Egypt, (for it was his arm, 1 Cor. x.) he showed that he was able to deliver us from spiritual Egypt. The charge of Mediator to expiate sin, vanquish hell, form a church, conduct and perfect it, are not to be effected by a person of less ability than infinite. Let this almightiness of His be the bottom, wherein to cast and fix the anchor of our hopes.

Instruct. 2. Hence may be inferred the Deity of the Holy Ghost. Works of omnipotency are ascribed to the Spirit of God: by the motion of the wings of this Spirit, as a bird over her eggs, was that rude and unshapen mass hatched into a comely world.[r] The stars, —or perhaps the angels, are meant by the "garnishing of the heavens" in the verse before the text,—were brought forth in their comeliness and dignity, as the ornaments of the upper world, by this Spirit; " By his Spirit he hath garnished the heavens." To this Spirit Job ascribes the formation both of the body and soul, under the title of Almighty (Job xxxiii. 4), " The Spirit of God hath made me, and the breath of the Almighty hath given me life." Resurrection, another work of omnipotency, is attributed to him (Rom. viii. 11). The conception of our Saviour in the womb; the miracles that he wrought, were by the power of the Spirit in him. Power is a title belonging to him, and sometimes both are put together (1 Thess. i. 5, and other places). And that great power of changing the heart, and sanctifying a polluted nature, a work greater than creation, is frequently acknowledged in the Scripture to be the peculiar act of the Holy Ghost. The Father, Son, Spirit, are one principle in creation, resurrection, and all the works of omnipotence.

Instruct. 3. Inference from the doctrine. The blessedness of God is hence evidenced. If God be Almighty, he can want nothing; all want speaks weakness. If he doth what he will, he cannot be miserable; all misery consists in those things which happen contrary to our will. There is nothing can hinder his happiness, because no-

r Gen. i. 2. So the word "moved" properly signifies.

thing can resist his power. Since he is omnipotent, nothing can hurt him, nothing can strip him of what he hath, of what he is.[s] If he can do whatsoever he will, he cannot want anything that he wills. He is as happy, as great, as glorious, as he will; for he hath a perfect liberty of will to will, and a perfect power to attain what he will; his will cannot be restrained, nor his power meted. It would be a defect in blessedness, to will what he were not able to do: sorrow is the result of a want of power, with a presence of will. If he could will anything which he could not effect, he would be miserable, and no longer God: he can do whatsoever he pleases, and therefore can want nothing that pleases him.[t] He cannot be happy, the original of whose happiness is not in himself: nothing can be infinitely happy, that is limited and bounded.

Instruct. 4. Hence is the ground for the immutability of God. As he is incapable of changing his resolves, because of his infinite wisdom, so he is incapable of being forced to any change, because of his infinite power. Being almighty, he can be no more changed from power to weakness; than, being all-wise, he can be changed from wisdom to folly; or, being omniscient, from knowledge to ignorance. He cannot be altered in his purposes, because of his wisdom; nor in the manner and method of his actions, because of his infinite strength. Men, indeed, when their designs are laid deepest, and their purposes stand firmest, yet are forced to stand still, or change the manner of the execution of their resolves, by reason of some outward accidents that obstruct them in their course; for, having not wisdom to foresee future hindrances, they have not power to prevent them, or strength to remove them, when they unexpectedly interpose themselves between their desire and performance; but no created power has strength enough to be a bar against God. By the same act of his will that he resolves a thing, he can puff away any impediments that seem to rise up against him. He that wants no means to effect his purposes, cannot be checked by anything that riseth up to stand in his way; heaven, earth, sea, the deepest places, are too weak to resist his will (Ps. cxxxv. 6). The purity of the angels will not, and the devil's malice cannot, frustrate his will; the one voluntarily obeys the beck of his hand, and the other is vanquished by the power of it. What can make him change his purposes; who (if he please) can dash the earth against the heavens in the twinkling of an eye, untying the world from its centre, clap the stars and elements together into one mass, and blow the whole creation of men and devils into nothing? Because he is almighty, therefore he is immutable.

Instruct. 5. Hence is inferred the providence of God, and his government of the world. His power, as well as his wisdom, gives him a right to govern: nothing can equal him, therefore nothing can share the command with him; since all things are his works, it is fittest they should be under his order: he that frames a work, is fittest to guide and govern it. God hath the most right to govern, because he hath knowledge to direct his power, and power to execute the results of his wisdom: he knows what is convenient to or-

* Sabunde, Tit. 39.   t Pont. Part VI. med. 16. p. 531.

der, and hath strength to effect what he orders. As his power would be oppressive without goodness and wisdom, so his goodness and wisdom would be fruitless without power. An artificer that hath lost his hands may direct, but cannot make an engine : a pilot that hath lost his arms may advise the way of steerage, but cannot hold the helm; something is wanting in him to be a complete governor : but since both counsel and power are infinite in God, hence results an infinite right to govern, and an infinite fitness, because his will cannot be resisted, his power cannot be enfeebled or diminished; he can quicken and increase the strength of all means as he pleases. He can hold all things in the world together, and preserve them in those functions wherein he settled them, and conduct them to those ends for which he designed them. Every artificer, the more excellent he is, and the more excellency of power appears in his work, is the more careful to maintain and cherish it. Those that deny Providence, do not only ravish from him the bowels of his goodness, but strip him of a main exercise of his power, and engender in men a suspicion of weariness and feebleness in him; as though his strength had been spent in making them, that none is left to guide them. They would make him headless in regard of his wisdom, and bowelless in regard of his goodness, and armless in regard of his strength. If he did not, or were not able to preserve and provide for his creatures, his power in making them would be, in a great part, an invisible power; if he did not preserve what he made, and govern what he preserves, it would be a kind of strange and rude power, to make, and suffer it to be dashed in pieces at the pleasure of others. If the power of God should relinquish the world, the life of things would be extinguished, the fabric would be confounded, and fall into a deplorable chaos. That which is composed of so many various pieces, could not maintain its union, if there were not a secret virtue binding them together and maintaining those varieties of links. Well, then, since God is not only so good, that he cannot will anything but what is good; so wise, that he cannot err or mistake; but also so able, that he cannot be defeated or mated; he hath every way a full ability to govern the world: where those three are infinite, the right and fitness resulting from thence is unquestionable : and, indeed, to deny God this active part of his power, is to render him weak, foolish, cruel, or all.

Instruct. 6. Here is a ground for the worship of God. Wisdom and power are the grounds of the respect we give to men; they being both infinite in God, are the foundation of a solemn honor to be returned to him by his creatures. If a man makes a curious engine, we honor him for his skill; if another vanquish a vigorous enemy, we admire him for his strength: and shall not the efficacy of God's power in creation, government, redemption, enflame us with a sense of the honor of his name and perfections? We admire those princes that have vast empires, numerous armies, that have a power to conquer their enemies, and preserve their own people in peace. How much more ground have we to pay a mighty reverence to God, who, without trouble and weariness, made and manages this vast empire of the world by a word and beck! What sensible thoughts have we of the noise of thunder, the power of the sun, the storms of the sea! These things that have no understanding have struck men with such a reverence, that many have adored them as gods. What reverence and adoration doth this mighty power, joined with an infinite wisdom in God, demand at our hands! All religion and worship stands especially upon two pillars, goodness, and power in God; if either of these were defective, all religion would faint away. We can expect no entertainment with him without goodness, nor any benefit from him without power. This God prefaceth to the command to worship him, the benefit his goodness had conferred upon them, and the powerful manner of conveyance of it to them (2 Kings xvii. 36): "The Lord brought you up from the land of Egypt with great power, and an out-stretched arm; him shall you fear, and him shall you worship, and to him shall you do sacrifice. Because this attribute is a main foundation of prayer, the Lord's Prayer is concluded with a doxology of it, "For thine is the kingdom, the power, and the glory." As he is rich, possessing all blessings; so he is powerful, to confer all blessings on us, and make them efficacious to us. The Jews repeat many times in their prayers, some say an hundred times, מלך העולם, "The King of the world;" it is both an awe and an encouragement.[u] We could not, without consideration of it, pray in faith of success; nay, we could not pray at all, if his power were defective to help us, and his mercy too weak to relieve us. Who would solicit a lifeless, or lie a prostrate suppliant, to a feeble arm? Upon this ability of God, our Saviour built his petitions (Heb. v. 7): "He offered up strong cries unto Him that was able to save him from death." Abraham's faith hung upon the same string (Rom. iv. 21), and the captived church supplicates God to act according to the greatness of his power (Ps. lxxix. 11). In all our addresses this is to be eyed and considered; God is able to help, to relieve, to ease me, let my misery be never so great, and my strength never so weak (Matt. viii. 2): "If thou wilt, thou canst make me clean, was the consideration the leper had when he came to worship Christ; he was clear in his power, and therefore worshipped him, though he was not equally clear in his will. All worship is shot wrong that is not directed to, and conducted by, the thoughts of this attribute, whose assistance we need. When we beg the pardon of our sins, we should eye mercy and power; when we beg his righting us in any case where we are unjustly oppressed, we do not eye righteousness without power; when we plead the performance of his promise, we do not regard his faithfulness only without the prop of his power. As power ushers in all the attributes of God in their exercise and manifestation in the world, so should it be the butt our eyes should be fixed upon in all our acts of worship: as without his power his other attributes would be useless, so without due apprehensions of his power our prayers will be faithless and comfortless. The title in the Lord's prayer directs us to a prospect both of his goodness and power; his goodness in the word Father, his greatness, excellency, and power, in the word Heaven. The heedless consideration of the infiniteness of this per-

[u] Capel. in 1 Tim. i. 17.

fection roots up piety in the midst of us, and makes us so careless in worship. Did we more think of that Power that raised the world out of nothing, that orders all creatures by an act of his will, that performed so great an exploit as that of our redemption, when masterless sin had triumphed over the world, we should give God the honor and adoration which so great an excellency challengeth and deserves at our hands, though we ourselves had not been the work of his hands, or the monuments of his strength; how could any creature engross to itself that reverence from us which is due to the powerful Creator, of whom it comes infinitely short in strength as well as wisdom?

Instruct. 7. From this we have a ground for the belief of the resurrection. God aims at the glory of his power, as well as the glory of any other attribute. Moses else would not have culled out this as the main argument, in his pleading with God, for the sheathing the sword which he began to draw out against them in the wilderness (Numb. xiv. 16): "The nations will say, Because the Lord was not able to bring these people into the land which he sware to them," &c. As the finding out the particulars of the dust of our bodies discovers the vastness of his knowledge, so to raise them will manifest the glory of his power as much as creation; bodies that have mouldered away into multitudes of atoms, been resolved into the elements, passed through varieties of changes, been sometimes the matter to lodge the form of a plant, or been turned into the substance of a fish or fowl, or vapored up into a cloud, and been part of that matter which hath compacted a thunder-bolt, disposed of in places far distant, scattered by the winds, swallowed and concocted by beasts; for these to be called out from their different places of abode, to meet in one body, and be restored to their former consistency, in a marriage union, in the "twinkling of an eye" (1 Cor. xv. 22), it is a consideration that may justly amaze us, and our shallow understandings are too feeble to comprehend it. But is it not credible, since all the disputes against it may be silenced by reflections on Infinite Power, which nothing can oppose, for which nothing can be esteemed too difficult to effect, which doth not imply a contradiction in itself? It was no less amazing to the blessed virgin to hear a message that she should conceive a Son without knowing a man; but she is quickly answered, by the angel, with a "Nothing is impossible to God" (Luke i. 34, 37). The distinct parts off our bodies cannot be hid from his all-seeing eye, wherever they are lodged, and in all the changes they pass through, as was discoursed when the Omniscience of God was handled; shall, then, the collection of them together be too hard for his invincible power and strength, and the uniting all those parts into a body, with new dispositions to receive their several souls, be too big and bulky for that Power which never yet was acquainted with any bar? Was not the miracle of our Saviour's multiplying the loaves, suppose it had not been by a new creation, but a collection of grain from several parts, very near as stupendous as this? Had any one of us been the only creatures made just before the matter of the world, and beheld that inform chaos covered with a thick darkness, mentioned Gen. i. 2, would not the report, that from this dark deep, next to nothing, should be raised such a multitude of comely creatures, with such innumerable varieties of members, voices, colors, motions, and such numbers of shining stars, a bright sun, one uniform body of light from this darkness, that should, like a giant, rejoice to run a race, for many thousands of years together, without stop or weariness; would not all these have seemed as incredible as the collection of scattered dust? What was it that erected the innumerable host of heaven, the glorious angels, and glittering stars, for aught we know more numerous than the bodies of men, but an act of the Divine will? and shall the power that wrought this sink under the charge of gathering some dispersed atoms, and compacting them into a human body? Can you tell how the dust of the ground was kneaded by God into the body of man, and changed into flesh, skin, hair, bones, sinews, veins, arteries, and blood, and fitted for so many several activities, when a human soul was breathed into it?[x] Can you imagine how a rib, taken from Adam's side, a lifeless bone, was formed into head, hands, feet, eyes? Why may not the matter of men, which have been, be restored, as well as that which was not, be first erected? Is it harder to repair those things which were, than to create those things which were not? Is there not the same Artificer? Hath any disease or sickliness abated his power? Is the Ancient of Days grown feeble? or shall the elements, and other creatures, that alway yet obeyed his command, ruffle against his raising voice, and refuse to disgorge those remains of human bodies they have swallowed up in their several bowels? Did the whole world, and all the parts of it, rise at his word? and shall not some parts of the world, the dust of the dead, stand up out of the graves at a word of the same mighty efficacy? Do we not annually see those marks of power which may stun our incredulity in this concern? Do you see in a small acorn, or little seed, any such sights, as a tree with body, bark, branches, leaves, flowers, fruit—where can you find them? Do you know the invisible corners where they lurk in that little body? And yet these you afterwards view rising up from this little body, when sown in the ground, that you could not possibly have any prospect of when you rolled it in your hand, or opened its bowels. And why may not all the particulars of our bodies, however disposed as to their distinct natures invisibly to us, remain distinct, as well as if you mingle a thousand seeds together? they will come up in their distinct kinds, and preserve their distinct virtues. Again, is not the making heaven and earth, the union of the Divine and human nature, eternity and infirmity, to make a virgin conceive a Son, bear the Creator, and bring forth the Redeemer, to form the blood of God of the flesh of a virgin, a greater work than the calling together and uniting the scattered parts of our bodies, which are all of one nature and matter? And since the power of God is manifested in pardoning innumerable sins, is not the scattering our transgressions, as far as the east is from the west, as the expression is, Ps. ciii. 12, and casting such numbers into the depths of the sea, which is God's power over himself, a greater argument of

[x] Lingend. Tom. III. pp. 779, 780.

might than the recalling and repairing the atoms of our bodies from their various receptacles? It is not hard for them to believe this of the resurrection, that have been sensible of the weight and force of their sins, and the power of God in pardoning and vanquishing that mighty resistance which was made in their hearts against the power of his renewing and sanctifying grace. The consideration of the infinite power of God is a good ground of the belief of the resurrection.

Instruct. 8. Since the power of God is so great and incomprehensible, how strange is it that it should be contemned and abused by the creatures as it is! The power of God is beaten down by some, outraged by others, blasphemed by many, under their sufferings. The stripping God of the honor of his creation, and the glory of his preservation of the world, falls under this charge: thus do they that deny his framing the world alone, or thought the first matter was not of God's creation, and such as fancied an evil principle, the author of all evil, as God is the author of all good, and so exempt from the power of God, that it could not be vanquished by him. These things have formerly found defenders in the world; but they are, in themselves, ridiculous and vain, and have no footing in common reason, and are not worthy of debate in a christian auditory.

In general, all idolatry in the world did arise from the want of a due notion of this Infinite Power. The heathen thought one God was not sufficient for the managing all things in the world, and therefore they feigned several gods, that had several charges; as Ceres presided over the fruits of the earth; Esculapius over the cure of distempers; Mercury for merchandise and trade; Mars for war and battles; Apollo and Minerva for learning and ingenious arts; and Fortune for casual things. Whence doth the other sort of idolatry, the adoring our bags and gold, our dependencies on, and trusting in, creatures for help arise, but from ignorance of God's power, or mean and slender apprehensions of it? First, there is a contempt of it. Secondly, An abuse of it.

1. It is contemned in every sin, especially in obstinacy in sin. All sin whatsoever is built upon some false notion or monstrous conception of one or other of God's perfections, and in particular of this. It includes a secret and lurking imagination, that we are able to grapple with Omnipotence, and enter the lists with Almightiness; what else can be judged of the apostle's expression (1 Cor. x. 22), "Do we provoke the Lord to jealousy; are we stronger than he?" Do we think we have an arm too powerful for that justice we provoke, and can repel that vengeance we exasperate? Do we think we are an even match for God, and are able to despoil him of his Divinity? To despise his will, violate his order, practise what he forbids with a severe threatening, and pawns his power to make it good, is to pretend to have an arm like God, and be able to thunder with a voice equal or superior to him, as the expression is (Job xl. 9). All security in sin is of this strain; when men are not concerned at Divine threatenings, nor staggered in their sinful race, they intimate, that the declarations of Divine Power are but vain-glorious boastings; that God is not so strong and able as he

reports himself to be; and therefore they will venture it, and dare him to try, whether the strength of his arm be as forcible as the words of his mouth are terrible in his threats; this is to believe themselves Creators, not creatures. We magnify God's power in our wants, and debase it in our rebellions; as though Omnipotence were only able to supply our necessities, and unable to revenge the injuries we offer him.

2. This power is contemned in distrust of God. All distrust is founded in a doubting of his truth, as if he would not be as good as his word; or of his omniscience, as if he had not a memory to retain his word; or of his power, as if he could not be as great as his word. We measure the infinite power of God by the short line of our understandings, as if infinite strength were bounded within the narrow compass of our finite reason; as if he could do no more than we were able to do. How soon did those Israelites lose the remembrance of God's outstretched arm, when they uttered that atheistical speech (Ps. lxxviii. 19), "Can God furnish a table in the wilderness?" As if he that turned the dust of Egypt into lice, for the punishment of their oppressors, could not turn the dust of the wilderness into corn, for the support of their bodies! As if he that had miraculously rebuked the Red Sea, for their safety, could not provide bread, for their nourishment! Though they had seen the Egyptians with lost lives in the morning, in the same place where their lives had been miraculously preserved in the evening, yet they disgrace that experimental power, by opposing to it the stature of the Anakims, the strength of their cities, and the height of their walls (Numb. xiii. 32). And (Numb. xiv. 3). "Wherefore hath the Lord brought us into this land to fall by the sword?" As though the giants of Canaan were too strong for Him, for whom they had seen the armies of Egypt too weak. How did they contract the almightiness of God into the littleness of a little man, as if he must needs sink under the sword of a Canaanite? This distrust must arise either from a flat atheism, a denial of the being of God, or his government of the world; or unworthy conceits of a weakness in him, that he had made creatures too hard for himself; that he were not strong enough to grapple with those mighty Anakims, and give them the possession of Canaan against so great a force. Distrust of him implies either that he was always destitute of power, or that his power is exhausted by his former works, or that it is limited, and near a period : it is to deny him to be the Creator that moulded heaven and earth. Why should we, by distrust, put a slight upon that power which he hath so often expressed, and which, in the minutest works of his hands, surmount the force of the sharpest understanding?

3. It is contemned in too great a fear of man, which ariseth from a distrust of Divine power. Fear of man is a crediting the might of man with a disrepute of the arm of God, it takes away the glory of his might, and renders the creature stronger than God; and God more feeble than a mortal; as if the arm of man were a rod of iron, and the arm of God a brittle reed. How often do men tremble at the threatenings and hectorings of ruffians, yet will stand as stakes

against the precepts and threatenings of God, as though he had less
power to preserve us, than enemies had to destroy? With what disdain doth God speak to men infected with this humor (Isa. li. 12, 13)?
"Who art thou, that art afraid of a man that shall die, and the
Son of man that shall be made as grass; and forgettest the Lord
thy Maker, that hath stretched forth the heavens, and laid the foundation of the earth; and hast feared continually every day, because
of the fury of the oppressor?" To fear man that is as grass, that
cannot think a thought without a Divine concourse, that cannot
breathe, but by a Divine power, nor touch a hair without license
first granted from heaven; this is forgetfulness, and consequently a
slight of that Infinite Power, which hath been manifested in founding the earth and garnishing the heavens. All fear of man, in the
way of our duty, doth in some sort thrust out the remembrance,
and discredit the great actions of the Creator. Would not a mighty
prince think it a disparagement to him, if his servant should decline
his command for fear of one of his subjects? and hath not the
great God just cause to think himself disgraced by us, when we deny
him obedience for fear of a creature: as though he had but an
infant ability too feeble to bear us out in duty, and incapable to
balance the strength of an arm of flesh?

4. It is contemned by trusting in ourselves, in means, in man,
more than in God. When in any distress we will try every creature
refuge, before we have recourse to God; and when we apply ourselves to him, we do it with such slight and perfunctory frames,
and with so much despondency, as if we despaired either of his
ability or will to help us; and implore him with cooler affections
than we solicit creatures: or, when in a disease we depend upon
the virtue of the medicine, the ability of the physician, and reflect
not upon that power that endued the medicine with that virtue, and
supports the quality in it, and concurs to the operation of it. When
we depend upon the activity of the means, as if they had power
originally in themselves, and not derivatively; and do not eye the
power of God animating and assisting them. We cannot expect relief from anything with a neglect of God, but we render it in our
thoughts more powerful than God: we acknowledge a greater
fulness in a shallow stream, than in an eternal spring; we do, in
effect, depose the true God, and create to ourselves a new one; we
assert, by such a kind of acting, the creature, if not superior, yet
equal with God, and independent on him. When we trust in our
own strength, without begging his assistance; or boast of our own
strength, without acknowledging his concurrence, as the Assyrian;
"By the strength of my hand have I done this; I have put down
the inhabitants like a valiant man" (Isa. x. 13). It is, as if the axe
should boast itself against him that hews therewith, and thinks
itself more mighty than the arm that wields it (ver. 15), when we
trust in others more than in God. Thus God upbraids those by the
prophet, that sought help from Egypt, telling them (Isa. xxxi. 3),
"The Egyptians were men, and not gods; intimating, that by their
dependence on them, they rendered them gods and not men, and
advanced them from the state of creatures to that of almighty

deities. It is to set a pile of dust, a heap of ashes, above Him that created and preserves the world. To trust in a creature, is to make it as infinite as God; to do that which is impossible in itself to be done. God himself cannot make a creature infinite, for that were to make him God. It is also contemned when we ascribe what we receive to the power of instruments, and not to the power of God. Men, in whatsoever they do for us, are but the tools whereby the Creator works. Is it not a disgrace to the limner to admire his pencil, and not himself; to the artificer, to admire his file and engines, and not his power? "It is not I," saith Paul, "that labor, but the grace, the efficacious grace of God, which is in me." Whatsoever good we do is from him, not from ourselves; to ascribe it to ourselves, or to instruments, is to overlook and contemn his power.

5. Unbelief of the gospel is a contempt and disowning Divine power. This perfection hath been discovered in the conception of Christ, the union of the two natures, his resurrection from the grave, the restoration of the world, and the conversion of men, more than in the creation of the world: then what a disgrace is unbelief to all that power that so severely punished the Jews for the rejecting the gospel: turned so many nations from their beloved superstitions; humbled the power of princes and the wisdom of philosophers; chased devils from their temples by the weakness of fishermen; planted the standard of the gospel against the common notions and inveterate customs of the world! What a disgrace is unbelief to this power which hath preserved Christianity from being extinguished by the force of men and devils, and kept it flourishing in the midst of sword, fire, and executioners; that hath made the simplicity of the gospel overpower the eloquence of orators, and multiplied it from the ashes of martyrs, when it was destitute of all human assistances! Not heartily to believe and embrace that doctrine, which hath been attended with such marks of power, is a high reflection upon this Divine perfection, so highly manifested in the first publication, propagation, and preservation of it.

Secondly, The power of God is abused, as well as contemned. 1. When we make use of it to justify contradictions. The doctrine of transubstantiation is an abuse of this power. When the maintainers of it cannot answer the absurdities alleged against it, they have recourse to the power of God. It implies a contradiction, that the same body should be on earth and in heaven at the same instant of time; that it should be at the right hand of God, and in the mouth and stomach of a man; that it should be a body of flesh, and yet bread to the eye and to the taste; that it should be visible and invisible, a glorious body, and yet gnawn by the teeth of a creature; that it should be multiplied in a thousand places, and yet an entire body in every one, where there is no member to be seen, no flesh to be tasted; that it should be above us in the highest heavens, and yet within us in our lower bowels; such contradictions as these are an abuse of the power of God. Again, we abuse this power when we believe every idle story that is reported, because God is able to make it so if he pleased. We may as well believe Æsop's Fables to be true, that birds spake, and beasts reasoned, because the power of

God can enable such creatures to such acts. God's power is not the rule of our belief of a thing without the exercise of it in matter of fact, and the declaration of it upon sufficient evidence.

2. The power of God is abused by presuming on it, without using the means he hath appointed. When men sit with folded arms, and make a confidence in his power a glorious title to their idleness and disobedience, they would have his strength do all, and his precept should move them to do nothing ; this is a trust of his power against his command, a pretended glorifying his power with a slight of his sovereignty. Though God be almighty, yet, for the most part, he exerciseth his might in giving life and success to second causes and lawful endeavors. When we stay in the mouth of danger, without any call ordering us to continue, and against a door of providence opened for our rescue, and sanctuary ourselves in the power of God without any promise, without any providence conducting us ; this is not to glorify the Divine might, but to neglect it, in neglecting the means which his power affords to us for our escape ; to condemn it to our humors, to work miracles for us according to our wills, and against his own.ʸ God could have sent a worm to be Herod's executioner when he sought the life of our Saviour, or employed an angel from heaven to have tied his hands or stopped his breath, and not put Joseph upon a flight to Egypt with our Saviour ; yet had it not been an abuse of the power of God, for Joseph to have neglected the precept, and slighted the means God gave him for the preserving his own life and that of the child's ? Christ himself, when the Jews consulted to destroy him, presumed not upon the power of God to secure him, but used ordinary means for his preservation, by walking no more openly, but retiring himself into a city near the wilderness till the hour was come, and the call of his Father manifest" (John xi. 53, 54). A rash running upon danger, though for the truth itself, is a presuming upon, and consequently an abuse of, this power ; a proud challenging it to serve our turns against the authority of his will, and the force of his precept ; a not resting in his ordinate power, but demanding his absolute power to pleasure our follies and presumptions ; concluding and expecting more from it than what is authorized by his will.

Instruct. 9. If infinite power be a peculiar property of God, how miserable will all wicked rebels be under this power of God ! Men may break his laws, but not impair his arm ; they may slight his word, but cannot resist his power. If he swear that he will sweep a place with the besom of destruction, " as he hath thought, so shall it come to pass ; and as he hath purposed, so shall it stand," (Isa. xiv. 23, 24). Rebels against an earthly prince may exceed him in strength, and be more powerful than their sovereign ; none can equal God, much less exceed him. As none can exercise an act of hostility against him without his permissive will, so none can struggle from under his hand without his positive will. He hath an arm not to be moved, a hand not to be wrung aside. God is represented on his throne like a " jasper stone" (Rev. iv. 3), as one of invincible power when he comes to judge ; the jasper is a stone which withstands the greatest force.[z] Though men resist the order of his laws, they cannot the sentence of their punishment, nor the execution of it. None can any more exempt themselves from the arm of his strength, than they can from the authority of his dominion. As they must bow to his sovereignty, so must they sink under his force. A prisoner in this world may make his escape, but a prisoner in the world to come cannot (Job x. 7). " There is none that can deliver out of thine hand." There is none to deliver when he tears in pieces" (Ps. l. 22). His strength is uncontrollable; hence his throne his represented as a "fiery flame" (Dan. vii. 9). As a spark of fire hath power to kindle one thing after another, and increase till it consumes a forest, a city, swallow up all combustible matter till it consumes a world, and many worlds, if they were in being, what power hath the tree to resist the fire, though it seems mighty, when it outbraves the winds? What man, to this day, hath been able to free himself from that chain of death God clapped upon him for his revolt? And if he be too feeble to rescue himself from a temporal, much less from an eternal death. The devils have, to this minute, groaned under the pile of wrath, without any success in delivering themselves by all their strength, which much surmounts all the strength of mankind, nor have they any hopes to work their rescue to eternity. How foolish is every sinner! Can we poor worms strut it out against Infinite Power? We cannot resist the meanest creatures when God commissions them, and puts a sword into their hands. They will not, no, not the worms, be startled at the glory of a king, when they have the Creator's warrant to be his executioners (Acts xii. 23). Who can withstand him, when he commands the waves and inundations of the sea to leap over the shore; when he divides the ground in earthquakes, and makes it gape wide to swallow the inhabitants of it; when the air is corrupted to breed pestilences; when storms and showers, unseasonably falling, putrify the fruits of the earth; what created power can mend the matter, and, with a prevailing voice, say to him, What dost thou? There are two attributes God will make glister in hell to the full; his wrath and his power (Rom. ix. 22): "What if God, willing to show his wrath, and to make his power known, endured with much long suffering the vessels of wrath fitted for destruction?" If it were mere wrath, and no power to second it, it were not so terrible; but it is wrath and power: both are joined together. It is not only a sharp sword, but a powerful arm; and not only that, for then it were well for the damned creature. To have many sharp blows, and from a strong arm, this may be without putting forth the highest strength a man hath; but in this God makes it his design to make his power known and conspicuous; he takes the sword, as it were, in both hands, that he may show the strength of his arm in striking the harder blow; and therefore the apostles calls it (2 Thess. i. 9) "the glory of his power," which puts a sting into his wrath; and it is called (Rev. xix. 15) "the fierceness of the wrath of the Almighty." God will do it in such a manner as to make men sensible of his almightiness in every stroke.

[z] Grot. *in loc.*

How great must that vengeance be, that is backed by all the strength of God! When there will be a powerful wrath, without a powerful compassion; when all his power shall be exercised in punishing, and not the least mite of it exercised in pitying; how irresistible will be the load of such a weighty hand! How can the dust of the balance break the mighty bars, or get out of the lists of a powerful vengeance, or hope for any grain of comfort? O, that every obstinate sinner would think of this, and consider his unmeasurable boldness in thinking himself able to grapple with Omnipotence! What force can any have to resist the presence of Him, before whom rocks melt, and the heavens, at length, shall be shrivelled up as a parchment by the last fire! As the light of God's face is too dazzling to be beheld by us, so the arm of his power is too mighty to be opposed by us. His almightiness is above the reach of our potsherd strength, as his infiniteness is above the capacity of our purblind understanding. God were not omnipotent, if his power could be rendered ineffectual by any.

Use II. A second use of this point, from the consideration of the infinite power of God, is of comfort. As Omnipotence is an ocean that cannot be fathomed, so the comforts from it are streams that cannot be exhausted. What joy can be wanting to him that finds himself folded in the arms of Omnipotence? This perfection is made over to believers in the covenant, as well as any other attribute; "I am the Lord, your God;" therefore, that power, which is as essential to the Godhead as any other perfection of his nature, is, in the rights and extent of it, assured unto you. Nay, may we not say, it is made over more than any other, because it is that which animates every other perfection; and is the Spirit that gives them motion and appearance in the world. If God had expressed himself in particular, as, "I am a true God, a wise God, a loving God, a righteous God, I am yours;" what would all, or any of those, have signified, unless the other also had been implied, as, "I am an almighty God, I am your God?" In God's making over himself in any particular attribute, this of his power is included in every one, without which, all his other grants would be insignificant. It is a comfort that power is in the hands of God; it can never be better placed, for he can never use his power to injure his confiding creature; if it were in our own hands, we might use it to injure ourselves. It is a power in the hands of an indulgent Father, not a hard-hearted tyrant; it is a just power; "His right hand is full of righteousness" (Ps. xlviii. 10); because of his righteousness he can never use it ill, and because of his wisdom he can never use it unseasonably. Men that have strength, often misplace the actings of it, because of their folly; and sometimes employ it to base ends, because of their wickedness; but this power in God is always awakened by goodness, and conducted by wisdom; it is never exercised by self-will and passion, but according to the immutable rule of his own nature, which is righteousness. How comfortable is it to think, that you have a God that can do what he pleases; nothing so difficult but he can effect, nothing so strong but he can overrule! You need not dread men, since you have One to restrain them; nor fear devils, since you have One to chain them; no creature but is acted by this power; no creature but must fall upon the withdrawing of this power. It was not all laid out in creation; it is not weakened by his preservation of things; he yet hath a fullness of power, and a residue of Spirit; for whom should that eternal arm of the Lord be displayed, and that incomprehensible thunder of his power be shot out, but for those for whose sake and for whose comfort it is revealed in his word? In particular,

1. Here is comfort in all afflictions and distresses. Our evils can never be so great to oppress us, as his power is great to deliver us. The same power that brought a world out of a chaos, and constituted, and hath hitherto preserved, the regular motion of the stars, can bring order out of our confusions, and light out of our darkness. When our Saviour was in the greatest distress, and beheld the face of his Father frowning, while he was upon the cross, in his complaint to him, he exerciseth faith upon his power (Matt. xxvii. 46): "Eli, Eli: My God, my God, why hast thou forsaken me?" that this, My strong, my strong; El, is a name of power, belonging to God; he comforts himself in his power, while he complains of his frowns. Follow his pattern, and forget not that power that can scatter the clouds, as well as gather them together. The Psalmist's support in his distress, was in the creative power of God (Ps. cxxi. 2): "My help comes from the Lord, which made heaven and earth."

2. It is comfort in all strong and stirring corruptions and mighty temptations. It is by this we may arm ourselves, and "be strong in the power of his might" (Eph. vi. 10); by this we may conquer principalities and powers, as dreadful as hell, but not so mighty as heaven; by this we may triumph over lusts within, too strong for an arm of flesh; by this the devils that have possessed us may be cast out; the battered walls of our souls may be repaired; and the sons of Anak laid flat. That power that brought light out of darkness, and overmastered the deformity of the chaos, and set bounds to the ocean, and dried up the Red Sea by a rebuke, can quell the tumults in our spirits, and level spiritual Goliahs by his word. When the disciples heard that terrifying speech of our Saviour, concerning rich men, that it was "easier for a camel to go through the eye of a needle, than for a rich man to enter into the kingdom of God" (Matt. xix. 24), to entertain the gospel, which commanded self-denial; and that, because of the allurements of the world, and the strong habits in their soul; Christ refers them to the power of God (ver. 26), who could expel those ill habits, and plant good ones: "With men this is impossible, but with God all things are possible." There is no resistance, but he can surmount; no strong-hold, but he can demolish; no tower, but he can level.

3. It is comfort from hence, that all promises shall be performed. Goodness is sufficient to make a promise, but power is necessary to perform a promise. Men that are honest, cannot often make good their words, because something may intervene that may shorten their ability: but nothing can disable God, without diminishing his godhead. He hath an infiniteness of power to accomplish his word, as well as an infiniteness of goodness to make and utter his word.

That might whereby he made heaven and earth, and his keeping truth forever, are joined together (Ps. cxlvi. 5, 6); his Father's faithfulness, and his creative power are linked together. It is upon this basis the covenant, and every part of it, is established, and stands as firm as the almightiness of God, whereby he sprung up the earth, and reared the heavens. "No power can resist his will" (Rom. ix. 19); "Who can disannul his purpose, and turn back his hand when it is stretched out" (Isa. xiv. 27)? His word is unalterable, and his power is invincible. He could not deceive himself, for he knew his own strength when he promised: no unexpected event can change his resolution, because nothing can happen without the compass of his foresight. No created strength can stop him in his action, because all creatures are ready to serve him at his command; not the devils in hell, nor all the wicked men on earth, since he hath strength to restrain them, and an arm to punish them. What can be too hard for Him that created heaven and earth? Hence it was, that when God promised anything anciently to his people, he used often the name of the Almighty, the Lord that created heaven and earth, as that which was an undeniable answer to any objection, against anything that might be made against the greatness and stupendousness of any promise; by that name, in all his works of grace, was he known to them (Exod. vi. 3). When we are sure of his will, we need not question his strength, since he never over-engaged himself above his ability. He that could not be resisted by anything in creation, nor vanquished by devils in redemption, can never want power to glorify his faithfulness in his accomplishment of whatsoever he hath promised.

4. From this infiniteness of power in God, we have ground of assurance for perseverance. Since conversion is resembled to the works of creation and resurrection, two great marks of his strength, he doth not surely employ himself in the first of changing the heart, to let any created strength baffle that power which he began and intends to glorify. It was this might that struck off the chain, and expelled that strong one that possessed you. What, if you are too weak to keep him out of his lost possession, will God lose the glory of his first strength, by suffering his foiled adversary to make a re-entry, and regain his former usurpation? His out-stretched arm will not do less by his spiritual, than it did by his national Israel: it guarded them all the way to Canaan, and left them not to shift for themselves after he had struck off the fetters of Egypt, and buried their enemies in the Red Sea (Deut. i. 31). This greatness of the Father, above all, our Saviour makes the ground of believers' continuance forever, against the blasts of hell and engines of the world (John x. 29). "My Father is greater than all, and none is able to pluck them out of my Father's hands." Our keeping is not in our own weak hands, but in the hands of Him who is mighty to save. That power of God keeps us which intends our salvation. In all fears of falling away, shelter yourselves in the power of God: "He shall be holden up," saith the apostle, speaking concerning one weak in faith; and no other reason is rendered by him but this, "For God is able to make him to stand" (Rom. xiv. 4).

5. From this attribute of the infinite power of God, we have a ground of comfort in the lowest estate of the church. Let the state of the church be never so deplorable, the condition never so desperate, that Power that created the world, and shall raise the bodies of men, can create a happy state for the church, and raise her from an overwhelming grave; though the enemies trample upon her, they cannot upon the arm that holds her, which by the least motion of it, can lift her up above the heads of her adversaries, and make them feel the thunder of that Power that none can understand: by the " blast of God they perish, and by the breath of his nostrils they are consumed" (Job iv. 9); they "shall be scattered as chaff before the wind." If once he "draw his hand out of his bosom," all must fly before him, or sink under him (Ps. lxxiv. 11): and when there is " none to help, his own arm sustains him, and brings salvation, and his fury doth uphold him" (Isa. lxiii. 5). What if the church totter under the underminings of hell? What if it hath a sad heart and wet eyes? In what a little moment can he make the night turn into day, and make the Jews, that were preparing for death in Shushan, triumph over the necks of their enemies, and march in one hour with swords in their hands, that expected the last hour "ropes about their necks (Esth. ix. 1, 5)? If Israel be pursued by Pharaoh, the sea shall open its arms to protect them: if they be thirsty, a rock shall spout out water to refresh them: if they be hungry, heaven shall be their granary for manna: if Jerusalem be besieged, and hath not force enough to encounter Sennacherib, an angel shall turn the camp into an Aceldema, a field of blood. His people shall not want deliverances, till God want a power of working miracles for their security: he is more jealous of his power, than the church can be of her safety. And if we should want other arguments to press him, we may implore him by virtue of his power: for when there is nothing in the church as a motive to him to save it, there is enough in his own name, and "the illustration of his power" (Ps. cvi. 8). Who can grapple with the omnipotency of that God, who is jealous of, and zealous for, the honor of it? And therefore God, for the most part, takes such opportunities to deliver, wherein his almightiness may be most conspicuous, and his counsels most admirable. He awakened not himself to deliver Israel, till they were upon the brink of the Red Sea; nor to rescue the three children, till they were in the fiery furnace; nor Daniel, till he was in the lion's den. It is in the weakness of his creature that his strength is perfected, not in a way of addition of perfectness to it, but in a way of manifestation of the perfection of it; as it is the perfection of the sun to shine and enlighten the world, not that the sun receives an increase of light by the darting of his beams, but discovers his glory to the admiration of men, and pleasure of the world. If it were not for such occasions, the world would not regard the mightiness of God, nor know what power were in him. It traverses the stage in its fulness and liveliness upon such occasions, when the enemies are strong, and their strength edged with an intense hatred, and but little time between the contrivance and execution. It is a great comfort that the lowest distresses of the church are a fit scene for the discovery of this attribute, and that the

glory of God's omnipotence, and the church's security, are so straitly linked together. It is a promise that will never be forgotten by God, and ought never to be forgotten by us, that "in this mountain the hand of the Lord shall rest" (Isa. xxv. 10); that is, the power of the Lord shall abide; and Moab "shall be trodden under him, even as straw is trodden down for the dunghill." And the "plagues of Babylon shall come in one day, death, and mourning, and famine; for strong is the Lord who judgeth her" (Rev. xviii. 8).

Use III. The third use is for exhortation.

1. Meditate on this power of God, and press it often upon your minds. We conclude many things of God that we do not practically suck the comfort of, for want of deep thoughts of it, and frequent inspection into it. We believe God to be true, yet distrust him; we acknowledge him powerful, yet fear the motion of every straw. Many truths, though assented to in our understandings, are kept under hatches by corrupt affections, and have not their due influence, because they are not brought forth into the open air of our souls by meditation. If we will but search our hearts, we shall find it is the power of God we often doubt of. When the heart of Ahaz and his subjects trembled at the combination of the Syrian and Israelitish kings against him, for want of a confidence in the power of God, God sends his prophet with commission to work a miraculous sign at his own choice, to rear up his fainting heart; and when he refused to ask a sign out of diffidence of that almighty Power, the prophet complains of it as an affront to his Master (Isa. vii. 12, 13). Moses, so great a friend of God, was overtaken with this kind of unbelief, after all the experiments of God's miraculous acts in Egypt; the answer God gives him manifests this to be at the core: "Is the Lord's hand waxed short" (Numb. xi. 23)? For want of actuated thoughts of this, we are many times turned from our known duty by the blast of a creature; as though man had more power to dismay us, than God hath to support us in his commanded way. The belief of God's power is one of the first steps to all religion; without settled thoughts of it, we cannot pray lively and believingly for the obtaining the mercies we want, or the averting the evils we fear; we should not love him, unless we are persuaded he hath a power to bless us; nor fear him, unless we were persuaded of his power to punish us. The frequent thoughts of this would render our faith more stable, and our hopes more stedfast; it would make us more feeble to sin, and more careful to obey. When the virgin staggered at the message of the angel, that she should "bear a Son," he, in his answer, turns her to the creative power of God (Luke i. 35), "The power of the Highest shall overshadow thee;" which seems to be in allusion to the Spirit's moving upon the face of the deep, and bringing a comely world out of a confused mass. Is it harder for God to make a virgin conceive a Son by the power of his Spirit, than to make a world? Why doth he reveal himself so often under the title of Almighty, and press it upon us, but that we should press it upon ourselves? And shall we be forgetful of that which every thing about us, everything within us, is a mark of? How come we by a power of seeing and hearing, a faculty, and act of understanding

and will, but by this power framing us, this power assisting us? What though the thunder of his power cannot be understood, no more can any other perfection of his nature; shall we, therefore, seldom think of it? The sea cannot be fathomed, yet the merchant excuseth not himself from sailing upon the surface of it. We cannot glorify God without due consideration of this attribute; for his power is his glory as much as any other, and called both by the name of glory (Rom. vi. 4), speaking of Christ's resurrection by the glory of the Father; and also "the riches of his glory" (Eph. iii. 16). Those that have strong temptations in their course and over-pressing corruptions in their hearts, have need to think of it out of interest, since nothing but this can relieve them. Those that have experimented the working of it in their new creation, are obliged to think of it out of gratitude. It was this mighty power over himself that gave rise to all that pardoning grace already conferred, or hereafter expected; without it our souls had been consumed, the world overturned; we could not have expected a happy heaven, but have lain yelling in an eternal hell, had not the power of his mercy exceeded that of his justice, and his infinite power executed what his infinite wisdom had contrived for our redemption. How much also should we be raised in our admirations of God, and ravish ourselves in contemplating that might that can raise innumerable worlds in those infinite imaginary spaces without this globe of heaven and earth, and exceed inconceivably what he hath done in the creation of this?

2. From the pressing the consideration of this upon ourselves, let us be induced to trust God upon the account of his power. The main end of the revelation of his power to the patriarchs, and of the miraculous operations of it in Egypt, was to induce them to an entire reposing themselves in God: and the Psalmist doth scarce speak of the Divine Omnipotence without making this inference from it; and scarce exhorts to a trust in God, but backs it with a consideration of his power in creation, it being the chief support of the soul (Ps. cxlvi. 1): "Happy is he whose hope is in the Lord his God, which made heaven and earth, the sea, and all that therein is." That Power is invincible that drew the world out of nothing: nothing can happen to us harder than the making the world without the concurrence of instruments: no difficulty can nonplus that strength, that hath drawn all things out of nothing, or out of a confused matter next to nothing: no power can rifle what we commit to him (2 Tim. i. 12). He is all power, above the reach of all power; all other powers in the world flowing from him, or depending on him, he is worthy to be trusted, since we know him true, without ever breaking his word; and Omnipotent, never failing of his purpose; and a confidence in it is the chief act whereby we can glorify this power, and credit his arm. A strong God, and a weak faith in omnipotence, do not suit well together. Indeed, we are more engaged to a trust in Divine power than the ancient patriarchs were; they had the verbal declaration of his power, and many of them little other evidence of it, than in the creation of the world; and their faith in God being established in this first discovery of his omnipotence, drew out itself further to believe, that whatsoever God promised by his word, he

was able to perform, as well as the creation of the world out of
nothing; which seems to be the intendment of the apostle (Heb. xi. 3);
not barely to speak of the creation of the world by God, which was
a thing the Hebrews understood well enough from their ancient
oracles; but to show the foundation of the patriarch's faith, *viz.*
God making the world by his Word, and what use they made of the
discovery of his power in that, to lead them to believe the promise
of God concerning the Seed of the woman to be brought into the
world. But we have not only the same foundation, but superadded
demonstrations of this attribute in the conception of our Saviour, the
union of the two natures, the glorious redemption, the propagation
of the gospel, and the new creation of the world. They relied upon
the naked power of God, without those more illustrious appearances
of it, which have been in the ages since, and arrived to their notice;
we have the wonderful effects of that which they had but obscure expectations of.

(1.) Consider, trust in God can never be without taking in God's
power as a concurrent foundation with his truth. It is the main
ground of trust, and so set forth in the prophet (Isa. xxvi. 4);
" Trust ye in the Lord for ever, for in the Lord Jehovah is everlasting strength." And the faith of the ancients so recommended (Heb.
xi), had this chiefly for its ground; and the faith in gospel times is
called a " trusting on his arm" (Isa. li. 5.) All the attributes of God
are the objects of our veneration, but they do not equally contribute
to the producing trust in our hearts; his eternity, simplicity, infiniteness, ravish and astonish our minds when we consider them; but
there is no immediate tendency in their nature to allure us to a confidence in him, no, not in an innocent state, much less in a lapsed
and revolted condition: but the other perfections of his nature, as
his holiness, righteousness, mercy, are amiable to us in regard of the
immediate operations of them upon and about the creature, and so
have something in their own nature to allure us to repose ourselves
in him; but yet those cannot engage to an entire trust in him without reflecting upon his ability, which can only render those useful
and successful to the creature.[a] For whatsoever bars stand in the
way of his holy, righteous, and merciful proceedings towards his
creatures, are not overmastered by those perfections, but by that
strength of his which can only relieve us in concurrence with the
other attributes. How could his mercy succor us without his arm,
or his wisdom guide us without his hand, or his truth perform promises to us without his strength? As no attribute can act without
it, so in our addresses to him upon the account of any particular
perfection in the Godhead according to our indigency, our eye must
be perpetually fixed upon this of his power, and our faith would be
feeble and dispirited without eyeing this: without this, his holiness,
which hates sin, would not be regarded; and his mercy, pitying a
grieving sinner, would not be valued. As this power is the ground
of a wicked man's fear, so it is the ground of a good man's trust.
This was that which was the principal support of Abraham, not
barely his promise, but his ability to make it good (Rom. iv. 21);

[a] Amyrant Moral. Tom. V. p. 170.

and when he was commanded to sacrifice Isaac, the ability of God to raise him up again (Heb. xi. 19). All faith would droop, and be in the mire, without leaning upon this; all those attributes which we consider as moral in God, would have no influence upon us without this, which we consider physically in God. Though we value the kindness men may express to us in our distresses, yet we make them not the objects of our confidence, unless they have an ability to act what they express. There can be no trust in God without an eye to his power.

(2.). Sometimes the power of God is the sole object of trust. As when we have no promise to assure us of his will, we have nothing else to pitch upon but his ability ; and that not his absolute power, but his ordinate, in the way of his providence; we must not trust in it so as to expect he should please our humor with fresh miracles, but rest upon his power, and leave the manner to his will. Asa, when ready to conflict with the vast Ethiopian army, pleaded nothing else but this power of God (2 Chron. xiv. 11). And the three children, who had no particular promise of deliverance (that we read of) stuck to God's ability to preserve them against the king's threatening, and owned it in the face of the king, yet with some kind of inward intimations in their own spirits, that he would also deliver them (Dan. iii. 17). "Our God, whom we serve, is able to deliver us from the burning fiery furnace." And accordingly the fire burnt the cords that tied them, without singeing any thing else about them. But when this power hath been exercised upon like occasions, it is a precedent he hath given us to rest upon. Precedents in law are good pleas, and strong encouragements to the client to expect success in his suit. "Our fathers trusted in thee, and thou didst deliver them," saith David (Ps. xxii. 4). And Jehoshaphat, in a case of distress (2 Chron. xx. 7), "Art not thou our God, that didst drive out the inhabitants of this land before thy people Israel?" When we have not any statute law and promise to plead, we may plead his power, together with the former precedents and act of it. The centurion had nothing else to act his faith upon but the power of Christ, and some evidences of it in the miracles reported of him ; but he is silent in the latter, and casts himself only upon the former, acknowledging that Christ had the same command over diseases, as himself had over his soldiers (Matt. viii. 10). And our Saviour, when he receives the petition of the blind men, requires no more of them in order to a cure, but a belief of his ability to perform it (Matt. ix. 28). "Believe you that I am able to do this?" His will is not known but by revelation, but his power is apprehended by reason, as essentially and eternally linked with the notion of a God. God also is jealous of the honor of this attribute ; and since it is so much virtually discredited, he is pleased when any do cordially own it, and entirely resign themselves to the assistance of it. Well, then, in all duties where faith is particularly to be acted, forget not this as the main prop of it : do you pray for a flourishing and triumphing grace? Consider him "as able to make all grace to abound in you" (2 Cor. ix. 8). Do you want comfort and reviving under your contritions and godly sorrow ? Consider him, as he declares himself, "the high and lofty One' (Isa. lvii. 15). Are you under pressing distresses? take Eliphaz's advice to Job, when he tells him what he himself would do if he were in his case (Job v. 8), "I would seek unto God, and unto God would I commit my cause:" but observe under what consideration (ver. 9) as to one "that doth great things, and unsearchable; marvellous things without number." When you beg of him the melting your rocky hearts, the dashing in pieces your strong corruptions, the drawing his beautiful image in your soul, the quickening your dead hearts, and reviving your drooping spirits, and supplying your spiritual wants, consider him as one "able to do abundantly," not only "above what you can ask," but "above what you can think" (Eph. iii. 20). Faith will be spiritless, and prayer will be liveless, if power be not eyed by us in those things which cannot be done without an arm of Omnipotence.

3. This doctrine teacheth us humility and submission. The vast disproportion between the mightiness of God, and the meanness of a creature, inculcates the lesson of humility in his presence. How becoming is humility under a mighty hand (1 Pet. v. 6)! What is an infant in a giant's hand, or a lamb in a lion's paw? Submission to irresistible power is the best policy, and the best security; this gratifies and draws out goodness, whereas murmuring and resistance exasperates and sharpens power. We sanctify his name, and glorify his strength, by falling down before it; it is an acknowledgment of his invisible strength, and our inability to match it. How low should we therefore lie before him, against whose power our pride and murmuring can do no good, who can out-wrestle us in our contests, and alway overcome when he judges (Rom. iii. 4)!

4. This doctrine teacheth us not to fear the pride and force of man. How unreasonable is it to fear a limited, above an unbounded power! How unbecoming is the fear of man in him, who hath an interest in a strength able to curb the strongest devils! Who would tremble at the threats of a dwarf, that hath a mighty and watchful giant for his guard? If God doth but arise, his enemies are scattered (Ps. lxviii. 1): the least motion makes them fly before him: it is no difficult thing for Him, that made them by a word, to unmake their designs, and shiver them in pieces by the breath of his mouth: "He brings princes to nothing, and makes the judges of the earth vanity; they wither when he blows upon them, and their stock shall not take root in the earth. He can command a whirlwind to take them away as stubble" (Isa. xl. 23, 24); yea, with the "shaking of his hand he makes servants to become rulers of those that were their masters (Zech. ii. 9). Whole nations are no more in his hands than a "morning cloud,' or the "dew upon the ground," or "the chaff before the wind," or the smoke against the motion of the air, which, though it appear out of a chimney like a black invincible cloud, is quickly dispersed, and becomes invisible (Hos. xiii. 3). How inconsiderable are the most mighty to this strength, which can puff away a whole world of proud grasshoppers, and a whole sky of daring clouds! He that by his word masters the rage of the sea, can overrule the pride and power of men. Where is the fury of the oppressor? It cannot overleap the bounds he hath set it, nor march an inch

beyond the point he hath prescribed it. Fear not the confederacies of man, but "sanctify the Lord of hosts; let him be your fear, and let him be your dread" (Isa. viii. 13). To fear men is to dishonor the name of God, and regard him as a feeble Lord, and not as the Lord of hosts, who is mighty in strength, so that they that harden themselves against him shall not prosper.

5. Therefore this doctrine teacheth us the fear of God. The prophet Jeremiah counts it as an impossible thing for men to be destitute of the fear of God, when they seriously consider his name to be great and mighty (Jer. x. 6, 7): "Thou art great, and thy name is great in might: who would not fear thee, O thou King of nations?" Shall we not tremble at his presence, who hath placed the "sand for the bound of the sea by a perpetual decree;" that though the waves thereof toss themselves, yet they cannot prevail (Jer. v. 22). He can arm the weakest creature for our destruction, and disarm the strongest creatures which appear for our preservation. He can command a hair, a crumb, a kernel, to go awry, and strangle us. He can make the heavens brass over our head, stop close the bottles of the clouds, and make the fruit of the fields droop, when there is a small distance to the harvest; he can arm men's wit, wealth, hands, against themselves; he can turn our sweet morsels into bitter, and our own consciences into devouring lions; he can root up cities by moles, and conquer the proudest by lice and worms. The omnipotence of God is not only the object of a believer's trust, but a believer's fear. It is from the consideration of this power only, that our Saviour presses his disciples, whom he entitles his friends, to fear God; which lesson he presses by a double repetition, and with a kind of asseveration, without rendering any other reason than this of the ability of God to cast into hell (Luke xii. 5). We are to fear Him because he can; but bless his goodness because he will not. In regard of his omnipotence, he is to be reverenced, not only by mortal men, but by the blessed angels, who are past the fear of any danger by his power, being confirmed in a happy state by his unalterable grace: when they adore him for his holiness, they reverence him for his power with covered faces: the title of the "Lord of hosts" is joined in their reverential praise with that of his holiness (Isa. vi. 3), "Holy, holy, holy is the Lord of hosts." How should we adore that Power which can preserve us, when devils and men conspire to destroy us! How should we stand in awe of that Power which can destroy us, though angels and men should combine to preserve us! The parts of his ways which are discovered, are sufficient motives to an humble and reverential adoration: but who can fear and adore him according to the vastness of his power, and his excellent greatness, since "the thunder of his power who can understand?"

DISCOURSE XI

ON THE HOLINESS OF GOD

Exodus xv. 11.—Who is like unto thee, O Lord, among the gods? Who is like thee, glorious in holiness, fearful in praises, doing wonders?

THIS verse is one of the loftiest descriptions of the majesty and excellency of God in the whole Scripture.[b] It is a part of Moses' 'Επινίκιον, or "triumphant song," after a great and real, and a typical victory; in the womb of which all the deliverances of the church were couched. It is the first song upon holy record, and it consists of gratulatory and prophetic matter; it casts a look backward to what God did for them in their deliverance from Egypt; and a look forward to what God shall do for the church ·in future ages. That deliverance was but a rough draught of something more excellent to be wrought towards the closing up of the world; when his plagues shall be poured out upon the anti-christian powers, which should revive the same song of Moses in the church, as fitted so many ages before for such a scene of affairs (Rev. xv. 2, 3). It is observed, therefore, that many words in this song are put in the future tense, noting a time to come; and the very first word, ver. 1, "Then sang Moses and the children of Israel this song;" ישיר, shall sing; implying, that it was composed and calculated for the celebrating some greater action of God's, which was to be wrought in the world.[c] Upon this account, some of the Jewish rabbins, from the consideration of this remark, asserted the doctrine of the resurrection to be meant in this place; that Moses and those Israelites should rise again to sing the same song, for some greater miracles God should work, and greater triumphs he should bring forth, exceeding those wonders at their deliverance from Egypt.

It consists of, 1. A preface (ver. 1); "I will sing unto the Lord."[d] 2. An historical narration of matter of fact (ver. 3, 4), "Pharaoh's chariots and his host hath he cast into the Red Sea;" which he solely ascribes to God (ver. 6), "Thy right hand, O Lord, is become glorious in power: thy right hand, O Lord, hath dashed in pieces the enemy;" which he doth prophetically, as respecting something to be done in after-times; or further for the completing of that deliverance; or, as others think, respecting their entering into Canaan; for the words, in these two verses, are put in the future tense. The manner of the deliverance is described (ver. 8); "The floods stood up-

b Trap. in loc.   c Manass. ben Israel, de Resurr. lib. 1, cap. 1, p. 7.
d Pareus in Exod. xv.

right as an heap, and the depths were congealed in the heart of the sea." In the 9th verse, he magnifies the victory from the vain glory and security of the enemy; "The enemy said, I will pursue, I will overtake, I will divide the spoil," &c. And ver. 16, 17, He prophetically describes the fruit of this victory, in the influence it shall have upon those nations, by whose confines they were to travel to the promised land; "Fear and dread shall fall upon them; by the greatness of thy arm they shall be as still as a stone, till thy people pass over which thou hast purchased." The phrase of this and the 17th and 18th verses, seems to be more magnificent than to design only the bringing the Israelites to the earthly Canaan; but seems to respect the gathering his redeemed ones together, to place them in the spiritual sanctuary which he had established, wherein the Lord should reign forever and ever, without any enemies to disturb his royalty; "The Lord shall reign forever and ever" (ver. 18). The prophet, in the midst of his historical narrative, seems to be in an ecstasy, and breaks out in a stately exaltation of God in the text.

Who is like unto thee, O Lord, among the gods? &c. Interrogations are, in Scripture, the strongest affirmations or negations; it is here a strong affirmation of the incomparableness of God, and a strong denial of the worthiness of all creatures to be partners with him in the degrees of his excellency; it is a preference of God before all creatures in holiness, to which the purity of creatures is but a shadow in desert of reverence and veneration, he being "fearful in praises." The angels cover their faces when they adore him in his particular perfections.

Amongst the gods. Among the idols of the nations, say some; others say,[e] it is not to be found that the Heathen idols are ever dignified with the title of "strong or mighty," as the word translated gods, doth import; and therefore understand it of the angels, or other potentates of the world; or rather inclusively, of all that are noted for, or can lay claim to, the title of strength and might upon the earth or in heaven. God is so great and majestic, that no creature can share with him in his praise.

Fearful in praises. Various are the interpretations of this passage: to be "reverenced in praises;" his praise ought to be celebrated with a religious fear. Fear is the product of his mercy as well as his justice; "He hath forgiveness that he may be feared" (Ps. cxxx. 4). Or, "fearful in praises;" whom none can praise without amazement at the considerations of his works. None can truly praise him without being affected with astonishment at his greatness.[f] Or, "fearful in praises;" whom no mortal can sufficiently praise, since he is above all praise.[g] Whatsoever a human tongue can speak, or an angelical understanding think of the excellency of his nature and the greatness of his works, falls short of the vastness of the Divine perfection. A creature's praises of God are as much below the transcendent eminency of God, as the meanness of a creature's being is below the eternal fulness of the Creator. Or, rather, "fearful," or terrible, "in praises;" that is, in the matter of thy praise: and the learned Rivet concurs with me in

e Rivet.   f Calvin.   g Munster.

this sense. The works of God, celebrated in this song, were terrible; it was the miraculous overthrow of the strength and flower of a mighty nation; his judgments were severe, as well as his mercy was seasonable. The word נורא signifies glorious and illustrious, as well as terrible and fearful. No man can hear the praise of thy name, for those great judicial acts, without some astonishment at thy justice, the stream, and thy holiness, the spring of those mighty works. This seems to be the sense of the following words, " doing wonders :" fearful in the matter of thy praise; they being wonders which thou hast done among us and for us.

Doing wonders. Congealing the waters by a wind, to make them stand like walls for the rescue of the Israelites ; and melting them by a wind, for the overthrow of the Egyptians, are prodigies that challenge the greatest adorations of that mercy which delivered the one, and that justice which punished the other; and of the arm of that power whereby he effected both his gracious and righteous purposes.

Whence observe, that the judgments of God upon his enemies, as well as his mercies to his people, are matters of praise. The perfections of God appear in both. Justice and mercy are so linked together in his acts of providence, that the one cannot be forgotten whilst the other is acknowledged. He is never so terrible as in the assemblies of his saints, and the deliverance of them (Ps. lxxxix. 7). As the creation was erected by him for his glory ; so all the acts of his government are designed for the same end : and his creatures deny him his due, if they acknowledge not his excellency in whatsoever dreadful, as well as pleasing garbs, it appears in the world. His terror as well as his righteousness appears, when he is a God of salvation (Ps. lxv. 5). " By terrible things in righteousness wilt thou answer us, O God of our salvation." But the expression I pitch upon in the text to handle, is *glorious in holiness.* He is magnified or honorable in holiness; so the word נאדר is translated (Isa. xlii. 21). " He will magnify the law, and make it honorable." Thy holiness hath shone forth admirably in this last exploit, against the enemies and oppressors of thy people. The holiness of God is his glory, as his grace is his riches : holiness is his crown, and his mercy is his treasure. This is the blessedness and nobleness of his nature ; it renders him glorious in himself, and glorious to his creatures, that understand any thing of this lovely perfection. Holiness is a glorious perfection belonging to the nature of God. Hence he is in Scripture styled often the Holy One, the Holy One of Jacob, the Holy One of Israel ; and oftener entitled Holy, than Almighty, and set forth by this part of his dignity more than by any other. This is more affixed as an epithet to his name than any other : you never find it expressed, His mighty name, or his His wise name; but His great name, and most of all, His holy name. This is his greatest title of honor; in this doth the majesty and venerableness of his name appear. When the sinfulness of Sennacherib is aggravated, the Holy Ghost takes the rise from this attribute (2 Kings xix. 22). " Thou hast lift up thine eyes on high, even against the Holy One of Israel ;" not against the wise, mighty, &c., but against the Holy One of Israel, as that wherein the majesty of God was most illustrious. It is upon this account he is called light, as impurity is called darkness; both in this sense are opposed to one another: he is a pure and unmixed light, free from all blemish in his essence, nature, and operations.

1. Heathens have owned it. Proclus calls him, the undefiled Governor of the world.[h] The poetical transformations of their false gods, and the extravagancies committed by them, was—in the account of the wisest of them—an unholy thing to report and hear.[i] And some vindicate Epicurus from the atheism wherewith he was commonly charged; that he did not deny the being of God, but those adulterous and contentious deities the people worshipped, which were practices unworthy and unbecoming the nature of God.[k] Hence they asserted, that virtue was an imitation of God, and a virtuous man bore a resemblance to God: if virtue were a copy from God, a greater holiness must be owned in the original. And when some of them were at a loss how to free God from being the author of sin in the world, they ascribe the birth of sin to matter, and run into an absurd opinion, fancying it to be uncreated, that thereby they might exempt God from all mixture of evil; so sacred with them was the conception of God, as a Holy God.

2. The absurdest heretics have owned it. The Maniches and Marchionites, that thought evil came by necessity, yet would salve God's being the author of it, by asserting two distinct eternal principles, one the original of evil, as God was the fountain of good: so rooted was the notion of this Divine purity, that none would ever slander goodness itself with that which was so disparaging to it.[l]

3. The nature of God cannot rationally be conceived without it. Though the power of God be the first rational conclusion, drawn from the sight of his works, wisdom the next, from the order and connexion of his works, purity must result from the beauty of his works: that God cannot be deformed by evil, who hath made every thing so beautiful in its time. The notion of a God cannot be entertained without separating from him whatsoever is impure and bespotting both in his essence and actions. Though we conceive him infinite in Majesty, infinite in essence, eternal in duration, mighty in power, and wise and immutable in his counsels; merciful in his proceedings with men, and whatsoever other perfections may dignify so sovereign a Being, yet if we conceive him destitute of this excellent perfection, and imagine him possessed with the least contagion of evil, we make him but an infinite monster, and sully all those perfections we ascribed to him before; we rather own him a devil than a God. It is a contradiction to be God and to be darkness, or to have one mote of darkness mixed with his light. It is a less injury to him to deny his being, than to deny the purity of it; the one makes him no god, the other a deformed, unlovely, and a detestable god. Plutarch said not amiss, That he should count himself less injured by that man, that should deny that there was such a man as Plutarch, than by him that should affirm that there was such

---

[h] Ἄχραντος ἡγεμών. p. 393.
[i] οὐδ' ἀκούειν ὅσιον. Ammon. in Plut. de 'Eι apud Delphos,
[k] Gassend. Tom. I, Phys. § 1, lib. 4, cap. 2, p. 289.
[l] Petav. Theol. Dogmat. Tom. I. lib. 6, cap. 5, p. 415.

a one indeed, but he was a debauched fellow, a loose and vicious person. It is a less wrong to God to discard any acknowledgments of his being, and to count him nothing, than to believe him to exist, but imagine a base and unholy Deity : he that saith, God is not holy, speaks much worse than he that saith, There is no God at all. Let these two things be considered.

I. If any, this attribute hath an excellency above his other perfections. There are some attributes of God we prefer, because of our interest in them, and the relation they bear to us : as we esteem his goodness before his power, and his mercy whereby he relieves us, before his justice whereby he punisheth us; as there are some we more delight in, because of the goodness we receive by them ; so there are some that God delights to honor, because of their excellency.

1. None is sounded out so, loftily, with such solemnity, and so frequently by angels that stand before his throne, as this. Where do you find any other attribute trebled in the praises of it, as this (Isa. vi. 3)? " Holy, holy, holy is the Lord of hosts, the whole earth is full of his glory ;" and (Rev. iv. 8), " The four beasts rest not day and night, saying, Holy, holy, holy, Lord God Almighty," &c. His power or sovereignty, as Lord of hosts, is but once mentioned, but with a ternal repetition of his holiness. Do you hear, in any angelical song, any other perfection of the Divine Nature thrice repeated? Where do we read of the crying out Eternal, eternal, eternal; or, Faithful, faithful, faithful, Lord God of Hosts? Whatsoever other attribute is left out, this God would have to fill the mouths of angels and blessed spirits for ever in heaven.

2. He singles it out to swear by (Ps. lxxxix. 35): " Once have I sworn by my holiness, that I will not lie unto David :" and (Amos iv. 2), " The Lord will swear by his holiness :" he twice swears by his holiness; once by his power (Isa. lxii. 8) ; once by all, when he swears by his name (Jer. xliv. 26). He lays here his holiness to pledge for the assurance of his promise, as the attribute most dear to him, most valued by him, as though no other could give an assurance parallel to it in this concern of an everlasting redemption which is there spoken of : he that swears, swears by a greater than himself ; God having no greater than himself, swears by himself: and swearing here by his holiness, seems to equal that single one to all his other attributes, as if he were more concerned in the honor of it, than of all the rest. It is as if he should have said, Since I have not a more excellent perfection to swear by, than that of my holiness, I lay this to pawn for your security, and bind myself by that which I will never part with, were it possible for me to be stripped of all the rest. It is a tacit imprecation of himself, If I lie unto David, let me never be counted holy, or thought righteous enough to be trusted by angels or men. This attribute he makes most of.

3. It is his glory and beauty. Holiness is the honor of the creature ; sanctification and honor are linked together (1 Thess. iv. 4); much more is it the honor of God; it is the image of God in the creature (Eph. iv. 24). When we take the picture of a man, we draw the most beautiful part, the face, which is a member of the greatest excellency. When God would be drawn to the life, as much

as can be, in the spirit of his creatures, he is drawn in this attribute, as being the most beautiful perfection of God, and most valuable with him. Power is his hand and arm; omniscience, his eye; mercy, his bowels; eternity, his duration; his holiness is his beauty (2 Chron. xx. 21);—"should praise the beauty of holiness." In Ps. xxvii. 4, David desires "to behold the beauty of the Lord, and inquire in his holy temple;" that is, the holiness of God manifested in his hatred of sin in the daily sacrifices. Holiness was the beauty of the temple (Isa. xlvi. 11); holy and beautiful house are joined together; much more the beauty of God that dwelt in the sanctuary. This renders him lovely to all his innocent creatures, though formidable to the guilty ones. A heathen philosopher could call it the beauty of the Divine essence, and say, that God was not so happy by an eternity of life, as by an excellency of virtue.[m] And the angels' song intimate it to be his glory (Isa. vi. 3); "The whole earth is full of thy glory;" that is, of his holiness in his laws, and in his judgments against sin, that being the attribute applauded by them before.

4. It is his very life. So it is called (Eph. iv. 18), "Alienated from the life of God," that is, from the holiness of God: speaking of the opposite to it, the uncleanness and profaneness of the Gentiles. We are only alienated from that which we are bound to imitate; but this is the perfection alway set out as the pattern of our actions, "Be ye holy, as I am holy;" no other is proposed as our copy; alienated from that purity of God, which is as much as his life, without which he could not live. If he were stripped of this, he would be a dead God, more than by the want of any other perfection. His swearing by it intimates as much; he swears often by his own life; "As I live, saith the Lord:" so he swears by his holiness, as if it were his life, and more his life than any other. Let me not live, or let me not be holy, are all one in his oath. His Deity could not outlive the life of his purity.

II. As it seems to challenge an excellency above all his other perfections, so it is the glory of all the rest. As it is the glory of the Godhead, so it is the glory of every perfection in the Godhead. As his power is the strength of them, so his holiness is the beauty of them. As all would be weak, without almightiness to back them, so all would be uncomely without holiness to adorn them. Should this be sullied, all the rest would lose their honor and their comfortable efficacy: as, at the same instant that the sun should lose its light, it would lose its heat, its strength, its generative and quickening virtue. As sincerity is the lustre of every grace in a Christian, so is purity the splendor of every attribute in the Godhead. His justice is a holy justice; his wisdom a holy wisdom; his arm of power a holy arm (Ps. xcviii. 1); his truth or promise a holy promise (Ps. cv. 42). Holy and true go hand in hand (Rev. vi. 10). His name, which signifies all his attributes in conjunction, is holy (Ps. ciii. 1); yea, he is "righteous in all his ways, and holy in all his works" (Ps. cxlv. 17): it is the rule of all his acts, the source of all his punishments. If every attribute of the Deity were a distinct member, purity would be the form, the soul, the spirit to animate them. Without it, his

m Plutarch Eugubin. de Perenni Phil. lib. 6, cap. 6.

patience would be an indulgence to sin, his mercy a fondness, his wrath a madness, his power a tyranny, his wisdom an unworthy subtilty. It is this gives a decorum to all. His mercy is not exercised without it, since he pardons none but those that have an interest, by union, in the obedience of a Mediator, which was so delightful to his infinite purity. His justice, which guilty man is apt to tax with cruelty and violence in the exercise of it, is not acted out of the compass of this rule. In acts of man's vindictive justice there is something of impurity, perturbation, passion, some mixture of cruelty; but none of these fall upon God in the severest acts of wrath. When God appears to Ezekiel, in the resemblance of fire, to signify his anger against the house of Judah for their idolatry, "from his loins downward" there was "the appearance of fire ;" but, from the loins upward, "the appearance of brightness, as the color of amber" (Ezek. viii. 2). His heart is clear in his most terrible acts of vengeance; it is a pure flame, wherewith he scorcheth and burns his enemies: he is holy in the most fiery appearance. This attribute, therefore, is never so much applauded, as when his sword hath been drawn, and he hath manifested the greatest fierceness against his enemies. The magnificent and triumphant expression of it in the text, follows just upon God's miraculous defeat and ruin of the Egyptian army: "The sea covered them; they sank as lead in the mighty waters:" then it follows, "Who is like unto thee, O Lord, glorious in holiness ?" And when it was so celebrated by the seraphims (Isa. vi. 3), it was when the "posts moved, and the house was filled with smoke" (ver. 4), which are signs of anger (Ps. xviii. 7, 8). And when he was about to send Isaiah upon a message of spiritual and temporal judgments, that he would make the "heart of that people fat, and their ears heavy, and their eyes shut; waste their cities without inhabitant, and their houses without man, and make the land desolate" (ver. 9–12): and the angels which here applaud him for his holiness, are the executioners of his justice, and here called seraphims, from burning or fiery spirits, as being the ministers of his wrath. His justice is part of his holiness, whereby he doth reduce into order those things that are out of order. When he is consuming men by his fury, he doth not diminish, but manifest purity (Zeph. iii. 5); "The just Lord is in the midst of her; he will do no iniquity." Every action of his is free from all tincture of evil. It is also celebrated with praise, by the four beasts about his throne, when he appears in a covenant garb with a rainbow about his throne, and yet with thunderings and lightnings shot against his enemies (Rev. iv. 8, compared with ver. 3, 5), to show that all his acts of mercy, as well as justice, are clear from any stain. This is the crown of all his attributes, the life of all his decrees, the brightness of all his actions: nothing is decreed by him, nothing is acted by him, but what is worthy of the dignity, and becoming the honor, of this attribute.

For the better understanding this attribute, observe, I. The nature of this holiness. II. The demonstration of it. III. The purity of his nature in all his acts about sin. IV. The use of all to ourselves.

I. The nature of Divine holiness *in general.* The holiness of God *negatively,* is a perfect and unpolluted freedom from all evil. As we call gold pure that is not embased by any dross, and that garment clean that is free from any spot, so the nature of God is estranged from all shadow of evil, all imaginable contagion. *Positively,* It is the rectitude or integrity of the Divine nature, or that conformity of it, in affection and action, to the Divine will, as to his eternal law, whereby he works with a becomingness to his own excellency, and whereby he hath a delight and complacency in everything agreeable to his will, and an abhorrency of everything contrary thereunto. As there is no darkness in his understanding, so there is no spot in his will: as his mind is possessed with all truth, so there is no deviation in his will from it. He loves all truth and goodness; he hates all falsity and evil. In regard of his righteousness, he loves righteousness (Ps. xi. 7); " The righteous Lord loveth righteousness," and " hath no pleasure in wickedness" (Ps. v. 4). He values purity in his creatures, and detests all impurity, whether inward or outward. We may, indeed, distinguish the holiness of God from his righteousness in our conceptions: holiness is a perfection absolutely considered in the nature of God; righteousness, a perfection, as referred to others, in his actions towards them and upon them.[n]

In particular, this property of the Divine nature is, 1. An essential and necessary perfection: he is essentially and necessarily holy. It is the essential glory of his nature: his holiness is as necessary as his being; as necessary as his omniscience: as he cannot but know what is right, so he cannot but do what is just. His understanding is not as created understanding, capable of ignorance as well as knowledge; so his will is not as created wills, capable of unrighteousness, as well as righteousness. There can be no contradiction or contrariety in the Divine nature, to know what is right, and to do what is wrong; if so, there would be a diminution of his blessedness, he would not be a God alway blessed, " blessed forever," as he is (Rom. ix. 5). He is as necessarily holy, as he is necessarily God; as necessarily without sin, as without change. As he was God from eternity, so he was holy from eternity. He was gracious, merciful, just in his own nature, and also holy; though no creature had been framed by him to exercise his grace, mercy, justice, or holiness upon.[o] If God had not created a world, he had, in his own nature, been Almighty, and able to create a world. If there never had been anything but himself, yet he had been omniscient, knowing everything that was within the verge and compass of his infinite power; so he was pure in his own nature, though he never had brought forth any rational creature whereby to manifest this purity. These perfections are so necessary, that the nature of God could not subsist without them. And the acts of those, *ad intra,* or within himself, are necessary; for being omniscient in nature, there must be an act of knowledge of himself and his own nature. Being infinitely holy, an act of holiness in infinitely loving himself, must necessarily flow from this perfection.[p] As the Divine will cannot but be perfect, so it cannot be wanting to render the highest love to itself, to its goodness, to the Divine nature, which is due to him. Indeed, the acts of those, *ad*

[n] Martin. de Deo, p. 86.   [o] Turretin. de Satisfact. p. 28,
[p] Ochino, Predic. Part III. Bodic. 51, pp. 347, 348.

extra, are not necessary, but upon a condition. To love righteousness, without himself, or to detect sin, or inflict punishment for the committing of it, could not have been, had there been no righteous creature for him to love, no sinning creature for him to loathe, and to exercise his justice upon, as the object of punishment. Some attributes require a condition to make the acts of them necessary; as it is at God's liberty, whether he will create a rational creature, or no; but when he decrees to make either angel or man, it is necessary, from the perfection of his nature, to make them righteous. It is at God's liberty whether he will speak to man, or no; but if he doth, it is impossible for him to speak that which is false, because of his infinite perfection of veracity. It is at his liberty whether he will permit a creature to sin; but if he sees good to suffer it, it is impossible but that he should detest that creature that goes cross to his righteous nature. His holiness is not solely an act of his will, for then he might be unholy as well as holy; he might love iniquity and hate righteousness; he might then command that which is good, and afterwards command that which is bad and unworthy; for what is only an act of his will, and not belonging to his nature, is indifferent to him. As the positive law he gave to Adam, of not eating the forbidden fruit, was a pure act of his will, he might have given him liberty to eat of it, if he had pleased, as well as prohibited him. But what is moral and good in its own nature, is necessarily willed by God, and cannot be changed by him, because of the transcendent eminency of his nature, and righteousness of his will. As it is impossible for God to command his creature to hate him, or to dispense with a creature for not loving him,—for this would be to command a thing intrinsically evil, the highest ingratitude, the very spirit of all wickedness, which consists in the hating God,—yet, though God be thus necessarily holy, he is not so by a bare and simple necessity, as the sun shines, or the fire burns; but by a free necessity, not compelled thereunto, but inclined from the fulness of the perfection of his own nature and will; so as by no means he can be unholy, because he will not be unholy; it is against his nature to be so.

2. God is only absolutely holy; "There is none holy as the Lord" (1 Sam. ii. 2); it is the peculiar glory of his nature; as there is none good but God, so none holy but God. No creature can be essentially holy, because mutable; holiness is the substance of God, but a quality and accident in a creature. God is infinitely holy, creatures finitely holy. He is holy from himself, creatures are holy by derivation from him. He is not only holy, but holiness; holiness in the highest degree, is his sole prerogative. As the highest heaven is called the heaven of heavens, because it embraceth in its circle all the heavens, and contains the magnitude of them, and hath a greater vastness above all that it encloseth, so is God the Holy of holies; he contains the holiness of all creatures put together, and infinitely more. As all the wisdom, excellency, and power of the creatures if compared with the wisdom, excellency, and power of God, is but folly, vileness, and weakness; so the highest created purity, if set in parallel with God, is but impurity and uncleanness (Rev. xv. 4): "Thou only art holy." It is like the light

of a glow-worm to that of the sun (Job xiii. 15); "The heavens are not pure in his sight, and his angels he charged with folly" (Job iv. 18). Though God hath crowned the angels with an unspotted sanctity, and placed them in a habitation of glory, yet, as illustrious as they are, they have an unworthiness in their own nature to appear before the throne of so holy a God; their holiness grows dim and pale in his presence. It is but a weak shadow of that Divine purity, whose light is so glorious, that it makes them cover their faces out of weakness to behold it, and cover their feet out of shame in themselves. They are not pure in his sight, because, though they love God (which is a principle of holiness) as much as they can, yet, not so much as he deserves; they love him with the intensest degree, according to their power; but not with the intensest degree, according to his own amiableness; for they cannot infinitely love God, unless they were as infinite as God, and had an understanding of his perfections equal with himself, and as immense as his own knowledge. God, having an infinite knowledge of himself, can only have an infinite love to himself, and, consequently, an infinite holiness without any defect; because he loves himself according to the vastness of his own amiableness, which no finite being can. Therefore, though the angels be exempt from corruption and soil, they cannot enter into comparison with the purity of God, without acknowledgment of a dimness in themselves. Besides, he charges them with folly, and puts no trust in them; because they have the power of sinning, though not the act of sinning; they have a possible folly in their own nature to be charged with. Holiness is a quality separable from them, but it is inseparable from God. Had they not at first a mutability in their nature, none of them could have sinned, there had been no devils; but because some of them sinned, the rest might have sinned. And though the standing angels shall never be changed, yet they are still changeable in their own nature, and their standing is due to grace, not to nature; and though they shall be for ever preserved, yet they are not, nor ever can be, immutable by nature, for then they should stand upon the same bottom with God himself; but they are supported by grace against that changeableness of nature which is essential to a creature; the Creator only hath immortality, that is, immutability (1 Tim. iii. 16). It is as certain a truth, that no creature can be naturally immutable and impeccable, as that God cannot create any anything actually polluted and imperfect. It is as possible that the highest creature may sin, as it is possible that it may be annihilated; it may become not holy, as it may become not a creature, but nothing. The holiness of a creature may be reduced into nothing, as well as his substance; but the holiness of the Creator cannot be diminished, dimmed, or overshadowed (James i. 17): "He is the Father of lights, with whom is no variableness or shadow of turning." It is as impossible his holiness should be blotted, as that his Deity should be extinguished: for whatsoever creature hath essentially such or such qualities, cannot be stripped of them, without being turned out of its essence. As a man is essentially rational; and if he ceaseth to be rational, he ceaseth to be man. The sun is essentially luminous; if it should become dark in its own body, it would cease to be the sun. In regard to this absolute and only holiness of God, it is thrice repeated by the seraphims (Isa. vi. 3). The three-fold repetition of a word notes the certainty or absoluteness of the thing, or the irreversibleness of the resolve; as (Ezek. xxi. 27), "I will overturn, overturn, overturn," notes the certainty of the judgment; also, (Rev. viii. 8), "Woe, woe, woe;" three times repeated, signifies the same. The holiness of God is so absolutely peculiar to him, that it can no more be expressed in creatures, than his omnipotence, whereby they may be able to create a world; or his omniscience, whereby they may be capable of knowing all things, and knowing God as he knows himself.

3. God is so holy, that he cannot possibly approve of any evil done by another, but doth perfectly abhor it; it would not else be a glorious holiness (Ps. v. 3). "He hath no pleasure in wickedness." He doth not only love that which is just, but abhor, with a perfect hatred, all things contrary to the rule of righteousness. Holiness can no more approve of sin than it can commit it: to be delighted with the evil in another's act, contracts a guilt, as well as the commission of it; for approbation of a thing is a consent to it. Sometimes the approbation of an evil in another is a more grievous crime than the act itself, as appears in Rom. i. 32, who knowing the judgment of God, "not only" do the same, but have pleasure in them that do it;" where the "not only" manifests it to be a greater guilt to take pleasure in them. Every sin is aggravated by the delight in it; to take pleasure in the evil of another's action, shows a more ardent affection and love to sin, than the committer himself may have. This, therefore, can as little fall upon God, as to do an evil act himself; yet, as a man may be delighted with the consequences of another's sin, as it may occasion some public good, or private good to the guilty person, as sometimes it may be an occasion of his repentance, when the horridness of a fact stares him in the face, and occasions a self-reflection for that, and other crimes, which is attended with an indignation against them, and sincere remorse for them; so God is pleased with those good things his goodness and wisdom bring forth upon the occasion of sin. But in regard of his holiness, he cannot approve of the evil, whence his infinite wisdom drew forth his own glory, and his creature's good. His pleasure is not in the sinful act of the creature, but in the act of his own goodness and skill, turning it to another end than what the creature aimed at.

(1.) He abhors it necessarily. Holiness is the glory of the Deity, therefore necessary. The nature of God is so holy, that he cannot but hate it (Hab. i. 13): "Thou art of purer eyes than to behold evil, and canst not look on iniquity:" he is more opposite to it than light to darkness, and, therefore, it can expect no countenance from him. A love of holiness cannot be without a hatred of everything that is contrary to it. As God necessarily loves himself, so he must necessarily hate everything that is against himself: and as he loves himself for his own excellency and holiness, he must necessarily detest whatsoever is repugnant to his holiness, because of the evil of it. Since he is infinitely good, he cannot but love goodness, as it is a resemblance to himself, and cannot but abhor unrighteousness, as being most distant from him, and contrary to him. If he have any esteem for his own perfections, he must needs have an implacable aversion to all that is so repugnant to him, that would, if it were possible, destroy him, and is a point directed, not only against his glory, but against his life. If he did not hate it, he would hate himself: for since righteousness is his image, and sin would deface his image; if he did not love his image, and loathe what is against his image, he would loathe himself, he would be an enemy to his own nature. Nay, if it were possible for him to love it, it were possible for him not to be holy, it were possible then for him to deny himself, and will that he were no God, which is a palpable contradiction.q Yet this necessity in God of hating sin, is not a brutish necessity, such as is in mere animals, that avoid, by a natural instinct, not of choice, what is prejudicial to them; but most free, as well as necessary, arising from an infinite knowledge of his own nature, and of the evil nature of sin, and the contrariety of it to his own excellency, and the order of his works.

(2.) Therefore intensely. Nothing do men act for more than their glory. As he doth infinitely, and therefore perfectly know himself, so he infinitely, and therefore perfectly knows what is contrary to himself, and, as according to the manner and measure of his knowledge of himself, is his love to himself, as infinite as his knowledge, and therefore inexpressible and unconceivable by us: so, from the perfection of his knowledge of the evil of sin, which is infinitely above what any creature can have, doth arise a displeasure against it suitable to that knowledge. In creatures the degrees of affection to, or aversion from a thing, are suited to the strength of their apprehensions of the good or evil in them. God knows not only the workers of wickedness, but the wickedness of their works (Job xi. 11), for "he knows vain men, he sees wickedness also." The vehemency of this hatred is expressed variously in Scripture; he loathes it so, that he is impatient of beholding it; the very sight of it affects him with detestation (Hab. i. 13); he hates the first spark of it in the imagination (Zech. viii. 17); with what variety of expressions doth he repeat his indignation at their polluted services (Amos v. 21, 22); "I hate, I detest, I despise, I will not smell, I will not regard; take away from me the noise of thy songs, I will not hear!" So, (Isa. i. 14), "My soul hates, they are a trouble to me, I am weary to bear them." It is the abominable thing that he hates (Jer. xliv. 4); he is vexed and fretted at it (Isa. lxiii. 10; Ezek. xvi. 33). He abhors it so, that his hatred redounds upon the person that commits it. (Ps. v. 5), "He hates all workers of iniquity." Sin is the only primary object of his displeasure: he is not displeased with the nature of man as man, for that was derived from him; but with the nature of man as sinful, which is from the sinner himself. When a man hath but one object for the exercise of all his anger, it is stronger than when diverted to many objects: a mighty torrent, when diverted into many streams, is weaker than when it comes in a full body upon one place only. The infinite anger and hatred of

q Turretin. de Satisfact. pp. 35, 36.

God, which is as infinite as his love and mercy, has no other object, against which he directs the mighty force of it, but only unright eousness. He hates no person for all the penal evils upon him, though they were more by ten thousand times than Job was struck with, but only for his sin. Again, sin being only evil, and an unmixed evil, there is nothing in it that can abate the detestation of God, or balance his hatred of it; there is not the least grain of goodness in it, to incline him to the least affection to any part of it. This hatred cannot but be intense; for as the more any creature is sanctified, the more is he advanced in the abhorrence of that which is contrary to holiness; therefore, God being the highest, most absolute and infinite holiness, doth infinitely, and therefore intensely, hate unholiness; being infinitely righteous, doth infinitely abhor unrighteousness; being infinitely true, doth infinitely abhor falsity, as it is the greatest and most deformed evil. As it is from the righteousness of his nature that he hath a content and satisfaction in righteousness (Ps. xi. 7), "The righteous Lord loveth righteousness;" so it is from the same righteousness of his nature, that he detests whatsoever is morally evil: as his nature therefore is infinite, so must his abhorrence be.

(3.) Therefore universally, because necessarily and intensely. He doth not hate it in one, and indulge it in another, but loathes it wherever he finds it; not one worker of iniquity is exempt from it (Ps. v. 5): "Thou hatest all workers of iniquity." For it is not sin, as in this or that person, or as great or little; but sin, as sin is the object of his hatred; and, therefore, let the person be never so great, and have particular characters of his image upon him, it secures him not from God's hatred of any evil action he shall commit. He is a jealous God, jealous of his glory (Exod. xx. 5); a metaphor, taken from jealous husbands, who will not endure the least adultery in their wives, nor God the least defection of man from his law. Every act of sin is a spiritual adultery, denying God to be the chief good, and giving that prerogative by that act to some vile thing. He loves it no more in his own people than he doth in his enemies; he frees them not from his rod, the testimony of his loathing their crimes: whosoever sows iniquity, shall reap affliction. It might be thought that he affected their dross, if he did not refine them, and loved their filth, if he did not cleanse them; because of his detestation of their sin, he will not spare them from the furnace, though because of love to their persons in Christ, he will exempt them from Tophet. How did the sword ever and anon drop down upon David's family, after his unworthy dealing in Uriah's case, and cut off ever and anon some of the branches of it? He doth sometimes punish it more severely in this life in his own people, than in others. Upon Jonah's disobedience a storm pursues him, and a whale devours him, while the profane world lived in their lusts without control. Moses, for one act of unbelief, is excluded from Canaan, when greater sinners attained that happiness. It is not a light punishment, but a vengeance he takes on their inventions (Ps. xcix, 8), to manifest that he hates sin as sin, and not because the worst persons commit it. Perhaps, had a profane man touched the ark, the hand of God had not so suddenly reached him; but when Uzzah, a man zealous for him, as may be supposed by his care for the support of the tottering ark, would step out of his place, he strikes him down for his disobedient action, by the side of the ark, which he would indirectly (as not being a Levite) sustain (2 Sam. vi. 7). Nor did our Saviour so sharply reprove the Pharisees, and turn so short from them as he did from Peter, when he gave a carnal advice, and contrary to that wherein was to be the greatest manifestation of God's holiness, *viz.* the death of Christ (Matt. xvi. 23). He calls him Satan, a name sharper than the title of the devil's children wherewith he marked the Pharisees, and given (besides him) to none but Judas, who made a profession of love to him, and was outwardly ranked in the number of his disciples. A gardener hates a weed the more for being in the bed with the most precious flowers. God's hatred is universally fixed against sin, and he hates it as much in those whose persons shall not fall under his eternal anger, as being secured in the arms of a Redeemer, by whom the guilt is wiped off, and the filth shall be totally washed away: though he hates their sin, and cannot but hate it, yet he loves their persons, as being united as members to the Mediator and mystical Head. A man may love a gangrened member, because it is a member of his own body, or a member of a dear relation, but he loathes the gangrene in it more than in those wherein he is not so much concerned. Though God's hatred of believers' persons is removed by faith in the satisfactory death of Jesus Christ, yet his antipathy against sin was not taken away by that blood; nay, it was impossible it should. It was never designed, nor had it any capacity to alter the unchangeable nature of God, but to manifest the unspottedness of his will, and his eternal aversion to anything that was contrary to the purity of his Being, and the righteousness of his laws.

(4.) Perpetually: this must necessarily follow upon the others. He can no more cease to hate impurity than he can cease to love holiness: if he should in the least instant approve of anything that is filthy, in that moment he would disapprove of his own nature and being; there would be an interruption in his love of himself, which is as eternal as it is infinite. How can he love any sin which is contrary to his nature, but for one moment, without hating his own nature, which is essentially contrary to sin? Two contraries cannot be loved at the same time; God must first begin to hate himself before he can approve of any evil which is directly opposite to himself. We, indeed, are changed with a temptation, sometimes bear an affection to it, and sometimes testify an indignation against it; but God is always the same without any shadow of change, and "is angry with the wicked every day" (Ps. vii. 11), that is, uninterruptedly in the nature of his anger, though not in the effects of it. God indeed may be reconciled to the sinner, but never to the sin; for then he should renounce himself, deny his own essence and his own divinity, if his inclinations to the love of goodness, and his aversion from evil, could be changed, if he suffered the contempt of the one, and encouraged the practice of the other.

4. God is so holy, that he cannot but love holiness in others.

Not that he owes anything to his creature, but from the unspeakable holiness of his nature, whence affections to all things that bear a resemblance of him do flow; as light shoots out from the sun, or any glittering body: it is essential to the infinite righteousness of his nature to love righteousness wherever he beholds it (Ps. xi. 7): "The righteous Lord loveth righteousness." He cannot, because of his nature, but love that which bears some agreement with his nature, that which is the curious draught of his own wisdom and purity: he cannot but be delighted with a copy of himself: he would not have a holy nature, if he did not love holiness in every nature: his own nature would be denied by him, if he did not affect everything that had a stamp of his own nature upon it. There was indeed nothing without God, that could invite him to manifest such goodness to man, as he did in creation: but after he had stamped that rational nature with a righteousness convenient for. it, it was impossible but that he should ardently love that impression of himself, because he loves his own Deity, and consequently all things which are any sparks and images of it: and were the devils capable of an act of righteousness, the holiness of his nature would incline him to love it, even in those dark and revolted spirits.

5. God is so holy, that he cannot positively will or encourage sin in any. How can he give any encouragement to that which he cannot in the least approve of, or look upon without loathing, not only the crime, but the criminal? Light may sooner be the cause of darkness than holiness itself be the cause of unholiness, absolutely contrary to it: it is a contradiction, that he that is the Fountain of good should be the source of evil; as if the same fountain should bubble up both sweet and bitter streams, salt and fresh (James iii. 11); since whatsoever good is in man acknowledges God for its author, it follows that men are evil by their own fault. There is no need for men to be incited to that to which the corruption of their own nature doth so powerfully bend them. Water hath a forcible principle in its own nature to carry it downward; it needs no force to hasten the motion: "God tempts no man, but every man is drawn away by his own lust" (James i. 13, 14). All the preparations for glory are from God (Rom. ix. 23); but men are said to "be fitted to destruction" (ver. 22); but God is not said to fit them; they, by their iniquities, fit themselves for ruin, and he, by his long-suffering, keeps the destruction from them for awhile.

(1.) God cannot command any unrighteousness. As all virtue is summed up in a love to God, so all iniquity is summed up in an enmity to God: every wicked work declares a man an enemy to God (Col. i. 21): "enemies in your minds by wicked works." If he could command his creature anything which bears an enmity in its nature to himself, he would then implicitly command the hatred of himself, and he would be, in some measure, a hater of himself: he that commands another to deprive him of his life, cannot be said to bear any love to his own life. God can never hate himself, and therefore cannot command anything that is hateful to him and tends to a hating of him, and driving the creature further from him; in that very moment that God should command such a thing, he would cease to be good. What can be more absurd to imagine, than that Infinite Goodness should enjoin a thing contrary to itself, and contrary to the essential duty of a creature, and order him to do anything that bespeaks an enmity to the nature of the Creator, or a deflouring and disparaging his works? God cannot but love himself, and his own goodness; he were not otherwise good; and, therefore, cannot order the creature to do anything opposite to this goodness, or anything hurtful to the creature itself, as unrighteousness is.

(2.) Nor can God secretly inspire any evil into us. It is as much against his nature to incline the heart to sin as it is to command it: as it is impossible but that he should love himself, and therefore impossible to enjoin anything that tends to a hatred of himself; by the same reason it is as impossible that he should infuse such a principle in the heart, that might carry a man out to any act of enmity against him. To enjoin one thing, and incline to another, would be an argument of such insincerity, unfaithfulness, contradiction to itself, that it cannot be conceived to fall within the compass of the Divine nature (Deut. xxxii. 4), who is a " God without iniquity," because " a God of truth" and sincerity, "just and right is he." To bestow excellent faculties upon man in creation, and incline him, by a sudden impulsion, to things contrary to the true end of him, and induce an inevitable ruin upon that work which he had composed with so much wisdom and goodness, and pronounced good with so much delight and pleasure, is inconsistent with that love which God bears to the creature of his own framing: to incline his will to that which would render him the object of his hatred, the fuel for his justice, and sink him into deplorable misery, it is most absurd, and unchristian-like to imagine.

(3.) Nor can God necessitate man to sin. Indeed sin cannot be committed by force; there is no sin but is in some sort voluntary; voluntary in the root, or voluntary in the branch; voluntary by an immediate act of the will, or voluntary by a general or natural inclination of the will. That is not a crime to which a man is violenced, without any concurrence of the faculties of the soul to that act; it is indeed not an act, but a passion; a man that is forced is not an agent, but a patient under the force: but what necessity can there be upon man from God, since he hath implanted such a principle in him, that he cannot desire anything but what is good, either really or apparently; and if a man mistakes the object, it is his own fault; for God hath endowed him with reason to discern, and liberty of will to choose upon that judgment. And though it is to be acknowledged that God hath an absolute sovereign dominion over his creature, without any limitation, and may do what he pleases, and dispose of it according to his own will, as a "potter doth with his vessel" (Rom. ix. 21); according as the church speaks (Isa. lxiv. 8), " We are the clay, and thou our potter; and we all are the work of thy hand;" yet he cannot pollute any undefiled creature by virtue of that sovereign power, which he hath to do what he will with it; because such an act would be contrary to the foundation and right of his dominion, which consists in the excellency of his nature, his immense wisdom, and unspotted purity; if God should therefore do any such act, he would expunge the right of his dominion by blotting out that nature which renders him fit for that dominion, and the exercise of it.[r] Any dominion which is exercised without the rules of goodness, is not a true sovereignty, but an insupportable tyranny. God would cease to be a rightful Sovereign if he ceased to be good; and he would cease to be good, if he did command, necessitate, or by any positive operation, incline inwardly the heart of a creature directly to that which were morally evil, and contrary to the eminency of his own nature. But that we may the better conceive of this, let us trace man in his first fall, whereby he subjected himself and all his posterity to the curse of the law and hatred of God; we shall find no footsteps, either of precept, outward force, or inward impulsion.[s] The plain story of man's apostasy dischargeth God from any interest in the crime as an encouragement, and excuseth him from any appearance of suspicion, when he showed him the tree he had reserved, as a mark of his sovereignty, and forbad him to eat of the fruit of it; he backed the prohibition with the threatening the greatest evil, *viz.* death; which could be understood to imply nothing less than the loss of all his happiness; and in that couched an assurance of the perpetuity of his felicity, if he did not, rebelliously, reach forth his hand to take and "eat of the fruit" (Gen. ii. 16, 17). It is true God had given that fruit an excellency, "a goodness for food, and a pleasantness to the eye" (Gen. iii. 6). He had given man an appetite, whereby he was capable of desiring so pleasant a fruit; but God had, by creation, arranged it under the command of reason, if man would have kept it in its due obedience; he had fixed a severe threatening to bar the unlawful excursions of it; he had allowed him a multitude of other fruits in the garden, and given him liberty enough to satisfy his curiosity in all, except this only. Could there be anything more obliging to man, to let God have his reserve of that one tree, than the grant of all the rest; and more deterring from any disobedient attempt than so strict a command, spirited with so dreadful a penalty? God did not solicit him to rebel against him; a solicitation to it, and a command against it, were inconsistent. The devil assaults him, and God permitted it, and stands, as it were, a spectator of the issue of the combat. There could be no necessity upon man to listen to, and entertain the suggestions of the serpent; he had a power to resist him, and he had an answer ready for all the devil's arguments, had they been multiplied to more than they were; the opposing the order of God had been a sufficient confutation of all the devil's plausible reasonings; that Creator, who hath given me my being, hath ordered me not to eat of it. Though the pleasure of the fruit might allure him, yet the force of his reason might have quelled the liquorishness of his sense; the perpetual thinking of, and sounding out, the command of God, had silenced both Satan and his own appetite; had disarmed the tempter, and preserved his sensitive part in its due subjection. What inclination can we suppose there could be from the Creator, when, upon the very first offer of the temptation, Eve opposes to the tempter the prohibition and threatening of God, and strains it to a higher peg than we find God had

[r] Amyrald. Disert. pp. 103, 104.   [s] Amyrald. Defens. de Calvin. pp. 151, 152.

delivered it in? For in Gen. ii. 17, it is, "You shall not eat of it;" but she adds (Gen. iii. 3), "Neither shall you touch it;" which was a remark that might have had more influence to restrain her. Had our first parents kept this fixed upon their understandings and thoughts, that God had forbidden any such act as the eating of the fruit, and that he was true to execute the threatening he had uttered, of which truth of God they could not but have a natural notion, with what ease might they have withstood the devil's attack, and defeated his design! And it had been easy with them, to have kept their understandings by the force of such a thought, from entertaining any contrary imagination. There is no ground for any jealousy of any encouragements, inward impulsions, or necessity from God in this affair. A discharge of God from this first sin will easily induce a freedom of him from all other sins which follow upon it. God doth not then encourage, or excite, or incline to sin. How can he excite to that which, when it is done, he will be sure to condemn? How can he be a righteous Judge to sentence a sinner to misery for a crime acted by a secret inspiration from himself? Iniquity would deserve no reproof from him, if he were any way positively the author of it. Were God the author of it in us, what is the reason our own consciences accuse us for it, and convince us of it? that, being God's deputy, would not accuse us of it, if the sovereign power by which it acts, did incline us to it. How can he be thought to excite to that which he hath enacted such severe laws to restrain, or incline man to that which he hath so dreadfully punished in his Son, and which it is impossible but the excellency of his nature must incline him eternally to hate? We may sooner imagine, that a pure flame shall engender cold, and darkness be the offspring of a sunbeam, as imagine such a thing as this. "What shall we say, is there unrighteousness with God? God forbid." The apostle execrates such a thought (Rom. ix. 14.)

6. God cannot act any evil, in or by himself. If he cannot approve of sin in others, nor excite any to iniquity, which is less, he cannot commit evil himself, which is greater; what he cannot positively will in another, can never be willed in himself; he cannot do evil through ignorance, because of his infinite knowledge; nor through weakness, because of his infinite power; nor through malice, because of his infinite rectitude. He cannot will any unjust thing, because, having an infinitely perfect understanding, he cannot judge that to be true which is false; or that to be good which is evil: his will is regulated by his wisdom. If he could will any unjust and irrational thing, his will would be repugnant to his understanding; there would be a disagreement in God, will against mind, and will against wisdom; he being the highest reason, the first truth, cannot do an unreasonable, false, defective action. It is not a defect in God that he cannot do evil, but a fulness and excellency of power; as it is not a weakness in the light, but the perfection of it, that it is unable to produce darkness; "God is the Father of lights, with whom is no variableness" (James i. 17). Nothing pleases him, nothing is acted by him, but what is beseeming the infinite excellency of his own nature; the voluntary necessity whereby God cannot be unjust,

renders him a God blessed forever; he would hate himself for the chief good, if, in any of his actions, he should disagree with his goodness. He cannot do any unworthy thing, not because he wants an infinite power, but because he is possessed of an infinite wisdom, and adorned with an infinite purity; and being infinitely pure, cannot have the least mixture of impurity. As if you can suppose fire infinitely hot, you cannot suppose it to have the least mixture of coldness; the better anything is, the more unable it is to do evil; God being the only goodness, can as little be changed in his goodness as in his essence.

II. The next inquiry is, The proof that God is holy, or the manifestation of it. Purity is as requisite to the blessedness of God, as to the being of God; as he could not be God without being blessed, so he could not be blessed without being holy. He is called by the title of Blessed, as well as by that of holy (Mark xiv. 61); " Art thou the Christ, the son of the Blessed?" Unrighteousness is a misery and turbulency in any spirit wherein it is; for it is a privation of an excellency which ought to be in every intellectual being, and what can follow upon the privation of an excellency but unquietness and grief, the moth of happiness? An unrighteous man, as an unrighteous man, can never be blessed, though he were in a local heaven. Had God the least spot upon his purity, it would render him as miserable in the midst of his infinite sufficiency, as iniquity renders a man in the confluence of his earthly enjoyments. The holiness and felicity of God are inseparable in him. The apostle intimates that the heathen made an attempt to sully his blessedness, when they would liken him to corruptible, mutable, impure man (Rom. i. 23, 25): "They changed the glory of the incorruptible God into an image, made like to corruptible man;" and after, he entitles God a "God blessed forever." The gospel is therefore called, "The glorious gospel of the blessed God" (1 Tim. i. 11), in regard of the holiness of the gospel precepts, and in regard of the declaration of the holiness of God in all the streams and branches, wherein his purity, in which his blessedness consists, is as illustrious as any other perfection of the Divine Being. God hath highly manifested this attribute in the state of nature; in the legal administration; in the dispensation of the gospel. His wisdom, goodness, and power, are declared in creation; his sovereign authority in his law; his grace and mercy in the gospel, and his righteousness in all. Suitable to this threefold state, may be that eternal repetition of his holiness in the prophecy (Isa. vi. 3); holy, as Creator and Benefactor; holy, as Lawgiver and Judge; holy, as Restorer and Redeemer.

First, His holiness appears, as he is Creator, in framing man in a perfect uprightness. Angels, as made by God, could not be evil; for God beheld his own works with pleasure, and could not have pronounced them all good, had some been created pure, and others impure; two moral contrarieties could not be good. The angels had a first estate, wherein they were happy (Jude 6); and had they not left their own habitation and state, they could not have been miserable. But, because the Scripture speaks only of the creation of man, we will consider, that the human nature was well strung and tuned by God, according to the note of his own holiness (Eccles. vii. 29); "God hath made man upright:" he had declared his power in other creatures, but would declare in his rational creature, what he most valued in himself; and, therefore, created him upright, with a wisdom which is the rectitude of the mind, with a purity which is the rectitude of the will and affections. He had declared a purity in other creatures, as much as they were capable of, viz. in the exact tuning them to answer one another. And that God, who so well tuned and composed other creatures, would not make man a jarring instrument, and place a cracked creature to be Lord of the rest of his earthly fabric. God, being holy, could not set his seal upon any rational creature, but the impression would be like himself, pure and holy also; he could not be created with an error in his understanding; that had been inconsistent with the goodness of God to his rational creature; if so, the erroneous motion of the will, which was to follow the dictates of the understanding, could not have been imputed to him as his crime, because it would have been, not a voluntary, but a necessary effect of his nature; had there been an error in the first wheel, the error of the next could not have been imputed to the nature of that, but to the irregular motion of the first wheel in the engine. The sin of men and angels, proceeded not from any natural defect in their understandings, but from inconsideration; he that was the author of harmony in his other creatures, could not be the author of disorder in the chief of his works. Other creatures were his footsteps, but man was his image (Gen. i. 26, 27): "Let us make man in our image, after our likeness;" which, though it seems to imply no more in that place, than an image of his dominion over the creatures, yet the apostle raises it a peg higher, and gives us a larger interpretation of it (Col. iii. 10): "And have put on the new man, which is renewed in knowledge after the image of Him that created him;" making it to consist in a resemblance to his righteousness. Image, say some, notes the form, as man was a spirit in regard of his soul; likeness, notes the quality implanted in his spiritual nature; the image of God was drawn in him, both as he was a rational, and as he was a holy creature. The creatures manifested the being of a superior power, as their cause, but the righteousness of the first man evidenced, not only a sovereign power, as the donor of his being, but a holy power, as the pattern of his work. God appeared to be a holy God in the righteousness of his creature, as well as an understanding God in the reason of his creature, while he formed him with all necessary knowledge in his mind and·all necessary uprightness in his will. The law of love to God, with his whole soul, his whole mind, his whole heart and strength, was originally written upon his nature; all the parts of his nature were framed in a moral conformity with God, to answer this law, and imitate God in his purity, which consists in a love of himself, and his own goodness and excellency. Thus doth the clearness of the stream point us to the purer fountain, and the brightness of the beam evidence a greater splendor in the sun which shot it out.

Secondly, His holiness appears in his laws, as he is a Lawgiver and a Judge. Since man was bound to be subject to God, as a creature, and had a capacity to be ruled by the law, as an understanding and willing creature; God gave him a law, taken from the depths of his holy nature, and suited to the original faculties of man. The rules which God hath fixed in the world, are not the resolves of bare will, but result particularly from the goodness of his nature; they are nothing else but the transcripts of his infinite detestation of sin, as he is the unblemished governor of the world. This being the most adorable property of his nature, he hath impressed it upon that law which he would have inviolably observed as a perpetual rule for our actions, that we may every moment think of this beautiful perfection. God can command nothing but what hath some similitude with the rectitude of his own nature; all his laws, every paragraph of them, therefore, scent of this, and glitter with it (Deut. iv. 8): "What nation hath statutes and judgments so righteous as all this law I set before you this day?" and, therefore, they are compared to fine gold, that hath no speck or dross (Ps. xix. 10).

This purity is evident—1. In the moral law, or law of nature. 2. In the ceremonial law. 3. In the allurements annexed to it, for keeping it, and the affrightments to restrain from the breaking of it. 4. In the judgments inflicted for the violation of it.

1. In the moral law: which is therefore dignified with the title of Holy, twice in one verse (Rom. vii. 12): "Wherefore, the law is holy, and the commandment is holy, just, and good;" it being the express image of God's will, as our Saviour was of his person, and bearing a resemblance to the purity of his nature. The tables of this law were put into the ark, that, as the mercy seat was to represent the grace of God, so the law was to represent the holiness of God (Ps. xix. 1). The Psalmist, after he had spoken of the glory of God in the heavens, wherein the power of God is exposed to our view, introduceth the law, wherein the purity of God is evidenced to our minds (ver. 7, 8, &c.): "Perfect, pure, clean, righteous," are the titles given to it. It is clearer in holiness than the sun is in brightness; and more mighty in itself, to command the conscience, than the sun is to run its race. As the holiness of the Scripture demonstrates the divinity of its Author; so the holiness of the law doth the purity of the Lawgiver.

(1.) The purity of this law is seen in the matter of it. It prescribes all that becomes a creature towards God, and all that becomes one creature towards another of his own rank and kind. The image of God is complete in the holiness of the first table, and the righteousness of the second; which is intimated by the apostle (Eph. iv. 24), the one being the rule of what we owe to God, the other being the rule of what we owe to man: there is no good but it enjoins, and no evil but it disowns. It is not sickly and lame in any part of it; not a good action, but it gives it its due praise; and not an evil action, but it sets a condemning mark upon. The commands of it are frequently in Scripture called judgments, because they rightly judge of good and evil; and are a clear light to inform the judgment of man in the knowledge of both. By this was the understanding of David enlightened to know every false way, and to "hate it" (Ps. cxix. 104). There is no case can happen, but may meet with a determination from it; it teaches men the noblest manner of living a life like God himself; honorably for the Lawgiver, and joyfully for the subject. It directs us to the highest end ; sets us at a distance from all base and sordid practices ; it proposeth light to the understanding, and goodness to the will. It would tune all the strings, set right all the orders of mankind : it censures the least mote, countenanceth not any stain in the life. Not a wanton glance can meet with any justification from it (Matt. v. 28) ; not a rash anger but it frowns upon (ver. 22). As the Lawgiver wants nothing as an addition to his blessedness, so his law wants nothing as a supplement to its perfection (Deut. iv. 2). What our Saviour seems to add, is not an addition to mend any defects, but a restoration of it from the corrupt glosses, wherewith the Scribes and Pharisees had eclipsed the brightness of it : they had curtailed it, and diminished part of its authority, cutting off its empire over the least evil, and left its power only to check the grosser practices. But Christ restores it to the due extent of its sovereignty, and shows it those dimensions in which the holy men of God considered it as " exceeding broad"(Ps. cxix. 96), reaching to all actions, all motions, all circumstances attending them ; full of inexhaustible treasures of righteousness. And though this law, since the fall, doth irritate sin, it is no disparagement, but a testimony to the righteousness of it ; which the apostle manifests by his " Wherefore (Rom. vii. 8), sin, taking occasion by the commandment, wrought in me all manner of concupiscence ;" and repeating the same sense (ver. 11), subjoins a " Wherefore" (ver. 12), " Wherefore the law is holy." The rising of men's sinful hearts against the law of God, when it strikes with its preceptive and minatory parts upon their consciences, evidenceth the holiness of the law and the Lawgiver. In its own nature it is a directing rule, but the malignant nature of sin is exasperated by it ; as an hostile quality in a creature will awaken itself at the appearance of its enemy. The purity of this beam, and transcript of God, bears witness to a greater clearness and beauty in the sun and original. Undefiled streams manifest an untainted fountain.

(2.) It is seen in the manner of its precepts. As it prescribes all good, and forbids all evil, so it doth enjoin the one, and banish the other as such. The laws of men command virtuous things ; not as virtuous in themselves, but as useful for human society ; which the magistrate is the conservator of, and the guardian of justice.[t] The laws of men contain not all the precepts of virtue, but only such as are accommodated to their customs, and are useful to preserve the ligaments of their government. The design of them is not so much to render the subjects good men, as good citizens : they order the practice of those virtues that may strengthen civil society, and discountenance those vices only which weaken the sinews of it : but God, being the guardian of universal righteousness, doth not only enact the observance of all righteousness, but the observance of it as righteousness. He commands that which is just in itself, enjoins virtues as virtues, and prohibits vices as vices : as they are profitable or injurious to ourselves, as well as to others. Men command temperance and justice ; not as virtues in themselves, but as they pre-

[t] Ames de Consc. lib. v. cap. 1. quest. 7.

vent disorder and confusion in a commonwealth ; and forbid adultery and theft, not as vices in themselves, but as they are intrenchments upon property ; not as hurtful to the person that commits them, but as hurtful to the person against whose right they are committed. Upon this account, perhaps, Paul applauds the holiness of the law of God in regard of its own nature, as considered in itself, more than he doth the justice of it in regard of man, and the goodness and conveniency of it to the world (Rom. vii. 12) ; the law is holy twice, and just and good but once.

(3.) In the spiritual extent of it. The most righteous powers of the world do not so much regard in their laws what the inward affections of their subjects are : the external acts are only the objects of their decrees, either to encourage them if they be useful, or discourage them if they be hurtful to the community. And, indeed, they can do no other, for they have no power proportioned to inward affections, since the inward disposition falls not under their censure ; and it would be foolish for any legislative power to make such laws, which it is impossible for it to put in execution. They can prohibit the outward acts of theft and murder, but they cannot command the love of God, the hatred of sin, the contempt of the world ; they cannot prohibit unclean thoughts, and the atheism of the heart. But the law of God surmounts in righteousness all the laws of the best-regulated commonwealths in the world : it restrains the licentious heart, as well as the violent hand ; it damps the very first bubblings of corrupt nature, orders a purity in the spring, commands a clean fountain, clean streams, clean vessels. It would frame the heart to an inward, as well as the life to an outward righteousness, and make the inside purer than the outside. It forbids the first belchings of a murderous or adulterous intention : it obligeth a man as a rational creature, and therefore exacts a conformity of every rational faculty, and of whatsoever is under the command of them. It commands the private closet to be free from the least cobweb, as well as the outward porch to be clean from mire and dirt. It frowns upon all stains and pollutions of the most retired thoughts : hence the apostle calls it a "spiritual law" (Rom. vii. 14), as not political, but extending its force further than the frontiers of the man; placing its ensigns in the metropolis of the heart and mind, and curbing with its sceptre the inward motions of the spirit, and commanding over the secrets of every man's breast.

(4). In regard of the perpetuity of it. The purity and perpetuity of it are linked together by the Psalmist (Ps. xix. 9) : "The fear of the Lord is clean, enduring for ever;" the fear of the Lord, that is, that law which commands the fear and worship of God, and is the rule of it. And, indeed, God values it at such a rate, that rather than part with a tittle, or let the honor of it lie in the dust, he would not only let "heaven and earth pass away," but expose his Son to death for the reparation of the wrong it had sustained. So holy it is, that the holiness and righteousness of God cannot dispense with it, cannot abrogate it, without despoiling himself of his own being: it is a copy of the eternal law. Can he ever abrogate the command of love to himself, without showing some contempt of his own excellency and very being? Before he can enjoin a creature not to love him, he must make himself unworthy of love, and worthy of hatred; this would be the highest unrighteousness, to order us to hate that which is only worthy of our highest affections. So God cannot change the first command, and order us to worship many gods; this would be against the excellency and unity of God: for God cannot constitute another God, or make anything worthy of an honor equal with himself.[u] Those things that are good, only because they are commanded, are alterable by God: those things that are intrinsically and essentially good, and therefore commanded, are unalterable as long as the holiness and righteousness of God stand firm. The intrinsic goodness of the moral law, the concern God hath for it; the perpetuity of the precepts of the first table, and the care he hath had to imprint the precepts of the second upon the minds and consciences of men, as the Author of nature for the preservation of the world, manifests the holiness of the Lawmaker and Governor.

2. His holiness appears in the ceremonial law: in the variety of sacrifices for sin, wherein he writ his detestation of unrighteousness in bloody characters. His holiness was more constantly expressed in the continual sacrifices, than in those rarer sprinklings of judgments now and then upon the world; which often reached, not the worst, but the most moderate sinners, and were the occasions of the questioning of the righteousness of his providence both by Jews and Gentiles. In judgments his purity was only now and then manifest: by his long patience, he might be imagined by some reconciled to their crimes, or not much concerned in them; but by the morning and evening sacrifice he witnessed a perpetual and uninterrupted abhorrence of whatsoever was evil. Besides those, the occasional washings and sprinklings upon ceremonial defilements, which polluted only the body, gave an evidence, that everything that had a resemblance to evil, was loathsome to him. Add, also, the prohibitions of eating such and such creatures that were filthy; as the swine that wallowed in the mire, a fit emblem for the profane and brutish sinner; which had a moral signification, both of the loathsomeness of sin to God, and the aversion themselves ought to have to everything that was filthy.

3. This holiness appears in the allurements annexed to the law for keeping it, and the affrightments to restrain from the breaking of it. Both promises and threatenings have their fundamental root in the holiness of God, and are both branches of this peculiar perfection. As they respect the nature of God, they are declarations of his hatred of sin, and his love of righteousness; the one belong to his threatenings, the other to his promises; both join together to represent this divine perfection to the creature, and to excite to an imitation in the creature. In the one, God would render sin odious, because dangerous, and curb the practice of evil, which would otherwise be licentious; in the other, he would commend righteousness, and excite a love of it, which would otherwise be cold. By there God suits the two great affections of men, fear and hope;

[u] Suarez.

both the branches of self-love in man: the promises and threatenings are both the branches of holiness in God. The end of the
promises is the same with the exhortation the apostle concludes from
them (2 Cor. vii. 1); "Having these promises, let us cleanse ourselves from all filthiness of flesh and spirit, perfecting holiness in
the fear of God." As the end of precept is to direct, the end of
threatenings is to deter from iniquity, so that the promises is to
allure to obedience. Thus God breathes out his love to righteousness in every promise; his hatred of sin in every threatening. The
rewards offered in the one, are the smiles of pleased holiness; and
the curses thundered in the other, are the sparklings of enraged
righteousness.

4. His holiness appears in the judgment inflicted for the violation
of this law. Divine holiness is the root of Divine justice, and Divine
justice is the triumph of Divine holiness. Hence both are expressed
in Scripture by one word of righteousness, which sometimes signifies the rectitude of the Divine nature, and sometimes the vindicative
stroke of his arm (Ps. ciii. 6); "The Lord executeth righteousness
and judgment for all that are oppressed." So (Dan. ix. 7) "Righteousness (that is, justice) belongs to thee." The vials of his wrath
are filled from his implacable aversion to iniquity. All penal evils
shower down upon the heads of wicked men, spread their root in,
and branch out from, this perfection. All the dreadful storms and
tempests in the world are blown up by it. Why doth he "rain
snares, fire and brimstone, and a horrible tempest!" Because "the
righteous Lord loveth righteousness" (Ps. xi. 6, 7). And, as was
observed before, when he was going about the dreadfulest work that
ever was in the world, the overturning the Jewish state, hardening
the hearts of that unbelieving people, and cashiering a nation, once
dear to him, from the honor of his protection; his holiness, as the
spring of all this, is applauded by the seraphims (Isa. vi. 3, compared with ver. 9—11), &c. Impunity argues the approbation of a
crime, and punishment the abhorrency of it. The greatness of the
crime, and the righteousness of the Judge, are the first natural sentiments that arise in the minds of men upon the appearance of Divine judgments in the world, by those that are near them;[x] as, when
men see gibbets erected, scaffolds prepared, instruments of death
and torture provided, and grievous punishments inflicted, the first
reflection in the spectator is the malignity of the crime, and the detestation the governors are possessed with.

(1). How severely hath he punished his most noble creatures for
it! The once glorious angels, upon whom he had been at greater
cost than upon any other creatures, and drawn more lively lineaments of his own excellency, upon the transgression of his law, are
thrown into the furnace of justice, without any mercy to pity them
(Jude 6). And though there were but one sort of creatures upon
the earth that bore his image, and were only fit to publish and keep
up his honor below the heavens, yet, upon their apostasy, though
upon a temptation from a subtle and insinuating spirit, the man,
with all his posterity, is sentenced to misery in life, and death at

ˣ Amirant. Moral. Tom. V. p. 388.

last; and the woman, with all her sex, have standing punishments inflicted on them, which, as they begun in their persons, were to reach as far as the last member of their successive generations. So holy is God, that he will not endure a spot in his choicest work. Men, indeed, when there is a crack in an excellent piece of work, or a stain upon a rich garment, do not cast it away; they value it for the remaining excellency, more than hate it for the contracted spot; but God saw no excellency in his creature worthy regarding, after the image of that which he most esteemed in himself was defaced.

(2). How detestable to him are the very instruments of sin! For the ill use the serpent, an irrational creature, was put to by the devil, as an instrument in the fall of man, the whole brood of those animals are cursed (Gen. iii. 14), "cursed above all cattle, and above every beast of the field." Not only the devil's head is threatened to be for ever bruised, and, as some think, rendered irrecoverable upon this further testimony of his malice in the seduction of man, who, perhaps, without this new act, might have been admitted into the arms of mercy, notwithstanding his first sin; "though the Scripture gives us no account of this, only this is the only sentence we read of pronounced against the devil, which puts him into an irrecoverable state by a mortal bruising of his head." But, I say, he is not only punished, but the organ, whereby he blew in his temptation, is put into a worse condition than it was before. Thus God hated the sponge, whereby the devil deformed his beautiful image: thus God, to manifest his detestation of sin, ordered the beast, whereby any man was slain, to be slain as well as the malefactor (Lev. xx. 15). The gold and silver that had been abused to idolatry, and were the ornaments of images, though good in themselves, and incapable of a criminal nature, were not to be brought into their houses, but detested and abhorred by them, because they were cursed, and an abomination to the Lord. See with what loathing expressions this law is enjoined to them (Deut. vii. 25, 26). So contrary is the holy nature of God to every sin, that it curseth everything that is instrumental in it.

(3.) How detestable is everything to him that is in the sinner's possession! The very earth, which God had made Adam the proprietor of, was cursed for his sake (Gen. iii. 17, 18). It lost its beauty, and lies languishing to this day; and, notwithstanding the redemption by Christ, hath not recovered its health, nor is it like to do, till the completing the fruits of it upon the children of God (Rom. viii. 20–22). The whole lower creation was made subject to vanity, and put into pangs, upon the sin of man, by the righteousness of God detesting his offence. How often hath his implacable aversion from sin been shown, not only in his judgments upon the offender's person, but by wrapping up, in the same judgment, those which stood in a near relation to them! Achan, with his children and cattle, are overwhelmed with stones, and burned together (Josh. vii. 24, 25). In the destruction of Sodom, not only the grown malefactors, but the young spawn, the infants, at present incapable of the same wickedness, and their cattle, were burned up by the same fire from heaven; and the place where their habitations stood, is, at this day, partly a heap of ashes, and partly an infectious lake, that chokes any fish that swims into it from Jordan, and stifles, as is related, by its vapor, any bird that attempts to fly over it.   O, how detestable is sin to God, that causes him to turn a pleasant land, as the " garden of the Lord" (as it is styled Gen. xiii. 10), into a lake of sulphur ; to make it, both in his word and works, as a lasting monument of his abhorence of evil !

(4.) What design hath God in all these acts of severity and vin-dictive justice, but to set off the lustre of his holiness ?   He testifies himself concerned for those laws, which he hath set as hedges and limits to the lusts of men ; and, therefore, when he breathes forth his fiery indignation against a people, he is said to get himself hon-or : as when he intended the Red Sea should swallow up the Egyp-tian army (Exod. xiv. 17, 18), which Moses, in his triumphant song, echoes back again (Exod. xv. 1): " Thou hast triumphed glorious-ly ;" gloriously in his holiness, which is the glory of his nature, as Moses himself interprets it in the text.   When men will not own the holiness of God, in a way of duty, God will vindicate it in a way of justice and punishment.   In the destruction of Aaron's sons, that were will-worshippers, and would take strange fire, " sanctified" and " glorified" are coupled (Lev. x. 3): he glorified himself in that act, in vindicating his holiness before all the people, declaring that he will not endure sin and disobedience.   He doth therefore, in this life, more severely punish the sins of his people, when they presume upon any act of disobedience, for a testimony that the nearness and dearness of any person to him shall not make him unconcerned in his holiness, or be a plea for impurity.   The end of all his judg-ments is to witness to the world his abominating of sin.   To punish and witness against men, are one and the same thing (Micah i. 2): " The Lord shall witness against you ;" and it is the witness of God's holiness (Hos. v. 5): " And the pride of Israel doth testify to his face :" one renders it the excellency of Israel, and understands it of God : the word גאון, which is here in our translation, " pride," is rendered " excellency" (Amos viii. 7): " The Lord God hath sworn by his excellency ;" which is interpreted " holiness" (Amos iv. 2): "The Lord God hath sworn by his holiness."   What is the issue or end of this swearing by "holiness," and of his "excellency" testify-ing against them ?   In all those places you will find them to be sweeping judgments: in one, Israel and Ephraim shall " fall in their iniquity ;" in another, he will " take them away with hooks," and " their posterity with fish-hooks ;" and in another, he would " never forget any of their works."   He that punisheth wickedness in those he before used with the greatest tenderness, furnisheth the world with an undeniable evidence of the detestableness of it to him.   Were not judgments sometimes poured out upon the world, it would be believed that God were rather an approver than an enemy to sin. To conclude, since God hath made a stricter law to guide men, an-nexed promises above the merit of obedience to allure them, and threatenings dreadful enough to affright men from disobedience, he cannot be the cause of sin, nor a lover of it.   How can he be the author of that which he so severely forbids ; or love that which he delights to punish ; or be fondly indulgent to any evil, when he hates the ignorant instruments in the offences of his reasonable creatures?

Thirdly. The holiness of God appears in our restoration. It is in the glass of the gospel we behold the " glory of the Lord" (2 Cor. iii. 18); that is, the glory of the Lord, into whose image we are changed; but we are changed into nothing, as the image of God, but into holiness: we bore not upon us by creation, nor by regeneration, the image of any other perfection: we cannot be changed into his omnipotence, omniscience, &c., but into the image of his righteousness. This is the pleasing and glorious sight the gospel mirror darts in our eyes. The whole scene of redemption is nothing else but a discovery of judgment and righteousness (Isa. i. 27): " Zion shall be redeemed with judgment, and her converts with righteousness."

1. This holiness of God appears in the manner of our restoration, *viz.* by the death of Christ. Not all the vials of judgments, that have, or shall be poured out upon the wicked world, nor the flaming furnace of a sinner's conscience, nor the irreversible sentence pronounced against the rebellious devils, nor the groans of the damned creatures, give such a demonstration of God's hatred of sin, as the wrath of God let loose upon his Son. Never did Divine holiness appear more beautiful and lovely, than at the time our Saviour's countenance was most marred in the midst of his dying groans. This himself acknowledges in that prophetical psalm (xxii. 1, 2), when God had turned his smiling face from him, and thrust his sharp knife into his heart, which forced that terrible cry from him, " My God, my God, why hast thou forsaken me?" He adores this perfection of holiness (ver. 3), " But thou art holy;" thy holiness is the spring of all this sharp agony, and for this thou inhabitest, and shalt forever inhabit, the praises of all thy Israel. Holiness drew the veil between God's countenance and our Saviour's soul. Justice indeed gave the stroke, but holiness ordered it. In this his purity did sparkle, and his irreversible justice manifested that all those that commit sin are worthy of death; this was the perfect index of his " righteousness" (Rom. iii. 25), that is, of his holiness and truth; then it was that God that is holy, was " sanctified in righteousness" (Isa. v. 16). It appears the more, if you consider,

(1.) The dignity of the Redeemer's person. One that had been from eternity; had laid the foundations of the world; had been the object of the Divine delight: he that was God blessed forever, become a curse; he who was blessed by angels, and by whom God blessed the world, must be seized with horror; the Son of eternity must bleed to death! When did ever sin appear so irreconcileable to God? Where did God ever break out so furiously in his detestation of iniquity? The Father would have the most excellent person, one next in order to himself, and equal to him in all the glorious perfections of his nature (Phil. ii. 6), die on a disgraceful cross, and be exposed to the flames of Divine wrath, rather than sin should live, and his holiness remain forever disparaged by the violations of his law.

(2.) The near relation he stood in to the Father. He was his " own Son that he delivered up" (Rom. viii. 32); his essential image, as dearly beloved by him as himself; yet he would abate nothing of his hatred of those sins imputed to one so dear to him, and who never had done anything contrary to his will. The strong cries uttered by him could not cause him to cut off the least fringe of this royal garment, nor part with a thread the robe of his holiness was woven with. The torrent of wrath is opened upon him, and the Father's heart beats not in the least notice of tenderness to sin, in the midst of his Son's agonies. God seems to lay aside the bowels of a father, and put on the garb of an irreconcileable enemy,ʸ upon which account, probably, our Saviour in the midst of his passion gives him the title of God; not of Father, the title he usually before addressed to him with, (Matt. xxvii. 46), "My God, my God;" not, My Father, my Father; "why hast thou forsaken me?" He seems to hang upon the cross like a disinherited son, while he appeared in the garb and rank of a sinner. Then was his head loaded with curses, when he stood under that sentence of "Cursed is every one that hangs upon a tree" (Gal. iii. 13), and looked as one forlorn and rejected by the Divine purity and tenderness. God dealt not with him as if he had been one in so near a relation to him. He left him not to the will only of the instruments of his death; he would have the chiefest blow himself of bruising of him (Isa. liii. 10): "It pleased the Lord to bruise him:" the Lord, because the power of creatures could not strike a blow strong enough to satisfy and secure the rights of infinite holiness. It was therefore a cup tempered and put into his hands by his Father; a cup given him to drink. In other judgments he lets out his wrath against his creatures; in this he lets out his wrath, as it were, against himself, against his Son, one as dear to him as himself. As in his making creatures, his power over nothing to bring it into being appeared; but in pardoning sin he hath power over himself; so in punishing creatures, his holiness appears in his wrath against creatures, against sinners by inherency; but by punishing sin in his Son, his holiness sharpens his wrath against him who was his equal, and only a reputed sinner; as if his affection to his own holiness surmounted his affection to his Son: for he chose to suspend the breakings out of his affections to his Son, and see him plunged in a sharp and ignominious misery, without giving him any visible token of his love, rather than see his holiness lie groaning under the injuries of a transgressing world.

(3.) The value he puts upon his holiness appears further, in the advancement of this redeeming person, after his death. Our Saviour was advanced, not barely for his dying, but for the respect he had in his death to this attribute of God (Heb. i. 9): "Thou hast loved righteousness, and hated iniquity: therefore God, even thy God, hath anointed thee with the oil of gladness," &c. By righteousness is meant this perfection, because of the opposition of it to iniquity. Some think "therefore" to be the final cause; as if this were the sense, "Thou art anointed with the oil of gladness, that thou mightest love righteousness and hate iniquity." But the Holy Ghost seeming to speak in this chapter not only of the Godhead of Christ but of his exaltation; the doctrine whereof he had begun in ver. 3, and prosecutes in the following verses, I would rather understand "therefore," for "this cause, or reason, hath God anointed thee;" not "to

ʸ Lingend. Tom. III. pp. 699, 700.

this end." Christ indeed had an unction of grace, whereby he was fitted for his mediatory work; he had also an unction of glory, whereby he was rewarded for it. In the first regard, it was a qualifying him for his office; in the second regard, it was a solemn inaugurating him in his royal authority. And the reason of his being settled upon a "throne for ever and ever," is, "because he loved righteousness." He suffered himself to be pierced to death, that sin, the enemy of God's purity, might be destroyed, and the honor of the law, the image of God's holiness, might be repaired and fulfilled in the fallen creature. He restored the credit of Divine holiness in the world, in manifesting, by his death, God an irreconcileable enemy to all sin; in abolishing the empire of sin, so hateful to God, and restoring the rectitude of nature, and new framing the image of God in his chosen ones. And God so valued this vindication of his holiness, that he confers upon him, in his human nature, an eternal royalty and empire over angels and men. Holiness was the great attribute respected by Christ in his dying, and manifested in his death; and for his love to this, God would bestow an honor upon his person, in that nature wherein he did vindicate the honor of so dear a perfection. In the death of Christ, he showed his resolution to preserve its rights; in the exaltation of Christ, he evinced his mighty pleasure for the vindication of it; in both, the infinite value he had for it, as dear to him as his life and glory.

(4.) It may be further considered, that in this way of redemption, his holiness in the hatred of sin seems to be valued above any other attribute. He proclaims the value of it above the person of his Son; since the Divine nature of the Redeemer is disguised, obscured, and vailed, in order to the restoring the honor of it. And Christ seems to value it above his own person, since he submitted himself to the reproaches of men, to clear this perfection of the Divine nature, and make it illustrious in the eyes of the world. You heard before, at the beginning of the handling this argument, it was the beauty of the Deity, the lustre of his nature, the link of all his attributes, his very life; he values it equal with himself, since he swears by it, as well as by his life; and none of his attributes would have a due decorum without it; it is the glory of power, mercy, justice, and wisdom, that they are all holy; so that though God had an infinite tenderness and compassion to the fallen creature, yet it should not extend itself in his relief to the prejudice of the rights of his purity: he would have this triumph in the tenderness of his mercy, as well as the severities of his justice. His mercy had not appeared in its true colors, nor attained a regular end, without vengeance on sin. It would have been a compassion that would, in sparing the sinner, have encouraged the sin, and affronted holiness in the issues of it: had he dispersed his compassions about the world, without the regard to his hatred of sin, his mercy had been too cheap, and his holiness had been contemned; his mercy would not have triumphed in his own nature, whilst his holiness had suffered; he had exercised a mercy with the impairing his own glory; but now, in this way of redemption, the rights of both are secured, both have their due lustre: the odiousness of sin is equally discovered with the greatest of his compassions; an infinite abhorrence of sin, and an infinite love to the world, march hand in hand together. Never was so much of the irreconcileableness of sin to him set forth, as in the moment he was opening his bowels in the reconciliation of the sinner. Sin is made the chiefest mark of his displeasure, while the poor creature is made the highest object of Divine pity. There could have been no motion of mercy, with the least injury to purity and holiness. In this way mercy and truth, mercy to the misery of the creature, and truth to the purity of the law, "have met together;" the righteousness of God, and the peace of the sinner, "have kissed each other" (Ps. lxxxv. 10).

2. The holiness of God in his hatred of sin appears in our justification, and the conditions he requires of all that would enjoy the benefit of redemption. His wisdom hath so tempered all the conditions of it, that the honor of his holiness is as much preserved, as the sweetness of his mercy is experimented by us; all the conditions are records of his exact purity, as well as of his condescending grace. Our justification is not by the imperfect works of creatures, but by an exact and infinite righteousness, as great as that of the Deity which had been offended: it being the righteousness of a Divine person, upon which account it is called the righteousness of God; not only in regard of God's appointing it, and God's accepting it, but as it is a righteousness of that person that was God, and is God. Faith is the condition God requires to justification; but not a dead, but an active faith, such a "faith as purifies the heart" (James ii. 20; Acts xv. 9). He calls for repentance, which is a moral retracting our offences, and an approbation of contemned righteousness and a violated law; an endeavor to gain what is lost, and to pluck out the heart of that sin we have committed. He requires mortification, which is called crucifying; whereby a man would strike as full and deadly a blow at his lusts, as was struck at Christ upon the cross, and make them as certainly die, as the Redeemer did. Our own righteousness must be condemned by us, as impure and imperfect: we must disown everything that is our own, as to righteousness, in reverence to the holiness of God, and the valuation of the righteousness of Christ. He hath resolved not to bestow the inheritance of glory without the root of grace. None are partakers of the Divine blessedness that are not partakers of the Divine nature: there must be a renewing of his image before there be a vision of his face (Heb. xii. 14). He will not have men brought only into a relative state of happiness by justification, without a real state of grace by sanctification; and so resolved he is in it, that there is no admittance into heaven of a starting, but a persevering holiness (Rom. ii. 7), "a patient continuance in well-doing:" patient, under the sharpness of affliction, and continuing, under the pleasures of prosperity. Hence it is that the gospel, the restoring doctrine, hath not only the motives of rewards to allure to good, and the danger of punishments to scare us from evil, as the law had; but they are set forth in a higher strain, in a way of stronger engagement; the rewards are heavenly, and the punishments eternal: and more powerful motives besides, from the choicer expressions of God's love in the death of his Son. The whole design of

it is to reinstate us in a resemblance to this Divine perfection ; whereby he shows what an affection he hath to this excellency of his nature, and what a detestation he hath of evil, which is contrary to it.

3. It appears in the actual regeneration of the redeemed souls, and a carrying it on to a full perfection. As election is the effect of God's sovereignty, our pardon the fruit of his mercy, our knowledge a stream from his wisdom, our strength an impression of his power; so our purity is a beam from his holiness. The whole work of sanctification, and the preservation of it, our Saviour begs for his disciples of his Father, under this title (John xvii. 11, 17): "Holy Father, keep them through thy own name," and "sanctify them through thy truth ;" as the proper source whence holiness was to flow to the creature: as the sun is the proper fountain whence light is derived, both to the stars above, and the bodies here below. Whence He is not only called Holy, but the Holy One of Israel (Isa. xliii. 15), " I am the Lord your Holy One, the Creator of Israel :" displaying his holiness in them, by a new creation of them as his Israel. As the rectitude of the creature at the first creation was the effect of his holiness, so the purity of the creature, by a new creation, is a draught of the same perfection. He is called the Holy One of Israel more in Isaiah, that evangelical prophet, in erecting Zion, and forming a people for himself, than in the whole Scripture besides. As he sent Jesus Christ to satisfy his justice for the expiation of the guilt of sin, so he sends the Holy Ghost for the cleansing of the filth of sin, and overmastering the power of it : Himself is the fountain, the Son is the pattern, and the Holy Ghost the immediate imprinter of this stamp of holiness upon the creature. God hath such a value for this attribute, that he designs the glory of this in the renewing the creature, more than the happiness of the creature ; though the one doth necessarily follow upon the other, yet the one is the principal design, and the other the consequent of the former: whence our salvation is more frequently set forth, in Scripture, by a redemption from sin, and sanctification of the soul, than by a possession of heaven.ᶻ Indeed, as God could not create a rational creature, without interesting this attribute in a special manner, so he cannot restore the fallen creature without it. As in creating a rational creature, there must be holiness to adorn it, as well as wisdom to form the design, and power to effect it; so in the restoration of the creature, as he could not make a reasonable creature unholy, so he cannot restore a fallen creature, and put him in a meet posture to take pleasure in him, without communicating to him a resemblance of himself. As God cannot be blessed in himself without this perfection of purity, so neither can a creature be blessed without it. As God would be unlovely to himself without this attribute, so would the creature be unlovely to God, without a stamp and mark of it upon his nature. So much is this perfection one with God, valued by him, and interested in all his works and ways!

III. The third thing I am to do, is to lay down some proposition in the defence of God's holiness in all his acts, about, or concerning

ᶻ Tit. ii. 11—14, and many other places.

sin. It was a prudent and pious advice of Camero, not to be too busy and rash in inquiries and conclusions about the reason of God's providence in the matter of sin. The Scripture hath put a bar in the way of such curiosity, by telling us, that the ways of God's wisdom and righteousness in his judgments are "unsearchable" (Rom. xi. 33): much more the ways of God's holiness, as he stands in relation to sin, as a Governor of the world; we cannot consider those things without danger of slipping: our eyes are too weak to look upon the sun without being dazzled: too much curiosity met with a just check in our first parent. To be desirous to know the reason of all God's proceedings in the matter of sin, is to second the ambition of Adam, to be as wise as God, and know the reason of his actings equally with himself. It is more easy, as the same author saith, to give an account of God's providence since the revolt of man, and the poison that hath universally seized upon human nature, than to make guesses at the manner of the fall of the first man. The Scripture hath given us but a short account of the manner of it, to discourage too curious inquiries into it. It is certain that God made man upright; and when man sinned in paradise, God was active in sustaining the substantial nature and act of the sinner while he was sinning, though not in supporting the sinfulness of the act: he was permissive in suffering it: he was negative in witholding that grace which might certainly have prevented his crime, and consequently his ruin; though he withheld nothing that was sufficient for his resistance of that temptation wherewith he was assaulted. And since the fall of man, God, as a wise governor, is directive of the events of the transgression, and draws the choicest good out of the blackest evil, and limits the sins of men, that they creep not so far as the evil nature of men would urge them to; and as a righteous Judge, he takes away the talent from idle servants, and the light from wicked ones, whereby they stumble and fall into crimes, by the inclinations and proneness of their own corrupt natures, leaves them to the bias of their own vicious habits, denies that grace which they have forfeited, and have no right to challenge, and turns their sinful actions into punishments, both to the committers of them and others.

Prop. I. God's holiness is not chargeable with any blemish for his creating man in a mutable state. It is true, angels and men were created with a changeable nature; as though there was a rich and glorious stamp upon them by the hand of God, yet their natures were not incapable of a base and vile stamp from some other principle: as the silver which bears upon it the image of a great prince, is capable of being melted down, and imprinted with no better an image than that of some vile and monstrous beast. Though God made man upright, yet he was capable of seeking "many inventions" (Eccl. vii. 29); yet the hand of God was not defiled by forming man with such a nature. It was suitable to the wisdom of God to give the rational creature, whom he had furnished with a power of acting righteously, the liberty of choice, and not fix him in an unchangeable state without a trial of him in his natural; that if he did obey, his obedience might be the more valuable; and if he did freely offend, his offence might be more inexcusable.

1. No creature can be capable of immutability by nature. Mutability is so essential to a creature, that a creature cannot be supposed without it; you must suppose it a Creator, not a creature, if you allow it to be of an immutable nature. Immutability is the property of the Supreme Being. God "only hath immortality" (1 Tim. vi. 16); immortality, as opposed not only to a natural, but to a sinful death; the word *only* appropriates every sort of immortality to God, and excludes every creature, whether angel or man, from a partnership with God in this by nature. Every creature, therefore, is capable of a death in sin. "None is good but God," and none is naturally free from change but God, which excludes every creature from the same prerogative; and certainly, if one angel sinned, all might have sinned, because there was the same root of mutability in one as well as another. It is as possible for a creature to be a Creator, as for a creature to have naturally an incommunicable property of the Creator. All things, whether angels or men, are made of nothing, and therefore, capable of defection;[a] because a creature being made of nothing, cannot be good, *per essentiam*, or essentially good, but by participation from another. Again, every rational creature, being made of nothing, hath a superior which created him and governs him, and is capable of a precept; and, consequently, capable of disobedience as well as obedience to the precept, to transgress it, as well as obey it. God cannot sin, because he can have no superior to impose a precept on him. A rational creature, with a liberty of will and power of choice, cannot be made by nature of such a mould and temper, but he must be as well capable of choosing wrong, as of choosing right; and, therefore, the standing angels, and glorified saints, though they are immutable, it is not by nature that they are so, but by grace, and the good pleasure of God; for though they are in heaven, they have still in their nature a remote power of sinning, but it shall never be brought into act, because God will always incline their wills to love him, and never concur with their wills to any evil act. Since, therefore, mutability is essential to a creature as a creature, this changeableness cannot properly be charged upon God as the author of it; for it was not the term of God's creating act, but did necessarily result from the nature of the creature, as unchangeableness doth result from the essence of God. The brittleness of a glass is no blame to the art of him that blew up the glass into such a fashion; that imperfection of brittleness is not from the workman, but the matter; so, though unchangeableness be an imperfection, yet it is so necessary a one, that no creature can be naturally without it; besides, though angels and men were mutable by creation, and capable to exercise their wills, yet they were not necessitated to evil, and this mutability did not infer a necessity that they should fall, because some angels, which had the same root of changeableness in their natures with those that fell, did not fall, which they would have done, if capableness of changing, and necessity of changing, were one and the same thing.

2. Though God made the creature mutable, yet he made him not

[a] Suarez, Vol. II. p. 548.

evil. There could be nothing of evil in him that God created after his own image, and pronounced "good" (Gen. i. 27, 31). Man had an ability to stand, as well as a capacity to fall: he was created with a principal of acting freely, whereby he was capable of loving God as his chief good, and moving to him as his last end; there was a beam of light in man's understanding to know the rule he was to conform to, a harmony between his reason and his affections, an original righteousness: so that it seemed more easy for him to determine his will to continue in obedience to the precept, than to swerve from it; to adhere to God as his chief good, than to listen to the charms of Satan. God created him with those advantages, that he might with more facility have kept his eyes fixed upon the Divine beauty, than turn his back upon it, and with greater ease have kept the precept God gave him, than have broken it. The very first thought darted, or impression made, by God, upon the angelical or human nature, was the knowledge of himself as their Author, and could be no more than such whereby both angels and men might be excited to a love of that adorable Being, that had framed them so gloriously out of nothing; and if they turned their wills and affections to another object it was not by the direction of God, but contrary to the impression God had made upon them, or the first thought he flashed into them. They turned themselves to the admiring their own excellency, or affecting an advantage distinct from that which they were to look for only from God (1 Tim. iii. 6). Pride was the cause of the condemnation of the devil. Though the wills of angels and men were created mutable, and so were imperfect, yet they were not created evil. Though they might sin, yet they might not sin, and, therefore, were not evil in their own nature. What reflection, then, could this mutability of their nature be upon God? So far is it from any, that he is fully cleared, by storing up in the nature of man sufficient provision against his departure from him. God was so far from creating him evil, that he fortified him with a knowledge in his understanding, and a strength in his nature to withstand any invasion. The knowledge was exercised by Eve, in the very moment of the serpent's assaulting her (Gen. iii. 3); Eve said to the serpent, "God hath said, ye shall not eat of it:" and had her thoughts been intent upon this, "God hath said," and not diverted to the motions of the sensitive appetite and liquorish palate, it had been sufficient to put by all the passes the devil did, or could have made at her. So that you see, though God made the creature mutable, yet he made him not evil. This clears the holiness of God.

3. Therefore it follows, That though God created man changeable, yet he was not the cause of his change by his fall. Though man was created defectible, yet he was not determined by God influencing his will by any positive act to that change and apostasy. God placed him in a free posture, set life and happiness before him on the one hand, misery and death on the other; as he did not draw him into the arms of perpetual blessedness, so he did not drive him into the gulf of his misery.[b] He did not incline him to evil. It was repugnant

---

[b] Amyr. Moral. Tom. I. pp. 615, 616.

to the goodness of God to corrupt the righteousness of those faculties he had so lately beautified him with. It was not likely he should deface the beauty of that work he had composed with so much wisdom and skill. Would he, by any act of his own, make that bad, which, but a little before, he had acquiesced in as good? Angels and men were left to their liberty and conduct of their natural faculties; and if God inspired them with any motions, they could not but be motions to good, and suited to that righteous nature he had endued them with. But it is most probable that God did not, in a supernatural way, act inwardly upon the mind of man, but left him wholly to that power, which he had, in creation, furnished him with. The Scripture frees God fully from any blame in this, and lays it wholly upon Satan, as the tempter, and upon man, as the determiner of his own will (Gen. iii. 6); Eve "took of the fruit, and did eat;" and Adam took from her of the fruit, "and did eat." And Solomon (Eccles. vii. 29) distinguisheth God's work in the creation of man "upright," from man's work in seeking out those ruining inventions. God created man in a righteous state, and man cast himself into a forlorn state. As he was a mutable creature, he was from God; as he was a changed and corrupted creature, it was from the devil seducing, and his own pliableness in admitting. As silver, and gold, and other metals, were created by God in such a form and figure, yet capable of receiving other forms by the industrious art of man; when the image of a man is put upon a piece of metal, God is not said to create that image, though he created the substance with such a property, that it was capable of receiving it; this capacity is from the nature of the metal by God's creation of it, but the carving the figure of this or that man is not the act of God, but the act of man. As images, in Scripture, are called the work of men's hands, in regard of the imagery, though the matter, wood or stone, upon which the image was carved, was a work of God's creative power. When an artificer frames an excellent instrument, and a musician exactly tunes it, and it comes out of their hands without a blemish, but capable to be untuned by some rude hand, or receive a crack by a sudden fall, if it meet with a disaster, is either the workman or musician to be blamed? The ruin of a house, caused by the wastefulness or carelessness of the tenant, is not to be imputed to the workman that built it strong, and left it in a good posture.

Prop. II. God's holiness is not blemished by enjoining man a law, which he knew he would not observe.

1. The law was not above his strength. Had the law been impossible to be observed, no crime could have been imputed to the subject, the fault had lain wholly upon the Governor; the non-observance of it had been from a want of strength, and not from a want of will. Had God commanded Adam to fly up to the sun, when he had not given him wings, Adam might have a will to obey it, but his power would be too short to perform it. But the law set him for a rule, had nothing of impossibility in it; it was easy to be observed; the command was rather below, than above his strength; and the sanction of it was more apt to restrain and scare him from the breach of it, than encourage any daring attempts against it; he had as much

power, or rather more, to conform to it, than to warp from it; and greater arguments and interest to be observant of it, than to violate it; his all was secured by the one, and his ruin ascertained by the other. The commands of God are not grievous (1 John v. 3); from the first to the last command, there is nothing impossible, nothing hard to the original and created nature of man, which were all summed up in a love to God, which was the pleasure and delight of man, as well as his duty, if he had not, by inconsiderateness, neglected the dictates and resolves of his own understanding. The law was suited to the strength of man, and fitted for the improvement and perfection of his nature; in which respect, the apostle calls it " good," as it refers to man, as well as "holy," as it refers to God (Rom. vii. 12). Now, since God created man a creature capable to be governed by a law, and as a rational creature endued with understanding and will, not to be governed, according to his nature, without a law; was it congruous to the wisdom of God to respect only the future state of man, which, from the depth of his infinite knowledge, he did infallibly foresee would be miserable, by the wilful defection of man from the rule? Had it been agreeable to the wisdom of God, to respect only this future state, and not the present state of the creature; and therefore leave him lawless, because he knew he would violate the law? Should God forbear to act like a wise governor, because he saw that man would cease to act like an obedient subject? Shall a righteous magistrate forbear to make just and good laws, because he foresees, either from the dispositions of his subjects, their ill-humor, or some circumstances which will intervene, that multitudes of them will incline to break those laws, and fall under the penalty of them? No blame can be upon that magistrate who minds the rule of righteousness, and the necessary duty of his government, since he is not the cause of those turbulent affections of men, which he wisely foresees will rise up against his just edicts.

2. Though the law now be above the strength of man, yet is not the holiness of God blemished by keeping it up. It is true, God hath been graciously pleased to mitigate the severity and rigor of the law, by the entrance of the gospel; yet where men refuse the terms of the gospel, they continue themselves under the condemnation of the law, and are justly guilty of the breach of it, though they have no strength to observe it. The law, as I said before, was not above man's strength, when he was possessed of original righteousness, though it be above man's strength, since he was stripped of original righteousness. The command was dated before man had contracted his impotency, when he had a power to keep it as well as to break it. Had it been enjoined to man only after the fall, and not before, he might have had a better pretence to excuse himself, because of the impossibility of it; yet he would not have had sufficient excuse, since the impossibility did not result from the nature of the law, but from the corrupted nature of the creature. It was "weak through the flesh" (Rom. viii. 3), but it was promulged when man had a strength proportioned to the commands of it. And now, since man hath unhappily made himself incapable of obeying it, must God's holiness in his law be blemished for enjoining it? Must he abrogate those commands, and prohibit

what before he enjoined, for the satisfaction of the corrupted creature? Would not this be his "ceasing to be holy," that his creature might be unblameably unrighteous? Must God strip himself of his holiness, because man will not discharge his iniquity? He cannot be the cause of sin, by keeping up the law, who would be the cause of all the unrighteousness of men, by removing the authority of it. Some things in the law that are intrinsically good in their own nature, are indispensable, and it is repugnant to the nature of God not to command them. If he were not the guardian of his indispensable law, he would be the cause and countenancer of the creatures' iniquity. So little reason have men to charge God with being the cause of their sin, by not repealing his law to gratify their impotence, that he would be unholy if he did. God must not lose his purity, because man hath lost his, and cast away the right of his sovereignty, because man hath cast away his power of obedience.

3. God's foreknowledge that his law would not be observed, lays no blame upon him. Though the foreknowledge of God be infallible, yet it doth not necessitate the creature in acting. It was certain from eternity, that Adam would fall, that men would do such and such actions, that Judas would betray our Saviour; God foreknew all those things from eternity; but, it is as certain that this foreknowledge did not necessitate the will of Adam, or any other branch of his posterity, in the doing those actions that were so foreseen by God; they voluntarily run into such courses, not by any impulsion. God's knowledge was not suspended between certainty and uncertainty; he certainly foreknew that his law would be broken by Adam; he foreknew it in his own decree of not hindering him, by giving Adam the efficacious grace which would infallibly have prevented it; yet Adam did freely break this law, and never imagined that the foreknowledge of God did necessitate him to it; he could find no cause of his own sin, but the liberty of his own will; he charges the occasion of his sin upon the woman, and consequently upon God in giving the woman to him (Gen. iii. 12). He could not be so ignorant of the nature of God, as to imagine him without a foresight of future things: since his knowledge of what was to be known of God by creation, was greater than any man's since, in all probability. But, however, if he were not acquainted with the notion of God's foreknowledge, he could not be ignorant of his own act; there could not have been any necessity upon him, any kind of constraint of him in his action, that could have been unknown to him; and he would not have omitted a plea of so strong a nature, when he was upon his trial for life or death; especially when he urgeth so weak an argument, to impute his crime to God, as the gift of the woman; as if that which was designed him for a help, were intended for his ruin. If God's prescience takes away the liberty of the creature, there is no such thing as a free action in the world (for there is nothing done but is foreknown by God, else we render God of a limited understanding), nor ever was, no, not by God himself, *ad extra ;* for whatsoever he hath done in creation, whatsoever he hath done since the creation, was foreknown by him : he resolved to do it, and, therefore, foreknew that he would do it. Did God do it,

therefore, necessarily, as necessity is opposed to liberty? As he freely decrees what he will do, so he effects what he freely decreed. Foreknowledge is so far from intrenching upon the liberty of the will, that predetermination, which in the notion of it speaks something more, doth not dissolve it; God did not only foreknow, but determine the suffering of Christ (Acts iv. 27, 28). It was necessary, therefore, that Christ should suffer, that God might not be mistaken in his foreknowledge, or come short of his determinate decree; but did this take away the liberty of Christ in suffering? (Eph. v. 2): "Who offered himself up to God;" that is, by a voluntary act, as well as designed to do it by a determinate counsel. It did infallibly secure the event, but did not annihilate the liberty of the action, either in Christ's willingness to suffer, or the crime of the Jews that made him suffer. God's prescience is God's provision of things arising from their proper causes; as a gardener foresees in his plants the leaves and the flowers that will arise from them in the spring, because he knows the strength and nature of their several roots which lie under ground; but his foresight of these things is not the cause of the rise and appearance of those flowers. If any of us see a ship moving towards such a rock or quicksand, and know it to be governed by a negligent pilot, we shall certainly foresee that the ship will be torn in pieces by the rock, or swallowed up by the sands; but is this foresight of ours from the causes, any cause of the effect; or can we from hence be said to be the authors of the miscarriage of the ship, and the loss of the passengers and goods? The fall of Adam was foreseen by God to come to pass by the consent of his free will, in the choice of the proposed temptation. God foreknew Adam would sin, and if Adam would not have sinned, God would have foreknown that he would not sin. Adam might easily have detected the serpents fraud, and made a better election; God foresaw that he would not do it; God's foreknowledge did not make Adam guilty or innocent: whether God had foreknown it or no, he was guilty by a free choice, and a willing neglect of his own duty. Adam knew that God foreknew that he might eat of the fruit, and fall and die, because God had forbidden him; the foreknowledge that he would do it, was no more a cause of his action, than the foreknowledge that he might do it. Judas certainly knew that his Master foreknew that he would betray him, for Christ had acquainted him with it (John xiii. 21, 26); yet he never charged this foreknowledge of Christ with any guilt of his treachery.

Prop. III. The holiness of God is not blemished by decreeing the eternal rejection of some men. Reprobation, in its first notion, is an act of preterition, or passing by. A man is not made wicked by the the act of God; but it supposeth him wicked; and so it is nothing else but God's leaving a man.in that guilt and filth wherein he beholds him. In its second notion, it is an ordination, not to a crime, but to a punishment (Jude 4): "an ordaining to condemnation." And though it be an eternal act of God, yet, in order of nature, it follows upon the foresight of the transgression of man, and supposeth the crime. God considers Adam's revolt, and views the whole mass of his corrupted posterity, and chooses some to reduce to himself by his grace, and leaves others to lie sinking in their ruins. Since all mankind fell by the fall of Adam, and have corruption conveyed to them successively by that root, whereof they are branches; all men might justly be left wallowing in that miserable condition to which they are reduced by the apostasy of their common head; and God might have passed by the whole race of man, as well as he did the fallen angels, without any hope of redemption. He was no more bound to restore man, than to restore devils, nor bound to repair the nature of any one son of Adam; and had he dealt with men as he dealt with the devils, they had had, all of them, as little just ground to complain of God; for all men deserved to be left to themselves, for all were concluded under sin; but God calls out some to make monuments of his grace, which is an act of the sovereign mercy of that dominion, whereby "he hath mercy on whom he will have mercy" (Rom. ix. 18); others he passes by, and leaves them remaining in that corruption of nature wherein they were born. If men have a power to dispose of their own goods, without any unrighteousness, why should not God dispose of his own grace, and bestow it upon whom he pleases; since it is a debt to none, but a free gift to any that enjoy it? God is not the cause of sin in this, because his operation about this is negative; it is not an action, but a denial of action, and therefore cannot be the cause of the evil actions of men.[c] God acts nothing, but withholds his power; he doth not enlighten their minds nor incline their wills so powerfully, as to expel their darkness, and root out those evil habits which possess them by nature. God could, if he would, savingly enlighten the minds of all men in the world, and quicken their hearts with a new life by an invincible grace; but in not doing it, there is no positive act of God, but a cessation of action. We may with as much reason say, that God is the cause of all the sinful actions that are committed by the corporation of devils, since their first rebellion, because he leaves them to themselves, and bestows not a new grace upon them,—as say, God is the cause of the sins of those that he overlooks and leaves in that state of guilt wherein he found them. God did not pass by any without the consideration of sin; so that this act of God is not repugnant to his holiness, but conformable to his justice.

Prop. IV. The holiness of God is not blemished by his secret will to suffer sin to enter into the world. God never willed sin by his preceptive will. It was never founded upon, or produced by any word of his, as the creation was. He never said, Let there be sin under the heaven, as he said, "Let there be water under the heaven." Nor doth he will it by infusing any habit of it, or stirring up inclinations to it; no, "God tempts no man" (James i. 13). Nor doth he will it by his approving will; it is detestable to him, nor ever can he be otherwise; he cannot approve it either before commission or after.

1. The will of God is in some sort concurrent with sin. He doth not properly will it, but he wills not to hinder it, to which, by his omnipotence, he could put a bar. If he did positively will it, it might be wrought by himself, and so could not be evil. If he did

[c] Amyral. Defence de Calv. p. 145.

in no sort will it, it would not be committed by his creature; sin entered into the world, either God willing the permission of it, or not willing the permission of it. The latter cannot be said; for then the creature is more powerful than God, and can do that which God will not permit. God can, if he be pleased, banish all sin in a moment out of the world: he could have prevented the revolt of angels, and the fall of man; they did not sin whether he would or no: he might, by his grace, have stepped in the first moment, and made a special impression upon them of the happiness they already possessed, and the misery they would incur by any wicked attempt. He could as well have prevented the sin of the fallen angels, and confirmed them in grace, as of those that continued in their happy state: he might have appeared to man, informed him of the issue of his design, and made secret impressions upon his heart, since he was acquainted with every avenue to his will. God could have kept all sin out of the world, as well as all creatures from breathing in it; he was as well able to bar sin forever out of the world, as to let creatures lie in the womb of nothing, wherein they were first wrapped. To say God doth will sin as he doth other things, is to deny his holiness; to say it entered without anything of his will, is to deny his omnipotence. If he did necessitate Adam to fall, what shall we think of his purity? If Adam did fall without any concern of God's will in it, what shall we say of his sovereignty? The one taints his holiness, and the other clips his power. If it came without anything of his will in it, and he did not foresee it, where is his omniscience? If it entered whether he would or no, where is his omnipotence (Rom. ix. 19)? "Who hath resisted his will?" There cannot be a lustful act in Abimelech, if God will withhold his power (Gen. xx. 6); "I withheld thee:" nor a cursing word in Balaam's mouth, unless God give power to speak it (Numb. xxii. 38): "Have I now any power at all to say anything? The word that God puts in my mouth, that shall I speak." As no action could be sinful, if God had not forbidden it; so no sin could be committed, if God did not will to give way to it.

2. God doth not will directly, and by an efficacious will. He doth not directly will it, because he hath prohibited it by his law, which is a discovery of his will: so that if he should directly will sin, and directly prohibit it, he would will good and evil in the same manner, and there would be contradictions in God's will: to will sin absolutely, is to work it (Ps. cxv. 3): "God hath done whatsoever he pleased." God cannot absolutely will it, because he cannot work it. God wills good by a positive decree, because he hath decreed to effect it.[d] He wills evil by a private decree, because he hath decreed not to give that grace which would certainly prevent it. God doth not will sin simply, for that were to approve it, but he wills it, in order to that good his wisdom will bring forth from it.[e] He wills not sin for itself, but for the event. To will sin as sin, or as purely evil, is not in the capacity of a creature, neither of man nor devil. The will of a rational creature cannot will anything but under the appearance of good, of some good in the sin itself, or some good in the issue of it.

---

[d] Rispolis.   [e] Bradward. lib. i. cap. 34. "God wills it *secundum quid*."

Much more is this far from God, who, being infinitely good, cannot will evil as evil; and being infinitely knowing, cannot will that for good which is evil.[f] Infinite wisdom can be under no error or mistake: to will sin as sin, would be an unanswerable blemish on God; but to will to suffer it in order to good, is the glory of his wisdom; it could never have peeped up its head, unless there had been some decree of God concerning it. And there had been no decree of God concerning it, had he not intended to bring good and glory out of it. If God did directly will the discovery of his grace and mercy to the world, he did in some sort will sin, as that without which there could not have been any appearance of mercy in the world; for an innocent creature is not the object of mercy, but a miserable creature: and no rational creature but must be sinful before it be miserable.

3. God wills the permission of sin. He doth not positively will sin, but he positively wills to permit it. And though he doth not approve of sin, yet he approves of that act of his will, whereby he permits it. For since that sin could not enter into the world without some concern of God's will about it, that act of his will that gave way to it, could not be displeasing to him: God could never be displeased with his own act: "He is not as man, that he should repent" (1 Sam. xv. 29). What God cannot repent of, he cannot but approve of: it is contrary to the blessedness of God to disapprove of, and be displeased with any act of his own will. If he hated any act of his own will, he would hate himself, he would be under a torture: every one that hates his own acts, is under some disturbance and torment for them. That which is permitted by him, is in itself, and in regard of the evil of it, hateful to him: but as the prospect of that good which he aims at in the permission of it is pleasing to him, so that act of his will, whereby he permits it, is ushered in by an approving act of his understanding. Either God approved of the permission, or not; if he did not approve his own act of permission, he could not have decreed an act of permission. It is inconceivable that God should decree such an act which he detested, and positively will that which he hated. Though God hated sin, as being against his holiness, yet he did not hate the permission of sin, as being subservient by the immensity of his wisdom to his own glory. He could never be displeased with that which was the result of his eternal counsel, as this decree of permitting sin was, as well as any other decree, resolved upon in his own breast. For as God acts nothing in time, but what he decreed from eternity, so he permits nothing in time but what he decreed from eternity to permit. To speak properly, therefore, God doth not will sin, but he wills the permission of it, and this will to permit is active and positive in God.

4. This act of permission is not a mere and naked permission, but such an one as is attended with a certainty of the event. The decrees of God to make use of the sin of man for the glory of his grace in the mission and passion of his Son, hung upon this entrance of sin. Would it consist with the wisdom of God to decree such great and stupendous things, the event whereof should depend upon an uncertain foundation which he might be mistaken in? God would have

[f] Aquin. cont. Gent. lib. i. cap. 95.

sat in counsel from eternity to no purpose, if he had only permitted those things to be done, without any knowledge of the event of this permission. God would not have made such provision for redemption to no purpose, or an uncertain purpose, which would have been, if man had not fallen; or if it had been an uncertainty with God whether he would fall or no. Though the will of God about sin was permissive, yet the will of God about that glory he would promote by the defect of the creature, was positive; and, therefore, he would not suffer so many positive acts of his will to hang upon an uncertain event; and, therefore, he did wisely and righteously order all things to the accomplishment of his great and gracious purposes.

5. This act of permission doth not taint the holiness of God. That there is such an act as permission, is clear in Scripture (Acts xiv. 16): "Who in times past suffered all nations to walk in their own ways." But that it doth not blemish the holiness of God, will appear,

1st. From the nature of this permission.

1. It is not a moral permission, a giving liberty of toleration by any law to commit sin with impunity; when, what one law did forbid, another law doth leave indifferent to be done or not, as a man sees good in himself. As when there is a law made among men, that no man shall go out of such a city or country without license; to go out without license is a crime by the law; but when that law is repealed by another, that gives liberty for men to go and come at their pleasure, it doth not make their going or coming necessary, but leaves those which were before bound, to do as they see good in themselves. Such a permission makes a fact lawful, though not necessary; a man is not obliged to do it, but he is left to his own discretion to do as he pleases, without being chargeable with a crime for doing it. Such a permission there was granted by God to Adam of eating of the fruits of the garden, to choose any of them for food, except the tree of "knowledge of good and evil." It was a precept to him, not to "eat of the fruit of the tree of knowledge of good and evil;" but the other was a permission, whereby it was lawful for him to feed upon any other that was most agreeable to his appetite: but there is not such a permission in the case of sin; this had been an indulgence of it, which had freed man from any crime, and, consequently, from punishment; because, by such a permission by law, he would have had authority to sin if he pleased. God did not remove the law, which he had before placed as a bar against evil, nor ceased that moral impediment of his threatening: such a permission as this, to make sin lawful or indifferent, had been a blot upon God's holiness.

2. But this permission of God, in the case of sin, is no more than the not hindering a sinful action, which he could have prevented. It is not so much an action of God, as a suspension of his influence, which might have hindered an evil act, and a forbearing to restrain the faculties of man from sin; it is, properly, the not exerting that efficacy which might change the counsels that are taken, and prevent the action intended; as when one man sees another ready to fall, and can preserve him from falling by reaching out his hand, he per-

mits him to fall, that is, he hinders him not from falling. So God describes his act about Abimelech (Gen. xx. 6); " I withheld thee from sinning against me, therefore suffered I thee not to touch her." If Abimelech had sinned, he had sinned by God's permission; that is, by God's not hindering, or not restraining him by making any impressions upon him. So that permission is only a withholding that help and grace, which, if bestowed, would have been an effectual remedy to prevent a crime; and it is rather a suspension, or cessation, than properly a permission, and sin may be said to be committed, not without God's permission, rather than by his permission. Thus, in the fall of man, God did not hold the reins strict upon Satan, to restrain him from laying the bait, nor restrain Adam from swallowing the bait: he kept to himself that efficacious grace which he might have darted out upon man to prevent his fall. God left Satan to his malice of tempting, and Adam to his liberty of resisting, and his own strength, to use that sufficient grace he had furnished him with, whereby he might have resisted and overcome the temptation. As he did not drive man to it, so he did not secretly restrain him from it. So, in the Jews crucifying our Saviour, God did not imprint upon their minds, by his Spirit, a consideration of the greatness of the crime, and the horror of his justice due to it; and, being without those impediments, they run furiously, of their own accord, to the commission of that evil; as, when a man lets a wolf or dog out upon his prey, he takes off the chain which held them, and they presently act according to their natures.[g]   In the fall of angels and men, God's act was leaving them to their own strength; in sins after the fall, it is God's giving them up to their own corruption; the first is a pure suspension of grace; the other hath the nature of a punishment (Ps. lxxxi. 12): " So I gave them up to their own hearts' lusts." The first object of this permissive will of God was to leave angels and men to their liberty, and the use of their free will, which was natural to them,[h] not adding that supernatural grace which was necessary, not that they should not at all sin, but that they should infallibly not sin : they had a strength sufficient to avoid sin, but not sufficient infallibly to avoid sin; a grace sufficient to preserve them, but not sufficient to confirm them.

3. Now this permission is not the cause of sin, nor doth blemish the holiness of God. It doth not intrench upon the freedom of men, but supposeth it, establisheth it, and leaves man to it. God acted nothing, but only ceased to act; and therefore could not be the efficient cause of man's sin. As God is not the author of good, but by willing and effecting it, so he is not the author of evil, but by willing and effecting it, : but he doth not positively will evil, nor effect it by any efficacy of his own. Permission is no action, nor the cause of that action which is permitted; but the will of that person who is permitted to do such an action is the cause.[i]   God can no more be said to be the cause of sin, by suffering a creature to act as it will, than he can be said to be the cause of the not being of any creature, by denying it being, and letting it remain nothing; it is not from God that it is nothing, it is nothing in itself. Though God be said

  ^g Lawson, p. 64.   ^h Suarez, Vol. IV. p. 414.   ⁱ Suarez, de Legib. p. 43.

to be the cause of creation, yet he is never by any said to be the cause of that nothing which was before creation. This permission of God is not the cause of sin, but the cause of not hindering sin. Man and angels had a physical power of sinning from God, as they were created with freewill, and supported in their natural strength; but the moral power to sin was not from God; he counselled them not to it, laid no obligation upon them to use their natural power for such an end; he only left them to their freedom, and not hindered them in their acting what he was resolved to permit.

2d. The holiness of God is not tainted by this, because he was under no obligation to hinder their commission of sin. Ceasing to act, whereby to prevent a crime or mischief, brings not a person permitting it under guilt, unless where he is under an obligation to prevent it; but God, in regard of his absolute dominion, cannot be charged with any such obligation. One man, that doth not hinder the murder of another, when it is in his power, is guilty of the murder in part; but, it is to be considered, that he is under a tie by nature, as being of the same kind, and being the other's brother, by a communion of blood, also under an obligation of the law of charity, enacted by the common Sovereign of the world: but what tie was there upon God, since the infinite transcendancy of his nature, and his sovereign dominion, frees him from any such obligation (Job ix. 12)? "If he takes away, who shall say, What dost thou?" God might have prevented the fall of men and angels; he might have confirmed them all in a state of perpetual innocency; but where is the obligation? He had made the creature a debtor to himself, but he owed nothing to the creature. Before God can be charged with any guilt in this case, it must be proved, not only that he could, but that he was bound to hinder it. No person can be justly charged with another's fault, merely for not preventing it, unless he be bound to prevent it; else, not only the first sin of angels and man would be imputed to God, as the Author, but all the sins of men. He could not be obliged by any law, because he had no superior to impose any law upon him; and it will be hard to prove that he was obliged, from his own nature, to prevent the entrance of sin, which he would use as an occasion to declare his own holiness, so transcendent a perfection of his nature, more than ever it could have been manifested by a total exclusion of it, *viz.* in the death of Christ. He is no more bound, in his own nature, to preserve, by supernatural grace, his creature from falling, after he had framed him with a sufficient strength to stand, than he was obliged, in his own nature, to bring his creature into being when it was nothing. He is not bound to create a rational creature, much less bound to create him with supernatural gifts; though, since God would make a rational creature, he could not but make him with a natural uprightness and rectitude. God did as much for angels and men as became a wise governor: he had published his law, backed it with severe penalties, and the creature wanted not a natural strength to observe and obey it. Had not man power to obey all the precepts of the law, as well as one? How was God bound to give him more grace, since what he had already was enough to shield him, and keep up his resistance against all the power of hell? It had been enough to have pointed his will against the temptation, and he had kept off the force of it. Was there any promise past to Adam of any further grace which he could plead as a tie upon God? No such voluntary limit upon God's supreme dominion appears upon record. Was anything due to man which he had not? anything promised him which was not performed? What action of debt, then, can the creature bring against God? Indeed, when man began to neglect the light of his own reason, and became inconsiderate of the precept, God might have enlightened his understanding by a special flash, a supernatural beam, and imprinted upon him a particular consideration of the necessity of his obedience, the misery he was approaching to by his sin, the folly of any apprehension of an equality in knowledge; he might have convinced him of the falsity of the serpent's arguments, and uncased to him the venom that lay under those baits. But how doth it appear that God was bound to those additional acts when he had already lighted up in him a "spirit, which was the candle of the Lord" (Prov. xx. 27), whereby he was able to discern all, if he had attended to it. It was enough that God did not necessitate man to sin, did not counsel him to it; that he had given him sufficient warning in the threatening, and sufficient strength in his faculties, to fortify him against temptation. He gave him what was due to him as a creature of his own framing; he withdrew no help from him, that was due to him as a creature, and what was not due he was not bound to impart. Man did not beg preserving grace of God, and God was not bound to offer it, when he was not petitioned for it especially: yet if he had begged it, God having before furnished him sufficiently, might, by the right of his sovereign dominion, have denied it without any impeachment of his holiness and righteousness. Though he would not in such a case have dealt so bountifully with his creature as he might have done, yet he could not have been impleaded, as dealing unrighteously with his creature. The single word that God had already uttered, when he gave him his precept, was enough to oppose against all the devil's wiles, which tended to invalidate that word: the understanding of man could not imagine that the word of God was vainly spoken; and the very suggestion of the devil, as if the Creator should envy his creature, would have appeared ridiculous, if he had attended to the voice of his own reason. God had done enough for him, and was obliged to do no more, and dealt not unrighteously in leaving him to act according to the principles of his nature. To conclude, if God's permission of sin were enough to charge it upon God, or if God had been obliged to give Adam supernatural grace, Adam, that had so capacious a brain, could not be without that plea in his mouth, "Lord thou mightest have prevented it; the commission of it by me could not have been without thy permission of it:" or, "Thou hast been wanting to me, as the author of my nature." No such plea is brought by Adam into the court, when God tried and cast him; no such pleas can have any strength in them. Adam had reason enough to know, that there was sufficient reason to overrule such a plea.

Since the permission of sin casts no dirt upon the holiness of God, as I think hath been cleared, we may under this head consider two things more.

1. That God's permission of sin is not so much as his restraint or limitation of it. Since the entrance of the first sin into the world by Adam, God is more a hinderer than a permitter of it. If he hath permitted that which he could have prevented, he prevents a world more, that he might, if he pleased, permit: the hedges about sin are larger than the outlets; they are but a few streams that glide about the world, in comparison of that mighty torrent he dams up both in men and devils. He that understands what a lake of Sodom is in every man's nature, since the universal infection of human nature, as the apostle describes it (Rom. iii. 9, 10, &c.), must acknowledge, that if God should cast the reins upon the necks of sinful men, they would run into thousands of abominable crimes, more than they do: the impression of all natural laws would be rased out, the world would be a public stew, and a more bloody slaughter house; human society would sink into a chaos; no starlight of commendable morality would be seen in it; the world would be no longer an earth, but an hell, and have lain deeper in wickedness than it doth. If God did not limit sin, as he doth the sea, and put bars to the waves of the heart, as well as those of the waters, and say of them, "Hitherto you shall go, and no further;" man hath such a furious ocean in him, as would overflow the banks; and where it makes a breach in one place, it would in a thousand, if God should suffer it to act according to its impetuous current. As the devil hath lust enough to destroy all mankind, if God did not bridle him; deal with every man as he did with Job, ruin their comforts, and deform their bodies with scabs; infect religion with a thousand more errors; fling disorders into commonwealths, and make them as a fiery furnace, full of nothing but flame; if he were not chained by that powerful arm, that might let him loose to fulfil his malicious fury; what rapines, murders, thefts, would be committed, if he did not stint him! Abimelech would not only lust after Sarah, but deflour her; Laban not only pursue Jacob, but rifle him; Saul not only hate David, but murder him; David not only threaten Nabal, but root him up, and his family, did not God girdle in the wrath of man :[k] a greater remainder of wrath is pent in, than flames out, which yet swells for an outlet. God may be concluded more holy in preventing men's sins, than the author of sin in permitting some; since, were it not for his restraints by the pull-back of conscience, and infused motions and outward impediments, the world would swarm more with this cursed brood.

2. His permission of sin is in order to his own glory, and a greater good. It is no reflection upon the Divine goodness to leave man to his own conduct, whereby such a deformity as sin sets foot in the world; since he makes his wisdom illustrious in bringing good out of evil, and a good greater than that evil he suffered to spring up.[l] God did not permit sin, as sin, or permit it barely for itself. As sin is not lovely in its own nature, so neither is the permission of sin intrinsically good or amiable for itself, but for those ends aimed at in

_____
[k] Ps. lxxvi. 10, as the word "restrain" signifies.   [l] *Majus bonum*, saith Bradward.

the permission of it. God permitted sin, but approved not of the object of that permission, sin; because that, considered in its own nature, is solely evil: nor can we think that God could approve of the act of permission, considered only in itself as an act; but as it respected that event which his wisdom would order by it. We cannot suppose that God should permit sin, but for some great and glorious end: for it is the manifestation of his own glorious perfections he intends in all the acts of his will (Prov. xvi. 4), "The Lord hath made all things for himself"—בעל hath wrought all things; which is not only his act of creation, but ordination: "for himself," that is, for the discovery of the excellency of his nature, and the communication of himself to his creature. Sin indeed, in its own nature, hath no tendency to a good end; the womb of it teems with nothing but monsters; it is a spurn at God's sovereignty, and a slight of his goodness: it both deforms and torments the person that acts it; it is black and abominable, and hath not a mite of goodness in the nature of it. If it ends in any good, it is only from that Infinite transcendency of skill, that can bring good out of evil, as well as light out of darkness. Therefore God did not permit it as sin, but as it was an occasion for the manifestation of his own glory. Though the goodness of God would have appeared in the preservation of the world, as well as it did in the creation of it, yet his mercy could not have appeared without the entrance of sin, because the object of mercy is a miserable creature; but man could not be miserable as long as he remained innocent. The reign of sin opened a door for the reign and triumph of grace (Rom. v. 21), "As sin hath reigned unto death, so might grace reign through righteousness to eternal life;" without it, the bowels of mercy had never sounded, and the ravishing music of Divine grace could never have been heard by the creature. Mercy, which renders God so amiable, could never else have beamed out to the world. Angels and men upon this occasion beheld the stirrings of Divine grace, and the tenderness of Divine nature, and the glory of the Divine persons in their several functions about the redemption of man, which had else been a spring shut up, and a fountain sealed; the song of glory to God, and good will to men in a way of redemption had never been sung by them. It appears in his dealing with Adam, that he permitted his fall, not only to show his justice in punishing, but principally his mercy in rescuing; since he proclaims to him first the promise of a Redeemer to "bruise the serpent's head," before he settled the punishment he should smart under in the world (Gen. iii. 15—17). And what fairer prospect could the creature have of the holiness of God, and his hatred of sin, than in the edge of that sword of justice, which punished it in the sinner; but glittered more in the punishment of a Surety so near allied to him? Had not man been criminal, he could not have been punishable, nor any been punishable for him: and the pulse of Divine holiness could not have beaten so quick, and been so visible, without an exercise of his vindicative justice. He left man's mutable nature, to fall under righteousness, that thereby he might commend the righteousness of his own nature (Rom. iii. 7). Adam's sin in its nature tended to the ruin of the world, and God takes an occasion from it for the glory of his grace in the redemption of the world; he brings forth thereby a new scene of wonders from heaven, and a surprising knowledge on earth; as the sun breaks out more strongly after a night of darkness and tempest. As God in creation framed a chaos by his power, to manifest his wisdom in bringing order out of disorder, light out of darkness, beauty out of confusion and deformity, when he was able by a word to have made all creatures stand up in their beauty, without the precedency of a chaos; so God permitted a moral chaos to manifest a greater wisdom in the repairing a broken image, and restoring a deplorable creature, and bringing out those perfections of his nature, which had else been wrapt up in a perpetual silence in his own bosom. It was therefore very congruous to the holiness of God to permit that which he could make subservient for his own glory, and particularly for the manifestation of this attribute of holiness, which seems to be in opposition to such a permission.[m]

Prop. V. The holiness of God is not blemished by his concurrence with the creature in the material part of a sinful act. Some to free God from having any hand in sin, deny his concurrence to the actions of the creature; because, if he concurs to a sinful action, he concurs to the sin also: not understanding how there can be a distinction between the act, and the sinfulness or viciousness of it; and how God can concur to a natural action, without being stained by that moral evil which cleaves to it. For the understanding of this, observe,

1. There is a concurrence of God to all the acts of the creature (Acts xvii. 28); "in him we live, and move, and have our being." We depend upon God in our acting as well as in our being: there is as much an efficacy of God in our motion as in our production; as none have life without his power in producing it, so none have any operation without his providence concurring with it. In him, or by him, that is, by his virtue preserving and governing our motions, as well as by his power bringing us into being. Hence man is compared to an axe (Isa. x. 15), an instrument that hath no action, without the co-operation of a superior agent handling it: and the actions of the second causes are ascribed to God; the grass, that is, the product of the sun, rain, and earth, he is said to make to grow upon the mountains (Ps. cxlvii. 8); and the skin and flesh, which is by natural generation, he is said to clothe us with (Job x. 5), in regard of his co-working with second causes, according to their natures. As nothing can exist, so nothing can operate without him; let his concurrence be removed, and the being and action of the creature cease; remove the sun from the horizon, or a candle from a room, and the light which flowed from either of them ceaseth. Without God's preserving and concurring power, the course of nature would sink, and the creation be in vain. All created things depend upon God as agents, as well as beings, and are subordinate to him in a way of action, as well as in a way of existing.[n] If God suspend his influence from their action, they would cease to act, as the fire did from

---

[m] But of the wisdom of God in the permitting sin in order to redemption, I have handled in the attribute of "Wisdom."   [n] Suarez, Metaph. Part I. p. 552.

burning the three children, as well as if God suspend his influence from their being, they would cease to be. God supports the nature whereby actions are wrought, the mind where actions are consulted, and the will where actions are determined, and the motive-power whereby actions are produced. The mind could not contrive, nor the hand act, a wickedness, if God did not support the power of the one in designing, and the strength of the other in executing a wicked intention. Every faculty in its being, and every faculty in its motion, hath a dependence upon the influence of God. To make the creature independent upon God in anything which speaks perfection, as action considered as action is, is to make the creature a sovereign being. Indeed, we cannot imagine the concurrence of God to the good actions of men since the fall, without granting a concurrence of God to evil actions; because there is no action so purely good but hath a mixture of evil in it, though it takes its denomination of good from the better part (Eccles. vii. 20), "There is no man that doth good, and sins not."

2. Though the natural virtue of doing a sinful action be from God, and supported by him, yet this doth not blemish the holiness of God; while God concurs with them in the act, he instils no evil into men.

(1.) No act, in regard of the substance of it, is evil. Most of the actions of our faculties, as they are actions, might have been in the state of innocency. Eating is an act Adam would have used if he had stood firm, but not eating to excess. Worship was an act that should have been performed to God in innocence, but not hypocritically. Every action is good by a physical goodness, as it is an act of the mind or hand, which have a natural goodness by creation; but every action is not morally good: the physical goodness of the action depends on God, the moral evil on the creature. There is no action, as a corporeal action, is prohibited by the law of God; but as it springs from an evil disposition, and is tainted by a venomous temper of mind.[o] There is no action so bad, as attended with such objects and circumstances; but if the objects and circumstances were changed, might be a brave and commendable action: so that the moral goodness or badness of an act is not to be esteemed from the substance of the act, which hath always a physical goodness; but from the objects, circumstances, and constitution of the mind in the doing of it. Worship is an act good in itself; but the worship of an image is bad in regard of the object. Were that act of worship directed to God that is paid to a statue, and offered up to him with a sincere frame of mind, it would be morally good. The act, in regard of its substance, is the same in both, and considered as separated from the object to which the worship is directed, hath the same real goodness in regard of the substance; but when you consider this action in relation to the different objects, the one hath a moral goodness, and the other a moral evil. So in speaking: speaking being a motion of the tongue in the forming of words, is an excellency belonging to a reasonable creature; an endowment bestowed, continued, and supported by God. Now, if the same tongue

[o] Amyrald. de Libero arbit. pp. 98, 99.

forms words whereby it curseth God this minute, and forms words whereby it blesses and praises God the next minute, the faculty of speaking is the same, the motion of the tongue is the same in pronouncing the name of God either in a way of cursing or blessing (James iii. 9, 10); it is the " same mouth that blesseth and curseth;" and the motion of it is naturally good in regard of the substance of the act in both; it is the use of an excellent power God hath given, and which God preserves, in the use of it. But the estimation of the moral goodness or evil is not from the act itself, but from the disposition of the mind. Once more: killing, as an act is good; nor is it unlawful as an act; for if so, God would never have commanded his people Israel to wage any war, and justice could not be done upon malefactors by the magistrate. A man were bound to sacrifice his life to the fury of an invader, rather than secure it by dispatching that of an enemy; but killing an innocent, or killing without authority, or out of revenge, is bad. It is not the material part of the act, but the object, manner, and circumstance, that makes it good or evil. It is no blemish to God's holiness to concur to the substance of an action, without having any hand in the immorality of it; because, whatsoever is real in the substance of the action might be done without evil. It is not evil as it is an act, as it is a motion of the tongue or hand, for then every motion of the tongue or hand would be evil.

(2.) Hence it follows, that an act, as an act, is one thing, and the viciousness another. The action is the efficacy of the faculty, extending itself to some outward object; but the sinfulness of an act consists in a privation of that comeliness and righteousness which ought to be in an action; in a want of conformity of the act with the law of God, either written in nature, or revealed in the Word.[p] Now, the sinfulness of an action is not the act itself, but is considered in it as it is related to the law, and is a deviation from it; and so it is something cleaving to the action, and therefore to be distinguished from the act itself, which is the subject of the sinfulness. When we say such an action is sinful, the action is the subject, and the sinfulness of the action is that which adheres to it. The action is not the sinfulness, nor the sinfulness the action; they are distinguished as the member, and a disease in the member, the arm and the palsy in it: the arm is not the palsy, nor is the palsy the arm; but the palsy is a disease that cleaves to the arm: so sinfulness is a deformity that cleaves to an action. The evil of an action is not the effect of an action, nor attends it as it is an action, but as it is an action so circumstantiated, and conversant about this or that object; for the same action done by two several persons, may be good in one, and bad in the other; as when two judges are in joint commission for the trial of a malefactor, both upon the appearance of his guilt condemn him. This action in both, considered as an action, is good; for it is an adjudging a man to death, whose crime deserves such a punishment. But this same act, which is but one joint act of both, may be morally good in one judge, and morally evil in the other: morally good in him that condemns him out of an unbiassed consideration of the demerit of his fact, obedience to the law, and conscious of the duty of his place; and morally evil in the other, who hath no respect to those considerations, but joins in the act of condemnation, principally moved by some private animosity against the prisoner, and desire of revenge for some injury he hath really received, or imagines that he hath received from him. The act in itself is the same materially in both; but in one it is an act of justice, and in the other an act of murder, as it respects the principles and motives of it in the two judges; take away the respect of private revenge, and the action in the ill judge had been as laudable as the action of the other. The substance of an act, and the sinfulness of an act, are separable and distinguishable; and God may concur with the substance of an act, without concurring with the sinfulness of the act: as the good judge, that condemned the prisoner out of conscience, concurred with the evil judge, who condemned the prisoner out of private revenge; not in the principle and motive of condemnation, but in the material part of condemnation. So God assists in that action of a man wherein sin is placed, but not in that which is the formal reason of sin, which is a privation of some perfection the action ought morally to have.

(3.) It will appear further in this, that hence it follows that the action, and the viciousness of the action, may have two distinct causes. That may be a cause of the one that is not the cause of the other, and hath no hand in the producing of it. God concurs to the act of the mind as it counsels, and to the external action upon that counsel, as he preserves the faculty, and gives strength to the mind to consult, and the other parts to execute; yet he is not in the least tainted with the viciousness of the action. Though the action be from God as a concurrent cause, yet the ill quality of the action is solely from the creature with whom God concurs. The sun and the earth concur to the production of all the plants that are formed in the womb of the one, and midwifed by the other. The sun distributes heat, and the earth communicates sap; it is the same heat dispersed by the one, and the same juice bestowed by the other: it hath not a sweet juice for one, and a sour juice for another. This general influx of the sun and earth is not the immediate cause that one plant is poisonous, and another wholesome; but the sap of the earth is turned by the nature and quality of each plant: if there were not such an influx of the sun and earth, no plant could exert that poison which is in its nature; but yet the sun and earth are not the cause of that poison which is in the nature of the plant. If God did not concur to the motions of men, there could be no sinful action, because there could be no action at all; yet this concurrence is not the cause of that venom that is in the action, which ariseth from the corrupt nature of the creature, no more than the sun and earth are the cause of the poison of the plant, which is purely the effect of its own nature upon that general influx of the sun and earth. The influence of God pierceth through all subjects; but the action of man done by that influence is vitiated according to the nature of its own corruption. As the sun equally shines through all the quarrels in the window; if the glass be bright and clear, there is a pure splendor; if it be red or green, the splendor is from the sun; but the discoloring of that light upon the wall, is from the quality of the glass. But to be yet plainer: the soul is the image of God, and by the acts of the soul, we may come to the knowledge of the acts of God; the soul gives motion to the body and every member of it, and no member could move without a concurrent virtue of the soul; if a member be paralytic or gouty, whatsoever motion that gouty member hath, is derived to it from the soul; but the goutiness of the member was not the act of the soul, but the fruit of ill humors in the body; the lameness of the member, and the motion of the member, have two distinct causes; the motion is from one cause, and ill motion from another.q As the member could not move irregularly without some ill humor or cause of that distemper, so it could not move at all without the activity of the soul: so, though God concur to the act of understanding, willing, and execution, why can he not be as free from the irregularity in all those, as the soul is free from the irregularity of the motion of the body, while it is the cause of the motion itself? There are two illustrations generally used in this case, that are not unfit; the motion of the pen in writing is from the hand that holds it, but the blurs by the pen are from some fault in the pen itself: and the music of the instrument is from the hand that touches it, but the jarring from the faultiness of the strings; both are the causes of the motion of the pen and strings, but not the blurs or jarrings.

(4). It is very congruous to the wisdom of God, to move his creatures according to their particular natures; but this motion makes him not the cause of sin. Had our innocent nature continued, God had moved us according to that innocent nature; but when the state was changed for a corrupt one, God must either forbear all concourse, and so annihilate the world, or move us according to that nature he finds in us. If he had overthrown the world upon the entrance of sin, and created another upon the same terms, sin might have as soon defaced his second work, as it did the first; and then it would follow, that God would have been alway building and demolishing. It was not fit for God to cease from acting as a wise governor of his creature, because man did cease from his loyalty as a subject. Is it not more agreeable to God's wisdom as a governor, to concur with his creature according to his nature, than to deny his concurrence upon every evil determination of the creature? God concurred with Adam's mutable nature in his first act of sin; he concurred to the act, and left him to his mutability. If Adam had put out his hand to eat of any other unforbidden fruit, God would have supported his natural faculty then, and concurred with him in his motion. When Adam would put out his hand to take the forbidden fruit, God concurred to that natural action, but left him to the choice of the object, and to the use of his mutable nature: and when man became apostate, God concurs with him according to that condition wherein he found him, and cannot move him otherwise, unless he should alter that nature man had contracted. God moving the creature as he found him, is no cause of the ill

q Zanch. Tom. II. lib. iii. cap. 4, quest. iv. p. 226.

motion of the creature: as when a wheel is broken the space of a foot, it cannot but move ill in that part till it be mended. He that moves it, uses the same motion (as it is his act) which he would have done had the wheel been sound; the motion is good in the mover, but bad in the subject: it is not the fault of him that moves it, but the fault of that wheel that is moved, whose breaches came by some other cause. A man doth not use to lay aside his watch for some irregularity, as long as it is capable of motion, but winds it up: why should God cease from concurring with his creature in its vital operations and other actions of his will, because there was a flaw contracted in that nature, that came right and true out of his hand? And as he that winds up his disordered watch, is in the same manner the cause of its motion then, as he was when it was regular, yet, by that act of his, he is not the cause of the false motion of it. but that is from the deficiency of some part of the watch itself: so, though God concurs to that action of the creature, whereby the wickedness of the heart is drawn out, yet is not God therefore as unholy as the heart.

(5.) God hath one end in his concurrence, and man another in his action: so that there is a righteous, and often a gracious end in God, when there is a base and unworthy end in man. God concurs to the substance of the act; man produceth the circumstance of the act, whereby it is evil. God orders both the action wherein he concurs, and the sinfulness over which he presides, as a governor, to his own ends. In Joseph's case, man was sinful, and God merciful; his brethren acted "envy," and God designed "mercy" (Gen. xlv. 4, 5). They would be rid of him as an eye-sore, and God concurred with their action to make him their preserver (Gen. l. 20), "Ye thought evil against me, but God meant it unto good." God concurred to Judas his action of betraying our Saviour; he supported his nature while he contracted with the priests, and supported his members while he was their guide to apprehend him; God's end was the manifestation of his choicest love to man, and Judas' end was the gratification of his own covetousness. The Assyrian did a divine work against Jerusalem, but not with a Divine end (Isa. x. 5—7). He had a mind to enlarge his empire, enrich his coffers with the spoil, and gain the title of a conqueror; he is desirous to invade his neighbors, and God employs him to punish his rebels; but he means not so, nor doth his heart think so; he intended not as God intended. The axe doth not think what the carpenter intends to do with it. But God used the rapine of ambitious nature as an instrument of his justice; as the exposing malefactors to wild beasts was an ancient punishment, whereby the magistrates intended the execution of justice, and to that purpose used the natural fierceness of the beasts to an end different from what those ravaging creatures aimed at. God concurred with Satan in spoiling Job of his goods, and scarifying his body; God gave Satan licence to do it, and Job acknowledges it to be God's act (Job i. 12—21); but their ends were different; God concurred with Satan for the clearing the integrity of his servant, when Satan aimed at nothing but the provoking him to curse his Creator. The physician applies leeches to suck the superfluous blood, but the leeches suck to glut themselves, without any regard to the intention of the physician, and the welfare of the patient.   In the same act where men intend to hurt, God intends to correct; so that his concurrence is in a holy manner, while men commit unrighteous actions.   A judge commands the executioner to execute the sentence of death, which he hath justly pronounced against a malefactor, and admonisheth him to do it out of love to justice ; the executioner hath the authority of the judge for his commission, and the protection of the judge for his security ; the judge stands by to countenance and secure him in the doing of it; but if the executioner hath not the same intention as the judge, *viz.* a love to justice in the performance of his office, but a private hatred to the offender, the judge, though he commanded the fact of the executioner, yet did not command this error of his in it; and though he protects him in the fact, yet he owns not this corrupt disposition in him in the doing what was enjoined him, as any act of his own.

To conclude this.   Since the creature cannot act without God, cannot lift up a hand, or move his tongue, without God's preserving and upholding the faculty, and preserving the power of action, and preserving every member of the body in its actual motion, and in every circumstance of its motion, we must necessarily suppose God to have such a way of concurrence as doth not intrench upon his holiness.   We must not equal the creature to God, by denying his dependence on him ; nor must we imagine such a concurrence to the sinfulness of an act, as stains the Divine purity, which is, I think, sufficiently salved by distinguishing the matter of the act from the evil adhering to it ; for since all evil is founded in some good, the evil is distinguishable from the good, and the deformity of the action from the action itself; which, as it is a created act, hath a dependence on the will and influence of God; and as it is a sinful act, is the product of the will of the creature.

Prop. VI. The holiness of God is not blemished by proposing objects to a man, which he makes use of to sin.   There is no object proposed to man, but is directed by the providence of God, which influenceth all the motions in the world; and there is no object proposed to man, but his active nature may, according to the goodness or badness of his disposition, make a good or an ill use of.   That two men, one of a charitable, the other of a hard-hearted disposition, meet with an indigent and necessitous object, is from the providence of God ; yet this indigent person is relieved by the one, and neglected by the other.   There could be no action in the world, but about some object ; there could be no object offered to us but by Divine Providence ; the active nature of man would be in vain, if there were not objects about which it might be exercised.   Nothing could present itself to man as an object, either to excite his grace, or awaken his corruption, but by the conduct of the Governor of the world.   That David should walk upon the battlements of his palace, and Bathsheba be in the bath at the same time, was from the Divine Providence which orders all the affairs of the world (2 Sam. xi. 7); and so some understand (Jer. vi. 21): "Thus saith the Lord, I will lay stumbling-blocks before this people, and the fathers and sons together shall fall upon them." Since they have offered sacrifices without those due qualifications in their hearts, which were necessary to render them acceptable to me, I will lay in their way such objects, which their corruption will use ill to their farther sin and ruin; so (Ps. cv. 25), "He turned their heart to hate his people;" that is, by the multiplying his people, he gave occasion to the Egyptians of hating them, instead of caressing them, as they had formerly done. But God's holiness is not blemished by this; for,

1. This proposing or presenting of objects invades not the liberty of any man. The tree of the knowledge of good and evil, set in the midst of the garden of Eden, had no violent influence on man to force him to eat of it; his liberty to eat of it, or not, was reserved entire to himself; no such charge can be brought against any object whatsoever. If a man meet accidentally at a table with meat that is grateful to his palate, but hurtful to the present temper of his body, doth the presenting this sort of food to him strip him of his liberty to decline it, as well as to feed of it? Can the food have any internal influence upon his will, and lay the freedom of it asleep whether he will or no? Is there any charm in that, more than in other sorts of diet? No; but it is the habit of love which he hath to that particular dish, the curiosity of his fancy, and the strength of his own appetite, whereby he is brought into a kind of slavery to that particular meat, and not anything in the food itself. When the word is proposed to two persons, it is embraced by the one, rejected by the other; is it from the word itself, which is the object, that these two persons perform different acts? The object is the same to both, but the manner of acting about the object is not the same; is there any invasion of their liberty by it? Is the one forced by the word to receive it, and the other forced by the word to reject it? Two such contrary effects cannot proceed from one and the same cause; outward things have only an objective influence, not an inward; if the mere proposal of things did suspend or strike down the liberty of man, no angels in heaven, no man upon earth, no, not our Saviour himself, could do anything freely, but by force; objects that are ill used are of God's creation, and though they have allurements in them, yet they have no compulsive power over the will.[r] The fruit of the tree of knowledge of good and evil was pleasing to the sight; it had a quality to allure; there had not else needed a prohibition to bar the eating of it; but it could not have so much power to allure, as the Divine threatening to deter.

2. The objects are good in themselves, but the ill use of them is from man's corruption. Bathsheba was, by God's providence, presented to David's sight, but it was David's disposition moved him to so evil an act; what if God knew that he would use that object ill? yet he knew he had given him a power to refrain from any ill use of it; the objects are innocent, but our corruption poisons them. The same object hath been used by one to holy purposes and holy improvements, that hath been used by another to sinful ends; when a charitable object is presented to a good man, and a cruel man, one

[r] Amyral. de Libero arbit. p. 224.

relieves him, the other reviles him; the object was rather an occasion to draw out the charity of one, as well as the other; but the refusing to reach out a helping hand, was not from the person in calamity, but the disposition of the refuser to whom he was presented; it is not from the nature of the object that men do good or evil, but from the disposition of the person; what is good in itself, is made bad by our corruption. As the same meat which nourishes and strengthens a sound constitution, cherisheth the disease of another that eats at the same table, not from any unwholesome quality in the food, but the vicious quality of the humors lodging in the stomach, which turn the diet into fuel for themselves, which in its own nature was apt to engender a wholesome juice. Some are perfected by the same things whereby others are ruined. Riches are used by some, not only for their own, but the advantage of others in the world; by others only for themselves, and scarcely so much as their necessities require. Is this the fault of the wealth, or the dispositions of the persons, who are covetous instead of being generous? It is a calumny, therefore, upon God to charge him with the sin of man upon this account. The rain that drops from the clouds upon the plants is sweet in itself, but when it moistens the root of any venomous plant, it is turned into the juice of the plant, and becomes venomous with it. The miracles that our Saviour wrought, were applauded by some, and envied by the Pharisees; the sin arose not from the nature of the miracles, but the malice of their spirits. The miracles were fitter in their own nature to have induced them to an adoration of our Saviour, than to excite so vile a passion against one that had so many marks from heaven to dignify him, and proclaim him worthy of their respect. The person of Christ was an object proposed to the Jews; some worship him, others condemn and crucify him, and according to their several vices and base ends they use this object. Judas to content his covetousness, the Pharisees to glut their revenge, Pilate for his ambition, to preserve himself in his government, and avoid the articles the people might charge him with of countenancing an enemy to Cæsar. God at that time put into their minds a rational and true proposition which they apply to ill purposes.[s] Caiaphas said, that "it was expedient for one man to die for the people," which "he spake not of himself" (John xi. 50, 51). God put it into his mind; but he might have applied it better than he did, and considered, though the maxim was commendable, whether it might justly be applied to Christ, or whether there was such a necessity that he must die, or the nation be destroyed by the Romans. The maxim was sound and holy, decreed by God; but what an ill use did the high-priest make of it to put Christ to death as a seditious person, to save the nation from the Roman fury!

3. Since the natural corruption of men will use such objects ill, may not God, without tainting himself, present such objects to them in subserviency to his gracious decrees? Whatsoever God should present to men in that state, they would make an ill use of; hath not God, then, the sovereign prerogative to present what he pleases, and suppress others? To offer that to them which may serve his

* Amyrald, Ironic. p. 337.

holy purpose, and hide other things from them which are not so conducing to his gracious ends, which would be as much the occasions of exciting their sin, as the others which he doth bring forth to their view? The Jews, at the time of Christ, were of a turbulent and seditious humor; they expected a Messiah, a temporal king, and would readily have embraced any occasion to have been up in arms to have delivered themselves from the Roman yoke; to this purpose the people attempted once to make him king: and probably the expectation they had that he had such a design to head them, might be one reason of their "hosannas;" because without some such conceit it was not probable they should so soon change their note, and vote him to the cross in so short a time, after they had applauded him as if he had been upon a throne; but their being defeated of strong expectations, usually ended in a more ardent fury. This turbulent and seditious humor God directs in another channel, suppresseth all occurrences that might excite them to a rebellion against the Romans, which, if he had given way to, the crucifying Christ, which was God's design to bring about at that time, had not probably been effected, and the salvation of mankind been hindered or stood at a stay for a time. God, therefore, orders such objects and occasions, that might direct this seditious humor to another channel, which would else have run out in other actions, which had not been conducing to the great design he had then in the world. Is it not the right of God, and without any blemish to his holiness, to use those corruptions which he finds sown in the nature of his creature by the hand of Satan, and to propose such objects as may excite the exercise of them for his own service? Sure God hath as much right to serve himself of the creature of his own framing, and what natures soever they are possessed with, and to present objects to that purpose, as a falconer hath to offer this or that bird to his hawk to exercise his courage, and excite his ravenousness, without being termed the author of that ravenousness in the creature. God planted not those corruptions in the Jews, but finds them in those persons over whom he hath an absolute sovereignty in the right of a Creator, and that of a Judge for their sins: and by the right of that sovereignty may offer such objects and occasions, which, though innocent in themselves, he knows they will make use of to ill purposes, but which by the same decree that he resolves to present such occasions to them, he also resolves to make use of them for his own glory. It is not conceivable by us what way that death of Christ, which was necessary for the satisfaction of Divine justice, could be brought about without ordering the evil of some men's hearts by special occasions to effect his purpose; we cannot suppose that Christ can be guilty of any crime that deserved death by the Jewish law; had he been so a criminal, he could not have been a Redeemer: a perfect innocence was necessary to the design of his coming.[t] Had God himself put him to that death, without using instruments of wickedness in it, by some remarkable hand from heaven, the innocence of his nature had been forever eclipsed, and the voluntariness of his sacrifice had been obscured: the strangeness of such a judgment would have made his

[t] This I have spoken of before, but it is necessary now.

innocence incredible; he could not reasonably have been proposed as an object of faith. What, to believe in one that was struck dead by a hand from heaven? The propagation of the doctrine of redemption had wanted a foundation; and though God might have raised him again, the certainty of his death had been as questionable as his innocence in dying, had he not been raised. But God orders everything so as to answer his own most wise and holy ends, and maintain his truth, and the fulfilling the predictions of the minutest concerns about them, and all this by presenting occasions innocent in themselves, which the corruptions of the Jews took hold of, and whereby God, unknown to them, brought about his own decrees: and may not this be conceived without any taint upon God's holiness? for when there are seeds of all sin in man's nature, why may not God hinder the sprouting up of this or that kind of seed, and leave liberty to the growth of the other, and shut up other ways of sinning, and restrain men from them, and let them loose to that temptation which he intends to serve himself of, hiding from them those objects which were not so serviceable to his purpose, wherein they would have sinned, and offer others, which he knew their corruption would use ill, and were serviceable to his ends; since the depravation of their natures would necessarily hurry them to evil without restraining grace, as a scale will necessarily rise up when the weight in it, which kept it down, is taken away?

Prop. VII. The holiness of God is not blemished by withdrawing his grace from a sinful creature, whereby he falls into more sin. That God withdraws his grace from men, and gives them up sometimes to the fury of their lusts, is as clear in Scripture as anything (Deut. xxix. 4): " Yet the Lord hath not given you a heart to perceive, and eyes to see, and ears to hear," &c. Judas was delivered to Satan after the sop, and put into his power, for despising former admonitions. He often leaves the reins to the devil, that he may use what efficacy he can in those that have offended the Majesty of God; he withholds further influences of grace, or withdraws what before he had granted them. Thus he withheld that grace from the sons of Eli, that might have made their father's pious admonitions effectual to them (I Sam. ii. 25): "They hearkened not to the voice of their father, because the Lord would slay them." He gave grace to Eli to reprove them, and withheld that grace from them, which might have enabled them against their natural corruption and obstinacy to receive that reproof. But the holiness of God is not blemished by this.

1. Because the act of God in this is only negative.[u] Thus God is said to "harden" men: not by positive hardening, or working anything in the creature, but by not working, not softening, leaving a man to the hardness of his own heart, whereby it is unavoidable by the depravation of man's nature, and the fury of his passions, but that he should be further hardened, and "increase unto more ungodliness," as the expression is (2 Tim. ii. 19). As a man is said to give another his life, when he doth not take it away when it lay at his mercy; so God is said to "harden" a man, when he doth not

---

[u] Testard, de Natur, et Grat. Thes. 150, 151. Amy on Divers Texts, p. 311.

mollify him when it was in his power, and inwardly quicken him with that grace whereby he might infallibly avoid any further provoking of him. God is said to harden men when he removes not from them the incentives to sin, curbs not those principles which are ready to comply with those incentives, withdraws the common assistances of his grace, concurs not with counsels and admonitions to make them effectual; flasheth not in the convincing light which he darted upon them before. If hardness follows upon God's withholding his softening grace, it is not by any positive act of God, but from the natural hardness of man. If you put fire near to wax or rosin, both will melt; but when that fire is removed, they return to their natural quality of hardness and brittleness; the positive act of the fire is to melt and soften, and the softness of the rosin is to be ascribed to that; but the hardness is from the rosin itself, wherein the fire hath no influence, but only a negative act by a removal of it: so, when God hardens a man, he only leaves him to that stony heart which he derived from Adam, and brought with him into the world. All men's understandings being blinded, and their wills perverted in Adam, God's withdrawing his grace is but a leaving them to their natural pravity, which is the cause of their further sinning, and not God's removal of that special light he before afforded them, or restraint he held over them. As when God withdraws his preserving power from the creature, he is not the efficient, but deficient cause of the creature's destruction; so, in this case, God only ceaseth to bind and dam up that sin which else would break out.

2. The whole positive cause of his hardness is from man's corruption. God infuseth not any sin into his creatures, but forbears to infuse his grace, and restrain their lusts, which, upon the removal of his grace, work impetuously: God only gives them up to that which he knows will work strongly in their hearts. And, therefore, the apostle wipes off from God any positive act in that uncleanness the heathens were given up to (Rom. i. 24, " Wherefore God gave them up to uncleanness, through the lusts of their own hearts." And, ver. 26, God gave them up to " vile affections;" but they were their own affections, none of God's inspiring,) by adding, " through the lusts of their own hearts." God's giving them up was the logical cause, or a cause by way of argument; their own lusts were the true and natural cause; their own they were, before they were given up to them, and belonging to none, as the author, but themselves, after they were given up to them. The lust in the heart, and the temptation without, easily close and mix interests with one another: as the fire in a coal pit will with the fuel, if the streams derived into it for the quenching it be dammed up: the natural passions will run to a temptation, as the waters of a river tumble towards the sea. When a man that hath bridled in a high-mettled horse from running out, gives him the reins; or a huntsman takes off the string that held the dog, and lets him run after the hare,—are they the immediate cause of the motion of the one, or the other?—no, but the mettle and strength of the horse, and the natural inclination of the hound, both which are left to their own motions to pursue their own natural instincts. Man doth as naturally tend to sin as a stone to

the centre, or as a weighty thing inclines to a motion to the earth: it is from the propension of man's nature that he "drinks up iniquity like water:" and God doth no more when he leaves a man to sin, by taking away the hedge which stopped him, but leave him to his natural inclination. As a man that breaks up a dam he hath placed, leaves the stream to run in their natural channel; or one that takes away a prop from a stone to let it fall, leaves it only to that nature which inclines it to a descent; both have their motion from their own nature, and man is sin from his own corruption. The withdrawing the sunbeams is not the cause of darkness, but the shadiness of the earth; nor is the departure of the sun the cause of winter, but the coldness of the air and earth, which was tempered and beaten back into the bowels of the earth by the vigor of the sun, upon whose departure they return to their natural state: the sun only leaves the earth and air as it found them at the beginning of the spring or the beginning of the day.[x] If God do not give a man grace to melt him, yet he cannot be said to communicate to him that nature which hardens him, which man hath from himself. As God was not the cause of the first sin of Adam, which was the root of all other, so he is not the cause of the following sins, which, as branches, spring from that root; man's free-will was the cause of the first sin, and the corruption of his nature by it the cause of all succeeding sins. God doth not immediately harden any man, but doth propose those things, from whence the natural vice of man takes an occasion to strengthen and nourish itself. Hence, God is said to "harden Pharaoh's heart" (Exod. vii. 13), by concurring with the magicians in turning their rods into serpents, which stiffened his heart against Moses, conceiving him by reason of that, to have no more power than other men, and was an occasion of his father hardening: and Pharaoh is said to "harden himself" (Exod. viii. 32); that is, in regard of his own natural passion.

3. God is holy and righteous, because he doth not withdraw from man, till man deserts him. To say, that God withdrew that grace from Adam, which he had afforded him in creation, or anything that was due to him, till he had abused the gifts of God, and turned them to an end contrary to that of creation, would be a reflection upon the Divine holiness. God was first deserted by man before man was deserted by God; and man doth first contemn and abuse the common grace of God, and those relics of natural light, that "enlighten every man that comes into the world" (John i. 9); before God leaves him to the hurry of his own passions. Ephraim was first joined to idols, before God pronounced the fatal sentence, "Let him alone" (Hos. iv. 17): and the heathens first changed the glory of the incorruptible God, before God withdrew his common grace from the corrupted creature (Rom. i. 23, 24); and they first "served the creature more than the Creator," before the Creator gave them up to the slavish chains of their vile affections (ver. 25, 26). Israel first cast off God before God cast off them; but then "he gave them up to their own hearts' lusts, and they walked in their own counsels"

[x] Amyrald, de Prædest. p. 107.

(Ps. lxxxi. 11, 12). Since sin entered into the world by the fall of Adam, and the blood of all his posterity was tainted, man cannot do anything that is formally good; not for want of faculties, but for the want of a righteous habit in those faculties, especially in the will; yet God discovers himself to man in the works of his hands; he hath left in him footsteps of natural reason; he doth attend him with common motions of his Spirit; corrects him for his faults with gentle chastisements. He is near unto all in some kind of instructions: he puts many times providential bars in their way of sinning; but when they will rush into it as the horse into the battle, when they will rebel against the light, God doth often leave them to their own course, sentence him that is "filthy to be filthy still" (Rev. xxii. 11), which is a righteous act of God, as he is rector and governor of the world. Man's not receiving, or not improving what God gives, is the cause of God's not giving further, or, taking away his own, which before he had bestowed; this is so far from being repugnant to the holiness and righteousness of God, that it is rather a commendable act of his holiness and righteousness, as the rector of the world, not to let those gifts continue in the hand of a man who abuses them contrary to his glory. Who will blame a father, that, after all the good counsels he hath given to his son to reclaim him, all the corrections he hath inflicted on him for his irregular practice, leaves him to his own courses, and withdraws those assistances which he scoffed at, and turned the deaf ear unto? Or, who will blame the physician for deserting the patient, who rejects his counsel, will not follow his prescriptions, but dasheth his physic against the wall? No man will blame him, no man will say that he is the cause of the patient's death, but the true cause is the fury of the distemper, and the obstinacy of the diseased person, to which the physician left him. And who can justly blame God in this case, who yet never denied supplies of grace to any that sincerely sought it at his hands; and what man is there that lies under a hardness, but first was guilty of very provoking sins? What unholiness is it to deprive men of those assistances, because of their sin, and afterwards to direct those counsels and practices of theirs, which he hath justly given them up unto, to serve the ends of his own glory in his own methods?

4. Which will appear further by considering, that God is not obliged to continue his grace to them. It was at his liberty whether he could give any renewing grace to Adam after his fall, or to any of his posterity: he was at his own liberty to withhold it or communicate it: but, if he were under any obligation then, surely he must be under less now, since the multiplication of sin by his creatures: but, if the obligation were none just after the fall, there is no pretence now to fasten any such obligation on God. That God had no obligation at first, hath been spoken to before; he is less obliged to continue his grace after a repeated refusal, and a peremptory abuse, than he was bound to proffer it after the first apostasy. God cannot be charged with unholiness in withdrawing his grace after we have received it, unless we can make it appear that his grace was a thing due to us, as we are his creatures, and as he is governor of the world. What prince looks upon himself as obliged to reside in any particu-

lar place of his kingdom? But suppose he be bound to inhabit in one particular city, yet after the city rebels against him, is he bound to continue his court there, spend his revenue among rebels, endanger his own honor and security, enlarge their charter, or maintain their ancient privileges? Is it not most just and righteous for him to withdraw himself, and leave them to their own tumultuousness and sedition, whereby they should eat the fruit of their own doings? If there be an obligation on God as a governor, it would rather lie on the side of justice to leave man to the power of the devil whom he courted, and the prevalency of those lusts he hath so often caressed; and wrap up in a cloud all his common illuminations, and leave him destitute of all common workings of his Spirit.

Prop. VIII. God's holiness is not blemished by his commanding those things sometimes which seem to be against nature, or thwart some other of his precepts; as when God commanded Abraham with his own hand to sacrifice his son (Gen. xxii. 2), there was nothing of unrighteousness in it. God hath a sovereign dominion over the lives and beings of his creatures, whereby as he creates one day, he might annihilate the next; and by the same right that he might demand the life of Isaac, as being his creature, he might demand the obedience of Abraham, in a ready return of that to him, which he had so long enjoyed by his grant. It is true, killing is unjust when it is done without cause, and by a private authority; but the authority of God surmounts all private and public authority whatsoever. Our lives are due to him when he calls for them; and they are more than once forfeit to him by reason of transgression. But, howsoever the case is, God commanded him to do it for the trial of his grace, but suffered him not to do it in favor to his ready obedience; but had Isaac been actually slain and offered, how had it been unrighteous in God, who enacts laws for the regulation of his creature, but never intended them to the prejudice of the rights of his sovereignty? Another case is that of the Israelites borrowing jewels of the Egyptians, by the order of God (Exod. xi. 2, 3; xii. 36). Is not God Lord of men's goods, as well as their lives? What have any, they have not received? and that not as proprietors independent on God, but his stewards; and may not he demand a portion of his steward to bestow upon his favorite? He that had power to dispose of the Egyptians' goods, had power to order the Israelites to ask them. Besides, God acted the part of a just judge in ordering them their wages for their service in this method, and making their task-masters give them some recompense for their unjust oppression so many years; it was a command from God, therefore, rather for the preservation of justice (the basis of all those laws which link human society), than any infringement of it. It was a material recompense in part, though not a formal one in the intention of the Egyptians; it was but in part a recompense; it must needs come short of the damage the poor captives had sustained by the tyranny of their masters, who had enslaved them contrary to the rules of hospitality; and could not make amends for the lives of the poor infants of Israel, whom they had drowned in the river. He that might for the unjust oppression of his people have taken away all their lives, destroyed the whole nation, and put the Israelites into the possession of their lands, could, without any unrighteousness, dispose of part of their goods; and it was rather an act of clemency to leave them some part, who had doubly forfeited all. Again, the Egyptians were as ready to lend by God's influence, as the Israelites were to ask by God's order: and though it was a loan, God, as Sovereign of the world, and Lord of the earth, and the fulness thereof, alienated the property by assuming them to the use of the tabernacle, to which service, most, if not all of them, were afterwards dedicated. God, who is lawgiver, hath power to dispense with his own law, and make use of his own goods, and dispose of them as he pleases; it is no unholiness in God to dispose of that which he hath a right unto. Indeed, God cannot command that which is in its own nature intrinsically evil; as to command a rational creature not to love him, not to worship him, to call God to witness to a lie; these are intrinsically evil; but for the disposing of the lives and goods of his creatures, which they have from him in right, and not in absolute propriety, is not evil in him, because there is no repugnancy in his own nature to such acts, nor is it anything inconsistent with the natural duty of a creature, and in such cases he may use what instruments he please. The point was, that holiness is a glorious perfection of the nature of God. We have showed the nature of this holiness in God; what it is; and we have demonstrated it, and proved that God is holy, and must needs be so; and also the purity of his nature in all his acts about sin: let us now improve it by way of use.

IV. Is holiness a transcendent perfection belonging to the nature of God? The first use shall be of instruction and information.

Inform. 1. How great and how frequent is the contempt of this eminent perfection in the Deity! Since the fall, this attribute, which renders God most amiable in himself, renders him most hateful to his apostate creature. It is impossible that he that loves iniquity, can affect that which is irreconcileably contrary to the iniquity he loves. Nothing so contrary to the sinfulness of man as the holiness of God, and nothing is thought of by the sinner with so much detestation. How do men account that which is the most glorious perfection of the Divinity, unworthy to be regarded as an accomplishment of their own souls! and when they are pressed to an imitation of it, and a detestation of what is contrary to it, have the same sentiment in their heart which the devil had in his language to Christ, Why art thou come to torment us before our time? What an enmity the world naturally hath to this perfection, I think is visible in the practice of the heathen, who among all their heroes which they deified, elevated none to that dignity among them for this or that moral virtue that came nearest to it, but for their valor or some usefulness in the concerns of this life. Æsculapius was deified for his skill in the cure of diseases; Bacchus, for the use of the grape; Vulcan, for his operations by fire; Hercules, for his destroying of tyrants and monsters; but none for their mere virtue; as if anything of purity were unworthy their consideration in the frame of a Deity, when it is the glory of all other perfections; so essential it is, that when men reject the imitation of this, God regards it as a total rejection of himself,

though they own all the other attributes of his nature (Ps. lxxxi. 11):
" Israel would none of me :" why ? because " they walked not in his
ways" (ver. 13); those ways wherein the purity of the Divine nature
was most conspicuous; they would own him in his power, when they
stood in need of a deliverance; they would own him in his mercy,
when they were plunged in distress; but they would not imitate
him in his holiness.   This being the lustre of the Divine nature, the
contempt of it is an obscuring all his other perfections, and a dashing a blot upon his whole escutcheon.   To own all the rest, and deny
him this, is to frame him as an unbeautiful monster,—a deformed
power.   Indeed, all sin is against this attribute ; all sin aims in general at the being of God, but in particular at the holiness of his Being.   All sin is a violence to this perfection ; there is not an iniquity
in the world, but directs its venomous sting against the Divine purity ; some sins are directed against his omniscience, as secret wickedness ; some against his providence, as distrust ; some against his
mercy, as unbelief ; some against his wisdom, as neglecting the
means instituted by him, censuring his ways and actings ; some
against his power, as trusting in means more than in God, and the
immoderate fear of men more than of God ; some against his truth,
as distrusting his promise, or not fearing his threatening ; but all
agree together in their enmity against this, which is the peculiar
glory of the Deity : every one of them is a receding from the Divine
image ; and the blackness of every one is the deeper, by how much
the distance of it from the holiness of God is the greater.   This contrariety to the holiness of God, is the cause of all the absolute atheism (if there be any such) in the world ; what was the reason " the
fool hath said in his heart, There is no God," but because the fool is
" corrupt, and hath done abominable work" (Ps, xiv. 1) ?   If they
believe the being of a God, their own reason will enforce them to
imagine him holy ; therefore, rather than fancy a holy God, they
would fain fancy none at all.—In particular,

1. The holiness of God is injured, in unworthy representations of
God, and imaginations of him in our own minds.   The heathen fell
under this guilt, and ascribed to their idols those vices which their
own sensuality inclined them to, unworthy of a man, much more unworthy of a God, that they might find a protection of their crimes in
the practice of their idols.   But is this only the notion of the heathens ? may there not be many among us whose love to their lusts,
and desires of sinning without control, move them to slander God in
their thoughts, rather than reform their lives, and are ready to frame,
by the power of their imaginative faculty, a God, not only winking,
but smiling, at their impurities?   I am sure God charges the impieties of men upon this score, in that Psalm (l. 21) which seems to
be a representation of the day of judgment, as some gather from ver.
6, when God sums up all together: " These things hast thou done,
and I kept silence ; thou thoughtest that I was altogether such an
one as thyself;" not a detester, but approver of thy crimes: and the
Psalmist seems to express God's loathing of sin in such a manner, as
intimates it to be contrary to the ideas and resemblances men make
of him in their minds (Ps. v. 4); " For thou art not a God that hast

pleasure in wickedness;" as we say, in vindication of a man, he is not such a man as you imagine him to be; thou art not such a God as the world commonly imagines thee to be, a God taking pleasure in iniquity. It is too common for men to fancy God not as he is, but as they would have him; strip him of his excellency for their own security. As God made man after his image, man would dress God after his own modes, as may best suit the content of his lusts, and encourage him in a course of sinning; for, when they can frame such a notion of God, as if he were a countenancer of sin, they will derive from thence a reputation to their crimes, commit wickedness with an unbounded licentiousness, and crown their vices with the name of virtues, because thay are so like to the sentiments of that God they fancy: from hence (as the Psalmist, in the Psalm before mentioned) ariseth that mass of vice in the world; such conceptions are the mother and nurse of all impiety. I question not but the first spring is some wrong notion of God, in regard of his holiness: we are as apt to imagine God as we would have him, as the black Ethiopians were to draw the image of their gods after their own dark hue, and paint him with their own color: as a philosopher in Theodoret speaks; If oxen and lions had hands, and could paint as men do, they would frame the images of their gods according to their own likeness and complexion. Such notions of God render him a swinish being, and worse than the vilest idols adored by the Egyptians, when men fancy a God indulgent to their appetites and most sordid lusts.

2. In defacing the image of God in our own souls. God, in the first draught of man, conformed him to his own image, or made him an image of himself; because we find that in regeneration this image is renewed (Eph. iv. 24); "The new man, which, after God, is created in righteousness and true holiness. He did not take angels for his pattern, in the first polishing the soul, but himself. In defacing this image we cast dirt upon the holiness of God, which was his pattern in the framing of us, and rather choose to be conformed to Satan, who is God's grand enemy, to have God's image wiped out of us, and the devil's pictured in us: therefore, natural men, in an unregenerate state, may justly be called devils, since our Saviour called the worst man, Judas, so (John vi. 1), and Peter, one of the best (Matt. xvi. 23): and if this title be given, by an infallible Judge, to one of the worst, and one of the best, it may, without wrong to any, be ascribed to all men that wallow in their sin, which is directly contrary to that illustrious image God did imprint upon them. How often is it seen that men control the light of their own nature, and stain the clearest beams of that candle of the Lord in their own spirits, that fly in the face of their own consciences, and say to them, as Ahab to Micaiah, Thou didst "never prophesy good to me;" thou didst never encourage me in those things that are pleasing to the flesh; and use it at the same rate as the wicked king did the prophet, "imprison it in unrighteousness" (Rom. i. 18), because it starts up in them sometimes sentiments of the holiness of God, which it represents in the soul of man! How jolly are many men when the exhalations of their sensitive part rise up to cloud the exactest principle of moral nature in their minds, and render the mon-

strous principles of the law of corruption more lively! Whence ariseth the wickedness which hath been committed with an open face in the world, and the applause that hath been often given to the worst of villanies? Have we not known, among ourselves, men to glory in their shame, and esteem that a most gentle accomplishment of man, which is the greatest blot upon his nature, and which, if it were upon God, would render him no God, but an impure devil; so that to be a gentleman among us hath been the same as to be an incarnate devil; and to be a man, was to be no better, but worse, than a brute? Vile wretches! is not this a contempt of Divine holiness, to kill that Divine seed which lies languishing in the midst of corrupted nature; to cut up any sprouts of it as weeds unworthy to grow in their gardens, and cultivate what is the seed of hell; prefer the rotten fruits of Sodom, marked with a Divine curse, before those relics of the fruits of Eden, of God's own planting?

3. The holiness of God is injured in charging our sin upon God. Nothing is more natural to men, than to seek excuses for their sin, and transfer it from themselves to the next at hand, and rather than fail, shift it upon God himself; and if they can bring God into a society with them in sin, they will hug themselves in a security that God cannot punish that guilt wherein he is a partner. Adam's children are not of a different disposition from Adam himself, who, after he was arraigned and brought to his trial, boggles not at flinging his dirt in the face of God, his Creator, and accuseth him as if he had given him the woman, not to be his help, but his ruin (Gen. iii. 12); "And the man said, The woman whom thou gavest to be with me, she gave me of the tree, and I did eat." He never supplicates for pardon, nor seeks a remedy, but reflects his crime upon God: Had I been alone, as I was first created, I had not eaten; but the woman, whom I received as a special gift from thee, hath proved my tempter and my bane. When man could not be like God in knowledge, he endeavored to make God like him in his crime; and when his ambition failed of equalizing himself with God, he did, with an insolence too common to corrupted nature, attempt, by the imputation of his sin, to equal the Divinity with himself. Some think Cain had the same sentiment in his answer to God's demand where his brother was (Gen. ii. 9); "Am I my brother's keeper?" Art not thou the Keeper and Governor of the world? why didst not thou take care of him, and hinder my killing him, and drawing this guilt upon myself, and terror upon my conscience? David was not behind, when, after the murder of Uriah, he sweeps the dirt from his own door to God's (2 Sam. xi. 25); "The sword devoureth one as well as another;" fathering that solely upon Divine Providence which was his own wicked contrivance: though afterwards he is more ingenuous in clearing God, and charging himself (Ps. li. 4): "Against thee, thee only have I sinned;" and he clears God in his judgment too. It is too common for the "foolishness of man to pervert his way;" and then "his heart frets against the Lord" (Prov. xix. 3). He studies mischief, runs in a way of sin, and when he hath conjured up troubles to himself, by his own folly, he excuseth himself, and, with indignation, charges God as the author both of his sin and misery,

and sets his mouth against the heavens. It is a more horrible thing to accuse God as a principal or accessary in our guilt, than to conceive him to be a favorer of our iniquity; yet both are bad enough.

4. The holiness of God is injured when men will study arguments from the holy word of God to color and shelter their crimes. When men will seek for a shelter for their lies, in that of the midwives to preserve the children, or in that of Rahab to save the spies, as if, because God rewarded their fidelity, he countenanced their sin. How often is Scripture wrested to be a plea for unbecoming practices, that God, in his word, may be imagined a patron for their iniquity? It is not unknown that some have maintained their quaffing and carousing (from Eccles. viii. 11), "That a man hath no better thing under the sun than to eat, drink, and be merry:" and their gluttony (from Matt. v. 11), "That which goes into the belly defiles not a man." The Jesuits' morals are a transcript of this. How often hath the Passion of our Saviour, the highest expression of God's holiness, been employed to stain it, and encourage the most debauched practices! Grace hath been turned into wantonness, and the abundance of grace been used as a blast to increase the flames of sin, as if God had no other aim in that work of redemption, but to discover himself more indulgent to our sensual appetites, and by his severity with his Son, become more gracious to our lusts; this is to feed the roots of hell with the dews of heaven, to make grace a pander for the abuse of it, and to employ the expressions of his holiness in his word to be a sword against the essential holiness of his nature: as if a man should draw an apology for his treason out of that law that was made to forbid, not to protect, his rebellion. Not the meanest instrument in the temple was to be alienated from the use it was by Divine order appointed to, nor was it to be employed in any common use; and shall the word of God, which is the image of his holiness, be transferred by base interpretations to be an advocate for iniquity? Such an ill use of his word reflects upon that hand which imprinted those characters of purity and righteousness upon it: as the misinterpretation of the wholesome laws of a prince, made to discourage debauchery, reflects upon his righteousness and sincerity in enacting them.

5. The holiness of God is injured, when men will put up petitions to God to favor them in a wicked design. Such there are, and taxed by the apostle (James iv. 3), "Ye ask amiss, that you may consume it upon your lusts," who desired mercies from God, with an intent to make them instruments of sin, and weapons of unrighteousness; as it is reported of a thief, that he always prayed for the success of his robbery. It hath not been rare in the world to appoint fasts and prayers for success in wars manifestly unjust, and commenced upon breaches of faith. Many covetous men petition God to prosper them in their unjust gain; as if the blessed God sat in his pure majesty upon a throne of grace, to espouse unjust practices, and make iniquity prosperous. There are such as "offer sacrifice with an evil mind" (Prov. xxi. 27), to barter with God for a divine blessing to spirit a wicked contrivance. How great a contempt of the holiness of God is this! How inexcusable would it be for a favorite to address him-

self to a just prince with this language: Sir, I desire a boon of such lands that lie near me, for an addition to my estate, that I may have supports for my debauchery, and be able to play the villain more powerfully among my neighbors! Hereby he implies that his prince is a friend to such crimes and wickedness he intends his petition for. Is not this the language of many men's hearts in the immediate presence of God? The order of prayer runs thus, " Hallowed be thy name;" first to have a deep sense of the holiness of the Divine nature, and an ardent desire for the glory of it. This order is inverted by asking those things which are not agreeable to the will of God, not meet for us to ask, and not meet for God to give; or asking things agreeable to the will of God, but with a wicked intention. This is, in effect, to desire God to strip himself of his holiness, and commit sacrilege upon his own nature to gratify our lusts.

6. The purity of God is contemned, in hating and scoffing at the holiness which is in a creature. Whoever looks upon the holiness of a creature as an unlovely thing, can have no good opinion of the amiableness of Divine purity. Whosoever hates those qualities and graces that resemble God in any person, must needs contemn the original pattern, which is more eminent in God. If there be no comeliness in a creature's holiness, to render it grateful to us, we should say of God himself, were he visible among us, with those in the prophet (Isa. liii.), "There is no beauty in him, that we should desire him." Holiness is beautiful in itself. If God be the most lovely Being, that which is a likeness to him, so far as it doth resemble him, must needs be amiable, because it partakes of God; and, therefore, those that see no beauty in an inferior holiness, but contemn it because it is a purity above them, contemn God much more. He that hates that which is imperfect merely for that excellency which is in it, doth much more hate that which is perfect, without any mixture or stain. Holiness being the glory of God, the peculiar title of the Deity, and from him derived unto the nature of a creature, he that mocks this in a person, derides God himself; and, when he cannot abuse the purity in the Deity, he will do it in his image; as rebels that cannot wrong the king in his person, will do it in his picture, and his subjects that are loyal to him. He that hates the picture of a man, hates the person represented by it much more; he that hates the beams, hates the sun; the holiness of a creature is but a beam from that infinite Sun, a stream from that eternal Fountain. Where there is a derision of the purity of any creature, there is a greater reflection upon God in that derision, as he is the Author of it. If a mixed and stained holiness be more the subject of any man's scoffs than a great deal of sin, that person hath a disposition more roundly to scoff at God himself, should he appear in that unblemished and unspotted purity which infinitely shines in his nature. O! it is a dangerous thing to scoff and deride holiness in any person, though never so mean; such do deride and scoff at the most holy God.

7. The holiness of God is injured by our unprepared addresses to him, when, like swine, we come into the presence of God with all our mire reeking and steaming upon us. A holy God requires a holy worship; and if our best duties, having filth in every part, as

performed by us, are unmeet for God, how much more unsuitable are dead and dirty duties to a living and immense holiness! Slight approaches and drossy frames speak us to have imaginations of God as of a slight and sottish being. This is worse than the heathens practised, who would purge their flesh before they sacrificed, and make some preparations in a seeming purity, before they would enter into their temples. God is so holy, that were our services as refined as those of angels, we could not present him with a service meet for his holy nature (Josh. xxiv. 19). We contemn, then, this perfection, when we come before him without due preparation; as if God himself were of an impure nature, and did not deserve our purest thoughts in our applications to him; as if any blemished and polluted sacrifice were good enough for him, and his nature deserved no better. When we excite not those elevated frames of spirit which are due to such a being, when we think to put him off with a lame and imperfect service, we worship him not according to the excellency of his nature, but put a slight upon his majestic sanctity. When we nourish in our duties those foolish imaginations which creep upon us; when we bring into, and continue our worldly, carnal, debauched fancies in his presence, worse than the nasty servants, or bemired dogs, a man would blush to be attended with in his visits to a neat person. To be conversing with sordid sensualities, when we are at the feet of an infinite God, sitting upon the throne of his holiness, is as much a contempt of him, as it would be of a prince, to bring a vessel full of nasty dung with us, when we come to present a petition to him in his royal robes; or as it would have been to God, if the high priest should have swept all the blood and excrements of the sacrifices from the foot of the altar into the Holy of holies, and heaped it up before the mercy-seat, where the presence of God dwelt between the cherubims, and afterwards shovelled it up into the ark, to be lodged with Aaron's rod and the pot of manna.

8. God's holiness is slighted in depending upon our imperfect services to bear us out before the tribunal of God. This is too ordinary. The Jews were often infected with it (Rom. iii. 10), who, not well understanding the enormity of their taansgressions, the interweaving of sin with their services, and the unspottedness of the Divine purity, mingled an opinion of merit with their sacrifices, and thought, by the cutting the throat of a beast, and offering it upon God's altar, they had made a sufficient compensation to that holiness they had offended. Not to speak of many among the Romanists who have the same notion, thinking to make satisfaction to God by erecting an hospital, or endowing a church, as if this injured perfection could be contented with the dregs of their purses, and the offering of an unjust mammon, more likely to mind God of the injury they have done him, than contribute to the appeasing of him. But is it not too ordinary with miserable men, whose consciences accuse them of their crimes, to rely upon the mumbling of a few formal prayers, and in the strength of them, to think to stand before the tremendous tribunal of God, and meet with a discharge upon this account from any accusation this Divine perfection can present against them? Nay, do not the best Christians sometimes

find a principle in them, that makes them stumble in their goings
forth to Christ, and glorifying the holiness of God in that method
which he hath appointed?   Sometimes casting an eye at their
grace, and sticking awhile to this or that duty, and gazing at the
glory of the temple-building, while they should more admire the
glorious Presence that fills it.   What is all this but a villifying of
the holiness of the Divine nature, as though it would be well enough
contented with our impurities and imperfections, because they look
like a righteousness in our estimation?   As though dross and dung,
which are the titles the apostles gives to all the righteousness of a
fallen creature (Phil. iii. 8), were valuable in the sight of God, and
sufficient to render us comely before him.   It is a blasphemy against
this attribute, to pretend that anything so imperfect, so daubed, as
the best of our services are, can answer to that which is infinitely
perfect, and be a ground of demanding eternal life: it is at best, to
set up a gilded Dagon, as a fit companion for .the ark of his Holiness; our own righteousness as a suitable mate for the righteousness
of God: as if he had repented of the claim he made by the law to an
exact conformity, and thrown off the holiness of his nature for the
fondling of a corrupted creature.   Rude and foolish notions of the
Divine purity are clearly evidenced by any confidence in any righteousness of our own, though never so splendid.   It is a rendering
the righteousness of God as dull and obscure as that of men; a
mere outside, as their own; as blind as the heathens pictured their
Fortune, that knew as little how to discern the nature and value of
the offerings made to her, as to distribute her gifts, as if it were all
one to them, to have a dog or a lamb presented in sacrifice.   As if
God did not well understand his own nature, when he enacted so
holy a law, and strengthened it with so severe a threatening; which
must follow upon our conceit, that he will accept a righteousness
lower than that which bears some suitableness to the holiness of his
own nature, and that of his law ; and that he could easily be put off
with a pretended and counterfeit service.   What are the services of
the generality of men, but suppositions, that they can bribe God to
an indulgence of them in their sins, and by an oral sacrifice, cause
him to divest himself of his hatred of their former iniquities, and
countenance their following practises.   As the harlot, that would
return fresh to her uncleanness, upon the confidence that her peace
offering had contented the righteousness of God (Prov. vii. 14): as
though a small service could make him wink at our sins, and lay
aside the glory of his nature; when, alas! the best duties in the
most gracious persons in this life, are but as the steams of a spiced
dung-hill, a composition of myrrh and froth, since there are swarms
of corruptions in their nature, and secret sins that they need a
cleansing from.
     9. It is a contemning the holiness of God, when we charge the
law of God with rigidness.   We cast dirt upon the holiness of God
when we blame the law of God, because it shackles us, and prohibit our desired pleasures; and hate the law of God, as they did
the prophets, because they did not prophesy smooth things; but
called to them, to " get" them " out of the way, and turn aside out

of the path, and cause the Holy One of Israel to cease from before them" (Isa. xxx. 10, 11). Put us no more in mind of the holiness of God, and the holiness of his law; it is a troublesome thing for us to hear of it: let him be gone from us, since he will not countenance our vices, and indulge our crimes; we would rather hear there is a God, than you would tell us of a holy one. We are contrary to the law, when we wish it were not so exact; and, therefore, contrary to the holiness of God, which set the stamp of exactness and righteousness upon it. We think him injurious to our liberty, when, by his precept he thwarts our pleasure; we wish it of another frame, more mild, more suitable to our minds: it is the same, as if we should openly blame God for consulting with his own righteousness, and not with our humors, before he settled his law; that he should not have drawn from the depths of his righteous nature, but squared it to accommodate our corruption. This being the language of such complaints, is a reproving God, because he would not be unholy, that we might be unrighteous with impunity. Had the Divine law been suited to our corrupt state, God must have been unholy to have complied with his rebellious creature. To charge the law with rigidness, either in language or practice, is the highest contempt of God's holiness; for it is an implicit wish, that God were as defiled, polluted, disorderly, as our corrupted selves.

10. The holiness of God is injured opinionatively. (1). In the opinion of venial sins. The Romanists divide sins into venial and mortal: mortal, are those which deserve eternal death; venial, the lighter sort of sins, which rather deserve to be pardoned than punished; or if punished, not with an eternal, but temporal punishment. This opinion hath no foundation in, but is contrary to, Scripture. How can any sin be in its own nature venial, when the due "wages of every sin is death" (Rom. vi. 23)? and he who "continues not in every thing that the law commands," falls under a "curse" (Gal. iii. 10). It is a mean thought of the holiness and majesty of God to imagine, that any sin which is against an infinite majesty, and as infinite a purity both in the nature of God and the law of God, should not be considered as infinitely heinous. All sins are transgressions of the eternal law, and in every one the infinite holiness of God is some way slighted. (2). In the opinion of works of supererogation. That is, such works as are not commanded by God, which yet have such a dignity and worth in their own nature, that the performers of them do not only merit at God's hands for themselves, but fill up a treasure of merits for others, that come short of fulfilling the precepts God hath enjoined. It is such a mean thought of God's holiness, that the Jews, in all the charges brought against them in Scripture, were never guilty of. And if you consider what pitiful things they are, which are within the compass of such works, you have sufficient reason to bewail the ignorance of man, and the low esteem he hath of so glorious a perfection. The whipping themselves often in a week, extraordinary watchings, fastings, macerating their bodies, wearing a capuchin's habit, &c. are pitiful things to give content to an Infinite Purity. As if the pre-

cept of God required only the inferior degrees of virtue, and the counsels the more high and excellent; as if the law of God, which the Psalmist counts "perfect" (Ps. xix. 7), did not command all good, and forbid all evil; as if the holiness of God had forgotten itself in the framing the law, and made it a scanty and defective rule; and the righteousness of a creature were not only able to make an eternal righteousness, but surmount it.   As man would be at first as knowing as God, so some of his posterity would be more holy than God; set up a wisdom against the wisdom of God, and a purity above the Divine purity.   Adam was not so presumptuous; he intended no more than an equalling God in knowledge; but those would exceed him in righteousness, and not only presume to render a satisfaction for themselves to the holiness they have injured, but to make a purse for the supply of others that are indigent, that they may stand before the tribunal of God with a confidence in the imaginary righteousness of a creature.   How horrible is it for those that come short of the law of God themselves, to think that they can have enough for a loan to their neighbors!   An unworthy opinion.

Inform. 2. It may inform us, how great is our fall from God, and how distant we are from him.   View the holiness of God, and take a prospect of the nature of man, and be astonished to see a person created in the Divine image, degenerated into the image of the devil. We are as far fallen from the holiness of God, which consists in a hatred of sin, as the lowest point of the earth is from the highest point of the heavens.   The devil is not more fallen from the rectitude of his nature and likeness to God, than we are; and that we are not in the same condition with those apostate spirits, is not from anything in our nature, but from the mediation of Christ, upon which account God hath indulged in us a continuance of some remainders of that which Satan is wholly deprived of.   We are departed from our original pattern; we were created to live the "life of God," that that is, a life of "holiness;" but now we are "alienated from the life of God" (Eph. iv. 18), and of a beautiful piece we are become deformed, daubed over with the most defiling mud: we "work uncleanness with greediness," according to our ability, as creatures; as God doth work "holiness" with affection and ardency, according to his infiniteness, as Creator.   More distant we are from God by reason of sin, than the vilest creature, the most deformed toad, or poisonous serpent, is from the highest and most glorious angel.   By forsaking our innocence, we departed from God as our original copy.   The apostle might well say (Rom. iii. 23), that by sin "we are come short of the glory of God."   Interpreters trouble themselves much about that place, "Man is come short of the glory of God," that is, of the holiness of God, which is the glory of the Divine nature, and was pictured in the rational, innocent creature.   By the "glory of God," is meant the holiness of God; (as 1 Cor. iii. 18), "Beholding, as in a glass, the glory of the Lord, we are changed into the same image from glory to glory;" that is the glory of God in the text, into the image of which we are changed; but the Scripture speaks of no other image of God, but that of holiness; "we are come short of the glory of God;" of the holiness of God, which is the glory of God; and the image of it, which was the glory of man. By sin, which is particular in opposition to the purity of God, man was left many leagues behind any resemblance to God; he stripped off that which was the glory of his nature, and was the only means of glorifying God as his Creator. The word ὑστεροῦνται, the apostle uses, is very significant,—postponed by sin an infinite distance from any imitation of God's holiness, or any appearance before him in a garb of nature pleasing to him. Let us lament our fall and distance from God.

Inform. 3. All unholinesss is vile, and opposite to the nature of God. It is such a loathsome thing, that the "purity of God's eye is averse from beholding" (Hab. i. 3). It is not said there, that he will not, but he cannot, look on evil; there cannot be any amicableness between God and sin, the natures of both are so directly and unchangeably contrary to one another. Holiness is the life of God; it endures as long as his life; he must be eternally averse from sin, he can live no longer than he lives in the hatred and loathing of it. If he should for one instant cease to hate it, he would cease to live. To be a holy God, is as essential to him, as to be a living God; and he would not be a living God, but a dead God, if he were in the least point of time an unholy God. He cannot look on sin without loathing it; he cannot look on sin but his heart riseth against it; it must needs be most odious to him, as that which is against the glory of his nature, and directly opposite to that which is the lustre and varnish of all his other perfections. It is the "abominable thing which his soul hates" (Jer. xliv. 4); the vilest terms imaginable are used to signify it. Do you understand the loathsomeness of a miry swine, or the nauseousness of the vomit of a dog? these are emblems of sin (2 Peter ii. 22). Can you endure the steams of putrefied carcasses from an open sepulchre (Rom. iii. 23)? is the smell of the stinking sweat or excrements of a body delightful? the word ῥυπαρία in James i. 21, signifies as much. Or is the sight of a body overgrown with scabs and leprosy grateful to you? So vile, so odious is sin, in the sight of God. It is no light thing, then, to fly in the face of God; to break his eternal law; to dash both the tables in pieces: to trample the transcript of God's own nature under our feet; to cherish that which was inconsistent with his honor; to lift up our heels against the glory of his nature; to join issue with the devil in stabbing his heart, and depriving him of his life. Sin, in every part of it, is an opposition to the holiness of God, and consequently an envying him a being and life, as well as a glory. If sin be such a thing, "ye that love the Lord, hate evil."

Inform. 4. Sin cannot escape a due punishment. A hatred of unrighteousness, and consequently a will to punish it, is as essential to God as a love of righteousness. Since he is not as an heathen idol, but hath eyes to see, and purity to hate every iniquity, he will have an infinite justice to punish whatsoever is against infinite holiness. As he loves everything that is amiable, so he loathes everything that is filthy, and that constantly, without any change; his whole nature is set against it; he abhors nothing but this. It is not the devil's knowledge or activity that his hatred is terminated in, but the malice and unholiness of his nature; it is this only is the object of his severity; it is in the recompense of this only that there can be a manifestation of his justice. Sin must be punished; for,

1. This detestation of sin must be manifested. How should we certainly know his loathing of it, if he did not manifest, by some act, how ungrateful it is to him? As his love to righteousness would not appear, without rewarding it; so his hatred of iniquity would be as little evidenced, without punishing it; his justice is the great witness to his purity. The punishment, therefore, inflicted on the wicked, shall be, in some respect, as great as the rewards bestowed upon the righteous. Since the hatred of sin is natural to God, it is as natural to him to show, one time or other, his hatred of it. And since men have a conceit that God is like them in impurity, there is a necessity of some manifestation of himself to be infinitely distant from those conceits they have of him (Ps. l. 21); "I will reprove thee, and set them in order before thine eyes." He would else encourage the injuries done to his holiness, favor the extravagances of the creature, and condemn, or at least slight, the righteousness both of his own nature, and his sovereign law. What way is there for God to manifest his hatred, but by threatening the sinner? and what would this be but a vain affrightment, and ridiculous to the sinner, if it were never to be put in execution? There is an indissoluble connection between his hatred of sin, and punishment of the offender (Ps. xi. 5, 6); "The wicked, his soul hates. Upon the wicked he shall rain snares, fire, and brimstone," &c. He cannot approve of it without denying himself; and a total impunity would be a degree of approbation. The displeasure of God is eternal and irreconcileable against sin; for sin being absolutely contrary to his holy nature, he is eternally contrary to it; if there be not, therefore, a way to separate the sin from the sinner, the sinner must lie under the displeasure of God; no displeasure can be manifested without some marks of it upon the person that lies under that displeasure. The holiness of God will right itself of the wrongs done to it, and scatter the profaners of it at the greatest distance from him, which is the greatest punishment that can be inflicted; to be removed far from the Fountain of Life is the worst of deaths; God can as soon lay aside his purity, as always forbear his displeasure against an impure person; it is all one not to hate it, and not to manifest his hatred of it.

2. As his holiness is natural and necessary, so is the punishment of unholiness necessary to him. It is necessary that he should abominate sin, and therefore necessary he should discountenance it. The severities of God against sin are not vain scare-crows; they have their foundation in the righteousness of his nature; it is because he is a righteous and holy God, that he "will not forgive our transgressions and sins" (Josh. xxiv. 19), that is, that he will punish them. The throne of his "holiness is a fiery flame" (Dan. vii. 9); there is both a pure light and a scorching heat. Whatsoever is contrary to the nature of God, will fall under the justice of God; he would else violate his own nature, deny his own perfection, seem to be out of love with his own glory and life. He doth not hate it out of choice, but from the immutable propension of his nature; it is not so free an act of his will, as the creation of man and angels, which he might

have forborne as well as effected. As the detestation of sin results from the universal rectitude of his nature, so the punishment of sin follows upon that, as he is the righteous Governor of the world: it is as much against his nature not to punish it, as it is against his nature not to loathe it; he would cease to be holy if he ceased to hate it, and he would cease to hate it if he ceased to punish it. Neither the obedience of our Saviour's life, nor the strength of his cries, could put a bar to the cup of his passion; God so hated sin, that when it was but imputed to his Son, without any commission of it, he would bring a hell upon his soul. Certainly if God could have hated sin without punishing it, his Son had never felt the smart of his wrath; his love to his Son had been strong enough to have caused him to forbear, had not the holiness of his nature been stronger to move him to inflict a punishment according to the demerit of his sin. God cannot but be holy, and therefore cannot but be just, because injustice is a part of unholiness.

3. Therefore there can be no communion between God and unholy spirits. How is it conceivable, that God should hate the sin, and cherish the sinner, with all his filth in his bosom? that he should eternally detest the crime, and eternally fold the sinner in his arms? Can less be expected from the purity of his nature, than to separate an impure soul, as long as it remains so? Can there be any delightful communion between those whose natures are contrary? Darkness and light may as soon kiss each other, and become one nature: God and the devil may as soon enter into an eternal league and covenant together. For God to have pleasure in wickedness, and to admit evil to dwell with him, are equally impossible to his nature (Ps. v. 4): while he hates impurity, he cannot have communion with an impure person. It may as soon be expected, that God should hate himself, offer violence to his own nature, lay aside his purity as an abominable thing, and blot his own glory, as love an impure person, entertain him as his delight, and set him in the same heaven and happiness with himself, and his holy angels. He must needs loathe him, he must needs banish him from his presence, which is the greatest punishment. God's holiness and hatred of sin necessarily infer the punishment of it.

Inform. 5. There is, therefore, a necessity of the satisfaction of the holiness of God by some sufficient mediator. The Divine purity could not meet with any acquiescence in all mankind after the fall: sin was hated; the sinner would be ruined, unless some way were found out to repair the wrongs done to the holiness of God; either the sinner must be condemned for ever, or some satisfaction must be made, that the holiness of the Divine nature might eternally appear in its full lustre. That it is essential to the nature of God to hate all unrighteousness, as that which is absolutely repugnant to his nature, none do question. That the justice of God is so essential to him, as that sin could not be pardoned without satisfaction, some do question; though this latter seems rationally to follow upon the former.ʸ That holiness is essential to the nature of God, is evident; because, else, God may as much be conceived without purity, as he might be

ʸ Turretin. de Satisfac. p. 8.

conceived without the creating the sun or stars. No man can, in his right wits, frame a right notion of a Deity without purity. It would be less blasphemy against the excellency of God, to conceit him not knowing, than to imagine him not holy : and, for the essentialness of his justice, Joshua joins both his holiness and his jealousy as going hand in hand together (Josh. xxiv. 19); " He is a holy God, he is a jealous God, he will not forgive your sin." But consider only the purity of God, since it is contrary to sin, and, consequently, hating the sinner; the guilty person cannot be reduced to God, nor can the holiness of God have any complacency in a filthy person, but as fire hath in stubble, to consume it. How the holy God should be brought to delight in man without a *salvo* for the rights of his holiness, is not to be conceived without an impeachment of the nature of God. The law could not be abolished; that would reflect, indeed, upon the righteousness of the Lawgiver: to abolish it, because of sin, would imply a change of the rectitude of his nature. Must he change his holiness for the sake of that which was against his holiness, in a compliance with a profane and unrighteous creature ? This should engage him rather to maintain his law, than to null it; and to abrogate his law as soon as he had enacted it, since sin stepped into the world presently after it, would be no credit to his wisdom. There must be a reparation made of the honor of God's holiness; by ourselves it could not be without condemnation; by another it could not be without a sufficiency in the person : no creature could do it. All the creatures being of a finite nature, could not make a compensation for the disparagements of Infinite Holiness. He must have despicable and vile thoughts of this excellent perfection, that imagines that a few tears, and the glavering fawnings at the death of a creature, can be sufficient to repair the wrongs, and restore the rights of this attribute. It must, therefore, be such a compensation as might be commensurate to the holiness of the Divine nature and the Divine law, which could not be wrought by any, but Him that was possessed of a Godhead to give efficacy and exact congruity to it. The Person designed and appointed by God for so great an affair, was "one in the form of God, one equal with God," (Phil. ii. 6), who could not be termed by such a title of dignity, if he had not been equal to God in the universal rectitude of the Divine nature, and therefore in his holiness. The punishment due to sin is translated to that person for the righting Divine holiness, and the righteousness of that Person is communicated to the sinner for the pardon of the offending creature. If the sinner had been eternally damned, God's hatred of sin had been evidenced by the strokes of his justice; but his mercy to a sinner had lain in obscurity. If the sinner had been pardoned and saved without such a reparation, mercy had been evident; but his holiness had hid its head for ever in his own bosom. There was therefore a necessity of such a way to manifest his purity, and yet to bring forth his mercy : that mercy might not alway sigh for the destruction of the creature, and that holiness might not mourn for the neglect of its honor.

Inform. 6. Hence it will follow, there is no justification of a sinner by any thing in himself. After sin had set foot in the world, man could present nothing to God acceptable to him, or bearing any proportion to the holiness of his law, till God set forth a Person, upon whose account the acceptation of our persons and services is founded (Eph. i. 6), "Who hath made us accepted in the Beloved." The Infinite purity of God is so glorious, that it shames the holiness of angels, as the light of the sun dims the light of the fire; much more will the righteousness of fallen man, who is vile, and "drinks up iniquity like water," vanish into nothing in his presence. With what self-abasement and abhorrence ought he to be possessed that comes as short of the angels in purity, as a dunghill doth of a star! The highest obedience that ever was performed by any mere man, since lapsed nature, cannot challenge any acceptance with God, or stand before so exact an inquisition. What person hath such a clear innocence, and unspotted obedience in such a perfection, as in any degree to suit the holiness of the Divine nature? (Ps. cxliii. 2): "Enter not into judgment with thy servant, for in thy sight shall no man living be justified." If God should debate the case simply with a man in his own person, without respecting the Mediator, he were not able to "answer one of a thousand." Though we are his servants, as David was, and perform a sincere service, yet there are many little motes and dust of sin in the best works, that cannot lie undiscovered from the eye of his holiness; and if we come short in the least of what the law requires, we are "guilty of all" (James ii. 10). So that "In thy sight shall no man living be justified;" in the sight of thy infinite holiness, which hates the least spot; in the sight of thy infinite justice, which punishes the least transgression. God would descend below his own nature, and vilify both his knowledge and his purity, should he accept that for a righteousness and holiness which is not so in itself; and nothing is so, which hath the least stain upon it contrary to the nature of God. The most holy saints in Scripture, upon a prospect of his purity, have cast away all confidence in themselves; every flash of the Divine purity has struck them into a deep sense of their own impurity and shame for it (Job xlii. 6), "Wherefore I abhor myself in dust and ashes." What can the language of any man be that lies under a sense of infinite holiness and his own defilement in the least, but that of the prophet (Isa. vi. v), "Woe is me, I am undone?" And what is there in the world can administer any other thought than this, unless God be considered in Christ, "reconciling the world to himself?" As a holy God, so righted, as that he can dispense with the condemnation of a sinner, without dispensing with his hatred of sin; pardoning the sin in the criminal, because it hath been punished in the Surety. That righteousness which God hath "set forth" for justification, is not our own, but a "righteousness which is of God" (Phil. iii. 9, 10), of God's appointing, and of God's performing; appointed by the Father, who is God, and performed by the Son, who is one with the Father; a righteousness surmounting that of all the glorious angels, since it is an immutable one which can never fail, an "everlasting righteousness" (Dan. ix. 24); a righteousness wherein the holiness of God can acquiesce, as considered in itself, because it is a righteousness of one equal with God. As we therefore dishonor the Divine Majesty when we insist upon our own bemired righteousness for our justification (as if a "a mortal man were as just as God," and a "man as pure as his Maker" (Job iv. 17), so we highly honor the purity of his nature, when we charge ourselves with folly, acknowledge ourselves unclean, and accept of that righteousness which gives a full content to his infinite purity. There can be no justification of a sinner by anything in himself.

Inform. 7. If holiness be a glorious perfection of the Divine nature, then the Deity of Christ might be argued from hence. He is indeed dignified with the title of the "Holy One" (Acts iii. 14, 16), a title often given to God in the Old Testament; and he is called the "Holy of holies" (Dan. ix. 24); but because the angels seemed to be termed "Holy ones" (Dan. iv. 13, 17), and the most sacred place in the temple was also called the "Holy of holies," I shall not insist upon that. But you find our Saviour particularly applauded by the angels, as "holy," when this perfection of the Divine nature, together with the incommunicable name of God, are linked together, and ascribed to him (Isa. vi. 3): "Holy, holy, holy is the Lord of Hosts; and the whole earth is full of his glory;" which the apostle interprets of "Christ" (John xii. 39, 41). Isaiah, again: "He hath blinded their eyes, and hardened their hearts, that they should not see with their eyes, nor understand with their hearts, and be converted, and I should heal them." These things said Isaiah, when he saw his glory, and spake of him. He that Isaiah saw environed with the seraphims, in a reverential posture before his face, and praised as most holy by them, was the true and eternal God; such acclamations belong to none but the great Jehovah, God, blessed forever; but, saith John, it was the "glory of Christ" that Isaiah saw in this vision; Christ, therefore, is "God blessed forever," of whom it was said, "Holy, holy, holy Lord of Hosts."[z] The evangelist had been speaking of Christ, the miracles which he wrought, the obstinacy of the Jews against believing on him; his glory, therefore, is to be referred to the subject he had been speaking of. The evangelist was not speaking of the Father, but of the Son, and cites those words out of Isaiah; not to teach anything of the Father, but to show that the Jews could not believe in Christ. He speaks of him that had wrought so many miracles; but Christ wrought those miracles: he speaks of him whom the Jews refused to believe on; but Christ was the person they would not believe on, while they acknowledged God. It was the glory of this person Isaiah saw, and this person Isaiah spake of, if the words of the evangelist be of any credit. The angels are too holy to give acclamations belonging to God, to any but him that is God.

Inform. 8. God is fully fit for the government of the world. The righteousness of God's nature qualifies him to be Judge of the world; if he were not perfectly righteous and holy, he were incapable to govern and judge the world (Rom. iii. 5): "If there be unrighteousness with God, how shall he judge the world?" "God will not do wickedly, neither will the Almighty pervert judgment" (Job xxxiv.

<hr>

[z] Placeus, de Deitat. Christi, *in loc.*

12). How despicable is a judge that wants innocence! As omniscience fits God to be a judge, so holiness fits him to be a righteous judge (Ps. i. 6): "The Lord knows," that is, loves, "the way of the righteous; but the way of the ungodly shall perish."

Inform. 9. If holiness be an eminent perfection of the Divine nature, the Christian religion is of a Divine extraction: it discovers the holiness of God, and forms the creature to a conformity to him. It gives us a prospect of his nature, represents him in the "beauty of holiness" (Ps. cx. 3), more than the whole glass of the creation. It is in this evangelical glass the glory of the Lord is beheld, and rendered amiable and imitable (2 Cor. iii. 18). It is a doctrine "according to godliness" (1 Tim. vi. 3), directing us to live the life of God; a life worthy of God, and worthy of our first creation by his hand. It takes us off from ourselves, fixeth us upon a noble end, points our actions, and the scope of our lives to God. It quells the monsters of sin, discountenanceth the motes of wickedness; and it is no mean argument for the divinity of it, that it sets us no lower a pattern for our imitation, than the holiness of the Divine Majesty. God is exalted upon the throne of his holiness in it, and the creature advanced to an image and resemblance of it (1 Pet. i. 16): "Be ye holy, for I am holy."

Use 2. The second use is for comfort. This attribute frowns upon lapsed nature, but smiles in the restorations made by the gospel. God's holiness, in conjunction with his justice, is terrible to a guilty sinner; but now, in conjunction with his mercy, by the satisfaction of Christ, it is sweet to a believing penitent. In the "first covenant," the purity of his nature was joined with the rigors of his justice; in the "second covenant," the purity of his nature is joined with the sweetness and tenderness of his mercy. In the one, justice flames against the sinner in the right of injured holiness; in the other, mercy yearns towards a believer, with the consent of righted holiness. To rejoice in the holiness of God is the true and genuine spirit of a renewed man: "My heart rejoiceth in the Lord;"—what follows?—"There is none holy as the Lord" (1 Sam. ii. 1, 2). Some perfections of the Divine nature are astonishing, some affrighting; but this may fill us both with astonishment at it, and a joy in it.

1. By covenant, we have an interest in this attribute, as well as any other. In that clause of "God's being our God," entire God with all his glory, all his perfections are passed over as a portion, and a gracious soul is brought into union with God, as his God; not with a part of God, but with God in the simplicity, extent, integrity of his nature; and therefore in this attribute. And, upon some account, it may seem more in this attribute than in any other; for if he be our God, he is our God in his life and glory, and therefore in his purity especially, without which he could not live; he could not be happy and blessed. Little comfort will it be to have a dead God, or a vile God, made over to us; and as, by this covenant, he is our Father, so he gives us his nature, and communicates his holiness in all his dispensations; and in those that are severest, as well as those that are sweetest (Heb. xii. 10): "But he corrects us for our profit, that we might be partakers of his holiness." Not simply "partak-

ers of holiness," but of "his holiness;" to have a portraiture of it in our nature, a medal of it in our hearts, a spark of the same nature with that immense splendor and flame in himself. The holiness of a covenant soul is a resemblance of the holiness of God, and formed by it; as the picture of the sun in a cloud is a fruit of his beams, and an image of its author. The fulness of the perfection of holiness remains in the nature of God, as the fulness of the light doth in the sun; yet there are transmissions of light from the sun to the moon, and it is a light of the same nature both in the one and in the other. The holiness of a creature is nothing else but a reflection of the Divine holiness upon it; and to make the creature capable of it, God takes various methods, according to his covenant grace.

2. This attribute renders God a fit object for trust and dependence. The notion of an unholy and unrighteous God, is an uncomfortable idea of him, and beats off our hands from laying any hold of him. It is upon this attribute the reputation and honor of God in the world is built; what encouragement can we have to believe him, or what incentives could we have to serve him, without the lustre of this in his nature? The very thought of an unrighteous God is enough to drive men at the greatest distance from him; as the honesty of a man gives a reputation to his word, so doth the holiness of God give credit to his promise. It is by this he would have us stifle our fears and fortify our trust (Isa. xli. 14): "Fear not, thou worm Jacob, and ye men of Israel; I will help thee, saith the Lord, and thy Redeemer, the Holy One of Israel:" he will be in his actions what he is in his nature. Nothing shall make him defile his own excellency; unrighteousness is the ground of mutability; but the promise of God doth never fail, because the rectitude of his nature doth never languish: were his attributes without the conduct of this, they would be altogether formidable. As this is the glory of all his other perfections, so this only renders him comfortable to a believing soul. Might we not fear his power to crush us, his mercy to overlook us, his wisdom to design against us, if this did not influence them? What an oppression is power without righteousness in the hand of a creature; destructive, instead of protecting! The devil is a mighty spirit, but not fit to be trusted, because he is an impure spirit. When God would give us the highest security of the sincerity of his intentions, he swears by this attribute (Ps. viii. 35): his holiness, as well as his truth, is laid to pawn for the security of his promise. As we make God the judge between us and others, when we swear by him, so he makes his holiness the judge between himself and his people, when he swears by it.

(1.) It is this renders him fit to be confided in for the answer of our prayers. This is the ground of his readiness to give. "If you, being evil, know how to give good gifts, how much more shall your Father which is in heaven give good gifts to them that ask him" (Matt. vii. 11)! Though the holiness of God be not mentioned, yet it is to be understood; the emphasis lies on these words, "if you, being evil:" God is then considered in a disposition contrary to this, which can be nothing but his righteousness. If you that are unholy, and have so much corruption in you, to render you cruel, can bestow upon your children the good things they want, how much more shall God, who is holy, and hath nothing in him to check his mercifulness to his creatures, grant the petitions of his supplicants! It was this attribute edged the fiduciary importunity of the souls under the altar, for the revenging their blood unjustly shed upon the earth: "How long, O Lord, holy and true, dost thou not avenge our blood on them that dwell on the earth" (Rev. vi. 10)? Let not thy holiness stand with folded arms, as careless of the eminent sufferings of those that fear thee; we implore thee by the holiness of thy nature, and the truth of thy word.

(2.) This renders him fit to be confided in for the comfort of our souls in a broken condition. The reviving the hearts of the spiritually afflicted, is a part of the holiness of his nature; "Thus saith the high and lofty One that inhabits eternity, whose name is Holy; I dwell in the high and holy place, with him also that is of a contrite and humble spirit, to revive the spirit of the humble" (Isa. lvii. 15). He acknowledgeth himself the lofty One; they might therefore fear he would not revive them; but he is also the holy One, and therefore he will refresh them; he is not more lofty than he is holy; besides, the argument of the immutability of his promise, and the might of his power, here is the holiness of his nature moving him to pity his drooping creature: his promise is ushered in with the name of power, "high and lofty One," to bar their distrust of his strength, and with a declaration of his holiness, to check any despair of his will: there is no ground to think I should be false to my word, or misemploy my power, since that cannot be, because of the holiness of my name and nature.

(3.) This renders him fit to be confided in for the maintenance of grace, and protection of us against our spiritual enemies. What our Saviour thought an argument in prayer, we may well take as a ground of our confidence. In the strength of this he puts up his suit, when in his mediatory capacity he intercedes for the preservation of his people (John xvii. 11); "Holy Father, keep through thy own name those that thou hast given me, that they may be one as we are." "Holy Father," not merciful Father, or powerful, or wise Father, but "holy;" and (ver. 25), "righteous Father." Christ pleads that attribute for the performance of God's word, which was laid to pawn when he passed his word: for it was by his holiness that he swore, that "his seed should endure forever, and his throne as the sun before him" (Ps. lxxxix. 36); which is meant of the perpetuity of the covenant which he made with Christ, and is also meant of the preservation of the mystical seed of David, and the perpetuating his loving-kindness to them (ver. 32, 33). Grace is an image of God's holiness, and, therefore, the holiness of God is most proper to be used as an argument to interest and engage him in the preservation of it. In the midst of church-provocations, he will not utterly extinguish, because he is the "Holy One" in the midst of her (Hos. xi. 9): nor in the midst of judgments will he condemn his people to death, because he is "their Holy One" (Hab. i. 12); but their enemies shall be ordained for judgment, and established for correction. One prophet assures them in the name of the Lord, upon the strength of this perfection; and the other, upon the same ground, is confident of the protection of the church, because of God's holiness engaged in an inviolable covenant.

3. *Comfort.* Since holiness is a glorious perfection of the nature of God, "he will certainly value every holy soul." It is of a greater value with him than the souls of all men in the world, that are destitute of it: "wicked men are the worst of vilenesses," mere dross and dunghill.[a] Purity, then, which is contrary to wickedness, must be the most precious thing in his esteem; he must needs love that quality which he is most pleased with in himself, as a father looks with most delight upon the child which is possessed with those dispositions he most values in his own nature. "His countenance doth behold the upright" (Ps. xi. 7). He looks upon them with a full and open face of favor, with a countenance clear, unmasked, and smiling with a face full of delight. Heaven itself is not such a pleasing object to him as the image of his own uncreated holiness in the created holiness of men and angels: as a man esteems that most which is most like him, of his own generation, more than a piece of art, which is merely the product of his wit or strength. And he must love holiness in the creature, he would not else love his own image, and, consequently, would undervalue himself. He despiseth the image the wicked bears (Ps. lxxiii. 20), but he cannot disesteem his own stamp on the godly; he cannot but delight in his own work, his choice work, the master-piece of all his works, the new creation of things; that which is next to himself, as being a Divine nature like himself (2 Pet. i. 4). When he overlooks strength, parts, knowledge, he cannot overlook this: he "sets apart him that is godly for himself" (Ps. iv. 3), as a peculiar object to take pleasure in; he reserves such for his own complaceny, when he leaves the rest of the world to the devil's power; he is choice of them above all his other works, and will not let any have so great a propriety in them as himself. If it be so dear to him here in its imperfect and mixed condition, that he appropriates it as a peculiar object for his own delight, how much more will the unspotted purity of glorified saints be infinitely pleasing to him! so, that he will take less pleasure in the material heavens than in such a soul. Sin only is detestable to God; and when this is done away, the soul becomes as lovely in his account, as before it was loathsome.

4. It is comfort, upon this account, that "God will perfect holiness in every upright soul." We many times distrust God, and despond in ourselves, because of the infinite holiness of the Divine nature, and the dunghill corruption in our own; but the holiness of God engageth him to the preservation of it, and, consequently, to the perfection of it, as appears by our Saviour's argument (John xvii. 11), "Holy Father, keep through thy own name, those whom thou hast given me;"—to what end?—"that they may be one as we are;" one with us, in the resemblances of purity. And the holiness of the soul is used as an argument by the Psalmist (Ps. lxxxvi. 2), "Preserve my soul, for I am holy;" that is, I have an ardent desire to holiness: thou hast separated me from the mass of the cor-

<hr>

[a] Ps. xii. 8. The vilest men.

rupted world, preserve and perfect me with the assembly of the glorified choir. The more holy any are, the more communicative they are; God being most holy, is most communicative of that which he most esteems in himself, and delights to see in his creature : he is, therefore, more ready to impart his holiness to them that beg for it, than to communicate his knowledge or his power. Though he were holy, yet he let Adam fall, who never petitioned his holiness to preserve him; he let him fall, to declare the holiness of his own nature, which had wanted its due manifestation without it : but since that cannot be declared in a higher manner than it hath been already in the death of the Surety, that bore our guilt, there is no fear he should cast the work out of his hands, since the design of the permission of man's apostasy, in the discovery of the perfections of his nature, has been fully answered. The "finishing the good work he hath begun," hath a relation to the glory of Christ; and his own glory in Christ to be manifested in the day of his appearing (Phil. i. 6), wherein the glory, both of his own holiness, and the holiness of the Mediator, are to receive their full manifestation. As it is a part of the holiness of Christ to "sanctify his church" (Eph. v. 26, 27) till not a wrinkle or spot be left, so it is the part of God not to leave that work imperfect which his holiness hath attempted a second time to beautify his creature with. He will not cease exalting this attribute, which is the believers' by the new covenant, till he utters that applauding speech of his own work (Cant. iv. 7), "Thou art all fair, my love ; there is no spot in thee."

Use 3, is for Exhortation. Is holiness an eminent perfection of the Divine nature? then—

Exhort. 1. Let us get and preserve right and strong apprehensions of this Divine perfection. Without a due sense of it, we can never exalt God in our hearts; and the more distinct conceptions we have of this, and the rest of his attributes, the more we glorify him. When Moses considered God as "his strength and salvation," he would exalt him (Exod. xv. 2); and he could never break out in so admirable a doxology as that in the text, without a deep sense of the glory of his purity, which he speaks of with so much admiration. Such a sense will be of use to us.

1. In promoting genuine convictions. A deep consideration of the holiness of God cannot but be followed with a deep consideration of our impure and miserable condition by reason of sin : we cannot glance upon it without reflections upon our own vileness. Adam no sooner heard the voice of a holy God in the garden, but he considered his own nakedness with shame and fear (Gen. iii. 10); much less can we fix our minds upon it, but we must be touched with a sense of our own uncleanness. The clear beams of the sun discover that filthiness in our garments and members, which was not visible in the darkness of the night. Impure metals are discerned by comparing them with that which is pure and perfect in its kind. The sense of guilt is the first natural result upon a sense of this excellent perfection; and the sense of the imperfection of our own righteousness is the next. Who can think of it, and reflect upon

himself as an object fit for Divine love? Who can have a due thought of it, without regarding himself as stubble before a consuming fire? Who can, without a confusion of heart and face, glance upon that pure eye which beholds with detestation the foul motes, as well as the filthier and bigger spots? When Isaiah saw his glory, and heard how highly the angels exalted God for this perfection, he was in a cold sweat, ready to swoon, till a seraphim, with a coal from the altar, both purged and revived him (Isa. vi. 5, 7). They are sound and genuine convictions, which have the prospect of Divine purity for their immediate spring, and not a foresight of our own misery; when it is not the punishment we have deserved, but the holiness we have offended, most grates our hearts. Such convictions are the first rude draughts of the Divine image in our spirits, and grateful to God, because they are an acknowledgment of the glory of this attribute, and the first mark of honor given to it by the creature. Those that never had a sense of their own vileness, were always destitute of a sense of God's holiness. And, by the way, we may observe, that those that scoff at any for hanging down the head under the consideration and conviction of sin (as is too usual with the world), scoff at them for having deeper apprehensions of the purity of God than themselves, and consequently make a mock of the holiness of God which is the ground of those convictions; a sense of this would prevent such a damnable reproaching.

2. A sense of this will render us humble in the possession of the greatest holiness a creature were capable of. We are apt to be proud, with the Pharisee, when we look upon others wallowing in the mire of base and unnatural lusts: but let any clap their wings, if they can, in a vain boasting and exaltation, when they view the holiness of God. What torch, if it had reason, would be proud, and swagger in its own light, if it compared itself with the sun? "Who can stand before this holy Lord God?" is the just reflection of the holiest person, as it was of those (1 Sam. vi. 20) that had felt the marks of his jealousy after their looking into the ark, though likely out of affection to it, and triumphant joy at its return. When did the angels testify, by the covering of their faces, their weakness to bear the lustre of his majesty, but when they beheld his glory? When did they signify, by their covering their feet, the shame of their own vileness, but when their hearts were fullest of the applaudings of this perfection (Isa. vi. 2, 3)? Though they found themselves without spot, yet not with such a holiness that they could appear either with their faces or feet unvailed and unmasked in the presence of God. Doth the immense splendor of this attribute engender shaming reflections in those pure spirits? What will it, what should it, do in us, that dwell in houses of clay, and creep up and down with that clay upon our backs, and too much of it in our hearts? The stars themselves, which appear beautiful in the night, are masked at the awaking of the sun. What a dim light is that of a glow-worm to that of the sun! The apprehensions of this made the elders humble themselves in the midst of their glory, by "casting down their crowns before his throne" (Rev. iv. 8, 10); a meta-

phor taken from the triumphing generals among the Romans, who hung up their victorious laurels in the Capitol, dedicating them to their gods, acknowledging them their superiors in strength, and authors of their victory. This self-emptiness at the consideration of Divine purity, is the note of the true church, represented by the twenty-four elders, and a note of a true member of the church; whereas boasting of perfection and merit is the property of the antichristian tribe, that have mean thoughts of this adorable perfection, and think themselves more righteous than the unspotted angels. What a self-annihilation is there in a good man, when the sense of Divine purity is most lively in him! yea, how detestable is he to himself! There is as little proportion between the holiness of the Divine Majesty, and that of the most righteous creature, as there is between a nearness of a person that stands upon a mountain, to the sun, and of him that beholds him in a vale; one is nearer than the other, but it is an advantage not to be boasted of, in regard of the vast distance that is between the sun and the elevated spectator.

3. This would make us full of an affectionate reverence in all our approaches to God. By this perfection God is rendered venerable, and fit to be reverenced by his creature; and magnificent thoughts of it in the creature would awaken him to an actual reverence of the Divine majesty (Ps. iii. 9): "Holy and reverend is his name;" a good opinion of this would engender in us a sincere respect towards him; we should then "serve the Lord with fear," as the expression is (Ps. ii. 11), that is, be afraid to cast anything before him that may offend the eyes of his purity. Who would venture rashly and garishly into the presence of an eminent moralist, or of a righteous king upon his throne? The fixedness of the angels arose from the continual prospect of this. What if we had been with Isaiah when he saw the vision, and beheld him in the same glory, and the heavenly choir in their reverential posture in the service of God; would it not have barred our wanderings, and staked us down to our duty? Would not the fortifying an idea of it in our minds produce the same effect? It is for want of this we carry ourselves so loosely and unbecomingly in the Divine presence, with the same, or meaner, affections than those wherewith we stand before some vile creature that is our superior in the world; as though a piece of filthy flesh were more valuable than this perfection of the Divinity. How doth the Psalmist double his exhortation to men to sing praise to God (Ps. xlvii. 6): "Sing praises to God, sing praises; sing praises unto our King, sing praises;" because of his majesty, and the purity of his dominion! and (ver. 8), "God reigneth over the heathen, God sitteth upon the throne of his holiness." How would this elevate us in praise, and prostrate us in prayer, when we praise and pray with an understanding and insight of that nature we bless or implore; as he speaks (ver. 7), "Sing ye praises with understanding." The holiness of God in his government and dominion, the holiness of his nature, and the holiness of his precepts, should beget in us an humble respect in our approaches. The more we grow in a sense of this, the more shall we advance in the true performance of all our duties. Those nations which adored the sun, had they at first seen his brightness wrapped

and masked in a cloud, and paid a veneration to it, how would their adorations have mounted to a greater point, after they had seen it in its full brightness, shaking off those vails, and chasing away the mists before it! what a profound reverence would they have paid it, when they beheld it in its glory and meridian brightness![b]   Our reverence to God in all our addresses to him will arrive to greater degrees, if every act of duty be ushered in, and seasoned with the thoughts of God as sitting upon a throne of holiness; we shall have a more becoming sense of our own vileness, a greater ardor to his service, a deeper respect in his presence, if our understanding be more cleared, and possessed with notions of this perfection.   Thus take a view of God in this part of his glory, before you fall down before his throne, and assure yourselves you will find your hearts and services quickened with a new and lively spirit.

4. A due sense of this perfection in God would produce in us a fear of God, and arm us against temptation and sin.   What made the heathen so wanton and loose, but the representations of their gods as vicious?   Who would stick at adulteries, and more prodigious lusts, that can take a pattern for them from the person he adores for a deity?   Upon which account Plato would have poets banished from his commonwealth, because, by dressing up their gods in wanton garbs in their poems, they encouraged wickedness in the people.   But if the thoughts of God's holiness were impressed upon us, we should regard sin with the same eye, mark it with the same detestation in our measures, as God himself doth.   So far as we are sensible of the Divine purity, we should account sin vile as it deserves; we should hate it entirely, without a grain of love to it, and hate it perpetually (Ps. cxix. 104): "Through thy precepts I get understanding, therefore I hate every false way."   He looks into God's statute-book, and thereby arrives to an understanding of the purity of his nature, whence his hatred of iniquity commenced. This would govern our motion, check our vices; it would make us tremble at the hissing of a temptation: when a corruption did but peep out, and put forth its head, a look to the Divine Purity would be attended with a fresh convoy of strength to resist it.   There is no such fortification, as to be wrapped up in the sense of this: this would fill us with an awe of God; we should be ashamed to admit any filthy thing into us, which we know is detestable to his pure eye.   As the approach of a grave and serious man makes children hasten their trifles out of the way; so would a consideration of this attribute make us cast away our idols, and fling away our ridiculous thoughts and designs.

5. A due sense of this perfection would inflame us with a vehement desire to be conformed to Him.   All our desires would be ardent to regulate ourselves according to this pattern of holiness and goodness, which is not to be equalled; the contemplating it as it shines forth in the face of Christ, will "transform us into the same image" (2 Cor. iii. 19).   Since our lapsed state, we cannot behold the holiness of God in itself without affrightment; nor is it an object of imitation, but as tempered in Christ to our view.   When we cannot, without blinding ourselves, look upon the sun in its brightness, we

[b] Amyrald. Moral. Tom. V. p. 462.

may behold it through a colored glass, whereby the lustre of it is moderated, without dazzling our eyes. The sense of it will furnish us with a greatness of mind, that little things will be contemned by us; motives of a greater alloy would have little influence upon us; we should have the highest motives to every duty, and motives of the same strain which influence the angels above. It would change us, not only into an angelical nature, but a divine nature: we should act like men of another sphere; as if we had received our original in another world, and seen with angels the ravishing beauties of heaven. How little would the mean employments of the world sink us into dirt and mud! How often hath the meditation of the courage of a valiant man, or acuteness and industry of a learned person, spurred on some men to an imitation of them, and transformed them into the same nature! as the looking upon the sun imprints an image of the sun upon our eye, that we seem to behold nothing but the sun a while after. The view of the Divine purity would fill us with a holy generosity to imitate him, more than the examples of the best men upon earth. It was a saying of a heathen, that "if virtue were visible, it would kindle a noble flame of love to it in the heart, by its ravishing beauty." Shall the infinite purity of the Author of all virtue come short of the strength of a creature? Can we not render that visible to us by frequent meditation, which, though it be invisible in his nature, is made visible in his law, in his ways, in his Son? It would make us ready to obey him, since we know he cannot command anything that is sinful, but what is holy, just, and good: it would put all our affections in their due place, elevate them above the creature, and subject them to the Creator.

6. It would make us patient and contented under all God's dispensations. All penal evils are the fruits of his holiness, as he is Judge and Governor of the world: he is not an arbitrary Judge, nor doth any sentence pronounced, nor warrant for execution issue from him, but what bears upon it a stamp of the righteousness of his nature; he doth nothing by passion or unrighteousness, but according to the eternal law of his own unstained nature, which is the rule to him in his works, the basis and foundation of his throne and sovereign dominion (Ps. lxxxix. 14): "Justice," or righteousness, "and judgment are the habitation of thy throne;" upon these his sovereign power is established: so that there can be no just complaint or indictment brought against any of his proceedings with men. How doth our Saviour, who had the highest apprehensions of God's holiness, justify God in his deepest distresses, when he cried, and was not answered in the particular he desired, in that prophetic Psalm of him (Ps. xxii. 2, 3), "I cry day and night, but thou hearest not!" Thou seemest to be deaf to all my petitions, afar off "from the words of my roaring; but thou art holy;" I cast no blame upon thee: all thy dealings are squared by thy holiness: this is the only law to thee; in this I acquiesce. It is part of thy holiness to hide thy face from me, to show thereby thy detestation of sin. Our Saviour adores the Divine purity in his sharpest agony, and a like sense of it would guide us in the same steps to acknowledge and glorify it, in our greatest desertions and afflictions; especially since as they are the

fruit of the holiness of his nature, so they are the means to impart to us clearer stamps of holiness, according to that in himself, which is the original copy (Heb. xii. 10). He melts us down as gold, to fit us for the receiving a new impression, to mortify the affections of the flesh, and clothe us with the graces of his Spirit. The due sense of this would make us to submit to his stroke, and to wait upon him for a good issue of his dealings.

Exhort. 2. Is holiness a perfection of the Divine nature? Is it the glory of the Deity? Then let us glorify this holiness of God. Moses glorifies it in the text, and glorifies it in a song, which was a copy for all ages. The whole corporation of seraphims have their mouths filled with the praises of it. The saints, whether militant on earth, or triumphant in heaven, are to continue the same acclamation, " Holy, holy, holy, Lord God of hosts" (Rev. iv. 8). Neither angels nor glorified spirits exalt at the same rate the power which formed them creatures, nor goodness which preserves them in a blessed immortality, as they do holiness, which they bear some beams of in their own nature, and whereby they are capacitated to stand before His throne. Upon the account of this, a debt of praise is demanded of all rational creatures by the Psalmist (Ps. xcix. 3), " Let them praise thy great and terrible name, for it is holy." Not so much for the greatness of his Majesty, or the treasures of his justice; but as they are considered in conjunction with his holiness, which renders them beautiful; " for it is holy." Grandeur and majesty, simply in themselves, are not objects of praise, nor do they merit the acclamations of men, when destitute of righteousness : this only renders everything else adorable ; and this adorns the Divine greatness with an amiableness (Isa. xii. 6): " Great is the Holy One of Israel in the midst of thee ;" and makes his might worthy of praise (Luke i. 49). In honoring this, which is the soul and spirit of all the rest, we give a glory to all the perfections which constitute and beautify his nature : and without the glorifying this we glorify nothing of them, though we should extol every other single attribute a thousand times. He values no other adoration of his creatures, unless this be interested, nor accepts anything as a glory from them (Lev. x. 3). "I will be sanctified in them that come near me, and I will be glorified:" as if he had said, In manifesting my name to be holy, you truly, you only honor me. And as the Scripture seldom speaks of this perfection without a particular emphasis, it teaches us not to think of it without a special elevation of heart: by this act only, while we are on earth, can we join consort with the angels in heaven ; he that doth not honor it, delight in it, and in the meditation of it, hath no resemblance of it ; he hath none of the image, that delights not in the original. Everything of God is glorious, but this most of all. If he built the world principally for anything, it was for the communication of his goodness, and display of his holiness. He formed the rational creature to manifest his holiness in that law whereby he was to be governed: then deprive not God of the design of his own glory. We honor this attribute,

1. When we make it the ground of our love to God. Not because he is gracious to us, but holy in himself. As God honors it,

in loving himself for it, we should honor it, by pitching our affections upon him chiefly for it. What renders God amiable to himself, should render him lovely to all his creatures (Isa. xlii. 21): "The Lord is well pleased for his righteousness' sake." If the hatred of evil be the immediate result of a love to God, then the peculiar object or term of our love to God, must be that perfection which stands in direct opposition to the hatred of evil (Ps. xcvii. 10): "Ye that love the Lord, hate evil." When we honor his holiness in every stamp and impression of it : his law, not principally because of its usefulness to us, its accommodateness to the order of the world, but for its innate purity ; and his people, not for our interest in them, so much as for bearing upon them this glittering mark of the Deity, we honor then the purity of the Lawgiver, and the excellency of the Sanctifier.

2. We honor it, when we regard chiefly the illustrious appearance of this in his judgments in the world. In a case of temporal judgment, Moses celebrates it in the text ; in a case of spiritual judgments, the angels applaud it in Isaiah. All his severe proceedings are nothing but the strong breathings of this attribute. Purity is the flash of his revenging sword. If he did not hate evil, his vengeance would not reach the committers of it. He is a "refiner's fire" in the day of his anger (Mal. iii. 2). By his separating judgments, "he takes away the wicked of the earth like dross" (Ps. cxix. 119). How is his holiness honored, when we take notice of his sweeping out the rubbish of the world ; how he suits punishment to sin, and discovers his hatred of the matter and circumstances of the evil, in the matter and circumstances of the judgment. This perfection is legible in every stroke of his sword ; we honor it when we read the syllables of it, and not by standing amazed only at the greatness and severity of the blow, when we read how holy he is in his most terrible dispensations : for as in them God magnifies the greatness of his power, so he sanctifies himself ; that is, declares the purity of his nature as a revenger of all impiety (Ezek. xxxviii. 22, 23) ; "And I will plead against him with pestilence, and with blood : and I will rain upon him, and upon his bands, and upon the people that are with him, an overflowing rain and great hailstones ; fire, and brimstone. Thus will I magnify myself, and sanctify myself."

3. We honor this attribute, when we take notice of it in every accomplishment of his promise, and every grant of a mercy. His truth is but a branch of his righteousness, a slip from this root. He is glorious in holiness in the account of Moses, because he "led forth his people whom he had redeemed" (Exod. xv. 13); his people by a covenant with their fathers, being the God of Moses, the God of Israel, and the God of their fathers (ver. 2). "My God, and my father's God, I will exalt thee." For what? for his faithfulness to his promise. The holiness of God, which Mary (Luke i. 49) magnifies, is summed up in this, the help he afforded his servant Israel in the "remembrance of his mercy, as he spake to our fathers, to Abraham and his seed forever" (ver. 54, 55). The certainty of his covenant mercy depends upon an unchangeableness of his holiness. What are "sure mercies," (Isa. lv. 3), are holy mercies in the Septua-

gint, and in Acts xiii. 34, which makes that translation canonical. His nearness to answer us, when we call upon him for such mercies, is a fruit of the holiness of his name and nature (Ps. clxv. 17). "The Lord is holy in all his works; the Lord is nigh to all them that call upon him." Hannah, after a return of prayer, sets a particular mark upon this, in her song (1 Sam. ii. 2); "There is none holy as the Lord;" separated from all dross, firm to his covenant, and righteous in it to his suppliants, that confide in him, and plead his word. When we observe the workings of this in every return of prayer, we honor it; it is a sign the mercy is really a return of prayer, and not a mercy of course, bearing upon it only the characters of a common providence. This was the perfection David would bless, for the catalogue of mercies in Ps. ciii. 1, &c.; "Bless his holy name." Certainly, one reason why sincere prayer is so delightful to him, is because it puts him upon the exercise of this his beloved perfection, which he so much delighteth to honor. Since God acts in all those as the governor of the world, we honor him not, unless we take notice of that righteousness which fits him for a governor, and is the inward spring of all his motions (Gen. xviii. 25). "Shall not the Judge of all the earth do right?" It was his design in his pity to Israel, as well as the calamities he intended against the heathens, to be "sanctified in them; that is, declared holy in his merciful as well as his judicial procedure (Ezra xxxvi. 21, 23). Hereby God credits his righteousness, which seemed to be forgotten by the one, and contemned by the other;[c] he removes, by this, all suspicion of unfaithfulness in him.

4. We honor this attribute, when we trust his covenant, and promise against outward appearances. Thus our Saviour, in the prophecy of him (Ps. xxii. 2–4), when God seemed to bar up the gates of his palace against the entry of any more petitions, this attribute proves the support of the Redeemer's soul; "But thou art holy, O thou that inhabitest the praises of Israel:" as it refers to what goes before, it has been twice explained; as it refers to what follows, it is a ground of trust; "Thou inhabitest the praises of Israel:" thou hast had the praises of Israel for many ages, for thy holiness. How? "Our fathers trusted in thee, and thou didst deliver them;" they honored thy holiness by their trust, and thou didst honor their faith by a deliverance; thou always hadst a purity that would not shame nor confound them. I will trust in thee as thou art holy, and expect the breaking out of this attribute for my good as well as my predecessors; "Our fathers trusted in thee," &c.

5. We honor this attribute, when we show a greater affection to the marks of his holiness in times of the greatest contempt of it. As the Psalmist (Ps. cxix. 126, 127); "They have made void thy law, therefore I love thy commandments above gold;" while they spurn at the purity of thy law, I will value it above the gold they possess; I will esteem it as gold, because others count it as dross; by their scorn of it, my love to it shall be the warmer; and my hatred of iniquity shall be the sharper: the disdain of others should inflame us with a zeal and fortitude to appear in behalf of his despised honor.

---

[c] Sanct. *in loc.*

We honor this holiness many other ways; by preparation for our addresses to him, out of a sense of his purity; when we imitate it: as He honors us by "teaching us his statutes" (Ps. cxix. 135), so we honor him by learning and observing them. When we beg of him to show himself a refiner of us, to make us more conformable to him in holiness, and bless him for any communication of it to us, it renders us beautiful and lovely in his sight. To conclude: to honor it, is the way to engage it for us; to give it the glory of what it hath done, by the arm of power for our rescue from sin, and beating down our corruptions at his feet, is the way to see more of its marvellous works, and behold a clearer brightness. As unthankfulness makes him withdraw his grace (Rom. i. 21, 24), so glorifying him causes him to impart it. God honors men in the same way they honor him; when we honor him by acknowledging his purity, he will honor us by communicating of it to us. This is the way to derive a greater excellency to our souls.

Exhort. 3. Since holiness is an eminent perfection of the Divine nature, let us labor after a conformity to God in this perfection. The nature of God is presented to us in the Scripture, both as a pattern to imitate, and a motive to persuade the creature to holiness (1 John iii. 3; Matt. v. 48; Lev. xi. 44; 1 Pet. i. 15, 16). Since it is, therefore, the nature of God, the more our natures are beautified with it, the more like we are to the Divine nature. It is not the pattern of angels, or archangels, that our Saviour, or his apostle, proposeth for our imitation; but the original of all purity, God himself; the same that created us, to be imitated by us. Nor is an equal degree of purity enjoined us; though we are to be pure, and perfect, and merciful as God is, yet not essentially so; for that would be to command us an impossibility in itself; as much as to order us to cease to be creatures, and commence gods. No creature can be essentially holy but by participation from the chief Fountain of Holiness; but we must have the same kind of holiness, the same truth of holiness. As a short line may be as straight as another, though it parallel it not in the immense length of it; a copy may have the likeness of the original, though not the same perfection; we cannot be good, without eyeing some exemplar of goodness as the pattern. No pattern is so suitable as that which is the highest goodness and purity. That limner that would draw the most excellent piece, fixes his eyes upon the most perfect pattern. He that would be a good orator, or poet, or artificer, considers some person most excellent in each kind, as the object of his imitation. Who so fit as God to be viewed as the pattern of holiness, in our intendment of, and endeavor after holiness? The Stoics, one of the best sects of philosophers, advised their disciples to pitch upon some eminent example of virtue, according to which to form their lives; as Socrates, &c. But true holiness doth not only endeavor to live the life of a good man, but chooses to live a divine life; as before the man was "alienated from the life of God" (Eph. iv. 19), so, upon his return, he aspires after the life of God. To endeavor to be like a good man is to make one image like another; to set our clocks by other clocks, without regarding the sun: but true holiness consists in a likeness to the most exact sampler. God

being the first purity, is the rule as well as the spring of all purity
in the creature, the chief and first object of imitation.   We disown
ourselves to be his creatures, if we breathe not after a resemblance to
him in what he is imitable.   There was in man, as created according
to God's image, a natural appetite to resemble God: it was at first
planted in him by the Author of his nature.   The devil's temptation
of him by that motive to transgress the law, had been as an arrow
shot against a brazen wall, had there not been a desire of some likeness to his Creator engraven upon him (Gen. iii. 5): it would have
had no more influence upon him, than it could have had upon a
mere animal.   But man mistook the term; he would have been like
God in knowledge, whereas, he should have affected a greater resemblance of him in purity.   O that we could exemplify God in our
nature!   Precepts may instruct us more, but examples affect us more;
one directs us, but the other attracts us.   What can be more attractive of our imitation, than that which is the original of all purity,
both in men and angels?   This conformity to him consists in an
imitation of him,

    1. In his law.   The purity of his nature was first visible in this
glass; hence, it is called a "holy" law (Rom. vii. 12); a "pure" law
(Ps. xix. 8).   Holy and pure, as it is a ray of the pure nature of the
Lawgiver.   When our lives are a comment upon his law, they are
expressive of his holiness: we conform to his holiness when we regulate ourselves by his law, as it is a transcript of his holiness: we do
not imitate it, when we do a thing in the matter of it agreeable to
that holy rule, but when we do it with respect to the purity of the
Lawgiver beaming in it.   If it be agreeable to God's will, and convenient for some design of our own, and we do anything only with
a respect to that design, we make not God's holiness discovered in
the law our rule, but our own conveniency: it is not a conformity to
God, but a conformity of our actions to *self*.   As in abstinence from
intemperate courses, not because the holiness of God in his law hath
prescribed it, but because the health of our bodies, or some noble
contentments of life, require it; then it is not God's holiness that is
our rule, but our own security, conveniency, or something else which
we make a God to ourselves.   It must be a real conformity to the
law: our holiness should shine as really in the practice, as God's
purity doth in the precept.   God hath not a pretence of purity in his
nature, but a reality: it is not only a sudden boiling up of an admiration of him, or a starting wish to be like him, from some sudden
impression upon the fancy, which is a mere temporary blaze, but a
settled temper of soul, loving everything that is like him, doing
things out of a firm desire to resemble his purity in the copy he hath
set; not a resting in negatives, but aspiring to positives; holy and
harmless are distinct things: they were distinct qualifications in our
High Priest in his obedience to the law (Heb. vii. 26), so they must
be in us.

    2. In his Christ.   As the law is the transcript, so Christ is the
image of his holiness: the glory of God is too dazzling to be beheld
by us: the acute eye of an angel is too weak to look upon that
bright sun without covering his face: we are much too weak to take

our measures from that purity which is infinite in his nature. But he hath made his Son like us, that by the imitation of him in that temper, and shadow of human flesh, we may arrive to a resemblance of him (2 Cor. iii. 18). Then there is a conformity to him, when that which Christ did is drawn in lively colors in the soul of a Christian; when, as he died upon the cross, we die to our sins; as he rose from the grave, we rise from our lusts; as he ascended on high, we mount our souls thither; when we express in our lives what shined in his, and exemplify in our hearts what he acted in the world, and become one with him, as he was separate from sinners. The holiness of God in Christ is our ultimate pattern: as we are not only to believe in Christ, but " by Christ in God" (John xiv. 1), so we are not only to imitate Christ, but the holiness of God as discovered in Christ. And, to enforce this upon us, let us consider,

(1.) It is this only wherein he commands our imitation of him. We are not commanded to be mighty and wise, as God is mighty and wise: but " be holy, as I am holy." The declarations of his power are to enforce our subjection; those of his wisdom, to encourage our direction by him; but this only to attract our imitation. When he saith, " I am holy," the immediate inference he makes, is, " Be ye so too," which is not the proper instruction from any other perfection.[d] Man was created by Divine power, and harmonized by Divine wisdom, but not after them, or according to them, as the true image; this was the prerogative of Divine holiness, to be the pattern of his rational creature:[e] wisdom and power were subservient to this, the one as the pencil, the other as the hand that moved it. The condition of a creature is too mean to have the communications of the Divine essence; the true impressions of his righteousness and goodness we are only capable of. It is only in those moral perfections we are said to resemble God. The devils, those impure and ruined spirits, are nearer to him in strength and knowledge than we are; yet in regard of that natural and intellectual perfection, never counted like him, but at the greatest distance from him, because at the greatest distance from his purity. God values not a natural might, nor an acute understanding, nor vouchsafes such perfections the glorious title of that of his image. Plutarch saith, God is angry with those that imitate his thunder or lightning, his works of majesty, but delighted with those that imitate his virtue.[f] In this only we can never incur any reproof from him, but for falling short of him and his glory. Had Adam endeavored after an imitation of this, instead of that of Divine knowledge, he had escaped his fall, and preserved his standing; and had Lucifer wished himself like God in this, as well as his dominion, he had still been a glorious angel, instead of being now a ghastly devil: to reach after a union with the Supreme Being, in regard of holiness, is the only generous and commendable ambition.

(2.) This is the prime way of honoring God. We do not so glorify God by elevated admirations, or eloquent expressions, or pompous services of him, as when we aspire to a conversing with him with unstained spirits, and live to him in living like him. The angels are

---

[d] " In this," saith Plato, " God is ἐν μέσῳ παράδειγμα.   [e] Eph. iv. 24. Col. iii. 10.
[f] Eugub. inde Perenni Philoso. lib. vi. cap. 6.

not called holy for applauding his purity, but conforming to it. The more perfect any creature is in the rank of beings, the more is the Creator honored; as it is more for the honor of God to create an angel or man, than a mere animal; because there are in such clearer characters of Divine power and goodness, than in those that are inferior. The more perfect any creature is morally, the more is God glorified by that creature; it is a real declaration, that God is the best and most amiable Being; that nothing besides him is valuable, and worthy to be object of our imitation. It is a greater honoring of him, than the highest acts of devotion, and the most religious bodily exercise, or the singing this song of Moses in the text, with a triumphant spirit; as it is more the honor of a father to be imitated in his virtues by his son, than to have all the glavering commendations by the tongue or pen of a vicious and debauched child. By this we honor him in that perfection which is dearest to him, and counted by him as the chiefest glory of his nature. God seems to accept the glorifying this attribute, as if it were a real addition to that holiness which is infinite in his nature, and because infinite, cannot admit of any increase: and, therefore, the word sanctified is used instead of glorified. (Isa. viii. 13), "Sanctify the Lord of Hosts himself, and let him be your fear, and let him be your dread." And (Isa. xxix. 23), "They shall sanctify the holy One of Jacob, and fear the God of Israel." This sanctification of God is by the fear of him, which signifies in the language of the Old Testament, a reverence of him, and a righteousness before him. He doth not say, when he would have his power or wisdom glorified, Empower me or make me wise; but when he would have his holiness glorified by the creature, it is, Sanctify me; that is, manifest the purity of my nature by the holiness of your lives: but he expresseth it in such a term, as if it were an addition to this infinite perfection; so acceptable it is to him, as if it were a contribution from his creature for the enlarging an attribute so pleasing to him, and so glorious in his eye. It is, as much as in the creature lies, a preserving the life of God, since this perfection is his life; and that he would as soon part with his life as part with his purity. It keeps up the reputation of God in the world, and attracts others to a love of him; whereas, unworthy carriages defame God in the eyes of men, and bring up an ill report of him, as if he were such an one as those that profess him, and walk unsuitably to their profession, appear to be.

(3.) This is the excellency and beauty of a creature. The title of "beauty" is given to it in Ps. cx. 3; "beauties," in the plural number, as comprehending it in all other beauties whatsoever. What is a Divine excellency cannot be a creature's deformity: the natural beauty of it is a representation of the Divinity; and a holy man ought to esteem himself excellent in being such in his measure as his God is, and puts his principal felicity in the possession of the same purity in truth. This is the refined complexion of the angels that stand before his throne. The devils lost their comeliness when they fell from it. It was the honor of the human nature of our Saviour, not only to be united to the Deity, but to be sanctified by it. He was "fairer than all the children of men," because he had a holiness above the children of men: "grace was poured into his lips" (Ps. xlv. 2). It was the jewel of the reasonable nature in paradise: conformity to God was man's original happiness in his created state; and what was naturally so, cannot but be immutably so in its own nature. The beauty of every copied thing consists in its likeness to the original; everything hath more of loveliness, as it hath greater impressions of its first pattern: in this regard holiness hath more of beauty on it than the whole creation, because it partakes of a greater excellency of God than the sun, moon, and stars. No greater glory can be, than to be a conspicuous and visible image of the invisible, and holy, and blessed God. As this is the splendor of all the Divine attributes, so it is the flower of all a christian's graces, the crown of all religion: it is the glory of the Spirit. In this regard the king's daughter is said to be "all glorious within" (Ps. xlv. 13). It is more excellent than the soul itself, since the greatest soul is but a deformed piece without it: a "diamond without lustre."[g] What are the noble faculties of the soul without it, but as a curious rusty watch, a delicate heap of disorder and confusion? It is impossible there can be beauty where there are a multitude of "spots and wrinkles" that blemish a countenance (Eph. v. 27). It can never be in its true brightness but when it is perfect in purity; when it regains what it was possessed of by creation, and dispossessed of by the fall, and recovers its primitive temper. We are not so beautiful by being the work of God, as by having a stamp of God upon us. Worldly greatness may make men honorable in the sight of creeping worms. Soft lives, ambitious reaches, luxurious pleasures, and a pompous religion, render no man excellent and noble in the sight of God: this is not the excellency and nobility of the Deity which we are bound to resemble; other lines of a Divine image must be drawn in us to render us truly excellent.

(4.) It is our life. What is the life of God is truly the life of a rational creature.[h] The life of the body consists not in the perfection of its members, and the integrity of its organs; these remain when the body becomes a carcass; but in the presence of the soul, and its vigorous animation of every part to perform the distinct offices belonging to each of them. The life of the soul consists not in its being, or spiritual substance, or the excellency of its faculties of understanding and will, but in the moral and becoming operations of them. The spirit is only "life because of righteousness" (Rom. viii. 10). The faculties are turned by it, to acquit themselves in their functions, according to the will of God; the absence of this doth not only deform the soul, but, in a sort, annihilate it, in regard of its true essence and end. Grace gives a Christian being, and a want of it is the want of a true being (1 Cor. xv. 10). When Adam divested himself of his original righteousness, he came under the force of the threatening, in regard of a spiritual death; every person is "morally dead while he lives" an unholy life (1 Tim. v. 6). What life is to the body, that is righteousness to the spirit; and the greater measure of holiness it hath, the more of life it hath, because it is in a

g Vaughan pp. 4, 5.   h Amirald. in Heb. pp. 101, 102.

greater nearness, and partakes more fully of the fountain of life. Is
not that the most worthy life, which God makes most account of,
without which his life could not be a pleasant and blessed life, but a
life worse than death ?   What a miserable life is that of the men of
the world, that are carried, with greedy inclinations, to all manner
of unrighteousness, whither their interests or their lusts invite them!
The most beautiful body is a carcass, and the most honorable person
hath but a brutish life (Ps. xlix. 20); miserable creatures when their
life shall be extinct without a Divine rectitude, when all other things
will vanish as the shadows of the night at the appearance of the sun !
Holiness is our life.

(5.) It is this only fits us for communion with God.   Since it is
our beauty and our life, without it what communion can an excellent
God have with deformed creatures ; a living God with dead creatures ?
" Without holiness none shall see God" (Heb. xii. 14).   The creature
must be stripped of his unrighteousness, or God of his purity, before
they can come together.   Likeness is the ground of communion, and
of delight in it: the opposition between God and unholy souls is as
great as that between "light and darkness" (1 John i. 6). Divine fruition
is not so much by a union of presence as a union of nature.   Heaven
is not so much an outward as an inward life ; the foundation of glory is
laid in grace ; a resemblance to God is our vital happiness, without
which the vision of God would not be so much as a cloudy and shadowy
happiness, but rather a torment than a felicity ; unless we be of a
like nature to God, we cannot have a pleasing fruition of him.
Some philosophers think that if our bodies were of the same nature
with the heavens, of an ethereal substance, the nearness to the sun
would cherish, not scorch us.   Were we partakers of a Divine
nature, we might enjoy God with delight ; whereas, remaining in
our unlikeness to him, we cannot think of him, and approach to
him without terror.   As soon as sin had stripped man of the image
of God, he was an exile from the comfortable presence of God, unworthy for God to hold any correspondence with : he can no more
delight in a defiled person that a man can take a toad into intimate
converse with him ; he would hereby discredit his own nature, and
justify our impurity.   The holiness of a creature only prepares him
for an eternal conjunction with God in glory.   Enoch's walking
with God was the cause of his being so soon wafted to the place
of a full fruition of him ; he hath as much delight in such as in
heaven itself; one is his habitation as well as the other ; the one is
his habitation of glory, and the other is the house of his pleasure :
if he dwell in Zion, it must be a " holy mountain" (Joel iii. 17), and
the members of Zion must be upheld in their rectitude and integrity
before they be " set before the face of God forever" (Ps. xli. 12.)
Such are styled his jewels, his portion, as if he lived upon them, as
a man upon his inheritance.   As God cannot delight in us, so neither
can we delight in God without it.   We must purify ourselves " as
he is pure," if we expect to " see him as he is," in the comfortable
glory and beauty of his nature (1 John iii. 2, 3), else the sight of
God would be terrible and troublesome : we cannot be satisfied with
the likeness of God at the resurrection, unless we have a righteous-

ness wherewith to "behold his face" (Ps. xvii. 15). It is a vain imagination in any to think that heaven can be a place of happiness to him, in whose eye the beauty of holiness which fills and adorns it, is an unlovely thing; or that any can have a satisfaction in that Divine purity which is loathsome to him in the imitations of it. We cannot enjoy him, unless we resemble him; nor take any pleasure in him, if we were with him, without something of likeness to him. Holiness fits us for communion with God.

(6.) We can have no evidence of our election and adoption without it. Conformity to God, in purity, is the fruit of electing love (Eph. i. 4); "He hath chosen us that we should be holy." The goodness of the fruit evidenceth the nature of the root: this is the seal that assures us the patent is the authentic grant of the Prince. Whatsoever is holy, speaks itself to be from God; and whosoever is holy, speaks himself to belong to God. This is the only evidence that "we are born of God" (1 John ii. 29). The subduing our souls to him, the forming us into a resemblance to himself, is a more certain sign we belong to him, than if we had, with Isaiah, seen his glory in the vision, with all his train of angels about him. This justifies us to be the seed of God, when he hath, as it were, taken a slip from his own purity, and engrafted it in our spirits: he can never own us for his children without his mark, the stamp of holiness. The devil's stamp is none of God's badge. Our spiritual extraction from him is but pretended, unless we do things worthy of so illustrious a birth, and becoming the honor of so great a Father: what evidence can we else have of any child-like love to God, since the proper act of love is to imitate the object of our affections? And that we may be in some measure like to God in this excellent perfection.

1st. Let us be often viewing and ruminating on the holiness of God, especially as discovered in Christ. It is by a believing meditation on him, that we are "changed into the same image" (2 Cor. iii. 18). We can think often of nothing that is excellent in the world, but it draws our faculties to some kind of suitable operation; and why should not such an excellent idea of the holiness of God in Christ perfect our understandings, and awaken all the powers of our souls to be formed to actions worthy of him? A painter employed in the limning some excellent piece, has not only his pattern before his eyes, but his eye frequently upon the pattern, to possess his fancy to draw forth an exact resemblance. He that would express the image of God, must imprint upon his mind the purity of his nature; cherish it in his thoughts, that the excellent beauty of it may pass from his understanding to his affections, and from his affections to his practice. How can we arise to a conformity to God in Christ, whose most holy nature we seldom glance upon, and more rarely sink our souls into the depths of it by meditation! Be frequent in the meditation of the holiness of God.

2d. Let us often exericse ourselves in acts of love to God, because of this perfection. The more adoring thoughts we have of God, the more delightfully we shall aspire to, and more ravishingly catch after, anything that may promote the more full draught of his Divine image in our hearts. What we intensely affect, we desire to

be as near to as we can, and to be that very thing, rather than ourselves. All imitations of others arise from an intense love to their
persons or excellency. When the soul is ravished with this perfection of God, it will desire to be united with it; to have it drawn in
it, more than to have its own being continued to it: it will desire
and delight in its own being, in order to this heavenly and spiritual
work. The impressions of the nature of God upon it, and the imitations of the nature of God by it, will be more desirable than any
natural perfection whatsoever. The will in loving is rendered like
the object beloved; is turned into its nature,[i] and imbibes its qualities. The soul, by loving God, will find itself more and more transformed into the Divine image; whereas, slighted ensamples are never
thought worthy of imitation.

3d. Let us make God our end. Every man's mind forms itself to
a likeness to that which it makes its chief end. An earthly soul is
as drossy as the earth he gapes for; an ambitious soul is as elevated
as the honor he reaches at; the same characters that are upon the
thing aimed at, will be imprinted upon the spirit of him that aims
at it. When God and his glory are made our end, we shall find a
silent likeness pass in upon us; the beauty of God will by degrees
enter upon our souls.

4th. In every deliberate action, let us reflect upon the Divine
purity as a pattern. Let us examine whether anything we are
prompted unto bear an impression of God upon it; whether it looks
like a thing that God himself would do in that case, were he in our
natures and in our circumstances. See whether it hath the livery of
God upon it, how congruous it is to his nature; whether, and in
what manner, the holiness of God can be glorified thereby; and let
us be industrious in all this; for can such an imitation be easy which
is resisted by the constant assaults of the flesh, which is discouraged
by our own ignorance, and depressed by our faint and languishing
desires after it? O! happy we, if there were such a heart in us!

Exhort. 4. If holiness be a perfection belonging to the nature of
God; then, where there is some weak conformity to the holiness of
God, let us labor to grow up in it, and breathe after fuller measures
of it. The more likeness we have to him, the more love we shall
have from him. Communion will be suitable to our imitation;
his love to himself in his essence, will cast out beams of love to
himself in his image. If God loves holiness in a lower measure,
much more will he love it in a higher degree, because then his
image is more illustrious and beautiful, and comes nearer to the
lively lineaments of his own infinite purity. Perfection in anything
is more lovely and amiable than imperfection in any state; and the
nearer anything arrives to perfection, the further are those things
separated from it which might cool an affection to it. An increase
in holiness is attended with a manifestation of his love (John xiv.
21): "He that hath my commandments, and keeps them, he it is
that loves me, and he shall be loved of my Father, and I will love
him, and I will manifest myself to him." It is a testimony of love
to God, and God will not be behind-hand with the creature in kind-

---

[i] Amor naturam induit, et mores imbibit rei amatæ.

ness; he loves a holy man for some resemblance to him in his nature; but when there is an abounding in sanctified dispositions suitable to it, there is an increase of favor; the more we resemble the original, the more shall we enjoy the blessedness of that original: as any partake more of the Divine likeness, they partake more of the Divine happiness.

Exhort. 5. Let us carry ourselves holily, in a spiritual manner, in all our religious approaches to God (Ps. xciii. 5); "Holiness becomes thy house, O Lord, for ever." This attribute should work in us a deep and reverential respect to God. This is the reason rendered why we should "worship at his footstool," in the lowest posture of humility prostrate before him, because "he is holy" (Ps. xcix. 5). Shoes must be put off from our feet (Exod. iii. 5), that is, lusts from our affections, everything that our souls are clogged and bemired with, as the shoe is with dirt. He is not willing we should offer to him an impure soul, mired hearts, rotten carcasses, putrefied in vice, rotten in iniquity; our services are to be as free from profaneness, as the sacrifices of the law were to be free from sickliness or any blemish. Whatsoever is contrary to his purity, is abhorred by him, and unlovely in his sight; and can meet with no other success at his hands, but a disdainful turning away both of his eye and ear (Isa. i. 15). Since he is an immense purity, he will reject from his presence, and from having any communion with him, all that which is not conformable to him; as light chases away the darkness of the night, and will not mix with it. If we "stretch out" our "hands towards him," we must "put iniquity far away from us" (Job xi. 13, 14); the fruits of all service will else drop off to nothing. "Then shall the offering of Judah and Jerusalem be pleasant to the Lord": when? when the heart is purged by Christ sitting as a "purifier of silver" (Mal. iii. 3, 4). Not all the incense of the Indies yield him so sweet a savor, as one spiritual act of worship from a heart estranged from the vileness of the world, and ravished with an affection to, and a desire of imitating, the purity of his nature.

Exhort. 6. Let us address for holiness to God, the fountain of it. As he is the author of bodily life in the creature, so he is the author of his own life, the life of God in the soul. By his holiness he makes men holy, as the sun by his light enlightens the air. He is not only the Holy One, but our Holy One (Isa. xliii. 15); "The Lord that sanctifies us" (Levit. xx. 8). As he hath mercy to pardon us, so he hath holiness to purify us, the excellency of being a sun to comfort us, and a shield to protect us, giving "grace and glory" (Ps. lxxiv. 11). Grace whereby we may have communion with him to our comfort, and strength against our spiritual enemies for our defence; grace as our preparatory to glory, and grace growing up till it ripen in glory. He only can mould us into a Divine frame; the great original can only derive the excellency of his own nature to us. We are too low, too lame, to lift up ourselves to it; too much in love with our own deformity, to admit of this beauty without a heavenly power inclining our desires for it, our affections to it, our willingness to be partakers of it. He can as soon set the beauty of holiness in a deformed heart, as the beauty of harmony in a confused mass, when he made the world. He can as soon cause the light of purity to rise out of the darkness of corruption, as frame glorious spirits out of the insufficiency of nothing. His beauty doth not decay; he hath as much in himself now as he had in his eternity; he is as ready to impart it, as he was at the creation; only we must wait upon him for it, and be content to have it by small measures and degrees. There is no fear of our sanctification, if we come to him as a God of holiness, since he is a God of peace, and the breach made by Adam is repaired by Christ (1 Thess. v. 23): "And the very God of peace sanctify you wholly," &c. He restores the sanctifying Spirit which was withdrawn by the fall, as he is a God pacified, and his holiness righted by the Redeemer. The beauty of it appears in its smiles upon a man in Christ, and is as ready to impart itself to the reconciled creature, as before justice was to punish the rebellious one. He loves to send forth the streams of this perfection into created channels, more than any else. He did not design the making the creature so powerful as he might, because power is not such an excellency in his own nature, but as it is conducted and managed by some other excellency. Power is indifferent, and may be used well or ill, according as the possessor of it is righteous or unrighteous. God makes not the creature so powerful as he might, but he delights to make the creature that waits upon him as holy as it can be; beginning it in this world, and ripening it in the other. It is from him we must expect it, and from him that we must beg it, and draw arguments from the holiness of his nature, to move him to work holiness in our spirits; we cannot have a stronger plea. Purity is the favorite of his own nature, and delights itself in the resemblances of it in the creature. Let us also go to God, to preserve what he hath already wrought and imparted. As we cannot attain it, so we cannot maintain it without him. God gave it Adam, and he lost it; when God gives it us, we shall lose it without his influencing and preserving grace; the channel will be without a stream, if the fountain do not bubble it forth; and the streams will vanish, if the fountain doth not constantly supply them. Let us apply ourselves to him for holiness, as he is a God glorious in holiness; by this we honor God, and advantage ourselves.

DISCOURSE XII

ON THE GOODNESS OF GOD

MARK x. 18.—And Jesus said unto him, Why callest thou me good? There is none good but one, that is, God.

THE words are part of a reply of our Saviour to the young man's petition to him: a certain person came in haste, "running'" as being eager for satisfaction, to entreat his directions, what he should do to inherit everlasting life; the person is described only in general (ver. 17), "There came one," a certain man: but Luke describes him by his dignity (Luke xviii. 18), "A certain ruler;" one of authority among the Jews. He desires of him an answer to a legal question, "What he should do?" or, as Matthew hath it, "What good thing shall I do, that I may have eternal life" (Matt. xix. 16)? He imagined everlasting felicity was to be purchased by the works of the law; he had not the least sentiments of faith: Christ's answer implies, there was no hopes of the happiness of another world by the works of the law, unless they were perfect, and answerable to every divine precept. He doth not seem to have any ill, or hypocritical intent in his address to Christ; not to tempt him, but to be instructed by him. He seems to come with an ardent desire, to be satisfied in his demand; he performed a solemn act of respect to him, he kneeled to him, γονυπετήσας, prostrated himself upon the ground; besides, Christ is said (ver. 21) to love him, which had been inconsistent with the knowledge Christ had of the hearts and thoughts of men, and the abhorrence he had of hypocrites, had he been only a counterfeit in this question. But the first reply Christ makes to him, respects the title of "Good Master," which this ruler gave him in his salutation.

1st, Some think, that Christ hereby would draw him to an acknowledgment of him as God; you acknowledge me "good;" how come you to salute me with so great a title, since you do not afford it to your greatest doctors? Lightfoot, *in loc.* observes, that the title of *Rabbi bone* is not in all the Talmud. You must own me to be God, since you own me to be "good:" goodness being a title only due, and properly belonging, to the Supreme Being. If you take me for a common man, with what conscience can you salute me in a manner proper to God? since no man is "good," no, not one, but the heart of man is evil continually. The Arians used this place, to back their denying the Deity of Christ: because, say they, he did not acknowledge himself "good," therefore he did not acknowledge himself God. But he doth not here deny his Deity, but reproves him for calling him good, when he had not yet confessed him to be more than a man.[k]   You behold my flesh, but you consider not the fulness of my Deity; if you account me "good," account me God, and imagine me not to be a simple and a mere man.[l] He disowns not his own Deity, but allures the young man to a confession of it.   Why callest thou me good, since thou dost not discover any apprehensions of my being more than a man?   Though thou comest with a greater esteem to me than is commonly entertained of the doctors of the chair, why dost thou own me to be "good," unless thou own me to be God?   If Christ had denied himself in this speech to be "good," he had rather entertained this person with a frown and a sharp reproof for giving him a title due to God alone, than have received him with that courtesy and complaisance as he did.[m]   Had he said, there is none "good" but the Father, he had excluded himself; but in saying, there is none "good" but God, he comprehends himself.

2d. Others say, that Christ had no intention to draw him to an acknowledgment of his Deity, but only asserts his divine authority or mission from God.   For which interpretation Maldonat calls Calvin an Arianizer.[n]   He doth not here assert the essence of his Deity, but the authority of his doctrine; as if he should have said, You do without ground give me the title of "good," unless you believe I have a Divine commission for what I declare and act.   Many do think me an impostor, an enemy of God, and a friend to devils; you must firmly believe that I am not so, as your rulers report me, but that I am sent of God, and authorized by him; you cannot else give me the title of good, but of wicked.   And the reason they give for this interpretation, is, because it is a question, whether any of the apostles understood him, at this time, to be God, which seems to have no great strength in it; since not only the devil had publicly owned him to be the "Holy One of God" (Luke iv. 34), but John the Baptist had borne record, that he was the "Son of God" (John i. 32, 34); and before this time Peter had confessed him openly, in the hearing of the rest of the disciples, that he was "the Christ, the Son of the living God" (Matt. xvi. 16).   But I think Paræus' interpretation is best, which takes in both those; either you are serious or deceitful in this address; if you are serious, why do you call me "good," and make bold to fix so great a title upon one you have no higher thoughts of than a mere man?   Christ takes occasion from hence, to assert God to be only and sovereignly "good:"   "There is none good but God."[o] God only hath the honor of absolute goodness, and none but God merits the name of "good."   A heathen could say much after the same manner; All other things are far from the nature of good; call none else good but God, for this would be a profane error: other things are only good in opinion, but have not the true substance of goodness: he is "good" in a more excellent way than any creature can be denominated "good."[p]

1. God is only originally good, good of himself.   All created goodness is a rivulet from this fountain, but Divine goodness hath

  k Erasm. in loc.   l Augustin.   m Hensius in Matt.   n Calvin in loc.
  o Trismegist. Pœmœnd. cap. 2.   p Eugubin. de Peron. Philos. lib. v. cap. 9.

no spring; God depends upon no other for his goodness; he hath it in, and of, himself: man hath no goodness from himself, God hath no goodness from without himself: his goodness is no more derived from another than his being: if we were good by any external thing, that thing must be in being before him, or after him; if before him, he was not then himself from eternity; if after him, he was not good in himself from eternity. The end of his creating things, then, was not to confer a goodness upon his creatures, but to partake of a goodness from his creatures. God is good by and in himself, since all things are only good by him; and all that goodness which is in creatures, is but the breathing of his own goodness upon them: they have all their loveliness from the same hand they have their being from. Though by creation God was declared good, yet he was not made good by any, or by all the creatures. He partakes of none, but all things partake of him. He is so good, that he gives all, and receives nothing; only good, because nothing is good but by him: nothing hath a goodness but from him.

2. God only is infinitely good. A boundless goodness that knows no limits, a goodness as infinite as his essence, not only good, but best; not only good, but goodness itself, the supreme inconceivable goodness. All things else are but little particles of God, small sparks from this immense flame, sips of goodness to this fountain. Nothing that is good by his influence can equal him who is good by himself: derived goodness can never equal primitive goodness. Divine goodness communicates itself to a vast number of creatures in various degrees; to angels, glorified spirits, men on earth, to every creature; and when it hath communicated all that the present world is capable of, there is still less displayed, than left to enrich another world. All possible creatures are not capable of exhausting the wealth, the treasures, that Divine bounty is filled with.

3. God is only perfectly good, because only infinitely good. He is good without indigence, because he hath the whole nature of goodness, not only some beams that may admit of increase of degree. As in him is the whole nature of entity, so in him is the whole nature of excellency. As nothing hath an absolute perfect being but God, so nothing hath an absolutely perfect goodness but God; as the sun hath a perfection of heat in it, but what is warmed by the sun is but imperfectly hot, and equals not the sun in that perfection of heat wherewith it is naturally endued. The goodness of God is the measure and rule of goodness in everything else.

4. God only is immutably good. Other things may be perpetually good by supernatural power, but not immutably good in their own nature. Other things are not so good, but they may be bad; God is so good, that he cannot be bad. It was the speech of a philosopher, that it was a hard thing to find a good man, yea, impossible; but though it were possible to find a good man, he would be good but for some moment, or a short time: for though he should be good at this instant, it was above the nature of man to continue in a habit of goodness, without going awry and warping.q But "the goodness of God endureth forever" (Ps. lii. 1). God always glitters in good-

q Eugubin. de Peron. Philos. lib. v. cap. 9. p. 97. col.

ness, as the sun, which the heathens called the visible image of the Divinity, doth with light.   There is not such a perpetual light in the sun as there is a fulness of goodness in God; "no variableness" in him, as he is the "Father of Lights" (James i. 17).

Before I come to the doctrine, that is, the chief scope of the words, some remarks may be made upon the young man's question and carriage: "What must I do to inherit eternal life?"

1. The opinion of gaining eternal life by the outward observation of the law, will appear very unsatisfactory to an inquisitive conscience.   This ruler affirmed, and certainly did confidently believe, that he had fulfilled the law (ver. 20): "All this have I observed from my youth;" yet he had not any full satisfaction in his own conscience; his heart misgave, and started upon some sentiments in him, that something else was required, and what he had done might be too weak, too short to shoot heaven's lock for him.   And to that purpose he comes to Christ, to receive instructions for the piecing up whatsoever was defective.   Whosoever will consider the nature of God, and the relation of a creature, cannot with reason think, that eternal life was of itself due from God as a recompense to Adam, had he persisted in a state of innocence.   Who can think so great a reward due, for having performed that which a creature in that relation was obliged to do?   Can any man think another obliged to convey an inheritance of a thousand pounds per annum upon his payment of a few farthings, unless any compact appears to support such a conceit?   And if it were not to be expected in the integrity of nature, but only from the goodness of God, how can it be expected since the revolt of man, and the universal deluge of natural corruption?   God owes nothing to the holiest creature; what he gives is a present from his bounty, not the reward of the creature's merit.   And the apostle defies all creatures, from the greatest to the least, from the tallest angel to the lowest shrub, to bring out any one creature that hath first given to God (Rom. xi. 35); "Who hath first given to him, and it shall be recompensed to him again?"   The duty of the creature, and God's gift of eternal life, is not a bargain and sale.   God gives to the creature, he doth not properly repay; for he that repays hath received something of an equal value and worth before.   When God crowns angels and men, he bestows upon them purely what is his own, not what is theirs by merit and and natural obligation: though indeed, what God gives by virtue of a promise made before, is, upon the performance of the condition, due by gracious obligation.   God was not indebted to man in innocence, but every man's conscience may now mind him that he is not upon the same level as in the state of integrity; and that he cannot expect anything from God, as the salary of his merit, but the free gift of Divine liberality.   Man is obliged to the practice of what is good, both from the excellency of the Divine precepts, and the duty he owes to God; and cannot, without some declaration from God, hope for any other reward, than the satisfaction of having well acquitted himself.[r]

2. It is the disease of human nature, since its corruption, to hope for eternal life by the tenor of the covenant of works.   Though this

[r] Amyrant, Morale.

ruler's conscience was not thoroughly satisfied with what he had done, but imagined he might, for all that, fall short of eternal life, yet he still hugs the imagination of obtaining it by doing (ver. 17); "What shall I do, that I may inherit eternal life?" This is natural to corrupted man. Cain thought to be accepted for the sake of his sacrifice; and, when he found his mistake, he was so weary of seeking happiness by doing, that he would court misery by murdering. All men set too high a value upon their own services. Sinful creatures would fain make God a debtor to them, and be purchasers of felicity: they would not have it conveyed to them by God's sovereign bounty, but by an obligation of justice upon the value of their works. The heathens thought God would treat men according to the merit of their services; and it is no wonder they should have this sentiment, when the Jews, educated by God in a wiser school, were wedded to that notion. The Pharisees were highly fond of it: it was the only argument they used in prayer for Divine blessing. You have one of them boasting of his frequency in fasting, and his exactness in paying his tithes (Luke xix. 12); as if God had been beholden to him, and could not, without manifest wrong, deny him his demand. And Paul confesseth it to be his own sentiment before his conversion; he accounted this "righteousness of the law gain to him" (Phil. iii. 7); he thought, by this, to make his market with God. The whole nation of the Jews affected it,[s] compassing sea and land to make out a righteousness of their own, as the Pharisees did to make proselytes. The Papists follow their steps, and dispute for justification by the merit of works, and find out another key of works of supererogation, to unlock heaven's gate, than whatever the Scripture informed us of. It is from hence, also, that men are so ready to make faith, as a work, the cause of our justification. Man foolishly thinks he hath enough to set up himself after he hath proved bankrupt, and lost all his estate. This imagination is born with us, and the best Christians may find some sparks of it in themselves, when there are springings up of joy in their hearts, upon the more close performance of one duty than of another; as if they had wiped off their scores, and given God a satisfaction for their former neglects. "We have forsaken all, and followed thee," was the boast of his disciples: "What shall we have, therefore?" was a branch of this root (Matt. xix. 27). Eternal life is a gift, not by any obligation of right, but an abundance of goodness; it is owing, not to the dignity of our works, but the magnificent bounty of the Divine nature, and must be sued for by the title of God's promise, not by the title of the creature's services. We may observe,

3. How insufficient are some assents to Divine truth, and some expressions of affection to Christ, without the practice of christian precepts. This man addressed Christ with a profound respect, acknowledging him more than an ordinary person, with a more reverential carriage than we read any of his disciples paid to him in the days of his flesh; he fell down at his feet, kissed his knees, as the custom was, when they would testify the great respect they had to any eminent person, especially to their rabbins. All this some think to be

[s] Rom. x. 3. "Going about to establish their own righteousness."

included in the word γονυπετήσας.[t] He seems to acknowledge him
the Messiah by giving him the title of " Good," a title they did not
give to their doctors of the chair; he breathes out his opinion, that
he was able to instruct him beyond the ability of the law ; he came
with a more than ordinary affection to him, and expectation of advantage from him, evident by his departing sad, when his expectations were frustrated by his own perversity ; it was a sign he had a
high esteem of him from whom he could not part without marks of
his grief.   What was the cause of his refusing the instructions he pretended such an affection to receive? He had possessions in the world.
How soon do a few drops of worldly advantages quench the first sparks
of an ill-grounded love to Christ ! How vain is a complimental and
cringing devotion, without a supreme preference of God, and valuation
of Christ above every outward allurement. We may observe this,
    4. We should never admit anything to be ascribed to us, which is
proper to God. " Why callest thou me good ? There is none good
but one, that is, God." If you do not acknowledge me God, ascribe
not to me the title of Good. It takes off all those titles which fawning flatterers give to men, " mighty," " invincible" to princes, "holiness" to the pope. We call one another good, without considering
how evil ; and wise, without considering how foolish ; mighty, without considering how weak, and knowing, without considering how
ignorant. No man, but hath more of wickedness than goodness ;
of ignorance than knowledge ; of weakness than strength. God is
a jealous God of his own honor ; he will not have the creature share
with him in his royal titles. It is a part of idolatary to give men
the titles which are due to God; a kind of a worship of the creatnre
together with the Creator. Worms will not stand out, but assault
Herod in his purple, when he usurps the prerogative of God, and
prove stiff and invincible vindicators of their Creator's honor, when
summoned to arms by the Creator's word (Acts xii. 22, 23).
    Doctrine. The observation which I intend to prosecute, is this:—
Pure and perfect goodness is only the royal prerogative of God ;
goodness is a choice perfection of the Divine nature. This is the
true and genuine character of God ; he is good, he is goodness, good
in himself, good in his essence, good in the highest degree, possessing
whatsoever is comely, excellent, desirable ; the highest good, because
first good : whatsoever is perfect goodness, is God ; whatsoever is
truly goodness in any creature, is a resemblance of God.[u] All the
names of God are comprehended in this one of good. All gifts, all
variety of goodness, are contained in him as one common good. He
is the efficient cause of all good, by an overflowing goodness of his
nature ; he refers all things to himself, as the end, for the representation of his own goodness; "Truly God is good" (Ps. lxxiii. 1).
Certainly, it is an undoubted truth ; it is written in his works of nature, and his acts of grace (Exod. xxxiv. 6). " He is abundant in
goodness." And every thing is a memorial, not of some few sparks,
but of his greater goodness (Ps. cxlv. 7). This is often celebrated in
the Psalms, and men invited more than once, to sing forth the
praises of it (Ps. cvii. 8, 15, 21, 31). It may better be admired than

    [t] Ver. 17. Lightfoot *in loc.*   [u] Ficin. in Dionys. de Divin. Nom. cap. 511.

sufficiently spoken of, or thought of, as it merits. It is discovered in all his works, as the goodness of a tree in all its fruits; it is easy to be seen, and more pleasant to be contemplated. In general,

1. All nations in the world have acknowledged God good; Τὸ Ἀγαθὸν was one of the names the Platonists expressed him by; and good and God, are almost the same words in our language. All as readily consented in the notion of his goodness, as in that of his Deity. Whatsoever divisions or disputes there were among them in the other perfections of God, they all agreed in this without dispute, saith Synesius. One calls him Venus, in regard of his loveliness.[x] Another calls him Ἔρωτα love, as being the band which ties all things together.[y] No perfection of the Divine nature is more eminently, nor more speedily visible in the whole book of the creation, than this. His greatness shines not in any part of it, where his goodness doth not as gloriously glister: whatsoever is the instrument of his work, as his power; whatsoever is the orderer of his work, as his wisdom; yet nothing can be adored as the motive of his work, but the goodness of his nature. This only could induce him to resolve to create: his wisdom then steps in, to dispose the methods of what he resolved; and his power follows to execute, what his wisdom hath disposed, and his goodness designed. His power in making, and his wisdom in ordering, are subservient to his goodness; and this goodness, which is the end of the creation, is as visible to the eyes of men, as legible to the understanding of men, as his power in forming them, and his wisdom in tuning them. And as the book of creation, so the records of his government must needs acquaint them with a great part of it, when they have often beheld him, stretching out his hand, to supply the indigent, relieve the oppressed, and punish the oppressors, and give them, in their distresses, what might " fill their hearts with food and gladness." It is this the apostle (Rom. i. 20, 21,) means by his Godhead, which he links with his eternity and power, as clearly seen in the things that are made, as in a pure glass, " For the invisible things of him from the creation of the world, are clearly seen, being understood by the things that are made, even his eternal power and Godhead." The Godhead which comprehends the whole nature of God as discoverable to his creatures, was not known, yea, was impossible to be known, by the works of creation. There had been nothing then reserved to be manifested in Christ: but his goodness, which is properly meant there by his Godhead, was as clearly visible as his power. The apostle upbraids them with their unthankfulness, and argues their inexcusableness, because the arm of his power in creation made no due impression of fear upon their spirits, nor the beams of his goodness wrought in them sufficient sentiments of gratitude. Their not glorifying God, was a contempt of the former; and their not being thankful, was a slight of the latter. God is the object of honor, as he is powerful, and the object of thankfulness properly as he is bountiful. All the idolatry of the heathens, is a clear testimony of their common sentiment of the goodness of God: since the more eminently useful any person was in some advantageous invention for the benefit of mankind, they thought he

[x] Empedocles. [y] Hesiod.

merited a rank in the number of their deities. The Italians esteemed
Pithagoras a god, because he was Φιλαιθρωπόιατος :[z] to be good and
useful, was an approximation to the Divine nature. Hence it was,
that when the Lystrians saw a resemblance of the Divine goodness
in the charitable and miraculous cure of one of their crippled citizens, presently they mistook Paul and Barnabas for gods, and inferred from thence their right to divine worship, inquiring into nothing else but the visible character of their goodness and usefulness,
to capacitate them for the honor of a sacrifice (Acts xiv. 8–11).
Hence it was, that they adored those creatures that were a common
benefit, as the sun and moon, which must be founded upon a pre-
existent notion, not only of a Being, but of the bounty and goodness of God, which was naturally implanted in them, and legible in
all God's works. And the more beneficial anything was to them,
and the more sensible advantages they received from it, the higher
station they gave it in the rank of their idols, and bestowed upon it
a more solemn worship : an absurd mistake to think everything that
was sensibly good to them, to be God, clothing himself in such a
form to be adored by them. And upon this account the Egyptians
worshipped God under the figure of an ox; and the East Indians,
in some parts of their country, deify a heifer, intimating the goodness of God, as their nourisher and preserver, in giving them corn,
whereof the ox is an instrument in serving for ploughing, and preparing the ground.

2. The notion of goodness is inseparable from the notion of a
God. We cannot own the existence of God, but we must confess
also the goodness of his nature. Hence, the apostle gives to his
goodness the title of his Godhead, as if goodness and godhead were
convertible terms (Rom. i. 20). As it is indissolubly linked with the
being of a Deity, so it cannot be severed from the notion of it : we
as soon undeify him by denying him good, as by denying him great:
Optimus, Maximus, the best, greatest, was the name whereby the Romans entitled Him. His nature is as good, as it is majestic; so doth
the Psalmist join them (Ps. cxlv. 6, 7), " I will declare my greatness ; they shall abundantly utter the memory of thy great goodness." They considered his goodness before his greatness, in putting
Optimus before *Maximus ;* greatness without sweetness, is an unruly
and affrighting monster in the world ; like a vast turbulent sea, always casting out mire and dirt. Goodness is the brightness and loveliness of our majestical Creator. To fancy a God without it, is to
fancy a miserable, scanty, narrow-hearted, savage God, and so an
unlovely, and horrible being : for he is not a God that is not good ;
he is not a God that is not the highest good : infinite goodness is
more necessary to, and more straitly joined with an infinite Deity,
than infinite power and infinite wisdom: we cannot conceive him
God, unless we conceive him the highest good, having nothing superior to himself in goodness, as he hath nothing superior to himself
in excellency and perfection. No man can possibly form a notion
of God in his mind, and yet form a notion of something better than
God ; for whoever thinks anything better than God, fancieth a God

[z] Iamblych. Vit. Pythag. lib. i. col. 6. p. 43.

with some defect: by how much the better he thinks that thing to be, by so much the more imperfect he makes God in his thoughts. This notion of the goodness of God was so natural, that some philosophers and others, being startled at the evil they saw in the world, fancied, besides a good God, an evil principle, the author of all punishments in the world. This was ridiculous; for those two must be of equal power, or one inferior to the other; if equal, the good could do nothing, but the evil one would restrain him; and the evil one could do nothing, but the good one would contradict him; so they would be always contending, and never conquering: if one were inferior to the other, then there would be nothing but what that superior ordered. Good, if the good one were superior; and nothing but evil, if the bad one were superior. In the prosecution of this, let us see.

I What this goodness is. II. Some propositions concerning the nature of it. III. That God is good. IV. The manifestation of it in creation, providence, and redemption. V. The use.

I. What this goodness is. There is a goodness of being, which is the natural perfection of a thing; there is the goodness of will, which is the holiness, and righteousness of a person; there is the goodness of the hand, which we call liberality, or beneficence, a doing good to others.

1. We mean not by this, the goodness of his essence, or the perfection of his nature. God is thus good, because his nature is infinitely perfect; he hath all things requisite to the completing of a most perfect and sovereign Being. All good meets in his essence, as all water meets in the ocean. Under this notion all the attributes of God, which are requisite to so illustrious a Being, are comprehended. All things that are, have a goodness of being in them, derived to them by the power of God, as they are creatures; so the devil is good, as he is a creature of God's making: he hath a natural goodness, but not a moral goodness: when he fell from God, he retained his natural goodness as a creature; because he did not cease to be, he was not reduced to that nothing, from whence he was drawn; but he ceased to be morally good, being stripped of his righteousness by his apostasy; as a creature, he was God's work; as a creature, he remains still God's work; and, therefore, as a creature, remains still good, in regard of his created being. The more of being anything hath, the more of this sort of natural goodness it hath; and so the devil hath more of this natural goodness than men have; because he hath more marks of the excellency of God upon him, in regard of the greatness of his knowledge, and the extent of his power, the largeness of his capacity, and the acuteness of his understanding, which are natural perfections belonging to the nature of an angel, though he hath lost his moral perfections. God is sovereignly and infinitely good in this sort of goodness. He is unsearchably perfect (Job xi. 7); nothing is wanting to his essence, that is necessary to the perfection of it; yet this is not that which the Scripture expresseth under the term of goodness, but a perfection of God's nature as related to us, and which he poureth forth upon all his creatures, as goodness which flows from this natural perfection of the Deity.

2. Nor is it the same with the blessedness of God, but something flowing from his blessedness. Were he not first infinitely blessed, and full in himself, he could not be infinitely good and diffusive to us; had he not an infinite abundance in his own nature, he could not be overflowing to his creatures; had not the sun a fulness of light in itself, and the sea a vastness of water, the one could not enrich the world with its beams, nor the other fill every creek with its waters.

3. Nor is it the same with the holiness of God. The holiness of God is the rectitude of his nature, whereby he is pure, and without spot in himself; the goodness of God is the efflux of his will, whereby he is beneficial to his creatures: the holiness of God is manifest in his rational creatures; but the goodness of God extends to all the works of his hands. His holiness beams most in his law; his goodness reacheth to everything that had a being from him (Ps. cxlv. 9): "The Lord is good to all." And though he be said in the same Psalm (ver. 17) to be "holy in all his works," it is to be understood of his bounty, bountiful in all his works; the Hebrew word signifying both holy and liberal, and the margin of the Bible reads it "merciful' or "bountiful."

4. Nor is this goodness of God the same with the mercy of God. Goodness extends to more objects than mercy; goodness stretcheth itself out to all the works of his hands; mercy extends only to a miserable object; for it is joined with a sentiment of pity, occasioned by the calamity of another. The mercy of God is exercised about those that merit pnnishment; the goodness of God is exercised upon objects that have not merited anything contrary to the acts of his bounty. Creation is an act of goodness, not of mercy; providence in governing some part of the world, is an act of goodness, not of mercy.[a] The heavens, saith Austin, need the goodness of God to govern them, but not the mercy of God to relieve them; the earth is full of the misery of man, and the compassions of God; but the heavens need not the mercy of God to pity them, because they are not miserable; though they need the goodness and power of God to sustain them; because, as creatures, they are impotent without him. God's goodness extends to the angels, that kept their standing, and to man in innocence, who in that state stood not in need of mercy. Goodness and mercy are distinct, though mercy be a branch of goodness; there may be a manifestation of goodness, though none of mercy. Some think Christ had been incarnate, had not man fallen: had it been so, there had been a manifestation of goodness to our nature, but not of mercy, because sin had not made our natures miserable. The devils are monuments of God's creating goodness, but not of his pardoning compassions. The grace of God respects the rational creature; mercy the miserable creature; goodness all his creatures, brutes, and the senseless plants, as well as reasonable man.

5. By goodness, is meant the bounty of God. This is the notion of goodness in the world; when we say a good man, we mean either a holy man in his life, or a charitable and liberal man in the man-

---

[a] Lombard lib. iv. distinct. 46. p. 286.

agement of his goods.   A righteous man, and a good man, are distinguished (Rom. v. 7).   "For scarcely for a righteous man will one die; yet for a good man one would even dare to die;" for an innocent man, one as innocent of the crime as himself would scarce venture his life; but for a good man, a liberal, tender-hearted man, that had been a common good in the place where he lived, or had done another as great a benefit as life itself amounts to, a man out of gratitude might dare to die.   "The goodness of God is his inclination to deal well and bountifully with his creatures."[b]   It is that whereby he wills there should be something besides himself for his own glory.   God is good himself, and to himself, *i. e.* highly amiable to himself; and, therefore, some define it a perfection of God, whereby he loves himself and his own excellency; but as it stands in relation to his creatures, it is that perfection of God whereby he delights in his works, and is beneficial to them.   God is the highest goodness, because he doth not act for his own profit, but for his creatures' welfare, and the manifestation of his own goodness.   He sends out his beams, without receiving any addition to himself, or substantial advantage from his creatures.   It is from this perfection that he loves whatsoever is good, and that is whatsoever he hath made, "for every creature of God is good" (1 Tim. iv. 4); every creature hath some communications from him, which cannot be without some affection to them; every creature hath a footstep of Divine goodness upon it; God, therefore, loves that goodness in the creature, else he would not love himself.   God hates no creature, no, not the devils and damned, as creatures; he is not an enemy to them, as they are the works of his hands; he is properly an enemy, that doth simply and absolutely wish evil to another; but God doth not absolutely wish evil to the damned; that justice that he inflicts upon them, the deserved punishment of their sin, is part of his goodness, as shall afterwards be shown.[c]   This is the most pleasant perfection of the Divine nature; his creating power amazes us; his conducting wisdom astonisheth us; his goodness, as furnishing us with all conveniences, delights us; and renders both his amazing power, and astonishing wisdom, delightful to us.   As the sun, by effecting things, is an emblem of God's power; by discovering things to us, is an emblem of his wisdom; but by refreshing and comforting us, is an emblem of his goodness; and without this refreshing virtue it communicates to us, we should take no pleasure in the creatures it produceth, nor in the beauties it discovers.   As God is great and powerful, he is the object of our understanding; but as good and bountiful, he is the object of our love and desire.

6. The goodness of God comprehends all his attributes.   All the acts of God are nothing else but the effluxes of his goodness, distinguished by several names, according to the objects it is exercised about.   As the sea, though it be one mass of water, yet we distinguish it by several names, according to the shores it washeth, and beats upon; as the British and German Ocean, though all be one sea.   When Moses longed to see his glory, God tells him, he would give him a prospect of his goodness (Ex. xxxiii. 19): "I will make

[b] Coccei. sum. p. 50.   [c] Cajetan in secund. secunda. Qu. 34. Ar. 3.

all my goodness to pass before thee." His goodness is his glory and Godhead, as much as is delightfully visible to his creatures, and whereby he doth benefit man: "I will cause my goodness," or "comeliness," as Calvin renders it, "to pass before thee;" what is this, but the train of all his lovely perfections springing from his goodness? the whole catalogue of mercy, grace, long-suffering, abundance of truth, summed up in this one word (Ex. xxxiv. 6). All are streams from this fountain; he could be none of this, were he not first good. When it confers happiness without merit, it is grace; when it bestows happiness against merit, it is mercy; when he bears with provoking rebels, it is long-suffering; when he performs his promise, it is truth; when it meets with a person to whom it is not obliged, it is grace; when he meets with a person in the world, to which he hath obliged himself by promise, it is truth;[d] when it commiserates a distressed person, it is pity; when it supplies an indigent person, it is bounty; when it succors an innocent person, it is righteousness; and when it pardons a penitent person, it is mercy; all summed up in this one name of goodness; and the Psalmist expresseth the same sentiment in the same words (Ps. cxlv. 7, 8): "They shall abundantly utter the memory of thy great goodness, and shall sing of thy righteousness. The Lord is gracious and full of compassion, slow to anger, and of great mercy; the Lord is good to all, and his tender mercies are over his works." He is first good, and then compassionate. Righteousness is often in Scripture taken, not for justice, but charitableness; this attribute, saith one,[e] is so full of God, that it doth deify all the rest, and verify the adorableness of him. His wisdom might contrive against us, his power bear too hard upon us; one might be too hard for an ignorant, and the other too mighty for an impotent creature; his holiness would scare an impure and guilty creature, but his goodness conducts them all for us, and makes them all amiable to us; whatever comeliness they have in the eye of a creature, whatever comfort they afford to the heart of a creature, we are obliged for all to his goodness. This puts all the rest upon a delightful exercise; this makes his wisdom design for us, and this makes his power to act for us; this veils his holiness from affrighting us, and this spirits his mercy to relieve us: all his acts towards man, are but the workmanship of this.[f] What moved him at first to create the world out of nothing, and erect so noble a creature as man, endowed with such excellent gifts; was it not his goodness? what made him separate his Son to be a sacrifice for us, after we had endeavored to rase out the first marks of his favor; was it not a strong bubbling of goodness? What moves him to reduce a fallen creature to the due sense of his duty, and at last bring him to an eternal felicity; is it not, only his goodness? This is the captain attribute that leads the rest to act. This attends them, and spirits them in all his ways of acting. This is the complement and perfection of all his works; had it not been for this, which set all the rest on work, nothing of his wonders had been seen in creation, nothing of his compassions had been seen in redemption,

---

[d] Herle upon Wisdom, cap. 5. pp. 41, 42. [e] Ingelo Bentivolio, and Uran. Book IV. pp. 260, 261. [f] Daille, Melang. Part II. pp. 704, 705.

II. The second thing is, some propositions to explain the nature of this goodness.

1. He is good by his own essence. God is not only good in his essence, but good by his essence ; the essence of " every created being is good ;" so the unerring God pronounced everything which he had made (Gen. i. 31). The essence of the worst creatures, yea, of the impure and savage devils, is good ; but they are not good *per essentiam*, for then they could not be bad, malicious, and oppressive. God is good, as he is God ; and therefore good by himself, and from himself, not by participation from another ; he made everything good, but none made him good ; since his goodness was not received from another, he is good by his own nature. He could not receive it from the things he created, they are later than he ; since they received all from him, they could bestow nothing on him ; and no God preceded him, in whose inheritance and treasures of goodness, he could be a successor ; he is absolutely his own goodness, he needed none to make him good ; but all things needed him, to be good by him. Creatures are good by being made so by him, and cleaving to him ; he is good without cleaving to any goodness without him. Goodness is not a quality in him, but a nature ; not a habit added to his essence, but his essence itself ; he is not first God, and then afterwards good ; but he is good as he is God ; his essence, being one and the same, is formally and equally God and good.⁶ 'Αυτάγαθον, "good of himself," was one of the names the Platonists gave him. He is essentially good in his own nature, and not by any outward action which follows his essence. He is an independent Being, and hath nothing of goodness or happiness from anything without him, or anything he doth act about. If he were not good by his essence, he could not be eternally good, he could not be the first good ; he would have something before him, from whence he derived that goodness wherewith he is possessed ; nor could he be perfectly good, for he could not be equally good to that from whom he derived his goodness ; no star, no splendid body, that derives light from the sun, doth equal that sun by which it is enlightened. Hence his goodness must be infinite, and circumscribed by no limits ; the exercise of his goodness may be limited by himself ; but his goodness, the principle, cannot ; for since his essence is infinite, and his goodness is not distinguished from his essence, it is infinite also ; if it were limited, it were finite ; he cannot be bounded by anything without him ; if so, then he were not God, because he would have something superior to him, to put bars in his way ; if there were anything to fix him, it must be a good or evil being ; good it cannot be, for it is the property of goodness to encourage goodness, not to bound it ; evil it cannot be, for then it would extinguish goodness, as well as limit it ; it would not be content with the circumscribing it, without destroying it ; for it is the nature of every contrary, to endeavor the destruction of its opposite. He is essentially good by his own essence ; therefore, good of himself ; therefore, eternally good ; and therefore, abundantly good.

2. God is the prime and chief goodness. Being good *per se*, and

⁶ Ficini. Epist. lib. xi. epist. 30.

by his own essence, he must needs be the chief goodness, in whom there can be nothing but good, from whom there can proceed nothing but good, to whom all good whatsoever must be referred, as the final cause of all good. As he is the chief Being, so he is the chief good; and as we rise by steps from the existence of created things, to acknowledge one Supreme Being, which is God, so we mount by steps from the consideration of the goodness of created things, to acknowledge one Infinite Ocean of sovereign goodness, whence the streams of created goodness are derived. When we behold things that partake of goodness from another, we must acquiesce in one that hath goodness by participation from no other, but originally from himself, and therefore supremely in himself above all other things: so that, as nothing greater and more majestic can be imagined, so also nothing better and more excellent can be conceived than God. Nothing can add to him, or make him better than he is; nothing can detract from him, to make him worse; nothing can be added to him, nothing can be severed from him; no created good can render him more excellent; no evil, from any creature, can render him less excellent; " our goodness extends not to him" (Ps. xvi. 2); " wickedness may hurt a man, as we are, and our righteousness may profit the son of man; but, if we be righteous, what give we to Him, or what receives he at our hands" (Job xxxv. 7, 8)? as he hath no superior in place above him, so, being chief of all, he cannot be made better by any inferior to him. How can he be made better by any that hath from himself all that he hath? The goodness of a creature may be changed, but the goodness of the Creator is immutable; he is always like himself, so good that he cannot be evil, as he is so blessed that he cannot be miserable. Nothing is good but God, because nothing is of itself but God; as all things, being from nothing, are nothing in comparison of God, so all things, being from nothing, are scanty and evil in comparison of God. If anything had been, *ex Deo*, God being the matter of it, it had been as good as God is; but since the principle, whence all things were drawn, was nothing, though the efficient cause by which they were extracted from nothing was God, they are as nothing in goodness, and not estimable in comparison of God (Ps. lxxiii. 25): " Whom have I in heaven but thee?" &c. God is all good; every creature hath a distinct variety of goodness: God distinctly pronounced every day's work in the creation " good." Food communicates the goodness of its nourishing virtue to our bodies; flowers the goodness of their odors to our smell; every creature a goodness of comeliness to our sight; plants the goodness of healing qualities for our cure; and all derive from themselves a goodness of knowledge, objectively to our understandings. The sun, by one sort of goodness, warms us; metals enrich us; living creatures sustain us, and delight us by another; all those have distinct kinds of goodness, which are eminently summed up in God, and are all but parts of his immense goodness. It is he that enlightens us by his sun, nourisheth us by bread (Matt. iv. 4): " It is not by bread alone that we live, but by the word of God." It is all but his own supreme goodness, conveyed to us through those varieties of conduit-pipes. " God is all good;" other things are good in their kind; as, a good man, a good angel, a good tree, a good plant; but God hath a good of all kinds eminently in his nature. He is no less all-good, than he is almighty, and all-knowing; as the sun contains in it all the light, and more light than is in all the clearest bodies in the world, so doth God contain in himself all the good, and more good than is in the richest creatures. Nothing is good, but as it resembles him; as nothing is hot, but as it resembles fire, the prime subject of heat. God is omnipotent, therefore no good can be wanting to him. If he were destitute of any which he could not have, he were not almighty: he is so good, that there is no mixture of anything which can be called not good in him; everything besides him wants some good, which others have. Nothing can be so evil as God is good. There can be no evil but there is some mixture of good with it; no nature so evil but there is some spark of goodness in it: but God is a good which hath no taint of evil; nothing can be so supreme an evil as God is supreme goodness. He is only good, without capacity of increase; he is all good, and unmixedly good; none good but God: a goodness, like the sun, that hath all light, and no darkness. That is the second thing; he is the supreme and chief goodness.

3. This goodness is communicative. None so communicatively good as God. As the notion of God includes goodness, so the notion of goodness includes diffusiveness; without goodness he would cease to be a Deity, and without diffusiveness he would cease to be good. The being good is necessary to the being God; for goodness is nothing else, in the notion of it, but a strong inclination to do good; either to find or make an object, wherein to exercise itself, according to the propension of its own nature; and it is an inclination of communicating itself, not for its own interest, but the good of the object it pitcheth upon. Thus God is good by nature; and his nature is not without activity; he acts conveniently to his own nature (Ps. cxix. 68): "Thou art good, and dost good." And nothing accrues to him, by the communications of himself to others, since his blessedness was as great before the frame of any creature as ever it was since the erecting of the world; so that the goodness of Christ himself increaseth not the lustre of his happiness (Ps. xvi. 2): "My goodness extends not to thee." He is not of a niggardly and envious nature; he is too rich to have any cause to envy, and too good to have any will to envy; he is as liberal as he is rich, according to the capacity of the object about which his goodness is exercised. The Divine goodness, being the supreme goodness, is goodness in the highest degree of activity; not an idle, enclosed, pent up goodness, as a spring shut up, or a fountain sealed, bubbling up within itself, but bubbling out of itself: a fountain of gardens to water every part of his creation; "He is an ointment poured forth" (Cant. i. 3): nothing spreads itself more than oil, and takes up a larger space wheresoever it drops. It may be no less said of the goodness of God, as it is of the fulness of Christ (Eph. i. 23); "He fills all in all:" he fills rational creatures with understanding, sensitive nature with vigor and motion, the whole world with beauty and sweetness. Every taste, every touch of a creature, is a taste and

touch of Divine goodness. Divine goodness offers itself in one spark in this creature, in another spark in the other creature, and altogether make up a goodness inconceivable by any creature. The whole mass, and extracted spirit of it, is infinitely short of the goodness of the Divine nature, imperfect shadows of that goodness which is in himself. Indeed, the more excellent anything is, the more nobly it acts; how remotely doth light, that excellent brightness of the creation, disperse itself! How doth that glorious creature, which God hath set in the heavens, spread its wings over heaven and earth, roll itself about the world, cast its beams upward and downward, insinuate into all corners, pierce the depths, and shoot up its rays into the heights, encircle the higher and lower creatures in its arms, reach out its communications to influence everything under the earth, as well as dart its beams of light and heat on things above, or upon the earth! "Nothing is hid from it" (Ps. xix. 6); not from its power, nor from its sweetness. How communicative also is water, a necessary and excellent creature! How active is it in a river, to nourish the living creatures engendered in its womb! refresheth every shore it runs by; promotes the propagation of fruits for the nourishment, and bestows a verdure upon the ground, for the delight of man; and where it cannot reach the higher ground in its substance, it doth by its vapors, mounted up and concocted by the sun, and gently distilled upon the earth, for the opening its womb to bring forth its fruits. God is more prone to communicate himself, than the sun to spread its wings, or the earth to mount up its fruits, or the water to multiply living creatures.[h] Goodness is his nature. Hence were there internal communications of himself from eternity; diffusions of himself, without himself, in time, in the creation of the world, like a full vessel running over. He created the world that he might impart his goodness to something without him, and diffuse larger measures of his goodness, after he had laid the first foundation of it in his being; and therefore he created several sorts of creatures, that they might be capable of various and distinct measures of his liberality, according to the distinct capacities of their nature, but imparted most to the rational creature, because that is only capable of an understanding to know him, and will to embrace him. He is the highest goodness, and therefore a communicative goodness, and acts excellently according to his nature.

4. God is necessarily good. None is necessarily good but God; he is as necessarily good, as he is necessarily God. His goodness is as inseparable from his nature as his holiness. He is good by nature, not only by will; as he is holy by nature, not only by will, he is good in his nature, and good in his actions; and as he cannot be bad in his nature, so he cannot be bad in his communications; he can no more act contrary to this goodness in any of his actions, than he can un-God himself. It is not necessary that God should create a world; he was at his own choice whether he would create or no; but when he resolves to make a world, it is necessary that he should make it good, because he is goodness itself, and cannot act against his own nature. He could not create anything without goodness in the very

[h] Tom. II. p. 926.

act; the very act of creation, or communicating being to anything without himself, is in itself an act of goodness, as well as an act of power; had he not been good in himself, nothing could have been endued with any goodness by him. In the act of giving being, he is liberal; the being he bestows is a displaying his own liberality; he could not confer what he needs not, and which could not be deserved, without being bountiful; since what was nothing, could not merit to be brought into being, the very act of giving to nothing a being, was an act of choice goodness. He could not create anything without goodness as the motive, and the necessary motive; his goodness could not necessitate him to make the world, but his goodness could only move him to resolve to make a world; he was not bound to erect and fashion it because of his goodness, but he could not frame it without his goodness as the moving cause. He could not create anything, but he must create it good. It had been inconsistent with the supreme goodness of his nature, to have created only murderous, ravenous, injurious creatures; to have created a bedlam rather than a world: a mere heap of confusion would have been as inconsistent with his Divine goodness, as with his Divine wisdom. Again, when his goodness had moved him to make a creature, his goodness would necessarily move him to be beneficial to his creature; not that this necessity results from any merit in the creature, which he had framed; but from the excellency and diffusiveness of his own nature, and his own glory; the end for which he formed it, which would have been obscure, yea, nothing, without some degrees of his bounty. What occasion of acknowledgments and praise could the creature have for its being, if God had given him only a miserable being, while it was innocent in action? The goodness of God would not suffer him to make a creature, without providing conveniences for it, so long as he thought good to maintain its being, and furnishing it with that which was necessary to answer that end for which he created it; and his own nature would not suffer him to be unkind to his rational creature, while it was innocent. It had been injustice to inflict evil upon the creature, that had not offended, and had no relation to an offending creature; the nature of God could not have brought forth such an act: and, therefore, some say, that God, after he had created man, could not presently annihilate him, and take away his life and being.[i] As a sovereign, he might do it; as Almighty, he was able to do it, as well as create him; but in regard of his goodness, he could not morally do it: for had he annihilated man as soon as ever he had made him, he had not made man for himself, and for his own glory; to be loved, worshipped, sought, and acknowledged by him. He would not then have been the end of man; he had created him in vain, and the world in vain, which he assures us he did not (Isa. xlv. 18, 19). And, certainly, if the gifts of God be without repentance, man could not have been annihilated after his creation, without repentance in God, without any cause, had not sin entered into the world. If God did not say to man, after sin had made its entrance into the world, " Seek ye me in vain," he could not, because of his goodness, have said so to man in his inno-

i Cocceii sum Theolog. p. 91.

cence.   As God is necessarily mind, so he is necessarily will; as he is necessarily knowing, so he is necessarily loving.   He could not be blessed, if he did not know himself, and his own perfection; nor good, if he did not delight in himself, and his own perfections. And this goodness whereby he delights in himself, is the source of his delight in his creatures, wherein he sees the footsteps of himself. If he loves himself, he cannot but love the resemblance of himself, and the image of his own goodness.   He loves himself, because he is the highest goodness and excellency; and loves everything as it resembles himself, because it is an efflux of his own goodness; and as he doth necessarily love himself, and his own excellency, so he doth necessarily love anything that resembles that excellency, which is the primary object of his esteem.   But,

5. Though he be necessarily good, yet he is also freely good.   The necessity of the goodness of his nature hinders not the liberty of his actions; the matter of his acting is not at all necessary, but the manner of his acting in a good and bountiful way, is necessary, as well as free.[k]   He created the world and man freely, because he might choose whether he would create it, but he created them good necessarily, because he was first necessarily good in his nature, before he was freely a Creator.   When he created man, he freely gave him a positive law, but necessarily a wise and righteous law; because he was necessarily wise, and righteous, before he was freely a Lawgiver. When he makes a promise, he freely lets the word go out of his lips, but when he hath made it, he is necessarily a faithful performer; because he was necessarily true and righteous in his nature, before he was freely a promiser.   God is necessarily good in his nature, but free in his communications of it; to make him necessarily to communicate his goodness in the first creation of the creature, would render him but impotent, good without liberty and without will; if the communications of it be not free, the eternity of the world must necessarily be concluded, which some anciently asserted from the naturalness of God's goodness, making the world flow from God as light from the sun.   God, indeed, is necessarily good, *affectivé* in regard of his nature, but freely good, *affectivé*, in regard of the effluxes of it to this or that particular subject he pitcheth on.   He is not so necessarily communicative of his goodness as the sun of his light, or a tree of its cooling shade, that chooseth not its objects, but enlightens all indifferently, without any variation or distinction; this were to make God of no more understanding than the sun, to shine not where it pleaseth, but where it must.   He is an understanding agent, and hath a sovereign right to choose his own subjects; it would not be a supreme goodness, if it were not a voluntary goodness.   It is agreeable to the nature of the highest good, to be absolutely free, to dispense his goodness in what methods and measures he pleaseth, according to the free determinations of his own will, guided by the wisdom of his mind, and regulated by the holiness of his nature. He is not to " give an account of any of his matters" (Job xxxiii. 13); " He will have mercy on whom he will have mercy, and he will have compassion on whom he will have compassion" (Rom. ix.

[k] Gilbert de Dei Dominio, p. 6.

15); and he will be good, to whom he will be good; when he doth act, he cannot but act well, so it is necessary; yet he may act this good or that good, to this or that degree, so it is free. As it is the perfection of his nature, it is necessary; as it is the communication of his bounty, it is voluntary. The eye cannot but see if it be open, yet it may glance upon this or that color, fix upon this or that object, as it is conducted by the will. God necessarily loves himself, because he is good, yet not by constraint, but freedom; because his affection to himself is from a knowledge of himself. He necessarily loves his own image, because it is his image; yet freely, because not blindly, but from motions of understanding and will. What necessity could there be upon him, to resolve to communicate his goodness? It could not be to make himself better by it, for he had a goodness incapable of any addition; he confers a goodness on his creatures, but reaps not a harvest of goodness to his own essence from his creatures. What obligation could there be from the creature, to confer a goodness on him to this or that degree, for this or that duration? If he had not created a man, nor angel, he had done them no wrong; if he had given them only a simple being, he had manifested a part of his goodness, without giving them a right to challenge any more of him; if he had taken away their beings after a time when he had answered his end, he had done them no injury: for what law obliged him to enrich them, and leave them in that being wherein he had invested them, but his sole goodness? Whatever sparks of goodness any creature hath, are the free effusions of God's bounty, the offspring of his own inclination to do well, the simple favor of the donor; not purchased, not merited by the creature. God is as unconstrained in his liberty, in all his communications, as infinite in his goodness, the fountain of them.

6. This goodness is communicative with the greatest pleasure. Moses desired to see his glory, God assures him he should see his goodness (Exod. xxxiii. 18, 19); intimating that his goodness is his glory, and his glory his delight also. He sends not forth his blessings with an ill will; he doth not stay till they are squeezed from him; he prevents men with his blessings of goodness (Ps. xxi. 3); he is most delighted when he is most diffusive; and his pleasure in bestowing, is larger than his creature's in possessing. He is not covetous of his own treasures. He lays up his goodness in order to laying it out with a complacency wholly divine. The jealousy princes have of their subjects makes them sparing of their gifts, for fear of giving them materials for rebellion: God's foresight of the ill use men would make of his benefits damped him not in bestowing his largesses. He is incapable of envy; his own happiness can no more be diminished, than it can be increased. None can over-top him in goodness, because nothing hath any good but what is derived from him; his gifts are without repentance: sorrow hath no footing in him, who is infinitely happy, as well as infinitely good. Goodness and envy are inconsistent. How unjustly, then, did the devil accuse God! What God gives out of goodness, he gives with joy and gladness. He did not only will that we should be, but rejoice that he had brought us into being; he rejoiced in his works (Ps. civ. 31),

and his wisdom stood by him, " delighting in the habitable parts of
the earth" (Prov. viii. 31). He beheld the world after its creation
with a complacency, and still governs it with the same pleasure
wherewith he reviewed it. Infinite cheerfulness attends infinite
goodness. He would not give, if he had not a pleasure that others
should enjoy his goodness; since he is better than anything, and
more communicative than anything; he is more joyful in giving
out, than the sun can be to run its race, in pouring forth light. He
is said only to repent, and grieve, when men answer not the obligations and ends of his goodness; which would be their own felicity,
as well as his glory. Though he doth not force greater degrees of
his goodness upon those that neglect it, yet he denies them not to
those that solicit him for it: it is always greater pleasure to him to
impart upon the importunities of the creatures, than it is to a mother to reach out her breast to her crying and longing infant. He is
not wearied by the solicitations of men; he is pleased with their
prayers, because he is pleased with the imparting of his own goodness: he seems to be in travail with it, longing to be delivered of it
into the lap of his creature. He is as much delighted with petitions
for his liberality in bestowing his best goodness, as princes are weary
of the craving of their subjects. None can be so desirous to squeeze
those that are under them, as God is delighted to enlarge his hand
towards them. It is the nature of his goodness to be glad of men's
solicitations for it, because they are significant valuations of it, and
therefore fit occasions for him to bestow it. Since he doth not delight in the unhappiness of any of his creatures, he certainly delights in what may conduce unto their felicity. He doth with the
same delight multiply the effects of his goodness where his wisdom
sees it convenient, as he beheld the first-fruits of his goodness with
a complacency upon laying the top-stone of the creation.

7. The displaying of this goodness was the motive and end of all
his works of creation and providence.[1] God being infinitely wise,
would not act without the highest reason, and for the highest end.
The reason that induced him to create, must be of as great an eminency as himself: the motive could not be taken without him, because there was nothing but himself in being; it must be taken,
therefore, from within himself, and from some one of those most excellent perfections whereby we conceive him. But, upon the exact
consideration of all of them, none can seem to challenge that honor
of being the motive of them, to resolve the setting forth any work,
but his own goodness; this being the first thing manifest in his creation, seems to be the first thing moving him to a resolution to create.
Wisdom may be considered as directing, power considered as acting, but it is natural to reflect upon goodness as moving the one to
direct, and the other to act. Power was the principle of his action,
wisdom the rule of his action, goodness the motive of his action;
principle and rule are awakened by the motive, and subservient to
the end. That which is the most amiable perfection in the Divine
nature, and that which he first took notice of, as the footsteps of
them, in the distinct view of every day's work, and the general view

[1] Amyr. Moral. Tom. I. p. 260.

of the whole frame, seems to claim the best right to be entitled the motive and end of his creation of things. God could have no end but himself, because there was nothing besides himself. Again, the end of every agent is that which he esteems good, and the best good for that kind of action: since nothing is to be esteemed good but God, nothing can be the ultimate end of God but himself, and his own goodness. What a man wills chiefly is his end; but God cannot will any other thing but himself as his end, because there is nothing superior to himself in goodness. He cannot will anything that supremely serves himself and his own goodness as his end; for, if he did, that which he wills must be superior to himself in goodness, and then he is not God; or inferior to him in goodness, and then he would not be righteous, in willing that which is a lower good before a higher. God cannot will anything as his end of acting, but himself, without undeifying himself. God's will being infinitely good, cannot move for anything but what is infinitely good; and, therefore, whatsoever God made, he made for himself (Prov. xvi. 4), that whatsoever he made might bear a badge of this perfection upon it, and be a discovery of his wonderful goodness: for the making things for himself doth not signify any indigence in God, that he made anything to increase his excellency (for that is capable of no addition), but to manifest his excellency. God possessing everything eminently in himself, did not create the world for any need he had of it; finite things were unable to make any accession to that which is infinite. Man, indeed, builds a house to be a shelter to him against wind and weather, and makes clothes to secure him from cold, and plants gardens for his recreation and health. God is above all those little helps; he did not make the world for himself in such a kind, but for himself, *i. e.* the manifestation of himself and the riches of his nature; not to make himself blessed, but to discover his own blessedness to his creatures, and to communicate something of it to them. He did not garnish the world with so much bounty, that he might live more happily than he did before, but that his rational creatures might have fit conveniences. As the end for which God demands the performance of our duty is not for his own advantage, but for our good (Deut. x. 13), so the end why he conferred upon us the excellency of such a being was for our good, and the discovery of his goodness to us; for had not God created the world, he had been wholly unknown to any but himself; he produced creatures, that he might be known: as the sun shines not only to discover other things, but to be seen itself in its beauty and brightness. God would create things, because he would be known in his glory and liberality; hence is it that he created intellectual creatures, because without them the rest of the creation could not be taken notice of: it had been in some sort in vain; for no nature lower than an understanding nature, was able to know the marks of God in the creation, and acknowledge him as God. In this regard, God is good above all creatures, because he intends only to communicate his goodness in creation, not to acquire any goodness, or excellency from them, as men do in their framing of things. God is all, and is destitute of nothing, and, therefore, nothing accrues to him by the creation, but the acknowledgment of his goodness. This goodness, therefore, must be the motive and end of all his works.

III. The third thing, that God is good.

1. The more excellent anything is in nature, the more of goodness and kindness it hath. For we see more of love and kindness in creatures that are endued with sense, to their descendants, than in plants, that have only a principle of growth. Plants preserve their seeds whole that are enclosed in them; animals look to their young only after they are dropped from them; yet, after some time, take no more notice of them than of a stranger that never had any birth from them. But man, that hath a higher principle of reason, cherisheth his offspring, and gives them marks of his goodness while he lives, and leaves not the world at the time of his death without some testimonies of it: much more must God, who is a higher principle than sense or reason, be "good" and bountiful to all his offspring. The more perfect anything is, the more it doth communicate itself. The sun is more excellent than the stars, and, therefore, doth more sensibly, more extensively, disperse its liberal beams than the stars do. And the better any man is, the more charitable he is; God being the most excellent nature, having nothing more excellent than himself, because nothing more ancient than himself, who is the Ancient of Days: there is nothing, therefore, better and more bountiful than himself.

2. He is the cause of all created goodness; he must therefore himself be the Supreme Good. What good is in the heavens, is the product of some Being above the earth; and those varieties of goodness in the earth, and several creatures, are somewhere in their fulness and union: that, therefore, which possesses all those scattered goodnesses in their fulness, must be all good, all that good which is displayed in creatures; therefore sovereignly best. Whatsoever natural or moral goodness there is in the world, in angels, or men, or inferior creatures, is a line drawn from that centre, the bubblings of that fountain. God cannot but be better than all, since the goodness that is in creatures is the fruit of his own. If he were not good, he could produce no good: he could not bestow what he had not. If the creature be "good," as the apostle says "every creature is" (1 Tim. iv. 4), he must needs be better than all, because they have nothing but what is derived to them from him; and much more goodness than all, because finite beings are not capable of receiving into them, and containing in themselves, all that goodness which is in an Infinite Being; when we search for good in creatures, they come short of that satisfaction which is in God (Ps. iv. 6). As the certainty of a first principle of all things, is necessarily concluded from the being of creatures, and the upholding and sustaining power and virtue of God is concluded from the mutability of those things in the world; whence we infer, that there must be some stable foundation of those tottering things, some firm hinge upon which those changeable things do move, without which there would be no stability in the kinds of things, no order, no agreement, or union among them: so from the goodness of everything, and their usefulness to us, we must conclude

him good, who made all those things. And since we find distinct goodnesses in the creature, we must conclude that one principle whence they did flow, excels in the glory of goodness: all those little glimmerings of goodness which are scattered in the creatures, as the image in the glass, represent the face, posture, motion of him whose image it is, but not in the fulness of life and spirit, as in the original; it is but a shadow at the best, and speaks something more excellent in the copy. As God hath an infiniteness of being above them, so he hath a supremacy of goodness beyond them: what they have, is but a participation from him; what he hath, must be infinitely supereminent above them. If anything be good by itself, it must be infinitely good, it would set itself no bounds; we must make as many gods, as particulars of goodness in the world: but being good by the bounty of another, that from whence they flow must be the chief goodness. It is God's excellency and goodness, which, like a beam, pierceth all things: he decks spirits with reason, endues matter with form, furnisheth everything with useful qualities.[m] As one beam of the sun illustrates fire, water, earth; so one beam of God enlightens and endows minds, souls, and universal nature: nothing in the world had its goodness from itself, any more than it had its being from itself. The cause must be richer than the effect.

But that which I intend is *the defence of this goodness.*

First, The goodness of God is not impaired by suffering sin to enter into the world, and man to fall thereby. It is rather a testimony of God's goodness, that he gave man an ability to be happy, than any charge against his goodness, that he settled man in a capacity to be evil. God was first a benefactor to man, before man could be a rebel against God. May it not be inquired, whether it had not been against the wisdom of God, to have made a rational creature with liberty, and not suffer him to act according to the nature he was endowed with, and to follow his own choice for some time? Had it been wisdom to frame a free creature, and totally to restrain that creature from following its liberty? Had it been goodness, as it were, to force the creature to be happy against its will? God's goodness furnished Adam with a power to stand; was it contrary to his goodness, to leave Adam to a free use of that power? To make a creature, and not let that creature act according to the freedom of his nature, might have been thought to have been a blot upon his wisdom, and a constraint upon the creature, not to make use of that freedom of his nature, which the Divine goodness had bestowed upon him. To what purpose did God make a law, to govern his rational creature, and yet resolve that creature should not have his choice, whether he would obey it or no? Had he been really constrained to observe it, his observation of it could no more have been called obedience, than the acts of brutes that have a kind of natural constraint upon them by the instinct of their nature, can be called obedience: in vain had God endowed a creature with so great and noble a principle as liberty. Had it been goodness in God, after he had

---

[m] Ficinus in Con. Amor. Orat. 2. cap. p. 1326.

made a reasonable creature, to govern him in the same manner as he does brutes by a necessary instinct? It was the goodness of God to the nature of men and angels, to leave them in such a condition, to be able to give him a voluntary obedience, a nobler offering than the whole creation could present him with; and shall this goodness be undervalued, and accounted mean, because man made an ill use of it, and turned it into wantonness? As the unbelief of man doth not diminish the redeeming grace of God (Rom. iii. 3), so neither doth the fall of man lessen the creating goodness of God. Besides, why should the permission of sin be thought more a blemish to his goodness, than the providing a way of redemption for the destroying the works of sin and the devil, be judged the glory of it, whereby he discovered a goodness of grace that surpassed the bounds of nature? If this were a thing that might seem to obscure or deface the goodness of God, in the permission of the fall of angels and Adam, it was in order to bring forth a greater goodness in a more illustrious pomp, to the view of the world (Rom. xi. 32): "God hath concluded them all in unbelief, that he might have mercy upon all." But if nothing could be alleged for the defence of his goodness in this, it were most comely for an ignorant creature not to impeach his goodness, but adore him in his proceedings, in the same language the apostle doth (ver. 33): "O the depth of the riches both of the wisdom and knowledge of God! How unsearchable are his judgments, and his ways past finding out!"

Secondly, Nor is his goodness prejudiced, by not making all things the equal subjects of it.

1. It is true all things are not subjects of an equal goodness. The goodness of God is not so illustriously manifested in one thing as another. In the creation he hath dropped goodness upon some, in giving them beings and sense, and poured it upon others in endowing them with understanding and reason. The sun is full of light, but it hath a want of sense; brutes excel in the vigor of sense, but they are destitute of the light of reason; man hath a mind and reason conferred on him, but he hath neither the acuteness of mind, nor the quickness of motion equal with an angel. In providence also he doth give abundance, and opens his hand to some; to others he is more sparing: he gives greater gifts of knowledge to some, while he lets others remain in ignorance; he strikes down some, and raiseth others; he afflicts some with a continual pain, while he blesseth others with an uninterrupted health; he hath chosen one nation wherein to set up his gospel sun, and leaves another benighted in their own ignorance. "Known was God in Judea; they were a peculiar people alone of all the nations of the earth" (Deut. xiv. 2). He was not equally good to the angels: he held forth his hand to support some in their happy habitation, while he suffered others to sink in irreparable ruin; and he is not so diffusive here of his goodness to his own as he will be in heaven. Here their sun is sometimes clouded, but there all clouds and shades will be blown away, and melted into nothing: instead of drops here, there will be above rivers of life. Is any creature destitute of the open marks of his goodness, though all are not enriched with those signal characters which he vouchsafes to

others? He that is unerring, pronounced everything good distinctly in its production, and the whole good in its universal perfection (Gen. i. 4, 10, 12, 18, 21, 25, 31). Though he made not all things equally good, yet he made nothing evil; and though one creature in regard of its nature may be better than another, yet an inferior creature, in regard of its usefulness in the order of the creation, may be better than a superior. The earth hath a goodness in bringing forth fruits, and the waters in the sea a goodness in multiplying food. That any of us have a being is goodness; that we have not so healthful a being as others is unequal, but not unjust goodness. He is good to all, though not in the same degree: "The whole earth is full of his mercy" (Ps. cxix. 64). A good man is good to his cattle, to his servants; he makes a provision for all, but he bestows not those floods of bounty upon them that he doth upon his children. As there are various gifts, but one Spirit (1 Cor. xii. 4), so there are various distributions, but from one goodness; the drops, as well as the fuller streams, are of the same fountain, and relish of the nature of it; and though he do not make all men partake of the riches of his grace after the corruption of their nature, is his goodness disgraced hereby? or doth he merit the title of cruelty? Will any diminish the goodness of a father for his not setting up his son after he hath foolishly and wilfully proved bankrupt; or not rather admire his liberality in giving him so large a stock to trade with when he first set him up in the world?

2. The goodness of God to creatures, is to be measured by their distinct usefulness to the common end. It were better for a toad or serpent to be a man, i. e. better for the creature itself, as it were advanced to a higher degree of being, but not better for the universe: he could have made every pebble a living creature, and every living creature a rational one; but that he made everything as we see, it was a goodness to the creature itself; but that he did not make it of a higher elevation in nature, was a part of his goodness to the rational creature. If all were rational creatures, there would have been wanting creatures of an inferior nature for their conveniency; there would have wanted the manifestation of the variety and "fulness of his goodness." Had all things in the world been rational creatures, much of that goodness which he hath communicated to rational creatures would not have appeared: how could man have showed his skill in taming and managing creatures more mighty than himself? What materials would there have been to manifest the goodness of God, bestowed upon the reasonable creatures for framing excellent works and inventions? Much of the goodness of God had lain wrapt up from sense and understanding. All other things partake not of so great a goodness as man; yet they are so subservient to that goodness poured forth on man, that little of it could have been seen without them. Consider man, every member in his body hath a goodness in itself; but a greater goodness as referred to the whole, without which the goodness of the more noble part would not be manifested. The head is the most excellent member, and hath greater impressions of Divine goodness upon it, in regard that it is the organ of understanding:

were every member of the body a head, what a deformed monster would man be! If he were all head, where would be feet for motion, and arms for action? Man would be fit only for thought, and not for exercise. The goodness of God in giving man so noble a part as the head, could not be known without a tongue, whereby to express the conception of his mind; and without feet and hands whereby to act much of what he conceives, and determines, and execute the resolves of his will; all those have a goodness in themselves, an honor, a comeliness from the goodness of God (1 Cor. xii. 22, 23), but not so great a goodness as the nobler part: yet, if you consider them in their functions, and refer them to that excellent member which they serve, their inferior goodness is absolutely necessary to the goodness of the other; without which, the goodness of the head and understanding would lie in obscurity, be insignificant to the whole world, and, in a great measure, to the person himself that wants such members.

3. "The goodness of God is more seen in this inequality." If God were equally good to all, it would destroy commerce, unity, the links of human society, damp charity, and render that useless which is one of the noblest and delightfulest duties to be exercised here; it would cool prayer, which is excited by wants, and is a necessary demonstration of the creature's dependence on God. But in this inequality every man hath enough in his enjoyments for praise, and in his wants, matter for his prayer. Besides the inequality of the creature is the ornament of the world; what pleasure could a garden afford if there were but one sort of flowers, or one sort of plants? far less than when there is variety to please the sight, and every other sense. Again, the freedom of Divine goodness, which is the glory of it, is evident hereby; had he been alike good to all, it would have looked like a necessary, not a free act; but by the inequality, it is manifest that he doth not do it by a natural necessity as the sun shines, but by a voluntary liberty, as being the entire Lord, and free disposer of his own goods; and that is the gift of the pleasure of his will, as well as the efflux of his nature, that he hath not a goodness without wisdom, but a wisdom as rich as his bounty.

4. The goodness of God could not be equally communicated to all, after their settlement in their several beings,—because they have not a capacity in their natures for it: he doth bestow the marks of his goodness according to that natural capacity of fitness he perceives in his creatures; as the water of the sea fills every creek and gulf with different measures, according to the compass each have to contain it; and as the sun doth disperse light to the stars above, and the places below, to some more, to some less, according to the measures of their reception. God doth not do good to all creatures according to the greatness of his own power, and the extent of his own wealth, but according to the capacity of the subject; not so much good as he can do, but so much good as the creature can receive. The creature would sink, if God would pour out all his goodness upon it; as Moses would have perished, if God should have shown him all his glory (Exod. xxxiii. 18, 20). He doth

manifest more good to his reasonable creatures, because they are more capable of acknowledging, and setting forth his goodness.

5. God ought to be allowed the free disposal of his own goodness. Is not God the Lord of his own gifts; and will you not allow him the privilege of having some more peculiar objects of his love and pleasure, which you allow without blame to man, and use yourself without any sense of a crime? Is a prince esteemed good, though he be not equally bountiful to all his servants, nor equally gracious in pardoning all his rebels; and shall the goodness of the great Sovereign of the world be impeached, notwithstanding those mighty distributions of it, because he will act according to his own wisdom and pleasure, and not according to men's fancies and humors? Must purblind reason be the judge and director how God shall dispose of his own, rather than his own infinite wisdom and sovereign will? Is God less good, because there are numberless nothings, which he is able to bring into being? He could create a world of more creatures than he hath done: doth he, therefore, wish evil to them, by letting them remain in that nothing from whence he could draw them? No; but he denies that good to them, which he is able, if he pleased, to confer upon them. If God doth not give that good to a creature which it wants by its own demerit, can he be said to wish evil to it; or, only to deny that goodness which the creature hath forfeited, and which is at God's liberty to retain or disperse?[n] Though God cannot but love his own image where he finds it, yet when this image is lost, and the devil's image voluntary received, he may choose whether he will manifest his goodness to such a one or no. Will you not account that man liberal, that distributes his alms to a great company, though he rejects some? Much more will you account him good, if he rejects none that implore him, but dispenseth his doles to every one upon their petition: and is he not good, because he will not bestow a farthing upon those that address not themselves to him? God is so good, that he denies not the best good to those that seek him: he hath promised life and happiness to them that do so. Is he less good, because he will not distribute his goodness to those that despise him? Though he be good, yet his wisdom is the rule of dispensing his goodness.

6. The severe punishment of offenders, and the afflictions he inflicts upon his servants, are no violations of his goodness. The notion of God's vindictive justice is as naturally inbred, and implanted in the mind of man, as that of his goodness, and those two sentiments never shocked one another. The heathen never thought him bad, because he was just; nor unrighteous, because he was good. God being infinitely good, cannot possibly intend or act anything but what is good: "Thou art good, and thou doest good;" i. e. whatsoever thou dost is good, whatsoever it be, pleasant or painful to the creature (Ps. cxix. 68): punishments themselves are not a moral evil in the person that inflicts, though they are a natural evil in the person that suffers them.[o] In ordering punishment to the wicked, good is added to evil; in ordering im-

[n] Camero, p. 30.   [o] Boetius.

punity to the wicked, evil is added to evil. To punish wickedness is right, therefore good : to leave men uncontrolled in their wickedness, is unrighteous, and therefore bad. But, again, shall his justice in some few judgments in the world, impeach his goodness, more than his wonderful patience to sinners is able to silence the calumnies against him? Is not his hand fuller of gracious doles, than of dreadful thunderbolts? Doth he not oftener seem forgetful of his justice, when he pours out upon the guilty the streams of his mercy, than to be forgetful of his goodness, when he sprinkles in the world some drops of his wrath ?

First, God's judgments in the world, do not infringe his goodness; for,

1. The justice of God is a part of the goodness of his nature. God himself thought so, when he told Moses he would make all his goodness pass before him (Exod. xxxiii. 19): he leaves not out in that enumeration of the parts of it, his resolution, by no means to clear the guilty, but to visit the iniquity of the fathers upon the children (Exod. xxxiv. 7). It is a property of goodness to hate evil, and, therefore, a property of goodness to punish it : it is no less righteousness to give according to the deserts of a person in a way of punishment, than to reward a person that obeys his precepts in a way of recompense. Whatsoever is righteous is good ; sin is evil; and, therefore, whatsoever doth witness against it, is good ; his goodness, therefore, shines in his justice, for without being just he could not be good. Sin is a moral disorder in the world : every sin is injustice : injustice breaks God's order in the world ; there is a necessity therefore of justice to put the world in order. Punishment orders the person committing the injury, who, when he will not be in the order of obedience, must be in the order of suffering for God's honor. The goodness of all things which God pronounced so, consisted in their order and beneficial helpfulness to one another : when this order is inverted, the goodness of the creature ceaseth : if it be a bad thing to spoil this order, is it not a part of Divine goodness to reduce them into order, that they may be reduced in some measure to their goodness? Do we ever account a governor less in goodness, because he is exact in justice, and punisheth that which makes a disorder in his government ? and is it a diminution of the Divine goodness, to punish that which makes a disorder in the world ? As wisdom without goodness would be a serpentine craft, and issue in destruction ; so goodness without justice would be impotent indulgence, and cast things into confusion. When Abel's blood cried out for engeance against Cain, it spake a good thing; Christ's blood speaking better things than the blood of Abel, implies that Abel's blood spake a good thing ; the comparative implies a positive (Heb. xii. 24). If it were the goodness of that innocent blood to demand justice, it could not be a badness in the Sovereign of the world to execute it. How can God sustain the part of a good and righteous judge, if he did not preserve human society ? and how would it be preserved, without manifesting himself by public judgments against public wrongs ? Is there not as great a necessity that goodness should have instruments of judgment, as that there should be

prisons, bridewells, and gibbets, in a good commonwealth? Did not the thunderbolts of God sometimes roar in the ears of men, they would sin with a higher hand than they do, fly more in the face of God, make the world as much a moral, as it was at first a natural chaos: the ingenuity of men would be damped, if there were not something to work upon their fears, to keep them in their due order. Impunity of the innocent person is worse than any punishment. It is a misery to want medicines for the cure of a sharp disease; and a mark of goodness in a prince to consult for the security of the political body, by cutting off a gangrened and corrupting member: and what prince would deserve the noble title of good, if he did not restrain, by punishment, those evils which impair the public welfare? Is it not necessary that the examples of sin, whereby others have been encouraged to wickedness, should be made examples of justice, whereby the same persons and others may be discouraged from what before they were greedily inclined unto? Is not a hatred of what is bad and unworthy, as much a part of Divine goodness, as a love to what is excellent, and bears a resemblance to himself? Could he possibly be accounted good, that should bear the same degree of affection to a prodigious vice, as to a sublime virtue? and should behave himself in the same manner of carriage to the innocent and culpable? could you account him good, if he did always with pleasure behold evil, and perpetually suffer the oppressions of the innocent under unpunished wickedness? How should we know the goodness of the Divine nature, and his affection to the goodness of his creature, if he did not by some acts of severity witness his implacable aversion against sin, and his care to preserve the good government of the world? If corrupted creatures should always be exempt from the effects of his indignation, he would declare himself not to be infinitely good, because he would not be really righteous. No man thinks it a natural vice in the sun, by the power of its scorching heat, to dry up and consume the unwholesome vapors of the air; nor are the demonstrations of Divine justice any blots upon his goodness, since they are both for the defence and glory of his holiness, and for the preservation of the beauty and order of the world.

2. Is it not part of the goodness of God to make laws, and annex threatenings; and shall it be an impeachment of his goodness to support them? The more severe laws are made for deterring evil, the better is that prince accounted in making such provision for the welfare of the community. The design of laws, and the design of upholding the honor of those laws by the punishment of offenders, is to promote goodness and restrain evil; the execution of those laws must be therefore pursuant to the same design of goodness which first settled them. Would it not be contrary to goodness, to suffer that which was designed for the support of goodness, to be scorned and slighted? It would neither be prudence nor goodness, but folly and vice, to let laws, which were made to promote virtue, be broken with impunity. Would not this be to weaken virtue, and give a new life and vigor to vice? Not only the righteousness of the law itself, but the wisdom of the Lawgiver would be exposed

to contempt, if the violations of it remained uncontrolled, and the violence offered by men passed unpunished. None but will acknowledge the Divine precepts to be the image of the righteousness of God, and beneficial for the common good of the world (Rom. vii. 12): "The law is holy, just, and good," and so is every precept of it; the law is for no other end, but to keep the creature in subjection to, and dependence on God; this dependence could not be preserved without a law, nor that law be kept in reputation, without a penalty; nor would that penalty be significant without an execution. Every law loseth the nature of a law, without a penalty; and the penalty loseth its vigor, without the infliction of it: how can those laws attain their end, if the transgressions of them be not punished? Would not the wickedness of the men's hearts be encouraged by such a kind of uncomely goodness? and all the threatenings be to no other end, than to engender vain and fruitless fears in the minds of men? Is it good for the majesty of God to suffer itself to be trampled on by his vassals? to suffer men, by their rebellion, to level his law with the wickedness of their own hearts; and by impunity slight his own glory, and encourage their disobedience? Who would give any man, any prince, any father, that should do so, the name of a good governor? If it were a fruit of Divine goodness to make laws, is it contrary to goodness to support the honor of them? It is every whit as rational and as good to vindicate the honor of his laws by justice, as at first to settle them by authority; as much goodness to vindicate it from contempt, as at first to enact it; as it is as much wisdom to preserve a law, as at first to frame it: shall his precepts be thought by him unworthy of a support, that were not thought by him unworthy to be made? The same reason of goodness that led him to enjoin them, will lead him to revenge them. Did evil appear odious to him, while he enacted this law; and would not his goodness, as well as his wisdom, appear odious to him, if he did never execute it? Would it not be a denial of his own goodness, to be led by the foolish and corrupt judgment of his creatures, and slight his own law, because his rebels spurn at it? Since he valued it before they could actually contemn it, would he not misjudge his own law and his own wisdom, discount from the true value of them, condemn his own acts, censure his precepts as unrighteous, and therefore evil and injurious? remove the differences between good and evil, look upon vice as virtue, and wickedness as righteousness, if he thought his commands unworthy a vindication? How can there be any support to the honor of his precepts, without sometimes executing the severity of his threatenings? And as to his threatenings of punishment for the breach of his laws, are they not designed to discourage wickedness, as the promises of reward were designed to encourage goodness? Hath he not multiplied the one, to scare men from sin, as well as the other, to allure men to obedience? Is not the same truth engaged to support the one, as well as the other; and how could he be abundant in goodness, if he were not abundant in truth (Exod. xxxiv. 6)? both are linked together; if he neglected his truth, he would be out of love with his own goodness; since it cannot be manifested in performing the promises to the obedient, if

it be not also manifested in executing his threatenings upon the rebellious. Had not God annexed threatenings to his laws, he would
have had no care of his own goodness. The order between God and
the creature, wherein the declaration of his goodness consisted, might
have been easily broken by his creature; man would have freed
himself from subjection to God; been unaccountable to him, had
this consisted with that infinite goodness whereby he loves himself,
and loves his creatures. As therefore the annexing threatenings to
his law, was a part of his goodness; the execution of them is so far
from being a blemish, that it is the honor of his goodness. The rewards of obedience, and the punishment of disobedience, refer to the
same end, *viz.* the due manifestation of the valuation of his own law,
the glorifying his own goodness, which enjoined so beneficial a law
for man, and the support of that goodness in the creatures, which by
that law he demands righteously and kindly of them.

3. Hence it follows, That not to punish evil, would be a want of
goodness to himself. The goodness of God is an indulgent goodness, in a way of wisdom and reason; not a fond goodness, in a
way of weakness and folly: would it not be a weakness, always to
bear with the impenitent? a want of expressing a goodness to goodness itself? Would not goodness have more reason to complain, for
a want of justice to rescue it, than men have reason to complain, for
the exercise of justice in the vindication of it? If God established
all things in order, with infinite wisdom and goodness, and God
silently beheld, forever, this order broken, would he not either
charge himself with a want of power, or a want of will, to preserve
the marks of his own goodness? Would it be a kindness to himself
to be careless of the breaches of his own orders? His throne would
shake, yea, sink from under him, if justice, whereby he sentenceth,
and judgment, whereby he executes his sentence, were not the supports of it (Ps. lxxxix. 14). "Justice and judgment are the habitation of thy throne, הכון, the stability or foundation of thy throne.
So, Ps. xcii. 2. Man would forget his relation to God; God would
be unknown to be sovereign of the world, were he careless of the
breaches of his own order (Ps. ix. 16). "The Lord is known by the
judgments which he executes;" is it not a part of his goodness, to
preserve the indispensable order between himself and his creatures?
His own sovereignty, which is good, and the subjection of the creature to him as sovereign, which is also good; the one would not be
maintained in its due place, nor the other restrained in due limits,
without punishment. Would it be a goodness in him to see goodness itself trampled upon constantly, without some time or other
appearing for the relief of it? Is it not a goodness to secure his own
honor, to prevent further evil? Is it not a goodness to discourage
men by judgments, sometimes, from a contempt and ill use of his
bounty; as well as sometimes patiently to bear with them, and wait
upon them for a reformation? Must God be bad to himself, to be
kind to his enemies? And shall it be acounted an unkindness, and
a mark of evil in him, not to suffer himself to be always outraged
and defied? The world is wronged by sin, as well as God is injured
by it. How could God be good to himself, if he righted not his

own· honor? or be a good governor of the world, if he did not some-times witness against the injuries it receives sometimes from the works of his hands? Would he be good to himself, as a God, to be careless of his own honor? or good, as the Rector of the world, and be regardless of the world's confusion? That God should give an eternal good to that creature that declines its duty, and despiseth his sovereignty, is not agreeable to the goodness of his wisdom, or that of his righteousness. It is a part of God's goodness to love him-self. Would he love his sovereignty, if he saw it daily slighted, without sometimes discovering how much he values the honor of it? Would he have any esteem for his own goodness, if he beheld it trampled upon, without any will to vindicate it? Doth mercy de-serve the name of cruelty, because it pleads against a creature that hath so often abused it, and hath refused to have any pity exercised towards it in a righteous and regular way? Is sovereignty destitute of goodness, because it preserves its honor against one that would not have it reign over him? Would he not seem, by such a regard-lessness, to renounce his own essence, undervalue and undermine his own goodness, if he had not an implacable aversion to whatso-ever is contrary to it? If men turn grace into wantonness, is it not more reasonable he should turn his grace into justice? All his attri-butes, which are parts of his goodness, engage him to punish sin; without it, his authority would be vilified, his purity stained, his power derided, his truth disgraced, his justice scorned, his wisdom slighted; he would be thought to have dissembled in his laws; and be judged, according to the rules of reason, to be void of true goodness.

4. Punishment is not the primary intention of God. It is his goodness that he hath no mind to punish; and therefore he hath put a bar to evil, by his prohibitions and threatenings, that he might prevent sin, and, consequently, any occasions of severity against his creature.ᵖ The principal intention of God, in his law, was to encourage goodness, that he might reward it; and when, by the commission of evil, God is provoked to punish, and takes the sword into his hand, he doth not act against the nature of his goodness, but against the first intention of his goodness in his pre-cepts, which was to reward; as a good judge principally intends, in the exercise of his office, to protect good men from violence, and maintain the honor of the laws, yet, consequently, to punish bad men, without which the protection of the good would not be secured, nor the honor of the law be supported; and a good judge, in the ex-ercise of his office, doth principally intend the encouragement of the good, and wisheth there were no wickedness that might occasion punishment; and, when he doth sentence a malefactor, in order to the execution of him, he doth not act against the goodness of his nature, but pursuant to the duty of his place, but wisheth he had no occasion for such severity. Thus God seems to speak of himself (Isa. xxviii. 21); he calls the act of his wrath his " strange work, his strange act;" a work, not against his nature, as the Governor of the world, but against his first intention, as Creator, which was to mani-fest his goodness; therefore he moves with a slow pace in those acts,

ᵖ Zarnovecius, de Satisfact. Part I. cap. i. pp. 3, 4.

brings out his judgments with relentings of heart, and seems to cast out his thunderbolts with a trembling hand: " He doth not afflict willingly, nor grieve the children of men" (Lam. iii. 33); and therefore he " delights not in the death of a sinner" (Ezek. xxxiii. 11); not in death, as death; in punishment, as punishment; but as it reduceth the suffering creature to the order of his precept, or reduceth him into order under his power, or reforms others who are spectators of the punishment upon a criminal of their own nature; God only hates the sin, not the sinner; he desires only the destruction of the one, not the misery of the other; the nature of a man doth not displease him, because it is a work of his own goodness, but the nature of the sinner displeaseth him, because it is a work of the sinner's own extravagance.q Divine goodness pitcheth not its hatred primarily upon the sinner, but upon the sin: but since he cannot punish the sin without punishing the subject to which it cleaves, the sinner falls under his lash. Whoever regards a good judge as an enemy to the malefactor, but as an enemy to his crime, when he doth sentence and execute him?

5. Judgments in the world have a goodness in them, therefore they are no impeachments of the goodness of God.

(1.) A goodness in their preparations. He sends not judgments without giving warnings; his justice is so far from extinguishing his goodness, that his goodness rather shines out in the preparations of his justice; he gives men time, and sends them messengers, to persuade them to another temper of mind, that he may change his hand, and exercise his liberality where he threatened his severity. When the heathen had presages of some evil upon their persons or countries, they took them for invitations to repentance, excited themselves to many acts of devotion, implored his favor, and often experimented it. The Ninevites, upon the proclamation of the destruction of their city by Jonah, fell to petitioning him, whereby they signified, that they thought him good, though he were just, and more prone to pity than severity; and their humble carriage caused the arrows he had ready against them to drop out of his hands (Jonah iii. 9, 10). When he brandisheth his sword, he wishes for some to stand in that gap, to mollify his anger, that he might not strike the fatal blow (Ezek. xxxii. 30); " I sought for a man among them that should make up the hedge, and stand in the gap before me in the land, that I should not destroy it." He was desirous that his creatures might be in a capacity to receive the marks of his bounty.r This he signified, not obscurely, to Moses (Exod. xxxii. 10), when he spoke to him to let him alone, that his anger might wax hot against the people, after they had made a golden calf and worshipped it. " Let me alone," said God: not that Moses restrained him, saith Chrysostom, who spake nothing to him, but stood silent before him, and knew nothing of the people's idolatry; but God would give him an occasion of praying for them, that he might exercise his mercy towards them; yet in such a manner, that the people, being struck with a sense of their crime, and the horror of Divine justice, they might be amended for the future, when they should understand that their death was not averted by their own merit or intercession, but by Moses, his patronage of them, and pleading for them; as we see sometimes masters and fathers angry with their servants and children, and preparing themselves to punish them, but secretly wish some friend to intercede for them, and take them out of their hands: there is a goodness shining in the preparations of his judgments.

2. A goodness in the execution of them. They are good, as they shew God disaffected to evil, and conduce to the glory of his holiness, and deter others from presumptuous sins (Deut. x. 3): " I will be glorified in all that draw near unto me ;—in his judgment upon Nadab and Abihu, the sons of Aaron, for offering strange fire. By them God preserves the excellent footsteps of his own goodness in his creation and his law, and curbs the licentiousness of men, and contains them within the bounds of their duty. "Thy judgments are good," saith the Psalmist (Ps. cxix; xxxix); i. e. thy judicial proceedings upon the wicked; for he desires God there to turn away, by some signal act, the reproach the wicked cast upon him. Can there be any thing more miserable than to live in a world full of wickedness, and void of the marks of Divine goodness and justice to repress it? Were there not judgments in the world, men would forget God, be insensible of his government of the world, neglect the exercises of natural and christian duties; religion would be at its last gasp, and expire among them, and men would pretend to break God's precepts by God's authority. Are they not good, then, as they restrain the creature from further evils; affright others from the same crimes which they were inclinable to commit? He strikes some, to reform others that are spectators; as Apollonius tamed pigeons by beating dogs before them. Punishments are God's gracious warnings to others, not to venture upon the crimes which they see attended with such judgments. The censers of Corah, Dathan, and Abiram, were to be wrought into plates for a covering of the altar, to abide there as a memento to others, not to approach to the exercise of the priestly office without an authoritative call from God (Numb. xvi. 38, 40); and those judgments exercised in the former ages of the world, were intended by Divine goodness for warnings, even in evangelical times. Lot's wife was turned into a pillar of salt, to prevent men from apostasy ; that use Christ himself makes of it, in the exhortation against " turning back" (Luke xvii. 32, 33). And (Ps. lviii. 10): " The righteous shall wash his feet in the blood of the wicked." When God shall drench his sword in the blood of the wicked, the righteous shall take occasion from thence, to purify themselves, and reform their ways, and look to the paths of their feet. Would not impunity be hurtful to the world, and men receive encouragement to sin, if severities sometimes did not bridle them from the practice of their inclinations ? Sometimes the sinner himself is reformed, and sometimes removed from being an example to others. Though thunder be an affrightening noise, and lightning a scaring flash, yet they have a liberal goodness in them, in shattering and consuming those contagious vapors which burden and infect the air, and thereby render it more clear and healthful. Again, there are few acts of Divine justice upon a people, but are in

the very execution of them attended with demonstrations of his goodness to others; he is a protector of his own, while he is a revenger on his enemies; when he rides upon his horses in anger against some, his chariots are "chariots of salvation" to others (Hab. iii. 8). Terror makes way for salvation; the overthrow of Pharaoh and the strength of his nation, completed the deliverance of the Israelites. Had not the Egyptians met with their destruction, the Israelites had unavoidably met with their ruin, against all the promises God had made to them, and to the defamation of his former justice, in the former plagues upon their oppressors. The death of Herod was the security of Peter, and the rest of the maliced christians. The gracious deliverance of good men is often occasioned by some severe stroke upon some eminent persecutor; the destruction of the oppressor is the rescue of the innocent. Again, where is there a judgment but leaves more criminals behind than it sweeps away, that deserved to be involved in the same fate with the rest? More Egyptians were left behind to possess and enjoy the goodness of their fruitful land, than they were that were hurried into another world by the overflowing waves; is not this a mark of goodness as well as severity? Again, is it not a goodness in Him not to pour out judgments according to the greatness of his power? to go gradually to work with those whom he might in a moment blow to destruction with one breath of his mouth? Again, he sometimes exerciseth judgments upon some, to form a new generation for himself; he destroyed an old world, to raise a new one more righteous, as a man pulls down his old buildings to erect a sounder and more stately fabric. To sum up what hath been said in this particular; how could God be a friend to goodness, if he were not an enemy to evil? how could he shew his enmity to evil, without revenging the abuse and contempt of his goodness? God would rather have the repentance of a sinner than his punishment; but the sinner would rather expose himself to the severest frowns of God, than pursue those methods wherein he hath settled the conveyances of his kindness; "You will not come to me that you might have life," saith Christ. How is eternity of punishment inconsistent with the goodness of God? nay, how can God be good without it? If wickedness always remain in the nature of man, is it not fit the rod should always remain on the back of men? Is it a want of goodness that keeps an incorrigible offender in chains in a bridewell? While sin remains, it is fit it should be punished; would not God else be an enemy to his own goodness, and shew favor to that which doth abuse it, and is contrary to it? He hath threatened eternal flames to sinners, that he might the more strongly excite them to a reformation of their ways, and a practice of his precepts. In those threatenings he hath manifested his goodness; and can it be bad in him to defend what his goodness hath commanded, and execute what his goodness hath threatened? His truth is also a part of his goodness; for it is nothing but his goodness performing that which it obliged him to do. That is the first thing; severe judgments in the world are no impeachments of his goodness.

Secondly, The afflictions God inflicts upon his servants, are no violations of his goodness. Sometimes God afflicts men for their temporal and eternal good; for the good of their grace, in order to the good of their glory; which is a more excellent good, than afflictions can be an evil. The heathens reflected upon Ulysses' hardship, as a mark of Jupiter's goodness and love to him, that his virtue might be more conspicuous. By strong persecutions brought upon the church, her lethargy is cured, her chaff purged, the glorious fruit of the gospel brought forth in the lives of her children; the number of her proselytes multiply, and the strength of her weak ones is increased, by the testimonies of courage and constancy which the stronger present to them in their sufferings. Do these good effects speak a want of goodness in God, who brings them into this condition? By those he cures his people of their corruptions, and promotes their glory, by giving them the honor of suffering for the truth, and raiseth their spirits to a divine pitch. The epistles of Paul to the Ephesians, Philippians, and Colossians, wrote by him while he was in Nero's chains, seem to have a higher strain than some of those he wrote when he was at liberty. As for afflictions, they are marks of a greater measure of fatherly goodness than he discovers to those that live in an uninterrupted prosperity, who are not dignified with that glorious title of sons, as those are that "he chasteneth" (Heb. xii. 6, 7). Can any question the goodness of the father that corrects his child to prevent his vice and ruin, and breed him up to virtue and honor? It would be a cruelty in a father leaving his child without chastisement, to leave him to that misery an ill education would reduce him to: "God judges us that we might not be condemned with the world" (1 Cor. xi. 32). Is it not a greater goodness to separate us from the world to happiness by his scourge, than to leave us to the condemnation of the world for our sins? Is it not a greater goodness to make us smart here, than to see us scorched hereafter? As he is our Shepherd, it is no part of his enmity or ill-will to us, to make us feel sometimes the weight of his shepherd's crook, to reduce us from our struggling. The visiting our transgressions with rods, and our iniquities with stripes, is one of the articles of the covenant of grace, wherein the greatest lustre of his goodness appears (Ps. lxxxix. 33). The advantage and gain of our afflictions is a greater testimony of his goodness to us, than the pain can be of his unkindness; the smart is well recompensed by the accession of clearer graces. It is rather a high mark of goodness, than an argument for the want of it, that he treats us as his children, and will not suffer us to run into that destruction we are more ambitious of, than the happiness he hath prepared for us, and by afflictions he fits us for the partaking of, by "imparting his holiness," together with the inflicting his rod (Heb. xii. 10). That is the third thing, God is good.

IV. The fourth thing is the manifestation of this goodness in *Creation, Redemption*, and *Providence*.

First, In *Creation*. This is apparent from what hath been said before, that no other attribute could be the motive of his creating, but his goodness; his goodness was the cause that he made any thing, and his wisdom was the cause that he made every thing in order and harmony. He pronounced "every thing good," *i. e.* such as became his goodness to bring forth into being, and rested in them more, as they were stamps of his goodness, than as they were marks of his power, or beams of his wisdom. And if all creatures were able to answer to this question, What that was which created them? the answer would be, Almighty power, but employed by the motion of infinite goodness.[s] All the varieties of creatures are so many apparitions of this goodness. Though God be one, yet he cannot appear as a God but in variety. As the greatness of power is not manifest but in variety of works, and an acute understanding not discovered but in variety of reasonings, so an infinite goodness is not so apparent as in variety of communications.

1. The creation proceeds from goodness. It is the goodness of God to extract such multitutes of things from the depths of nothing. Because God is good, things have a being; if he had not been good, nothing could have been good; nothing could have imparted that which it possessed not; nothing but goodness could have communicated to things an excellency, which before they wanted. Being is much more excellent than nothing. By this goodness, therefore, the whole creation was brought out of the dark womb of nothing; this formed their natures, this beautified them with their several ornaments and perfections, whereby everything was enabled to act for the good of the common world. God did not create things because he was a living Being, but because he was a good Being. No creature brought forth anything in the world merely because it is, but because it is good, and by a communicated goodness fitted for such a production. If God had been the creating principle of things only as he was a living Being, or as he was an understanding Being, then all things should have partaken of life and understanding, because all things were to bear some characters of the Deity upon them. If by understanding, solely, God were the Creator of all things, all things should have borne the mark of the Deity upon them, and should have been more or less understanding; but he created things as he was good, and by goodness he renders all things more or less like himself: hence everything is accounted more noble, not in regard of its being, but in regard of the beneficialness of its nature. The being of things was not the end of God in creating, but the goodness of their being. God did not rest from his works because they were his works, *i. e.* because they had a being; but because they had a good being (Gen. i.); because they were naturally useful to the universe: nothing was more pleasing to him, than to behold those shadows and copies of his own goodness in his works.

2. Creation was the first act of goodness without himself. When he was alone from eternity, he contented himself with himself, abounding in his own blessedness, delighting in that abundance; he was incomprehensively rich in the possession of an unstained felicity.[t] This creation was the first efflux of his goodness without himself: for the work of creation cannot be called a work of mercy.[u] Mercy supposeth a creature miserable, but that which hath no being is sub-

[s] Cusan, p. 228.   [t] Petav. Theolog. Dogmat. Tom. i. p. 402.
[u] Lessius, de Perfect. Div, p. 100.

ject to no misery; for to be miserable supposeth a nature in being, and deprived of that good which belongs to the pleasure and felicity of nature ; but since there was no being, there could be no misery. The creation, therefore, was not an act of mercy, but an act of sole goodness ; and, therefore, it was the speech of an heathen, that when God first set upon the creation of the world, he transformed himself into love and goodness, Εἰς ἔρωτα μεταβλῆθαι τὸν θεὸν μέλλοιτα δημιουργεῖν.[x] This led forth, and animated his power, the first moment it drew the universe out of the womb of nothing.   And,

3. There is not one creature but hath a character of his goodness. The whole world is a map to represent, and a herald to proclaim this perfection.   It is as difficult not to see something of it in every creature with the eye of our minds, as it is not to see the beams of the shining sun with those off our bodies.   " He is good to all" (Ps. cxlv. 9); he is, therefore, good in all; not a drop of the creation, but is a drop of his goodness.   These are the colors worn upon the heads of every creature.   As in every spark the light of the fire is manifested, so doth every grain of the creation wear the visible badges of this perfection.   In all the lights, the Father of Lights hath made the riches of goodness apparent; no creature is silent in it; it is legible to all nations in every work of his hands.   That, as it is said of Christ (Ps. xl. 7), " In the volume of thy book it is written of me:" In the volume of the book of the Scripture it is written of me, and my goodness in redemption : so it may be said of God, In the volume of the book of the creature it is written of me, and my goodness in creation.   Every creature is a page in this book, whose "line is gone through all the earth, and their words to the end of the world" (Ps. xix. 4); though, indeed, the less goodness in some is obscured by the more resplendent goodness he hath imparted unto others. What an admirable piece of goodness is it to communicate life to a fly !   How should we stand gazing upon it, till we turn our eye inwards, and view our own frame, which is much more ravishing !

But let us see the goodness of God in the creation of man,—*in the being and nature of man*.   God hath, with a liberal hand, conferred upon every creature the best being it was capable of in that station and order, and conducing to that end and use in the world he intended it for.   But when you have run over all the measures of goodness God hath poured forth upon other creatures, you will find a greater fulness of it in the nature of man, whom he hath placed in a more sublime condition, and endued with choicer prerogatives, than other creatures : he was made but little lower than the angels, and much more loftily crowned with glory and honor than other creatures (Ps. viii. 5).   Had it not been for Divine goodness, that excellent creature had lain wrapt up in the abyss of nothing ; or if he had called it out of nothing, there might have been less of skill and less of goodness displayed in the forming of it, and a lesser kind of being imparted to it, than what he hath conferred.

1. How much of goodness is visible in his body !   God drew out some part of the dust of the ground, and copied out this perfection, as well as that of his power, on that mean matter, by erecting it into

x Pherecydes.

the form of a man, quickening that earth by the inspiration of a
"living soul" (Gen. ii. 7) : of this matter he composed an excellent
body, in regard of the majesty of the face, erectness of its stature,
and grace of every part.   How neatly hath he wrought this "tabernacle of clay, this earthly house," as the apostle calls it (2 Cor. v. 1) !
a curious wrought piece of needle-work, a comely artifice (Ps. cxxxix.
15), an embroidered case for an harmonious lute.   What variety of
members, with a due proportion, without confusion, beautiful to
sight, excellent for use, powerful for strength!   It hath eyes to
conduct its motion, to serve in matter for the food, and delight of
the understanding ; ears to let in the pleasure of sound, to convey
intelligence of the affairs of the world, and the counsels of heaven,
to a more noble mind.   It hath a tongue to express and sound forth
what the learned inhabitant in it thinks ; and hands to act what the
inward counseller directs; and feet to support the fabric.   It is tempered with a kindly heat, and an oily moisture for motion, and endued with conveyances for air, to qualify the fury of the heat, and
nourishment to supply the decays of moisture.   It is a cabinet fitted
by Divine goodness for the enclosing a rich jewel; a palace made
of dust, to lodge in it the viceroy of the world ; an instrument disposed for the operations of the nobler soul which he intended to
unite to that refined matter.   What is there in the situation of every
part, in the proportion of every member, in the usefulness of every
limb and string to the offices of the body, and service of the soul ;
what is there in the whole structure that doth not inform us of the
goodness of God ?

2. But what is this to that goodness which shines in the nature of
the soul ?   Who can express the wonders of that comeliness that is
wrapped up in this mask of clay ?   A soul endued with a clearness
of understanding and freedom of will : faculties no sooner framed,
but they were able to produce the operation they were intended for ;
a soul that excelled the whole world, that comprehended the whole
creation ; a soul that evidenced the extent of its skill in giving
names to all that variety of creatures which had issued out of the
hand of Divine Power (Gen. ii. 19); a soul able to discover the nature of other creatures, and manage and conduct their motions.   In
the ruins of a palace we may see the curiosity displayed, and the cost
expended in the building of it ; in the ruins of this fallen structure,
we still find it capable of a mighty knowledge ; a reason able to regulate affairs, govern states, order more mighty and massy creatures,
find out witty inventions; there is still an understanding to irradiate
the other faculties, a mind to contemplate its own Creator, a judgment to discern the differences between good and evil, vice and virtue, which the goodness of God hath not granted to any lower creature.   These excellent faculties, together with the power of self-reflection, and the swiftness of the mind in running over the things of
the creation, are astonishing gleams of the vast goodness of that Divine Hand which ennobled this frame.   To the other creatures of
this world, God had given out some small mites from his treasury ;
but in the perfections of man, he hath opened the more secret parts

of his exchequer, and liberally bestowed those doles, which he hath not expended upon the other creatures on earth.

3. Besides this, he did not only make man so noble a creature in his frame, but " he made him after his own image in holiness." He imparted to him a spark of his own comeliness, in order to a communion with himself in happiness, had man stood his ground in his trial, and used those faculties well, which had been the gift of his Bountiful Creator: he " made man after his image," after his own image (Gen. i. 26, 27); that as a coin bears the image of the prince, so did the soul of man the " image of God :" not the image of angels, though the speech be in the plural number: " Let us make man." It is not to a creature, but to a Creator; let " us," that are his makers, make him in the image of his makers. God created man, angels did not create him; God created man in his " own" image, not, therefore, in the image of angels: the nature of God, and the nature of angels, are not the same. Where, in the whole Scripture, is man said to be made after the image of angels? God made man not in the image of angels, to be conformed to them as his prototype, but in the image of the blessed God, to be conformed to the Divine nature : that as he was conformed to the image of his holiness, he might also partake of the image of his blessedness, which, without it, could not be attained: for as the felicity of God could not be clear without an unspotted holiness, so neither can there be a glorious happiness without purity in the creature; this God provided for in his creation of man, giving him such accomplishments in those two excellent pieces of soul and body, that nothing was wanting to him but his own will, to instate him in an invariable felicity. He was possessed with such a nature by the hand of Divine Goodness, such a loftiness of understanding, and purity of faculties, that he might have been for ever happy as well as the standing angels: and he was placed in such a condition, that moved the envy of fallen spirits; he had as much grace bestowed upon him, as was proportionable to that covenant God then made with him : the tenor of which was, that his life should continue so long as his obedience, and his happiness endure so long as his integrity: and as God, by creation, had given him an integrity of nature, so he had given him a power to persist in it, if he would. Herein is the goodness of God displayed, that he made man after his own image.

4. As to the life of man in this world, God, by an immense goodness, copied out in him the whole creation, and made him an abridgment of the higher and lower world,—a little world in a greater one. The link of the two worlds, of heaven and earth, as the spiritual and corporeal natures are united in him, the earth in the dust of his body, and the heavens in the crystal of his soul: he hath the upper springs of the life of angels in his reason, and the nether springs of the life of animals in his sense. God displayed those virtues in man, which he had discovered in the rest of the lower creation; but, besides the communication which he had with earth in his nature, God gave him a participation with heaven in his spirit. A mere bodily being he·hath given to the heavens, earth, elements; a vegetative life, or a life of growth, he hath vouchsafed to the plants of the ground: he

hath stretched out his liberality more to animals and beasts, by giving them sense.   All these hath his goodness linked in man, being, life, sense, with a richer dole than any of those creatures have received in a rational, intellectual life, whereby he approacheth to the nature of angels.   This some of the Jews understood (Gen. ii. 7) : "God breathed into his nostrils the breath of life, and man became a living soul," חיים, breath of lives, in the Hebrew ; not one sort of life, but that variety of lives which he had imparted to other creatures : all the perfections scattered in other creatures do unitedly meet in man : so that Philo might well call him "every creature, the model of the whole creation :" his soul is heaven, and his body is earth.ʸ   So that the immensity of his goodness to man, is as great as all that goodness you behold in sensitive and intelligible things.

5. All this was free goodness.   God eternally possessed his own felicity in himself, and had no need of the existence of anything without himself for his satisfaction.   Man, before his being, could have no good qualities to invite God to make him so excellent a fabric : for, being nothing, he was as unable to allure and merit, as to bring himself into being ; nay, he created a multitude of men, who, he foresaw would behave themselves in as ungrateful a manner, as if they had not been his creatures, but had bestowed that rich variety upon themselves without the hand of a superior Benefactor. How great is this goodness, that hath made us models of the whole creation, tied together heaven and earth in our nature, when he might have ranked us among the lower creatures of the earth, made us mere bodies as the stones, or mere animals as the brutes, and denied us those capacious souls, whereby we might both know him and enjoy him !   What could man have been more, unless he had been the original, which was impossible?   He could not be greater than to be an image of the Deity, an epitome of the whole.   Well may we cry out with the Psalmist (Ps. viii. 1, 4), " O Lord, our Lord, how excellent is thy name," the name of thy goodness, " in all the earth !"   How, more particularly in man !   " What is man that thou art mindful of him?"   What is a little clod of earth and dust, that thou shouldst ennoble him with so rich a nature, and engrave upon him such characters of thy immense Being?

6. The goodness of God appears in the conveniences he provided for, and gave to man.   As God gave him a being morally perfect in regard of righteousness, so he gave him a being naturally perfect in regard of delightful conveniences, which was the fruit of excellent goodness ; since there was no quality in man, to invite God to provide him so rich a world, nor to bestow upon him so comely a being.

(1). The world was made for man.   Since angels have not need of anything in this world, and are above the conveniences of earth and air, it will follow, that man, being the noblest creature on the earth, was the more immediate end of the visible creation.   All inferior things are made to be subservient to those that have a more excellent prerogative of nature ; and, therefore, all things for man, who exceeds all the rest in dignity : as man was made for the honor of God, so the world was made for the support and delight of man,

ʸ Eugubin, lib. v. cap. 9.

in order to his performing the service due from him to God. The empire God settled man in as his lieutenant over the works of his hands, when he gave him possession of paradise, is a clear manifestation of it: God put all things under his feet, and gave him a deputed dominion over the rest of the creatures under himself, as the absolute sovereign (Ps. viii. 6—8); "Thou madest him to have dominion over the works of thy hands; thou hast put all things under his feet, all sheep and oxen; yea, and the beasts of the field, the fowl of the air, and the fish of the sea; yea, and whatsoever passeth over the paths of the sea." What less is witnessed to by the calamity all creatures were subjected to by the corruption of man's nature? Then was the earth cursed, and a black cloud flung upon the beauty of the creation, and the strength and vigor of it languisheth to this day under the curse of God (Gen. ii. 17, 18), and groans under that vanity the sin of man subjected it to (Rom. viii. 20, 22). The treasons of man against God brought misery upon that which was framed for the use of man: as when the majesty of a prince is violated by the treason and rebellion of his subjects, all that which belongs to them, and was, before the free gift of the prince to them, is forfeit; their habitations, palaces, cattle, all that belongs to them bear the marks of his sovereign fury: had not the delicacies of the earth been made for the use of man, they had not fallen under the indignation of God upon the sin of man. God crowned the earth with his goodness to gratify man; gave man a right to serve himself of the delightful creatures he had provided (Gen. i. 28—30); yea, and after man had forfeited all by sin, and God had washed again the creature in a deluge, he renews the creation, and delivers it again into the hand of man, binding all creatures to pay a respect to him, and recognise him as their Lord, either spontaneously, or by force; and commissions them all to fill the heart of man with "food and gladness" (Gen. ix. 2, 3): and he loves all creatures as they conduce to the good of, and are serviceable to, his prime creature, which he set up for his own glory: and therefore, when he loves a person, he loves what belongs to him: he takes care of Jacob and his cattle: of penitent Nineveh and their cattle (Jonah iv. 11): as when he sends judgments upon men he destroys their goods.

2. God richly furnished the world for man. He did not only erect a stately palace for his habitation, but provided all kind of furniture as a mark of his goodness, for the entertainment of his creature, man: he arched over his habitation with a bespangled heaven, and floored it with a solid earth, and spread a curious wrought tapestry upon the ground where he was to tread, and seemed to sweep all the rubbish of the chaos to the two uninhabitable poles. When at the first creation of the matter the waters covered the earth, and rendered it uninhabitable for man, God drained them into the proper channels he had founded for them, and set a bound that they might not pass over, that they turn not again to "cover the earth" (Gen i. 9.) They fled and hasted away to their proper stations (Ps. civ. 7—9), as if they were ambitious to deny their own nature, and content themselves with an imprisonment for the convenient habitation of Him who was to be appointed Lord of the world. He hath set up stand-

ing lights in the heaven, to direct our motion, and to regulate the seasons: the sun was created, that man might see to "go forth to his labor" (Ps. civ. 22, 23): both sun and moon, though set in the heaven, were formed to "give light" on the earth (Gen. i. 15, 17). The air is his aviary, the sea and rivers his fish-ponds, the valleys his granary, the mountains his magazine; the first afford man creatures for nourishment, the other metals for perfection: the animals were created for the support of the life of man ; the herbs of the ground were provided for the maintenance of their lives; and gentle dews, and moistening showers, and, in some places, slimy floods appointed to render the earth fruitful, and capable to offer man and beast what was fit for their nourishment. He hath peopled every element with a variety of creatures both for necessity and delight; all furnished with useful qualities for the service of man. There is not the most despicable thing in the whole creation but it is endued with a nature to contribute something for our welfare : either as food to nourish us when we are healthful ; or as medicine to cure us when we are distempered ; or as a garment to clothe us when we are naked, and arm us against the cold of the season ; or as a refreshment when we are weary ; or as a delight when we are sad : all serve for necessity or ornament, either to spread our table, beautify our dwellings, furnish our closets, or store our wardrobes (Ps. civ. 24): " The whole earth is full of his riches." Nothing but by the rich goodness of God is exquisitely accommodated, in the numerous brood of things, immediately or mediately for the use of man ; all, in the issue, conspire together to render the world a delightful residence for man ; and, therefore, all the living creatures were brought by God to attend upon man after his creation, to receive a mark of his dominion over them, by the "imposition of their names" (Gen. ii. 19, 20). He did not only give variety of senses to man, but provided variety of delightful objects in the world for every sense; the beauties of light and colors for our eye, the harmony of sounds for our ear, the fragrancy of odors for our nostrils, and a delicious sweetness for our palates : some have qualities to pleasure ; all, everything, a quality to pleasure, one or other: he doth not only present those things to our view, as rich men do in ostentation their goods, he makes us the enjoyers as well as the spectators, and gives us the use as well as the sight ; and, therefore, he hath not only given us the sight, but the knowledge of them : he hath set up a sun in the heavens, to expose their outward beauty and conveniences to our sight; and the candle of the Lord is in us, to expose their inward qualities and conveniences to our knowledge, that we might serve ourselves of, and rejoice in, all this furniture wherewith he hath garnished the world, and have wherewithal to employ the inquisitiveness of our reason, as well as gratify the pleasures of our sense; and, particularly, God provided for innocent man a delightful mansion-house, a place of more special beauty and curiosity, the garden of Eden, a delightful paradise, a model of the beauties and pleasures of another world, wherein he had placed whatsoever might contribute to the felicity of a rational and animal life, the life of a creature composed of mire and dust, of sense and reason (Gen. ii. 9). Besides the other delicacies consigned, in that place, to the use of man, there was a tree of life provided to maintain his being, and nothing denied, in the whole compass of that territory, but one tree, that of the knowledge of good and evil, which was no mark of an ill-will in his Creator to him, but a reserve of God's absolute sovereignty, and a trial of man's voluntary obedience. What blur was it to the goodness of God, to reserve one tree for his own propriety, when he had given to man, in all the rest, such numerous marks of his rich bounty and goodness? What Israel, after man's fall, enjoyed sensibly, Nehemiah calls "great goodness" (Neh. ix. 25). How inexpressible, then, was that goodness manifested to innocent man, when so small a part of it, indulged to the Israelites after the curse upon the ground, is called, as truly it merits, such great goodness! How can we pass through any part of this great city, and cast our eyes upon the well-furnished shops, stored with all kinds of commodities, without reflections upon this goodness of God starting up before our eyes in such varieties, and plainly telling us that he hath accommodated all things for our use, suited things, both to supply our need, content a reasonable curiosity, and delight us in our aims at, and passage to, our supreme end!

(3.) The goodness of God appears in the laws he hath given to man, the covenant he hath made with him. It had not been agreeable to the goodness of God to let a creature, governable by a law, be without a law to regulate him; his goodness then which had broke forth in the creation, had suffered an eclipse and obscurity in his government. As infinite goodness was the motive to create, so infinite goodness was the motive of his government. And this appears,

[1.] In the fitting the law to the nature of man. It was rather below than above his strength; he had an integrity in his nature to answer the righteousness of the precept. God created "man upright" (Eccles. vii. 29); his nature was suited to the law, and the law to his nature; it was not above his understanding to know it, nor his will to embrace it, nor his passions to be regulated by it. The law and his nature were like to exact straight lines, touching one another in every part when joined together. God exacted no more by his law than what was written by nature in his heart: he had a knowledge by creation to observe the law of his creation, and he fell not for want of a righteousness in his nature: he was enabled for more than was commanded him, but wilfully indisposed to less than he was able to perform. The precepts were easy, not only becoming the authority of a sovereign to exact, but the goodness of a father to demand, and the ingenuity of a creature and a son to pay. "His commands are not grievous" (1 John v. 3); the observance of them had filled the spirit of man with an extraordinary contentment. It had been no less a pleasure and a delightful satisfaction to have kept the law in a created state, than it is to keep it in some measure in a renewed state. The renewed nature finds a suitableness in the law to kindle a "delight" (Ps. i. 2): it could not then have anywise shook the nature of an upright creature, nor have been a burden too heavy for his shoulders to bear. Though he had not a grace

given him above nature, yet he had not a law given him that surmounted his nature : it did not exceed his created strength, and was
suited to the dignity and nobility of a rational nature. It was a
"just law" (Rom. vii. 12), and, therefore, not above the nature of
the subject that was bound to obey it. And had it been impossible
to be observed, it had been unrighteous to be enacted : it had not
been a matter of Divine praise, and that seven times a day ; as it is,
"Seven times a day do I praise thee, because of thy righteous judgments" (Ps. cxix. 164). The law was so righteous, that Adam had
every whit as much reason to bless God in his innocence for the
righteousness of it, as David had with the relics of enmity against
it : his goodness shines so much in his law, as merits our praise of
him, as he is a sovereign Lawgiver, as well as a gracious Benefactor,
in the imparting to us a being.

[2.] In fitting it for the happiness of man. For the satisfaction
of his soul, which finds a reward in the very act of keeping it, (Ps.
cxix. 165), "Great peace in the loving it ;" for the preservation of
human society, wherein consists the external felicity of man. It
had been inconsistent with the Divine goodness to enjoin man anything that should be oppressive and uncomfortable. Bitterness cannot come from that which is altogether sweet : goodness would not
have obliged the creature to anything, but what is not only free from
damaging him, but wholly conducing to his welfare, and perfective
of his nature. Infinite wisdom could not order anything but what
was agreeable to infinite goodness. As his laws are the most rational, as being the contrivance of infinite wisdom ; so they are the best,
as being the fruit of infinite goodness. His laws are not only the
acts of his sovereign authority, but the effluxes of his loving-kindness, and the conductors of man to an enjoyment of a greater bounty :
he minds as well the promotion of his creatures' felicity, as the asserting his own authority ; as good princes make laws for their subjects' benefit as well as their own honor. What was said of a more
difficult and burdensome law long after man's fall, may much more
be said of the easy law of nature in the state of man's innocence,
that it was "for our good" (Deut. x. 12, 13). He never pleaded
with the Israelites for the observation of his commands upon the
account of his authority, so much as upon the score of their benefit
by them (Deut. iv. 40 ; xii. 28). And when his precepts were
broken, he seems sometimes to be more grieved for men's impairing
their own felicity by it, than for their violating his authority : "O,
that thou hadst hearkened to my commandments, then had thy peace
been as a river !" (Isa. xlviii. 18). Goodness cannot prescribe a
thing prejudicial : whatsoever it enjoins, is beneficial to the spiritual
and eternal happiness of the rational creature : this was both the
design of the law given, and the end of the law. Christ, in his answer to the young man's question, refers him to the moral law,
which was the law of nature in Adam, as that whereby eternal life
was to be gained : which evidenceth, that when the law was first
given as the covenant of works, it was for the happiness of man ;
and the end of giving it was, that man might have eternal life by
it : there would else be no strength or truth in that answer of Christ

to that Ruler. And, therefore, Stephen calls the law given by Moses, which was the same with the law of nature in Adam, "the living oracles" (Acts vii. 38). He enjoined men's services to them not simply for his own glory, but his glory in men's welfare: as if there were any being better than himself, his goodness and righteousness would guide him to love that better than himself; because it is good and righteous to love that best which is most amiable: so, if there were any that could do us more good, and shower down more happiness upon us than himself, he would be content we should obey that as sovereign, and steer our course according to his laws: "If God be God, follow him; but if Baal, then follow him" (1 Kings xviii. 21). If the observance of the precepts of Baal be more beneficial to you; if you can advance your nature by his service, and gain a more mighty crown of happiness than by mine, follow him with all my heart: I never intended to enjoin you anything to impair, but increase your happiness. The chief design of God in his law is the happiness of the subject; and obedience is intended by him as a means for the attaining of happiness, as well as preserving his own sovereignty: this is the reason why he wished that Israel had walked in his ways, "that their time might have endured forever" (Ps. lxxxi. 13, 15, 16). And by the same reason, this was his intendment in his law given to man, and his covenant made with man at the creation, that he might be fed with the finest part of his bounty, and be satisfied with honey out of the eternal Rock of Ages. To paraphrase his expression there :—The goodness of God appears further,

[3]. In engaging man to obedience by promises and threatenings. A threatening is only mentioned (Gen. ii. 17), but a promise is implied: if eternal death were fixed for transgression, eternal life was thereby designed for obedience: and that it was so, the answer of Christ to the Ruler evidenceth, that the first intendment of the precept was the eternal life of the subject, ordered to obey it.

1st. God might have acted, in settling his law, only as a sovereign. Though he might have dealt with man upon the score of his absolute dominion over him as his creature, and signified his pleasure upon the right of his sovereignty, threatening only a penalty if man transgressed, without the promising a bountiful acknowledgment of his obedience by a reward as a benefactor: yet he would treat with man in gentle methods, and rule him in a track of sweetness as well as sovereignty: he would preserve the rights of his dominion in the authority of his commands, and honor the condescensions of his goodness in the allurements of a promise. He that might have solely demanded a compliance with his will, would kindly article with him, to oblige him to observe him out of love to himself as well as duty to his Creator; that he might have both the interest of avoiding the threatened evil to affright him, and the interest of attaining the promised good to allure him to obedience. How doth he value the title of Benefactor above that of a Lord, when he so kindly solicits, as well as commands; and engageth to reward that obedience which he might have absolutely claimed as his due, by enforcing fears of the severest penalty!

His sovereignty seems to stoop below itself for the elevation of his goodness; and he is pleased to have his kindness more taken notice of than his authority. Nothing imported more condescension than his bringing forth his law in the nature of a covenant, whereby he seems to humble himself, and veil his superiority to treat with man as his equal, that the very manner of his treatment might oblige him in the richest promises he made to draw him, and the startling threatenings he pronounced to link him to his obedience: and, therefore, is it observable, that when after the transgression of Adam God comes to deal with him, he doth not do it in that thundering rigor, which might have been expected from an enraged sovereign, but in a gentle examination (Gen. iii. 11, 13): "Hast thou eaten of the tree whereof I commanded thee that thou shouldst not eat?" To the woman, he said no more than, "What is this that thou hast done?" And in the Scripture we find, when he cites the Israelites before him for their sin, he expostulates with them not so much upon the absolute right he had to challenge their obedience, as upon the equity and reasonableness of his law which they had transgressed; that by the same argument of sweetness, wherewith he would attract them to their duty, he might shame them after their offence (Isa. i. 2; Ezek. xviii. 25).

2d. By the threatenings he manifests his goodness as well as by his promises. He promises that he might be a rewarder, and threatens that he might not be a punisher; the one is to elevate our hope, and the other to excite our fear, the two passions whereby the nature of man is managed in the world. He imprints upon man sentiments of a misery by sin, in his thundering commination, that he might engage him the more to embrace and be guided by the motives of sweetness in his gracious promises. The design of them was to preserve man in his due bounds, that God might not have occasion to blow upon him the flames of his justice; to suppress those irregular passions, which the nature of man (though created without any disorder) was capable of entertaining upon the appearance of suitable objects; and to keep the waves from swelling upon any turning wind, that so man, being modest in the use of the goodness God had allowed him, might still be capable of fresh streams of Divine bounty, without ever falling under his righteous wrath for any transgression. What a prospect of goodness is in this proceeding, to disclose man's happiness to be as durable as his innocence; and set before a rational creature the extremest misery due to his crime, to affright him from neglecting his Creator, and making unworthy returns to his goodness! What could be done more by goodness to suit that passion of fear which was implanted in the nature of man, than to assure him he should not degenerate from the righteousness of his nature, and violate the authority of his Creator, without falling from his own happiness, and sinking into the most deplorable calamity!

3d. The reward he promised manifests yet further his goodness to man. It was his goodness to intend a reward to man; no necessity could oblige God to reward man, had he continued obedient in his created state: for in all rewards which are truly merited, beside

some kind of equality to be considered between the person doing
service and the person rewarding, and also between the act performed and the reward bestowed, there must also be considered the
condition of the person doing the service, that he is not obliged to
do it as a duty, but is at his own choice whether to offer it or no.
But man, being wholly dependent on God in his being and preservation, having nothing of his own, but what he had received from
the hands of Divine bounty, his service was due by the strongest
obligation to God (1 Cor. iv. 7). But there was no natural engagement on God to return a reward to him ; for man could return nothing of his own but that only which he had received from his
Creator. It must be pure goodness that gives a gracious reward for
a due debt, to receive his own from man, and return more than he
had received. A Divine reward doth far surmount the value of a
rational service. It was, therefore, a mighty goodness to stipulate
with man, that upon his obedience he should enjoy an immortality
in that nature. The article on man's part was obedience, which
was necessarily just, and founded in the nature of man ; he had
been unjust, ungrateful, and violated all laws of righteousness, had
he committed any act unworthy of one that had been so great a
subject of Divine liberality.[z] But the article on God's part, of giving a perpetual blessedness to innocent man, was not founded upon
rules of strict justice and righteousness, for that would have argued
God to be a debtor to man ; but that God cannot be to the work of
his hands, that had received the materials of his being and acting
from him, as the vessel doth from the potter. But this was founded
only on the goodness of the Divine nature, whereby he cannot but
be kind to an innocent and holy creature. The nature of God inclined him to it by the rules of goodness, but the service of man
could not claim it by the rules of justice without a stipulation ; so
that the covenant whereby God obliged himself to continue the
happiness of man upon the continuance of his obedience, in the
original of it, springs from pure goodness ; though the performance
of it, upon the fulfilling condition required in the creature, was
founded upon the rules of righteousness and truth, after Divine
goodness had brought it forth. God did create man for a reward
and happiness ; now God's implanting in the nature of man a desire
after happiness, and some higher happiness than he had in creation
invested him in, doth evidence that God did not create man only
for his own service, but for his attaining a greater happiness. All
rational creatures are possessed with a principle of seeking after
good, the highest good, and God did not plant in man this principle
in vain ; it had not been goodness to put this principle in man, if
he had designed never to bestow a happiness on man for his obedience : this had been repugnant to the goodness and wisdom of
God ; and the Scripture doth very emphatically express the felicity
of man to be the design of God in the first forming him and moulding him a creature, as well as working him a new creature ; " He
that hath wrought us for the self-same thing is God" (2 Cor. v. 1, 5) :
he framed this earthly tabernacle for a residence in an eternal habi-

z Amyral. Dissertat. pp. 637, 638.

tation, and a better habitation than an earthly paradise. What we expect in the resurrection, that very same thing God did in creation intend us for; but since the corruption of our natures, we must undergo a dissolution of our bodies, and may have just reason of a despondency, since sin hath seemed to change the course of God's bounty, and brought us under a curse. He hath given us the earnest of his Spirit, as an assurance that he will perform that very self-same thing, the conferring that happiness upon renewed creatures for which he first formed man in creation, when he compacted his earthly tabernacle of the dust of the ground, and reared it up before him.

4th. It was a mighty goodness that God should give man an eternal reward. That an eternity of reward was promised, is implied in the death that was threatened upon transgression: whatsoever you conceive the threatened death to be, either for nature, or duration upon transgression; of the same nature and duration you must suppose the life to be, which is implied upon his constancy in his integrity. As sin would render him an eternal object of God's hatred, so his obedience would render him an eternally amiable object to his Creator, as the standing angels are preserved and confirmed in an entire felicity and glory. Though the threatening be only expressed by God (Gen. ii. 17), yet the other is implied, and might easily be concluded from it by Adam. And one reason why God only expressed the threatening, and not the promise, was, because man might collect some hopes and expectations of a perpetual happiness from that image of God which he beheld in himself, and from the large provision he had made for him in the world, and the commission given him to increase and multiply, and to rule as a lord over his other works; whereas he could not so easily have imagined himself capable of being exposed to such an extraordinary calamity as an eternal death, without some signification of it from God. It is easily concludable, that eternal life was supposed to be promised, to be conferred upon him if he stood, as well as eternal death to be inflicted on him if he rebelled.[a] Now this eternal life was not due to his nature, but it was a pure beam, and gift of Divine goodness; for there was no proportion between man's service in his innocent estate, and a reward so great both for nature and duration: it was a higher reward than can be imagined either due to the nature of man, or upon any natural right claimable by his obedience. All that could be expected by him was but a natural happiness, not a supernatural: as there was no necessity upon the account of natural righteousness, so there was no necessity upon the account of the goodness of God to elevate the nature of man to a supernatural happiness, merely because he created him: for though it be necessary for God, when he would create, in regard of his wisdom, to create for some end, yet it was not necessary that end should be a supernatural end and happiness, since a natural blessedness had been sufficient for man. And though God, in creating angels and men intellectual and rational creatures, did make them necessary for himself and his own glory, yet it was not necessarily for him to

[a] Suarez. de Gratia, Vol. I. pp. 126, 127.

order either angels or men to such a felicity as consists in a clear vision, and so high a fruition, of himself: for all other things are made by him for himself, and yet not for the vision of himself, God might have created man only for a natural happiness, according to the perfection of his natural faculties, and had dealt bountifully with him, if he had never intended him a supernatural blessedness and an eternal recompense: but what a largeness of goodness is here, to design man, in his creation, for so rich a blessedness as an eternal life, with the fruition of himself! He hath not only given to man all things which are necessary, but designed for man that which the poor creature could not imagine: he garnished the earth for him, and garnished him for an eternal felicity, had he not, by slighting the goodness of God, stripped himself of the present, and forfeited his future blessedness.

Secondly, The manifestation of this goodness in *Redemption*. The whole gospel is nothing but one entire mirror of Divine goodness: the whole of redemption is wrapped up in that one expression of the angels' song (Luke ii. 14), "Good-will towards men." The angels sang but one song before, which is upon record, but the matter of it seems to be the wisdom of God chiefly in creation (Job xxxviii. 7; compare chap. ix. 5, 6, 8, 9). The angels are there meant by the "morning stars;" the visible stars of heaven were not distinctly formed when the foundations of the earth were laid: and the title of the sons of God verifies it, since none but creatures of understanding are dignified in Scripture with that title. There they celebrate his wisdom in creation ; here his goodness in redemption, which is the entire matter of the song.

i. Goodness was the spring of redemption. All and every part of it owes only to this perfection the appearance of it in the world. This only excited wisdom to bring forth from so great an evil as the apostacy of man, so great a good as the recovery of him. When man fell from his created goodness, God would evidence that he could not fall from his infinite goodness: that the greatest evil could not surmount the ability of his wisdom to contrive, nor the riches of his bounty to present us a remedy for it. Divine Goodness would not stand by a spectator, without being reliever of that misery man had plunged himself into; but by astonishing methods it would recover him to happiness, who had wrested himself out of his hands, to fling himself into the most deplorable calamity: and it was the greater, since it surmounted those natural inclinations, and those strong provocations which he had to shower down the power of his wrath. What could be the source of such a procedure, but this excellency of Divine nature, since no violence could force him, nor was there any merit to persuade to such a restoration? This, under the name of his "love," is rendered the sole cause of the redeeming death of the Son: it was to commend his love with the highest gloss, and in so singular a manner that had not its parallel in nature, nor in all his other works, and reaches in the brightness of it beyond the manifested extent of any other attribute (Rom. v. 8). It must be only a miraculous goodness that induced him to expose the life of his Son to those difficulties in the world, and death upon the cross, for the freedom of sordid rebels: his great end was to give such a demonstration of the liberality of his nature, as might be attractive to his creature, remove its shakings and tremblings, and encourage its approaches to him. It is in this he would not only manifest his love, but assume the name of "Love." By this name the Holy Ghost calls him, in relation to this good will manifested in his Son (1 John iv. 8, 9), "God is love." In this is manifested the love of God towards us, because that God sent his only-begotten Son into the world, that we might "live through him." He would take the name he never expressed himself in before. He was Jehovah, in regard of the truth of his promise; so he would be known of old: he is Goodness, in regard of the grandeur of his affection in the mission of his Son: and, therefore, he would be known by the name of Love now, in the days of the gospel.

ii. It was a pure goodness. He was under no obligation to pity our misery, and repair our ruins: he might have stood to the terms of the first covenant, and exacted our eternal death, since we had committed an infinite transgression: he was under no tie to put off the robes of a judge for the bowels of a father, and erect a mercy-seat above his tribunal of justice.[b] The reparation of man had no necessary connexion with his creation; it follows not, that because Goodness had extracted us from nothing by a mighty power, that it must lift us out of wilful misery by a mighty grace. Certainly that God who had no need of creating us, had far less need of redeeming us: for, since he created one world, he could have as easily destroyed it, and reared another. It had not been unbecoming the Divine Goodness or Wisdom, to have let man perpetually wallow in that sink wherein he had plunged himself, since he was criminal by his own will, and, therefore, miserable by his own fault: nothing could necessitate this reparation. If Divine Goodness could not be obliged by the angelical dignity to repair that nature, he is further from any obligation by the meanness of man to repair human nature. There was less necessity to restore man than to restore the fallen angels. What could man do to oblige God to a reparation of him, since he could not render him a recompense for his goodness manifested in his creation? He must be much more impotent to render him a debtor for the redemption of him from misery. Could it be a salary for anything we had done? Alas! we are so far from meriting it, that by our daily demerits, we seem ambitious to put a stop to any further effusions of it: we could not have complained of him, if he had left us in the misery we had courted, since he was bound by no law to bestow upon us the recovery we wanted. When the apostle speaks of the gospel of "redemption," he giveth it the title of the "gospel of the blessed God" (2 Tim. i. 11). It was the gospel of a God abounding in his own blessedness, which received no addition by man's redemption; if he had been blessed by it, it had been a goodness to himself, as well as to the creature: it was not an indigent goodness needing the receiving anything from us; but it was a pure goodness, streaming out of itself, without bringing anything into itself for the perfection of it: there was no goodness in

[b] Rada. Controvers. Part III. p. 363.

us to be the motive of his love, but his goodness was the fountain of our benefit.

iii. It was a distinct goodness of the whole Trinity. In the creation of man we find a general consultation (Gen. i. 26), without those distinct labors and offices of each person, and without those raised expressions and marks of joy and triumph as at man's restoration. In this there are distinct functions; the grace of the Father, the merit of the Son, and the efficacy of the Spirit. The Father makes the promise of redemption, the Son seals it with his blood, and the Spirit applies it. The Father adopts us to be his children, the Son redeems us to be his members, and the Spirit renews us to be his temples. In this the Father testifies himself well-pleased in a voice; the Son proclaims his own delight to do the will of God, and the Spirit hastens, with the wing of a dove, to fit him for his work, and afterwards, in his apparition in the likeness of fiery tongues, manifests his zeal for the propagation of the redeeming gospel.

iv. The effects of it proclaim His great goodness. It is by this we are delivered from the corruption of our nature, the ruin of our happiness, the deformity of our sins, and the punishment of our transgressions; he frees us from the ignorance wherewith we were darkened and from the slavery wherein we were fettered. When he came to make Adam's process after his crime, instead of pronouncing the sentence of death he had merited, he utters a promise that man could not have expected; his kindness swells above his provoked justice, and, while he chaseth him out of paradise, he gives him hopes of regaining the same, or a better habitation; and is, in the whole, more ready to prevent him with the blessings of his goodness, than charge him with the horror of his crimes (Gen. iii. 15). It is a goodness that pardons us more transgressions than there are moments in our lives, and overlooks as many follies as there are thoughts in our heart: he doth not only relieve our wants, but restores us to our dignity. It is a greater testimony of goodness to instate a person in the highest honors, than barely to supply his present necessity: it is an admirable pity whereby he was inclined to redeem us, and an incomparable affection whereby he was resolved to exalt us. What can be desired more of him than his goodness hath granted? He hath sought us out when we were lost, and ransomed us when we were captives; he hath pardoned us when we were condemned, and raised us when we were dead. In creation he reared us from nothing, in redemption he delivers our understanding from ignorance and vanity, and our wills from impotence and obstinacy, and our whole man from a death worse than that nothing he drew us from by creation.

v. Hence we may consider the height of this goodness in redemption to exceed that in creation. He gave man a being in creation, but did not draw him from inexpressible misery by that act. His liberality in the gospel doth infinitely surpass what we admire in the works of nature; his goodness in the latter is more astonishing to our belief, than his goodness in creation is visible to our eye. There is more of his bounty expressed in that one verse, " So God loved the world, that he gave his only begotten Son" (John iii. 16), than there is in the whole volume of the world : it is an incomprehensible *so;* a *so* that all the angels in heaven cannot analyse; and few comment upon, or understand, the dimensions of this *so.* In creation he formed an innocent creature of the dust of the ground; in redemption he restores a rebellious creature by the blood of his Son : it is greater than that goodness manifested in creation.

1st. In regard of the difficulty in effecting it. In creation, mere nothing was vanquished to bring us into being; in redemption, sullen enmity was conquered for the enjoyment of our restoration ; in creation, he subdued a nullity to make us creatures; in redemption, his goodness overcomes his omnipotent justice to restore us to felicity. A word from the mouth of Goodness inspired the dust of men's bodies with a living soul; but the blood of his Son must be shed, and the laws of natural affection seems to be overturned, to lay the foundation of our renewed happiness. In the first, heaven did but speak, and the earth was formed; in the second, heaven itself must sink to earth, and be clothed with dusty earth, to reduce man's dust to its original state.

2d. This goodness is greater than that manifested in creation, in regard of its cost. This was a more expensive goodness than what was laid out in creation. "The redemption of one soul is precious" (Ps. xlix. 8), much more costly than the whole fabric of the world, or as many worlds as the understandings of angels in their utmost extent can conceive to be created. For the effecting of this, God parts with his dearest treasure, and his Son eclipses his choicest glory. For this, God must be made man, Eternity must suffer death, the Lord of angels must weep in a cradle, and the Creator of the world must hang like a slave ; he must be in a manger in Bethlehem, and die upon a cross on Calvary ; unspotted righteousness must be made sin, and unblemished blessedness be made a curse. He was at no other expense than the breath of his mouth to form man ; the fruits of the earth could have maintained innocent man without any other cost; but his broken nature cannot be healed without the invaluable medicine of the blood of God. View Christ in the womb and in the manger, in his weary steps and hungry bowels, in his prostrations in the garden, and in his clodded drops of bloody sweat; view his head pierced with a crown of thorns, and his face besmeared with the soldiers' slabber ; view him in his march to Calvary, and his elevation on the painful cross, with his head hanged down, and his side streaming blood; view him pelted with the scoffs of the governors, and the derisions of the rabble; and see, in all this, what cost Goodness was at for man's redemption ! In creation, his power made the sun to shine upon us, and, in redemption, his bowels sent a Son to die for us.

3d. This goodness of God in redemption is greater than that manifested in creation, in regard of man's desert of the contrary. In the creation, as there was nothing without him to allure him to the expressions of his bounty, so there was nothing that did damp the inclinations of his goodness : the nothing from whence the world was drawn, could never merit, nor demerit a being, because it was nothing; as there was nothing to engage him, so there was nothing to disoblige him ; as his favor could not be merited, so neither could his anger be deserved. But in this he finds ingratitude against the former marks of his goodness, and rebellion against the sweetness of his sovereignty,—crimes unworthy of the dews of goodness, and worthy of the sharpest strokes of vengeance ; and therefore the Scripture advanceth the honor of it above the title of mere goodness, to that of "grace" (Rom. i. 2; Titus ii. 11); because men were not only unworthy of a blessing, but worthy of a curse. An innocent nothing more deserves creation, than a culpable creature deserves an exemption from destruction. When man fell, and gave occasion to God to repent of his created work, his ravishing goodness surmounted the occasions he had of repenting, and the provocations he had to the destruction of his frame.

4th. It was a greater goodness than was expressed towards the angels.

1. A greater goodness than was expressed towards the standing angels. The Son of God did no more expose his life for the confirmation of those that stood, than for the restoration of those that fell ; the death of Christ was not for the holy angels, but for simple man ; they needed the grace of God to confirm them, but not the death of Christ to restore or preserve them ; they had a beloved holiness to be established by the powerful grace of God, but not any abominable sin to be blotted out by the blood of God ; they had no debt to pay but that of obedience; but we had both a debt of obedience to the precepts, and a debt of suffering to the penalty, after the fall. Whether the holy angels were confirmed by Christ, or no, is a question: some think they were, from Colos. i. 20, where " things in heaven" are said to be " reconciled ;" but some think, that place signifies no more than the reconciliation of things in heaven, if meant of the angels, to things on earth, with whom they were at enmity in the cause of their Sovereign ; or the reconciliation of things in heaven to God, is meant the glorified saints, who were once in a state of sin, and whom the death of Christ upon the cross reached, though dead long before. But if angels were confirmed by Christ, it was by him not as a slain sacrifice, but as a sovereign Head of the whole creation, appointed by God to gather all things into one ; which some think to be the intendment of Eph. i. 10, where all things, as well those in heaven, as those in earth, are said to be " gathered together in one, in Christ." Where is a syllable in Scripture of his being crucified for angels, but only for sinners ? Not for the confirmation of the one, but the reconciliation of the other ; so that the goodness whereby God continued those blessed spirits in heaven, through the effusions of his grace, is a small thing to the restoring us to our forfeited happiness, through the streams of Divine blood. The preserving a man in life is a little thing, and a smaller benefit than the raising a man from death. The rescuing a man from an ignominious punishment, lays a greater obligation than barely to prevent him from committing a capital crime. The preserving a man standing upon the top of a steep hill, is more easy than to bring a crippled and phthisical man, from the bottom to the top. The continuance God gave to the angels, is not so signal a mark of

his goodness as the deliverance he gave to us; since they were not sunk into sin, nor by any crime fallen into misery.

2. His goodness in redemption is greater than any goodness expressed to the fallen angels. It is the wonder of his goodness to us, that he was mindful of fallen man, and careless of fallen angels; that he should visit man, wallowing in death and blood, with the dayspring from on high, and never turn the Egyptian darkness of devils into cheerful day; when they sinned, Divine thunder dashed them into hell; when man sinned, Divine blood wafts the fallen creature from his misery: the angels wallow in their own blood forever, while Christ is made partaker of our blood, and wallows in his blood, that we might not forever corrupt in ours; they tumbled down from heaven, and Divine goodness would not vouchsafe to catch them; man tumbles down, and Divine goodness holds out a hand drenched in the blood of Him, that was from the foundations of the world, to lift us up (Heb. ii. 16). He spared not those dignified spirits, when they revolted; and spared not punishing his Son for dusty man, when he offended; when he might as well forever have let man lie in the chains wherein he had entangled himself, as them. We were as fit objects of justice as they, and they as fit objects of goodness as we; they were not more wretched by their fall than we; and the poverty of our nature rendered us more unable to recover ourselves, than the dignity of theirs did them; they were his Reuben, his first-born; they were his might, and the beginning of his strength; yet those elder sons he neglected, to prefer the younger; they were the prime and golden pieces of creation, not laden with gross matter, yet they lie under the ruins of their fall, while man, lead in comparison of them, is refined for another world. They seemed to be fitter objects of Divine goodness, in regard of the eminency of their nature above the human; one angel excelled in endowments of mind and spirit, vastness of understanding, greatness of power, all the sons of men; they were more capable to praise him, more capable to serve him; and because of the acuteness of their comprehension, more able to have a due estimate of such a redemption, had it been afforded them; yet that goodness which had created them so comely, would not lay itself out in restoring the beauty they had defaced. The promise was of bruising the serpent's head for us, not of lifting up the serpent's head with us; their nature was not assumed, nor any command given them to believe or repent; not one devil spared, not one apostate spirit recovered, not one of those eminent creatures restored; every one of them hath only a prospect of misery, without any glimpse of recovery; they were ruined under one sin, and we repaired under many. All His redeeming goodness was laid out upon man (Ps. cxliv. 3); "What is man that thou takest knowledge of him; and the Son of man, that thou makest account of him?" Making account of him above angels; as they fell without any tempting them, so God would leave them to rise, without any assisting them. I know the schools trouble themselves to find out the reasons of this peculiarity of grace to man, and not to them; because the whole human nature fell, but only a part of the angelical; the one sinned by a seduction, and the other

by a sullenness, without any tempter; every angel sinned by his own proper will, whereas Adam's posterity sinned by the will of the first man, the common root of all.   God would deprive the devil of any glory in the satisfaction of his envious desire to hinder man from attainment and possession of that happiness which himself had lost. The weakness of man below the angelical nature might excite the Divine mercy; and since all the things of the lower world were created for man, God would not lose the honor of his works, by losing the immediate end for which he framed them.   And finally, because in the restoration of angels, there would have been only a restoration of one nature, that was not comprehensive of the nature of inferior things; but after all such conjectures, man must sit down, and acknowledge Divine goodness to be the only spring, without any other motive.   Since Infinite Wisdom could have contrived a way for redemption for fallen angels, as well as for fallen man, and restored both the one and the other; why might not Christ have assumed their nature as well as ours, into the unity of the Divine person, and suffered the wrath of God in their nature for them, as well as in his human soul for us?   It is as conceivable that two natures might have been assumed by the Son of God, as well as three souls be in man distinct, as some think there are.

3. To enhance this goodness yet higher; it was a greater goodness to us, than was for a time manifested to Christ himself.   To demonstrate his goodness to man, in preventing his eternal ruin, he would for a while withhold his goodness from his Son, by exposing his life as the price of our ransom; not only subjecting him to the derisions of enemies, desertions of friends, and malice of devils, but to the inexpressible bitterness of his own wrath in his soul, as made an offering for sin.   The particle *so* (John iii. 16), seems to intimate this supremacy of goodness; He "so loved the world, that he gave his only begotten Son."   He so loved the world, that he seemed for a time not to love his Son in comparison of it, or equal with it.   The person to whom a gift is given is, in that regard, accounted more valuable than the gift or present made to him: thus God valued our redemption above the worldly happiness of the Redeemer, and senteneth him to an humiliation on earth, in order to our exaltation in heaven; he was desirous to hear him groaning, and see him bleeding, that we might not groan under his frowns, and bleed under his wrath; he spared not him, that he might spare us; refused not to strike him, that he might be well pleased with us; drenched his sword in the blood of his Son, that it might not forever be wet with ours, but that his goodness might forever triumph in our salvation; he was willing to have his Son made man, and die, rather than man should perish, who had delighted to ruin himself; he seemed to degrade him for a time from what he was.[c]   But since he could not be united to any but to an intellectual creature, he could not be united to any viler and more sordid creature than the earthly nature of man: and when this Son, in our nature, prayed that the cup might pass from him, Goodness would not suffer it, to show how it valued

c Lingend de Eucharist, pp. 84, 85.

the manifestation of itself, in the salvation of man, above the preservation of the life of so dear a person.

In particular, wherein this goodness appears:—

1st. The first resolution to redeem, and the means appointed for redemption, could have no other inducement but Divine goodness. We cannot too highly value the merit of Christ; but we must not so much extend the merit of Christ, as to draw a value to eclipse the goodness of God; though we owe our redemption and the fruits of it to the death of Christ, yet we owe not the first resolutions of redemption, and assumption of our nature, the means of redemption, to the merit of Christ. Divine goodness only, without the association of any merit, not only of man, but of the Redeemer himself, begat the first purpose of our recovery; he was singled out, and predestinated to be our Redeemer, before he took our nature to merit our redemption. "God sent his Son," is a frequent expression in the Gospel of St. John (John iii. 34; v. 24; xvii. 3). To what end did God send Christ, but to redeem? The purpose of redemption, therefore, preceded the pitching upon Christ as the means and procuring cause of it, i. e. of our actual redemption, but not of the redeeming purpose; the end is always in intention before the means.[d] "God so loved the world, that he gave his only begotten Son;" the love of God to the world was first in intention, and the order of nature, before the will of giving his Son to the world. His intention of saving was before the mission of a Saviour; so that this affection rose, not from the merit of Christ, but the merit of Christ was directed by this affection. It was the effect of it, not the cause. Nor was the union of our nature with his merited by him; all his meritorious acts were performed in our nature; the nature, therefore, wherein he performed it, was not merited; that grace which was not, could not merit what it was; he could not merit that humanity, which must be assumed before he could merit anything for us, because all merit for us must be offered in the nature which had offended. It is true "Christ gave himself," but by the order of Divine goodness; he that begat him, pitched upon him, and called him to this great work (Heb. v. 5); he is therefore called "the Lamb of God," as being set apart by God to be a propitiating and appeasing sacrifice. He is the "Wisdom of God," since from the Father he reveals the counsel and order of redemption. In this regard he calls God "his God" in the prophet (Isa. xlix. 4), and in the evangelist (John xx. 17); though he was big with affection for the accomplishment, yet he came not to do his "own will," but the will of Divine goodness; his own will it was, too, but not principally, as being the first wheel in motion, but subordinate to the eternal will of Divine bounty. It was by the will of God that he came, and by his will he drank the dreggy cup of bitterness. Divine justice laid "upon him the iniquity of us all," but Divine goodness intended it for our rescue; Divine goodness singled him out, and set him apart; Divine goodness invited him to it; Divine goodness commanded him to effect it, and put a law into his heart, to bias him in the performing of it; Divine goodness sent him, and Divine goodness moved justice to bruise him; and, after

[d] Lessius.

his sacrifice, Divine goodness accepted him, and caressed him for it. So earnest was it for our redemption, as to give out special and irreversible orders : death was commanded to be endured by him for us, and life commanded to be imparted by him to us (John x. 16, 18). If God had not been the mover, but had received the proposal from another, he might have heard it, but was not bound to grant it ; his sovereign authority, was not under any obligation to receive another's sponsion for the miserable criminal. As Christ is the head of man, so "God is the head of Christ" (1 Cor. xi. 3); he did nothing but by his directions, as he was not a Mediator, but by the constitution of Divine goodness. As a "liberal man deviseth liberal things" (Isa. ii. 8), so did a bountiful God devise a bountiful act, wherein his kindness and love as a Saviour appeared : he was possessed with the resolutions to manifest his goodness in Christ, "in the beginning of his way" (Prov. viii. 22, 23), before he descended to the act of creation. This intention of goodness preceded his making that creature man, who, he foresaw, would fall, and, by his fall, disjoint and entangle the whole frame of the world, without such a provision.

2d. In God's giving Christ to be our Redeemer, he gave the highest gift that it was possible for Divine goodness to bestow. As there is not a greater God than himself to be conceived, so there is not a greater gift for this great God to present to his creatures : never did God go farther, in any of his excellent perfections, than this. It is such a dole that cannot be transcended with a choicer ; he is, as it were, come to the last mite of his treasure ; and though he could create millions of worlds for us, he cannot give a greater Son to us. He could abound in the expressions of his power, in new creations of worlds, which have not yet been seen, and in the lustre of his wisdom in more stately structures ; but if he should frame as many worlds as there are mites of dust and matter in this, and make every one of them as bright and glorious as the sun, though his power and wisdom would be more signalized, yet his goodness could not, since he hath not a choicer gift to bless those brighter worlds withal, than he hath conferred upon this : nor can immense goodness contrive a richer means to conduct those worlds to happiness, than he hath both invented for this world, and presented it with. It cannot be imagined, that it can extend itself farther than to give a gift equal with himself ; a gift as dear to him as himself. His wisdom, had it studied millions of eternities (excuse the expression, since eternity admits of no millions, it being an interminable duration), it could have found out no more to give ; this goodness could have bestowed no more, and our necessity could not have required a greater offering for our relief. When God intended, in redemption, the manifestation of his highest goodness, it could not be without the donation of the choicest gift; as, when he would insure our comfort, he swears "by himself," because he cannot swear "by a greater" (Heb. vi. 13): so, when he would insure our happiness, he gives us his Son, because he cannot give a greater, being equal with himself. Had the Father given himself in person, he had given one first in order, but not greater in essence and glorious perfections : it could have been no more than the life of God, and should then have been laid down for us; and so it was now, since the human nature did not subsist but in his Divine person.

1. It is a greater gift than worlds, or all things purchased by him. What was this gift but "the image of his person, and the brightness of his glory" (Heb. i. 3)? What was this gift but one as rich as eternal blessedness could make him? What was this gift, but one that possessed the fulness of earth, and the more immense riches of heaven? It is a more valuable present, than if he presented us with thousands of worlds of angels and inferior creatures, because his person is incomparably greater, not only than all conceivable, but inconceivable, creations; we are more obliged to him for it, than if he had made us angels of the highest rank in heaven, because it is a gift of more value than the whole angelical nature, because he is an infinite person, and therefore infinitely transcends whatsoever is finite, though of the highest dignity. The wounds of an Almighty God for us are a greater testimony of goodness, than if we had all the other riches of heaven and earth. This perfection had not appeared in such an astonishing grandeur, had it pardoned us without so rich a satisfaction; that had been pardon to our sin, not a God of our nature. "God so loved the world" that he pardoned it, had not sounded so great and so good, as God so loved the world, that he "gave his only-begotten Son." *Est aliquid in Christo formosius Servatore.* There is something in Christ more excellent and comely than the office of a Saviour; the greatness of his person is more excellent, than the salvation procured by his death: it was a greater gift than was bestowed upon innocent Adam, or the holy angels. In the creation, his goodness gave us creatures for our use: in our redemption, his goodness gives us what was dearest to him for our service, our Sovereign in office to benefit us, as well as in a royalty to govern us.

2. It was a greater gift, because it was his own Son, not an angel. It had been a mighty goodness to have given one of the lofty seraphims; a greater goodness to have given the whole corporation of those glorious spirits for us, those children of the Most High: but he gave that Son, whom he commands "all the angels to worship" (Heb. i. 6), and all men to adore, and pay the "lowest homage to" (Ps. ii. 12); that Son that is to be honored by us, as we "honor the Father" (John v. 23); that Son which was his "delight" (Prov. viii. 30); his delights in the Hebrew, wherein all the delights of the Father were gathered in one, as well as of the whole creation; and not simply a Son, but an only-begotten Son, upon which Christ lays the stress with an emphasis (1 John iii. 16). He had but one Son in heaven or earth, one Son from an unviewable eternity, and that one Son he gave for a degenerate world; this son he consecrated for "evermore a Priest" (Heb. vii. 28). "The word of the oath makes the Son;" the peculiarity of his Sonship heightens the goodness of the Donor. It was no meaner a person that he gave to empty himself of his glory, to fulfil an obedience for us, that we might be rendered happy partakers of the Divine nature. Those that know the natural affection of a father to a son, must judge the affection of God the Father to the Son infinitely greater, than the affection of an earthly

father to the son of his bowels. It must be an unparalleled goodness, to give up a Son that he loved with so ardent an affection, for the redemption of rebels: abandon a glorious Son to a dishonorable death, for the security of those that had violated the laws of righteousness, and endeavored to pull the sovereign crown from his head. Besides, being an only Son, all those affections centered in him, which in parents would have been divided among a multitude of children: so, then, as it was a testimony of the highest faith and obedience in "Abraham to offer up his only-begotten son to God" (Heb. xi. 17); so it was the triumph of Divine goodness, to give so great, so dear a person, for so little a thing as man; and for such a piece of nothing and vanity, as a sinful world.

3. And this Son given to rescue us by his death. It was a gift to us; for our sakes he descended from his throne, and dwelt on earth; for our sakes he was "made flesh," and infirm flesh; for our sakes he was "made a curse," and scorched in the furnace of his Father's wrath; for our sakes he went naked, armed only with his own strength, into the lists of that combat with the devils, that led us captive. Had he given him to be a leader for the conquest of some earthly enemies, it had been a great goodness to display his banners, and bring us under his conduct; but he sent him to lay down his life in the bitterest and most inglorious manner, and exposed him to a cursed death for our redemption from that dreadful curse, which would have broken us to pieces, and irreparably have crushed us. He gave him to us, to suffer for us as a man, and redeem us as a God; to be a sacrifice to expiate our sin by translating the punishment upon himself, which was merited by us. Thus was he made low to exalt us, and debased to advance us, "made poor to enrich us" (2 Cor. viii. 9); and eclipsed to brighten our sullied natures, and wounded, that he might be a physician for our languishments. He was ordered to taste the bitter cup of death, that we might drink of the rivers of immortal life and pleasures: to submit to the frailties of the human nature, that we might possess the glories of the divine: he was ordered to be a sufferer, that we might be no longer captives; and to pass through the fire of Divine wrath, that he might purge our nature from the dross it had contracted. Thus was the righteous given for sin, the innocent for criminals, the glory of heaven for the dregs of earth, and the immense riches of a Deity expended to restock man.

4. And a Son that was exalted for what he had done for us by the order of Divine goodness. The exaltation of Christ was no less a signal mark of his miraculous goodness to us, than of his affection to him: since he was obedient by Divine goodness to die for us, his advancement was for his obedience to those orders. The name given to him "above every name" (Phil. ii. 8, 9), was a repeated triumph of this perfection; since his passion was not for himself, he was wholly innocent, but for us who were criminal. His advancement was not only for himself as Redeemer, but for us as redeemed: Divine goodness centered in him, both in his cross and in his crown; for it was for the "purging our sins, he sat down on the right hand of the Majesty on high" (Heb. i. 3): and the whole blessed society

of principalities and powers in heaven admire this goodness of God, and ascribe to him "honor, glory, and power" for advancing the "Lamb slain" (Rev. v. 11–13). Divine goodness did not only give him to us, but gave him power, riches, strength, and honor, for manifesting this goodness to us, and opening the passages for its fuller conveyances to the sons of men. Had not God had thoughts of a perpetual goodness, he would not have settled him so near him, to manage our cause, and testified so much affection to him on our behalf. This goodness gave him to be debased for us, and ordered him to be enthroned for us: as it gave him to us bleeding, so it would give him to us triumphing; that as we have a share by grace in the merits of his humiliation, we might partake also of the glories of his coronation; that, from first to last, we may behold nothing but the triumphs of Divine goodness to fallen man.

5. In bestowing this gift on us, Divine goodness gives whole God to us. Whatsoever is great and excellent in the Godhead, the Father gives us, by giving us his Son: the Creator gives himself to us in his Son Christ. In giving creatures to us, he gives the riches of earth; in giving himself to us, he gives the riches of heaven, which surmount all understanding: it is in this gift he becomes our God, and passeth over the title of all that he is for our use and benefit, that every attribute in the Divine nature may be claimed by us; not to be imparted to us whereby we may be deified, but employed for our welfare, whereby we may be blessed. He gave himself in creation to us in the image of his holiness; but, in redemption, he gave himself in the image of his person: he would not only communicate the goodness without him, but bestow upon us the infinite goodness of his own nature; that that which was his own end and happiness might be our end and happiness, viz. himself. By giving his Son, he hath given himself; and in both gifts he hath given all things to us. The Creator of all things is eminently all things: "He hath given all things into the hands of his Son" (John iii. 35); and, by consequence, given all things into the hands of his redeemed creatures, by giving them Him to whom he gave all things; whatsoever we were invested in by creation, whatsoever we were deprived of by corruption, and more, he hath deposited in safe hands for our enjoyment: and what can Divine goodness do more for us? What further can it give unto us, than what it hath given, and in that gift designed for us?

3d. This goodness is enhanced by considering the state of man in the first transgression, and since.

1. Man's first transgression. If we should rip up every vein of that first sin, should we find any want of wickedness to excite a just indignation? What was there but ingratitude to Divine bounty, and rebellion against Divine sovereignty? The royalty of God was attempted; the supremacy of Divine knowledge above man's own knowledge envied; the riches of goodness, whereby he lived and breathed, slighted. There is a discontent with God upon an unreasonable sentiment, that God had denied a knowledge to him which was his right and due, when there should have been an humble acknowledgment of that unmerited goodness, which had not only

given him a being above other creatures, but placed him the governor and lord of those that were inferior to him.   What alienation
of his understanding was there from knowing God, and of his will
from loving him! A debauch of all his faculties; a spiritual adultery,
in preferring, not only one of God's creatures, but one of his desperate enemies, before him; thinking him a wiser counsellor than
Infinite Wisdom, and imagining him possessed with kinder affections
to him than that God who had newly created him.   Thus he joins
in league with hell against heaven, with a fallen spirit against his
bountiful Benefactor, and enters into society with rebels that just
before commenced a war against his and their common Sovereign:
he did not only falter in, but cast off, the obedience due to his Creator; endeavored to purloin his glory, and actually murdered all those
that were virtually in his loins. "Sin entered into the world" by
him, "and death by sin, and passed upon all men" (Rom. v. 12),
taking them off from their subjection to God, to be slaves to the
damned spirits, and heirs of their misery: and, after all this, he adds
a foul imputation on God, taxing him as the author of his sin, and
thereby stains the beauty of his holiness.   But, notwithstanding all
this, God stops not up the flood-gates of his goodness, nor doth he
entertain fiery resolutions against man, but brings forth a healing
promise; and sends not an angel upon commission to reveal it to
him, but preaches it himself to this forlorn and rebellious creature
(Gen. iii. 15).
     2. Could there be anything in this fallen creature to allure God to
the expression of his goodness?   Was there any good action in all
his carriage that could plead for a re-admission of him to his former
state?   Was there one good quality left, that could be an orator to
persuade Divine goodness to such a gracious procedure?   Was there
any moral goodness in man, after this debauch, that might be an
object of Divine love?   What was there in him, that was not rather
a provocation than an allurement?   Could you expect that any perfection in God should find a motive in this ungrateful apostate to
open a mouth for him, and be an advocate to support him, and bring
him off from a just tribunal? or, after Divine goodness had begun to
pity and plead for man, is it not wonderful that it should not discon-
tinue the plea, after it found man's excuse to be as black as his crime
(Gen. iii. 12), and his carriage, upon his examination, to be as dis-
obliging as his first revolt?   It might well be expected, that all the
perfections in the Divine nature would have entered into an association eternally to treat this rebel according to his deserts.   What attractives were there in a silly worm, much less in such complete
wickedness, inexcusable enmity, infamous rebellion, to design a Redeemer for him, and such a person as the Son of God to a fleshy
body, an eclipse of glory, and an ignominious cross? The meanness
of man was further from alluring God to it, than the dignity of
angels.
     3. Was there not a world of demerit in man, to animate grace as
well as wrath against him?   We were so far from deserving the
opening any streams of goodness, that we had merited floods of devouring wrath.   What were all men but enemies to God in a high

manner? Every offence was infinite, as being committed against a being of infinite dignity; it was a stroke at the very being of God, a resistance of all his attributes; it would degrade him from the height and perfection of his nature; it would not, by its good will, suffer God to be God. If he that hates his brother is a murderer of his brother (1 John iii. 15), he that hates his Creator is a murderer of the Deity, and every "carnal mind is enmity to God" (Rom. viii. 7): every sin envies him his authority, by breaking his precept; and envies him his goodness, by defacing the marks of it: every sin comprehends in it more than men or angels can conceive: that God who only hath the clear apprehensions of his own dignity, hath the sole clear apprehensions of sin's malignity. All men were thus by nature: those that sinned before the coming of the Redeemer had been in a state of sin; those that were to come after him would be in a state of sin by their birth, and be criminals as soon as ever they were creatures. All men, as well the glorified, as those in the flesh at the coming of the Redeemer, and those that were to be born after, were considered in a state of sin by God, when he bruised the Redeemer for them; all were filthy and unworthy of the eye of God; all had employed the faculties of their souls, and the members of their bodies, which they enjoyed by his goodness, against the interest of his glory. Every rational creature had made himself a slave to those creatures over whom he had been appointed a lord, subjected himself as a servant to his inferior, and strutted as a superior against his liberal Sovereign, and by every sin rendered himself more a child of Satan, and enemy of God, and more worthy of the curses of the law, and the torments of hell. Was it not, now, a mighty goodness that would surmount those high mountains of demerit, and elevate such creatures by the depression of his Son? Had we been possessed of the highest holiness, a reward had been the natural effect of goodness. It was not possible that God should be unkind to a righteous and innocent creature; his grace would have crowned that which had been so agreeable to him. He had been a denier of himself, had he numbered innocent creatures in the rank of the miserable; but to be kind to an enemy, to run counter to the vastness of demerit in man, was a superlative goodness, a goodness triumphing above all the provocations of men, and pleas of justice: it was an abounding goodness of grace; "where sin abounded, grace did much more abound" (Rom. v. 20), ὑπερεπερίσσευσεν; it swelled above the heights of sin, and triumphed more than all his other attributes.

4. Man was reduced to the lowest condition. Our crimes had brought us to the lowest calamity; we were brought to the dust, and prepared for hell. Adam had not the boldness to request, and therefore we may judge he had not the least hopes of pardon; he was sunk under wrath, and could have expected no better an entertainment than the tempter, whose solicitations he submitted to. We had cast the diadem from our heads, and lost all our original excellency; we were lost to our own happiness, and lost to our Creator's service, when he was so kind as to send his Son to seek us (Matt. xviii. 11), and so liberal as to expend his blood for our cure and preservation. How great was that goodness that would not abandon us in our mis-

ery, but remit our crimes, and rescue our persons, and ransom our souls by so great a price from the rights of justice, and horrors of hell, we were so fitted for?

5. Every age multiplied provocations; every age of the world proved more degenerate. The traditions, which were purer and more lively among Adam's immediate posterity, were more dark among his further descendants; idolatry, whereof we have no marks in the old world before the deluge, was frequent afterwards in every nation: not only the knowledge of the true God was lost, but the natural reverential thoughts of a Deity were expelled. Hence gods were dubbed according to men's humors; and not only human passions, but brutish vices, ascribed to them: as by the fall we were become less than men, so we would fancy God no better than a beast, since beasts were worshipped as gods (Rom. i. 21); yea, fancied God no better than a devil, since that destroyer was worshipped instead of the Creator, and a homage paid to the powers of hell that had ruined them, which was due to the goodness of that Benefactor, who had made them and preserved them in the world. The vilest creatures were deified; reason was debased below common sense; and men adored one end of a "log," while they "warmed themselves with the other" (Isa. xliv. 14, 16, 17); as if that which was ordained for the kitchen were a fit representation for God in the temple. Thus were the natural notions of a Deity depraved; the whole world drenched in idolatry; and though the Jews were free from that gross abuse of God, yet they were sunk also into loathsome superstitions, when the goodness of God brought in his designed Redeemer and redemption into the world.

6. The impotence of man enhanceth this goodness. Our own eye did scarce pity us, and it was impossible for our own hands to relieve us; we were insensible of our misery, in love with our death; we courted our chains, and the noise of our fettering lusts were our music, "serving divers lusts and pleasures" (Tit. iii. 3). Our lusts were our pleasures; Satan's yoke was as delightful to us to bear, as to him to impose: instead of being his opposers in his attempts against us, we were his voluntary seconds, and every whit as willing to embrace, as he was to propose, his ruining temptations. As no man can recover himself from death, so no man can recover himself from wrath; he is as unable to redeem, as to create himself; he might as soon have stripped himself of his being, as put an end to his misery; his captivity would have been endless, and his chains remediless, for anything he could do to knock them off, and deliver himself; he was too much in love with the sink of sin, to leave wallowing in it, and under too powerful a hand, to cease frying in the flames of wrath. As the law could not be obeyed by man, after a corrupt principle had entered into him, so neither could justice be satisfied by him after his transgression. The sinner was indebted, but bankrupt; as he was unable to pay a mite of that obedience he owed to the precept, because of his enmity, so he was unable to satisfy what he owed to the penalty, because of his feebleness: he was as much without love to observe the one, as "without strength" to bear the other: he could not, because of his "enmity, be subject to

the law" (Rom. viii. 7), or compensate for his sin, because he was
" without strength" (Rom. v. 6). His strength to offend was great ;
but to deliver himself a mere nothing. Repentance was not a thing
known by man after the fall, till he had hopes of redemption ; and
if he had known and exercised it, what compensation are the tears
of a malefactor for an injury done to the crown, and attempting the
life of his prince ? How great was Divine goodness, not only to
pity men in this state, but to provide a strong Redeemer for them !
" O Lord, my strength, and my Redeemer !" said the Psalmist (Ps.
xix. 14) : when he found out a Redeemer for our misery, he found
out a strength for our impotency. To conclude this : behold the
" goodness of God," when we had thus unhandsomely dealt with
him ; had nothing to allure his goodness, multitudes of provocations
to incense him, were reduced to a condition as low as could be, fit
to be the matter of his scoffs, and the sport of Divine justice, and so
weak that we could not repair our own ruins ; then did he open a
fountain of fresh goodness in the death of his Son, and sent forth
such delightful streams, as in our original creation we could never
have tasted ; not only overcame the resentments of a provoked justice, but magnified itself by our lowness, and strengthened itself by
our weakness. His goodness had before created an innocent, but
here it saves a malefactor ; and sends his Son to die for us, as if the
Holy of holies were the criminal, and the rebel the innocent. It had
been a pompous goodness to have given him as a king ; but a goodness of greater grandeur to expose him as a sacrifice for slaves and
enemies. Had Adam remained innocent, and proved thankful for
what he had received, it had been great goodness to have brought
him to glory ; but to bring filthy and rebellious Adam to it, surmounts, by inexpressible degrees, that sort of goodness he had experimented before ; since it was not from a light evil, a tolerable
curse unawares brought upon us, but from the yoke we had willingly submitted to, from the power of darkness we had courted, and the
furnace of wrath we had kindled for ourselves. What are we dead
dogs, that he should behold us with so gracious an eye ? This goodness is thus enhanced, if you consider the state of man in his first
transgression, and after.

4th. This goodness further appears in the high advancement of our
nature, after it had so highly offended. By creation, we had an
affinity with animals in our bodies, with angels in our spirits, with
God in his image ; but not with God in our nature, till the incarnation of the Redeemer. Adam, by creation, was the son of God
(Luke iii. 38), but his nature was not one with the person of God :
he was his son, as created by him, but had no affinity to him by virtue of union with him : but now man doth not only see his nature in
multitudes of men on earth, but, by an astonishing goodness, beholds his nature united to the Deity in heaven : that as he was the
son of God by creation, he is now the brother of God by redemption ; for with such a title doth that Person, who was the Son of God
as well as the Son of man, honor his disciples (John xx. 17) : and
because he is of the same nature with them, he " is not ashamed to
call them brethren" (Heb. ii. 11). Our nature, which was infinitely

distant from, and below the Deity, now makes one person with the Son of God. What man sinfully aspired to, God hath graciously granted, and more : man aspired to a likeness in knowledge, and God hath granted him an affinity in union. It had been astonishing goodness to angelize our natures ; but in redemption Divine goodness hath acted higher, in a sort to deify our natures. In creation, our nature was exalted above other creatures on earth ; in our redemption, our nature is exalted above all the host of heaven : we were higher than the beasts, as creatures, but "lower than the angels" (Ps. viii. 5); but, by the incarnation of the Son of God, our nature is elevated many steps above them. After it had sunk itself by corruption below the bestial nature, and as low as the diabolical, the "fulness of the Godhead dwells in our nature bodily" (Col. ii. 9), but never in the angels, angelically. The Son of God descended to dignify our nature, by assuming it; and ascended with our nature to have it crowned above those standing monuments of Divine power and goodness (Eph. i. 20, 21). That Person that descended in our nature into the grave, and in the same nature was raised up again, is, in that same nature, set at the right hand of God in heaven, "far above all principality, and power, and might, and dominion, and every name that is named." Our refined clay, by an indissoluble union with this Divine Person, is honored to sit forever upon a throne above all the tribes of seraphims and cherubims ; and the Person that wears it, is the head of the good angels, and the conqueror of the bad ; the one are put under his feet, and the other commanded to adore him, "that purged our sins in our nature" (Heb. i. 3, 6): that Divine Person in our nature receives adoration from the angels ; but the nature of man is not ordered to pay any homage and adorations to the angels. How could Divine goodness, to man, more magnify itself? As we could not have a lower descent than we had by sin, how could we have a higher ascent than by a substantial participation of a divine life, in our nature, in the unity of a Divine Person ? Our earthly nature is joined to a heavenly Person; our undone nature united to "one equal with God" (Phil. ii. 6). It may truly be said, that man is God, which is infinitely more glorious for us, than if it could be said, man is an angel. If it were goodness to advance our innocent nature above other creatures, the advancement of our degenerate nature above angels deserves a higher title than mere goodness. It is a more gracious act, than if all men had been transformed into the pure spiritual nature of the loftiest cherubims.

5th. This goodness is manifest in the covenant of grace made with us, whereby we are freed from the rigor of that of works. God might have insisted upon the terms of the old covenant, and required of man the improvement of his original stock; but God hath condescended to lower terms, and offered man more gracious methods, and mitigated the rigor of the first, by the sweetness of the second.

1. It is goodness, that he should condescend to make another covenant with man. To stipulate with innocent and righteous

Adam for his obedience, was a stoop of his sovereignty; though he gave the precept as a sovereign Lord, yet in his covenanting, he seems to descend to some kind of equality with that dust and ashes with whom the treated. Absolute sovereigns do not usually covenant with their people, but exact obedience and duty, without binding themselves to bestow a reward; and if they intend any, they reserve the purpose in their own breasts, without treating their subjects with a solemn declaration of it. There was no obligation on God to enter into the first covenant, much less, after the violation of the first, to the settlement of a new. If God seemed in some sort to equal himself to man in the first, he seemed to descend below himself in treating with a rebel upon more condescending terms in the second. If his covenant with innocent Adam was a stoop of his sovereignty, this with rebellious Adam seems to be a stripping himself of his majesty in favor of his goodness; as if his happiness depended upon us, and not ours upon him. It is a humiliation of himself to behold the things in heaven, the glorious angels, as well as things on earth, mortal men (Ps. cxiii. 6); much more to bind himself in gracious bonds to the glorious angels; and much more if to rebel man. In the first covenant there was much of sovereignty as well as goodness; in the second there is less of sovereignty, and more of grace: in the first there was a righteous man for a holy God; in the second a polluted creature for a pure and provoked God: in the first he holds his sceptre in his hand, to rule his subjects; in the second he seems to lay by his sceptre, to court and espouse a beggar (Hosea ii. 18—20): in the first he is a Lord; in the second a husband; and binds himself upon gracious conditions to become a debtor. How should this goodness fill us with an humble astonishment, as it did Abraham, when he "fell on his face," when he heard God speaking of making a covenant with him! (Gen. xvii. 2, 3). And if God speaking to Israel out of the fire, and making them to hear his voice out of heaven, that he might instruct them, was a consideration whereby Moses would heighten their admiration of Divine goodness, and engage their affectionate obedience to him (Deut. iv. 32, 36, 40), how much more admirable is it for God to speak so kindly to us through the pacifying blood of the covenant, that silenced the terrors of the old, and settled the tenderness of the new!

2. His goodness is seen in the nature and tenor of the new covenant. There are in this richer streams of love and pity. The language of one was, Die, if thou sin; that of the other, Live, if thou believest:[e] the old covenant was founded upon the obedience of man; the new one is not founded upon the inconstancy of man's will, but the firmness of Divine love, and the valuable merit of Christ. The head of the first covenant was human and mutable; the Head of the second is divine and immutable. The curse due to us by the breach of the first, is taken off by the indulgence of the second: we are by it snatched from the jaws of the law, to be wrapped up in the bosom of grace (Rom. viii. 1). "For you are not under the law, but under grace" (Rom. vi. 14); from the curse

[e] Turreti, Ser. p. 33.

and condemnation of the law, to the sweetness and forgiveness of grace. Christ bore the one, being "made a curse for us" (Gal. iii. 13), that we might enjoy the sweetness of the other; by this we are brought from Mount Sinai, the mount of terror, to Mount Sion, the mount of sacrifice, the type of the great Sacrifice (Heb. xii. 18, 22). That covenant brought in death upon one offence, this covenant offers life after many offences (Rom. v. 16, 17): that involves us in a curse, and this enricheth us with a blessing; the breaches of that expelled us out of Paradise, and the embracing of this admits us into heaven. This covenant demands, and admits of that repentance whereof there was no mention in the first; that demanded obedience, not repentance upon a failure; and though the exercise of it had been never so deep in the fallen creature, nothing of the law's severity had been remitted by any virtue of it. Again, the first covenant demanded exact righteousness, but conveyed no cleansing virtue, upon the contracting any filth. The first demands a continuance in the righteousness conferred in creation; the second imprints a gracious heart in regeneration. "I will pour clean water upon you; I will put a new spirit within you," was the voice of the second covenant, not of the first. Again, as to pardon: Adam's covenant was to punish him, not to pardon him, if he fell; that threatened death upon transgression, this remits it; that was an act of Divine sovereignty, declaring the will of God; this is an act of Divine grace, passing an act of oblivion on the crimes of the creature: that, as it demanded no repentance upon a failure, so it promised no mercy upon guilt; that convened our sin, and condemned us for it; this clears our guilt, and comforts us under it. The first covenant related us to God as a Judge; every transgression against it forfeited his indulgence as a Father: the second delivers us from God as a condemning Judge, to bring us under his wing, as an affectionate Father; in the one there was a dreadful frown to scare us; in the other, a healing wing to cover and relieve us. Again, in regard of righteousness: that demanded our performance of a righteousness in and by ourselves, and our own strength; this demands our acceptance of a righteousness higher than ever the standing angels had; the righteousness of the first covenant was the righteousness of a man, the righteousness of the second is the righteousness of a God (2 Cor. v. 21). Again, in regard of that obedience it demands: it exacts not of us, as a necessary condition, the perfection of obedience, but the sincerity of obedience; an uprightness in our intention, not an unspottedness in our action; an integrity in our aims, and an industry in our compliance with divine precepts: "Walk before me, and be thou perfect" (Gen. xvii. 1); i. e. sincere. What is hearty in our actions, is accepted; and what is defective, is overlooked, and not charged upon us, because of the obedience and righteousness of our Surety. The first covenant rejected all our services after sin; the services of a person under the sentence of death, are but dead services: this accepts our imperfect services, after faith in it; that administered no strength to obey, but supposed it; this supposeth our inability to obey, and confers some strength for it: "I will put my spirit within you, and cause you to walk in my statutes" (Ezek. xxxvi. 27). Again, in regard of the promises: the old covenant had good, but the new hath "better promises" (Heb. viii. 6), of justification after guilt and sanctification after filth, and glorification at last of the whole man. In the first, there was provision against guilt, but none for the removal of it: provision against filth, but none for the cleansing of it; promise of happiness implied, but not so great a one as that "life and immortality" in heaven, "brought to light by the gospel" (2 Tim. i. 10). Why said to be "brought to light by the gospel?" because it was not only buried, upon the fall of man under the curses of the law, but it was not so obvious to the conceptions of man in his innocent state. Life indeed was implied to be promised upon his standing, but not so glorious an immortality disclosed, to be reserved for him, if he stood: as it is a covenant of better promises, so a covenant of sweeter comforts; comforts more choice, and comforts more durable; an "everlasting consolation, and a good hope" are the fruits of "grace," *i. e.* the covenant of grace (2 Thess. ii. 16). In the whole there is such a love disclosed, as cannot be expressed; the apostle leaves it to every man's mind to conceive it, if he could, "What manner of love the Father hath bestowed upon us, that we should be called the sons of God" (1 John iii. 1). It instates us in such a manner of the love of God as he bears to his Son, the image of his person (John xvii. 23): "That the world may know that thou hast loved them, as thou hast loved me."

3. This goodness appears in the choice gift of himself which he hath made over in this covenant (Gen. xvii. 7). You know how it runs in Scripture: "I will be their God, and they shall be my people" (Jer. xxxii. 38): a propriety in the Deity is made over by it. As he gave the blood of his Son to seal the covenant, so he gave himself as the blessing of the covenant; "He is not ashamed to be called their God" (Heb. xi. 16). Though he be environed with millions of angels, and presides over them in an inexpressible glory, he is not ashamed of his condescensions to man, and to pass over himself as the propriety of his people, as well as to take them to be his. It is a diminution of the sense of the place, to understand it of God, as Creator; what reason was there for God to be ashamed of the expressions of his power, wisdom, goodness, in the works of his hands? But we might have reason to think there might be some ground in God to be ashamed of making himself over in a deed of gift to a mean worm and filthy rebel; this might seem a disparagement to his majesty; but God is not ashamed of a title so mean, as the God of his despised people; a title below those others, of the "Lord of hosts, glorious in holiness, fearful in praises, doing wonders, riding on the wings of the wind, walking in the circuits of heaven." He is no more ashamed of this title of being our God, than he is of those other that sound more glorious; he would rather have his greatness veil to his goodness, than his goodness be confined by his majesty; he is not only our God, but our God as he is the God of Christ: he is not ashamed to be our propriety, and Christ is not ashamed to own his people in a partnership with him in this propriety (John xx.

17): "I ascend to my God, and your God." This of God's being our God, is the quintessence of the covenant, the soul of all the promises: in this he hath promised whatsoever is infinite in him, whatsoever is the glory and ornament of his nature, for our use; not a part of him, or one single perfection, but the whole vigor and strength of all. As he is not a God without infinite wisdom, and infinite power, and infinite goodness, and infinite blessedness, &c., so he passes over, in this covenant, all that which presents him as the most adorable Being to his creatures; he will be to them as great, as wise, as powerful, as good as he is in himself; and the assuring us, in this covenant, to be our God, imports also that he will do as much for us, as we would do for ourselves, were we furnished with the same goodness, power, and wisdom : in being our God, he testifies it is all one, as if we had the same perfections in our own power to employ for our use ; for he being possessed with them, it is as much as if we ourselves were possessed with them, for our own advantage, according to the rules of wisdom, and the several conditions we pass through for his glory. But this must be taken with a relation to that wisdom, which he observes in his proceedings with us as creatures, and according to the several conditions we pass through for his glory. Thus God's being ours is more than if all heaven and earth were ours besides ; it is more than if we were fully our own, and at our own dispose ; it makes " all things that God hath ours" (1 Cor. iii. 22) ; and therefore, not only all things he hath created, but all things that he can create ; not only all things that he hath contrived, but all things that he can contrive : for in being ours, his power is ours, his possible power as well as his active power; his power, whereby he can effect more than he hath done, and his wisdom, whereby he can contrive more than he hath done ; so that if there were need of employing his power to create many worlds for our good, he would not stick at it ; for if he did, he would not be our God, in the extent of his nature, as the promise intimates. What a rich goodness, and a fulness of bounty, is there in this short expression, as full as the expression of a God can make it, to be intelligible, to such creatures as we are !

4. This goodness is further manifest in the confirmation of the covenant. His goodness did not only condescend to make it for our happiness, after we had made ourselves miserable, but further condescended to ratify it in the solemnest manner for our assurance, to overrule all the despondencies unbelief could raise up in our souls. The reason why he confirmed it by an oath, was to show the immutability of his glorious counsel, not to tie himself to keep it, for his word and promise is in itself as immutable as his oath; they were " two immutable things, his word and his oath," one as unchangeable as the other; but for the strength of our consolation, that it might have no reason to shake and totter (Heb. vi. 17, 18): he would condescend as low as was possible for a God to do for the satisfaction of the dejected creature. When the first covenant was broken, and it was impossible for man to fulfil the terms of it, and mount to happiness thereby, he makes another; and, as if we had reason to distrust him in the first, he solemnly ratifies it in a higher manner than

he had done the other, and swears by himself that he will be true to it, not so much out of an election of himself, as the object of the oath (Heb. vi. 13): "Because he could not swear by a greater, he swears by himself;" whereby the apostle clearly intimates, that Divine goodness was raised to such a height for us, that if there had been anything else more sacred than himself, or that could have punished him if he had broken it, that he would have sworn by, to silence any diffidence in us, and confirm us in the reality of his intentions. Now if it were a mighty mark of goodness for God to stoop to a covenanting with us, it was more for a sovereign to bind himself so solemnly to be our debtor in a promise, as well as he was our sovereign in the precept, and stoop so low in it to satisfy the distrust of that creature, that deserved for ever to lie soaking in his own ruins, for not believing his bare word.   What absolute prince would ever stoop so low as to article with rebellious subjects, whom he could in a moment set his foot upon and crush ; much less countenance a causeless distrust of his goodness by the addition of his oath, and thereby bind his own hands, which were unconfined before, and free to do what he pleased with them ?

5. This goodness of God is remarkable also in the condition of this covenant which is faith.   This was the easiest condition, in its own nature, that could be imagined ; no difficulty in it but what proceeds from the pride of man's nature, and the obstinacy of his will.   It was not impossible in itself ; it was not the old condition of perfect obedience.   It had been mighty goodness to set us up again upon our old stock, and restore us to the tenor and condition of the covenant of works, or to have required the burdensome ceremonies of the law. Nor is it an exact knowledge he requires of us ; all men's understandings being of a different size, they had not been capable of this. It was the most reasonable condition, in regard of the excellency of the things proposed, and the effects following upon it; nay, it was necessary.   It had been a want of goodness to himself and his own honor; he had cast that off, had he not insisted on this condition of faith, it being the lowest he could condescend to with a *salvo* for his glory.   And it was a goodness to us ; it is nothing else he requires, but a willingness to accept what he hath contrived and acted for us : and no man can be happy against his will; without this belief, at least, man could never voluntarily have arrived to his happiness. The goodness of God is evidenced in that.

[1st.] It is an easy condition, not impossible.   1. It was not the condition of the old covenant.   The condition of that was an entire obedience to every precept with a man's whole strength, and without any flaw or crack.   But the condition of the evangelical covenant is a sincere, though weak, faith ; He hath suited this covenant to the misery of man's fallen condition; he considers our weakness, and that we are but dust, and therefore exacts not of us an entire, but a sincere, obedience.   Had God sent Christ to expiate the crime of Adam, restore him to his paradise estate, and repair in man the ruined image of holiness, and after this to have renewed the covenant of works for the future, and settled the same condition in exacting a complete obedience for the time to come ; Divine goodness had been above any accusation, and had deserved our highest admiration in the pardon of former transgressions, and giving out to us our first stock. But Divine goodness took larger strides: he had tried our first condition, and found his mutable creature quickly to violate it: had he demanded the same now, it is likely it had met with the same issue as before, in man's disobedience and fall; we should have been as men, as Adam (Hos. vi. 7), "transgressing the covenant;" and then we must have lain groaning under our disease, and wallowing in our blood, unless Christ had come to die for the expiation of our new crimes; for every transgression had been a violation of that covenant, and a forfeiture of our right to the benefits of it. If we had broke it but in one tittle, we had rendered ourselves incapable to fulfil it for the future; that one transgression had stood as a bar against the pleas of after-obedience. But God hath wholly laid that condition aside as to us, and settled that of faith, more easy to be performed, and to be renewed by us. It is infinite grace in him, that he will accept of faith in us, instead of that perfect obedience he required of us in the covenant of works. 2. It is easy, not like the burdensome ceremonies appointed under the law. He exacts not now the legal obedience, expensive sacrifices, troublesome purifications, and abstinences, that "yoke of bondage" (Gal. v. 1) which they were "not able to bear" (Acts xv. 10). He treats us not as servants, or children, in their nonage, under the elements of the world, nor requires those innumerable bodily exercises that he exacted of them: he demands not "a thousand of lambs," and "rivers of oil;" but he requires a sincere confession and repentance, in order to our absolution; an "unfeigned faith," in order to our blessedness, and elevation to a glorious life. He requires only that we should believe what he saith, and have so good an opinion of his goodness and veracity, as to persuade ourselves of the reality of his intentions, confide in his word, and rely upon his promise, cordially embrace his crucified Son, whom he hath set forth as the means of our happiness, and have a sincere respect to all the discoveries of his will. What can be more easy than this? Though some in the days of the apostles, and others since have endeavored to introduce a multitude of legal burdens, as if they envied God the expressions of his goodness, or thought him guilty of too much remissness, in taking off the yoke, and treating man too favorably. 3. Nor is it a clear knowledge of every revelation, that is the condition of this covenant. God in his kindness to man hath made revelations of himself, but his goodness is manifested in obliging us to believe him, not fully to understand him. He hath made them, by sufficient testimonies, as clear to our faith, as they are incomprehensible to our reason: he hath revealed a Trinity of Persons, in their distinct offices, in the business of redemption, without which revelation of a Trinity we could not have a right notion and scheme of redeeming grace. But since the clearness of men's understanding is sullied by the fall, and hath lost its wings to fly up to a knowledge of such sublime things as that of the Trinity, and other mysteries of the Christian religion, God hath manifested his goodness in not obliging us to understand them but to believe them; and hath given us reason enough

to believe it to be his revelation, (both from the nature of the revelation itself, and the way and manner of propagating it, which is
wholly divine, exceeding all the methods of human art,) though he
hath not extended our understandings to a capacity to know them,
and render a reason of every mystery. He did not require of every
Israelite, or of any of them that were stung by the fiery serpents,
that they should understand, or be able to discourse of the nature
and qualities of that brass of which the serpent upon the pole was
made, or by what art that serpent was formed, or in what manner
the sight of it did operate in them for their cure; it was enough that
they did believe the institution and precept of God, and that their
own cure was assured by it: it was enough if they cast their eyes
upon it according to the direction. The understandings of men are
of several sizes and elevations, one higher than another: if the condition of this covenant had been a greatness of knowledge, the most
acute men had only enjoyed the benefits of it. But it is "faith,"
which is as easy to be performed by the ignorant and simple, as by
the strongest and most towering mind: it is that which is within the
compass of every man's understanding. God did not require that
every one within the verge of the covenant should be able to discourse of it to the reasons of men; he required not that every man
should be a philosopher, or an orator, but a believer. What could
be more easy than to lift up the eye to the brazen serpent, to be
cured of a fiery sting? What could be more facile than a glance,
which is done without any pain, and in a moment? It is a condition
may be performed by the weakest as well as the strongest: could
those that were bitten in the most vital part cast up their eyes, though
at the last gasp, they would arise to health by the expulsion of the
venom.

[2d.] As it is easy, so it is reasonable. Repent and believe, is
that which is required by Christ and the apostles for the enjoyment
of the kingdom of heaven. It is very reasonable that things so great
and glorious, so beneficial to men, and revealed to them by so sound
an authority, and an unerring truth, should be believed. The excellency of the thing disclosed could admit of no lower a condition
than to be believed and embraced. There is a sort of faith, that is
a natural condition in everything: all religion in the world, though
never so false, depends upon a sort of it; for unless there be a belief of future things, there would never be a hope of good, or a fear
of evil, the two great hinges upon which religion moves. In all
kinds of learning, many things must be believed before a progress
can be made. Belief of one another is necessary in all acts of human life; without which human society would be unlinked and dissolved. What is that faith that God requires of us in this covenant,
but a willingness of soul to take God for our God, Christ for our
Mediator, and the procurer of our happiness (Rev. xxii. 17)? What
prince could require less upon any promise he makes his subjects,
than to be believed as true, and depended on as good; that they
should accept his pardon, and other gracious offers, and be sincere
in their allegiance to him, avoiding all things that may offend him,
and pursuing all things that may please him? Thus God, by so

small and reasonable a condition as faith, lets in the fruits of Christ's death into our soul, and wraps us up in the fruition of all the privileges purchased by it. So much he hath condescended in his goodness, that upon so slight a condition we may plead his promise, and humbly challenge, by virtue of the covenant, those good things he hath promised in his word. It is so reasonable a condition, that if God did not require it in the covenant of grace, the creature were obliged to perform it: for the publishing any truth from God, naturally calls for credit to be given it by the creature, and an entertainment of it in practice. Could you offer a more reasonable condition yourselves, had it been left to your choice? Should a prince proclaim a pardon to a profligate wretch, would not all the world cry shame of him, if he did not believe it upon the highest assurances? and if ingenuity did not make him sorry for his crimes, and careful in the duty of a subject, surely the world would cry shame of such a person.

[3d.] It is a necessary condition. 1. Necessary for the honor of God. A prince is disparaged if his authority in his law, and if his graciousness in his promises, be not accepted and believed. What physician would undertake a cure, if his precepts may not be credited? It is the first thing in the order of nature, that the revelation of God should be believed, that the reality of his intentions in inviting man to the acceptance of those methods he hath prescribed for their attaining their chief happiness, should be acknowledged. It is a debasing notion of God, that he should give a happiness, purchased by Divine blood, to a person that hath no value for it, nor any abhorrency of those sins that occasioned so great a suffering, nor any will to avoid them: should he not vilify himself, to bestow a heaven upon that man that will not believe the offers of it, nor walk in those ways that lead to it? that walks so, as if he would declare there was no truth in his word, nor holiness in his nature? Would not God by such an act verify a truth in the language of their practice, *viz.* that he were both false and impure, careless of his word, and negligent of his holiness? As God was so desirous to ensure the consolation of believers, that if there had been a greater Being than himself to attest, and for him to be responsible to, for the confirmation of his promise, he would willingly have submitted to him, and have made him the umpire, " He swore by himself, because he could not swear by a greater" (Heb. vi. 19); by the same reason, had it stood with the majesty and wisdom of God to stoop to lower conditions in this covenant, for the reducing of man to his duty and happiness, he would have done it; but his goodness could not take lower steps, with the preservation of the rights of his majesty, and the honor of his wisdom. Would you have had him wholly submitted to the obstinate will of a rebellious creature, and be ruled only by his terms? Would you have had him received men to happiness, after they had heightened their crimes by a contempt of his grace, as well as of his creating goodness, and have made them blessed under the guilt of their crimes without an acknowledgment? Should he glorify one that will not believe what he hath revealed, nor repent of what himself hath committed; and so save a man after a repeated unthankfulness to the most immense grace that ever was, or can be, discovered and offered, without a detestation of his ingratitude, and a voluntary acceptance of his offers? It is necessary, for the honor of God, that man should accept of his terms, and not give laws to him to whom he is obnoxious as a guilty person, as well as subject as a creature. Again, it was very equitable and necessary for the honor of God, that since man fell by an unbelief of his precept and threatening, he should not rise again without a belief of his promise, and casting himself upon his truth in that: since he had vilified the honor of his truth in the threatening; since man in his fall would lean to his own understanding against God, it is fit that, in his recovery, the highest powers of his soul, his understanding and will, should be subjected to him in an entire resignation. Now, whereas knowledge seems to have a power over its object, faith is a full submission to that which is the object of it. Since man intended a glorying in himself, the evangelical covenant directs its whole battery against it, that men may "glory in nothing but Divine goodness" (1 Cor. i. 29—31). Had man performed exact obedience by his own strength, he had had something in himself as the matter of his glory. And though, after the fall, grace had made itself illustrious in setting him up upon a new stock, yet had the same condition of exact obedience been settled in the same manner, man would have had something to glory in, which is struck off wholly by faith; whereby man in every act must go out of himself for a supply, to that Mediator which Divine goodness and grace hath appointed. 2. It is necessary for the happiness of man. That can be no contenting condition wherein the will of man doth not concur. He that is forced to the most delicious diet, or to wear the bravest apparel, or to be stored with abundance of treasure, cannot be happy in those things without an esteem of them, and delight in them: if they be nauseous to him, the indisposition of his mind is a dead fly in those boxes of precious ointment. Now, faith being a sincere willingness to accept of Christ, and to come to God by him, and repentance being a detestation of that which made man's separation from God, it is impossible he could be voluntarily happy without it: man cannot attain and enjoy a true happiness without an operation of his understanding about the object proposed, and the means appointed to enjoy it. There must be a knowledge of what is offered, and of the way of it, and such a knowledge as may determine the will to affect that end, and embrace those means; which the will can never do, till the understanding be fully persuaded of the truth of the offerer, and the goodness of the proposal itself, and the conveniency of the means for the attaining of it. It is necessary, in the nature of the thing, that what is revealed should be believed to be a Divine revelation. God must be judged true in the promising justification and sanctification, the means of happiness; and if any man desires to be partaker of those promises, he must desire to be sanctified; and how can he desire that which is the matter of those promises, if he wallow in his own lusts, and desire to do so, a thing repugnant to the promise itself? Would you have God force man to be happy against his will? Is it not very reasonable he should demand the consent of his reasonable creature to that blessedness he offers him? The new covenant is a "marriage covenant" (Hos. ii. 16, 19, 20), which implies a consent on our parts, as well as a consent on God's part; that is no marriage that hath not the consent of both parties. Now faith is our actual consent, and repentance and sincere obedience are the testimonies of the truth and reality of this consent.

6th. Divine goodness is eminent in his methods of treating with men to embrace this covenant. They are methods of gentleness and sweetness: it is a wooing goodness, and a bewailing goodness; his expressions are with strong motions of affection: he carrieth not on the gospel by force of arms: he doth not solely menace men into it, as worldly conquerors have done; he doth not, as Mahomet, plunder men's estates, and wound their bodies, to imprint a religion on their souls: he doth not erect gibbets, and kindle faggots, to scare men to an entering into covenant with him. What multitudes might he have raised by his power, as well as others! What legions of angels might he have rendezvoused from heaven, to have beaten men into a profession of the gospel! Nor doth he only interpose his sovereign authority in the precept of faith, but useth rational expostulations, to move men voluntarily to comply with his proposals (Isa. i. 18), " Come now, and let us reason together," saith the Lord. He seems to call heaven and earth to be judge, whether he had been wanting in any reasonable ways of goodness, to overcome the perversity of the creature; (Isa. i. 2), " Hear, O heavens, and give ear, O earth, I have nourished and brought up children." What various encouragements doth he use agreeable to the nature of men, endeavoring to persuade them with all tenderness, not to despise their own mercies, and be enemies to their own happiness! He would allure us by his beauty, and win us by his mercy. He uses the arms of his own excellency and our necessity to prevail upon us, and this after the highest provocations. When Adam had trampled upon his creating goodness, it was not crushed; and when man had cast it from him, it took the higher rebound: when the rebel's provocation was fresh in his mind, he sought him out with a promise in his hand, though Adam fled from him out of enmity as well as fear (Gen. iii). And when the Jews had outraged his Son, whom he loved from eternity, and made the Lord of heaven and earth bow down his head like a slave on the cross, yet in that place, where the most horrible wickedness had been committed, must the gospel be preached: the law must go forth out of that Sion, and the apostles must not stir from thence till they had received the promise of the Spirit, and published the word of grace in that ungrateful city, whose inhabitants yet swelled with indignation against the Lord of Life, and the doctrine he had preached among them (Luke xxiv. 47 ; Acts i. 4, 5). He would overlook their indignities out of tenderness to their souls, and expose the apostles to the peril of their lives, rather than expose his enemies to the fury of the devil.

1. How affectionately doth he invite men! What multitudes of alluring promises and pressing exhortations are there everywhere sprinkled in the Scripture, and in such a passionate manner, as if God were solely concerned in our good, without a glance on his own

glory! How tenderly doth he woo flinty hearts, and express more
pity to them than they do to themselves! With what affection do
his bowels rise up to his lips in his speech in the prophet, Isa. li. 4,
"Hearken to me, O my people, and give ear unto me, O my nation!"
"My people," "my nation!"—melting expressions of a tender God
soliciting a rebellious people to make their retreat to him. He never
emptied his hand of his bounty, nor divested his lips of those charitable expressions. He sent Noah to move the wicked of the old
world to an embracing of his goodness, and frequent prophets to the
provoking Jews; and as the world continued, and grew up to a
taller stature in sin, he stoops more in the manner of his expressions. Never was the world at a higher pitch of idolatry than at
the first publishing the gospel; yet, when we should have expected
him to be a punishing, he is a beseeching God. The apostle fears
not to use the expression for the glory of ⸱ivine goodness; "We
are ambassadors for Christ, as though God did beseech you by us"
(2 Cor. v. 20). The beseeching voice of God is in the voice of the
ministry, as the voice of the prince is in that of the herald: it is as
if Divine goodness did kneel down to a sinner with ringed hands
and blubbered cheeks, entreating him not to force him to re-assume
a tribunal of justice in the nature of a Judge, since he would treat
with man upon a throne of grace in the nature of a Father; yea, he
seems to put himself into the posture of the criminal, that the offending creature might not feel the punishment due to a rebel. It is not
the condescension, but the interest, of a traitor to creep upon his
knees in sackcloth to his sovereign, to beg his life; but it is a miraculous goodness in the sovereign to creep in the lowest posture to the
rebel, to importune him, not only for an amity to him, but a love for
his own life and happiness: this He doth, not only in his general
proclamations, but in his particular wooings, those inward courtings
of his Spirits, soliciting them with more diligence (if they would observe it) to their happiness, than the devil tempts them to the ways
of their misery: as he was first in Christ, reconciling the world,
when the world looked not after him, so he is first in his Spirit,
wooing the world to accept of that reconciliation, when the world
will not listen to him. How often doth he flash up the light of nature and the light of the word in men's hearts, to move them not to
lie down in sparks of their own kindling, but to aspire to a better
happiness, and prepare them to be subject to a higher mercy, if they
would improve his present entreaties to such an end! And what
are his threatenings designed for, but to move the wheel of our
fears, that the wheel of our desire and love might be set on motion
for the embracing his promise? They are not so much the thunders of his justice, as the loud rhetoric of his good will, to prevent
men's misery under the vials of wrath: it is his kindness to scare
men by threatenings, that justice might not strike them with the
sword: it is not the destruction, but the preserving reformation, that
he aims at: he hath no pleasure in the death of the wicked; this he
confirms by his oath. His threatenings are gracious expostulations
with them: "Why will ye die, O house of Israel" (Ezek. xxxiii.
11)? They are like the noise a favorable officer makes in the street,

to warn the criminal he comes to seize upon, to make his escape : he
never used his justice to crush men, till he had used his kindness to
allure them.   All the dreadful descriptions of a future wrath, as well
as the lively descriptions of the happiness of another world, are designed to persuade men ; the honey of his goodness is in the bowels
of those roaring lions : such pains doth Goodness take with men, to
make them candidates for heaven.

2. How readily doth he receive men when they do return ! We
have David's experience for it (Ps. xxxii. 5) ; " I said, I will confess
my transgressions unto the Lord ; and thou forgavest the iniquity
of my sin.   Selah."   A sincere look from the creature draws out his
arms, and opens his bosom ; he is ready with his physic to heal us,
upon a resolution to acquaint him with our disease, and by his medicines prevents the putting our resolution into a petition.   The
Psalmist adds a " Selah" to it, as a special note of thankfulness for
Divine goodness.   He doth not only stand ready to receive our petitions while we are speaking, but answers us before we call (Isa.
lxv. 24) ; listening to the motions of our heart, as well as to the supplications of our lips.   He is the true Father, that hath a quicker
pace in meeting, than the prodigal hath in returning ; who would
not have his embraces and caresses interrupted by his confession
(Luke xv. 20—22) ; the confession follows, doth not precede, the
Father's compassion.   How doth he rejoice in having an opportunity to express his grace, when he hath prevailed with a rebel to
throw down his arms, and lie at his feet ; and this because " he delights in mercy" (Micah. vii. 18) !   He delights in the expressions of
it from himself, and the acceptance of it by his creature.

3. How meltingly doth he bewail man's wilful refusal of his goodness !   It is a mighty goodness to offer grace to a rebel; a mighty
goodness to give it him after he hath a while stood off from the
terms ; an astonishing goodness to regret and lament his wilful perdition.   He seems to utter those words in a sigh, " O that my people
had hearkened unto me, and Israel had walked in my way" (Ps.
lxxxi. 13) !   It is true, God hath not human passions, but his affections cannot be expressed otherwise in a way intelligible to us ; the
excellency of his nature is above the passions of men ; but such expressions of himself manifest to us the sincerity of his goodness : and
that, were he capable of our passions, he would express himself in
such a manner as we do : and we find incarnate Goodness bewailing
with tears and sighs the ruin of Jerusalem (Luke xix. 42).   By the
same reason that when a sinner returns there is joy in heaven, upon
his obstinacy there is sorrow in earth.   The one is, as if a prince
should clothe all his court in triumphant scarlet, upon a rebel's repentance ; and the other, as if a prince put himself and his court in
mourning for a rebel's obstinate refusal of a pardon, when he lies at
his mercy.   Are not now these affectionate invitations, and deep be-
wailings of their perversity, high testimonies of Divine goodness ?
Do not the unwearied repetitions of gracious encouragements deserve
a higher name than that of mere goodness?   What can be a stronger
evidence of the sincerity of it, than the sound of his saving voice in
our enjoyments, the motion of his Spirit in our hearts, and his grief

for the neglect of all? These are not testimonies of any want of goodness in his nature to answer us, or unwillingness to express it to his creature. Hath he any mind to deceive us, that thus intreats us? The majesty of his nature is too great for such shifts; or, if it were not, the despicableness of our condition would render him above the using any. Who would charge that physician with want of kindness, that freely offers his sovereign medicine, importunes men, by the love they have to their health, to take it, and is dissolved into tears and sorrow when he finds it rejected by their peevish and conceited humor?

7th. Divine goodness is eminent in the sacraments he hath affixed to this covenant, especially the Lord's supper. As he gave himself in his Son, so he gives his Son in the sacrament; he doth not only give him as a sacrifice upon the cross for the expiation of our crimes, but as a feast upon the table for the nourishment of our souls: in the one he was given to be offered; in this he gives him to be partaken of, with all the fruits of his death; under the image of the sacramental signs, every believer doth eat the flesh, and drink the blood of the great Mediator of the covenant. The words of Christ, " This is my body, and this is my blood," are true to the end of the world (Matt. xxvi. 26, 28). This is the most delicious viand of heaven, the most exquisite dainty food God can feed us with : the delight of the Deity, the admiration of angels; a feast with God is great, but a feast on God is greater. Under those signs that body is presented; that which was conceived by the Spirit, inhabited by the Godhead, bruised by the Father to be our food, as well as our propitiation, is presented to us on the table. That blood which satisfied justice, washed away our guilt on the cross, and pleads for our persons at the throne of grace; that blood which silenced the curse, pacified heaven, and purged earth, is given to us for our refreshment. This is the bread sent from heaven, the true manna; the cup is "the cup of blessing," and, therefore, a cup of goodness (1 Cor. x. 15). It is true, bread doth not cease to be bread, nor the wine cease to be wine; neither of them lose their substance, but both acquire a sanctification, by the relation they have to that which they represent, and give a nourishment to that faith that receives them. In those God offers us a remedy for the sting of sin, and troubles of conscience; he gives us not the blood of a mere man, or the blood of an incarnate angel, but of God blessed forever; a blood that can secure us against the wrath of heaven, and the tumults of our consciences; a blood that can wash away our sins, and beautify our souls; a blood that hath more strength than our filth, and more prevalency than our accuser; a blood that secures us against the terrors of death, and purifies us for the blessedness of heaven. The goodness of God complies with our senses, and condescends to our weakness; he instructs us by the eye, as well as by the ear; he lets us see, and taste, and feel him, as well as hear him; he veils his glory under earthly elements, and informs our understanding in the mysteries of salvation by signs familiar to our senses; and because we cannot with our bodily eyes behold him in his glory, he presents him to the eyes of our minds in elements, to affect our understandings in the

representations of his death. The body of Christ crucified is more
visible to our spiritual sense, than the invisible Deity could be visible
in his flesh upon earth ; and the power of his body and blood is as
well experimented in our souls, as the power of his Divinity was
seen by the Jews in his miraculous actions in his body in the world.
It is the goodness of God, to mind us frequently of the great things
Christ hath purchased ; that as himself would not let them be out
of his mind, to communicate them to us, so he would give us means
to preserve them in our minds, to adore him for them, and request
them of him ; whereby he doth evidence his own solicitousness, that
we should not be deprived by our own forgetfulness of that grace
Christ hath purchased for us ; it was to remember the Redeemer,
" and show his death till he came" (1 Cor. xi. 25, 26).

1. His goodness is seen in the end of it, which is a sealing the covenant of grace.   The common nature and end of sacraments is to
seal the covenant they belong to, and the truths of the promises of
it.[f] The legal sacraments of circumcision and the passover sealed the
legal promises and the covenant in the Judicial administration of it ;
and the evangelical sacraments seal the evangelical promises, as a
ring confirms a contract of marriage, and a seal the articles of a
compact ; by the same reason, circumcision is called a "seal of the
righteousness of faith" (Rom. iv. 11) ; other sacraments may have
the same title ; God doth attest, that he will remain firm in his promise, and the receiver attests he will remain firm in his faith.   In all
reciprocal covenants, there are mutual engagements, and that which
serves for a seal on the part of the one, serves for a seal also on the
part of the other ; God obligeth himself to the performance of the
promise, and man engageth himself to the performance of his duty.
The thing confirmed by this sacrament is the perpetuity of this covenant in the blood of Christ, whence it is called "the New Testament," or covenant "in the blood of Christ" (Luke xxii. 20).   In
every repetition of it, God, by presenting, confirms his resolution to
us, of sticking to this covenant for the merit of Christ's blood ; and
the receiver, by eating the body and drinking the blood, engageth
himself to keep close to the condition of faith, expecting a full salvation and a blessed immortality upon the merit of the same blood
alone.   This sacrament could not be called the " New Testament, or
Covenant," if it had not some relation to the covenant ; and what it
can be but this, I do not understand.   The covenant itself was confirmed " by the death of Christ" (Heb. ix. 15), and thereby made unchangeable both in the benefits to us, and the condition required of
us ; but he seals it to our sense in a sacrament, to give us strong consolation ; or, rather, the articles of the covenant of redemption between the Father and the Son, agreed on from eternity, were accomplished on Christ's part by his death, on the Father's part by his
resurrection ; Christ performed what he promised in the one, and God
acknowledgeth the validity of it, and performs what he had promised
in the other.   The covenant of grace, founded upon this covenant of
redemption, is sealed in the sacrament ; God owns his standing to the
terms of it, as sealed by the blood of the Mediator, by presenting

.[f] Amyral. Irenicum. pp. 16, 17.

him to us under those signs, and gives us a right upon faith to the enjoyment of the fruits of it. As the right of a house is made over by the delivery of the key, and the right of land translated by the delivery of a turf; whereby he gives us assurance of his reality, and a strong support to our confidence in him; not that there is any virtue and power of sealing in the elements themselves, no more than there is in a turf to give an enfeoffment in a parcel of land; but as the power of one is derived from the order of the law, so the confirming power of the sacrament is derived from the institution of God; as the oil wherewith kings were annointed, did not of itself confer upon them that royal dignity, but it was a sign of their investiture into office, ordered by Divine institution. We can with no reason imagine, that God intended them as naked signs or pictures, to please our eyes with the image of them, to represent their own figures to our eyes, but to confirm something to our understanding by the efficacy of the Spirit accompanying them:[g] they convey to the believing receiver what they represent, as the great seal of a prince, fixed to the parchment, doth the pardon of a rebel as well as its own figure. Christ's death, and the grace of the covenant is not only signified, but the fruits and merit of that death communicated also. Thus doth Divine goodness evidence itself, not only in making a gracious covenant with us, but fixing seals to it; not to strengthen his own obligation, which stood stronger than the foundations of heaven and earth, upon the credit of his word, but to strengthen our weakness, and support our security, by something which might appear more formal and solemn than a bare word. By this, the Divine goodness provides against our spiritual faintings, and shows us by real signs as well as verbal declarations, that the covenant sealed by the blood of Christ, is unalterable; and thereby would fortify and mount our hopes to degrees in some measure suitable to the kindness of the covenant, and the dignity of the Redeemer's blood. And it is yet a further degree of this goodness, that he hath appointed us so often to celebrate it, whereby he shows how careful he is to keep up our tottering faith, and preserve us constant in our obedience; obliging himself to the performance of his promise, and obliging us to the payment of our duty.

2. His goodness is seen in the sacrament in giving us in it an union and communion with Christ. There is not only a commemoration of Christ dying, but a communication of Christ living. The apostle strongly asserts it by way of interrogation (1 Cor. x. 16), "The cup of blessing which we bless, is it not the communion of the blood of Christ? the bread which we break, is it not the communion of the body of Christ?" In the cup there is a communication of the blood of Christ, a conveyance of a right to the merits of his death, and the blessedness of his life: we are not less by this made one body with Christ than we are by baptism (1 Cor. xii. 13): and "put on Christ" living in this, as well as in baptism (Gal. iii. 27); that as his taking our infirm flesh was a real incarnation, so the giving us his flesh to eat is a mystical incarnation in believers, whereby they become one body with him as crucified, and one body with

[g] Daille, Melang. Part I, p. 253.

him as risen; for if Christ himself be received by faith in the word
(Col. ii. 6), he is no less received by faith in the sacrament. When
the Holy Ghost is said to be received, the graces or gifts of the Holy
Ghost are received; so when Christ is received, the fruits of his
death are really partaken of. The Israelites that ate of the sacrifices,
did "partake of the altar" (1 Cor. x. 18), *i. e.* had a communion with
the God of Israel, to whom they had been sacrificed; and those that
"ate of the sacrifices" offered to idols, had a "fellowship with devils,"
to whom those sacrifices were offered (ver. 20). Those that partake
of the sacraments in a due manner, have a communion with that
God to whom it was sacrificed, and a communion with that body
which was sacrificed to God; not that the substance of that body
and blood is wrapped up in the elements, or that the bread and wine
are transformed into the body and blood of Christ, but as they represent him, and by virtue of the institution are, in estimation himself, his own body and blood; by the same reason as he is called
"Christ our passover," he may be called "Christ our supper" (1 Cor.
v. 7): for as they are so reckoned to an unworthy receiver, as if
they were the real body and blood of Christ, because by his not discerning the Lord's body in it, or making light of it as common bread,
he is judged "guilty of the body and blood of Christ," guilty of treating him in as base a manner as the Jews did when they crowned him
with thorns (1 Cor. xi. 27, 29): by the same reason they must be
reckoned to a worthy receiver, as the very body and blood of Christ:
so that as the unworthy receiver "eats and drinks damnation," the
worthy receiver "eats and drinks" salvation. It would be an empty
mystery, and unworthy of an institution by Divine goodness, if there
were not some communion with Christ in it: there would be some
kind of deceit in the precept, "Take, eat, and drink, this is my body
and blood," if there were not a conveyance of spiritual vital influences to our souls: for the natural end of eating and drinking is the
nourishment and increase of the body, and preservation of life, by
that which we eat and drink. The infinite wise, gracious, and true
God, would never give us empty figures without accomplishing that
which is signified by them, and suitable to them. How great is this
goodness of God! he would have his Son in us, one with us, straitly
joined to us, as if we were his proper flesh and blood: in the incarnation Divine goodness united him to our nature; in the sacrament,
it doth in a sort unite him with his purchased privileges to our persons; we have not a communion with a part or a member of his
body, or a drop of his blood, but with his whole body and blood, represented in every part of the elements. The angels in the heaven
enjoy not so great a privilege; they have the honor to be under him
as their Head, but not that of having him for their food; they behold him, but they do not taste him. And, certainly, that goodness
that hath condescended so much to our weakness, would impart it to
us in a very glorious manner, were we capable of it. But, because
a man cannot behold the light of the sun in its full splendor by reason of the infirmities of his eyes, he must behold it by the help of a
glass, and such a communication through a colored and opaque glass,
is as real from the sun itself, though not so glorious, but more shrouded

and obscure; it is the same light that shines through that medium, as spreads itself gloriously in the open air, though the one be masked, and the other open-faced. To conclude this, by the way, we may take notice of the neglect of this ordinance: if it be a token of Divine goodness to appoint it, it is no sign of our estimation of Divine goodness to neglect it. He that values the kindness of his friend, will accept of his invitation, if there be not some strong impediments in the way, or so much familiarity with him that his refusal upon a light occasion would not be unkindly taken. But though God put on the disposition of a friend to us, yet he looseth not the authority of a sovereign; and the humble familiarity he invites us to, doth not diminish the condition and duty of a subject. A sovereign prince would not take it well, if a favorite should refuse the offered honor of his table. The viands of God are not to be slighted. Can we live better upon our poor pittance than upon his dainties? Did not Divine goodness condescend in it to the weakness of our faith, and shall we conceit our faith stronger than God thinks it? If he thought fit by those seals to make a deed of gift to us, shall we be so unmannerly to him, and such enemies to the security he offers us over and above his word, as not to accept it? Are we unwilling to have our souls inflamed with love, our hearts filled with comfort, and armed against the attempts of our enemies? It is true, there is a guilt of the body and blood of Christ contracted by a slightness in the manner of attending; is it not also contracted by a refusal and neglect? What is the language of it? If it speaks not the death of Christ in vain, it speaks the institution of this ordinance as a remembrance of his death, to be a vanity, and no mark of Divine goodness. Let us, therefore, put such a value upon Divine goodness in this affair, as to be willing to receive the conveyances of his love, and fresh engagements of our duty; the one is due from us to the kindness of our friend, and the other belongs to our duty as his subjects.

vi. By this redemption God restores us to a more excellent condition than Adam had in innocence. Christ was sent by Divine goodness, not only to restore the life Adam's sin had stripped us of, but to give it more abundantly than Adam's standing could have conveyed it to us (John x. 10), "I am come that they might have life, and that they might have it more abundantly." More abundantly for strength, more abundantly for duration, a life abounding with greater felicity and glory: the substance of those better promises of the new covenant than what attended the old. There are fuller streams of grace by Christ than flowed to Adam, or could flow from Adam. As Christ never restored any to health and strength while he was in the world, but he gave them a greater measure of both than they had before; so there is the same kindness, no question, manifested in our spiritual condition. Adam's life might have preserved us, but Adam's death could not have rescued either himself or his posterity; but, in our redemption, we have a Redeemer, who hath "died to expiate our sins," and so crowned with life to save, and forever preserve our persons (Rom. v. 10), "Because I live, ye shall live also:" so that by redeeming goodness the life of a believer is as perpetual as the life of the Redeemer Christ (John xiv. 19). Adam, though innocent, was under the danger of perishing; a believer, though culpable, is above the fears of mutability. Adam had a holiness in his nature, but capable of being lost; by Christ believers have a holiness bestowed, not capable of being rifled, but which will remain till it be at last fully perfected : though they have a power to change in their nature, yet they are above an actual final change by the indulgence of Divine grace. Adam stood by himself; believers stand in a root, impossible to be shaken or corrupted : by this means the "promise is sure to all the seed" (Rom. iv. 16). Christ is a stronger person than Adam, who can never break covenant with God, and the truth of God will never break covenant with him. We are united to a more excellent Head than Adam: instead of a root merely human, we have a root Divine as well as human. In him we had the righteousness of a creature merely human; in this we have a righteousness divine, the righteousness of God-man; the stock is no longer in our own hands, but in the hands of One that cannot embezzle it, or forfeit it : Divine goodness hath deposited it strongly for our security. The stamp we receive, by the Divine goodness, from the second Adam, is more noble than that we should have received from the first, had he remained in his created state : Adam was formed of the dust of the earth, and the new man is formed by the incorruptible seed of the word; and at the resurrection, the body of man shall be endued with better qualities than Adam had at creation : they shall be like that glorious Body which is in heaven, in union with the person of the "Son of God" (Phil. iii. 21). Adam, at the best, had but an earthly body, but the Lord from heaven hath a "heavenly body," the image of which shall be borne by the redeemed ones, as they have borne the image of the earthly (1 Cor. xv. 47—49). Adam had the society of beasts; redeemed ones expect, by Divine goodness in redemption, a commerce with angels; as they are reconciled to them by his death, they shall certainly come to converse with them at the consummation of their happiness; as they are made of one family, so they will have a peculiar intimacy : Adam had a paradise, and redeemed ones a heaven provided for them; a happier place with a richer furniture. It is much to give so complete a paradise to innocent Adam; but more to give heaven to an ungrateful Adam, and his rebellious posterity : it had been abundant goodness to have restored us to the same condition in that paradise from whence we were ejected; but a superabundant goodness to bestow upon us a better habitation in heaven, which we could never have expected. How great is that goodness, when by sin we were fallen to be worse than nothing, that He should raise us to be more than what we were ; that restored us, not to the first step of our creation, but to many degrees of elevation beyond it ! not only restores us, but prefers us; not only striking off our chains, to set us free, but clothing us with a robe of righteousness, to render us honorable; not only quenching our hell, but preparing a heaven; not re-garnishing an earthly, but providing a richer palace : his goodness was so great, that, after it had rescued us, it would not content itself with the old furniture, but makes all new for us in another world; a new wine to drink; a new heaven to dwell in; a more magnificent structure for our habitation: thus hath Goodness prepared for us a straiter union, a stronger life, a purer righteousness, an unshaken standing, and a fuller glory; all more excellent than was within the compass of innocent Adam's possession.

vii. This goodness in redemption extends itself to the lower creation. It takes in, not only man, but the whole creation, except the fallen angels, and gives a participation of it to insensible creatures; upon the account of this redemption the sun, and all kind of creatures, were preserved, which otherwise had sunk into destruction upon the sin of man, and ceased from their being, as man had utterly ceased from his happiness (Colos. i. 17): "By him all things consist." The fall of man brought, not only a misery upon himself, but a vanity upon the creature; the earth groaned under a curse for his sake. They were all created for the glory of God, and the support of man in the performance of his duty, who was obliged to use them for the honor of Him that created them both. Had man been true to his obligations, and used the creatures for that end to which they were dedicated by the Creator; as God would have then rejoiced in his works, so his works would have rejoiced in the honor of answering so excellent an end: but when man lost his integrity, the creatures lost their perfection; the honor of them was stained when they were debased to serve the lusts of a traitor, instead of supporting the duty of a subject, and employed in the defence of the vices of men against the precepts and authority of their common Sovereign. This was a vilifying the creature, as it would be a vilifying the sword of a prince, which is, for the maintenance of justice, to be used for the murder of an innocent; and a dishonoring a royal mansion, to make it a storehouse for a dunghill. Had those things the benefit of sense, they would groan under this disgrace, and rise up in indignation against them that offered them this affront, and turned them from their proper end. When sin entered, the heavens that were made to shine upon man, and the earth that was made to bear and nourish an innocent creature, were now subjected to serve a rebellious creature; and as man turned against God, so he made those instruments against God, to serve his enmity, luxury, sensuality. Hence the creatures are said to groan (Rom. viii. 22); "The whole creation groans and travails in pain together until now." They would really groan, had they understanding to be sensible of the outrage done them. "The whole creation."—It is the pang of universal nature, the agony of the whole creation, to be alienated from the original use for which they were intended, and be disjointed from their end to serve the disloyalty of a rebel. The drunkard's cup, and the glutton's table, the adulterer's bed, and the proud man's purple, would groan against the abuser of them. But when all the fruits of redemption shall be completed, the goodness of God shall pour itself upon the creatures, deliver them from the "bondage of corruption into the glorious liberty of the children of God" (Rom. viii. 21); they shall be reduced to their true end, and returned in their original harmony. As the creation doth passionately groan under its vanity, so it doth "earnestly expect and wait for its deliverance at the time of the manifestation of the sons of God" (ver. 19). The manifestation of the sons of God is the attainment of the liberty of the creature. They shall be freed from the vanity under which they are enslaved; as it entered by sin, it shall vanish upon the total removal of sin. What use they were designed for in paradise they will have afterwards, except that of the nourishment of men, who shall be as "angels, neither eating nor drinking:" the glory of God shall be seen and contemplated in them. It can hardly be thought that God made the world to be little a moment after he had reared it, sullied by the sin of man, and turned from its original end, without thoughts of a restoration of it to its true end, as well as man to his lost happiness. The world was made for man: man hath not yet enjoyed the creature in the first intention of them; sin made an interruption in that fruition. As redemption restores man to his true end, so it restores the creatures to their true use. The restoration of the world to its beauty and order was the design of the Divine goodness in the coming of Christ, as it is intimated in Isa. xi. 6–9; as he "came not to destroy the law, but to fulfil it," so he came not to destroy the creatures, but to repair them: to restore to God the honor and pleasure of the creation, and restore to the creatures their felicity in restoring their order: the fall corrupted it, and the full redemption of men restores it. The last time is called, not a time of destruction, but a "time of restitution," and that "of all things" (Acts iii. 21) of universal nature, the main part of the creation at least. All those things which were the effects of sin will be abolished; the removal of the cause beats down the effect. The disorder and unruliness of the creature, arising from the venom of man's transgression, all the fierceness of one creature against another shall vanish. The world shall be nothing but an universal smile; nature shall put on triumphant vestments: there shall be no affrighting thunders, choking mists, venomous vapors, or poisonous plants. It would not else be a restitution of all things. They are now subject to be wasted by judgments for the sin of their possessor, but the perfection of man's redemptions shall free them from every misery. They have an advancement at the present, for they are under a more glorious Head, as being the possession of Christ, the heavenly Adam, much superior to the first: as it is the glory of a person to be a servant to a prince, rather than a peasant. And afterwards, they shall be elevated to a better state, sharing in man's happiness, as well as they did in his misery: as servants are interested in the good fortune of their master, and bettered by his advance in his prince's favor. As man in his first creation was mutable and liable to sin, so the creatures were liable to vanity; but as man by grace shall be freed from the mutability, so shall the creatures be freed from the fears of an invasion, by the vanity that sullied them before. The condition of the servants shall be suited to that of their Lord, for whom they were designed: hence, all creatures are called upon to rejoice upon the perfection of salvation, and the appearance of Christ's royal authority in the world. If they were to be destroyed, there would be no ground to invite them to triumph (Ps. xcvi. 11, 12; cxviii. 7, 8). Thus doth Divine goodness spread its kind arms over the whole creation.

Thirdly. The third thing is the goodness of God in his *Government.* That goodness that despised not their creation, doth not despise their conduct. The same goodness that was the head that framed them, is the helm that guides them; his goodness hovers over the whole frame, either to prevent any wild disorders unsuitable to his creating end, or to conduct them to those ends which might illustrate his wisdom and goodness to his creatures. His goodness doth no less incline him to provide for them, than to frame them. It is the natural inclination of man to love what is purely the birth of his own strength or skill. He is fond of preserving his own inventions, as well as laborious in inventing them. It is the glory of a man to preserve them, as well as to produce them. God loves everything which he hath made, which love could not be without a continued diffusiveness to them, suitable to the end for which he made them. It would be a vain goodness, if it did not interest itself in managing the world, as well as erecting it: without his government everything in the world would jostle against one another: the beauty of it would be more defaced, it would be an unruly mass, a confused chaos rather than a Κόσμος, a comely world. If Divine goodness respected it when it was nothing, it would much more respect it when it was something, by the sole virtue of his power and good-will to it, without any motive from anything else than himself, because there was nothing else but himself. But since he sees his own stamp in things without himself in the creature, which is a kind of motive or moving object to Divine goodness to preserve it, when there was nothing without himself that could be any motive to Him to create it: as when God hath created a creature, and it falls into misery, that misery of the creature, though it doth not necessitate his mercy, yet meeting with such an affection as mercy in his nature, is a moving object to excite it; as the repentance of Nineveh drew forth the exercise of his pity and preserving goodness. Certainly, since God is good, he is bountiful; and if bountiful, he is provident. He would seem to envy and malign his creatures, if he did not provide for them, while he intends to use them: but infinite goodness cannot be effected with envy; for all envy implies a want of that good in ourselves, which we regard with so evil an eye in another. But God, being infinitely blessed, hath not the want of any good that can be a rise to such an uncomely disposition. The Jews thought that Divine goodness extended only to them in an immediate and particular care, and left all other nations and things to the guidance of angels. But the Psalmist (Ps. cvii. a psalm calculated for the celebration of this perfection, in the continued course of his providence throughout all ages of the world) ascribes to Divine goodness immediately all the advantages men meet with. He helps them in their actions, presides over their motions, inspects their several conditions, labors day and night in a perpetual care of them. The whole life of the world is linked together by Divine goodness. Everything is ordered by him in the place where he hath set it, without which the world would be stripped of that excellency it hath by creation.

1st. This goodness is evident in the care he hath of all creatures. There is a peculiar goodness to his people; but this takes not away his general goodness to the world : though a master of a family hath a choicer affection to those that have an affinity to him in nature, and stand in a nearer relation, as his wife, children, servants ; yet he hath a regard to his cattle, and other creatures he nourisheth in his house. All things are not only before his eyes, but in his bosom ; he is the nurse of all creatures, supplying their wants, and sustaining them from that nothing they tend to. The "earth is full of his riches" (Ps. civ 24) ; not a creek or cranny but partakes of it. Abundant goodness daily hovers over it, as well as hatched it. The whole world swims in the rich bounty of the Creator, as the fish do in the largeness of the sea, and birds in the spaciousness of the air.[h] The goodness of God is the river that waters the whole earth. As a lifeless picture casts its eye upon every one in the room, so doth a living God upon everything in the world. And as the sun illuminates all things which are capable of partaking of its light, and diffuseth its beams to all things which are capable of receiving them, so doth God spread his wings over the whole creation, and neglects nothing, wherein he sees a mark of his first creating goodness.

1. His goodness is seen, in preserving all things. "O Lord, thou preservest man and beast" (Ps. xxxvi. 6). Not only man, but beasts, and beasts as well as men ; man, as the most excellent creature, and beasts as being serviceable to man, and instruments of his worldly happiness. He continues the species of all things, concurs with them in their distinct offices, and quickens the womb of nature. He visits man every day, and makes him feel the effects of his providence, in giving him "fruitful seasons, and filling his heart with food and gladness" (Acts xiv. 17), as witnesses of his liberality and kindness to man. "The earth is visited and watered by the river of God. He settles the furrows of the earth, and makes it soft with showers," that the corn may be nourished in its womb, and spring up to maturity. "He crowns the year with his goodness, and his paths drop fatness. The little hills rejoice on every side ; the pastures are clothed with flocks, and the valleys are covered over with corn," as the Psalmist elegantly says (Ps. lxv. 9, 10 ; cvii. 35, 36). He waters the ground by his showers, and preserves the little seed from the rapine of animals. "He draws not out the evil arrows of famine," as the expression is (Ezek. v. 16). Every day shines with new beams of his Divine goodness. The vastness of this city, and the multitudes of living souls in it, is an astonishing argument. What streams of nourishing necessaries are daily conveyed to it! Every mouth hath bread to sustain it ; and among all the number of poor in the bowels and skirts of it, how rare is it to hear of any starved to death for want of it! Every day he "spreads a table" for us, and that with varieties, and "fills our cups" (Ps. xxiii. 5). He shortens not his hand, nor withdraws his bounty : the increase of one year by his blessing, restores what was spent by the former. He is the "strength of our life" (Ps. xxvii. 1), continuing the vigor of our limbs, and the health of our bodies ; secures us from "terrors by night, and the arrows of diseases that fly by day" (Ps. xci. 5) ;

h Gulielmus Parasien. p. 184.

"sets a hedge about our estates" (Job i. 10), and defends them against the attempts of violence; preserves our houses from flames that might consume them, and our persons from the dangers that lie in wait for them; watcheth over us "in our goings out, and our comings in" (Ps. cxxi. 8), and way-lays a thousand dangers we know not of: and employs the most glorious creatures in heaven in the service of mean "men upon earth" (Ps. xci. 11): not by a faint order, but a pressing charge over them, to "keep them in all his ways." Those that are his immediate servants before his throne, he sends to minister to them that were once his rebels. By an angel he conducted the affairs of Abraham (Gen. xxiv. 7): and by an angel secured the life of Ishmael (Gen. xxi. 17): glorious angels for mean man, holy angels for impure man, powerful angels for weak man. How in the midst of great dangers, doth his sudden light dissipate our great darkness, and create a deliverance out of nothing! How often is he found a present help in time of trouble! When all other assistance seems to stand at a distance, he flies to us beyond our expectations, and raises us up on the sudden from the pit of our dejectedness, as well as that of our danger, exceeding our wishes, and shooting beyond our desires as well as our deserts. How often, in the time of confusion, doth he preserve an indefensible place from the attacks of enemies, like a bark in the midst of a tempestuous sea! the rage falls upon other places round about them, and, by a secret efficacy of Divine goodness, is not able to touch them. He hath peculiar preservations for his Israel in Egypt, and his Lots in Sodom, his Daniels in the lions' dens, and his children in a fiery furnace. He hath a tenderness for all, but a peculiar affection to those that are in covenant with him.

2. The goodness of God is seen in taking care of the animals and and inanimate things. Divine goodness embraceth in its arms the lowest worm as well as the loftiest cherubim: he provides food for the "crying ravens" (Ps. cxlvii. 9), and a prey for the appetite of the "hungry lion" (Ps. civ. 21): "He opens his hand, and fills with good those innumerable creeping things, both small and great beasts; they are all waiters upon him, and all are satisfied by their bountiful Master" (Ps. civ. 25—28). They are better provided for by the hand of heaven, than the best favorite is by an earthly prince: for "they are filled with good." He hath made channels in the wildest deserts, for the watering of beasts, and trees for the nests and "habitation of birds" (Ps. civ. 10, 12, 17). As a Lawgiver to the Jews, he took care that the poor beast should not be abused by the cruelty of man: he provided for the ease of the laboring beast in that command of the Sabbath, wherein he provided for his own service: the cattle was to do "no work" on it (Exod. xx. 10). He ordered that the mouth of the ox should not be muzzled while it trod out the corn (Deut. xxv. 4, it being the manner of those countries to separate the corn from the stalk by that means, as we do in this by thrashing), regarding it as a part of cruelty to deprive the poor beast of tasting, and satisfying itself with that which he was so officious by his labor to prepare for the use of man. And when any met with a nest of young birds, though

they might take the young to their use, they were forbidden to seize upon the dam, that she might not lose the objects of her affection and her own liberty in one day (Deut. xxii. 6).

And see how God enforceth this precept with a threatening of a shortness of life, if they transgressed it (Deut. xxii. 7)! "Thou shalt let the dam go, that it may be well with thee, and that thou mayest prolong thy days." He would revenge the cruelty to dumb creatures with the shortness of the oppressor's life: nor would he have cruelty used to creatures that were separated for his worship: he therefore provides that a cow, or an ewe, and their young ones, should "not be killed for sacrifice in one day" (Lev. xxii. 28). All which precepts, say the Jews, are to teach men mercifulness to their beasts; so much doth Divine goodness bow down itself, to take notice of those mean creatures, which men have so little regard to, but for their own advantage; yea, he is so good, that he would have worship declined for a time in favor of a distressed beast; the "helping a sheep, or an ox, or an ass, out of a pit," was indulged them even "on the Sabbath-day," a day God had peculiarly sanctified and ordered for his service (Matt. xii. 11; Luke xiv. 5): in this case he seems to remit for a time the rights of the Deity for the rescue of a mere animal. His goodness extends not only to those kind of creatures that have life, but to the insensible ones; he clothes the grass, and "arrays the lilies of the field" with a greater glory than Solomon had upon his throne (Matt. vi. 28, 29); and such care he had of those trees which bore fruit for the maintenance of man or beast, that he forbids any injury to be offered to them, and bars the rapine and violence, which by soldiers used to be practised (Deut. xx. 19), though it were to promote the conquest of their enemy. How much goodness is it, that he should think of so small a thing as man! How much more that he should concern himself in things that seem so petty as beasts and trees! Persons seated in a sovereign throne, think it a debasing of their dignity to regard little things: but God, who is infinitely greater in majesty above the mightiest potentate, and the highest angel, yet is so infinitely good, as to employ his divine thoughts about the meanest things. He who possesses the praises of angels, leaves not off the care of the meanest creatures: and that majesty that dwells in a pure heaven, and an inconceivable light, stoops to provide for the ease of those creatures that lie and lodge in the dirt and dung of the earth. How should we be careful not to use those unmercifully, which God takes such care of in his law, and not to distrust that goodness, that opens his hand so liberally to creatures of another rank!

3. The goodness of God is seen in taking care of the meanest rational creatures; as servants and criminals. He provided for the liberty of slaves, and would not have their chains continue longer than the seventh year, unless they would voluntarily continue under the power of their masters; and that upon pain of his displeasure, and the withdrawing his blessing (Deut. xv. 18). And though, by the laws of many nations, masters had an absolute power of life and death over their servants, yet God provided that no member should be lamed, not an eye, no, nor a tooth, struck out, but the master was

to pay for his folly and fury the price of the "liberty of his servant" (Exod. xxi. 26, 27): he would not suffer the abused servant to be any longer under the power of that man that had not humanity to use him as one of the same kindred and blood with himself. And though those servants might be never so wicked, yet, when unjustly afflicted, God would interest himself as their guardian in their protection and delivery. And when a poor slave had been provoked, by the severity of his master's fury, to turn fugitive from him, he was, by Divine order, not to be delivered up again to his master's fury, but dwell in that city, and with that person, to whom he had "fled for refuge" (Deut. xxiii. 15, 16). And when public justice was to be administered upon the lesser sort of criminals, the goodness of God ordered the "number of blows" not to exceed forty, and left not the fury of man to measure out the punishment to excess (Deut. xxv. 3). And in any just quarrel against a provoking and injuring enemy, he ordered them not to ravage with the sword till they had summoned a rendition of the place (Deut. xx. 10). And as great a care he took of the poor, that they should have the gleanings both of the vineyard and field (Lev. xix. 10; xxiii. 22), and not be forced to pay "usury for the money lent them (Exod. xxii. 25).

4. His goodness is seen in taking care of the wickedest persons. "The earth is full of his goodness" (Ps. xxxvii. 5). The wicked as well as the good enjoy it; they that dare lift up their hands against heaven in the posture of rebels, as well as those that lift up their eyes in the condition of suppliants. To do good to a criminal, far surmounts that goodness that flows down upon an innocent object: now God is not only good to those that have some degrees of goodness, but to those that have the greatest degrees of wickedness, to men that turn his liberality into affronts of him, and have scarce an appetite to anything but the violation of his authority and goodness. Though, upon the fall of Adam, we have lost the pleasant habitation of paradise, and the creatures made for our use are fallen from their original excellency and sweetness; yet he hath not left the world utterly incommodious for us, but yet stores it with things not only for the preservation, but delight of those that make their whole lives invectives against this good God. Manna fell from heaven for the rebellious as well as for the obedient Israelites. Cain as well as Abel, and Esau as well as Jacob, had the influences of his sun, and the benefits of his showers. The world is yet a kind of paradise to the veriest beasts among mankind; the earth affords its riches, the heavens its showers, and the sun its light, to those that injure and blaspheme him: "He makes his sun to rise on the evil and on the good, and sends rain on the just and on the unjust" (Matt. v. 45). The wickedest breathe in his air, walk upon his earth, and drink of his water, as well as the best. The sun looks with as pleasant and bright an eye upon a rebellious Absalom, as a righteous David; the earth yields its plants and medicines to one as well as to the other; it is seldom that He deprives any of the faculties of their souls, or any members of their bodies. God distributes his blessings where he might shoot his thunders; and darts his light on those who deserve an eternal darkness; and presents the good things of the earth to those

that merit the miseries of hell; for "the earth, and the fulness thereof, is the Lord's" (Ps. xxiv. 1); everything in it is his in propriety, ours in trust; it is his corn, his wine (Hos. ii. 8); he never divested himself of the propriety, though he grants us the use; and by those good things he supports multitudes of wicked men, not one or two, but the whole shoal of them in the world; for he is "the Saviour of all men," *i. e.* is the preserver of all men (1 Tim. iv. 10). And as he created them, when he foresaw they would be wicked; so he provides for them, when he beholds them in their ungodliness. The ingratitude of men stops not the current of his bounty, nor tires his liberal hand; howsoever unprofitable and injurious men are to him, he is liberal to them; and his goodness is the more admirable, by how much the more the unthankfulness of men is provoking: he sometimes affords to the worst a greater portion of these earthly goods; they often swim in wealth, when others pine away their lives in poverty. And the silk-worm yields its bowels to make purple for tyrants, while the oppressed scarce have from the sheep wool enough to cover their nakedness; and though he furnish men with those good things, upon no other account than what princes do, when they nourish criminals in a prison till the time of their execution, it is a mark of his goodness. Is it not the kindness of a prince to treat his rebels deliciously? to give them the liberty of the prison, and the enjoyments of the delights of the place, rather than to load their legs with fetters, and lodge them in a dark and loathsome dungeon, till he orders them, for their crime, to be conducted to the scaffold or gibbet? Since God is thus kind to the vilest men, whose meanness, by reason of sin, is beyond that of any other creature, as to shoot such rays of goodness upon them; how inexpressible would be the expressions of his goodness, if the Divine image were as pure and bright upon them as it was upon innocent Adam!

2d. His goodness is evident in the preservation of human society. It belongs to his power that he is able to do it, but to his goodness that he is willing to do it.

1. This goodness appears in prescribing rules for it. The moral law consists but of ten precepts, and there are more of them ordered for the support of human society, than for the adoration and honor of himself (Exod. xx. 1, 2); four for the rights of God, and six for the rights of man, and his security in his authority, relations, life, goods, and reputation; superiors not to be dishonored, life not to be invaded, chastity not to be stained, goods not to be filched, good name not to be cracked by false witness, nor anything belonging to our neighbor to be coveted; and in the whole Scripture, not only that which was calculated for the Jews, but compiled for the whole world; he hath fixed rules for the ordering all relations, magistrates, and subjects; parents and children; husbands and wives; masters and servants; rich and poor, find their distinct qualifications and duties. There would be a paradisiacal state, if men had a goodness to observe what God hath had a goodness to order for the strengthening the sinews of human society; the world would not groan under oppressing tyrants, nor princes tremble under discontented subjects, or mighty rebels; children would not be provoked to anger by the unreasonableness

of their parents, nor parents sink under grief by the rebellion of their children; masters would not tyrannize over the meanest of their servants, nor servants invade the authority of their masters.

2. The goodness of God in the preserving human society, is seen in setting a magistracy to preserve it. Magistracy is from God in its original; the charter was drawn up in paradise; civil subordination must have been had man remained in innocence; but the charter was more explicitly renewed and enlarged at the restoration of the world after the deluge, and given out to man under the broad seal of heaven; "Whoso sheds man's blood, by man shall his blood be shed" (Gen. ix. 6). The command of shedding the blood of a murderer was a part of his goodness, to secure the lives of those that bore his image. Magistrates are "the shields of the earth," but they "belong to God" (Ps. xlvii. 9). They are fruits of his goodness in their original, and authority; were there no magistracy, there would be government, no security to any man under his own vine and fig tree; the world would be a den of wild beasts preying upon one another; every one would do what seems good in his eyes; the loss of government is a judgment God brings upon a nation when men become "as the fishes of the sea," to devour one another, because they "have no ruler over them" (Hab. i. 14). Private dissensions will break out into public disorders and combustions.

3. The goodness of God in the preservation of human society, is seen in the restraints of the passions of men. He sets bounds to the passions of men as well as to the rollings of the sea; "He stilleth the noise of the waves, and the tumults of the people" (Ps. lxv. 7). Though God hath erected a magistracy to stop the breaking out of those floods of licentiousness, which swell in the hearts of men; yet, if God should not hold stiff reins on the necks of those tumultuous and foaming passions, the world would be a place of unruly confusion, and hell triumph upon earth; a crazy state would be quickly broke in pieces by boisterous nature. The tumults of a people could no more be quelled by the force of man, than the rage of the sea by a puff of breath; without Divine goodness, neither the wisdom nor watchfulness of the magistrates, nor the industry of officers, could preserve a state. The laws of men would be too slight to curb the lusts of men, if the goodness of God did not restrain them by a secret hand, and interweave their temporal security with observance of those laws. The sons of Belial did murmur when Saul was chosen king; and that they did no more was the goodness of God, for the preservation of human society. If God did not restrain the impetuousness of men's lusts, they would be the entire ruin of human society; their lusts would render them as bad as beasts, and change the world into a savage wilderness.

4. The goodness of God is seen in the preservation of human society, in giving various inclinations to men for public advantage. If all men had an inclination to one science or art, they would all stand idle spectators of one another; but God hath bestowed various dispositions and gifts upon men, for the promoting the common good, that they may not only be useful to themselves, but to society. He

will have none idle, none unuseful, but every one acting in a due place, according to their measures, for the good of others.

5. The goodness of God is seen in the witness he bears against those sins that disturb human society. In those cases he is pleased to interest himself in a more signal manner, to cool those that make it their business to overturn the order he hath established for the good of the earth. He doth not so often in this world punish those faults committed immediately against his own honor, as those that put the world into a hurry and confusion: as a good governor is more merciful to crimes against himself, than those against his community. It is observed that the most turbulent seditious persons in a state come to most violent ends, as Corah, Adonijah, Zimri: Ahithopel draws Absalom's sword against David and Israel, and the next is, he twists a halter for himself: Absalom heads a party against his father, and God, by a goodness to Israel, hangs him up, and prevents not its safety by David's indulgence, and a future rebellion, had life been spared by the fondness of his father. His providence is more evident in discovering disturbers, and the causes that move them, in defeating their enterprises, and digging the contrivers out of their caverns and lurking holes: in such cases, God doth so act, and use such methods, that he silenceth any creature from challenging any partnership with him in the discovery. He doth more severely in this world correct those actions that unlink the mutual assistance between man and man, and the charitable and kind correspondence he would have kept up. The sins for which the "wrath of God comes upon the children of disobedience" (Col. iii. 5, 6) in this world are of this sort; and when princes will be oppressing the people, God will be "pouring contempt on the princes, and set the poor on high from affliction" (Ps. cvii. 40, 41). An evidence of God's care and kindness in the preserving human society, is those strange discoveries of murders, though never so clandestine and subtilly committed, more than of any other crime among men: Divine care never appears more than in bringing those hidden and injurious works of darkness to light, and a due punishment.

6. His goodness is seen in ordering mutual offices to one another against the current of men's passions. Upon this account he ordered, in his laws for the government of the Israelites, that a man should reduce the wandering beast of his enemy to the hand of his rightful proprietor, though he were a provoking enemy; and also "help the poor beast that belonged to one that hated him, when he saw him sink under his burden" (Exod. xxiii. 4, 5). When mutual assistance was necessary, he would not have men considered as enemies, or considered as wicked, but as of the same blood with ourselves, that we might be serviceable to one another for the preservation of life and goods.

7. His goodness is seen in remitting something of his own right, for the preserving a due dependence and subjection. He declines the right he had to the vows of a minor, or one under the power of another, waving what he might challenge by the voluntary obligation of his creature, to keep up the due order between parents and children, husbands and wives, superiors and inferiors; those that

were under the power of another, as a child under his parents, or a wife under her husband, if they had "vowed a vow unto the Lord," which concerned his honor and worship, it was void without the approbation of that person under whose charge they were (Num. xxx. 3, 4, &c.). Though God was the Lord of every man's goods, and men but his stewards; and though he might have taken to himself what another had offered by a vow, since whatsoever could be offered was God's own, though it was not the parties' own who offered it; yet God would not have himself adored by his creature to the prejudice of the necessary ties of human society; he lays aside what he might challenge by his sovereign dominion, that there might not be any breach of that regular order which was necessary for the preservation of the world. If Divine goodness did not thus order things, he would not do the part of a Rector of the world; the beauty of the world would be much defaced, it would be a confused mass of men and women, or rather, beasts and bedlams. Order renders every city, every nation, yea, the whole earth, beautiful: this is an effect of Divine goodness.

3d. His goodness is evident in encouraging anything of moral goodness in the world. Though moral goodness cannot claim an eternal reward, yet it hath been many times rewarded with a temporal happiness; he hath often signally rewarded acts of honesty, justice, and fidelity, and punished the contrary by his judgments, to deter man from such an unworthy practice, and encourage others to what was comely, and of a general good report in the world. Ahab's humiliation put a demurrer to God's judgments intended against him; and some ascribe the great victories and success of the Romans to that justice which was observed among themselves. Baruch was but an amanuensis to the Prophet Jeremy to write his prophecy, and very despondent of his own welfare (Jer. xlv. 13); God upon that account provides for his safety, and rewards the industry of his service with the security of his person; he was not a statesman, to declare against the corrupt counsels of them that sat at the helm, nor a prophet, to declare against their profane practices, but the prophet's scribe; and as he writes in God's service the prophecies revealed to the prophet, God writes his name in the roll of those that were designed for preservation in that deluge of judgments which were to come upon that nation. Epicurus complained of the administration of God, that the virtuous moralist had not sufficient smiles of Divine favor, nor the swinish sensualist frowns of Divine indignation. But what if they have not always that confluence of outward wealth and pleasures, but remain in the common level? yet they have the happiness and satisfaction of a clear reputation, the esteem of men, and the secret applauses of their very enemies, besides the inward ravishments upon an exercise of virtue, and the commendatory subscription of their own hearts, a dainty the vicious man knows not of; they have an inward applause from God as a reward of Divine goodness, instead of those racks of conscience upon which the profane are sometimes stretched. He will not let the worst men do him any service (though they never intended in the act of service him, but themselves) without giving them their wages: he will not let them hit him in the teeth as if he were beholden to them. If Nebu-chadnezzar be the instrument of God's judgments against Tyrus and Israel, he will not only give him that rich city, but a richer country, Egypt, the granary for her neighbors, a wages above his work. In this is Divine goodness eminent, since, in the most moral actions, as there is something beautiful, so there is something mixed, hateful to the infinitely exact holiness of the Divine nature; yet he will not let that which is pleasing to him go unrewarded, and defeat the expectations of men, as men do with those they employ, when, for one flaw in an action, they deny them the reward due for the other part. God encouraged and kept up morality in the cities of the Gentiles for the entertainment of a further goodness in the doctrine of the gospel when it should be published among them.

4th. Divine goodness is eminent in providing a Scripture as a rule to guide us, and continuing it in the world. If man be a rational creature, governable by a law, can it be imagined there should be no revelation of that law to him? Man, by the light of reason, must needs confess himself to be in another condition than he was by creation, when he came first out of the hands of God; and can it be thought, that God should keep up the world under so many sins against the light of nature, and bestow so many providential influences, to invite men to return to him, and acquaint no men in the world with the means of that return? Would he exact an obedience of men, as their consciences witness he doth, and furnish them with no rules to guide them in the darkness they cannot but acknowledge that they have contracted? No; Divine goodness hath otherwise provided: this Bible we have is his word and rule. Had it been a falsity and imposture, would that goodness, that watches over the world, have continued it so long? That goodness that overthrew the burdensome rites of Moses, and expelled the foolish idolatry of the Pagans, would have discovered the imposture of this, had it not been a transcript of his own will. Whatever mistakes he suffers to remain in the world, what goodness had there been to suffer this anciently amongst the Jews, and afterwards to open it to the whole world, to abuse men in religion and worship, which so nearly concerned himself and his own honor, that the world should be deceived by the devil without a remedy in the morning of its appearance? It hath been honored and admired by some heathens, when they have cast their eyes upon it, and their natural light made them behold some footsteps of a Divinity in it. If this, therefore, be not a Divine prescript, let any that deny it, bring as good arguments for any book else, as can be brought for this. Now, the publishing this is an argument of Divine goodness: it is designed to win the affections of beggarly man, to be espoused to a God of eternal blessedness and immense riches. It speaks words in season: no doubts but it resolves; no spiritual distemper but it cures; no condition but it hath a comfort to suit it. It is a garden which the hand of Divine bounty hath planted for us; in it he condescends to shadow himself in those expressions that render him in some manner intelligible to us. Had God wrote in a loftiness of style suitable to the greatness of his majesty, his writing had been as little understood by us, as the brightness of his glory can be beheld by us. But he draws phrases from our affairs, to express his mind to us; he incarnates himself in his word to our minds, before his Son was incarnate in the flesh to the eyes of men: he ascribes to himself eyes, ears, hands, that we might have, from the consideration of ourselves, and the whole human nature, a conception of his perfections: he assumes to himself the members of our bodies, to direct our understandings in the knowledge of his Deity; this is his goodness. Again, though the Scripture was written upon several occasions, yet in the dictating of it, the goodness of God cast his eye upon the last ages of the world (1 Cor. x. 11): "They are written for our admonition, upon whom the ends of the world are come." It was given to the Israelites, but Divine goodness intended it for the future Gentiles. The old writings of the prophets were thus designed, much more the later writings of the apostles. Thus did Divine goodness think of us, and prepare his records for us, before we were in the world: these he hath written plain for our instruction, and wrapped up in them what is necessary for our salvation: it is clear to inform our understanding, and rich to comfort us in our misery; it is a light to guide us, and a cordial to refresh us; it is a lamp to our feet, and a medicine for our diseases; a purifier of our filth, and a restorer of us in our faintings. He hath by his goodness sealed the truth of it, by his efficacy on multitudes of men: he hath made it the "word of regeneration" (James i. 18). Men, wilder and more monstrous than beasts, have been tamed and changed by the power of it: it hath raised multitudes of dead men from a grave fuller of horror than any earthly one. Again, Goodness was in all ages sending his letters of advice and counsel from heaven, till the canon of the Scripture was closed; sometimes he wrote to chide a froward people, sometimes to cheer up an oppressed and disconsolate people, according to the state wherein they were; as we may observe by the several seasons wherein parts of Scripture were written. It was His goodness that he first revealed anything of his will after the fall; it was a further degree of goodness, that he would add more cubits to its stature; before he would lay aside his pencil, it grew up to that bulk wherein we have it. And his goodness is further seen in the preserving it; he hath triumphed over the powers that opposed it, and showed himself good to the instruments that propagated it: he hath maintained it against the blasts of hell, and spread it in all languages against the obstructions of men and devils. The sun of his word is by his kindness preserved in our horizon, as well as the sun in the heavens. How admirable is Divine goodness! He hath sent his Son to die for us, and his written word to instruct us, and his Spirit to edge it for an entrance into our souls: he hath opened the womb of the earth to nourish us, and sent down the records of heaven to direct us in our pilgrimage: he hath provided the earth for our habitation, while we are travellers, and sent his word to acquaint us with a felicity at the end of our journey, and the way to attain in another world what we want in this, *viz.* a happy immortality.

5th. His goodness in his government is evident, in conversions of men. Though this work be wrought by his power, yet his power

was first solicited by his goodness.   It was his rich goodness that he
would employ his power to pierce the scales of a heart as hard as
those of the "leviathan."   It was this that opened the ears of men
to hear him, and draws them from the hurry of worldly cares, and
the charms of sensual pleasures, and, which is the top of all, the impostures and cheats of their own hearts.   It is this that sends a spark
of his wrath into men's consciences, to put them to a stand in sin,
that he might not send down a shower of brimstone eternally to consume their persons.   This it was that first showed you the excellency
of the Redeemer, and brought you to taste the sweetness of his blood,
and find your security in the agonies of his death.   It is his goodness to call one man and not another, to turn Paul in his course, and
lay hold of no other of his companions.   It is his goodness to call
any, when he is not bound to call one.

1. It is his goodness to pitch upon mean and despicable men in
the eye of the world ; to call this poor publican, and overlook that
proud Pharisee, this man that sits upon a dunghill, and neglect him
that glisters in his purple.   His majesty is not enticed by the lofty
titles of men, nor, which is more worth, by the learning and knowledge of men.   "Not many wise, not many mighty," not many doctors, not many lords, though some of them ; but his goodness condescends to the "base things" of the world, and things which are
"despised" (1 Cor. i. 26–28).   "The poor receive the gospel" (Matt.
xi. 5), when those that are more acute, and furnished with a more
apprehensive reason, are not touched by it.

2. The worst men.   He seizeth sometimes upon men most soiled,
and neglects others that seem more clean and less polluted.   He turns
men in their course in sin, that, by their infernal practices, have
seemed to have gone to school to hell, and to have sucked in the sole
instructions of the devil.   He lays hold upon some when they are
most under actual demerit, and snatches them as fire-brands out of
the fire, as upon Paul when fullest of rage against him ; and shoots
a beam of grace, where nothing could be justly expected but a thunderbolt of wrath.   It is his goodness to visit any, when they lie putrefying in their loathsome lusts ; to draw near to them who have
been guilty of the greatest contempt of God, and the light of nature;
the murdering Manassehs, the persecuting Sauls, the Christ-crucify-
ing Jews,—persons in whom lusts had had a peaceable possession
and empire for many years.

3. His goodness appears in converting men possessed with the
greatest enmity against him, while he was dealing with them.   All
were in such a state, and framing contrivances against him, when
Divine goodness knocked at the door (Col. i. 21).   He looked after
us when our backs were turned upon him, and sought us when we
slighted him, and were a "gainsaying people" (Rom. x. 21); when we
had shaken off his convictions, and contended with our Maker, and
mustered up the powers of nature against the alarms of conscience ;
struggled like wild bulls in a net, and blunted those darts that stuck
in our souls.   Not a man that is turned to him, but had lifted up
the heel against his gospel grace, as well as made light of his creating
goodness.   Yet it hath employed itself about such ungrateful

wretches, to polish those knotty and rugged pieces for heaven; and so invincibly, that he would not have his goodness defeated by the fierceness and rebellion of the flesh. Though the thing was more difficult in itself (if anything may be said to have a difficulty to omnipotency) than to make a stone live, or to turn a straw into a marble pillar. The malice of the flesh makes a man more unfit for the one, than the nature of the straw unfits it for the other.

4. His goodness appears in turning men, when they were pleased with their own misery, and unable to deliver themselves; when they preferred a hell before him, and were in love with their own vileness; when his call was our torment, and his neglect of us had been accounted our felicity. Was it not a mighty goodness to keep the light close to our eyes, when we endeavored to blow it out; and the corrosive near to our hearts, when we endeavored to tear it off, being more fond of our disease than the remedy? We should have been scalded to death with the Sodomite, had not God laid his good hand upon us, and drawn us from the approaching ruin we affected, and were loath to be freed from. And had we been displeased with our state, yet we had been as unable spiritually to raise ourselves from sin to grace, as to raise ourselves naturally from nothing to being. In this state we were when his goodness triumphed over us; when he put a hook into our nostrils, to turn us in order to our salvation; and drew us out of the pit which we had digged, when he might have left us to sink under the rigors of his justice we had merited. Now this goodness in conversion is greater than that in creation; as in creation there is nothing to oppose him, so there was nothing to disoblige him; creation was terminated to the good of a mutable nature, and conversion tends to a supernatural good. God pronounced all creatures good at first, and man among the rest, but did not pronounce any of them, or man himself, his "portion," his "inheritance," his "segullah," his "house," his "diadem." He speaks slightly of all those things which he made, the noblest heavens, as well as the lowest earth, in comparison of a true convert: "All those things hath mine hand made, and all those things have been: but to this man will I look, to him that is of a contrite spirit" (Isa. lxvi. 1, 2). It is more goodness to give the espousing grace of the covenant, than the completing glory of heaven; as it is more for a prince to marry a beggar, than only to bring her to live deliciously in his courts. All other benefits are of a meaner strain, if compared with this; there is little less of goodness in imparting the holiness of his nature, than imputing the righteousness of his Son.

6th. The Divine goodness doth appear in answering prayers. He delights to be familiarly acquainted with his people, and to hear them call upon him. He indulgeth them a free access to him, and delights in every address of an "upright man" (Prov. xv. 8). The wonderful efficacy of prayer depends not upon the nature of our petitions or the temper of our soul, but the goodness of God to whom we address. Christ establisheth it upon this bottom: when he exhorts to ask in his name, he tells them the spring of all their grants is the Father's love: "I say not, I will pray the Father for you, for the Father himself loves you" (John xvi. 26, 27). And since it is of itself incredible, that a Majesty, exalted above the cherubims, should stoop so low as to give a miserable and rebellious creature admittance to him, and afford him a gracious hearing, and a quick supply, Christ ushers in the promise of answering prayer with a note of great assurance: "I say unto you, Ask, and it shall be given you" (Luke xi. 9, 10). I, that know the mind of my Father, and his good disposition, assure you your prayer shall not be in vain. Perhaps you will not be so ready of yourselves to imagine so great a liberality; but take it upon my word, it is true, and so you will find it. And his bounty travels, as it were, in birth, to give the greatest blessings, upon our asking, rather than the smallest: "your heavenly Father shall give his Holy Spirit to them that ask him" (ver. 13): which in Matt. vii. 11, is called, "good things." Of all the good and rich things Divine goodness hath in his treasury, he delights to give the best upon asking, because God doth act so as to manifest the greatness of his bounty and magnificence to men; and, therefore, is delighted when men, by their petitioning him, own such a liberal disposition in him, and put him upon the manifesting it. He would rather you should ask the greatest things heaven can afford, than the trifles of this world; because his bounty is not discovered in meaner gifts: he loves to have an opportunity to manifest his affection above the liberality and tenderness of worldly fathers. He doth more wait to give in a way of grace, than we to beg; and, "therefore, will the Lord wait, that he may be gracious unto you" (Isa. xxx. 18). He stands expecting your suits, and employs his wisdom in pitching upon the fittest seasons, when the manifestation of his goodness may be most gracious in itself, and the mercy you want most welcome to you; as it follows, "for the Lord is a God of judgment." He chooseth the time wherein his doles may be most acceptable to his suppliants; "In an acceptable time have I heard thee" (Isa. xlix. 8). He often opens his hand while we are opening our lips, and his blessings meet our petitions at the first setting out upon their journey to heaven: "While they are yet speaking, I will hear" (Isa. lxv. 24). How often do we hear a secret voice within us, while we are praying, saying, "Your prayer is granted;" as well as hear a voice behind us, while we are erring, saying, "This is the way, walk in it!" And his liberality exceeds often our desires, as well as our deserts; and gives out more than we had the wisdom or confidence to ask. The apostle intimates it in that doxology, "Unto Him who is able to do abundantly above all that we ask or think" (Eph. iii. 20). This power would not have been so strong an argument of comfort, if it were never put in practice; he is more liberal than his creatures are craving. Abraham petitioned for the life of Ishmael, and God promiseth him the "birth of Isaac" (Gen. xvii. 18, 19). Isaac asks for a "child," and God gives him "two" (Gen. xxv. 21, 22). Jacob desires "food" to eat, and "raiment" to put on; God confines not his bounty within the narrow limits of his petition, but instead of a "staff," wherewith he passed Jordan, makes him repass it with "two bands" (Gen. xxviii. 20). David asked life of God, and he gave him "life," and a "crown" to boot (Ps. xxi. 2—5). The

Israelites would have been contented with a free life in Egypt; they only cried to have their chains struck off; God gave them that, and adopts them to be his "peculiar people," and raises them into a famous state. It is a wonder that God should condescend so much, that he should hear prayers so weak, so cold, so wandering, and gather up our sincere petitions from the dung of our distractions and diffidence. David vents his astonishment at it; "Blessed be God, for he hath shown me marvellous kindness. I said in my haste, I am cut off from before thine eyes: nevertheless, thou heardest the voice of my supplication" (Ps. xxxi 21, 22). How do we wonder at the goodness of a petty man, in granting our desires; how much more should we at the humility and goodness of the most sovereign Majesty of heaven and earth!

7th. The goodness of God is seen in bearing with the infirmities of his people, and accepting imperfect obedience. Though Asa had many blots in his escutcheon, yet they are overlooked, and this note set upon record by Divine goodness, that his heart was perfect towards the Lord all his days; "But the high places were not removed: nevertheless, Asa's heart was perfect with the Lord all his days" (1 Kings, xv. 14). He takes notice of a sincere, though chequered obedience, to reward it, which could claim nothing but a slight from him, if he were extreme to mark what is done amiss. When there is not an opportunity to work, but only to will, he accepts the will, as if it had passed into work and act. He sees no iniquity in Jacob (Numb. xxiii. 21), i. e. He sees it not so as to cast off a respect to their persons, and the acceptance of their services: his omniscience knows their sins, but his goodness doth not reject their persons. He is of so good a disposition, that he delights in a weak obedience of his servants, not in the imperfection, but in the obedience (Ps. xxxvii. 23); "He delights in the way of a good man," though he sometimes slips in it: he accepts a poor man's pigeon, as well as a rich man's ox: he hath a bottle for the tears, and a book for the "services of the upright," as well as for the most perfect obedience of angels (Ps. lvi. 8): he preserves their tears, as if they were a rich and generous wine, as the vine-dresser doth the expressions of the grape.

8th. The goodness of God is seen in afflictions and persecutions. If it be "good for us to be afflicted," for which we have the psalmist's vote (Ps. cxix. 71), then goodness in God is the principal cause and orderer of the afflictions. It is his goodness to snatch away that whence we fetch supports for our security, and encouragements for our insolence against him: he takes away the thing which we have some value for, but such as his infinite wisdom sees inconsistent with our true happiness. It is no ill-will in the physician to take away the hurtful matter the patient loves, and prescribe bitter potions, to advance that health which the other impaired; nor any mark of unkindness in a friend, to wrest a sword out of a madman's hand, wherewith he was about to stab himself, though it were beset with the most orient pearls. To prevent what is evil, is to do us the greatest good. It is a kindness to prevent a man from falling down a precipice, though it be with a violent blow, that lays him flat upon the ground at some distance from the edge of it. By afflictions he often snaps asunder those chains which fettered us, and quells those passions which ravaged us : he sharpens our faith, and quickens our prayers; he brings us in the secret chamber of our own heart, which we had little mind before to visit by a self-examination. It is such a goodness that he will vouchsafe to correct man in order to his eternal happiness, that Job makes it one part of his astonishment (Job. vii. 17); "What is man, that thou shouldest magnify him? that thou shouldest set thy heart upon him? and that thou shouldest visit him every morning, and try him every moment?" His strokes are often the magnifyings and exaltings of man. He sets his heart upon man, while he inflicts the smart of his rod: he shows thereby, what a high account he makes of him, and what a special affection he bears to him. When he might treat us with more severity after the breach of his covenant, and make his jealousy flame out against us in furious methods, he will not destroy his relation to us, and leave us to our own inclinations, but deal with us as a father with his children ; and when he takes this course with us, it is when it cannot be avoided without our ruin : his goodness would not suffer him to do it, if our badness did not force him to it (Jer. ix. 7), "I will melt them and try them, for how shall I do for the daughter of my people?" What other course can I take but this, according to the nature of man? The goldsmith hath no other way to separate the dross from the metal, but by melting it down. And when the impurities of his people necessitate him to this proceeding, "he sits as a refiner" (Mal. iii. 3): he watches for the purifying the silver, not for his own profit as the goldsmith, but out of a care of them, and good will to them; as himself speaks (Isa. xlviii. 10), "I have refined thee, but not with silver ;" or, as some read it, "not for sil-ver." As when he scatters his people abroad for their sin, he will not leave them without his presence for their "sanctuary" (Ezek. xi. 16): he would by his presence with them supply the place of ordi-nances, or be an ark to them in the midst of the deluge : his hand that struck them, is never without a goodness to comfort them and pity them. When Jacob was to go into Egypt, which was to prove a furnace of affliction to his offspring, God promises to go down with him, and to "bring him up again" (Gen. xlvi. 4) : a promise not only made to Jacob in his person, but to Jacob in his posterity. He re-turned not out of Egypt in his person, but as the father of a nu-merous posterity. He that would go down with their root, and afterwards bring up the branches, was certainly with them in all their oppressions: "I will go down with thee." "Down," saith one; what a word is that for a Deity ! into Egypt, idolatrous Egypt; what a place is that for his holiness![i] Yet O, the goodness of God ! He never thinks himself low enough to do his people good, nor any place too bad for his society with them. So when he had sent away into captivity the people of Israel by the hand of the Assyrian, his bowels yearn after them in their affliction (Isa. lii. 4, 5); the Assy-rian "oppressed them without cause," i. e. without a just cause in the conqueror to inflict so great an evil upon them, but not without

¹ Harwood's Sermon at Oxford, p. 5.

cause from God, whom they had provoked. "Now, therefore, what have I here, saith the Lord?" What do I here? I will not stay behind them. What do I longer here? for I will redeem again those jewels the enemy hath carried away. That chapter is a prophecy of redemption: God shows himself so good to his people in their persecutions, that he gives them occasion to glorify him in the very fires, as the Divine order is (Isa. xxiv. 15), "Wherefore glorify the Lord in the fires."

9th. The goodness of God is seen in temptations. In those he takes occasion to show his care and watchfulness, as a father uses the distress of a child as an opportunity for manifesting the tenderness of his affection. God is at the beginning and end of every temptation; he measures out both the quality and quantity: he exposeth them not to temptation beyond the ability he had already granted them, or will at the time, or afterwards multiply in them. He hath promised his people that "the gate of hell shall not prevail against them" (1 Cor. x. 13): that "in all things" they shall be "more than conquerors through Him that loved them:" that the most raging malice of hell shall not wrest them out of his hands. His goodness is not less in performing than it was in promising: and as the care of his providence extends to the least as well as the greatest, so the watchfulness of his goodness extends to us in the least as well as in the greatest temptations.

1. The goodness of God appears in shortening temptations. None of them can go beyond their "appointed times" (Dan. xi. 35): the strong blast Satan breathes cannot blow, nor the waves he raises rage one minute beyond the time God allows them; when they have done their work, and come to the period of their time, God speaks the word, and the wind and sea of hell must obey him, and retire into their dens. The more violent temptations are, the shorter time doth God allot to them. The assaults Christ had at the time of his death were of the most pressing and urging nature: the powers of darkness were all in arms against him; the reproaches and scorns put upon him, questioning his sonship, were very sharp; yet a little before his suffering he calls it but an hour (Luke xxii. 53), "This is your hour, and the power of darkness." A short time that men and devils were combined against him; and the time of temptation that is to come upon all the world for their trial, is called but an "hour" (Rev. iii. 10). In all such attempts, the greatness of the rage is a certain prognostic of the shortness of the season (Rev. xii. 12).

2. The goodness of God appears in strengthening his people under temptations. If he doth not restrain the arm of Satan from striking, he gives us a sword to manage the combat, and a shield to bear off the blow (Eph. vi. 16, 17). If he obscures his goodness in one part, he clears and brightens it in another: he either binds the strong man that he shall not stir, or gives us armor to render us victorious. If we fall, it is not for want of provision from him, but for want of our "putting on the armor of God" (Eph. vi. 11, 13). When we have not a strength by nature, he gives it us by grace: he often quells those passions within which would join hands with, and second the temptation without. He either qualifies the temptation

suitably to the force we have, or else supplies us with a new strength
to mate the temptation he intends to let loose against us; he knows
we are but dust, and his goodness will not have us unequally match-
ed. The Jews that in Antiochus' time were under great temptation
to apostasy by reason of the violence of their persecutions, were,
"out of weakness, made strong" for the combat (Heb. xi. 34). The
Spirit came more strongly upon Sampson when the Philistines most
furiously and confidently assaulted him. His Spirit is sent to
strengthen his people before the devil is permitted to tempt them
(Matt. iv. 2); "Then was Jesus led up of the Spirit." Then; When?
When the Spirit had in an extraordinary manner descended upon
him (Matt. iii. 16), "then," and not before. As the angels appeared
to Christ, after his temptation, to minister to him, so they appeared
to him before his passion, the time of the strongest powers of darkness, to strengthen him for it: he is so good, that when he knows
our potsherd strength too weak, he furnisheth our recruits from his
own omnipotence (Eph. vi. 10); "Be strong in the Lord, and in the
power of his might." He doth, as it were, breathe in something of
his own almightiness, to assist us in our wrestling against principalities and powers, and make us capable to sustain the violent storms
of the enemies.

3. The goodness of God is seen in temptations, in giving great
comforts in or after them. The Israelites had a more immediate
provision of manna from heaven when they were in the wilderness.
We read not that the Father spake audibly to the Son, and gave him
so loud a testimony, that he was his "beloved Son, in whom he was
well pleased," till he was upon the brink of strong temptations
(Matt. iii. 17): nor sent angels to minister immediately to his person, till after his success (Matt. iv. 11). Job never had such evidences of Divine love till after he had felt the sharp strokes of Satan's malice; he had heard of God before, by the "hearing of the
ear," but afterwards is admitted into greater familiarity (Job. xlii.
5): he had more choice appearances, clearer illuminations, and more
lively instructions. And, though his people fall into temptation,
yet, after their rising, they have more signal marks of his favor than
others have, or themselves, before they fell. Peter had been the
butt of Satan's rage, in tempting him to deny Christ, and he had
shamefully complied with the temptation; yet, to him particularly,
must the first news of the Redeemer's resurrection be carried, by
God's order, in the mouth of an angel (Mark xvi. 7); "Go your
ways, tell his disciples, and Peter." We have the greatest communion with God after a victory; the most refreshing truths after the
devil hath done his worst. God is ready to furnish us with strength
in a combat, and cordials after it.

4. The goodness of God is seen in temptations, in discovering and
advancing inward grace by this means. The issue of a temptation
of a Christian is often like that of Christ's, the manifesting a greater
vigor of the Divine nature, in affections to God, and enmity to sin.
Spices perfume not the air with their scent till they are invaded by
the fire: the truth of grace is evidenced by them. The assault of
an enemy revives, and actuates that strength and courage which is

in a man, perhaps unknown to himself, as well as others, till he meets with an adversary: many seem good, not that they are so in themselves, but for want of a temptation: this many times verifies a virtue, which was owned upon trust before, and discovers that we had more grace than we thought we had. The solicitations of Joseph's mistress cleared up his chastity: we are many times under temptation, as a candle under the snuffer; it seems to be out, but presently burns the clearer. Afflictions are like those clouds which look black, and eclipse the sun from the earth, but yet, when they drop, refresh that ground they seem to threaten, and multiply the grain on the earth, to serve for our food; and so our troubles, while they wet us to the skin, wash much of that dust from our graces which in a clearer day had been blown upon us. Too much rest corrupts; exercise teacheth us to manage our weapons: the spiritual armor would grow rusty, without opportunity to furbish it up; faith receives a new heart by every combat, and by every victory; like a fire, it spreads itself further, and gathers strength by the blowing of the wind. While the gardener commands his servant to shake the tree, he intends to fasten its roots, and settle it firmer in its place; and is this an ill-will to the plant?

5. His goodness is seen in temptations, in preventing sin which we were likely to fall into. Paul's thorn in the flesh was to prevent the pride of his spirit, and let out the windiness of his heart (2 Cor. xii. 7), lest it should be exalted above measure. The goodness of God makes the devil a polisher, while he intends to be a destroyer. The devil never works, but suitably to some corruption lurking in us: Divine goodness makes his fiery darts a means to discover, and so to prevent the treachery of that perfidious inmate in our hearts; humility is a greater benefit than a putrefying pride; if God brings us into a wilderness to be tempted of the devil, it is to bring down our loftiness, to starve our carnal confidence, and expel our rusting "security" (Deut. viii. 2); we many times fly under a temptation to God, from whom we sat too loose before. Is it not goodness to use those means that may drive us into his own arms? It is not a want of goodness to soap the garment, in order to take away the spots; we have reason to bless God for the assaults from hell, as well as pure mercies from heaven; and it is a sin to overlook the one as well as the other, since Divine goodness shines in both.

6. The goodness of God is seen in temptations, in fitting us more for his service. Those whom God intends to make choice instruments in his service, are first seasoned with strong temptations, as timber reserved for the strong beams of a building is first exposed to sun and wind, to make it more compact for its proper use. By this men are brought to answer the end of their creation, the service of God, which is their proper goodness. Peter was, after his foil by a temptation, more courageous in his Master's cause than before, and the more fitted to strengthen his brethren.

Thus the goodness of God appears in all parts of his government.

V. I shall now come to the *Use*. First, Of instruction.

1. If God be so good, how unworthy is the contempt or abuse of his goodness! (1.) The contempt and abuse of Divine goodness is

frequent and common; it began in the first ages of the world, and commenced a few moments after the creation; it hath not to this day diminished its affronts; Adam began the dance, and his posterity have followed him; the injury was directed against this, when he entertained the seducer's notion of God's being an envious Deity, in not indulging such a knowledge as he might have afforded him (Gen. iii. 5): "God doth know, that you shall be as gods, knowing good and evil." The charge of envy is utterly inconsistent with pure goodness. What was the language of this notion, so easily entertained by Adam, but that the tempter was better than God, and the nature of God as base and sordid as the nature of a devil? Satan paints God with his own colors, represents him as envious and malicious as himself; Adam admires, and believes the picture to be true, and hangs it up as a beloved one in the closet of his heart. The devil still drives on the same game, fills men's hearts with the same sentiments, and by the same means he murdered our first parents, he redoubles the stabs to his posterity. Every violation of the Divine law is a contempt of God's goodness, as well as his sovereignty, because his laws are the products both of the one and the other. Goodness animates them, while sovereignty enjoys them: God hath commanded nothing but what doth conduce to our happiness. All disobedience implies, that his law is a snare to entrap us, and make us miserable, and not an act of kindness, to render us happy, which is a disparagement to this perfection, as if he had commanded what would promote our misery, and prohibited what would conduce to our blessedness: to go far from him, and walk after vanity, is to charge him with our iniquity, and unrighteousness, baseness, and cruelty, in his commands: God implies it by his speech (Jer. ii. 5), "What iniquity have your fathers found in me, that they are gone far from me, and walked after vanity?" as if, like a tyrant, he had consulted cruelty in the composure of them, and designed to feast himself with the blood and misery of his creatures. Every sin is, in its own nature, a denial of God to be the chiefest good and happiness, and implies that it is no great matter to lose him: it is a forsaking him as the Fountain of Life, and a preferring a cracked and "empty cistern" as the chief happiness before him (Jer. ii. 13). Though sin is not so evil as God is good, yet it is the greatest evil, and stands in opposition to God as the greatest good. Sin disorders the frame of the world; it endeavored to frustrate all the communications of Divine goodness in creation, and to stop up the way of any further streams of it to his creatures.

(2.) The abuse and contempt of the Divine goodness is base and disingenious. It is the highest wickedness, because God is the highest goodness, pure goodness that cannot have anything in him worthy of our contempt. Let men injure God under what notion they will, they injure his goodness; because all his attributes are summed up in this one, and all, as it were, deified by it. For whatsoever power or wisdom he might have, if he were destitute of this he were not God: the contempt of his goodness implies him to be the greatest evil, and worst of beings. Badness, not goodness, is the proper object of contempt: as respect is a propension of mind to something that is good, so contempt is an alienation of the mind from something as evil, either simply or supposedly evil in its nature, or base or unworthy in its action towards that person that contemns it. As men desire nothing but what they apprehend to be good, so they slight nothing but what they apprehend to be evil: since nothing, therefore, is more contemned by us than God, nothing more spurned at by us than God, it will follow that we regard him as the most loathsome and despicable being, which is the greatest baseness. And our contempt of him is worse than that of the devils; they injure him under the inevitable strokes of his justice, and we slight him when we are surrounded with the expressions of his bounty; they abuse him under vials of wrath, and we under a plenteous liberality: they malice him, because he inflicts on them what is hurtful; and we despise him, because he commands what is profitable, holy, and honorable, in its own nature, though not in our esteem. They are not under those high obligations as we; they abuse his creating, and we his redeeming goodness: he never sent his Son to shed a drop of blood for their recovery; they can expect nothing but the torment of their persons, and the destruction of their works; but we abuse that goodness that would rescue us since we are miserable, as well as that righteousness which created us innocent. How base is it to use him so ill, that is not once or twice, but a daily, hourly Benefactor to us; whose rain drops upon the earth for our food, and whose sun shines upon the earth for our pleasure as well as profit: such a Benefactor as is the true Proprietor of what we have, and thinks nothing too good for them that think everything too much for his service! How unworthy is it to be guilty of such base carriage towards him, whose benefits we cannot want, nor live without! How disingenious both to God and ourselves, to " despise the riches of his goodness, that are designed to lead us to repentance" (Rom. ii. 4), and by that to happiness! And more heinous are the sins of renewed men upon this account, because they are against his " goodness" not only offered to them, but tasted by them; not only against the notion of goodness, but the experience of goodness, and the relished sweetness of choicest bounty.

(3). God takes this contempt of his goodness heinously. He never upbraids men with anything in the Scripture, but with the abuse of the good things he hath vouchsafed them, and the unmindfulness of the obligations arising from them. This he bears with the greatest regret and indignation. Thus he upbraids Eli with the preference of him to the priesthood above other families (1 Sam. ii. 28): and David with his exaltation to the crown of Israel (2 Sam. xii. 7—9), when they abused those honors to carelessness and licentiousness. All sins offend God, but sins against his goodness do more disparage him; and, therefore, his fury is the greater, by how much the more liberally his benefits have been dispensed. It was for abuse of Divine goodness, as soon as it was tasted, that some angels were hurled from their blessed habitation and more happy nature: it was for this Adam lost his present enjoyments, and future happiness, for the abuse of God's goodness in creation. For the abuse of God's goodness the old world fell under the fury

of the flood; and for the contempt of the Divine goodness in redemption, Jerusalem, once the darling city of the infinite Monarch
of the world, was made an Aceldema, a field of blood.   For this
cause it is, that candlesticks have been removed, great lights put
out, nations overturned, and ignorance hath triumphed in places
bright before with the beams of heaven.   God would have little care
of his own goodness, if he always prostituted the fruits of it to our
contempt.   Why should we expect he should always continue that
to us which he sees we will never use to his service?   When the
Israelites would dedicate the gifts of God to the service of Baal,
then he would return, and take away his corn, and his wine, and
make them know by the loss, that those things were his in dominion, which they abused, as if they had been sovereign lords of
them (Hos. ii. 8, 9).   Benefits are entailed upon us no longer than
we obey (Josh. xxiv. 20): " If you forsake the Lord, he will do you
hurt, after he hath done you good."   While we obey, his bounty
shall shower upon us : and when we revolt, his justice shall consume us.   Present mercies abused, are no bulwarks against independent judgments.   Got hath curses as well as blessings ; and they
shall light more heavy when his blessings have been more weighty:
justice is never so severe as when it comes to right goodness, and
revenge its quarrel for the injuries received.

A convenient inquiry may be here, How God's goodness is contemned or abused?

1st. By a forgetfulness of his benefits.   We enjoy the mercies,
and forget the Donor; we take what he gives, and pay not the
tribute he deserves ; the " Israelites forgot God their Saviour, which
had done great things in Egypt" (Ps. cvi. 21).   We send God's
mercies where we would have God send our sins, into the land of
forgetfulness, and write his benefits where himself will write the
names of the wicked, in the dust, which every wind defaceth : the
remembrance soon wears out of our minds, and we are so far from
remembering what we had before, that we scarce think of that hand
that gives, the very instant wherein his benefits drop upon us.
Adam basely forgot his Benefactor, presently after he had been
made capable to remember him, and reflect upon him ; the first remark we hear of him, is of his forgetfulness, not a syllable of his
thankfulness.   We forget those souls he hath lodged in us, to acknowledge his favors to our bodies; we forget that image wherewith he beautified us, and that Christ he exposed as a criminal to
death for our rescue, which is such an act of goodness as cannot be
expressed by the eloquence of the tongue, or conceived by the
acuteness of the mind.   Those things which are so common, that
they cannot be invisible to our eyes, are unregarded by our minds ;
our sense prompts our understanding, and our understanding is deaf
to the plain dictates of our sense.   We forget his goodness in the
sun, while it warms us, and his showers while they enrich us ; in
the corn, while it nourisheth us, and the wine while it refresheth
us ; " She did not know that I gave her corn, and wine, and oil"
(Hos. ii. 8) : she that might have read my hand in every bit of
bread, and every drop of drink, did not consider this.   It is an in-

justice to forget the benefits we receive from man; it is a crime of a higher nature to forget those dispensed to us by the hand of God, who gives us those things that all the world cannot furnish us with, without him. The inhabitants of Troas will condemn us, who worshipped mice, in a grateful remembrance of the victory they had made easy for them, by gnawing their enemies' bow-strings. They were mindful of the courtesy of animals, though unintended by those creatures; and we are regardless of the fore-meditated bounty of God. It is in God's judgment a brutishness beyond that of a stupid ox, or a duller ass; "The ox knows his owner, and the ass his master's crib: but Israel doth not know, my people do not consider" (Isa. i. 3). The ox knows his owner that pastures him, and the ass his master that feeds him; but man is not so good as to be like to them, but so bad as to be inferior to them: he forgets Him that sustains him, and spurns at him, instead of valuing him for the benefits conferred by him. How horrible is it, that God should lose more by his bounty, than he would do by his parsimony! If we had blessings more sparingly, we should remember him more gratefully. If he had sent us a bit of bread in a distress by a miracle, as he did to Elijah by the ravens, it would have stuck longer in our memories; but the sense of daily favors soonest wears out of our minds, which are as great miracles as any in their own nature, and the products of the same power; but the wonder they should beget in us, is obscured by their frequency.

2d. The goodness of God is contemned by an impatient murmuring. Our repinings proceed from an inconsideration of God's free liberality, and an ungrateful temper of spirit. Most men are guilty of this. It is implied in the commendation of Job under his pressures (Job i. 22): "In all this Job sinned not, nor charged God foolishly," as if it were a character peculiar to him, whereby he verified the eulogy God had given of him before (ver. 8), that there was "none like him in the earth, a perfect and an upright man." What is implied by the expression? but that scarce a man is to be found without unjust complaints of God, and charging him under their crosses with cruelty; when in the greatest they have much more reason to bless him for his bounty in the remainder. Good men have not been innocent. Baruch complains of God for adding grief to his sorrow, not furnishing him with those "great things" he expected (Jer. xlv. 3, 4); whereas, he had matter of thankfulness in God's gift of his life as a prey. But his master chargeth God in a higher strain: "O Lord, thou hast deceived me, and I was deceived: I am in derision daily" (Jer. xx. 7). When he met with reproach instead of success in the execution of his function, he quarrels with God, as if he had a mind to cheat him into a mischief, when he had more reason to bless him for the honor of being employed in his service. Because we have not what we expect, we slight his goodness in what we enjoy. If he cross us in one thing, he might have made us successless in more: if he take away some things, he might as well have taken away all. The unmerited remainder, though never so little, deserves our acknowledgements more than the deserved loss can justify our repining. And for that which is snatched from us, there is more cause to be thankful, that we have enjoyed it so long, than to murmur that we possess it no longer. Adam's sin implies a repining: he imagined God had been short in his goodness, in not giving him a knowledge he foolishly conceived himself capable of, and would venture a forfeiture of what already had been bountifully bestowed upon him. Man thought God had envied him, and ever since man studies to be even with God, and envies him the free disposal of his own doles: all murmuring, either in our own cause or others, charges God with a want of goodness, because there is a want of that which he foolishly thinks would make himself or others happy. The language of this sin is, that man thinks himself better than God; and if it were in his power, would express a more plentiful goodness than his Maker. As man is apt to think himself " more pure than God" (Job iv. 17), so of a kinder nature also than an infinite goodness. The Israelites are a wonderful example of this contempt of Divine goodness; they had been spectators of the greatest miracles, and partakers of the choicest deliverance: he had solicited their redemption from captivity; and when words would not do, he came to blows for them, musters up his judgments against their enemies, and, at last, as the Lord of hosts and God of battles, totally defeats their pursuers, and drowns them and their proud hopes of victory in the Red Sea. Little account was made of all this by the redeemed ones; "they lightly esteemed the rock of their salvation," and launch into greater unworthiness, instead of being thankful for the breaking their yoke: they are angry with him, that he had done so much for them: they repented that ever they had complied with him, for their own deliverance, and had a regret that they had been brought out of Egypt: they were angry that they were freemen, and that their chains had been knocked off: they were more desirous to return to the oppression of their Egyptian tyrants, than have God for their governor and caterer, and be fed with his manna. " It was well with us in Egypt: Why came we forth out of Egypt?" which is called a " despising the Lord" (Numb. xi. 18, 20). They were so far from rejoicing in the expectation of the future benefits promised them, that they murmured that they had not enjoyed less; they were so sottish, as to be desirous to put themselves into the irons whence God had delivered them: they would seek a remedy in that Egypt, which had been the prison of their nation, and under the successors of that Pharaoh, who had been the invader of their liberties; they would snatch Moses from the place where the Lord, by an extraordinary providence, hath established him; they would stone those that minded them of the goodness of God to them, and thereupon of their crime and their duty (Numb. xvi. 3, 9—11); they rose against their benefactors, and "murmured against God," that had strengthened the hands of their deliverers; they "despised the manna" he had sent them, and "despised the pleasant land" he intended them (Ps. cvi. 24): all which was a high contempt of God and his unparalleled goodness and care of them. All murmuring is an accusation of Divine goodness.

3d. By unbelief and impenitency. What is the reason we come not to Him when he calls us; but some secret imagination that he is of an ill nature, means not as he speaks, but intends to mock us, instead of welcoming us? When we neglect his call, spurn at his bowels, slight the riches of his grace; as it is a disparagement to his wisdom to despise his counsel, so it is to his goodness to slight his offers, as though you could make better provision for yourselves than he is able or willing to do. It disgraceth that which is designed to the praise of the glory of his grace, and renders God cruel to his own Son, as being an unnecessary shedder of his blood. As the devil by his temptation of Adam, envied God the glory of his creating goodness, so unbelief envies God the glory of his redeeming grace: it is a bidding defiance to him, and challenging him to muster. up the legions of his judgments, rather than have sent his Son to suffer for us, or his Spirit to solicit us. Since the sending his Son was the greatest act of goodness that God could express, the refusal of him must be the highest reproach of that liberality God designed to commend to the world in so rare a gift: the ingratitude in this refusal must be as high in the rank of sins, as the person slighted is in the rank of beings, or rank of gifts. Christ is a gift (Rom. v. 16), the royalest gift, an unparalleled gift, springing from inconceivable treasures of goodness (John iii. 16). What is our turning our backs upon this gift but a low opinion of it? as though the richest jewel of heaven were not so valuable as a swinish pleasure on earth, and deserved to be treated at no other rate than if mere offals had been presented to us. The plain language of it is, that there were no gracious intentions for our welfare in this present; and that he is not as good, in the mission of his Son, as he would induce us to imagine. Impenitence is also an abuse of this goodness, either by presumption, as if God would entertain rebels that bid defiance against him with the same respect that he doth his prostrate and weeping suppliants; that he will have the same regard to the swine as to the children, and lodge them in the same habitation; or it speaks a suspicion of God as a deceitful Master, one of a pretended, not a real goodness, that makes promises to mock men, and invitations to delude them: that he is an implacable tyrant, rather than a good Father; a rigid, not a kind Being, delightful only to mark our faults, and overlook our services.

4th. The goodness of God is contemned by a distrust of his providence. As all trust in him supposeth him good, so all distrust of him supposeth him evil; either without goodness to exert his power, or without power to display his goodness. Job seems to have a spice of this in his complaint (Job xxx. 20), "I cry unto thee, and thou dost not hear me; I stand up, and thou regardest me not." It is a fume of the serpent's venom, first breathed into man, to suspect him of cruelty, severity, regardlessness, even under the daily evidences of his good disposition: and it is ordinary not to believe him when he speaks, nor credit him when he acts; to question the goodness of his precepts, and misinterpret the kindness of his providence; as if they were designed for the supports of a tyranny, and the deceit of the miserable. Thus the Israelites thought their miraculous deliverance from Egypt, and the placing them in security in the wilderness, was intended only to pound them up for a slaughter (Numb. xiv. 3): thus they defiled the lustre of Divine goodness which they had so highly experimented, and placed not that confidence in him which was due to so frequent a Benefactor, and thereby crucified the rich kindness of God, as Genebrard translates the word "limited" (Ps. lxxviii. 41). It is also a jealousy of Divine goodness, when we seek to deliver ourselves from our straits by unlawful ways, as though God had not kindness enough to deliver us without committing evil. What! did God make a world, and all creatures in it, to think of them no more, not to concern himself in their affairs? If he be good, he is diffusive, and delights to communicate himself; and what subjects should there be for it, but those that seek him, and implore his assistance? It is an indignity to Divine bounty to have such mean thoughts of it, that it should be of a nature contrary to that of his works, which, the better they are, the more diffusive they are. Doth a man distrust that the sun will not shine any more, or the earth not bring forth its fruit? Doth he distrust the goodness of an approved medicine for the expelling his distemper? If we distrust those things, should we not render ourselves ridiculous and sottish? and if we distrust the Creator of those things, do we not make ourselves contemners of his goodness? If his caring for us be a principal argument to move us to cast our care upon him, as it is 1 Pet. v. 7, "Casting your care upon him, for he cares for you;" then, if we cast not our care upon him, it is a denial of his gracious care of us, as if he regarded not what becomes of us.

5th. We do contemn or abuse his goodness by omissions of duty. These sometimes spring from injurious conceits of God, which end in desperate resolutions. It was the crime of a good prophet in his passion (2 Kings vi. 33): "This evil is of the Lord, why should I wait on the Lord any longer?" God designs nothing but mischief to us, and we will seek him no longer. And the complaint of those in Malachi (Mal. iii. 14) is of the same nature; "Ye have said, It is vain to serve God; and what profit is it that we have kept his ordinances?" We have all this while served a hard Master, not a Benefactor, and have not been answered with advantages proportionable to our services; we have met with a hand too niggardly to dispense that reward which is due to the largeness of our offerings. When men will not lift up their eyes to heaven, and solicit nothing but the contrivance of their own brain, and the industry of their own heads, they disown Divine goodness, and approve themselves as their own gods, and the spring of their own prosperity. Those that run not to God in their necessity, to crave his support, deny either the arm of his power, or the disposition of his will, to sustain and deliver them: they must have very mean sentiments, or none at all, of this perfection, or think him either too empty to fill them, or too churlish to relieve them; that he is of a narrow and contracted temper, and that they may sooner expect to be made better and happier by anything else than by him: and as we contemn his goodness by a total omission of those duties which respect our own advantage and supply, as prayer; so we contemn him as the chiefest good, by an omission of the due manner of any act of worship which is designed purely for the acknowledgment of him. As every omission of the material part of a duty is a denial of his sovereignty as commanding it, so every omission of the manner of it, not performing it with due esteem and valuation of him, a surrender of all the powers of our soul to him, is a denial of him as the most amiable object. But certainly to omit those addresses to God which his precept enjoins, and his excellency deserves, speaks this language, that they can be well enough, and do well enough, without God, and stand in no need of his goodness to maintain them. The neglect or refusal in a malefactor to supplicate for his pardon, is a wrong to, and contempt of, the prince's goodness: either implying that he hath not a goodness in his nature worthy of an address, or that he scorns to be obliged to him for any exercise of it.

6th. The goodness of God is contemned, or abused, in relying upon our services to procure God's good will to us. As, when we stand in need either of some particular mercy, or special assistance; when pressures are heavy, and we have little hopes of ease in an ordinary way; when the devotions in course have not prevailed for what we want; we engage ourselves by extraordinary vows and promises to God, hereby to open that goodness which seems to be locked up from us.[k] Sometimes, indeed, vows may proceed from a sole desire to engage ourselves to God, from a sense of the levity and inconstancy of our spirits; binding ourselves to God by something more sacred and inviolable than a common resolution. But many times the vowing the building of a temple, endowing a hospital, giving so much in alms if God will free them from a fit of sickness, and spin out the thread of their lives a little longer (as hath been frequent among the Romanists), arises from an opinion of laziness and a selfishness in the Divine goodness; that it must be squeezed out by some solemn promises of returns to him, before it will exercise itself to take their parts. Popular vows are often the effects of an ignorance of the free and bubbling nature of this perfection of the generousness and royalty of Divine goodness: as if God were of a mean and mechanic temper, not to part with anything unless he were in some measure paid for it; and of so bad a nature as not to give passage to any kindness to his creature without a bribe. It implies also that he is of an ignorant as well as contracted goodness; that he hath so little understanding, and so much weakness of judgment, as to be taken with such trifles, and ceremonial courtships, and little promises; and meditated only low designs, in imparting his bounty: it is just as if a malefactor should speak to a prince,—Sir, if you will but bestow a pardon upon me, and prevent the death I have merited for this crime, I will give you this rattle. All vows made with such a temper of spirit to God, are as injurious and abusive to his goodness, as any man will judge such an offer to be to a majestic and gracious prince; as if it were a trading, not a free and royal goodness.

7th. The goodness of God is abused when we give up our souls and affections to those benefits we have from God; when we make

[k] Amyral. Moral. Tom. IV. p. 291.

those things God's rivals, which were sent to woo us for him, and offer those affections to the presents themselves, which they were sent to solicit for the Master. This is done, when either we place our trust in them, or glue our choicest affections to them. This charge God brings against Jerusalem, the trusting in her own beauty, glory, and strength, though it was a comeliness put upon her by God (Ezek. xvi. 14, 15). When a little sunshine of prosperity breaks out upon us, we are apt to grasp it with so much eagerness and closeness, as if we had no other foundation to settle ourselves upon, no other being that might challenge from us our sole dependence. And the love of ourselves, and of creatures above God, is very natural to us: "Lovers of themselves, and lovers of pleasure more than of God" (2 Tim. iii. 2, 4). Self-love is the root, and the love of pleasures the top branch, that mounts its head highest against heaven. It is for the love of the world that the dangers of the sea are passed over, that men descend into the bowels of the earth, pass nights without sleep, undertake suits without intermission, wade through many inconveniences, venture their souls, and contemn God; in those things men glory, and foolishly grow proud by them, and think themselves safe and happy in them.[1] Now to love ourselves above God, is to own ourselves better than God, and that we transcend him in an amiable goodness; or, if we love ourselves equal with God, it at least manifests that we think God no better than ourselves; and think ourselves our own chief good, and deny anything above us to outstrip us in goodness, whereby to deserve to be the centre of our affections and actions, and to love any other creature above him, is to conclude some defect in God; that he hath not so much goodness in his own nature as that creature hath, to complete our felicity; that God is a slighter thing than that creature. It is to account God, what all the things in the world are,—an imaginary happiness, a goodness of clay; and them what God is,—a Supreme Goodness. It is to value the goodness of a drop above that of the spring, and the goodness of the spark above that of the sun. As if the bounty of God were of a less alloy than the advantages we immediately receive from the hands of a silly worm. By how much the better we think a creature to be, and place our affections chiefly upon it, by so much the more deficient and indigent we conclude God; for God wants so much in our conception, as the other thing hath goodness above him in our thoughts. Thus is God lessened below the creature, as if he had a mixture of evil in him, and were capable of an imperfect goodness. He that esteems the sun that shines upon him, the clothes that warm him, the food that nourisheth him, or any other benefit above the Donor, regards them as more comely and useful than God himself; and behaves himself as if he were more obliged to them than to God, who bestowed those advantageous qualities upon them.

8th. The Divine goodness is contemned, in sinning more freely upon the account of that goodness, and employing God's benefits in a drudgery for our lusts. This is a treachery to his goodness, to make his benefits serve for an end quite contrary to that for which

[1] Cressol. Antholog. Part II. p. 29.

ON THE GOODNESS OF GOD

he sent them.   As if God had been plentiful in his blessings, to hire them to be more fierce in their rebellions, and fed them to no other purpose, but that they might more strongly kick against him; this is the fruit which corrupt nature produceth.   Thus the Egyptians, who had so fertile a country, prove unthankful to the Creator, by adoring the meanest creatures, and putting the sceptre of the Monarch of the world into the hands of the sottishest and cruellest beasts. And the Romans multiply their idols, as God multiplied their victories.   This is also the complaint of God concerning Israel: "She did not know that I gave her corn, and wine, and oil, and multiplied her silver and gold, which they prepared for Baal" (Hos. ii. 8). They ungratefully employed the blessings of God in the worship of an idol against the will of the Donor.   So in Hos. x. 1; "According to the multitude of his fruit, he hath increased the altars; according to the goodness of his land, they have made goodly images."   They followed their own inventions with the strength of my outward blessings; as their wealth increased, they increased the ornaments of their images; so that what were before of wood and stone, they advanced to gold and silver.   And the like complaint you may see Ezek. 16, 17.   Thus,

[1.]   The benefits of God are abused to pride, when men standing upon a higher ground of outward prosperity, vaunt it loftily above their neighbors; the common fault of those that enjoy a worldly sunshine, which the apostle observes in his direction to Timothy; "Charge them that are rich in this world, that they be not high-minded" (1 Tim. vi. 17).   It is an ill use of Divine blessings to be filled by them with pride and wind.   Also,

[2.]   When men abuse plenty to ease; because they have abundance, spend their time in idleness, and make no other use of Divine benefits than to trifle away their time, and be utterly useless to the world.

[3.]   When they also abuse peace and other blessing to security; as they which would not believe the threatenings of judgment, and the storm coming from a far country, because the Lord was in Sion, and her King in her; "Is not the Lord in Sion, is not her King in her" (Jer. viii. 19)? thinking they might continue their progress in their sin, because they had the temple, the seat of the Divine glory, Sion, and the promise of an everlasting kingdom to David; abusing the promise of God to presumption and security, and turning the grace of God into wantonness.

[4.]   Again, when they abuse the bounty of God to sensuality and luxury, misemploying the provisions God gives them, in resolving to live like beasts, when by a good improvement of them, they might attain the life of angels.   Thus is the light of the sun abused to conduct them, and the fruits of the earth abused to enable them to their prodigious debauchery: as we do, saith one, with the Thames, which brings us in provision, and we soil it with our rubbish.[m]   The more God sows his gifts, the more we sow our cockle and darnel.   Thus we make our outward happiness the most unhappy part of our lives, and by the strength of Divine blessings, exceed all laws of reason and religion too.   How unworthy a carriage is this, to use the express-

[m] Young, of Affliction, p. 34.

ions of Divine goodness as occasions of a greater outrage and affront of him ; when we stab his honor by those instruments he puts into our hands to glorify him ! as if a favorite should turn that sword into the bowels of his prince, wherewith he knighted him ; and a servant, enriched by a lord, should hire by that wealth, murderers to take away his life ! How brutish is it, the more God courts us with his blessings, the more to spurn at him with our feet ; like the mule that lifts up his heel against the dam, as soon as ever it hath sucked her ! We never beat God out of our hearts, but by his own gifts ; he receives no blows from men, but by those instruments he gave them to promote their happiness. While man is an enjoyer, he makes God a loser, by his own blessings ; inflames his rebellion by those benefits which should kindle his love ; and runs from him by the strength of those favors which should endear the donor to him : " Do you thus requite the Lord, O foolish people, and unwise ?" is the expostulation (Deut. xxxii. 6.) Divine goodness appears in the complaint of the abuse of it, in giving them titles below their crime, and complaining more of their being unfaithful to their own interest, than enemies to his glory : " foolish and unwise" in neglecting their own happiness ; a charge below the crime, which deserved to be " abominable, ungrateful people to a prodigy." All this carriage towards God, is as if a man should knock the chirurgeon on the head, as soon as he hath set and bound up his dislocated members. So God compares the ungrateful behavior of the Israelites against him : " Though I have bound and strengthened their arms, yet do they imagine mischief against me" (Hos. vii. 15) : a metaphor taken from a chirurgeon that applies corroborating plasters to a broken limb.

9th. We contemn the goodness of God, in ascribing our benefits to other causes than Divine goodness. Thus Israel ascribed her felicity, plenty, and success, to her idols, as " rewards which her lovers had given her" (Hos. ii. 5, 12). And this charge Daniel brought home upon Belshazzar : " Thou hast praised the gods of silver, and gold, and brass, and iron ; and the God in whose hand is thy breath, and whose are all thy ways, hast thou not glorified" (Dan. v. 23). The God who hath given success to the arms of thy ancestors, and conveyed by their hands so large a dominion to thee, thou hast not honored in the same rank with the sordidest of thy idols. It is the same case, when we own him not as the author of any success in our affairs, but by an overweening conceit of our own sagacity, applaud and admire ourselves, and overlook the hand that conducted us, and brought our endeavors to a good issue. We eclipse the glory of Divine goodness, by setting the crown that is due to it upon the head of our own industry ; a sacrilege worse than Belshazzar's drinking of wine with his lords and concubines in the sacred vessels pilfered from the temple ; as in that place of Daniel. This was the proud vaunt of the Assyrian conqueror, for which God threatens to punish the fruit of his stout heart : " By the strength of my hand, I have done it, and by my wisdom ; for I am prudent ;" and, " I have removed the bounds of the people, and have robbed their treasures ;" and, " I have put down the inhabitants like a valiant man" (Isa. x. 12–14). Not a word of Divine goodness and assistance in all this, but applauding

his own courage and conduct.   This is a robbing of God, to set up
ourselves, and making Divine goodness a footstool, to ascend into
his throne.   And as it is unjust, so it is ridiculous, to ascribe to ourselves, or instruments, the chief honor of any work; as ridiculous
as if a soldier, after a victory, should erect an altar to the honor of
his sword; or an artificer offer sacrifices to the tools whereby he completed some excellent and useful invention : a practice that every
rational man would disdain, where he should see it.   It is a discard-
ing any thoughts of the goodness of God, when we imagine, that
we chiefly owe anything in this world to our own industry or wit,
to friends or means, as though Divine goodness did not open its hand
to interest itself in our affairs, support our ability, direct our counsels, and mingle itself with anything we do.   God is the principal
author of any advantage that accrues to us, of any wise resolution
we fix upon, or any proper way we take to compass it ; no man can
be wise in opposition to God, act wisely, or well without him ; his
goodness inspires men with generous and magnificent counsels, and
furnisheth them with fit and proportionable means ; when he withdraws his hand, men's heads grow foolish, and their hands feeble ;
folly and weakness drop upon them, as darkness upon the world
upon the removal of the sun ; it is an abuse of Divine goodness not
to own it, but erect an idol in its place.   Ezra was of another mind
when he ascribed to the good hand of God the " providing ministers
for the temple," and not to his own care and diligence (chap. viii. 18) ;
and Nehemiah, the "success he had with the king" in the behalf of
his nation, and not solely to his favor with the prince, or the arts he
used to please him (chap. ii. 8).
   2.   The second information is this : If God be so good, it is a certain argument that man is fallen from his original state.   It is the
complaint of man, sometimes, that other creatures have more of
earthly happiness than men have ; live freer from cares and trouble,
and are not racked with that solicitousness and anxiety as man is :
have not such distempers to embitter their lives.   It is a good ground
for man to look into himself, and consider whether he hath not, some
ways or other, disobliged God more than other creatures can possibly do.   We often find that the creatures men have need of in this
state, do not answer the expectation of man : "Cursed be the ground
for thy sake" (Gen. iii. 17).   A fruitful land is made barren ; thorns
and thistles triumph upon the face of the earth, instead of good fruit.
Is it likely that that goodness, which is as infinite as his power, and
knows no more limits than his Almightiness, should imprint so many
scars upon the world, if he had not been heinously provoked by some
miscarriage of his creature?   Infinite Goodness could never move
Infinite Justice to inflict punishment upon creatures, if they had not
highly merited it ; we cannot think that any creature was blemished
with a principle of disturbance, as it came first out of the hand of
God.   All things were certainly settled in a due order and dependence upon one another ; nothing could be ungrateful and unuseful
to man by the original law of their creation ; if there had, it had not
been goodness, but evil and baseness, that had created the world.
When we see, therefore, the course of nature overturned, the order

Divine goodness had placed, disturbed; and the creatures pronounced good and useful to man, employed as instruments of vengeance against him; we must conclude some horrible blot upon human nature, and very odious to a God of infinite goodness; and that this blot was dashed upon man by himself, and his own fault; for it is repugnant to the infinite goodness of God to put into the creature a sinning nature, to hurry him into sin, and then punish him for that which he had impressed upon him. The goodness of God inclines him to love goodness wherever he finds it; and not to punish any that have not deserved it by their own crimes. The curse we therefore see the creatures groan under, the disorders in nature, the frustrating the expectations of man in the fruits of the earth and plentiful harvests, the trouble he is continually exposed to in the world, which tedders down his spirit from more generous employments, shows that man is not what he was when Divine goodness first erected him; but hath admitted into his nature something more uncomely in the eye of God; and so heinous, that it puts his goodness sometimes to a stand, and makes him lay aside the blessings his hand was filled with, to take up the arms of vengeance, wherewith to fight against the world. Divine goodness would have secured his creatures from any such invasions, and never used those things against man, which he designed in the first frame for man's service, were there not some detestable disorder risen in the nature of man which makes God withhold his liberality and change the dispensation of his numerous benefits into legions of judgments. The consideration of the Divine goodness, which is a notion that man naturally concludes to be inseparable from the Deity, would, to an unbiassed reason, verify the history of those punishments settled upon man in the third chapter of Genesis, and make the whole seem more probable to reason at the first relation. This instruction naturally flows from the doctrine of Divine goodness: if God be so good, it is a certain argument that man is fallen from his original state.

3. The third information is this: If God be infinitely good, there can be no just complaint against God, if men be punished for abusing his goodness. Man had nothing, nay, it was impossible he could have anything, from Infinite Goodness to disoblige him, but to engage him. God never did, nay, never could, draw his sword against man, till man had slighted him and affronted him by the strength of his own bounty. It is by this God doth justify his severest proceedings against men, and very seldom charges them with any else as the matter of their provocations (Hos. ii. 9): "Therefore will I return, and take away my corn in the time thereof, and my wine in the season thereof, and will recover my wool and my flax." And in Ezek. xvi., after he had drawn out a bill of complaint against them, and inserted only the abuse of his benefits, as a justification of what he intended to do; he concludes (ver. 27), "Behold, therefore, I have stretched out my hand over thee, and diminished thy ordinary food, and delivered thee unto the will of them that hate thee." When men suffer, they suffer justly; they were not constrained by any violence, or forced by any necessity, nor provoked by any ill usage, to turn head against God, but broke the bands of

the strongest obligations and most tender allurements. What man, what devil, can justly blame God for punishing them, after they had been so intolerably bold, as to fly in the face of that goodness that had obliged them, by giving them beings of a higher elevation than to inferior creatures, and furnishing them with sufficient strength to continue in their first habitation? Man seems to have less reason to accuse God of rigor than devils; since, after his unreasonable revolt, a more express goodness than that which created him hath solicited him to repentance, courted him by melting promises and expostulations, added undeniable arguments of bounty, and drawn out the choicest treasures of heaven, in the gift of his Son, to prevail over men's perversity. And yet man, after he might arrive to the height and happiness of an angel, will be fond of continuing in the meanness and misery of a devil; and more strongly link himself to the society of the damned spirits, wherein, by his first rebellion, he had incorporated himself. Who can blame God for vindicating his own goodness from such desperate contempts, and the extreme ingratitude of man? If God be good, it is our happiness to adhere to him; if we depart from him, we depart from goodness; and if evil happen to us, we cannot blame God, but ourselves, for our departure.[n] Why are men happy? because they cleave to God. Why are men miserable? because they recede from God. It is then our own fault that we are miserable; God cannot be charged with any injustice if we be miserable, since his goodness gave means to prevent it, and afterwards added means to recover us from it, but all despised by us. The doctrine of Divine goodness justifies every stone laid in the foundation of hell, and every spark in that burning furnace, since it is for the abuse of infinite goodness that it was kindled.

4. The fourth information: Here is a certain argument, both for God's fitness to govern the world, and his actual government of it.

(1.) This renders him fit for the government of the world, and gives him a full title to it. This perfection doth the Psalmist celebrate throughout the 107th Psalm, where he declares God's works of providence (ver. 8, 15, 21, 32). Power without goodness would deface, instead of preserving; ruin is the fruit of rigor without kindness; but God, because of his infinite and immutable goodness, cannot do anything unworthy of himself, and uncomely in itself, or destructive to any moral goodness in the creature. It is impossible he should do anything that is base, or act anything but for the best, because he is essentially and naturally, and, therefore, necessarily good. As a good tree cannot bring forth bad fruit, so a good God cannot produce evil acts, no more than a pure beam of the sun can engender so much as a mite of darkness, or infinite heat produce any particle of cold. As God is so much light, that he can be no darkness, so he is so much good, that he can have no evil; and because there is no evil in him, nothing simply evil can be produced by him. Since he is good by nature, all evil is against his nature, and God can do nothing against his nature; it would be a part of impotence in him to will that which is evil; and, therefore, the misery man

[n] Petav. Theolog. Dogmat. Vol. I. p. 407.

feels, as well as the sin whereby he deserves that misery, are said to
be from himself (Hos. xiii. 9): "O Israel, thou hast destroyed thyself!" And though God sends judgments upon the world, we have
shown these to be intended for the support and vindication of his
goodness. And Hezekiah judged no otherwise, when, after the
threatening of the devastation of his house, the plundering his treasures, and captivity of his posterity, he replies, "Good is the word of
the Lord, which thou hast spoken" (Isa. xxxix. 8). God cannot act
anything that is base and cruel, because his goodness is as infinite as
his power, and his power acts nothing but what his wisdom directs,
and his goodness moves him to. Wisdom is the head in government,
omniscience the eye, power the arm, and goodness the heart and
spirit in them, that animates all.

(2.) As goodness renders Him fit to govern the world, so God doth
actually govern the world. Can we understand this perfection aright,
and yet imagine that he is of so morose a disposition as to neglect
the care of his creatures? that his excellency, which was displayed
in framing the world, should withdraw and wrap up itself in his own
bosom, without looking out, and darting itself out in the disposal
of them? Can that which moved him first to erect a world, suffer
him to be unmindful of his own work? Would he design first to
display it in creation, and afterwards obscure the honor of it? That
cannot be entitled an infinite permanent goodness, which should be
so indifferent as to let the creatures tumble together as they please,
without any order, after he had moulded them in his hand. If goodness be diffusive and communicative of itself, can it consist with the
nature of it, to extend itself to the giving the creatures being, and
then withdraw and contract itself, not caring what becomes of them?
It is the nature of goodness, after it hath communicated itself, to enlarge its channels; that fountain that springs up in a little hollow
part of the earth, doth in a short progress increase its streams, and
widen the passages through which it runs; it would be a blemish to
Divine goodness, if it did desert what it made, and leave things to
wild confusions, which would be, if a good hand did not manage
them, and a good mind preside over them. This is the lesson intended to us by all his judgments (Dan. iv. 17), "That the living
may know that the Most High rules in the kingdoms of men." If
he doth not actually govern the world, he must have devolved it
somewhere, either to men or angels; not to men, who naturally want
a goodness and wisdom to govern themselves, much more to govern
others exactly. And, besides the misinterpretations of actions, they
are liable to the want of patience, to bear with the provocations of
the world; since some of the best at one time in the world, and, in the
greatest example of meekness and sweetness, would have kindled a
fire in heaven to have consumed the Samaritans, for no other affront
than a non-entertainment of their Master and themselves (Luke ix.
54). Nor hath he committed the disposal of things to angels, either
good or bad; though he useth them as instruments in his government, yet they are not the principal pilots to steer the world. Bad
angels certainly are not; they would make continual ravages, meditate ruin, never defeat their own counsels, which they manage by the

wicked as the instruments in the world, nor fill their spirits with disquiet and restlessness when they are engaged in some ruinous design, as often is experienced: nor hath he committed it to the good angels, who, for aught we know, are not more numerous than the evil ones are; but besides, we can scarcely think their finite nature capable of so much goodness, as to bear the innumerable debaucheries, villanies, blasphemies, vented in one year, one week, one day, one hour, throughout the world; their zeal for their Creator might well be supposed to move them to testify their affection to him in a constant and speedy righting of his injured honor upon the heads of the offenders. The evil angels have too much cruelty, and would have no care of justice, but take pleasure in the blood of the most innocent, as well as the most criminal; and the good angels have too little tenderness to suffer so many crimes: since the world, therefore, continues without those floods of judgments, which it daily merits; since, notwithstanding all the provocations, the order of it is preserved; it is a testimony that an Infinite Goodness holds the helm in his hands, and spreads its warm wings over it.

5. The fifth information is this: Hence we may infer the ground of all religion; it is this perfection of goodness. As the goodness of God is the lustre of all his attributes, so it is the foundation and link of all true religious worship: the natural religion of the heathens was introduced by the consideration of Divine goodness, in the being he had bestowed upon them, and the provisions that were made for them. Divine bounty was the motive to erect altars, and present sacrifices, though they mistook the object of their worship, and offered the dues of the Creator to the instruments whereby he conveyed his benefits to them: and you find, that the religion instituted by him among the Jews, was enforced upon them by the consideration of their miraculous deliverance from Egypt, the preservation of them in the wilderness, and the enfeoffing them in a land flowing with milk and honey. Every act of bounty and success the heathens received, moved them to appoint new feasts, and repeat their adorations of those deities they thought the authors and promoters of their victories and welfare. The devil did not mistake the common sentiment of the world in Divine service, when he alleged to God, that "Job did not fear him for nought," i. e. worship him for nothing (Job i. 9). All acts of devotion take their rise from God's liberality, either from what they have or from what they hope; praise speaks the possession, and prayer the expectation, of some benefit from his hand: though some of the heathens made fear to be the prime cause of the acknowledgment and worship of a deity, yet surely something else besides and beyond this established so great a thing as religion in the world; an ingenuous religion could never have been born into the world without a notion of goodness, and would have gaped its last as soon as this notion should have expired in the minds of men. What encouragement can fear of power give, without sense of goodness? just as much as thunder hath, to invite a man to the place where it is like to fall, and crush him. The nature of "fear" is to drive from, and the nature of "goodness" to allure to, the object: the Divine thunders, prodigies, and other armies

of his justice in the world, which are the marks of his power, could conclude in nothing but a slavish worship: fear alone would have made men blaspheme the Deity; instead of serving him, they would have fretted against him; they might have offered him a trembling worship; but they could never have, in their minds, thought him worthy of an adoration; they would rather have secretly complained of him, and cursed him in their heart, than inwarly have admired him: the issue would have been the same, which Job's wife advised him to, when God withdrew his protection from his goods and body: "Curse God, and die" (Job ii. 9). It is certainly the common sentiment of men, that he that acts cruelly and tyrannically, is not worthy of an integrity to be retained towards him in the hearts of his subjects; but Job fortifies himself against this temptation from his bosom friend, by the consideration of the good he had received from God, which did more deserve a worship from him than the present evil had reason to discourage it. Alas! what is only feared, is hated, not adored. Would any seek to an irreconcileable enemy? would any person affectionately list himself in the service of a man void of all good disposition? would any distressed person put up a petition to that prince, who never gave any experiment of the sweetness of his nature, but always satiated himself with the blood of the meanest criminals? All affection to service is rooted up when hopes of receiving good are extinguished: there could not be a spark of that in the world, which is properly called religion, without a notion of goodness; the existence of God is the first pillar, and the goodness of God in rewarding the next, upon which coming to him (which includes all acts of devotion) is established (Heb. xi. 6); "He that comes unto God, must believe that he is, and that he is a rewarder of them that diligently seek him:" if either of those pillars be not thought to stand firm, all religion falls to the ground. It is this, as the most agreeable motive, that the apostle James uses, to encourage men's approach to God, because "he gives liberally, and upbraideth not" (James i. 5). A man of a kind heart and a bountiful hand shall have his gate thronged with suppliants, who sometimes would be willing to lay down their lives; "for a good man one would even dare to die:" when one of a niggardly or tyrannical temper shall be destitute of all free and affectionate applications. What eyes would be lifted up to heaven? what hands stretched out, if there were not a knowledge of goodness there to enliven their hopes of speeding in their petitions? Therefore Christ orders our prayers to be directed to God as a Father, which is a title of tenderness, as well as a "Father in heaven," a mark of his greatness; the one to support our confidence, as well as the other to preserve our distance. God could not be ingenuously adored and acknowledged, if he were not liberal as well as powerful; the goodness of God is the foundation of all ingenuous religion, devotion and worship.

6. The sixth instruction: The goodness of God renders God amiable. His goodness renders him beautiful, and his beauty renders him lovely; both are linked together (Zech. ix. 17): "How great is his goodness! and how great is his beauty!" This is the most powerful attractive, and masters the affections of the soul: it

is goodness only supposed, or real, that is thought worthy to demerit our affections to anything. If there be not a reality of this, or at least an opinion and estimation of it in an object, it would want a force and vigor to allure our will. This perfection of God is the loadstone to draw us, and the centre for our spirits to rest in.

1. This renders God amiable to himself. His goodness is his " Godhead" (Rom. i. 20): by his Godhead is meant his goodness; if he loves his Godhead for itself, he loves his goodness for itself; he would not be good, if he did not love himself; and if there were anything more excellent, and had a greater goodness than himself, he would not be good if he did not love that greater goodness above himself; for not only a hatred of goodness is evil, but an indifferent or cold affection to goodness hath a tincture of evil in it. If God were not good, and yet should love himself in the highest manner, he would be the greatest evil, and do the greatest evil in that act; for he would set his love upon that which is not the proper object of such an affection, but the object of aversion: his own infinite excellency, and goodness of his nature, renders him lovely and delightful to himself; without this he could not love himself in a commendable and worthy way, and becoming the purity of a Deity; and he cannot but love himself for this; for, as creatures, by not loving him as the supreme good, deny him to be the choicest good, so God would deny himself, and his own goodness, if he did not love himself, and that for his goodness. But the apostle tells us, that " God cannot deny himself" (2 Tim. ii. 13). Self-love, upon this account, is the only prerogative of God, because there is not anything better than himself that can lay any just claim to his affections: he only ought to love himself, and it would be an injustice in him to himself, if he did not. He only can love himself for this: an infinite goodness ought to be infinitely loved, but he only being infinite, can only love himself according to the due merit of his own goodness. He cannot be so amiable to any man, to any angel, to the highest seraphim, as he is to himself; because he is only capable in regard of his infinite wisdom, to know the infiniteness of his own goodness. And no creature can love him as he ought to be loved, unless it had the same infinite capacity of understanding to know him, and of affection to embrace him. This first renders God amiable to himself.

2. It ought therefore to render him amiable to us. What renders him lovely to his own eye, ought to render him so to ours; and since, by the shortness of our understandings, we cannot love him as he merits, yet we should be induced by the measures of his bounty, to love him as we can. If this do not present him lovely to us, we own him rather a devil than a God: if his goodness moved him to frame creatures, his goodness moved him also to frame creatures for himself and his own glory. It is a mighty wrong to him not to look with a delightful eye upon the marks of it, and return an affection to God in some measure suitable to his liberality to us; we are descended as low as brutes, if we understand him not to be the perfect good; and we are descended as low as devils, if our affections are not attracted by it.

(1.) If God were not infinitely good, he could not be the object of supreme love. If he were finitely good, there might be other things as good as God, and then God in justice could not challenge our choicest affections to him above anything else: it would be a defect of goodness in him to demand it, because he would despoil that which were equally good with him, of its due and right to our affections, which it might claim from us upon the account of its goodness: God would be unjust to challenge more than was due to him; for he would claim that chiefly to himself which another had a lawful share in. Nothing can be supremely loved that hath not a triumphant excellency above all other things; where is an equality of goodness, neither can justly challenge a supremacy, but only an equality of affection.

(2.) This attribute of goodness renders him more lovely than any other attribute. He never requires our adoration of him so much as the strongest or wisest, but as the best of beings: he uses this chiefly to constrain and allure us. Why would he be feared or worshipped, but because " there is forgiveness with him" (Ps. cxxx. 4)? it is for his goodness' sake that he is sued to by his people in distress (Ps. xxv. 7), " For thy goodness' sake, O Lord." Men may be admired because of their knowledge, but they are affected because of their goodness: the will, in all the variety of objects it pursues, centres in this one thing of good as the term of its appetite. All things are beloved by men, because they have been bettered by them. Severity can never conquer enmity, and kindle love: were there nothing but wrath in the Deity, it would make him be feared, but render him odious, and that to an innocent nature. As the spouse speaks of Christ (Cant. v. 10, 11), so we may of God: though she commends him for his head, the excellency of his wisdom; his eyes, the extent of his omniscience; his hands, the greatness of his power; and his legs, the swiftness of his motions and ways to and for his people; yet the " sweetness of his mouth," in his gracious words and promises, closes all, and is followed with nothing but an exclamation, that " he is altogether lovely" (ver. 16). His mouth, in pronouncing pardon of sin, and justification of the person, presents him most lovely. His power to do good is admirable, but his will to do good is amiable: this puts a gloss upon all his other attributes. Though he had knowledge to understand the depth of our necessities, and power to prevent them, or rescue us from them, yet his knowledge would be fruitless, and his power useless, if he were of a rigid nature, and not touched with any sentiments of kindness.

(3.) This goodness therefore lays a strong obligation upon us. It is true he is lovely in regard of his absolute goodness, or the goodness of his nature, but we should hardly be persuaded to return him an affection without his relative goodness, his benefits to his creatures; we are obliged by both to love him.

[1.] By his absolute goodness, or the goodness of his nature. Suppose a creature had drawn its original from something else wherein God had no influx, and had never received the least mite of a benefit from him, but from some other hand, yet the infinite excellency and goodness of his nature would merit the love of that creature, and it would act sordidly and disingenuously if it did not discover a mighty respect for God : for what ingenuity could there be in a rational creature, that were possessed with no esteem for any nature filled with unbounded goodness and excellency, though he had never been obliged to him for any favor? That man is accounted odious, and justly despicable by man, that reproaches and disesteems, nay, that doth not value a person of a high virtue in himself, and an universal goodness and charity to others, though himself never stood in need of his charity, and never had any benefit conveyed from his hands, nor ever saw his face, or had any commerce with him : a value of such a person is but a just due to the natural claim of virtue.   And, indeed, the first object of love is God in the excellency of his own nature, as the first object of love in marriage is the person ; the portion is a thing consequent upon it.   To love God only for his benefits, is to love ourselves first, and him secondarily : to love God for his own goodness and excellency, is a true love of God ; a love of him for himself.   That flaming fire in his own breast, though we have not a spark of it, hath a right to kindle one in ours to him.

[2.] By his relative goodness, or that of his benefits.   Though the excellency of his own nature, wherein there is a combination of goodness, must needs ravish an apprehensive mind ; yet a reflection upon his imparted kindness, both in the beings we have from him, and the support we have by him, must enhance his estimation.   When the excellency of his nature, and the expressions of his bounty are in conjunction, the excellency of his own nature renders him estimable in a way of justice, and the greatness of his benefits renders him valuable in a way of gratitude : the first ravisheth, and the other allures and melts : he hath enough in his nature to attract, and sufficient in his bounty to engage our affections.   The excellency of his nature is strong enough of itself to blow up our affections to him, were there not a malignity in our hearts that represents him under the notion of an enemy ; therefore in regard of our corrupt state, the consideration of Divine largesses comes in for a share in the elevation of our affections.   For, indeed, it is a very hard thing for a man to love another, though never so well qualified, and of an eminent virtue, while he believes him to be his enemy, and one that will severely handle him, though he hath before received many good turns from him ; the virtue, valor, and courtesy of a prince, will hardly make him affected by those against whom he is in arms, and that are daily pilfered by his soldiers, unless they have hopes of a reparation from him, and future security from injuries.   Christ, in the repetition of the command to "love God with all our mind, with all our heart, and with all our soul," i. e. with such an ardency above all things which glitter in our eye, or can be created by him, considers him as "our God" (Matt. xxii. 37).   And the Psalmist considers him as one that had kindly employed his power for him, in the eruption of his love (Ps. xviii. 1), "I will love thee, O Lord, my strength ;" and so in Ps. cxvi. 1, "I love the Lord, because he hath heard the voice of my supplications." An esteem of the benefactor is inseparable from gratitude for the received benefits: and should not then the unparalleled kindness of God advance him in our thoughts, much more than slighter courtesies do a created benefactor in ours? It is an obligation on every man's nature to answer bounty with gratitude, and goodness with love. Hence you never knew any man, nor can the records of eternity produce any man, or devil, that ever hated any person, or anything as good in itself: it is a thing absolutely repugnant to the nature of any rational creature. The devils hate not God because he is good, but because he is not so good to them as they would have him; because he will not unlock their chains, turn them into liberty, and restore them to happiness; *i. e.* because he will not desert the rights of abused goodness. But how should we send up flames of love to that God, since we are under his direct beams, and enjoy such plentiful influences! If the sun is comely in itself, yet it is more amiable to us, by the light we see, and the warmth we feel.

1st. The greatness of his benefits have reason to affect us with a love to him. The impress he made upon our souls when he extracted us from the darkness of nothing; the comeliness he hath put upon us by his own breath; the care he took of our recovery, when we had lost ourselves; the expense he was at for our regaining our defaced beauty; the gift he made of his Son; the affectionate calls we have heard to over-master our corrupt appetites, move us to repentance, and make us disaffect our beloved misery; the loud sound of his word in our ears, and the more inward knockings of his Spirit in our heart; the offering us the gift of himself, and the everlasting happiness he courts us to, besides those common favors we enjoy in the world, which are all the streams of his rich bounty: the voice of all is loud enough to solicit our love, and the merit of all ought to be strong enough to engage our love: " there is none like the God of Jeshurun, who rides upon the heaven in thy help, and in his excellency on the sky" (Deut. xxxiii. 26).

2d. The unmeritedness of them doth enhance this. It is but reason to love him who hath loved us first (1 John iv. 19). Hath he placed his delight upon any when they were nothing, and after they were sinful; and shall he set his delight upon such vile persons, and shall not we set our love upon so excellent an object as himself? How base are we, if his goodness doth not constrain us to affect him who hath been so free in his favor to us, who have merited the quite contrary at his hands? If "his tender mercies are over all his works" (Ps. cxlv. 9), he ought for it to be esteemed by all his works that are capable of a rational estimation.

3d. Goodness in creatures makes them estimable, much more should the goodness of God render him lovely to us. If we love a little spark of goodness in this or that creature, if a drop be so delicious to us, shall not the immense Sun of goodness, the ever-flowing Fountain of all, be much more delightful? The original excellency always outstrips what is derived from it; if so mean and contracted an object as a little creature deserves estimation for a little mite communicated to it, so great and extended a goodness as is in the Creator much more merits it at our hands: he is good after the infinite methods of a Deity: a weak resemblance is lovely; much more amiable, then, must be the incomprehensible original of that. beauty. We love creatures for what we think to be good in them, though it may be hurtful; and shall we not love God, who is a real and unblemished goodness, and from whose hand are poured out all those blessings that are conveyed to us by second causes? The object that delights us, the capacity we have to delight in it, are both from him; our love, therefore, to him should transcend the affection we bear to any instruments he moves for our welfare. "Among the gods, there is none like thee, O Lord, neither are there any works like unto thy works" (Ps. lxxxvi. 8): among the pleasantest creatures there is none like the Creator, nor any goodness like unto his goodness. Shall we love the food that nourisheth us, and the medicine that cures us, and the silver whereby we furnish ourselves with useful commodities? Shall we love a horse, or dog, for the benefits we have by them? and shall not the spring of all those draw our souls after it, and make us aspire to the honor of loving and embracing Him who hath stored every creature with that which may pleasure us? But, instead of endeavoring to parallel our affection with his kindness, we endeavor to make our disingenuity as extensive and towering as his Divine goodness.

4th. This is the true end of the manifestation of his goodness, that he might appear amiable, and have a return of affection. Did God display his goodness only to be thought of, or to be loved? It is the want of such a return, that he hath usually aggravated, from the benefits he hath bestowed upon men. Every thought of him should be attended with a motion suitable to the excellency of his nature and works. Can we think those nobler spirits, the angels, look upon themselves, or those frames of things in the heavens and earth, without starting some practical affection to him for them? Their knowledge of his excellency and works cannot be a lazy contemplation: it is impossible their wills and affections should be a thousand miles distant from their understandings in their operations. It is not the least part of his condescending goodness to court in such methods the affections of us worms, and manifest his desire to be beloved by us. Let us give him, then, that affection he deserves, as well as demands, and which cannot be withheld from him without horrible sacrilege. There is nothing worthy of love besides him; let no fire be kindled in our hearts, but what may ascend directly to him.

7. The seventh instruction is this: This renders God a fit object of trust and confidence. Since none is good but God, none can be a full and satisfactory ground or object of confidence but God: as all things derive their beings, so they derive their helpfulness to us from God; they are not, therefore, the principal objects of trust, but that goodness alone that renders them fit instruments of our support; they can no more challenge from us a stable confidence, than they can a supreme affection. It is by this the Psalmist allures men to a trust in him; "Taste and see how good the Lord is:" what is the consequence? "Blessed is the man that trusts in thee" (Ps. xxxiv. 8). The voice of Divine goodness sounds nothing more intelligibly,

and a taste of it produceth nothing more effectually, than this.   As the vials of his justice are to make us fear him, so the streams of his goodness are to make us rely on him: as his patience is designed to broach our repentance, so his goodness is most proper to strengthen our assurance in him: that goodness which surmounted so many difficulties, and conquered so many motions that might be made against any repeated exercise of it, after it had been abused by the first rebellion of man; that goodness that after so much contempt of it, appeared in such a majestic tenderness, and threw aside those impediments which men had cast in the way of Divine inclinations: this goodness is the foundation of all reliance upon God.   Who is better than God? and, therefore, who more to be trusted than God? As his power cannot act anything weakly, so his goodness cannot act anything unbecomingly, and unworthy of his infinite majesty. And here consider,

(1.) Goodness is the first motive of trust.   Nothing but this could be the encouragement to man, had he stood in a state of innocence, to present himself before God; the majesty of God would have constrained him to keep his due distance, but the goodness of God could only hearten his confidence: it is nothing else now that can preserve the same temper in us in our lapsed condition.   To regard him only as the Judge of our crimes, will drive us from him; but only the regard of him as the Donor of our blessings, will allure us to him. The principal foundation of faith is not the word of God, but God himself, and God as considered in this perfection.   As the goodness of God in his invitations and providential blessings "leads us to repentence" (Rom. ii. 4), so, by the same reason, the goodness of God by his promises leads us to reliance.   If God be not first believed to be good, he would not be believed at all in anything that he speaks or swears: if you were not satisfied in the goodness of a man, though he should swear a thousand times, you would value neither his word nor oath as any security.   Many times, where we are certain of the goodness of a man, we are willing to trust him without his promise.   This Divine perfection gives credit to the Divine promises; they of themselves would not be a sufficient ground of trust, without an apprehension of his truth; nor would his truth be very comfortable without a belief of his good will, whereby we are assured that what he promises to give, he gives liberally, free, and without regret.   The truth of the promiser makes the promise credible, but the goodness of the promiser makes it cheerfully relied on. In Ps. lxxiii.   (Asaph's penitential psalm for his distrust of God,) he begins the first verse with an assertion of this attribute (ver. 1), "Truly God is good to Israel;" and ends with this fruit of it (ver. 28), "I will put my trust in the Lord God."   It is a mighty ill nature that receives not with assurance the dictates of Infinite Goodness, (that cannot deceive or frustrate the hopes we conceive of him) that is inconceivably more abundant in the breast and inclinations of the promiser, than expressible in the words of his promise, "All true faith works by love" (Gal. v. 6), and, therefore, necessarily includes a particular eyeing of this excellency in the Divine nature, which renders him amiable, and is the motive and encouragement of a love to him.   His power indeed is a foundation of trust, but his goodness is the principal motive of it. His power without good-will would be dangerous, and could not allure affection; and his good-will without power would be useless; and though it might merit a love, yet could not create a confidence; both in conjunction are strong grounds of hope, especially since his goodness is of the same infinity with his wisdom and power; and that he can be no more wanting in the effusions of this upon them that seek him, than in his wisdom to contrive, or his power to effect, his designs and works.

(2.) This goodness is more the foundation and motive of trust under the gospel, than under the law. They under the law had more evidences of Divine power, and their trust eyed that much; though there was an eminency of goodness in the frequent deliverances they had, yet the power of God had a more glorious dress than his goodness, because of the extraordinary and miraculous ways whereby he brought those deliverances about.   Therefore, in the catalogue of believers in Heb. xi. you shall find the power of God to be the centre of their rest and trust; and their faith was built upon the extraordinary marks of Divine power, which were frequently visible to them.   But under the gospel, goodness and love was intended by God to be the chief object of trust; suitable to the excellency of that dispensation, he would have an exercise of more ingenuity in the creatures: therefore, it is said (Hos. iii. 5), a promise of gospel-times, "They shall fear God and his goodness in the latter days," when they shall return to "seek the Lord, and David their king." It is not said, they shall fear God, and his power, but the Lord and his goodness, or the Lord for his goodness: fear is often in the Old Testament taken for faith, or trust.   This Divine goodness, the object of faith, is that goodness discovered in David their king; the Messiah, our Jesus. God, in this dispensation, recommends his goodness and love, and reveals it more clearly than other attributes, that the soul might have more prevailing and sweeter attractives to confide in him.

(3.) A confidence in him gives him the glory of his goodness. Most nations that had nothing but the light of nature, thought it a great part of the honor that was due to God, to implore his goodness, and cast their cares upon it.   To do good, is the most honorable thing in the world, and to acknowledge a goodness in a way of confidence, is as high an honor as we can give to it, and a great part of gratitude for what it hath already expressed.   Therefore we find often, that an acknowledgment of one benefit received, was attended with a trust in him for what they should in the future need (Ps. lvi. 13): "Thou hast delivered my soul from death, wilt thou not deliver my feet from falling? So, 2 Cor. i. 10: and they who have been most eminent for their trust in him, have had the greatest eulogies and commendations from him.   As a diffidence doth disparage this perfection, thinking it meaner and shallower than it is, so confidence highly honors it.   We never please him more, than when we trust in him; "The Lord takes pleasure in them that fear him, in them that hope in his mercy" (Ps. cxlvii. 11).   He takes it for an honor to have this attribute exalted by such a carriage of his

creature. He is no less offended when we think his heart straitened, as if he were a parsimonious God; than when we think his arm
shortened, as if he were an impotent and feeble God. Let us, therefore, make this use of his goodness, to hearten our faith. When we
are scared by the terrors of his justice, when we are dazzled by the
arts of his wisdom, and confounded by the splendor of his majesty,
we may take refuge in the sanctuary of his goodness; this will encourage us, as well as astonish us; whereas, the consideration of his
other attributes would only amaze us, but can never refresh us, but
when they are considered marching under the conduct and banners
of this. When all the other perfections of the Divine nature are
looked upon in conjunction with this excellency, each of them send
forth ravishing and benign influences upon the applying creature.
It is more advantageous to depend upon Divine bounty, than our
own cares; we may have better assurance upon this account in his
cares for us, than in ours for ourselves. Our goodness for ourselves
is finite; and besides, we are too ignorant: his goodness is infinite,
and attended with an infinite wisdom; we have reason to distrust
ourselves, not God. We have reason to be at rest, under that kind
influence we have so often experimented; he hath so much goodness, that he can have no deceit: his goodness in making the promise, and his goodness in working the heart to a reliance on it, are
grounds of trust in him; "Remember thy word to thy servant,
upon which thou hast caused me to hope" (Ps. cxix. 49). If his
promise did not please him, why did he make it? If reliance on
the promise did not please him, why did his goodness work it? It
would be inconsistent with his goodness to mock his creature, and it
would be the highest mockery to publish his word, and create a temper in the heart of his supplicant, suited to his promise which he
never intended to satisfy. He can as little wrong his creature, as
wrong himself; and, therefore, can never disappoint that faith which
in his own methods casts itself into the arms of his kindness, and
is his own workmanship, and calls him Author. That goodness that
imparted itself so freely in creation, will not neglect those nobler
creatures that put their trust in him. This renders God a fit object
for trust and confidence.

8. The eighth instruction: This renders God worthy to be obeyed and honored. There is an excellency in God to allure, as well as
sovereignty to enjoin obedience: the infinite excellency of his nature is so great, that if his goodness had promised us nothing to encourage our obedience, we ought to prefer him before ourselves, devote ourselves to serve him, and make his glory our greatest content; but much more when he hath given such admirable expressions of his liberality, and stored us with hopes of richer and fuller
streams of it. When David considered the absolute goodness of
his nature, and the relative goodness of his benefits, he presently
expresseth an ardent desire to be acquainted with the Divine
statutes, that he might make ingenious returns in a dutiful observance; "Thou art good, and thou dost good; teach me thy statutes"
(Ps. cxix. 68). As his goodness is the original, so the acknowledgment of it is the end of all, which cannot be without an observance

of his will. His goodness requires of us an ingenuous, not a servile obedience. And this is established upon two foundations.

[1.] Because the bounty of God hath laid upon us the strongest obligations. The strength of an obligation depends upon the greatness and numerousness of the benefits received. The more excellent the favors are which are conferred upon any person, the more right hath the benefactor to claim an observance from the person bettered by him. Much of the rule and empire which hath been in several ages conferred by communities upon princes, hath had its first spring from a sense of the advantages they have received by them, either in protecting them from their enemies, or rescuing them from an ignoble captivity; in enlarging their territories, or increasing their wealth. Conquest hath been the original of a constrained, but beneficence always the original of a voluntary and free subjection.º Obedience to parents is founded upon their right, because they are instrumental in bestowing upon us being and life; and because this of life is so great a benefit, the law of nature never dissolves this obligation of obeying and honoring parents; it is as long-lived as the law of nature, and hath an universal practice, by the strength of that law, in all parts of the world: and those rightful chains are not unlocked, but by that which unties the knot between soul and body: much more hath God a right to be obeyed and reverenced, who is the principal Benefactor, and moved all those second causes to impart to us, what conduced to our advantage. The just authority of God over us results from the superlativeness of his blessings he hath poured down upon us, which cannot be equalled, much less exceeded, by any other. As therefore upon this account he hath a claim to our choicest affections, so he hath also to most exact obedience; and neither one nor other can be denied him, without a sordid and disingenuous ingratitude; God therefore aggravates the rebellion of the Jews from the cares he had in the bringing them up (Isa. ii. 2), and the miraculous deliverance from Egypt (Jer. xi. 7, 8); implying that those benefits were strong obligations to an ingenuous observance of him.

[2.] It is established upon this, that God can enjoin the observance of nothing but what is good. He may by the right of his sovereign dominion, command that which is indifferent in its own nature: as in positive laws, the not eating the fruit of the tree of the knowledge of good and evil, which had not been evil in itself, set aside the command of God to the contrary; and likewise in those ceremonial laws he gave the Jews: but in regard to the transcendent goodness and righteousness of his nature, he will not, he cannot command anything that is evil in itself, or repugnant to the true interest of his creature; and God never obliged the creature to anything but what was so free from damaging it, that it highly conduced to its good and welfare: and therefore it is said, that "his commands are not grievous" (1 John v. 3): not grievous in their own nature, nor grievous to one possessed with a true reason. The command given to Adam in Paradise was not grievous in itself, nor could he ever have thought it so, but upon a false supposition instilled into him by the tempter. There is a pleasure results from the law of God

º Amyrald. Dissert. p. 65.

to a holy rational nature, a sweetness tasted both by the understanding and by the will, for they both "rejoice the heart and enlighten the eyes" of the mind (Ps. xix. 8). God being essentially wisdom and goodness, cannot deviate from that goodness in any orders he gives the creature; whatsoever he enacts must be agreeable to that rule, and therefore he can will nothing but what is good and excellent, and what is good for the creature; for since he hath put originally into man a natural instinct to desire that which is good, he would never enact any thing for the creature's observance,[p] that might control that desire imprinted by himself, but what might countenance that impression of his own hand; for if God did otherwise, he would contradict his own natural law, and be a deluder of his creatures, if he impressed upon them desires one way, and ordered directions another. The truth is, all his moral precepts are comely in themselves, and they receive not their goodness from God's positive command, but that command supposeth their goodness; if everything were good because God loves it, or because God wills it, i. e. that God's loving it or willing it made that good which was not good before, then, as Camero well argues somewhere, God's goodness would depend upon his loving himself; he was good because he loved himself, and was not good till he loved himself; whereas, indeed, God's loving himself, doth not make him good, but supposeth him good: he was good in the order of nature before he loved himself; and his being good was the ground of his loving himself, because, as was said before, if there were anything better than God, God would love that; for it is inconsistent with the nature of God and infinite goodness not to love that which is good, and not to love that supremely which is the supreme good. Further to understand it, you may consider, if the question be asked, why God loves himself? you would think it a reasonable answer to say, because he is good. But if the question be asked, why God is good? you would think that answer, because he loves himself, would be destitute of reason; but the true answer would be, because his nature is so, and he could not be God if he were not good: therefore God's goodness is in order of our conception before his self-love, and not his self-love before his goodness; so the moral things God commands, are good in themselves before God commands them; and such, that if God should command the contrary, it would openly speak him evil and unrighteous. Abstract from Scripture, and weigh things in your own reason; could you conceive God good, if he should command a creature not to love him? could you preserve the notion of a good nature in him, if he did command murder, adultery, tyranny, and cutting of throats? You would wonder to what purpose he made the world, and framed it for society, if such things were ordered, that should deface all comeliness of society: the moral commands given in the word, appeared of themselves very beautiful to mere reason, that had no knowledge of the written law; they are good, and because they are so, his goodness had moved his sovereign authority strictly to enjoin them. Now this goodness, whereby he cannot oblige a

---

[p] "As a heathen," Maximus Tyrius, Dissert. 22, p. 220. Οὐ γὰρ θέμις Διὶ βούλεσθαι ἄλλο τι ἤ τὸ κάλλιστον.

creature to anything that is evil, speaks him highly worthy of our observance, and our disobedience to his law to be full of inconceivable malignity : that is the last thing.

Second Use is of comfort. He is a good without mixture, good without weariness—none good but God, none good purely, none good inexhaustibly, but God; because he is good, we may, upon our speaking, expect his instruction; "Good is the Lord, therefore will he teach sinners in his way" (Ps. xxv. 8). His goodness makes him stoop to be the tutor to those worms that lie prostrate before him; and though they are sinners full of filth, he drives them not from his school, nor denies them his medicines, if they apply themselves to him as a physician. He is good in removing the punishment due to our crimes, and good in bestowing benefits not due to our merits; because he is good, penitent believers may expect forgiveness; "Thou, Lord, art good, and ready to forgive" (Ps. lxxxvi. 5). He acts not according to the rigor of the law, but willingly grants his pardon to those that fly into the arms of the Mediator; his goodness makes him more ready to forgive, than our necessities make us desirous to enjoy; he charged not upon Job his impatient expressions in cursing the day of his birth; his goodness passed that over in silence, and extols him for speaking the thing that is right, right in the main, when he charges his friends for not speaking of him the thing that is right, as his servant Job had done (Job xlii. 7). He is so good, that if we offer the least thing sincerely, he will graciously receive it; if we have not a lamb to offer, a pigeon or turtle shall be accepted upon his altar; he stands not upon costly presents, but sincerely tendered services. All conditions are sweetened by it; whatsoever any in the world enjoy, is from a redundancy of this goodness; but whatsoever a good man enjoys, is from a propriety in this goodness.

1. Here is comfort in our addresses to him. If he be a fountain and sea of goodness, he cannot be weary of doing good, no more than a fountain or sea are of flowing. All goodness delights to communicate itself; infinite goodness hath then an infinite delight in expressing itself; it is a part of his goodness not to be weary of showing it; he can never, then, be weary of being solicited for the effusions of it; if he rejoices over his people to do them good, he will rejoice in any opportunities offered to him to honor his goodness, and gladly meet with a fit subject for it; he therefore delights in prayer. Never can we so delight in addressing, as he doth in imparting; he delights more in our prayers than we can ourselves; goodness is not pleased with shyness. To what purpose did his immense bounty bestow his Son upon us, but that we should be "accepted" both in our persons and petitions (Eph. i. 6)? "His eyes are upon the righteous, and his ears are open to their cry" (Ps. xxxiv. 15); he fixes the eye of his goodness upon them, and opens the ears of his goodness for them; he is pleased to behold them, and pleased to listen to them, as if he had no pleasure in anything else; he loves to be sought to, to give a vent to his bounty; "Acquaint thyself with God, and thereby good shall come unto thee" (Job xxii. 21). The word signifies, to accustom ourselves to God; the more we accustom ourselves in speaking, the more he will accustom himself in giving; he loves not

to keep his goodness close under lock and key, as men do their treasures. If we knock, he opens his exchequer (Matt. vii. 7); his goodness is as flexible to our importunities, as his power is invincible by the arm of a silly worm; he thinks his liberality honored by being applied to, and your address to be a recompense for his expense. There is no reason to fear, since he hath so kindly invited us, but he will as heartily welcome us; the nature of goodness is to compassionate and communicate, to pity and relieve, and that with a heartiness and cheerfulness; man is weary of being often solicited, because he hath a finite, not a bottomless, goodness: he gives sometimes to be rid of his suppliant, not to encourage him to a second approach. But every experience God gives us of his bounty, is a motive to solicit him afresh, and a kind of obligation he hath laid upon himself to " renew it" (1 Sam. xvii. 37): it is one part of his goodness that it is boundless and bottomless; we need not fear the wasting of it, nor any weariness in him to bestow it. The stock cannot be spent, and infinite kindness can never become niggardly; when we have enjoyed it, there is still an infinite ocean in Him to refresh us, and as full streams as ever to supply us. What an encouragement have we to draw near to God! We run in our straits to those that we think have most good will, as well as power to relieve and protect us. The oftener we come to him, and the nearer we approach to him, the more of his influences we shall feel: as the nearer the sun, the more of its heat insinuates itself into us. The greatness of God, joined with his goodness, hath more reason to encourage our approach to him, than our flight from him, because his greatness never goes unattended with his goodness; and if we were not so good, he would not be so great in the apprehensions of any creature. How may his goodness, in the great gift of his Son, encourage us to apply to him: since he hath set him as a day's-man between himself and us, and appointed him an Advocate to present our requests for us, and speed them at the throne of grace; and he never leaves till Divine goodness subscribes a *fiat* to our believing and just petitions!

2. Here is comfort in afflictions. What can we fear from the conduct of Infinite Goodness? Can his hand be heavy upon those that are humble before him? They are the hands of Infinite Power indeed, but there is not any motion of it upon his people, but is ordered by a goodness as infinite as his power, which will not suffer any affliction to be too sharp or too long. By what ways soever he conveys grace to us here, and prepares us for glory hereafter, they are good, and those are the good things he hath chiefly obliged himself to give (Ps. lxxxiv. 11): " Grace and glory" will he " give, and no good thing will he withhold from them that walk uprightly." This David comforted himself with, in that which his devout soul accounted the greatest calamity, his absence from the courts and house of God (ver. 2). Not an ill will, but a good will, directs his scourges; he is not an idle spectator of our combats; his thoughts are fuller of kindness than ours, in any case, can be of trouble: and because he is good, he wills the best good in everything he acts; in exercising virtue, or correcting vice. There is no affliction without some apparent mixtures of goodness; when he speaks how he had smitten

Israel (Jer. ii. 30), he presently adds (ver. 31), "Have I been a wilderness to Israel, a land of darkness?" Though he led them through a desert, yet he was not a desert to them; he was no land of darkness to them; while they marched through a land of barrenness, he was a caterer to provide them "manna," and a place of "broad rivers" and streams. How often hath Divine goodness made our afflictions our consolations; our diseases, our medicines, and his gentle strokes, reviving cordials! How doth he provide for us above our deserts, even while he doth punish us beneath our merits! Divine goodness can no more mean ill, than Divine wisdom can be mistaken in its end, or Divine power overruled in its actions. "Charity thinks no evil" (1 Cor. xiii. 5); charity in the stream doth not, much less doth charity in the fountain. To be afflicted by a hand of goodness hath something comfortable in it, when to be afflicted by an evil hand is very odious. Elijah, who was loth to die by the hand of a whorish idolatrous Jezebel, was very desirous to die by the hand of God (1 Kings, xix. 2—4). He accounted it a misery to have died by her hand, who hated him, and had nothing but cruelty; and, therefore, fled from her, when he wished for death, as a desirable thing by the hand of that God who had been good to him, and could not but be good in whatsoever he acted.

3. The third comfort flowing from this doctrine of the goodness of God, is, it is a ground of assurance of happiness. If God be so good, that nothing is better, and loves himself, as he is good, he cannot be wanting in love to those that resemble his nature, and imitate his goodness: he cannot but love his own image of goodness; wherever he finds it, he cannot but be bountiful to it; for it is impossible there can be any love to any object, without wishing well to it, and doing well for it. If the soul loves God as its chiefest good, God will love the soul as his pious servant: as he hath offered to them the highest allurements, so he will not withhold the choicest communications. Goodness cannot be a deluding thing; it cannot consist with the nobleness and largeness of this perfection to invite the creature to him, and leave the creature empty of him when it comes. It is inconsistent with this perfection to give the creature a knowledge of himself, and a desire of enjoyment larger than that knowledge; a desire to know, and enjoy him perpetually, yet never intend to bestow an eternal communication of himself upon it. The nature of man was erected by the goodness of God, but with an enlarged desire for the highest good, and a capacity of enjoying it. Can goodness be thought to be deceitful, to frustrate its own work, be tired with its own effusions, to let a gracious soul groan under its burden, and never resolve to ease him of it; to see delightfully the aspirings of the creature to another state, and resolve never to admit him to a happy issue of those desires? It is not agreeable to this inconceivable perfection to be unconcerned in the longings of his creature, since their first longings were placed in them by that goodness which is so free from mocking the creature, or falling short of its well-grounded expectations or desires, that it infinitely exceeds them. If man had continued in innocence, the goodness of God, without question, would have continued him in happiness: and,

since he hath had so much goodness to restore man, would it not be dishonorable to that goodness to break his own conditions, and defeat the believing creature of happiness, after it hath complied with his terms? He is a believer's God in covenant, and is a God in the utmost extent of this attribute, as well as of any other; and, therefore, will not communicate mean and shallow benefits, but according to the grandeur of it, sovereign and divine, such as the gift of a happy immortality. Since he had no obligation upon him, to make any promise, but the sweetness of his own nature, the same is as strong upon him to make all the words of his grace good; they cannot be invalid in any one tittle of them as long as his nature remains the same; and his goodness cannot be diminished without the impairing of his Godhead, since it is inseparable from it. Divine goodness will not let any man serve God for nought; he hath promised our weak obedience more than any man in his right wits can say it merits (Matt. x. 42): " A cup of cold water shall not lose its reward." He will manifest our good actions as he gave so high a testimony to Job, in the face of the devil, his accuser: it will not only be the happiness of the soul, but of the body, the whole man, since soul and body were in conjunction in the acts of righteousness; it consists not with the goodness of God to reward the one, and to let the other lie in the ruins of its first nothing: to bestow joy upon the one for its being principal, and leave the other without any sentiments of joy, that was instrumental in those good works, both commanded and approved by God: he that had the goodness to pity our original dust, will not want a goodness to advance it: and if we put off our bodies, it is but afterwards to put them on repaired and fresher. From this goodness, the upright may expect all the happiness their nature is capable of.

4. It is a ground of comfort in the midst of public dangers. This hath more sweetness in it to support us, than the malice of enemies hath to deject us; because he is " good," he is " a stronghold in the day of trouble" (Nah. i. 7). If his goodness extends to all his creatures, it will much more extend to those that honor him: if the earth be full of his goodness, that part of heaven which he hath upon earth shall not be empty of it. He hath a goodness often to deliver the righteous, and a justice to put the wicked in his stead (Prov. xi. 8). When his people have been under the power of their enemies, he hath changed the scene, and put the enemies under the power of his people: he hath clapped upon them the same bolts which they did upon his servants. How comfortable is this goodness that hath yet maintained us in the midst of dangers, preserved us in the mouth of lions, quenched kindled fire; hitherto rescued us from designed ruin subtilly hatched, and supported us in the midst of men very passionate for our destruction; how hath this watchful goodness been a sanctuary to us in the midst of an upper hell!

Third Use is of exhortation.

1. How should we endeavor after the enjoyment of God as good! How earnestly should we desire him! As there is no other goodness worthy of our supreme love, so there is no other goodness worthy our most ardent thirst. Nothing deserves the name of a desirable

good, but as it tends to the attainment of this : here we must pitch our desires, which otherwise will terminate in nullities or incon ceivable disturbances.

(1.) Consider, nothing but good can be the object of a rational appetite. The will cannot direct its motion to anything under the notion of evil, evil in itself, or evil to it; whatsoever courts it must present itself in the quality of a good in its own nature, or in its present circumstances to the present state and condition of the desire ; it will not else touch or affect the will. This is the language of that faculty : " Who will show me any good ?" (Ps. iv. 6), and good is as inseparably the object of the will's motion, as truth is of the understanding's inquiry. Whatsoever a man would allure another to comply with, he must propose to the person under the notion of some beneficialness to him in point of honor, profit, or pleasure. To act after this manner is the proper character of a rational creature; and though that which is evil is often embraced instead of that which is good, and what we entertain as conducing to our felicity proves our misfortune, yet that is from our ignorance, and not from a formal choice of it as evil; for what evil is chosen it is not possible to choose under the conception of evil, but under the appearance of a good, though it be not so in reality. It is inseparable from the wills of all men to propose to themselves that which in the opinion and judgment of their understandings or im agination is good, though they often mistake and cheat themselves.

(2.) Since that good is the object of a rational appetite, the purest, best, and most universal good, such as God is, ought to be most sought after. Since good only is the object of a rational appetite, all the motions of our souls should be carried to the first and best good : a real good is most desirable ; the greatest excellency of the creatures cannot speak them so, since, by the corruption of man, they are "subjected to vanity" (Rom. viii. 20). God is the most excellent good without any shadow ; a real something without that nothing which every creature hath in its nature (Isa. xl. 17). A perfect good can only give us content : the best goodness in the creature is but slender and imperfect; had not the venom of corruption infused a vanity into it, the make of it speaks it finite, and the best qualities in it are bounded, and cannot give satisfaction to a rational appetite which bears in its nature an imitation of Divine infiniteness, and therefore can never find an eternal rest in mean trifles. God is above the imperfection of all creatures ; creatures are but drops of goodness, at best but shallow streams ; God is like a teeming ocean, that can fill the largest as well as the narrowest creek. He hath an accumulative goodness ; several creatures answer several necessities, but one God can answer all our wants: he hath an universal fulness, to overtop our universal emptiness: he contains in himself the sweetness of all other goods, and holds in his bosom plentifully what creatures have in their natures sparingly. Creatures are uncertain goods ; as they begin to exist, so they may cease to be; they may be gone with a breath, they will certainly languish if God blows upon them (Isa. xl. 24): the same breath that raised them can blast them ; but who can rifle God of the least part of his excellency? Mutability is inherent in the nature of every creature, as a creature. All sublunary things are as gourds, that refresh us one moment with their presence, and the next fret us with their absence; like fading flowers, strutting to-day, and drooping to-morrow (Isa. xl. 6): while we possess them, we cannot clip their wings, that may carry them away from us, and may make us vainly seek what we thought we firmly held. But God is as permanent a good as he is a real one: he hath wings to fly to them that seek him, but no wings to fly from them forever, and leave them. God is an universal good; that which is good to one may be evil to another; what is desirable by one may be refused as inconvenient for another: but God being an universal, unstained good, is useful for all, convenient to the natures of all but such as will continue in enmity against him. There is nothing in God can displease a soul that desires to please him; when we are in darkness, he is a light to scatter it; when we are in want, he hath riches to relieve us; when we are in spiritual death, he is a Prince of life to deliver us; when we are defiled, he is holiness to purify us: it is in vain to fix our hearts anywhere but on him, in the desire of whom there is a delight, and in the enjoyment of whom there is an inconceivable pleasure.

(3.) He is most to be sought after, since all things else that are desirable had their goodness from him. If anything be desirable because of its goodness, God is much more desirable because of his, since all things are good by a participation, and nothing good but by his print upon it: as what being creatures have was derived to them by God, so what goodness they are possessed with they were furnished with it by God; all goodness flowed from him, and all created goodness is summed up in him. The streams should not terminate our appetite without aspiring to the fountain. If the waters in the channel, which receive mixture, communicate a pleasure, the taste of the fountain must be much more delicious; that original Perfection of all things hath an inconceivable beauty above those things it hath framed. Since those things live not by their own strength, nor nourish us by their own liberality, but by the "word of God" (Matt. iv. 4), that God that speaks them into life, and speaks them into usefulness, should be most ardently desired as the best. If the sparkling glory of the visible heavens delight us, and the beauty and bounty of the earth please and refresh us, what should be the language of our souls upon those views and tastes but that of the Psalmist, "Whom have I in heaven but thee? and there is none upon earth that I can desire beside thee" (Ps. lxxiii. 25). No greater good can possibly be desired, and no less good should be ardently desired. As he is the supreme good, so we should bear that regard to him as supremely, and above all, to thirst for him: as he is good, he is the object of desire; as the choicest and first goodness, he is desirable with the greatest vehemency. "Give me children, or else I die" (Gen. xxx. 1), was an uncomely speech; the one was granted, and the other inflicted; she had children, but the last cost her her life: but, Give me God, or I will not be content, is a gracious speech, wherein we cannot miscarry; all that God demands of us is, that we should long for him, and look for our happiness only in him. That is the first thing, endeavor after the enjoyment of God as good.

2. Often meditate on the goodness of God. What was man produced for, but to settle his thoughts upon this? What should have been Adam's employment in innocence, but to read over all the lines of nature, and fix his contemplations on that good hand that drew them? What is man endued with reason for, above all other animals, but to take notice of this goodness spread over all the creatures, which they themselves, though they felt it, could not have such a sense of as to make answerable returns to their Benefactor? Can we satisfy ourselves in being spectators of it, and enjoyers of it, only in such a manner as the brutes are? The beasts behold things as well as we, they feel the warm beams of this goodness as well as we, but without any reflection upon the Author of them. Shall Divine blessings meet with no more from us but a brutish view and beholding of them? What is more just, than to spend a thought upon Him who hath enlarged his hand in so many benefits to us? Are we indebted to any more than we are to him? Why should we send our souls to visit anything more than him in his works? That we are able to meditate on him is a part of his goodness to us, who hath bestowed that capacity upon us; and, if we will not, it is a great part of our ingratitude. Can anything more delightful enter into us, than that of the kind and gracious disposition of that God who first brought us out of the abyss of an unhappy nothing, and hath hitherto spread his wings over us? Where can we meet with a nobler object than Divine goodness? and what nobler work can be practised by us than to consider it? What is more sensible in all the operations of his hands than his skill, as they are considered in themselves, and his goodness, as they are considered in relation to us? It is strange that we should miss the thoughts of it; that we should look upon this earth, and everything in it, and yet overlook that which it is most full of, viz. Divine goodness (Ps. xxxiii. 5); it runs through the whole web of the world; all is framed and diversified by goodness; it is one entire single goodness, which appears in various garbs and dresses in every part of the creation. Can we turn our eyes inward, and send our eyes outward, and see nothing of a Divinity in both worthy of our deepest and seriousest thoughts? Is there anything in the world we can behold, but we see his bounty, since nothing was made but is one way or other beneficial to us? Can we think of our daily food, but we must have some reflecting thoughts on our great Caterer? Can the sweetness of the creature to our palate obscure the sweetness of the Provider to our minds? It is strange that we should be regardless of that wherein every creature without us, and every sense within us and about us, is a tutor to instruct us! Is it not reason we should think of the times wherein we were nothing, and from thence run back to a never-begun eternity, and view ourselves in the thoughts of that goodness, to be in time brought forth upon this stage, as we are at present? Can we consider but one act of our understandings, but one thought, one blossom, one spark of our souls mounting upwards, and not reflect upon the goodness of God to us, who, in that faculty that

sparkles out rational thoughts, has advanced us to a nobler state, and endued us with a nobler principle, than all the creatures we see on earth, except those of our own rank and kind? Can we consider but one foolish thought, one sinful act, and reflect upon the guilt and filth of it, and not behold goodness in sparing us, and miracles of goodness in sending his Son to die for us, for the expiation of it? This perfection cannot well be out of our thoughts, or at least it is horrible it should, when it is writ in every line of the creation, and in a legible rubric, in bloody letters, in the cross of his Son. Let us think with ourselves, how often he hath multiplied his blessings, when we did deserve his wrath! how he hath sent one unexpected benefit upon the heel of another, to bring us with a swift pace the tidings of good-will to us! how often hath he delivered us from a disease that had the arrows of death in its hand ready to pierce us! how often hath he turned our fears into joys, and our distempers into promoters of our felicity! how often hath he mated a temptation, sent seasonable supplies in the midst of a sore distress, and prevented many dangers which we could not be so sensible of, because we were, in a great measure, ignorant of them! How should we meditate upon his goodness to our souls, in preventing some sins, in pardoning others, in darting upon us the knowledge of his gospel, and of himself, in the face of his Son Christ! This seems to stick much upon the spirit of Paul, since he doth so often sprinkle his epistles with the titles of the "grace of God, riches of grace, unsearchable riches of God, riches of glory," and cannot satisfy himself, with the extolling of it. Certainly, we should bear upon our heart a deep and quick sense of this perfection; as it was the design of God to manifest it, so it would be acceptable to God for us to have a sense of it: a dull receiver of his blessings is no less nauseous to him than a dull dispenser of his alms; he loves a "cheerful giver" (2 Cor. ix. 7); he doth himself what he loves in others; he is cheerful in giving, and he loves we should be serious in thinking of him, and have a right apprehension and sense of his goodness.

(1.) A right sense of his goodness would dispose us to an ingenuous worship of God. It would damp our averseness to any act of religion; what made David so resolute and ready to "worship towards his holy temple" but the sense of his "loving kindness?" (Ps. cxxxviii. 2). This would render him always in our mind a worthy object of our devotion, a stable prop of our confidence. We should then adore him, when we consider him as "our God," and ourselves as "the people of his pasture, and the sheep of his hand" (Ps. xcv. 7): we should send up prayers with strong faith and feeling, and praises with great joy and pleasure. The sense of his goodness would make us love him, and our love to him would quicken our adoration of him; but if we regard not this, we shall have no mind to think of him, no mind to act anything towards him; we may tremble at his presence, but not heartily worship him; we shall rather look upon him as a tyrant, and think no other affection due to him than what we reserve for an oppressor, viz. hatred and ill-will.

(2.) A sense of it will keep us humble. A sense of it would effect that for which itself was intended; *viz.* bring us to a repentance for our crimes, and not suffer us to harden ourselves against him. When we should deeply consider how he hath made the sun to shine upon us, and his rain to fall upon the earth for our support; the one to supple the earth, and the other to assist the juice of it to bring forth fruits; how would it reflect upon us our ill requitals, and make us hang down our heads before him in a low posture, pleasing to him, and advantageous to ourselves! What would the first charge be upon ourselves, but what Moses brings in his expostulation against the Israelites (Deut. xxxii. 6): "Do I thus requite the Lord?" What is this goodness for me, who am so much below him; for me, who have so much incensed him; for me, who have so much abused what he hath allowed? It would bring to remembrance the horror of our crimes, and set us a blushing before him, when we should consider the multitude of his benefits, and our unworthy behaviour, that hath not constrained him even against the inclination of his goodness, to punish us: how little should we plead for a further liberty in sin, or palliate our former faults! When we set Divine goodness in one column, and our transgressions in another, and compare together their several items, it would fill us with a deep consciousness of our own guilt, and divest us of any worth of our own in our approaches to him; it would humble us, that we cannot love so obliging a God as much as he deserves to be loved by us; it would make us humble before men. Who would be proud of a mere gift which he knows he hath not merited? How ridiculous would that servant be, that should be proud of a rich livery, which is a badge of his service, not a token of his merit, but of his master's magnificence and bounty, which, though he wear this day, he may be stripped of to-morrow, and be turned out of his master's family!

(3.) A sense of the Divine goodness would make us faithful to him. The goodness of God obligeth us to serve him, not to offend him; the freeness of his goodness should make us more ready to contribute to the advancement of his glory. When we consider the benefits of a friend proceed out of kindness to us, and not out of self ends and vain applause, it works more upon us, and makes us more careful of the honor of such a person. It is a pure bounty God hath manifested in creation and providence, which could not be for himself, who, being blessed forever, wanted nothing from us: it was not to draw a profit from us, but to impart an advantage to us; "Our goodness extends not to him" (Ps. xvi. 2). The service of the benefactor is but a rational return for benefits; whence Nehemiah aggravates the sins of the Jews (Neh. ix. 35): "They have not served thee in thy great goodness that thou gavest them;" *i. e.* which thou didst freely bestow upon them. How should we dare to spend upon our lusts that which we possess, if we considered by whose liberality we came by it? how should we dare to be unfaithful in the goods he hath made us trustees of? A deep sense of Divine goodness will ennoble the creature, and make it act for the most glorious and noble end; it would strike Satan's temptation dead at a blow; it would pull off the false mask and vizor from what he presents to us, to draw us from the service of our Benefactor; we could not, with a sense of this, think him kinder to us than God hath, and will be, which is the great motive of men to join hands with him, and turn their backs upon God.

(4.) A sense of the Divine goodness would make us patient under our miseries. A deep sense of this would make us give God the honor of his goodness in whatsover he doth, though the reason of his actions be not apparent to us, nor the event and issue of his proceedings foreseen by us. It is a stated case, that goodness can never intend ill, but designs good in all its acts "to them that love God" (Rom. viii. 28): nay, he always designs the best; when he bestows anything upon his people, he sees it best they should have it; and when he removes anything from them, he sees it best they should lose it. When we have lost a thing we loved, and refuse to be comforted, a sense of this perfection, which acts God in all, would keep us from misjudging our sufferings, and measuring the intention of the hand that sent them, by the sharpness of what we feel. What patient, fully persuaded of the affection of the physician, would not value him, though that which is given to purge out the humors, racks his bowels? When we lose what we love, perhaps it was some outward lustre tickled our apprehensions, and we did not see the viper we would have harmed ourselves by; but God seeing it, snatched it from us, and we mutter as if he had been cruel, and deprived us of the good we imagined, when he was kind to us, and freed us from the hurt we should certainly have felt. We should regard that which in goodness he takes from us, at no other rate than some gilded poison and lurking venom; the sufferings of men, though upon high provocations, are often followed with rich mercies, and many times are intended as preparations for greater goodness. When God utters that rhetoric of his bowels, "How shall I give thee up, O Ephraim, I will not execute the fierceness of my anger!" (Hos. xi. 8), he intended them mercy in their captivity, and would prepare them by it, to walk after the Lord. And it is likely the posterity of those ten tribes were the first that ran to God, upon the publishing the gospel in the places where they lived; he doth not take away himself when he takes away outward comforts; while he snatcheth away the rattles we play with, he hath a breast in himself for us to suck. The consideration of his goodness would dispose us to a composed frame of spirit. If we are sick, it is goodness, it is a disease, and not a hell. It is goodness, that it is a cloud, and not a total darkness. What if he transfers from us what we have? he takes no more than what his goodness first imparted to us; and never takes so much from his people as his goodness leaves them: if he strips them of their lives, he leaves them their souls, with those faculties he furnished them with at first, and removes them from those houses of clay to a richer mansion. The time of our sufferings here, were it the whole course of our life, bears not the proportion of a moment to that endless eternity wherein he hath designed to manifest his goodness to us. The consideration of Divine goodness would teach us to draw a calm even from storms, and distil balsam from rods. If the reproofs of the righteous be an excellent oil (Ps.

cxlv. 5), we should not think the corrections of a good God to have a less virtue.

(5.) A sense of the Divine goodness would mount us above the world. It would damp our appetites after meaner things; we should look upon the world not as a God, but a gift from God, and never think the present better than the Donor. We should never lie soaking in muddy puddles were we always filled with a sense of the richness and clearness of this Fountain, wherein we might bathe ourselves; little petty particles of good would give us no content, when we were sensible of such an unbounded ocean. Infinite goodness, rightly apprehended, would dull our desires after other things, and sharpen them with a keener edge after that which is best of all. How earnestly do we long for the presence of a friend, of whose good will towards us we have full experience.

(6.) It would check any motions of envy: it would make us joy in the prosperity of good men, and hinder us from envying the outward felicity of the wicked. We should not dare with an evil eye to censure his good hand (Matt. xx. 15), but approve of what he thinks fit to do, both in the matter of his liberality and the subjects he chooseth for it. Though if the disposal were in our hands, we should not imitate him, as not thinking them subjects fit for our bounty; yet since it is in his hands, we be to approve of his actions and not have an ill will towards him for his goodness, or towards those he is pleased to make the subject of it. Since all his doles are given to "invite man to repentance" (Rom. ii. 4), to envy them those goods God hath bestowed upon them, is to envy God the glory of his own goodness, and them the felicity those things might move them to aspire to; it is to wish God more contracted, and thy neighbor more miserable: but a deep sense of his sovereign goodness would make us rejoice in any marks of it upon others, and move us to bless him instead of censuring him.

(7.) It would make us thankful. What can be the most proper, the most natural reflection, when we behold the most magnificent characters he hath imprinted upon our souls; the conveniency of the members he hath compacted in our bodies, but a praise of him? Such motion had David upon the first consideration: "I will praise thee, for I am fearfully and wonderfully made" (Ps. cxxxix. 14). What could be the most natural reflection, when we behold the rich prerogatives of our natures above other creatures, the provision he hath made for us for our delight in the beauties of heaven, for our support in the creatures on earth? What can reasonably be expected from uncorrupted man, to be the first motion of his soul, but an extolling the bountiful hand of the invisible donor, whoever he be? This would make us venture at some endeavors of a grateful acknowledgment, though we should despair of rendering anything proportionable to the greatness of the benefit; and such an acknowledgment of our own weakness would be an acceptable part of our gratitude. Without a due and deep sense of Divine goodness, our praise of it, and thankfulness for it, will be but cold, formal, and customary; our tongues may bless him, and our heart slight him: and this will lead us to the third exhortation:

3. Which is that of thankfulness for Divine goodness. The absolute goodness of God, as it is the excellency of his nature, is the object of praise: the relative goodness of God, as he is our benefactor, is the object of thankfulness. This was always a debt due from man to God; he had obligations in the time of his integrity, and was then to render it; he is not less, but more obliged to it in the state of corruption; the benefits being the greater, by how much the more unworthy he is of them by reason of his revolt. The bounty bestowed upon an enemy that merits the contrary, ought to be received with a greater resentment than that bestowed on a friend, who is not unworthy of testimonies of respect. Gratitude to God is the duty of every creature that hath a sense of itself; the more excellent being any enjoy the more devout ought to be the acknowledgment. How often doth David stir up, not only himself, but summon all creatures, even the insensible ones, to join in the concert! He calls to the "deeps, fire, hail, snow, mountains and hills," to bear a part in this work of praise (Ps. cxlviii); not that they are able to do it actively, but to show that man is to call in the whole creation to assist him passively, and should have so much charity to all creatures, as to receive what they offer, and so much affection to God, as to present to him what he receives from him. Snow and hail cannot bless and praise God, but man ought to praise God for those things wherein there is a mixture of trouble and inconvenience, something to molest our sense, as well as something that improves the earth for fruit. This God requires of us: for this he instituted several offerings, and required a little portion of fruits to be presented to him, as an acknowledgment they held the whole from his bounty. And the end of the festival days among the Jews was to revive the memory of those signal acts wherein his power for them, and his goodness to them, had been extraordinarily evident; it is no more but our mouths to praise him, and our hand to obey him, that he exacts at our hands. He commands us not to expend what he allows us in the erecting stately temples to his honor; all the coin he requires to be paid with for his expense is the "offering of thanksgiving" (Ps. l. 14): and this we ought to do as much as we can, since we cannot do it as much as he merits, for "who can show forth all his praise?" (Ps. cvi. 2.) If we have the fruit of his goodness, it is fit he should have the "fruit of our lips" (Heb. xiii. 15): the least kindness should inflame our souls with a kindly resentment. Though some of his benefits have a brighter, some a darker, aspect towards us, yet they all come from this common spring; his goodness shines in all; there are the footsteps of goodness in the least, as well as the smiles of goodness in the greatest; the meanest therefore is not to pass without a regard of the Author. As the glory of God is more illustrious in some creatures than in others, yet it glitters in all, and the lowest as well as the highest administers matter of praise; but they are not only little things, but the choicer favors he has bestowed upon us. How much doth it deserve our acknowledgment, that he should contrive our recovery, when we had plotted our ruin! that when he did from eternity behold the crimes wherewith we would incense him, he should not, according to the rights of justice, cast us into hell, but prize us at

the rate of the blood and life of his only Son, in value above the blood of men and lives of angels! How should we bless that God, that we have yet a gospel among us, that we are not driven into the utmost regions, that we can attend upon him in the face of the sun, and not forced to the secret obscurities of the night! Whatsoever we enjoy, whatsoever we receive, we must own him as the Donor, and read his hand in it. Rob him not of any praise to give to an instrument. No man hath wherewithal to do us good, nor a heart to do us good, nor opportunities of benefitting us without him. When the cripple received the soundness of his limbs from Peter, he praised the hand that sent it, not the hand that brought it (Acts iii 6): he "praised God" (ver. 8). When we want anything that is good, let the goodness of Divine nature move us to David's practice, to "thirst after God" (Ps. xlii. 1): and when we feel the motions of his goodness to us, let us imitate the temper of the same holy man (Ps. ciii. 2): "Bless the Lord, O my soul, and forget not all his benefits." It is an unworthy carriage to deal with him as a traveller doth with a fountain, kneel down to drink of it when he is thirsty, and turn his back upon it, and perhaps never think of it more after he is satisfied.

4. And, lastly, Imitate this goodness of God. If his goodness hath such an influence upon us as to make us love him, it will also move us with an ardent zeal to imitate him in it. Christ makes this use from the doctrine of Divine goodness (Matt. v. 44, 45): "Do good to them that hate you, that you may be the children of your Father which is in heaven; for he makes his sun to rise on the evil and on the good." As holiness is a resemblance of God's purity, so charity is a resemblance of God's goodness; and this our Saviour calls perfection (ver. 48): "Be ye therefore perfect, even as your Father, which is in heaven, is perfect." As God would not be a perfect God without goodness, so neither can any be a perfect Christian without kindness; charity and love being the splendor and loveliness of all Christian graces, as goodness is the splendor and loveliness of all Divine attributes. This and holiness are ordered in the Scripture to be the grand patterns of our imitation. Imitate the goodness of God in two things.

(1.) In relieving and assisting others in distress. Let our heart be as large in the capacity of creatures, as God's is in the capacity of a Creator. A large heart from him to us, and a strait heart from us to others, will not suit: let us not think any so far below us as to be unworthy of our care, since God thinks none that are infinitely distant from him too mean for his. His infinite glory mounts him above the creature, but his infinite goodness stoops him to the meanest works of his hands. As he lets not the transgressions of prosperity pass without punishment, so he lets not the distress of his afflicted people pass him without support. Shall God provide for the ease of beasts, and shall not we have some tenderness towards those that are of the same blood with ourselves, and have as good blood to boast of as runs in the veins of the mightiest monarch on earth; and as mean, and as little as they are, can lay claim to as ancient a pedigree as the stateliest prince in the world, who cannot ascend to

ancestors beyond Adam ? Shall we glut ourselves with Divine be·
neficence to us, and wear his livery only on our own backs, forgetting the afflictions of some dear Joseph ; when God, who hath an
unblemished felicity in his own nature, looks out of himself to view
and relieve the miseries of poor creatures ?   Why hath God increased
the doles of his treasures to some more than others?   Was it merely
for themselves, or rather that they might have a bottom to attain the
honor of imitating him ?   Shall we embezzle his goods to our own
use, as if we were absolute proprietors, and not stewards entrusted
for others ?   Shall we make a difficulty to part with something to
others, out of that abundance he hath bestowed upon any of us?
Did not his goodness strip his Son of the glory of heaven for a time
to enrich us ? and shall we shrug when we are to part with a little
to pleasure him ?   It is not very becoming for any to be backward
in supplying the necessities of others with a few morsels, who have
had the happiness to have had their greatest necessities supplied with
his Son's blood.   He demands not that we should strip ourselves of
all for others, but of a pittance, something of superfluity, which will
turn more to our account than what is vainly and unprofitably consumed on our backs and bellies.   If he hath given much to any of
us, it is rather to lay aside part of the income for his service ; else
we would monopolize Divine goodness to ourselves, and seem to distrust under our present experiments his future kindness, as though
the last thing he gave us was attended with this language, Hoard up
this, and expect no more from me ; use it only to the glutting your
avarice, and feeding your ambition : which would be against the
whole scope of Divine goodness.   If we do not endeavor to write
after the comely copy he hath set us, we may provoke him to harden himself against us, and in wrath bestow that on the fire, or on
our enemies, which his goodness hath imparted to us for his glory,
and the supplying the necessities of poor creatures.   And, on the
contrary, he is so delighted with this kind of imitation of him, that
a cup of cold water, when there is no more to be done, shall not be
unrewarded.

(2.) Imitate God in his goodness, in a kindness to our worst enemies.   The best man is more unworthy to receive anything from God
than the worst can be to receive from us.   How kind is God to those
that blaspheme him, and gives them the same sun, and the same
showers, that he doth to the best men in the world !   Is it not more
our glory to imitate God in "doing good to those that hate us," than
to imitate the men of the world in requiting evil, by a return of a
sevenfold mischief?   This would be a goodness which would vanquish the hearts of men, and render us greater than Alexanders and
Cæsars, who did only triumph over miserable carcasses ; yea, it is to
triumph over ourselves in being good against the sentiments of corrupt nature.   Revenge makes us slaves to our passions, as much as
the offenders, and good returns render us victorious over our adverl
saries (Rom. xii. 21) : "Be not overcome of evil, but overcome evi-
with good."   When we took up our arms against God, his goodness
contrived not our ruin, but our recovery.   This is such a goodness
of God as could not be discovered in an innocent state ; while man

had continued in his duty, he could not have been guilty of an enmity ; and God could not but affect him, unless he had denied himself : so this of being good to our enemies could never have been practised in a state of rectitude ; since, where was a perfect innocence, there could be no spark of enmity to one another. It can be no disparagement to any man's dignity to cast his influences on his greatest opposers, since God, who acts for his own glory, thinks not himself disparaged by sending forth the streams of his bounty on the wickedest persons, who are far meaner to him than those of the same blood can be to us. Who hath the worse thoughts of the sun, for shining upon the earth, that sends up vapors to cloud it? it can be no disgrace to resemble God ; if his hand and bowels be open to us, let not ours be shut to any.

DISCOURSE XIII

ON GOD'S DOMINION

PSALM ciii. 19.—The Lord hath prepared his throne in the heavens: and his kingdom ruleth over all.

THE Psalm begins with the praise of God, wherein the penman excites his soul to a right and elevated management of so great a duty (ver. 1): "Bless the Lord, O my soul: and all that is within me, bless his holy name:" and because himself and all men were insufficient to offer up a praise to God answerable to the greatness of his benefits, he summons in the end of the psalm the angels, and all creatures, to join in concert with him. Observe,

1. As man is too shallow a creature to comprehend the excellency of God, so he is too dull and scanty a creature to offer up a due praise to God, both in regard of the excellency of his nature, and the multitude and greatness of his benefits.

2. We are apt to forget Divine benefits: our souls must therefore be often jogged, and roused up. "All that is within me," every power of my rational, and every affection of my sensitive part: all his faculties, all his thoughts. Our souls will hang back from God in every duty, much more in this, if we lay not a strict charge upon them. We are so void of a pure and entire love to God, that we have no mind to those duties. Wants will spur us on to prayer, but a pure love to God can only spirit us to praise. We are more ready to reach out a hand to receive his mercies, than to lift up our hearts to recognize them after the receipt. After the Psalmist had summoned his own soul to this task, he enumerates the Divine blessings received by him, to awaken his soul by a sense of them to so noble a work. He begins at the first and foundation mercy to himself, the pardon of his sin and justification of his person, the renewing of his sickly and languishing nature (ver. 3): "Who forgives all thy iniquities, and heals all thy diseases." His redemption from death, or eternal destruction; his expected glorification thereupon, which he speaks of with that certainty, as if it were present (ver. 4): "Who redeems thy life from destruction, who crowns thee with loving-kindness and tender mercies." He makes his progress to the mercy manifested to the church in the protection of it against, or delivery of it from, oppressions (ver. 6): "The Lord executeth righteousness and judgment for all that are oppressed." In the discovery of his will and law, and the glory of his merciful name to it (ver. 7, 8): "He made known his ways unto Moses, and his acts unto the children of Israel. The Lord is merciful and gracious, slow to anger, and plenteous in mercy:"

which latter words may refer also to the free and unmerited spring of the benefits he had reckoned up: *viz.*, the mercy of God, which he mentions also (ver. 10): "He hath not dealt with us after our sins, nor rewarded us according to our iniquities;" and then extols the perfection of Divine mercy, in the pardoning of sin (ver. 11, 12); the paternal tenderness of God (ver. 13); the eternity of his mercy (ver. 17); but restrains it to the proper object (ver. 11, 17), "to them that fear him;" *i. e.* to them that believe in him. *Fear* being the word commonly used for *faith* in the Old Testament, under the legal dispensation, wherein the spirit of bondage was more eminent than the spirit of adoption, and their fear more than their confidence. Observe,

1. All true blessings grow up from the pardon of sin (ver. 3): "Who forgives all thine iniquities." That is the first blessing, the top and crown of all other favors, which draws all other blessings after it, and sweetens all other blessings with it. The principal intent of Christ was expiation of sin, redemption from iniquity; the purchase of other blessings was consequent upon it. Pardon of sin is every blessing virtually, and in the root and spring it flows from the favor of God, and is such a gift as cannot be tainted with a curse, as outward things may.

2. Where sin is pardoned, the soul is renewed (ver. 3): "Who heals all thy diseases." Where guilt is remitted, the deformity and sickness of the soul is cured. Forgiveness is a teeming mercy; it never goes single; when we have an interest in Christ, as bearing the chastisement of our peace, we receive also a balsam from his blood, to heal the wounds we feel in our nature. (Isa. liii. 5): "The chastisement of our peace was upon him, and with his stripes we are healed." As there is a guilt in sin, which binds us over to punishment, so there is a contagion in sin, which fills us with pestilent diseases; when the one is removed, the other is cured. We should not know how to love the one without the other. The renewing the soul is necessary for a delightful relish of the other blessings of God. A condemned malefactor, infected with a leprosy, or any other loathsome distemper, if pardoned, could take little comfort in his freedom from the gibbet without a cure of his plague.

3. God is the sole and sovereign Author of all spiritual blessings: "Who forgives all thy iniquities, and heals all thy diseases." He refers all to God, nothing to himself in his own merit and strength. All, not the pardon of one sin merited by me, not the cure of one disease can I owe to my own power, and the strength of my free-will, and the operations of nature. He, and he alone is the Prince of pardon, the Physician that restores me, the Redeemer that delivers me; it is a sacrilege to divide the praise between God and ourselves. God only can knock off our fetters, expel our distempers, and restore a deformed soul to its decayed beauty.

4. Gracious souls will bless God as much for sanctification as for justification. The initials of sanctification (and there are no more in this life) are worthy of solemn acknowledgment. It is a sign of growth in grace when our hymns are made up of acknowledgments of God's sanctifying, as well as pardoning grace. In blessing God

for the one, we rather show a love to ourselves; in blessing God for the other, we cast out a pure beam of love to God : because, by purifying grace, we are fitted to the service of our Maker, prepared to every good work which is delightful to him; by the other, we are eased in ourselves. Pardon fills us with inward peace, but sanctification fills us with an activity for God. Nothing is so capable of setting the soul in a heavenly tune, as the consideration of God as a pardoner and as a healer.

5. Where sin is pardoned, the punishment is remitted (ver. 3, 4): " Who forgives all thy iniquities, and redeems thy life from destruction." A malefactor's pardon puts an end to his chains, frees him from the stench of the dungeon, and fear of the gibbet. Pardon is nothing else but the remitting of guilt, and guilt is nothing else but an obligation to punishment as a penal debt for sin. A creditor's tearing a bond frees the debtor from payment and rigor.

6. Growth in grace is always annexed to true sanctification. So that " thy youth is renewed like the eagle's" (ver. 5). Interpreters trouble themselves much about the manner of the eagle's renewing its youth, and regaining its vigor: he speaks best that saith, the Psalmist speaks only according to the opinion of the vulgar, and his design was not to write a natural history.q Growth always accompanies grace, as well as it doth nature in the body; not that it is without its qualms and languishing fits, as children are not, but still their distempers make them grow. Grace is not an idle, but an active principle. It is not like the Psalmist means it of the strength of the body, or the prosperity and stability of his government, but the vigor of his grace and comfort, since they are spiritual blessings here that are the matter of his song. The healing the disease conduceth to the sprouting up and flourishing of the body. It is the nature of grace to go from strength to strength.

7. When sin is pardoned, it is perfectly pardoned. " As far as the east is from the west, so far hath He removed our transgressions from us" (ver. 11, 12). The east and west are the greatest distance in the world; the terms can never meet together. When sin is pardoned, it is never charged again; the guilt of it can no more return, than east can become west, or west become east.

8. Obedience is necessary to an interest in the mercy of God. " The mercy of the Lord is to them that fear him, to them that remember his commandments, to do them" (ver. 17). Commands are to be remembered in order to practice; a vain speculation is not the intent of the publication of them.

After the Psalmist had enumerated the benefits of God, he reflects upon the greatness of God, and considers him on his throne encompassed with the angels, the ministers of his providence. " The Lord hath prepared his throne in the heavens and his kingdom rules over all" (ver. 19). He brings in this of his dominion just after he had largely treated of his mercy. Either,

1. To signify, That God is not only to be praised for his mercy, but for his majesty, both for the height and extent of his authority.

2. To extol the greatness of his mercy and pity. What I have

q Amyrald. in loc.

said now, O my soul, of the mercy of God, and his paternal pity, is commended by his majesty; his grandeur hinders not his clemency: though his throne be high, his bowels are tender. He looks down upon his meanest servants from the height of his glory. Since his majesty is infinite, his mercy must be as great as his majesty. It must be a greater pity lodging in his breast, than what is in any creature, since it is not damped by the greatness of his sovereignty.

3. To render his mercy more comfortable. The mercy I have spoken of, O my soul, is not the mercy of a subject, but of a sovereign. An executioner may torture a criminal, and strip him of his life, and a vulgar pity cannot relieve him, but the clemency of the prince can perfectly pardon him. It is that God who hath none above him to control him, none below him to resist him, that hath performed all the acts of grace to thee. If God by his supreme authority pardons us, who can reverse it? If all the subjects of God in the world should pardon us, and God withhold his grant, what will it profit us? Take comfort, O my soul, since God from his throne in the highest, and that God who rules over every particular of the creation, hath granted and sealed thy pardon to thee. What would his grace signify, if he were not a monarch, extending his royal empire over everything, and swaying all by his sceptre?

4. To render the Psalmist's confidence more firm in any pressures. Ver. 15, 16. He had considered the misery of man in the shortness of his life; his place should know him no more; he should never return to his authority, employments, opportunities, that death would take from him; but, howsoever, the mercy and majesty of God were the ground of his confidence. He draws himself from poring upon any calamities which may assault him, to heaven, the place where God orders all things that are done on the earth. He is able to protect us from our dangers, and to deliver us from our distresses; whatsoever miseries thou mayest lie under, O my soul, cast thy eye up to heaven, and see a pitying God in a majestic authority: a God who can perform what he hath promised to them that fear him, since he hath a throne above the heavens, and bears sway over all that envy thy happiness, and would stain thy felicity: a God whose authority cannot be curtailed and dismembered by any. When the prophet solicits the sounding of the Divine bowels, he urgeth him by his dwelling in heaven, the habitation of his holiness (Isa. lxiii. 15). His kingdom ruleth over all: there is none therefore hath any authority to make him break his covenant, or violate his promise.

5. As an incentive to obedience. The Lord is merciful, saith he, to them "that remember his commandments to do them" (ver. 17, 18): and then brings in the text as an encouragement to observe his precepts. He hath a majesty that deserves it from us, and an authority to protect us in it. If a king in a small spot of earth is to be obeyed by his subjects, how much more is God, who is more majestic than all the angels in heaven, and monarchs on earth; who hath a majesty to exact our obedience, and a mercy to allure it! We should not set upon the performance of any duty, without an eye lifted up to God as a great king. It would make us willing to serve him; the more noble the person, the more honorable and

powerful the prince, the more glorious is his service. A view of God upon his throne will make us think his service our privilege, his precepts our ornaments, and obedience to him the greatest honor and nobility. It will make us weighty and serious in our performances: it would stake us down to any duty. The reason we are so loose and unmannerly in the carriage of our souls before God, is because we consider him not as a " great King" (Mal. i. 14). " Our Father, which art in heaven," in regard of his majesty, is the preface to prayer.

Let us now consider the words in themselves. " The Lord hath prepared his throne in the heavens, and his kingdom rules over all."

The Lord hath prepared.—The word signifies " established," as well as " prepared," and might so be rendered. Due preparation is a natural way to the establishment of a thing: hasty resolves break and moulder. This notes, 1. The infiniteness of his authority. He prepares it, none else for him. It is a dominion that originally resides in his nature, not derived from any by birth or commission; he alone prepared it. He is the sole cause of his own kingdom; his authority therefore is unbounded, as infinite as his nature : none can set laws to him, because none but himself prepared his throne for him. As he will not impair his own happiness, so he will not abridge himself of his own authority. 2. Readiness to exercise it upon due occasions. He hath prepared his throne : he is not at a loss; he needs not stay for a commission or instructions from any how to act. He hath all things ready for the assistance of his people ; he hath rewards and punishments ; his treasures and axes, the great marks of authority lying by him, the one for the good, the other for the wicked. His " mercy he keeps by him for thousands" (Exod. xxxiv. 7). His " arrows" he hath prepared by him for rebels (Ps. vii. 13). 3. Wise management of it. It is prepared ; preparations imply prudence ; the government of God is not a rash and heady authority. A prince upon his throne, a judge upon the bench, manages things with the greatest discretion, or should be supposed so to do. 4. Successfulness and duration of it. He hath prepared or established. It is fixed, not tottering ; it is an immovable dominion ; all the strugglings of men and devils cannot overturn it, nor so much as shake it. It is established above the reach of obstinate rebels ; he cannot be deposed from it, he cannot be mated in it. His dominion, as himself, abides forever. And as his counsel, so his authority, shall stand, and " he will do all his pleasure" (Isa. xlvi. 10).

His throne in the heavens.—This is an expression to signify the authority of God; for as God hath no member properly, though he be so represented to us, so he hath properly no throne. It signifies his power of reigning and judging. A throne is proper to royalty, the seat of majesty in its excellency, and the place where the deepest respect and homage of subjects is paid, and their petitions presented. That the throne of God is in the heavens, that there he sits as Sovereign, is the opinion of all that acknowledge a God ; when they stand in need of his authority to assist them, their eyes are lifted up, and their heads stretched out to heaven ; so his Son Christ prayed ; he " lifted up his eyes to heaven," as the place where his Father sat in majesty, as the most adorable object (John xvii. 1). Heaven hath the title of his "throne," as the earth hath that of his "footstool" (Isa. lxvi. 1.) And, therefore, heaven is sometimes put for the authority of God (Dan. iv. 26). "After that thou shalt have known that the heavens do rule," *i. e.* that God, who hath his throne in the heavens, orders earthly princes and sceptres as he pleases, and rules over the kingdoms of the world. His throne in the heavens notes, 1. The glory of his dominion. The heavens are the most stately and comely pieces of the creation. His majesty is there most visible, his glory most splendid (Ps. xix. 1). The heavens speak out with a full mouth his glory. It is therefore called "the habitation" of his "holiness and of his glory" (Isa. lxiii. 15). There is the greater glister and brightness of his glory. The whole earth, indeed, is full of his glory, full of the beams of it; the heaven is full of the body of it; as the rays of the sun reach the earth, but the full glory of it is in the firmament. In heaven his dominion is more acknowledged by the angels standing at his beck, and by their readiness and swiftness obeying his commands, going and returning as a flash of lightning (Ezek. i. 14). His throne may well be said to be in the heavens, since his dominion is not disputed there by the angels that attend him, as it is on earth by the rebels that arm themselves against him. 2. The supremacy of his empire. The heavens are the loftiest part of the creation, and the only fit palace for him; it is in the heavens his majesty and dignity are so sublime, that they are elevated above all earthly empires. 3. Peculiarity of this dominion. He rules in the heavens alone. There is some shadow of empire in the world. Royalty is communicated to men as his substitutes. He hath disposed a vicarious dominion to men in his footstool, the earth; he gives them some share in his authority; and, therefore, the title of his name (Ps. lxxxii. 6): "I have said, ye are gods;" but in heaven he reigns alone without any substitutes; his throne is there. He gives out his orders to the angels himself; the marks of his immediate sovereignty are there most visible. He hath no vicars-general of that empire. His authority is not delegated to any creature; he rules the blessed spirits by himself; but he rules men that are on his footstool by others of the same kind, men of their own nature. 4. The vastness of his empire. The earth is but a spot to the heavens; what is England in a map to the whole earth, but a spot you may cover with your finger? much less must the whole earth be to the extended heavens; it is but a little point or atom to what is visible; the sun is vastly bigger than it, and several stars are supposed to be of a greater bulk than the earth; and how many, and what heavens are beyond, the ignorance of man cannot understand. If the "throne" of God be there, it is a larger circuit he rules in than can well be conceived. You cannot conceive the many millions of little particles there are in the earth; and if all put together be but as one point to that place where the throne of God is seated, how vast must his empire be! He rules there over the angels, which "excel in strength" those "hosts" of his "which do his pleasure," in comparison of whom all the men in the world, and the power of the greatest potentates, is no more than the strength of an ant or fly; multitudes of them encircle his throne, and listen to his orders without roving, and execute them without disputing. And since his throne is in the heavens, it will follow, that all things under the heaven are parts of his dominion; his throne being in the highest place, the inferior things of earth cannot but be subject to him; and it necessarily includes his influence on all things below: because the heavens are the cause of all the motion in the world, the immediate thing the earth doth naturally address to for corn, wine, and oil, above which there is no superior but the Lord (Hos. ii. 21, 22): "The earth hears the corn, wine, and oil; the heavens hear the earth, and the Lord hears the heavens." 5. The easiness of managing this government. His throne being placed on high, he cannot but behold all things that are done below; the height of a place gives advantage to a pure and clear eye to behold things below it. Had the sun an eye, nothing could be done in the open air out of its ken. The "throne" of God being in heaven, he easily looks from thence upon all the children of men (Ps. xiv. 2): "The Lord looked down from heaven upon the children of men, to see if there were any that did understand." He looks not down from heaven as if he were in regard of his presence confined there: but he looks down majestically, and by way of authority, not as the look of a bare spectator, but the look of a governor, to pass a sentence upon them as a judge. His being in the heavens renders him capable of doing "whatsoever he pleases" (Ps. cxv. 3). His "throne" being there, he can by a word, in stopping the motions of the heavens, turn the whole earth into confusion. In this respect, it is said, "He rides upon the heaven in thy help" (Deut. xxxiii. 26); discharges his thunders upon men, and makes the influences of it serve his people's interest. By one turn of a cock, as you see in grottoes, he can cause streams from several parts of the heavens to refresh, or ruin the world. 6. Duration of it. The heavens are incorruptible; his throne is placed there in an incorruptible state. Earthly empires have their decays and dissolutions. The throne of God outlives the dissolution of the world.

His kingdom rules over all.—He hath an absolute right over all things within the circuit of heaven and earth; though his throne be in heaven, as the place where his glory is most eminent and visible, his authority most exactly obeyed, yet his kingdom extends itself to the lower parts of the earth. He doth not muffle and cloud up himself in heaven, or confine his sovereignty to that place, his royal power extends to all visible, as well as invisible things: he is proprietor and possessor of all (Deut. x. 14): "The heaven and the heaven of heavens is the Lord's thy God, the earth also, with all that is there." He hath right to dispose of all as he pleases. He doth not say, his kingdom rules all that fear him, but, "over all;" so that it is not the kingdom of *grace* he here speaks of, but his *natural* and universal kingdom. Over angels and men; Jews and Gentiles; animate and inanimate things.

The Psalmist considers God here as a great monarch and general, and all creatures as his hosts and regiments under him, and takes notice principally of two things. 1. The establishment of his throne together with the seat of it. *He hath prepared his throne in the heavens.* 2. The extent of his empire.—*His kingdom rules over all.* This text, in all the parts of it, is a fit basis for a discourse upon the dominion of God, and the observation will be this.

Doctrine.—God is sovereign Lord and King, and exerciseth a dominion over the whole world, both heaven and earth. This is so clear, that nothing is more spoken of in Scripture. The very name, "Lord," imports it; a name originally belonging to gods, and from them translated to others. And he is frequently called "the Lord of Hosts," because all the troops and armies of spiritual and corporeal creatures are in his hands, and at his service: this is one of his principal titles. And the angels are called his "hosts" (ver. 21, following the text) his camp and militia: but more plainly (1 Kings, xxii. 19), God is presented upon his throne, encompassed with all the "hosts of heaven" standing on his right hand and on his left, which can be understood of no other than the angels, that wait for the commands of their Sovereign, and stand about, not to counsel him, but to receive his orders. The sun, moon, and stars, are called his "hosts" (Deut. iv. 19); appointed by him for the government of inferior things: he hath an absolute authority over the greatest and the least creatures; over those that are most dreadful, and those that are most beneficial; over the good angels that willingly obey him, over the evil angels that seem most incapable of government. And as he is thus "Lord of hosts," he is the "King of glory," or a glorious King (Ps. xxiv. 10). You find him called a "great King," the "Most High" (Ps. xcii. 1), the Supreme Monarch, there being no dignity in heaven or earth but what is dim before him, and infinitely inferior to him; yea, he hath the title of "Only King" (1 Tim. vi. 15). The title of royalty truly and properly only belongs to him: you may see it described very magnificently by David, at the free-will offering for the building of the temple (1 Chron. xxix. 11, 12): "Thine, O Lord, is the greatness, and the power, and the glory, and the victory, and the majesty; thine is the kingdom, O God, and thou art exalted as Head above all: both riches and honor come of thee, and thou reignest over all; and in thy hand is power and might; and in thy hand it is to make great, and to give strength to all." He hath an eminency of power or authority above all: all earthly princes received their diadems from him, yea, even those that will not acknowledge him, and he hath a more absolute power over them than they can challenge over their meanest vassals: as God hath a knowledge infinitely above our knowledge, so he hath a dominion incomprehensibly above any dominion of man; and, by all the shadows drawn from the authority of one man over another, we can have but weak glimmerings of the authority and dominion of God.

There is a threefold dominion of God. 1. Natural, which is absolute over all creatures, and is founded in the nature of God as Creator. 2. Spiritual, or gracious, which is a dominion over his church as redeemed, and founded in the covenant of grace. 3. A glorious kingdom, at the winding up of all, wherein he shall reign over all, either in the glory of his mercy, as over the glorified saints, or in the glory of his justice, in the condemned devils and men. The first dominion is founded in nature; the second in grace; the third in regard of the blessed in grace; in regard of the damned, in demerit in them, and justice in him. He is Lord of all things, and always in regard of propriety (Ps. xxiv. 1): "The earth is the Lord's, and the fulness thereof; the world, and all that dwell therein." The earth, with the riches and treasures in the bowels of it; the habitable world, with everything that moves upon it, are his; he hath the sole right, and what right soever any others have is derived from him. In regard also of possession (Gen. xiv. 22): "The Most High God, possessor of heaven and earth:" in respect of whom, man is not the proprietary nor possessor, but usufructuary at the will of this grand Lord.

In the prosecution of this, I. I shall lay down some general propositions for the clearing and confirming it. II. I shall show wherein this right of dominion is founded. III. What the nature of it is. IV. Wherein it consists; and how it is manifested.

I. Some general propositions for the clearing and confirming of it.

1. We must know the difference between the might or power of God and his authority. We commonly mean by the power of God the strength of God, whereby he is able to effect all his purposes; by the authority of God, we mean the right he hath to act what he pleases: omnipotence is his physical power, whereby he is able to do what he will; dominion is his moral power, whereby it is lawful for him to do what he will. Among men, strength and authority are two distinct things; a subject may be a giant, and be stronger than his prince, but he hath not the same authority as his prince: worldly dominion may be seated, not in a brawny arm, but a sickly and infirm body. As knowledge and wisdom are distinguished; knowledge respects the matter, being, and nature of a thing; wisdom respects the harmony, order, and actual usefulness of a thing; knowledge searcheth the nature of a thing, and wisdom employs that thing to its proper use: a man may have much knowledge, and little wisdom; so a man may have much strength, and little or no authority; a greater strength may be settled in the servant, but a greater authority resides in the master; strength is the natural vigor of a man: God hath an infinite strength, he hath a strength to bring to pass whatsover he decrees; he acts without fainting and weakness (Isa. xl. 28), and impairs not his strength by the exercise of it: as God is Lord, he hath a right to enact; as he is almighty, he hath a power to execute; his strength is the executive power belonging to his dominion: in regard of his sovereignty, he hath a right to command all creatures; in regard of his almightiness, he hath power to make his commands be obeyed, or to punish men for the violation of them: his power is that whereby he subdues all creatures under him; his dominion is that whereby he hath a right to subdue all creatures under him. This dominion is a right of making what he pleases, of possessing what he made, of disposing of what he doth possess; whereas his power is an ability to make what he hath a right to create, to hold what he doth possess, and to execute the manner wherein he resolves to dispose of his creatures.

2. All the other attributes of God refer to this perfection of domi-

nion. They all bespeak him fit for it, and are discovered in the exercise of it (which hath been manifested in the discourses of those attributes we have passed through hitherto). His goodness fits him for it, because he can never use his authority but for the good of the creatures, and conducting them to their true end: his wisdom can never be mistaken in the exercise of it; his power can accomplish the decrees that flow from his absolute authority. What can be more rightful than the placing authority in such an infinite Goodness, that hath bowels to pity, as well as a sceptre to sway his subjects? that hath a mind to contrive, and a will to regulate his contrivances for his own glory and his creatures' good, and an arm of power to bring to pass what he orders? Without this dominion, some perfections, as justice and mercy, would lie in obscurity, and much of his wisdom would be shrouded from our sight and knowledge.

3. This of dominion, as well as that of power, hath been acknowledged by all. The high priest was to "waive the offering," or shake it to and fro (Exod. xxix. 24), which the Jews say was customarily from east to west, and from north to south, the four quarters of the world, to signify God's sovereignty over all the parts of the world; and some of the heathens, in their adorations, turned their bodies to all quarters, to signify the extensive dominion of God throughout the whole earth. That dominion did of right pertain to the Deity, was confessed by the heathen in the name "Baal," given to their idols, which signifies Lord; and was not a name of one idol, adored for a god, but common to all the eastern idols. God hath interwoven the notion of his sovereignty in the nature and constitution of man, in the noblest and most inward acts of his soul, in that faculty or act which is most necessary for him, in his converse in this world, either with God or man: it is stamped upon the consicence of man, and flashes in his face in every act of self-judgment conscience passes upon a man: every reflection of conscience implies an obligation of man to some law "written in his heart" (Rom. ii. 15). This law cannot be without a legislator, nor this legislator without a sovereign dominion; these are but natural and easy consequences in the mind of man from every act of conscience. The indelible authority of conscience in man, in the whole exercise of it, bears a respect to the sovereignty of God, clearly proclaims not only a supreme Being, but a supreme Governor, and points man directly to it, that a man may as soon deny his having such a reflecting principle within him, as deny God's dominion over him, and consequently over the whole world of rational creatures.

4. This notion of sovereignty is inseparable from the notion of a God. To acknowledge the existence of a God, and to acknowledge him a rewarder, are linked together (Heb. xi. 6). To acknowledge him a rewarder, is to acknowledge him a governor; rewards being the marks of dominion. The very name of God includes in it a supremacy and an actual rule. He cannot be conceived as God, but he must be conceived as the highest authority in the world. It is as possible for him not to be God as not to be supreme. Wherein can the exercise of his excellencies be apparent, but in his soverign rule?

To fancy an infinite power without a supreme dominion, is to fancy a mighty senseless statue, fit to be beheld, but not fit to be obeyed; as not being able or having no right to give out orders, or not caring for the exercise of it. God cannot be supposed to be the chief being, but he must be supposed to give laws to all, and receive laws from none. And if we suppose him with a perfection of justice and righteousness (which we must do, unless we would make a lame and imperfect God) we must suppose him to have an entire dominion, without which he could never be able to manifest his justice. And without a supreme dominion he could not manifest the supremacy and infiniteness of his righteousness.

(1.) We cannot suppose God a Creator, without supposing a sovereign dominion in him. No creature can be made without some law in its nature; if it had not law, it would be created to no purpose, to no regular end. It would be utterly unbecoming an infinite wisdom to create a lawless creature, a creature wholly vain; much less can a rational creature be made without a law: if it had no law, it were not rational: for the very notion of a rational creature implies reason to be a law to it, and implies an acting by rule. If you could suppose rational creatures without a law, you might suppose that they might blaspheme their Creator, and murder their fellow-creatures, and commit the most abominable villanies destructive to human society, without sin; for " where there is no law, there is no transgression."[r] But those things are accounted sins by all mankind, and sins against the Supreme Being: so that a dominion, and the exercise of it, is so fast linked to God, so entirely in him, so intrinsic in his nature, that it cannot be imagined that a rational creature can be made by him, without a stamp and mark of that dominion in his very nature and frame; it is so inseparable from God in his very act of creation.

(2.) It is such a dominion as cannot be renounced by God himself. It is so intrinsic and connatural to him, so inlaid in the nature of God, that he cannot strip himself of it, nor of the exercise of it, while any creature remains. It is preserved by him, for it could not subsist of itself; it is governed by him, it could not else answer its end. It is impossible there can be a creature, which hath not God for its Lord. Christ himself, though in regard of his Deity equal with God, yet in regard of his created state, and assuming our nature, was God's servant, was governed by him in the whole of his office, acted according to his command and directions; God calls him his servant (Isa. xlii. 1): and Christ, in that prophetic psalm of him, calls God his Lord (Ps. xvi. 2): " O my soul, thou hast said unto the Lord, Thou art my Lord." It was impossible it should be otherwise; justice had been so far from being satisfied, that it had been highly incensed if the order of things in the due subjection to God had been broke, and his terms had not been complied with. It would be a judgment upon the world if God should give up the government to any else, as it is when he gives " children to be princes" (Isa. iii. 4); i. e. children in understanding.

(3.) It is so inseparable, that it cannot be communicated to any creature. No creature is able to exercise it; every creature is unable to perform all the offices that belong to this dominion. No creature can impose laws upon the consciences of men: man knows not the inlets into the soul, his pen cannot reach the inwards of man. What laws he hath power to propose to conscience, he cannot see executed; because every creature wants omniscience; he is not able to perceive all those breaches of the law which may be committed at the same time in so many cities, so many chambers. Or, suppose an angel, in regard to the height of his standing, and the insufficiency of walls, and darkness, and distance to obstruct his view, can behold men's actions, yet he cannot know the internal acts of men's minds and wills, without some outward eruption and appearance of them. And if he be ignorant of them, how can he execute his laws? If he only understand the outward fact without the inward thought, how can he dispense a justice proportionable to the crime? he must needs be ignorant of that which adds the greatest aggravation sometimes to a sin, and inflicts a lighter punishment upon that which receives a deeper tincture from the inward posture of the mind, than another fact may do, which in the outward act may appear more base and unjust; and so while he intends righteousness, may act a degree of injustice. Besides, no creature can inflict a due punishment for sin; that which is due to sin, is a loss of the vision and sight of God; but none can deprive any of that but God himself; nor can a creature reward another with eternal life, which consists in communion with God, which none but God can bestow.[s]

II. Wherein the dominion of God is founded.

1. On the excellency of his nature. Indeed, a bare excellency of nature bespeaks a fitness for government, but doth not properly convey a right of government. Excellency speaks aptitude, not title: a subject may have more wisdom than the prince, and be fitter to hold the reins of government, but he hath not a title to royalty. A man of large capacity and strong virtue is fit to serve his country in parliament, but the election of the people conveys a title to him. Yet a strain of intellectual and moral abilities beyond others, is a foundation for dominion. And it is commonly seen that such eminences in men, though they do not invest them with a civil authority, or an authority of jurisdiction, yet they create a veneration in the minds of men; their virtue attracts reverence, and their advice is regarded as an oracle. Old men by their age, when stored with more wisdom and knowledge by reason of their long experience, acquire a kind of power over the younger in their dictates and councils, so that they gain, by the strength of that excellency, a real authority in the minds of those men they converse with, and possess themselves of a deep respect for them. God therefore being an incomprehensible ocean of all perfection, and possessing infinitely all those virtues that may lay a claim to dominion, hath the first foundation of it in his own nature. His incomparable and unparalleled excellency, as well as the greatness of his work, attracts the voluntary worship of him as a sovereign Lord (Ps. lxxxvi. 8): " Among the gods, there is none like unto thee; neither are there any works

* Maccov. Colleg. Theolog. Disput. 18, pp. 12, 13.

like unto thy work.   All nations shall come and worship before thee." Though his benefits are great engagements to our obedience and affection, yet his infinite majesty and perfection requires the first place in our acknowledgements and adorations.   Upon this account God claims it (Isa. xlvi. 9): "I am God, and there is none like me; I will do all my pleasure:" and the prophet Jeremiah upon the same account acknowledgeth it (Jer. x. 6, 7): "Forasmuch as there is none like unto thee, O Lord, thou art great, and thy name is great in might: who would not fear thee, O King of nations? for to thee doth it appertain: forasmuch as there is none like unto thee."   And this is a more noble title of dominion, it being an uncreated title, and more eminent than that of creation or preservation. This is the natural order God hath placed in his creatures, that the more excellent should rule the inferior.[t]   He committed not the government of lower creatures to lions and tigers, that have a delight in blood, but no knowledge of virtue; but to man, who had an eminence in his nature above other creatures, and was formed with a perfect rectitude, and a height of reason to guide the reins over them. In man, the soul being of a more sublime nature, is set of right to rule over the body; the mind, the most excellent faculty of the soul, to rule over the other powers of it: and wisdom, the most excellent habit of the mind, to guide and regulate that in its determinations; and when the body and sensitive appetite control the soul and mind, it is an usurpation against nature, not a rule according to nature. The excellency, thereof, of the Divine nature is the natural foundation for his dominion.   He hath wisdom to know what is fit for him to do, and an immutable righteousness whereby he cannot do any thing base and unworthy: he hath a foreknowledge whereby he is able to order all things to answer his own glorious designs and the end of his government, that nothing can go awry, nothing put him to a stand, and constrain him to meditate new counsels.   So that if it could be supposed that the world had not been created by him, that the parts of it had met together by chance, and been compacted into such a body, none but God, the supreme and most excellent Being in the world, could have merited, and deservedly challenged the government of it; because nothing had an excellency of nature to capacitate it for it, as he hath, or to enter into a contest with him for a sufficiency to govern.[u]

2. It is founded in his act of creation.   He is the sovereign Lord, as he is the almighty Creator.   The relation of an entire Creator induceth the relation of an absolute Lord; he that gives being, motion, that is the sole cause of the being of a thing, which was before nothing, that hath nothing to concur with him, nothing to assist him, but by his sole power commands it to stand up into being, is the unquestionable Lord and proprietor of that thing that hath no dependence but upon him; and by this act of creation, which extended to all things, he became universal Sovereign over all things: and those that waive the excellency of his nature as the foundation of his government, easily acknowledge the sufficiency of it upon his actual creation.   His dominion of jurisdiction results from creation.

[t] Raynaud, Theolog. Nat. p. 757.   [u] Camero. p. 371. Amyrald, Dissert. pp. 72, 73.

When God himself makes an oration in defence of his sovereignty (Job xxxviii.), his chief arguments are drawn from creation; and (Ps. xcv. 3, 5), "The Lord is a great King above all gods; the sea is his, and he made it:" and so the apostle, in his sermon to the Athenians. As he "made the world, and all things therein," he is styled, "Lord of heaven and earth" (Acts xvii. 24). His dominion, also, of property stands upon this basis: "The heavens are thine, the earth also is thine: as for the world, and the fulness thereof, thou hast founded them" (Ps. lxxxix. 11). Upon this title of forming Israel as a creature, or rather as a church, he demands their service to him as their Sovereign: "O Jacob and Israel, thou art my servant, I have formed thee: thou art my servant, O Israel" (Isa. xliv. 21). The sovereignty of God naturally ariseth from the relation of all things to himself as their entire Creator, and their natural and inseparable dependence upon him in regard of their being and well-being. It depends not upon the election of men; God hath a natural dominion over us as creatures, before he hath a dominion by consent over us as converts: as soon as ever anything began to be a creature, it was a vassal to God, as a Lord. Every man is acknowledged to have a right of possessing what he hath made, and a power of dominion over what he hath framed: he may either cherish his own work, or dash it in pieces; he may either add a greater comeliness to it, or deface what he hath already imparted. He hath a right of property in it: no other man can, without injury, pilfer his own work from him. The work hath no propriety in itself; the right must lie in the immediate framer, or in the person that employed him. The first cause of everything hath an unquestionable dominion of propriety in it upon the score of justice. By the law of nations, the first finder of a country is esteemed the rightful possessor and lord of that country, and the first inventor of an art hath a right of exercising it. If a man hath a just claim of dominion over that thing whose materials were not of his framing, but from only the addition of a new figure from his skill; as a limner over his picture, the cloth whereof he never made, nor the colors wherewith he draws it were never endued by him with their distinct qualities, but only he applies them by his art, to compose such a figure; much more hath God a rightful claim of dominion over his creatures, whose entire being, both in matter and form, and every particle of their excellency, was breathed out by the word of his mouth. He did not only give the matter a form, but bestowed upon the matter itself a being; it was formed by none to his hand, as the matter is on which an artist works. He had the being of all things in his own power, and it was at his choice whether he would impart it or no; there can be no juster and stronger ground of a claim than this. A man hath a right to a piece of brass or gold by his purchase, but when by his engraving he hath formed it into an excellent statue, there results an increase of his right upon the account of his artifice. God's creation of the matter of man gave him a right over man; but his creation of him in so eminent an excellency, with reason to guide him, a clear eye of understanding to discern light from darkness, and truth from falsehood, a freedom of will to act accordingly, and an original righteousness as the varnish and beauty of all; here is the strongest foundation for a claim of authority over man, and the strongest obligation on man for subjection to God. If all those things had been past over to God by another hand, he could not be the supreme Lord, nor could have an absolute right to dispose of them at his pleasure: that would have been the invasion of another's right. Besides, creation is the only first discovery of his dominion. Before the world was framed there was nothing but God himself, and, properly, nothing is said to have dominion over itself; this is a relative attribute, reflecting on the works of God.[x] He had a right of dominion in his nature from eternity, but before creation he was actually Lord only of a nullity; where there is nothing it can have no relation; nothing is not the subject of possession nor of dominion. There could be no exercise of this dominion without creation: what exercise can a sovereign have without subjects? Sovereignty speaks a relation to subjects, and none is properly a sovereign without subjects. To conclude: from hence doth result God's universal dominion; for being Maker of all, he is the ruler of all, and his perpetual dominion; for as long as God continues in the relation of Creator, the right of his sovereignty as Creator cannot be abolished.

3. As God is the final cause, or end of all, he is Lord of all. The end hath a greater sovereignty in actions than the actor itself: the actor hath a sovereignty over others in action, but the end for which any one works hath a sovereignty over the agent himself: a limner hath a sovereignty over the picture he is framing, or hath framed, but the end for which he framed it, either his profit he designed from it, or the honor and credit of skill he aimed at in it, hath a dominion over the limner himself: the end moves and excites the artist to work; it spirits him in it, conducts him in his whole business, possesses his mind, and sits triumphant in him in all the progress of his work; it is the first cause for which the whole work is wrought.[y] Now God, in his actual creation of all, is the sovereign end of all; "for thy pleasure they are and were created" (Rev. iv. 11); "The Lord hath made all things for himself" (Prov. xvi. 4). Man, indeed, is the subordinate and immediate end of the lower creation, and therefore had the dominion over other creatures granted to him: but God being the ultimate and principal end, hath the sovereign and principal dominion; all things as much refer to him, as the last end, as they flow from him as the first cause. So that, as I said before, if the world had been compacted together by a jumbling chance, without a wise hand, as some have foolishly imagined, none could have been an antagonist with God for the government of the world; but God, in regard of the excellency of his nature, would have been the Rector of it, unless those atoms that had composed the world had had an ability to govern it. Since there could be no universal end of all things but God, God only can claim an entire right to the government of it; for though man be the end of the lower creation, yet man is not the end of himself and his own being; he is not the end of the creation of the supreme

[x] Stoughton's "Righteous Man's Plea," Serm. VI. p. 28
[y] Vid. Lessium de Perfect. Divin. pp. 77, 78.

heavens; he is not able to govern them; they are out of his ken, and out of his reach. None fit in regard of the excellency of nature, to be the chief end of the whole world but God; and therefore none can have a right to the dominion of it but God: in this regard God's dominion differs from the dominion of all earthly potentates. All the subjects in creation were made for God as their end, so are not people for rulers, but rulers made for people for their protection, and the preservation of order in societies.

4. The dominion of God is founded upon his preservation of things. (Ps. xcv. 3, 4); " The Lord is a great King above all gods:" why? " In his hand are all the deep places of the earth." While his hand holds things, his hand hath a dominion over them. He that holds a stone in the air, exerciseth a dominion over its natural inclination in hindering it from falling. The creature depends wholly upon God in its preservation ; as soon as that Divine hand which sustains everything were withdrawn, a languishment and swooning would be the next turn in the creature. He is called Lord, *Adonai*, in regard of his sustentation of all things by his continual influx; the word coming of אדן, which signifies a basis or pillar, that supports a building. God is the Lord of all, as he is the sustainer of all by his power, as well as the Creator of all by his word. The sun hath a sovereign dominion over its own beams, which depend upon it, so that if he withdraws himself, they all attend him, and the world is left in darkness. God maintains the vigor of all things, conducts them in their operations; so that nothing that they are, nothing that they have, but is owing to his preserving power. The Master of this great family may as well be called the Lord of it, since every member of it depends upon him for the support of that being he first gave them, and holds of his empire. As the right to govern resulted from creation, so it is perpetuated by the preservation of things.

5. The dominion of God is strengthened by the innumerable benefits he bestows upon his creatures: the benefits he confers upon us after creation, are not the original ground of his dominion. A man hath not authority over his servant from the kindness he shows to him, but his authority commenceth before any act of kindness, and is founded upon a right of purchase, conquest, or compact. Dominion doth not depend upon mere benefits; then inferiors might have dominions over superiors. A peasant may save the life of a prince to whom he was not subject; he hath not therefore a right to step up into his throne and give laws to him: and children that maintain their parents in their poverty, might then acquire an authority over them which they can never climb to; because the benefits they confer cannot parallel the benefits they have received from the authors of their lives. The bounties of God to us add nothing to the intrinsic right of his natural dominion; they being the effects of that sovereignty, as he is a rewarder and governor ; as the benefits a prince bestows upon his favorite increases not that right of authority which is inherent in the crown, but strengthens that dominion as it stands in relation to the receiver, by increasing the obligation of the favorite to an observance of him, not only as

his natural prince, but his gracious benefactor. The beneficence of God adds, though not an original right of power, yet a foundation of a stronger upbraiding the creature, if he walks in a violation and forgetfulness of those benefits, and pull in pieces the links of that ingenuous duty they call for; and an occasion of exercising of justice in punishing the delinquent, which is a part of his empire (Isa. i. 2): " Hear, O heavens, and give ear, O earth, the Lord hath spoken; I have nourished children, and they have rebelled against me." Thus the fundamental right as Creator is made more indisputable by his relation as a benefactor, and more as being so after a forfeiture of what was enjoyed by creation. The benefits of God are innumerable, and so magnificent that they cannot meet with any compensation from the creature; and, therefore, do necessarily require a submission from the creature, and an acknowledgment of Divine authority. But that benefit of redemption doth add a stronger right of dominion to God; since he hath not only as a Creator given them being and life as his creatures, but paid a price, the price of his Son's blood, for their rescue from captivity; so that he hath a sovereignty of grace as well as nature, and the ransomed ones belong to him as Redeemer as well as Creator (1 Cor. vi. 19, 20): " Ye are not your own, for ye are bought with a price;" therefore your body and your spirit are God's. By this he acquired a right of another kind, and bought us from that uncontrollable lordship we affected over ourselves by the sin of Adam, that he might use us as his own peculiar for his own glory and service. By this redemption there results to God a right over our bodies, over our spirits, over our services, as well as by creation; and to show the strength of this right, the apostle repeats it, " you are bought;" a purchase cannot be without a price paid; but he adds price also, " bought with a price." To strengthen the title, purchase gave him a new right, and the greatness of the price established that right. The more a man pays for a thing, the more usually we say, he deserves to have it, he hath paid enough for it; it was, indeed, price enough, and too much for such vile creatures as we are.

III. The third thing is, The nature of this dominion.

1. This dominion is independent. His throne is in the heavens; the heavens depend not upon the earth, nor God upon his creatures. Since he is independent in regard of his essence, he is so in his dominion, which flows from the excellency and fulness of his essence; as he receives his essence from none, so he derives his dominion from none; all other dominion except paternal authority is rooted originally in the wills of men. The first title was the consent of the people, or the conquest of others by the help of those people that first consented; and in the exercise of it, earthly dominion depends upon assistance of the subjects, and the members being joined with the head carry on the work of government, and prevent civil dissensions; in the support of it, it depends upon the subjects' contributions and taxes; the subjects in their strength are the arms, and in their purses the sinews of government; but God depends upon none in the foundation of his government; he is not a Lord by the votes

of his vassals.[z] Nor is it successively handed to him by any predecessor, nor constituted by the power of a superior; nor forced he his way by war and conquest, nor precariously attained it by suit or flattery, or bribing promises. He holds not the right of his empire from any other; he hath no superior to hand him to his throne, and settle him by commission; he is therefore called "King of kings, and Lord of lords," having none above him; "A great King above all gods" (Ps. xcv. 3): needing no license from any when to act, nor direction how to act, or assistance in his action; he owes not any of those to any person; he was not ordered by any other to create, and therefore received not orders from any other to rule over what he hath created. He received not his power and wisdom from another, and therefore is not subject to any for the rule of his government. He only made his own subjects, and from himself hath the sole authority; his own will was the cause of their beings, and his own will is the director of their actions. He is not determined by his creatures in any of his motions, but determines the creatures in all; his actions are not regulated by any law without him, but by a law within him, the law of his own nature. It is impossible he can have any rule without himself, because there is nothing superior to himself, nor doth he depend upon any in the exercise of his government; he needs no servants in it, when he uses creatures: it is not out of want of their help, but for the manifestation of his wisdom and power. What he doth by his subjects, he can do by himself: "The government is upon his shoulder" (Isa. ix. 6), to show that he needs not any supporters. All other governments flow from him, all other authorities depend upon him; *Dei Gratiâ*, or *Dei Providentiâ*, is in the style of princes. As their being is derived from his power, so their authority is but a branch of his dominion. They are governors by Divine providence; God is governor by his sole nature. All motions depend upon the first heaven, which moves all; but that depends upon nothing. The government of Christ depends upon God's uncreated dominion, and is by commision from him; Christ assumed not this honor to himself, "But he that said unto him, Thou art my Son," bestowed it upon him. "He put all things under his feet," but not himself (1 Cor. xv. 27). "When he saith, All things are put under him, he is excepted, which did put all things under him." He sits still as an independent governor upon his throne.

2. This dominion is absolute. If his throne be in the heavens, there is nothing to control him. If he be independent, he must needs be absolute; since he hath no cause in conjunction with him as Creator, that can share with him in his right, or restrain him in the disposal of his creature. His authority is unlimited; in this regard the title of "Lord" becomes not any but God properly. Tiberius, though none of the best, though one of the subtilest princes, accounted the title of "Lord" a reproach to him: since he was not absolute."[a]

1st. Absolute in regard of freedom and liberty. (1.) Thus creation is a work of his mere sovereignty; he created, because it was his plea-

[z] Raynaud, Theolog. Natural, pp. 760—762.
[a] Sueton. de Tiberio, cap. 27.

sure to create (Rev. iv. 11). He is not necessitated to do this or that. He might have chosen whether he would have framed an earth and heavens, and laid the foundations of his chambers in the waters. He was under no obligation to reduce things from nullity to existence. (2.) Preservation is the fruit of his sovereignty. When he had called the world to stand out, he might have ordered it to return into its dark den of nothingness, ripped up every part of its foundation, or have given being to many more creatures then he did. If you consider his absolute sovereignty, why might he not have divested Adam presently of those rational perfections wherewith he had endowed him? And might he not have metamorphosed him into some beast, and elevated some beast into a rational nature? Why might he not have degraded an angel to a worm, and advanced a worm to the nature and condition of an angel? Why might he not have revoked that grant of dominion, which he had passed to man over all creatures? It was free to him to permit sin to enter into the earth, or to have excluded it out of he earth, as he doth out of heaven. (3.) Redemption is a fruit of his sovereignty. By his absolute sovereignty he might have confirmed all the angels in their standing by grace, and prevented the revolt of any of their members from him; and when there was a revolt both in heaven and earth, it was free to him to have called out his Son to assume the angelical, as well as the human, nature, or have exercised his dominion in the déstruction of men and devils, rather than in the redemption of any; he was under no obligation to restore either the one or the other. (4.) May he not impose what terms he pleases? May he not impose what laws he pleases, and exact what he will of his creature without promising any rewards? May he not use his own for his own honor, as well as men use for their credit what they do possess by his indulgence? (5.) Affliction is an act of his sovereignty. By this right of sovereignty, may not God take away any man's goods, since they were his doles? As he was not indebted to us when he bestowed them, so he cannot wrong us when he removes them. He takes from us what is more his own than it is ours, and was never ours but by his gift, and that for a time only, not forever. By this right he may determine our times, put a period to our days when he pleases, strip us of one member, and lop off another. Man's being was from him, and why should he not have a sovereignty to take what he had a sovereignty to give? Why should this seem strange to any of us, since we ourselves exercise an absolute dominion over those things in our possession, which have sense and feeling, as well as over those that want it? Doth not every man think he hath an absolute authority over the utensils of his house, over his horse, his dog, to preserve or kill him, to do what he please with him, without rendering any other reason than, *It is my own?* May not God do much more? Doth not his dominion over the work of his hands transcend that which a man can claim over his beast that he never gave life unto? He that dares dispute against God's absolute right, fancies himself as much a god as his Creator: understands not the vast difference between the Divine nature and his own; between the sovereignty of God and his own, which is all the theme

God himself discourseth upon in those stately chapters (Job. xxxviii. xxxix. &c.); not mentioning a word of Job's sin, but only vindicating the rights of his own authority. Nor doth Job, in his reply (Job xl. 4), speak of his sin, but of his natural vileness as a creature in the presence of his Creator. By this right, God unstops the bottles of heaven in one place, and stops them in another, causing it "to rain upon one city, and not upon another" (Amos iv. 7); ordering the clouds to move to this or that quarter where he hath a mind to be a benefactor or a judge. (6.) Unequal dispensations are acts of his sovereignty. By this right he is patient toward those whose sins, by the common voice of men, deserve speedy judgments, and pours out pain upon those that are patterns of virtue to the world. By this he gives sometimes the worst of men an ocean of wealth and honor to swim in, and reduceth an useful and exemplary grace to a scanty poverty. By this he "rules the kingdoms of men," and sets a crown upon the head of the basest of men (Dan. iv. 17), while he deposeth another that seemed to deserve a weightier diadem. This is, as he is the Lord of the ammunition of his thunders, and the treasures of his bounty. (7.) He may inflict what torments he pleases. Some say, by this right of sovereignty he may inflict what torments he pleaseth upon an innocent person; which, indeed, will not bear the nature of a punishment as an effect of justice, without the supposal of a crime; but a torment, as an effect of that sovereign right he hath over his creature, which is as absolute over his work as the "potter's" power is "over his own clay" (Jer. xviii. 6; Rom. ix. 21). May not the potter, after his labor, either set his "vessel" up to adorn his house, or knock it in pieces, and fling it upon the dunghill; separate it to some noble use, or condemn it to some sordid service?[b] Is the right of God over his creatures less than that of the potter over his vessel, since God contributed all to his creature, but the potter never made the clay, which is the substance of the vessel, nor the water which was necessary to make it tractable, but only moulded the substance of it into such a shape? The vessel that is framed, and the potter that frames it, differ only in life: the body of the potter, whereby he executes his authority, is of no better a mould than the clay, the matter of his vessel. Shall he have so absolute a power over that which is so near him, and shall not God over that which is so infinitely distant from him? The "vessel," perhaps, might plead for itself that it was once part of the body of a man, and as good as the "potter" himself; whereas no creature can plead it was part of God, and as good as God himself. Though there be no man in the world but deserves affliction, yet the Scripture sometimes lays affliction upon the score of God's dominion, without any respect to the sin of the afflicted person. Speaking of a sick person (James v. 15), "If he have committed sins, they shall be forgiven him;" whereby is implied, that he might be struck into sickness by God, without any respect to a particular sin, but in a way of trial; and that his affliction sprung not from any exercise of Divine justice, but from his absolute sovereignty; and so, in the case of the blind man, when the disciples asked for what sin it was,

[b] Lessius de Perfect. Divin. pp. 66, 67.

whether for his "own," or his "parents sin," he was born blind?
(John ix. 3), "Neither hath this man sinned, nor his parents;" which
speaks, in itself, not against the whole current of Scripture; but the
words import thus much, that God, in this blindness from the birth,
neither respected any sin of the man's own, nor of his parents, but
he did it as an absolute sovereign, to manifest his own glory in that
miraculous cure which was wrought by Christ. Though afflictions
do not happen without the desert of the creature, yet some afflictions may be sent without any particular respect to that desert,
merely for the manifestation of God's glory, since the creature was
made for God himself, and his honor, and therefore may be used in
a serviceableness to the glory of the Creator.

2d. His dominion is absolute in regard of unlimitedness by any
law without him. He is an absolute monarch that makes laws for
his subjects, but is not bound by any himself, nor receives any rules
and laws from his subjects, for the management of his government.
But most governments in the world are bounded by laws made by
common consent. But when kings are not limited by the laws of
their kingdoms, yet they are bounded by the law of nature, and by
the providence of God. But God is under no law without himself;
his rule is within him, the rectitude and righteousness of his own
nature; he is not under that law he hath prescribed to man. The
law was not made for a "righteous man" (1 Tim. i. 9), much less for
a righteous God. God is his own law; his own nature is his rule,
as his own glory is his end; himself is his end, and himself is his
law. He is moved by nothing without himself; nothing hath the
dominion of a motive over him but his own will, which is his rule
for all his actions in heaven and earth. (Dan. iv. 32), "He rules in
the kingdom of men, and gives it to whomsoever he will." And,
(Rom. ix. 18,) "He hath mercy on whom he will have mercy;" as
all things are wrought by him according to his own eternal ideas in
his own mind, so all is wrought by him according to the inward
motive in his own will, which was the manifestation of his own
honor. The greatest motives, therefore, that the best persons have
used, when they have pleaded for any grant from God, was his
own glory, which would be advanced by an answer of their petition.

3d. His dominion is absolute in regard of supremacy and uncon-
trollableness. None can implead him, and cause him to render a
reason of his actions. He is the sovereign King, "Who may say
unto him, What dost thou?" (Eccles. viii. 4.) It is an absurd thing
for any to dispute with God. (Rom. xi. 20), "Who art thou, O man,
that repliest against God?" Thou, a man, a piece of dust, to argue
with a God incomprehensibly above thy reason, about the reason of
his works! Let the potsherds strive with the potsherds of the earth,
but "not with Him that fashioned them" (Isa. xlv. 9). In all the
desolations he works, he asserts his own supremacy to silence men.
(Ps. xlvi. 10), "Be still, and know that I am God!" Beware of any
quarrelling motions in your minds; it is sufficient than I am God,
that is supreme, and will not be impleaded, and censured, or worded
with by any creature about what I do. He is not bound to render a

reason of any of his proceedings. Subjects are accountable to their princes, and princes to God, God to none; since he is not limited by any superior, his prerogative is supreme.

4th. His dominion is absolute in regard of irresistibleness. Other governments are bounded by law; so that what a governor hath strength to do, he hath not a right to do; other governors have a limited ability, that what they have a right to do, they have not always a strength to do; they may want a power to execute their own counsels. But God is destitute of neither; he hath an infinite right, and an infinite strength; his word is a law; he commands things to stand out of nothing, and they do so. " He commanded," or spake, ὁ εἰπὼν, "light to shine out of darkness" (2 Cor. iv. 6). There is no distance of time between his word: " Let there be light; and there was light" (Gen. i. 3). Magistrates often use not their authority, for fear of giving occasion to insurrections, which may overturn their empire. But if the Lord will work, " who shall let it?" (Isa. xliii. 19): and if God will not work, who shall force him? He can check and overturn all other powers; his decrees cannot be stopped, nor his hand held back by any: if he wills to dash the whole world in pieces, no creature can maintain its being against his order. He sets the ordinances of the heavens, and the dominion thereof in the earth; and sends lightnings, that they may go, and say unto him, " Here we are" (Job. xxxviii. 33, 34).

3. Yet this dominion, though it be absolute, is not tyrannical, but it is managed by the rules of wisdom, righteousness, and goodness. If his throne be in the heavens, it is pure and good: because the heavens are the purest parts of the creation, and influence by their goodness the lower earth. Since he is his own rule, and his nature is infinitely wise, holy, and righteous, he cannot do a thing but what is unquestionably agreeable with wisdom, justice, and purity. In all the exercises of his sovereign right, he is never unattended with those perfections of his nature. Might not God, by his absolute power, have pardoned men's guilt, and thrown the invading sin out of his creatures? but in regard of his truth pawned in his threatening, and in regard of his justice, which demanded satisfaction, he would not. Might not God, by his absolute sovereignty, admit a man into his friendship, without giving him any grace? but in regard of the incongruity of such an act to his wisdom and holiness, he will not. May he not, by his absolute power, refuse to accept a man that desires to please him, and reject a purely innocent creature? but in regard of his goodness and righteousness, he will not. Though innocence be amiable in its own nature, yet it is not necessary in regard of God's sovereignty, that he should love it; but in regard of his goodness it is necessary, and he will never do otherwise. As God never acts to the utmost of his power, so he never exerts the utmost of his sovereignty: because it would be inconsistent with those other properties which render him perfectly adorable to the creature. As no intelligent creature, neither angel nor man, can be framed without a law in his nature, so we cannot imagine God without a law in his own nature, unless we would fancy him a rude, tyrannical, foolish being, that hath nothing of holiness,

goodness, righteousness, wisdom. If he "made the heavens in wisdom" (Ps. cxxxvi. 5), he made them by some rule, not by a mere will, but a rule within himself, not without. A wise work is never the result of an absolute unguided will.

(1.) This dominion is managed by the rule of wisdom. What may appear to us to have no other spring than absolute sovereignty, would be found to have a depth of amazing wisdom, and accountable reason, were our short capacities long enough to fathom it. When the apostle had been discoursing of the eternal counsels of God, in seizing upon one man, and letting go another, in neglecting the Jews, and gathering in the Gentiles, which appears to us to be results only of an absolute dominion, yet he resolves not those amazing acts into that, without taking it for granted that they were governed by exact wisdom, though beyond his ken to see and his line to sound. "O, the depth of the riches, both of the wisdom and knowledge of God; how unsearchable are his judgments, and his ways past finding out" (Rom. ii. 33)! There are some things in matters of state, that may seem to be acts of mere will, but if we were acquainted with the *arcana imperii*, the inward engines which moved them, and the ends aimed at in those undertakings, we might find a rich vein of prudence in them, to incline us to judge otherwise than bare arbitrary proceedings. The other attributes of power and goodness are more easily perceptible in the works of God than his wisdom. The first view of the creation strikes us with this sentiment, that the Author of this great fabric was mighty and beneficial; but his wisdom lies deeper than to be discerned at the first glance, without a diligent inquiry; as at the first casting our eyes upon the sea, we behold its motion, color, and something of its vastness, but we cannot presently fathom the depth of it, and understand those lower fountains that supply that great ocean of waters. It is part of God's sovereignity, as it is of the wisest princes, that he hath a wisdom beyond the reach of his subjects; it is not for a finite nature to understand an Infinite Wisdom, nor for a foolish creature that hath lost his understanding by the fall, to judge of the reason of the methods of a wise Counsellor. Yet those actions that savor most of sovereignty, present men with some glances of his wisdom. Was it mere will, that he suffered some angels to fall? But his wisdom was in it for the manifestation of his justice, as it was also in the case of Pharaoh. Was it mere will, that he suffered sin to be committed by man? Was not his wisdom in this for the discovery of his mercy, which never had been known without that, which should render a creature miserable? "He hath concluded them all in unbelief, that he might have mercy upon all" (Rom. xi. 32). Though God had such an absolute right, to have annihilated the world as soon as ever he had made it, yet how had this consisted with his wisdom, to have erected a creature after his own image one day, and despised it so much the next, as to cashier it from being? What wisdom had it been to make a thing only to destroy it; to repent of his work as soon as ever it came out of his hands, without any occasion offered by the creature? If God be supposed to be Creator, he must be supposed to have an end in creation; what end can that be but himself and his own glory, the manifestation of the perfections of his nature? What perfection could have been discovered in so quick an annihilation, but that of his power in creating, and of his sovereignty in snatching away the being of his rational creature, before it had laid the methods of acting? What wisdom to make a world, and a reasonable creature for no use; not to praise and honor him, but to be broken in pieces, and destroyed by him?

(2.) His sovereignty is managed according to the rule of righteousness. Worldly princes often fancy tyranny and oppression to be the chief marks of sovereignty, and think their sceptres not beautiful till died in blood, nor the throne secure till established upon slain carcasses. But "justice and judgment" are the foundation of the throne of God (Ps. lxxxix. 14); alluding perhaps to the supporters of arms and thrones, which among princes are the figures of lions, emblems of courage, as Solomon had (1 Kings, x. 19). But God makes not so much might, as right, the support of his. He sits on a "throne of holiness" (Ps. xlvii. 8). As he reigns over the heathens, referring to the calling of the Gentiles after the rejecting of the Jews; the Psalmist here praising the righteousness of it, as the Apostle had the unsearchable wisdom of it (Rom. xi. 33). "In all his ways he is righteous" (Ps. cxlv. 17): in his ways of terror as well as those of sweetness; in those works wherein little else but that of his sovereignty appears to us. It is always linked with his holiness, that he will not do by his absolute right anything but what is conformable to it: since his dominion is founded upon the excellency of his nature, he will not do anything but what is agreeable to it, and becoming his other perfections. Though he be an absolute sovereign, he is not an arbitrary governor; "Shall not the Judge of all the earth do right" (Gen. xviii. 25)? i. e. it is impossible but he should act righteously in every punctilio of his government, since his righteousness capacitates him to be a judge, not a tyrant, of all the earth. The heathen poets represented their chief god Jupiter with Themis, or Right, sitting by him upon his throne in all his orders. God cannot by his absolute sovereignty command some things, because they are directly against unchangeable righteousness; as to command a creature to hate or blaspheme the Creator, not to own him nor praise him. It would be a manifest unrighteousness to order the creature not to own him, upon whom he depends both in its being and well-being; this would be against that natural duty which is indispensably due from every rational creature to God. This would be to order him to lay aside his reason, while he retains it; to disown him to be the Creator, while man remains his creature. This is repugnant to the nature of God, and the true nature of the creature; or to exact anything of man, but what he had given him a capacity, in his original nature, to perform. If any command were above our natural power, it would be unrighteous; as to command a man to grasp the globe of the earth, to stride over the sea, to lave out the waters of the ocean; these things are impossible, and become not the righteousness and wisdom of God to enjoin. There can be no obligation on man to an impossibility. God had a free dominion over nullity before the creation; he could call it out into the being of man and beast, but he could not do anything in creation foolishly, because of his infinite wisdom; nor could he by the right of his absolute sovereignty make man sinful, because of his infinite purity. As it is impossible for him not to be sovereign, it is impossible for him to deny his Deity and his purity. It is lawful for God to do what he will, but his will being ordered by the righteousness of his nature, as infinite as his will, he cannot do anything but what is just; and therefore in his dealing with men, you find him in Scripture submitting the reasonableness and equity of his proceedings to the judgment of his depraved creatures, and the inward dictates of their own conscience. "And now, O inhabitants of Jerusalem, and men of Judah, judge, I pray you, between me and my vineyard" (Isa. v. 3). Though God be the great Sovereign of the world, yet he acts not in a way of absolute sovereignty. He rules by law; he is a "Lawgiver" as well as a "King" (Isa. xxxiii. 22). It had been repugnant to the nature of a rational creature to be ruled otherwise; to be governed as a beast, this had been to frustrate those faculties of will and understanding which had been given him. To conclude this: when we say, God can do this or that, or command this or that, his authority is not bounded and limited properly. Who can reasonably detract from his almightiness, because he cannot do anything which savors of weakness; and what detracting is it from his authority, that he cannot do anything unseemly for the dignity of his nature? It is rather from the infiniteness of his righteousness than the straitness of his authority; at most it is but a voluntary bounding his dominion by the law of his own holiness.

(3.) His sovereignty is managed according to the rule of goodness. Some potentates there have been in the world, that have loved to suck the blood, and drink the tears, of their subjects; that would rule more by fear than love; like Clearchus, the tyrant of Heraclea, who bore the figure of a thunderbolt instead of a sceptre, and named his son Thunder, thereby to tutor him to terrify his subjects.[c] But as God's throne is a throne of holiness, so it is a "throne of grace" (Heb. iv. 16), a throne encircled with a rainbow: "In sight like to an emerald" (Rev. iv. 23): an emblem of the covenant, that hath the pleasantness of a green color, delightful to the eye, betokening mercy. Though his nature be infinitely excellent above us, and his power infinitely transcendent over us, yet the majesty of his government is tempered with an unspeakable goodness. He acts not so much as an absolute Lord, as a gracious Sovereign and obliging Benefactor. He delights not to make his subjects slaves; exacts not from them any servile and fearful, but a generous and cheerful, obedience. He requires them not to fear, or worship him so much for his power, as his goodness. He requires not of a rational creature anything repugnant to the honor, dignity, and principles of such a nature; not anything that may shame, disgrace it, and make it weary of its own being, and the service it owes to its Sovereign. He draws by the cords of a man; his goodness renders his laws as sweet as honey or the honey-comb to an unvitiated palate and a renewed mind. And though it be granted he hath a full dispose of his creature, as the

c Causin, Poly-Histor. lib. iv. cap. 22.

potter of his vessel, and might by his absolute sovereignty inflict upon an innocent an eternal torment, yet his goodness will never permit him to use this sovereign right to the hurt of a creature that deserves it not. If God should cast an innocent creature into the furnace of his wrath, who can question him? But who can think that his goodness will do so, since that is as infinite as his authority? As not to punish the sinner would be a denial of his justice, so to torment an innocent would be a denial of his goodness. A man hath an absolute power over his beast, and may take away his life, and put him to a great deal of pain; but that moral virtue of pity and tenderness would not permit him to use this right, but when it conduceth to some greater good than that can be evil; either for the good of man, which is the end of the creature, or for the good of the poor beast itself, to rid him of a greater misery; none but a savage nature, a disposition to be abhorred, would torture a poor beast merely for his pleasure. It is as much against the nature of God to punish one eternally, that hath not deserved it, as it is to deny himself, and act anything foolishly and unbeseeming his other perfections, which render him majestical and adorable. To afflict an innocent creature for his own good, or for the good of the world, as in the case of the Redeemer, is so far from being against goodness, that it is the highest testimony of his tender bowels to the sons of men. God, though he be mighty, "withdraws not his eyes," *i. e.* his tender respect, "from the righteous" (Job, xxxvi. 5, 7—10). And if he "bind them in fetters," it is to "show them their transgressions," and "open their ear to discipline," and renewing commands, in a more sensible strain, "to depart from iniquity." What was said of Fabritius, "You may as soon remove the sun from its course, as Fabritius from his honesty," may be of God: you may as soon dash in pieces his throne, as separate his goodness from his sovereignty.

4. This sovereignty is extensive over all creatures. He rules all, as the heavens do over the earth. He is "King of worlds, King of ages," as the word translated "eternal" signifies (1 Tim. i. 17), τῷ δὲ βασιλεῖ τῶν αἰώνων: and the same word is so translated (Heb. i. 2), "By whom also he made the worlds." The same word is rendered "worlds" (Heb. xi. 3): "The worlds were framed by the Word of God." God is King of ages or worlds, of the invisible world and the sensible; of all from the beginning of their creation, of whatsoever is measured by a time. It extends over angels and devils, over wicked and good, over rational and irrational creatures; all things bow down under his hand; nothing can be exempted from him: because there is nothing but was extracted by him from nothing into being. All things essentially depend upon him; and, therefore, must be essentially subject to him; the extent of his dominion flows from the perfection of his essence; since his essence is unlimited, his royalty cannot be restrained. His authority is as void of any imperfection as his essence is; it reaches out to all points of the heaven above, and the earth below. Other princes reign in a spot of ground. Every worldly potentate hath the confines of his dominions. The Pyrenean mountains divide France from Spain, and the Alps, Italy from France. None are called kings absolutely, but kings of this or

that place. But God is the King; the spacious firmament limits
not his dominion ; if we could suppose him bounded by any place,
in regard of his presence, yet he could never be out of his own dominion ; whatsoever he looks upon, wheresoever he were, would be
under his rule. Earthly kings may step out of their own country
into the territory of a neighbor prince; and as one leaves his country,
so he leaves his dominion behind him; but heaven and earth, and
every particle of both, is the territory of God. "He hath prepared
his throne in the heavens, and his kingdom rules over all."

(1.) The heaven of angels, and other excellent creatures, belong to
his authority. He is principally called "The Lord of Hosts," in relation to his entire command over the angelical legions : therefore,
ver. 21, following the text, they are called his "hosts," and "ministers that do his pleasure." Jacob called him so before (Gen. xxxii.
1, 2). When he met the angels of God, he calls them "the host of
God;" and the Evangelist, long after, calls them so (Luke, ii. 13):
"A multitude of the heavenly host, praising God ;" and all this host
he commands (Isa. xlv. 12): "My hands have stretched out the
heavens, and all their host have I commanded." He employs them
all in his service; and when he issues out his orders to them to do
this or that, he finds no resistance of his will. And the inanimate
creatures in heaven are at his beck; they are his armies in heaven,
disposed in an excellent order in their several ranks (Ps. cxlvii. 4):
"He calls the stars by name;" they render a due obedience to him as
servants to their master, when he singles them out, "and calls them
by name," to do some special service; he calls them out to their
several offices, as the general of an army appoints the station of
every regiment in a battalia. Or "he calls them by name," *i. e.* he
imposeth names upon them, a sign of dominion : the giving names
to the inferior creatures being the first act of Adam's derivative dominion over them. These are under the sovereignty of God. The
stars, by their influences, fight against Sisera (Judges, v. 20). And
the sun holds in its reins, and stands stone still, to light Joshua to a
complete victory (Josh. x. 12). They are all marshalled in their
ranks to receive his word of command, and fight in close order, as
being desirous to have a share in the ruin of the enemies of their
Sovereign. And those creatures which mount up from the earth,
and take their place in the lower heavens, vapors, whereof hail and
snow are formed, are part of the army, and do not only receive, but
fulfil, his word of command (Ps. cxlviii. 8). These are his stores
and magazines of judgment against a time of trouble, and "a day of
battle and war" (Job, xxxviii. 22. 23). The sovereignty of God is
visible in all their motions, in their going and returning. If he says,
Go, they go ; if he say, Come, they come ; if he say, do this, they
gird up their loins, and stand stiff to their duty.

(2.) The hell of devils belong to his authority. They have cast
themselves out of the arms of his grace into the furnace of his justice; they have, by their revolt, forfeited the treasure of his goodness, but cannot exempt themselves from the sceptre of his dominion ;
when they would not own him as a Lord Father, they are under
him as a Lord Judge; they are cast out of his affection, but not

freed from his yoke. He rules over the good angels as his subjects, over the evil ones as his rebels. In whatsoever relation he stands, either as a friend or enemy, he never loses that of a Lord. A prince is the lord of his criminals as well as of his loyalest subjects. By this right of his sovereignty, he uses them to punish some, and be the occasion of benefit to others : on the wicked he employs them as instruments of vengeance; towards the godly, as in the case of Job, as an instrument of kindness for the manifestation of his sincerity against the intention of that malicious executioner. Though the devils are the executioners of his justice, it is not by their own authority, but God's ; as those that are employed either to rack or execute a malefactor, are subjects to the prince not only in the quality of men, but in the execution of their function. The devil, by drawing men to sin, acquires no right to himself over the sinner: for man by sin offends not the devil, but God, and becomes guilty of punishment under God.[d] When, therefore, the devil is used by God for the punishment of any, it is an act of his sovereignty for the manifestation of the order of his justice. And as most nations use the vilest persons in offices of execution, so doth God those vile spirits. He doth not ordinarily use the good angels in those offices of vengeance, but in the preservation of his people. When he would solely punish, he employs " evil angels" (Ps. lxxviii. 49), a troop of devils. His sovereignty is extended over the "deceiver and the deceived" (Job, xii. 16); over both the malefactor and the executioner, the devil and his prisoner. He useth the natural malice of the devils for his own just ends, and by his sovereign authority orders them to be the executioners of his judgments upon their own vassals, as well as sometimes inflicters of punishments upon his own servants.

(3.) The earth of men and other creatures belongs to his authority (Ps. xlvii. 7). God is King of "all the earth," and rules to the "ends" of it (Ps. lix. 13). Ancient atheists confined God's dominion to the heavenly orbs, and bounded it within the circuit of the celestial sphere (Job, xxii. 14): " He walks in the circuit of heaven," *i. e.* he exerciseth his dominion only there. *Pedum positio* was the sign of the possession of a piece of land, and the dominion of the possessor of it ; and land was resigned by such a ceremony, as now, by the delivery of a twig or turf.[e] But his dominion extends,

1st. Over the least creatures. All the creatures of the earth are listed in Christ's muster-roll, and make up the number of his regiments. He hath an host on earth as well as in heaven (Gen. ii. 1): " The heavens and earth were finished, and all the host of them." And they are " all his servants" (Ps. cxiv. 91), and move at his pleasure. And he vouchsafes the title of his army to the locust, caterpillar, and palmer worm (Joel, ii. 25); and describes their motions by military words, " climbing the walls, marching, not breaking their ranks" (ver. 7). He hath the command, as a great general, over the highest angel and the meanest worm ; all the kinds of the smallest insects he presseth for his service. By this sovereignty he muzzled the devouring nature of the fire to preserve the three children, and let it loose to consume their adversaries ; and if he speaks the word,

d Suarez. Vol. II. lib. viii. cap, 20. p. 736.   e Bolduc. *in loc.*

the stormy waves are hushed, as if they had no principle of rage within them (Ps. lxxxix. 9). Since the meanest creature attains its end, and no arrow that God hath by his power shot into the world but hits the mark he aimed at, we must conclude, that there is a sovereign hand that governs all: not a spot of earth, or air, or water in the world, but is his possession; not a creature in any element but is his subject.

2d. His dominion extends over men. It extends over the highest potentate, as well as the meanest peasant; the proudest monarch is no more exempt than the most languishing beggar. He lays not aside his authority to please the prince, nor strains it up to terrify the indigent. "He accepts not the persons of princes, nor regards the rich more than the poor; for they are all the work of his hand" (Job, xxxiv. 19). Both the powers and weaknesses, the gallantry and peasantry of the earth, stand and fall at his pleasure. Man, in innocence, was under his authority as his creature; and man, in his revolt, is further under his authority as a criminal: as a person is under the authority of a prince, as a governor, while he obeys his laws; and further under the authority of the prince, as a judge, when he violates his laws. Man is under God's dominion in everything, in his settlement, in his calling, in the ordering his very habitation (Acts, xvii. 26): "He determines the bounds of their habitations." He never yet permitted any to be universal monarch in the world, nor over the fourth part of it, though several, in the pride of their heart, have designed and attempted it: the pope, who hath bid the fairest for it in spirituals, never attained it; and when his power was most flourishing, there were multitudes that would never acknowledge his authority.

3d. But especially this dominion, in the peculiarity of its extent, is seen in the exercise of it over the spirits and hearts of men. Earthly governors have, by his indulgence, a share with him in a dominion over men's bodies, upon which account he graceth princes and judges with the title of "gods" (Ps. lxxxii. 6); but the highest prince is but a prince "according to the flesh," as the apostle calls masters in relation to their servants (Col. iii. 22).

God is the sovereign; man rules over the beast in man, the body; and God rules over the man in man, the soul. It sticks not in the outward surface, but pierceth to the inward marrow. It is impossible God should be without this; if our wills were independent of him, we were in some sort equal with himself, in part gods, as well as creatures. It is impossible a creature, either in whole or in part, can be exempted from it; since he is the fashioner of hearts as well as of bodies. He is the Father of spirits, and therefore hath the right of a paternal dominion over them. When he established man lord of the other creatures, he did not strip himself of the propriety; and when he made man a free agent, and lord of the acts of his will, he did not divest himself of the sovereignty. His sovereignty is seen,

[1.] In gifting the spirits of men. Earthly magistrates have hands too short to inspire the hearts of their subjects with worthy sentiments: when they confer an employment, they are not able to convey an ability with it fit for the station: they may as soon frame a statue of liquid water, and gild, or paint it over with the costliest colors, as impart to any a state-head for a state-ministry. But when God chooseth a Saul from so mean an employment as seeking of asses, he can treasure up in him a spirit fit for government; and fire David, in age a stripling, and by education a shepherd, with courage to encounter, and skill to defeat, a massy Goliath. And when he designs a person for glory, to stand before his throne, he can put a new and a royal spirit into him (Ezek. xxxvi. 26). God only can infuse habits into the soul, to capacitate it to act nobly and generously.

[2.] His sovereignty is seen in regard of the inclinations of men's wills. No creature can immediately work upon the will, to guide it to what point he pleaseth, though mediately it may, by proposing reasons which may master the understanding, and thereby determine the will. But God bows the hearts of men, by the efficacy of his dominion, to what centre he pleaseth. When the more overweening sort of men, that thought their own heads as fit for a crown as Saul's, scornfully despised him; yet God touched the hearts of a band of men to follow and adhere to him (1 Sam. x. 26, 27). When the antichristian whore shall be ripe for destruction, God shall " put it into the heart" of the ten horns or kings, " to hate the whore, burn her with fire, and fulfil his will" (Rev. xvii. 16, 17). He "fashions the hearts" alike, and tunes one string to answer another, and both to answer his own design (Ps. xxxiii. 15). And while men seem to gratify their own ambition and malice, they execute the will of God, by his secret touch upon their spirits, guiding their inclinations to serve the glorious manifestation of truth. While the Jews would, in a reproachful disgrace to Christ, crucify two thieves with him, to render him more incapable to have any followers, they accomplished a prophecy, and brought to light a mark of the Messiah, whereby he had been charactered in one of their prophets, that he should be "numbered among transgressors" (Isa. liii. 12). He can make a man of not willing, willing; the wills of all men are in his hand; *i. e.* under the power of his sceptre, to retain or let go upon this or that errand, to bend this or that way; as water is carried by pipes to what house or place the owner of it is pleased to order. "The king's heart is in the hand of the Lord, as the rivers of waters; he turns it whithersoever he will" (Prov. xxi. 1) without any limitation. He speaks of the heart of princes; because, in regard of their height, they seem to be more absolute, and impetuous as waters; yet God holds them in his hand, under his dominion; turns them to acts of clemency or severity, like waters, either to overflow and damage, or to refresh and fructify. He can convey a spirit to them, or "cut it off" from them (Ps. lxxvi. 12). It is with reference to his efficacious power, in graciously turning the heart of Paul, that the apostle breaks off his discourse of the story of his conversion, and breaks out into a magnifying and glorifying of God's dominion. "Now unto the King eternal," &c. "be honor and glory forever and ever" (1 Tim. i. 17). Our hearts are more subject to the Divine sovereignty than our members in their motions are subject to our own wills. As we can move our hand east or west to any quarter of the world, so can God bend our wills to what mark he pleases. The second cause in every motion depends upon the first; and that will, being a second cause, may be furthered or hindered in its inclinations or executions by God; he can bend or unbend it, and change it from one actual inclination to another. It is as much under his authority and power to move, or hinder, as the vast engine of the heavens is in its motion or standing still, which he can affect by a word. The work depends upon the workman; the clock upon the artificer for the motions of it.

[3.] His dominion is seen in regard of terror or comfort. The heart or conscience is God's special throne on earth, which he hath reserved to himself, and never indulged human authority to sit upon it. He solely orders this in ways of conviction or comfort. He can flash terror into men's spirits in the midst of their earthly jollities, and put death into the pot of conscience, when they are boiling up themselves in a high pitch of worldly delights, and can raise men's spirits above the sense of torment under racks and flames. He can draw a hand-writing not only in the outward chamber, but the inward closet; bring the rack into the inwards of a man. None can infuse comfort when he writes bitter things, nor can any fill the heart with gall, when he drops in honey. Men may order outward duties, but they cannot unlock the conscience, and constrain men to think them duties which they are forced, by human laws, outwardly to act: and as the laws of earthly princes are bounded by the outward man, so do their executions and punishments reach no further than the case of the body: but God can run upon the inward man, as a giant, and inflict wounds and gashes there.

5. It is an eternal dominion. In regard of the exercise of it, it was not from eternity, because there was not from eternity any creature under the government of it; but in regard of the foundation of it, his essence, his excellency, it is eternal; as God was from eternity almighty, but there was no exercise or manifestation of it till he began to create. Men are kings only for a time; their lives expire like a lamp, and their dominion is extinguished with their lives; they hand their empire by succession to others, but many times it is snapped off before they are cold in their graves. How are the famous empires of the Chaldeans, Medes, Persians, and Greeks, mouldered away, and their place knows them no more! and how are the wings of the Roman eagle cut, and that empire which overspread a great part of the world, hath lost most of its feathers, and is confined to a narrower compass! The dominion of God flourisheth from one generation to another: "He sits King forever" (Ps. xxix. 10). His "session" signifies the establishment, and "forever" the duration; and he "sits now," his sovereignty is as absolute, as powerful as ever. How many lords and princes hath this or that kingdom had! in how many families hath the sceptre lodged! when as God hath had an uninterrupted dominion; as he hath been always the same in his essence, he hath been always glorious in his sovereignty: among men, he that is lord to-day, may be stripped of it to-morrow; the dominions in the world vary; he that is a prince may see his royalty upon the wings, and feel himself laden with fetters; and a prisoner may be "lifted from his dungeon" to a throne. But there can be no diminution of God's government; "His throne is from generation

to generation" (Lam. v. 19); it cannot be shaken: his sceptre, like Aaron's rod, is always green; it cannot be wrested out of his hands; none raised him to it, none therefore can depose him from it; it bears the same splendor in all human affairs; he is an eternal, an "immortal King" (1 Tim. i. 17); as he is eternally mighty, so he is eternally sovereign; and, being an eternal King, he is a King that gives not a momentary and perishing, but a durable and everlasting life, to them that obey him: a durable and eternal punishment to them that resist him.

IV. Wherein this dominion and sovereign consists, and how it is manifested.

First. The first act of sovereignty is the making laws. This is essential to God; no creature's will can be the first rule to the creature, but only the will of God: he only can prescribe man his duty, and establish the rule of it; hence the law is called "the royal law" (James, ii. 8): it being the first and clearest manifestation of sovereignty, as the power of legislation is of the authority of a prince. Both are joined together in Isa. liii. 22: "The Lord is our Lawgiver; the Lord is our King;" legislative power being the great mark of royalty. God, as King, enacts his laws by his own proper authority, and his law is a declaration of his own sovereignty, and of men's moral subjection to him, and dependence on him. His sovereignty doth not appear so much in his promises as in his precepts: a man's power over another is not discovered by promising, for a promise doth not suppose the promiser either superior or inferior to the person to whom the promise is made.[f] It is not an exercising authority over another, but over a man's self; no man forceth another to the acceptance of his promise, but only proposeth and encourageth to an embracing of it. But commanding supposeth always an authority in the person giving the precept; it obligeth the person to whom the command is directed; a promise obligeth the person by whom the promise is made. God, by his command, binds the creature; by his promise he binds himself; he stoops below his sovereignty, to lay obligations upon his own majesty; by a precept he binds the creature, by a promise he encourageth the creature to an observance of his precept: what laws God makes, man is bound, by virtue of his creation, to observe; that respects the sovereignty of God: what promises God makes, man is bound to believe; but that respects the faithfulness of God. God manifested his dominion more to the Jews than to any other people in the world; he was their Lawgiver, both as they were a church and a commonwealth: as a church, he gave them ceremonial laws for the regulating their worship; as a state, he gave them judicial laws for the ordering their civil affairs; and as both, he gave them moral laws, upon which both the laws of the church and state were founded. This dominion of God, in this regard, will be manifest,

(1.) In the supremacy of it. The sole power of making laws doth originally reside in him (James, iv. 12); "There is one Lawgiver, who is able to save, and to destroy." By his own law he judges of the eternal states of men, and no law of man is obligatory, but as it

---

[f] Suarez. de Legib. p. 23.

is agreeable to the laws of this supreme Lawgiver, and pursuant to his righteous rules for the government of the world. The power that the potentates of the world have to make laws is but derivative from God. If their dominion be from him, as it is, for "by him kings reign" (Prov. viii. 15), their legislative power, which is a prime flower of their sovereignty, is derived from him also: and the apostle resolves it into this original when he orders us to be "subject to the higher powers, not only for wrath, but for conscience sake" (Rom. xiii. 5). Conscience, in its operations, solely respects God; and therefore, when it is exercised as the principle of obedience to the laws of men, it is not with respect to them, singly considered, but as the majesty of God appears in their station and in their decrees. This power of giving laws was acknowledged by the heathen to be solely in God by way of original; and therefore the greatest lawgivers among the heathen pretended their laws to be received from some deity or supernatural power, by special revelation: now, whether they did this seriously, acknowledging themselves this part of the dominion of God,—for it is certain that whatsoever just orders were issued out by princes in the world, was by the secret influence of God upon their spirits (Prov. viii. 15): "By me princes decree justice;" by the secret conduct of Divine wisdom,—or whether they pretended it only as a public engine, to enforce upon people the observance of their decrees, and gain a greater credit to their edicts, yet this will result from it, that the people in general entertained this common notion, that God was the great Lawgiver of the world. The first founders of their societies could never else have so absolutely gained upon them by such a pretence. There was always a revelation of a law from the mouth of God in every age: the exhortation of Eliphaz to Job (Job, xxii. 22), of receiving a "law from the mouth" of God, at the time before the moral law was published, had been a vain exhortation had there been no revelation of the mind of God in all ages.

(2.) The dominion of God is manifest in the extent of his laws. As he is the Governor and Sovereign of the whole world, so he enacts laws for the whole world. One prince cannot make laws for another, unless he makes him his subject by right of conquest; Spain cannot make laws for England, or England for Spain; but God having the supreme government, as King over all, is a Lawgiver to all, to irrational, as well as rational creatures. The "heavens have their ordinances" (Job, xxxviii. 33); all creatures have a law imprinted on their beings; rational creatures have Divine statutes copied in their heart: for men, it is clear (Rom. ii. 14), every son of Adam, at his coming into the world, brings with him a law in his nature, and when reason clears itself up from the clouds of sense, he can make some difference between good and evil; discern something of fit and just. Every man finds a law within him that checks him if he offends it: none are without a legal indictment and a legal executioner within them; God or none was the Author of this as a sovereign Lord, in establishing a law in man at the same time, wherein, as an Almighty Creator, he imparted a being. This law proceeds from God's general power of governing, as he is the Author of nature, and binds not barely as it is the reason of man, but by the authority of God, as it is a law engraven on his conscience: and no doubt but a law was given to the angels; God did not govern those intellectual creatures as he doth brutes, and in a way inferior to his rule of man. Some sinned; all might have sinned in regard to the changeableness of their nature. Sin cannot be but against some rule; "where there is no law, there is no transgression;" what that law was is not revealed; but certainly it must be the same in part with the moral law, so far as it agreed with their spiritual natures; a love to God, a worship of him, and a love to one another in their societies and persons.

(3.) The dominion of God is manifest in the reason of some laws, which seem to be nothing else than purely his own will. Some laws there are for which a reason may be rendered from the nature of the thing enjoined, as to love, honor, and worship God: for others, none but this, God will have it so: such was that positive law to Adam of "not eating of the tree of knowledge of good and evil" (Gen. ii. 17), which was merely an asserting his own dominion, and was different from that law of nature God had written in his heart. No other reason of this seems to us, but a resolve to try man's obedience in a way of absolute sovereignty, and to manifest his right over all creatures, to reserve what he pleased to himself, and permit the use of what he pleased to man, and to signify to man that he was to depend on him, who was his Lord, and not on his own will. There was no more hurt in itself, for Adam to have eaten of that, than of any other in the garden; the fruit was pleasant to the eye, and good for food; but God would show the right he had over his own goods, and his authority over man, to reserve what he pleases of his own creation from his touch; and since man could not claim a propriety in anything, he was to meddle with nothing but by the leave of his Sovereign, either discovered by a special or general license. Thus God showed himself the Lord of man, and that man was but his steward, to act by his orders. If God had forbidden man the use of more trees in the garden, his command had been just; since, as a sovereign Lord, he might dispose of his own goods; and when he had granted him the whole compass of that pleasant garden, and the whole world round about for him and his posterity, it was a more tolerable exercise of his dominion to reserve this "one tree," as a mark of his sovereignty, when he had left "all others" to the use of Adam. He reserved nothing to himself, as Lord of the manor, but this; and Adam was prohibited nothing else but this one, as a sign of his subjection. Now for this no reason can be rendered by any man but merely the will of God; this was merely a fruit of his dominion. For the moral laws a reason may be rendered; to love God hath reason to enforce it besides God's will; viz., the excellency of his nature, and the greatness and multitudes of his benefits. To love our neighbor hath enforcing reasons; viz., the conjunction in blood, the preservation of human society, and the need we may stand in of their love ourselves: but no reason can be assigned of this positive command about the tree of knowledge of good and evil, but the pleasure of God. It was a branch of his pure dominion to

but merely the pleasure of God. It was a branch of his pure dominion
to try man's obedience, and a mark of his goodness to try it by so
and light a precept, when he might have extended his authority
further. Had not God given this or the like order, his absolute
dominion had not been so conspicuous. It is true, Adam had a law
of nature in him, whereby he was obliged to perpetual obedience;
and though it was a part of God's dominion to implant it in him, yet
his supreme dominion over the creatures had not been so visible to
man but by this, or a precept of the same kind. What was commanded or prohibited by the law of nature, did bespeak a comeliness
in itself, it appeared good or evil to the reason of man; but this was
neither good nor evil in itself, it received its sole authority from the
absolute will of God, and nothing could result from the fruit itself,
as a reason why man should not taste it, but only the sole will of
God. And as God's dominion was most conspicuous in this precept,
so man's obedience had been most eminent in observing it: for in
his obedience to it, nothing but the sole power and authority of God,
which is the proper rule of obedience, could have been respected, not
any reason from the thing itself. To this we may refer some other
commands, as that of appointing the time of solemn and public worship, the *seventh day;* though the worship of God be a part of the
law of nature, yet the appointing a particular day, wherein he would
be more formally and solemnly acknowledged than on other days,
was grounded upon his absolute right of legislation: for there was
nothing in the time itself that could render that day more holy than
another, though God respected his " finishing the work of creation"
in his institution of that day (Gen. ii. 3).   Such were the ceremonial
commands of sacrifices and washings under the law, and the commands of sacraments under the gospel: the one to last till the first
coming of Christ and his passion; the other to last till the second
coming of Christ and his triumph.   Thus he made natural and unavoidable uncleannesses to be sins, and the touching a dead body to
be pollution, which in their own nature were not so.

(4.) The dominion of God appears in the moral law, and his
majesty in publishing it.   As the law of nature was writ by his own
fingers in the nature of man, so it was engraven by his own finger
in the " tables of stone" (Exod. xxxi. 18), which is very emphatically expressed to be a mark of God's dominion. " And the tables
were the work of God, and the writing was the writing of God engraven upon the tables" (Exod. xxxii. 16); and when the first tables
were broken, though he orders Moses to frame the tables, yet the
writing of the law he reserves to himself (Exod. xxxiv. 1).   It is
not said of any part of the Scripture, that it was writ by the finger
of God, but only of the Decalogue: herein he would have his sovereignty eminently appear; it was published by God in state, with
a numerous attendance of his heavenly militia (Deut. xxxii. 2); and
the artillery of heaven was shot off at the solemnity; and therefore
it is called a fiery law, coming from his right hand, *i. e.* his sovereign
power.   It was published with all the marks of supreme majesty.

(5.) The dominion of God appears in the obligation of the law,
which reacheth the conscience.   The laws of every prince are fram-

ed for the outward conditions of men; they do not by their authority bind the conscience; and what obligations do result from them
upon the conscience, is either from their being the same immediately
with Divine laws, or as they are according to the just power of the
magistrate, founded on the law of God. Conscience hath a protection from the King of kings, and cannot be arrested by any human
power. God hath given man but an authority over half the man,
and the worst half too, that which is of an earthly original; but reserved the authority over the better and more heavenly half to himself. The dominion of earthly princes extends only to the bodies of
men; they have no authority over the soul, their punishment and
rewards cannot reach it: and therefore their laws, by their single
authority, cannot bind it, but as they are coincident with the law of
God, or as the equity of them is subservient to the preservation of
human society, a regular and righteous thing, which is the divine
end in government; and so they bind, as they have relation to God
as the supreme magistrate. The conscience is only intelligible to
God in its secret motions, and therefore only guidable by God; God
only pierceth into the conscience by his eye, and therefore only can
conduct it by his rule. Man cannot tell whether we embrace this
law in our heart and consciences, or only in appearance; "He only
can judge it" (Luke xii. 3, 4), and therefore he only can impose
laws upon it; it is out of the reach of human penal authority, if
their laws be transgressed inwardly by it. Conscience is a book in
some sort as sacred as the Scripture; no addition can be lawfully
made to it, no subtraction from it. Men cannot diminish the duty
of conscience, or raze out the law God hath stamped upon it. They
cannot put a *supersedeas* to the writ of conscience, or stop its mouth
with a *noli prosequi*. They can make no addition by their authority
to bind it; it is a flower in the crown of Divine sovereignty only.

2. His sovereignty appears in a power of dispensing with his own
laws. It is as much a part of his dominion to dispense with his
laws, as to enjoin them; he only hath the power of relaxing his
own right, no creature hath power to do it; that would be to usurp
a superiority over him, and order above God himself. Repealing or
dispensing with the law is a branch of royal authority. It is true,
God will never dispense with those moral laws which have an eternal reason in themselves and their own nature; as for a creature to
fear, love, and honor God; this would be to dispense with his own
holiness, and the righteousness of his nature, to sully the purity of
his own dominion; it would write folly upon the first creation of
man after the image of God, by writing mutability upon himself, in
framing himself after the corrupted image of man; it would null
and frustrate the excellency of the creature, wherein the image of
God mostly shines; nay, it would be to dispense with a creature's
being a Creator, and make him independent upon the Sovereign of
the world in moral obedience. But God hath a right to dispense
with the ordinary laws of nature in the inferior creatures; he hath
a power to alter their course by an arrest of miracles, and make
them come short, or go beyond his ordinances established for them.
He hath a right to make the sun stand still, or move backward; to

bind up the womb of the earth, and bar the influences of the clouds;
bridle in the rage of the fire, and the fury of lions; make the liquid
waters stand like a wall, or pull up the dam, which he hath set to
the sea, and command it to overflow the neighboring countries: he
can dispense with the natural laws of the whole creation, and strain
everything beyond its ordinary pitch. Positive laws he hath revers-
ed; as the ceremonial law given to the Jews. The very nature, indeed, of that law required a repeal, and fell of course; when that
which was intended by it was come, it was of no longer significancy;
as before it was a useful shadow, it would afterwards have been an
empty one: had not God took away this, Christianity had not, in
all likelihood, been propagated among the Gentiles. This was the
"partition wall between Jews and Gentiles" (Eph. xii. 14); which
made them a distinct family from all the world, and was the occasion of the enmity of the Gentiles against the Jews. When God
had, by bringing in what was signified by those rites, declared his
decree for the ceasing of them; and when the Jews, fond of those
Divine institutions, would not allow him the right of repealing what
he had the authority of enacting; he resolved, for the asserting his
dominion, to bury them in the ruins of the temple and city, and
make them forever incapable of practising the main and essential
parts of them; for the temple being the pillar of the legal service,
by demolishing that, God hath taken away their rights of sacrificing,
it being peculiarly annexed to that place; they have no altar dignified with a fire from heaven to consume their sacrifices, no legal
high-priest to offer them. God hath by his providence changed his
own law as well as by his precept; yea, he hath gone higher, by virtue
of his sovereignty, and changed the whole scene and methods of his
government after the fall, from King Creator to King Redeemer.
He hath revoked the law of works as a covenant; released the
penalty of it from the believing sinner, by transferring it upon the
Surety, who interposed himself by his own will and Divine designa-
tion. He hath established another covenant upon other promises
in a higher root, with greater privileges, and easier terms. Had
not God had this right of sovereignty, not a man of Adam's posterity could have been blessed; he and they must have lain groaning under the misery of the fall, which had rendered both himself
and all in his loins unable to observe the terms of the first covenant.
He hath, as some speak, dispensed with his own moral law in some
cases; in commanding Abraham to sacrifice his son, his only son,
a righteous son, a son whereof he had the promise, that "in Isaac
should his seed be called;" yet he was commanded to sacrifice him
by the right of his absolute sovereignty as the supreme Lord of the
lives of his creatures, from the highest angel to the lowest worm,
whereby he bound his subjects to this law, not himself. Our lives
are due to him when he calls for them, and they are a just forfeit
to him, at the very moment we sin, at the very moment we come
into the world, by reason of the venom of our nature against him,
and the disturbance the first sin of man (whereof we are inheritors)
gave to his glory. Had Abraham sacrificed his son of his own
head, he had sinned, yea, in attempting it; but being authorized

from heaven, his act was obedience to the Sovereign of the world, who had a power to dispense with his own law; and with this law he had before dispensed, in the case of Cain's murder of Abel, as to the immediate punishment of it with death, which, indeed, was settled afterwards by his authority, but then omitted because of the paucity of men, and for the peopling the world; but settled after-wards, when there was almost, though not altogether, the like occasion of omitting it for a time.

3. His sovereignty appears in punishing the transgression of his law.

(1.) This is a branch of God's dominion as lawgiver. So was the vengeance God would take upon the Amalekites (Exod. xvii. 16): "The Lord hath sworn, that the Lord will have war;" the Hebrew is, "The hand upon the throne of the Lord," as in the margin: as a "lawgiver" he "saves or destroys" (James, iv. 12). He acts according to his own law, in a congruity to the sanction of his own precepts; though he be an arbitrary lawgiver, appointing what laws he pleases, yet he is not an arbitrary judge. As he commands nothing but what he hath a right to command, so he punisheth none but whom he hath a right to punish, and with such punishment as the law hath denounced. All his acts of justice and inflictions of curses are the effects of this sovereign dominion (Ps. xxix. 10): "He sits King upon the floods;" upon the deluge of waters wherewith he drowned the world, say some. It is a right belonging to the authority of magistrates to pull up the infectious weeds that corrupt a commonwealth; it is no less the right of God, as the lawgiver and judge of all the earth, to subject criminals to his vengeance, after they have rendered themselves abominable in his eyes, and carried themselves unworthy subjects of so great and glorious a King. The first name whereby God is made known in Scripture, is Elohim (Gen. i. 1): "In the beginning God created the heaven and earth;" a name which signifies his power of judging, in the opinion of some critics; from him it is derived to earthly magistrates; their judgment is said, therefore, to be the "judgment of God" (Deut. i. 17). When Christ came, he proposed this great motive of repentance from the "kingdom of heaven being at hand;" the kingdom of his grace, whereby to invite men; the kingdom of his justice in the punishment of the neglecters of it, whereby to terrify men. Punishments as well as rewards belong to royalty; it issued accordingly; those that believed and repented came under his gracious sceptre, those that neglected and rejected it fell under his iron rod; Jerusalem was destroyed, the temple demolished, the inhabitants lost their lives by the edge of the sword, or lingered them out in the chains of a miserable captivity. This term of "judge," which signifies a sovereign right to govern and punish delinquents, Abraham gives him, when he came to root out the people of Sodom, and make them the examples of his vengeance (Gen. xviii. 25).

(2.) Punishing the transgressions of his law. This is a necessary branch of dominion. His sovereignty in making laws would be a trifle, if there were not also an authority to vindicate those laws from contempt and injury; he would be a Lord only spurned at by rebels. Sovereignty is not preserved without justice. When the Psalmist speaks of the majesty of God's kingdom, he tells us, that "righteousness and judgment are the habitation of his throne" (Ps. xcvii. 1, 2). These are the engines of Divine dignity which render him glorious and majestic. A legislative power would be trampled on without executive; by this the reverential apprehensions of God are preserved in the world. He is known to be Lord of the world "by the judgments which he executes" (Ps. ix. 16). When he seems to have lost his dominion, or given it up in the world, he recovers it by punishment. When he takes some away "with a whirlwind, and in his wrath," the natural consequence men make of it, is this: "Surely there is a God that judgeth the earth" (Ps. lviii. 9, 11). He reduceth the creature, by the lash of his judgments, that would not acknowledge his authority in his precepts. Those sins which disown his government in the heart and conscience, as pride, inward blasphemy, &c., he hath reserved a time hereafter to reckon for. He doth not presently shoot his arrows into the marrow of every delinquent, but those sins which traduce his government of the world, and tear up the foundations of human converse, and a public respect to him, he reckons with particularly here, as well as hereafter, that the life of his sovereignty might not always faint in the world.

(3.) This of punishing was the second discovery of his dominion in the world. His first act of sovereignty was the giving a law; the next, his appearance in the state of a judge. When his orders were violated, he rescues the honor of them by an execution of justice. He first judged the angels, punishing the evil ones for their crime: the first court he kept among them as a governor, was to give them a law; the second court he kept was as a judge trying the delinquents, and adjudging the offenders to be "reserved in chains of darkness" till the final execution (Jude, 6); and, at the same time probably, he confirmed the good ones in their obedience by grace. So the first discovery of his dominion to man, was the giving him a precept, the next was the inflicting a punishment for the breach of it. He summons Adam to the bar, indicts him for his crime, finds him guilty by his own confession, and passeth sentence on him, according to the rule he had before acquainted him with.

(4.) The means whereby he punisheth shows his dominion. Sometimes he musters up hail and mildew; sometimes he sends regiments of wild beasts; so he threatens Israel (Lev. xxvi. 22). Sometimes he sends out a party of angels to beat up the quarters of men, and make a carnage among them (2 Kings, xix. 35). Sometimes he mounts his thundering battery, and shoots forth his ammunition from the clouds, as against the Philistines (1 Sam. vii. 10). Sometimes he sends the slightest creatures to shame the pride and punish the sin of man, as "lice, frogs, locusts," as upon the Egyptians (Exod. viii.—x.).

Secondly. This dominion it manifested by God as a proprietor and Lord of his creatures and his own goods. And this is evident,

1. In the choice of some persons from eternity. He hath set apart some from eternity, wherein he will display the invincible efficacy of his grace, and thereby infallibly bring them to the fruition

of glory (Eph. i. 4, 5): "According as he hath chosen us in him before the foundation of the world, that we should be holy and without blame before him in love, having predestinated us to the adoption of children by Jesus Christ to himself, according to the good pleasure of his will." Why doth he write some names in the "book of life," and leave out others? Why doth he enrol some, whom he intends to make denizens of heaven, and refuse to put others in his register? The apostle tells us, it is the pleasure of his will. You may render a reason for many of God's actions, till you come to this, the top and foundation of all; and under what head of reason can man reduce this act but to that of his royal prerogative? Why doth God save some, and condemn others at last? because of the faith of the one, and unbelief of the other. Why do some men believe? because God hath not only given them the means of grace, but accompanied those means with the efficacy of his Spirit. Why did God accompany those means with the efficacy of his Spirit in some, and not in others? because he had decreed by grace to prepare them for glory. But why did he decree, or choose some, and not others? Into what will you resolve this but into his sovereign pleasure? Salvation and condemnation at the last upshot, are acts of God as the Judge, conformable to his own law of giving life to believers, and inflicting death upon unbelievers; for those a reason may be rendered; but the choice of some, and preterition of others, is an act of God as he is a sovereign monarch, before any law was actually transgressed, because not actually given. When a prince redeems a rebel, he acts as a judge according to law; but when he calls some out to pardon, he acts as a sovereign by a prerogative above law; into this the apostle resolves it (Rom. ix. 13, 15). When he speaks of God's loving Jacob and hating Esau, and that before they had done either good or evil, it is, "because God will have mercy on whom he will have mercy, and compassion on whom he will have compassion." Though the first scope of the apostle, in the beginning of the chapter, was to declare the reason of God's rejecting the Jews, and calling in the Gentiles; had he only intended to demolish the pride of the Jews, and flat their opinion of merit, and aimed no higher than that providential act of God; he might, convincingly enough to the reason of men, have argued from the justice of God, provoked by the obstinacy of the Jews, and not have had recourse to his absolute will; but, since he asserts this latter, the strength of his argument seems to lie thus: if God by his absolute sovereignty may resolve, and fix his love upon Jacob and estrange it from Esau, or any other of his creatures, before they have done good or evil, and man have no ground to call his infinite majesty to account, may he not deal thus with the Jews, when their demerit would be a bar to any complaints of the creature against him?[g] If God were considered here in the quality of a judge, it had been fit to have considered the matter of fact in the criminal; but he is considered as a sovereign, rendering no other reason of his action but his own will; "whom he will he hardens" (ver. 18). And then the apostle concludes (ver. 20), "Who art thou, O man, that repliest against God?" If the reason drawn

[g] Amyrald, Dissert. pp. 101, 102.

from God's sovereignty doth not satisfy in this inquiry, no other reason can be found wherein to acquiesce : for the last condemnation there will be sufficient reason to clear the justice of his proceedings. But, in this case of election, no other reason but what is alleged, *viz.*, the will of God, can be thought of, but what is liable to such knotty exceptions that cannot well be untied.

(1.) It could not be any merit in the creature that might determine God to choose him. If the decree of election falls not under the merit of Christ's passion, as the procuring cause, it cannot fall under the merit of any part of the corrupted mass. The decree of sending Christ did not precede, but followed, in order of nature, the determination of choosing some. When men were chosen as the subjects for glory, Christ was chosen as the means for the bringing them to glory (Eph. i. 4) : " Chosen us in him, and predestinated us to the adoption of children by Jesus Christ." The choice was not merely in Christ as the moving cause ; that the apostle asserts to be " the good pleasure of his will ;" but in Christ, as the means of conveying to the chosen ones the fruits of their election. What could there be in any man that could invite God to this act, or be a cause of distinction of one branch of Adam from another ? Were they not all hewed out of the same rock, and tainted with the same corruption in blood ? Had it been possible to invest them with a power of merit at the first, had not that venom, contracted in their nature, degraded all of power for the future ? What merit was there in any but of wrathful punishment, since they were all considered as criminals, and the cursed brood of an ungrateful rebel ? What dignity can there be in the nature of the purest part of clay, to be made a vessel of honor, more than in another part of clay, as pure as that which was formed into a vessel for mean and sordid use ? What had any one to move his mercy more than another, since they were all children of wrath, and equally daubed with original guilt and filth ? Had not all an equal proportion of it to provoke his justice ? What merit is there in one dry bone more than another, to be inspired with the breath of a spiritual life ? Did not all lie wallowing in their own filthy blood ? and what could the steam and noisomeness of that deserve at the hands of a pure Majesty, but to be cast into a sink furthest from his sight ? Were they not all considered in this deplorable posture, with an equal proportion of poison in their nature, when God first took his pen, and singled out some names to write in the book of life ? It could not be merit in any one piece of this abominable mass, that should stir up that resolution in God to set apart this person for a vessel of glory, while he permitted another to putrefy in his own gore. He loved Jacob, and hated Esau, though they were both parts of the common mass, the seed of the same loins, and lodged in the same womb.

(2.) Nor could it be any foresight of works to be done in time by them, or of faith, that might determine God to choose them. What good could he foresee resulting from extreme corruption, and a nature alienated from him ? What could he foresee of good to be done by them, but what he resolved in his own will, to bestow an ability upon them to bring forth ? His choice of them was to a holiness, not for a holiness preceding his determination (Eph. i. 4). He hath chosen us, "that we might be holy" before him; he ordained us "to good works," not for them (Eph. ii. 10). What is a fruit cannot be a moving cause of that whereof it is a fruit: grace is a stream from the spring of electing love; the branch is not the cause of the root, but the root of the branch; nor the stream the cause of the spring, but the spring the cause of the stream. Good works suppose grace, and a good and right habit in the person, as rational acts suppose reason. Can any man say that the rational acts man performs after his creation were a cause why God created him? This would make creation, and everything else, not so much an act of his will, as an act of his understanding. God foresaw no rational act in man, before the act of his will to give him reason; nor foresees faith in any, before the act of his will determining to give him faith: "Faith is the gift of God" (Eph. ii. 8). In the salvation which grows up from this first purpose of God, he regards not the works we have done, as a principal motive to settle the top-stone of our happiness, but his own purpose, and the grace given in Christ; "who hath saved us, and called us with a holy calling, not according to our own works, but according to his own purpose and grace, which was given to us in Christ, before the world began" (2 Tim. i. 9). The honor of our salvation cannot be challenged by our works, much less the honor of the foundation of it. It was a pure gift of grace, without any respect to any spiritual, much less natural, perfection. Why should the apostle mention that circumstance, when he speaks of God's loving Jacob, and hating Esau, "when neither of them had done good or evil" (Rom. ix. 11), if there were any foresight of men's works as the moving cause of his love or hatred? God regarded not the works of either as the first cause of his choice, but acted by his own liberty, without respect to any of their actions which were to be done by them in time. If faith be the fruit of election, the prescience of faith doth not influence the electing act of God. It is called "the faith of God's elect" (Tit. i. 1): "Paul, an apostle of Jesus Christ, according to the faith of God's elect;" *i. e.* settled in this office to bring the elect of God to faith. If men be chosen by God upon the foresight of faith, or not chosen till they have faith, they are not so much God's elect, as God their elect; they choose God by faith, before God chooseth them by love: it had not been the faith of God's elect, *i. e.* of those already chosen, but the faith of those that were to be chosen by God afterwards. Election is the cause of faith, and not faith the cause of election; fire is the cause of heat, and not the heat of fire; the sun is the cause of the day, and not the day the cause of the rising of the sun. Men are not chosen because they believe, but they believe because they are chosen: the apostle did ill, else, to appropriate that to the elect which they had no more interest in, by virtue of their election, than the veriest reprobate in the world.[h] If the foresight of what works might be done by his creatures was the motive of his choosing them, why did he not choose the devils to redemption, who could have done him better service, by the strength of their nature, than the

[h] Daille, *in loc.*

whole mass of Adam's posterity? Well, then, there is no possible way to lay the original foundation of this act of election and preterition in anything but the absolute sovereignty of God. Justice or injustice comes not into consideration in this case. There is no debt which justice or injustice always respects in its acting: if he had pleased, he might have chosen all; if he had pleased, he might have chosen none. It was in his supreme power to have resolved to have left all Adam's posterity under the rack of his justice; if he determined to snatch out any, it was a part of his dominion, but without any injury to the creatures he leaves under their own guilt. Did he not pass by the angels, and take man? and, by the same right of dominion, may he pick out some men from the common mass, and lay aside others to bear the punishment of their crimes. Are they not all his subjects? all are his criminals, and may be dealt with at the pleasure of their undoubted Lord and Sovereign. This is a work of arbitrary power; since he might have chosen none, or chosen all, as he saw good himself. It is at the liberty of the artificer to determine his wood or stone to such a figure, that of a prince, or that of a toad; and his materials have no right to complain of him, since it lies wholly upon his own liberty. They must have little sense of their own vileness, and God's infinite excellency above them by right of creation, that will contend that God hath a lesser right over his creatures than an artificer over his wood or stone. If it were at his liberty whether to redeem man, or send Christ upon such an undertaking, it is as much at his liberty, and the prerogative is to be allowed him, what person he will resolve to make capable of enjoying the fruits of that redemption. One man was as fit a subject for mercy as another, as they all lay in their original guilt: why would not Divine mercy cast its eye upon this man, as well as upon his neighbor? There was no cause in the creature, but all in God; it must be resolved into his own will: yet not into a will without wisdom. God did not choose hand over head, and act by mere will, without reason and understanding; an Infinite Wisdom is far from such a kind of procedure; but the reason of God is inscrutable to us, unless we could understand God as well as he understands himself; the whole ground lies in God himself, no part of it in the creature; "not in him that wills, nor in him that runs, but in God that shows mercy" (Rom. ix. 15, 16). Since God hath revealed no other cause than his will, we can resolve it into no other than his sovereign empire over all creatures. It is not without a stop to our curiosity, that in the same place where God asserts the absolute sovereignty of his mercy to Moses, he tells him he could not see his face: "I will be gracious to whom I will be gracious;" and he said, "Thou canst not see my face" (Exod. xxxiii. 19, 20): the rays of his infinite wisdom are too bright and dazzling for our weakness. The apostle acknowledged not only a wisdom in this proceeding, but a riches and treasure of wisdom; not only that, but a depth and vastness of those riches of wisdom; but was unable to give us an inventory and scheme of it (Rom. xi. 33). The secrets of his counsels are too deep for us to wade into; in attempting to know the reason of those acts, we should find ourselves swallowed up into a bottomless gulf: though the understanding be above our capacity, yet the admiration of his authority and submission to it are not. " We should cast ourselves down at his feet, with a full resignation of ourselves to his sovereign pleasure."[i] This is a more comely carriage in a Christian than all the contentious endeavors to measure God by our line.

2. In bestowing grace where he pleases. God in conversion and pardon works not as a natural agent, putting forth strength to the utmost, which God must do, if he did renew man naturally, as the sun shines, and the fire burns, which always act, *ad extremum virium*, unless a cloud interpose to eclipse the one, and water to extinguish the other. But God acts as a voluntary agent, which can freely exert his power when he please, and suspend it when he please. Though God be necessarily good, yet he is not necessitated to manifest all the treasures of his goodness to every subject ; he hath power to distil his dews upon one part, and not upon another. If he were necessitated to express his goodness without a liberty, no thanks were due to him. Who thanks the sun for shining on him, or the fire for warming him ? None ; because they are necessary agents, and can do no other. What is the reason he did not reach out his hand to keep all the angels from sinking, as well as some, or recover them when they were sunk ? What is the reason he engrafts one man into the true Vine, and lets the other remain a wild olive ? Why is not the efficacy of the Spirit always linked with the motions of the Spirit ? Why does he not mould the heart into a gospel frame when he fills the ear with a gospel sound ? Why doth he strike off the chains from some, and tear the veil from the heart, while he leaves others under their natural slavery and Egyptian darkness ? Why do some lie under the bands of death, while another is raised to a spiritual life ? What reason is there for all this but his absolute will ? The apostle resolves the question, if the question be asked, why he begets one and not another ? Not from the will of the creature, but " his own will," is the determination of one (James, i. 18). Why doth he work in one "to will and to do," and not in another ? Because of "his good pleasure," is the answer of another (Phil. ii. 13). He could as well new create every one, as he at first created them, and make grace as universal as nature and reason, but it is not his pleasure so to do.

(1.) It is not from want of strength in himself. The power of God is unquestionably able to strike off the chains of unbelief from all ; he could surmount the obstinacy of every child of wrath, and inspire every son of Adam with faith as well as Adam himself. He wants not a virtue superior to the greatest resistance of his creature ; a victorious beam of light might be shot into their understandings, and a flood of grace might overspread their wills with one word of his mouth, without putting forth the utmost of his power. What hindrance could there be in any created spirit, which cannot be easily pierced into and new moulded by the Father of spirits ? Yet he only breathes this efficacious virtue into some, and leaves others under that insensibility and hardness which they love, and suffer them to continue in their benighting ignorance, and consume them-

[i] This was Dr. Goodwin's speech when he was in trouble.

selves in the embraces of their dear, though deceitful Delilahs. He
could have conquered the resistance of the Jews, as well as chased
away the darkness and ignorance of the Gentiles. No doubt but he
could overpower the heart of the most malicious devil, as well as
that of the simplest and weakest man. But the breath of the Almighty Spirit is in his own power, to breathe "where he lists"
(John, iii. 8). It is at his liberty whether he will give to any the
feelings of the invincible efficacy of his grace ; he did not want
strength to have kept man as firm as a rock against the temptation
of Satan, and poured in such fortifying grace, as to have made him
impregnable against the powers of hell, as well as he did secure the
standing of the angels against the sedition of their fellows : but it
was his will to permit it to be otherwise.

(2.) Nor is it from any prerogative in the creature. He converts
not any for their natural perfection, because he seizeth upon the
most ignorant ; nor for their moral perfection, because he converts
the most sinful ; nor for their civil perfection, because he turns the
most despicable.

[1.] Not for their natural perfection of knowledge. He opened
the minds and hearts of the more ignorant. Were the nature of
the Gentiles better manured than that of the Jews, or did the tapers of their understandings burn clearer ? No; the one were skilled
in the prophecies of the Messiah, and might have compared the predictions they owned with the actions and sufferings of Christ, which
they were spectators of. He let alone those that had expectations
of the Messiah, and expectations about the time of Christ's appearance, both grounded upon the oracles wherewith he had entrusted
them. The Gentiles were unacquainted with the prophets, and
therefore destitute of the expectations of the Messiah (Eph. ii. 12):
they were " without Christ;" without any revelation of Christ, because "aliens from the commonwealth of Israel, and strangers to the
covenant of promise, having no hope, and without God in the
world," without any knowledge of God, or promises of Christ. The
Jews might sooner, in a way of reason, have been wrought upon
than the Gentiles, who were ignorant of the prophets, by whose
writings they might have examined the truth of the apostles' declarations. Thus are they refused that were the kindred of Christ, according to the flesh, and the Gentiles, that were at a greater distance
from him, brought in by God; thus he catcheth not at the subtle and
mighty devils, who had an original in spiritual nature more like to
him, but at weak and simple man.

[2.] Not for any moral perfection, because he converts the most
sinful : the Gentiles, steeped in idolatry and superstition. He sow-
ed more faith among the Romans than in Jerusalem ; more faith in
a city that was the common sewer of all the idolatry of the nations
conquered by them, than in that city which had so signally been
owned by him, and had not practised any idolatry since the Babylonish captivity. He planted saintship at Corinth, a place notorious
for the infamous worship of Venus, a superstition attended with the
grossest uncleanness ; at Ephesus, that presented the whole world
with a cup of fornication in their temple of Diana ; among the Colos-

sians, votaries to Cybele in a manner of worship attended with beastly and lascivious ceremonies. And what character had the Cretians from one of their own poets, mentioned by the apostle to Titus, whom he had placed among them to further the progress of the gospel, but the vilest and most abominable? (Titus i. 12): "liars," not to be credited; "evil beasts," not to be associated with; "slow bellies," fit for no service. What prerogative was there in the nature of such putrefaction? as much as in that of a toad to be elevated to the dignity of an angel. What steam from such dung-hills could be welcome to him, and move him to cast his eye on them, and sweeten them from heaven? What treasures of worth were here to open the treasures of his grace! Were such filthy snuffs fit of themselves to be kindled by, and become a lodging for, a gospel beam? What invitements could he have from lying, beastliness, gluttony, but only from his own sovereignty? By this he plucked firebrands out of the fire, while he left straighter and more comely sticks to consume to ashes.

[3.] Not for any civil perfection, because he turns the most des-picable. He elevates not nature to grace upon the account of wealth, honor, or any civil station in the world: he dispenseth not ordi-narily those treasures to those that the mistaken world foolishly ad-mire and dote upon (1 Cor. i. 26); "Not many mighty, not many noble:" a purple robe is not usually decked with this jewel; he takes more of mouldy clay than refined dust to cast into his image, and lodges his treasures more in the earthly vessels than in the world's golden ones; he gives out his richest doles to those that are the scorn and reproach of the world. Should he impart his grace most to those that abound in wealth or honor, it had been some founda-tion for a conception that he had been moved by those vulgarly es-teemed excellencies to indulge them more than others. But such a conceit languisheth when we behold the subjects of his grace as void originally of any allurements, as they are full of provocations. Hereby he declares himself free from all created engagements, and that he is not led by any external motives in the object.

[4.] It is not from any obligation which lies upon him. He is in-debted to none: disobliged by all. No man deserves from him any act of grace, but every man deserves what the most deplorable are left to suffer. He is obliged by the children of wrath to nothing else but showers of wrath; owes no more a debt to fallen man, than to fallen devils, to restore them to their first station by a superlative grace. How was he more bound to restore them, than he was to preserve them; to catch them after they fell, than to put a bar in the way of their falling? God, as a sovereign, gave laws to men, and a strength sufficient to keep those laws. What obligation is there upon God to repair that strength man wilfully lost, and extract him out of that condition into which he voluntarily plunged him-self? What if man sinned by temptation, which is a reason alleged by some, might not many of the devils do so too? Though there was a first of them that sinned without a temptation, yet many of them might be seduced into rebellion by the ringleader. Upon that account he is no more bound to give grace to all men, than to devils.

If he promised life upon obedience, he threatened death upon transgression.   By man's disobedience God is quit of his promise, and
owes nothing but punishment upon the violation of his law.   Indeed
man may pretend to a claim of sufficient strength from him by creation, as God is the author of nature, and he had it; but since he hath
extinguished it by his sin, he cannot in the least pretend any obligation on God for a new strength.   If it be a "peradventure" whether
he will "give repentance," as it is 2 Tim. ii. 25, there is no tie in
the case; a tie would put it beyond a peradventure with a God that
never forfeited his obligation.   No husbandman thinks himself
obliged to bestow cost and pains, manure and tillage, upon one field
more than another; though the nature of the ground may require
more, yet he is at his liberty whether he will expend more upon one
than another.[k]   He may let it lie fallow as long as he please.
God is less obliged to till and prune his creatures, than man is obliged
to his field or trees.   If a king proclaim a pardon to a company of
rebels, upon the condition of each of them paying such a sum of
money; their estates before were capable of satisfying the condition,
but their rebellion hath reduced them to an indigent condition; the
proclamation itself is an act of grace, the condition required is not
impossible in itself: the prince, out of a tenderness to some, sends
them that sum of money, he hath by his proclamation obliged them
to pay, and thereby enabled them to answer the condition he requires; the first he doth by a sovereign authority, the second he
doth by a sovereign bounty.   He was obliged to neither of them;
punishment was a debt due to all of them; if he would remit it upon
condition, he did relax his sovereign right; and if he would by his
largess make any of them capable to fulfil the condition, by sending
them presently a sufficient sum to pay the fine, he acted as proprietor of his own goods, to dispose of them in such a quantity to those
to whom he was not obliged to bestow a mite.

[5.] It must therefore be an act of his mere sovereignty.   This
can only sit arbitrator in every gracious act.   Why did he give
grace to Abel and not to Cain, since they both lay in the same
womb, and equally derived from their parents a taint in their nature; but that he would show a standing example of his sovereignty
to the future ages of the world in the first posterity of man?   Why
did he give grace to Abraham, and separate him from his idolatrous
kindred, to dignify him to be the root of the Messiah?   Why did
he confine his promise to Isaac, and not extend it to Ishmael, the
seed of the same Abraham by Hagar, or to the children he had by
Keturah after Sarah's death?   What reason can be alleged for this but
his sovereign will?   Why did he not give the fallen angels a moment
of repentance after their sin, but condemned them to irrevocable
pains?   Is it not as free for him to give grace to whom he please, as
create what worlds he please; to form this corrupted clay into his
own image, as to take such a parcel of dust from all the rest of the
creation whereof to compact Adam's body?   Hath he not as much
jurisdiction over the sinful mass of his creatures in a new creation,
as he had over the chaos in the old?   And what reason can be ren-

k Claude, sur la Parabole des Noces, p. 29.

dered, of his advancing this part of matter to the nobler dignity of a star, and leaving that other part to make up the dark body of the earth; to compact one part into a glorious sun, and another part into a hard rock, but his royal prerogative? What is the reason a prince subjects one malefactor to punishment, and lifts up another to a place of trust and profit? that Pharaoh honored the butler with an attendance on his person, and remitted the baker to the hands of the executioner? It was his pleasure. And is not as great right due to God, as is allowed to the worms of the earth? What is the reason he hardens a Pharaoh, by a denying him that grace which should mollify him, and allows it to another? It is because he will. "Whom he will he hardens" (Rom. ix. 18). Hath not man the liberty to pull up the sluice, and let the water run into what part of the ground he pleases? What is the reason some have not a heart to understand the beauty of his ways? Because the Lord doth not give it them (Deut. xxix. 4). Why doth he not give all his converts an equal measure of his sanctifying grace? some have mites and some have treasures. Why doth he give his grace to some sooner, to some later? some are inspired in their infancy, others not till a full age, and after; some not till they have fallen into some gross sin, as Paul; some betimes, that they may do him service: others later, as the thief upon the cross, and presently snatcheth them out of the world? Some are weaker, some stronger in nature, some more beautiful and lovely, others more uncomely and sluggish. It is so in supernaturals. What reason is there for this, but his own will? This is instead of all that can be assigned on the part of God. He is the free disposer of his own goods, and as a Father may give a greater portion to one child than to another. And what reason of complaint is there against God? may not a toad complain that God did not make it a man, and give it a portion of reason? or a fly complain that God did not make it an angel, and give it a garment of light; had they but any spark of understanding; as well as man complain that God did not give him grace as well as another? Unless he sincerely desired it, and then was denied it, he might complain of God, though not as a sovereign, yet as a promiser of grace to them that ask it. God doth not render his sovereignty formidable; he shuts not up his throne of grace from any that seek him; he invites man; his arms are open, and the sceptre stretched out; and no man continues under the arrest of his lusts, but he that is unwilling to be otherwise, and such a one hath no reason to complain of God.

3. His sovereignty is manifest in disposing the means of grace to some, not to all. He hath caused the sun to shine bright in one place, while he hath left others benighted and deluded by the devil's oracles. Why do the evangelical dews fall in this or that place, and not in another? Why was the gospel published in Rome so soon, and not in Tartary? Why hath it been extinguished in some places, as soon almost as it had been kindled in them? Why hath one place been honored with the beams of it in one age, and been covered with darkness the next? One country hath been made a sphere for this star, that directs to Christ, to move in; and afterwards it hath been taken away, and placed in another; sometimes

more clearly it hath shone, sometimes more darkly, in the same place; what is the reason of this? It is true something of it may be referred to the justice of God, but much more to the sovereignty of God. That the gospel is published later, and not sooner, the apostle tell us is "according to the commandment of the everlasting God" (Rom. xvi. 26).

(1.) The means of grace, after the families from Adam became distinct, were never granted to all the world. After that fatal breach in Adam's family by the death of Abel, and Cain's separation, we read not of the means of grace continued among Cain's posterity; it seems to be continued in Adam's sole family, and not published in societies till the time of Seth. "Then began men to call upon the name of the Lord" (Gen. iv. 26). It was continued in that family till the deluge, which was 1523 years after the creation, according to some, or 1656 years, according to others. After that, when the world degenerated, it was communicated to Abraham, and settled in the posterity that descended from Jacob; though he left not the world without a witness of himself, and some sprinklings of revelations in other parts, as appears by the Book of Job, and the discourses of his friends.

(2.) The Jews had this privilege granted them above other nations, to have a clearer revelation of God. God separated them from all the world to honor them with the *depositum* of his oracles (Rom. iii. 2): "To them were committed the oracles of God." In which regard all other nations are said to be "without God" (Eph. ii. 12), as being destitute of so great a privilege. The Spirit blew in Canaan when the lands about it felt not the saving breath of it. "He hath not dealt so with any nation; and as for his judgments, they have not known them" (Ps, cxlvii. 20). The rest had no warnings from the prophets, no dictates from heaven, but what they had by the light of nature, the view of the works of creation, and the administration of Providence, and what remained among them of some ancient traditions derived from Noah, which, in tract of time, were much defaced. We read but of one Jonah sent to Nineveh, but frequent alarms to the Israelites by a multitude of prophets commissioned by God. It is true, the door of the Jewish church was open to what proselytes would enter themselves, and embrace their religion and worship; but there was no public proclamation made in the world; only God, by his miracles in their deliverance from Egypt (which could not but be famous among all the neighbor nations), declared them to be a people favored by heaven: but the tradition from Adam and Noah was not publicly revived by God in other parts, and raised from that grave of forgetfulness wherein it had lain so long buried. Was there any reason in them for this indulgence? God might have been as liberal to any other nation, yea, to all the nations in the world, if it had been his sovereign pleasure: any other people were as fit to be entrusted with his oracles, and be subjects for his worship, as that people; yet all other nations, till the rejection of the Jews, because of their rejection of Christ, were strangers from the covenant of promise. These people were part of the common mass of the world: they had no prerogative in nature above Adam's posterity. Were they the extract of an innocent part of his loins, and all the other nations drained out of his putrefaction? Had the blood of Abraham, from whom they were more immediately descended, any more precious tincture than the rest of mankind? They, as well as other nations, were made of "one blood" (Acts xvii. 26); and that corrupted both in the spring and in the rivulets. Were they better than other nations, when God first drew them out of their slavery? We have Joshua's authority for it, that they had complied with the Egyptian idolatry, "and served other gods," in that place of their servitude (Josh. xxiv. 14). Had they had an abhorrency of the superstition of Egypt, while they remained there, they could not so soon have erected a golden calf for worship, in imitation of the Egyptian idols. All the rest of mankind had as inviting reasons to present God with, as those people had. God might have granted the same privilege to all the world, as well as to them, or denied it them, and endowed all the rest of the world with his statutes: but the enriching such a small company of people with his Divine showers, and leaving the rest of the world as a barren wilderness in spirituals, can be placed upon no other account originally than that of his unaccountable sovereignty, of his love to them: there was nothing in them to merit such high titles from God as his first-born, his peculiar treasure, the apple of his eye. He disclaims any righteousness in them, and speaks a word sufficient to damp such thoughts in them, by charging them with their wickedness, while he "loaded them with his benefits" (Deut. ix. 4, 6). The Lord "gives thee not" this land for "thy righteousness;" for thou art a stiff-necked people. It was an act of God's free pleasure to "choose them to be a people to himself" (Deut. vii. 6).

(3.) God afterwards rejected the Jews, gave them up to the hardness of their hearts, and spread the gospel among the Gentiles. He hath cast off the children of the kingdom, those that had been enrolled for his subjects for many ages, who seemed, by their descent from Abraham, to have a right to the privileges of Abraham; and called men from the east and from the west, from the darkest corners in the world, to "sit down with Abraham, Isaac, and Jacob, in the kingdom of heaven," i. e. to partake with them of the promises of the gospel (Matt. viii. 11). The people that were accounted accursed by the Jews enjoy the means of grace, which have been hid from those that were once dignified this 1600 years; that they have neither ephod, nor teraphim, nor sacrifice, nor any true worship of God among them (Hos. iii. 4). Why he should not give them grace to acknowledge and own the person of the Messiah, to whom he had made the promises of him for so many successive ages, but let their "heart be fat," and "their ears heavy" (Isa. vi. 10)?—why the gospel at length, after the resurrection of Christ, should be presented to the Gentiles, not by chance, but pursuant to the resolution and prediction of God, declared by the prophets that it should be so in time? —why he should let so many hundreds of years pass over, after the world was peopled, and let the nations all that while soak in their idolatrous customs?—why he should not call the Gentiles without rejecting the Jews, and bind them both up together in the bundle of life?—why he should acquaint some people with it a little after the publishing it in Jerusalem, by the descent of the Spirit, and others not a long time after?—some in the first ages of Christianity enjoyed it; others have it not, as those in America, till the last age of the world;—can be referred to nothing but his sovereign pleasure. What merit can be discovered in the Gentiles? There is something of justice in the case of the Jews' rejection, nothing but sovereignty in the Gentiles' reception into the church. If the Jews were bad, the Gentiles were in some sort worse: the Jews owned the one true God, without mixture of idols, though they owned not the Messiah in his appearance, which they did in a promise; but the Gentiles owned neither the one nor the other. Some tell us, it was for the merit of some of their ancestors. How comes the means of grace, then, to be taken from the Jew, who had (if any people ever had) meritorious ancestors for a plea? If the merit of some of their former progenitors were the cause, what was the reason the debt due to their merit was not paid to their immediate progeny, or to themselves, but to a posterity so distant from them, and so abominably depraved as the Gentile world was at the day of the gospel-sun striking into their horizon? What merit might be in their ancestors (if any could be supposed in the most refined rubbish), it was so little for themselves, that no oil could be spared out of their lamps for others. What merit their ancestors might have, might be forfeited by the succeeding generations. It is ordinarily seen, that what honor a father deserves in a state for public service, may be lost by the son, forfeited by treason, and himself attainted. Or was it out of a foresight that the Gentiles would embrace it, and the Jews reject it; that the Gentiles would embrace it in one place, and not in another? How did God foresee it, but in his own grace, which he was resolved to display in one, not in another? It must be then still resolved into his sovereign pleasure. Or did he foresee it in their wills and nature? What, were they not all one common dross? Was any part of Adam, by nature, better than another? How did God foresee that which was not, nor could be, without his pleasure to give ability, and grace to receive? Well, then, what reason but the sovereign pleasure of God can be alleged, why Christ forbade the apostles, at their first commission, to preach to the Gentiles (Matt. x. 15), but, at the second and standing commission, orders them to preach to "every creature?" Why did he put a demur to the resolutions of Paul and Timothy, to impart light to Bithynia, or order them to go into Macedonia? Was that country more worthy upon whom lay a great part of the blood of the world shed in Alexander's time (Acts xvi. 6, 7, 9, 10)? Why should Corazin and Bethsaida enjoy those means that were not granted to the Tyrians and Sidonians, who might probably have sooner reached out their arms to welcome it (Matt. xi. 21)? Why should God send the gospel into our island, and cause it to flourish so long here, and not send it, or continue it, in the furthest eastern parts of the world? Why should the very profession of Christianity possess so small a compass of ground in the world, but five parts in thirty, the Mahometans holding six parts, and the other nineteen overgrown with Paganism, where either the gospel was never planted, or else since rooted up? To whom will you refer this, but to the same cause our Saviour doth the revelation of the gospel to babes, and not to the wise—even to his Father? "For so it seemed good in thy sight" (Matt. xi. 25, 26); "For so was thy good pleasure before thee" (as in the original); it is at his pleasure whether he will give any a clear revelation of his gospel, or leave them only to the light of nature. He could have kept up the first beam of the gospel in the promise in all nations among the apostasies of Adam's posterity, or renewed it in all nations when it began to be darkened, as well as he first published it to Adam after his fall; but it was his sovereign pleasure to permit it to be obscured in one place, and to keep it lighted in another.

4. His sovereignty is manifest in the various influences of the means of grace. He saith to these waters of the sanctuary, as to the floods of the sea, "Hitherto you shall go, and no further." Sometimes they wash away the filth of the flesh and outward man, but not that of the spirit; the gospel spiritualizeth some, and only moralizeth others; some are by the power of it struck down to conviction, but not raised up to conversion; some have only the gleams of it in their consciences, and others more powerful flashes; some remain in their thick darkness under the beaming of the gospel every day in their face, and after a long insensibleness are roused by its light and warmth; sometimes there is such a powerful breath in it, that it levels the haughty imaginations of men, and lays them at its feet that before strutted against it in the pride of their heart. The foundation of this is not in the gospel itself, which is always the same, nor in the ordinances, which are channels as sound at one time as at another, but Divine sovereignty that spirits them as he pleaseth, and "blows when and where it lists." It has sometimes conquered its thousands (Acts, ii. 41); at another time scarce its tens; sometimes the harvest hath been great, when the laborers have been but few; at another time it hath been small, when the laborers have been many; sometimes whole sheaves; at another time scarce gleanings. The evangelical net hath been sometimes full at a cast, and at every cast; at another time many have labored all night, and day too, and catched nothing (Acts, ii. 47): "The Lord added to the church daily." The gospel chariot doth not always return with captives chained to the sides of it, but sometimes blurred and reproached, wearing the marks of hell's spite, instead of imprinting the marks of its own beauty. In Corinth it triumphed over many people (Acts, xviii. 10); in Athens it is mocked, and gathers but a few clusters (Acts, xvii. 32, 34). God keeps the key of the heart, as well as of the womb. The apostles had a power of publishing the gospel, and working miracles, but under the Divine conduct; it was an instrumentality *durante bene placito*, and as God saw it convenient. Miracles were not upon every occasion allowed to them to be wrought, nor success upon every administration granted to them; God sometimes lent them the key, but to take out no more treasure than was allotted to them. There is a variety in the time of gospel operation; some rise out of their graves of sin, and beds of sluggishness, at the first appearance of this sun; others lie snorting

longer. Why doth not God spirit it at one season as well as at another, but set his distinct periods of time, but because he will show his absolute freedom?   And do we not sometimes experiment that after the most solemn preparations of the heart, we are frustrated of those incomes we expected?   Perhaps it was because we thought Divine returns were due to our preparations, and God stops up the channel, and we return drier than we came, that God may confute our false opinion, and preserve the honor of his own sovereignty. Sometimes we leap with John Baptist in the womb at the appearance of Christ; sometimes we lie upon a lazy bed when he knocks from heaven; sometimes the fleece is dry, and sometimes wet, and God withholds to drop down his dew of the morning upon it.   The dews of his word, as well as the droppings of the clouds, belong to his royalty; light will not shine into the heart, though it shine round about us, without the sovereign order of that God " who command-ed light to shine out of the darkness" of the chaos (2 Cor. iv. 6). And is it not seen also in regard of the refreshing influences of the word? sometimes the strongest arguments, and clearest promises, prevail nothing towards the quelling black and despairing imagi-nations ; when, afterwards, we have found them frighted away by an unexpected word, that seemed to have less virtue in it itself than any that passed in vain before it.   The reasonings of wisdom have dropped down like arrows against a brazen wall, when the speech of a weaker person hath found an efficacy.   It is God by his sovereignty spirits one word and not another; sometimes a secret word comes in, which was not thought of before, as dropped from heaven, and gives a refreshing, when emptiness was found in all the rest.   One word from the lips of a sovereign prince is a greater cordial than all the harangues of subjects without it; what is the reason of this variety, but that God would increase the proofs of his own sover-eignty ? that as it was a part of his dominion to create the beauty of a world, so it is no less to create the peace as well as the grace of the heart (Isa. lvii. 19): " I create the fruit of the lips, peace."   Let us learn from hence to have adoring thoughts of, not murmuring fancies against, the sovereignty of God; to acknowledge it with thankfulness in what we have; to implore it with a holy submission in what we want.   To own God as a sovereign in a way of depend-ence, is the way to be owned by him as subjects in a way of favor.

5. His sovereignty is manifested in giving a greater measure of knowledge to some than to others.   What parts, gifts, excellency of nature, any have above others, are God's donative; " He gives wis-dom to the wise, and knowledge to them that know understanding" (Dan. ii. 21); wisdom, the habit, and knowledge, the right use of it, in discerning the right nature of objects, and the fitness of means conducing to the end; all is but a beam of Divine light; and the different degrees of knowledge in one man above another, are the effects of his sovereign pleasure.   He enlightens not the minds of all men to know every part of his will; one " eats with a doubtful conscience," another in " faith," without any staggering (Rom. xiv. 2).   Peter had a desire to keep up circumcision, not fully understand-ing the mind of God in the abolition of the Jewish ceremonies;

while Paul was clear in the truth of that doctrine. A thought comes into our mind that, like a sunbeam, makes a Scripture truth visible in a moment, which before we were poring upon without any success; this is from his pleasure. One in the primitive times had the gift of knowledge, another of wisdom, one the gift of prophecy, another of tongues, one the gift of healing, another that of discerning spirits; why this gift to one man, and not to another? Why such a distribution in several subjects? Because it is his sovereign pleasure. "The Spirit divides to every man severally as he will" (1 Cor. xii. 11). Why doth he give Bezaleel and Aholiab the gift of engraving, and making curious works for the tabernacle (Exod. xxxi. 3), and not others? Why doth he bestow the treasures of evangelical knowledge upon the meanest of earthen vessels, the poor Galileans, and neglect the Pharisees, stored with the knowledge both of naturals and morals? Why did he give to some, and not to others, "to know the mysteries of the kingdom of heaven?" (Matt. xiii. 11.) The reason is implied in the words, "Because it was the mystery of his kingdom," and therefore was the act of his sovereignty. How would it be a kingdom and monarchy if the governor of it were bound to do what he did? It is to be resolved only into the sovereign right of propriety of his own goods, that he furnisheth babes with a stock of knowledge, and leaves the wise and prudent empty of it (Matt. xi. 26): "Even so, Father: for so it seemed good in thy sight." Why did he not reveal his mind to Eli, a grown man, and in the highest office in the Jewish church, but open it to Samuel, a stripling? why did the Lord go from the one to the other? Because his motion depends upon his own will. Some are of so dull a constitution, that they are incapable of any impression, like rocks too hard for a stamp; others like water; you may stamp what you please, but it vanisheth as soon as the seal is removed. It is God forms men as he pleaseth: some have parts to govern a kingdom, others scarce brains to conduct their own affairs; one is fit to rule men, and another scarce fit to keep swine; some have capacious souls in crazy and deformed bodies, others contracted spirits and heavier minds in a richer and more beautiful case. Why are not all stones alike? some have a more sparkling light, as gems, more orient than pebbles;—some are stars of first, and others of a less magnitude; others as mean as glow-worms, a slimy lustre:—it is because he is the sovereign Disposer of what belongs to him; and gives here, as well as at the resurrection, to one "a glory of the sun;" to another that of the "moon;" and to a third a less, resembling that of a "star" (1 Cor. xv. 40). And this God may do by the same right of dominion, as he exercised when he endowed some kinds of creatures with a greater perfection than others in their nature. Why may he not as well garnish one man with a greater proportion of gifts, as make a man differ in excellency from the nature of a beast? or frame angels to a more purely spiritual nature than a man? or make one angel a cherubim or seraphim, with a greater measure of light than another? Though the foundation of this is his dominion, yet his wisdom is not uninterested in his sovereign disposal; he garnisheth those with a greater ability whom he intends for greater service, than those that he intends for less, or none at all; as an artificer bestows more labor, and carves a more excellent figure upon those stones that he designs for a more honorable place in the building. But though the intending this or that man for service be the motive of laying in a greater provision in him than in others, yet still it is to be referred to his sovereignty, since that first act of culling him out for such an end was the fruit solely of his sovereign pleasure: as when he resolved to make a creature actively to glorify him, in wisdom he must give him reason; yet the making such a creature was an act of his absolute dominion.

6. His sovereignty is manifest in the calling some to a more special service in their generation. God settles some in immediate offices of his service, and perpetuates them in those offices, with a neglect of others, who seem to have a greater pretence to them. Moses was a great sufferer for Israel, the solicitor for them in Egypt, and the conductor of them from Egypt to Canaan; yet he was not chosen to the high priesthood, but that was an office settled upon Aaron, and his posterity after him, in a lineal descent; Moses was only pitched upon for the present rescue of the captived Israelites, and to be the instrument of Divine miracles; but notwithstanding all the success he had in his conduct, his faithfulness in his employment, and the transcendent familiarity he had with the great Ruler of the world, his posterity were left in the common level of the tribe of Levi, without any special mark of dignity upon them above the rest for all the services of that great man. Why Moses for a temporary magistrate, Aaron for a perpetual priesthood, above all the rest of the Israelites? hath little reason but the absolute pleasure of God, who distributes his employments as he pleaseth; and as a master orders his servant to do the noblest work, and another to labor in baser offices, according to his pleasure. Why doth he call out David, a shepherd, to sway the Jewish sceptre, above the rest of the brothers, that had a fairer appearance, and had been bred in arms, and inured to the toils and watchings of a camp? Why should Mary be the mother of Christ, and not some other of the same family of David, of a more splendid birth, and a nobler education? Though some other reasons may be rendered, yet that which affords the greatest acquiescence, is the sovereign will of God. Why did Christ choose out of the meanest of the people the twelve apostles, to be heralds of his grace in Judea, and other parts of the world; and afterwards select Paul before Gamaliel, his instructor, and others of the Jews, as learned as himself, and advance him to be the most eminent apostle, above the heads of those who had ministered to Christ in the days of his flesh? Why should he preserve eleven of those he first called to propagate and enlarge his kingdom, and leave the other to the employment of shedding his blood? Why, in the times of our reformation, he should choose a Luther out of a monastery, and leave others in their superstitious nastiness, to perish in the traditions of their fathers? Why set up Calvin, as a bulwark of the gospel, and let others as learned as himself wallow in the sink of popery? It is his pleasure to do so. The potter hath power to separate this part of the clay to form a vessel

for a more public use, and another part of the clay to form a vessel for a more private one. God takes the meanest clay to form the most excellent and honorable vessels in his house. As he formed man, that was to govern the creatures of the same clay and earth whereof the beasts were formed, and not of that nobler element of water, which gave birth to the fish and birds: so he forms some, that are to do him the greatest service, of the meanest materials, to manifest the absolute right of his dominion.

7. His sovereignty is manifest in the bestowing much wealth and honor upon some, and not vouchsafing it to the more industrious labors and attempts of others. Some are abased, and others are elevated; some are enriched, and others impoverished; some scarce feel any cross, and others scarce feel any comfort in their whole lives; some sweat and toil, and what they labor for runs out of their reach; others sit still, and what they wish for falls into their lap. One of the same clay hath a diadem to beautify his head, and another wants a covering to protect him from the weather. One hath a stately palace to lodge in, and another is scarce master of a cottage where to lay his head. A sceptre is put into one man's hand, and a spade into another's; a rich purple garnisheth one man's body, while another wraps himself in dunghill rags. The poverty of some, and the wealth of others, is an effect of the Divine sovereignty, whence God is said to be the Maker of the "poor as well as the rich" (Prov. xxii. 2), not only of their persons, but of their conditions. The earth, and the fulness thereof, is his propriety; and he hath as much a right as Joseph had to bestow changes of raiment upon what Benjamins he please. There is an election to a greater degree of worldly felicity, as there is an election of some to a greater degree of supernatural grace and glory: as he makes it "rain upon one city, and not upon another" (Amos iv. 7), so he causeth prosperity to distil upon the head of one and not upon another; crowning some with earthly blessings, while he crosseth others with continual afflictions: for he speaks of himself as a great proprietor of the corn that nourisheth us, and the wine that cheers us, and the wood that warm us (Hos. ii. 8, 9): "I will take away," not your corn and wine, but "my corn, my wine, my wool." His right to dispose of the goods of every particular person is unquestionable. He can take away from one, and pass over the propriety to another. Thus he devolved the right of the Egyptian jewels to the Israelites, and bestowed upon the captives what before he had vouchsafed to the oppressors; as every sovereign state demands the goods of their subjects for the public advantage in a case of exigency, though none of that wealth was gained by any public office, but by their private industry, and gained in a country not subject to the dominion of those that require a portion of them. By this right he changes strangely the scene of the world; sometimes those that are high are reduced to a mean and ignominious condition, those that are mean are advanced to a state of plenty and glory. The counter, which in accounting signifies now but a penny, is presently raised up to signify a pound. The proud ladies of Israel, instead of a girdle of curious needlework, are brought to make use

of a cord; as the vulgar translates *rent*, a rag, or list of cloth (Isa. iii. 24), and sackcloth for a stomacher instead of silk.   This is the sovereign act of God, as he is Lord of the world (Ps. lxxv. 6, 7): " Promotion cometh neither from the east, nor from the west, nor from the south, but God is the Judge: he putteth down one, and setteth up another."   He doth no wrong to any man, if he lets him languish out his days in poverty and disgrace: if he gives or takes away, he meddles with nothing but what is his own more than ours: if he did dispense his benefits equally to all, men would soon think it their due.   The inequality and changes preserve the notion of God's sovereignty, and correct our natural unmindfulness of it.   If there were no changes, God would not be feared as the " King of all the earth" (Ps. lv. 19): to this might also be referred his investing some countries with greater riches in their bowels, and on the surface; the disposing some of the fruitful and pleasant regions of Canaan or Italy, while he settles others in the icy and barren parts of the northern climates.

8. His sovereignty is manifest in the times and seasons of dispensing his goods.   He is Lord of the times when, as well as of the goods which, he doth dispose of to any person; these " the Father hath put in his own power" (Acts i. 7).   As it was his sovereign pleasure to restore the kingdom to Israel, so he would pitch upon the time when to do it, and would not have his right invaded, so much as by a question out of curiosity.   This disposing of opportunities, in many things, can be referred to nothing else but his sovereign pleasure.   Why should Christ come at the twilight and evening of the world? at the fulness, and not at the beginning, of time?   Why should he be from the infancy of the world so long wrapt up in a promise, and not appear in the flesh till the last times and gray hairs of the world, when so many persons, in all nations, had been hurried out of the world without any notice of such a Redeemer?   What was this but his sovereign will?   Why the Gentiles should be left so long in the devil's chains, wallowing in the sink of their abominable superstitions, since God had declared his intention by the prophets to call multitudes of them, and reject the Jews;—why he should defer it so long, can be referred to nothing but the same cause.   What is the reason the veil continues so long upon the heart of the Jews, that is promised, one time or other, to be taken off?   Why doth God delay the accomplishment of those glorious predictions of the happiness and interest of that people?   Is it because of the sin of their ancestors,—a reason that cannot bear much weight?   If we cast it upon that account, their conversion can never be expected, can never be effected ; if for the sins of their ancestors, is it not also for their own sins?   Do their sins grow less in number, or less venomous, or provoking in quality, by this delay ?   Is not their blasphemy of Christ as malicious, their hatred of him as strong and rooted, as ever?   Do they not as much approve of the bloody act of their ancestors, since so many ages are past, as their ancestors did applaud it at the time of the execution? Have they not the same disposition and will, discovered sufficiently by the scorn of Christ, and of those that profess his name, to act the

same thing over again, were Christ now in the same state in the world, and they invested with the same power of government? If their conversion were deferred one age after the death of Christ for the sins of their preceding ancestors, is it to be expected now; since the present generation of the Jews in all countries have the sins of those remote, the succeeding, and their more immediate ancestors, lying upon them? This, therefore, cannot be the reason; but as it was the sovereign pleasure of God to foretell his intention to overcome the stoutness of their hearts, so it is his sovereign pleasure that it shall not be performed till the "fulness of the Gentiles be come in" (Rom. xi. 25). As he is the Lord of his own grace, so he is the Lord of the time when to dispense it. Why did God create the world in six days, which he could have erected and beautified in a moment? Because it was his pleasure so to do. Why did he frame the world when he did, and not many ages before? Because he is Master of his own work. Why did he not resolve to bring Israel to the fruition of Canaan till after four hundred years? Why did he draw out their deliverance to so long time after he began to attempt it? Why such a multitude of plagues upon Pharaoh to work it, when he could have cut short the work by one mortal blow upon the tyrant and his accomplices? It was his sovereign pleasure to act so, though not without other reasons intelligible enough by looking into the story. Why doth he not bring man to a perfection of stature in a moment after his birth, but let him continue in a tedious infancy, in a semblance to beasts, for the want of an exercise of reason? Why doth he not bring this or that man, whom he intends for service, to a fitness in an instant, but by long tracts of study, and through many meanders and labyrinths? Why doth he transplant a hopeful person in his youth to the pleasures of another world, and let another, of an eminent holiness, continue in the misery of this, and wade through many floods of afflictions? What can we chiefly refer all these things to but his sovereign pleasure? The "times are determined by God" (Acts, xvii. 26).

Thirdly. The dominion of God is manifested as a governor, as well as a lawgiver and proprietor.

1. In disposing of states and kingdoms. (Ps. lxxv. 7): "God is Judge; he puts down one, and sets up another." "Judge" is to be taken not in the same sense that we commonly use the word, for a judicial minister in a way of trial, but for a governor; as you know the extraordinary governors raised up among the Jews were called judges, whence one entire book in the Old Testament is so denominated, the Book of Judges. God hath a prerogative to "change times and seasons" (Dan. ii. 21), *i. e.* the revolutions of government, whereby times are altered. How many empires, that have spread their wings over a great part of the world, have had their carcasses torn in pieces; and unheard-of nations plucked off the wings of the Roman eagle, after it had preyed upon many nations of the world; and the Macedonian empire was as the dew that is dried up a short time after it falls.[1] He erected the Chaldean monarchy, used Nebuchadnezzar to overthrow and punish the ungrateful Jews, and, by a

---

[1] Mr. Mede, in one of his letters.

sovereign act, gave a great parcel of land into his hands; and what
he thought was his right by conquest, was God's donative to him.
You may read the charter to Nebuchadnezzar, whom he terms his
servant (Jer. xxvii. 6): "And now I have given all those lands" (the
lands are mentioned ver. 3), "into the hands of Nebuchadnezzar, the
king of Babylon, my servant:" which decree he pronounceth after
his asserting his right of sovereignty over the whole earth (ver. 5).
After that, he puts a period to the Chaldean empire, and by the same
sovereign authority decrees Babylon to be a spoil to the nations of
the north country, and delivers her up as a spoil to the Persian (Jer.
l. 9, 10): and this for the manifestation of his sovereign dominion,
that he was the Lord, that made peace, and created evil (Isa. xlv. 6,
7). God afterwards overthrows that by the Grecian Alexander, prophesied of under the figure of a goat, with "one horn between his
eyes" (Dan. viii.): the swift current of his victories, as swift as his
motion, showed it to be from an extraordinary hand of heaven, and
not either from the policy or strength of the Macedonian. His
strength, in the prophet, is described to be less, being but one horn
running against the Persian, described under the figure of a ram with
two horns:[m] and himself acknowledged a Divine motion exciting
him to that great attempt, when he saw Joddus, the high-priest, coming out in his priestly robes, to meet him at his approach to Jerusalem, whom he was about to worship, acknowledging that the vision
which put him upon the Persian war appeared to him in such a garb.
What was the reason Israel was rent from Judah, and both split into
two distinct kingdoms? Because Rehoboam would not hearken to
sober and sound counsels, but follow the advice of upstarts. What
was the reason he did not hearken to sound advice, since he had so
advantageous an education under his father Solomon, the wisest
prince of the world? "The cause was from the Lord" (1 Kings, xii.
15), that he might perform what he had before spoke. In this he
acted according to his royal word; but, in the first resolve, he acted
as a sovereign lord, that had the disposal of all nations in the world.
And though Ahab had a numerous posterity, seventy sons to inherit
the throne after him, yet God by his sovereign authority gives them
up into the hands of Jehu, who strips them of their lives and hopes
together: not a man of them succeeded in the throne, but the crown
is transferred to Jehu by God's disposal. In wars, whereby flourishing kingdoms are overthrown, God hath the chief hand; in reference to which it is observed that, in the two prophets, Isaiah and
Jeremiah, God is called "the Lord of Hosts" one hundred and thirty
times. It is not the sword of the captain, but the sword of the Lord,
bears the first rank; "the sword of the Lord and of Gideon" (Judges,
vii. 18). The sword of a conquerer is the sword of the Lord, and
receives its charge and commission from the great Sovereign (Jer.
xlvii. 6, 7). We are apt to confine our thoughts to second causes,
lay the fault upon the miscarriages of persons, the ambition of the
one, and the covetousness of another, and regard them not as the
effects of God's sovereign authority, linking second causes together
to serve his own purpose. The skill of one man may lay open the

[m] Josephus.

folly of a counsellor; an earthly force may break in pieces the power of a mighty prince: but Job, in his consideration of those things, refers the matter higher: "He looseth the bond of kings, and girdeth their loins with a girdle" (Job, xii. 18). "He looseth the bonds of kings," *i. e.* takes off the yokes they lay upon their subjects, "and girds their loins with a girdle" (a *cord,* as the vulgar); he lays upon them those fetters they framed for others; such a girdle, or band, as is the mark of captivity, as the words, ver. 19, confirm it: "He leads princes away spoiled, and overthrows the mighty." God lifts up some to a great height, and casts down others to a disgraceful ruin. All those changes in the face of the world, the revolutions of empires, the desolating and ravaging wars, which are often immediately the birth of the vice, ambition, and fury of princes, are the royal acts of God as Governor of the world. All government belongs to him; he is the Fountain of all the great and the petty dominions in the world; and, therefore, may place in them what substitutes and vice-gerents he pleaseth, as a prince may remove his officers at pleasure, and take their commissions from them. The highest are settled by God *durante bene placito,* and not *quamdiu bene se gesserint.* Those princes that have been the glory of their country have swayed the sceptre but a short time, when the more wolvish ones have remained longer in commission, as God hath seen fit for the ends of his own sovereign government. Now, by the revolutions in the world, and changes in governors and government, God keeps up the acknowl-edgment of his sovereignty, when he doth arrest grand and public offenders that wear a crown by his providence, and employ it, by their pride, against him that placed it there. When he arraigns such by a signal hand from heaven, he makes them the public examples of the rights of his sovereignty, declaring thereby, that the cedars of Lebanon are as much at his foot, as the shrubs of the valley; that he hath as sovereign an authority over the throne in the palace, as over the stool in the cottage.

2. The dominion of God is manifested in raising up and ordering the spirits of men according to his pleasure. He doth, as the Father of spirits, communicate an influence to the spirits of men, as well as an existence; he puts what inclinations he pleaseth into the will, stores it with what habits he please, whether natural or supernatural, whereby it may be rendered more ready to act according to the Di-vine purpose. The will of man is a finite principle, and therefore subject to Him who hath an infinite sovereignty over all things; and God, having a sovereignty over the will, in the manner of its acting, causeth it to will what he wills, as to the outward act, and the out-ward manner of performing it. There are many examples of this part of his sovereignty. God, by his sovereign conduct, ordered Moses a protectoress as soon as his parents had formed an "ark of bul-rushes," wherein to set him floating on the river (Exod. ii. 3–6): they expose him to the waves, and the waves expose him to the view of Pharoah's daughter, whom God, by his secret ordering her motion, had posted in that place; and though she was the daughter of a prince that inveterately hated the whole nation, and had, by various arts, endeavored to extirpate them, yet God inspires the royal lady

with sentiments of compassion to the forlorn infant, though she knew him to be one of the Hebrews' children (ver. 6), *i. e.* one of that race whom her father had devoted to the hands of the executioner; yet God, that doth by his sovereignty rule over the spirits of all men, moves her to take that infant into her protection, and nourish him at her own charge, give him a liberal education, adopt him as her son, who, in time, was to be the ruin of her race, and the saviour of his nation. Thus he appointed Cyrus to be his shepherd, and gave him a pastoral spirit for the restoration of the city and temple of Jerusalem (Isa. xliv. 28): and Isaiah (chap. xlv. 5) tells them, in the prophecy, that he had girded him, though Cyrus had not known him, *i. e.* God had given him a military spirit and strength for so great an attempt, though he did not know that he was acted by God for those divine purposes. And when the time came for the house of the Lord to be rebuilt, the spirits of the people were raised up, not by themselves, but by God (Ezra, i. 5), "Whose spirit God had raised to go up;" and not only the spirit of Zerubbabel, the magistrate, and of Joshua, the priest, but the spirit of all the people, from the highest to the meanest that attended him, were acted by God to strengthen their hands, and promote the work (Hag. i. 14). The spirits of men, even in those works which are naturally desirable to them, as the restoration of the city and rebuilding of the Temple was to those Jews, are acted by God, as the Sovereign over them, much more when the wheels of men's spirits are lifted up above their ordinary temper and motion. It was this empire of God good Nehemiah regarded, as that whence he was to hope for success; he did not assure himself so much of it, from the favor he had with the king, nor the reasonableness of his intended petition, but the absolute power God had over the heart of that great monarch; and, therefore, he supplicates the heavenly, before he petitioned the earthly, throne (Neh. ii. 4): "So I prayed to the God of heaven." The heathens had some glance of this; it is an expression that Cicero hath somewhere, "That the Roman commonwealth was rather governed by the assistance of the Supreme Divinity over the hearts of men, than by their own counsels and management." How often hath the feeble courage of men been heightened to such a pitch as to stare death in the face, which before were damped with the least thought or glance of it! This is a fruit of God's sovereign dominion.

3. The dominion of God is manifest in restraining the furious passions of men, and putting a block in their way. Sometimes God doth it by a remarkable hand, as the Babel builders were diverted from their proud design by a sudden confusion of their language, and rendering it unintelligible to one another; sometimes by ordinary, though unexpected, means; as when Saul, like a hawk, was ready to prey upon David, whom he had hunted as a partridge upon the mountains, he had another object presented for his arms and fury by the Philistines' sudden invasion of a part of his territory (1 Sam. xxiii. 26—28). But it is chiefly seen by an inward curbing mutinous affections, when there is no visible cause. What reason but this can be rendered, why the nations bordering on Canaan, who bore no good will to the Jews, but rather wished the whole race of

them rooted out from the face of the earth, should not invade their country, pillage their houses, and plunder their cattle, while they were left naked of any human defence, the males being annually employed at one time at Jerusalem in worship; what reason can be rendered, but an invisible curb God put into their spirits? What was the reason not a man, of all the buyers and sellers in the Temple, should rise against our Saviour, when, with a high hand, he began to whip them out, but a Divine bridle upon them? though it appears, by the questioning his authority, that there were Jews enough to have chased out him and his company (John, ii. 15, 18). What was the reason that, at the publishing the gospel by the apostles at the first descent of the Spirit, those that had used the Master so barbarously a few days before, were not all in a foam against the servants, that, by preaching that doctrine, upbraided them with the late murder? Had they better sentiments of the Lord, whom they had put to death? Were their natures grown tamer, and their malignity expelled? No; but that Sovereign who had loosed the reins of their malicious corruption, to execute the Master for the purchase of redemption, curbed it from breaking out against the servants, to further the propagation of the doctrine of redemption. He that restrains the roaring lion of hell, restrains also his whelps on earth; he and they must have a commission before they can put forth a finger to hurt, how malicious soever their nature and will be. His empire reaches over the malignity of devils, as well as the nature of beasts. The lions out of the den, as well as those in the den, are bridled by him in favor of his Daniels. His dominion is above that of principalities and powers; their decrees are at his mercy, whether they shall stand or fall; he hath a vote above their stiffest resolves: his single word, *I will*, or, *I forbid*, outweighs the most resolute purposes of all the mighty Nimrods of the earth in their rendezvouses and cabals, in their associations and counsels (Isa. viii. 9, 10): "Associate yourselves, O ye people, and ye shall be broken in pieces; take counsel together, and it shall come to nought." "When the enemy shall come in like a flood," with a violent and irresistible force, intending nothing but ravage and desolation, "the Spirit of the Lord shall lift up a standard against them" (Isa. lix. 19), shall give a sudden check, and damp their spirits, and put them to a stand. When Laban furiously pursued Jacob, with an intent to do him an ill turn, God gave him a command to do otherwise (Gen. xxxi. 24). Would Laban have respected that command any more than he did the light of nature when he·worshipped idols, had not God exercised his authority in inclining his will to observe it, or laying restraints upon his natural inclinations, or denying his concourse to the acting those ill intentions he had entertained? The stilling the principles of commotion in men, and the noise of the sea, are arguments of the Divine dominion; neither the one nor the other is in the power of the most sovereign prince without Divine assistance: as no prince can command a calm to a raging sea, so no prince can order stillness to a tumultuous people; they are both put together as equally parts of the Divine prerogative (Ps. lxv. 7), which "stills the noise of the sea, and tumult of the people:" and David owns God's sovereignty more than his own, "in subduing the people under him" (Ps. xviii. 47). In this his empire is illustrious (Ps. xxix. 10): "The Lord sitteth upon the floods, yea, the Lord sitteth King for ever;" a King impossible to be deposed, not only on the natural floods of the sea, that would naturally overflow the world, but the metaphorical floods or tumults of the people, the sea in every wicked man's heart, more apt to rage morally than the sea to foam naturally. If you will take the interpretation of an angel, waters and floods, in the prophetic style, signify the inconstant and mutable people (Rev. xvii. 1, 5): "The waters where the whore sits are people, and multitudes, and nations, and tongues:" so the angel expounds to John the vision which he saw (ver. 1). The heathens acknowledged this part of God's sovereignty in the inward restraints of men: those apparitions of the gods and goddesses in Homer, to several of the great men when they were in a fury, were nothing else, in the judgment of the wisest philosophers, than an exercise of God's sovereignty in quelling their passions, checking their uncomely intentions, and controlling them in that which their rage prompted them to. And, indeed, did not God set bounds to the storms in men's hearts, we should soon see the funeral, not only of religion, but civility; the one would be blown out, and the other torn up by the roots.

4. The dominion of God is manifest in defeating the purposes and devices of men. God often makes a mock of human projects, and doth as well accomplish that which they never dreamt of, as disappoint that which they confidently designed. He is present at all cabals, laughs at men's formal and studied counsels, bears a hand over every egg they hatch, thwarts their best compacted designs, supplants their contrivances, breaks the engines they have been many years rearing, diverts the intentions of men, as a mighty wind blows an arrow from the mark which the archer intended. (Job, v. 12): "He disappointeth the devices of the crafty, so that their hands cannot perform their enterprise; he taketh the wise in their own craftiness, and the counsel of the froward is carried headlong." Enemies often draw an exact scheme of their intended proceedings, marshal their companies, appoint their rendezvous, think to make but one morsel of those they hate; God, by his sovereign dominion, turns the scale, changeth the gloominess of the oppressed into a sunshine, and the enemies' sunshine into darkness. When the nations were gathered together against Sion, and said, "Let her be defiled, and let our eye look upon Sion" (Micah, iv. 11), what doth God do in this case? (ver. 12), "He shall gather them," *i. e.* those conspiring nations, as "sheaves into the floor." Then he sounds a trumpet to Sion: "Arise, and thresh, O daughter of Sion, for I will make thy horn iron, and thy hoofs brass, and thou shalt beat in pieces many people; and I will consecrate their gain unto the Lord, and their substance unto the Lord of the whole earth." I will make them and their counsels, them and their strength, the monuments and signal marks of my empire over the whole earth. When you see the cunningest designs baffled by some small thing intervening; when you see men of profound wisdom infatuated, mistake their way, and "grope in the noon-day as in the night" (Job, v. 14), bewildered in

a plain way ; when you see the hopes of mighty attempters dashed into despair, their triumphs turned into funerals, and their joyful expectations into sorrowful disappointments ; when you see the weak, devoted to destruction, victorious, and the most presumptuous defeated in their purposes, then read the Divine dominion in the desolation of such devices. How often doth God take away the heart and spirit of grand designs, and burst a mighty wheel, by snatching but one man out of the world! How often doth he "cut off the spirits of princes" (Ps. lxxvi. 12), either from the world by death, or from the execution of their projects by some unforeseen interruption, or from favoring those contrivances, which before they cherished by a change of their minds! How often hath confidence in God, and religious prayer, edged the weakest and smallest number of weapons to make a carnage of the carnally confident! How often hath presumption been disappointed, and the contemned enemy rejoiced in the spoils of the proud expectant of victory! Phidias made the image of Nemesis, or Revenge, at Marathon, of that marble which the haughty Persians, despising the weakness of the Athenian forces, brought with them, to erect a trophy for an expected, but an ungained, victory.[n] Haman's neck, by a sudden turn, was in the halter, when the Jews' necks were designed to the block; Julian designed the overthrow of all the Christians, just before his breast was pierced by an unexpected arrow; the Powder-traitors were all ready to give fire to the mine, when the sovereign hand of Heaven snatched away the match. Thus the great Lord of the world cuts off men on the pinnacle of their designs, when they seem to threaten heaven and earth; puts out the candle of the wicked, which they thought to use to light them to the execution of their purposes; turns their own counsels into a curse to themselves, and a blessing to their adversaries, and makes his greatest enemies contribute to the effecting his purposes. How may we take notice of God's absolute disposal of things in private affairs, when we see one man, with a small measure of prudence and little industry, have great success, and others, with a greater measure of wisdom, and a greater toil and labor, find their enterprises melt between their fingers! It was Solomon's observation, "That the race was not to the swift, nor the battle to the strong, neither bread to the wise, nor riches to men of understanding, nor yet favor to men of skill" (Eccles. ix. 11). Many things might interpose to stop the swift in his race, and damp the courage of the most valiant : things do not happen according to men's abilities, but according to the overruling authority of God: God never yet granted man the dominion of his own way, no more than to be lord of his own time: " The way of man is not in himself, it is not in him that walketh to direct his steps" (Jer. x. 23). He hath given man a power of acting, but not the sovereignty to command success. He makes even those things which men intended for their security to turn to their ruin; Pilate delivered up Christ to be accounted a friend to Cæsar, and Cæsar soon after proves an enemy to him, removes him from his government, and sends him into banishment. The Jews imagined by the crucifying Christ to keep the Roman ensigns at a

[n] Causin. Symb. lib. ii. cap. 65.

distance from them, and this hasted their march, by God's sovereign disposal, which ended in a total desolation. "He makes the judges fools" (Job, xxii. 17), by taking away his light from their understanding, and suffering them to go on in the vanity of their own spirits, that his sovereignty in the management of things may be more apparent; for then he is known to be Lord, when he "snares the wicked in the work of his own hands" (Ps. ix. 16). You have seen much of this doctrine in your experience, and, if my judgment fail me not, you will yet see much more.

5. The dominion of God is manifest in sending his judgments upon whom he please. "He kills and makes alive; he wounds and heals" whom he pleaseth: his thunders are his own, and he may cast them upon what subjects he thinks good: he hath a right, in a way of justice, to punish all men; he hath his choice, in a way of sovereignty, to pick out whom he please, to make the examples of it. Might not some nations be as wicked as those of Sodom and Gomorrah, yet have not been scorched with the like dreadful flames? Zoar was untouched, while the other cities, her neighbors, were burnt to ashes. Were there never any places and persons successors in Sodom's guilt? Yet those only by his sovereign authority are separated by him to be the examples of his "eternal vengeance" (Jude, 7). Why are not sinners as Sodom, like as those ancient ones, scalded to death by the like fiery drops? It is because it is his pleasure; and the same reason is to be rendered, why he would in a way of justice cut off the Jews for their sins, and leave the Gentiles untouched in the midst of their idolatries. When the church was consumed because of her iniquities, they acknowledged God's sovereignty in this. "We are the clay, and thou art our Potter, and we all the work of thy hands" (Isa. lxiv. 7, 8); thou hast a liberty to break or preserve us. Judgments move according to God's order. When the sword hath a charge against Ashkelon and the sea-shore, thither it must march, and touch not any other place or person as it goes, though there may be demerit enough for it to punish. When the prophet had spake to the sword, "O thou sword of the Lord, how long will it be ere thou be quiet? put up thyself into thy scabbard, rest and be still;" the prophet answers for the sword, "How can it be quiet, seeing the Lord hath given it a charge against Ashkelon? there hath he appointed it" (Jer. xlvii. 6, 7). If he hath appointed a judgment against London or Westminster, or any other place, there it shall drop, there it shall pierce, and in no other place without a like charge. God, as a sovereign, gives instructions to every judgment, when, and against whom, it shall march, and what cities, what persons, it shall arrest; and he is punctually obeyed by them, as a sovereign Lord. All creatures stand ready for his call, and are prepared to be executioners of his vengeance, when he speaks the word; they are his hosts by creation, and in array for his service: at the sound of his trumpet, or beat of his drum, they troop together with arms in their hands, to put his orders exactly in execution.

6. The dominion of God is manifest in appointing to every man his calling and station in the world. If the hairs of every man's head fall under his sovereign care, the calling of every man, wherein

he is to glorify God and serve his generation, which is of a greater concern than the hairs of the head, falls under his dominion. He is the master of the great family, and divides to every one his work as he pleaseth. The whole work of the Messiah, the time of every action, as well as the hour of his passion, was ordered and appointed by God. The separation of Paul to the preaching of the gospel, was by the sovereign disposal of God (Rom. i. 1). By the same exercise of his authority, that he "sets every man the bounds of his habitation" (Acts, xvii. 26), he prescribes also to him the nature of his work. He that ordered Adam, the father of mankind, his work, and the place of it, the "dressing the garden" (Gen. ii. 15), doth not let any of his posterity be their own choosers, without an influence of his sovereign direction on them. Though our callings are our work, yet they are by God's order, wherein we are to be faithful to our great Master and Ruler.

7. The dominion of God is manifest in the means and occasions of men's conversion. Sometimes one occasion, sometimes another; one word lets a man go, another arrests him, and brings him before God and his own conscience; it is as God gives out the order. He lets Paul be a prisoner at Jerusalem, that his cause should not be determined there; moves him to appeal to Cæsar, not only to make him a prisoner, but a preacher, in Cæsar's court, and render his chains an occasion to bring in a harvest of converts in Nero's palace. His bonds in or for Christ are "manifest in all the palace" (Phil. i. 12, 13); not the bare knowledge of his bonds, but the sovereign design of God in those bonds, and the success of them; the bare knowledge of them would not make others more confident for the gospel, as it follows, ver. 14, without a providential design of them. Onesimus, running from his master, is guided by God's sovereign order into Paul's company, and thereby into Christ's arms; and he who came a fugitive, returns a Christian (Philem. 10, 15). Some, by a strong affliction, have had by the Divine sovereignty their understandings awakened to consider, and their wills spirited to conversion. Monica being called Meribibula, or toss-pot, was brought to consider her way, and reform her life. A word hath done that at one time, which hath often before fallen without any fruit. Many have come to suck in the eloquence of the minister, and have found in the honey for their ears a sting for their consciences. Austin had no other intent in going to hear Ambrose but to have a taste of his famous oratory. But while Ambrose spake a language to his ear, God spake a heavenly dialect to his heart. No reason can be rendered of the order, and timing, and influence of those things, but the sovereign pleasure of God, who will attend one occasion and season with his blessing, and not another.

8. The dominion of God is manifest in disposing of the lives of men. He keeps the key of death, as well as that of the womb, in his own hand; he hath given man a life, but not power to dispose of it, or lay it down at his pleasure; and therefore he hath ordered man not to murder, not another, not himself; man must expect his call and grant, to dispose of the life of his body. Why doth he cut the thread of this man's life, and spin another's out to a longer term?

Why doth one die an inglorious death, and another more honorable? One silently drops away in the multitude, while another is made a sacrifice for the honor of God, or the safety of his country. This is a mark of honor he gives to one and not to another. "To you it is given" (Phil. i. 29). The manner of Peter's death was appointed (John, xxi. 19). Why doth a small and slight disease against the rules of physic, and the judgment of the best practitioners, dislodge one man's soul out of his body, while a greater disease is mastered in another, and discharges the patient, to enjoy himself a longer time in the land of the living? Is it the effect of means so much as of the Sovereign Disposer of all things? If means only did it, the same means would always work the same effect, and sooner master a dwarfish than a giant-like distemper. "Our times are only in God's hands" (Ps. xxxi. 15); either to cut short or continue long. As his sovereignty made the first marriage knot, so he reserves the sole authority to himself to make the divorce.

Fourthly. The dominion of God is manifest in his being a Redeemer, as well as Lawgiver, Proprietor, and Governor. His sovereignty was manifest in the creation, in bestowing upon this or that part of matter a form more excellent than upon another. He was a Lawgiver to men and angels, and prescribed them rules according to the counsel of his own will. These were his creatures, and perfectly at his disposal. But in redemption a sovereignty is exercised over the Son, the Second person in the Trinity, one equal with the Father in essence and works, by whom the worlds were created, and by whom they do consist. The whole gospel is nothing else but a declaration of his sovereign pleasure concerning Christ, and concerning us in him; it is therefore called "the mystery of his will" (Eph. i. 9); the will of God is distinct from the will of Christ, a purpose in himself, not moved thereunto by any; the whole design was framed in the Deity, and as much the purpose of his sovereign will as the contrivance of his immense wisdom. He decreed, in his own pleasure, to have the Second Person assume our nature for to deliver mankind from that misery whereinto it was fallen. The whole of the gospel, and the privileges of it, are in that chapter resolved into the will and pleasure of God. God is therefore called "the head of Christ" (1 Cor. xi. 3). As Christ is superior to all men, and the man superior to the woman, so is God superior to Christ, and of a more eminent dignity; in regard of the constituting him mediator, Christ is subject to God, as the body to the head. "Head" is a title of government and sovereignty, and magistrates were called the "heads" of the people. As Christ is the head of man, so is God the head of Christ; and as man is subject to Christ, so is Christ subject to God; not in regard of the Divine nature, wherein there is an equality, and consequently no dominion of jurisdiction; nor only in his human nature, but in the economy of a Redeemer, considered as one designed, and consenting to be incarnate, and take our flesh; so that after this agreement, God had a sovereign right to dispose of him according to the articles consented to. In regard of his undertaking, and the advantage he was to bring to the elect of God upon the earth, he calls God by the solemn title of "his Lord" in that prophetic psalm of him (Ps. xvi. 2): "O my soul, thou hast said unto the Lord, Thou art my Lord: my goodness extends not unto thee, but unto the saints that are in the earth." It seems to be the speech of Christ in heaven, mentioning the saints on earth as at a distance from him. I can add nothing to the glory of thy majesty, but the whole fruit of my meditation and sufferings will redound to the saints on earth. And it may be observed, that God is called the Lord of Hosts in the evangelical prophets, Isaiah, Haggai, Zachariah, and Malachi, more in reference to this affair of redemption, and the deliverance of the church, than for any other works of his providence in the world.

1. This sovereignty of God appears, in requiring satisfaction for the sin of man. Had he indulged man after his fall, and remitted his offence without a just compensation for the injury he had received by his rebellion, his authority had been vilified, man would always have been attempting against his jurisdiction, there would have been a continual succession of rebellions on man's part; and if a continual succession of indulgences on God's part, he had quite disowned his authority over man, and stripped himself of the flower of his crown; satisfaction must have been required some time or other from the person thus rebelling, or some other in his stead; and to require it after the first act of sin, was more preservative to the right of the Divine sovereignty, than to do it after a multitude of repeated revolts. God must have laid aside his authority if he had laid aside wholly the exacting punishment for the offence of man.

2. This sovereignty of God appears, in appointing Christ to this work of redemption. His sovereignty was before manifest over angels and men by the right of creation; there was nothing wanting to declare the highest charge of it, but his ordering his own Son to become a mortal creature; the Lord of all things to become lower than those angels that had, as well as all other things, received their being and beauty from him, and to be reckoned in his death among the dust and refuse of the world: he by whom God created all things, not only became a man, but a crucified man, by the will of his Father (Gal. i. 4), "who gave himself for our sins according to the will of God;" to which may refer that expression (Prov. viii. 22), of his being "possessed by God in the beginning of his way." Possession is the dominion of a thing invested in the possessor; he was possessed, indeed, as a Son by eternal generation; he was possessed also in the beginning of his way or works of creation, as a Mediator by special constitution: to this the expression seems to refer, if you read on to the end of ver. 31, wherein Christ speaks of his "rejoicing in the habitable part of his earth," the earth of the great God, who hath designed him to this special work of redemption. He was a Son by nature, but a Mediator by Divine will; in regard of which Christ is often called God's servant, which is a relation to God as a Lord. God being the Lord of all things, the dominion of all things inferior to him is inseparable from him; and in this regard, the whole of what Christ was to do, and did actually do, was acted by him as the will of God, and is expressed so by himself in the prophecy (Ps. xl. 7), "Lo, I come;" (ver. 8), "I delight to do

thy will;" which are put together (Heb. x. 7), "Lo, I come to do thy will, O God." The designing Christ to this work was an act of mercy, but founded on his sovereignty. His compassionate bowels might have pitied us without his being sovereign, but without it could not have relieved us. It was the council of his own will, as well as of his bowels: none was his counsellor or persuader to that mercy he showed: (Rom. xi. 34), "Who hath been his counsellor?" for it refers to that mercy in "sending the Deliverer out of Sion" (ver. 26), as well as to other things the apostle had been discoursing of. As God was at liberty to create, or not to create, so he was at liberty to redeem or not to redeem, and at his liberty whether to appoint Christ to this work, or not to call him out to it. In giving this order to his Son, his sovereignty was exercised in a higher manner than in all the orders and instructions he hath given out to men or angels, and all the employments he ever sent them upon. Christ hath names which signify an authority over him: he is called "an Angel," and a "Messenger" (Mal. iii. 1); an "Apostle" (Heb. iii. 1): declaring thereby, that God hath as much authority over him as over the angels sent upon his messages, or over the apostles commissioned by his authority, as he was considered in the quality of Mediator.

3. This sovereignty of God appears in transferring our sins upon Christ. The supreme power in a nation can only appoint or allow of a commutation of punishment; it is a part of sovereignty to transfer the penalty due to the crime of one upon another, and substitute a sufferer, with the sufferer's own consent, in the place of a criminal, whom he had a mind to deliver from a deserved punishment. God transferred the sins of men upon Christ, and inflicted on him a punishment for them. He summed up the debts of man, charged them upon the score of Christ, imputing to him the guilt, and inflicting upon him the penalty. (Isa. liii. 6): "The Lord hath laid upon him the iniquity of us all;" he made them all to meet upon his back: "He hath made him to be sin for us" (2 Cor. v. 21); he was made so by the sovereign pleasure of God: a punishment for sin, as most understand it, which could not be righteously inflicted, had not sin been first righteously imputed, by the consent of Christ, and the order of the Judge of the world. This imputation could be the immediate act of none but God, because he was the sole creditor. A creditor is not bound to accept of another's suretyship, but it is at his liberty whether he will or no; and when he doth accept of him, he may challenge the debt of him, as if he were the principal debtor himself. Christ made himself sin for us by a voluntary submission; and God made him sin for us by a full imputation, and treated him penally, as he would have done those sinners in whose stead he suffered. Without this act of sovereignty in God, we had forever perished: for if we could suppose Christ laying down his life for us without the pleasure and order of God, he could not have been said to have borne our punishment. What could he have undergone in his humanity but a temporal death? But more than this was due to us, even the wrath of God, which far exceeds the calamity of a mere bodily death. The soul being principal in the crime, was to

be principal in the punishment. The wrath of God could not have dropped upon his soul, and rendered it so full of agonies, without the hand of God: a creature is not capable to reach the soul, neither as to comfort nor terror; and the justice of God could not have made him a sufferer, if it had not first considered him a sinner by imputation, or by inherency, and actual commission of a crime in his own person. The latter was far from Christ, who was holy, harmless, and undefiled. He must be considered then in the other state of imputation, which could not be without a sovereign appointment, or at least concession of God: for without it, he could have no more authority to lay down his life for us, than Abraham could have had to have sacrificed his son, or any man to expose himself to death without a call; nor could any plea have been entered in the court of heaven, either by Christ for us, or by us for ourselves. And though the death of so great a person had been meritorious in itself, it had not been meritorious for us, or accepted for us; Christ is "delivered up by him" (Rom. viii. 32), in every part of that condition wherein he was, and suffered; and to that end, that "we might become the righteousness of God in him" (2 Cor. v. 21): that we might have the righteousness of him that was God imputed to us, or that we might have a righteousness as great and proportioned to the righteousness of God, as God required. It was an act of Divine sovereignty to account him that was righteous a sinner in our stead, and to account us, who were sinners, righteous upon the merit of his death.

4. This was done by the command of God; by God as a Lawgiver, having the supreme legislative and preceptive authority: in which respect, the whole work of Christ is said to be an answer to a law, not one given him, but put into his heart, as the law of nature was in the heart of man at first. (Ps. xl. 7, 8): "Thy law is within my heart." This law was not the law of nature or moral law, though that was also in the heart of Christ, but the command of doing those things which were necessary for our salvation, and not a command so much of doing, as of dying. The moral law in the heart of Christ would have done us no good without the mediatory law; we had been where we were by the sole observance of the precepts of the moral law, without his suffering the penalty of it: the law in the heart of Christ was the law of suffering, or dying, the doing that for us by his death which the blood of sacrifices was unable to effect. Legal "sacrifices thou wouldest not; thy law is within my heart;" i. e. thy law ordered me to be a sacrifice; it was that law, his obedience to which was principally accepted and esteemed, and that was principally his passive, his obedience to death (Phil. ii. 8); this was the special command received from God, that he should die (John x. 18). It is not so clearly manifested when this command was given, whether after the incarnation of Christ, or at the point of his constitution as Mediator, upon the transaction between the Father and the Son concerning the affair of redemption: the promise was given "before the world began" (Tit. i. 2). Might not the precept be given, before the world began, to Christ, as considered in the quality of Mediator and Redeemer? Precepts and promises usually attend one another; every covenant is made up of both. Christ, considered

here as the Son of God in the Divine nature, was not capable of a command or promise; but considered in the relation of Mediator between God and man, he was capable of both. Promises of assistance were made before his actual incarnation, of which the Prophets are full : why not precepts for his obedience, since long before his incarnation this was his speech in the Prophet, " Thy law is within my heart !" however, a command, a law it was, which is a fruit of the Divine sovereignty ; that as the sovereignty of God was impeached and violated by the disobedience of Adam, it might be owned and vindicated by the obedience of Christ ; that as we fell by disloyalty to it, we might rise by the highest submission to it in another head, infinitely superior in his person to Adam, by whom we fell.

5. This sovereignty of God appears in exalting Christ to such a sovereign dignity as our Redeemer. Some, indeed, say, that this sovereignty of Christ's human nature was natural, and the right of it resulted from its union with the Divine ; as a lady of mean condition, when espoused and married to a prince, hath, by virtue of that, a natural right to some kind of jurisdiction over the whole kingdom, because she is one with the king.° But to waive this ; the Scripture placeth wholly the conferring such an authority upon the pleasure and will of God. As Christ was a gift of God's sovereign will to us, so this was a gift of God's sovereign will to Christ (Matt. xxviii. 28) : " All power is given me." And he " gave him to be head over all things to the church" (Eph. i. 22) ; "God gave him a name above every name" (Phil. ii. 9) ; and, therefore, his throne he sits upon is called "The throne of his Father" (Rev. iii. 21). And he " committed all judgment to the Son," i. e. all government and dominion ; an empire in heaven and earth (John, v. 22) ; and that because he is " the Son of Man" (ver. 27) ; which may understood, that the Father hath given him authority to exercise that judgment and government as the Son of Man, which he originally had as the Son of God ; or rather, because he became a servant, and humbled himself to death, he gives him this authority as the reward of his obedience and humility, conformable to Phil. ii. 9. This is an act of the high sovereignty of God, to obscure his own authority in a sense, and take into association with him, or vicarious subordination to him, the human nature of Christ as united to the Divine ; not only lifting it above the heads of all the angels, but giving that person in our nature an empire over them, whose nature was more excellent than ours : yea, the sovereignty of God appears in the whole management of this kingly office of Christ ; for it is managed in every part of it according to God's order (Ezek. xxxvii. 24, 25) : "David, my servant, shall be king over them," and " my servant David shall be their prince forever :" he shall be a prince over them, but my servant in that principality, in the exercise and duration of it. The sovereignty of God is paramount in all that Christ hath done as a priest, or shall do as a king.

Use I. For instruction.

1. How great is the contempt of this sovereignty of God ! Man

° Lessius, de Perfect. Divin. lib. x. p. 65.

naturally would be free from God's empire, to be a slave under the dominion of his own lust; the sovereignty of God, as a Lawgiver, is most abhorred by man (Lev. xxvi. 43). The Israelites, the best people in the world, were apt, by nature, not only to despise, but abhor, his statutes; there is not a law of God but the corrupt heart of man hath an abhorrency of: how often do men wish that God had not enacted this or that law that goes against the grain! and, in wishing so, wish that he were no sovereign, or not such a sovereign as he is in his own nature, but one according to their corrupt model. This is the great quarrel between God and man, whether he or they shall be the Sovereign Ruler. He should not, by the will of man, rule in any one village in the world; God's vote should not be predominant in any one thing. There is not a law of his but is exposed to contempt by the perverseness of man (Prov. i. 21): "Ye have set at nought all my counsel, and would have none of my reproof:" *Septuag.* "Ye have made all my counsels without authority." The nature of man cannot endure one precept of God, nor one rebuke from him; and for this cause God is at the expense of judgments in the world, to assert his own empire to the teeth and consciences of men (Ps. lix. 13): "Lord, consume them in wrath, and let them know that God rules in Jacob, to the ends of the earth." The dominion of God is not slighted by any creature of this world but man; all others observe it by observing his order, whether in their natural motions or preternatural irruptions; they punctually act according to their commission. Man only speaks a dialect against the strain of the whole creation, and hath none to imitate him among all the creatures in heaven and earth, but only among those in hell: man is more impatient of the yoke of God than of the yoke of man. There are not so many rebellions committed by inferiors against their superiors and fellow-creatures, as are committed against God. A willing and easy sinning is an equalling the authority of God to that of man (Hos. vi. 7): "They, like men, have transgressed my covenant;" they have made no more account of breaking my covenant than if they had broken some league or compact made with a mere man; so slightly do they esteem the authority of God; such a disesteem of the Divine authority is a virtual undeifying of him.ᵖ To slight his sovereignty is to stab his Deity; since the one cannot be preserved without the support of the other, his life would expire with his authority. How base and brutish is it for vile dust and mouldering clay to lift up itself against the majesty of God, whose throne is in the heavens, who sways his sceptre over all parts of the world—a Majesty before whom the devils shake, and the highest cherubims tremble! It is as if the thistle, that can presently be trod down by the foot of a wild beast, should think itself a match for the cedar of Lebanon, as the phrase is, 2 Kings, xiv. 9.

Let us consider this in general; and, also, in the ordinary practice of men. *First,* In general.

(1.) All sin in its nature is a contempt of the Divine dominion. As every act of obedience is a confirmation of the law, and consequently a subscription of the authority of the Lawgiver (Deut. xxvii.

ᵖ Munster.

26), so every breach to it is a conspiracy against the sovereignty of the Lawgiver; setting up our will against the will of God is an articling against his authority, as setting up our reason against the methods of God is an articling against his wisdom; the intendment of every act of sin is to wrest the sceptre out of God's hand. The authority of God is the first attribute in the Deity which it directs its edge against; it is called, therefore, a " transgression of his law" (1 John, iii. 4), and, therefore, a slight, or neglect, of the majesty of God; and the not keeping his commands is called a " forgetting God" (Deut. viii. 11), *i. e.* a forgetting him to be our absolute Lord. As the first notion we have of God as a Creator is that of his sovereignty, so the first perfection that sin struck at, in the violation of the law, was his sovereignty as a Lawgiver. "Breaking the law is a dishonoring God" (Rom. ii. 23), a snatching off his crown; to obey our own wills before the will of God, is to prefer ourselves as our own sovereigns before him. Sin is a wrong, and injury to God, not in his essence, that is above the reach of a creature, nor in anything profitable to him, or pertaining to his own intrinsic advantage; not an injury to God in himself, but in his authority, in those things which pertain to his glory; a disowning his due right, and not using his goods according to his will. Thus the whole world may be called, as God calls Chaldea, " a land of rebels" (Jer. 1, 21): " Go up against the land of Merathaim," or rebels : rebels, not against the Jews, but against God. The mighty opposition in the heart of man to the supremacy of God is discovered emphatically by the apostle (Rom. viii. 7) in that expression, " The carnal mind is enmity against God, *i. e.* against the authority of God, because " it is not subject to the law of God, neither indeed can be." It refuseth not subjection to this or that part, but to the whole; to every mark of Divine authority in it; it will not lay down its arms against it, nay, it cannot but stand upon its terms against it; the law can no more be fulfilled by a carnal mind, than it can be disowned by a sovereign God. God is so holy, that he cannot alter a righteous law, and man is so averse, that he cares not for, nay, cannot fulfil, one title; so much doth the nature of man swell against the majesty of God. Now an enmity to the law, which is in every sin, implies a perversity against the authority of God that enacted it.

(2.) All sin, in its nature, is the despoiling God of his sole sovereignty, which was probably the first thing the devil aimed at. That pride was the sin of the devil, the Scripture gives us some account of, when the apostle adviseth not a novice, or one that hath but lately embraced the faith, to be chosen a bishop (1 Tim. iii. 6), " Lest, being lifted up with pride, he fall into the condemnation of the devil;" lest he fall into the same sin for which the devil was condemned. But in what particular thing this pride was manifest, is not so easily discernible; the ancients generally conceived it to be an affecting the throne of God, grounding it on Isa. xiv. 12 : " How art thou fallen, O Lucifer, son of the morning! for thou hast said in thy heart, I will ascend into heaven, I will exalt my throne above the stars of God." It is certain the prophet speaks there of the king of Babylon, and taxeth him for his pride, and gives to him the title of "Lucifer," perhaps likening him in his pride to the devil, and then it notes plainly the particular sin of the devil, attempting a share in the sovereignty of God; and some strengthen their conjecture from the name of the archangel who contended against Satan (Jude, 9), which is Michael, which signifies, "Who as God?" or, "Who like God?" the name of the angel giving the superiority to God, intimating the contrary disposition in the devil, against whom he contended. It is likely his sin was an affecting equality with God in empire, or a freedom from the sovereign authority of God; because he imprinted such a kind of persuasion on man at his first temptation: "Ye shall be as gods" (Gen. iii. 5); and though it be restrained to the matter of knowledge, yet that being a fitness for government, it may be extended to that also. But it is plainly a persuading them, that they might be, in some sort, equal with God, and independent on him as their superior. What he had found so fatal to himself, he imagined would have the same success in the ruin of man. And since the devil hath, in all ages of the world, usurped a worship to himself which is only due to God, and would be served by man, as if he were the God of the world; since all his endeavor was to be worshipped as the Supreme God on earth, it is not unreasonable to think, that he invaded the supremacy of God in heaven, and endeavored to be like the Most High before his banishment, as he hath attempted to be like the Most High since. And since the devil and antichrist are reputed by John, in the Revelation, to be so near of kin, and so like in disposition, why might not that, which is the sin of antichrist, the image of him, be also the sin of Satan, "to exalt himself above all that is called God" (2 Thess. ii. 4), and "sit as God in his temple," affecting a partnership in his throne and worship? Whether it was this, or attempting an unaccountable dominion over created things, or because he was the prime angel, and the most illustrious of that magnificent corporation, he might think himself fit to reign with God over all things else? Or if his sin were envy, as some think, at the felicity of man in paradise, it was still a quarrelling with God's dominion, and right of disposing his own goods and favors; he is, therefore, called "Belial" (2 Cor. vi. 14, 15): "What concord hath Christ with Belial?" i. e. with the devil, one "without yoke," as the word "Belial" signifies.

(3.) It is more plain, that this was the sin of Adam. The first act of Adam was to exercise a lordship over the lower creatures, in giving names to them,—a token of dominion (Gen. ii. 19). The next was to affect a lordship over God, in rebelling against him. After he had writ the first mark of his own delegated dominion, in the names he gave the creatures, and owned their dependence on him as their governor, he would not acknowledge his own dependence on God. As soon as the Lord of the world had put him into possession of the power he had allotted him, he attempted to strip his Lord of that which he had reserved to himself; he was not content to lay a yoke upon the other creatures, but desirous to shake off the Divine yoke from himself, and be subject to none but his own will; hence Adam's sin is more particularly called "disobedience" (Rom. v. 19): for, in the eating the apple, there was no moral evil in itself, but a contradiction to the positive command and order of God, whereby he did disown God's right of commanding him, or reserving anything from him to his own use. The language all his posterity speaks, " Let us break his bands, and cast away his cords from us" (Ps. ii. 3), was learned from Adam in that act of his. The next act we read of, was that of Cain's murdering Abel, which was an invading God's right, in assuming an authority to dispose of the life of his brother, —a life which God had given him, and reserved the period of it in his own hands. And he persists in the same usurpation when God came to examine him, and ask him where his brother was ; how scornful was his answer ! (Gen. iv. 9) : " Am I my brother's keeper?" as much as if he had said, What have you to do to examine me ? or, What obligation is there upon me to render an account of him ? or, as one saith, it is as much as if he had said, " Go, look for him yourself."q The sovereignty of God did not remain undisturbed as soon as ever it appeared in creation ; the devils rebelled against it in heaven, and man would have banished it from the earth.

(4.) The sovereignty of God hath not been less invaded by the usurpations of men. One single order of the Roman episcopacy hath endeavored to usurp the prerogatives of God; the Pope will prohibit what God hath allowed ; the marriage of priests ; the receiving of the cup, as well as of the bread, in the sacrament; the eating of this or that sort of meat at special times, meats which God hath sanctified ; and forbid them, too, upon pain of damnation. It is an invasion of God's right to forbid the use of what God hath granted, as though the earth, and the fulness thereof, were no longer the Lord's, but the Pope's ; much more to forbid what God hath commanded, as if Christ overreached his own authority, when he enjoined all to drink of the sacramental wine, as well as eat of the sacramental bread. No lord but will think his right usurped by that steward who shall permit to others what his lord forbids, and forbid that which his master allows, and act the lord instead of the servant. Add to this the pardons of many sins, as if he had the sole key to the treasures of Divine mercy ; the disposing of crowns and dominions at his pleasure, as if God had divested himself of the title of King of kings, and transferred it upon the see of Rome. The allowing public stews, dispensing with incestuous marriages, as if God had acted more the part of a tyrant than of a righteous Sovereign in forbidding them, depriving the Jews of the propriety in their estates upon their conversion to Christianity, as if the pilfering men's goods were the way to teach them self-denial, the first doctrine of Christian religion ; and God shall have no honor from the Jew without a breach of his law by theft from the Christian. Granting many years' indulgences upon slight performances, the repeating so many *Ave-Marias* and *Pater-Nosters* in a day, canonizing saints, claiming the keys of heaven, and disposing of the honors and glory of it, and proposing creatures as objects of religious worship, wherein he answers the character of the apostle (2 Thess. ii. 4), "showing himself that he is God," in challenging that power which is only the right of Divine sovereignty ; exalting himself above God, in indulging

q Trap. *in loc.*

those things which the law of God never allowed, but hath severely prohibited. This controlling the sovereignty of God, not allowing him the rights of his crown, is the soul and spirit of many errors. Why are the decrees of election and preterition denied? Because men will not acknowledge God the Sovereign Disposer of his creature. Why is effectual calling and efficacious grace denied? Because they will not allow God the proprietor and distributer of his own goods. Why is the satisfaction of Christ denied? Because they will not allow God a power to vindicate his own law in what way he pleaseth. Most of the errors of men may be resolved into a denial of God's sovereignty; all have a tincture of the first evil sentiment of Adam.

Secondly. The sovereignty of God is contemned in the practices of men—(1.) As he is a *Lawgiver.*

[1.] When laws are made, and urged in any state contrary to the law of God. It is part of God's sovereignty to be a Lawgiver; not to obey his law is a breach made upon his right of government; but it is treason in any against the crown of God, to mint laws with a stamp contrary to that of heaven, whereby they renounce their due subjection, and vie with God for dominion, snatch the supremacy from him, and account themselves more lords than the Sovereign Monarch of the world. When men will not let God be the judge of good and evil, but put in their own vote, controlling his to establish their own; such are not content to be as gods, subordinate to the supreme God, to sit at his feet; nor co-ordinate with him, to sit equal upon his throne; but paramount to him, to over-top and shadow his crown;—a boldness that leaves the serpent, in the first temptation, under the character of a more commendable modesty; who advised our first parents to attempt to be as gods, but not above him, and would enervate a law of God, but not enact a contrary one to be observed by them. Such was the usurpation of Nebuchadnezzar, to set up a golden image to be adored (Dan. iii.), as if he had power to mint gods, as well as to conquer men; to set the stamp of a Deity upon a piece of gold, as well as his own effigies upon his current coin. Much of the same nature was that of Darius, by the motion of his flatterers, to prohibit any petition to be made to God for the space of thirty days, as though God was not to have a worship without a license from a doting piece of clay (Dan. vi. 7). So Henry the Third of France, by his edict, silenced masters of families from praying with their households.[r] And it is a farther contempt of God's authority, when good men are oppressed by the sole weight of power, for not observing such laws, as if they had a real sovereignty over the consciences of men, more than God himself.[s] When the apostles were commanded by an angel from God, to preach in the Temple the doctrine of Christ (Acts, v. 19, 20), they were fetched from thence with a guard before the council (ver. 6). And what is the language of those statesmen to them? as absolute as God himself could speak to any transgressors of his law. " Did not we straitly command you, that you should not teach in this name?" (ver. 28). It is sufficient that we gave yuo a command to be silent, and publish

r Trap. *in loc.*   s Faucheur, Vol. II. pp. 663, 664.

no more this doctrine of Jesus; it is not for you to examine our decrees, but rest in our order as loyal subjects, and comply with your rulers; they might have added,—though it be with the damnation of your souls. How would those overrule the apostles by no other reason but their absolute pleasure! And though God had espoused their cause, by delivering them out of the prison, wherein they had locked them the day before, yet not one of all this council had the wit or honesty to entitle it a fighting against God, but Gamaliel (ver. 29). So foolishly fond are men to put themselves in the place of God, and usurp a jurisdiction over men's consciences: and to presume that laws made against the interest and command of God, must be of more force than the laws of God's enacting.

[2.] The sovereignty of God is contemned in making additions to the laws of God. The authority of a sovereign Lawgiver is invaded and vilified when an inferior presumes to make orders equivalent to his edicts. It is a *præmunire* against heaven to set up an authority distinct from that of God, or to enjoin anything as necessary in matter of worship for which a Divine commission cannot be shown. God was always so tender of this part of his prerogative, that he would not have anything wrought in the tabernacle, not a vessel, not an instrument, but what himself had prescribed. "According to all that I show thee, after the pattern of the tabernacle, and the pattern of all the instruments thereof, even so shall ye make it" (Exod. xxv. 9); which is strictly urged again, ver. 40: "Look that thou make them after their pattern;" look to it, beware of doing anything of thine own head, and justling with my authority. It was so afterwards in the matter of the temple, which succeeded the tabernacle; God gave the model of it to David, and made him "understand in writing by his hand upon him, even all the works of this pattern" (1 Chron. xxviii. 19). Neither the royal authority in Moses, who was king in Jesurun; nor in David, who was a man after God's own heart, and called to the crown by a special and extraordinary providence; nor Aaron, and the high priests his successors, invested in the sacerdotal office, had any authority from God, to do anything in the framing the tabernacle or temple of their own heads. God barred them from anything of that nature, by giving them an exact pattern, so dear to him was always this flower of his crown. And afterwards, the power of appointing officers and ordinances in the church was delegated to Christ, and was among the rest of those royalties given to him, which he fully completed "for the edifying of the body" (Eph. iv. 11, 12); and he hath the eulogy by the Spirit of God, to be "faithful as Moses was in all his house, to Him that appointed him" (Heb. iii. 2). Faithfulness in a trust implies a punctual observing directions; God was still so tender of this, that even Christ, the Son, should no more do anything in this concern without appointment and pattern, than "Moses, a servant" (ver. 5, 6). It seems to be a vote of nature to refer the original of the modes of all worship to God; and therefore in all those varieties of ceremonies among the heathens, there was scarce any but were imagined by them to be the dictates and orders of some of their pretended deities, and not the resolves of mere human authority. What intrusion upon God's right hath the papacy made in regard of officers, cardinals, patriarchs, &c., not known in any Divine order? In regard of ceremonies in worship, pressed as necessary to obtain the favor of God, holy water, crucifixes, altars, images, cringings, reviving many of the Jewish and Pagan ceremonies, and adopting them into the family of Christian ordinances; as if God had been too absolute and arbitrary in repealing the one, and dashing in pieces the other. When God had by his sovereign order framed a religion for the heart, men are ready to usurp an authority to frame one for the sense, to dress the ordinances of God in new and gaudy habits, to take the eye by a vain pomp; thus affecting a Divine royalty, and acting a silly childishness; and after this, to impose the observation of those upon the consciences of men, is a bold ascent into the throne of God; to impose laws upon the conscience, which Christ hath not imposed, hath deservedly been thought the very spirit of antichrist; it may be called also the spirit of anti-god. God hath reserved to himself the sole sovereignty over the conscience, and never indulged men any part of it; he hath not given man a power over his own conscience, much less one man a power over another's conscience. Men have a power over outward things to do this or that, where it is determined by the law of God, but not the least authority to control any dictate or determination of conscience: the sole empire of that is appropriate to God, as one of the great marks of his royalty. What an usurpation is it of God's right to make conscience a slave to man, which God hath solely, as the Father of spirits, subjected to himself!—an usurpation which, though the apostles, those extraordinary officers, might better have claimed, yet they utterly disowned any imperious dominion over the faith of others (2 Cor. i. 24). Though in this they do not seem to climb up above God, yet they set themselves in the throne of God, envy him an absolute monarchy, would be sharers with him in his legislative power, and grasp one end of his sceptre in their own hands. They do not pretend to take the crown from God's head, but discover a bold ambition to shuffle their hairy scalps under it, and wear part of it upon their own, that they may rule with him, not under him; and would be joint lords of his manor with him, who hath, by the apostle, forbidden any to be "lords of his heritage" (1 Pet. v. 3): and therefore they cannot assume such an authority to themselves till they can show where God hath resigned this part of his authority to them. If their exposition of that place (Matt. xvi. 18), "Upon this rock I will build my church," be granted to be true, and that the person and successors of Peter are meant by that rock, it could be no apology for their usurpations; it is not Peter and his successors shall build, but "I will build;" others are instruments in building, but they are to observe the directions of the grand Architect.

[3.] The sovereignty of God is contemned when men prefer obedience to men's laws before obedience to God. As God hath an undoubted right, as the Lawgiver and Ruler of the world, to enact laws without consulting the pleasure of men, or requiring their consent to the verifying and establishing his edicts, so are men obliged, by their allegiance as subjects, to observe the laws of their Creator, without consulting whether they be agreeable to the laws of his revolted creatures. To consult with flesh and blood whether we should obey, is to authorize flesh and blood above the purest and most sovereign Spirit. When men will obey their superiors, without taking in the condition the apostle prescribes to servants (Col. iii. 22), " In singleness of heart fearing God," and postpone the fear of God to the fear of man, it is to render God of less power with them than the drop of a bucket, or dust of the balance. When we, out of fear of punishment, will observe the laws of men against the laws of God, it is like the Egyptians, to worship a ravenous crocodile instead of a Deity; when we submit to human laws, and stagger at Divine, it is to set man upon the throne of God, and God at the footstool of man; to set man above, and God beneath; to make him the tail, and not the head, as God speaks in another case of Israel (Deut. xxviii. 13). When we pay an outward observation to Divine laws, because they are backed by the laws of man, and human authority is the motive of our observance, we subject God's sovereignty to man's anthority; what he hath from us, is more owing to the pleasure of men than any value we have for the empire of God: when men shall commit murders, and imbrue their hands in blood by the order of a grandee; when the worst sins shall be committed by the order of papal dispensations; when the use of his creatures, which God hath granted and sanctified, shall be abstained from for so many days in the week, and so many weeks in the year, because of a Roman edict, the authority of man is acknowledged, not only equal, but superior, to that of God; the dominion of dust and clay is preferred before the undoubted right of the Soverign of the world; the commands of God are made less than human, and the orders of men more authoritative than Divine, and a grand rebel's usurpation of God's right is countenanced. When men are more devout in observance of uncertain traditions, or mere human inventions, than at the hearing of the unquestionable oracles of God; when men shall squeeze their countenances into a more serious figure, and demean themselves in a more religious posture, at the appearance of some mock ceremony, clothed in a Jewish or Pagan garb, which hath unhappily made a rent in the coat of Christ, and pay a more exact reverence to that which hath no Divine, but only a human stamp upon it, than to the clear and plain word of God, which is perhaps neglected with sleepy nods, or which is worse, entertained with profane scoffs;—this is to prefer the authority of man employed in trifles, before the authority of the wise Lawgiver of the world: besides, the ridiculousness of it is as great as to adore a glow-worm, and laugh at the sun; or for a courtier to be more exact in his cringes and starched postures before a puppet than before his sovereign prince. In all this we make not the will and authority of God our rule, but the will of man; disclaim our dependence on God, to hang upon the uncertain breath of a creature. In all this God is made less than man, and man more than God; God is deposed, and man enthroned; God made a slave, and man a sovereign above him. To this we may refer the solemn addresses of some for the maintenance of the Protestant religion according to law, the law of man; not so much minding the law of God, resolving to make the law, the church, the state, the rule of their religion, and change that if the laws be changed, steering their opinions by the compass of the magistrate's judgment and interest.

(2.) The dominion of God, as a *Proprietor*, is practically contemned.

[1.] By envy. When we are not flush and gay, as well spread and sparkling as others, this passion gnaws our souls, and we become the executioners to rack ourselves, because God is the executor of his own pleasure, The foundation of this passion is a quarrel with God; to envy others the enjoyment of their propriety is to envy God his right of disposal, and, consequently, the propriety of his own goods; it is a mental theft committed against God; we rob him of his right in our will and wish; it is a robbery to make ourselves equal with God when it is not our due, which is implied (Phil. ii. 6), when Christ is said "to think it no robbery to be equal with God." We would wrest the sceptre out of his hand, wish he were not the conductor of the world, and that he would resign his sovereignty, and the right of the distribution of his own goods, to the *capricios* of our humor, and ask our leave to what subjects he should dispense his favors. All envy is either a tacit accusation of God as an usurper, and assuming a right to dispose of that which doth not belong to him, and so it is a denial of his propriety, or else charges him with a blind or unjust distribution, and so it is a bespattering his wisdom and righteousness. When God doth punish envy, he vindicates his own sovereignty, as though this passion chiefly endeavored to blast this perfection (Ezek. xxv. 11, 12): "As I live, saith the Lord, I will do according to thy anger, and according to thy envy, and thou shall know that I am the Lord." The sin of envy in the devils was immediately against the crown of God, and so was the sin of envy in the first man, envying God the sole prerogative in knowledge above himself. This base humor in Cain, at the preference of Abel's sacrifice before his, was the cause that he deprived him of his life: denying God, first his right of choice and what he should accept, and then invading God's right of propriety, in usurping a power over the life and being of his brother, which solely belonged to God.

[2.] The dominion of God, as a proprietor, is practically contemned by a violent or surreptitious taking away from any what God hath given him the possession of. Since God is the Lord of all, and may give the possession and dominion of things to whom he pleaseth, all theft and purloining, all cheating and cozening another of his right, is not only a crime against the true possessor, depriving him of what he is entrusted with, but against God, as the absolute and universal proprietor, having a right thereby to confer his own goods upon whom he pleaseth, as well as against God as a Lawgiver, forbidding such a violence: the snatching away what is another's, denies man the right of possession, and God the right of donation: the Israelites taking the Egyptians' jewels had been theft had it not been by a Divine license and order, but cannot be slandered with such a term, after the Proprietor of the whole world had altered the title, and alienated them by his positive grant from the Egyptians, to confer them upon the Israelites.

[3.] The dominion of God, as a proprietor, is practically contemned

by not using what God hath given us for those ends for which he
gave them to us.   God passeth things over to us with a condition to
use that for his glory which he hath bestowed upon us by his bounty: he is Lord of the end for which he gives, as well as Lord of what
he gives; the donor's right of propriety is infringed when the lands
and legacies he leaves to a particular use are not employed to those
ends to which he bequeathed them: the right of the lord of a manor
is violated when the copyhold is not used according to the condition
of the conveyance.   So it is an invasion of God's sovereignty not to
use the creatures for those ends for which we are entrusted with
them: when we deny ourselves a due and lawful support from them;
hence covetousness is an invasion of his right: or when we unneces-
sarily waste them; hence prodigality disowns his propriety: or when
we bestow not anything upon the relief of others; hence uncharita-
bleness comes under the same title, appropriating that to ourselves,
as if we were the lords, when we were but the usufructuaries for ourselves, and stewards for others; this is to be " rich to ourselves, not
to God" (Luke xii. 21), for so are they who employ not their wealth
for the service, and according to the intent, of the donor.   Thus the
Israelites did not own God the true proprietor of their corn, wine,
and oil, which God had given them for his worship, when they prepared offerings for Baal out of his stock: " For she did not know
that I gave her corn, and wine, and oil, and multiplied her gold and
silver, which they prepared for Baal" (Hos. ii. 8); as if they had been
sole proprietors, and not factors by commission, to improve the
goods for the true owner.   It is the same invasion of God's right to
use the parts and gifts that God hath given us, either as fuel for our
pride, or advancing self, or a witty scoffing at God and religion;
when we use not religion for the honor of our Sovereign, but a stool
to rise by, and observe his precepts outwardly, not out of regard to
his authority, but as a stale to our interest, and furnishing self with
a little concern and trifle; when men will wrest his word for the favor
of their lusts, which God intended for the checking of them, and
make interpretations of it according to their humors, and not according
to his will discovered in the Scripture, this is to pervert the use of the
best goods and *depositum* he hath put into our hands, even Divine
revelations.   Thus hypocrisy makes the sovereignty of God a nullity.

(3.) The dominion of God, as a *Governor*, is practically contemned.

[1.] In idolatry.   Since worship is an acknowledgment of God's
sovereignty, to adore any creature instead of God, or to pay to anything that homage of trust and confidence which is due to God,
though it be the highest creature in heaven or earth, is to acknowledge that sovereignty to pertain to a creature, which is challenged
by God; as to set up the greatest lord in a kingdom in the government, instead of the lawful prince, is rebellion and usurpation;
and that woman incurs the crime of adultery, who commits it with
a person of great port and honor, as well as with one of a mean
condition.   While men create anything a god, they own themselves
supreme above the true God, yea, and above that which they account a god; for, by the right of creation, they have a superiority,

as it is a deity blown up by the breath of their own imagination. The authority of God is in this sin acknowledged to belong to an idol; it is called loathing of God as a husband (Ezek. xvi. 45), all the authority of God as a husband and Lord over them: so when we make anything or any person in the world the chief object and prop of our trust and confidence, we act the same part. Trust in an idol is the formal part of idolatry; "so is every one that trusts in them" (Ps. cxv. 8), *i. e.* in idols: whatsoever thing we make the object of our trust, we rear as an idol. It is not unlawful to have the image of a creature, but to bestow divine adoration upon it; it was not unlawful for the Egyptians to possess and use oxen, but to dub them gods to be adored, it was: it is not unlawful to have wealth and honor, nor to have gifts and parts, they are the presents of God; but to love them above God, to fix our reliance upon them more than upon God, is to rob God of his due, who, being our Creator, ought to be our confidence. What we want we are to desire of him, and expect from him. When we confide in anything else we deny God the glory of his creation; we disown him to be Lord of the world; imply that our welfare is in the hands of, and depends upon, that thing wherein we confide; it is not only to "equal it to God" in sovereign power, which is his own phrase (Isa. xl. 25), but to prefer it before him in a reproach of him. When the hosts of heaven shall be served instead of the Lord of those hosts; when we shall lackey after the stars, depend barely upon their influences, without looking up to the great Director of the sun, it is to pay an adoration unto a captain in a regiment which is due to the general. When we shall "make gold our hope, and say to the fine gold, Thou art my confidence," it is to deny the supremacy of that God that is above; as well as if we kiss our hands, in a way of adoration, to the sun in its splendor, or "the moon walking in its brightness," for Job couples them together (ch. xxxi. 25—28); it is to prefer the authority of earth before that of heaven, and honor clay above the Sovereign of the world: as if a soldier should confide more in the rag of an ensign, or the fragment of a drum, for his safety, than in the orders and conduct of his general; it were as much as is in his power to uncommission him, and snatch from him his commander's staff. When we advance the creature in our love above God, and the altar of our soul smokes with more thoughts and affections to a petty interest than to God, we lift up that which was given us as a servant in the place of the Sovereign, and bestow that throne upon it which is to be kept undefiled for the rightful Lord, and subject the interest of God to the demands of the creature. So much respect is due to God, that none should be placed in the throne of our affections equal with him, much less anything to perk above him.

[2.] Impatience is a contempt of God as a governor. When we meet with rubs in the way of any design, when our expectations are crossed, we will break through all obstacles to accomplish our projects, whether God will or no. When we are too much dejected at some unexpected providence, and murmur at the instruments of it, as if God divested himself of his prerogative of conducting human affairs; when a little cross blows us into a mutiny, and swells us into a sauciness to implead God, or make us fret against him (as the expression is, Isa. viii. 21), wishing him out of his throne; no sin is so devilish as this; there is not any strikes more at all the attributes of God than this, against his goodness, righteousness, holiness, wisdom, and doth as little spare his sovereignty as any of the rest: what can it be else, but an impious invasion of his dominion, to quarrel with him for what he doth, and to say, What reason hast thou to deal thus with me? This language is in the nature of all impatience, whereby we question his sovereignty, and parallel our dominion with his. When men have not that confluence of wealth or honor they greedily desired, they bark at God, and revile his government: they are angry God doth not more respectfully observe them, as though he had nothing to do in their matters, and were wanting in that becoming reverence which they think him bound to pay to such great ones as they are; they would have God obedient to their minds, and act nothing but what he receives a commission for from their wills. When we murmur, it is as if we would command his will, and wear his crown; a wresting the sceptre out of his hands to sway it ourselves; we deny him the right of government, disown his power over us, and would be our own sovereigns: you may find the character of it in the language of Jehoram (as many understand it), "Behold, this evil is of the Lord; what should I wait for the Lord any longer?" (2 Kings, vi. 33). This is an evil of such a nature, that it could come from none but the hand of God; why should I attend upon him, as my Sovereign, that delights to do me so much mischief, that throws curses upon me when I expected blessings? I will no more observe his directions, but follow my own sentiments, and regard not his authority in the lips of his doting prophet. The same you find in the Jews, when they were under God's lash; "And they said, There is no hope: but we will walk after our own devices, and we will every one do the imagination of his evil heart" (Jer. xviii. 12): we can expect no good from him, and therefore we will be our own sovereigns, and prefer the authority of our own imaginations before that of his precepts. Men would be their own carvers, and not suffer God to use his right; as if a stone should order the mason in what manner to hew it, and in what part of the building to place it. We are not ordinarily concerned so much at the calamities of our neighbors, but swell against heaven at a light drop upon ourselves. We are content God should be the sovereign of others, so that he will be a servant to us: let him deal as he will himself with others, so he will treat us, and what relates to us, as we will ourselves. We would have God resign his authority to our humors, and our humors should be in the place of a God to him, to direct him what was fit to do in our cause. When things go not according to our vote, our impatience is a wish that God was deposed from his throne, that he would surrender his seat to some that would deal more favorably, and be more punctual observers of our directions. Let us look to ourselves in regard of this sin, which is too common, and the root of much mischief. This seems to be the first bubbling of Adam's will; he was not content with the condition wherein God had placed him, but affected another, which ended in the ruin of himself, and of mankind.

[3.] Limiting God in his way of working to our methods, is another part of the contempt of his dominion. When we will prescribe him methods of acting, that he should deliver us in this or that way, we would not suffer him to be the Lord of his own favors, and have the privilege to be his own director. When we will limit him to such a time, wherein to work our deliverance, we would rob him of the power of times and seasons, which are solely in his hand. We would regulate his conduct according to our imaginations, and assume a power to give laws to our Sovereign. Thus the Israelites "limited the Holy One of Israel" (Ps. lxxviii. 41): they would control his absolute dominion, and, of a sovereign, make him their slave. Man, that is God's vassal, would set bounds to his Lord, and cease to be a servant, and commence master, when he would give, not take, directions from him. When God had given them manna, and their fancies were weary of that delicious food, they would prescribe heaven to rain down some other sort of food for them. When they wanted no sufficient provision in the wilderness, they quarrelled with God for bringing them out of Egypt, and not presently giving them a place of seed, of figs, vines, and pomegranates (Numb. xx. 5), which is called a "striving with the Lord" (ver. 13), a contending with him for his Lordship. When we tempt God, and require a sign of him as a mark of his favor, we circumscribe his dominion; when we will not use the means he hath appointed, but father our laziness upon a trust in his providence, as if we expected he should work a miracle for our relief; when we censure him for what he hath done in the course of his providence; when we capitulate with him, and promise such a service, if he will do us such a good turn according to our platform, we would bring down his sovereign pleasure to our will, we invade his throne, and expect a submissive obedience from him. Man that hath not wit enough to govern himself, would be governing God, and those that cannot be their own sovereigns, affect a sovereignty over heaven.

[4.] Pride and presumption is another invasion of his dominion. When men will resolve to go to-morrow to such a city, to such a fair and market, to traffic, and get gain, without thinking of the necessity of a Divine license, as if ourselves were the lords of our time and of our lives, and God were to lackey after us (James iv. 13, 15): "Ye that say, To-day we will go into such a city, and buy and sell, whereas ye ought to say, If the Lord will, we shall live;" as if they had a freehold, and were not tenants at will to the Lord of the manor. When we presume upon our own strength or wit to get the better of our adversaries; as the Germans (as Tacitus relates) assured themselves, by the numerousness of their army, of a victory against the Romans, and prepared chains to fetter the captives before the conquest, which were found in their camp after their defeat;—when we are peremptory in expectations of success according to our will; as Pharaoh (Exod. xv. 9), "I will pursue, I will overtake, I will divide the spoil, my lust shall be satisfied upon them, I will draw my sword, my hand shall destroy them:" he speaks more like a god than a man, as if he were the sovereign power, and God only his vicar and lieutenant; how he struts, without thinking of a superior power to curb him!—when men ascribe to themselves what is the sole fruit of God's sovereign pleasure; as the king of Assyria speaks a language fit only to be spoken by God (Isa. x. 13, 14, &c.), " I have removed the bounds of the people; my hand hath found as a nest the riches of the people; I have gathered all the earth ;" which God declares to be a wrong to his sovereignty by the title wherewith he prefaceth his threatening against him (ver. 16): " Therefore shall the Lord, the Lord of hosts, send among his fat ones leanness," &c. It is indeed a rifling, if not of his crown, yet of the most glittering jewel of it, his glory. " He that mocks the poor reproacheth his Maker" (Prov. xvii. 5). He never thinks that God made them poor, and himself rich; he owns not his riches to be dropped upon him by the Divine hand. Self is the great invader of God's sovereignty; doth not only spurn at it, but usurp it, and assume divine honors, payable only to the universal Sovereign. The Assyrian was not so modest as the Chaldean, who would impute his power and victories to his idol (Hab. i. 11), whom he thought to be God, though yet robbing the true God of his authority; and so much was signified by their names, Nebuchadnezzar, Evil-Merodach, Belshazzar, Nebo, Merodach, Bel, being the Chaldean idols, and the names signifying, Lord of wealth, Giver of riches, and the like.— When we behave ourselves proudly towards others, and imagine ourselves greater than our Maker ever meant us ;—when we would give laws to others, and expect the most submissive observances from them, as if God had resigned his authority to us, and made us, in his stead, the rightful monarchs of the world. To disdain that any creature should be above us, is to disdain God's sovereign disposition of men, and consequently, his own superiority over us. A proud man would govern all, and would not have God his Sovereign, but his subject; to overvalue ourselves, is to undervalue God.

[5.] Slight and careless worship of God is another contempt of his sovereignty. A prince is contemned, not only by a neglect of those reverential postures which are due to him, but in a reproachful and scornful way of paying them. To behave ourselves uncomely or immodestly before a prince, is a disesteem of majesty. Sovereignty requires awe in every address, where this is wanting there is a disrepect of authority. We contemn God's dominion when we give him the service of the lip, the hand, the knee, and deny him that of the heart; as they in Ezekiel, xxxiii. 31, as though he were the Sovereign only of the body, and not of the soul. To have devout figures of the face, and uncomely postures of the soul, is to exclude his dominion from our spirits, while we own it only over our outward man ; we render him an insignificant Lord, not worthy of any higher adorations from us than a senseless statue; we demean not ourselves according to his majestical authority over us, when we present him not with the cream and quintessence of our souls. The greatness of God required a great house, and a costly palace (1 Chron. xxix. 11, 16); David speaks it in order to the building God a house and a temple ; God being a great King expects a male the best of our flock (Mal. i. 14), a masculine and vigorous service. When we present him with a sleepy, sickly rheumatic service, we betray our conceptions of him to be as mean as if he were some petty lord, whose dominion were of no larger extent than a mole-hill, or some inconsiderable village.

[6.] Omission of the service he hath appointed is another contempt of his sovereignty. This is a contempt of his dominion, whereby he hath a right to appoint what means and conditions he pleaseth, for the enjoyment of his proffered and promised benefits. It is an enmity to his sceptre not to accept of his terms after a long series of precepts and invitations made for the restoring us to that happiness we had lost, and providing all means necessary thereunto, nothing being wanting but our own concurrence with it, and acceptance of it, by rendering that easy homage he requires. By withholding from him the service he enjoins, we deny that we hold anything of him; as he that pays not the quit rent, though it be never so small, disowns the sovereignty of the lord of the manor; it implies, that he is a miserable poor lord, having no right, or destitute of any power, to dispose of anything in the world to our advantage (Job, xxii. 17): "They say unto God, Depart from us, what can the Almighty do for them?" They will have no commerce with him in a way of duty, because they imagine him to have no sovereign power to do anything for them in way of benefit, as if his dominion were an empty title, and as much destitute of any authority to command a favor for them as any idol. They think themselves to have as absolute a disposal of things, as God himself. What can he do for us? what can he confer upon us, that we cannot invest ourselves in? as though they were sovereigns in an equality with God. Thus men live "without God in the world" (Eph. ii. 12), as if there were no Supreme Being to pay a respect to, or none fit to receive any homage at their hands; withholding from God the right of his time and the right of his service, which is the just claim of his sovereignty.

[7.] Censuring others is a contempt of his sovereignty. When we censure men's persons or actions by a rash judgment; when we will be judges of the good and evil of men's actions, where the law of God is utterly silent, we usurp God's place, and invade his right; we claim a superiority over the law, and judge God defective, as the Rector of the world, in his prescriptions of good and evil. (James, iv. 11, 12), "He that speaks evil of his brother, and judgeth his brother, speaks evil of the law, and judgeth the law; there is one Lawgiver who is able to save, and to destroy: who art thou that judgest another? Do you know what you do in judging another? You take upon you the garb of a sovereign, as if he were more your servant than God's, and more under your authority than the authority of God; it is a setting thyself in God's tribunal, and assuming his rightful power of judging; thy brother is not to be governed by thy fancy, but by God's law, and his own conscience.

2. *Information.* Hence it follows, that God doth actually govern the world. He hath not only a right to rule, but "he rules over all," so saith the text. He is "King of kings, and Lord of lords,"—

what, to let them do what they please, and all that their lusts prompt them to? hath God an absolute dominion? Is it good, and is it wise? Is it then a useless prerogative of the Divine nature? Shall so excellent a power lie idle, as if God were a lifeless image? Shall we fancy God like some lazy monarch, that solaceth himself in the gardens of his palace, or steeps himself in some charming pleasures, and leaves his lieutenants to govern the several provinces, which are all members of his empire, according to their own humor? Not to exercise this dominion is all one as not to have it; to what purpose is he invested with this sovereignty, if he were careless of what were done in the world, and regarded not the oppressions of men? God keeps no useless excellency by him; he actually reigns over the heathen (Ps. xlvii. 8), and those as bad, or worse than heathens. It had been a vanity in David to call upon the heavens to be glad, and the earth to rejoice, under the rule of a "sleepy Deity" (1 Chron. xvi. 31). No; his sceptre is full of eyes, as it was painted by the Egyptians; he is always waking, and always more than Ahasuerus, reading over the records of human actions. Not to exercise his authority, is all one as not to regard whether he keep the crown upon his head, or continue the sceptre in his hand. If his sovereignty were exempt from care, it would be destitute of justice; God is more righteous than to resign the ensigns of his authority to blind and oppressive man; to think that God hath a power, and doth not use it for just and righteous ends, is to imagine him an unrighteous as well as a careless Sovereign; such a thing in a man renders him a base man, and a worse governor; it is a vice that disturbs the world, and overthrows the ends of authority, as to have a power, and use it well, is the greatest virtue of an earthly sovereign. What an unworthy conception is it of God, to acknowledge him to be possessed of a greater authority than the greatest monarch, and yet to think that he useth it less than a petty lord; that his crown is of no more value with him than a feather? This represents God impotent, that he cannot, or unrighteous and base, that he will not administer the authority he hath for the noblest and justest end. But can we say, that he neglects the government of the world? How come things then to remain in their due order? How comes the law of nature yet to be preserved in every man's soul? How comes conscience to check, and cite, and judge? If God did not exercise his authority, what authority could conscience have to disturb man in unlawful practices, and to make his sports and sweetness so unpleasant and sour to him? Hath he not given frequent notices and memorials, that he holds a curb over corrupt inclinations, puts rubs in the way of malicious attempters, and often oversets the disturbers of the peace of the world?

3. *Information.* God can do no wrong, since he is absolute Sovereign. Man may do wrong, princes may oppress and rifle, but it is a crime in them so to do: because their power is a power of government, and not of propriety, in the goods or lives of their subjects; but God cannot do any wrong, whatsoever the clamors of creatures are, because he can do nothing but what he hath a sovereign right to do. If he takes away your goods, he takes not

away anything that is yours more than his own, since though he entrusted you with them, he divested not himself of the propriety. When he takes away our lives, he takes what he gave us by a temporary donation, to be surrendered at his call: we can claim no right in anything but by his will. He is no debtor to us: and since he owes us nothing, he can wrong us in nothing that he takes away. His own sovereignty excuseth him in all those acts which are most distasteful to the creature. If we crop a medicinal plant for our use, or a flower for our pleasure, or kill a lamb for our food, we do neither of them any wrong: because the original of them was for our use, and they had their life, and nourishment, and pleasing qualities for our delight and support. And are not we much more made for the pleasure and use of God, than any of those can be for us? "Of him and to him are all things" (Rom. xi. 36): hath not God as much right over any one of us, as over the meanest worm? Though there be a vast difference in nature between the angels in heaven and the worms on earth, yet they are all one in regard of subjection to God; he is as much the Lord of the one as the other; as much the Proprietor of the one as the other; as much the Governor of one as the other;—not a cranny in the world is exempt from his jurisdiction;—not a mite or grain of a creature exempt from his propriety. He is not our Lord by election; he was a Lord before we were in being; he had no terms put upon him who capitulated with him, and set him in his throne by covenant. What oath did he take to any subject at his first investiture in his authority? His right is as natural, as eternal as himself: as natural as his existence, and as necessary as his Deity. Hath he any law but his own will? What wrong can he do that breaks no law, that fulfils his law in everything he doth, by fulfilling his own will, which as it is absolutely sovereign, so it is infinitely righteous? In whatsoever he takes from us, then, he cannot injure us; it is no crime in any man to seize upon his own goods to vindicate his own honor; and shall it be thought a wrong in God to do such things, besides the occasion he hath from every man, and that every day provoking him to do it? He seems rather to wrong himself by forbearing such a seizure, than wrong us by executing it.

4. *Information.* If God have a sovereignty over the whole world, then merit is totally excluded. His right is so absolute over all creatures, that he neither is, nor can be, a debtor to any; not to the undefiled holiness of the blessed angels, much less to poor earthly worms; those blessed spirits enjoy their glory by the title of his sovereign pleasure, not by virtue of any obligation devolving from them upon God. Are not the faculties, whereby they and we perform any act of obedience, his grant to us? Is not the strength, whereby they and we are enabled to do anything pleasing to him, a gift from him? Can a vassal merit of his lord, or a slave of his master, by using his tools, and employing his strength in his service, though it was a strength he had naturally, not by donation from the man in whose service it is employed? God is Lord of all—all is due to him; how can we oblige him by giving him what

is his own, more his to whom it is presented, than ours by whom it is offered? He becomes not a debtor by receiving anything from us, but by promising something to us.[t]

5. *Information.* If God hath a sovereign dominion over the whole world, then hence it follows, that all magistrates are but sovereigns under God. He is King of kings, and Lord of lords; all the potentates of the world are no other than his lieutenants, movable at his pleasure, and more at his disposal than their subjects are at theirs. Though they are dignified with the title of "gods," yet still they are at an infinite distance from the supreme Lord; gods under God, not to be above him, not to be against him. The want of the due sense of their subordination to God hath made many in the world act as sovereigns above him more than sovereigns under him. Had they all bore a deep conviction of this upon their spirits, such audacious language had never dropped from the mouth of Pharaoh: "Who is the Lord, that I should obey his voice, to let Israel go?" (Exod. v. 2), presuming that there was no superior to control him, nor any in heaven able to be a match for him; Darius had never published such a doting edict, as to prohibit any petition to God; Nero had never fired Rome, and sung at the sight of the devouring flames; nor ever had he ripped up his mother's belly, to see the womb where he first lodged, and received a life so hateful to his country. Nor would Abner and Joab, the two generals, have accounted the death of men but a sport and interlude. "Let the young men arise and play before us" (2 Sam. ii. 14); what play it was, the next verse acquaints you with; thrusting their swords into one another's sides. They were no more troubled at the death of thousands, than a man is to kill a fly, or a flea. Had a sense of this but hovered over their souls, people in many countries had not been made their foot-balls, and used worse than their dogs! Nor had the lives of millions, worth more than a world, been exposed to fire and sword, to support some sordid lust, or breach of faith upon an idle quarrel, and for the depredation of their neighbors' estates; the flames of cities had not been so bright, nor the streams of blood so deep, nor the cries of innocents so loud. In particular,

(1). If God be Sovereign, all under-sovereigns are not to rule against him, but to be obedient to his orders. If they "rule by his authority" (Prov. viii. 15), they are not to rule against his interest; they are not to imagine themselves as absolute as God, and that their laws must be of as sovereign authority against his honor, as the Divine are for it. If they are his lieutenants on earth, they ought to act according to his orders. No man but will account a governor of a province a rebel, if he disobeys the orders sent to him by the sovereign prince that commissioned him. Rebellion against God is a crime of princes, as well as rebellion against princes a crime of subjects. Saul is charged with it by Samuel in a high manner for an act of simple disobedience, though intended for the service of God, and the enriching his country with the spoils of the Amalekites. "Rebellion is as the sin of witchcraft" (1 Sam. xv. 23); like witchcraft or covenanting with the devil, acting as if he had

[t] Austin.

received his commission not from God, but from Satan. Magistrates, as commissioned by God, ought to act for him. Doth human authority ever give a commission to any to rebel against itself? did God ever depute any earthly sovereignty against his glory, and give them leave to outlaw his laws, to introduce their own? No; when he gave the vicarious dominion to Christ, he calls upon the kings of the earth to be instructed, and be wise, and "kiss the Son" (Ps. ii. 10, 12), *i. e.* to observe his orders, and pay him homage as their Governor. What a silly doltish thing is it to resist that Supreme Authority, to which the archangels submit themselves, and regulate their employments punctually by their instructions! Those excellent creatures exactly obey him in all the acts of their subordinate government in the world; those in whose hand the greatest monarch is no more than a silly fly between the fingers of a giant. A contradiction to the interest of God hath been fatal to kings. The four monarchies have had their wings clipped, and most of them have been buried in their own ashes; they have all, like the imitators of Lucifer's pride, fallen from the heaven of their glory to the depth of their shame and misery. All governors are bound to be as much obedient to God, as their subjects are bound to be submissive to them. Their authority over men is limited; God's authority over them is absolute and unbounded. Though every soul ought to be subject to the higher powers, yet there is a higher Power of all, to which those higher powers are to subject themselves; they are to be keepers of both the tables of the law of God, and are then most sovereigns when they set in their own practice an example of obedience to God, for their subjects to write after.

(2.) They ought to imitate God in the exercise of their sovereignty in ways of justice and righteousness. Though God be an absolute sovereign, yet his government is not tyrannical, but managed accord ing to the rules of righteousness, wisdom, and goodness. If God, that created them as well as their subjects, doth so exercise his government, it is a duty incumbent upon them to do the same; since they are not the creators of their people, but the conductors. As God's government tends to the good of the world, so ought theirs to the good of their countries. God committed not the government of the world to the Mediator in an unlimited way, but for the good of the church, in order to the eternal salvation of his people. "He gave him to be head over all things to the church" (Eph. i. 22). He had power over the devils to restrain them in their temptation and malice; power over the angels to order their ministry for the heirs of salvation. So power is given to magistrates for the civil preservation of the world and of human society; they ought therefore to consider for what ends they were placed over the rest of mankind, and not exercise their authority in a licentious way, but conformable to that justice and righteousness wherein God doth administer his government, and for the preservation of those who are committed to them.

(3.) Magistrates must then be obeyed when they act according to God's order, and within the bounds of the Divine commission. They are no friends to the sovereignty of God, that are enemies to magistracy, his ordinance. Saul was a good governor, though none of the best men, and the despisers of his government after God's choice, were the sons of Belial (1 Sam. x. 27). Christ was no enemy to Cæsar. To pull down a faithful magistrate, such an one as Zerubbabel, is to pluck a signet from the hand of God; for in that capacity he accounts him (Hag. ii. 23). God's servants stand or fall to their own Master; how doth he check Aaron and Miriam for speaking against Moses, his servant? "Were you not afraid to speak against my servant Moses?" (Numb. xii. 8); against Moses as related to you in the capacity of a governor; against Moses as related to you in the capacity of my servant? To speak anything against them, as they act by God's order, is an invasion of God's sovereign right, who gave them their commission. To act against just power, or the justice of an earthly power, is to act against God's ordinance, who ordained them in the world, but not any abuse, or ill use of their power.

Use II. How dreadful is the consideration of this doctrine to all rebels against God! Can any man that hath brains in his head, imagine it an inconsiderable thing to despise the Sovereign of the world? It was the sole crime of disobedience to that positive law, whereby God would have a visible memorial of his sovereignty preserved in the eye of man, that showered down that deluge of misery, under which the world groans to this day. God had given Adam a soul, whereby he might live as a rational creature; and then gives him a law, whereby he might live as a dutiful subject: for God forbidding him to eat of the fruit of the tree of knowledge of good and evil, declared his own supremacy over Adam, and his propriety in the pleasant world he had given him by his bounty; he let him know hereby, that man was not his own lord, nor was to live after his own sentiments, but the directions of a superior. As when a great lord builds a magnificent palace, and brings in another to inhabit it, he reserves a small duty to himself, not of an equal value with the house, but for an acknowledgment of his own right, that the tenant may know he is not the lord of it, but hath this grant by the liberality of another.[u] God hereby gave Adam matter for a pure obedience, that had no foundation in his own nature by any implanted law; he was only in it to respect the will of his Sovereign, and to understand that he was to live under the power of a higher than himself. There was no more moral evil in the eating of this fruit, as considered distinct from the command, than in eating of any other fruit in the garden: had there been no prohibition, he might with as much safety have fed upon it as upon any other. No law of nature was transgressed in the act of eating of it, but the sovereignty of God over him was denied by him; and for this the death threatened was inflicted on his posterity: for though divines take notice of other sins in the fall of Adam, yet God, in his trial, chargeth him with none but this, and doth put upon his question an emphasis of his own authority: "Hast thou eaten of the tree whereof I commanded ye that thou shouldst not eat?" (Gen. iii. 11). This I am pleased with, that thou shouldest disown my dominion over thyself, and this garden. This was the inlet to all the other sins: as the acknowledgment of God's sovereignty is the first step to the practice of all the

u Chrysost. in Gen. Hom. 16.

duties of a creature, so the disowning his sovereignty is the first spring of all the extravagances of a creature. Every sin against the sovereign Lawgiver is worthy of death : the transgression of this command deserved death, and procured it to spread itself over the face of the world. God's dominion cannot be despised without meriting the greatest punishment.

1. Punishment necessarily follows upon the doctrine of sovereignty. It is a faint and a feeble sovereignty that cannot preserve itself, and vindicate its own wrongs against rebellious subjects ; the height of God's dominion infers a vengeance on the contemners of it : if God be an eternal King, he is an eternal Judge. Since sin unlinks the dependence between God the Sovereign, and man the subject, if God did not vindicate the rights of his sovereignty, and the authority of his law, he would seem to despise his own dominion, be weary of it, and not act the part of a good governor. But God is tender of his prerogative, and doth most bestir himself when men exalt themselves proudly against him : " In the thing wherein they dealt proudly, he will be above them" (Exod. xviii. 11). When Pharaoh thought himself a mate for God, and proudly rejected his commands, as if they had been the messages of some petty Arabian lord, God rights his own authority upon the life of his enemy by the ministry of the Red Sea. He turned a great king into a beast, to make him know that the Most High ruled in the kingdoms of men : " The demand is by the word of the holy ones, to the intent that the living may know that the Most High ruleth in the kingdoms of men" (Dan. iv, 16, 17); and that by the petitions of the angels, who cannot endure that the empire of God should be obscured and diminished by the pride of man. Besides the tender respect he hath to his own glory, he is constantly presented with the solicitations of the angels to punish the proud ones of the earth, that darken the glory of his majesty : it is necessary for the rescue of his honor, and necessary for the satisfaction of his illustrious attendants, who would think it a shame to them to serve a Lord that were always unconcerned in the rebellions of his creatures, and tamely suffer their spurns at his throne ; and therefore there is a day wherein the haughtiness of man shall be bowed down, the cedars of Lebanon overthrown, and high mountains levelled, that " God may be exalted in that day" (Isa. ii. 11, 12), &c. Pride is a sin that immediately swells against God's authority ; this shall be brought down that God may be exalted ; not that he should have a real exaltation, as if he were actually deposed from his government, but that he shall be manifested to be the Sovereign of the whole world. It is necessary there should be a day to chase away those clouds that are upon his throne, that the lustre of his majesty may break forth to the confusion of all the children of pride that vaunt against him. God hath a dominion over us as a Lawgiver, as we are his creatures; and a dominion over us in a way of justice, as we are his criminals.

2. This punishment is unavoidable.

(1.) None can escape him. He hath the sole authority over hell and death, the keys of both are in his hand : the greatest Cæsar can no more escape him than the meanest peasant : " Who art thou, O

great mountain, before Zerubbabel?" (Zech. iv. 7). The height of
angels is no match for him, much less that of the mortal grandees of
the world; they can no more resist him than the meanest person;
but are rather, as the highest steeples, the fittest marks for his crushing thunder. If he speaks the word, the principalities of men come
down, and "the crown of their glory" (Jer. xiii. 18). He can "take
the mighty away in a moment," and that "without hands," *i. e.*
without instruments (Job, xxxi.v 20). The strongest are like the
feet of Nebuchadnezzar's image, iron and clay; iron to man, but clay
to God, to be crumbled to nothing.

(2.) What comfort can be reaped from a creature, when the Sovereign of the world arms himself with terrors, and begins his visitation?
"What will you do in the day of visitation, to whom will you flee
for help, and where will you leave your glory?" (Isa. x. 3). The
torments from a subject may be relieved by the prince, but where
can there be an appeal from the Sovereign of the world? Where is
there any above him to control him, if he will overthrow us? Who
is there to call him to account, and say to him, What dost thou?
He works by an uncontrollable authority; he needs not ask leave
of any; "he works, and none can let it" (Isa. xliii. 13): as when he
will relieve, none can afflict; so when he will wound, none can relieve. If a king appoint the punishment of a rebel, the greatest
favorite in the court cannot speak a comfortable word to him: the
most beloved angel in heaven cannot sweeten and ease the spirit of
a man that the Sovereign Power is set against to make the butt of
his wrath. The devils lie under his sentence, and wear their chains
as marks of their condemnation, without hope of ever having them
filed off, since they are laid upon them by the authority of an unaccountable Sovereign.

(3.) By his sovereign authority God can make any creature the
instrument of his vengeance. He hath all the creatures at his beck,
and can commission any of them to be a dreadful scourge. Strong
winds and tempests fulfil his word (Ps. cxlviii. 8); the lightnings
answer him at his call, and cry aloud, "Here are we" (Job, xxxviii.
35). By his sovereign authority he can render locusts as mischievous
as lions, forge the meanest creatures into swords and arrows, and
commission the most despicable to be his executioners. He can cut
off joy from our spirits, and make our own hearts be our tormentors,
our most confident friends our persecutors, our nearest relations to
be his avengers; they are more his, who is their Sovereign, than
ours, who place a vain confidence in them. Rather than Abraham
shall want children, he can raise up stones, and adopt them into his
family; and rather than not execute his vengeance, he can array the
stones in the streets, and make them his armed subjects against us.
If he speak the word, a hair shall drop from our heads to choke us,
or a vapor, congealed into rheum in our heads, shall drop down and
putrefy our vitals. He can never want weapons, who is Sovereign
over the thunders of heaven and stones of the earth, over every
creature; and can, by a sovereign word, turn our greatest comforts
into curses.

3. This punishment must be terrible. How doth David, a great

king, sound in his body, prosperous in his crown, and successful in his conquests, settled in all his royal conveniences, groan under the wrathful touch of a greater King than himself (Ps. vi. xxxviii., and his other penitential Psalms), not being able to give himself a writ of ease by all the delights of his palace and kingdom! "If the wrath of a king be as the roaring of a lion" (Prov. xix. 10) to a poor subject, how great is the wrath of the King of kings, that cannot be set forth by the terror of all the amazing volleys of thunder that have been since the creation, if the noise of all were gathered into one single crack! As there is an inconceivable ground of joy in the special favor of so mighty a King, so is there of terror in his severe displeasure: he is "terrible to the kings of the earth; with God is terrible majesty" (Ps. lxxvi. 12). What a folly is it, then, to rebel against so mighty a Sovereign!

Use III. Of comfort. The throne of God drops honey and sweetness, as well as dread and terror; all his other attributes afford little relief without this of his dominion and universal command. When, therefore, he speaks of his being the God of his people, he doth often preface it with "the Lord thy God;" his sovereignty, as a Lord, being the ground of all the comfort we can take in his federal relation as our God; thy God, but superior to thee; thy God, not as thy cattle and goods are thine, in a way of sole propriety, but a Lord too, in a way of sovereignty, not only over thee, but over all things else for thee. As the end of God's settling earthly governments was for the good of the communities over which the governors preside, so God exerciseth his government for the good of the world, and more particularly for the good of the church, over which he is a peculiar Governor.

1. His love to his people is as great as his sovereignty over them. He stands not upon his dominion with his people so much as upon his affection to them; he would not be called "Baali, my Lord," *i. e.* he would not be known only by the name of sovereignty, but "Ishi, my husband," a name of authority and sweetness together (Hos. ii. 16, 19, &c.): he signifies that he is not only the Lord of our spirits and bodies, but a husband by a marriage knot, admitting us to a nearness to him, and communion of goods with him. Though he majestically sits upon a high throne, yet it is a throne "encircled with a rainbow" (Ezek. i. 28), to show that his government of his people is not only in a way of absolute dominion, but also in a way of federal relation; he seems to own himself their subject rather than their Sovereign, when he gives them a charter to command him in the affairs of his church (Isa. xlv. 11); "Ask of me things to come concerning my sons, and concerning the work of my hands command you me." Some read it by way of question, as a corrective of a sauciness: Do you ask me of things to come, and seem to command me concerning the works of my hands, as if you were more careful of my interest among my people than I am, who have formed them? But if this were the sense, it would seem to discourage an importunity of prayer for public deliverance; and therefore, to take it according to our translation, it is an exhortation to prayer, and a mighty encouragement in the management and exercise of it. Urge

me with my promise, in a way of humble importunity, and you shall find me as willing to perform my word, and gratify your desires, as if I were rather under your authority, than you under mine: as much as to say, If I be not as good as my word, to satisfy those desires that are according to my promise, implead me at my own throne, and, if I be failing in it, I will give judgment against myself: almost like princes' charters, and gracious grants, "We grant such a thing against us and our heirs," giving the subject power to implead them if they be not punctually observed by them. How is the love of God seen in his condescension below the majesty of earthy governors! He that might command, by the absoluteness of his authority, doth not only do that, but entreats, in the quality of a subject, as if he had not a fulness to supply us, but needed something from us for a supply of himself (2 Cor. v. 20): "As though God did beseech you by us." And when he may challenge, as a due by the right of his propriety, what we bestow upon his poor, which are his subjects as well as ours, he reckons it as a loan to him, as if what we had were more our own than his (Prov. xix. 17). He stands not upon his dominion so much with us, when he finds us conscientious in paying the duty we owe to him; he rules as a Father, by love as well as by authority; he enters into a peculiar communion with poor earthly worms, plants his gracious tabernacle among the troops of sinners, instructs us by his word, invites us by his benefits, admits us into his presence, is more desirous to bestow his smiles than we to receive them, and acts in such a manner as if he were willing to resign his sceptre into the hands of any that were possessed with more love and kindness to us than himself: this is the comfort of believers.

2. In his being Sovereign, his pardons carry in them a full security. He that hath the keys of hell and death, pardons the crime, and wipes off the guilt. Who can repeal the act of the chief Governor? what tribunal can null the decrees of an absolute throne? (Isa. xliii. 25), "I, even I, am he that blots out thy transgressions, for my name's sake." His sovereign dominion renders his mercy comfortable. The clemency of a subject, though never so great, cannot pardon; people may pity a criminal, while the executioner tortures him, and strips him of his life; but the clemency of the Supreme Prince establisheth a pardon. Since we are under the dominion of God, if he pardons, who can reverse it? if he doth not, what will the pardons of men profit us in regard of an eternal state? If God be a King forever, then he whom God forgives, he in whom God reigns, shall live forever; else he would want subjects on earth, and have none of his lower creatures, which he formed upon the earth, to reign over after the dissolution of the world; if his pardons did not stand secure, he would, after this life, have no voluntary subjects that had formerly a being upon the earth; he would be a King only over the damned creatures.

3. Corruptions will certainly be subdued in his voluntary subjects. The covenant, "I will be your God," implies protection, government, and relief, which are all grounded upon sovereignty; that, therefore, which is our greatest burden, will be removed by his sovereign power (Mic. vii. 19): "He will subdue our iniquities." If the

outward enemies of the church shall not bear up against his dominion, and perpetuate their rebellions unpunished, those within, his people, shall as little bear up against his throne, without being destroyed by him; the billows of our own hearts, and the raging waves within us, are as much at his beck as those without us; and his sovereignty is more eminent in quelling the corruptions of the heart, than the commotions of the world in reigning over men's spirits, by changing them, or curbing them, more than over men's bodies, by pinching and punishing them. The remainders of Satan's empire will moulder away before him, since He that is in us is a greater Sovereign "than he that is in the world" (1 John, iv. 4). His enemies will be laid at his feet, and so never shall prevail against him, when his kingdom shall come. He could not be Lord of any man, as a happy creature, if he did not, by his power, make them happy; and he could not make them happy, unless, by his grace, he made them holy: he could not be praised, as a Lord of glory, if he did not make some creatures glorious to praise him; and an earthly creature could not praise him perfectly, unless he had every grain of enmity to his glory taken out of his heart. Since God is the only Sovereign, he only can still the commotions in our spirits, and pull down all the ensigns of the devil's royalty; he can waste him by the powerful word of his lips.

4. Hence is a strong encouragement for prayer. "My King," was the strong compellation David used in prayer, as an argument of comfort and confidence, as well as that of "my God" (Ps. v. 2): "Hearken to the voice of my cry, my King and my God." To be a king is to have an office of government and protection: he gives us liberty to approach to him as the "Judge of all" (Heb. xii. 23), *i.e.* as the Governor of the world; we pray to one that hath the whole globe of heaven and earth in his hand, and can do whatsoever he will: though he be higher than the cherubims, and transcendently above all in majesty, yet we may soar up to him with the wings of our soul, faith and love, and lay open our cause, and find him as gracious as if he were the meanest subject on earth, rather than the most sovereign God in heaven. He hath as much of tenderness as he hath of authority, and is pleased with prayer, which is an acknowledgment of his dominion, an honoring of that which he delights to honor; for prayer, in the notion of it, imports thus much—that God is the Rector of the world, that he takes notice of human affairs, that he is a careful, just, wise Governor, a storehouse of blessing, a fountain of goodness to the indigent, and a relief to the oppressed. What have we reason to fear when the Sovereign of the world gives us liberty to approach to him and lay open our case? that God, who is King of the whole earth, not only of a few villages or cities in the earth, but the whole earth; and not only King of this dreggy place of our dross, but of heaven, having prepared, or established, his throne in the most glorious place of the creation.

5. Here is comfort in affliction. As a sovereign, he is the author of afflictions; as a sovereign, he can be the remover of them; he can command the waters of affliction to go so far and no farther. If he speaks the word, a disease shall depart as soon as a servant shall

from your presence with a nod; if we are banished from one place, he can command a shelter for us in another; if he orders Moab, a nation that had no great kindness for his people, to let "his outcasts dwell with them," they shall entertain them, and afford them sanctuary (Isa. xvi. 4). Again, God chasteneth as a "Sovereign," but teacheth as a "Father" (Ps. xcix. 12); the exercise of his authority is not without an exercise of his goodness; he doth not correct for his own pleasure, or the creature's torment, but for the creature's instruction; though the rod be in the hand of a sovereign, yet it is tinctured with the kindness of Divine bowels: he can order them as a sovereign to mortify our flesh, and try our faith. In the severest tempest, the Lord that raised the wind against us, which shattered the ship, and tore its rigging, can change that contrary wind for a more happy one, to drive us into the port.

6. It is a comfort against the projects of the church's adversaries in times of public commotions. The consideration of the Divine sovereignty may arm us against the threatenings of mighty ones, and the menaces of persecutors. God hath authority above the crowns of men, and a wisdom superior to the cabals of men; none can have a step without him; he hath a negative voice upon their counsels, a negative hand upon their motions; their politic resolves must stop at the point he hath prescribed them; their formidable strength cannot exceed the limits he hath set them; their overreaching wisdom expires at the breath of God: "There is no wisdom nor understanding nor counsel against the Lord" (Prov. xxi. 30); not a bullet can be discharged, nor a sword drawn, a wall battered, nor a person despatched out of the world, without the leave of God, by the mightiest in the world. The instruments of Satan are no more free from his sovereign restraint than their inspirer; they cannot pull the hook out of their nostrils, nor cast the bridle out of their mouths; this Sovereign can shake the earth, rend the heavens, overthrow mountains, the most mountainous opposers of his interest. Though the nations rush in against his people like the rushing of many waters, "God shall rebuke them, they shall be chased as the chaff of the mountains before the wind, and like a rolling thing before the whirlwind" (Isa. xvii. 13); so doth he often burst in pieces the most mischievous designs, and conducts the oppressed to a happy port: he often turns the severest tempests into a calm, as well as the most peaceful calm into a horrible storm. How often hath a well-rigged ship, that seemed to spurn the sea under her feet, and beat the waves before her to a foam, been swallowed up into the bowels of that element, over whose back she rode a little before! God never comes to deliver his church as a governor, but in a wrathful posture (Ezek. xx. 33): "Surely, saith the Lord, with a mighty hand, and with an outstretched arm, and with fury poured out, will I rule over you;" not with fury poured out upon the church, but fury poured out upon her enemies, as the words following evidence: the church he would bring out from the countries where she was scattered, and bring the people into the bond of the covenant. He sometimes "cuts off the spirits of princes" (Ps. lxxvi. 12), i. e. cuts off their designs as men do the pipes of a water-course. The hearts of all are as open to him

as the riches of heaven, where he resides; he can slip an inclination into the heart of the mighty, which they dreamed not of before; and if he doth not change their projects, he can make them abortive, and waylay them in their attempts. Laban marched with fury, but God put a padlock on his passion against Jacob (Gen. xxxi. 24, 29); the devils, which ravage men's minds, must be still when he gives out his sovereign orders. This Sovereign can make his people find favor in the eyes of the cruel Egyptians, which had so long oppressed them (Exod. xi. 3); and speak a good word in the heart of Nebuchadnezzar for the prophet Jeremiah, that he should order his captain to take him into his special protection, when he took Zedekiah away prisoner in chains, and "put out his eyes" (Jer. xxxix. 11). His people cannot want deliverance from Him who hath all the world at his command, when he is pleased to bestow it; he hath as many instruments of deliverance as he hath creatures at his beck in heaven or earth, from the meanest to the highest. As he is the Lord of hosts, the church hath not only an interest in the strength he himself is possessed with, but in the strength of all the creatures that are under his command, in the elements below, and angels above. In those armies of heaven, and in the inhabitants of the earth, he doth " what he will" (Dan. iv. 35); they are all in order and array at his command. There are angels to employ in a fatal stroke, lice and frogs to quell the stubborn hearts of his enemies; he can range his thunders and lightnings, the cannon and granadoes of heaven, and the worms of the earth in his service; he can muzzle lions, calm the fury of the fire, turn his enemies' swords into their own bowels, and their artillery on their own breasts; set the wind in their teeth, and make their chariot-wheels languish; make the sea enter a quarrel with them, and wrap them in its waves till it hath stifled them in its lap. The angels have storms, and tempests, and wars in their hands, but at the disposal of God; when they shall cast them out against the empire of antichrist (Rev. vii. 1, 2), then shall Satan be discharged from his throne, and no more seduce the nations; the everlasting gospel shall be preached, and God shall reign gloriously in Sion. Let us, therefore, shelter ourselves in the Divine sovereignty, regard God as the most high in our dangers and in our petitions. This was David's resolution (Ps. lvii. 1, 2): " I will cry unto God most high;" this dominion of God is the true "tower of David, wherein there are a thousand shields" for defence and encouragement (Cant. iv. 4).

Use IV. If God hath an extensive dominion over the whole world, this ought to be often meditated on, and acknowledged by us. This is the universal duty of mankind. If he be the Sovereign of all, we should frequently think of our great Prince, and acknowledge ourselves his subjects, and him our Lord. God will be acknowledged the Lord of the whole earth; the neglect of this is the cause of the judgments which are sent upon the world. All the prodigies were to this end, that they might know, or acknowledge, that "God was the Lord" (Exod. x. 2); as God was proprietor, he demanded the first-born of every Jew, and the first-born of every beast; the one was to be redeemed, and the other sacrificed; this was the quit rent they were to pay to him for their fruitful land. The first-fruits of the earth were ordered to be paid to him, as a homage due to the landlord, and an acknowledgment they held all in chief of him. The practice of offering first-fruits for an acknowledgment of God's sovereignty, was among many of the heathens, and very ancient; hence they dedicated some of the chief of their spoils, owning thereby the dominion and goodness of God, whereby they had gained the victory; Cain owned this in offering the fruits of the earth, and it was his sin he owned no more, *viz.*, his being a sinner, and meriting the justice of God, as his brother Abel did in his bloody sacrifice. God was a sovereign Proprietor and Governor while man was in a state of innocence; but when man proved a rebel, the sovereignty of God bore another relation towards him, that of a Judge, added to the other. The first-fruits might have been offered to God in a state of innocence, as a homage to him as Lord of the manor of the world; the design of them was to own God's propriety in all things, and men's dependence on him for the influences of heaven in producing the fruits of the earth, which he had ordered for their use. The design of sacrifices, and placing beasts instead of the criminal, was to acknowledge their own guilt, and God as a sovereign Judge; Cain owned the first, but not the second; he acknowledged his dependence on God as a Proprietor, but not his obnoxiousness to God as a Judge; which may be probably gathered from his own speech, when God came to examine him, and ask him for his brother (Gen. iv. 9): " Am I my brother's keeper?" Why do you ask me? though I own thee as the Lord of my land and goods, yet I do not think myself accountable to thee for all my actions. This sovereignty of God ought to be acknowledged in all the parts of it, in all the manifestattons of it to the creature; we should bear a sense of this always upon our spirits, and be often in the thoughts of it in our retirements; we should fancy that we saw God upon his throne in his royal garb, and great attendants about him, and take a view of it, to imprint an awe upon our spirits. The meditation of this would,

1. Fix us on him as an object of trust. It is upon his sovereign dominion as much as upon anything, that safe and secure confidence is built; for if he had any superior above him to control him in his designs and promises, his veracity and power would be of little efficacy to form our souls to a close adherency to him. It were not fit to make him the object of our trust that can be gainsayed by a higher than himself, and had not a full authority to answer our expectations; if we were possessed with this notion fully and believingly, that God were high above all, that "his kingdom rules over all," we should not catch at every broken reed, and stand gaping for comforts from a pebble stone. He that understands the authority of a king, would not waive a reliance on his promise to depend upon the breath of a changeling favorite. None but an ignorant man would change the security he may have upon the height of a rock, to expect it from the dwarfishness of a molehill. To put confidence in any inferior lord more than in the prince, is a folly in civil converse, but a rebellion in divine; God only being above all, can only rule all; can command things to help us, and check other things which we depend on, and make them fall short of our expectations.

The due consideration of this doctrine would make us pierce through second causes to the first, and look further than to the smaller sort of sailors, that climb the ropes, and dress the sails, to the pilot that sits at the helm, the master, that, by an indisputable authority, orders all their notions. We should not depend upon second causes for our support, but look beyond them to the authority of the Deity, and the dominion he hath over all the works of his hands (Zech. x. 1): "Ask ye of the Lord rain in the time of the latter rain;" when the seasons of the year conspire for the producing such an effect, when the usual time of rain is wheeled about in the year, stop not your thoughts at the point of the heavens whence you expect it, but pierce the heavens, and solicit God, who must give order for it before it comes. The due meditation of all things depending on the Divine dominion would strike off our hands from all other holds, so that no creature would engross the dependence and trust which is due to the First Cause; as we do not thank the heavens when they pour out rain, so we are not to depend upon them when we want it; God is to be sought to when the womb of second causes is opened to relieve us, as well as when the womb of second causes is barren, and brings not forth its wonted progeny.

2. It would make us diligent in worship. The consideration of God, as the Supreme Lord, is the foundation of all religion: "Our Father, which art in heaven," prefaceth the Lord's prayer; "Father" is a name of authority; "in heaven," the place where he hath fixed his throne, notes his government; not "my Father," but "our Father," notes the extent of this authority. In all worship we acknowledge the object of our worship our Lord, and ourselves his vassals; if we bear a sense that he is our Sovereign King, it would draw us to him in every exigence, and keep us with him in a reverential posture, in every address; when we come, we should be careful not to violate his right, but render him the homage due to his royalty. We should not appear before him with empty souls, but filled with holy thoughts: we should bring him the best of our flock, and present him with the prime of our strength; were we sensible we hold all of him, we should not withhold anything from him which is more worthy than another. Our hearts would be framed into an awful regard of him, when we consider that glorious and "fearful name, the Lord our God" (Deut. xxviii. 58). We should look to our feet when we enter into his house; if we considered him in heaven upon his throne, and ourselves on earth at his footstool (Eccles. v. 2), lower before him than a worm before an angel, it would hinder garnishness and lightness. The Jews, saith Capel, on 1 Tim. i. 17, repeat this expression, מלך העולם, King of worlds, or Eternal King; probably the first original of it might be to stake them down from wandering. When we consider the majesty of God, clothed with a robe of light, sitting upon his high throne, adorned with his royal ensigns, we should not enter into the presence of so great a Majesty with the sacrifice of fools, with light motions and foolish thoughts, as if he were one of our companions to be drolled with. We should not hear his word as if it were the voice of some ordinary peasant. The consideration of majesty would engender reverence in our ser-

vice; it would also make us speak of God with honor and respect, as of a great and glorious king, and not use defaming expressions of him, as if he were an infamous being.   And were he considered as a terrible majesty, he would not be frequently solicited by some to pronounce a damnation upon them upon every occasion.

3. It would make us charitable to others.   Since he is our Lord, the great Proprietor of the world, it is fit he should have a part of our goods, as well as our time : he being the Lord both of our goods and time.   The Lord is to be honored with our substance (Prov. iii. 9); kings were not to be approached to without a present; tribute is due to kings: but because he hath no need of any from us to bear up his state, maintain the charge of his wars, or pay his military officers and hosts, it is a debt due to him to acknowledge him in his poor, to sustain those that are a part of his substance; though he stands in no need of it himself, yet the poor, that we have always with us, do; as a seventh part of our weekly time, so some part of our weekly gains, are due to him.   There was to be a weekly laying by in store somewhat of what God had prospered them, for the relief of others (1 Cor. xvi. 1, 2); the quantity is not determined, that is left to every man's conscience, "according as God hath prospered him" that week.   If we did consider God as the Donor and Proprietor, we should dispose of his gifts according to the design of the true owner, and act in our places as stewards entrusted by him, and not purse up his part, as well as our own, in our coffers.   We should not deny him a small quit rent, as an acknowledgement that we have a greater income from him; we should be ready to give the inconsiderable pittance he doth require of us, as an acknowledgment of his propriety, as well as liberality.

4. It would make us watchful, and arm us against all temptations. Had Eve stuck to her first argument against the serpent, she had not been instrumental to that destruction which mankind yet feel the smart of (Gen. iii. 3) : "God hath said, Ye shall not eat of it;" the great Governor of the world hath laid his sovereign command upon us in this point.   The temptation gained no ground till her heart let go the sense of this for the pleasure of her eye and palate.   The repetition of this, the great Lord of the world hath said or ordered, had both unargumented and disarmed the tempter.   A sense of God's dominion over us would discourage a temptation, and put it out of countenance; it would bring us with a vigorous strength to beat it back to a retreat.   If this were as strongly urged as the temptation, it would make the heart of the tempted strong, and the motion of the tempter feeble.

5. It would make us entertain afflictions as they ought to be entertained, *viz.*, with a respect to God.   When men make light of any affliction from God, it is a contempt of his sovereignty, as to contemn the frown, displeasure, and check of a prince, is an affront to majesty : it is as if they did not care a straw what God did with them, but dare him to do his worst.   There is a "despising the chastening of the Almighty" (Job, v. 17).   To be unhumbled under his hand, is as much, or more, affront to him, than to be impatient under it.   Afflictions must be entertained as a check from heaven,

as a frown from the great Monarch of the world; under the feeling of every stroke, we are to acknowledge his sovereignty and bounty; to despise it, is to make light of his authority over us; as to despise his favors is to make light of his kindness to us. A sense of God's dominion would make us observe every check from him, and not diminish his authority by casting off a due sense of his correction.

6. This dominion of God would make us resign up ourselves to God in everything. He that considers himself a thing made by God, a vassal under his authority, would not expostulate with him, and call him to an account why he hath dealt so or so with him. It would stab the vitals of all pleas against him. We should not then contest with him, but humbly lay our cause at his feet, and say with Eli, (1 Sam. iii. 18), "It is the Lord, let him do what seems good." We should not commence a suit against God, when he doth not answer our prayers presently, and send the mercy we want upon the wings of the wind; he is the Lord, the Sovereign. The consideration of this would put an end to our quarrels with God; should I expect that the Monarch of the world should wait upon me; or I, a poor worm, wait upon him? Must I take state upon me before the throne of heaven, and expect the King of kings should lay by his sceptre, to gratify my humor? Surely Jonah thought God no more than his fellow, or his vassal, at that time when he told him to his face he did well to be angry, as though God might not do what he pleased with so small a thing as a gourd; he speaks as if he would have sealed a lease of ejectment, to exclude him from any propriety in anything in the world.

7. This dominion of God would stop our vain curiosity. When Peter was desirous to know the fate of John, the beloved disciple, Christ answereth no more than this: (John, xxi. 22), "If I will that he tarry till I come, what is that to thee? follow thou me." Consider your duty, and lay aside your curiosity, since it is my pleasure not to reveal it. The sense of God's absolute dominion would silence many vain disputes in the world. What if God will not reveal this or that? the manner and method of his resolves should humble the creature under intruding inquiries.

Use V. Of exhortation.

1. The doctrine of the dominion of God may teach us humility. We are never truly abased, but by the consideration of the eminence and excellency of the Deity. Job never thought himself so pitiful a thing, so despicable a creature, as after God's magnificent declamation upon the theme of his own sovereignty (Job, xlii. 5, 6). When God's name is regarded as the most excellent and sovereign name in all the earth, then is the soul in the fittest temper to lie low, and cry out, What is man, that so great a Majesty should be mindful of him? When Abraham considers God as the supreme Judge of all the earth, he then owns "himself but dust and ashes" (Gen. xviii. 25, 27). Indeed, how can vile and dusty man vaunt before God, when angels, far more excellent creatures, cannot stand before him, but with a veil on their faces? How little a thing is man in regard of all the earth! How mean a thing is the earth in regard of the vaster heavens! How poor a thing is the whole

world in comparison of God! How pitiful a thing is man, if compared with so excellent a Majesty! There is as great a distance between God and man, as between being and not being; and the more man considers the Divine royalty, the more disesteem he will have of himself; it would make him stoop and disrobe himself, and fall low before the throne of the King of kings, throwing down before his throne any crown he gloried in (Rev. iv. 10).

(1). In regard of authority. How unreasonable is pride in the presence of majesty! How foolish is it for a country justice of peace to think himself as great as his prince that commissioned him! How unreasonable is pride in the presence of the greatest sovereignty! What, is human greatness before Divine? The stars discover no light when the sun appears, but in a humble posture withdraw in their lesser beams, to give the sole glory of enlightening the world to the sun, who is, as it were, the sovereign of those stars, and imparts a light unto them. The greatest prince is infinitely less, if compared with God, than the meanest scullion in his kitchen can be before him. As the wisdom, goodness, and holiness of a man is a mere mote compared to the goodness and holiness of God, so is the authority of a man a mere trifle in regard of the sovereignty of God: and who but a simple child would be proud of a mote or trifle? Let man be as great as he can, and command others, he is still a subject to One greater than himself. Pride would then vanish like smoke at the serious consideration of this sovereignty. One of the kings of this country did very handsomely shame the flattery of his courtiers, that cried him up as lord of sea and land, by ordering his chair to be set on the sand of the sea shore, when the tide was coming in, and commanding the waters not to touch his feet, which when they did without any regard to his authority, he took occasion thereby to put his flatterers out of countenance, and instruct himself in a lesson of humility. "See," saith he, "how I rule all things, when so mean a thing as the water will not obey me!" It is a ridiculous pride that the Turk and Persian discover in their swelling titles. What poor sovereigns are they, that cannot command a cloud, give out an effectual order for a drop of rain, in a time of drought, or cause the bottles of heaven to turn their mouth another way in a time of too much moisture! Yet their own prerogatives are so much in their minds, that they jostle out all thoughts of the supreme prerogative of God, and give thereby occasion to frequent rebellions against him.

(2). In regard of propriety. And this doctrine is no less an abatement of pride in the highest, as well as in the meanest; it lowers pride in point of propriety, as well as in point of authority. Is any proud of his possessions? how many lords of those possessions have gone before you! how many are to follow you![x] Your dominion lasts but a short time, too short to be a cause of any pride and glory in it. God by a sovereign power can take you from them, or them from you, when he pleaseth. The traveller refresheth himself in the heat of summer under a shady tree; how many have done so before him the same day he knows not, and

[x] Raynard, de Deo, p. 766.

how many will have the benefit after before night comes, he is as much ignorant of; he, and the others that went before him and follow after him, use it for their refreshment, but none of them can say, that they are the lords of it; the property is invested in some other person, whom perhaps they know not. The propriety of all you have is in God, not truly in yourselves. Doth not that man deserve scorn from you, who will play the proud fool in gay clothes and attire, which are known to be none of his own, but borrowed? Is it not the same case with every proud man, though he hath a property in his goods by the law of the land? Is anything you have your own truly? Is it not lent you by the great Lord? Is it not the same vanity in any of you, to be proud of what you have as God's loan to you, as for such a one to be proud of what he hath borrowed of man? And do you not make yourselves as ridiculous to angels and good men, who know that though it is yours in opposition to man, yet it is not yours in opposition to God? they are granted you only for your use, as the collar of esses and sword, and other ensigns of the chief magistrate in the city, pass through many hands in regard of the use of them, but the propriety remains in the community and body of the city: or as the silver plate of a person that invites you to a feast is for your use during the time of the invitation. What ground is there to be proud of those things you are not the absolute lords and proprietors of, but only have the use of them granted to you during the pleasure of the Sovereign of the world!

2. Praise and thankfulness result from this doctrine of the sovereignty of God.

(1). He is to be praised for his royalty. (Ps. cxlv. 1), "I will extoll thee, my God, O King." The Psalmist calls upon men five times to sing praise to him as King of all the earth. (Ps. xlvii. 6, 7), "Sing praises to God, sing praises: sing praises to our king, sing praises: for God is the King of all the earth; sing ye praises with understanding." All creatures, even the inanimate ones, are called upon to praise him because of the excellency of his name and the supremacy of his glory, in the 148th Psalm throughout, and ver. 13. That Sovereign Power that gave us hearts and tongues, deserves to have them employed in his praises, especially since he hath by the same hand given us so great matter for it. As he is a Sovereign we owe him thankfulness; he doth not deal with us in a way of absolute dominion; he might then have annihilated us, since he hath as full a dominion to reduce us to nothing. Consider the absoluteness of his sovereignty in itself, and you must needs acknowledge that he might have multiplied precepts, enjoined us the observance of more than he hath done; he might have made our tether much shorter; he might exact obedience, and promise no reward for it; he might dash us against the walls, as a potter doth his vessel, and no man have any just reason to say, What dost thou? or, Why dost thou use me so? A greater right is in him to use us in such a manner as we do sensible as well as insensible things. And if you consider his dominion as it is capable to be exercised in a way of unquestionable justice, and submitted to the reason and judgments of creatures, he might have dealt with us in a smarter way than he hath hitherto done; instead of one affliction, we might have had a thousand: he might have shut his own hands from pouring out any good upon us, and ordered innumerable scourges to be prepared for us; but he deals not with us according to the rights of his dominion. He doth not oppress us by the greatness of his majesty; he enters into covenant with us, and allures us by the chords of a man, and shows himself as much a merciful as an absolute Sovereign.

(2.) As he is a Proprietor, we owe him thankfulness. He is at his own choice whether he will bestow upon us any blessings or no; the more value, therefore, his benefits deserve from us, and the Donor the more sincere returns. If we have anything from the creature to serve our turn, it is by the order of the chief Proprietor. He is the spring of honor, and the fountain of supplies: all creatures are but as the conduit pipes in a great city, which serve several houses with water, but from the great spring. All things are conveyed originally from his own hand, and are dispensed from his exchequer. If this great Sovereign did not order them, you would have no more supplies from a creature than you could have nourishment from a chip: it is the Divine will in everything that doth us good; every favor from creatures is but a smile from God, an evidence of his royalty to move us to pay a respect to him as the great Lord. Some heathens had so much respect for God, as to conclude that his will, and not their prudence, was the chief conductor of their affairs. His goodness to us calls for our thankfulness, but his sovereignty calls for a higher elevation of it: a smile from a prince is more valued, and thought worthy of more gratitude, than a present from a peasant; a small gift from a great person is more gratefully to be received than a larger from an inferior person: the condescension of royalty magnifies the gift. What is man, that thou, so great a Majesty, art mindful of him, to bestow this or that favor upon him?—is but a due reflection upon every blessing we receive. Upon every fresh blessing we should acknowledge the Donor and true Proprietor, and give him the honor of his dominion: his property ought to be thankfully owned in everything we are capable of consecrating to him; as David, after the liberal collection he had made for the building of the temple, owns in his dedication of it to that use the propriety of God: "Who am I, and what is my people, that we should be able to offer so willingly after this sort? for all things come of thee, and of thine own have we given thee" (1 Chron. xxix. 14): it was but a return of God's own to him, as the waters of the river are no other than the return to the sea of what was taken from it. Praise and thankfulness is a rent due from all mankind, and from every creature, to the great Landlord, since all are tenants, and hold by him at his will. "Every creature in heaven and earth, and under the earth, and in the sea," were heard, by John, to ascribe "blessing, honor, glory, and power, to Him that sits on the throne" (Rev. v. 13). We are as much bound to the sovereignty of God for his preservation of us, as for his creation of us; we are no less obliged to him that preserves our beings when exposed to dangers, than we are for bestowing a being upon us when we were not capable of danger. Thankfulness is due to this Sovereign for public concerns. Hath he not preserved the ship of his church in the midst of whistling winds and roaring waves; in the midst of the combats of men and devils; and rescued it often when it hath been near shipwrecked?

3. How should we be induced from hence to promote the honor of this Sovereign! We should advance him as supreme, and all our actions should concur in his honor: we should return to his glory what we have received from his sovereignty, and enjoy by his mercy: he that is the superior of all, ought to be the end of all. This is the harmony of the creation; that which is of an inferior nature is ordered to the service of that which is of a more excellent nature; thus water and earth, that have a lower being, are employed for the honor and beauty of the plants of the earth, who are more excellent in having a principle of a growing life: these plants are again subservient to the beasts and birds, which exceed them in a principle of sense, which the others want: those beasts and birds are ordered for the good of man, who is superior to them in a principle of reason, and is invested with a dominion over them. Man having God for his superior, ought as much to serve the glory of God, as other things are designed to be useful to man. Other governments are intended for the good of the community, the chief end is not the good of the governors themselves: but God being every way sovereign, the sovereign Being, giving being to all things, the sovereign Ruler, giving order and preservation to all things, is also the end of all things, to whose glory and honor all things, all creatures, are to be subservient; "for of him, and through him, and to him, are all things, to whom be glory for ever" (Rom. xi. 36): *of* him, as the efficient cause; *through* him, as the preserving cause; *to* him, as the final cause. All our actions and thoughts ought to be addressed to his glory; our whole beings ought to be consecrated to his honor, though we should have no reward but the honor of having been subservient to the end of our creation: so much doth the excellency and majesty of God, infinitely elevated above us, challenge of us. Subjects use to value the safety, honor, and satisfaction of a good prince above their own: David is accounted worth ten thousand of the people; and some of his courtiers thought themselves obliged to venture their lives for his satisfaction in so mean a thing as a little water from the well of Bethlehem. Doth not so great, so good a Sovereign as God, deserve the same affection from us? "Do we swear," saith a heathen, "to prefer none before Cæsar, and have we not greater reason to prefer none before God?"y It is a justice due from us to God to maintain his glory, as it is a justice to preserve the right and property of another. As God would lay aside his Deity if he did deny himself, so a creature acts irregularly, and out of the rank of a creature, if it doth not deny itself for God. He that makes himself his own end, makes himself his own sovereign. To napkin up a gift he hath bestowed upon us, or to employ what we possess solely to our own glory, to use anything barely for ourselves, without respect to God, is to apply it to a wrong use, and to injure

y Arrian in Epictet.

God in his propriety, and the end of his donation. What we have ought to be used for the honor of God: he retains the dominion and lordship, though he grants us the use: we are but stewards, not proprietors, in regard to God, who expects an account from us, how we have employed his goods to his honor. The kingdom of God is to be advanced by us: we are to pray that his kingdom may come: we are to endeavor that his kingdom may come, that is, that God may be known to be the chief Sovereign; that his dominion, which was obscured by Adam's fall, may be more manifested; that his subjects, which are suppressed in the world, may be supported; his laws, which are violated by the rebellions of men, may be more obeyed; and his enemies be fully subdued by his final judgment, the last evidence of his dominion in this state of the world; that the empire of sin and the devil may be abolished, and the kingdom of God perfected, that none may rule but the great and rightful Sovereign. Thus while we endeavor to advance the honor of his throne, we shall not want an honor to ourselves. He is too gracious a Sovereign to neglect them that are mindful of his glory; "those that honor him, he will honor" (1 Sam. ii. 30).

4. Fear and reverence of God in himself, and in his actions, is a duty incumbent on us from this doctrine (Jer. x. 7): "Who would not fear thee, O King of nations?" The ingratitude of the world is taxed in not reverencing God as a great king, who had given so many marks of his royal government among them. The prophet wonders there was no fear of so great a King in the world, since, "among all the wise men of the nations, and among all their kings, there is none like unto this;" no more reverence of him, since none ruled so wisely, nor any ruled so graciously. The dominion of God is one of the first sparks that gives fire to religion and worship, considered with the goodness of this Sovereign (Ps. xii. 27, 28): "All the nations shall worship before thee, for the kingdom is the Lord's, and he is Governor among the nations." Epicurus, who thought God careless of human affairs, leaving them at hap-hazard, to the conduct of men's wisdom and mutability of fortune, yet acknowledged that God ought to be worshipped by man for the excellency of his nature, and the greatness of his majesty. How should we reverence that God, that hath a throne encompassed with such glorious creatures as angels, whose faces we are not able to behold, though shadowed in assumed bodies! how should we fear the Lord of Hosts, that hath so many armies at his command in the heavens above, and in the earth below, whom he can dispose to the exact obedience of his will! how should men be afraid to censure any of his actions, to sit judge of their Judge, and call him to an account at their bar! how should such an earth-worm, a mean animal as man, be afraid to speak irreverently of so great a King among his pots and strumpets! Not to fear him, not to reverence him, is to pull his throne from under him, and make him of a lower authority than ourselves, or any creature that we reverence more.

5. Prayer to God, and trust in him, is inferred from his sovereignty. If he be the supreme Sovereign, holding heaven and earth in his hand, disposing all things here below, not committing everything

to the influence of the stars or the humors of men, we ought, then, to apply ourselves to him in every case, implore the exercise of his authority; we hereby own his peculiar right over all things and persons. He only is the supreme Head in all causes, and over all persons: "Thine is the kingdom" (Matt. vi. 13), concludes the Lord's prayer, both as a motive to pray, and a ground to expect what we want. He that believes not God's government will think it needless to call upon him, will expect no refuge under him in a strait, but make some creature-reed his support. If we do not seek to him, but rely upon the dominion we have over our own possessions, or upon the authority of anything else, we disown his supremacy and dominion over all things; we have as good an opinion of ourselves, or of some creatures, as we ought to have of God; we think ourselves, or some natural cause we seek to or depend upon, as much sovereigns as he, and that all things which concern us are as much at the dispose of an inferior, as of the great Lord. It is, indeed, to make a god of ourselves, or of the creature; when we seek to him, upon all occasions, we own this Divine eminency, we acknowledge that it is by him men's hearts are ordered, the world governed, all things disposed; and God, that is jealous of his glory, is best pleased with any duty in the creature that doth acknowledge and desire the glorification of it, which prayer and dependence on him doth in a special manner, desiring the exercise of his authority, and the preservation of it in ordering the affairs of the world.

6. Obedience naturally results from this doctrine. As his justice requires fear, his goodness thankfulness, his faithfulness trust, his truth belief, so his sovereignty, in the nature of it, demands obedience: as it is most fit he should rule, in regard of his excellency, so it is most fit we should obey him in regard of his authority: he is our Lord, and we his subjects; he is our Master, and we his servants; it is righteous we should observe him, and conform to his will: he is everything that speaks an authority to command us, and that can challenge an humility in us to obey. As that is the truest doctrine that subjects us most to God, so he is the truest Christian that doth, in his practice, most acknowledge this subjection; and as sovereignty is the first notion a creature can have of God, so obedience is the first and chief thing conscience reflects upon the creature. Man holds all of God; and therefore owes all the operations capable to be produced by those faculties to that Sovereign Power that endowed him with them. Man had no being but from him; he hath no motion without him; he should, therefore, have no being but for him; and no motion but according to him: to call him Lord, and not to act in subjection to him, is to mock and put a scorn upon him (Luke vi. 46): "Why call you me Lord, Lord, and do not the things that I say?" It is like the crucifying Christ under the title of a King. It is not by professions, but by observance of the laws of a prince, that we manifest a due respect to him: by that we reverence that authority that enacted them, and the prudence that framed them.

This doctrine affords us motives to obey, and directs us to the manner of obedience.

1st. Motives to obey,

(1.) It is comely and orderly. Is it not a more becoming thing to be ruled by the will of our Sovereign than by that of our lusts?—to observe a wise and gracious Authority, than to set up inordinate appetites in the room of his law? Would not all men account it a disorder to be abominated, to see a slave or vassal control the just orders of his lord, and endeavor to subject his master's will to his own? much more to expect God should serve our humor rather than we be regulated by his will. It is more orderly that subjects should obey their governors, than governors their subjects; that passion should obey reason, than reason obey passion. When good governors are to conform to subjects, and reason veil to passion, it is monstrous! the one disturbs the order of a community, and the other defaceth the beauty of the soul. Is it a comely thing for God to stoop to our meanness, or for us to stoop to his greatness?

(2.) In regard of the Divine sovereignty, it is both honorable and advantageous to obey God. It is, indeed, the glory of a superior to be obeyed by his inferior; but where the sovereign is of transcendent excellency and dignity, it is an honor to a mean person to be under his immediate commands, and enrolled in his service. It is more honor to be God's subject than to be the greatest worldly monarch; his very service is an empire, and disobedience to him is a slavery. It is a part of his sovereignty to reward any service done him.[z] Other lords may be willing to recompense the service of their subjects, but are often rendered unable; but nothing can stand in the way of God to hinder your reward, if nothing stand in your way to hinder your obedience (Lev. xviii. 5): "If you keep my statutes, you shall live in them; I am the Lord." Is there anything in the world can recompense you for rebellion against God, and obedience to a lust? Saul cools the hearts of his servants from running after David, by David's inability to give them fields and vineyards (1 Sam. xxii. 7): "Will the son of Jesse give every one of you fields and vineyards, and make you captains of thousands, and captains of hundreds, that you have conspired against me?" But God hath a dominion to requite, as well as an authority to command your obedience; he is a great Sovereign, to bear you out in your observance of his precepts against all reproaches and violence of men, and at last to crown you with eternal honor. If he should neglect vindicating, one time or other, your loyalty to him, he will neglect the maintaining and vindicating his own sovereignty and greatness.

(3.) God, in all his dispensations to man, was careful to preserve the rights of his sovereignty in exacting obedience of his creature. The second thing he manifested his sovereignty in was that of a Lawgiver to Adam, after that of a Proprietor in giving him the possession of the garden; one followed immediately the other (Gen. ii. 15, 16): "The Lord God took the man, and put him into the garden of Eden, to dress it; and the Lord God commanded the man, saying, Of every tree of the garden thou mayest freely eat, but of the tree of the knowledge of good and evil thou shalt not eat of it,"

---

[z] Servire, Deo regnare est.

&c. Nothing was to be enjoyed by man but upon the condition of obedience to his Lord; and it is observed that in the description of the creation, God is not called "Lord" till the finishing of the creation, and particularly in the forming of man. "And the Lord God formed man" (Gen. ii. 7). Though he was Lord of all creatures, yet it was in man he would have his sovereignty particularly manifested, and by man have his authority specially acknowledged. The law is prefaced with this title: "I am the Lord thy God" (Exod. xx. 2): authority in Lord, sweetness in God, the one to enjoin, the other to allure obedience; and God enforceth several of the commands with the same title. And as he begins many precepts with it, so he concludes them with the same title, "I am the Lord," Lev. xix. 37, and in other places. In all his communications of his goodness to man in ways of blessing them, he stands upon the preservation of the rights of his sovereignty, and manifests his graciousness in favor of his authority. "I am the Lord your God," your God in all my perfections for your advantage, but yet your Sovereign for your obedience. In all his condescension he will have the rights of this untouched and unviolated by us. When Christ would give the most pregnant instance of his condescending and humble kindness, he urgeth his authority to ballast their spirits from any presumptuous eruptions because of his humility. "You call me Master, and Lord; and you say well: for so I am" (John, xiii. 13). He asserts his authority, and presseth them to their duty, when he had seemed to lay it by for the demeanor of a servant, and had, below the dignity of a master, put on the humility of a mean underling, to wash the disciples feet; all which was to oblige them to perform the command he then gave them (ver. 14), and in obedience to his authority, and imitation of his example.

(4.) All creatures obey him. All creatures punctually observe the law he hath imprinted on their nature, and in their several capacities acknowledge him their Sovereign; they move according to the inclinations he imprinted on them. The sea contains itself in its bounds, and the sun steps out of its sphere; the stars march in their order, "they continue this day according to thy ordinance, for all are thy servants" (Ps. cxix. 91). If he orders things contrary to their primitive nature, they obey him. When he speaks the word, the devouring fire becomes gentle, and toucheth not a hair of the children he will preserve; the hunger-starved lions suspend their ravenous nature, when so good a morsel as Daniel is set before them; and the sun, which had been in perpetual motion since its creation, obeys the writ of ease God sent it in Joshua's time, and stands still. Shall insensible and sensible creatures be punctual to his orders, passively acknowledge his authority? shall lions and serpents obey God in their places?—and shall not man, who can, by reason, argue out the sovereignty of God, and understand the sense and goodness of his laws, and actively obey God with that will he hath enriched him with above other creatures? Yet the truth is, every sensitive, yea, every senseless creature, obeys God more than his rational, more than his gracious creatures in this world. The rational creatures since the fall have a prevailing principle of corruption. Let the obedience of other creatures incite us more to imitate them, and shame our remissness in not acknowledging the dominion of God, in the just way he prescribes us to walk in. Well then, let us not pretend to own God as our Lord, and yet act the part of rebels; let us give him the reverence, and pay him that obedience, which of right belongs to so great a King. Whatsoever he speaks as a true God, ought to be believed; whatsoever he orders as a sovereign God, ought to be obeyed ; let not God have less than man, nor man have more than God. It is a common principle writ upon the reason of all men, that respect and observance is due to the majesty of a man, much more to the Majesty of God as a Lawgiver.

2d. As this doctrine presents us motives, so it directs us to the manner and kind of our obedience to God.

(1.) It must be with a respect to his authority. As the veracity of God is the formal object of faith, and the reason why we believe the things he hath revealed; so the authority of God is the formal object of our obedience, or the reason why we observe the things he hath commanded. There must be a respect to his will as the rule, as well as to his glory as the end. It is not formally obedience that is not done with regard to the order of God, though it may be materially obedience, as it answers the matter of the precept. As when men will abstain from excess and rioting, because it is ruinous to their health, not because it is forbidden by the great Lawgiver; this is to pay a respect to our own conveniency and interest, not a conscientious observance to God; a regard to our health, not to our Sovereign ; a kindness to ourselves, not a justice due to the rights of God. There must not only be a consideration of the matter of the precept as convenient, but a consideration of the authority of the Lawgiver as obligatory. "Thus saith the Lord," ushers in every order of his, directing our eye to the authority enacting it; Jeroboam did God's will of prophecy in taking the kingdom of Israel; and the devils may be subservient in God's will or providence; but neither of them are put upon the account of obedience, because not done intentionally with any conscience of the sovereignty of God. God will have this owned by a regular respect to it; so much he insists upon the honor of it, that the sacrifice of Christ, God-man, was most agreeable to him, not only as it was great and admirable in itself, but also for that ravishing obedience to his will, which was the life and glory of his sacrifice, whereby the justice of God was not only owned in the offering, but the sovereignty of God owned in the obedience. "He became obedient unto death ; wherefore God highly exalted him" (Phil. ii. 8).

(2.) It must be the best and most exact obedience. The most sovereign authority calls for the exactest and lowest observance; the highest Lord for the deepest homage; being, he is, a "great King, he must have the best in our flock" (Mal. i. 14). Obedience is due to God, as King, and the choicest obedience is due to him, as he is the most excellent King. The more majestic and noble any man is, the more careful we are in our manner of service to him. We are bound to obey God, not only under the title of a "Lord" in regard of jurisdiction and political subjection, but under the title of a true

"Lord and Master," in regard of propriety; since we are not only his subjects but his servants, the exactest obedience is due to God, *jure servitutis;* "When you have done all, say you are unprofitable servants" (Luke, xvii. 10), because we can do nothing which we owe not to God.

(3.) Sincere and inward obedience. As it is a part of his sovereignty to prescribe laws not only to man in his outward state, but to his conscience, so it is a part of our subjection to receive his laws into our will and heart. The authority of his laws exceeds human laws in the extent and riches of them, and our acknowledgment of his sovereignty cannot be right, but by subjecting the faculties of our soul to the Lawgiver of our souls; we else acknowledge his authority to be as limited as the empire of man; when his will not only sways the outward action, but the inward motion, it is a giving him the honor of his high throne above the throne of mortals. The right of God ought to be preserved undamaged in affection, as well as action.

(4.) It must be sole obedience. We are ordered to serve him only; "Him only shalt thou serve" (Matt. iv. 10): as the only Supreme Lord, as being the highest Sovereign, it is fit he should have the highest obedience before all earthly sovereigns, and as being unparalleled by any among all the nations, so none must have an obedience equal to him. When God commands, if the highest power on earth countermands it, the precept of God must be preferred before the countermand of the creature. "Whether it be right in the sight of God, to hearken unto you more than unto God, judge ye" (Acts, iv. 18, 19). We must never give place to the authority of all the monarchs in the world, to the prejudice of that obedience we owe to the Supreme Monarch of heaven and earth; this would be to place the throne of God at the footstool of man, and debase him below the rank of a creature. Loyalty to man can never recompense for the mischief accruing from disloyalty to God. All the obedience we are to give to man, is to be paid in obedience to God, and with an eye to his precept: therefore, what servants do for their masters, they must do "as to the Lord" (Col. iii. 23); and children are to obey their parents "in the Lord" (Eph. vi. 1). The authority of God is to be eyed in all the services payable to man; proper and true obedience hath God solely for its principal and primary object; all obedience to man that interferes with that, and would justle out obedience to God, is to be refused. What obedience is due to man, is but rendered as a part of obedience to God, and a stooping of his authority.

(5.) It must be universal obedience. The laws of man are not to be universally obeyed; some may be oppressing and unjust: no man hath authority to make an unjust law, and no subject is bound to obey an unrighteous law; but God being a righteous Sovereign, there is not one of his laws but doth necessarily oblige us to obedience. Whatsoever this Supreme Power declares to be his will, it must be our care to observe; man, being his creature, is bound to be subject to whatsoever laws he doth impose to the meanest as well as to the greatest: they having equally a stamp of Divine authority upon them. We are not to pick and choose among his precepts: this is to pare away part of his authority, and render him a half sovereign. It must be universal in all places. An Englishman in Spain is bound to obey the laws of that country wherein he resides: and so not responsible there for the breach of the laws of his native country. In the same condition is a Spaniard in England. But the laws of God are to be obeyed in every part of the world; wheresoever Divine Providence doth cast us, it casts us not out of the places where he commands, nor out of the compass of his own empire. He is Lord of the world, and his laws oblige in every part of the world; they were ordered for a world, and not for a particular climate and territory.

(6.) It must be indisputable obedience. All authority requires readiness in the subject; the centurion had it from his soldiers; they went when he ordered them, and came when he beckoned to them (Matt. viii. 9). It is more fit God should have the same promptness from his subjects. We are to obey his orders, though our purblind understanding may not apprehend the reason of every one of them. It is without dispute that he is sovereign, and therefore it is without dispute that we are bound to obey him, without controlling his conduct. A master will not bear it from his slave, why should God from his creature? Though God admits his creatures sometimes to treat with him about the equality of his justice, and also about the reason of some commands, yet sometimes he gives no other reason but his own sovereignty, "Thus saith the Lord;" to correct the malapertness of men, and exact from them an entire obedience to his unlimited and absolute authority. When Abraham was commanded to offer Isaac, God acquaints him not with the reason of his demand till after (Gen. xxii. 2, 12), nor did Abraham enter any demur to the order, or expostulate with God, either from his own natural affection to Isaac, the hardness of the command, it being, as it were, a ripping up of his own bowels, nor the quickness of it after he had been a child of the promise, and a Divine donation above the course of nature. Nor did Paul confer with flesh and blood, and study arguments from nature and interest to oppose the Divine command, when he was sent upon his apostolical employment (Gal. i. 16). The more indisputable his right is to command, the stronger is our obligation to obey, without questioning the reason of his orders.

(7.) It must be joyful obedience. Men are commonly more cheerful in their obedience to a great prince than to a mean peasant; because the quality of the master renders the service more honorable. It is a discredit to a prince's government, when his subjects obey him with discontent and dejectedness, as though he were a hard master, and his laws tyrannical and unrighteous. When we pay obedience but with a dull and feeble pace, and a sour and sad temper, we blemish our great Sovereign, imply his commands to be grievous, void of that peace and pleasure he proclaims to be in them; that he deserves no respect from us, if we obey him because we must, and not because we will. Involuntary obedience deserves not the title: it is rather submission than obedience, an act of the body, not of the mind: a mite of obedience with cheerfulness, is better than a talent without it. In the little Paul did, he comforts himself in this, that with the " mind he served the law of God" (Rom. vii. 25); the testimonies of God were David's delight (Ps. cxix. 24). Our understandings must take pleasure in knowing him, our wills delightfully embrace him, and our actions be cheerfully squared to him. This credits the sovereignty of God in the world, makes others believe him to be a gracious Lord, and move them to have some veneration for his authority.

(8.) It must be a perpetual obedience. As man is a subject as soon as he is a creature, so he is a subject as long as he is a creature. God's sovereignty is of perpetual duration, as long as he is God; man's obedience must be perpetual, while he is a man. God cannot part with his sovereignty, and a creature cannot be exempted from subjection; we must not only serve him, but cleave to him (Deut. xiii. 4). Obedience is continued in heaven, his throne is established in heaven, it must be bowed to in heaven, as well as in earth. The angels continually fulfil his pleasure.

7. *Exhortation.* Patience is a duty flowing from this doctrine. In all strokes upon ourselves, or thick showers upon the church, "the Lord reigns," is a consideration to prevent muttering against him, and make us quietly wait to see what the issue of his Divine pleasure will be. It is too great an insolence against the Divine Majesty to censure what he acts, or quarrel with him for what he inflicts. Proud clay doth very unbecomingly swell against an infinite superior. If God be our Sovereign, we ought to subscribe to his afflicting will without debates, as well as to his liberal will with affectionate applauses. We should be as full of patience under his sharper, as of praise under his more grateful, dispensations, and be without reluctancy against his penal, as well as his preceptive, pleasure. It is God's part to inflict, and the creature's part to submit.

This doctrine affords us motives, and shows us the nature of patience. 1. Motives to it.

(1.) God, being Sovereign, hath an absolute right to dispose of all things. His title to our persons and possessions is, upon this account, stronger than our own can be; we have as much reason to be angry with ourselves, when we assert our worldly right against others, as to be angry with God for asserting the right of his dominion over us. Why should we enter a charge against him, because he hath not tempered us so strong in our bodies, drawn us with as fair colors, embellished our spirits with as rich gifts as others? Is he not the Sovereign of his own goods, to impart what, and in what measure, he pleaseth? Would you be content your servants should check your pleasure in dispensing your own favors? It is an unreasonable thing not to leave God to the exercise of his own dominion. Though Job were a pattern of patience, yet he had deep tinctures of impatience; he often complains of God's usage of him as too hard, and stands much upon his own integrity; but when God comes, in the latter chapters of that book, to justify his carriage towards him, he chargeth him not as a criminal, but considers him only as his vassal. He might have found flaws enough in Job's carriage, and corruption enough in Job's nature, to clear the equity of his proceeding as a judge; but he useth no other medium to convince him, but the greatness of his Majesty, the unlimitedness of his sovereignty, which so appals the good man, that he puts his finger on his mouth and stands mute with a self-abhorrency before him, as a Sovereign, rather than as a Judge. When he doth pinch us, and deprive us of what we most affect, his right to do it should silence our lips and calm our hearts from any boisterous uproars against him.

(2.) The property of all still remains in God, since he is sovereign. He did not divest himself of the property when he granted us the use; the earth is his, not ours; the fulness any of us have, as well as the fulness others have. After he had given the Israelites corn, wine, and oil, he calls them all *his*, and emphatically adds *my*, to every one of them (Hos. ii. 9). His right is universal over every mite we have, and perpetual too; he may, therefore, take from us what he please. He did but deposit in our hands for awhile the benefits we enjoy, either children, friends, estate, or lives; he did not make a total conveyance of them, and alienate his own property, when he put them into our hands; we can show no patent for them, wherein the full right is passed over to us, to hold them against his will and pleasure, and implead him if he offer to re-assume them: he reserved a power to dispossess us upon a forfeiture, as he is the Lord and Governor. Did any of us yet answer the condition of his grant? it was his indulgence to allow them so long; there is reason to submit to him, when he re-assumes what he lent us, and rather to thank him that he lent it so long, and did not seize upon it sooner.

(3.) Other things have more reason to complain of our sovereignty over them, than we of God's exercise of his sovereignty over us. Do we not exercise an authority over our beasts, as to strike them when we please, and merely for our pleasure; and think we merit no reproof for it, because they are our own, and of a nature inferior to ours? And shall not God, who is absolute, do as much with us, who are more below him than the meanest creatures are below us? They are creatures as well as we, and we no more creatures than they; they were framed by Omnipotence as well as we; there is no more difference between them and us in the notion of creatures. As there is no difference between the greatest monarch on earth, and the meanest beggar on the dunghill, in the notion of a man; the beggar is a man, as well as the monarch, and as much a man; the difference consists in the special endowments we have above them by the bounty of their and our common Creator. We are less, if compared with God, than the worst, meanest, and most sordid creature can be, if compared with us. Hath not a bird or a hare (if they had a capacity) more reason to complain of men's persecuting them by their hawks and their dogs? but would their complaints appear reasonable, since both were made for the use of man, and man doth but use the nature of the one to attain a benefit by the other? Have we any reason to complain of God if he lets loose other creatures, the devouring hounds of the world, to bite and afflict us? We must not open our lips against him, nor let our heart swell against his scourge, since both they and we were made for his use, as well as other creatures for our; this is a reason to stifle all complaints against God, but not to make us careless of preventing afflictions, or emerging out of them by all just ways. The hare hath a nature to shift for itself by its winding and turning, and the bird by its flight; and neither of them could be blamed, if they were able, should the one scratch out the eyes of the hounds, and the other sacrifice the hawk to its own fury.

(4.) It is a folly not to submit to him. Why should we strive against him, since he is an unaccountable Sovereign, and "gives no account of any of his matters?" (Job, xxxiii. 13.) Who can disannul the judgment God gives? There is no appeal from the supreme court; a higher court can repeal or null the sentence of an inferior court, but the sentence of the highest stands irreversible, but by itself and its own authority. It is better to lower our sails, than to grapple with one that can shoot us under water; to submit to that Sovereign whom we cannot subdue.

2. It shows us the true nature of patience in regard of God: it is a submission to God's sovereignty. As the formal object of obedience is the authority of God enacting the law, so the formal object of patience is the authority of God inflicting the punishment: as his right of commanding is to be eyed in the one, so his right of punishing is to be considered in the other. This was Eli's condition, when he had received a message that might put flesh and blood into a mutiny, the rending the priesthood from his family, and the ruin of his house: yet this consideration, "It is the Lord," calms him into submission, and a willing compliance with the Divine pleasure (1 Sam. iii. 18): "It is the Lord, let him do what seems good in his sight." Job was of the same strain (Job, i. 21): "The Lord gives, and the Lord hath taken away, blessed be the name of the Lord;" he considers God as a sovereign, who was not to be reproached, or have anything uncomely uttered of him, for what he had done. To be patient because we cannot avoid it, or resist it, is a violent, not a loyal patience; but to submit because it is the will of God to inflict; to be silent, because the sovereignty of God doth order it, is a patience of a true complexion. The other kind of patience is no other than that of an enemy that will free himself as soon as he can, and by any way, though never so violent, that offers itself. This sort of patience is that of a subject acknowledging the supreme authority over him, and that he ought to be ordered by the will, and to the glory of God, more than by his own will, and for his own ease; " I was dumb, I opened not my mouth" (Ps. xxxix. 10); not because I could not help it, but "because thou didst it," thou who art my sovereign Lord. The greatness of God claims an awful and inviolable respect from his creatures in what way soever he doth dispose of them; this is due to him; since his kingdom ruleth over all, his kingdom should be acknowledged by all, and his royal authority submitted to in all that he doth.

DISCOURSE XIV

ON GOD'S PATIENCE

NAHUM, I. 3.—The Lord is slow to anger, and great in power, and will not at all acquit the wicked: the Lord hath his way in the whirlwind and in the storm, and the clouds are the dust of his feet.

THE subject of this prophecy is God's sentence against Nineveh, the head and metropolis of the Assyrian empire: a city famous for its strength, and thickness of its walls, and the multitude of its towers for defence against an enemy. The forces of this empire did God use as a scourge against the Israelites, and by their hands ruined Samaria, the chief city of the ten tribes, and transplanted them as captives into another country (2 Kings, xvii. 5, 6), about six years after Hezekiah came to the crown of Judah (2 Kings, xviii. compared with chap. xvii. 6), in whose time, or, as some think, later, Nahum uttered this prophecy. The name, *Nahum*, signifies Comforter; though the matter of his prophecy be dreadful to Nineveh, it was comfortable to the people of God: for a promise is made, (ver. 7), "The Lord is good, a stronghold in the day of trouble; and he knoweth them that trust in him." And an encouragement to Judah, to keep their solemn feasts, (ver. 15: and also in chap. ii. 3), with a declaration of the misery of Nineveh, and the destruction of it. Observe,

1. In all the fears of God's people, God will have a Comforter for them. Judah might well be dejected with the calamity of their brethren, not knowing but it might be their own turn shortly after. They knew not where the ambition of the Assyrian would stop; but God by his prophets calms their fears of their furious neighbor, by predicting to them the ruin of their feared adversary.

2. The destruction of the church's enemies is the comfort of the church. By that God is glorified in his justice, and the church secured in its worship.

3. The victories of persecutors secure them not from being the triumphs of others. The Assyrians that conquered and captived Israel, were themselves to be conquered and captived by the Medes. The whole oppressing empire is threatened with destruction in the ruin of their chief city; accordingly it was accomplished, and the empire extinguished by a greater power. God burns the rod when it hath done the work he appointed it for; and the wisp of straw wherewith the vessels are scoured, is flung into the fire, or upon the dunghill.

Nahum begins his prophecy majestically, with a description of the wrath and fury of God. (Ver. 2), "God is jealous, and the Lord revengeth; the Lord revengeth, and is furious: the Lord will take vengeance on his adversaries, and reserveth wrath for his enemies." And therefore the whole of it is called (ver. 1), "The burden of Nineveh," as those prophecies are, which are composed of threatenings of judgments, which lie as a mighty weight upon the heads and backs of sinners.

God is jealous—jealous of his glory and worship, and jealous for his people, and their security. He cannot long bear the oppressions of his people, and the boasts of his enemies. He is jealous for himself, and is jealous for you of Judah, who retain his worship. He is not forgetful of those that remember him, nor of the danger of those that are desirous to maintain his honor in the world. In this first expression, the prophet uses the covenant name, God; the covenant runs, "I am your God," or "the Lord your God;" mostly God without Lord, never Lord without God: and, therefore, his jealousy here is meant of the care of his people, and the relation that his actions against his enemies have to his servants. He is a lover of his own, and a revenger on his enemies.

The Lord revengeth, and is furious.—He now describes God by a name of sovereignty and power, when he describes him in his wrath and fury, and is furious. *Heb.* כעל חמה, *Lord of hot anger.* God will vindicate his own glory, and have his right on his enemies in a way of punishment, if they will not give it him in a way of obedience. It is three times repeated, to show the certainty of the judgment;[a] and the name of "Lord" added to every one, to intimate the power wherewith the judgment should be executed. It is not a fatherly correction of children in a way of mercy, but an offended Sovereign's destruction of his enemies in a way of vengeance. There is an anger of God with his own people, which hath more of mercy than wrath; in this his rod is guided by his bowels. There is a fury of God against his enemies, where there is sole wrath without any tincture of mercy; when his sword is all edge, without any balsam drops upon it. Such a fury as David deprecates (Ps. vi. 1): "O Lord, rebuke me not in thy anger, nor chasten me in thy sore displeasure," with a fury untempered with grace, and insupportable wrath.

He reserves wrath for his enemies.—He lays it up in his treasury, to be brought out and expended in a due season. "Wrath" is supplied by our translators, and is not in the Hebrew. He reserves, what?— that which is too sharp to be expressed, too great to be conceived: a vengeance it is. And רגוטד היא, *He reserves it.* He that hath an infinite wrath, he reserves it; that hath a strength and power to execute it.

(Ver. 3.) *The Lord is slow to anger, Heb.* ארך אפים, *of broad nostrils.* The anger of God is expressed by this word, which signifies "nostrils:" as, Job, ix. 13, "If God will not withdraw his anger," *Heb.* "his nostrils." And the anger whereby the wicked are consumed, is called the "breath of nostrils" (Job, iv. 9); and when he is angry, smoke and fire are said to go out of his nostrils (2 Sam. ii. 9); and in Psalm lxxiv. 1, "Why doth thy anger smoke?" *Heb.* "Why do

a Ribera, *in loc.*

thy nostrils smoke?" So the rage of a horse, when he is provoked in battle, is called the glory of his nostrils (Job, xxxix. 20). He breathes quick fumes, and neighs with fury. And slowness to anger is here expressed by the phrase of "long or wide nostrils:" because in a vehement anger, the blood boiling about the heart, exhales men's spirit, which fume up, and break out in dilated nostrils. But where the passages are straighter the spirits have not so quick a vent, and therefore raise more motions within; or, because the wider the nostrils are, the more cool air is drawn in to temper the heat of the heart, where the angry spirits are gathered; and so the passion is allayed, and sooner calmed. God speaks of himself in Scripture often after the rate of men; Jeremiah prays (ch. xv. 15) that God would not take him away in his long-suffering, *Heb.* "in the length of his nostrils," *i. e.* Be not slow and backward in thy anger against my persecutors, as to give them time and opportunity to destroy me. The nostrils, as well as other members of a human body, are ascribed to God. He is slow to anger; he hath anger in his nature, but is not always in the execution of it.

And great in power.—This may refer to his patience as the cause of it, or as a bar to the abuse of it.

1. "He is slow to anger, and great in power," *i. e.* his power moderates his anger; he is not so impotent as to be at the command of his passions, as men are; he can restrain his anger under just provocations to exercise it. His power over himself is the cause of his slowness to wrath, as Numb. xiv. 17: "Let the power of my Lord be great," saith Moses, when he pleads for the Israelites' pardon. Men that are great in the world are quick in passions, and are not so ready to forgive an injury, or bear with an offender, as one of a meaner rank. It is a want of a power over a man's self that makes him do unbecoming things upon a provocation. A prince that can bridle his passion, is a king over himself, as well as over his subjects. God is slow to anger, because great in power: he hath no less power over himself than over his creatures: he can sustain great injuries without an immediate and quick revenge: he hath a power of patience, as well as a power of justice.

2. Or thus: "He is slow to anger and great in power." He is slow to anger, but not for want of power to revenge himself; his power is as great to punish, as his patience to spare. It seems thus, that slowness to anger is brought in as an objection against the revenge proclaimed. What do you tell us of vengeance, vengeance, nothing but such repetitions of vengeance?—as though we were ignorant that God is slow to anger. It is true, saith the prophet, I acknowledge it as much as you, that God is slow to anger; but withal, great in power. His anger certainly succeeds his abused patience; he will not always bridle in his wrath, but one time or other let it march out in fury against his adversaries. The Assyrians, who had captived the ten tribes, and been victorious a little against the Jews, might think that the God of Israel had been conquered by their gods, as well as the people professing him had been subdued by their arms; that God had lost all his power; and the Jews might argue, from God's patience to his enemies, against the credit

of the prophet's denouncing revenge. The prophet answers, to the terror of the one, and the comfort of the other, that this indulgence to his enemies, and not accounting with them for their crimes, proceeded from the greatness of his patience, and not from any debility in his power. As it refers to the Assyrian, it may be rendered thus: You Ninevites, upon your repentance after Jonah's thundering of judgments, are witnesses of the slowness of God to anger, and had your punishments deferred; but, falling to your old sins, you shall find a real punishment, and that he hath as much power to execute his ancient threatenings, as he had then compassion to recall them; his patience to you then was not for want of power to ruin you, but was the effect of his goodness towards you. As it refers to the Jews, it may be thus paraphrased: Do not despise this threatening against your enemies because of the greatness of their might, the seeming stability of their empire, and the terror they possess all the nations with round about them: it may be long before it comes, but assure yourselves the threatening I denounce shall certainly be executed; though he hath patience to endure them a hundred and thirty-five years (for so long as it was before Nineveh was destroyed after this threatening, as Ribera, *in loc.*[b] computes from the years of the reign of the kings of Judah), yet he hath also power to verify his word, and accomplish his will: assure yourselves, he will not at all acquit the wicked.

He will not acquit the wicked.—He will not always account the criminal an innocent, as he seems to do by a present sparing of them, and dealing with them as if they were destitute of any provoking carriage towards him, and he void of any resentment of it. He will "not acquit the wicked;" how is this? Who then can be saved? Is there no place for remission? He will "not acquit the wicked." *i. e.* he will not acquit obstinate sinners. As he hath patience for the wicked, so he hath mercy for the penitent. The wicked are the subjects of his long-suffering, but not of his acquitting grace; he doth not presently punish their sins, because he is slow to anger; but without their repentance he will not blot out their sins, because he is righteous in judgment: if God should acquit them without repentance for their crimes, he must himself repent of his own law and righteous sanction of it. "He will not acquit," *i. e.* he will not go back from the thing he hath spoken, and forbear, at long run, the punishment he hath threatened.

The Lord hath his way in the whirlwind.—The way of God signifies sometimes the law of God, sometimes the providential operations of God: "Is not my way equal?" (Ezek. xviii. 25). It seems there to take in both.

And in the storm, and the clouds are the dust of his feet.—The prophet describes here the fight of God with the Assyrians, as if he rushed upon them with a mighty noise of an army, raising the dust with the feet of their horses, and motion of their chariots.[c] Symbolically, it signifies the multitude of the Chaldean and Median forces, invading, besieging, and storming the city. It signifies,

1. The rule of providence. The way of God is in every motion

of the creature; he rules all things, whirlwinds, storms, and clouds; his way is in all their walks, in the whirlings and blusterings of the one, in the raising and dissolving the other. He blows up the winds, and compacts the clouds, to make them serviceable to his designs.

2. The management of wars by God. His way is in the storm: as he was the Captain of the Assyrians against Samaria, so he will be the Captain of the Medes against Nineveh: as Israel was not so much wasted by the Assyrians as by the Lord, who levied and armed their forces; so Nineveh shall be subverted, rather by God, than by the arms of the Medes. Their force is described not to be so much from human power as Divine. God is President in all the commotions of the world, his way is in every whirlwind.

3. The easiness of executing the judgment. He is of so great power that he can excite tempests in the air, and overthrow them with the clouds, which are the dust of his feet: he can blind his enemies, and avenge himself on them: he is Lord of clouds, and can fill their womb with hail, lightnings, and thunders, to burst out upon those he kindles his anger against: he is of so great force, that he needs not use the strength of his arm, but the dust of his feet, to effect his destroying purpose.

4. The suddenness of the judgment. Whirlwinds come suddenly, without any harbingers to give notice of their approach: clouds are swift in their motion; "Who are those that fly as a cloud?" (Isa. lx. 8), i. e. with a mighty nimbleness. What God doth, he shall do on the sudden, come upon them before they are aware, be too quick for them in his motion to overrun and overreach them. The winds are described with wings, in regard of the quickness of their motion.

5. The terror of judgments. "The Lord hath his way in the whirlwind," i. e. in great displeasure. The anger of the Lord is often compared to a storm; he shall bring clouds of judgments upon them, many and thick, as terrible as when a day is turned into night, by the mustering of the darkest clouds that interpose between the sun and the earth. "Clouds and darkness are round about him, and a fire goes before him," when he "burns up his enemies" (Ps. xcvii. 2, 3). The judgments shall have terror without mercy, as clouds obscure the light, and are dark masks before the face and glory of the sun, and cut off its refreshing beams from the earth. Clouds note multitude and obscurity; God could crush them without a whirlwind, beat them to powder with one touch, but he will bring his judgments in the most surprising and amazing manner to flesh and blood, so that all their glory shall be changed into nothing but terror, by the noise of the bellowing winds, and the clouds, like ink, blacking the heavens.

6. The confusion of the offenders upon God's proceeding. A whirlwind is not only a boisterous wind, that hurls and rolls everything out of its place, but, by its circular motion, by its winding to all points of the compass, it confounds things, and jumbles them together. It keeps not one point, but, by a circumgyration, toucheth upon all. Clouds, like dust, shall be blown in their face, and gum up their eyes: they shall be in a posture of confusion, not know what counsels to take, what motions to resolve upon. Let them look

to every point of heaven and earth, they shall meet with a whirlwind to confound them, and cloudy dust to blind them.

7. The irresistibleness of the judgment. Winds have more than a giant-like force, a torrent of compacted air, that, with an invincible wilfulness, bears all before it, displaceth the firmest trees, and levels the tallest towers, and pulls up bodies from their natural place. Clouds also are over our heads, and above our reach; when God places them upon his people for defence they are an invincible security (Isa. iv. 5); and when he moves them, as his chariot, against a people, they end in an irresistible destruction. Thus the ruin of the wicked is described (Prov. x. 25): "As the whirlwind passes, so is the wicked no more:" it blows them down, sweeps them away, they irrecoverably fall before the force of it. What heart can endure, and what hands can be strong, in the days wherein God doth deal with them! (Ezek. xxii. 14). Thus is the judgment against Nineveh described: God hath his way in the whirlwind, to thunder down their strongest walls, which were so thick that chariots could march abreast upon them; and batter down their mighty towers, which that city had in multitudes upon their walls.

They are the first words I intend to insist upon, to treat of the Patience of God described in those words, "The Lord is slow to anger."

Doctrine. Slowness to anger, or admirable patience, is the property of the Divine nature. As patience signifies suffering, so it is not in God. The Divine nature is impassible, incapable of any impair, it cannot be touched by the violences of men, nor the essential glory of it be diminished by the injuries of men; but as it signifies a willingness to defer, and an unwillingness to pour forth his wrath upon sinful creatures, he moderates his provoked justice, and forbears to revenge the injuries he daily meets with in the world. He suffers no grief by men's wronging him, but he restrains his arm from punishing them according to their merits; and thus there is patience in every cross a man meets with in the world, because, though it be a punishment, it is less than is merited by the unrighteous rebel, and less than may be inflicted by a righteous and powerful God. This patience is seen in his providential works in the world: "He suffered the nations to walk in their own way," and the witness of his providence to them was his "giving them rain and fruitful seasons, filling their heart with food and gladness" (Acts, xvi. 17). The heathens took notice of it, and signified it by feigning their god Saturn, to be bound a whole year in a soft cord, a cord of wool, and expressed it by this proverb: "The mills of the gods grind slowly;" *i. e.* God doth not use men with that severity that they deserve; the mills being usually turned by criminals condemned to that work.[d] This, in Scripture, is frequently expressed by a slowness to anger (Ps. ciii. 8), sometimes by long-suffering, which is a patience with duration (Ps. cxlv. 8; Joel, ii. 13). He is slow to anger, he takes not the first occasions of a provocation; he is long-suffering (Rom. ix. 22), and (Ps. lxxxvi. 15) he forbears punishment upon many occasions offered him. It is long before he consents to give fire to his wrath,

d Rhodigi. lib. vi. c. 14.

and shoot out his thunderbolts. Sin hath a loud cry, but God seems
to stop his ears, not to hear the clamor it raises and the charge it
presents. He keeps his sword a long time in the sheath ; one calls
the patience of God the sheath of his sword, upon those words (Ezek.
xxi. 3), "I will draw forth my sword out of his sheath." This is one
remarkable letter in the name of God ; he himself proclaims it (Exod.
xxxiv. 6): "The Lord, the Lord God, merciful, gracious, and long-
suffering." And Moses pleads it in the behalf of the people (Numb.
xiv. 18), where he placeth it in the first rank ; the Lord is "long-
suffering and of great mercy :" it is the first spark of mercy, and ushers it to its exercises in the world.[c] In the Lord's proclamation, it is
put in the middle link, mercy and truth together ; mercy could have
no room to act if patience did not prepare the way ; and his truth
and goodness, in his promise of the Redeemer, would not have been
manifest to the world if he had shot his arrows as soon as men committed their sins, and deserved his punishment. This perfection is
expressed by other phrases, as "keeping silence" (Ps. l. 21): "These
things hast thou done, and I kept silence," אלת עשית והחר שחר ; it
signifies to behave one's self as a deaf or dumb man. I did not fly
in thy face, as some do, with a great noise upon a light provocation, as if their life, honor, estates, were at the stake ; I did not
presently call thee to the bar, and pronounce judicial sentence upon
thee according to the law, but demeaned myself as if I had been
ignorant of thy crimes, and had not been invested with the power
of judging thee for them. *Chald.* "I waited for thy conversion."
God's patience is the silence of his justice, and the first whisper of
his mercy. It is also expressed by not laying folly to men (Job, xxiv.
12) ; men groan under the oppressions of others, yet God lays not
folly to them, *i. e.* to the oppressors ; God suffers them to go on with
impunity. He doth not deliver his people because he would try
them, and takes not revenge upon the unrighteous, because in patience he doth bear with them : patience is the life of his providence
in this world. He chargeth not men with their crimes here, but reserves them, upon impenitency, for another trial. This attribute is
so great a one, that it is signally called by the name of "Perfection"
(Matt. v. 45, 48). He had been speaking of Divine goodness, and
patience to evil men, and he concludes, "Be you perfect," &c., implying it to be an amazing perfection of the Divine nature, and worthy of imitation.

In the prosecution of this, I. Let us consider the nature of this patience. II. Wherein it is manifested. III. Why God doth exercise
so much patience. IV. The Use.

I. The nature of this patience.

1. It is part of the Divine goodness and mercy, yet differs from
both. God being the greatest goodness, hath the greatest mildness.
Mildness is always the companion of true goodness, and the greater
the goodness the greater the mildness. Who so holy as Christ, and
who so meek? God's slowness to anger is a branch or slip from his
mercy (Ps. cxlv. 8): "The Lord is full of compassion, slow to anger."

---

[c] Δῆλον δὲ ὅτι ἐγχειρίδιον τὴν τιμωρίαν καλεῖ, κολέον δὲ τουτέστι τὴν θήκην του ἐγχειριδίου
μακροθυμίαν ὀνομάζει. Theodoret, *in loc.*

It differs from mercy in the formal consideration of the object; mercy respects the creature as miserable, patience respects the creature as criminal; mercy pities him in his misery, and patience bears with the sin which engendered that misery, and is giving birth to more. Again, mercy is one end of patience; his long-suffering is partly to glorify his grace: so it was in Paul (1 Tim. i. 16). As slowness to anger springs from goodness, so it makes mercy the butt and mark of its operations (Isa. xxx. 18): "He waits that he may be gracious." Goodness sets God upon the exercise of patience, and patience sets many a sinner on running into the arms of mercy. That mercy which makes God ready to embrace returning sinners, makes him willing to bear with them in their sins, and wait their return. It differs also from goodness, in regard of the object. The object of goodness is every creature, angels, men, all inferior creatures, to the lowest worm that crawls upon the ground. The object of patience is, primarily, man, and secondarily, those creatures that respect men's support, conveniency, and delight; but they are not the objects of patience, as considered in themselves, but in relation to man, for whose use they were created; and therefore God's patience to them is properly his patience with man. The lower creatures do not injure God, and therefore are not the objects of his patience, but as they are forfeited by man, and man deserves to be deprived of them; as man in this regard falls under the patience of God, so do those creatures which are designed for man's good. That patience which spares man, spares other creatures for him, which were all forfeited by man's sin, as well as his own life, and are rather the testimonies of God's patience, than the proper objects of it. The object of God's goodness, then, is the whole creation; not a devil in hell, but as a creature, is a mark of his goodness, but not of his patience. There is a kind of sparing exercised to the devils, in deferring their complete punishment, and hitherto keeping off the day wherein their final sentence is to be pronounced; yet the Scripture never mentions this by the name of slowness to anger, or long-suffering. It can no more be called patience, than a prince's keeping a malefactor in chains, and not pronouncing a condemning sentence, or not executing a sentence already pronounced, can be called a patience with him, when it is not out of kindness to the offender, but for some reasons of state. God's sparing the devils from their total punishment—which they have not yet, but are "reserved in chains, under darkness for it" (Jude, 6)—is not in order to repentance, or attended with any invitations from God, or hopes in them; and, therefore, cannot come under the same title as God's sparing man: where there is no proposal of mercy, there is no exercise of patience. The fallen angels had no mercy reserved for them, nor any sacrifices prepared for them; God "spared not the angels" (2 Pet. ii. 4), "but delivered them into chains of darkness, to be reserved unto judgment," *i. e.* he had no patience for them; for patience is properly a temporary sparing a person, with a waiting of his relenting, and a change of his injurious demeanor. The object of goodness is more extensive than that of patience: nor do they both consider the object under the same relation. Goodness respects things in a capacity, or in a state of creation, and brings them forth into creation, and nurseth and supports them as creatures. Patience considers them already created, and fallen short of the duty of creatures; it considers them as sinners, or in relation to sinners. Had not sin entered, patience had never been exercised; but goodness had been exercised, had the creature stood firm in its created state without any transgression; nay, creation could not have been without goodness, because it was goodness to create; but patience had never been known without an object, which could not have been without an injury. Where there is no wrong, no suffering, nor like to be any, patience hath no prospect of any operation. So, then, goodness respects persons as creatures, patience as transgressors; mercy eyes men as miserable and obnoxious to punishment; patience considers men as sinful, and provoking to punishment.

2. Since it is a part of goodness and mercy, it is not an insensible patience. What is the fruit of pure goodness cannot be from a weakness of resentment; he is "slow to anger;" the prophet doth not say, he is incapable of anger, or cannot discern what is a real object of anger; it implies, that he doth consider every provocation, but he is not hasty to discharge his arrows upon the offenders; he sees all, while he bears with them; his omniscience excludes any ignorance; he cannot but see every wrong; every aggravation in that wrong, every step and motion from the beginning to the completing it; for he knows all our thoughts; he sees the sin and the sinner at the same time; the sin with an eye of abhorrency, and the sinner with an eye of pity. His eye is upon their iniquities, and his hatred edged against them; while he stands with arms open, waiting a penitent return. When he publisheth his patience in his keeping silence, he publisheth also his resolution, to set sin in order before their eyes (Ps. l. 21): "I will reprove thee, and set them in order before thy eyes." Think me not such a piece of phlegm, and so dull as not to resent your insolences; you shall see, in my final charge, when I come to judge, that not a wry look escaped my knowledge, that I had an eye to behold, and a heart to loathe every one of your transgressions. The church was ready to think that God's slowness to deliver her, and his bearing with her oppressors, was not from any patience in his nature, but a drowsy carelessness, a senseless lethargy (Ps. xliv. 23): "Awake, why sleepest thou, O Lord?" We must conclude him an inapprehensive God, before we can conclude him an insensible God. As his delaying his promise is not slackness to his people (2 Pet. iii. 9), so his deferring of punishment is not from a stupidity under the affronts offered him.

3. Since it is a part of his mercy and goodness, it is not a constrained or faint-hearted patience. It is not a slowness to anger, arising from a despondency of his own power to revenge. He hath as much power to punish as he hath to forbear punishment. He that created a world in six days, and that by a word, wants not a strength to crush all mankind in one minute; and with as much ease as a word imports, can give satisfaction to his justice in the blood of the offender. Patience in man is many times interpreted, and truly too, a cowardice, a feebleness of spirit, and a want of strength. But it is

not from the shortness of the Divine arm, that he cannot reach us, nor from the feebleness of his hand, that he cannot strike us. It is not because he cannot level us with the dust, dash us in pieces like a potter's vessel, or consume us as a moth. He can make the mightiest to fall before him, and lay the strongest at his feet the first moment of their crime. He that did not want a powerful word to create a world, cannot want a powerful word to dissolve the whole frame of it, and raze it out of being. It is not, therefore, out of a distrust of his own power, that he hath supported a sinful world for so many ages, and patiently borne the blasphemies of some, the neglects of others, and the ingratitude of all, without inflicting that severe justice which righteously he might have done; he wants no thunder to crush the whole generation of men, nor waters to drown them, nor earth to swallow them up. How easy is it for him to single out this or that particular person to be the object of his wrath, and not of his patience! What he hath done to one, he may to another; any signal judgment he hath sent upon one, is an evidence that he wants not power to inflict it upon all. Could he not make the motes in the air to choke us at every breath, rain thunderbolts instead of drops of water, fill the clouds with a consuming lightning, take off the reverence and fear of man, which he hath imprinted upon the creature, spirit our domestic ·beasts to be our executioners, unloose the tiles from the house-top to brain us, or make the fall of a house to crush us? It is but taking out the pins, and giving a blast, and the work is done. And doth he want a power to do any of those things? It is not then a faint-hearted, or feeble patience, that he exerciseth towards man.

4. Since it is not for want of power over the creature, it is from a fulness of power over himself. This is in the text, "The Lord is slow to anger, and great in power;" it is a part of his dominion over himself, whereby he can moderate, and rule his own affections according to the holiness of his own will. As it is the effect of his power, so it is an argument of his power; the greatness of the effect demonstrates the fulness and sufficiency of the cause. The more feeble any man is in reason the less command he hath over his passions, and he is the more heady to revenge. Revenge is a sign of a childish mind; the stronger any man is in reason, the more command he hath over himself. "He that is slow to anger is better than the mighty; and he that rules his own spirit, than he that takes a city" (Prov. xvi. 32); he that can restrain his anger, is stronger than the Cæsars and Alexanders of the world, that have filled the earth with slain carcasses and ruined cities. By the same reason, God's slowness to anger is a greater argument of his power than the creating a world, or the power of dissolving it by a word; in this he hath a dominion over creatures, in the other over himself; this is the reason he will not return to destroy; because "I am God, and not man" (Hos. xi. 9); I am not so weak and impotent as man, that cannot restrain his anger. This is a strength possessed only by a God, wherein a creature is no more able to parallel him, than in any other; so that he may be said to be the Lord of himself; as it is in the verse before the text, that he is the Lord of anger, in the Hebrew, instead of

"furious," as we translate it; so he is the Lord of patience. The end why God is patient, is to show his power. "What if God, willing to show his wrath, and to make his power known, endured with much long-suffering the vessels of wrath fitted to destruction?" (Rom. ix. 22). To show his wrath upon sinners, and his power over himself in bearing such indignities, and forbearing punishment so long, when men were vessels of wrath fitted for destruction, of whom there was no hopes of amendment. Had he immediately broken in pieces those vessels, his power had not so eminently appeared as it hath done, in tolerating them so long, that had provoked him to take them off so often; there is indeed the power of his anger, and there is the power of his patience; and his power is more seen in his patience than in his wrath: it is no wonder that He that is above all, is able to crush all; but it is a wonder, that he that is provoked by all, doth not, upon the first provocation, rid his hands of all. This is the reason why he did bear such a weight of provocations from vessels of wrath, prepared for ruin, that he might γνωρίσαι τὸ δυνατὸν αὐτοῦ, show what he was able to do, the lordship and royalty he had over himself. The power of God is more manifest in his patience to a multitude of sinners, than it would be in creating millions of worlds out of nothing; this was the δυνατὸν αὐτοῦ, a power over himself.

5. This patience being a branch of mercy, the exercise of it is founded in the death of Christ. Without the consideration of this, we can give no account why Divine patience should extend itself to us, and not to the fallen angels. The threatening extends itself to us as well as to the fallen angels; the threatening must necessarily have sunk man, as well as those glorious creatures, had not Christ stepped in to our relief. Had not Christ interposed to satisfy the justice of God, man upon his sin had been actually bound over to punishment, as well as the fallen angels were upon theirs, and been fettered in chains as strong as those spirits feel.[f] The reason why man was not hurled into the same deplorable condition upon his sin, as they were, is Christ's promise of taking our nature, and not theirs. Had God designed Christ's taking their nature, the same patience had been exercised towards them, and the same offers would have been made to them, as are made to us. In regard to these fruits of this patience, Christ is said to buy the wickedest apostates from him: "Denying the Lord that bought them" (1 Pet. ii. 1). Such were bought by him, as "bring upon themselves just destruction, and whose damnation slumbers not" (ver. 3); he purchased the continuance of their lives, and the stay of their execution, that offers of grace might be made to them. This patience must be either upon the account of the law, or the gospel; for there are no other rules, whereby God governs the world. A fruit of the law it was not; that spake nothing but curses after disobedience; not a letter of mercy was writ upon that, and therefore nothing of patience; death and wrath were denounced; no slowness to anger intimated. It must be therefore upon account of the gospel, and a fruit of the covenant of grace, whereof Christ was Mediator. Besides this perfection

f Testard. de Natur. et Grat. Thess. 119.

being God's " waiting that he might be gracious" (Isa. xxx. 18), that
which made way for God's grace made way for his waiting to manifest it.   God discovered not his grace, but in Christ; and therefore
discovered not his patience but in Christ; it is in him he met with
the satisfaction of his justice, that he might have a ground for the
manifestation of his patience. And the sacrifices of the law, wherein
the life of a beast was accepted for the sin of man, discovered the
ground of his forbearance of them to be the expectation of the great
Sacrifice, whereby sin was to be completely expiated (Gen. viii. 21).
The publication of his patience to the end of the world is presently
after the sweet savor he found in Noah's sacrifice. The promised
and designed coming of Christ, was the cause of that patience God
exercised before in the world; and his gathering the elect together,
is the reason of his patience since his death.

6. The naturalness of his veracity and holiness, and the strictness
of his justice, are no bars to the exercise of his patience.

(1.) His veracity. In those threatenings where the punishment is
expressed, but not the time of inflicting it prefixed and determined
in the threatening, his veracity suffers no damage by the delaying
execution; so it be once done, though a long time after, the credit
of his truth stands unshaken : as when God promises a thing without fixing the the time, he is at liberty to pitch upon what time he
pleases for the performance of it, without staining his faithfulness to
his word, by not giving the thing promised presently. Why should
the deferring of justice upon an offender be any more against his
veracity than his delaying an answer to the petitions of a suppliant?
But the difference will lie in the threatening. " In the day thou eatest thereof, thou shalt die the death" (Gen. ii. 17). The time was
there settled ; " in that day thou shalt die;" some refer " day" to
eating, not to dying; and render the sentence thus : I do not prohibit thee the eating this fruit for a day or two, but continually. In
whatsoever day thou eatest thereof, thou shalt die; but not understanding his dying that very day he should eat of it; referring
" day" to the extensiveness of the prohibition, as to time. But to
leave this as uncertain, it may be answered, that as in some threatenings a condition is implied, though not expressed, as in that positive denouncing of the destruction of Ninevah : " Yet forty days,
and Ninevah shall be destroyed" (Jonah, iii. 4), the condition is implied; unless they humble themselves, and repent; for upon their
repentance, the sentence was deferred. So here, " in the day thou
eatest thereof, thou shalt die the death," or certainly die, unless there
be a way found for the expiation of thy crime, and the righting my
honor.   This condition, in regard of the event, may as well be asserted to be implied in this threatening, as that of repentance was in
the other; or rather, " thou shalt die," thou shalt die spiritually, thou
shalt lose that image of mine in thy nature, that righteousness which
is as much the life of thy soul as thy soul is the life of thy body;
that righteousness whereby thou art enabled to live to me and thy
own happiness. What the soul is to the body, a quickening soul,
that the image of God is to the soul, a quickening image. Or "thou
shalt die the death," or certainly die; thou shalt be liable to death.

And so it is to be understood, not of an actual death of the body, but the merit of death, and the necessity of death; thou wilt be obnoxious to death, which will be avoided, if thou dost forbear to eat of the forbidden fruit; thou shalt be a guilty person, and so under a sentence of death, that I may, when I please, inflict it on thee.[g] Death did come upon Adam that day, because his nature was vitiated; he was then also under an expectation of death, he was obnoxious to it, though that day it was not poured out upon him in the full bitterness and gall of it: as when the apostle saith, "The body is dead because of sin" (Rom. viii. 10), he speaks to the living, and yet tells them the body was dead because of sin; he means no more than that it was under a sentence, and so a necessity of dying, though not actually dead; so thou shalt be under the sentence of death that day, as certainly as if that day thou shouldst sink into the dust: and as by his patience towards man, not sending forth death upon him in all the bitter ingredients of it, his justice afterwards was more eminent upon man's surety, than it would have been if it had been then employed in all its severe operations upon man. So was his veracity eminent also in making good this threatening, in inflicting the punishment included in it upon our nature assumed by a mighty Person, and upon that Person in our nature, who was infinitely higher than our nature.

(2.) His justice and righteousness are not prejudiced by his patience. There is a hatred of the sin in his holiness, and a sentence past against the sin in his justice, though the execution of that sentence be suspended, and the person reprieved by patience, which is implied (Eccles. viii. 11): "Because sentence against an evil work is not executed speedily; therefore, the heart of the sons of men is fully set in them to do evil;" sentence is past, but a speedy execution is stopped. Some of the heathens, who would not imagine God unjust, and yet, seeing the villanies and oppressions of men in the world remain unpunished, and frequently beholding prosperous wickedness, to free him from the charge of injustice, denied his providence and actual government of the world; for if he did take notice of human affairs, and concern himself in what was done upon the earth, they could not think an Infinite Goodness and Justice could be so slow to punish oppressors, and relieve the miserable, and leave the world in that disorder under the injustice of men: they judged such a patience as was exercised by him, if he did govern the world, was drawn out beyond the line of fit and just. Is it not a presumption in men to prescribe a rule of righteousness and conveniency to their Creator? It might be demanded of such, whether they never injured any in their lives; and when certainly they have one way or another, would they not think it a very unworthy, if not unjust, thing, that a person so injured by them should take a speedy and severe revenge on them?—and if every man should do the like, would there not be a speedy despatch made of mankind? Would not the world be a shambles, and men rush forwards to one another's destructions, for the wrongs they have mutually received? If it be accounted a virtue in man, and no unrighteousness, not pre-

[g] Perer, *in loc.*

sently to be all on fire against an offence; by what right should any question the inconsistency of God's patience with his justice? Do we praise the lenity of parents to children, and shall we disparage the long-suffering of God to men? We do not censure the righteousness of physicians and chirurgeons, because they cut not off a corrupt member this day as well as to-morrow? And is it just to asperse God, because he doth defer his vengeance which man assumes to himself a right to do? We never account him a bad governor that defers the trial, and consequently the condemnation and execution of a notorious offender for important reasons, and beneficial to the public, either to make the nature of his crime more evident, or to find out the rest of his complices by his discovery. A governor, indeed, were unjust, if he commanded that which were unrighteous, and forbade that which were worthy and commendable; but if he delays the execution of a convict offender for weighty reasons, either for the benefit of the state whereof he is the ruler, or for some advantage to the offender himself, to make him have a sense of, and a regret for his offence, we account him not unjust for this. God doth not by his patience dispense with the holiness of his law, nor cut off anything from its due authority. If men do strengthen themselves by his long-suffering against his law, it is their fault, not any unrighteousness in him; he will take a time to vindicate the righteousness of his own commands, if men will wholly neglect the time of his patience, in forbearing to pay a dutiful observance to his precept. If justice be natural to him, and he cannot but punish sin, yet he is not necessitated to consume sinners, as the fire doth stubble put into it, which hath no command over its own qualities to restrain them from acting; but God is a free agent, and may choose his own time for the distribution of that punishment his nature leads him to. Though he be naturally just, yet it is not so natural to him, as to deprive him of a dominion over his own acts, and a freedom in the exerting them what time he judgeth most convenient in his wisdom. God is necessarily holy, and is necessarily angry with sin; his nature can never like it, and cannot but be displeased with it; yet he hath a liberty to restrain the effects of this anger for a time, without disgracing his holiness, or being interpreted to act unrighteously; as well as a prince or state may suspend the execution of a law, which they will never break, only for a time and for a public benefit. If God should presently execute his justice, this perfection of patience, which is a part of his goodness, would never have an opportunity of discovery; part of his glory, for which he created the world, would lie in obscurity from the knowledge of his creature; his justice would be signal in the destruction of sinners, but this stream of his goodness would be stopped up from any motion. One perfection must not cloud another; God hath his seasons to discover all, one after another: "The times and seasons are in his own power" (Acts, i. 7): the seasons of manifesting his own perfections as well as other things; succession of them, in their distinct appearance, makes no invasion upon the rights of any. If justice should complain of an injury from patience, because it is delayed, patience hath more reason to complain of an injury from justice, that by such a plea it would be wholly obscured and inactive: for this perfection hath the shortest time to act its part of any, it hath no stage but this world to move in; mercy hath a heaven, and justice a hell, to display itself to eternity, but long-suffering hath only a short-lived earth for the compass of its operation. Again, justice is so far from being wronged by patience, that it rather is made more illustrious, and hath the fuller scope to exercise itself; it is the more righted for being deferred, and will have stronger grounds than before for its activity; the equity of it will be more apparent to every reason, the objections more fully answered against it, when the way of dealing with sinners by patience hath been slighted. When this dam of long-suffering is removed, the floods of fiery justice will rush down with more force and violence; justice will be fully recompensed for the delay, when, after patience is abused, it can spread itself over the offender with a more unquestionable authority; it will have more arguments to hit the sinner in the teeth with, and silence him; there will be a sharper edge for every stroke; the sinner must not only pay for the score of his former sins, but the score of abused patience, so that justice hath no reason to commence a suit against God's slowness to anger: what it shall want by the fulness of mercy upon the truly penitent, it will gain by the contempt of patience on the impenitent abusers. When men, by such a carriage, are ripened for the stroke of justice, justice may strike without any regret in itself, or pull-back from mercy; the contempt of long-suffering will silence the pleas of the one, and spirit the severity of the other. To conclude: since God hath glorified his justice on Christ, as a surety for sinners, his patience is so far from interfering with the rights of his justice, that it promotes it; it is dispensed to this end, that God might pardon with honor, both upon the score of purchased mercy and contented justice; that by a penitent sinner's return his mercy might be acknowledged free, and the satisfaction of his justice by Christ be glorified in believing: for he is long-suffering from an unwillingness "that any should perish, but that all should come to repentance" (2 Pet. iii. 9); i. e. all to whom the promise is made, for to such the apostle speaks, and calls it " long-suffering to us-ward ;" and repentance being an acknowledgment of the demerit of sin, and a breaking off unrighteousness, gives a particular glory to the freeness of mercy, and the equity of justice.

II. The second thing, How this patience or slowness to anger is manifested.

1. To our first parents. His slowness to anger was evidenced in not directing his artillery against them, when they first attempted to rebel. He might have struck them dead when they began to bite at the temptation, and were inclinable to a surrender; for it was a degree of sinning, and a breach of loyalty as well, though not so much as the consummating act. God might have given way to the floods of his wrath at the first spring of man's aspiring thoughts, when the monstrous motion of being as God began to be curdled in his heart; but he took no notice of any of their embryo sins till they came to a ripeness, and started out of the womb of their minds into the open

air: and after he had brought his sin to perfection, God did not presently send that death upon him, which he had merited, but continued his life to the space of 930 years (Gen. v. 5). The sun and stars were not arrested from doing their office for him. Creatures were continued for his use, the earth did not swallow him up, nor a thunderbolt from heaven raze out the memory of him. Though he had deserved to be treated with such a severity for his ungrateful demeanor to his Creator and Benefactor, and affecting an equality with him, yet God continued him with a sufficiency for his content, after he turned rebel, though not with such a liberality as when he remained a loyal subject; and though he foresaw that he would not make an end of sinning, but with an end of living, he used him not in the same manner as he had used the devils. He added days and years to him, after he had deserved death, and hath for this 5,000 years continued the propagation of mankind, and derived from his loins an innumerable posterity, and hath crowned multitudes of them with hoary heads. He might have extinguished human race at the first; but since he hath preserved it till this day, it must be interpreted nothing else but the effect of an admirable patience.

2. His slowness to anger is manifest to the Gentiles. What they were, we need no other witness than the apostle Paul, who sums up many of their crimes (Rom. i. 29—32). He doth preface the catalogue with a comprehensive expression, "Being filled with all unrighteousness;" and concludes it with a dreadful aggravation, "They not only do the same, but have pleasure in them that do them." They were so soaked and naturalized in wickedness, that they had no delight, and found no sweetness in anything else but what was in itself abominable; all of them were plunged in idolatry and superstition; none of them but either set up their great men, or creatures, beneficial to the world, and some the damned spirits in his stead, and paid an adoration to insensible creatures or devils, which was due to God. Some were so depraved in their lives and actions, that it seemed to be the interest of the rest of the world, that they should have been extinguished for the instruction of their contemporaries and posterity. The best of them had turned all religion into a fable, coined a world of rites, some unnatural in themselves, and most of them unbecoming a rational creature to offer, and a Deity to accept: yet he did not presently arm himself against them with fire and sword, nor stopped the course of their generations, nor tear out all those relics of natural light which were left in their minds. He did not do what he might have done, but he winked at the "times of that ignorance" (Acts, xvii. 30), their ignorant idolatry; for that it refers to (ver. 29): "They thought the Godhead was like to gold or silver, or stone graven by art, and men's device; ὑπεριδὼν, overlooking them. He demeaned himself so, as if he did not take notice of them. He winked as if he did not see them, and would not deal so severely with them: the eye of his justice seemed to wink, in not calling them to an account for their sin.

3. His slowness to anger is manifest to the Israelites. You know how often they are called a "stiff-necked people;" they are said to do evil "from their youth;" i. e. from the time wherein they were

erected a nation and commonwealth; and that "the city had been a provocation of his anger, and of his fury, from the day that they built it, even to this day;" *i. e.* the day of Jeremiah's prophecy, "that he should remove it from before his face" (Jer. xxxii. 31): from the days of Solomon, say some, which is too much a curtailing of the text, as though their provocations had taken date no higher than from the time of Solomon's rearing the temple, and beautifying the city, whereby it seemed to be a new building.   They began more early ; they scarce discontinued their revolting from God ; they were a " grief to him forty years together in the wilderness" (Ps. xcv. 10), "yet he suffered their manners" (Acts, xiii. 18).   He bore with their ill-behaviour and sauciness towards him ; and no sooner was Joshua's head laid, and the elders, that were their conductors, gathered to their fathers, but the next generation forsook God, and smutted themselves with the idolatry of the nations (Judges, ii. 7, 10, 11): and when he punished them by prospering the arms of their enemies against them, they were no sooner delivered upon their cry and humiliation, but they began a new scene of idolatry ; and though he brought upon them the power of the Babylonian empire, and laid chains upon them to bring them to their right mind.   And at seventy years' end he struck off their chains, by altering the whole posture of affairs in that part of the world for their sakes: overturning one empire, and settling another for their restoration to their ancient city. And though they did not after disown him for their God, and set up "Baal in his throne," yet they multiplied foolish traditions, whereby they impaired the authority of the law ; yet he sustained them with a wonderful patience, and preferred them before all other people in the first offers of the gospel; and after they had outraged not only his servants, the prophets, but his Son, the Redeemer, yet he did not forsake them, but employed his apostles to solicit them, and publish among them the doctrine of salvation : so that his treating this people might well be called "much long-suffering," it being above 1500 years, wherein he bore with them, or mildly punished them, far less than their deserts; their coming out of Egypt being about the year of the world 2450, and their final destruction as a commonwealth, not till about forty years after the death of Christ ; and all this while his patience did sometimes wholly restrain his justice, and sometimes let it fall upon them in some few drops, but made no total devastation of their country, nor wrote his revenge in extraordinary bloody characters, till the Roman conquest, wherein he put a period to them both as a church and state.   In particular this patience is manifest,

1st. In his giving warnings of judgments, before he orders them to go forth.   He doth not punish in a passion, and hastily ; he speaks before he strikes, and speaks that he may not strike.   Wrath is published before it is executed, and that a long time ; an hundred and twenty years' advertisement was given to a debauched world before the heavens were opened, to spout down a deluge upon them.   He will not be accused of coming unawares upon a people ; he inflicts nothing but what he foretold either immediately to the people that provoke him, or anciently to them that have been their forerunners in the same provocation (Hos. vii. 12), "I will chastise them, as their congregation hath heard." Many of the leaves of the Old Testament are full of those presages and warnings of approaching judgment. These make up a great part of the volume of it in various editions, according to the state of the several provoking times. Warnings are given to those people that are most abominable in his sight (Zeph. ii. 1, 2); "Gather yourselves together, yea, gather together, O nation not desired,"—it is a *Meiosis*, O nation abhorred,—"before the decree bring forth." He sends his heralds before he sends his armies; he summons them by the voice of his prophets, before he confounds them by the voice of his thunders. When a parley is beaten, a white flag of peace is hung out, before a black flag of fury is set up. He seldom cuts down men by his judgments, before he hath "hewed them by his prophets" (Hos. vi. 5). Not a remarkable judgment but was foretold: the flood to the old world by Noah; the famine to Egypt by Joseph; the earthquake by Amos (ch. i. 1); the storm from Chaldea by Jeremiah; the captivity of the ten tribes by Hosea; the total destruction of Jerusalem and the Temple by Christ himself. He hath chosen the best persons in the world to give those intimations; Noah, the most righteous person on the earth, for the old world; and his Son, the most beloved person in heaven, for the Jews in the later time: and in other parts of the world, and in the later times, where he hath not warned by prophets, he hath supplied it by prodigies in the air and earth; histories are full of such items from heaven. Lesser judgments are forewarners of greater, as lightnings before thunder are messengers to tell us of a succeeding clap.

(1). He doth often give warning of judgments. He comes not to extremity, till he hath often shaken the rod over men; he thunders often, before he crusheth them with his thunderbolt; he doth not till after the first and second admonition punish a rebel, as he would have us reject a heretic. "He speaks once, yea, twice" (Job, xxxiii. 14), "and man perceives it not;" he sends one message after another, and waits the success of many messages before he strikes. Eight prophets were ordered to acquaint the whole world with approaching judgment (2 Pet. ii. 5): he saved "Noah, the eighth person, a preacher of righteousness, bringing in the flood upon the world of the ungodly," called "the eighth" in respect of his preaching, not in regard of his preservation; he was the eighth preacher in order, from the beginning of the world, that endeavored to restore the world to the way of righteousness. Most, indeed, consider him here as the eighth person saved, so do our translators; and, therefore, add *person*, which is not in the Greek. Some others consider him here as the eighth preacher of righteousness, reckoning Enoch, the son of Seth, the first, grounding it upon Gen. iv. 26: "Then began men to call upon the name of the Lord," *Heb.* "Then it was began to call in the name of the Lord," τὸ ὄνομα τοῦ Κυρίου Θεοῦ. *Sept.* "He began to call in the name of the Lord," which others render, "He began to preach, or call upon men in the name of the Lord." The word קָרָא signifies to preach, or to call upon men by preaching (Prov. i. 21): "Wisdom crieth," or "preaches;" and if this be so, as it is very probable, it is easy to reckon him the eighth preacher, by numbering the successive heads of the generations (Gen. v.), beginning at Enoch, the first preacher of righteousness. So many there were before God choked the old world with water, and swept them away. It is clear he often did admonish, by his prophets, the Jews of their sin, and the wrath which should come upon them.[h] One prophet, Hosea, prophesied seventy years; for he prophesied in the days of four kings of Judah, and one of Israel, Jeroboam, the son of Joash (Hos. i. 1), or Jeroboam, the second of that name. Uzziah, king of Judah, in whose reign Hosea prophesied, lived thirty-eight years after the death of Jeroboam. The second Jotham, Uzziah's successor, reigned sixteen years; Ahaz sixteen; Hezekiah twenty-nine years. Now, take nothing of Hezekiah's time, and date the beginning of his prophecy from the last year of Jeroboam's reign, and the time of Hosea's prophecy will be seventy years complete; wherein God warned those people, and waited the return particularly of Israel;[i] and not less than five of those we call the Lesser Prophets, were sent to foretell the destruction of the ten tribes, and to call them to repentance,—Hosea, Joel, Amos, Micah, Jonah; and though we have nothing of Jonah's prophecy in this concern of Israel, yet that he lived in the time of the same Jeroboam, and prophesied things which are not upon record in the book of Jonah, is clear (2 Kings, xiv. 25). And besides those, Isaiah prophesied also in the reign of the same kings as Hosea did (Isa. i. 1); and it is God's usual method to send forth his servants, and when their admonitions are slighted he commissions others, before he sends out his destroying armies (Matt. xxii. 3, 4, 7).

(2). He doth often give warning of judgments, that he might not pour out his wrath. He summons them to a surrender of themselves, and a return from their rebellion, that they might not feel the force of his arms. He offers peace before he shakes off the dust of his feet, that his despised peace might not return in vain to him to solicit a revenge from his anger. He hath a right to punish upon the first commission of a crime, but he warns men of what they have deserved, of what his justice moves him to inflict, that by having recourse to his mercy he might not exercise the rights of his justice. God sought to kill Moses for not circumcising his son (Exod. iv. 24). Could God, that sought it, miss a way to do it? Could a creature lurch, or fly from him? God put on the garb of an enemy, that Moses might be discouraged from being an instrument of his own ruin : God manifested an anger against Moses for his neglect, as if he would then have destroyed him, that Moses might prevent it by casting off his carelessness, and doing his duty. He sought to kill him by some evident sign, that Moses might escape the judgment by his obedience. He threatens Nineveh, by the prophet, with destruction, that Nineveh's repentance might make void the prophecy. He fights with men by the sword of his mouth, that he might not pierce them by the sword of his wrath. He threatens, that men might prevent the execution of his threatening; he terrifies, that he might not destroy, but that men by humi-

---

[h] Vid. Gell's Ἀγγελοκατία.   [i] Sanctius. Prolegom. in Hosea, Prolog. III.

liation may lie prostrate before him, and move the bowels of his mercy to a louder sound than the voice of his anger. He takes time to whet his sword, that men may turn themselves from the edge of it. He roars like a lion, that men, by hearing his voice, may shelter themselves from being torn by his wrath. There is patience in the sharpest threatening, that we may avoid the scourge. Who can charge God with an eagerness to revenge, that sends so many heralds, and so often before he strikes, that he might be prevented from striking? His threatenings have not so much of a black flag as of an olive branch. He lifts up his hand before he strikes, that men might see and avert the stroke (Isa. xxvi. 11).

2d. His patience is manifest in long delaying his threatened judgments, though he finds no repentance in the rebels. He doth sometimes delay his lighter punishments, because he doth not delight in torturing his creatures; but he doth longer delay his destroying punishments, such as put an end to men's happiness, and remit them to their final and unchangeable state; because he "doth not delight in the death of a sinner." While he is preparing his arrows, he is waiting for an occasion to lay them aside, and dull their points, that he may with honor march back again, and disband his armies. He brings lighter smarts sooner, that men might not think him asleep, but he suspends the more terrible judgments that men might be led to repentance. He scatters not his consuming fires at the first, but brings on ruining vengeance with a "slow pace; sentence against an evil work is not speedily executed" (Eccles. viii. 11). The Jews therefore say, that Michael, the minister of justice, flies with one wing, but Gabriel, the minister of mercy, with two. An hundred and twenty years did God wait upon the old world, and delay their punishment all the time the "ark was preparing" (1 Pet. iii. 20); wherein that wicked generation did not enjoy only a bare patience, but a striving patience (Gen. vi. 3): "My Spirit shall not always strive with man, yet his days shall be one hundred and twenty years," the days wherein I will strive with him; that his long-suffering might not lose all its fruit, and remit the objects of it into the hands of consuming justice. It was the tenth generation of the world from Adam, when the deluge overflowed it, so long did God bear with them: and the tenth generation from Noah wherein Sodom was consumed. God did not come to keep his assizes in Sodom, till "the cry of their sins was very strong," that it had been a wrong to his justice to have restrained it any longer. The cry was so loud that he could not be at quiet, as it were, on his throne of glory for the disturbing noise (Gen. xviii. 20, 21). Sin transgresseth the law; the law being violated, solicits justice; justice, being urged, pleads for punishment; the cry of their sins did, as it were, force him from heaven to come down, and examine what cause there was for that clamor. Sin cries loud and long before he takes his sword in hand. Four hundred years he kept off deserved destruction from the Amorites, and deferred making good his promise to Abraham, of giving Canaan to his posterity, out of his long-suffering to the Amorites (Gen. xv. 16). In the fourth generation they shall come hither again, "for the iniquity of the Amorites is not yet full." Their measure was filling then, but not so full as to put a stop to any further patience till four hundred years after. The usual time in succeeding generations, from the denouncing of judgments to the execution, is forty years; this some ground upon Ezek. iv. 6, "Thou shalt bear the iniquity of the house of Judah forty days," taking each day for a year. Though Hosea lived seventy years, yet from the beginning of his prophesying judgments against Israel to the pouring them out upon that idolatrous people, it was forty years. Hosea, as was mentioned before, prophesied against them in the days of Jeroboam the Second, in whose time God did wonderfully deliver Israel (2 Kings, xiv. 26, 27). From that time, till the total destruction of the ten tribes, it was forty years, as may easily be computed from the story (2 Kings, xv.—xvi.), by the reign of the succeeding kings. So forty years after the most horrid villany that ever was committed in the face of the sun, *viz.*, the crucifying the Son of God, was Jerusalem destroyed, and the inhabitants captived; so long did God delay a visible punishment for such an outrage. Sometimes he prolongs sending a threatened judgment upon a mere shadow of humiliation; so he did that denounced against Ahab. He turned it over to his posterity, and adjourned it to another season (1 Kings, xxi. 29). He doth not issue out an arrest upon one transgression; you often find him not commencing a suit against men till "three and four transgressions." The first of Amos, all along that chapter and the second chapter, for "three and four," *i. e.* "seven;" a certain number for an uncertain. He gives not orders to his judgments to march till men be obstinate, and refuse any commerce with him; he stops them till "there be no remedy" (2 Chron. xxxvi. 16). It must be a great wickedness that gives vent to them (Hos. x. 15); *Heb.* "Your wickedness of wickedness." He is so "slow to anger," and stays the punishment his enemies deserve, that he may seem to have forgot his "kindness to his friends" (Ps. xliv. 24): "Wherefore hidest thou thy face, and forgettest our affliction and oppression?" He lets his people groan under the yoke of their enemies, as if he were made up of kindness to his enemies, and anger against his friends. This delaying of punishment to evil men is visible in his suspending the terrifying acts of conscience, and supporting it only in its checking, admonishing, and controlling acts. The patience of a governor is seen in the patient mildness of his deputy: David's conscience did not terrify him till nine months after his sin of murder. Should God set open the mouth of this power within us, not only the earth, but our own bodies and spirits, would be a burden to us: it is long before God puts scorpions into the hands of men's consciences to scourge them: he holds back the rod, waiting for the hour of our return, as if that would be a recompense for our offences and his forbearance.

3d. His patience is manifest in his unwillingness to execute his judgments when he can delay no longer. "He doth not afflict willingly, nor grieve the children of men" (Lam. iii. 33): *Heb.* "He doth not afflict from his heart:" he takes no pleasure in it, as he is Creator. The height of men's provocations, and the necessity of the preserving his rights, and vindicating his laws, obligeth him to it, as he is the Governor of the world; as a judge may willingly condemn a malefactor to death out of affection to the laws, and desire to preserve the order of government, but unwillingly, out of compassion to the offender himself. When he resolved upon the destruction of the old world, he spake it as a God grieved with an occasion of punishment (Gen. vi. 6, 7, compared together). When he came to reckon with Adam, " he walked," he did not run with his sword in his hand upon him, as a mighty man with an eagerness to destroy him (Gen. iii. 8), and that "in the cool of the day," a time when men, tired in the day, are unwilling to engage in a hard employment. His exercising judgment is a " coming out of his place" (Isa. xxvi. 21 ; Mic. i. 3) : he comes out of his station to exercise judgment; a throne is more his place than a tribunal. Every prophecy, loaded with threatenings, is called the " burden of the Lord ;" a burden to him to execute it, as well as to men to suffer it. Though three angels came to Abraham about the punishment of Sodom, whereof one Abraham speaks to as to God, yet but two appeared at the destruction of Sodom, as if the Governor of the world were unwilling to be present at such dreadful work (Gen. xix. 1) : and when the man, that had the ink-horn by his side, that was appointed to mark those that were to be preserved in the common destruction, returned to give an account of the performing his commission (Ezek. ix. 10), we read not of the return of those that were to kill, as if God delighted only to hear again of his works of mercy, and had no mind to hear again of his severe proceedings. The Jews, to show God's unwillingness to punish, imagine that hell was created the second day, because that day's work is not pronounced good by God as all the other days' works are[k] (Gen. i. 8).

(1.) When God doth punish he doth it with some regret. When he hurls down his thunders, he seems to do it with a backward hand, because with an unwilling heart.[l] He created, saith Chrysostom, the world in six days, but was seven days in destroying one city, Jericho, which he had before devoted to be razed to the ground. What is the reason, saith he, that God is so quick to build up, but slow to pull down ? His goodness excites his power to the one, but is not earnest to persuade him to the other : when he comes to strike, he doth it with a sigh or groan (Isa. i. 24): " Ah! I will ease me of my adversaries, and avenge me on my enemies," הוֹי, Ah! a note of grief. So Hos. vi. 4, " O Ephraim! what shall I do unto thee? O Judah! what shall I do unto thee?" It is an *addubitatio*, a figure in rhetoric, as if God were troubled that he must deal so sharply with them, and give them up to their enemies:—I have tried all means to reclaim you ; I have used all ways of kindness, and nothing prevails ; what shall I do? my mercy invites me to spare them, and their ingratitude provokes me to ruin them. God had borne with that people of Israel almost three hundred years, from the setting up of the calves at Dan and Bethel ; sent many a prophet to warn them, and spent many a rod to reform them : and when he comes to execute his threatenings, he doth with a conflict in himself (Hos. xi. 8) : " How

<hr>

[k] Mercer in Gen.   [l] Cressol. Decad. II. p. 163.

shall I give thee up, O Ephraim? how shall I deliver thee, Israel?" as if there were a pull-back in his own bowels. He solemnizeth their approaching funeral with a hearty groan, and takes his farewell of the dying malefactor with a pang in himself. How often, in former times, when he had signed a warrant for their execution, did he call it back? (Ps. lxxviii. 38): "Many a time turned he his anger away." Many a time he recalled or ordered his anger to return again, as the word signifies, as if he were irresolute what to do: he recalled it, as a man doth his servant, several times, when he is sending him upon an unwelcome message; or as a tender-hearted prince wavers and trembles when he is to sign a writ for the death of a rebel that hath been before his favorite, as if, when he had signed the writ, he blotted out his name again, and flung away the pen. And his method is remarkable when he came to punish Sodom; though the cry of their sin had been fierce in his ears, yet when he comes to make inquisition, he declares his intention to Abraham, as if he were desirous that Abraham should have helped him to some arguments to stop the outgoings of his judgment. He gave liberty to the best person in the world to stand in the gap, and enter into a treaty with him, to show, saith one,[m] how willingly his mercy would have compounded with his justice for their redemption; and Abraham interceded so long, till he was ashamed for pleading the cause of patience and mercy to the wrong of the rights of Divine justice. Perhaps, had Abraham had the courage to ask, God would have had the compassion to grant a reprieve just at the time of execution.

(2.) His patience is manifest in that when he begins to send out his judgments, he doth it by degrees. His judgments are "as the morning light," which goes forth by degrees in the hemisphere (Hos. vi. 5). He doth not shoot all his thunders at once, and bring his sharpest judgments in array at one time, but gradually, that a people may have time to turn to him (Joel, i. 4). First the palmer-worm, then the locust, then the canker-worm, then the caterpillar; what one left, the other was to eat, if there were not a timely return. A Jewish writer[n] saith, these judgments came not all in one year, but one year after another. The palmer-worm and locust might have eaten all, but Divine patience set bounds to the devouring creatures. God had been first as a moth to Israel (Hos. v. 12): "Therefore will I be to the house of Ephraim as a moth;" Rivet translates it, "I have been;" in the Hebrew it is "I," without adding "I have been," or "I will be," and more probably "I have been;" I was as a moth, which makes little holes in a garment, and consumes it not all at once; and as "rottenness to the house of Judah," or a worm that eats into wood by degrees. Indeed, this people had consumed insensibly, partly by civil combustions, change of governors, foreign invasions, yet they were as obstinate in their idolatry as ever; at last God would be no longer to them as a moth, but as a lion, tear and go away (ver. 14): so Hos. ii., God had disowned Israel for his spouse (ver. 2), "She is not my wife, neither am I her husband;" yet he had not taken away her ornaments, which by the right of divorce he might have done, but still expected her reformation, for

[m] Pierce, Sinner Implead. p. 227.   [n] Kimchi.

that the threatening intimates (ver. 3); let her put away her whoredom, "lest I strip her naked, and set her as in the day when she was born." If she returned, she might recover what she had lost; if not, she might be stripped of what remained: thus God dealt with Judah (Ezek. ix. 3). The glory of God goes first from the cherub to the threshold of the house, and stays there, as if he had a mind to be invited back again; then it goes from the threshold of the house, and stands over the cherubims, as if upon a penitent call it would drop down again to its ancient station and seat, over which it hovered (Ezek. x. 18); and when he was not solicited to return, he departs out of the city, and stood upon the mountain, which is on the east part of the city (Ezek. xi. 23), looking still towards, and hovering about the temple, which was on the east of Jerusalem, as if loth to depart, and abandon the place and people. He walks so leisurely, with his rod in his hand, as if he had a mind rather to fling it away than use it; his patience in not pouring out all his vials, is more remarkable than his wrath in pouring out one or two. Thus hath God made his slowness to anger visible to us in the gradual punishment of us; first, the pestilence on this city, then firing our houses, consumption of trade; these have not been answered with such a carriage as God expects, therefore a greater is reserved. I dare prognosticate, upon reasons you may gather from what hath been spoke before, if I be not much mistaken, the forty years of his usual patience are very near expired; he hath inflicted some, that he might be met with in a way of repentance, and omit with honor the inflicting the remainder.

4th. His patience is manifest, in moderating his judgments, when he sends them. Doth he empty his quiver of his arrows, or exhaust his magazines of thunder? No; he could roll one thunderbolt successively upon all mankind; it is as easy with him to create a perpetual motion of lightning and thunder, as of the sun and stars, and make the world as terrible by the one, as it is delightful by the other. He opens not all his store, he sends out a light party to skirmish with men, and puts not in array his whole army; "He stirs not up all his wrath" (Ps. lxxviii. 38); he doth but pinch, where he might have torn asunder; when he takes away much, he leaves enough to support us; if he had stirred up all his anger, he had taken away all, and our lives to boot. He rakes up but a few sparks, takes but one firebrand to fling upon men, when he might discharge the whole furnace upon them; he sends but a few drops out of the cloud, which he might make to break in the gross, and fall down upon our heads to overwhelm us; he abates much of what he might do. When he might sweep away a whole nation by deluges of water, corruption of the air, or convulsions of the earth, or by other ways that are not wanting at his order; he picks out only some persons, some families, some cities; sends a plague into one house, and not into another; here is patience to the stock of a nation, while he inflicts punishment upon some of the most notorious sinners in it. Herod is suddenly snatched away, being willingly flattered into the thoughts of his being a god; God singled out the chief in the herd for whose sake he had been affronted by the rabble (Acts xii. 22,

23). Some find him sparing them, while others feel him destroying them; he arrests some, when he might seize all, all being his debtors; and often in great desolations brought upon a people for their sin, he hath left a stump in the earth, as Daniel speaks (Dan. iv. 15), for a nation to grow upon it again, and arise to a stronger constitution. He doth punish "less than our iniquities deserve" (Ezra ix. 13), and rewards us "not according to our iniquities" (Ps. ciii. 10). The greatness of any punishment in this life, answers not the greatness of the crime. Though there be an equity in whatsoever he doth, yet there is not an equality to what we deserve; our iniquities would justify a severer treating of us; his justice goes not here to the end of its line, it is stopped in its progress, and the blows of it weakened by his patience; he did not curse the earth after Adam's fall, that it should bring forth no fruit, but that it should not bring forth fruit without the wearisome toil of man, and subjected him to distempers presently, but inflicted not death immediately; while he punished him, he supported him; and while he expelled him from paradise, he did not order him not to cast his eye towards it, and conceive some hopes of regaining that happy place.

5th. His patience is seen in giving great mercies after provocations. He is so slow to anger, that he heaps many kindnesses upon a rebel, instead of punishment. There is a prosperous wickedness, wherein the provoker's strength continues firm; the troubles, which like clouds drop upon others, are blown away from them, and they are "not plagued like other men," that have a more worthy demeanor towards God (Ps. lxxiii. 3—5). He doth not only continue their lives, but sends out fresh beams of his goodness upon them, and calls them by his blessings, that they may acknowledge their own fault and his bounty, which he is not obliged to by any gratitude he meets with from them, but by the richness of his own patient nature: for he finds the unthankfulness of men as great as his benefits to them. He doth not only continue his outward mercies, while we continue our sins, but sometimes gives fresh benefits after new provocations, that if possible he might excite an ingenuity in men. When Israel at the Red Sea flung dirt in the face of God, by quarrelling with his servant Moses for bringing them out of Egypt, and misjudging God in his design of deliverance, and were ready to submit themselves to their former oppressors (Exod. xiv. 11, 12), which might justly have urged God to say to them, Take your own course; yet he is not only patient under their unjust charge, but "makes bare his arm in a deliverance at the Red Sea," that was to be an amazing monument to the world in all ages; and afterwards, when they repiningly quarrelled with him in their wants in the wilderness, he did not only not revenge himself upon them, or cast off the conduct of them, but bore with them by a miraculous long-suffering, and supplied them with miraculous provision,—manna from heaven, and water from a rock. Food is given to support us, and clothes to cover us, and Divine patience makes the creature which we turn to another use than what they were at first intended for, serve us contrary to their own genius: for had they reason, no question but they would complain to be subjected to the service of man, who hath been so ungrateful to their Creator, and groan at the abuse of God's patience, in the abuse they themselves suffer from the hands of man.

6th. All this is more manifest, if we consider the provocations he hath. Wherein his slowness to anger infinitely transcends the patience of any creature; nay, the spirits of all the angels and glorified saints in heaven, would be too narrow to bear the sins of the world for one day, nay, not so much as the sins of churches, which is a little spot in the whole world; it is because he is the Lord, one of an infinite power over himself, that not only the whole mass of the rebellious world, but of the sons of Jacob (either considered as a church and nation springing from the loins of Jacob, or considered as the regenerate part of the world, sometimes called the seed of Jacob), "are not consumed" (Mal. iii. 6). A Jonah was angry with God, for recalling his anger from a sinful people; had God committed the government of the world to the glorified saints, who are perfect in love and holiness, the world would have had an end long ago; they would have acted that which they sue for at the hands of God, and is not granted them. "How long, Lord, holy and true, dost thou not avenge our blood on them that dwell on the earth?" (Rev. vi. 10). God hath designs of patience above the world, above the unsinning angels, and perfectly renewed spirits in glory. The greatest created long-suffering is infinitely disproportioned to the Divine: fire from heaven would have been showered down before the greatest part of a day were spent, if a created patience had the conduct of the world, though that creature were possessed with the spirit of patience, extracted from all the creatures which are in heaven, or are, or ever were upon the earth. Methinks Moses intimates this; for as soon as God had passed by, proclaiming his name gracious and long suffering, as soon as ever Moses had paid his adoration, he falls to praying that God would go with the Israelites; "For it is a stiff-necked people" (Exod. xxxiv. 8, 9). What an argument is here for God to go along with them! he might rather, since he had heard him but just before say "he would by no means clear the guilty," desire God to stand further off from them, for fear the fire of his wrath should burst out from him, to burn them as he did the Sodomites. But he considers, that as none but God had such anger to destroy them, so none but God had such a patience to bear with them; it is as much as if he should have said, Lord! if thou shouldest send the most tender-hearted angel in heaven to have the guidance of this people, they would be a lost people; a period will quickly be set to their lives, no created strength can restrain its power from crushing such a stiff-necked people; flesh and blood cannot bear them, nor any created spirit of a greater might.

(1.) Consider the greatness of the provocations. No light matter, but actions of a great defiance: what is the practical language of most in the world, but that of Pharoah? "Who is the Lord, that I should obey him?" How many questions his being, and more his authority? What blasphemies of him, what reproaches of his Majesty! Men "drinking up iniquity like water," and with a haste and ardency "rushing into sin, as the horse into the battle." What is there in the reasonable creature, that hath the quickest capacity, and the deepest obligation to serve him, but opposition and enmity, a slight of him in everything, yea, the services most seriously performed, unsuited to the royalty and purity of so great a Being? such provocations as dare him to his face, that are a burden to so righteous a Judge, and so great a lover of the authority and majesty of his laws; that were there but a spark of anger in him, it is a wonder it doth not show itself. When he is invaded in all his attributes, it is astonishing that this single one of patience and meekness should withstand the assault of all the rest of his perfections; his being, which is attacked by sin, speaks for vengeance; his justice cannot be imagined to stand silent without charging the sinner. His holiness cannot but encourage his justice to urge its pleas, and be an advocate for it. His omniscience proves the truth of all the charge, and his abused mercy hath little encouragement to make opposition to the indictment; nothing but patience stands in the gap to keep off the arrest of judgment from the sinner.

(2.) His patience is manifest, if you consider the multitudes of these provocations. Every man hath sin enough in a day to make him stand amazed at Divine patience, and to call it, as well as the apostle did, "all long-suffering" (1 Tim. i. 16). How few duties of a perfectly right stamp are performed! What unworthy considerations mix themselves, like dross, with our purest and sincerest gold! How more numerous are the respects of the worshippers of him to themselves, than unto him! How many services are paid him, not out of love to him, but because he should do us no hurt, and some service; when we do not so much design to please him, as to please ourselves by expectations of a reward from him! What master would endure a servant that endeavored to please him, only because he should not kill him? Is that former charge of God upon the old world yet out of date, "That the imagination of the thoughts of the heart of man was only evil, and that continually?" (Gen. vi. 5.) Was not the new world as chargeable with it as the old? Certainly it was (Gen. viii. 21); and is of as much force this very minute as it was then. How many are the sins against knowledge, as well as those of ignorance; presumptuous sins, as well as those of infirmity! How numerous those of omission and commission! It is above the reach of any man's understanding to conceive all the blasphemies, oaths, thefts, adulteries, murders, oppressions, contempt of religion, the open idolatries of Turks and heathens, the more spiritual and refined idolatries of others.[o] Add to those, the ingratitude of those that profess his name, their pride, earthliness, carelessness, sluggishness to Divine duties, and in every one of those a multitude of provocations; the whole man being engaged in every sin, the understanding contriving it, the will embracing it, the affections complying with it, and all the members of the body instruments in the acting the unrighteousness of it; every one of these faculties bestowed upon men by him, are armed against him in every act: and in every employment of them there is a distinct provocation, though centred in one sinful end and object. What are the offences all the

* Lessius, p. 152.

men of the world receive from their fellow-creatures, to the injuries God receives from men, but as a small dust of earth to the whole mass of earth and heaven too? What multitudes of sins is one profane wretch guilty of in the space of twenty, forty, fifty years? Who can compute the vast number of his transgressions, from the first use of reason to the time of the separation of his soul from his body, from his entrance into the world to his exit? What are those, to those of a whole village of the like inhabitants? What are those, to those of a great city? Who can number up all the foul-mouthed oaths, the beastly excess, the goatish uncleanness, committed in the space of a day, year, twenty years in this city, much less in the whole nation, least of all, in the whole world? Were it no more than the common idolatry of former ages, when the whole world turned their backs upon their Creator, and passed him by to sue to a creature, a stock or stone, or a degraded spirit? How provoking would it be to a prince to see a whole city under his dominion deny him a respect, and pay it to his scullion, or the common executioner he employs! Add to this the unjust invasion of kings, the oppressions exercised upon men, all the private and public sins that have been in the world ever since it began. The Gentiles were described by the apostle (Rom. i. 29—31), in a black character, "They were haters of God;" yet how did the "riches of his patience" preserve multitudes of such disingenuous persons, and how "many millions of such haters of him" breathe every day in his air, and are maintained by his bounty, have their tables spread, and their cups filled to the brim, and that, too, in the midst of reiterated belchings of their enmity against him? All are under sufficient provocations of him to the highest indignation. The presiding angels over nations could not forbear, in love and honor to their governor, to arm themselves to the destruction of their several charges, if Divine patience did not set them a pattern, and their obedience incline them to expect his orders, before they act what their zeal would prompt them to. The devils would be glad of a commission to destroy the world, but that his patience puts a stop to their fury, as well as his own justice.

(3.) Consider the long time of this patience. He spread out his hands "all the day" to a rebellious world (Isa. lxv. 2). All men's day, all God's day, which is a "thousand years," he hath borne with the gross of mankind, with all the nations of the world in a long succession of ages, for five thousand years and upwards already, and will bear with them till the time comes for the world's dissolution. He hath suffered the monstrous acts of men, and endured the contradictions of a sinful world against himself, from the first sin of Adam, to the last committed this minute. The line of his patience hath run along with the duration of the world to this day; and there is not any one of Adam's posterity but hath been expensive to him, and partaken of the riches of it.

(4.) All these he bears when he hath a sense of them. He sees every day the roll and catalogue of sin increasing; he hath a distinct view of every one, from the sin of Adam to the last filled up in his omniscience; and yet gives no order for the arrest of the world. He knows men fitted for destruction ; all the instants he exerciseth long-suffering towards them, which makes the apostle call it not simply long-suffering, without the addition of πολλῆ, "much long-suffering" (Rom. ix. 23). There is not a grain in the whole mass of sin, that he hath not a distinct knowledge of, and of the quality of it. He perfectly understands the greatness of his own majesty that is vilified, and the nature of the offence that doth disparage him. He is solicited by his justice, directed by his omniscience, and armed with judgments to vindicate himself, but his arm is restrained by patience. To conclude : no indignity is hid from him, no iniquity is beloved by him ; the hatred of their sinfulness is infinite, and the knowledge of the malice is exact. The subsisting of the world under such weighty provocations, so numerous, so long time, and with his full sense of every one of them, is an evidence of such a "forbearance and long-suffering," that the addition of riches which the apostle puts to it (Rom. ii. 4), labors with an insufficiency clearly to display it.

III. Why God doth exercise so much patience.

1. To show himself appeasable. God did not declare by his patience to former ages, or any age, that he was appeased with them, or that they were in his favor ; but that he was appeasable, that he was not an implacable enemy, but that they might find him favorable to them, if they did seek after him. The continuance of the world by patience, and the bestowing many mercies by goodness, were not a natural revelation of the manner how he would be appeased : that was made known only by the prophets, and after the coming of Christ by the apostles ; and had indeed been intelligible in some sort to the whole world, had there been a faithfulness in Adam's posterity, to transmit the tradition of the first promise to succeeding generations. Had not the knowledge of that died by their carelessness and neglect, it had been easy to tell the reason of God's patience to be in order to the exhibition of the "Seed of the woman to bruise the serpent's head." They could not but naturally know themselves sinners, and worthy of death ; they might, by easy reflections upon themselves, collect that they were not in that comely and harmonious posture now, as they were when God first wrought them with his own finger, and placed them as his lieutenants in the world ; they knew they did grievously offend him ; this they were taught by the sprinklings of his judgments among them sometimes. And since he did not utterly root up mankind, his sparing patience was a prologue of some further favors, or pardoning grace to be displayed to the world by some methods of God yet unknown to them. Though the earth was something impaired by the curse after the fall, yet the main pillars of it stood ; the state of the natural motions of the creature was not changed ; the heavens remained in the same posture wherein they were created ; the sun, and moon, and other heavenly bodies, continued their usefulness and refreshing influences to man.

The heavens did still "declare the glory of God, day unto day" did "utter speech ; their line is gone throughout all the earth, and their words to the end of the world" (Ps. xix. 1—4) : which declared God to be willing to do good to his creatures, and were as so many legible letters or rudiments, whereby they might read his patience, and that a further design of favor to the world lay hid in that patience. Paul applies this to the preaching of the gospel (Rom. x. 18): "Have they not heard the word of God? yes, verily, their sound went into all the earth, and their words unto the end of the world." Redeeming grace could not be spelled out by them in a clear notion, but yet they did declare that which is the foundation of gospel mercy. Were not God patient, there were no room for a gospel mercy, so that the heavens declare the gospel, not formally, but fundamentally, in declaring the long-suffering of God, without which no gospel had been framed, or could have been expected. They could not but read in those things favorable inclinations towards them : and though they could not be ignorant that they deserved a mark of justice, yet seeing themselves supported by God, and beholding the regular motions of the heavens from day to day, and the revolutions of the seasons of the year, the natural conclusions they might draw from thence was, that God was placable ; since he behaved himself more as a tender friend, that had no mind to be at war with them, than an enraged enemy. The good things which he gave them, and the patience whereby he spared them, were no arguments of an implacable disposition ; and, therefore, of a disposition willing to be appeased. This is clearly the design of the apostle's arguing with the Lystrians, when they would have offered sacrifices to Paul (Acts, xiv. 17). When God " suffered all nations to walk in their own ways, he did not leave himself without witness, giving rain from heaven, and fruitful seasons." What were those witnesses of? not only of the being of a God, by their readiness to sacrifice to those that were not gods, only supposed to be so in their false imaginations ; but witnesses to the tenderness of God, that he had no mind to be severe with his creatures, but would allure them by ways of goodness. Had not God's patience tended to this end, to bring the world under another dispensation, the apostle's arguing from it had not been suitable to his design, which seems to be a hindering the sacrifices they intended for them, and a drawing them to embrace the gospel, and therefore preparing the way to it, by speaking of the patience and goodness of God to them, as an unquestionable testimony of the reconcilableness of good to them, by some sacrifice which was represented under the common notion of sacrifices.ᴾ These things were not witnesses of Christ, or syllables whereby they could spell out the redeeming person ; but witnesses that God was placable in his own nature. When man abused those noble faculties God had given him, and diverted them from the use and service God intended them for, God might have stripped man of them the first time that he misemployed them ; and it would have seemed most agreeable to his wisdom and justice, not to suffer himself to be abused, and the world to go contrary to its natural end. But since he did not level the world with its first nothing, but healed the world so favorably, it was evident that his patience pointed the world to a further design of mercy and goodness in him. To imagine that God had no other design in his long-

ᴾ Amyrald, Dissert. pp. 191, 192.

suffering but that of vengeance, had been a notion unsuitable to the goodness and wisdom of God. He would never have pretended himself to be a friend, if he had harbored nothing but enmity in his heart against them. It had been far from his goodness to give them a cause to suspect such a design in him, as his patience certainly did, had he not intended it. Had he preserved men only for punishment, it is more like he would have treated men as princes do those they reserve for the axe or halter, give them only things necessary to up-hold their lives till the day of execution, and not have bestowed upon them so many good things to make their lives delightful to them, nor have furnished them with so many excellent means to please their senses, and recreate their minds; it had been a mocking of them to treat them at that rate, if nothing but punishment had been intended towards them. If the end of it, to lead men to re-pentance, were easily intelligible by them, as the apostle intimates (Rom. ii. 4)—which is to be linked with the former chapter, a dis-course of the Gentiles: "Not knowing," saith he, "that the riches of his forbearance and goodness leads thee to repentance"—it also gives them some ground to hope for pardon. For what other argu-ment can more induce to repentance than an expectation of mercy upon a relenting, and acknowledging the crime? Without a design of pardoning grace, his patience would have been in a great mea-sure exercised in vain : for by mere patience God is not reconciled to a sinner, no more than a prince to a rebel, by bearing with him. Nor can a sinner conclude himself in the favor of God, no more than a rebel can conclude himself in the favor of his prince; only, this he may conclude, that there is some hopes he may have the grant of a pardon, since he hath time to sue it out. And so much did the patience of God naturally signify that he was of a reconcilable tem-per, and was willing men should sue out their pardon upon repent-ance; otherwise, he might have magnified his justice, and con-demned men by the law of works.

(2.) He therefore exercised so much patience to wait for men's repentance. All the notices and warnings that God gives men, of either public or personal calamities, is a continual invitation to re-pentance. This was the common interpretation the heathens made of extraordinary presages and prodigies, which showed as well the delays as the approaches of judgments. What other notion but this, that those warnings of judgments witness a slowness to anger, and a willingness to turn his arrows another way, should move them to multiply sacrifices, go weeping to their temples, sound out prayers to their gods, and show all those other testimonies of a repentance which their blind understandings hit upon? If a prince should sometimes in a light and gentle manner punish a criminal, and then relax it, and show him much kindness, and afterwards inflict upon him another kind of punishment as light as the former, and less than was due to his crime, what could the malefactor suspect by such a way of proceeding, but that the prince, by those gently-repeated chastisements, had a mind to move him to a regret for his crime?q And what other thoughts could men naturally have of God's con-

q Amyraldus, Moral. Tom. II. p. 186.

duct, that he should warn them of great judgments, send light afflictions, which are testimonies rather of a patience than of a severe wrath, but that it was intended to move them to a relenting, and a breaking off their sins by working righteousness? Though Divine patience does not, in the event, induce men to repentance, yet the natural tendency of such a treatment is to mollify men's hearts, to overcome their obstinacy; and no man hath any reason to judge otherwise of such a proceeding. The "long-suffering of God is salvation," saith Peter (2 Pet. iii. 15), *i. e.* hath a tendency to salvation, in its being a solicitation of men to the means of it; for the apostle cites Paul for the confirmation of it,—" Even as our beloved brother, Paul, hath written unto you," which must refer to Rom, ii. 4: "it leads to repentance," ἄγει, it conducts, which is more than barely to invite; it doth, as it were, take us by the hand, and point us to the way wherein we should go; and for this end it was exercised, not only towards the Jews, but towards the Gentiles, not only towards those that are within the pale of the church, and under the dews of the gospel, but to those that are in darkness, and in the shadow of death; for this discourse of the apostle was but an inference from what he had treated of in the first chapter concerning the idolatry and ingratitude of the Gentiles; since the Gentiles were to be punished for the abuse of it as well as the Jews, as he intimates, ver. 9. It is plain that his patience, which is exercised towards the idolatrous Gentiles, was to allure them to repentance as well as others; and it was a sufficient motive in itself to persuade them to a change of their vile and gross acts, to such as were morally good: and there was enough in God's dealing with them, and in that light they had to engage them to a better course than what they usually walked in; and though men do abuse God's long-suffering, to encourage their impenitence, and persisting in their crimes, yet that they cannot reasonably imagine that to be the end of God is evident; their own gripes of conscience would acquaint them that it is otherwise. They know that conscience is a principle that God hath given them, as well as understanding, and will, and other faculties; that God doth not approve of that which the voice of their own consciences, and of the consciences of all men under natural light, are utterly against: and if there were really, in this forbearance of God, an approbation of men's crimes, conscience could not, frequently and universally in all men, check them for them. What authority could conscience have to do it? But this it doth in all men: as the apostle (Rom. i. 22), " They know the judgment of God, that those that do such things," which he had mentioned before, "are worthy of death." In this thing the consciences of all men cannot err: they could not, therefore, conclude from hence God's approbation of their iniquities, but his desire that their hearts should be touched with a repentance for them. The "sin of Ephraim is hid" (Hos. xiii. 12, 13); *i. e.* God doth not presently take notice of it, to order punishment; he lays it in a secret place from the eye of his justice, that Ephraim might not be his unwise son, and "stay long in the place of the breaking forth of children;" *i. e.* that he should speedily reclaim himself, and not continue in the way of destruction. God hath no need to abuse any; he doth not lie to the sons of men; if he would have men perish, he could easily destroy them, and have done it long ago: he did not leave the woman Jezebel in being, nor lengthened out her time, but as a space to repent (Rev. ii. 21), that she might reflect upon her ways, and devote herself seriously to his service, and her own happiness. His patience stands between the offending creature and eternal misery a long time, that men might not foolishly throw away their souls, and be damned for their impenitency; by this he shows himself ready to receive men to mercy upon their return. To what purpose doth he invite men to repentance, if he intended to deceive them, and damn them after they repent?

3. He doth exercise patience for the propagation of mankind. If God punished every sin presently, there would not only be a period put to churches, but to the world; without patience, Adam had sunk into eternal anguish the first moment of his provocation, and the whole world of mankind, in his loins, had perished with him, and never seen the light. If this perfection had not interposed after the first sin, God had lost his end in the creation of the world, which he "created not in vain, but formed it to be inhabited" (Isa. xlv. 18). It had been inconsistent with the wisdom of God to make a world to be inhabited, and destroy it upon sin, when it had but two principal inhabitants in it; the reason of his making this earth had been insignificant; he had not had any upon earth to glorify him, without erecting another world, which might have proved as sinful and as quickly wicked as this; God should have always been pulling down down and rearing up, creating and annihilating; one world would have come after another, as wave after wave in the sea. His patience stepped in to support the honor of God, and the continuance of men, without which one had been in part impaired, and the other totally lost.

4. He doth exercise patience for the continuance of the church. If he be not patient toward sinners, what stock would there be for believers to spring up from? He bears with the provoking carriage of men, evil men, because out of their loins he intends to extract others, which he will form for the glory of his grace. He hath some unborn that belong to the election of grace, which are to be the seed of the worst of men; Jeroboam, the chief incendiary of the Israelites to idolatry, had an Abijah, in whom was found "some good thing towards the Lord God of Israel" (1 Kings, xiv. 13). Had Ahaz been snapped in the first act of his wickedness, the Israelites had wanted so good a prince and so good a man as Hezekiah, a branch of that wicked predecessor. What gardener cuts off the thorns from the rose-brush till he hath gathered the roses? and men do not use to burn all the crab-tree, but preserve a stock to engraft some sweet fruit upon. There could not have been a saint in the earth, nor, consequently, in heaven, had it not been for this perfection: he did not destroy the Israelites in the wilderness, that he might keep up a church among them, and not extinguish the whole seed that were heirs of the promises and covenant made with Abraham. Had God punished men for their sins as soon as they had been committed,

none would have lived to have been better, none could have continued in the world to honor him by their virtues. Manasseh had never been a convert, and many brutish men had never been changed from beasts to angels, to praise and acknowledge their Creator. Had Peter received his due recompense upon the denial of his Master, he had never been a martyr for him; nor had Paul been a preacher of the gospel; nor any else : and so the gospel had not shined in any part of the world. No seed would have been brought into Christ; Christ is beholding immediately to this attribute for all the seed he hath in the world: it is for his name's sake that he doth defer his anger; and for his praise that he doth refrain from "cutting us off" (Isa. xlviii. 9): and in the next chapter follows a prophecy of Christ. To overthrow mankind for sin, were to prevent the spreading a church in the world: a woman that is guilty of a capital crime, and lies under a condemning sentence, is reprieved from execution for her being with child; it is for the child's sake the woman is respited, not for her own : it is for the elect's sake, in the loins of transgressors, that they are a long time spared, and not for their own (Isa. lxv. 8): "As the new wine is found in a cluster, and one saith, Destroy it not, for a blessing is in it, so will I do for my servants' sakes, that I may not destroy them all;" as a husbandman spares a vine for some good clusters in it. He had spoke of vengeance before, yet he would reserve some from whom he would bring forth those that should be "inheritors of his mountains," that he might make up his church of Judea; Jerusalem being a mountainous place, and the type of the church in all ages. What is the reason he doth not level his thunder at the heads of those for whose destruction he receives so many petitions from the "souls under the altar?" (Rev. vi. 9, 10). Because God had others to write a testimony for him in their own blood, and perhaps out of the loins of those for whom vengeance was so earnestly supplicated; and God, as the master of a vessel, lies patiently at anchor, till the last passenger he expects be taken in.[r]

5. For the sake of his church he is patient to wicked men. The tares are patiently endured till the harvest, for fear in the plucking up the one, there might be some prejudice done to the other. Upon this account he spares some, who are worse than others whom he crusheth by signal judgments: the Jews had committed sins worse than Sodom, for the confirmation of which we have God's oath (Ezek. xvi. 48); and more by half than Samaria, or the ten tribes had done (ver 51): yet God spared the Jews, though he destroyed the Sodomites. What was the reason, but a larger remnant of righteous persons, more clusters of good grapes, were found among them than grew in Sodom? (Isa. i. 9). A few more righteous in Sodom had damped the fire and brimstone designed for that place, and a "remnant of such in Judea" was a bar to that fierceness of anger, which otherwise would have quickly consumed them. Had there been but "ten righteous in Sodom," Divine patience had still bound the arms of Justice, that it should not have prepared its brimstone, notwithstanding the clamor of the sins of the multitude. Judea was ripe for the sickle, but God would put a lock upon the torrent of his

[r] Smith on the Creed, p. 404.

judgments, that they should not flow down upon that wicked place, to make them a desolation and a curse, as long as tender-hearted Josiah lived, "who had humbled himself" at the threatening, and wept before the Lord (1 Kings, xxii. 19, 20). Sometimes he bears with wicked men, that they might exercise the patience of the saints (Rev. xiv. 12): the whole time of the "forbearance of antichrist" in all his intrusions into the temple of God, invasions of the rights of God, usurpations of the office of Christ, and besmearing himself with the blood of the saints, was to give them an opportunity of patience. God is patient towards the wicked, that by their means he might try the righteous. He burns not the wisp till he hath scoured his vessels; nor lays by the hammer, till he hath formed some of his matter into an excellent fashion. He useth the worst men as rods to correct his people, before he sweeps the twigs out of his house. God sometimes uses the thorns of the world, as a hedge to secure his church, sometimes as instruments to try and exercise it. Howsoever he useth them, whether for security or trial, he is patient to them for his church's advantage.

6. When men are not brought to repentance by his patience, he doth longer exercise it, to manifest the equity of his future justice upon them. As wisdom is justified by her obedient children, so is justice justified by the rebels against patience; the contempt of the latter is the justification of the former. The "apostles were unto God a sweet savor of Christ in them that perish," as well as in them that were saved by the acceptation of their message (2 Cor. ii. 15). Both are fragrant to God; his mercy is glorified by the one's acceptance of it, and his justice freed from any charge against it by the other's refusal. The cause of men's ruin cannot be laid upon God, who provided means for their salvation, and solicited their compliance with him. What reason can they have to charge the Judge with any wrong to them, who reject the tenders he makes, and who hath forborne them with so much patience, when he might have censured them by his righteous justice, upon the first crime they committed, or the first refusal of his gracious offers? "*Quanto Dei magis judicium tardum est tanto magis justum.*"[s] After the despising of patience, there can be no suspicion of an irregularity in the acts of justice. Man hath no reason to fall foul in his charge upon God, if he were punished for his own sin, considering the dignity of the injured person, and the meanness of himself, the offender; but his wrath is more justified when it is poured out upon those whom he hath endured with much long-suffering. There is no plea against the shooting of his arrows into those, for whom this voice hath been loud, and his arms open for their return. As patience, while it is exercised, is the silence of his justice, so when it is abused, it silenceth men's complaints against his justice. The "riches of his forbearance" made way for the manifesting the "treasures of his wrath." If God did but a little bear with the insolencies of men, and cut them off after two or three sins, he would not have opportunity to show either the power of his patience, or that of his wrath; but when he hath a right to punish for one sin, and yet bears with them for many,

* Minuc. Felix, p. 41.

and they will not be reclaimed, the sinner is more inexcusable, Divine justice less chargeable, and his wrath more powerful. (Rom. ix. 22), " What if God, willing to show his wrath, and to make his power known, endured with much long-suffering the vessels of wrath fitted for destruction?" The proper and immediate end of his long-suffering is to lead men to repentance; but after they have by their obstinacy fitted themselves for destruction, he bears longer with them, to "magnify his wrath" more upon them; and if it is not the *finis operantis,* it is at least the *finis operis,* where patience is abused. Men are apt to complain of God, that he deals hardly with them; the Israelites seem to charge God with too much severity, to cast them off, when so many promises were made to the fathers for their perpetuity and preservation, which is intimated, Hos. ii. 2. " Plead with your mother, plead:" by the double repetition of the word " plead;" do not accuse me of being false or too rigorous, but accuse your mother, your church, your magistracy, your ministry, for their spiritual fornications which have provoked me; for their נאפופיה, intimating the greatness of their sins by the reduplication of the word, " lest I strip her naked." I have borne with her under many provocations, and I have not yet taken away all her ornaments, or said to her, according to the rule of divorce, *Res tuas tibi habeto.* God answers their impudent charge: " She is not my wife, nor am I her husband;" he doth not say first, I am not her husband, but she is not my wife; she first withdrew from her duty by breaking the marriage covenant, and then I ceased to be her husband. No man shall be condemned, but he shall be convinced of the due desert of his sin, and the justice of God's proceeding. God will lay open men's guilt, and repeat the measures of his patience to justify the severity of his wrath (Hos. vii. 10), " Sins will testify to their face." What is in its own nature a preparation for glory, men by their obstinacy make a preparation for a more indisputable punishment. We see many evidences of God's forbearance here, in sparing men under those blasphemies which are audible, and those profane carriages which are visible, which would sufficiently justify an act of severity; yet when men's secret sins, both in heart and action, and the vast multitude of them, far surmounting what can arrive to our knowledge here, shall be discovered, how great a lustre will it add to God's bearing with them, and make his justice triumph without any reasonable demur from the sinner himself! He is long-suffering here, that his justice may be more public hereafter.

Use IV. For instruction. How is this patience of God abused! The Gentiles abused those testimonies of it, which were written in showers and fruitful seasons. No nation was ever stripped of it, under the most provoking idolatries, till after multiplied spurns at it: not a person among us but hath been guilty of the abuse of it. How have we contemned that which demands a reverence from us! How have we requited God's waitings with rebellions, while he hath continued urging and expecting our return! Saul relented at David's forbearing to revenge himself, when he had his prosecuting and industrious enemy in his power. (1 Sam. xxiv. 17), " Thou art more righteous than I; thou hast rewarded me good, whereas I have rewarded thee evil :" and shall we not relent at God's wonderful long-suffering, and silencing his anger so much? He could puff away our lives, but he will not, and yet we endeavor to strip him of his being, though we cannot.

1. Let us consider the ways, how slowness to anger is abused.

(1.) It is abused by misinterpretations of it, when men slander his patience to be only a carelessness and neglect of his providence ; as Averroes argued from his slowness to anger, a total neglect of the government of the lower world : or when men from his long-suffering charge him with impurity, as if his patience were a consent to their crimes ; and because he suffered them, without calling them to account, he were one of their partisans, and as wicked as themselves (Ps. l. 21): " Because I kept silence, thou thoughtest I was altogether such a one as thyself." His silence makes them conclude him to be an abettor of, and a consort in their sins ; and think him more pleased with their iniquity than their obedience. Or when they will infer from his forbearance a want of his omniscience; because he suffers their sins, they imagine he forgets them (Ps. x. 11): " He hath said in his heart, God hath forgotten :" thinking his patience proceeds not from the sweetness of his nature, but a weakness of his mind. How base is it, instead of admitting him, to disparage him for it ; and because he stands in so advantageous a posture towards us, not to own the choicest prerogatives of his Deity! This is to make a perfection, so useful to us, to shadow and extinguish those others, which are the prime flowers of his crown.

(2.) His patience is abused by continuing in a course of sin under the influences of it. How much is it the practical language of men, Come, let us commit this or that iniquity; since Divine patience hath suffered worse than this at our hands! Nothing is remitted to their sensual pleasures, and eagerness in them. How often did the Israelites repeat their murmurings against him, as if they would put his patience to the utmost proof, and see how far the line of it could extend! They were no sooner satisfied in one thing, but they quarrelled with him about another, as if he had no other attribute to put in motion against them. They tempted him as often as he relieved them, as though the declaration of his name to Moses (Exod. xxxiv.), "to be a God gracious, and long-suffering," had been intended for no other purpose but a protection of them in their rebellions. Such a sort of men the prophet speaks of, that were " settled in their lees," or dregs (Zeph. i. 12): they were congealed, and frozen in their successful wickedness. Such an abuse of Divine patience is the very dregs of sin ; God chargeth it highly upon the Jews (Isa. lvii. 11): " I have held my peace, even of old, and thou fearest me not;" my silence made thee confident, yea, impudent in thy sin.

(3.) His patience is abused by repeating sin, after God hath, by an act of his patience, taken off some affliction from men. As metals melted in the fire remain fluid under the operations of the flames, yet when removed from the fire, they quickly return to their former hardness, and sometimes grow harder than they were before ; so men who, in their afflictions, seem to be melted, like Ahab confess their sins, lie prostrate before God, and seek him early ; yet, if they be brought from under the power of their afflictions, they return to their old nature, and are as stiff against God, and resist the blows of the Spirit as much as they did before. They think they have a new stock of patience to sin upon. Pharaoh was somewhat thawed under judgments, and frozen again under forbearance (Exod. ix. 27, 34). Many will howl when God strikes them, and laugh at him when he forbears them. Thus that patience which should melt us, doth often harden us, which is not an effect natural to his patience, but natural to our abusing corruption.

(4.) His patience is abused, by taking encouragement from it to mount to greater degrees of sin. Because God is slow to anger, men are more fierce in sin, and not only continue in their old rebellions, but heap new upon them. If he spare them for three transgressions, they will commit four, as is intimated in the first and second of Amos; "Men's hearts are fully set in them to do evil, because sentence against an evil work is not speedily executed" (Eccles. viii. 11). Their hearts are more desperately bent; before they had some waverings, and pull-backs, but after a fair sunshine of Divine patience, they entertain more unbridled resolutions, and pass forward with more liberty and licentiousness. They make his long-suffering subservient to turn out all those little relentings and regrets they had before, and banish all thoughts of barring out a temptation. No encouragement is given to men by God's patience, but they force it by their presumption. They invert God's order, and bind themselves stronger to iniquity by that which should bind them faster to their duty. A happy escape at sea makes men go more confidently into the deeps afterward. Thus we deal with God as debtors do with good-natured creditors : because they do not dun them for what they owe, they take encouragement to run more upon the score, till the sum amounts above their ability of payment.

But let it be considered, 1st. That this abuse of patience is a high sin. As every act of forbearance obligeth us to duty, so every act of it abused, increaseth our guilt. The more frequent its solicitations of us have been, the deeper aggravations our sin receives by it. Every sin, after an act of Divine patience, contracts a blacker guilt. The sparing us after the last sin we committed, was a superadded act of long-suffering, and a laying out more of his riches upon us : and, therefore, every new act committed is a despite against greater riches expended, and greater cost upon us, and against his preserving us from the hand of justice for the last transgression. It is disingenuous not to have a due resentment of so much goodness, and base to injure him the more, because he doth not right himself. Shall he receive the more wrongs from us, by how much the sweeter he is to us? No man's conscience but will tell him it is vile to prefer the satisfaction of a sordid lust, before the counsel of a God of so gracious a disposition. The sweeter the nature, the fouler is the injury that is done unto it. 2d. It is dangerous to abuse his patience. Contempt of kindness is most irksome to an ingenuous spirit; and he is worthy to have the arrows of God's indignation lodged in his heart, who despiseth the riches of his long-suffering. For,

[1.] The time of patience will have an end. Though his Spirit strives with man, yet it shall "not always strive" (Gen. vi. 3). Though there be a time wherein Jerusalem might "know the things that concerned her peace," yet there is another period wherein they should be "hid from her eyes" (Luke xix. 43): "O that thou hadst known in this thy day!" Nations have their day, and persons have their day; and the day of most persons is shorter than the day of nations. Jerusalem had her day of forty years; but how many particular persons were taken off before the last or middle hours of that day were arrived! "Forty years was God grieved" with the generation of the Israelites (Heb. iii. 11). One carcass dropped after another in that limited time, and at the end not a man but fell under the judicial stroke, except Caleb and Joshua. One hundred and twenty years was the term set to the mass of the old world, but not to every man in the old world; some fell while the ark was preparing, as well as the whole stock when the ark was completed. Though he be patient with most, yet he is not in the same degree with all; every sinner hath his time of sinning, beyond which he shall proceed no further, be his lusts never so impetuous, and his affections never so imperious. The time of his patience is, in Scripture, set forth sometimes by years; three years he came to find fruit on the fig-tree: sometimes by days; some men's sins are sooner ripe, and fall. There is a measure of sin (Jer. ii. 13), which is set forth by the ephah (Zech. v. 8), which, when it is filled, is sealed up, and a weight of lead cast upon the mouth of it. When judgments are preparing, once and twice the Lord is prevailed with by the intercession of the prophet: the prepared grass-hoppers are not sent to devour, and the kindled fire is not blown up to consume (Amos, vii. 1—8). But at last God takes the plumb-line, to suit and measure punishment to their sin, and would not pass by them any more; and when their sin was ripe, represented by a "basket of summer-fruit," God would withhold his hand no longer, but brought such a day upon them, wherein "the songs of the Temple should be howlings, and dead bodies be in every place" (Amos, viii. 2, 3). He lays by any further thoughts of patience to speed their ruin. God had borne long with the Israelites, and long it was before he gave them up. He would first brake the "bow in Jezreel" (Hos. i. 5); take away the strength of the nation by the death of Zechariah, the last of Jehu's race, which introduced civil dissentions and ambitious murders, for the throne, whereby in weakening one part they weakened the whole; or, as some think, alluding to Tiglah Pilezar, who carried captive two tribes and a half. If this would not reclaim them, then follows "Lo-ruhamah, I will not have mercy," I will sweep them out of the land (ver. 6). If they did not repent, they should be "Lo-ammi" (ver. 9), "You are not my people," and "I will not be your God." They should be discovenanted, and stripped of all federal relation. Here patience forever withdrew from them, and wrathful anger took its place. And, for particular persons, the time of life, whether shorter or longer, is the only time of long-suffering. It hath no other stage than the present state of things to act upon; there is none else to be expected after but giving account of what hath been done in the body, not of anything done after the soul is fled from the body:

the time of patience ends with the first moment of the soul's departure from the body. This time only is the " day of salvation ;" *i. e.* the day wherein God offers it, and the day wherein God waits for our acceptance of it : it is at his pleasure to shorten or lengthen our day, not at ours ; it is not our long-suffering, but his ; he hath the command of it.

[2.] God hath wrath to punish, as well as patience to bear. He hath a fury to revenge the outrages done to his meekness : when his messages of peace, sent to reclaim men, are slighted, his sword shall be whetted, and his instruments of war prepared (Hos. v. 3) : " Blow ye the cornet in Gibeah, and the trumpet in Ramah." As he deals gently, like a father, so he can punish capitally as a judge : though he holds his peace for a long time, yet at last he will go forth like a mighty man, and stir up jealousy, as a man of war, to cut in pieces his enemies. It is not said he hath no anger, but that he is "slow to anger," but sharp in it : he hath a sword to cut, and a bow to shoot, and arrows to pierce (Ps. xii. 13) : though he be long drawing the one out of its scabbard, and long fitting the other to his bow, yet, when they are ready, he strikes home, and hits the mark : though he hath a time of patience, yet he hath also a "day of rebuke" (Hos. v. 9) ; though patience overrules justice, by suspending it, yet justice will at last overrule patience, by an utter silencing it. God is Judge of the whole earth to right men, yet he is no less Judge of the injuries he receives to right himself. Though God awhile was pressed with the murmurings of the Israelites, after their coming out of Egypt, and seemed desirous to give them all satisfaction upon their unworthy complaints, yet, when they came to open hostility, in setting a golden calf in his throne, he commissions the " Levites to kill every man his brother and companion in the camp" (Exod. xxxii. 27) : and how desirous soever he was to content them before, they never murmured afterwards but they severely smarted for it. When once he hath begun to use his sword, he sticks it up naked, that it might be ready for use upon every occasion. Though he hath feet of lead, yet he hath hands of iron. It was long that he supported the peevishness of the Jews, but at last he captived them by the arms of the Babylonians, and laid them waste by the power of the Romans. He planted, by the apostles, churches in the east ; and when his goodness and long-suffering prevailed not with them, he tore them up by the roots. What Christians are to be found in those once famous parts of Asia but what are overgrown with much error and ignorance ?

[3.] The more his patience is abused, the sharper will be the wrath he inflicts. As his wrath restrained makes his patience long, so his compassions restrained will make his wrath severe ; as he doth transcend all creatures in the measures of the one, so he doth transcend all creatures in the sharpness of the other. Christ is described with "feet of brass," as if they burned in a furnace (Rev. i. 15), slow to move, but heavy to crush, and hot to burn. His wrath loseth nothing by delay ; it grows the fresher by sleeping, and strikes with greater strength when it awakes : all the time men are abusing his patience, God is whetting his sword, and the longer it is whetting the sharper will be the edge ; the longer he is fetching his blow, the smarter it will be. The heavier the cannons are, the more difficultly are they drawn to the besieged town; but, when arrived, they recompense the slowness of their march by the fierceness of their battery. "Because I have purged thee," *i. e.* used means for thy reformation, and waited for it, "and thou wast not purged, thou shalt not be purged from thy filthiness any more, till I have caused my fury to rest upon thee: I will not go back, neither will I spare; according to thy ways, and according to thy doings, shall they judge thee" (Ezek. xxiv. 13, 14). God will spare as little then as he spared much before; his wrath shall be as raging upon them as the sea of their wickedness was within them. When there is a bank to forbid the irruption of the streams, the waters swell; but when the bank is broke, or the lock taken away, they rush with the greater violence, and ravage more than they would have done had they not met with a stop: the longer a stone is in falling, the more it bruiseth and grinds to powder. There is a greater treasure of wrath laid up by the abuses of patience: every sin must have a just recompense of reward; and therefore every sin, in regard of its aggravations, must be more punished than a sin in the singleness and simplicity of its own nature. As treasures of mercy are kept by God for us, "he keeps mercy for thousands;" so are treasures of wrath kept by him to be expended, and a time of expense there must be: patience will account to justice all the good offices it hath done the sinner, and demand to be righted by justice; justice will take the account from the hands of patience, and exact a recompense for every disingenuous injury offered to it. When justice comes to arrest men for their debts, patience, mercy, and goodness, will step in as creditors, and clap their actions upon them, which will make the condition so much more deplorable.

[4.] When he puts an end to his abused patience, his wrath will make quick and sure work. He that is "slow to anger" will be swift in the execution of it. The departure of God from Jerusalem is described with "wings and wheels" (Ezek. xi. 23). One stroke of his hand is irresistible; he that hath spent so much time in waiting needs but one minute to ruin; though it be long ere he draws his sword out of his scabbard, yet, when once he doth it, he despatcheth men at a blow. Ephraim, or the ten tribes, had a long time of patience and prosperity, but now shall a "month devour him with his portion" (Hos. v. 7). One fatal month puts a period to the many years' peace and security of a sinful nation; his arrows wound suddenly (Ps. lxiv. 7); and while men are about to fill their bellies, he casts the fruits of his wrath upon them (Job, xx. 23), like thunder out of a cloud, or a bullet out of a cannon, that strikes dead before it is heard. God deals with sinners as enemies do with a town, batter it not by planted guns, but secretly undermines and blows up the walls, whereby they involve the garrison in a sudden ruin, and carry the town. God spared the Amalekites a long time after the injury committed against the Israelites, in their passage out of Egypt to Canaan; but when he came to reckon with them, he would waste them in a trice, and make an utter consumption of them (1 Sam. xv. 2, 3). He describes himself by a "travailing woman" (Isa. xxiv. 14), that hath borne long in her womb, and at last sends forth her birth with strong cries. Though he hath held his peace, been still, and refrained himself, yet, at last, he will destroy and devour at once: the Ninevites, spared in the time of Jonah for their repentance, are, in nature, threatened with a certain and total ruin, when God should come to bring them to an account for his length and patience, so much abused by them. Though God endured the murmuring Israelites so long in the wilderness, yet he paid them off at last, and took away the rebels in his wrath: he uttered their sentence with an irreversible oath, that "none of them should enter into his rest;" and he did as surely execute it as he had solemnly sworn it.

[5.] Though he doth defer his visible wrath, yet that very delay may be more dreadful than a quick punishment. He may forbear striking, and give the reins to the hardness and corruption of men's hearts; he may suffer them to walk in their own counsels, without any more striving with them, whereby they make themselves fitter fuel for his vengeance. This was the fate of Israel when they would not hearken to his voice; he "gave them up to their own hearts' lusts, and they walked in their own counsels" (Ps. lxxxi. 12). Though his sparing them had the outward aspect of patience, it was a wrathful one, and attended with spiritual judgments; thus many abusers of patience may still have their line lengthened, and the candle of prosperity to shine upon their heads, that they may increase their sins, and be the fitter mark at last for his arrows; they swim down the stream of their own sensuality with a deplorable security, till they fall into an unavoidable gulf, where, at last, it will be a great part of their hell to reflect on the length of Divine patience on earth, and their inexcusable abuse of it.

2. It informs us of the reason why he lets the enemies of his church oppress it, and defers his promise of the deliverance of it. If he did punish them presently, his holiness and justice would be glorified, but his power over himself in his patience would be obscured. Well may the church be content to have a perfection of God glorified, that is not like to receive any honor in another world by any exercise of itself. If it were not for this patience, he were incapable to be the Governor of a sinful world; he might, without it, be the Governor of an innocent world, but not of a criminal one; he would be the destroyer of the world, but not the orderer and disposer of the extravagancies and sinfulness of the world. The interest of his wisdom, in drawing good out of evil, would not be served, if he were not clothed with this perfection as well as with others. If he did presently destroy the enemies of his church upon the first oppression, his wisdom in contriving, and his power in accomplishing deliverance against the united powers of hell and earth, would not be visible, no, nor that power in preserving his people unconsumed in the furnace of affliction. He had not got so great a name in the rescue of his Israel from Pharaoh, had he thundered the tyrant into destruction upon his first edicts against the innocent. If he were not patient to the most violent of men, he might seem to be cruel. But when he offers peace to them under their rebellions, waits that they may be members of his church,

rather than enemies to it, he frees himself from any such imputation, even in the judgment of those that shall feel most of his
wrath; it is this renders the equity of his justice unquestionable,
and the deliverance of his people righteous in the judgment of
those from whose fetters they are delivered. Christ reigns in the
midst of his enemies, to show his power over himself, as well as
over the heads of his enemies, to show his power over his rebels. And though he retards his promise, and suffers a great interval of time between the publication and performance, sometimes
years, sometimes ages to pass away, and little appearance of any
preparation, to show himself a God of truth; it is not that he hath
forgotten his word, or repents that ever he passed it, or sleeps in a
supine neglect of it: but that men might not perish, but bethink
themselves, and come as friends into his bosom, rather than be
crushed as enemies under his feet (2 Pet. iii. 9): "The Lord is not
slack concerning his promise, but is long-suffering to us-ward, not
willing that any should perish, but that all should come to repentance." Hereby he shows, that he would be rather pleased with the
conversion, than the destruction, of men.

3. We see the reason why sin is suffered to remain in the regenerate; to show his patience towards his own; for since this attribute
hath no other place of appearance but in this world, God takes opportunity to manifest it; because, at the close of the world, it will
remain closed up in the Deity, without any further operation. As
God suffers a multitude of sins in the world, to evidence his patience to the wicked, so he suffers great remainders of sin in his
people, to show his patience to the godly. His sparing mercy is admirable, before their conversion, but more admirable in bearing with
them after so high an obligation as the conferring upon them special
converting grace.

Use 2. Of comfort. It is a vast comfort to any when God is pacified towards them; but it is some comfort to all, that God is yet patient towards them, though but very little to a refractory sinner.
His continued patience to all, speaks a possibility of the care of all,
would they not stand against the way of their recovery. It is a
terror that God hath anger, but it is a mitigation of that terror that
God is slow to it; while his sword is in his sheath there is some
hopes to prevent the drawing of it: alas! if he were all fire and
sword upon sin, what would become of us? We should find nothing else but overflowing deluges, or sweeping pestilences, or perpetual flashes of Sodom's fire and brimstone from heaven. He dooms
us not presently to execution, but gives us a long breathing time
after the crime, that by retiring from our iniquities, and having recourse to his mercy, he may be withheld forever from signing a warrant against us, and change his legal sentence into an evangelical
pardon. It is a special comfort to his people, that he is a "sanctuary to them" (Ezek. xi. 16); a place of refuge, a place of spiritual
communications; but it is some refreshment to all in this life, that
he is a defence to them: for so is his patience called (Numb. xiv.
9): "Their defence is departed from them;" speaking to the
Israelites, that they should not be afraid of the Canaanites, for

their defence is departed from them. God is no longer patient to them, since their sins be full and ripe. Patience, as long as it lasts, is a temporary defence to those that are under the wing of it; but to the believer it is a singular comfort; and God is called the "God of patience and consolation" in one breath (Rom. xv. 5): "The God of patience and consolation grant you to be like-minded;" all interpreters understand it effectively. The God that inspires you with patience, and cheers you with comfort, grant this to you. Why may it not be understood formally, of the patience belonging to the nature of God? and though it be expressed in the way of petition, yet it might also be proposed as a pattern for imitation, and so suits very well to the exhortation laid down (ver. 1), which was to "bear with the infirmities of the weak," which he presseth them to (ver. 3) by the example of Christ; and (ver. 5) by the patience of God to them, and so they are very well linked together. "God of patience and consolation" may well be joined, since patience is the first step of comfort to the poor creature. If it did not administer some comfortable hopes to Adam, in the interval between his fall and God's coming to examine him, I am sure it was the first discovery of any comfort to the creature, after the sweeping the destroying deluge out of the world (Gen. ix. 21); after the "savor of Noah's sacrifice," representing the great Sacrifice which was to be in the world, had ascended up to God, the return from him is a publication of his forbearing to punish any more in such a manner: and though he found man no better than he was before, and the imaginations of men's hearts as evil as before the deluge, that he would not again smite every living thing, as he had done. This was the first expression of comfort to Noah, after his exit from the ark; and declares nothing else but the continuance of patience to the new world above what he had shown to the old.

1. It is a comfort, in that it is an argument of his grace to his people. If he hath so rich a patience to exercise towards his enemies, he hath a greater treasure to bestow upon his friends. Patience is the first attribute which steps in for our salvation, and therefore called "salvation" (2 Pet. iii. 15). Something else is therefore built upon it, and intended by it, to those that believe. Those two letters of his name, "a God keeping mercy for thousands, and forgiving iniquity, transgressions and sin," follow the other letter of his long-suffering in the proclamation (Exod. xxxiv. 6, 7). He is "slow to anger," that he may be merciful, that men may seek, and receive their pardon. If he be long-suffering, in order to be a pardoning God, he will not be wanting in pardoning those who answer the design of his forbearance of them. You would not have had sparing mercy to improve, if God would have denied you saving mercy upon the improvement of his sparing goodness. If he hath so much respect to his enemies that provoke him, as to endure them with much long-suffering, he will surely be very kind to those that obey him, and conform to his will. If he hath much long-suffering to those that are "fitted for destruction" (Rom. ix. 22), he will have a muchness of mercy for those that are prepared for glory by faith and re-

pentance. It is but a natural conclusion a gracious soul may make, —If God had not a mind to be appeased towards me, he would not have had a mind to forbear me; but since he hath forborne me, and given me a heart to see, and answer the true end of that forbearance, I need not question, but that sparing mercy will end in saving, since it finds that repentance springing up in me, which that patience conducted me to.

2. His patience is a ground to trust in his promise. If his slowness to anger be so great when his precept is slighted, his readiness to give what he hath promised will be as great when his promise is believed. If the provocations of them meet with such an unwillingness to punish them, faith in him will meet with the choicest embraces from him. He was more ready to make the promise of redemption after man's apostasy, than to execute the threatening of the law. He doth still witness a greater willingness to give forth the fruits of the promise, than to pour out the vials of his curses. His slowness to anger is an evidence still, that he hath the same disposition, which is no slight cordial to faith in his word.

3. It is a comfort in infirmities. If he were not patient, he could not bear with so many peevishnesses and weaknesses in the hearts of his own. If he be patient to the grosser sins of his enemies, he will be no less to the lighter infirmities of his people. When the soul is a bruised reed, that can emit no sound at all, or one very harsh and ungrateful, he doth not break it in pieces, and fling it away in disdain, but waits to see whether it will fully answer his pains, and be brought to a better frame and sweeter note. He brings them not to account for every slip, but, "as a father, spares his son that serves him" (Mal. iii. 17). It is a comfort to us in our distracted services; for were it not for this slowness to anger, he would stifle us in the midst of our prayers, wherein there are as many foolish thoughts to disgust him, as there are petitions to implore him. The patientest angels would hardly be able to bear with the follies of good men in acts of worship.

Use 3. For exhortation.

1. Meditate often on the patience of God. The devil labors for nothing more than to deface in us the consideration and memory of this perfection. He is an envious creature; and since it hath reached out itself to us and not to him, he envies God the glory of it, and man the advantage of it: but God loves to have the volumes of it studied, and daily turned over by us. We cannot without an inexcusable wilfulness miss the thoughts of it, since it is visible in every bit of bread, and breath of air in ourselves, and all about us.

(1.) The frequent consideration of his patience would render God highly amiable to us. It is a more endearing argument than his mere goodness; his goodness to us as creatures, endowing us with such excellent faculties, furnishing us with such a commodious world, and bestowing upon us so many attendants for our pleasure and service, and giving us a lordship over his other works, deserves our affection: but his patience to us as sinners, after we have merited the greatest wrath, shows him to be of a sweeter disposition than creating goodness to unoffending creatures; and, consequently, speaks a greater love in him, and bespeaks a greater affection from us. His creating goodness discovered the majesty of his Being, and the greatness of his mind, but this the sweetness and tenderness of his nature. In this patience he exceeds the mildness of all creatures to us; and therefore should be enthroned in our affections above all other creatures. The consideration of this would make us affect him for his nature as well as for his benefits.

(2.) The consideration of his patience would make us frequent and serious in the exercise of repentance. In its nature it leads to it, and the consideration of it would engage us to it, and melt us in the exercise of it. Could we deeply think of it without being touched with a sense of the kindness of our forbearing Creditor and Governor? Could we gaze upon it, nay, could we glance upon it, without relenting at our offending one of so mild a nature, without being sensibly affected, that he hath preserved us so long from being loaded with those chains of darkness, under which the devils groan? This forbearance hath good reason to make sin and sinners ashamed. That you are in being, is not for want of advantages enough in his hand against you; many a forfeiture you have made, and many an engagement you have broke; he hath scarce met with any other dealing from us, than what had treachery in it. Whatsoever our sincerity is, we have no reason to boast of it, when we consider what mixtures there are in it, and what swarms of base motions taint it. Hath he not lain pressed and groaning under our sins, as a "cart is pressed with sheaves" (Amos, ii. 13), when one shake of himself, as Sampson, might have rid him of the burden, and dismissed us in his fury into hell? If we should often ask our consciences why have we done thus and thus against so mild a God, would not the reflection on it put us to the blush? If men would consider, that such a time they provoked God to his face, and yet not have felt his sword; such a time they blasphemed him, and made a reproach of his name, and his thunder did not stop their motion; such a time they fell into an abominable brutishness, yet he kept the punishment of devils, the unclean spirits, from reaching them; such a time he bore an open affront from them, when they scoffed at his word, and he did not send a destruction, and laugh at it: would not such a meditation work some strange kind of relentings in men? What if we should consider, that we cannot do a sinful act without the support of his concurring Providence? We cannot see, hear, move, without his concourse. All creatures we use for our necessity or pleasure, are supported by him in the very act of assisting to pleasure us; and when we abuse those creatures against him, which he supports for our use, how great is his patience to bear with us, that he doth not annihilate those creatures, or at least embitter their use! What issue could reasonably be expected from this consideration, but, "O wretched man that I am, to serve myself of God's power to affront him, and of his long-suffering to abuse him?" O infinite patience to employ that power to preserve me, that might have been used to punish me! He is my Creator, I could not have a being without him, and yet I offend him! He is my Preserver, I cannot maintain my being without him, and yet I affront him! Is this a worthy requital of God (Deut. xxxii. 6), "Do you thus requite the Lord?" would be the heart-breaking reflection. How would it give men a fuller prospect of the depravation of their nature than anything else; that their corruption should be so deep and strong, that so much patience could not overcome it! It would certainly make a man ashamed of his nature as well as his actions.

(3.) The consideration of his patience would make us resent more the injuries done by others to God. A patient sufferer, though a deserving sufferer, attracts the pity of men, that have a value for any virtue, though clouded with a heap of vice. How much more should we have a concern of God, who suffers so many abuses from others! and be grieved, that so admirable a patience should be slighted by men, who solely live by and under the daily influence of it! The impression of this would make us take God's part, as it is usual with men to take the part of good dispositions that lie under oppression.

(4.) It would make us patient under God's hand. His slowness to anger and his forbearance is visible, in the very strokes we feel in this life. We have no reason to murmur against him, who gives us so little cause, and in the greatest afflictions gives us more occasion of thankfulness than of repining. Did not slowness to the extremest anger moderate every affliction, it had been a scorpion instead of a rod. We have reason to bless Him, who, from his long-suffering, sends temporal sufferings, where eternal are justly due. (Ezra, ix. 13), "Thou hast punished us less than our iniquities do deserve." His indulgences towards us have been more than our corrections, and the length of his patience hath exceeded the sharpness of his rod. Upon the account of his long-suffering, our mutinies against God have as little to excuse them, as our sins against him have to deserve his forbearance. The consideration of this would show us more reason to repine at our own repinings, than at any of his smarter dealings; and the consideration of this would make us submissive under the judgments we expect. His undeserved patience hath been more than our merited judgments can possibly be thought to be. If we fear the removal of the gospel for a season, as we have reason to do, we should rather bless him, that by his waiting patience, he hath continued it so long, than murmur, that he threatens to take it away so late. He hath borne with us many a year, since the light of it was rekindled, when our ancestors had but six years' of patience between the rise of Edward the Sixth, and the ascent of Queen Mary, to the crown.

2. Exhortation is to admire and stand astonished at his patience, "and bless him for it." If you should have defiled your neighbor's bed, or sullied his reputation, or rifled his goods, would he have withheld his vengeance, unless he had been too weak to execute it? We have done worse to God than we can do to man, and yet he draws not that sword of wrath out of the scabbard of his patience, to sheath it in our hearts. It is not so much a wonder that any judgments are sent, as that there are no more, and sharper. That the world shall be fired at last, is not a thing so strange, as that fire doth not come down every day upon some part of it. Had the disciples, that saw such excellent patterns of mildness from their

Master, and were so often urged to learn of him that was lowly and meek, the government of the world, it had been long since turned into ashes, since they were too forward to desire him to open his magazine of judgments, and kindle a fire to consume a Samaritan village, for a slight affront in comparison of what he received from others, and afterwards from themselves in their forsaking of him (Luke, ix. 52—54). We should admire and praise that here which shall be praised in heaven; though patience shall cease as to its exercise after the consummation of the world, it shall not cease from receiving the acknowledgments of what it did, when it traversed the stage of this earth. If the name of God be glorified, and acknowledged in heaven, no question but this will also; since long-suffering is one of his Divine titles, a letter in his name, as well as "merciful, and gracious, abundant in goodness and truth." And there is good reason to think that the patience exercised towards some, before converting grace was ordered to seize upon them, will bear a great part in the anthems of heaven. The greater his long-suffering hath been to men, that lay covered with their own dung, a long time before they were freed by grace from their filth; the more admiringly and loudly they will cry up his mercy to them, after they have passed the gulf, and see a deserved hell at a distance from them, and many in that place of torment who never had the tastes of so much forbearance. If mercy will be praised there, that which began the alphabet of it, cannot be forgot. If Paul speak so highly of it in a damping world, and under the pull-backs of a "body of death," as he doth 1 Tim. i. 16, 17: "For this cause I obtained mercy; that Christ might show forth all long-suffering. Now unto the King eternal, immortal, invisible, the only wise God, be honor, and glory, for ever and ever. Amen." No doubt, but he will have a higher note for it, when he is surrounded with a heavenly flame, and freed from all remains of dulness. Shall it be praised above, and have we no notes for it here below? Admire Christ, too, who sued out your reprieve upon the account of his merit. As mercy acts not upon any but in Christ, so neither had patience borne with any but in Christ. The pronouncing the arrest of judgment (Gen. viii. 21) was when "God smelled a sweet savor from Noah's sacrifice," not from the beasts offered, but the anti-typical sacrifice represented. That we may be raised to bless God for it, let us consider,

(1.) The multitude of our provocations. Though some have blacker guilt than others, and deeper stains, yet let none wipe his mouth, but rather imagine himself to have but little reason to bless it. Are not all our offences as many as there have been minutes in our lives? All the moments of our continuance in the world have been moments of his patience and our ingratitude. Adam was punished for one sin, Moses excluded Canaan for a passionate unbelieving word. Ananias and Sapphira lost their lives for one sin against the Holy Ghost. One sin sullied the beauty of the world, defaced the works of God, and cracked heaven and earth in pieces, had not infinite satisfaction been proposed to the provoked Justice by the Redeemer; and not one sin committed, but is of the same venomous nature. How many of those contradictions against himself hath he borne with! Had we been only unprofitable to him, his forbearance of us had been miraculous; but how much doth it exceed a miracle, and lift itself above the meanness of a conjunction with such an epithet, since we have been provoking! Had there been no more than our impudent or careless rushings into his presence in worship; had they been only sins of omission, and sins of ignorance, it had been enough to have put a stand to any further operations of this perfection towards us. But add to those, sins of commission, sins against knowledge, sins against spiritual motions, sins against repeated resolutions, and pressing admonitions, the neglects of all the opportunities of repentance; put them all together, and we can as little recount them, as the sands on the sea-shore. But what, do I only speak of particular men? View the whole world, and if our own iniquities render it an amazing patience, what a mighty supply will be made to it in all the numerous and weighty provocations, under which he hath continued the world for so many revolutions of years and ages! Have not all those pressed into his presence with a loud cry, and demanded a sentence from justice? yet hath not the Judge been overcome by the importunity of our sins? Were the devils punished for one sin, a proud thought, and that not committed against the blood of Christ, as we have done numberless times; yet hath not God made us partakers in their punishment, though we have exceeded them in the quality of their sin. O admirable patience! that would bear with me under so many, while he would not bear with the sinning angels for one.[t]

(2.) Consider how mean things we are, who have provoked him. What is man but a vile thing, that a God, abounding with all riches, should take care of so abject a thing, much more to bear so many affronts from such a drop of matter, such a nothing creature! That he that hath anger at his command, as well as pity, should endure such a detestable, deformed creature by sin, to fly in his face! "What is man, that thou art mindful of him?" (Ps. viii.) אֱנוֹשׁ, miserable, incurable man, derived from a word, that signifies to be incurably sick. Man is "Adam," earth from his earthly original, and "Enoch," incurable from his corruption. Is it not worthy to be admired, that a God of infinite glory should wait on such Adams, worms of earth, and be, as it were, a servant, and attendant to such Enochs, sickly and peevish creatures?

(3.) Consider who it is that is thus patient. He it is that, with one breath, could turn heaven and earth, and all the inhabitants of both, into nothing; that could, by one thunderbolt, have razed up the foundations of a cursed world. He that wants not instruments without to ruin us, that can arm our own consciences against us, and can drown us in our own phlegm; and, by taking out one pin from our bodies, cause the whole frame to fall asunder. Besides, it is a God that, while he suffers the sinner, hates the sin more than all the holy men upon earth, or angels in heaven, can do; so that his patience for a minute transcends the patience of all creatures, from the creation to the dissolution of the world: because it is the patience of a

t Pont. Part I. p. 42.

God, infinitely more sensible to the cursed quality of sin, and infinitely more detesting it.

(4.) Consider how long he hath forborne his anger. A reprieve for a week or a month is accounted a great favor in civil states; the civil law enacts, "That if the emperor commanded a man to be condemned, the execution was to be deferred thirty days: because in that time the prince's anger might be appeased."[u] But how great a favor is it to be reprieved thirty years for many offences, every one of which deserves death more at the hands of God than any offence can at the hands of man! Paul was, according to the common account, but about thirty years old at his conversion; and how much doth he elevate Divine long-suffering! Certainly there are many who have more reason, as having larger quantities of patience cut out to them, who have lived to see their own gray hairs in a rebellious posture against God, before grace brought them to a surrender. We were all condemned in the womb; our lives were forfeited the first moment of our breath, but patience hath stopped the arrest; the merciful Creditor deserves to have acknowledgment from us, who hath laid by his bond so many years without putting it in suit against us. Many of your companions in sin have perhaps been surprised long ago, and haled to an eternal prison; nothing is remaining of them but their dust, and the time is not yet come for your funeral. Let it be considered, that that God that would not wait upon the fallen angels one instant after their sin, nor give them a moment's space of repentance, hath prolonged the life of many a sinner in the world to innumerable moments, to 420,000 minutes in the space of a year, to 8,400,000 minutes in the space of twenty years. The damned in hell would think it a great kindness to have but a year's, month's, nay, day's respite, as a space to repent in.

(5.) Consider also, how many have been taken away under shorter measures of patience : some have been struck into a hell of misery, while thou remainest upon an earth of forbearance. In a plague, the destroying angel hath hewed down others, and passed by us; the arrows have flew about our heads, passed over us, and stuck in the heart of a neighbor. How many rich men, how many of our friends and familiars, have been seized by death since the beginning of the year, when they least thought of it, and imagined it far from them! Have you not known some of your acquaintance snatched away in the height of a crime? Was not the same wrath due to you as well as to them! And had it not been as dreadful for you to be so surprised by Him as it was for them? Why should he take a less sturdy sinner out of thy company, and let thee remain still upon the earth? If God had dealt so with you, how had you been cut off, not only from the enjoyment of this life, but the hopes of a better! And if God had made such a providence beneficial for reclaiming you, how much reason have you to acknowledge him! He that hath had least patience, hath cause to admire; but those that have more, ought to exceed others in blessing him for it. If God had put an end to your natural life before you had made provision for eternal, how deplorable would your condition have been!

Consider also, whoever have been sinners formerly of a deeper note; might not God have struck a man in the embraces of his harlots, and choked him in the moment of his excessive and intemperate healths, or on the sudden have spurted fire and brimstone into a blasphemer's mouth? What if God had snatched you away, when you had been sleeping in some great iniquity, or sent you while burning in lust to the fire it merited? Might he not have cracked the string that linked your souls to your bodies, in the last sickness you had? And what then had become of you? What could have been expected to succeed your impenitent state in this world, but howlings in another? but he reprieved you upon your petitions, or the solicitations of your friends; and have you not broke your word with him? Have your hearts been steadfast; hath he not yet waited, expecting when you would put your vows and resolutions into execution? What need had he to cry out to any so loud and so long, O you fools, "how long will you love foolishness?" (Prov. i. 22), when he might have ceased his crying to you, and have by your death prevented your many neglects of him? Did he do all this that any of us might add new sins to our old; or rather, that we should bless him for his forbearance, comply with the end of it in reforming our lives, and having recourse to his mercy?

3. Exhortion; therefore presume not upon his patience. The exercise of it is not eternal; you are at present under his patience; yet, while you are unconverted, you are also under his anger (Ps. vii. 1·1), "God is angry with the wicked every day." You know not how soon his anger may turn his patience aside, and step before it. It may be his sword is drawn out of his scabbard, his arrows may be settled in his bow; and perhaps there is but a little time before you may feel the edge of the one or the point of the other: and then there will be no more time for patience in God to us, or petition from us to him. If we repent here he will pardon us. If we defer repentance, and die without it, he will have no longer mercy to pardon, nor patience to bear. What is there in our power but the present? the future time we cannot command, the past time we cannot recall; squander not then the present away. The time will come when "time shall be no more," and then long-suffering shall be no more. Will you neglect the time, wherein patience acts, and vainly hope for a time beyond the resolves of patience? Will you spend that in vain, which goodness hath allotted you for other purposes? What an estimate will you make of a little forbearance to respite death, when you are gasping under the stroke of its arrows! How much would you value some few days of those many years you now trifle away! Can any think God will be always at an expense with them in vain, that he will have such riches trampled under their feet, and so many editions of his patience be made waste paper? Do you know how few sands are yet to run in your glass? Are you sure that He that waits to-day, will wait as well to-morrow? How can you tell, but that God that is slow to anger to-day, may be swift to it the next? Jerusalem had but a day of peace, and the most careless sinner hath no more. When their day was done, they were destroyed by famine, pestilence, or sword, or led into a doleful

captivity. Did God make our lives so uncertain, and the duration of his forbearance unknown to us, that we should live in a lazy neglect of his glory, and our own happiness? If you should have more patience in regard of your lives, do you know whether you shall have the effectual offers of grace? As your lives depend upon his will, so your conversion depends solely upon his grace. There have been many examples of those miserable wretches, that have been left to a reprobate sense, after they have a long time abused Divine forbearance. Though he waits, yet he "binds up sin." (Hos. xiii. 12), "The sin of Ephraim is bound up," as bonds are bound up by a creditor till a fit opportunity: when God comes to put the bond in suit, it will be too late to wish for that patience we have so scornfully despised. Consider therefore the end of patience. The patience of God considered in itself, without that which it tends to, affords very little comfort; it is but a step to pardoning mercy, and it may be without it, and often is. Many have been reprieved that were never forgiven; hell is full of those that had patience as well as we, but not one that accepted pardoning grace went within the gates of it. Patience leaves men, when their sins have ripened them for hell; but pardoning grace never leaves men till it hath conducted them to heaven. His patience speaks him placable, but doth not assure us that he is actually appeased. Men may hope that a long-suffering tends to a pardon, but cannot be assured of a pardon, but by something else above mere long-suffering. Rest not then upon bare patience, but consider the end of it; it is not that any should sin more freely, but repent more meltingly; it is not to spirit rebellion, but give a merciful stop to it. Why should any be so ambitious of their ruin, as to constrain God to ruin them against the inclinations of his sweet disposition?

4. The fourth exhortation is, Let us imitate God's patience in our own to others. He is unlike God that is hurried, with an unruly impetus, to punish others for wronging him. The consideration of Divine patience should make us square ourselves according to that pattern. God hath exercised a long-suffering from the fall of Adam to this minute on innumerable subjects, and shall we be transported with desire of revenge upon a single injury? If God were not "slow to wrath," a sinful world had been long ago torn up from the foundation. And if revenge should be exercised by all men against their enemies, what man should have been alive, since there is not a man without an enemy? If every man were like Saul, breathing out threatenings, the world would not only be an aceldema, but a desert. How distant are they from the nature of God, who are in a flame upon every slight provocation from a sense of some feeble and imaginary honor, that must bloody their sword for a trifle, and write their revenge in wounds and death! When God hath his glory every day bespattered, yet he keeps his sword in his sheath; what a woe would it be to the world, if he drew it upon every affront! This is to be like brutes, dogs, or tigers, that snarl, bite, and devour, upon every slight occasion: but to be patient is to be divine, and to show ourselves acquainted with the disposition of God. "Be you therefore perfect, as your heavenly Father is perfect" (Matt. v. 48):

i. e. Be you perfect and good; for he had been exhorting them to bless them that cursed them, and to do good to them that hated them, and that from the example God had set them, in causing his sun to rise upon the evil as well as the good. "Be you therefore perfect." To conclude: as patience is God's perfection, so it is the accomplishment of the soul: and as his "slowness to anger" argues the greatness of his power over himself, so an unwillingness to revenge is a sign of a power over ourselves which is more noble than to be a monarch over others.

INDEX

---

ii. 123—125, 142, 143. How great it is,
ii. 480, 481. Doth not impeach God's
goodness, ii. ·231, 232. It is evident, ii.
325, 326 ; brought a curse on the creatures.—See *Creatures*.

Falls of God's children turned to their good,
i. 537—547.

Fear, not the cause of the belief of a God,
i. 41. Men that are under a slavish fear
of him wish there were no God, i. 98, 99.
Of man, a contempt of God's power, ii.
93, 94. Should be of God, and not of
the pride or force of man, ii. 106, 107.
God's sovereignty should cause it, ii. 462.

Features different in every man, and how
necessary it should be so, i. 66, 67, 520.

Fervency.—See *Activity*.

Flesh, the legal services so called, i. 213,
214.

Fools, wicked men are so, i. 23, 586, 587.

Folly, sin is so.—See *Sin*.

Forgetfulness of God, men naturally are
prone to it, i. 159, 160. Of his mercies
a great sin (see *Mercies*). How attributed to God, i. 421.

Foreknowledge in God of sin, no blemish to
his holiness, ii. 145, 146.—See *Knowledge
of God*.

Future things, men desirous to know them,
i. 476, 477. Known by God.—See *Knowledge of God*.

G

Gabriel, on what messages he was sent, ii.
75.

Generation, could not be from eternity, i.
44—46.

Gifts, God can bestow them on men, ii.
384, 385. His sovereignty seen in giving
greater measures to one than another, ii.
408—410.

Glory of all they do or have, men are apt
to ascribe to themselves, i. 139. Of God
little minded in many seemingly good
actions, i. 124—127. Men are more concerned for their own reputation than
God's glory, i. 140. Should be aimed at
in spiritual worship. i. 239—241. God's
permission of sin is in order to it, ii. 154
—156. Should be advanced by us, ii.
461, 462.

God, his existence known by the light of
nature, i. 86 ; by the creatures, i. 28, 29,
42—64. Miracles not wrought to prove
it, i. 29. Owned by the universal consent of all nations, i. 30, 31. Never disputed of old, i. 31, 32. Denied by very
few, if any, i. 32, 33. Constantly owned
in all changes of the world, i. 34 ; under
anxieties of conscience, *ib*. The devil
not able to root out the belief of it, i. 35.
Natural and innate, i. 35, 36. Not introduced merely by tradition, i. 37, 38 ; nor
policy, i. 38, 39 ; nor fear, i. 41. Witnessed to by the very nature of man, i.

63—75 ; and by extraordinary occurrences, i. 76, 77 ; impossible to demonstrate there is none, i. 81. Motives to
endeavor to be settled in the belief of it,
i. 84, 85. Directions, i. 86, 87. Men wish
there were none, and who they are, i. 96
—99. Two ways of describing him, negation and affirmation, i. 181, 182. Is
active and communicative, i. 201. Propriety in him a great blessedness (See
Covenant). Infinitely happy, ii. 86, 87.

Good, that which is materially so may be
done, and not formally, i. 120, 124—126.
Actions cannot be performed before conversion, i. 163, 164. The thoughts of
God's presence a spur to them, i. 404,
405. God only is so, ii. 210, 211.

Goodness, pure and perfect, the royal prerogative of God only, ii. 214. Owned by
all nations, ii. 215, 219. Inseparable
from the notion of God, ii. 216, 217.
What is meant by it, ii. 217. How distinguished from mercy, ii. 218, 219. Comprehends all his attributes, ii. 219, 220.
Is so by his essence, ii. 221, 222. The
chief, *ib*. It is communicative, ii. 223,
224 ; necessary to him, ii. 224—226 ;
voluntary, ii. 226, 227 ; communicative
with the greatest pleasure, ii. 227, 228 ;
the displaying of it, the motive and end of
all his works, ii. 228—230. Arguments
to prove it a property of God, ii 230,
231 ; vindicated from the objections made
against it, ii. 231—244 ; appears in creation, ii. 244—258 ; in redemption, ii. 258
—294 : in his government, ii. 295—313 ;
frequently contemned and abused, ii. 313,
314 ; the abuse and contempt of it, base
and disingenuous, ii. 314, 315 ; highly re-
sented by God, ii. 315, 316. How it is
contemned and abused, ii. 316—325. Men
justly punished for it, ii. 326, 327. Fits
God for the government of the world,
and engages him actually to govern it, ii.
327, 328. The ground of all religion, ii.
329, 330. Renders God amiable to himself, ii. 331. Should do so to us, and
why, ii. 332—335. Renders him a fit
object of trust, with motives to it, drawn
hence, ii. 335—338 ; and worthy to be
obeyed and honored, ii. 338—341. Comfortable to the righteous, and wherein, ii.
341—344. Should engage us to endeavor
after the enjoyment of him, with motives, ii. 344—347. Should be often
meditated on, and the advantages of so
doing, ii. 347—351. We should be thankful for it, ii. 351—353 ; and imitate it,
and wherein, ii. 353—355.

Gospel, men greater enemies to, than to the
law, i. 165. Its excellency, i. 167, 501,
502. Called spirit, i. 213. The only
means of establishment, i. 501. Of an
eternal resolution, though of a temporary revelation, i. 502. Mysterious, *ib*.
The first preachers of it (see *Apostles*).

A TABLE

OF THE

PLACES OF SCRIPTURE EXPLAINED IN THIS BOOK